GOWER'S

PRINCIPLES OF

MODERN COMPANY LAW

D0241092

AUSTRALIA
The Law Book Company
Sydney

CANADA
The Carswell Company
Toronto, Ontario

INDIA
N. M. Tripathi (Private) Ltd.
Bombay
and
Eastern Law House (Private) Ltd.
Calcutta
M.P.P. House
Bangalore
Universal Book Traders
Delhi

ISRAEL
Steimatzky's Agency Ltd.
Tel-Aviv

PAKISTAN
Pakistan Law House
Karachi

GOWER'S

PRINCIPLES OF

MODERN COMPANY LAW

FIFTH EDITION

By

L. C. B. GOWER, LL.M., F.B.A.

Solicitor

With contributions from

D. D. PRENTICE, M.A., LL.B., J.D.

Barrister

Allen & Overy Professor of Corporate Law

Fellow of Pembroke College, Oxford

and

B. G. PETTET, LL.B.

Barrister

Senior Lecturer in Laws

University College London

LONDON

SWEET & MAXWELL

1992

First Edition 1954
Second Edition 1957
Second Impression 1959
Third Impression 1961
Fourth Impression 1963
Fifth Impression 1965
Sixth Impression 1967
Seventh Impression 1968
Third Edition 1969
Fourth Edition 1979
First Supplement 1980
Second Supplement 1988
Fifth Edition 1992

Published in 1992 by
Sweet & Maxwell Ltd., South Quay Plaza,
183 Marsh Wall, London E14 9FT
Computerset by
P.B. Computer Typesetting, N. Yorks
Printed in Great Britain by
BPCC Hazells Ltd.,
Member of BPCC Ltd., Aylesbury, Bucks, England

A CIP catalogue record
for this book is available
from the British Library

ISBN 0 420 46390 9 hb
      0 420 46400 X pb

©
L.C.B. Gower
1992

PREFACE

This edition is virtually a new book. With the exception of the first three chapters nearly all that appeared in earlier editions has been re-written or discarded. Its aims, however, remain the same; namely to try to provide an interesting textbook primarily for those studying English Company Law in some depth. The reception afforded earlier editions suggests that at the dates of their publication there was a perceived need for such a book. But circumstances are now very different. The spate of companies' and related legislation in the 1980s and the ever-growing volume of case law have transformed the subject. The number of students studying it as an important part of the curriculum of every English Law School has vastly increased. And there are now several excellent textbooks which may well fully meet students' needs.

However it was urged upon me that there was still a place for this book and I thought that there might be—though not unless it was subjected to more drastic treatment than merely updating the 4th Edition. Accordingly when, at the end of 1987, I found myself free from other full-time commitments, I decided to embark on the task of re-writing in my dotage a book that I had written in my youth. This I could not have attempted had it not been for Ben Petter's excellent Second Cumulative Supplement to the 4th Edition. With its aid I hoped that I might be capable of completing the task in time for publication before the academic year 1991–92. What I had not bargained for was the Companies Act 1989 which, to an even greater extent than the Acts of 1980 and 1981, started life as a Bill of modest dimensions implementing EC Directives but, as a result of amendments, mostly at the late stages of its passage through Parliament, finally emerged in November 1989 as a major Companies Act, twice as long as the original Bill and making important changes to nearly every Part of the principal Act of 1985. As a result, most of what I had written prior to 1990 had to be scrapped. By the end of that year it became clear that if the work was to be finished in time even for the academic year 1992–93, I should have to persuade someone else to assume responsibility for what was clearly going to prove a particularly difficult and time-consuming chapter—that on Company Charges—in the light of the changes of the registration system made by the 1989 Act. This, to my great good fortune, I was able to persuade Professor Prentice to undertake. My debt to him is great; not only has he enabled me to finish the other chapters more or less on time, but it has meant that there is one chapter (Chapter 16) on which readers can confidently rely as an accurate and scholarly account of an important branch of Company Law.

v

Of the other chapters, for which I alone am responsible, I am acutely aware that they have many defects. I hope, however, that I have not wholly destroyed what was said to be the principal merit of earlier editions; namely that the book was relatively easy to read. If I have, the book does not deserve to survive and I would not want it to. Where I have unquestionably failed is in my ambition to reduce the size of this edition below that of the 4th; it is, I fear, even larger. The only excuse that I can offer is that, as it seems to me, English Company Law is in danger of becoming an unwieldy subject even if one treats Insolvency Law and Securities Regulation as discrete subjects needing to be dealt with in textbooks in Company Law only to the extent that some knowledge of them is essential for an understanding of Company Law itself. Faced with the increasing spate of legislation, primary and secondary, and of reported cases resulting from specialised series of Company Law reports, it is becoming increasingly difficult to deal with the subject within a reasonable compass and to extract its "principles" as this book purports to do. Particularly is this so now that those principles derive largely from legislation drafted in excessive detail. While I have tried not merely to summarise the effect of the legislation but to explain the reasons for it, even this I have not always succeeded in doing. The legislation normally results from Government policy and, as an unusually frank Secretary of State told me: "Government policy doesn't need to have reasons".

I fear, too, that I have aggravated the problems flowing from sporadic growth by self-indulgently spreading myself on topics which particularly interest me and on recent judicial and legislative developments which seem likely to be of interest to students and their teachers; and indeed, to practitioners. Although this book is not intended as a work of reference for practitioners some of them seem to have found its earlier editions helpful—not as they tell me, to remind them of what the established law is but to point them to possible lines of argument on areas in which the law is uncertain. Accordingly I have continued to stick my neck out in relation to such areas with greater readiness than seems to be regarded as appropriate and permissible in works of reference. If as a result, readers of this edition find it too argumentative that is a fault of which the book and its author have always been guilty. I have also accepted (albeit with a grain of salt) assurances from friends in the Department of Trade and Industry that earlier editions have been prescribed reading for new recruits to its Companies Division. Accordingly I have ventured to draw attention to what, rightly or wrongly, seem to me to be flaws in the present provisions of the Companies Acts, hoping thereby that some of them may be thought worthy of addition to the Division's "blood-bank" of desirable reforms.

Throughout this edition, it is assumed that all legislation enacted prior to the 1991-92 Session will have been brought into full operation (but with a warning when that is known to be unlikely) and, unless the context otherwise requires, references to "the Act" are to the Companies Act 1985 as thus amended. As regards case law, every effort has been made to refer to decisions of importance reported prior to the latest date logistically possible but, as regards those first reported in the last months of 1991 or later, there sometimes has had to be no more than a bare reference inserted at proof stage.

In conclusion, it is my pleasant duty to express heartfelt thanks to all those who responded so generously and helpfully to my pleas for information or allowed me to pick their brains, in the course of the preparation of this edition. I hope they will forgive me if I do not attempt to mention them by name; they include friends and former colleagues in the Department of Trade and Industry and the S.I.B. and the ever-helpful officials of The Stock Exchange, and the Panel on Takeovers and Mergers. I must, however, mention by name those whose help went still further. I have already expressed my indebtedness to Professor Prentice in relation to Chapter 16, and to Mr. Pettet, but for whose Second Cumulative Supplement to the 4th Edition I would never have embarked upon a 5th. In addition, each of them read the text either in manuscript, proof or both. But for Wedderburn, who had been a co-editor of the 3rd and 4th Editions, continued to offer help and encouragement throughout the preparation of this one and nobly found time to read most of the chapters at the proof stage. His criticisms and suggestions were invaluable. At a very late stage I belatedly had the sense to ask an insolvency expert, Mr. Harry Rajak of King's College, London, if he would look at the final Chapter 28 to which he responded in the most helpful manner possible. I am also most grateful to Professor R. B. Jack who first alerted me to the importance of Lord Prosser's judgment in the Scottish case, *Dawson v. Coats Patons*, sending me a transcript of the judgment and copies of the reports of the earlier stages. His offer to check the proofs to see that I had not made too many egregious errors in the course of my rare excursions into Scottish Company Law was one which I had hoped to take up; but when the proof stage was reached the time-table was so tight that I felt that it would be inexcusable to impose further on the kindness of one who has so many other commitments. I also wish to associate myself with the expressions of gratitude which I know that Professor Prentice has conveyed to his colleague, Dr. Fidelis Oditah of Merton College, Oxford, for his help in relation to Chapter 16.

At all stages the publishers have been unfailingly helpful and were it not for their house-rules which prohibit tributes to named members of their staff I would have expressed my warmest gratitude to the immensely efficient ladies who held my hand throughout this edition's gestation and but for whom it would never have appeared on time—if ever. That prohibition however does not extend to the three freelance experts whom they recruited to relieve me of the tasks which I had the sense to realise I was totally incapable of performing. Accordingly I offer my warmest thanks to Moira Greenhalgh, who has prepared the Index, Caroline Chambers, who prepared the Tables and Andrew Griffith, who prepared the Glossary of Terms.

Last but not least, I should like to express gratitude and sympathy to the many typists who converted my illegible handwriting into intelligible typescript (readers of a younger generation will be amazed to learn that anyone still writes in longhand—but that is the only way I know) and to the typesetters who did a remarkable job of deciphering my proof corrections.

L. C. B. Gower
April 16, 1992.

CONTENTS

Part One

INTRODUCTORY

ix

Contents

Part Four

A COMPANY'S SECURITIES

INVESTOR AND CREDITOR PROTECTION

Contents

Part Six

COMPANIES IN TRAUMA

Contents

Table of Cases

Table of Cases

Table of Statutes

Table of Statutes

TABLE OF STATUTORY INSTRUMENTS

TABLE OF RULES OF TAKE-OVER CODE

GLOSSARY OF TERMS

ACCOUNTING REFERENCE DATE

The date in each year which marks the end of the company's accounting reference period and thus its financial year and by reference to which the company must draw up its statutory accounts. A company may alter its accounting reference date from time to time subject to certain restrictions. See also "year end".

ACCOUNTING REFERENCE PERIOD

The period between the company's incorporation and its accounting reference date (which must be more than 6 months but less than 18 months) and thereafter the period between the company's accounting reference dates in each year. This determines the company's financial year.

ACTING IN CONCERT

Where two or more shareholders in a public company are acting together pursuant to some agreement, so that their liability to comply with disclosure requirements and the like is determined by the size of their aggregate holding. See also "concert party".

ADMINISTRATION

A special procedure for managing the affairs of an insolvent company for a limited period to determine whether the company's business can be salvaged or wound up more efficiently. This was introduced by the Insolvency Act 1985.

ADMINISTRATION ORDER

A court order putting a company into administration.

ADMINISTRATIVE RECEIVER

A receiver appointed to manage the affairs of a company by a secured creditor who has a floating charge covering most of the company's business and assets. Such a receiver now has wide powers under the Insolvency Act.

ADMINISTRATOR

A qualified insolvency practitioner appointed by the court to manage a company which is in administration.

ALLOTMENT

The issue of a share or shares by a company to the first holder(s) of the share(s). See also "issue".

Glossary of Terms

ANNUAL GENERAL MEETING (AGM)

A meeting of the members of a company which must be held every year.

ANNUAL RETURN

A form which a company is obliged to complete and file with the Registrar of Companies every year disclosing various details about the company, its members and its officers.

ARTICLES OF ASSOCIATION

A document which, together with the memorandum of association, comprises the constitution of a company. The articles contain detailed rules for the administration of the company's affairs and are often based on the model articles in Table A.

ASSOCIATED COMPANY

This term has different meanings. It is used to refer to companies which are in the same group as each other such as fellow subsidiaries. It is also used in connection with statutory duties and disabilities imposed by the Companies Act on directors: certain of these have been extended to apply to companies associated with or controlled by any director of the company, these terms being defined in s.346 Companies Act.

AUDITOR

A suitably qualified person or firm whom a company is obliged to appoint to audit its statutory accounts and report to the members on these every year.

AUTHORISED SHARE CAPITAL

The total number and nominal value of shares which a company is authorised to issue by its memorandum of association and by any subsequent resolution increasing its size and thus being the aggregate of the company's issued share capital and of any remaining shares which are unissued.

AUTOMATIC CRYSTALLISATION

The crystallisation of a floating charge which under the express terms of the charge will occur automatically upon the occurrence of certain specified events rather than upon the serving by the creditor of a notice of crystallisation.

BALANCE SHEET

Part of a company's statutory accounts, being a statement of its assets and liabilities.

BCC

British Company Cases (published by CCH).

BCLC

Butterworths Company Law Cases.

BOARD OF DIRECTORS

The body which has the prime responsibility for the management of a company, being the directors of the company acting collectively in accordance with its articles.

BONUS SHARE

A share which is issued to an existing shareholder of a company not in return for a payment from the shareholder but as an accounting exercise, such as to represent the capitalisation of net profits, whereby the company's issued share capital is increased by a transfer from some other item on its balance sheet.

CALL

The procedure whereby a shareholder is required to pay to the company the whole or part of any unpaid amount outstanding in respect of a share which has already been issued.

CALL OPTION

An option whereby the beneficiary is entitled, subject to specified conditions, to require someone to sell shares on specified terms.

CAPITAL

This term has different meanings in relation to a company according to the context. It can be used to refer to the company's issued share capital. It can also be used to refer to the finance which a company has raised being the aggregate of its equity capital and its loan capital. A further use of the term is in a less technical sense to distinguish a company's accumulated assets and resources from its flow of income.

CAPITAL REDEMPTION RESERVE

This is an item in a company's balance sheet. If a company purchases or redeems any of its shares in accordance with the relevant procedures in the Companies Act, it must transfer the nominal value of the shares purchased or redeemed to the capital redemption reserve and thereby maintain the size of its undistributable reserves.

CAPITALISATION

An accounting exercise whereby net profits which have been retained in a company and not paid out to shareholders can be used to increase the size of the company's paid-up share capital or its other undistributable reserves, usually by making a bonus issue of shares with a suitable aggregate nominal value to its existing shareholders.

Glossary of Terms

CERTIFICATE OF INCORPORATION

The document issued by the Registrar of Companies when a company is incorporated and which constitutes proof that the company has been duly incorporated.

CERTIFICATE OF INCORPORATION ON CHANGE OF NAME

An amended certificate of incorporation which is issued by the Registrar of Companies when a company has changed its name, the new name taking effect upon the issue of this certificate.

CHARGE

A form of security which a company may give over its assets to a creditor and which may be either a fixed charge or a floating charge.

CLASS RIGHTS

Special rights conferred by a company's articles on the holders of certain shares which usually have a special designation. Such rights may include priority to a dividend, enhanced voting strength or a power of veto and can only be cancelled or varied in accordance with a special procedure. The courts have also applied this term to include any special rights which the articles confer on a shareholder which are inextricably linked with the shareholder's holding of shares but are not attached to any shares in particular.

COMPANY LIMITED BY GUARANTEE

A type of registered company where the members have guaranteed to pay a specified contribution towards its debts and liabilities. The liability of its members is limited to the amount of this guarantee.

COMPANY LIMITED BY SHARES

A type of registered company whose members are issued with shares in the company in return for payment. The liability of its members is limited to paying to the company any unpaid amount outstanding on their shares.

COMPANY SECRETARY

An officer which every company must appoint who has various duties concerning the administration of the company and the filing of information with the Registrar of Companies.

CONCERT PARTIES

A group of two or more shareholders in a public company who have agreed to act together and who are therefore treated collectively for the purposes of certain disclosure requirements and the like. See also "acting in concert".

CONNECTED PERSON

Certain statutory duties and disabilities imposed by the Companies Act on a director have been extended to persons connected with any director of the company. This term is defined in s.346 Companies Act.

CONSOLIDATION

A method of accounting whereby certain groups of companies produce group accounts showing the financial affairs of the whole group rather than each group member simply producing separate statutory accounts. The Companies Act 1989 has largely restricted the requirement to produce accounts in this form to larger groups.

CONSTRUCTIVE NOTICE

A doctrine, also known as "deemed notice," whereby someone dealing with a company is treated as knowing everything about the company that could be discovered from an examination of its file at the Registry of Companies. Provision was made in the Companies Act 1989 for abolishing this doctrine.

CORPORATE PERSONALITY

The fact that the company is treated by the law as a separate person from its members and as having its own rights and liabilities.

CORPORATE VEIL

A term commonly used to describe the separation of the company's rights and liabilities from those of its members and in particular the fact that the members of a company will usually have no liability for the company's debts and liabilities.

CRYSTALLISATION

The transformation of a floating charge so that it settles upon the assets covered by the charge whereupon it takes on the characteristics of a fixed charge and the company is no longer free to deal with the assets charged. Crystallisation will occur in accordance with the terms of the instrument creating the charge and will usually require the serving of a notice of crystallisation by the creditor unless it is an automatic crystallisation.

DEFERRED SHARE

A share in a company which has inferior rights.

DERIVATIVE ACTION

An action which a minority shareholder may in certain circumstances be permitted to bring on behalf of the company in the interests of

Glossary of Terms

Derivative Action—cont. justice even though the action has not been authorised by the board or by a general meeting of the company.

Director An officer of the company, being a member of the board of directors or a sole director.

Dissenting Members Those shareholders who have voted against a resolution which has nevertheless been passed. For some resolutions, the Companies Act has given such a minority certain rights to apply to court.

Distributable Profits Those profits of a company which are available for distribution to its shareholders subject to the restrictions set by the Companies Act.

Dividends A payment to the shareholders from the distributable profits of the company and which is usually paid in proportion to the shareholders' shareholdings.

DTI The Department of Trade and Industry: This is a government department under the Secretary of State for Trade and Industry which has responsibility for regulating companies. See "Secretary of State".

DTI Inspectors Suitably qualified persons who may be appointed by the Secretary of State to investigate the affairs of a company in certain circumstances.

DTI Investigation An investigation of a company's affairs by DTI inspectors which may be instigated by the Secretary of State in certain circumstances as provided by the Companies Act.

EEIG European Economic Interest Grouping: a new type of association designed to facilitate co-operation between firms in different EC Member States.

Elective Regime The ability of private companies to achieve a measure of deregulation pursuant to the Companies Act 1989 by passing elective resolutions to reduce or remove certain administrative requirements.

Elective Resolution A resolution which a private company may pass to reduce or remove certain administrative requirements and which requires unanimous support from those members entitled to vote.

EQUITY CAPITAL

Finance raised by a company in return for a share of profits rather than that which is to be repaid with interest. It in effect refers to the proceeds of issues of shares as opposed to loan capital.

EXTRAORDINARY GENERAL MEETING

Any meeting of the members of a company other than the annual general meeting.

EXTRAORDINARY RESOLUTION

A resolution of the members of a company or of a class of members which can only be passed with the support of at least three quarters of the votes cast and which normally requires at least 14 days' notice.

FINANCIAL YEAR

The period for which a company must prepare its statutory accounts and provide an annual return and which is determined by its accounting reference period.

FIRM

This term has different meanings in different contexts. It can be used to refer to a partnership as distinct from a company. It can also be used to refer to a business organisation in general encompassing both companies and partnerships. In economic analysis, it refers to a unit of production.

FLOATING CHARGE

A form of security peculiar to a company whereby the company can continue dealing with the assets covered by the charge unless and until the charge crystallises.

FLOTATION

The process whereby a public company offers its shares for sale to the public on The Stock Exchange or a similar market in shares, having satisfied the relevant requirements of the market, and whereupon those shares can subsequently be traded on the particular market.

FRAUD ON THE MINORITY

This term is used in two distinct contexts. It refers to the abuse by a majority of the members of a company of any of their powers in relation to the affairs of the company and in particular of their power to alter the company's articles of association by special resolution. The term is also used to describe the circumstances in which a minority shareholder can bring a derivative action on behalf of a company.

F.S. ACT

The Financial Services Act 1986.

Glossary of Terms

GENERAL MEETING A duly convened meeting of the members of a company.

GROUP A group of related companies, usually consisting of a holding company and its subsidiaries, treated by the law collectively for certain purposes.

HOLDING COMPANY A parent company, being a company which controls another company, usually by owning a voting majority of shares. The term is defined in s.736(1) Companies Act 1985 which was expanded by the Companies Act 1989.

INCORPORATION The point at which a company comes into existence as a separate legal person and its certificate of incorporation is issued.

INSIDER DEALING Dealing in the shares of a company with the benefit of confidential or restricted information which the dealer has acquired through his position in relation to the company.

ISSUE The process by which a share or shares in a company is assigned to the first holder(s) of the share(s) in consideration of the nominal value of the share(s) and any premium which can be paid immediately or (subject to certain restrictions) left outstanding as a liability of the shareholder(s) to the company. See also "allotment".

ISSUED SHARE CAPITAL That portion of a company's authorised share capital which has been issued to its shareholders and the nominal value of this share capital.

LIFTING THE VEIL Where the courts disregard the corporate veil for some reason and do not consider the rights or liabilities of the company in complete isolation from those of its members. This term tends to be used interchangeably with "piercing the veil".

LIMITED LIABILITY The principle that a company is responsible for its own debts and liabilities and that the only liability which shareholders have in that respect is their liability to pay to the company any unpaid portion of the nominal value of their shares or any unpaid premium.

LIQUIDATION — The process whereby a company is wound up and dissolved.

LIQUIDATOR — The person in charge of the affairs of a company in liquidation.

LISTED ISSUE — An issue of shares which are listed on The Stock Exchange or some other recognised stock exchange and which can therefore be traded in that market.

LISTING PARTICULARS — Those details concerning an issue of shares and the company issuing them which must be provided to enable them to be traded on a recognised stock exchange.

LOAN CAPITAL — Finance which a company obtains by an issue of shares by borrowing rather than from issuing shares and is thus to be distinguished from "equity capital".

LOAN STOCK — An aggregation of loan capital raised by a company, which is often held on common terms set out in a common instrument.

MAINTENANCE OF CAPITAL — The theory that the law should protect the creditors of a company by restricting the payments that can be made from the company's assets to its shareholders and in particular by ensuring that a shareholder can only be repaid any amount paid up on a share (directly or indirectly) if specified conditions and formalities are complied with. This theory is based on the optimistic assumption that such restrictions will help preserve the value of a company's assets and ensure that the amount of a company's paid up share capital reflects this value more accurately. It underlies a number of common law and statutory rules applying to transactions involving shares.

MANAGING DIRECTOR — A director who is in overall charge of the day-to-day running of a company.

MEMORANDUM OF ASSOCIATION — The document which, together with the articles of association, comprises the constitution of a company. The memorandum will contain the company's objects clause and its main details.

MINIMUM SHARE CAPITAL — The minimum issued share capital which a company is obliged to have, being at present

Glossary of Terms

MINIMUM SHARE CAPITAL—*cont.* two shares of any value for a private company, and fifty thousand pounds (with at least a quarter paid up) for a public company.

MINORITY SHAREHOLDER(s) Shareholders who do not have a majority of votes on a particular issue or who are unable to block a particular resolution.

NEGATIVE PLEDGE An undertaking given by a company, usually as a term of a charge, not to create a further charge in favour of another creditor.

NOMINAL SHARE CAPITAL The face or par value of a company's authorised or issued share capital.

NOMINAL VALUE This means the face value or par value of a share which is determined when the share is authorised or issued and can only be changed by a special procedure thereafter. The nominal value of a share is not necessarily related to its market value. See also par value.

NOMINEE SHAREHOLDER A person who holds shares but does not have any beneficial interest in them but holds them on trust for some other person.

OBJECTS CLAUSE The clause in a company's memorandum of association which sets out the intended objectives of the company and the ancillary powers which it may require in pursuing them and which usually tends to be comprehensive and exhaustive.

OFFICERS The officers of a company such as its directors and its secretary.

OFF-MARKET TRANSACTION A sale of shares which does not take place on a recognised stock exchange.

OFFICIAL RECEIVER A public official who has a number of functions in relation to insolvent companies and individuals.

OPTION In relation to shares, an option is a right to buy shares or to sell shares on specified terms and subject to specified conditions, these rights being termed respectively a call option and a put option.

ORDINARY RESOLUTION A resolution of the members of a company which can be passed by a simple majority of the votes cast and which normally requires at least 14 days' notice.

ORDINARY SHARE

A share in a company which does not have any special or inferior rights attached to it.

OVERSEAS COMPANY

A company incorporated outside Great Britain but which has established a place of business within Great Britain and is required to file various particulars at the Registry of Companies under Part XXIII of the Companies Act 1985.

PAID-UP SHARE CAPITAL

The nominal value of that portion of a company's issued share capital which has been paid up by the shareholders.

PAR VALUE

The face or nominal value of a share as opposed to its market value. See also "nominal value".

PARENT COMPANY

A holding company. This term also means a company which is a parent undertaking for accounting purposes.

PARENT UNDERTAKING

A term introduced by the Companies Act 1989 for accounting purposes meaning an undertaking which controls another undertaking, its subsidiary undertaking, in any of the ways specified by the Act. The term applies to any holding company as defined by the Companies Act but encompasses a wider range of companies and undertakings as well.

PARTNERSHIP

A legal relationship which subsists between persons who are carrying on a business with a view to profit within the meaning of the Partnership Act 1890 and which may be deemed to exist between any persons who are sharing the profits of a business.

PIERCING THE VEIL

Where the courts disregard the corporate veil for some reason. This term tends to be used interchangeably with "lifting the veil" but connotes in particular the imposition of liability on a shareholder for a debt or liability of the company.

PLACING

The sale of shares in a company to selected purchasers by pre-arrangement as opposed to being offered for sale to the public generally.

POLL

A formal counting of votes cast by the members of a company at a general meeting whereby a member's votes will be determined

POLL—*cont.*

according to the size of the shareholding, or otherwise in accordance with the company's articles, and votes can be cast by proxy in the absence of a member.

PRE-EMPTION RIGHTS

The rights which the existing shareholders of a company may have that shares which are to be issued or transferred must first be offered to them in proportion to their shareholdings on specified terms before they can be issued or transferred elsewhere. Such rights are conferred by the Companies Act in relation to issues of shares and are often found in a private company's articles or in a shareholders' agreement.

PREFERENCE SHARES

Shares which have a right to dividends in priority to the other shareholders and may have a prior right to a repayment of capital as well. There is no standard formula for such shares and the terms of the preferential dividend and any other special rights or any inferior rights (for example as regards voting) must be set out in the company's articles of association.

PREFERENTIAL DEBTS

Certain unsecured debts due from a company which have a preferential right to repayment in a winding-up.

PRE-INCORPORATION CONTRACT

A contract made on behalf of a company before the company has been incorporated.

PREMIUM

Any amount payable for the issue of a share in addition to its nominal value.

PRIVATE COMPANY

Any registered company which is not a public company. Its name will usually end with the word "limited" or the abbreviation "ltd".

PROMOTER

A person who procures the formation of a company or the flotation of a public company.

PROSPECTUS

An offer to the public to subscribe for shares in a public company.

PROXY

Someone who has been authorised to attend a general meeting and vote on behalf of a member. Also applied to the document authorising him.

PUBLIC COMPANY

A registered company which states in its memorandum that it is to be a public company and which complies with the other

Public Company—
cont.

requirements of the Companies Act concerning public companies. Its name will usually end with the words "public limited company" or the abbreviation "plc".

Put Option

An option whereby the beneficiary is entitled, subject to specified conditions, to require someone to buy shares on specified terms.

Quorum

The minimum number of persons in attendance necessary for a valid meeting to take place.

Ratification

The procedure whereby an unauthorised action taken in the name of a company may be adopted and validated on behalf of the company by a person or body which does have the authority to do so.

Receiver

Someone appointed by a secured creditor of a company who has a fixed and/or floating charge over the assets of a company or any of them to deal with the assets covered by the charge pursuant to the terms of the charge. If the relevant charge covers most of the company's business and assets, the receiver will be an administrative receiver, secured creditor of a company.

Receivership

The procedure whereby a receiver or administrative receiver is appointed by a secured creditor to deal with or manage the whole or part of a company's business and assets pursuant to a charge.

Reconstruction

A process whereby the whole or part of a company's business is transferred to a new company. This may be done to reorganise the structure of the company's business or to reflect a change in control or as part of an arrangement to deal with the company's insolency.

Redeemable Share

A share which the company is entitled to buy from the shareholder or which the shareholder can require the company to buy on specified terms and subject to specified conditions, which will usually be set out in the company's articles of association.

Glossary of Terms

REDUCTION OF CAPITAL
The procedure whereby a company may reduce the amount of its issued share capital either by making a repayment to shareholders and reducing the nominal share value of their shares accordingly or by cancelling the whole or part of the nominal value of some or all of the company's shares.

REGISTERED COMPANY
A company which is formed by registration with the Registrar of Companies as opposed to being formed by Royal Charter or by an Act of Parliament.

REGISTRAR OF COMPANIES (THE REGISTRAR)
The public official in charge of the formation of registered companies, maintaining their public files and supervising their compliance with the various administrative and disclosure requirements imposed on companies by the Companies Act.

RESOLUTION
A formal decision made by the board of directors, the members or any class of the members of a company and complying with the relevant requirements for the particular decision.

RIGHTS ISSUE
An issue of shares in a company whereby existing shareholders are given pre-emption rights usually at a favourable price.

SCHEME OF ARRANGEMENT
A formal and properly sanctioned arrangement concerning the affairs of a company made between the company and its creditors or between the company and its members.

SECRETARY OF STATE
The Secretary of State of Trade and Industry who has various functions in relation to the regulation of companies under the Companies Act.

SECRET PROFIT
A profit made by a director or other fiduciary agent of a company from their position and where proper disclosure has not been made.

SECURED CREDITOR
A creditor of a company whose debt is secured by a charge over some or all of the assets of the company or by some other form of security.

SHADOW DIRECTOR
A person in accordance with whose directions or instructions the directors of a company are accustomed to act within the meaning of s.741(2) Companies Act 1985.

SHARE

A unit of the share capital of a company.

SHARE CAPITAL

The authorised and/or issued share capital of a company.

SHARE PREMIUM ACCOUNT

An item in a company's accounts representing the amount of any premium paid or payable on the company's issued share capital.

SHAREHOLDER

Someone who holds a share in a company and who is therefore a member of the company.

SHAREHOLDERS' AGREEMENT

An agreement among the shareholders of a company relating to the affairs of the company and which is in addition to the company's articles of association.

SHELF-COMPANY

A company which is formed and does not trade but is kept available for anyone who wishes to obtain a company quickly and does not have the time to wait for one to be formed in the usual way.

SHORT NOTICE

Extraordinary general meetings can be held and resolutions be put to such meetings at shorter notice than would otherwise be required provided that the requisite minimum of the members agree to such short notice. Special notice cannot be reduced in this way.

SOCIETAS EUROPEA (S.E.)

The proposed type of EC incorporated company.

SPECIAL NOTICE

A special period of 28 days' notice which must be given for certain resolutions including ones for the removal from office of a director or an auditor.

SPECIAL RESOLUTION

A resolution of the members of a company which can only be passed if it is supported by at least three quarters of the votes cast and which normally requires at least 21 days' notice.

STATUTORY ACCOUNTS

The accounts which a company is obliged by the Companies Act to produce in the requisite form and have audited each year.

SUBSIDIARY

A company which is controlled by another company, its parent or holding company, who usually holds a voting majority of its shares. The term is defined in s.736(1) Companies Act 1985 which was expanded by the Companies Act 1989.

SUBSIDIARY UNDERTAKING	A term introduced by the Companies Act 1989 for accounting purposes meaning an undertaking which is controlled by another undertaking in a way specified by the Act. The definition includes all companies which are subsidiaries under the Companies Act but encompasses a wider range of companies and undertakings as well.
TABLE A	A model set of articles of association for a company, currently set out in a statutory instrument and which has been amended from time to time.
TALISMAN	A computerised system for handling the transfer of shares on The Stock Exchange.
TAURUS	Transfer and Automated Registration of Unregistered Stock: A new computerised system for recording the transfer of shares on The Stock Exchange which will replace the use of stock transfer forms and share certificates.
TRADING CERTIFICATE	A certificate required by a company formed as a public company before it is entitled to commence trading. It is not required by a private company which re-registers as a public company.
TRANSMISSION OF SHARES	The vesting of shares in another person by operation of law rather than by transfer for example following the death or bankruptcy of the shareholder.
UCITS	"Undertakings for collective investment in transferable securities"; the EC name for unit trusts.
ULTRA VIRES	An act done by someone in the name of a company for which they lack the necessary power or authority. The term has traditionally been used in company law to refer to an act which the company itself has no capacity to do because it is beyond the scope of the company's objects clause or because it involves a breach of company law. There has been confusion as to the meaning of the term in company law because it has also been used to describe an act of the board of directors which is beyond the scope of their authority

ULTRA VIRES—*cont.*

to act on behalf of the company but which would have been within the capacity of the company itself.

UNDERTAKING

This term includes partnerships and unincorporated associations as well as companies and was introduced by the Companies Act 1989 for accounting purposes.

UNDISTRIBUTABLE
RESERVES

An accounting term meaning those items in a company's accounts such as its issued share capital and any share premium account which must be balanced by assets before the company can show a profit.

UNLIMITED COMPANY

A company whose members have unlimited liability for its debts and liabilities.

WINDING UP

The liquidation of a company being the formal process whereby a company's affairs are brought to a close and its liabilities settled and any surplus assets distributed to its members prior to its dissolution.

WRITTEN
RESOLUTION

A resolution passed by the members of a company by signing a written form of the resolution rather than by voting at a duly convened meeting. The Companies Act 1989 gave all private companies the ability to pass members' resolutions in this way, subject to certain safeguards, but many companies have a similar power in their articles though this may be less effective for certain purposes.

YEAR END

The date on which a company's financial year ends and by reference to which it must prepare its statutory accounts. See also accounting reference date.

Part One

INTRODUCTORY

CHAPTER 1

NATURE AND FUNCTIONS OF COMPANIES

SCOPE OF THE SUBJECT

ALTHOUGH company law is a well-recognised subject in the legal curriculum and the title of a voluminous literature, its exact scope is vague since "the word *company* has no strictly legal meaning."[1] It is clear, however, that in legal theory (though not, as we shall see, always in economic reality) the term implies an association[2] of a number[3] of people for some common object or objects. The purposes for which men and women may wish to associate are multifarious, ranging from those as basic as marriage and mutual protection against the elements to those as sophisticated as the objects of the Confederation of British Industry or the Atomic Energy Authority. But in common parlance the word "company" is normally reserved[4]; for those associated for economic purposes, *i.e.* to carry on a business for gain.

English law provides two main types of organisation for such associations; partnerships and companies. Although the word "company" is colloquially applied to both,[5] the modern English lawyer regards companies and company law as distinct from partnerships and partnership law. Partnership law, which is now largely codified in the Partnership Act 1890, is based on the law of agency, each partner becoming an agent of the others,[6] and it therefore affords a suitable framework for an association of a small body of persons having trust and confidence in each other. A more complicated form of association, with a large and fluctuating membership, requires a more elaborate organisation which ideally should confer corporate personality on the association, that is, should recognise that it constitutes a distinct legal person, subject to legal duties and entitled to legal rights separate from those of its

---

[1] *Per* Buckley J. in *Re Stanley* [1906] 1 Ch. 131 at p. 134.
[2] *Pace* James L.J. in *Smith* v. *Anderson* (1880) 15 Ch.D. 247 at p. 273: "The word 'association,' in the sense in which it is now commonly used, is etymologically inaccurate, for 'association' does not properly describe the thing formed, but properly and etymologically describes the act of association together, from which act of associating there is formed a company or partnership."
[3] The number need not be more than two, and of these the interest of one need not be more than nominal, as in the so-called "one-man company." Nor indeed does the "company" automatically cease merely because, in the course of time, the number of members is reduced to one or none.
[4] But not universally; we still talk about an infantry company, a livery company and the "glorious company of the Apostles."
[5] So that it is common for partners to carry on business in the name of "———— & Company."
[6] Partnership Act 1890, s.5.

3

members.[7] This the modern company can obtain easily and cheaply by being formed under a succession of statutes culminating in the principal Companies Act of 1985 as amended in particular by that of 1989.

Briefly what occurs is that the promoters of a company prepare certain documents expressing their desire to be formed into a company with a specified name and objects and these documents are lodged with the Registrar of Companies. If the documents are in order, they are registered, the Registrar grants a certificate of incorporation, and the company is formed. The essential feature is public registration and this type of company is therefore described as a registered company.

Although today there is a clear-cut legal distinction between partnerships and incorporated companies and although the latter can now be formed almost as easily and cheaply as the former, this is a relatively modern development. Little more than a century-and-a-half ago corporate personality could be acquired only by the dilatory and expensive process of promoting a special Act of Parliament or acquiring a Royal Charter. Hence, the business world tried to adapt the partnership form to an organisation with a large and fluctuating membership and, as we shall see,[8] thanks to the equitable doctrine of the trust, their efforts met with considerable success. It was from these "deed of settlement" companies (rather than from chartered corporations) that the modern company was developed. Nearly all these unincorporated companies[9] have now either been wound up, registered under the Companies Acts, or become incorporated by statute or charter, but until recently several important insurance companies remained as examples of the once normal earlier form.[10]

Choice of partnership or company

The distinction between partnerships and companies is often merely one of machinery and not of function. If a small number of persons

[7] It is outside the scope of this book to discuss whether this recognition is of a pre-existing fact (as contended by the Realist school, associated with the name of Gierke) or a legal fiction. Legal personality, in the sense of the capacity to be the subject of legal rights and duties, is necessarily the creation of law whether conferred upon a single human being or a group and the Realist and other theories are of no direct concern to the lawyer (as opposed to the political scientist) except in so far as they have influenced the judges in the development of the law. See further H. L. A. Hart, (1954) 70 L.Q.R. 37 at 49–60.

[8] Chaps. 2 and 3.

[9] An unincorporated company must not be confused with an unlimited incorporated company. The members may, if they wish, form an incorporated company but accept personal responsibility for its debts. In such a case they will reap all the other advantages of corporate personality which an unincorporated association necessarily lacks: see Chap. 5, below.

[10] The Sun Insurance Society and the General Life Assurance Company did not adopt the modern form until as late as 1926 and 1927 respectively. Insurance companies formed before 1844 or in 1855–1856 can lawfully remain organised in the old way, and it seems that a few mutual assurance societies still are.

wish to carry on business in common with a view to profit they may either form themselves into a partnership or a company. Normally the only restraint on their freedom of choice is that, if their numbers are too great for that mutual trust appropriate to a partnership, they must form a company. An arbitrary maximum of 20 is imposed by section 716(1) of the Companies Act 1985 (re-enacting similar provisions in the earlier Acts). However, this maximum does not apply to firms of solicitors, accountants qualified to audit company accounts or members of a recognised stock exchange[11]; and the Secretary of State may by regulations exempt other professions.[12] Several unincorporated firms of solicitors or accountants now have well over 100 partners.[13]

Types of company

Incorporation under the Companies Act is not the only way in which a company may be formed. Three types of company are recognised by section 716:[14]

(i) *Registered companies*

There is first the company formed under the Act in the manner briefly described above. This is the typical and infinitely the most important kind of company at the present day and that with which this book is primarily concerned.

(ii) *Statutory companies*

Bodies with special types of object which it has been thought desirable to encourage may be formed under general public Acts, such as the Friendly Societies, the Industrial and Provident Acts, and the Building Societies Acts. Although some of these bodies, particularly building societies, or co-operative societies formed under the Industrial and Provident Societies Acts, closely resemble companies, they fall outside the scope of this book. A company properly so called may, however, be formed by a special Act. In the past, statutory incorporation by private Acts, of public utilities, such

---

[11] s.716(2). There is a further exemption in subs. (5) of bodies approved for the purposes of the Marine and Aviation (War Risks) Act 1952 as re-insurers of war risks. In other cases Lloyd's underwriting syndicates are so organised as to avoid the implication that their members are "associated" in a business. Lloyd's itself is now a statutory corporation but does not itself undertake insurance business.

[12] By various Partnerships (Unrestricted Size) Regs. several types of partnership have been exempted. These include patent agents, surveyors, auctioneers, valuers, estate agents, actuaries, chartered engineers and architects. In practice, membership of, or recognition by, a professional association is a condition of exemption.

[13] Similar limits and exceptions apply to limited partnerships; see s.717.

[14] Earlier Acts referred also to a fourth type, "cost-book" companies engaged in working tin mines in the Cornish "Stanneries," but this reference was repealed by s.28 of the Companies Consolidation (Consequential Provisions) Act 1985, it having finally been concluded that no such companies now exist.

as railway, gas, water and electricity undertakings, was comparatively common since the undertakings would require powers and monopolistic rights which needed a special legislative grant. During the 19th century therefore public general Acts[15] were passed providing for standard clauses deemed to be incorporated into the private Acts, unless expressly excluded. As a result of post-war nationalisation measures, most of these statutory companies were taken over by public boards or corporations set up by public Acts (but many of them have now been "privatised" and become registered companies). These boards and corporations also fall outside the scope of this book. But some statutory companies remain and others may be formed. The statute under which they are formed need not incorporate them but today this is invariably done.

(iii) *Chartered companies*

Section 716 thirdly refers to companies formed in pursuance of "letters patent."[16] This relates to companies granted a charter by the Crown under the Royal Prerogative or special statutory powers.[17] Such a charter normally confers corporate personality, but, as it was regarded as dubious policy for the Crown to confer a full charter or incorporation on an ordinary trading concern, it was empowered by the Trading Companies Act 1834 and the Chartered Companies Act 1837 to confer by letters patent all or any of the privileges of incorporation without actually granting a charter.[18] Today an ordinary trading concern would not contemplate trying to obtain a Royal Charter,[19] for incorporation under the Companies Acts would be far quicker and cheaper. In practice, therefore, this method of incorporation is used only by organisations formed for charitable, or quasi-charitable, objects, such as learned and artistic societies, schools and colleges, which want the greater prestige that a charter is thought to confer.

---

[15] The Companies Clauses Acts 1845–1889. These Acts, containing the general corporate powers and duties, were supplemented in the case of particular utilities by various other "Clauses Acts," *e.g.* the Lands Clauses Consolidation and Railways Clauses Consolidation Acts 1845; the Electric Lighting (Clauses) Act 1899, and numerous Waterworks Clauses Acts, and Gasworks Clauses Acts.

[16] This is, of course, the same expression as is used in connection with inventions and historically the two are closely connected. Just as the Crown might grant a monopoly of an invention by grant under its letters patent, so might it grant a charter of incorporation and the charter might confer a monopoly of trading in a particular territory.

[17] Under many ad hoc statutes the Crown has been granted power to grant charters in cases falling outside its prerogative powers. Moreover, by the Chartered Companies Acts 1837 and 1884, the prerogative was extended by empowering the Crown to grant charters for a limited period and to extend them. Thus the B.B.C. charter was for 10 years and has been prolonged from time to time.

[18] The Stock Exchange, when revising its "deed of settlement" constitution in the light of the City of London's "Big Bang," at one time proposed to apply for privileges under the latter Act, but instead registered under Part XXII, Chap. II of the Act.

[19] There are, however, still a few old-established trading companies incorporated by charter.

Many such organisations remain unincorporated for, as Maitland pointed out in his famous essay *Trust and Corporation*,[20] until recent years England, in contrast with the Continental countries, made little use of corporations in connection with associations for purposes other than those of trade, preferring to rely on the English invention of the trust. By the trust, learned societies, clubs, and professional bodies (like the Inns of Court, Lloyd's and the Stock Exchange) could function satisfactorily without incorporation by vesting their property in a small body of trustees.[21] Many of the more important and wealthy, such as the leading public schools, colleges and universities, obtained Royal Charters, while others, as we have seen, became subject to special legislation. But many societies, clubs and professional bodies (including the Inns of Court) remain unincorporated to this day.[22]

Although this book is primarily concerned with companies registered under the Companies Act 1985 (or one of the earlier Companies Acts and thus subject to the provisions of the 1985 Act[23]) it should be pointed out that certain provisions of that Act may apply to the other types of company previously mentioned and, indeed, to other bodies as well. Thus under section 718, certain "unregistered companies" are subject to the provisions specified in Schedule 22 if incorporated and having a principal place of business in Great Britain. Further, under Part XXIII a company incorporated outside Great Britain which establishes a place of business here must comply with the obligations of that Part.[24]

The functions of company legislation

Company legislation has two main functions: (i) enabling and (ii) regulatory. The enabling function empowers people to do what they could not otherwise achieve—namely to create a body with a distinct corporate personality. The regulatory function prescribes the conditions which have to be complied with to obtain incorporation and the rules that thereafter have to be observed to protect members, creditors and the public against the dangers inherent in such a body.

In respect of neither function, and particularly the second, is the Companies Act 1985, despite its vast size,[25] a complete codification of

---

[20] *Collected Papers*, Vol. III, p. 321, *Selected Essays* (ed. Hazeltine), p. 141.
[21] Until the legislation of the late 19th century, so did building societies, friendly societies, industrial and provident societies and trade unions. Even now some of these remain unincorporated and still rely primarily on the trust.
[22] Lloyd's became incorporated by statute in 1871.
[23] See Part XXII of the Act.
[24] See Chap. 11 at pp. 193–295 below.
[25] It originally consisted of 747 sections and was supplemented by the Company Securities (Insider Dealing) Act (19 sections), Business Names Act (11 sections) and Companies Consolidation (Consequential Provisions) Act (35 sections and 2 Schedules) also enacted in 1985 as part of the consolidation exercise.

English Company Law.[26] It is merely a consolidation of statutory provisions in the former principal Act of 1948, and in four subsequent major Companies Acts and other legislation. And, unhappily, it immediately ceased to be even a complete consolidation because subsequent Acts repealed and replaced many of its provisions and added many more. Behind it is a residual body of law and equity where some of the fundamental principles are still to be found.[27] However, there are now few of those general principles which are not affected in some way by the extremely detailed provisions of the Act which exceeds in bulk that of the companies' legislation anywhere else and astonishes our partners in the EC. Their legislation is expressed in relatively general terms which the courts are left to interpret purposefully; ours, even to a greater extent than in other common law countries, is expressed in meticulous detail attempting to cover every conceivable eventuality, and thus to become "judge-proof" when interpreted literally. Contrary to what an earlier generation was taught at Law School, in the Civil Law countries judges have greater freedom to make law (albeit on the basis of codified general principles) while in the United Kingdom it is increasingly made by statute and judges are inhibited from developing new principles by the extent and detail of the statutory intervention.

THE FUNCTIONS OF COMPANIES

Inadequacy of legal definitions

At the beginning of this chapter it was said that "company" implied an association of a number of persons for a common object, that object normally being the economic gain of its members. But it is no longer practicable to restrict consideration to trading concerns. In the last 100 years incorporation has become so easy and so cheap that many non-profit-making bodies, which would hitherto have remained unincorporated, have become registered under the Companies Acts. Far from being designed to secure the economic profit of their members, these companies expressly prohibit it, and between them and normal trading companies there is nothing in common beyond the fact that they both adopt the same legal framework within which to function.[28]

[26] For an attempt at a complete codification in a Commonwealth country with a company law based on the English model, see Ghana's Companies Code 1963 (Act 179). This was based on a report by the author: *Final Report of the Commission of Enquiry into the Working and Administration of the Company Law of Ghana* (Accra 1961).

[27] In fact, since the Acts apply to Scotland as well as to England and Wales, the statutory rules are superimposed on two distinct common law systems. In some respects these differ widely. This book is primarily concerned with English (not Scottish) company law.

[28] As we shall see, the legal framework is modified slightly to meet their particular needs: below, p. 11.

Even as regards trading companies our description was legalistic rather than realistic. No doubt many of the smaller companies may properly be described as associations of a number of persons for the common object of mutual profit; if two partners convert their business into a limited company they may well continue to carry on business in common, just as they did before the incorporation. But this is not necessarily an accurate description even of small companies. A sole trader may convert his business into a company and, although he must initially bring in at least one other person,[29] that person need have no beneficial interest in the business and need take no part in running it. In such a case, the association of a number of persons is a legal fiction.

More remarkable is the unreality of this description when applied to large public companies. A holder of 100 shares in, say, Imperial Chemical Industries is a member of the company but it is fantasy to describe him as associating with the other members in running it. The running of the business is left to the directors, or probably to the managing directors, and the shareholder, although a member, is in economic reality but not in the eyes of the law, a mere lender of capital, on which he hopes for a return but without any effective control over the borrower.

The legal implications of this development were first explored in the United States by A. A. Berle and G. C. Means in their *The Modern Corporation and Private Property*,[30] which drew attention to the revolutionary change thus brought about in our traditional conceptions of the nature of property. Today the great bulk of industrial enterprise is in the hands not of individual entrepreneurs but of large public companies in which many individuals have property rights as shareholders and to the capital of which they have directly or indirectly contributed. Direct or indirect investment in companies probably constitutes the most important single item of property, but whether this property brings profit to its "owners" no longer depends on their energy and initiative but on that of the management from which they are divorced. The modern shareholder in a public company has ceased to be a quasi-partner and has become instead simply a supplier of capital. If he invests in the older forms of private property, such as a farm or his own shop, he becomes tied to that property.[31] The modern public company meets the need for a new type of property in which the relationship between the owner and the property plays little part, so that the owner can recover his wealth when he needs it without removing it from the enterprise which requires it indefinitely. "The separation of ownership from management and control in the corporate system has performed this

---

29 Some other countries have recognised that this is pointless and permit the formation of a one-man company as an EC Directive will require us to do.
30 New York, 1933 (reprinted in 1968 with a new preface).
31 *Berle & Means*, p. 284.

essential step in securing liquidity."[32] The modern public company is therefore one further piece of machinery (like the trust) whereby the property of individuals is managed by other individuals. In so far as there is any true association in the modern public company it is between management and workers rather than between the shareholders *inter se* or between them and the management. But the fact that the workers form an integral part of the company is largely ignored by the law.[33]

The three functions of the modern company

From a functional viewpoint there are today three distinct types of company:—

1. *Companies formed for purposes other than the profit of their members, i.e.* those formed for social, charitable or quasi-charitable purposes. In this case incorporation is merely a more modern and convenient substitute for the trust.

2. *Companies formed to enable a single trader or a small body of partners to carry on a business.* In these companies, incorporation is a device for personifying the business and, normally, divorcing its liability from that of its members despite the fact that the members retain control and share the profits.

3. *Companies formed in order to enable the investing public to share in the profits of an enterprise without taking any part in its management.* In this last type, which is economically (but not numerically) by far the most important, the company is again a device analogous to the trust, but this time it is designed to facilitate the raising and putting to use of capital by enabling a large number of owners to entrust it to a small number of expert managers.

For the first of these classes the Companies Act provides the company limited by guarantee. For the second and third it provides the company limited by shares. It also provides for the possibility of registering as an unlimited company (with or without a share capital) but as, in practice, great and perhaps exaggerated:[34] importance is placed on the advantage of limitation of liability this is rarely resorted to except where the nature of the business is such that though incorporation is permissible, limited liability is not.

[32] *Ibid.* 285.
[33] See, however, Companies Act 1985 ss.309 and 719, Insolvency Act 1986, s.187, and Chapter 4. at pp. 73, 74 below.
[34] The members of a private company (or such of them as are directors) will find that they will be required to give personal guarantees to those who grant formal credit facilities to the company—thus rendering the limitation on liability illusory.

Guarantee companies

The Companies Act does not permit a company to be created in which the members are free from any liability whatsoever, but, as an alternative to limiting their contribution to the amount payable on their shares, it enables them to agree that in the event of liquidation they will, if required, subscribe an agreed amount. The Act recognises two forms of company limited by guarantee, namely, the guarantee company without a share capital and the guarantee company with a share capital. The former is the guarantee company in its pure form, whereas the latter is something of a hybrid. Little use was made of the hybrid form and the power to form such a company, or for a pure guarantee company to convert to one with a share capital, was abolished by the Companies Act 1980.[35] But the pure form was, and is, widely used by charitable and quasi-charitable organisations (such as schools, colleges and the "Friends" of museums and picture galleries) since incorporation with limited liability is often more convenient and less risky than a trust. A division of the undertaking into shares is inappropriate since no sharing of profits is contemplated and the incorporators may not wish initially to put any money into the concern as they would have to if they subscribed for shares. The members are under no liability so long as the company remains a going concern; they are liable, to the extent of their guarantees[36] only if the company is wound up and a contribution is needed to enable its debts to be paid.[37]

Companies limited by shares

A guarantee company is, however, unsuitable where the primary object is to carry on a business for profit and to divide that profit among the members. Just as a partnership agreement will need to prescribe the shares of the partners, so will a company's constitution need to define the shares of its members, and if these shares are to be transferable it will be convenient for them to be expressed in comparatively small denominations. Thus if the initial capital is to be £1,000 this will normally be divided into 1000 shares of £1 each, even though there may initially be only two or three members. The members who subscribe for the shares will be under a duty to pay the company for them in money or money's worth, and the company is accordingly said to be "limited by shares," that is to say, the

[35] Now 1985 Act s.1(4). But a small number of such companies remain (for example theatre clubs and management companies for blocks of flats of which the tenants are members).
[36] Which, in practice, are minimal; usually only £1.
[37] In contrast, a member of one of the surviving guarantee companies with a share capital may be under a two-fold liability—as shareholder to pay up the price of his shares and, on winding up, as guarantor.

members' liability[38] to contribute towards the company's debts is limited to the nominal value of the shares for which they have subscribed, and once the shares have been "paid up" they are under no further liability. A fundamental distinction between this type of company and the pure guarantee company is that the law assumes that its working capital will be, to some extent at any rate, contributed by the members; their contributions float the company on its launching and are not a mere *tabula in naufragio* to which creditors may cling when the company sinks.

Public and private companies

The company limited by shares can be used whether the company is to be a small family concern or a large organisation to which the public is to be invited to contribute capital, but obviously some of the safeguards required in the latter case in the interests of the public investor, can be dispensed with in the former. In recognition of this the Companies (Consolidation) Act 1908 exempted from some of the normal requirements a "private company" which it defined as one which (a) limited the membership to 50, (b) restricted the right to transfer shares and (c) prohibited any invitation to the public of its shares. Companies not coming within this definition were normally described as "public companies."

This definition survived until the Companies Act 1980 although it had proved quite inadequate to distinguish small family concerns from other, so-called public, companies;[39] and although the two most prized advantages afforded private companies[40] had been removed by the Companies Act 1967.[41] However, the 1980 Act, implementing the EC Second Company Law Directive, adopted the more satisfactory approach of defining the public company as a company limited by shares (or by guarantee and having a share capital[42]) whose memorandum of association states that it is to be a public company and in relation to which the provisions of the Companies Act as to registration or re-registration are complied with.[43] These provisions

[38] In the case of private companies this liability may in practice be illusory as there is no minimum nominal value of shares or of total share capital. A company (estate agents) has been registered with a share capital of 1/2d. divided into two 1/4d. shares!

[39] A further attempt to achieve this aim was made by the Companies Act 1948, which sub-divided private companies into "exempt" and "non-exempt," but this produced hideous complications and capricious results and, in accordance with the recommendations of the Jenkins Committee (Cmnd. 1749, paras. 55–63), was abandoned by the 1967 Act, s.2.

[40] Exemption from filing accounts and from the prohibition on loans to directors.

[41] 1967 Act s.2. But the exemption from filing accounts continues to apply to unlimited companies unless they are part of a group with limited companies or are promoters of trading stamp schemes: 1985 Act, s.254 (as inserted by the 1989 Act). And now "small" limited companies need only file a modified balance sheet and no profit and loss account and "medium-sized" companies a balance sheet and a modified profit and loss account: 1985 Act ss.246–249 and Sched. 8 (as substituted by the 1989 Act).

[42] New companies of this type cannot be formed: see above.

[43] See now 1985 Act s.1(3).

prescribe that the suffix to its name must be "public limited company"[44] (or its abbreviation "plc"[45]) instead of "limited,"[46] and that before it can do business it must have a prescribed minimum issued and paid up share capital.[47] All other companies are private companies. They are not subject to the minimum capital requirements but normally it is a criminal offence to issue an advertisement offering their shares or debentures.[48] If limited companies, the traditional suffix "Limited" or "Ltd." normally remains mandatory.[49]

The result is that only some 11,100 companies are now registered as public ones while there are over 998,700 private companies.[50] Some of the latter are large both in assets and in number of members (for the former limit of 50 on that number has now gone and the attempt to restrict private companies to small family concerns has been finally abandoned). On the other hand, the differences in the legal rules relating to public and private companies, which had by 1980 become minimal, have grown as a result of the Acts of 1980, 1981 and 1989 and seem likely to become greater in the future.[51] Moreover the Act, in relation to financial disclosure, draws a three-fold distinction between large, medium and small companies.[52] This is part of a continuing effort to relieve small businesses of unnecessary burdens. Unhappily an attempt in 1981 to tackle the problem by providing a simpler form of incorporation for really small firms was abortive.[53]

THE COMPANY'S CONSTITUTION

Before proceeding further it may be useful to indicate in general terms the type of constitution adopted by companies to enable them to perform their economic or social functions as described above.

Today a company's original constitution is very much a matter for its promoters. This was not always so. When incorporation could be

44 s.25(1).
45 s.27.
46 Welsh equivalents can be adopted if its registered office is to be in Wales: ss.25(1) and 27.
47 ss.117 and 118.
48 Financial Services Act 1986 ss.143(3), 170 and 171(3) (which replace the repealed s.81 of the 1985 Act).
49 Once again with Welsh equivalents: 1985 ss.25(2) and 27.
50 *Companies in 1989-90* (HMSO), Table A2. But there has been a steady rise in the proportion of public companies since 1984 from 0.4 per cent. to 1.1 per cent.: *ibid.*
51 If only because some of the EC Company law Directives which we shall have to implement need be applied only to public companies.
52 See n. 41 above, and the de-regulatory steps taken by ss.113–117 of the 1989 Act in relation to private companies in general.
53 See *A New Form of Incorporation for Small Firms* (1981 Cmnd. 8171). It received insufficient support to encourage the Government to proceed further. But legislation on somewhat similar lines has been enacted in South Africa which appears to have led to a substantial increase in incorporations each year with twice as many opting for the new form of "close" rather than the traditional "private" company. It has also aroused interest in Australia.

obtained only through a special statute or charter the promoters could petition for what they wanted but it rested with the legislature or the Crown to decide what they should actually have. In theory, this is still the case so far as statutory and chartered companies are concerned, but in practice the initiative has shifted to the promoters, who will draft and promote their private Bill or append a draft charter to their petition, and, although this may be rejected or amended, they will probably either fail completely or obtain very much what they themselves have put forward. And as regards a company registered under the Companies Act—overwhelmingly the most common type—the promoters have almost complete freedom, provided that the constitution is set out in the statutory form. This is because the modern company—as we shall see in the next two chapters—developed mainly through the unincorporated partnership, the constitution of which naturally depended on the agreement of the partners.

The modern registered company has, however, inherited one feature from statutory and chartered corporations, namely that its constitution has to be set out in two separate documents, its memorandum of association (corresponding to the statute or charter) and its articles of association (corresponding to the bye-laws which, in practice, the statute or charter would empower the corporation to make to supplement its provisions). This makes sense if it is desired to ensure that the basic constitution of the body corporate shall be inflexible and not alterable without the consent of Parliament or the Crown. In theory that inflexibility applies to registered companies. The memorandum of association, laying down the company's basic constitution, is alterable only to the extent permitted by the Companies Act[54] and, under the early Companies Acts, the company itself had virtually no power to effect alterations. But today the constitution has become much more flexible and in one way or another every provision of the memorandum (except that fixing the country in which its registered office is to be situated) can be altered unless the memorandum expressly provides to the contrary. Moreover, the memorandum need only state the company's name, objects, domicile, share capital (if any) and, if such be the case, that the liability of the members is limited and that it is a public company. Everything else is regarded as a matter of administration to be dealt with in the second document, the articles of association. The provisions of this, subject to some ill-defined restraints on abuse,[55] are alterable by a special resolution of the company;[56] *i.e.* by a resolution in general meeting passed by a three-fourths majority of

---

[54] s.2(7).
[55] See Chaps. 20 and 22. These restraints stop far short of any principle that "bye-laws must be reasonable."
[56] s.9.

members voting after at least 21 days' notice has been given of the intention to pass it as a special resolution.[57]

The company's organs

The form of articles of association has become largely standardised under the influence of the model tables formerly appended to the Companies Acts and now prescribed by regulations[58] and of specialist company lawyers and books of precedents. They may, and do, contain regulations on many matters—on the share capital, meetings, dividends, accounts and the like—but the most important are those relating to the company's organs.

A company has two primary organs, the members in general meeting and the board of directors. Here, again, an analogy may be found in constitutional law. In a parliamentary democracy such as ours, legislative sovereignty rests with Parliament, while administration is left to the executive Government, subject to a measure of control by Parliament through its power to force a change of Government. It is much the same with a company; except, of course, that a company is not sovereign but has a limited competence only. Within these limits, supreme rule-making authority (in theory) rests with a general meeting of the members. Generally a simple majority vote suffices, but in some cases a larger majority or other special formalities may be required. Thus the Companies Act provides that certain things can only be done by an extraordinary resolution, which requires a three-fourths majority, and others by a special resolution which requires longer than the normal notice, and, again, a three-fourths majority, and the constitution may entrench certain rights still further by embodying them in the memorandum and providing that they shall be unalterable.[59]

Although it would be constitutionally possible for the company in general meeting to exercise all the powers of the company, it clearly would not be practicable (except in the case of a small company which is in reality an incorporated partnership or sole trader) for day-to-day administration to be undertaken by such a cumbersome piece of machinery. Hence the articles will provide for a board of directors[60] and will say what powers are to be performed by the

---

[57] s.378(2).

[58] Companies (Tables A to F) Regulations 1984 (S.I. No. 805 as slightly amended by S.I. No. 1052). These include also model memoranda of association but unless and until the Act is amended to provide (as some Commonwealth Acts do) that a registered company has the capacity of a natural person, no memorandum will be found with an "objects clause" as short and sweet as those in these models. But see s.3A, inserted by the 1989 Act, which is intended to encourage such brevity.

[59] s.17(2).

[60] The name "directors" will not necessarily be used; in many guarantee companies the equivalent officers will be called "governors"; see the definition of "directors" in s.741(1).

board and how it is to be appointed and changed. Like the Government, the directors will be answerable to the "Parliament" constituted by the general meeting, but in practice (again like the Government) they will exercise as much control over it as it exercises over them. And the modern practice is to confer on the directors the right to exercise all the company's powers, except such as the Act, the memorandum and articles or a special resolution expressly provide must be exercised in general meeting.[61]

Powers which are strictly legislative are not in general affected by this delegation, for the Companies Act in section 9 provides that an alteration of the articles requires a special resolution of the company in general meeting. Nevertheless, the dividing line between legislation and administration is difficult to draw, and just as the modern Legislature finds it necessary to delegate to the Executive many powers which are of a legislative nature, so will the directors of a modern company undertake considerably more than detailed administration; it is certainly they who will make most policy decisions. Indeed, their position *vis-à-vis* the company is, in many ways, more powerful then that of the Government *vis-à-vis* the Parliament at Westminster. The theory of parliamentary sovereignty means that Parliament could (in theory) override anything done by the Government notwithstanding that this was clearly within its competence as a matter of pure administration. So originally could the members in general meeting; in fact the directors seem to have been treated as their agents. The modern theory, however, is somewhat different, for, provided that the act is within the powers delegated to the directors, the members in general meeting normally cannot interfere with it.[62] The most they can do is to dismiss the directorate and appoint others in their place, or alter the articles so as to restrict the powers of the directors for the future.

This wide delegation of the company's powers is, however, to the directors acting as a board, not to the individual directors. But, here again, it will obviously be impractical in the case of large companies for day-to-day management to take place at formal board meetings which will probably be held not more than once a quarter. In the meantime other officers of the company will have to ensure that the decisions of the board are implemented and its policy carried out; under the board and directly or indirectly responsible to and appointed by the board will be found the management and secretariate. In all probability some at least of the managers and perhaps the secretary, will also be directors, for the normal practice today is to provide that directors may be appointed to other paid offices in the company.[63] And, in practice, these officers will do much

61 Table A, Art. 70.
62 See further Chap. 7, pp. 147–153, below.
63 Table A, Art. 84.

more than merely carry out the decisions and policy of the board; they will themselves make policy decisions. In fact, many, and perhaps most, of the company's powers which have been primarily delegated to the board will be subdelegated by them to the managing director or directors; a provision enabling this to be done has become common form in articles.[64]

It is in these managers that in reality we find the closest parallel to the executive government; this, indeed, is recognised by the common use of the expression "business executives" to describe, not directors as such, but the higher ranks of managers. The business of the directorate is coming more and more to be recognised as one of laying down policy in the most general terms and exercising an equally general supervision over the way in which it is carried out; everything else is left to the managers assisted by the secretariate.

These distinctions between the functions of members in general meeting, boards of directors and management must not be exaggerated. They are of importance only in the case of the public company or the larger private company. In the one- or two-man private company the factual position will be the same as in a partnership, with the same few people exercising all these functions.[65] In practice they will probably not clearly distinguish between their actions in their various capacities and normally this will not matter much.

One of the main problems facing company law is to provide in relation to public companies an adequate system of checks and balances between the various organs—and here again there is an obvious analogy in the field of government. For the present, however, it is only necessary to point out that this division of functions between separate organs is one of the features which distinguishes a company from a partnership and which enables the public company to fulfil its economic role.

Interpretation of the constitution

The analogies which have been drawn with constitutional law must not be taken to imply that the courts, in interpreting the constitution of a company, adopt the same "large and liberal interpretation" that may be regarded as appropriate when construing the written constitution of a state.[66] Though they will strive to adopt a construction which gives "business efficacy"[67] to the company's regulations, they are bound by the strict letter of the words used and,

64 Table A, Art. 72.
65 Hence it was not until 1948 that a private company was required to have any directors. Only one is essential in their case—public companies must have at least two: 1985 Act, s.282—but a sole director may not also be the secretary: s.283(2) and (4).
66 *Edwards* v. *Att.-Gen. for Canada* [1930] A.C. 124, P.C., at pp. 136-137.
67 *Holmes* v. *Keyes* [1959] Ch. 199, C.A., *per* Jenkins L.J. at p. 215.

if these words are unambiguous, an argument that they produce inconvenience,[68] or even absurdity, is unlikely to succeed.[69] The result is to produce even greater strictness than in normal cases of contract, for the written regulations cannot be rectified by the court even if they are not in accordance with the parties' intention.[70]

As already mentioned, the wording of clauses in memoranda and articles has become largely standardised and for this reason the courts will be reluctant to disturb a decision on construction which has stood for some time and upon which the title to property may depend.[71] This, however, has not always deterred them from overruling such a decision if satisfied that it is erroneous.[72]

[68] *Worcester Corsetry Ltd.* v. *Witting* [1936] Ch. 640, C.A., at p. 646.
[69] *Grundt* v. *Great Boulder Proprietary Mines Ltd.* [1948] Ch. 145, C.A. " 'Absurdity' . . . like public policy, is a very unruly horse": Greene M.R. at p. 158. See also Vaisey J. in *Rayfield* v. *Hands* [1960] Ch. 1 at p. 4 and *cf. Bushell* v. *Faith* [1970] A.C. 1099, H.L.
[70] *Scott* v. *Frank Scott (London) Ltd.* [1940] Ch. 794, C.A. Within limits they can, of course, be altered for the future if the necessary majority can be obtained for passing a special resolution.
[71] *Re Warden & Hotchkiss Ltd.* [1945] Ch. 270, C.A.
[72] For a strong example, see the overruling of *Re William Metcalfe Ltd.* [1933] Ch. 142, C.A. by *Scottish Insurance Corpn.* v. *Wilsons & Clyde Coal Co.* [1949] A.C. 462, H.L., and *Re Isle of Thanet Electricity Supply Co.* [1950] Ch. 161, C.A. See below, p. 371.

CHAPTER 2

HISTORY OF COMPANY LAW TO 1825

This book is concerned with modern company law, but there are some branches of modern English company law which cannot be properly understood without reference to their historical background, and company law is certainly one of them; indeed, of all branches of the law it is perhaps the one least readily understood except in relation to its historical development, and a somewhat extended account of which is therefore essential.[1] Such an account falls conveniently into three periods: (1) until 1720 when the Bubble Act was passed; (2) from 1720 until the Bubble Act was repealed in 1825; and (3) from 1825 until the present day. The present chapter deals with the first two of these periods.

Early forms of commercial association

Various forms of association were known to medieval law and as regards some of them the concept of incorporation was early recognised. At first, however, incorporation seems to have been used only in connection with ecclesiastical and public bodies, such as chapters, monasteries and boroughs, which had corporate personality conferred upon them by a charter from the Crown or were deemed by prescription to have received such a grant.[2]

[1] This account owes much to Formoy, *The Historical Foundations of Modern Company Law* (Lond. 1923); C. A. Cooke, *Corporation, Trust and Company* (Manchester, 1950); Holdsworth, *History of English Law* Vol. 8, pp. 192-222; *Anglo-American Essays in Legal History*, Vol. 3, pp. 161-255 (Boston, Mass. 1909); W. R. Scott, *Joint Stock Companies to 1720* (Camb. 1909-1912)—especially Vol. 1; C. T. Carr, *Law of Corporations* (Camb. 1905) and *Select Charters of Trading Corporations* (Selden Society, 1913); C. M. Schmitthoff, *The Origin of the Joint Stock Company* (1939) 3 Toronto L.J. 74-96; A. B. DuBois, *The English Business Company after the Bubble Act, 1720-1800* (N.Y. 1938); H. A. Shannon, *The Coming of General Limited Liability*, and *The First 5,000 Limited Companies and their Duration* (1931-1932) Econ. Hist., Vol. 11, 267 and 396; B. C. Hunt, *The Development of the Business Corporation in England, 1800-1867* (Harvard Economic Studies, 1936). The works of DuBois and Hunt are particularly fascinating accounts of the formative years which largely render obsolete earlier accounts of the periods to which they relate. Much old learning is to be found in J. Grant, *Law of Corporations* (Lond. 1850).

[2] While it is doubtful whether English law has ever unequivocally committed itself to the "fiction" theory of corporation, it seems to have fairly consistently adopted the "concession" theory—namely, that incorporation depends upon a State grant. But it has recognised the power of foreign States and it may be that until the Reformation a grant of incorporation could be conferred on an English religious body by the Pope. That incorporation might be granted by statute appears never to have been doubted (Holdsworth, H.E.L., Vol. 3, p. 476) but in fact it was not until the latter part of the 18th century that it became the practice for Acts of Parliament actually to effect the incorporation. Until then statutes were used only to amplify the royal prerogative by authorising the Crown to confer a charter of incorporation with privileges beyond those which the Crown alone could confer (this was done, for example, in the case of the Bank of England and the South Sea Co.). DuBois (*op. cit.* pp. 87 and 88) quotes examples of incorporation granted by Scottish burghs during the 18th century when the question also arose of the extent to which the royal

—continued on next page

In the commercial sphere the principal medieval associations were the guilds of merchants, organisations which had few resemblances to modern companies but corresponded roughly to our trade protection associations, with the ceremonial and mutual fellowship of which we can see relics in the modern Freemasons and Livery Companies. Many of these guilds in due course obtained charters from the Crown, mainly because this was the only effective method of obtaining for their members a monopoly of any particular commodity or branch of trade. Incorporation as a convenient method of distinguishing the rights and liabilities of the association from those of its members was hardly needed since each member traded on his own account subject only to obedience to the regulations of the guild.

Trading on joint account, as opposed to individual trading subject to the rules of the guild, was carried on through partnerships, of which two types were known to the medieval law merchant. The first of these, the *commenda*, was in fact a cross between a partnership and a loan whereby a financier advanced a sum of money to the active trader upon terms that he should share in the profits of the enterprise, his position being similar to that of a sleeping partner but with no liability beyond that of the capital originally advanced. In continental law the *commenda* developed into the *société en commandite*, a form of association which has played, and still plays, an important part in the commercial life of those countries which adopted it. But in England it never took root, possibly because we lagged behind the Continent in book-keeping technique.[3] Had it become an accepted institution of English law the history of our company law might well have been very different, but in fact it did not become legalised here until 1907[4] by which time complete limitation of liability could be obtained easily and cheaply by incorporation under the Companies Act.

The other type of partnership was the *societas*, a more permanent form of association which developed into the present-day partnership, each partner being an agent of the others and liable to the full extent of his private fortune for partnership debts. The full implications of the partnership relationship were not fully worked out by courts of equity until the eighteenth and nineteenth centuries but these two main elements of agency and unlimited liability were already appreciated during this period.

Merchant adventurers

The first type of English organisation to which the name "company" was generally applied was that adopted by merchant

---

[2] *continued from previous page*
prerogative could be delegated to colonial governors. As Sir Cecil Carr pointed out long ago (*Law of Corporations*, pp. 173 *et seq.*) the concession theory has worn somewhat thin now that incorporation can be obtained by mere registration.

[3] See Cooke, *op. cit.* p. 46.

[4] Limited Partnerships Act 1907. It was adopted in Ireland by statute in 1781 and it seemed for a time that it might take root in Scotland: DuBois, *op. cit.* pp. 224–225.

adventurers for trading overseas. Royal charters conferring privileges on such companies are found as early as the fourteenth century,[5] but it was not until the expansion of foreign trade and settlement in the sixteenth century that they become common. The earliest types were the so-called "regulated companies" which were virtually extensions of the guild principle into the foreign sphere and which retained much of the ceremonial and freemasonry of the domestic guilds. Each member traded with his own stock and on his own account, subject to obeying the rules of the company, and incorporation was not essential since the trading liability of each member would be entirely separate from that of the company and the other members. Charters were nevertheless obtained largely because of the need to acquire a monopoly of trade for members of the company and governmental power over the territory for the company itself.[6]

At a later stage, however, the partnership principle of trading on joint account was adopted by the regulated companies which became joint commercial enterprises instead of trade protection associations.[7] At first, in addition to the separate trading by each member with his own stock, and later instead of it, they started to operate on joint account and with a joint stock.

This process can be traced in the development of the famous East India Company,[8] which received its first charter in 1600, granting it a monopoly of trade with the Indies. Originally any member could carry on that trade privately, although there also existed a joint stock to which members could, if they wished, subscribe varying amounts. At first this joint stock and the profits made from it were redivided among the subscribers after each voyage. From 1614 onwards, however, the joint stock was subscribed for a period of years, and this practice subsisted until 1653 when a permanent joint stock was introduced. It was not until 1692 that private trading was finally forbidden to members. Until this date, therefore, the constitution of the East India Co. represents a compromise between a regulated company, formed primarily for the government of a particular trade, and the more modern type of company, designed to trade for the profits of its members. This new type was called a joint stock[9] company, a name which persists until the present day, although few of those who use it realise that it was adopted to distinguish the companies to which it relates from a once normal, but now obsolete, form.

---

[5] See C. T. Carr, *Select Charters of Trading Corporations* (Selden Society), pp. xi–xii.

[6] See the charter of the Levant Company (1600) in Hahlo, *A Casebook of Company Law* (2nd ed.), p. 8.

[7] For an account of this development and a comparison with similar developments on the Continent, see Schmitthoff (1939) 3 Toronto L.J., pp. 89–206.

[8] See Scott, *op. cit.* Vol. II, pp. 74 *et seq.*

[9] "Stock" is, of course, here used in the same sense as in "stock in trade" and not as in "stocks and shares."

Companies and incorporation

It was not until the second half of the seventeenth century that the differentiation between the two types of company was firmly established. Nor was there, until very much later, any clear distinction between unincorporated partnerships and incorporated companies. Many joint stock companies were originally formed as partnerships by agreement under seal, providing for the division of the undertaking into shares which were transferable by the original partners with greater or less freedom according to the terms of the partnership agreement. At this time there was no limit to the number of partners, but in fact they were generally small in number and additional capital was raised by "leviations," or calls on the existing members rather than by invitations to the public.

On the other hand, incorporation had certain clear advantages. A corporation was capable of existing in perpetuity, it could sue outsiders and its own members, and possession of a common seal facilitated the distinction between the acts of the company and those of its members. Although the transferability of shares was in practice procurable under a skilfully drafted deed of co-partnership, its legality, except under a power expressly conferred in a charter, was not free from doubt, for choses-in-action were not assignable at common law. However, the fact that shares were essentially a form of chose-in-action was not clearly recognised until later. The shares of the New River Company[10] were, for example, held to be realty,[11] and so they remained until the twentieth century.

Rather surprisingly the most important advantage of all those conferred by incorporation—limited liability—seems only to have been realised as an afterthought. The fact that an individual member of a corporation was not liable for its debts had been accepted in the case of non-trading corporations as early as the fifteenth century,[12] and, not without some doubts, it was eventually recognised at the end of this period in the case of trading companies.[13] But, although it

---

[10] Which originated in a statute of 1606 (3 Jac. 1, c. 18), was granted a charter in 1619, and became subject to no fewer than 13 later statutes culminating in the Metropolis Water Act 1902, which expressly preserved its shares as realty (s.9(1)) and which vested the water-supply part of the undertaking in the Metropolitan Water Board. In pursuance of a further statute the company registered under the Companies Acts in 1905 and later became an investment trust company. (The "new river," which it created still flows.) For a full history of the company, see Rudden, *The New River* (1985, Clarendon Press).

[11] *Townsend* v. *Ash* (1745) 3 Atk. 336. The theory seems to have been that a corporation held its assets on trust for its members; *cf Child* v. *Hudson's Bay Co.* (1723) 2 P. Wms. 207. Later equity went a stage further by recognising, both in partnerships and companies, an implied trust for conversion under which the shares became personalty irrespective of the nature of the firm's assets. In many charters and statutes of incorporation this conversion was expressly provided for; see Companies Clauses Consolidation Act 1845, s.7, and Companies Act 1985, s.182(1).

[12] Holdsworth, H.E.L., Vol. 3, 484.

[13] *Edmunds* v. *Brown & Tillard* (1668) 1 Lev. 237; *Salmon* v. *The Hamborough Co.* (1671) 1 Ch.Cas. 204, H.L.

was recognised, it appears at first to have been valued mainly because it avoided the risk of the company's property being seized in payment of the members' separate debts,[14] rather than as a method of enabling the members to escape liability for the company's debts. This doubtless was because many charters expressly conferred a power on the company to make "leviations" (or calls) on the members and it was by no means clear that a company did not have this power even in the absence of an express provision.[15] This being so, limited liability was illusory; the company as a person was liable to pay its debts and in order to raise money to do so it would make calls on its members. Moreover, the creditors, by a process resembling subrogation, could proceed directly against the members if the company refrained from taking the necessary action.[16] But legal ingenuity was not long in appreciating the possibilities of expressly excluding or limiting the company's power to make levies by agreement to that effect between the company and its members. Such agreements seem to have been in use by both incorporated and unincorporated companies, and the fact that they were effective only in the case of the former was probably not clearly grasped by lawyers and certainly not by investors.

Growth of domestic companies

By the middle of the seventeenth century powerful monopolistic companies were already coming to be regarded as anachronisms; it was realised that their governmental powers were properly the functions of the State itself and that their monopolies were an undue restraint on freedom of trade. Most of them atrophied; but some survived for a time by converting, as did the Levant and Russia companies, from the joint stock to the regulated form (a strange reversal of the normal trend designed to allow greater freedom to their members) and others, like the Royal Africa Company, by completely relinquishing their monopolies.[17] After the Revolution of 1688[18] it seems to have been tacitly assumed that the Crown's prerogative was limited to the right to grant a charter of

---

[14] See the common form provision in petitions for charters quoted by Carr, *Select Charters*, xvii, xviii.

[15] See DuBois, *op. cit.* 98 *et seq.*

[16] *Salmon v. The Hamborough Co.*, above. But for a criticism of this interpretation of the decision, see Jenkins [1975] Camb.L.J. 308.

[17] The Hudson's Bay Company did not do so until 1869 and still survives as a chartered company. The East India Co. also survived until the middle of the nineteenth century but as a State organ rather than as a trading concern.

[18] Previously it seems to have been assumed that the *Case of Monopolies* (1602) 11 Co.Rep. 84b, and the Statute of Monopolies 1623, had left unimpaired the Crown's power to grant a monopoly for the regulation of foreign trade and this power had been upheld by the H.L. in 1684 in *East India Co.* v. *Sandys*, 10 St.Tr. 371. But *cf. Horne* v. *Ivy* (1668) 1 Vent. 47, showing that the courts were already placing limitations on the extent of its exercise.

incorporation, and that any monopolistic or other special powers should be conferred by statute.[19]

The decline in the foreign-trading companies was, however, accompanied by an immense growth in those for domestic trade. Some of these were powerful corporations chartered under statutory powers (such as the Bank of England[20]) the objects of which resembled those of the public corporations of the present day, but most were public companies in the sense that they invited the participation of the investing public. As regards these, the close relation between incorporation and monopoly was still maintained, for most companies were incorporated in order to work a patent of monopoly granted to an inventor.[21]

By the end of the seventeenth century some idea had been gleaned of one of the primary functions of the company concept—the possibility of enabling the capitalist to combine with the entrepreneur. Share dealings were common and stock-broking was a recognised profession, the abuses of which the legislature sought to regulate as early as 1696.[22] But it would be entirely misleading to suggest that there was in any sense a company law; at the most there was an embryonic law of partnership which applied to those companies which had not become incorporated and, with modifications required by the terms of the charter and the nature of incorporation, to those which had. Both deeds of partnership (or "settlement," to use the later term) and charters owed much to the practices of the medieval guilds, particularly as regards the constitution of the governing body which generally consisted of a governor and assistant governors. From the end of the seventeenth century the term "directors" began to supersede "assistant governors." But the terminology varied and still varies.[23] It is interesting to note that although the invention of preference shares is generally attributed to the railway boom a century later, certain companies had already experimented with different classes of shares or of loan stock[24] (for the distinction between shares and debentures was not appreciated until much later).

The South Sea Bubble

The first and second decades of the eighteenth century were marked by an almost frenetic boom in company flotations which led

---

[19] Even earlier this had become the practice in the case of domestic companies requiring special powers; for example, the New River Co. (see n. 10, above).

[20] Incorporated, by charter preceded by statute, in 1694.

[21] See Cooke, *op. cit.* Chap. 4.

[22] 8 & 9 Wm. 3, c. 32. It is interesting to note that this legislation followed a report of the Commissioners for Trade (the forerunners of the Board (later the Department) of Trade;) which seems to be the first instance of this Department interesting itself in a branch of company law (see p. 35, below).

[23] Thus the Bank of England, the B.B.C. and most incorporated schools and colleges still employ the term "Governors," while some corporations use the expression "Managers."

[24] Scott, *op. cit.* Vol. I, pp. 364–365.

to the famous South Sea Bubble.[25] Most company promoters were not particularly fussy about whether they obtained charters (an expensive and dilatory process), and those who felt it desirable to give their projects this hallmark of respectability found it simpler and cheaper to acquire charters from moribund companies which were able to do a brisk trade therein.[26] An insurance company acquired the charters of the Mines Royal and the Mineral and Battery Works, and a company which proposed to lend money on land in Ireland and a banking partnership[27] in turn acquired the charter of the Sword Blade Company which had been formed to manufacture hollow sword blades.

Impetus was given to this boom by the grandiose scheme of the South Sea Company to acquire virtually the whole of the National Debt[28] (some £31m) by buying out the holders or persuading them to exchange their holdings for the company's stock, the theory being that the possession of an interest-bearing loan owed by the State was a basis upon which the company might raise vast sums to extend its trade. This theory was not necessarily unsound—it was indeed a logical extension of the principle upon which the Bank of England, and the South Sea Company itself, had been originally formed—but unfortunately the company had precious little trade to expand. Moreover, it had to pay dearly for its privileges by outbidding and outbribing the Bank of England.[29]

When the flood of speculative enterprises was at its height, Parliament decided to intervene to check the gambling mania which the Government had itself encouraged by sanctioning the South Sea Company's scheme. Its attempt was, however, somewhat inept. A House of Commons Resolution[30] of 27 April 1720 ignored the causes

[25] The literature on the Bubble crisis is, of course, immense; the most scholarly treatment is still that of Scott, *op. cit.* Vol. I, Chaps. XXI and XXII. For popular accounts, see Carswell, *The South Sea Bubble* (Lond. 1960), and Cowell, *The Great Swindle* (Lond. 1960).

[26] We cannot afford to scoff at our predecessors, for a trade is still done in dormant companies. Two centuries hence, a generation which, for tax reasons, was prepared to pay more for those with accumulated losses will probably appear just as ridiculous.

[27] Which thereupon issued "sword blade" notes and bonds, and acted as bankers for the South Sea Company.

[28] The company was originally formed, by charter preceded by statute, in 1711, to incorporate the holders of the floating debt in exchange for a monopoly of trade with South America, a right which the power of Spain rendered something of a *damnosa hereditas*. The extended scheme seems to have been inspired by the financial experiments known as the Mississippi System introduced in France, with equally disastrous results, by John Law.

[29] It is interesting to speculate on what might have happened had the Bank of England outbid the company. Perhaps it would have been the former whose bubble reputation was so soon pricked, and the latter which acquired the mantle of respectability (with the final canon of nationalisation) in fact worn by "the old lady of Threadneedle Street."

[30] H.C. Jour. XIX, 351. This resolution was based upon the Report of a Committee appointed on 22 Feb. to inquire into certain of the projects: for its Report, see *ibid.* pp. 341 *et seq.*

and merely emphasised the effects of the rash speculation by drawing attention to the numerous undertakings which were purporting to act as corporate bodies without legal authority, practices which "manifestly tend to the prejudices of the public trade and commerce of the Kingdom." This was followed by the so-called Bubble Act[31] of the same year, which also made no attempt to put joint stock companies on a proper basis so as to further industry and trade and protect investors. Exactly what it did is, however, somewhat obscure.

The main section, 18, repeated the Resolution of the House of Commons and provided that all such undertakings as were therein described, "tending to the common Grievance, Prejudice and Inconvenience of His Majesty's subjects," should be illegal and void. The section then proceeded to give particular examples, *viz.* the acting as a corporate body and the raising of transferable stock or the transfer of any shares therein without legal authority either by Act of Parliament or Crown charter, or acting or pretending to act under any obsolete charter. By section 21, brokers dealing in securities of illegal companies were to be liable to penalties. The remaining sections, however, exempted companies established before 24 June 1718 (which were therefore left to the common law, whatever that may have been), and also the East India and South Sea Companies and the two assurance companies authorised by the first part of the Act. Finally, in section 25, there was a vague proviso that nothing "shall extend . . . to prohibit or restrain the carrying on of any home or foreign trade in partnership in such manner as hath been hitherto usually and may be lawfully done according to the Laws of this Realm now in force."

This statute was our first attempt at a Companies Act[32] and it clearly reflected little credit on anyone concerned with it. As Holdsworth says,[33] "What was needed was an Act which made it easy for joint stock societies to adopt a corporate form and, at the same time, safeguarded both the shareholders in such societies and the public against frauds and negligence in their promotion and management. What was passed was an Act which deliberately made it difficult for joint stock societies to assume a corporate form and contained no rules at all for the conduct of such societies, if, and when, they assumed it." But in fact the authorities were faced with a new phenomenon and had no clear idea of the issues involved. Nor is it altogether fair to blame them; a further 120 years' experience was

[31] 31 6 Geo. 1, c. 18. This prolix and confusing statute, which, as Maitland said, "seems to scream at us from the Statute Book" (*Collected Papers*, Vol. 3, p. 390), is divided into two parts. The first (ss.1–17) authorised the incorporation of the London and Royal Exchange Assurance Companies with a monopoly of the corporate insurance of marine risks. It is with the later sections only that we are at present concerned.

[32] Or, perhaps, more properly, a Prevention of Fraud (Investments) Act, such as that of 1939 or 1958.

[33] H.E.L., Vol. 8, 219–220.

to be needed before anything on the right lines was enacted, and even today we find it necessary to amend our company law every few years. It was obviously too much to expect the Parliament of 1720 to rush through a Companies Act comparable to that of 1985 or even 1844. Where they seem most blameworthy is not for what they omitted to do, but for the vagueness of what they in fact did, and when the courts were called upon to interpret it they found it vague indeed. But this they were not called upon to do for many years.

The Bubble bursts

The passage of the Bubble Act, to which publicity was given by Royal Proclamation, and the events leading up to it must obviously have done much to sap public confidence. But what precipitated the disastrous collapse of 1720 was the institution of proceedings against some of the companies operating under obsolete charters with a view to these being forfeited.[34] This, as might perhaps have been foreseen,[35] led to a widespread panic from which the South Sea Company itself never fully recovered.[36] In June 1720 its stock had stood at over 1,000 per cent. and immediately before the issue of the writs it was still at 850 per cent. A month later it had fallen to 390 and by the end of the year it was quoted at 125. The Government was too much involved to allow the company to crash completely,[37] but the subsequent investigations disclosed fraud and corruption (in which members of the Government and the royal household were implicated) and it never fully recovered. With it fell many of its contemporaries, which, not being regularly chartered nor so fortunate as to have friends in high places, burst like the bubbles they were. But, although they disappeared, they were not forgotten, for public confidence in joint stock companies and their securities was destroyed so effectively that it was three-quarters of a century before there was a comparable boom. If the legislators had intended the Bubble Act to suppress companies they had succeeded beyond their reasonable expectations; if, as seems more probable, they had intended to

34 For an account of these proceedings and an attempted refutation of the generally accepted theory that they were instituted by the South Sea Company or its directors, see (1952) 68 L.Q.R. 214.

35 Although the legitimacy of the birth of the South Sea Company was beyond reproach, it was employing as its bankers a company incorporated under the Sword Blade Charter. The failure of these bankers was one of the factors which frustrated the efforts to arrest the panic by an agreement between the South Sea Company and the Bank of England.

36 The third volume of Scott, *op. cit.* contains a graph showing the fluctuations in the shares of the South Sea Company, the East India Company and the Bank of England between May and September 1720.

37 In the words of Holdsworth (H.E.L., Vol. 2, p. 210) it "dragged out a struggling existence till 1807; and the faded splendours of its South Sea House survived long enough to secure immortality in the Essays of Elia." Later that House became for a time the home of the Baltic Exchange, and a building in the City of London bearing the name South Sea House survived the blitz of the Second World War more successfully than the company survived the financial "blitz" of an earlier century.

protect investors from ruin and to safeguard the South Sea Company, they had failed miserably.

Prosecutions under the Act were few; only one[38] is reported until the beginning of the nineteenth century.[39] Nevertheless it is clear that the Bubble Act was for long a sword of Damocles which exercised a restraining influence as potent as the memory of the great slump. DuBois's researches[40] have shown how existing companies and the promoters of new enterprises took counsel's opinion on the application to them of the Act, and it is to this Act that he attributes the first traces of the dominant part subsequently played by lawyers in the development of company law and practice.

Effect on incorporations

Joint stock companies did not disappear completely. On the contrary, many regularly chartered companies and a few unincorporated ones[41] had survived the panic and were living examples of the advantages of this type of organisation. Others, too, still succeeded in obtaining charters; but not many, for a lasting effect of the Bubble Act and the crisis of 1720 was to make the Law Officers of the Crown chary of advising the grant of charters,[42] and to insist on restrictive conditions in those that were granted.[43]

Nor at first was Parliament any more complaisant. It was not until towards the end of the century, with the growth of canal building, which necessarily involved an application to Parliament for special powers, that Parliament became less strict in its requirements and that direct statutory incorporations became common.[44] It is to this statutory incorporation that we owe many of the features of modern companies: in particular the method of limiting liability of the members to the nominal value of their shares.

[38] *R. v. Cawood* (1724) 2 Ld.Raym. 1361. It decided nothing of importance on the interpretation of the Act.
[39] But contemporary news-sheets make it clear that others were instituted.
[40] *Op. cit.* pp. 3 *et seq.* He refers particularly to the influence of Sjt. Pengelly who is known to have delivered opinons (which still survive) on no fewer than 27 companies and whose views foreshadow the judicial interpretation adopted in the succeeding century. Dubois's book, to which the author is greatly indebted, is not as well-known as it deserves to be.
[41] Including the Sun Fire Office, established in 1709.
[42] For an account of the difficulties which company promoters had to surmount, see Dubois, *op. cit.* pp. 12 *et seq.* "The law officers of the Crown, mindful of [the Act's] provisions, hesitated to approve of applications for charters which contemplated the creation of large stocks of transferable shares. Consequently, not only were the operations of unincorporated joint stock companies restricted by the Act, but the Act was used as an expression of policy to restrain the formation of business corporations": *ibid.* p. 12.
[43] *Ibid.* To this period can be traced conditions restricting the amount of capital which the company might raise. A further restraint on joint enterprise arose from the habit, introduced after 1720, of inserting in patents of invention prohibitions on assignment to more than five persons; *ibid.* pp. 21–24.
[44] Over 100 statutory incorporations occurred during the last 40 years of the eighteenth century.

Hence throughout the century (and beyond) the shadow of 1720 retarded the development of incorporated companies. The official view is well represented by the oft-quoted words of Adam Smith,[45] writing as late as 1776, in which he stated that a joint stock company was an appropriate type of organisation only for those trades which could be reduced to a routine, namely, those of banking, fire and marine insurance, making and maintaining canals, and bringing water to cities; others, in his view, were bound to be inefficient as businesses as well as being contrary to the public interest. The great man thereby put the seal of his approval on the current legislative and administrative practice, for the authorities, in their wisdom, had incorporated precisely these four types and had (with rare exceptions) refused to incorporate others.

Resurgence of unincorporated companies

Had the authorities granted incorporation more readily, already in the eighteenth century incorporated companies might have become the dominant type of commercial enterprise. And had that policy been adopted, the Government, by its control over charters and statutes, could have shaped the development of company law 150 years earlier than it seriously attempted to do so. Instead, as we have seen, the authorities placed almost insuperable difficulties in the way of incorporation and left it to businessmen and their legal advisers to find an alternative device. This they found in the unincorporated association; paradoxically, the Bubble Act in the end caused a rebirth of the very type of association which it had sought to destroy. The history of the previous period had shown that it was perfectly feasible to trade with a joint stock without incorporation, and although the Bubble Act had struck at unincorporated companies it had expressly exempted partnerships carried on "in such manner as hath been hitherto usually and may be lawfully done."[46] This exemption clearly could not have covered every type of unincorporated company, for otherwise the Act became completely meaningless, but exactly how far partnerships could lawfully go was far from clear. The size of the membership could not be the decisive factor for at this time there was not and never had been any upper limit on numbers.[47] Professional opinion at the time[48] took the view, in fact adopted by the courts in the nineteenth century, that the basic test of illegality was the

[45] *Wealth of Nations*, V, Chap. 1, Pt. III, Art. 1.

[46] s.25.

[47] Except in the case of banking, as regards which the Bank of England's monopoly was protected by a prohibition, under a statute of 1708 (7 Anne, c. 30), of banking in England by more than five persons in association. And under the first part of the Bubble Act itself the London and Royal Exchange Assurances had a monopoly of insuring marine risks by companies or societies.

[48] See DuBois, *op. cit.* pp. 3 *et seq.*

existence of freely transferable shares and for a time such unincorporated associations as were formed (and the shock of the crash of 1720 caused there to be few for many years) were careful to place severe restrictions on transfers.[49] But from the middle of the century onwards it is clear that unincorporated joint stock companies, often with a large number of proprietors,[50] were operating to a gradually increasing extent and that (as the Bubble Act came to be regarded as a dead letter) complete freedom of transfer of shares was assumed to be permissible.

The deed of settlement company

Legal ingenuity enabled these unincorporated associations to operate with many of the advantages of incorporation by use of trusts.[51] The company would be formed under a "deed of settlement" (approximating to a cross between the modern articles of association and a trust deed for debentures or unit trusts) under which the subscribers would agree to be associated in an enterprise with a prescribed joint stock divided into a specified number of shares; the provisions of the deed would be variable with the consent of a specified majority of the proprietors; management would be delegated to a committee of directors; and the company's property would be vested in a separate body of trustees,[52] some of whom would often be directors also. Usually it would be provided that these trustees could sue or be sued on behalf of the company, and although the legal efficacy of such a provision was by no means clear, suit by the trustees in a court of equity seems to have been generally permitted.[53] As for the right to be sued, it will be appreciated that obscurity on this point was by no means an unmixed disadvantage from the point of view of the company.

Long before the end of the century certain types of commercial activity were dominated by companies organised on this basis, which, strangely enough, seems to have been encouraged rather than frowned upon by the Government, for frequent examples are found of refusal by the Law Officers to recommend charters of incorporation on the ground that "coparcenary" was a more appropriate form

---

[49] In the light of this it is interesting to note that unincorporated companies were often described as "private" companies, in contradistinction to the incorporated "public" company; restriction on transfer was until 1980 an essential feature of the 20th-century private company. Use of the term "public company" to describe those formally incorporated is found in a statute of 1767 (7 Geo. 3, c. 48), which struck at the practice of splitting shareholdings to increase voting power, by disqualifying members from voting until they had held their shares for six months.

[50] The true extent of the numbers was sometimes disguised by the device of sub-partnerships, *i.e.* the original few shares would be subsequently subdivided; see Dubois, *op. cit.* pp. 78–79.

[51] For details, see DuBois, *op. cit.* Chap. III.

[52] This was by no means unusual even in the case of incorporated companies: *ibid.* pp. 115–116.

[53] In practice considerable use was made of arbitration: *ibid.* 221.

of organisation.[54] Unincorporated associations had a virtual monopoly of the growing activity of non-marine[55] insurance, both by companies trading for the profit of their members (where the old Sun had formed the model for the Phoenix, Norwich General, Norwich Union and a host of others) and by mutual and friendly societies.[56] They were also used extensively in the metal industries and the theatre, and were even used at times in canal building where statutory incorporation was more common. Indeed, the researches of DuBois into the eighteenth-century company records and counsel's opinions have made it clear that the use of joint stock companies was far more widespread than had hitherto been supposed on the basis of the paucity of incorporations and of reported cases on unincorporated companies.

On the other hand, we have to wait until the nineteenth century for any outbreak of speculation in shares comparable to that of 1720. Although the mechanism of the stock market was well understood and several rather half-hearted attempts were made by the legislature to check its abuses,[57] company shares do not seem to have been generally regarded as suitable investments or gambling counters[58] for the lay public, but rather as means of enabling members of the mercantile community to acquire a permanent stake in enterprises with which they were familiar. But the picture changed at the turn of the century, when first the exigencies of war and then the growth of the railways led to an outbreak of company promotion and of general speculation comparable to that of the Bubble period. It was only then

---

54 Thus on the Equitable Assurance petition in 1761 the Att.-Gen. (Yorke) said: "If the Petitioners are so sure of success there is an easy method of making the experiment by entering into a voluntary partnership of which there are several instances now subsisting in the business of insuring": quoted in DuBois, *op. cit.* 30. Having regard to the size of these enterprises the Law Officers can hardly have been so naïve as to suppose that the "partnership" would be other than on a joint stock basis. Indeed petitions were often made by existing unincorporated companies and it was not unknown for such companies to take the opinion of the Law Officers on questions relating to their constitutions: *ibid.* p. 313, n. 35. (Law Officers at that time were not forbidden to undertake private practice).

55 The first part of the Bubble Act had given the London and Royal Exchange Assurance companies a monopoly of marine assurance by associations. During this period the value of this monopoly was diminished by individual insurances by underwriters who assembled at Lloyd's Coffee House and grew into the famous "Lloyd's of London" which was eventually incorporated, although policies continue to be underwritten not by the corporation but by individual underwriters.

56 Friendly Societies became so common that they were authorised by statute in 1793 (33 Geo. 3, c. 54), the first general authorising Act from which sprang not only the modern Friendly Society but also Industrial and Provident Societies, and Building Societies. Under the Act the rules had to be approved by the local justices, who probably enjoyed ratifying the rule of the Beneficent Society of Tinwold (1793) that "None shall be admitted into this Society who are suspected of being friendly to the new fangled doctrines of LIBERTY AND EQUALITY AND THE RIGHTS OF MAN as set forth by Thomas Paine and his adherents."

57 7 Geo. 1, stat. 2, No. 8 (1721); 7 Geo. 2, c. 8 (1733); and 10 Geo. 2, c. 8 (1736).

58 During the 18th century the lotteries met this need. Their abolition in 1826 under the Lotteries Act 1823 may well have encouraged share speculation. On these early lotteries, see J. Ashton, *A History of English Lotteries* (Lond. 1893) a most entertaining book.

that the inherent disadvantages of the unincorporated type became fully apparent.

Disadvantages of unincorporation

As we have seen, one difficulty related to the power to sue or be sued. In law, these unincorporated companies were partnerships,[59] and this was before the time when legislation permitted suit in the firm's name. Actions at law[60] had to be brought by or against all the partners, and the difficulties[61] which this caused (particularly when there had been changes in the shareholdings) can be imagined. The only satisfactory, but expensive, solution was the promotion of a private Act of Parliament permitting the company to sue or be sued in the name of one or more of its officials. Such Acts became common towards the end of this period,[62] and the right was conferred on friendly societies by the (Public) Act of 1793. As will be appreciated, the members of the company would probably be concerned only with the possibility of suing and would be happy to find obstacles in the way of being sued, particularly as they would be personally liable without limitation.

This brings us to the second and most important disadvantage of the absence of incorporation—the members could not limit their personal liability. Until late in the century limited liability still seems to have been regarded as only a secondary consideration; DuBois[63] finds the earliest clear recognition of it as the motive for incorporation in the petition for incorporation by the Warmley Company in 1768. But increasingly from then on it became openly recognised as a factor of prime importance and one which incorporation alone could fully achieve. Unincorporated companies could strive to approximate to it by expressly contracting in every case that liability should be limited to the funds of the company—a solution only practicable where the contracts were of a formal type such as insurance,[64] for it was generally believed that a statement to this effect in the deed of settlement would be ineffective even if the

[59] But even the law could not shut its eyes to all the differences between a large company and a simple partnership. A shareholder in the former could obviously not bind the company, as a partner could the firm; anyone dealing with the company must be deemed to know that powers of management were restricted to the directors. Here we can detect the germ of the later rule in *Royal British Bank v. Turquand*; see Chap. 8, below.

[60] As we have seen, equity was somewhat more lenient and, even at common law if the contract was with the trustees, they could sue on it for the benefit of the company: *Metcalfe v. Brian* (1810) 12 East 400.

[61] They are well described in *George on Companies* (1825), pp. 19 *et seq.*, quoted by Formoy, *op. cit.* pp. 33 *et seq.*

[62] DuBois, *op. cit.* p. 142, quotes an example as early as 1730 but this was exceptional.

[63] *Op. cit.* p. 95.

[64] In the 19th century these stipulations became customary in the policies of unincorporated offices. Such an express contract was ultimately held to be effective: *Hallet v. Dowdall* (1852) 21 L.J.Q.B. 98.

creditor had notice of it.[65] Or, of course, they could make a virtue of necessity, as did the Phoenix Assurance which, when its rival, the incorporated Royal Exchange Assurance, boasted of the advantages to policy-holders of a ready remedy against the corporate stock, retorted by emphasising the advantages to the public of the full responsibility of its members.[66]

In truth, however, unlimited liability, though a danger to the risk-taker, was often a snare and a delusion rather than a protection to the public and no handicap at all to the dishonest promoter. The difficulties of suing a fluctuating body and the even greater difficulties of levying execution[67] made the personal liability of the members largely illusory. Moreover, the investor was supposed to become a member by signing the deed of settlement and until he did so his identity would not be known by the creditors. But in fact "stags" would deal in allotment letters or scrip certificates to bearer without signing the deed and often before any formal deed was in existence, and dishonest promoters, who alone might be under any legal liability, might disappear with the subscription moneys.[68] Many promotions were still-born and others perished with the slumps[69] which followed each successive boom. Some intervention by the State was inevitable but the question was what form it should take.

State intervention

The first form was the characteristic English expedient of reviving an old remedy—in this case prosecution under the almost forgotten Bubble Act. In November 1807 the Attorney-General (at the instance of a private relator) sought a criminal information against two recently formed unincorporated companies,[70] both of which had freely transferable shares and advertised that the liability of the members would be limited. Lord Ellenborough[71] dismissed the applications because of the lapse of 87 years since the Act was previously invoked, but he issued a stern warning that no one in the future could pretend that the statute was obsolete and indicated that a "speculative project founded on joint stock or transferable shares"

[65] But statements alleging limited liability were commonplace in both deeds of settlement and prospectuses: see Hunt, *op. cit.* pp. 33–34, 72 and 99–101. They were eventually held to be ineffective in *Re Sea, Fire & Life Insurance Co.* (1854) 3 De G.M. & G. 459.

[66] DuBois, *op. cit.* p. 96.

[67] These difficulties are well explained in Formoy, *op. cit.* pp. 35 *et seq.* They did not disappear even if there was a private Act permitting the company to be sued in the name of its officers.

[68] The opportunities for fraud thus provided are immortalised by Charles Dickens's account of the "Anglo-Bengalee Disinterested Loan and Life Assurance Company" in the pages of *Martin Chuzzlewit*.

[69] These occurred particularly in 1808, 1825–1826, and 1844–1845: See Hunt, *op. cit. passim.*

[70] The London Paper Manufacturing Co. and the London Distillery Co.

[71] *R.* v. *Dodd* (1808) 9 East 516.

was prohibited.[72] Shortly afterwards two further associations were held illegal, apparently because their shares were transferable.[73]

These decisions caused alarm among investors and promoters and were probably contributory causes of the slump of 1808. However, despite further prosecutions, confidence was gradually restored and the years 1824–1825 witnessed a boom which was compared with that of 1719–1720 and which was followed by a similar slump. The various court cases[74] did little to clarify the law; the better view seemed to be that a company with freely transferable shares was illegal, but that one where the right to transfer was restricted was unlawful only if it had "a mischievous tendency." On the other hand there were many who were opposed to the whole concept of joint stock enterprise, both incorporated and unincorporated, and until the middle of the nineteenth century bitter debates continued in which the virtues of healthy private enterprise were contrasted with the dead hand of monopolistic companies.[75] Lord Eldon, in particular, attacked the latter in both his legislative and judicial capacity. In the former he announced his intention of introducing further restrictive legislation but finally dropped this idea on the ground that the law as it stood was sufficiently strict.[76] Had his view of it prevailed, it certainly would have been strict, for he was apparently prepared to hold that assuming to act as a corporation[77] was an offence at common law as well as under the Act.[78]

Finally, the Government felt compelled to do something to bring the law more into accord with the facts; but just as their predecessors in 1720 could think of nothing more constructive than the Bubble Act, so now they could think of nothing better than its repeal. In 1825, its Indian summer was finally ended. The repealing statute[79] was sponsored by Huskisson, the President of the Board of Trade,

[72] *Ibid.* pp. 526–528.
[73] *Buck v. Buck* (1808) 1 Camp. 547 and *R. v. Stratton* (1809) 1 Camp. 549n. As we have seen (above, p. 28, n. 40) this had been Sjt. Pengelly's view.
[74] They were summarised by Hunt, *op. cit.* Chaps. II and III, and in Cooke, *op. cit.* Chap. VII. The most instructive of those reported are: *R. v. Webb* (1811) 14 East 406; *Pratt v. Hutchinson* (1812) 15 East 511; *Josephs v. Pebrer* (1825) 3 B. & C. 639; and *Kinder v. Taylor* (1825) 3 L.J.Ch. 68. See further *Lindley on Companies*, (6th ed. 1902), pp. 180–184.
[75] Accounts of these will be found in Hunt, *op. cit. passim.* The arguments used by the supporters of "private" (as opposed to corporate) enterprise were astonishingly reminiscent of those later used by the opponents of nationalisation.
[76] Hunt, *op. cit.* pp. 38 and 39.
[77] But Eldon himself was unable to give any clear account of what this meant. The Inns of Court come close to acting as corporations, even to the extent, or so it is generally said, of using common seals and this seems to have impressed Eldon and acted as a restraining influence: see *Lloyd v. Loaring* (1802) 6 Ves. 773 at p. 779. But query if the Inns do, in fact, use common seals: see Lloyd, *Law of Unincorporated Associations*, p. 51, n. (c).
[78] He did not get a very good press; the Morning Chronicle said it confirmed their view that his opinions "as a Politician were seldom worth much": 30 March 1825, quoted by Hunt, *op. cit.* p. 39.
[79] 6 Geo. 4, c. 91. The marine insurance monopoly had been repealed a year earlier: 5 Geo. 4, c. 114.

and it is then that this Government Department first started to take an active part in the development of company law.

Influence of the Board of Trade

The Board[80] was the successor of the Commissioners for Trade and Plantations, the history of which, as an ad hoc or standing Committee of the Privy Council, can be traced back to the beginning of the seventeenth century and whose report on stock-jobbing in 1696 led to the first legislative attempt[81] to regulate brokers. Throughout the eighteenth century examples can be found of references to the Commissioners of petitions for charters of incorporation,[82] especially in cases where the object was colonial trade (for at this time the greater part of the Commissioners' work was concerned with the colonies rather than with domestic trade). But, in general, decisions were taken by the Law Officers[83] (which in practice must often have meant the Attorney-General's "devil"[84]) and it was not until the Board was re-created by Pitt in 1784 that the emphasis changed and that it gradually came to be recognised that the Board was the appropriate Government Department to advise on incorporations and to guide the development of company law. Since Huskisson repealed the Bubble Act a century-and-a-half ago the Board, until it ceased to have an independent existence in 1970,[85] was responsible for all company legislation and was entrusted with gradually increasing supervisory powers over joint stock enterprises. It is appropriate that its first major intervention should have been an act of liberation rather than of control, for its policy throughout had been to allow the greatest possible freedom to private enterprise. As its official historian[86] truly says: "Broadly speaking the part played by the Board of Trade in relation to the movement which has revolutionised

---

80 The influence of the Board has been largely ignored by writers on the history of company law. For accounts of the Board's development, which, however, say little about its functions in connection with companies, see Llewellyn Smith, *The Board of Trade* (The Whitehall Series, 1928) and Prouty, *The Transformation of the Board of Trade 1830–1855* (Lond. 1957).

81 8 & 9 Wm. 3, c. 32.

82 See DuBois, *op. cit.* pp. 13, 57, 58, 60, 62, 66, 69, 70, 89 and 172. There are also occasional examples of applications to the Commissioners for investigation of the affairs of existing companies: *ibid.* 126.

83 DuBois, *op. cit.* pp. 169–170 n. 135 says: "The usual procedure in the case of an application for incorporation was the presentation of a petition to the Privy Council. The Privy Council would refer the matter to a subcommittee, which, if it were favourably inclined to the plan after consideration, would submit the petition to the Attorney-General or Solicitor-General. On occasion the Commissioners of Trade and Plantations would be consulted."

84 Napier, *A Century of Law Reform* (Lond. 1901), p. 389.

85 On the creation of the Department of Trade and Industry in 1970 it absorbed the Board but left it in existence, the Secretary of State for Trade and Industry retaining the additional title of President of the Board: S.I. 1970 No. 1537. In 1974 the Department split into separate Departments of Trade and of Industry which combined again in 1983.

86 Llewellyn Smith, *op. cit.* p. 168.

the structure of industry has been that of a vigilant onlooker rather than of a continuous supervisor."

CHAPTER 3

HISTORY OF COMPANY LAW SINCE 1825

Twenty years' vacillation

THE repeal, like the enactment, of the Bubble Act was followed by a disastrous slump further emphasising the need for some constructive measures of control. These, however, were still lacking; the only real advance made by the 1825 Act was a provision[1] enabling the Crown to declare the extent of the member's liability on the grant of charters, so that charters were no longer necessarily accompanied by a complete absence of liability on the part of the members for the company's debts. This provision might have been expected to encourage greater freedom in the grant of charters, but in fact the authorities remained as strict as ever. Applications for statutory incorporation, stimulated by the boom in railway promotion, fared better but their expense was prohibitive except in the case of the largest concerns.[2]

Hence, most promoters were thrown back on the unincorporated form, the legality of which was still in doubt, especially as Eldon had secured the inclusion in the repealing Act of an express recital that undertakings should be adjudged and dealt with according to common law. It was not until 1843 that it became reasonably clear what their position was at common law,[3] and even then little had been done to remove the disadvantages under which they laboured. But, despite these handicaps, joint stock banks,[4] insurance companies and a host of other projects flourished as never before and joint stock companies came to play an important role in every part of

---

[1] s.2.

[2] Hunt, *op. cit.* p. 82, quotes two railway incorporations which cost £72,868 and £40,588. Even the fees for a charter amounted to at least £402 which was a substantial sum in those days: *ibid.* The Report on Investments for the Savings of the Middle and Working Classes (1850 B.P.P., Vol. XIX, 169) quoted a chartered incorporation costing £1,134 which was alleged (surely mistakenly?) to be "greater even than that of obtaining an Act of Parliament."

[3] *Garrard* v. *Hardey* (1843) 5 M. & G. 471; *Harrison* v. *Heathorn* (1843) 6 M. & G. 81; not following *Duvergier* v. *Fellows* (1828) 5 Bing. 248 and *Blundell* v. *Winsor* (1835) 8 Sim. 601. Brougham L.C. on the Bench took a more liberal view than his predecessor (*Walburn* v. *Ingilby* (1832) 1 Myl. & K. 61) although in the House he was almost equally reactionary on this matter and received an equally unfavourable press. "The commercial part of the community have little reason to thank God, with Cobbett, that there is a House of Lords, and above all a Lord Brougham": *Morning Chronicle*, 15 August 1838 (cited in Hunt, *op. cit.* p. 84)—a reference to the prosecution of Cobbett in 1831 for criminal libel when he subpoenaed six members of the House of Lords and secured an acquittal largely because of the evidence of Brougham L.C.

[4] Guided by the experience of Scotland (where joint stock banks had flourished in contrast with the failures of the English private concerns) the monopoly of the Bank of England was whittled away by Acts of 1826 (7 Geo. 4, c. 46) and 1833 (3 & 4 Wm. 4, c. 98). These Acts provided that banking companies could sue or be sued in the names of their officers and, in anticipation of the Act of 1844, provided for registration of certain essential particulars.

the country's economy. Clearly some steps had to be taken to remove the legal confusion.

The first step was taken by the Trading Companies Act of 1834, which was intended to extend slightly the availability of corporate advantages. It empowered the Crown to confer by letters patent any of the privileges of incorporation without actually granting a charter, thus, in particular, obviating the need for special Acts enabling companies to sue and be sued in the names of their officers.[5] The major importance of this compromise was that it was the first general Act requiring public registration of members, but it contained no express provision that the letters patent might limit the members' liability and, indeed, expressly provided that judgments against the company should, with leave of the court, be enforceable against every member until three years after he had ceased to be a member. Moreover, its practical value was much diminished by the restrictive rules which the Board of Trade laid down for the granting of petitions under it.[6]

In 1837 the Board of Trade instructed a Chancery barrister, H. Bellenden Ker, to prepare a report on the law of partnership with particular reference to the expediency of introducing limited partnerships on the continental model.[7] His report[8] was pigeon-holed and the only result was the re-enactment of the 1834 Act in the Chartered Companies Act of 1837 but with the valuable clarification that personal liability of members might be limited by the letters patent to a specified amount per share. In the ensuing 17 years some 50 companies did in fact form under this Act, but most still preferred to rely on the *de facto* protection from personal liability conferred by the difficulties of suing and levying execution on the members of a fluctuating body. Many of these were from their inception fraudulent shams, particularly the bogus assurance companies such as those pilloried by Dickens in *Martin Chuzzlewit*,[9] and it was primarily the existence of these which led the Board of Trade to secure the appointment in 1841 of a Parliamentary Committee on Joint Stock Companies. In 1843 Gladstone, who had become President of the Board of Trade, assumed the chairmanship of the Committee and

---

[5] The difficulties with which a suitor might otherwise be faced have already been stressed; they are well exemplified in *Van Sandau* v. *Moore* (1825) 1 Russell 441, in which Lord Eldon, at p. 472, gave this as his principal justification for holding unincorporated companies to be illegal.

[6] They are quoted by Hunt, *op. cit.* pp. 57–58. The progressive Huskisson had retired from the Board in 1827, and in 1830 had lost his life in an accident at the opening of the Liverpool and Manchester railway—a victim of the railway boom which he had himself done so much to promote. In the words of a contemporary poet:

"This fatal chance not only caused delay

But damped the joy that erst had crowned the day"!

T. Baker: *The Steam Engine*, canto X.

[7] John Austin was a staunch advocate of this proposal: see *1825 Parliamentary History and Review*, p. 711.

[8] 1837 B.P.P., Vol. XLIV, 399.

[9] First published in 1843.

widened the scope of its inquiries. Its epoch-making report[10] and the Joint Stock Companies Act 1844[11] which followed it, were mainly due to his genius and energy.

Gladstone's legislation of 1844 and 1845

The 1844 Act introduced three main principles which have constituted the basis of our company law from that time. In the first place it drew a clear distinction between private partnerships and joint stock companies by providing for the registration of all new companies with more than 25 members,[12] or with shares transferable without the consent of all the members. Secondly, it provided for incorporation by mere registration as opposed to a special Act or charter; but this it did by a system of provisional registration, which authorised the company to function for certain strictly limited preliminary purposes, followed by complete registration on filing a deed of settlement containing the prescribed particulars and other documents when for the first time the company became incorporated.[13] Thirdly, it provided for full publicity which ever since has been regarded as the most potent safeguard against fraud. It is to this Act, too, that we owe the Registrar of Companies[14] with whom particulars of companies' constitutions, and changes therein, and annual returns are filed.

Limited liability, however, was still excluded. Although the company became incorporated, the personal liability of the members was preserved,[15] but their liability was to cease three years after they had transferred their shares by registered transfer[16] and creditors had to proceed first against the assets of the company.[17] Existing companies were compelled to register certain particulars, but did not have the privileges conferred by the Act unless they amended their deeds of settlement so as to comply with its provisions.[18] Winding up was dealt with by a separate Act[19] of the same date which made

---

[10] 1844 B.P.P., Vol. VII.
[11] It contained 80 sections and nine Schedules and was by far the most elaborate piece of company legislation attempted in England up to that time. It did not apply to Scotland which was left to its common law (Scottish judges were distinctly more liberal than their English colleagues) until the Act of 1856.
[12] Reduced to the present 20 by the Act of 1856. This provision was based on Ker's report of 1837 which suggested a maximum of 15. New assurance companies were also required to register irrespective of the number of members or transferability of shares: s.2.
[13] We may detect resemblances to this "two-tier" arrangement in the present provisions for a "certificate of incorporation" followed later, in the case of a public company, by a "trading certificate" (Companies Act 1985, s.117) but there is no historical connection between the two sets of provisions.
[14] s.19.
[15] s.25.
[16] This provision was, of course, based on the Trading Companies Act 1834.
[17] s.66.
[18] ss.58–59.
[19] 7 & 8 Vict. c. 111.

companies subject to the bankruptcy law. Banking companies were also dealt with by a separate Act,[20] the provisions of which were generally similar except that the maximum number of members of an unregistered partnership was six[21] (instead of 25) and that there were stringent requirements for a minimum nominal and paid-up capital. It is perhaps surprising that these latter conditions did not then become general requirements of English company law for they constitute an essential feature of continental practice and appear to be a fair price to pay for the boon of simple and cheap incorporation by registration.[22]

Finally, Gladstone prepared and introduced the Bill which was passed under his successor as the Companies Clauses Consolidation Act 1845.[23] This set out the standard provisions normally included in private statutes of incorporation. These provisions were thereafter to be incorporated by reference, thus materially shortening and cheapening the process of statutory incorporation—still necessary in the case of public utilities requiring powers of compulsory acquisition.

Gladstone, therefore, during his tenure of office as President of the Board of Trade, succeeded for the first time in placing joint stock companies on a sound legal footing; he may fairly be regarded as the father of modern company law. His legislation, however, only solved the legal and not the commercial problems. It gave a company the legal status of a corporation but denied its members the most sought-after advantage of it—freedom from personal liability. In the latter respect the only advance was the recognition that the company itself was primarily liable and that its bankruptcy did not necessarily involve bankruptcy of its members.

The winding-up Acts

The legislation of 1844 was passed at the height of the "railway mania" and led to promotions in other fields, thus bringing the man in the street into contact with companies as never before, and to an expansion of the stock markets both in London and the Provinces.[24]

20 7 & 8 Vict. c. 113.
21 Later it became 10.
22 *cf.* O. Kahn-Freund: *Some Reflections on Company Law Reform* (1945) 7 M.L.R. 54 at pp. 57–59. Such provisions were, in fact, included in the Limited Liability Bill of 1855, but were struck out in Committee. They were reintroduced by the H.L. in an emasculated form but deleted in the Act of 1856. However, there have been special capital requirements in relation to certain types of business (*e.g.* banking and insurance) as there are now for all public companies.
23 A separate Act of the same date dealt with Scottish statutory companies (8 & 9 Vict. c. 17). These Acts contained the general corporate powers and duties and Table A of later Acts owed much to them. They were supplemented in the cases of particular types of utility by other Acts of the same and later years. As Cooke points out (*op. cit.* p. 119), these were illustrations of a wider tendency to bring under general legislation matters which had previously been left to private Bills; other examples will be found in the fields of divorce, naturalisation and municipal corporations.
24 Hunt, *op. cit.* pp. 104 *et seq.*

Inevitably, however, the boom was followed by a collapse a year later which changed the emphasis from promotions to liquidations. A winding-up Act applying to railway companies[25] was passed in 1846 and this was followed in 1848[26] and 1849[27] by Acts of general application conferring winding-up jurisdiction on the Court of Chancery. Unhappily the resulting conflicts of jurisdiction between the Courts of Bankruptcy and Chancery led to great confusion,[28] which, less unhappily, proved highly beneficial to the legal and the new-born accountancy professions.

At a later date the confusion was resolved by the total removal of incorporated companies from the bankruptcy jurisdiction[29] and by the discrete treatment of company insolvency in Companies Acts and of individuals in Bankruptcy Acts, a distinction which prevailed until they were reunited by the Insolvency Act 1986.

The struggle for limited liability

Several features of the Act of 1844 were open to criticism. In particular the cumbersome procedure of provisional and final registration[30] was attacked, but was left unaltered until 1856,[31] though frequently disregarded by unscrupulous promoters who dealt in scrip prior to complete registration.

But, of course, the main cause of complaint was the absence of limited liability, and the next 10 years saw the battle fairly joined on this issue. It is clear that public opinion began to harden in favour of the extension of limited liability, particularly when the slump of 1845–1848 drew poignant attention to the consequences of its absence. But it was less clear how and to what companies it should be extended. As a result of the 1844 Act there were three principal types[32] of commercial association:

25 9 & 10 Vict. c. 28.
26 11 & 12 Vict. c. 45.
27 12 & 13 Vict. c. 108.
28 Accounts appear in Formoy, *op. cit.* pp. 93 *et seq.*, and Cooke, *op. cit.* Chap. X. They illustrate their accounts principally by the Royal British Bank's liquidation (1856) 28 L.T.(o.s.) 224. It is, of course, to this company that we are indebted for the rule in *Royal British Bank v. Turquand* (below, Chap. 8).
29 The Joint Stock Companies Act 1856 and the Companies Winding Up (Amendment) Act 1857.
30 It is estimated that less than half the provisional registrations were ever followed by complete registration: Shannon (1931–1932) Econ. Hist., Vol. II, p. 397. See also *ibid.* pp. 281–282. The defects were emphasised in the Report of the Select Committee on Assurance Associations, 1852–1853, B.P.P., Vol. XXI.
31 A few amendments were made in 1847 (10 & 11 Vict. c. 78, notably the deletion of the need to file prospectuses, a retrograde step which was apparently taken without any reference to the Registrar: see his evidence before the Select Committee on Assurance Associations, above, at p. 13, Q. 160. It was not corrected until 1900.
32 There were also companies granted letters patent under the Trading Companies Act 1834 and Chartered Companies Act 1837, which were unincorporated (unless they registered under the 1844 Act) but with most of the advantages of chartered incorporation except limited liability.

1. Private partnerships of not more than 25 persons, and quasi-partnerships of unlimited size formed before 1844 which had not re-formed under the Act of that year. These were unincorporated and the liability of the members was necessarily unlimited.

2. Chartered and statutory companies, which were incorporated and the members of which were normally free from liability or had their liability limited to a prescribed sum per share.

3. Companies formed or registered under the Act of 1844 which were incorporated but with unlimited liability.

The first question therefore was whether limited liability should be extended to private partnerships on the lines of the continental *sociétés en commandite*, to registered companies, or to both.

Bellenden Ker's report of 1837 had been directed primarily to private partnerships and the desirability of the *société en commandite*. The 1844 Report had given birth to the third type of association but had not extended limited liability to it; the object of the Commission was to control companies and discourage frauds, not to stimulate promotions. The *société en commandite* was outside the terms of reference of the 1844 Commission but was the main subject of consideration by the Select Committee of 1850 on Investments for the Savings of the Middle and Working Classes, which reported[33] that "the difficulties which affected the law of partnership operate with increasing severity in proportion to the smallness of the sums subscribed and the number of persons included in the association. . . . Any measures for the removal of these difficulties would be particularly acceptable to the Middle and Working Classes and would tend to satisfy them that they are not excluded from fair competition by laws throwing obstacles in the way of men with small capitals." The result, as Hunt[34] says, was that the argument for limited liability acquired a "tinge of social amelioration." One can detect more than a slight whiff of humbug when one reads the evidence of Chancery barristers accepting the invitation of M.P.s to persuade them that limited liability was desirable in the interests of the poor. In truth, as the evidence of working-class witnesses makes plain, what the working man required was an improvement in the law of friendly societies, particularly as regards housing trusts, co-operative societies and building societies—and this in fact soon came about.[35] John Stuart Mill, more realistically, pointed out[36] that "the great value of

[33] 1850 B.P.P., Vol. XIX, 169.
[34] *Op. cit.* p. 120.
[35] Industrial and Provident Societies Acts 1852, 1854 and 1856; Building Societies Act 1874.
[36] In his evidence at p. 78.

a limit of responsibility as it relates to the working classes would be not so much to facilitate the investment of their savings, not so much to enable the poor to lend to those who are rich, as to enable the rich to lend to those who are poor."

A year later a similarly constituted Select Committee considered the law of partnership. On the major issue of limited liability its report[37] was non-committal; it recommended that this vexed question should be referred to a Royal Commission "of adequate legal and commercial knowledge." It did, however, make one firm recommendation, namely, that it should be permissible to lend money at a rate of interest varying with the profits of a business without becoming a partner in the business. At this time it was still supposed that such a loan automatically made the lender a partner[38]; the Committee proposed that instead he should be a deferred creditor in the event of bankruptcy and thus placed in a position not dissimilar to that of a limited partner.

In accordance with the recommendations of the Committee the question was referred to a strong Royal Commission[39] containing representatives from England, Scotland and Ireland.[40] They were, however, quite unable to reach unanimity. They had, they said, "been much embarassed by the great contrariety of opinion. . . . Gentlemen of great experience and talent have arrived at conclusions diametrically opposite; and in supporting these conclusions have displayed reasoning power of the highest order. It is difficult to say on which side the weight of authority in this country predominates." In the result a bare majority of five[41] signed a Report, opposing the general extension of limited liability to joint stock companies or the introduction of the *société en commandite*, and stating that they were unable to agree on the 1851 Committee's proposal regarding loans. Bramwell and Hodgson (a merchant banker), on the other hand, were wholeheartedly in favour of all three proposals. They came out uncompromisingly in favour of laissez-faire. "If ever," said Bramwell,[42] "there was a rule established by reason, authority and experience, it is that the interest of a community is best consulted by leaving to its members, as far as possible, the unrestricted and unfettered exercise of their own talents and industry." In his opinion the restraint on limited liability offended against this golden rule. He therefore recommended[43] that people should be allowed as of right

[37] 1851 B.P.P., Vol. XVIII, 1.
[38] *Grace v. Smith* (1775) 2 Wm.Bl. 997.
[39] 1854 B.P.P., Vol. XXVII, 445. The same Commission was to consider the assimilation of the mercantile laws of the various parts of the U.K.
[40] The English legal representatives were G. W. Bramwell Q.C. (afterwards Baron Bramwell), Cresswell J. and J. Anderson, Q.C. (afterwards an Official Referee).
[41] Including Cresswell J.
[42] *Ibid.* p. 23.
[43] *Ibid.* p. 29.

to form partnerships limiting the liability of all or some by private agreement followed by registration; and that where the liability of all was to be limited the partnership should be incorporated and the word "Limited" added after the name. The remaining member, Anderson, was against the introduction of limited liability and *sociétés en commandite*, but in favour of the 1851 Committee's proposal regarding loans.

Although the majority against limited liability was six out of eight, the House of Commons immediately passed, without a division, a motion in favour of limited partnerships.[44] On this occasion the Government remained non-committal,[45] but in the following Session they introduced two Bills, the Partnership Amendment Bill allowing profit-sharing loans without partnership, and the Limited Liability Bill which provided for limited liability in the case of companies securing complete registration under the 1844 Act subject to certain safeguards. Their bold action in introducing the latter is the more surprising since almost all the prior discussion had related to limited partnerships and not to incorporated companies.

Both Bills secured a second reading in the Commons[46] without a Division, but thereafter the former fell a victim to time pressure and proceeded no further. Nevertheless, the Government determined to press on with the Limited Liability Bill, which was rushed through the Commons and given a third reading, again without a Division.[47] It was then sent to the Lords who were asked to pass it that same Session as a matter of urgency. Certain Lords protested vigorously,[48] and certainly it is difficult to see why the Government, which had sat on the fence for so long, should suddenly regard this as a matter of the utmost urgency at the most critical time of the Crimean War. Doubtless it was true that public opinion, at any rate as represented by the Press,[49] had at last come to favour the measure, but this hardly explains the almost indecent haste with which it was pushed

[44] (1854) *Hansard*, 3rd Series, Vol. 134, at cols. 752 *et seq.*
[45] Commenting on the speech of Cardwell, the President of the Board of Trade, Cobden said (*ibid.* col. 779) that "all he could learn of the views of the right hon. gentleman was that he told them when he began that he would not offer an opinion, and he contrived very ingeniously to keep his word."
[46] *Hansard*, 3rd Series, Vol. 139, cols. 310 *et seq.*
[47] Cols. 1709 *et seq.* (for Committee Stage, see (*ibid.* cols. 1348, 1378, 1445 and 1517).
[48] Fourteen voted against and nine of them minuted a formal protest (*ibid.* col. 1918).
[49] By this time even *The Times*, formerly an uncompromising opponent, had come round. Lord Stanley of Alderley in introducing the measure in the House of Lords said that a hostile deputation had "candidly admitted that, with the exception of the Leeds Mercury, there was no journal in the Kingdom which would admit an article against the principle of limited liability" (*Hansard* 139, col. 1896). This seems to be an exaggeration so far as the legal Press was concerned, for the *Law Times* was still most hostile—even to the extent of describing the Bill as the "Rogues Charter"; see (1854) 24 L.T. 142; (1855) 25 L.T. 116 and 210; (1856) 26 L.T. 230; and (1858) 31 L.T. 14. Nor was it universally popular in business circles. The Manchester Chamber of Commerce declared it "so subversive of that high moral responsibility which has hitherto distinguished our Partnership Laws (!) as to call for their strongest disapproval": *Proceedings*, 13 June 1855, cited by Redford, *Manchester Merchants and Foreign Trade*, p. 215, and Cooke, *op. cit.* p. 157.

through,[50] particularly as the official view still seemed to be that it was a question of abstract principle rather than of practical importance.[51] The Lords, having made various amendments, finally passed the Bill without a Division.[52] The Commons[53] reluctantly accepted the Lords' amendments and the Bill was given the Royal Assent in August 1855.

The attainment of limited liability

The Act[54] provided for the limited liability of the members of a company on complete registration if (a) the company had at least 25 members holding £10 shares paid up to the extent of 20 per cent., (b) not less than three-fourths of the nominal capital was subscribed, (c) "Limited" was added to the company's name, and (d) the Board of Trade approved the auditors. The directors were to be personally liable if they paid a dividend knowing the company to be insolvent or made loans to the members, and the company had to wind up if three-fourths of the capital was lost.[55] Banks and insurance companies were excluded. The method of limitation was that already used for chartered companies under the Act of 1837 and for statutory companies under the Companies Clauses Act of 1845, namely, the restriction of members' liability to the nominal (unpaid) value of their shares.

The Limited Liability Act only remained in force for a few months, as it was repealed and incorporated in the Joint Stock Companies Act 1856.[56] This Act, of 116 sections and a Schedule of Tables and forms, was the first of the modern Companies Acts. It did away with provisional registration, superseded deeds of settlement by the modern memorandum and articles of association,[57] and incorporated provisions for winding up. Banks and insurance companies were still

50 John Bright told the Manchester Chamber of Commerce in 1856 that the Bill was rushed through because the Palmerston administration wanted to be able to say that something had been done besides voting money for the War (Redford and Cooke, *op. cit.*) But Bright (an opponent of the War) was perhaps not an impartial witness.
51 Both Pleydell-Bouverie (the Vice-President of the Board of Trade) in the Commons (col. 329), and Lord Stanley of Alderley (the President) in the Lords (col. 1919) said that they thought it would prove the wisdom of Adam Smith's view, "that in ordinary trading undertakings Joint Stock Companies could not compete with private traders", but that there ought to be no legal impediments in the way of competition.
52 Cols. 1895 *et seq.*, 2025 *et seq.*, and 2123 *et seq.*
53 Cols. 2127 *et seq.*
54 18 & 19 Vict. c. 133. It contained only 19 sections.
55 An existing company could take advantage of the new Act on complete registration under the 1844 Act if it made the necessary alterations to its deed of settlement by a resolution passed by a three-fourths majority of shareholders voting at a special meeting, and obtained a certificate of solvency from the Board of Trade.
56 The Government had reintroduced the Partnership Amendment Bill at the same time (*Hansard* 140, cols. 110 *et seq.*) but this ill-fated measure was ultimately withdrawn (*ibid.* col. 2201).
57 Model articles were appended in Table B which became the influential Table A of the 1862 and later Acts.

excluded but, unlike the earlier Acts, it applied to Scotland. Passed as it was in the heyday of laissez-faire it allowed incorporation with limited liability to be obtained with a freedom amounting almost to licence; all that was necessary was for seven or more persons to sign and register a memorandum of association. Virtually all the safeguards prescribed by the 1855 Act were deleted; there was no minimum nominal or paid-up capital or share value; only the provision for winding up on the loss of three-fourths of the capital was retained; and this too disappeared in 1862. Board of Trade approval of auditors was not required and even their appointment was no longer compulsory.[58] Directors were still to be liable if they paid dividends knowing the company to be insolvent, but the only other requirements were the use of the word "limited" and provisions for registration and publicity.

In effect, the legislature had adopted Lord Bramwell's[59] recommendations and accepted his view that those who dealt with companies knowing them to be limited had only themselves to blame if they burnt their fingers. The mystic word "Limited" was intended to act as a red flag warning the public of the perils which they faced if they had dealings with the dangerous new invention. It is because of the arbitrary coupling of personal liability and incorporation which had prevailed for 11 years that English companies still bear the label "Ltd."[60] instead of the more logical "Inc." of the United States.

The battle for incorporation with limited liability by simple registration was now won and the issue has never been seriously reopened, although the victory has at times been unpopular.[61] Its importance has sometimes been discounted. Certainly it is true that the various devices, already described, for acquiring de facto freedom from liability had become perfected, and this led The Economist[62] to regard the issue as of no great importance. Maitland[63] seems to have taken much the same view. "If," he said, "the State had not given way we should have had in England joint stock companies, unincorporated, but contracting with limited liability. We know

---

[58] Provisions regarding auditors were moved from the operative parts, where they had been in the Acts of 1844 and 1855, to the optional Table B. In fact these provisions continued to be adopted expressly or impliedly by most companies, so that the salutary practice of a professional audit remained customary although not again compulsory until 1900. It had been reintroduced as regards banks by the Companies Act 1879. For an account of the historical development of the accounting and auditing provisions of the Acts, see Littleton & Yamey (ed.), Studies in the History of Accounting, 356–379.

[59] He took great pride in having invented "Limited"; see his speech to the Institute of Bankers in 1888, Journal of Inst., Vol. 9, pp. 373 et seq, and especially p. 397. Llewellyn Smith (op. cit. p. 165) says that he even suggested playfully that the word should be inscribed on his tombstone.

[60] Or, now, "plc" in the case of public limited companies.

[61] The repeated bank failures during the second half of the 19th century caused renewed outbursts against limited liability; particularly on the failure of Overend Gurney Ltd. in 1866: see Hunt, op. cit. pp. 153 et seq.

[62] (1854) Vol. XII, 698.

[63] Trust and Corporation, Collected Papers, Vol. III, pp. 321, 392.

nowadays that men are not deterred from making contracts by the word "limited." "We have no reason to suppose that they would have been deterred if that word were expanded into four or five lines printed at the head of the company's letter paper." Nevertheless it is clear that without the legislative intervention, limited liability could never have been attained in a satisfactory and clear-cut fashion, and that it was this intervention which finally established companies as the major instrument in economic development. Of this the immediate and startling increase in promotions is sufficient proof.[64]

Subsequent developments

The subsequent history of companies belongs to the modern law and can be sketched more briefly.[65] Its main feature has been a movement away from the complete freedom allowed by the 1856 Act and the imposition of greater controls and increased provisions for publicity—the basic policy of Gladstone's Act of 1844 which had suffered partial eclipse in later Acts.

In 1857 the Act of the previous year was slightly amended,[66] banks were brought within its scope by the Joint Stock Banking Companies Act 1857, but without limited liability which was not conceded until the following year,[67] and legislation was passed dealing with frauds by directors.[68] In 1862 the various enactments were consolidated and amended in an Act which is the first to bear the short title of "Companies Act,"[69] and which, with numerous amendments,[70] remained the principal Act until 1908. It was considerably larger than the 1856 Act, consisting of no fewer than 212 sections and three Schedules. The additions were mainly amendments to the winding-up provisions and improved and more detailed drafting, but it included insurance companies[71] and also introduced the company limited by guarantee which, as already pointed out,[72]

[64] Between 1844 and 1856, 956 companies were completely registered under the 1844 Act; in the six years following the 1856 Act no fewer than 2,479 were registered and their paid-up capital in 1864 was over £31 m.; Shannon, *op. cit.* p. 290. For further details, see the Table at *ibid.* p. 421.

[65] Students of the history of this later period are referred to Dr. J. B. Jeffreys' London Ph.D. Thesis: *"Trends in Business Organisation in Great Britain Since 1856"* which is unfortunately unpublished but is available in the London University Library. It contains an excellent account of the major trends and an invaluable bibliography.

[66] 20 & 21 Vict. c. 14.

[67] 21 & 22 Vict. c. 91.

[68] 20 & 21 Vict. c. 54. See also Larceny Act 1861, ss.81–84.

[69] The poet W. H. Auden was somehow able to detect in this Act the symptoms of a modification of the pure liberal doctrine of laissez-faire: *Poets of the English Language*, Vol. 5, p. xxiii.

[70] The most important were the Companies Acts of 1867, 1879 and 1880, the Companies Winding Up Act 1890, the Directors' Liability Act 1890, and the Companies Act 1900.

[71] Hitherto governed by the 1844 Act which had been revived for their benefit: 20 & 21 Vict. c. 80.

[72] Above, Chap. 1, p. 11.

affords a convenient type of organisation for clubs and charitable or quasi-charitable associations.

Limited partnerships and private companies[73]

Hence by 1862 two of the three functions[73] of the modern company had been catered for. Capitalists were encouraged to lend their money to industry without having themselves to operate the enterprise, and non-trading bodies formed for social or philanthropic purposes could conveniently adopt the company rather than the trust as their *modus operandi*. But, or so it was thought, the need for limited liability within the field of the ordinary partnership or one-man business had still not been met. By the Partnership Amendment Act 1865[74] (commonly known as Bovill's Act) it was ultimately provided that sharing of profits should not be conclusive evidence of partnership but that lenders, or sellers of goodwill, in consideration of a share of profits should be deferred creditors. At the time it was thought that this had effected a substantial advance by legalising something in the nature of limited partnerships. In fact, as the courts soon held,[75] it did no such thing; it protected the creditor only where he was not in truth associated in the running of the business, for, if he was, he became fully liable as a partner notwithstanding that he was described as a contributor "under Bovill's Act." It therefore made no advance on the decision of the House of Lords in *Cox v. Hickman*[76] which had already overruled the rule in *Grace v. Smith*.[77] Far from protecting such lenders, the Act merely worsened their position by making them deferred creditors on bankruptcy.

When this was realised there was a renewed outbreak of attempts to introduce full-fledged limited partnerships on the continental model, and it was from one such abortive attempt[78] that the Partnership Act 1890 resulted, although this in its final form merely codified the existing law. In fact, however, the Companies Acts enabled all the advantages of limited partnerships, and more besides, to be obtained; for the requirement of seven members did not mean that so many as seven had to be beneficially interested—some could be bare nominees for the others and all could thus acquire the benefits of limited liability.[79] When this was established, as a result

[73] Above, Chap. 1, p. 10.

[74] This was an amended version of the ill-fated Partnership Bill of 1855.

[75] *Syers v. Syers* (1876) 1 App.Cas. 174, H.L.; *Pooley v. Driver* (1876) 5 Ch.D. 458.

[76] (1860) 8 H.L.C. 268.

[77] (1775) 2 Wm.Bl. 997, above.

[78] See the account by the original draftsman, Sir F. Pollock, in the preface to the 12th edition of his *Law of Partnership*.

[79] The result, as has been well said (by O. Kahn-Freund in his notes to Renner, *The Institutions of Private Law* (London 1948) at pp. 221 and 222) is that whereas in the 18th and early 19th centuries the law of partnership had been pressed into the service of joint stock enterprise, now the legal form of joint stock undertakings has come to annex the functions of the law of partnership. A similar reversal has taken place in the law of trusts into whose service the joint stock company is now pressed as a trust corporation: for a brief history of this development, see D. R. Marsh, "The Friendly Corporation," in (1951) IV Cambridge J. 451, and for a fuller account, the same author's *Corporate Trustees* (London 1952).

of the House of Lords decision in the famous case of *Salomon* v. *Salomon*[80] the need for limited partnerships had ceased, particularly as the legislature, far from discouraging "one-man" and other small "private companies," discriminated in their favour by the Companies Acts of 1900 and 1907 by exempting them from certain of the requirements of publicity.

Nevertheless, public opinion, in this instance lagging behind the law, caused limited partnerships to be legalised by the Limited Partnerships Act 1907. In practice this Act has not been much used because the private limited company involves little more trouble and expense to the members, and enables the liability of all of them to be limited, even if they take part in the management.

Case law developments

As already pointed out, the Companies Acts are far from being a complete code and it would be misleading to give an impression that the major developments during the nineteenth century were entirely statutory. On the contrary, the courts, building on the foundations of agency, trust and partnership law, had for the first time evolved a coherent and comprehensive body of company law. Many of the most fundamental principles were worked out by the courts with little or no help from the statutes though some, but still not all, have since been codified, amended, or eroded by later Companies Acts.

Twentieth-century reforms

By the end of the nineteenth century the Board of Trade had established the practice of appointing at intervals of about 20 years a Departmental Committee to review company law, implementing its recommendations by an amending Act with was then repealed and replaced by a consolidation of all company legislation in a Companies Act. This practice was followed during the first half of the twentieth century with new consolidations in 1908,[81] 1929[82] and 1948.[83] Thereafter it ran into difficulties. The latest, and probably the last, Company Law Committee (the Jenkins Committee) was appointed in 1960 and reported in 1962.[84] While it was sitting, legislation was passed introducing into Scottish law the valuable English concept of

[80] [1897] A.C. 22, H.L. Below, pp. 85–87.
[81] Companies (Consolidation) Act 1908 (implementing the Report of the Loreburn Committee: 1906 Cmnd. 3052).
[82] Companies Act 1929 (implementing the Report of the Greene Committee: 1926 Cmd. 2657, and an earlier Report of the the Wrenbury Committee: 1918 Cd. 9138).
[83] Companies Act 1948 (implementing the Report of the Cohen Committee: 1945 Cmd. 6659).
[84] 1962 Cmnd. 1749.

the floating charge,[85] and shortly thereafter there were two further Acts. One attempted to curb the abuses flowing from a growing practice, by companies which were not recognised banks, of inviting the public to deposit money with them[86] and the other simplified somewhat the process of transferring stocks and shares.[87] But thereafter successive Governments proved dilatory in implementing the Jenkins Committee's recommendations.

A first step was taken in the Companies Act 1967 which, in addition to tightening the prudential regulation of insurance companies, abolished the 1948 Act's distinction between "exempt" and other (non-exempt) private companies[88] and made a few other amendments relating to companies generally. This was intended by the then Labour Government as a prelude to "wider reforms in the structure and philosophy of our company law" after a re-examination of "the whole theory and purpose of the limited joint stock company, the comparative rights and obligations of shareholders, directors, creditors, employees and the community as a whole."[89] Nothing as ambitious had been attempted by any Company Law Committee or Royal Commission; nor has it been attempted since. The succeeding Conservative Government introduced a Bill in 1973 which would have implemented most of the other recommendations of the Jenkins Committee and, had it been enacted and followed by a reconsolidation, our company law would have been more intelligible both to us and to our Continental partners in the European Communities to which we had belatedly secured admission. Unfortunately the Bill lapsed with the defeat of the Conservative administration in the General Election of 1974 and was never resuscitated. An Insolvency Act and a further Companies Act, dealing mainly with accounts and audit, were passed in 1976, but thereafter the legislative programme was dominated by the need to comply with our EC obligations.

The European Commission has an ambitious programme for harmonising the company laws of the Member States, and the United Kingdom is faced by the need to implement by legislation[90] a continuing flow of Directives, many of which are specifically

[85] Companies (Floating Charges) (Scotland) Act 1961 (implementing a Report of the Scottish Law Reform Committee: (Cmnd. 1017). This, however, did not introduce receiverships which were also unknown to Scottish law. Following a Report of the Scottish Law Commission (1970 Cmnd. 4336) this omission was rectified by the Companies (Floating Charges and Receiverships) (Scotland) Act 1972.

[86] Protection of Depositors Act 1963 which was later superseded by the Banking Act 1979 and, now, 1987.

[87] Stock Transfer Act 1963. Further steps in this direction were later taken by the Stock Exchange (Completion of Bargains) Act 1976 and by s.207 of the Companies Act 1989 and, in relation to the stocks of public authorities, by the Stock Transfer Act 1982.

[88] See Chap. I at p. 12 n. 39, above.

[89] H.C.Debs., Vol. 741, Col. 359.

[90] The European Communities Act 1972 confers a limited power to use secondary legislation rather than an Act of Parliament but most Directives cannot be satisfactorily implemented except by the latter.

designated as Company Law Directives or impinge closely on company law.[91] The European Communities Act 1972 attempted to comply with our immediate obligations in this respect and, in its section 9, to implement the First Company Law Directive relating to publicity, pre-incorporation contracts, the *ultra vires* doctrine and the authority of directors. In 1980 and 1981 two major Companies Acts were passed, primarily to implement respectively the Second Company Law Directive, relating to the formation of public companies and the maintenance of their capital, and the Fourth relating to accounts.

The fact that compliance with our international obligations made it necessary to find a niche for these implementing measures in the legislative programme provided an opportunity to include also provisions unrelated to the Directives but thought to be desirable (and overdue) domestic reforms. This opportunity was seized to a greater extent than the Government had initially envisaged, with the result that in each case the Act emerged some 50 per cent. longer than the Bill as originally introduced. These Acts made very substantial changes relating, in particular, to duties of directors and conflicts of interest, insider dealing, remedies for members unfairly prejudiced, company names, acquisition by companies of their own shares,[92] providing financial assistance for the acquisition of their shares, and disclosure of interests in shares.

The 1985 consolidation

This spate of legislation made the need for a new consolidation of the Companies Acts an urgent necessity—our company legislation was in a worse state than at any time this century.[93] In achieving this mammoth task by 1985 the draftsman was assisted by prior use of the power, inserted in the Companies Act 1981,[94] for amendments, which the Law Commission and the Scottish Law Commission recommended as needed to produce a satisfactory consolidation, to be made by Orders in Council. He also had the courage not to follow slavishly the wording of the provisions to be consolidated and succeeded in improving both wording and arrangement. What emerged was a main Companies Act 1985, and three supplemental Acts of the same year, the Company Securities (Insider Dealing) Act,

[91] See Chap. 4, below.
[92] On which a Consultative Document, *The Purchase by a Company of its Own Shares*, had been published as 1980 Cmnd. 7944.
[93] By 1984 the Companies Acts 1948–1983 officially consisted of: the principal Act of 1948, Parts I and III of the Companies Act 1967, the Companies (Floating Charges and Receivers) (Scotland) Act 1972, s.9 of the European Communities Act 1972, ss.1 to 4 of the Stock Exchange (Completion of Bargains) Act 1976 (but not the Stock Transfer Acts 1963 and 1982), s.9 of the Insolvency Act 1976, the Companies Acts 1976, 1980 and 1981 and a short but highly technical Companies (Beneficial Interests) Act 1983.
[94] s.116.

the Business Names Act and the Companies Consolidation (Consequential Provisions) Act.

Unfortunately the consolidation could not include important pieces of legislation then in preparation. These were, first, the Insolvency Acts 1985 and 1986. The 1985 Act, implementing the Report of the Cork Committee[95]—though not as comprehensively as the Committee had hoped—made major reforms both to the law of individual bankruptcy and to company winding up. The second consolidated the new and the surviving earlier legislation on these subjects. The result was to remove from the Companies Act 1985 all the provisions relating to winding up and receiverships. This was followed by the Company Directors Disqualification Act 1986 which consolidated all the extant provisions empowering the courts to disqualify miscreants from acting as directors or being concerned in the management of companies—provisions which had previously been split between Insolvency Acts and Companies Acts. Secondly, there was the Financial Services Act 1986 which, in addition to repealing and replacing the Prevention of Fraud (Investments) Act 1958[96] by a detailed and sophisticated system of regulation of those professionally engaged in investment business, repealed and replaced all the "prospectus provisions" of the Companies Act, amended a number of its other provisions, particularly in relation to take-overs, and replaced some sections of the Company Securities (Insider Dealing) Act. This has left gaping holes in the Companies Act and unconsolidated Insider Dealing legislation. It has, however, also led to a major, and desirable, reclassification of subject-matter, distinguishing Company Law from Insolvency Law and from Securities Regulation.

Reclassification of Company Law

Hitherto the winding up of companies had been seen as a branch of company law divorced from the bankruptcy law relating to individuals. Now both need to be regarded as branches of a single subject—Insolvency Law. It is, perhaps, anomalous that members' voluntary winding up of solvent companies should be dealt with in the Insolvency Act; it might have been better if that had remained in the Companies Act (or, failing that, if the Insolvency Act had been entitled the Bankruptcy and Winding Up Act). But it is an advance to have recognised the essential unity of bankruptcy and insolvent liquidation and, accordingly, that Company Law should concentrate on the life, rather than the death and interment, of companies. That, of course, does not mean that companies (or books on Company Law) can wholly ignore what will happen if companies become insolvent.

[95] (1982) Cmnd. 8558.
[96] For an analysis of the defects of the 1958 Act: see Gower, *Review of Investor Protection: A discussion document* (1982, HMSO).

Even more important are the implications of the Financial Services Act.[97] Many other common law countries have long recognised that what most of them call Securities Regulation is a distinct and important subject (and, incidentally, one in which it is lucrative to specialise). We, however, had treated it, in so far as we recognised it at all, as an unimportant adjunct to Company Law. That has changed now that the primitive Prevention of Fraud (Investments) Act 1958 (which was virtually identical with the pre-War Act of the same name) has been replaced by an up-to-date system modelled to a large extent on that of the United States. By whatever name it is called—Securities Regulation, Investment Regulation, Financial Services Regulation or whatever—and wherever one draws its precise boundaries, it has become an important subject in its own right and one on which books will need to be written and courses conducted at Law Schools. Some books already have been written; but, as yet, mainly compilations and annotations of primary and secondary legislation and of the rules of the overseer regulatory authority—the Securities and Investments Board (SIB)—and those of its recognised self-regulatory organisations (SROs) and professional bodies (RPBs). Though valuable to practitioners, these books are not adequate as a basis for academic courses.

This book does not attempt to deal with the new subject in so far as that is concerned with the regulation of those who carry on investment business—the financial services industry. But it has to deal with some of the matters covered by the Financial Services Act. Public issues, take-overs and insider dealing are rightly dealt with in that Act since they relate to dealings with investments, whether or not these are the securities of companies. On the other hand, the most important types of investment in these respects are company securities. Hence such matters also have to be dealt with in books on Company Law and not left exclusively to those on Financial Services Regulation.

The Companies Act 1989

A further Companies Act[98] was passed in 1989. The primary purpose of this was to implement the Seventh EC Company Directive on consolidated accounts and the Eighth on audits, but,

[97] The Act was largely based on the Gower Report, *Review of Investor Protection, Part I* (1984 Cmnd. 9125) and Part II (1985, HMSO) and on a White Paper, *Financial Services in the United Kingdom: A new framework for investor protection:* 1985 Cmnd. 9432. For a brief (and "personal") account of the genesis of the Act and the main features of the regulatory system, see "*Big Bang" and City Regulation* (1988) 51 M.L.R. 1. Although in this area the influence of the EC had hitherto been less dominant, it had not been negligible (for example in relation to public issues). The EC has now embarked on a programme designed to lead to a unified European financial market by the end of 1992. Happily the U.K. with a more advanced system than many of its partners has been able to influence these developments to a greater extent than it has with the Company Law Directives.

[98] Of 216 sections and 24 Schedules!

once again, the opportunity was taken to include a number of domestic reforms (and to amend the Financial Services Act). The amendments to the Companies Act were substantial and, at the time of writing, there has not been an official reconsolidation.[99] Unless that is undertaken promptly after each new Companies Act (for others will undoubtedly have to be enacted to implement further Company Law Directives) much of the good work which culminated in the 1985 consolidation will have been in vain.

Reorganisation at the DTI

The Department of Trade and Industry (the DTI) is now the Government Department responsible, among many other matters, for Company Law, Insolvency and Financial Services Regulation. Under the Secretary of State there is usually an Under Secretary of State for Corporate Affairs. The Board of Trade has effectively ceased to exist as such—though its ghost haunts the Department's corridors and the Secretary of State sometimes wears his presidential hat on social occasions. What under the Board had been a single Companies and Insurance Division, has now become distinct Companies, Financial Services, Insolvency, Insurance and Investigations Divisions. The first of these is at present organised in four branches most of which are located in London. In 1988, the Companies Registration offices for England and Wales (located in Cardiff)[1] and for Scotland (located in Edinburgh) were converted into an Executive Agency[2] known as *Company House* with a view to affording them greater autonomy but without severing their relationship with the Department.

In 1978 the Department had re-established a standing Company Law Advisory Committee of outside experts but this was no more successful than earlier such efforts and it was disbanded in 1983.[3] The experiment of recruiting a part-time Adviser on Company Law, started in 1979, has now been replaced by the engagement of consultants to review specific subjects.

[99] But unless officialdom is prepared to allow this to be done on consolidation retaining the existing numbering of the sections, the professions would probably prefer this to be left to the commercial publishers. Other countries do not boggle at sections numbered 35A, 35B (etc.) and there is no valid reason why we should.

[1] But with search facilities still available in London, a facility which it is intended to extend to other cities. A programme of computerisation of the Registries is in hand but, at present, is less advanced than in some other common law countries; in Singapore, for example, a lawyer or accountant can make searches and file all documents (including all those required on original registration) via his own office computers.

[2] As did the Insolvency Service in 1990.

[3] But see the recent Memorandum of the Law Society's Company Law Committee (approved by the Law Reform Committee of the General Council of the Bar): *The Reform of Company Law* (July 1991 No. 255. This, rightly, is highly critical of the present procedures for keeping Company Law up-to-date. It suggests the establishment of an independent Company Law Commission on the lines of those in some other Commonwealth countries (and which have produced consultative documents and reports the likes of which the D.T.I. has been unable to match).

CHAPTER 4

THE FUTURE?

THE purpose of this chapter is to draw attention to the main developments in English Company Law that are likely to occur in the near future and to certain fundamental problems that are likely to continue to plague us. As has happened over the past two decades, future developments will depend to a large extent on developments in the relevant law of the European Community (the EC). Hence what is likely to occur there is dealt with first, prefaced by a brief overview[1] of the manner in which Community law becomes part of a member State's domestic law or effectively dictates the content of that State's domestic law.

THE IMPACT OF THE EC[1a]

Sources of Community law

The EC was established by the Treaty of Rome, negotiated between the original member States and acceded to by the United Kingdom when we secured admission in 1973.[2] Prior to our accession the Treaty and the Community legislation made under it were foreign law, affecting British individuals and companies only to the extent that they undertook operations in or with a member State of the Community.[3] Thereafter, sometimes directly as Community law or, more often, indirectly as United Kingdom legislation implementing Community obligations, they became part of our law capable of affecting operations even if these were exclusively within the United Kingdom.

[1] EC Law is now a well-established subject in the legal curriculum with a voluminous literature for which this "brief overview" is not intended as a substitute but merely as a "child's guide" for those who have not studied it.

[1a] It has not been possible to deal adequately with all the changes agreed at the Community's Summit meeting at Maastricht in December 1991 since the MS of this edition had been delivered to the publishers before that date. However an effort has been made to insert mentions of the most fundamental amendments.

[2] There were then (and at the time of writing still are) three Communities, i.e. the major European Economic Community (the EEC) the European Coal and Steel Community (the ECSC) and the European Atomic Energy Community (Euratom). But in practice they have operated as one and, as a result of the Treaty amendments agreed at the Maastricht Summit, they will officially become one EC.

[3] cf. Imperial Chemical Industries v. EC [1972] E.C.R. 619 (alleged violation of EC anti-trust law).

Community Law consists essentially of the Treaty (and any amending measures[4]), secondary legislation made thereunder, and decisions of the European Court of Justice. There are two main types of secondary EC legislation: Regulations and Directives. According to Article 189 of the Treaty, the distinction between them is that Regulations apply to member States generally and are binding and enforceable without any further action on their part, whereas Directives are binding only upon those member States to which they are addressed and only as to the results to be achieved, leaving the manner and form of implementing them to the member States concerned. That, however, is somewhat misleading. In practice, if Regulations are to be fully effective in member States some action by them is likely to be needed.[5] And, normally, Directives are addressed to all member States and prescribe the means as well as the ends to be achieved; moreover, under the jurisprudence of the European Court, provisions in them which are sufficiently clear and complete may have direct effect without implementing action by member States.[6]

The changes to our law thought to be necessary to comply with Community obligations at the date of our accession were made by the European Communities Act 1972, those relating to Company Law being in section 9.[7] In addition, the Act acknowledged our continuing responsibilities by providing, in section 2, for recognition and enforcement of all rights, obligations and remedies to which, under the Treaties, effect is to be given without further enactment,[8] and by declaring that legislation, passed or to be passed, was to be construed and have effect accordingly.[9] The section also facilitated implementation of Community legislation by enabling such implementation to be by secondary legislation,[10] subject to the limitations imposed by Schedule 2 to the Act.[11]

There are a number of ways in which a member State may fail to comply with its Treaty obligations. For example, it may fail to observe a provision of the Treaty or a Regulation or to implement a Directive within the time prescribed or to implement it fully. The

[4] Of which the most important at present is the so-called Single European Act (EC No. 12 of 1986). But the amendments, agreed at Maastricht, to almost every Part of the Treaty are so extensive as to have been described as "re-writing" it. And, under a Protocol, unanimously agreed, the 11 member States other than the U.K. will be enabled to proceed with the "social" Articles 117–122 with the U.K. excluded from further deliberations taken and from the application of measures taken as a result.
[5] The principal Regulation relevant to company law, Regulation No. 2137/85, on European Economic Interest Groupings (EEIGs)—see below p. 66—specifically leaves some matters to national laws. So does the Draft Regulation on the proposed Statute for the European Company: see below pp. 67–69.
[6] See below, pp. 57, 58.
[7] Now split between ss. 18, 35, 36, 42, 351, 711 and Sched. 22 of the Companies Act 1985.
[8] s.2(1).
[9] s.2(4).
[10] Order in Council or Ministerial regulation.
[11] Para. 2(1).

primary sanction then will be that the Commission[12] or another member State[13] may bring the offending State before the European Court. Generally the failure will not be of concern to individuals or companies. But questions of Community law may, and increasingly do, arise for decision in national courts, even in litigation between private individuals or companies. For example, in litigation in England, the interpretation of domestic legislation designed to implement an EC Directive may arise for decision.[14] If the domestic legislation is capable of being construed in a way which will effectively implement the Directive, the English court should so construe it.[14] Or a party may argue that a provision of the Treaty or secondary EC legislation has direct effect and gives rise to an enforceable community right on which he is entitled to rely.

In either event, a question of interpretation of Community legislation may arise. In the first example, the English judge may well find the Directive at least as difficult to construe as the English legislation. In the second, two questions are likely to arise: (i) does the Community legislation give rise to a directly enforceable right? (ii) If so, what is the extent of that right? If the case cannot be disposed of without answers to these questions, the English court may refer the matter to the European Court for a preliminary ruling,[15] which the English court must then follow.[16]

As a result of such references, the European Court has drawn a more subtle distinction between provisions of the Treaty or Regulations and those of Directives. The former are directly applicable and enforceable by or against member States or private individuals or companies if capable of being so construed.[17]

12 Treaty, Art. 169. Most member States (including the U.K.) have suffered this fate though the U.K. has a better record than most in implementing timeously—though not always fully.

13 Treaty, Art. 170.

14 *Garland* v. *British Rail Engineering Ltd.* [1983] 2 A.C. 751, H.L.; *Pickstone* v. *Freemans plc* [1989] A.C. 66, H.L.; and *Lister* v. *Forth Dry Dock* [1990] 1 A.C. 546, H.L.(Sc.) where this was done by adopting a purposive construction of a U.K. statutory instrument involving the deemed insertion of 19 words so as to make it consistent with a Directive as interpreted by the ECJ. But *cf. Duke* v. *Reliance Systems Ltd.*, [1988] A.C. 618 H.L.

15 Treaty, Art. 177 and European Communities Act s.3(1). The ECJ has decided that, in exceptional circumstances, it may, when first giving such an interpretation, place limitations on the extent to which this affects legal relationships previously established in good faith: see *Blaizot* v. *University of Liège* (Case 24/86) [1989] 1 C.M.L.R. 57, where it did so, and *Barra* v. *Belgian State* (Case 309/85) [1988] 2 C.M.L.R. 409, where it declined, the relevant interpretation having already been given without a limitation in *Gravier* v. *Ville de Liège* [1985] E.C.R. 593.

16 Pending receipt of the ECJ's ruling the English courts may be faced with the problem of how it should act to protect the position of the parties. The H.L. sought the guidance of the ECJ on this: R. v. *Secretary of State for Transport, ex p. Factortame Ltd.* [1990] 2 A.C. 85, H.L. In its reply the ECJ ruled that it was the duty of the English Courts to grant such interim relief as was needed to protect Community rights, disapplying any rule of English law that purported to preclude their doing so: *ibid.* (No. 2) [1991] 1 A.C. 603, H.L.

17 Thus a female employee discriminated against in respect of pay could rely, in the English courts, on Art. 119 of the Treaty, which has been held to be directly

—continued on next page

Directives, however, are addressed to member States and accordingly, although provisions in them, if sufficiently clear and precise, may have direct effect when a member State, to which they are addressed,[18] fails to implement them properly within the time allowed,[18] they are not directly enforceable by individuals or companies except against the defaulting member State or its organs or emanations.[19]

In respect of the obligation to give direct effect to Community Law, even if National Law is inconsistent with it, the jurisprudence of the European Court is becoming increasingly strict[19a] and will face the English Courts with questions in relation to company law matters; indeed it already has.[20] And some of the Company Law and related Directives are certainly sufficiently clear and precise to be capable of direct application,[21] the main problem being the increasing practice of allowing member States various prescribed options between which they may choose.

The single European market

A main objective of the EC is to bring about a single integrated Community-wide market. The principal mechanisms for achieving this

[17] *continued from previous page*
applicable (*Defrenne* v. *Sabena* [1978] E.C.R. 1365, ECJ), notwithstanding that she had no remedy under the Equal Pay Act 1970: *Macarthys* v. *Smith* [1981] Q.B.180, ECJ and C.A.

[18] A common occurrence.

[19] *Marshall* v. *Southampton and W. Hampshire A.H.A.* [1986] Q.B. 401, ECJ and C.A. (but see *ibid.* (No. 2)) [1991] E.C.R. 136 C.A. *Johnson* v. *Chief Constable of R.U.C.* [1967] Q.B. 129, ECJ, where the individual plaintiffs succeeded under what the English courts have described as "a principle akin to estoppel," the State being prevented from taking advantage of its failure to amend the national legislation: *Foster* v. *British Gas plc* [1991] 2 A.C. 306, H.L.. Contrast *Duke* v. *Reliance Systems Ltd.* [1988] A.C. 618, H.L., where the plaintiffs failed since the defendants were not regarded as "organs or emanations" of the State and the courts felt unable to construe the then U.K. legislation purporting to implement a Directive in a manner consistent with it. And see *Doughty* v. *Rolls-Royce plc, The Times*, where the C.A. held, with the like result, that Rolls-Royce, notwithstanding that it was wholly-owned by the State and provided services to the State, which were of importance to the defence of the realm, was not an organ or emanation of it but an independent commercial company against which these principles could not be invoked.

[19a] See *e.g. Francovich* v. *Italian Republic* (Cases C–6/90 and C–9/90) *The Times* Euro L.R, 20th Nov. 91; *Marleasing S.A.* v. *La Comercial S.A.* (Case 6–106/89) not yet reported but see [1991] C.M.L.L. Rw. 205–223. In the light of these ECJ decisions (and *Factortáme* above n. 16) that of the H.L. in *Duke* (n. 19) seems insupportable.

[20] *R.* v. *H.M. Treasury, ex p. Daily Mail & General Trust* [1989] Q.B. 446, ECJ, where an English court had referred to the European Court the preliminary question whether the refusal of the Treasury to consent (under the then s.482 of the Income and Corporation Taxes Act 1970) to the transfer of the company's central management and control from England to the Netherlands conflicted with Community law on freedom of establishment. See also *Lister* v. *Forth Dry Dock*, above n. 14.

[21] Initially the Listing Directives 79/279/EEC, 80/390/EEC and 82/121/EEC were implemented by appending them verbatim to The Stock Exchange (Listing) Regulations (1984 S.I. 716), which made them part of the U.K. law and repealed or disapplied such existing statutory provisions as were inconsistent with them: see below p. 65.

are envisaged as the abolition of restrictions on the right of establishment, measures ensuring freedom of capital movements, freedom to provide Community-wide services and, to the extent necessary, harmonisation of legal regulations throughout the Community. A new impetus was given to this programme in 1986 when the Governments of all member States subscribed to the Single European Act[22] which came into force on 1 July 1987. This Act added a number of new Articles to the Treaty and amended others with a view to ensuring the establishment, over a period expiring on 31 December 1992, of the internal market, defined as "an area without internal frontiers in which the free movement of goods, persons, services and capital is ensured ... [23] The main change designed to hasten progress was to permit the Council to adopt by a qualified majority[24] (instead of unanimously) proposals based on a considerable number of Articles of the Treaty as supplemented by the Act.[25]

Even so, and despite the considerable progress that had already been made in certain areas,[26] it is impossible to believe that the whole programme can be fully achieved before 1993. The process of EC legislation is lengthy and complicated. Draft proposals are initiated by the Commission and, normally, then discussed in a group, convened by it, of "experts" from member States. After adoption by the Commission as formal Proposals these are sent to the European Parliament and to the Economic and Social Committee (ECOSOC) and are communicated to the Council. In the light of the opinions expressed by the Parliament and the Committee, the Commission may amend the Proposals before presenting draft legislation to the Council where it is discussed by a working group of officials from member States. It is subsequently referred to the Committee of Permanent Representatives (COREPER) which remits it to the Council for final decision. Since the coming into force of the Single European Act, under a "cooperation procedure" designed to enhance the role of the Parliament, the latter at this stage, is given a second opportunity of expressing an opinion prior to final adoption of the measure by the Council.[26a]

All this may take years and, at any rate in the case of Directives, further years have to be allowed for implementation by member

22 EC No. 12. Supp. 2/86 to EC Bull. and (1986) Cmnd. 9758.
23 New Art. 8A. Among the Declarations annexed was one declaring the "firm political will to take, before 1 January 1993, the decisions necessary to complete the internal market ...... ";
24 The number of votes (76 in total) which member States have on the Council is weighted according to their size. Under the amended Art. 148 of the Treaty a qualified majority is one in which 54 votes are cast in favour (by at least eight members if, unusually, the vote is not on a Proposal of the Commission).
25 In particular, Arts. 7, 8A, 28, 54(2), 59 and 100A.
26 *e.g.* in the financial field, in relation to banking, insurance, company law, unit trusts and stock exchange listing.
26a And see n. 30 below for the future position resulting from the Maastricht Agreement.

States. Clearly, therefore, despite the head of steam behind it the programme is unlikely to be fully completed before the end of the century and company law developments in the United Kingdom will continue to be dominated by it well into the next.

Harmonisation of company and related Law[27]

As we have seen,[28] prior to the accession of the United Kingdom, the Commission had embarked upon an ambitious programme in relation to Company Law. An early effort was the drawing up of a Convention on the mutual recognition of companies and other profit-making bodies with legal personality[29] which Article 220 of the Treaty had specifically required member States to negotiate. Under the Act of Accession, the United Kingdom undertook to accede to the Convention which, however, has never come into force. The Netherlands did not ratify it and, on the enlargement of the Community, it was generally accepted that no Convention was needed since, in practice, all member States already afforded such recognition. Hence this particular project has, in effect, been abandoned. This, however, did not discourage activity on other fronts.

The Company Law Directives

The main action has been the series of Company Law Directives[30] designed to harmonise the laws of the member States to the extent necessary to achieve the aims of the Treaty. The Treaty seems to use indiscriminately the expressions "co-ordination," "harmonisation," and "approximation," all of which appear to bear the same meaning which clearly stops short of "unification"—at any rate unless the aims of the Treaty cannot be achieved without unification. That is unlikely to be the case in relation to Company Law; indeed some have queried whether "harmonisation" (the expression favoured in the two

[27] The Companies Division of the DTI produces (at present annually) a useful publication, *Harmonisation of Company and Related Law in the European Community: Progress of Draft Directives and other Proposals*, which indicates the progress made in the implementation of proposals in this area. The latest lists some 40 in the pipeline and this represents only a fraction of the total which will be needed for the completion of the internal market: see the Commission's White Paper, *Completing the Internal Market* (Com. (85) 310).

[28] pp. 50, 51 above.

[29] EC Bull. Supp. 2/1969.

[30] Hitherto these Directives have been made primarily under Art. 54(3)(*g*) of the Treaty. But under the Maastricht amendments they will in future normally be made under a new Art. 189B after consulting the Econ. and Social Committee. This Art. increases the role of the European Parliament and establishes a Conciliation Committee to resolve disputes between the Parliament and the Council. If that Committee fails to do so the Council by a qualified majority will get its way unless the Parliament, by an absolute majority, rejects it. Art. 100A under which directives are sometimes made, is similarly amended.

English-speaking States) can be really "necessary" (as opposed to desirable) in order to achieve the Treaty's aims. Nevertheless, Directives have tended to become more and more detailed in respect of method as well as aims and more like Regulations—which could achieve unification, at any rate to the extent possible without a single European language.

The First Company Law Directive, which had been adopted prior to our accession, was implemented by section 9 of the European Communities Act 1972, the Second Directive by the Companies Act 1980 and the Fourth Directive by the Companies Act 1981. Subsequently the Third Directive (78/855/EEC) relating to certain types of corporate mergers within a single member State and a later Sixth Directive (82/891/EEC) relating to a form of de-merger known on the Continent as a "scission," were implemented, under the powers conferred by section 2 of the European Communities Act 1972,[31] by the Companies (Mergers and Divisions) Regulations 1987.[32] Neither type of transaction was commonly undertaken in the United Kingdom but could have been under sections 425 to 427 of the Companies Act 1985. Accordingly the Regulations amended the Act to comply with the Directives by inserting in the Companies Act a new section 472A and a new Schedule (now 15B). The Seventh Directive (83/349/EEC), which supplements the provisions of the Fourth Directive by dealing with group accounts, and the Eighth Directive (84/253/EEC), which deals with the qualifications of auditors were implemented by the United Kingdom in the Companies Act 1989. Proposals for a Tenth Directive, facilitating mergers, of the types dealt with in the Third Directive, between companies in different member States, for an Eleventh, on disclosures to be made by branches of companies established in one member State and carrying on business in another and for a Thirteenth on Takeovers are proceeding through the Community's legislative processes. A Twelfth on single member private companies (not, one would have thought, a matter on which the need for harmonisation is self-evident) awaits implementation in the United Kingdom.[33] So does the important Directive 89/592/EEC (not in the numbered Company Law series) on Co-ordinating Regulations on Insider Dealing.[34] There are also implemented directives on accounts and auditors: see Chaps. 17 & 18.

Unfortunately, less progress has been made with two Draft Directives (the Fifth and the Ninth) which are of considerable importance and deserve individual treatment.

[31] See p. 56 above.
[32] 1987 S.I. No. 1991.
[33] A Consultation Document circulated by the DTI in Nov. 1991 indicates that it is proposed to implement it by a Statutory Instrument making the essential amendments to the Act.
[34] On which see Chap. 23 below.

The Draft Fifth Directive. Proposals for this directive on the structure of public limited companies, first emerged in 1972. It provided for harmonisation of such matters as the duties and liabilities of directors, the powers of the general meeting, the inter-relationship between the various organs of the company, the rights and remedies of shareholders and minorities, and the approval of annual accounts. Many of the proposals in these respects are valuable and not especially controversial. But what made the Draft highly controversial and caused it to get bogged-down was that is was originally based upon the inter-related concepts of two-tier boards of directors and "co-determination."

These concepts originated in Germany. Since 1861, German public companies have had a two-tier board structure: a supervisory board to control the basic policy of the company and a management board to manage its operations. The supervisory board appoints the management board but otherwise the two are distinct and a member of one may not be a member of the other. After the 1939–45 War, on the instigation of the occupation authorities in West Germany, representatives elected by the company's employees were, by law, given half the places on the supervisory boards of coal and steel companies and, in 1952, one third in the case of other large companies, a proportion increased to nearly one half in 1976. Representation at board level is under-pinned by works councils providing for formal consultation with employees at lower levels. Less far-reaching approaches to this system of *Mitbestimmung* or "co-determination" have been adopted in some other European countries.[35]

The first Draft proposed comparable harmonised provisions throughout the Community in the case of the larger public companies.[36] To this, however, some member States were strongly opposed. In the United Kingdom in the 1970s, under Labour Governments and when trade unions were more powerful, industrial democracy was the subject of heated debate and led to the appointment and report of the Bullock Committee[37] (which split three ways but with a majority favouring a unitary board and making detailed suggestions for worker representation) and to a Government White Paper proposing co-determination but under a two-tier board.[38] But the subsequent Conservative Government set its face firmly against worker participation other than on a voluntary basis,[39] and in the light of the weakened position of the trade unions,[39] co-

---

[35] The Netherlands, Luxemburg, Sweden and Denmark, while France permits optional two-tier boards (which very few of its companies have adopted).
[36] In the latest Draft it would apply only to public companies with more than 1000 employees.
[37] *Report of the Committee on Industrial Democracy.* (1977) Cmnd. 6076.
[38] *Industrial Democracy*, (1978) Cmnd. 7231.
[39] Whose attitude had always been somewhat ambivalent.

determination officially ceased to be regarded as a live issue. The pity is that whatever one's views may be on two-tier boards and co-determination, harmonisation is certainly desirable on many of the less controversial matters covered by the Draft. But there seemed to be little hope of making progress on them until a consensus in the Community was achieved regarding co-determination. However, later Drafts are no longer tied to the German concepts. *Compulsory* two-tier boards were abandoned in that published in 1983 and in the latest[40] all that is required is that a member State must make provision for either one or both of a one-tier or a two-tier system and that if it makes provision for both it may permit each company to choose which to adopt. Moreover worker-representation on the supervisory board, if there is one, or on the unitary board, if there is not, is not the only permitted method of providing worker-participation. There are three options: (i) board representation, (ii) a separate organ, representing employees only, with rights to be regularly given information and to be consulted, and (iii) a collective agreement concluded between the company (or an organisation representing the company) and an organisation representing the employees providing that the concluded agreement provides at least for (i) or (ii).[41] Since (ii) amounts to "consultation" rather than "co-determination," this is a far cry from the compulsory introduction of anything like the German system. It seems to be generally acceptable in most member States but the present United Kingdom Government remains implacably opposed, believing "that in the United Kingdom employee involvement depends on a spirit of cooperation rather than on formal machinery, and that it is best introduced voluntarily."[42] Hence whether the Draft Directives will now have a smoother ride may depend on the result of the United Kingdom General Election in 1992. Meanwhile some progress has been made on the less controversial matters in the Draft and the Maastricht Summit has shown that the Community is adroit in finding means of preventing the United Kingdom's opposition from wrecking a general consensus of other member States.

Hence, there now seems to be a real prospect that the Directive will be adopted reasonably soon—though its implementation by member States by 1993 is too much to hope for.

The Draft Ninth Directive. This Draft on Groups (as opposed to group *accounts*) was first discussed in the early 1970s and preliminary drafts were given a limited circulation by the Commission in 1974/5, 1981 and 1984. On the latest of these, the Department of Trade and

---

[40] 1988 Draft: appended to the D.T.I.'s Consultative Document of Jan. 1990.
[41] The introduction of this third option caused the British trade unions to swing in favour of its proposal: *cf.* n. 39 above.
[42] See para 4 of the D.T.I. Consultative Document (n. 40 above). But does the British experience suggest that really meaningful employee involvement will be introduced on any scale without compulsion?

Industry published a Consultative Document in 1985. The Draft deals with what have long been recognised as important questions and ones on which English Company Law has failed to answer satisfactorily,[43] namely: How far is the dominant company in a Group entitled to operate subsidiary companies for its benefit, or that of the Group as a whole, ignoring the interests of members of the subsidiaries? And, when, and to what extent, should it be legally liable to meet the debts of its insolvent subsidiaries? The Draft is based on the German answers to these questions—understandably so since Germany has always been the most advanced in recognising that "enterprise entity" is a more meaningful concept than "corporate entity." As such, however, it is widely regarded, even in Germany, as excessively complicated and inflexible.[44] and it has made no further progress.

Nevertheless, it seems clear that this is an area in which harmonisation is needed urgently. International conglomerates now dominate the supply of financial services and face the Community with grave problems in relation to the Single European Market; problems which will be aggravated while there remains "great diversity of concepts and regulation all over Europe."[45] Hence it is nonsensical for member States to argue, as the United Kingdom has done, that Groups present no serious legal problems and that, even if they did, there would be no need for harmonised regulation. What they should be doing is to seek to improve upon the solutions in the present Draft. It must surely be possible to accept and to implement more simply the basic principles on which the Draft is based, namely that if the parent company wishes to operate subsidiaries primarily in the interests of it or the group as a whole it must (1) give minority shareholders an opportunity of getting out,[46] (2) treat them fairly if they do not, and (3) accept liability for the debts of its insolvent subsidiaries.[47]

Other Community legislation

In addition to the above numbered Company Law Directives, there has been and continues to be a considerable volume of other Community legislation highly relevant to Company Law.

---

[43] See below, pp. 113, 114 and 122, 123.
[44] See Buxbaum & Hopt: *Legal Harmonisation and the Business Enterprise* (de Gruyter 1988) p. 188: "This German law on groups of companies should not be used as a model for other member States. Not only is it extraordinarily complicated and cumbersome, and therefore out of place in countries with different legal traditions (such as Britain and Belgium), but it is even questionable whether it meets its objectives."
[45] *Ibid.* p. 189.
[46] In the U.K. some recognition of this principle is afforded by the provisions of the Take-over Code on mandatory bids, and ss.428–430F of the Companies Act 1985; Chap. 27 below.
[47] The present English law seems to be that, unless there is a formal guarantee, there is no such liability notwithstanding a so-called, "letter of comfort": see *Kleinwort Benson Ltd.* v. *Malaysian Mining Corporation* [1989] 1 W.L.R. 379, C.A.

(a) *The Listing and Public Offering Directives*

Of particular importance have been the three harmonising Listing Directives, 79/279/EEC, 80/390/EEC and 82/121/EEC, relating respectively to admission of securities to official stock exchange listing, listing particulars to be published to lead to stock exchange listing, and continuing disclosure of information relating to listed securities.[48] These were initially implemented by the United Kingdom in haste and unsatisfactorily by Regulations[49] made under section 2 of the European Communities Act 1972.[50] Subsequently, and somewhat more satisfactorily, these Regulations were replaced by Part IV of the Financial Services Act 1986 and regulations made thereunder. The effect has been to produce very substantial changes—to the status of The Stock Exchange, and to the nature and contents of its *Yellow Book*, containing the detailed rules which supplement Part IV of the Financial Services Act.

A further Directives 89/298/EEC, dealing with prospectuses on public offerings generally, should logically have preceded the three listing Directives but it proved more controversial and was not in fact adopted until 1989. Its impact on Directives 80/390 and 87/345 is such that Part IV of the Financial Services Act and the rules and regulations made thereunder will have had to be revised, as will Part V of that Act (dealing with unlisted issues) before it can belatedly be brought into operation. An obstacle to rapid progress has been that a further amending Directive on mutual recognition was found to be needed to clear up an anomaly which had come to light and this Directive was not adopted until May 1990. Hence it is unlikely that the aim will be finally achieved before 1992.

(b) *The UCITS Directive*

Another Directive (85/611/EEC) relates to the co-ordination of laws and administrative provisions concerning what have come to be known here by the acronym UCITS ("undertakings for collective investment in transferable securities") *i.e.* the type of investment medium presently undertaken under United Kingdom law through unit trusts but, in some other countries, particularly the United States, more often through open-ended investment companies ("mutual funds"). The Directive contemplates the use of either the

---

[48] These were not included in the numbered Company Law Series since they relate to official listing of securities of other bodies as well as of companies.

[49] The Stock Exchange (Listing) Regulations (1984 S.I. no. 716).

[50] One unsatisfactory feature of this stop-gap solution had been that paragraph 1(c) of Sched. 2 of the Act does not enable Regulations to "confer any power to legislate by means of orders, rules, regulations or other subordinate instrument . . ." and The Stock Exchange, as "the competent authority" under the Directives needed such a power in order that the rules in its revised *Yellow Book* could be given legislative, instead of merely contractual, force.

trust or the corporate form. It has been implemented by Part 1, Chapter VIII of the Financial Services Act and regulations made thereunder, but without, as yet, providing for the formation in the United Kingdom of the corporate, (*i.e.* mutual fund) type. An amending Directive (88/220/EEC) resolves problems arising in some member States by the limits imposed by the principal Directive on the nature of permitted underlying investments.

(c) *The EEIGs Regulation*

In July 1985 a Regulation (No. 2137) was adopted providing for the establishment of an entity to be recognised throughout the Community and known as a European Economic Interest Grouping (or EEIG). Based on the model of the French *Groupement d'Interet Economique*, the EEIG is designed to enable existing business undertakings in different member States to form an autonomous body to provide common services ancillary to the primary activities of its members. Any profits it makes belong to its members and they are jointly and severally responsible for its liabilities.

The basic requirements for the formation of an EEIG are simply the conclusion of a written contract between the members and registration at a registry in the member State where it is to have its official address. The Regulation confers upon the EEIG full legal capacity, though whether it is afforded corporate personality is left to national law, which is also left with considerable scope to supplement the mandatory provisions of the Regulation. Hence, although the Regulation is directly applicable, it provided that EEIGs could not be set up before 1 July 1989 so as to allow member States time to get their houses in order and their registration offices established. The United Kingdom has supplemented the EC Regulations by the European Economic Interest Grouping Regulations 1989[51] which nominate the Companies Registrar as the registering authority and the Secretary of State as the "competent authority." A number of the sections of the Companies Act[52] and the Insolvency Act[53] are applied to an EEIG as if it was a company registered under the Companies Act and it may be wound up as an unregistered company under Part V of the Insolvency Act.[54]

What use English companies will make of this, to us, novel type of body remains to be seen. They may find themselves required to use it if they wish to collaborate in joint operations with companies established in countries, especially France, where it is not so novel. Some English solicitors (partnerships not companies) have already

---

[51] 1989 S.I. No. 638.
[52] Reg. 18 and Sched. 4.
[53] Reg. 19 which applies to them Part III of the Insolvency Act relating to receiverships.
[54] In which event the Company Directors Disqualification Act applies to their managers: Reg. 20.

adopted it as a means of collaboration with lawyers elsewhere in the Community.[55]

(d) *The "European Company" Proposals*

Of the many other Proposals which have not yet been adopted, one, which has long been on the stocks, bears some similarity to the EEIG but is much more ambitious. This is the Proposal for a Regulation for a European Company—*i.e.* one incorporated under Community Law and registered with a Community institution. This is generally regarded as the brain-child of Professor Pieter Sanders of the University of Rotterdam[56] who aired the idea in a speech in 1959 and, in 1965, was invited by the Commission, on the initiative of the French Government, to lead a team which produced, with remarkable speed, a draft Statute published in 1967. Subsequently, after further study, the Commission published a draft Regulation and a revised draft Statute. Thereafter the project was put on the back-burner where it remained until 1988, when the Commission, in a well-argued Memorandum, proposed its revival as a major contribu-tion to the Single European Market, and to its economic and social programmes, and as a possible means of resolving the vexed worker-participation problem. Most member States (but not the United Kingdom) favoured a resumption of work on the Statute and in August 1989 the Commission submitted formal Proposals to the Council for a Regulation[57] on a Statute for a European public limited company, to be known as a *Societas Europea* (SE),[58] and a complementary Directive regarding the involvement of employees in SEs. In December 1989 the Departments of Trade and Industry and of Employment circulated a Consultative Document which includes the texts of the Regulation and Directive[59] and the Commission's commentary thereon.[59a]

As the Directive's provisions regarding worker-participation are in substance identical with those in the latest draft of the Fifth Company Law Directive and raise the same issues[60] no more need be said here than that the United Kingdom Government's opposition to them is no less implacable[61] notwithstanding that they would relate to a

[55] The most useful English publication yet produced on EEIGs is that published by Jordans in 1990.

[56] Though the French claim co-paternity.

[57] COM (89) 268 final - SYN 218.

[58] COM (89) 268 final - SYN 219.

[59] The Regulation and the Directive form a composite whole and must be applied together: Commission's Commentary (appended as Annex B to the Government's Consultative Document) p.1.

[59a] A further Consultative Document on the latest (1991) Proposal was published by the DTI on 30 Jan. 1992 — too late for more than this mention.

[60] On which, particularly in the present context, see Wedderburn, *The Social Charter, European Company and Employment Rights* (1990, The Institute of Employment Rights).

[61] See para. 33 of its Consultative Document.

Community body and not a British one. But mention should be made of two further Commission initiatives in 1991 which are relevant in the context of worker participation whether under the draft Fifth Company Law Directive or the draft European Company Directive. The first, and more important, is a Proposal[62] for a Directive requiring works councils is every "undertaking[63] of European Scale," defined essentially as one which has 1,000 or more employees and at least 100 in each of two member States. It is designed to replace the now defunct *Vredeling* Draft Directive and it spells out workers' rights to information and consultation through works councils at various levels within the undertaking. The second Proposal[64] is for a Council Recommendation designed to encourage employees' profit sharing, share ownership and stock option schemes and to suggest the principles on which they should be based. This was circulated by the Department of Employment in January 1992 with a Consultation Document which concludes that "the Commission can make a constructive contribution in this area by disseminating information and promoting good practice"[65] but that "the Government will, however, want to ensure in negotiations that the recommendation does not in any way limit an organisation's freedom to choose the form of participation appropriate to its particular circumstances."[66]

Reverting now to the European Company Regulation on the Statute for SEs: while the United Kingdom Government see no need for this (but do not object in principle)[67] the Continental member States (and the Commission) regard it as needed if the EC enterprises large enough to compete effectively with those of America and Japan are to emerge. The 1988 Draft permitted the use of an SE only in a restrictive range of circumstances when two or more companies in different member States wished to merge[68] or to form a joint subsidiary or holding company. But subsequent discussions have culminated in an amended Proposal[69] whereby two or more companies of different member States may merge into an SE or a single company in one member State may convert itself or form an SE so long as it has a subsidiary or branch in another member State.[70]

[62] COM (91) 345 final.
[63] Whether or not a company.
[64] COM (91) 259 final.
[65] Para.11.
[66] Para.12. Both Proposals were made under Articles of the Treaty requiring unanimity but, should the U.K. exercise its veto, it would presumably be open to the other 11 Member States and the Commission to take them up under the Maastricht Protocol.
[67] Consultative Document on the 1988 Draft, paras.32 and 35.
[68] Under the Continental practice mergers are effected by merging undertakings (take-overs) of share capital are uncommon and hostile ones virtually impossible) but where the companies concerned are incorporated in different States this at present is impracticable.
[69] COM (91) 174 final - SYN 218.
[70] This comes close to the system in Canada where incorporators have the option of forming under the (federal) Canada Business Corporations Act or under the legislation of one of the Provinces. The ideal in a federation is federal pre-emption of

The draft Statute is, in effect, a skeletal Companies Act. It relies extensively on existing Community legislation (particularly the Company Law Directives which in some cases are incorporated by reference) and provides that matters not expressly mentioned shall be governed by the general principles on which the Regulation is based, and, if these do not provide a solution, by the law relating to public companies of the State in which the SE has its registered office. In the Government's Consultation Document on the 1988 Draft this reliance on national law was rightly identified as a serious flaw,[71] but the later amendments[72] increase the number of matters when that will be so. Nevertheless, as we have seen,[73] it is a feature common to many EC Regulations and though a flaw it does not seem to be a fatal one.

It therefore seems likely that the Regulation (as well as the Directive in one way or another) will eventually be adopted. The danger of this to the United Kindom seems to be that, if it maintains its hostility to the Directive and its apathy towards the Regulation, SEs are more likely to choose to have their headquarters elsewhere than in the United Kingdom, leading perhaps to some shift of the financial centre of the Community from London to, say, Frankfurt.

(e) *Other proposals*

Many other adopted or proposed Directives of direct relevance to Company Law will need to be implemented in the next few years. Among them are measures for harmonised regulation on disclosure of acquisitions or disposals of major holdings in listed companies,[74] and on investment services.[75] Nor can one ignore the action that has been taken, and is continuing, in areas unrelated to company law but which are of immense importance to the operation of companies and to their mobility throughout the Community. Pre-eminent among these are the efforts to promote monetary union and a single European currency, harmonisation of tax regimes and generally to strengthen by Directives or Regulations the Treaty's three fundamental and directly applicable freedoms—freedom of establishment, freedom to provide services and freedom of competition.

UNRESOLVED DOMESTIC PROBLEMS

It would be wrong to give the impression that no developments in English Company Law are likely to occur unless they are required in order to comply with our EC obligations. On the contrary, the

---

[71] *Company Law* (as Australia is at last likely to achieve). But this is not yet practical politics in the quasi-federal EC.
[72] Para.32.
[73] In COM (91) final - SYN 218.
[74] See p. 56 above.
[75] Directive 89/117/EEC.
The Draft Directive on which is proving controversial, particularly as regards provisions on the required capital adequacy of providers of financial services.

Department of Trade and Industry has a large "blood-bank" of needed reforms which it is anxious to transfuse into bodies corporate as opportunities arise. Efforts will undoubtedly be made to do so in Bills which find places in the legislative programme as a result of the obligation to implement EC Directives. It is unlikely, however, that this will result in any fundamental changes or to the resolution of any major questions.

The major questions still unresolved, and likely to remain unresolved, can really be reduced to one: Has our system of Company Law (evolved in the 19th Century) adapted itself adequately to the needs of the 20th and the likely challenges of the 21st? To suggest that it has not, may seem churlish. Unquestionably the limited liability company has been a major instrument in making possible the industrial and commercial developments which have occurred throughout the world. And our system of Company Law was, until recently, the model widely followed in the Common Law countries. That leading role has now been taken over by the United States[76] and we cannot hope to recover it. As a result of our membership of the EC, our Company Law is increasingly diverging from that in the non-European, Common Law world and all we can do is to strive harder to influence the harmonisation programme of the EC so as to ensure that the result preserves the best features of both the Common Law system and the Civil Law systems of our Continental partners.[77]

Nor can it be said that our company legislation has not reacted to changing conditions; legislation which grew from 212 sections and three schedules in the Companies Act 1862 to 747 sections and 25 Schedules in the Companies Act 1985[78] cannot be accused of stagnation.[79] But if one looks at the major developments this century and at the problems that these have thrown up, it is difficult to avoid the conclusion that there has been a reluctance to recognise their implications for Company Law and that, when those implications have been recognised, the reaction has been to add to the existing framework without ever re-examining its foundations to ensure that they are still sufficiently sound to bear the weight of the expanding superstructure.

That sad conclusion can be illustrated by a brief look[80] at five of those developments and at how our Company Law has reacted, or failed to react, to them.

[76] Whose Business Corporation Laws influence Canada, Australia and N. Zealand directly and the rest of the Common Law world mainly through the latter two.
[77] Perhaps other countries (Japan?) might then find it worthwhile to borrow from it.
[78] And this ignores the other three Acts forming part of the 1985 Consolidation and the many other enactments which compilations, such as Butterworth's *Company Law Handbook*, rightly include.
[79] A more legitimate criticism is that it has grown excessively; no other country's legislation goes into such detail.
[80] It must be brief, for the primary object of this book is to explain what the law is and not what ideally it ought to be.

1. *The growth of incorporated, and decline of unincorporated, businesses*

When incorporation with limited liability was introduced in the 19th Century it was envisaged that its use would be in relation to businesses for which entrepreneurs needed to raise capital for large-scale enterprises (*i.e.* in relation to what are now called public limited companies). By the end of that century it had been recognised that it could also be advantageously adopted by partnerships and sole traders. Today it is commonly used throughout industry and commerce, leaving the unincorporated form largely to the professions which, as professional rules are relaxed to permit incorporation, are now also adopting the corporate form. The implications of this have not been wholly ignored by Company Law. On the contrary, ever since the distinction between public and private companies was introduced efforts have been made to adjust the companies' legislation to the needs of small businesses. But these efforts led only to vacillating concessions in favour of "private," "exempt private," "small" and "medium-sized" companies. A belated effort was made in 1981[81] to arouse interest in a separate form of incorporation which would recognise that a company in which there was no separation of ownership and control was, in principle and in its needs, a different animal from a public company. But the attempt failed, and placebos continue to be preferred to major surgery. The most promising of these[82] arose from an initiative by the Institute of Directors which resulted in the D.T.I. in 1988 consulting on what came to be described as *The Elective Regime in Private Companies*. Under this, with the consent of the members, private companies would be enabled to contract out of the need to observe a number of provisions of the Companies Act, thus suspending their application to the company unless and until the members resolve to end that suspension. This proposal was adopted in the Companies Act 1989 under the rubric *De-regulation of Private Companies*[83] and is certainly a step in the right direction though it falls far short of giving such companies a simple Act of their own.

2. *"Corporate Governance"*

The increasing economic power of public companies and the implications of the separation, in their case, of ownership and control have thrown up a number of inter-related problems. Initially these were seen as restricted to finding means of ensuring that those who controlled and managed such companies did so for the benefit of the shareholders and were effectively accountable to them. This was

---

[81] *A New Form of Incorporation for Small Firms: A Consultative Document* (1981 Cmnd. 8171).

[82] And the least, that mooted in 1987 by the Inland Revenue and the DTI in a Consultative Document on "*Disincorporation*" suggesting that small incorporated businesses should be provided with facilities to convert to unincorporated form.

[83] 1989 Act, ss.113–117 inserting new provisions in the 1985 Act.

generally described, particularly in the American literature, as the quest for "stockholder democracy," but that expression is now heard less often as it has come to be accepted that Athenian democracy is not the way to govern a large public company. Instead, this and a wider range of problems have come to be debated under the rubric "*Corporate Governance*."[84] However, the quest for "accountability" to shareholders still continues and has always been recognised as a proper subject for Company Law. The traditional methods of seeking to secure it have mainly been by an increase both in the information which has to be disclosed to shareholders and in the matters that need to be ratified by them in general meeting. These methods can be effective only if the members (i) are sufficiently knowledgeable fully to understand the information, (ii) have large enough shareholdings to be able to influence decisions and (iii) are able and willing to resort to the courts if need be. In the United Kingdom the only shareholders likely to meet conditions (i) and (ii) are institutional investors—who today own some 80 per cent. of listed shares (another major transformation this century). But they rarely meet condition (iii) because, though able, they are usually unwilling to litigate[85] and prefer either to support the managers or to sell their shares if they have lost confidence in them.

The basic problem here is that accountability cannot be secured by legal prescriptions unless these are enforced—in the last resort by the courts. In England,[86] the cost of litigation, even if successful, is such that shareholders are not able and willing to resort to the courts. The major contribution that English Company Law has made in this area is to recognise that what is needed is a watchdog empowered to take action on their behalf (by investigations, inspections and the institution of civil and criminal proceedings).[87] In the company law field that watchdog is the Department of Trade and Industry but in the related field of financial services the role is delegated to a self-standing body (SIB). It is possible that one day its role may be extended to "corporate governance" also.

---

[84] In the U.S.A., the American Law Institute is at present undertaking a mammoth review designed to lead to the publication of *Principles of Corporate Governance: Analysis and Recommendations* (for an account by the A.L.I.'s President of its genesis and goals see (1987) 8 Cardozo L. Rev. 661). In the U.K. a "Committee on Corporate Governance," under the chairmanship of Sir Adrian Cadbury, was appointed in May 1991 but its aim seems to be the more modest one of reviewing the relationship between members, directors and auditors. In Europe the Draft Fifth Directive is frequently (and appropriately) described as one on *Corporate Governance.* For a comparative survey see Hopt & Teubner (Eds.) *Corporate Governance and Directors' Liabilities* (de Gruyter 1985).

[85] And it must be said that on the rare occasions when they have litigated on behalf of the shareholders as a whole they have received precious little encouragement from the English courts: see, *e.g. Prudential Assurance v. Chatterley-Whitfield Collieries* [1949] A.C. 512, H.L., and *Prudential Assurance v. Newman Industries Ltd.* (No. 2), [1982] Ch. 204, C.A.

[86] Contrast the U.S.A., where different rules relating to liability for costs and lawyers' ability and willingness to take cases on a contingent fee, enable litigation to be undertaken with less risk of bankruptcy.

[87] See Chap. 25 below.

Until the 1930s, and despite the fact that it had become commonplace for directors' reports to declare that they recognise that they owed duties not only to the shareholders but also the company's employees, customers, and the community, it had not occurred to company lawyers, at any rate in the Common Law world, that if there were any such duties they had anything to do with Company Law. Since then, however, stimulated by the writings of Berle and Means[88] and the debate between Berle and Dodds in the Harvard Law Review,[89] company lawyers have, often with misgivings, faced the possibility that these wider duties may be owed and that public companies may have developed social consciences.[90] This is coupled with a general recognition that public companies are not, in practice, carried on solely, or even mainly, with a view to the maximisation of profits for the benefit of shareholders but rather to increase the size and importance of the company and thereby the power and influence of its controllers and managers. And now these matters too are debated under the rubric "Corporate Governance."[91]

English Company Law, however, has proved resistant to the acceptance of such subversive notions. Although in the 1970s we toyed with the idea of "co-determination" in the sense of worker-participation in corporate decision-making, this has ceased to be regarded as a live issue here, and is unlikely to become one until Community action succeeds in reviving it.[92] However, two small steps towards recognising that the employees are part of a company, and not just servants of it, were taken by the Companies Act 1980. This declared that "the matters to which directors … shall have regard … shall include the interests of the company's employees in general as well as the interests of its members,"[93] though it carefully went on to ensure that employees, as such, had no power to enforce that duty.[94] And, perhaps more importantly, it declared that on the cessation or transfer of a company's business, the company might make provision for employees or former employees even though that might not be in the best interests of the company.[95] In general, however, the position

[88] *The Modern Corporation and Private Property* (1932) and revised edition (1968): see Chap. 1 p. 9 above.
[89] (1932) 43 Harvard L.Rev., 1049: (1932) 45 Harvard L.Rev. 1145.
[90] See, *e.g.* Berle, *The 20th Century Capitalist Revolution* (1954) and *Power without Property* (1959).
[91] The sub-title of Hopt & Teubner: *loc. cit.* n. 84, above, is "Legal, Economic and Sociological Analyses on Corporate Social Responsibilities." There is an immense literature on all these topics. Those wishing to explore them further will find an exhaustive bibliography at the end of each contribution in that book: see, especially, Herman: *Corporate Control, Corporate Power* (C.U.P. 1981). And, for more recent publications, see Wedderburn, *The Social Responsibility of Companies* (1985) 15 Melbourne University Law Review p. 4 and Trust, *Corporation and the Worker* (1985) 23 Osgoode Hall L.J. 203.
[92] See pp. 62, 63 above.
[93] s.46(1). Now Companies Act 1985, s.309(1).
[94] s.46(2). Now Companies Act 1985, s.309(2).
[95] s.74. Now Companies Act 1985 s.719 and Insolvency Act 1986, s.187. This reverses the effect of the decision in *Parke v. Daily News* [1962] Ch. 927. See p. 169 below.

of employees vis-a-vis the companies who employ them and on which their livelihood is likely to depend to a far greater extent than does that of the shareholders, is still not regarded as a matter for Company Law but for the Law of Master and Servant, latterly given the less Victorian name of Industrial or Labour Law. Voluntary employee share-ownership schemes have been encouraged by the Government by tax and other concessions. But these schemes stop far short of co-determination; if shareholders lack effective participation in decision making, workers are not helped in that regard by becoming shareholders—though that may perhaps lead them to take a greater interest in enhancing the company's prosperity.

So far as concerns the wider social duties of public companies, English Company Law has made no movement at all. Whatever directors themselves may say, the law says that their duties are owed to the company which for this purpose means the long-term interests of its members and, as a result of the recent grudging admissions, its employees. In the United Kingdom the possibility that this may be an anachronism is more widely debated by those who are not lawyers[96] than by those who are—and is less debated by anyone than it is in the USA.[97] And this despite the efforts of the Government to encourage wider business sponsorship of the arts and of other charitable activities.[98]

3. *Monopolies and mergers*

Another world-wide phenomenon has been the growth of monopolies and cartels. In the United States a recognition of the potential dangers led, as early as 1899, to "anti-trust" legislation designed to curb them. In the United Kingdom we tardily followed their example in 1948 by enacting the Monopolies and Restrictive Practices (Enquiry and Control) Act under which potentially dangerous situations, whether arising from mergers, or from restrictive trading agreements between firms, were subjected to an administrative investigation by a new body—the Monopolies Commission. However, by the Restrictive Trade Practices Act 1956, jurisdiction on restrictive agreements was transferred to a new judicial body, the Restrictive Trade Practices Court, and such agreements became illegal unless they could be shown to come within one or more of a limited number of "gateways." The main result of that has been the ending of overt retail price maintenance (except in

[96] See, *e.g.* the one-man crusade of George Goyder in his *The Future of Private Enterprise* (1951), *The Responsible Company* (1961), *The Responsible Worker* (1975) and *The Just Enterprise* (1987).
[97] But the lawyers' contributions are growing: see n. 91 above.
[98] Fortunately, boards of directors do not seem to experience much difficulty in persuading themselves that generosity in this respect is for the good of the company. But the extent of the generosity is minimal in comparison with that in the USA.

relation to books). The former system, however, has been maintained in relation to monopolies and mergers.

The present domestic legislation consists of the Fair Trading Act 1973 (as amended), the Restrictive Trade Practices Act 1976 and the Competition Act 1980.[99] In relation to mergers the position, in brief, is that prospective mergers over a prescribed size may, and in some circumstances must, be referred to the Monopolies and Mergers Commission and orders may be made prohibiting the mergers or otherwise remedying their adverse effects if that Commission finds that they are likely to be contrary to the public interest. An important role in deciding whether there shall be a reference is played by the Director-General of Fair Trading who subjects the proposals to preliminary scrutiny and recommends to the Secretary of State for Trade and Industry whether or not they should be referred. In practice, relatively few proposed mergers are referred and, of those that are, most are allowed through, often subject to undertakings—which, however, have proved difficult to enforce. Hence, in contrast with restrictive trading agreements, the system has had relatively minor effects. Nor, did the directly applicable rules of the Treaty of Rome bite particularly hard despite the efforts of the European Commission to supplement them by securing the adoption of comprehensive Regulations. However, Council Regulation 89/4064/EEC[1] has now led to a clearer division of responsibility between national authorities and the European Commission under a "one-stop" system whereby the latter will deal with major international mergers leaving the rest to the national authorities.

One weakness has been the ambivalent attitude both of the EC and of the United Kingdom Government. The declared present policy of both is to judge mergers and take-overs on whether they reduce competition in, respectively, the EC or the United Kingdom, and largely to ignore other public policy considerations. Even so, a countervailing consideration is also recognised; i.e. that European groups should be sufficiently large and powerful to be able to compete with the mammoth foreign-dominated multi-nationals, an objective which can often be achieved only with some reduction of domestic competition.

These developments have been ignored by United Kingdom Company Law; neither the Companies Act nor the City Code on Take-overs and Mergers[2] as such concerns itself with public policy considerations, whether on grounds of competition or otherwise. This, however, does not mean that the relevant legislation has not had a considerable effect on practice in relation to take-overs. The

[99] Modified, in relation to bodies recognised under the F.S. Act 1986, by Part I, Chap. XIV of that Act.
[1] Which came into force in Sept. 1990.
[2] On which see Chap. 27, below.

City Code requires offers, subject to possible reference to the Monopolies and Mergers Commission or action by the European Commission, to provide that the offer will lapse if there is such a reference or action. Hence it has come to be a recognised ploy in the case of a hostile take-over bid for the directors of the target company to lobby the Director-General of Fair Trading seeking to persuade him to recommend a reference[3]—action which might be thought contrary to the spirit of the Code's General Principles which proscribe action which could result in depriving shareholders of the opportunity to decide on the merits of the offer. In appropriate cases lobbying the EC Commission is also resorted to.[4]

4. *Mega-multinationals*

The growing number, and power, of multinational groups, operating in many countries and, possibly, dwarfing all of them, is another phenomenon which has caused alarm and led some countries to take protective measures. Once again, such action as has been taken in the United Kingdom has not been through companies' legislation. Indeed, except in relation to tax avoidance, very little has been done. The fact that large areas of British commerce and industry (including the national press and financial services) are now dominated by multinationals, whose ultimate control is outside both the United Kingdom and the EEC, is treated with apparent equanimity, except in some cases in relation to the privatisation of nationalised industries—the final development to which reference needs to be made.

5. *Nationalisation and privatisation*

In the United Kingdom the immediate post-War years were an era of nationalisation. Occasionally the Government achieved its aim by acquiring a controlling interest in the companies or groups whose business was being nationalised; more often a new type of corporate body, "the public corporation," was created by the nationalising statute and the undertakings and assets vested in that body. Either method produced material differences in "corporate governance"—particularly when the latter was adopted; any pretence that the directorate was answerable to the shareholders was abandoned since there were no shareholders. Instead the board became answerable to the appropriate Minister and he or she to Parliament. It was also hoped that nationalisation would lead to a more co-operative and less confrontational relationship between management and employees. In

[3] And for the board of the predator to seek to persuade him not to—as will both boards in the case of an agreed bid.
[4] On the British Airways/British Caledonian merger the EC Commission secured tougher undertakings than the U.K. Government had prescribed.

most cases the hoped-for advantages failed to materialise and we are now in an era of de-nationalisation or "privatisation."

When nationalisation had been achieved by acquisition by the Government of the share capital of the former companies, privatisation is a straightforward operation, not necessarily involving any legislative action; the Government merely has to dispose of the shares either by a public offering and listing on The Stock Exchange or by private deals. When the undertaking had been vested in a statutory public corporation the privatising *modus operandi* is somewhat more complicated; a new limited company has to be registered and the undertaking vested in it and, normally, a public offering made of its share capital. In either event, novel constitutional and legal questions are likely to arise.[5] This is principally because, although the Government may declare that it wishes to relinquish all political control, leaving the industry to the discipline of the market, this generally proves to be easier said than done, and because when, as in the case of public utilities, the company will have a monopoly, special arrangements need to be made to protect consumers.

Hence privatisation has led to interesting distortions of, and supplements to, Company Law. The distortions consist of special provisions in the company's articles of association (some of which would not be countenanced by The Stock Exchange in the case of normal listed companies) designed principally to enable the Government to prevent takeovers or other changes of control which it regards as undesirable. One such device[6] is the "golden share," retained by the Government, either for a limited period or indefinitely, and enabling it to outvote all others on certain types of resolution.[7] Another is a provision enabling the Government to nominate some of the directors. The supplements to Company Law, adopted to protect consumers in the cases where there is a monopoly, consist of consumer "watchdogs" independent of the company's management, the prototype being OFTEL which performs this role in relation to British Telecom.

Surprisingly, one constituency for which no special protective measures have been thought appropriate in the privatisation measures is that of the vastly increased body of individual, small, first-time investors whom the privatisation issues have been deliberately designed to attract—and with considerable success although most of them sell the shares once they have exhausted the special

---

[5] For a useful brief account, see Graham & Prosser, *Privatising Nationalised Industries* (1987) 50 M.L.R. 16.

[6] Others include provisions intended to ensure that no shareholder is beneficially entitled to an interest in more than a fixed proportion (say 15 per cent.) of voting shares and disenfranchising his shares if he does. So far none of these devices seems to have proved particularly effective.

[7] The legality of this device was upheld by the House of Lords in *Bushell* v. *Faith* [1970] A.C. 1099 which, ironically, the Government had proposed to over-rule in its aborted Companies Bill 1973.

inducements offered them. Shareholders have no greater protection than they would in other public listed companies; in so far as there is control over the management it will be by the Government, or institutional investors if and when they choose to exercise it in their own interests.

CONCLUSION

It seems inevitable that developments in our Company Law over the next 25 years will follow much the same pattern as that of the past twenty five. Reforms will be piecemeal without any review of the basic structure and with a marked reluctance to tackle fundamental problems except to the extent forced upon us by the EC. The latter's initiatives will result in major changes and if these are to be to our liking it behoves us to play a more constructive role in the preparatory stages of Community legislation than we generally have in the past. Domestically inspired changes to our companies' and related legislation are likely to be restricted mainly to technical matters, to the removal of flaws which have come to light in the legislation of 1985–86, and to the closing of loop-holes revealed by scandals as yet unforeseen. Our company legislation will continue to increase in length and, since changes in our style of legislative drafting are most unlikely, will become still more complex and opaque. But cheer up: all this should provide grist to the mills of company lawyers.

Part Two

THE CONSEQUENCES OF INCORPORATION

INTRODUCTION

As we have seen, today one of the outstanding features of a company is that it is an incorporated body. This Part explores the main consequences which flow from incorporation. Chapter 5 attempts to summarise the practical advantages and disadvantages of carrying on business as a registered company rather than as an unincorporated sole trader, or as a partnership (the alternative when a small body of persons wishes to "carry on business in common with a view of profit."[1]). Chapter 6 discusses the circumstances in which, despite the fact that the company is incorporated, the courts are willing to treat it as if it were not, sometimes to the advantage and sometimes to the disadvantage of its members. Chapters 7 to 10 deal with legal rules, peculiar to incorporated companies, in relation to their organs and officers, to their liability for the acts or omissions of their organs or officers, and to the raising and maintaining of their capital.

It must be stressed, however, that it does not follow that every unincorporated body lacks all the attributes which incorporation automatically provides. As we have seen,[2] statutes of the early nineteenth century enabled the Crown by letters patent to confer all or any of the advantages of incorporation without actually granting corporate personality, and similarly a statute may confer many of these privileges without actual incorporation. In fact, this has frequently been done, with the result that between the two extremes of an unincorporated club or society and a full-fledged corporation there are many hybrids, which, though formally unincorporated, possess a greater or lesser number of the attributes of a corporation. Among these hybrids even partnerships ought perhaps to be included for the partners can now sue or be sued in the firm's name, and if insolvent, can be wound up in much the same way as an incorporated company.

Originally the main examples of hybrids were those that sprang from the 19th Century's friendly societies, co-operative societies and trade unions. Most of these have now attained full corporate status (though still registered with the Registrar of Friendly Societies) and are subject to their own legislation and not regarded as "companies"—though in most cases they can be wound up as if they were. Thus co-operative societies and housing associations, formed under the Industrial and Provident Societies Acts, and building societies, formed under the Building Societies Acts, have full corporate

---

[1] Partnership is defined thus in s.1(1) of the Partnership Act 1890.
[2] Above, Chap. 3, p. 37.

personality. Indeed the latter, as a result of the Building Societies Act 1986, may now extend their roles way beyond their traditional ones of providing savings facilities and loans for house purchase and they are subject to the general supervision of a new Building Societies Commission and to that of the Securities and Investments Board in relation to their "investment business" activities.[3] Only friendly societies and trade unions remain, somewhat anomalously, formally unincorporated though for most purposes they are treated as if they were distinct legal entities[4] but with their property vested in trustees. This reliance on the trust concept rather than on that of de jure incorporation, also played a part in the development of trustee savings banks until they were merged and converted into a "privatised" public company under the Trustee Savings Banks Act 1985.[5]

Even more anomalous is the position of certain international bodies. This was vividly illustrated as a result of the sensational collapse in 1985 of the International Tin Council (the ITC) which led to a spate of litigation greatly to the advantage of City solicitors and a large proportion of the Bar.

The ITC was a body with headquarters in London established under a succession of treaties of which the latest, the Sixth International Tin Agreement (ITA6), was concluded between the Governments of twenty-three sovereign States (including the United Kingdom) and the EC (which was held not to be a sovereign State). ITA6 conferred legal personality under international law on the ITC and, under United Kingdom law,[6] it was expressly recognised as an "international organisation" within the meaning of the International Organisations Act 1968 with the legal capacities of a body corporate but enjoying immunity from suit (other than to enforce an arbitration award) unless it expressly submitted to the jurisdiction of a national court. On its collapse it had debts of hundreds of millions of pounds

---

[3] One has converted to a listed public limited company—not without experiencing some problems.

[4] An attempt was made by s.74 (I) of the Industrial Relations Act 1971 to require registered trade unions to become bodies corporate but this proved abortive as the unions refused to register under the Act. Accordingly the Trade Union and Labour Relations Act 1974 went to the opposite extreme by providing in s.2 that "a trade union . . . shall not be, or be treated as if it were, a body corporate" although it went on to say that the union could sue or be sued in its own name and that any judgment should be enforceable against its property "to the like extent and in like manner as if the union were a body corporate." As a result it has been held that although a union may sue in tort it cannot sue for libel because it no longer has a "personality" to be defamed: *EETPU v. The Times* [1980] Q.B. 285.

[5] An operation which revealed, to most people's surprise, that, in contrast with other associations, the statutory Savings Banks had no members, that their depositors' rights were contractual and not as beneficiaries under a trust, and that the banks' assets belonged to the State: *Ross v. Lord Advocate and Others* [1986] 1 W.L.R. 1077 (H.L.Sc. & E.). But the trust concept played and, in the United Kingdom, continues to play a major role in relation to unit trusts, for a brief account of which see pp. 247, 248 below.

[6] S.I. 1972 No. 120.

which its creditors sought vainly to recover, their attempts to do so being struck out as disclosing no cause of action justiciable in the English courts. Even those creditors who had obtained arbitration awards found that they had no effective way of enforcing them by winding up the ITC as an unregistered company or securing the appointment of a receiver. Nor could they, or any other creditors, bring direct actions against the members of the ITC; under English law the members of a body with a distinct legal personality were not, as such, liable either primarily or secondarily for its debts. These decisions were reached after protracted hearings of four groups of appeals by the Court of Appeal[7] and the House of Lords[8] in judgments of enormous length and impressive erudition.[9]

After years of bickering and procrastination the only consolation that the creditors received was that the repeated exhortations in the various judgments to the member Governments to meet their undoubted moral obligations, led to an offer of £182m in settlement of claims totalling approximately £500m, which, *faute de mieux*, was accepted.

As there is a growing number of similar international organisations operating in the United Kingdom[10] the implications are somewhat alarming. We seemingly have in our midst bodies immune from suit with members who are under no legal obligation to meet the bodies' debts. If they become insolvent there is no means of securing that there is an orderly distribution of their remaining assets by a qualified insolvency practitioner.[11] And their members, even if they are respectable sovereign States, cannot be relied on to meet their moral obligations.

However, some slight comfort can perhaps be derived from the subsequent decision of the House of Lords in *Arab Monetary Fund v.*

---

[7] Reported as *Rayner (Mincing Lane) Ltd. v. D.T.I.* [1989] Ch. 72; *Maclaine Watson & Co. v. ITC*, *ibid.* 253, *Maclaine Watson & Co. v. ITC (No. 2)*, *ibid.* 286, *Re International Tin Council*, *ibid.* 309.

[8] Reported as *Rayner (Mincing Lane) Ltd. v. D.T.I.* [1990] 2 A.C. 418 H.L. The length of the arguments led Lord Templeman to protest: "For the conduct of these appeals there were locked in battle 24 counsel supported by batteries of solicitors and legal experts, armed with copies of 200 authorities and 14 volumes of extracts, British and foreign, from legislation, books [including the 4th edition of this one] and articles. Ten counsel addressed the Appellate Committee for 26 days … In my opinion the length of oral argument permitted in future appeals should be subject to prior limitation by the Appellate Committee": at p. 483.

[9] See especially that of Kerr L.J. in [1989] Ch. at pp. 139–203 and that of Lord Oliver at [1990] 2 A.C. at pp. 484–522.

[10] The annex to Kerr L.J.'s judgment in [1989] Ch. at p. 203 lists over 60; but, fortunately, it is unlikely that many of them trade with the reckless abandon of the I.T.C.'s buffer-stock manager.

[11] When, in the inter-War years we were faced with an analogous situation (not of our own making) in relation to the pre-Revolution Russian banks operating in this country, we passed special legislation to make it clear that they could be wound up under the Companies Act notwithstanding that they had ceased to exist under the law of the USSR. The situation which now faces us is a result of our own legislation which, as Lord Griffiths pointed out (at [1990] 2 A.C. pp. 483–485) has produced consequences which Ministers had assured Parliament were "inconceivable".

Hashim (No. 3)[12] in which it distinguished its decision in the ITC litigation by holding that it had not decided what many of us[13] thought it had. Like the ITC, the Arab Monetary Fund had been established by an agreement between some 20 States (this time Arab or Palestinian) which agreement provided that the Fund should have "independent" juridical personality—and in particular the right to own, contract and litigate—and which required the member States to ratify it in accordance with their particular constitutional arrangement. This the United Arab Emirates (a sovereign State recognised by the United Kingdom) did by a federal decree which, it was held, had the effect of creating the Fund as a body corporate under the law of the U.A.E. and which the United Kingdom could and should recognise as such. Accordingly it could sue in the English courts. This is to be welcomed; but unfortunately it throws no light on the questions whether it could be sued here and, if so whether and how a judgment against it would be enforced. The recent Foreign Corporations Act 1991 deals only with a different problem; the status in the United Kingdom of a body incorporated, or formerly incorporated, under the laws of a foreign territory which has not been recognised by the United Kingdom as a sovereign State. Under this Act, so long as the territory has laws applied by "a settled court system in that territory" the status of the body will be governed by those laws.[14]

12 [1991] 2 A.C. 114 (Hoffman J.; C.A. & H.L.)
13 Including the majority in the C.A. and Lord Lowry who dissented in the H.L.
14 This should help to avoid problems which might otherwise arise as a result of the splitting up of the former USSR and Yugoslavia pending the recognition of the new States.

CHAPTER 5

ADVANTAGES AND DISADVANTAGES OF INCORPORATION

Legal entity distinct from its members

As already emphasised, the fundamental attribute of corporate personality—from which indeed all the other consequences flow—is that the corporation is a legal entity distinct from its members. Hence it is capable of enjoying rights and of being subject to duties which are not the same as those enjoyed or borne by its members. In other words, it has "legal personality" and is often described as an *artificial person* in contrast with a human being, a *natural person*.[1]

As we have seen, corporate personality became an attribute of the normal joint stock company only at a comparatively late stage in its development, and it was not until *Salomon v. Salomon & Co.*[2] at the end of the nineteenth century that its implications were fully grasped even by the courts. The facts of this justly celebrated case were as follows:

Salomon had for many years carried on a prosperous business as a leather merchant. In 1892 he decided to convert it into a limited company and for this purpose Salomon & Co. Ltd. was formed with Salomon, his wife and five of his children as members and Salomon as managing director. The company purchased the business as a going concern for £39,000—"a sum which represented the sanguine expectations of a fond owner rather than anything that can be called a businesslike or reasonable estimate of value."[3] The price was satisfied by £10,000 in debentures, conferring a charge over all the company's assets, £20,000 in fully paid £1 shares and the balance in cash. The result was that Salomon held 20,001 of the 20,007 shares issued, and each of the remaining six shares was held by a member of his family, apparently as a nominee for him. The company almost immediately ran into difficulties and only a year later the then holder of the debentures appointed a receiver and the company went into liquidation. Its assets were sufficient to discharge the debentures but nothing was left for the unsecured creditors. In these circumstances Vaughan Williams J. and a strong Court of Appeal held that the whole transaction was contrary to the true intent of the Companies Act and that the company was a mere sham, and an alias, agent, trustee or nominee for Salomon who remained the real proprietor of

---

[1] A company, even if it has only one member, is a "corporation aggregate" as opposed to the somewhat anomalous "corporation sole" in which an office, e.g. that of a bishop, is personified.

[2] [1897] A.C. 22, H.L.

[3] *Per* Lord Macnaghten at p 49.

the business. As such he was liable to indemnify the company against its trading debts. But the House of Lords unanimously reversed this decision. They held that the company has been validly formed since the Act merely required seven members holding at least one share each. It said nothing about their being independent, or that they should take a substantial interest in the undertaking, or that they should have a mind and will of their own, or that there should be anything like a balance of power in the constitution of the company. Hence the business belonged to the company and not to Salomon, and Salomon was *its* agent. In the blunt words of Lord Halsbury L.C.[4]

"Either the limited company was a legal entity or it was not. If it was, the business belonged to it and not to Mr. Salomon. If it was not, there was no person and no thing to be an agent at all; and it is impossible to say at the same time that there is a company and there is not."

Or, as Lord Macnaghten put it[5]:

"The company is at law a different person altogether from the subscribers . . ; and, though it may be that after incorporation the business is precisely the same as it was before, and the same persons are managers, and the same hands receive the profits, the company is not in law the agent of the subscribers or trustee for them. Nor are the subscribers, as members, liable in any shape or form, except to the extent and in the manner provided by the Act."[6]

Of course this decision does not mean that a promoter can with impunity defraud the company which he forms or swindle his existing creditors. In the *Salomon* case it was argued that the company was entitled to rescind in view of the wilful overvaluation of the business sold to it. But the House held that in fact there was no fraud at all since the shareholders were fully conversant with what was being done. Had Salomon made a profit which he concealed from his fellow shareholders the position would have been different.[7] Nor was there any fraud on Salomon's pre-incorporation creditors, all of whom were paid off in full out of the purchase price. Otherwise they or

[4] At p. 31.
[5] At p. 51.
[6] For an early statutory recognition of the same principle, see 22 Geo. 3 c. 45, which disqualified those holding Government contracts from election to Parliament but expressly provided (s.3) that the prohibition did not extend to members of incorporated companies holding such contracts.
[7] See below Chap. 12.

Salomon's trustee in bankruptcy might have been entitled to upset the sale.[8] And today, the charge securing the debenture might be invalidated if there was a successful petition for a winding-up or an administration order within two years.[9] But, in this particular case, Salomon seems to have been one of the victims rather than the villain of the piece for he had mortgaged his debentures and used the money to try to support the tottering company. However, the result would have been the same if he had not, and even if he had been the only creditor to receive anything from the business which was "his" in fact though not in law.

This decision opened up new vistas to company lawyers and the world of commerce. Not only did it finally establish the legality of the "one-man" company and showed that incorporation was as readily available to the small private partnership and sole trader as to the large public company, but it also revealed that it was possible for a trader not merely to limit his liability to the money which he put into the enterprise but even to avoid any serious risk to the major part of that by subscribing for debentures rather than shares. This result seems shocking, and the decision has been much criticised.[10] The only justification for it is that the public deal with a limited company at their peril and know, or should know, what to expect. In particular a search of the company's file at Companies House should reveal its latest annual accounts and whether there are any charges on the company's assets.[11] But the accounts will probably be months out of date and, in the case of a small or medium sized company, may be expurgated editions of those circulated to the members.[12] Nor does everyone having dealings with a company have the time or knowledge needed to search the file. The experienced business man with his trade protection associations can take care of himself, but the little man, whom the law should particularly protect, rarely has any idea of the risks he runs when he grants credit to a company with a high-sounding name,[13] impressive nominal capital (not paid up in cash), and with assets mortgaged up to the hilt.[14] Nor is it practical for the

[8] Under what are now ss.423 to 425 of the Insolvency Act 1986.

[9] Insolvency Act 1986, s.245.

[10] See, *e.g.* O. Kahn-Freund, *Some Reflections on Company Law Reform* (1944) 7 M.L.R. 54 (a thought-provoking article still well worth study) in which it is described as a "calamitous decision."

[11] But not necessarily the amount secured; most companies grant floating charges to their bankers to secure "all sums due or to become due" on their current overdrafts and the register of charges will not give any indication of the size of the overdraft at any particular time.

[12] Companies Act 1985 ss.247–251: see below Chap. 17.

[13] There are undoubtedly many who think that "Ltd." is an indication of size and stability (which "plc" may be but "Ltd" certainly is not) rather than a warning of irresponsibility.

[14] But no sympathy was wasted on him by the H.L. "A creditor who will not take the trouble to use the means which the statute provides for enabling him to protect himself must bear the consequences of his own negligence": per Lord Watson at p. 40.

unemployed workman, who is offered a job with a limited company, to decline it until he has first searched the company's file.[15]

Since the Salomon case, the complete separation of the company and its members has never been doubted. As we shall see later,[16] there are cases in which the legislature, and to a very small extent the courts, have allowed the veil of incorporation to be lifted, but in general it is opaque and impassable. The consequences, however, are not necessarily wholly beneficial to the members.[17] For example, if a trader incorporates his business he will cease to have an insurable interest in its assets even though he is the beneficial owner of all the shares. If therefore he forgets to assign the insurance policies, and to obtain any necessary consents of the insurers, nothing will be payable if the assets perish.[18] Similarly, a parent company will not have an insurable interest in the assets of its subsidiary companies even though wholly owned, for the rule that a company is distinct from its members applies equally to the separate companies of a group.[19] In Kahn-Freund's striking phrase[20] "sometimes corporate entity works like a boomerang and hits the man who was trying to use it."

(1) *Limited liability*

It follows from the fact that a corporation is a separate person that its members are not as such liable for its debts.[21] Hence in the absence of express provision to the contrary the members will be completely free from any personal liability. This is, in fact, the position as regards municipal and ecclesiastical corporations and the modern public corporations, and may be so as regards statutory and chartered companies, the members of which will be under personal liability only if, and to the extent that, the statute or charter so provides.

But as regards a company registered under the Companies Acts a complete absence of any liability is not permitted. Such a company can either be registered as unlimited, in which case the members are in effect guarantors of its obligations without any restriction on amount,[22] or it can be limited by shares or guarantee.[23] In the case of

---

[15] The likely result would be to lose him his unemployment benefit.

[16] Below Chap. 6.

[17] See especially Kiralfy, *Some Unforseen Consequences of Private Incorporation* in (1949) 65 L.Q.R. 231, and Kahn-Freund, *loc. cit.* and below, Chap. 6.

[18] *Macaura* v. *Northern Assurance Co.* [1925] A.C. 619, H.L.; *Levinger* v. *Licences, etc. Insurance Co.* (1936) 54 Ll.L.R. 68.

[19] As will be pointed out later, inroads have been made into this principle, but it still remains the general rule though for tax purposes "group relief" had drawn its sting.

[20] *Loc. cit.* p. 56.

[21] This sentence was quoted and relied on by Kerr L.J. in *Rayner (Mincing Lane) Ltd.* v. *Dept. of Trade* [1989] Ch. 72 at p. 176 as an accurate statement of English law although, as he pointed out, it is not accurate in relation to most Civil Law countries—including Scotland so far as partnerships are concerned—or to international law: at pp. 176–183.

[22] "In effect" because, of course, the *modus operandi* is different; the creditor has no direct right against the member, as he would have against a surety on default by the principal debtor.

[23] The Companies Acts (now 1985 Act, ss.306–307) have always provided that a limited company may have directors with unlimited liability. It is not surprising that these

a company limited by shares each member is liable to contribute when called upon to do so the full nominal value of the shares held by him in so far as this has not already been paid by him or any prior holder of those shares. In the case of a guarantee company each member is liable to contribute a specified amount to the assets of the company in the event of its being wound up while he is a member or within one year after he ceases to be a member. In effect, therefore, the member, without being directly liable to the company's creditors, is in both cases a limited guarantor of the company.

When, therefore, obligations are incurred on behalf of a company, the company is liable and not the members, though the company may ultimately be able to recover a contribution from them to enable it to discharge its obligations. If the company is an unlimited one their liability to contribute will be unlimited; if it is limited by shares their liability will be limited to the unpaid nominal value of their shares and in practice their shares are today likely to be fully paid up so that they will be under no further liability. If the company is limited by guarantee they will be under no liability until it is wound up, and then, in practice, only for a derisory sum.[24] In contrast an unincorporated association, not being a legal person, cannot be liable, and obligations entered into on its behalf can bind only the actual officials who purport to act on its behalf, or the individual members if the officials have actual or apparent authority to bind them. In either event the persons bound will be liable to the full extent of their property unless they expressly or impliedly restrict their responsibility to the extent of the funds of the association, as the officials may well do. Hence the extent to which the member will be liable depends on the terms of the contract of association. In the case of a club, and presumably the same applies to learned and scientific societies, there will generally be implied a term that the members are not personally liable for obligations incurred on behalf of the club. But very different is the position of members of a partnership, an association carrying on business for gain. Each partner is an agent of all the others and his acts done in "carrying on in the normal way business of the kind carried on by the firm" bind the partners.[25] Only if the creditor knows of the limitation placed on the partners' authority will the other members escape liability.[26] Moreover, an attempt to restrict the partners' liability to partnership funds by a provision to that effect in the partnership agreement will

24 See Chap. 1, p. 11 n. 36 above.
25 Partnership Act 1890, s.5. This applies equally to Scotland thus largely negativing the consequence of recognising the Scottish firm as a separate person.
26 *Ibid.* ss.5 and 8.

provisions have long been a dead letter except occasionally in relation to professions which permit their members to practise as incorporated companies but only if the directors accept personal liability.

be ineffective even if known to the creditors[27]; they will only be able to restrict their financial liability, in respect of acts otherwise authorised, by an express agreement to that effect with the creditor concerned.[28]

There is, it is true, now a method whereby liability can be limited without forming an incorporated company; namely, by a limited partnership under the Limited Partnerships Act 1907. But this has many disadvantages in comparison with a company. In particular, it is not possible to limit the personal liability of all the partners but only some of them.[29] Moreover, even the limited partners lose their privilege of limited liability if they take any part in the management of the business.[30] This latter rule is especially inconvenient, for although a person who puts money into a business may be happy to leave the running of it to his colleagues while all goes well, he will probably want to be able to intervene if things go wrong. If a limited partner does so, his attempt to salvage the wreck may well result in the whole of his fortune sinking with it.

Hence a limited company is generally found preferable. It enables the liability of all the members to be limited without restriction on the part which they play in the management, and, although it involves somewhat greater formality, publicity and expense, these are not very onerous. In practice, therefore, limited partnerships are used only where for some reasons an incorporated company is inappropriate (*e.g.* in the case of certain professions which companies are not allowed to practise) but one member of the firm is not prepared to accept full liability for its debts or the other partners do not want him to play any part in the management. This may occur on the retirement from active participation of a senior partner whom it is wished to retain as a consultant or for the prestige value of his name and reputation. Save in these rare cases where limited partnerships are appropriate, the only practical alternatives are either complete personal liability or limited liability through the medium of a company.

In the case of small private limited companies the members' freedom from personal liability may, in practice, prove to be largely illusory. Banks and others who grant the company formal credit facilities are likely to require the members, or such of them as are directors, personally to guarantee the company's indebtedness. If, then, the company becomes insolvent, members or directors face personal liabilities which may bankrupt them. Limited liability protects them only in respect of claims by trade creditors who have

---

[27] *Re Sea, Fire and Life Insurance Co.* (1854) 3 De G.M. & G. 459.
[28] *Hallett* v. *Dowdall* (1852) 21 L.J.Q.B. 98. It is a criminal offence to carry on business under a name ending with "Limited" unless duly incorporated with limited liability: Companies Act 1985 s.34.
[29] Limited Partnership Act 1907, s.4(2).
[30] *Ibid.* s.6(1). They may only "advise with the partners."

not been in a position to obtain personal guarantees and from claims in tort if they are not the particular tortfeasors who acted for the company. Moreover, in the case of any company, small or large, there is, as a result of sections 213–217 of the Insolvency Act 1986, discussed in the next chapter, increased risk that on the company's insolvent liquidation those who have taken part in its management may be ordered to contribute towards the payment of its debts.

(2) *Property*

One obvious advantage of corporate personality is that it enables the property of the association to be more clearly distinguished from that of its members. In an unincorporated society, the property of the association is the joint property of the members. The rights of the members therein differ from their rights to their separate property since the joint property must be dealt with according to the rules of the society and no individual member can claim any particular asset. By virtue of the trust the obvious complications can be minimised but not completely eradicated. And the complications cause particular difficulty in the case of a trading partnership both as regards the true nature of the interests of the partners[31] and as regards claims of creditors.[32]

On incorporation, the corporate property belongs to the company and members have no direct proprietary rights to it but merely to their "shares," in the undertaking.[33] A change in the membership, which causes inevitable dislocation to a partnership firm, leaves the company unconcerned; the shares may be transferred but the company's property will be untouched and no realisation or splitting up of its property will be necessary, as it will on a change in the constitution of a partnership firm. Similarly, the claims of the company's creditors will merely be against the company's property and the difficulties which can arise on bankruptcy of partners will not occur.

(3) *Suing and being sued*

Closely allied to questions of property are those relating to legal actions. The difficulties in the way of suing, or being sued by, an unincorporated association have been sufficiently stressed in the previous chapters, where it was pointed out that they were partially surmounted by the trust device and, more satisfactorily, by statutory

---

31 See Partnership Act 1890, ss.20–22; *Re Fuller's Contract* [1933] Ch. 652.
32 *Ibid*, s.23, and the Insolvent Partnerships Order 1986 (1986 S.I. No. 2142).
33 "Shareholders are not, in the eye of the law, part owners of the undertaking. The undertaking is something different from the totality of the shareholdings": *per* Evershed L.J. in *Short* v. *Treasury Commissioners* [1948] 1 K.B. 116, 122, C.A. (affd. [1948] A.C. 534 H.L.).

intervention. The problem is obviously of the greatest practical importance in connection with trading bodies and in fact it has now been solved in the case of partnerships by allowing a partnership to sue or be sued in the firm's name.[34] Hence, there is now no difficulty so far as the pure mechanics of suit are concerned—although there may still be complications in enforcing the judgment.

In the case of other unincorporated bodies (such as clubs and learned societies) not subject to special statutory provisions, the problems of suit are still serious. Sometimes its committee or other agents may be personally liable or authorised to sue. Otherwise, the only course is a "representative action" whereby, under certain conditions, one or more persons may sue or be sued on behalf of all the interested parties. But resort to this procedure[35] is available only subject to compliance with a number of somewhat ill-defined conditions, and the law, which has been inadequately explored,[36] is obscure and difficult. The result is apt to be embarrassing to the society when it wishes to enforce its rights (or, more properly, those of its members) though it has compensating advantages when it wishes to evade its duties.[37] Needless to say, none of these difficulties arises when an incorporated company is suing or being sued; the company as a legal person can take action to enforce its legal rights and can be sued for breach of its legal duties. The only disadvantage is that if a limited company is the plaintiff it may be ordered to give security for costs.[38]

(4) *Perpetual succession*

One of the obvious advantages of an artificial person is that it is not susceptible to "the thousand natural shocks that flesh is heir to." It cannot become incapacitated by illness, mental or physical, and it has not (or need not have) an allotted span of life.[39] This is not to say that the death or incapacity of its human members may not cause the company considerable embarrassment; obviously it will if all the

[34] R.S.C., Ord. 81. For the equivalent county court procedure, see C.C.R. Ord. 5 r. 9 and the County Courts Act 1984 s.48.
[35] Which is of considerable importance in company law, *e.g.* where a member, on behalf of himself and the other members is suing the company to restrain an alleged "fraud on the minority" (see Chap. 24 below) or where a debenture holder starts an action, on behalf of himself and the other debenture holders, to enforce the security (see Chap. 16 below).
[36] But see *Prudential Assurance Co. Ltd.* v. *Newman Industries Ltd.* [1981] Ch. 257; *E.M.I. Records Ltd.* v. *Riley* [1981] 1 W.L.R. 923.
[37] "An unincorporated association has certain advantages when litigation is desired against them": per Scrutton L.J. in *Bloom* v. *National Federation of Discharged Soldiers* (1918) 35 T.L.R. 50, 51, C.A.
[38] Companies Act 1985, s.726.
[39] s.84(1)(*a*) of the Insolvency Act 1986, replacing s.572 of the Companies Act 1985 and a similar provision in earlier Companies Acts, envisages that the period of the company's duration may be fixed in the articles, but this is never done in practice and even if it were the company would not automatically expire on the expiration of the term; an ordinary resolution would be necessary. It is otherwise with chartered companies: see Chap. 1, above p. 6.

directors die or are imprisoned or if there are too few surviving members to hold a valid meeting, or if the bulk of the members or directors become enemy aliens.[40] But the vicissitudes of the flesh have no direct effect on the disembodied company.[41] The death of a member leaves the company unmoved; members may come and go but the company can go on for ever.[42] The insanity of the managing director will not be calamitous to the company provided that he is removed promptly; he may be the company's brains but lobectomy is a simpler operation than on a natural person.

Once again, the disadvantages in the case of an unincorporated society can be minimised by the use of a trust. If the property of the association is vested in a small body of trustees, the death, disability or retirement of an individual member, other than one of the trustees, need not cause much trouble. But, of course, the trustees, if natural persons, will themselves need replacing at fairly frequent intervals and the need for constant appointment of new trustees is a nuisance if nothing worse. Indeed, it may be said that the trust never functioned at its simplest until it was able to enlist the aid of its own child, the incorporated company, to act as a trust corporation with perpetual succession.

Moreover, the trust obviates difficulties only when a member or his estate, has, under the constitution of the association, no right to be paid a share of the assets on death or retirement, which, of course, is the position with the normal club or learned society. But on the retirement or death of a partner, the partnership is automatically dissolved, so far at any rate as he is concerned,[43] and he or his estate will be entitled to be paid his share. The resulting dislocation of the firm's business can be reduced by special clauses in the articles of partnership, providing for an arbitrary basis of valuation of his share and for deferred payment, but cannot be eradicated altogether. With an incorporated company these problems do not arise. The member

---

[40] Cf. Daimler Co. v. Continental Tyre and Rubber Co. [1916] 2 A.C. 307, H.L.

[41] As Greer L.J. said in Stepney Corporation v. Osofsky [1937] 3 All E.R. 289, 291 C.A.: a corporate body has "no soul to be saved or body to be kicked.'" This epigram is believed to be of considerable antiquity. Glanville Williams, Criminal Law: The General Part (2nd ed.), p. 856, has traced it back to Lord Thurlow and an earlier variation to Coke. Cf. the decree of Pope Innocent IV forbidding the excommunication of corporations because, having neither minds nor souls, they could not sin: see Carr, Law of Corporation, at p. 73. In Rolloswin Investments Ltd. v. Chromolit Portugal S.A.R.L. [1970] 1 W.L.R. 912 it was held that since a company was incapable of public worship it was not a "person" within the meaning of the Sunday Observance Act 1677 so that a contract made by it on a Sunday was not void (the court was unaware that before the case was heard the Act had been repealed by the Statute Law (Repeals) Act 1969).

[42] During the 1939—45 War all the members of one private company, while in general meeting, were killed by a bomb. But the company survived; not even a hydrogen bomb could have destroyed it. And see the Australian case of Re Noel Tedman Holding Pty. Ltd. (1967) Qd.R. 561, Qd.Sup.Ct. where the only two members were killed in a road accident.

[43] And, in the absence of contrary agreement, as regards all the partners: Partnership Act 1890 s.33.

or his estate is not entitled to be paid out by the company. If he, or his personal representative, trustee in bankruptcy, or receiver, wishes to realise the value of his shares, these must be sold, whereupon the purchaser will, on entry in the share register, become a member in place of the former holder.[44]

Until the Companies Act 1981 it was not permissible for the company itself to be the purchaser and this could be disadvantageous both to the would-be seller and to the company and the other members, especially in the case of private companies. The seller might not be able to find a purchaser and the other members might not have sufficient free capital to purchase the shares. Now, subject to stringent conditions, purchase by the company is allowed[45] as it has long been under the laws of many other countries.

The continuing existence of a company, irrespective of changes in its membership, is helpful in other directions also. When an individual sells his business to another, difficult questions may arise regarding the performance of existing contracts by the new proprietor,[46] the assignment of rights of a personal nature,[47] and the validity of agreements made with customers ignorant of the change of proprietorship.[48] Similar problems may arise on a change in the constitution of a partnership.[49] Where the business is incorporated and the sale is merely of the shares, none of these difficulties arises. The company remains the proprietor of the business, performs the existing contracts and retains the benefits of them, and enters into future agreements. The difficulties attending vicarious performance, assignments and mistaken identity do not arise.

(5) *Transferable shares*

As was pointed out in Part I, incorporation, with the resulting separation of the business from its members, greatly facilitates the transfer of the members' interests. Even without formal incorporation much the same end was achieved through the device of the trust coupled with an agreement for transferability in the deed of settlement. But this end could only be approximately attained since the member, even after transfer, would remain liable for the firm's

[44] In practice, this may not be so easy as the company's articles may restrict transfer.
[45] Companies Act 1985, ss.162–181: see Chap. 9 below.
[46] *Robson v. Drummond* (1831) 2 B. & Ad. 303; *cf. British Waggon Co. v. Lea* (1880) 5 Q.B.D. 149.
[47] *Griffith v. Tower Publishing Co.* [1897] 1 Ch. 21 (publishing agreement held not assignable); *Kemp v. Baerselman* [1906] 2 K.B. 604, C.A. (agreement not assignable if question of one party's obligation depends on the other's "personal requirements"). *Cf. Tolhurst v. Associated Portland Cement* [1902] 2 K.B. 660, C.A.
[48] *Boulton v. Jones* (1857) 2 H. & N. 564.
[49] See *Brace v. Calder* (1895) 2 Q.B. 253, C.A. where the retirement of two partners was held to operate as the wrongful dismissal of a manager. And see also Partnership Act 1890 s.18. In practice such difficulties are often avoided by an implied novation.

debts incurred during the time when he was a member. Moreover, in the absence of limited liability his opportunities to transfer would in practice be much restricted.

With an incorporated company freedom to transfer, both legally and practically, can be readily attained. The company can be incorporated with its liability limited by shares, and these shares constitute items of property which are freely transferable in the absence of express provision to the contrary, and in such a way that the transferor drops out[50] and the transferee steps into his shoes. A partner has a proprietary interest which he can assign, but the assignment does not operate to divest him of his status or liability as a partner; it merely affords the assignee the right to receive whatever the firm distributes in respect of the assigning partner's share.[51] The assignee can be admitted into partnership in the place of the assignor only if the other partners agree[52] and the assignor will not be relieved of his existing liabilities as a partner unless the creditors agree, expressly or impliedly, to release him.[53]

Even in the case of an incorporated company the power to transfer may, of course, be subject to restrictions. In a private company some form of restriction was formerly essential in order to comply with its statutory definition[54] and it is still desirable if such a company is to retain its character of an incorporated private partnership. In practice these restrictions are usually so stringent as to make transferability largely illusory. Nor is there any legal objection to restrictions in the case of a public company, although such restrictions, except as regards partly paid shares, are unusual, and impracticable if the shares are to be marketed on The Stock Exchange.[55] But there is this fundamental difference: in a partnership transferability depends on express agreement and is subject to legal and practical limitations, whereas in a company it exists to the fullest extent in the absence of express restriction. The partnership relationship is essentially personal; and in practice this is maintained in the case of the private company which in economic reality is often a partnership though in law an incorporated company.[56] On the other hand, the relationship between members of a public company is, as we have seen[57]

---

50 Subject only to a possible liability under ss.74–76 of the Insolvency Act 1986 if liquidation follows within a year and the shares were not fully paid up.
51 Partnership Act 1980, s.31.
52 *Ibid.* s.24(7).
53 *Ibid.* s.17(2) and (3).
54 Companies Act 1948 s.28. Such restrictions are no longer obligatory under the new distinction between plcs and private companies resulting from the Companies Act 1980; see now Companies Act 1985 s.1 (3).
55 See *The Yellow Book* Section 9, Chap. 1, para. 1.2.
56 In recent years the courts have shown a welcome tendency to recognise the economic reality in applying the legal rules to such incorporated partnerships: see especially *Ebrahimi v. Westbourne Galleries Ltd.* [1973] A.C. 360, H.L.: see Chap. 24, p. 663 below.
57 See Chap. 1, above.

essentially impersonal and financial and hence there is usually no reason to restrict changes in membership.

(6) *Borrowing*

Hitherto we have considered only the advantages or disadvantages which flow inevitably, or at any rate naturally, from the fact of incorporation. There are, however, two further respects, borrowing and taxation, in which incorporation has important consequences.

At first sight one would suppose that a sole trader or partners, being personally liable, would find it easier than a company to raise money by borrowing. In practice, however, this is not so since a company is often able to grant a more effective charge to secure the indebtedness. The ingenuity of equity practitioners led to the evolution of an unusual but highly beneficial type of security known as the floating charge; *i.e.* a charge which floats like a cloud over the whole assets from time to time falling within a generic description, but without preventing the mortgagor from disposing of those assets in the usual course of business until something occurs to cause the charge to become crystallised or fixed. This type of charge is particularly suitable when a business has no fixed assets, such as land, which can be included in a normal mortgage, but carries a large and valuable stock-in-trade. Since this stock needs to be turned over in the course of business a fixed charge is impracticable because the consent of the mortgagee would be needed every time anything was sold and a new charge would have to be entered into whenever anything was bought. A floating charge obviates these difficulties; it enables the stock to be turned over but attaches to whatever it is converted into and to whatever new stock is acquired.

In theory there is no reason why such charges should not be granted by sole traders and partnerships as well as by incorporated companies. But, until recently, there have been two pieces of legislation which have effectively precluded that. The first was the "reputed ownership" provision in the bankruptcy legislation relating to individuals.[58] This, however, under the reforms resulting from the report of the Cork Committee,[59] was repealed and not replaced in the Insolvency Act 1986. It never applied to the winding-up of companies. The second, which still remains, is that the charge, in so far as it related to chattels, would be a bill of sale within the meaning of the Bills of Sale Acts 1878 and 1882 which apply only to individuals and not to companies.[60] Hence it would need to be

---

[58] Bankruptcy Act 1914, s.38(1)(*c*).

[59] (1982) Cmnd. 8558, Chap. 23. Its repeal had been recommended in the Report of the Blagden Committee 25 years earlier: (1957) Cmnd. 221.

[60] This was always accepted in relation to mortgages in the light of s.17 of the 1882 Act. It has now been held, after an exhaustive review of the conflicting authorities, that both Acts apply only to individuals: *Slavenburg's Bank v. International Natural Resources Ltd.* [1980] 1 W.L.R. 1076.

registered in the Bills of Sale Registry,[61] and, what is more important, as a mortgage bill it would need to be in the statutory form[62] which involves specifying the chattels in detail in a schedule. Compliance with the latter requirement is obviously impossible, since in a floating charge the chattels are, *ex hypothesi*, indeterminate and fluctuating.

When, belatedly, we get round to reforming, as many common law countries have done, our antiquated law relating to security interests in movables,[63] we shall be able to repeal the Bills of Sale Acts and thus make it practicable for unincorporated firms to borrow on the security of floating charges[64] or some comparable form of security on the lines of that provided by Article 9 of the American Uniform Commercial code.[65] In the meantime, use of this advantageous form of security is in practice restricted to bodies corporate. By virtue of it the lender can obtain an effective security on "all the undertaking and assets of the company both present and future" either alone or in conjunction with a fixed charge on its land.[66] If, in addition, the lender requires some personal security he can insist on the members, or some of them, (*e.g.* the directors) joining as guarantors. By so doing he can place himself in a far stronger position than if he merely had the personal security of the individual traders. It therefore happens not infrequently that a business is converted into a company solely in order to enable further capital to be raised by borrowing. And sometimes, as the *Salomon* case[67] shows, a trader by "selling" his business to a company which he has formed can give himself priority over his future creditors by taking a debenture, secured by a floating charge, for the purchase price.

(7) *Taxation*

If the public revenue was raised only by indirect taxes such as VAT, stamp duties, and customs and excise duties there would be no need for the tax treatment of companies and of individuals to differ;

---

[61] For some reason registration of a bill of sale against a tradesman destroys his credit, whereas registration of a debenture against a company does not. This can only be explained on the basis that the former is exceptional, whereas the latter is usual and familiarity has bred contempt.

[62] 1882 Act, s.9. Nor could it cover future goods: see s.5. s.6(2) allows a limited power of replacement but not anything as fluid as a floating charge.

[63] As recommended in the Crowther Report on Consumer Credit (1971 Cmnd. 4596). Part V, and in the Review of Security Interests in Property which the DTI commissioned from Professor A. L. Diamond (HMSO 1989).

[64] Farmers can already do so under the Agricultural Credits Act 1928 which permits individuals to grant to banks floating charges over farming stock and agricultural assets and excludes the application of the former reputed ownership provision and the Bills of Sale Acts: see ss.5 and 8(1), (2) and (4). Farming stock and agricultural assets are more readily distinguishable from a farmer's other assets (than, say, the stock of an antique dealer who lives over his shop) thus meeting the difficulty referred to under (2) above on p. 91.

[65] See the Reports referred to in n. 63 above.

[66] The implications of floating charges are discussed more fully in Chap. 16 below.

[67] [1897] A.C. 22, H.L. above p. 85.

nor, generally speaking, are they treated differently in relation to such taxes. But different treatment is inevitable in relation to direct taxes such as those on income and capital gains, especially when the rates are progressive and personal allowances are provided. In this country, where, since World War 1 until 1988, direct taxes have been levied at high rates, the different treatment and the real or imagined advantages of incorporation to the business and its members, have probably been the principal motives for incorporating. It would be inappropriate in this book to attempt to deal with taxation, a highly technical subject, the detailed rules of which are liable to change yearly and the basic principles not infrequently.[68] The summary account which follows is over-simplified and designed only to outline the major differences under the present system of annual taxation of income and capital gains.

Individuals are taxed (subject to various reliefs and personal allowances) on the whole of their annual income and realised capital gains exceeding prescribed minimum levels. In the case of income, the tax rates were progressive until 1988 when two rates only, were substituted. In so far as their income represents the profits of business carried on by them, expenses "wholly and exclusively" incurred for the purposes of the business are deductible in computing taxable income. In so far as income represents the emoluments of an employment, individuals are taxed on these (less expenses "wholly, exclusively *and necessarily*" incurred in the performance of their duties[69]) under the PAYE[70] system, whereby employers deduct from pay packets sums determined according to each employee's "code number" and account to the Revenue. Investment income is taxed in full but, to avoid double taxation, may give rise to a tax credit in so far as it consists of dividends or other income from which tax has been deducted at source.[71]

In contrast, incorporated companies are taxed on the whole of their income and capital gains, computed in accordance with principles, similar to those used in computing the profits and gains of a business carried on by individuals, under a single flat-rate Corporation Tax.[72] When a company pays a dividend, it also has to pay to the Revenue a prescribed fraction of the amount of that distribution as "advance corporation tax" (ACT) which, as its name implies, is treated as an advance tax payment which will be set-off against the company's corporation tax liability for the period in question. Each shareholder receiving a dividend is entitled to a tax credit representing his aliquot

---

68 There were major changes in 1965, 1972 and over subsequent years.
69 This does not include expenses incurred in travelling to and from work.
70 "Pay as you earn."
71 See below.
72 There is a slightly lower "small companies rate" for companies (whether large or small in turnover or membership) whose profits do not exceed a prescribed level.

share of the ACT paid. He will be subject to income tax at his personal rate on the grossed-up amount of the dividend, (*i.e.* the net amount paid plus the tax credit) but will be treated as having already paid the amount of that credit. In practice; the prescribed fraction of the distribution which is payable as ACT is adjusted when rates of income tax rise or fall so as to ensure that the tax credit corresponds to income tax payable by a lower-rate taxpayer on the gross amount of the distribution to him, thus obviating any need for subsequent adjustment in the case of a large class of tax-payers. If, however that shareholder is (a) below the income tax limit or (b) taxed at the higher rate he will be entitled to a refund in case (a) or liable to pay more in case (b). The complication that not all the shareholders will necessarily be individuals is dealt with by treating dividends paid to companies as "franked investment income" on which, in effect, they receive a credit against their liability for ACT on payment of their own dividends.

Individuals, in deciding whether or not it would be advantageous, tax-wise, to incorporate their business, will need to consider first whether the combined burden of tax borne by themselves and the company is likely to be less than if they carried on business without incorporation. If they are liable to tax at the higher rate (or think it likely that the business will flourish so that they will become thus liable) there would be obvious advantages in incorporating if profits could be retained in the business without the individuals being liable to income tax thereon. That, however, was such an obvious tax-avoidance device (and one even more attractive before capital gains tax was introduced) that it has long been controlled; now by provisions relating to what are called "close companies."[73] And these are defined so widely that almost any private company and many unlisted public ones are close companies. As such they were subject to a particularly rigorous regime (presently much relaxed) and the Revenue was empowered to apportion among the "participators" such part of the retained investment income as could not be shown to be necessarily retained for the purpose of its business and to tax them as if it had been distributed to them.[74] Except in the unlikely event that those incorporating the company are able and willing to "go public" straightaway[75]; the company will almost certainly start life as a close company and in the vast majority of cases will always remain a close company. These rules about apportionment used to apply not

[73] This expression, which is used in many English-speaking countries to describe private companies, has, in the U.K., been pre-empted by the tax legislation.
[74] "Participators" includes a wider class than shareholders and "distributions" includes more than just dividends, the intention being to catch extractions of profits by the participators however that may be disguised.
[75] The only *likely* examples of this are where a new company emerges as a result of a reconstruction or takes over the business or share capital of a nationalised concern under the present Government's privatisation programme.

just to investment income but to trading profits as well but trading profits have been taken out of the system so that now even a close company (unless it is an investment company[76]) can retain its trading profits subject only to paying corporation tax on them. This is, therefore, a considerable advantage vis-a-vis sole or partnership trading.

In practice the members of a small company will also try to reduce the company's taxable income by paying themselves directors' or other salaries, thereby reducing the company's taxable profits. This, within reason, even a close company can now do. Moreover, as we have seen, a company may find it easier than a sole trader or partnership to raise working capital by borrowing, and the interest which it pays will be an allowable charge in determining taxable profits and not a distribution unless paid to a "participator" who is also a director or related to a director. Furthermore, a company will find it easier to establish that expenses incurred were "wholly and exclusively" for business purposes. If, for example, a company decides to move its centre of operations from London to Leeds and to pay the expenses incurred by its executive directors and other employees in moving house, that, in principle, will be an allowable expense of the company. If, however, a sole trader or partnership decides to move, the expenses incurred by the trader or partners in moving homes will not be deductible. Hence in a recent case[77] where two partners in a large firm of chartered accountants were required by the firm to change their places of work to a branch in a different part of the country, their domestic removal expenses, borne by the firm, were held not to be deductible in assessing the firm's taxable profits. Similarly in an earlier case[78] it was held that a lady barrister (a sole trader—the Bar does not permit practice in partnership) could not deduct expenditure on sombre clothing suitable for court appearances. Notwithstanding that she would not be seen dead in it on other occasions, it nevertheless served her personal needs as well as her professional purposes and the expenditure was not "wholly and exclusively" for the latter.[79] Presumably the decision would have been the same in relation to her domestic removal expenses if she had decided to move to Chambers in another part of the country.

However, a partnership may be in a better position than either a sole trader or a company in relation to the complicated rules which apply on the cessation of a business. When that occurs the income of certain accounting periods may, in effect, be taxed twice over, while

[76] When apportionment of the whole income is automatic.
[77] *MacKinlay* v. *Arthur Young McCleland Moores & Co.* [1990] 2 A.C. 239 H.L., reversing C.A. ([1989] Ch. 454) which had thought that the fact that partnerships are taxed as if the firm was an "entity" meant that they should be treated as if the partners were employees of it.
[78] *Mallalieu* v. *Drummond* [1983] 2 A.C. 861, H.L.
[79] Though expenditure on replacing her wig and gown would be.

that of other periods escapes tax. Partners can, normally, elect whether the retirement of a partner is or is not treated as a cessation and may thereby be able to secure that one or more years of high profits drop out of the computation. This flexibility will not continue after the firm is incorporated since a retirement of a director and the disposal of his shares will not in itself be a cessation of the company's business.

It is probably true to say that were the future incidence of tax the only thing that needed to be considered, if the business is flourishing it would probably be advisable to incorporate. But that, of course, is not the only thing that needs to be considered. In addition, there are the costs of incorporating and of complying in future with the formalities which will have to be observed. These are summarised under (8) below. Formerly, among the initial costs there was an indirect tax—capital duty—that had to be paid at the rate of 1 per cent. on the share capital of the company or on the value of the net assets transferred by the incorporators to the company in return for shares if that was greater. When an existing business was incorporated this could, in itself, be an appreciable levy. It was, however, abolished in 1988. But, unless the only assets transferred are cash (which is unlikely except where incorporation is of a new business) the assets will have to be valued and professional fees may be incurred. Furthermore, the transfer of such assets as do not pass by manual delivery will require an assignment or conveyance involving additional legal costs and stamp duties. Nor should one ignore the effect of the incorporation on the incorporators' personal tax positions at the time of the incorporation. They will be concerned to ensure that they do not lose any existing reliefs or privileges, that they obtain any that may be available in relation to the transaction, and that they are not adversely affected by a deemed cessation of the former unincorporated business. If the assets transferred to the company have gone up in value since the incorporators acquired them, the transfer to the company may throw up a charge to capital gains tax unless detailed rules which remove this charge are exactly complied with. This is usually the biggest tax cost if they do not get it right and lawyers' and accountants' fees are likely to be incurred in setting up the transaction in such a way as to ensure that they do.

Hence the costs, initial and future, may be such as to reduce profits disproportionately—or even to produce losses. While this will certainly save tax it is not what the incorporators have in mind—unless they wish to adopt the only cast-iron means of tax avoidance, that of having no resources other than social security. And if they think that incorporation of a company or a number of inter-related companies is likely to provide a launch-pad for ingenious tax avoidance schemes, they deceive themselves. Statutory anti-avoidance provisions[80] and decisions of the House of Lords[81] have virtually put paid to that.

(8) *Formalities, publicity and expense*

Incorporation is necessarily attended with formalities, loss of privacy and expense greater than that which would normally apply to a sole trader or partnership. A sole trader is a person who already exists. A partnership cannot exist without some form of agreement, but this can be written on a half-sheet of notepaper or be an informal oral agreement. An unincorporated firm can conduct its affairs without any formality and publicity beyond that which may be prescribed by the regulations (if any) applying to the particular type of business. If the business is carried on under a name different from the true name of the sole trader or those of all the partners, it will have to comply with the provisions of the Business Names Act 1985 (as would a company trading under a pseudonym) but these are not onerous—registration in the former Business Names Register was abolished as a result of the Companies Act 1981. The business, unless it is insolvent, can eventually be wound up equally cheaply, privately and informally. An incorporated company, on the other hand, necessarily involves formalities, publicity and expenses at its birth, throughout its active life and on its final dissolution.

Private Companies. On the original formation of a private company, the incorporators[82] have only to complete and register a memorandum and articles of association and a few simple forms. These can be obtained at any law stationers, and Table A can be adopted as its articles.[83] Alternatively, a ready-made company can be bought "off-the-shelf" from one of the agencies which make a business of forming companies and selling them to all-comers.[84] The heaviest expenses on incorporation are likely to be capital gains tax (if the rules for

[80] Now mostly collected together in Part XVII of the Income and Corporation Taxes Act 1988. The initial "catch-all" section (s.703) springs from F.A. 1960, s.28.

[81] *Ramsay Ltd. v. Inland Revenue Commissioners* [1982] A.C. 300; *Furniss v. Dawson* [1984] A.C. 474; *cf. Craven v. White* [1989] A.C.398, H.L. These hold that transactions which are part of a "pre-ordained series of transactions", and have no business or commercial purpose other than tax avoidance are to be disregarded in determining tax liability. Incorporating, *per se*, even if the main motive was tax reduction, would not be such a transaction since, as we have seen, it has other "business or commercial purposes."

[82] There must be at least two (for no good reason) so a sole trader will have to recruit someone else (often his or her spouse) who will hold one share probably on trust for the quondam sole trader. But this will change when the Directive on single-member companies (see p. 61 above) is implemented.

[83] Or Table C or E if limited by guarantee or unlimited, Table A, without substantial deletions and additions is unlikely to be ideal for small private companies. The new s.8A (inserted by the 1989 Act) envisages a Table G for "partnership companies" but at the time of writing it seems unlikely that the needed Regulations will be made for some time.

[84] While they remain on the shelf they will be "dormant companies" able to take advantage of s. 250, (as substituted by 1989 Act) regarding accounts and audit; and the assets transferred to them (the £2 paid for two subscribers' shares) will be minimal and may need to be increased after the purchase.

exemption are not strictly complied with[85]) and professional fees—for it is rash to dispense with professional advice even if the intention is to buy a shelf company.

It is the formalities and costs of operating the company which, at present, are found excessively burdensome. Registers have to be maintained, documents filed at Companies House, and accounts kept and audited (but that should, and probably would, be done even if the business was not incorporated—though somewhat less elaborately and probably with the audit undertaken, more cheaply, by firm not recognised for the auditing of company accounts). Publicity will have to be given to the constitution and officers of the company and, in the normal case where the company has limited liability, to its balance sheets and profit and loss accounts.[86] And, until the 1989 Act, formal meetings (which had long-tended to be fictional in the case of small companies) ought to have been held. Finally, when the business of the company closes down it will have to be formally wound up (unless the Registrar can be persuaded to exercise his powers to strike it off the register[87]).

While the members of private companies cling to the protection of limited liability they cannot expect to be allowed to conduct their affairs with quite the same freedom as partnerships. Nevertheless it has long been realised that many of the requirements of the Act are unduly burdensome or inappropriate, at any rate in the cases of small companies, as most private ones are. Hence the Companies Act 1989 has at last made a serious effort to meet their needs. First it inserted new sections and a new Schedule 15A into the principal Act enabling them to dispense in most cases with formal meetings and with the pretence that they had held them when frequently they had not. By the new section 381A(1) it is provided that anything which may be done by a private company by a resolution of the company in general meeting or by a resolution of a meeting of a class of members may instead be done, without a meeting and without any previous notice being required, by a resolution in writing signed by or on behalf of all members entitled to vote on that resolution.[88] This applies to all types of resolution—ordinary, extraordinary, special or "elective"[89] except for resolutions to remove a director[90] or an auditor[91] before the expiration of his period of office.[92]

---

[85] See p. 101 above.
[86] Subject to concessions afforded to "small" or "medium-sized" companies: ss.246–247 as substituted by the 1989 Act: see Chap. 17 below.
[87] s.652. This he will generally do if satisfied that the company is moribund and without assets or liabilities: see Chap. 28 at pp. 774, 775 below.
[88] Signatures need not be on a single document provided that each is on a document which accurately sets out the proposed resolution: s.381B(4) applies when the last member signs (unless s.381A(2). It is deemed to be passed when it becomes affective under that subs.): s.381A(5).
[89] s.381A(6). On "elective resolutions" see p. 105 below.
[90] Under s.303: see p. 153, *et seq.*, below.
[91] Under s.391: see pp. 487–490 below.
[92] s.381A(7) and Sched. 15A Part I. Part II adapts certain sections of the Act which as drafted assume that a meeting will be held, so as to meet cases where a written resolution is used instead.

However, section 381B provides that a copy of any proposed written resolution has to be sent to the company's auditors.[93] If the resolution concerns the auditors as auditors,[94] they may, within seven days of the receipt of the copy, give notice to the company stating their opinion that the resolution should be considered at a meeting.[95] In that event, or if the company has omitted to send the copy, the written resolution will not be effective under section 381A unless the auditors notify the company that in their opinion the proposed resolution does not concern them as auditors, or does so concern them but need not be considered at a meeting, or if they do not give any notification within the seven days.[96]

This requirement always to notify the auditors has been criticised as perverse, novel, contradictory, cumbersome and destructive of the object of the reform.[97] That may be putting it too strongly. Clearly if the resolution does concern the auditors they ought to receive warning of it and to be able to demand a meeting at which they can be heard. And even if it does not directly concern them as auditors it might afford some protection against domineering directors pressurising the members to sign without allowing them time for adequate reflection. But neither aim is achieved unless failure to comply with the section renders the resolution invalid. In most cases that is not the result. As we shall see later,[98] case-law, has established that, with a possible exception when a statutory provision specifically precludes action unless a meeting is held[99] a unanimous agreement of all the members entitled to vote is equivalent to a resolution in general meeting. This the Act preserves: section 381C(2) provides that nothing in sections 381A and 381B affects any enactment or rule of law as to—

(a) things done otherwise than by passing a resolution, or
(b) cases in which a resolution is treated as having been passed, or a person is precluded from alleging that a resolution has not been duly passed."

Hence, if all the members have agreed, in most, if perhaps not all cases, the resolution will be effective even though section 381B is not complied with.

---

[93] s.381B(1).
[94] In the event of disagreement between the company and the auditors on whether or not it concerns them as auditors the ultimate decision will rest with the courts which, however, will doubtless be reluctant to disagree with the auditors' opinion.
[95] s.381B(2).
[96] s.381B(3) & (4).
[97] Sealy (1989) 10 Co.Law 210.
[98] See Chap. 6, pp. 134–138 below.
[99] As a result of s.381A(4) & (5) where a written resolution complies with s.381A there is no such exception. Nor can s.381A be affected by any provision in the company's memorandum or articles: s.381C(1).

Formalities and Expense

Proceeding by way of a written resolution does not obviate the need to record the resolution in the company's minute book[1] or to send a copy to the Registrar within 15 days after it is passed.[2] But the omission to do either does not affect the validity of the resolution though it makes the company and its officers in default liable to penalties[3] and, in the former case, deprives them of the presumption that all the requirements of the Act have been complied with.[4]

Furthermore, the 1989 Act has introduced an "elective regime" enabling private companies to dispense with or relax a number of the requirements of the principal Act. At present the requirements to which this applies[5] relate to the duration of the directors' authority to allot shares[6], laying accounts and reports before a general meeting,[7] the need to hold annual general meetings[8], the majority required to authorise short notice of a meeting,[9] and the need to appoint auditors each year[10]. In combination with section 381A, the effect is virtually to enable private companies to dispense completely with formal meetings if all the members want to. All that is needed is to pass an "elective resolution" in accordance with section 379A. On its face, this demands that the resolution shall be (a) passed at a general meeting of which at least 21 days' notice has been given stating that an elective resolution is to be proposed and setting out its terms and (b) agreed to at the meeting by all members entitled to attend and vote.[11] In fact, however, as a result of section 381A[12] it can be passed by a written resolution under that section unless the auditors are able to, and do, demand a meeting because it concerns them as auditors.[13] The elective resolution can be rescinded by an ordinary resolution[14] and ceases to have effect if the company re-registers as a public company.[15] A copy of any elective resolution, or ordinary resolution revoking it, has to be sent to the Registrar.[16]

---

[1] s.382A(1).
[2] s.380.
[3] s.382(5) and s.382A(3).
[4] s.382A(2).
[5] See s.379A(1) lists the relevant sections. Somewhat mysteriously, s.379A(5) says that the provisions of the section (1) have effect notwithstanding any contrary provision in the company's articles but, in conspicuous contrast with s.381C(1), do not say "memorandum or articles." Is the intention that a company can contract out of the ability to pass elective resolutions by a provision in the memorandum? Or is it an oversight? Or a deliberate omission on the basis that it is unthinkable that any company would do so?
[6] 1985 Act s.80A.
[7] ibid. s.252.
[8] ibid. s.366A.
[9] ibid. ss.369(4) and 378(3).
[10] s.386.
[11] s.379A(1) and (2).
[12] See s.381A(6) above.
[13] s.381B above.
[14] s.379A(3). Which again can be a written resolution under s.381A.
[15] s.379(4).
[16] s.380 as amended.

Finally, and, in the long term, perhaps most importantly, section 117 of the 1989 Act[17] empowers the Secretary of State to make provision by regulations[18] whereby additional requirements which appear to him "to relate primarily to the internal administration and procedure of companies" may be dispensed with or modified by elective resolutions[19] and to make consequential amendments to the principal Act.[20] If robust use is made of this power small companies may at long last be provided with a regime more suitable to their needs. While this will be less satisfactory than providing them with a separate Act (they will still have to plough through the mammoth Companies Act to ascertain what sections apply to them) it will be a major reform removing many of the disadvantages of incorporation.

Public companies. It is unusual initially to incorporate a company as a public limited company. In the rare circumstances where this is done, the initial costs will be heavy since the new company must have a prescribed minimum share capital[21] and, before commencing business, must obtain a certificate from the Registrar that it has complied with the strict conditions regarding the allotment of its capital.[22] Normally, companies start as private ones and become public only when they wish their shares to be offered to the public. On conversion they have to comply with similarly strict provisions relating to capital.[23] In either event, the company on going public will, in addition, have to incur the heavy expense of complying with Part IV or V of the Financial Services Act 1986 and with the rules in The Stock Exchange's *Yellow Book*, if the securities are to be listed.[24]

As we have seen,[25] a public company is essentially one which is designed to enable entrepreneurs to raise capital from the public and one in which there is a separation of ownership and control. Hence, throughout its life it will be subject to a regime somewhat stricter than that applying to a private company. But this, in practice, is unlikely to be found unduly burdensome in the light of its greater resources.

Other consequences of incorporation

In addition to the advantages and disadvantages discussed in this chapter, certain major consequences follow from incorporation, each

---

[17] This provision is not inserted in the principal Act but presumably will be if and when there is another official consolidation.
[18] Subject to an affirmative resolution of both Houses: s.117(5).
[19] s.117(1).
[20] s.117(2) and (3).
[21] s.11.
[22] ss.117, 118.
[23] 1985 Act ss.43–48.
[24] These Parts of the F.S. Act have replaced the former "prospectus" provisions of the Companies Act 1985: See Chap. 13 below.
[25] p. 10 above.

of which requires a chapter to itself. Incorporated companies are subject to technical legal rules (which do not apply to sole traders or partnerships) restricting the range of their activities (the *ultra vires* rule or what remains of it[26]) and regarding raising and maintaining their capital.[27] Though the *ultra vires* rule has virtually disappeared, the rules relating to capital have not and these are probably disadvantageous from the viewpoint of the members, since they prevent them from withdrawing their capital with the same ease as they could if the business was unincorporated (or unlimited). Pure agency principles which apply to partnerships (each partner being an agent of the firm) are modified in relation to incorporated companies—the members as such are not its agents.[28] This may sometimes be to the advantage of the members and sometimes to their disadvantage. But before turning to these matters we must look at the circumstances in which the law is prepared to ignore, in whole or in part, the normal consequences of the corporate entity principle by "lifting the veil" of incorporation.

26 Chap. 8 below.
27 Chaps. 9 and 10 below.
28 Chaps. 7 and 8 below.

CHAPTER 6

LIFTING THE VEIL

WHAT is generally described as "lifting the veil"[1] has until quite recently aroused little attention and less theoretical discussion in this country.[2] Nevertheless, it has always been recognised that "the legislature can forge a sledgehammer capable of cracking open the corporate shell"[3] and even without the aid of a legislative sledgehammer the courts have sometimes been prepared to have a crack. To various illustrations we now turn. In the cases where the veil is lifted, the law either goes behind the corporate personality to the individual members, or ignores the separate personality of each company in favour of the economic entity constituted by a group of associated companies. The latter situation is often merely an example of the former, the individual members being corporate, rather than human, beings but even when that is so the two situations are worth distinguishing since there seems to be a greater readiness to lift the veil in the latter.

Before dealing with exceptional situations in which the veil is lifted, it should be emphasised that the veil never means that the affairs of the company are completely concealed from view. On the contrary, the legislature has always made it an essential condition of the recognition of corporate personality with limited liability that it should be accompanied by wide publicity. Although third parties dealing with the company will normally have no right to resort against its members, they are nevertheless entitled to see who those members are, what shares they hold and, in the case of a listed company, the beneficial interests in those shares if substantial. They are also entitled to see who its officers are (so that they know with whom to deal), what its constitution is (so that they know what the company may do and how it may do it), and what its capital is and how it has been obtained (so that they know whether to trust it). And unless it is an unlimited company they are also entitled to see its

---

[1] Etymologically "mask" might have been a better metaphor, since "persona" is derived from the name for a mask worn by a player in the Greek theatre.

[2] It is a favourite topic in the U.S.A. where the veil is lifted more readily (see Whincup, *Inequitable Incorporation* (1981) 2 Co. Law 158) and there is now a considerable body of comparative literature in English; see, *e.g.* Cohn & Simitis, *Lifting the Veil in the Company Laws of the European Continent* (1963) 12 I.C.L.Q. 189; Schmitthoff, *Wholly Owned and Controlled Subsidiaries* [1978] J.B.L. 218; Wooldridge, *Groups of Companies: Britain, France and Germany* (I.A.L.S. 1981); Hopt (ed.), *Groups of Companies in European Laws* (de Gruyter 1982); Rixon, *Lifting Veils of Holding and Subsidiary Companies* (1986) 102 L.Q.R. 415, and Ottolenghi, *From Peeping behind the Corporate Veil to Ignoring it Completely:* (1990) 53 M.L.R. 338. Schmitthoff & Wooldridge (Eds.) *Groups of Companies* (1991).

[3] *Per* Devlin J. in *Bank voor Handel en Scheepvaart N.V.* v. *Slaford* [1953] 1 Q.B. 248 at 278.

accounts, or at least a modified version of them—again in order to know whether to trust it.

Normally, however, third parties are neither bound nor entitled to look behind such information as the law provides shall be made public; in addition to the veil of incorporation, there is something in the nature of a curtain formed by the company's public file, and what goes on behind it is concealed from the public gaze.[4] But sometimes this curtain also may be raised. For example, an inspector may be appointed to investigate the company's affairs,[5] in which case he will have the widest inquisitorial powers; indeed he may even be appointed for the purpose of going behind the company's registers to ascertain who are its true owners. It is not always easy to decide whether one is faced with a true example of lifting the veil or with a raising of the curtain and some of the examples[6] dealt with hereafter should perhaps be regarded as lifting the curtain (rather than the veil).

That, however, is not our primary concern, which is to examine the circumstances in which the fundamental principle of corporate personality itself is disregarded. Some of the major examples arising under the express words of a statute will be discussed first.

UNDER EXPRESS STATUTORY PROVISION

Reduction of number of members

Under what is now section 24 of the Companies Act, if a company carries on business for more than six months with less than two[7] members any person who is a member after that six months may become liable, jointly and severally with the company, for the payment of its debts. Hence, at present[7a] even in the case of the "one-man" company or the wholly-owned subsidiary of another company, it is advisable that there should continue to be at least one other member although he may hold his share as a nominee for the "one-man" or the parent company.

This section does not operate to destroy the separate personality of the company; it still remains an existing entity even though there is one member only,[8] or, indeed, although there is none.[9] And the rights which the section confers on creditors are severely limited. It is only the member who remains after the six months that can be sued

---

[4] *cf.* the rule in *Royal British Bank* v. *Turquand*, below, Chap. 8.
[5] See Chap. 25 below.
[6] *e.g.* the residence and ratification cases: see pp. 134–138 below.
[7] Prior to the Companies Act 1980 it was less then seven in the case of public companies.
[7a] But this will change on the implementation of the 12th Company Law Directive on single-member private companies.
[8] *Jarvis Motors (Harrow) Ltd.* v. *Carabott* [1964] 1 W.L.R. 1101. But the company can be wound up on this ground: Insolvency Act 1986, s.122(1)(e).
[9] Anomalously the section does not then bite, there being no member to make liable.

(not those whose withdrawal has led to the fall below the minimum[10]) and then only if he knows that it is carrying on business with only one member[11] and he is liable only in respect of debts contracted[12] after the six months and while he was a member. The crowning anomaly is that liability attaches only to a member and not to a director unless he is also a member.

Although the facts giving rise to a possible application of the section are of not infrequent occurrence[13] it seems rarely, if ever, to be invoked, doubtless because of the limitations considered, and it constitutes an exception to the general rule of theoretical interest rather than practical importance.

Fraudulent or wrongful trading

An example of far greater practical importance has long been afforded by provisions which, until 1986, were in section 332[14] of the Companies Act 1948. This created a specific but widely defined criminal offence of carrying on the business of a company with intent to defraud. It further provided that, if the company was in the course of winding up, the court could declare that the culprits were to be personally responsible, without limitation of liability, for all or any of the debts or other liabilities of the company to the extent that the court might direct. In the legislative reforms of 1985–86 the criminal offence became section 458[15] of the Companies Act but the civil sanction was moved to sections 213–215 of the Insolvency Act 1986 and, following the recommendations of the Cork Committee[16] extended to "wrongful trading" involving a lesser degree of moral

---

[10] Thus, if the members of a company are A. and B. and B. dies and his executors fail to become registered as members, A will be liable for debts contracted six months after B's death (unless C is admitted to membership), and there can be no resort against B's estate. It seems that the deceased B cannot be counted as a member, although the shares are registered in his name: *Re Bowling & Welby's Contract* [1895] 1 Ch. 663, C.A.

[11] Which, if he was not an officer of the company, he might not know.

[12] This presumably means only contractual pecuniary obligations and not other liabilities; *cf.* "debts or other liabilities" in the sections referred to below under *Fraudulent or Wrongful Trading.*

[13] *e.g.* in the circumstances suggested in n. 10. There may be complications in regularising the position especially if there are no surviving directors. It may then be necessary to apply to the court under s.371 to order a meeting and to direct that one member shall suffice. If all the members have died the position is still more difficult. The Jenkins Committee recommended that for the purposes of that section the personal representatives of deceased members should be treated as members (Cmnd. 1749, para. 26) but this has not yet been implemented. *cf. Re Noel Tedman Holding Pty. Ltd.* (1967) Qd.R.561 (Qd.Sup.Ct), where a still wider provision in Table A of the Australian Act enabled the executors prior to obtaining probate (but not administrators prior to obtaining letters of administration) to act at a meeting ordered by the court.

[14] As amended by s.96 of the Companies Act 1981 which reversed the effect of the decision in *DPP v. Schildkamp* [1971] A.C.I.(H.L.) holding that winding up of the company was an essential precondition to a criminal prosecution.

[15] Which, as did the amended s.332, applies whether or not the company is in liquidation.

[16] (1981) Cmnd. 8558, Chap. 44.

culpability. It is with the latter sections that we are here concerned[17] and they constitute what is probably the most extreme departure from the rule in *Salomon's* case yet achieved in the United Kingdom.

Section 213, dealing with fraudulent trading, is generally the same as the relevant provisions of the former section 332 and decisions on the latter remain relevant. It provides that:

"(1) If in the course of the winding up of a company it appears that any business of the company has been carried on[18] with intent to defraud creditors of the company[19] or creditors of any other person or for any fraudulent purpose . . . ."

then;

"(2) The court on the application of the liquidator may declare that any persons who were knowingly parties to the carrying on the business in [that] manner are to be liable to make such contributions (if any) to the company's assets as the court thinks proper."

Hence, unlike the criminal offence now in the Companies Act, it applies only if the company is in liquidation[20] and, in contrast with the former section 332,[21] applications for the declaration can be made only by the liquidator. But the class of persons against whom the declaration can be made is far wider than members or directors. Hence the Government[22] (even when less reluctant than it now is to rescue "lame ducks") and banks and parent companies have at times felt inhibited from providing finance to ailing companies, fearing that they may thereby fall foul of the provisions. Their fears, however, seem unfounded so long as they play no active role in running the company with fraudulent intent.[23]

---

[17] But the criminal sanction is a useful deterrent and prosecutions will doubtless continue to be frequent since it has been regarded as less confusing to juries to face them with a single charge of fraudulent trading rather than with numerous charges of individual acts of fraud: see *R. v. Kemp* [1988] Q.B. 645, C.A. (pet. dis. [1988] 1 W.L.R. 846, H.L.)

[18] It may be regarded as carrying on business notwithstanding that it has ceased active trading: *Re Sarflax Ltd.* [1979] Ch. 592.

[19] It suffices if only one creditor in the course of one transaction is defrauded: *Re Cooper Chemicals Ltd.* [1978] Ch. 262. Or if those defrauded are customers who are not actual, but only potential, creditors: *R. v. Kemp*, above. Or indeed if none is actually defrauded.

[20] But, in contrast with s.214 (below) not necessarily *insolvent* liquidation.

[21] Under which the application could also have been made by the official receiver, a creditor or a member.

[22] See Ganz, *Government and Industry* (1977) at pp. 97–100.

[23] In *Re Maidstone Building Provisions Ltd.* [1971] 1 W.L.R. 1085 an attempt to obtain a declaration against the company's secretary, who was also a partner in its auditors' firm, failed because, although he had given financial advice and had not attempted to prevent the company from trading, he had not taken "positive steps in the carrying on of the company's business in a fraudulent manner." In *Re Augustus Barnett & Son Ltd.* [1986] BCLC 170 an attempt against its parent company (Rumasa) failed on the same ground. But in *Re Cooper Chemicals Ltd.*, above, it was held that a declaration could be made against a creditor who refrained from pressing for repayment knowing that the business was being carried on in fraud of creditors and who accepted part payment out of money which he knew had been obtained by that fraud.

To establish that intent, what has to be shown is "actual dishonesty involving, according to current notions of fair trading among commercial men, real moral blame."[24] That may be inferred if "a company continues to carry on business and to incur debts at a time when there is, to the knowledge of the directors, no reasonable prospect of the creditors ever receiving payment of those debts,"[25] but cannot be inferred merely because they ought to have realised it. It is this need to prove subjective moral blame that had led the Jenkins Committee in 1962 vainly to recommend the introduction of a remedy for "reckless trading"[26] and the Cork Committee, 20 years later, successfully to promote it under the the name of "wrongful trading."

"*Wrongful trading*" is dealt with in section 214 of the Insolvency Act. It empowers the court to make a declaration similar to that under section 213[27] but only in one specific set of circumstances. It operates only when the company has gone into *insolvent* liquidation[28] and the declaration can be made only against a person who, at some time before the commencement of the winding up, was a director of the company and knew, or ought to have concluded, at that time,[29] that there was no reasonable prospect that the company would avoid going into insolvent liquidation.[30] But the declaration is not to be made if the court is satisfied that the person concerned thereupon took every step with a view to minimising the potential loss to the company's creditors as, on the assumption that he knew there was no reasonable prospect of avoiding insolvent liquidation, he ought to have taken.[31] In judging what facts he ought to have known or ascertained, what conclusions he should have drawn and what steps he should have taken, he is to be assumed to be a reasonably diligent person having both the general knowledge, skill and experience to be expected of a person carrying out his functions in relation to the company[32] and the general knowledge, skill and experience that he in fact has.[33]

24 *Re Patrick Lyon Ltd.* [1933] Ch. 786 at pp. 790, 791.
25 *Re William C. Leitch Ltd.* [1932] 2 Ch. 71, *per* Maugham J at p. 77. See also *R. v. Grantham* [1984] Q.B. 675, C.A., where the court upheld a direction to the jury that they might convict of fraudulent trading a person who had taken an active part in running the business if they were satisfied that he had helped to obtain credit knowing that there was no good reason for thinking that funds would become available to pay the debts when they became due or shortly thereafter.
26 Cmnd. 1749, para. 503(b).
27 Insolvency Act 1986, s.214(1).
28 *i.e.* when its assets are insufficient for the payment of its liabilities and the expenses of the winding up: *ibid.* s.214(6).
29 Which must be after 27 April 1986.
30 *Ibid.* s.214(2).
31 *Ibid.* s.214(3).
32 This includes functions entrusted to him even if he has not carried them out: *ibid.* s.214(5). If he has failed the objective test he cannot be excused by the court, under Companies Act 1985 s.727, on the ground that he has acted honestly: *Re Produce Marketing Consortium Ltd.* [1989] 1 W.L.R. 745.
33 *Ibid.* s.214(4).

The section therefore recognises that the person concerned may not be in a position himself to put the company into liquidation but that if, as a reasonable director, he ought to have known that it was heading towards insolvency he must have done something to seek to prevent its continuing to trade if he is to avoid the possibility of having to contribute to the payment of its debts. Moreover, and this of considerable importance for a number of reasons, for the purpose of section 214 "director" includes a "shadow director," [34] *i.e.* "a person in accordance with whose directions or instructions the directors of the company are accustomed to act. ... " [35] This considerably widens the class of persons against whom a declaration can be made. And in respect of shadow directors the action that they should have taken is clear. Although a single director may not be in a position to seek winding up, the board of directors can. [36] Hence a shadow director, once he knows or ought to have known that there was no reasonable prospect of avoiding insolvent liquidation, should direct or instruct the board to take that action. [37]

It also raises the very real prospect of invoking section 214 against the company's parent company. In the comparable definition of "shadow director" for the purposes of the Companies Act, [38] it is expressly provided that in relation to certain specified sections [39] of that Act:

"a body corporate is not to be treated as a shadow director of any of its subsidiary companies by reason only that the directors of the subsidiary are accustomed to act in accordance with its directions or instructions."

But there is no such exception in the Insolvency Act. Hence, if in a group of companies the directors of the subsidiaries are accustomed to act on the directions or instructions of the parent company, the parent will be a shadow director of the subsidiaries and liable to have a direction made against it if the other conditions are fulfilled. It should be easier to identify such a group (and to establish the parent's knowledge of the subsidiary's financial position [40]) than is likely to be the case with individuals who lurk in the shadows. Hence

34 *Ibid.* s.214(7).
35 *Ibid.* s.251. But not "by reason only that the directors act on advice given by him in a professional capacity,".
36 *Ibid.* s.124(1).
37 The directors themselves will be vulnerable to a declaration if they fail to show their customary obedience.
38 s.741(2).
39 ss.309, 319–322 and 330–346.
40 The parent of even the most loosely organised group is likely to require its subsidiaries to afford it monthly or quarterly financial statements. And normally its accounts and those of its subsidiaries will have to be consolidated annually: see p. 118 below.

a parent company will either have to allow the board of a subsidiary to act independently in the sole interest of the subsidiary,[41] free from directions or instructions from above, or face the possibility that it will have to contribute to the payment of the subsidiary's creditors if it allows the subsidiary to sink into insolvent liquidation. This is a considerable step in the direction of rationalising the legal position of groups.[42]

Section 214 is expressly stated to be "without prejudice" to section 213[43] and there may well be cases where the circumstances will justify an application by the liquidator under both. Indeed, section 215 contains certain procedural provisions common to both fraudulent and wrongful trading. Most of these repeat, in substance, provisions in the former section 332: for example, that on an application for a declaration the liquidator may give or call evidence[44] and that the court may add further directions for giving effect to any declaration it makes and, in particular, may direct that the liability of any person against whom the declaration is made shall be a charge on any debt due from the company to him or on any mortgage or charge in his favour on assets of the company.[45] And both sections 213 and 214 have effect notwithstanding that the person concerned may be criminally liable.[46] What is new and valuable is that section 215[47] also provides that the court may direct that the whole or any part of a debt, and interest thereon, owed by the company to a person against whom a declaration is made, shall be postponed to all other debts, and interest thereon, owed by the company.

Decisions on the former section 332[48] established that the amount of the contribution which the declaration makes should be a specific sum, not necessarily related or limited to amounts due to creditors shown to have been defrauded[49] and that money thus recovered forms part of the general assets of the company available to meet the claims of all creditors and not merely those whose debts were contracted during the time when the trading was fraudulent or wrongful. In one case[50] the Court of Appeal was divided on whether

[41] Which is probably what in law it is supposed to do anyway.
[42] But it is one which deals only with principle (3) of the Draft Ninth Directive (see p. 64 above) and stops short of full recognition of that principle.
[43] *Ibid.* s.214(8).
[44] *Ibid.* s.215(1).
[45] Including any assignees from that person: *ibid.* s.215(2) and (3).
[46] *Ibid.* s.215(5).
[47] Subs. (4).
[48] *Re William C. Leitch Ltd.*, above; *Re William C. Leitch Ltd. (No. 2)* [1933] Ch. 161; *Re Cyona Distributors Ltd.* [1967] Ch. 889, C.A.
[49] But in cases of wrongful trading, prima facie the contribution should be the amount by which the company's assets can be discerned to have been depleted by the director's conduct, and in the exercise of that discretion the absence of fraudulent intent should not be ignored: *Re Produce Marketing Consortium Ltd. (No. 2)* [1989] B.C.L.C. 520. For an analysis of this (the most important decision to date on s.214) and on the section generally, see Prentice (1990) 10 Ox.Jo.Leg. Studs. 265.
[50] *Re Cyona Distributors Ltd.*, above.

this was necessarily the case when the application was made by a creditor, but held that it certainly was if the application was by the liquidator. As, now, it can be made only by the liquidator, the disagreement seems to have been resolved.

Abuse of company names or employment of disqualified directors

The Insolvency Act 1986 added further examples of cases where the managers of a company may become liable for its debts and other liabilities. A common abuse had been for those responsible for the running of a company which had gone into insolvent liquidation to form another company, with an identical or very similar name[51] which bought the undertaking and assets from the original company's liquidator[52] and through which they continued to trade. At best this was likely to mislead and confuse customers[53]; at worst it was a deliberate fraud. Section 216 of the Insolvency Act now makes it an offence for anyone who was a director or shadow director of the original company at any time during the 12 months preceding its going into insolvent liquidation to be in any way concerned (except with the leave of the court or in such circumstances as may be prescribed) during the next five years in the formation or management of a company, or business, with a name by which the original company was known or one so similar as to suggest an association with that company. Moreover, under section 217, he becomes personally liable, jointly and severally with that company and any other person so liable, for the debts and other liabilities of that company incurred while he was concerned in its management in breach of section 216. So does anyone involved in its management who acts or is willing to act on the instructions given by a person whom he knows, at that time, to be in breach of section 216.[54]

Similar consequences apply to a person against whom a court order has been made under the Company Directors Disqualification Act 1986.[55] Section 15 of that Act provides that if such a person acts in the management of a company in contravention of the order, both he, and any other person concerned with the management of that

---

[51] The relaxation of the control over company names by the Companies Act 1981 (see pp. 268 below) facilitated this.

[52] Or from a receiver and manager appointed by a debenture holder. The sale was sometimes at a gross undervalue.

[53] Re-use of former names is not necessarily improper. So long as effective steps can be taken to avoid misleading future creditors of the second company, it may be justified if it enables such goodwill as the former company may have had to be preserved so that its undertaking can be sold at an enhanced price for the benefit of its creditors.

[54] For the purpose of both sections 216 and 217, "company" includes any company which may be wound up under Part V of the Insolvency Act, *i.e.* virtually any company or association: *ibid.* s.220.

[55] See Chap. 7 at, pp. 144–147 below.

company who is willing to act on his instructions despite knowing he is disqualified, are jointly and severally liable with the company for its debts contracted during that time.[56]

It will be observed that these sections, though similar in their consequences to sections 213–215 of the Insolvency Act, differ from them in that they apply without the need for an application to, and declaration by, the court—though the persons concerned may apply to the court to be granted leave. They differ also in that the sanctions apply to conduct, not in relation to the company that has gone into liquidation, but in relation to another company or business whether or not that goes into liquidation.

Misdescription of the company

On ordinary agency principles the officers of a company will, of course, make themselves personally liable, notwithstanding that they are acting for the company, if they choose to contract personally; for example by not disclosing that they are acting on behalf of the company. But the Companies Acts have gone further. What is now section 349(4) of the Companies Act 1985 provides that if any officer of the company or other person acting on its behalf:

"signs or authorises to be signed on behalf of the company any bill of exchange, promissory note, endorsement, cheque or order for money or goods[56a] in which the company's name is not mentioned [in legible characters] . . . he is . . . liable to a fine; and he is further personally liable to the holder of the bill of exchange, promissory note, cheque or order for money or goods for the amount of it (unless it is duly paid by the company)."

The result of this is that if the correct and full name of the company does not so appear, the signatory will be personally liable to pay if the company does not.[57] And it seems clear that it makes no difference that the third party concerned has not been misled by the description.[58] However, as a result of what is now section 27 of the

---

[56] And note s.14 as regards criminal sanctions.
[56a] But not, it seems, an order for the supply of services even if they involve supplying goods!
[57] See *Atkins* v. *Wardle* (1889) 5 T.L.R. 734, C.A.; *Scottish & Newcastle Breweries Ltd.* v. *Blair*, 1967 S.L.T. 72; *Civil Service Co-operative Society* v. *Chapman* [1914] 30 T.L.R. 679; *British Airways Board* v. *Parish* [1979] 2 Lloyd's Rep. 361. Contrast *Oshkosh B'Gosh Inc.* v. *Dan Marbel Inc. Ltd.* [1989] BCLC 507, C.A. where a director, who had authorised the issue of an unsigned order for goods on which an incorrect name of the company was printed (the company was in process of changing its name to that printed but had not actually done so) was held not liable; he had not "signed or authorised" any signature.
[58] In the Scottish case of *Scottish & Newcastle Breweries Ltd.* v. *Blair* (above) Lord Hunter (at p. 74) expressly approved this sentence.

Companies Act, the use of the authorised abbreviation, "Ltd." or "plc" instead of the full prescribed suffix "limited" or "public limited company" (or the Welsh equivalent) is permissible. And the abbreviation of "Company" to "Co." has been held to be acceptable.[59] Furthermore the holder's conduct may estop him from enforcing the liability of the signatory; for example where he has written the document with the misdescription and submitted it for signature.[60] In any event the liability of the signatory is important only if the company is insolvent. If the signatory is authorised to act on its behalf, it will not escape liability, although misdescribed, so long as its identity can be established[61] and, if the signatory is successfully sued, he will be entitled to be indemnified by the company. On the company's insolvency, however, it affords the holder a remedy which may be wholly unmeritorious. It might be a useful reform to amend the subsection by affording the signatory a defence if he could establish that the holder had not been misled by the misdescription; the recent decisions display a marked disinclination to apply the provision when that is so.[62]

Premature trading

Another example in the Companies Act is in section 117(8). Under the section, a public limited company, newly incorporated as such, must not "do business or exercise any borrowing powers" until it has obtained, from the Registrar of Companies, a certificate that it has complied with the provisions of the Act relating to the raising of the prescribed minimum share capital or until it has re-registered as a private company. If it enters into any transaction[63] in contravention of this provision, not only are the company, and its officers in default, liable to fines[64] but, if the company fails to comply with its obligations in that connection within 21 days of being called upon to do so,[65] the directors of the company are jointly and severally liable

59 *Banque de l'Indochine v. Euroseas Group Finance Co. Ltd.* [1981] 3 All E.R. 198.
60 In *Durham Fancy Goods Ltd. v. Michael Jackson (Fancy Goods) Ltd.* [1968] 2 Q.B. 839 it was held that the abbreviation of the "Michael" to "M" breached the section but that the plaintiffs could not rely on it as they had submitted the document to the defendants with that abbreviation. But, in *Blum v. O.C.P.s.a.* [1988] B.C.L.C. 170 at 175a May L.J. reserved his position on the correctness of the decision.
61 *Goldsmith (Sicklesmere) Ltd. v. Baxter* [1970] Ch. 85.
62 And when they feel compelled to do so, tend to blame Parliament: see *Lindholst v. Fowler* [1988] BCLC 166, C.A. and *Rafsanjan Pistachio Producers v. Reiss* [1990] BCLC 352.
63 The validity of which is not affected: subs. (8).
64 Subs. (7).
65 Subs. (8), the wording of which does not make it crystal clear whether this means its obligations under the transaction or its obligations under the section to obtain the certificate or to convert to a private company. It presumably means the former, if only because it would be absurd that someone who has entered into the transaction, in the belief that the company is a properly capitalised plc, entitled to do business as such, should forfeit any remedy against its directors if it succeeds in converting to a private company within the 21 days.

to indemnify the other party in respect of any loss or damage suffered by reason of the company's failure to comply.

Whether this is a true example of lifting the veil is questionable; technically it does not make the directors liable for the company's debts but rather penalises the directors for any loss the third parties suffer as a result of the directors' default in complying with the section. But the effect is much the same. It is, however, unlikely to be invoked often since it is unusual for companies to be formed initially as public ones.

Company groups

Reference has already been made to the growth of groups of companies and to the failure of English company legislation to adapt adequately to this phenomenon.[66] Nevertheless, it has long been recognised that, in relation to financial disclosure, the phenomenon cannot be ignored if a "true and fair" view of the overall position of the group is to be presented and that accordingly when one company (the parent or holding company[67]) controls others (the subsidiary and sub-subsidiary companies) the parent company must present group financial statements as well as its own individual statements, thus avoiding the misleading impression which the latter alone might give.[68]

Having taken this step and prescribed criteria for determining when a parent-subsidiary relationship was established, use of the concept was extended to other areas. A further complication arose when it was thought desirable to provide for financial disclosure regarding some companies over which the degree of control was not such as to make them "subsidiaries" within the meaning of the statutory definition.[69] This is not the place to describe in detail the highly

[66] See pp. 63, 64 but *cf.* pp. 113, 114 above.
[67] In practice the expressions "parent" and "holding" were used interchangeably. Until the Companies Act 1989, U.K. company legislation used the latter, but the EEC Company Law Directives the former, which seems preferable since "holding" suggests that the sole function of the parent is to control the operations of subsidiaries whereas it too may well be undertaking one or more of the trading activities of the group. Now, in the Act, they have different meanings: see p. 121 below.
[68] To take a simplified example: if a parent company A has two wholly owned subsidiaries, B and C, and in a financial year B makes a loss of £100,000 while C makes a distributable profit of £10,000 all of which it pays to A by way of dividend, the individual accounts of A (assuming it has broken even) will show a profit of £10,000 whereas in fact the group has made a loss of £90,000.
[69] At this stage nomenclature went haywire. The Fourth and Seventh Directives describe the main class of such companies as "associated companies", and so do the accountancy bodies in *Statements of Standard Accounting Practice* (SSAPs). But Sched. 4 to the Companies Act called them "related companies" (an expression generally used to describe companies within the same group of parent and subsidiaries—and so used in the contemporaneous Companies Securities (Insider Dealing) Act—but which Sched. 4 described as "group companies").

technical statutory provisions. It suffices to summarise, briefly and ignoring many refinements and qualifications, their general effect in the light of the changes resulting from the implementation of the Seventh Company Law Directive (83/349/EEC) by the Companies Act 1989,[70] which introduced a distinction between "parent and subsidiary undertakings" (relevant in relation to financial statements) and "holding company and subsidiaries" (relevant to other statutory provisions).

(i) *Financial statements*

Group accounts now have to be in the form of a consolidated balance sheet and a consolidated profit and loss account[71] for the parent and all its subsidiaries, so far as possible as if they were a single company and eliminating inter-group transactions.[72] Although this applies only if the parent is a company, a subsidiary may be any form of "undertaking," corporate or unincorporated (for example, a partnership).[73] Under section 258 and Schedule 10A (inserted by the Act of 1989) the parent-subsidiary relationship is established if any one (or more) of five criteria is met. Briefly summarised,[74] these criteria are that one undertaking (the parent):

(a) holds a majority of voting rights in another undertaking;

(b) is a member[75] of the other undertaking and has the right to appoint or remove a majority of its board of directors;

(c) by virtue of provisions in the constitution of the other undertaking or in a written "control contract," permitted by that constitution, has a right, recognised by the law under which that undertaking is established, to exercise a "dominant influence" over that undertaking (by giving directions to the directors of the undertaking on its operating and financial policies which those directors are obliged to comply with whether or not the directors are for the benefit of the undertaking)[76];

---

70 Which made substantial amendments to the relevant provisions in Part VII of the Act and added a new Sched. 4A on consolidated accounts.

71 Formerly they could be in another form if that was thought to be clearer but little use was made of this concession.

72 Companies Act 1985, s.227 and Sched. 4A (as substituted by the 1989 Act). There are certain exceptions specified in ss.228 and 229.

73 Formerly, subsidiaries had to be bodies corporate though not necessarily registered companies.

74 This summary, which ignores many of the detailed requirements, is of s.258 with such amplifications from ss.259, 260 and Sched. 10A as are needed to make it intelligible.

75 For the extended meaning of "member," see s.258(3).

76 s.258(2)(c) and Sched. 10A, paras. 4(1) and (2). It is difficult to see how a "control contract" could ever be regarded as "permitted by law" in relation to an English subsidiary: it would seem to be expressly forbidden by s.310: on which see Chap. 21 at pp. 572–575 below.

(d)   is a member of another undertaking and alone controls, pursuant to an agreement with other members, a majority of the voting rights in that undertaking;

(e)   has a "participating interest" in another undertaking (*i.e.* an interest in its shares which it holds for the purpose of securing a contribution to its (the parent's) own activities by the exercise of the control or influence arising from that interest)[77] and actually exercises a dominant influence over it[78] or there is unified management of both undertakings[79]

and sub-subsidiaries are to be treated as subsidiaries of the ultimate parent also.[80]

In addition to consolidating the figures so as to give, in the manner prescribed by Schedule 4A, a true and fair view of the parent and subsidiaries as a whole, details about the various undertakings have to be given in notes to the accounts.[81] In particular the parent company has to name all its subsidiaries, to state the countries where they are established and to specify the proportion of their shares or class of shares that it holds. And a subsidiary, in a note to its accounts, must name the body corporate[82] which its directors believe to be its ultimate parent and, if known to them, its country of incorporation.

However, as already mentioned, even though the parent-subsidiary relationship may not be established, some measure of financial disclosure, falling short of full consolidation, may be required. This is so in two sets of circumstances. The first is where the "quasi-parent" (to coin a name) has a "participating interest," as defined in section 260, in another undertaking.[83] That, under criterion (e) above, may cause that undertaking to become its subsidiary if it actually exercises its dominance. If it refrains from doing so, the undertaking will nevertheless be what the Act now calls "an associated undertaking",[84] and, in notes to the accounts, similar information to that required in the case of a subsidiary will have to be given. Moreover, separate figures relating to the quasi-parent's stake in it will have to be incorporated in its balance sheet and profit and loss account. The second circumstance is when the company owns 10 per cent. or more of an undertaking. Information regarding the undertaking will then

[77] This is presumed to be the purpose (unless the contrary is shown) if 20 per cent. or more of the shares are held: s.260(2).
[78] Whether or not by the means specified in criterion (c): see Sched. 10A, para. 4(3).
[79] ss.258(4) and 260.
[80] s.258(5).
[81] s.231 and Sched. 5, as substituted or amended by the Companies Act 1989. Part I of the Schedule specifies what has to be stated in the notes when the company is not required to prepare group accounts and Part II specifies what has to be stated when it is required to do so.
[82] Whether or not it is a "company" required to produce consolidated accounts.
[83] See above, n. 77.
[84] Thus coming into line with the Directives and SSAPs: see n. 69 above.

have to be given in notes to the accounts, the information varying according to whether more than 20 per cent. is owned.

(ii) *Extension to other matters*

The Companies Acts have long used the concept of the parent-subsidiary relationship in areas other than that of financial disclosure. Clearly if one is to ban or control certain types of transaction between a company and its directors it is essential to ensure that this cannot be easily evaded by effecting the transactions with or through another company in the group. Hence many of the sections in Part X (Enforcement of Fair Dealing by Directors) so provide.[85] Similarly, the prohibition on financial assistance for the purchase of a company's own shares extends to financial assistance by any of its subsidiaries.[86]

Until the Companies Act 1989 a common definition of the parent-subsidiary relationship applied to all references in the companies' legislation to holding or subsidiary companies. When, however, the Directives compelled us to change the definition for the purposes of accounts it was represented that to apply the whole of the extended definition to other cases would introduce an unreasonable degree of uncertainty.[87] Hence it was decided to omit two of the criteria in such cases and to use different terminology. As a result, in addition to the definition of parent and subsidiary undertakings for the purposes of consolidation[88] and related financial disclosure, we now have a simpler definition of holding and subsidiary companies which applies to other cases where we are not constrained by the Directives. While it is a pity that it was thought necessary to have different definitions for what are essentially the same concept, there is no doubt that both are considerable improvements on the previous definition[89] since they recognise that what counts is "control" and not majority shareholding which, because of non-voting shares or weighted voting, will not necessarily afford control.[90]

Under the substituted section 736(1) of the Companies Act 1985, the definition of "holding" and "subsidiary" company now is:

"A company is a subsidiary of another company, its 'holding' company, if that other company"

---

[85] See especially ss.319 (contracts of employment for more than five years), 320–332 (substantial property transactions), 323 (dealing in share options), 324–329 (disclosure of shareholdings) and 330–342 (loans and "quasi-loans").

[86] s.151.

[87] *e.g.* in relation to the prohibition on a subsidiary holding shares in its parent (s.23, as substituted by s.129 of the 1989 Act) and in the definition of "related company" in the Company Securities (Insider Dealing) Act 1985, s.11.

[88] For purposes of consolidation a measure of uncertainty is acceptable because, when in doubt, one can play safe and consolidate.

[89] 1948 Act, s.154.

[90] Under the former s.154(10)(a)(ii) holding more than half in nominal value of a company's equity share capital (voting or non-voting) made it a subsidiary.

(a) holds a majority of the voting rights in it, or
(b) is a member of it and has the right to appoint or remove a majority of its board of directors, or
(c) is a member of it and controls alone, pursuant to an agreement with other shareholders or members, a majority of the voting rights in it,

or if it is a subsidiary of a company which is itself a subsidiary of that other company."

The section goes on in subsection (2) to (7) to amplify and explain this definition and a new section 736A empowers the Secretary of State to amend the definition by regulations. The essential differences from "parent" and "subsidiaries" under section 158 are that section 736 applies only when both the holding company and the subsidiaries are "bodies corporate" and that, of the five criteria in section 258,[91] only (a), (b) and (d)—and not (c) or (e)—are included in section 736.

(iii) *Overall result*

Although we now have some measure of recognition of the economic unity of a group, it does nothing to solve the major problems referred to at page 64 above. The directors of each individual company in a group are still supposed to operate it in the best interests of that company and not in the interests of the group. And the creditors of each company can look only to that company for payment of its debts and cannot rely on the parent bailing them out. As Templeman L.J. (as he then was) said in 1979[92]:

"English company law possesses some curious features, which may generate curious results. A parent company may spawn a number of subsidiary companies, all controlled directly or indirectly by the shareholders of the parent company. If one of the subsidiary companies ... turns out to be the runt of the litter and declines into insolvency to the dismay of its creditors, the parent company and other subsidiary companies may prosper to the joy of the shareholders without any liability for the debts of the insolvent subsidiary."

Since 1979 the position has improved somewhat as a result of the Insolvency Act and, in particular, its provisions in relation to fraudulent or wrongful trading under which the parent may be liable as a shadow director.[93] How far it has improved will depend on how ready the courts will be to hold both (a) that the parent company was party to the carrying on of the subsidiary's business with the required

---

[91] pp. 119, 120 above.
[92] *Re Southard & Co. Ltd.* [1979] 1 W.L.R. 1198, C.A. at p. 1208.
[93] See above.

intent and knowledge, and (b) that the directors of the subsidiary were accustomed to act in accordance with the parent's directions.

Apart from that, it can be argued that the extended provisions regarding group disclosure have, in this respect, made matters worse rather than better for they are calculated to lead those who read group annual reports to assume that there is group liability. Why, otherwise, should a subsidiary's reports be required to name its ultimate holding company?[94]

Miscellaneous statutory examples

In addition to the foregoing examples culled from the companies and related legislation, scattered throughout the statute-book are to be found many examples of modification of the corporate entity principle. This is particularly the case in relation to taxation; the Revenue, not surprisingly, has been astute to secure the passage of legislation "capable of cracking open the corporate shell"[95] when this is being used for purposes of tax avoidance and has occasionally done so to mitigate the burden of taxation if a strict application of the corporate entity principle would be unduly harsh or inhibiting.[96]

Mostly, statutory inroads have been in relation to groups (using the Companies Acts' definition of holding and subsidiary companies or some lesser degree of common control) or to situations arising on a change of control. Illustrations of both occur in the employment legislation relating to redundancy and unfair dismissal,[97] under which changes of employment within the group from one company to another or as a result of mergers are not treated as breaking the period of continuous employment. Another illustration occurs in relation to rights under business tenancies. Under the Landlord and Tenant Act 1954, as amended by the Law of Property Act 1969, when either the landlord or the tenant is a company its rights under the Act may enure for the benefit of other companies in the group[98] and, reversing a decision in which the court had refused to lift the veil,[99] an individual landlord may be able to recover possession if he requires it for the purpose of a business carried on, not by him, but by a company which he controls.[1]

Nevertheless, the courts have generally been reluctant to construe a statute as lifting the veil unless compelled to do so by the clearest words of the statute. The classic illustration is the refusal of the

[94] It is fanciful to suppose that this requirement has been retained to assist those who wish to avoid having investments in, or dealings with, a company in a group with interests in S. Africa, tobacco or armaments.
[95] See p. 108 above.
[96] *e.g.* in relation to "group relief."
[97] Presently in the Employment Protection (Consolidation) Act 1978, Part VI.
[98] Landlord & Tenant Act 1954, s.42.
[99] *Tunstall* v. *Steigmann* [1962] 2 Q.B. 593, C.A.
[1] Landlord & Tenant Act 1954, s.30(3).

House of Lords in *Nokes v. Doncaster Amalgamated Collieries*[2] to construe what is now section 427 of the Companies Act 1985 as meaning that an order made thereunder transferring the property and liabilities of one company to another on a reconstruction could operate to transfer a contract of personal service; and this notwithstanding that the section specifically provides that "property" includes property, rights and powers of every description. To Lord Atkin the contrary interpretation would have been 'tainted with oppression and confiscation"[3] and would have subverted "the principle that a man is not to be compelled to serve a master against his will . . . [which] is deep-seated in the common law of this country."[4] Yet, had the whole share capital of the transferor company been transferred instead of the undertaking, the man would have been compelled to serve what, in reality, was a new master. The employee is better protected by recognising the continuation of the enterprise but providing him with rights to payments for redundancy or unfair dismissal if he is not kept on. And this is now recognised in respect of both transfers of the undertaking (where the effect of the *Nokes* decision has been reversed[5]) and changes of controlling shareholdings.[6]

UNDER CASE LAW

Efforts by the judges to lift the veil have, in general, been hamstrung by the *Salomon* case, which finally destroyed the possibility of regarding a "one-man company" as a mere alias of, or agent for, the principal shareholder. Perhaps the most extreme illustration of a refusal to lift the veil is afforded by *Lee v. Lee's Air Farming Ltd.*[7] There Lee, for the purpose of carrying on his business of aerial top-dressing, had formed a company of which he beneficially owned all the shares and was sole "governing director." He was also appointed chief pilot. Pursuant to the company's statutory obligations he caused the company to insure against liability to pay compensation under the Workmen's Compensation Act. He was killed in a flying accident. The Court of Appeal of New Zealand held that his widow was not entitled to compensation from the company, (*i.e.* from their insurers) since Lee could not be regarded as a "worker," (*i.e.* servant) within the meaning of the Act. But the Privy Council reversed that decision,

2 [1940] A.C. 1014, H.L. (reversing the unanimous decisions of the courts below.).
3 *Ibid.* at p. 1030.
4 *Ibid.* at p. 1033.
5 See the Transfer of Undertakings (Protection of Employment) Regs. 1981 (S.I. No. 1794) implementing Directive 77/187/EEC and construed by the House of Lords so as to give full effect to it: *Lister v. Forth Dry Dock* [1990] 1 A.C. 546, H.L. (Sc.).
6 Employment Protection (Consolidation) Act 1978, s.94.
7 [1961] A.C. 12, P.C.

holding that Lee and his company were distinct legal entities which had entered into contractual relationships under which he became, *qua* chief pilot, a servant of the company. In his capacity of governing director he could, on behalf of the company, give himself orders in his other capacity of pilot, and hence the relationship between himself, as pilot, and the company was that of servant and master. In effect the magic of corporate personality enabled him to be master and servant at the same time and to get all the advantages of both (and of limited liability).[8]

Nevertheless, there have been exceptional cases in which the courts have felt able to lift the veil and until recently there were perhaps signs of a greater willingness to do so. Indeed, as recently as 1985 a judgment of the Court of Appeal declared that:

"In our view the cases ... show that the court will use its power to pierce the corporate veil if it is necessary to achieve justice irrespective of the legal efficacy of the corporate structure ..."[9]

a view emphatically rejected by the Court of Appeal in the recent case of *Adams* v. *Cape Industries plc.*[10] In that important case the Court in a mammoth judgment, involving a number of issues, subjected lifting the veil to the most exhaustive treatment that it has yet received in the English (or Scottish) courts.

The facts of the case were somewhat complicated but for present purposes it suffices to say that what the Court had ultimately to determine was whether judgments obtained in the United States against Cape, an English registered company whose business was mining asbestos in S. Africa and marketing it worldwide, would be recognised and enforced by the English Courts. In the absence of submission to the foreign jurisdiction this depended on whether Cape could be said to have been "present" in the United States. The Court held that the English Courts will not treat a trading corporation incorporated under the law of one country as present within the jurisdiction of another unless (i) it has established and maintained at its own expense a fixed place of business there and for more than a minimal time carried on its business there by servants or agents or (ii) its representative has for more than a minimal time been carrying on its business there at or from some fixed place of business.[11]

In contending that Cape had been present in the United States the plantiffs raised three arguments.

---

[8] Note also *Underwood* v. *Bank of Liverpool* [1924] 1 K.B. 775, C.A., which shows that third parties who are so ill-advised as to regard the members as the same as the company will not only fail to make the members liable to them, but may sometimes incur liability to the company.

[9] *Re A Company* (1985) 1 BCC 99,421, C.A.

[10] [1990] Ch. 433, Scott J and C.A. (pet.dis. [1990] 2 W.L.R. 786, H.L.).

[11] At p. 530.

Lifting the Veil

The "single economic unit" argument

The first of these, described as the "single economic unit argument" proceeded as follows: Admittedly there is no general principle that all companies in a group of companies are to be regarded as one; on the contrary the fundamental principle is unquestionably that "each company in a group of companies . . . is a separate legal entity possessed of separate rights and liabilities."[12] Nevertheless, it was argued, the court will, in appropriate circumstances, ignore the distinction between them, treating them as one. For this proposition a number of authorities were cited.

The first of these was *The Roberta*,[13] in which bills of lading had been signed on behalf of a subsidiary company but a concession was made at the trial that the parent company was responsible for the bills. The judge described the concession as properly made since the subsidiary was a separate entity from the parent (which owned all its shares and supplied two out of three directors) "in name only and probably for the purposes of taxation."[14] The second was *Holdsworth & Co. v. Caddies*[15] in which it had been argued that Caddies who had been appointed managing director of Holdsworth, the parent company of the group, could not be ordered to devote his whole time solely to duties in relation to the affairs of the subsidiaries since these were separate legal entities under the control of their own boards of directors. This argument was rejected as too technical. Caddies' service agreement was "an agreement *in re mercatoria* and must be construed in light of the facts and realities of the situation."[16] The third authority was *Scottish Co-operative Wholesale Society Ltd v. Meyer*.[17] In that case it had been argued that the appellant could not be said to have conducted the affairs of the company in a manner oppressive to some part of the members within the meaning of section 210 of the Companies Act 1948[18] since it was not that company which had acted oppressively but a subsidiary which it had formed. The House of Lords had no hesitation in rejecting this argument since "every step taken by [the subsidiary] was determined by the policy of [the parent]"[19] and "the section warrants the courts in looking at the business realities of the situation and does not confine them to a narrow legalistic view."[20]

[12] At p. 532, quoting Roskill L.J. in *The Albazero* [1977] A.C. 744, C.A. and H.L., at 807.
[13] (1937) 58 Ll.L.R. 159.
[14] At p. 169.
[15] [1955] 1 W.L.R. 352, H.L.
[16] *Per* Lord Reid at p. 367.
[17] [1959] A.C. 324, H.L. (Sc.)
[18] Now replaced by ss.459–461 of the 1985 Act on which see Chap. 24 at pp. 662–668 below.
[19] *Per* Lord Simonds at p. 342.
[20] These words were of Lord President Cooper on the first hearing of the case and quoted with approval by Lord Simonds at p. 343.

The above three authorities related exclusively to the interpretation of statutes or documents, an area in which further authority to the like effect can be found.[21] The fourth case relied on in support of the "single economic unit argument", D.H.N. Food Distributors Ltd v. Tower Hamlets L.B.C.,[22] was rather different. D.H.N. had two wholly-owned subsidiaries in one of which the landed property of the group, was vested while D.H.N. carried on the business of the group, occupying the property as a licensee. According to the decision of the Lands Tribunal, on the compulsory purchase of the land, negligible compensation only was payable since D.H.N. had been deprived merely of a revocable license and the subsidiary had had no business to lose. The Court of Appeal reversed that decision on three grounds, the one relevant here[23] being expressed thus by Lord Denning M.R.:[24]

"This group is virtually the same as a partnership in which all the three companies are partners. They should not be treated separately so as to be defeated on a technical point ... They should not be deprived of the compensation which should justly be payable for disturbance. The three companies should, for present purposes, be treated as one and the parent company, D.H.N., should be treated as that one."

This, and the way in which it was put by Goff L.J.,[25] namely that:

"This is a case in which one is entitled to look at the realities of the situation and to pierce the corporate veil"

show, surely, that the Court did not regard itself as construing a document or statute but was relying on what, in the judgment in Cape, is dealt with under its next head, "the corporate veil" point. And, surely, it was on that assumption that in the later case of Woolfson v. Strathclyde Regional Council,[26] Lord Keith of Kirkel said, in reference to the D.H.N. case,[27]

---

21 See e.g. Bird & Co. v. Thos. Cook & Son Ltd [1937] 2 All E.R. 227, where the endorsement of a cheque in favour of Thos. Cook & Son Ltd. was treated as an endorsement in favour of a group company; Thos. Cook & Son (Bankers) Ltd.; and Amalgamated Investment & Property Co. v. Texas Commercial Bank [1982] Q.B. 84, C.A. (per dis [1982] 1 W.L.R.1. H.L.) where a guarantee of repayment of loans made by a bank was construed as covering those made by a wholly-owned subsidiary set up by the bank as its channel for making the loans.
22 [1976] 1 W.L.R. 852, C.A.
23 The others being (i) that the subsidiary held the property on a resulting trust for D.H.N. which had supplied the money for its purchase and (ii) that D.H.N. had an irrevocable licence.
24 At p. 860.
25 At p. 861 D. See also Shaw L.J. at pp. 867-868.
26 1978 S.L.T. 159, H.L.Sc.
27 At p. 161 in a speech with which Lords Wilberforce, Frazer of Tullybelton and Russell of Killowen agreed.

"I have some doubts whether ... the Court of Appeal properly applied the principle that is is appropriate to pierce the corporate veil only where special circumstances exist indicating that it is a mere façade concealing the true facts."

In none of the cases considered under the present heading[28] was the company concerned a "mere façade concealing the true facts". If it were only when that is so that the court, in construing a document or statute, could have regard to the economic realities there would be very few such cases.

It is therefore somewhat puzzling that the Court of Appeal in *Cape*, said:[29]

"the relevant parts of the judgments in the D.H.N. case ... must, we think, likewise be regarded as decisions on the relevant statutory provisions for compensation even though these parts were somewhat broadly expressed and the correctness of the decision was doubted by the House of Lords in *Woolfson* ..."

The true position, it is submitted, is that a façade concealing the true facts is *not* an essential element in interpretation cases; it is this which distinguishes them from the "corporate veil" cases considered under the next heading.

The fifth and sixth cases prayed in aid of the "single economic unit" argument clearly were cases of interpretation. In the first, *Revlon Inc v. Cripp & Lee Ltd*,[30] the question arose as to whether goods were "connected in the course of trade with the proprietor of the trademark," within the meaning of section 4(3) of the Trade Marks Act 1938. The proprietor of the trade mark was not Revlon Inc (Revlon) but Revlon Suisse S.A. (Suisse). In holding that the goods traded by Revlon were connected with Suisse, Buckley J., said:[31]

"Since ... all the relevant companies are wholly owned subsidiaries of Revlon, it is undoubted that the mark is, albeit remotely, an asset of Revlon and its exploitation is for the ultimate benefit of no one but Revlon ... The mark is an asset of the Revlon group of companies regarded as a whole, which all belong to Revlon. This view does not, in my opinion, constitute what is sometimes called piercing the corporate veil; it recognises the legal and factual position resulting from the mutual relationship of the various companies."

28 With the possible exception of *Scottish Co-operative v. Meyer*.
29 At p. 536 E.
30 [1980] F.S.R. 85.
31 At p. 105

The sixth authority considered by the Court was the advice of Advocate General Warner in two related cases[32] before the European Court of Justice (an illustration of the growing influence of EC law on English Law) on the question whether a parent company and its subsidiary were separate "undertakings" within the meaning of the competition Articles 85 and 86 of the Treaty. He pointed out[33] that neither article referred to "persons" but to "undertakings, a much wider and looser concept" and said that this is "what one would expect, because it would be inappropriate to apply rigidly in the sphere of competition law the doctrine referred to by English lawyers as that of *Salomon v. Salomon & Co Ltd.*" In his view that doctrine existed basically in order to preserve the principle of limited liability although it had been applied, "with more or less happy results in other spheres." But "to export it blindly into branches of the law where it had little relevance could serve only to divorce law from reality". If a company, established outside the E.C., carried on business from a branch office within the E.C. it would be amenable to the jurisdiction of the E.C. Commission and Court; it should make no difference if it did so through a subsidiary company whether wholly owned or not. He therefore concluded that:

(i) "there is a presumption that a subsidiary will act in accordance with the wishes of its parents because according to common experience they generally do so act; (ii) unless the presumption is rebutted, it is proper for the parent and the subsidiary to be treated as a single undertaking for the purposes of articles 85 and 86 . . ."

After reviewing these authorities the Court in *Cape* expressed some sympathy with the plaintiffs' submissions and agreed that:

"To the layman at least the distinction between the case where a company trades itself in a foreign country and the case where it trades in a foreign country through a subsidiary, whose activities it has power to control, may seem a slender one."[34]

It also accepted that the wording of a particular statute or document may justify the court in interpreting it so that a parent and subsidiary are treated as one unit at any rate for some purposes.[35] It seems therefore that in aid of interpretation the court may (and indeed should) have regard to the economic realities in relation to the companies concerned. But that now seems to be the extent to which the "single economic unit" argument can succeed.

---

[32] *Instituto Chemioterapico SpA and Commercial Solvents Corpn. v. The Commission* (Cases 6 and 7/73) [1974] E.C.R. 223.
[33] At pp. 263–264. Cited in *Cape* at 535–536.
[34] At p. 536 B.
[35] At p. 536 D.

The "corporate veil" point

However, the Court accepted that:

"Quite apart from the cases where statute or contract permits a broad interpretation to be given to references to members of a group of companies there is one-well recognised exception to the rule prohibiting the piercing of "the corporate veil."[36]

Since the House of Lords' decision in *Woolfson* v. *Strathclyde Regional Council*[37] this exception has generally been expressed (and was in *Cape*) as permitting it when the corporate structure is a "mere façade concealing the true facts" — "façade"[38] having replaced an assortment of epithets[39] which judges have employed in earlier cases. The difficulty is to know what precisely may make a company a "mere façade".

Of the earlier cases, the one which the Court found the most helpful in this connection[40] was *Jones* v. *Lipman*.[41] In that case Lipman, having entered into a contract to sell land to Jones attempted to defeat Jones' right to specific performance by forming a company and conveying the land to it. Russell J. made an order for specific performance against both Lipman and the company, holding that specific performance cannot be resisted by a vendor who has absolute ownership and control of the company in which the land is vested. This case showed, the Court held, that contrary to the views of Scott J. at first instance, where a façade is alleged the motives of the architects of the façade may be highly material.[42] It also shows that piercing the veil can be invoked against a controller of a company whether an individual or a company.[43]

Apart from *Jones* v. *Lipman* the Court felt that it was "left with rather sparse guidance as to the principles which should guide the court in determining whether or not the arrangements of a corporate group involve a façade …" but, unfortunately, it declined to "attempt a comprehensive definition of those principles."[44] It did, however, decide that one of Cape's wholly owned subsidiaries (AMC incorporated in Liechtenstein) was a façade in the relevant sense. Scott J. had found as a fact that arrangements made in 1979

---

36 At p. 539.
37 Above n.26.
38 Used, clearly in its secondary meaning (the primary one being "the face of a building") *i.e.* "an outward appearance or front, especially a deceptive one."
39 Such as "device," "sham," "creature," "stratagem," "mask," "puppet" and even (see *Re Bugle Press* [1961] Ch. 270, C.A., at 288) "a little hut."
40 See at p. 542.
41 [1962] 1 W.L.R. 832.
42 At pp. 540 C. and 542 C.
43 So could the "interpretation" exception (to which the "single economic unit" exception has been reduced) if that was a legitimate interpretation of the statute or document concerned.
44 At p. 543 D.

regarding AMC and other companies concerned in the marketing of Cape's asbestos "were part of one composite arrangement designed to enable Cape asbestos to continue to be sold into the United States while reducing, if not eliminating, the appearance of any involvement therein of Cape or its subsidiaries."[45] Although he had thought that motive was irrelevant, the Court of Appeal, as we have seen, thought it might be highly relevant, though apparently this particular motive alone would not have sufficed to make AMC a mere façade.[46] What seems to have been regarded as decisive was the fact that AMC was not only a wholly owned subsidiary of Cape but also no more than a corporate name which Cape or its subsidiaries used on invoices.[47] However the implications of that were not pursued because all the Court was concerned with was whether Cape could be regarded as present in the United States and "on the judge's undisputed findings AMC was not in reality carrying on any business in the United States,"[48] and therefore could not cause Cape to be regarded as present there. Presumably, however, those who, as a result of the invoices thought they were dealing with AMC would, if AMC failed to perform the contract, have been able to sue Cape.

What mattered in relation to establishing that Cape was present in the United States was whether another company, C.P.C., incorporated and carrying on business in the United States, was a façade. Despite the fact that C.P.C. was a party to the same arrangement as AMC, and that it probably had been incorporated at Cape's expense that did not in itself make it a mere façade. On the facts the Court was satisfied that it was an independent corporation, wholly owned by its chief executive and carrying on its own business in the States and not the business of Cape or its subsidiaries.

Moreover the Court, declared[49] that it did not accept that:

"as a matter of law the court is entitled to lift the corporate veil as against a defendant company which is the member of a corporate group, merely because the corporate structure has been used so as to ensure that the legal liability (if any) in respect of particular future activities of the group (and correspondingly the risk of enforcement of that liability) will fall on another member of the group rather than the defendant company. Whether or not this is desirable, the right to use a corporate structure in this manner is inherent in our corporate law."[50]

[45] At p. 478 F, approved by the C.A. at 541 G-H, 544 A and B.
[46] See the discussion, which follows, regarding another related company, C.P.C.
[47] At p. 479 E and 543 E.
[48] At p. 543 G.
[49] at p. 544 D, E.
[50] at p. 544 E. Hence Cape's *wholly owned* American subsidiary N.A.A.C. which, prior to the 1979 arrangements (when it was wound up) had performed a similar role to that undertaken thereafter by C.P.C. has equally to be regarded as a separate entity: see at p. 538.

And the Court added:[51]

"[Counsel for the plaintiffs] urged on us that the purpose of the operation was in substance that Cape would have the practical benefit of the group's asbestos trade in the United States … without the risks of tortious liability. This may be so. However, in our judgment Cape was in law entitled to organise the group's affairs in that manner and (save in the case of AMC to which special considerations apply) to expect that the court would apply the principle of [the *Salomon* case]."

The agency argument

A company having power to act as an agent may do so as agent for its parent company or indeed for all or any of its individual members if it or they authorise it to do so. If so, the parent company or the members will be bound by the acts of its agent so long as those acts are within the actual or apparent scope of the authority.[52] But there is no presumption of any such agency relationship and in the absence of an express agreement between the parties[53] it will be very difficult to establish one. In *Cape* the attempt to do so failed.[54] While it was clear that C.P.C. rendered services to Cape and in some cases acted as its agent in relation to particular transactions, that did not suffice to satisfy the conditions which the Court had held to be necessary if Cape was to be regarded as "present" in the United States.[55] C.P.C. had carried on its own business from its own fixed place of business in the United States.[56]

The end result

Where then does this leave "lifting of the veil"? Well, considerably more attenuated than some of us would wish. There seem to be three circumstances only in which the courts can do so. These are:

51 At p. 544 E, F.
52 See Chap. 7 below.
53 As in *Southern v. Watson* [1940] 3 All E.R. 439, C.A., where, on the conversion of a business into a private company, the sale agreement provided that the company should fulfil existing contracts of the business as agent of the sellers, and in *Rainham Chemical Works v. Belvedere* [1921] 2 A.C. 465, H.L. where the agreement provided that the newly formed company should take possession of land as agent of its vendor promoters.
54 Both in relation to C.P.C. (at pp. 547–549) and to its predecessor, N.A.A.C., (n. 50 above) despite the fact that it had been Cape's wholly owned subsidiary (at pp. 545–547).
55 See above.
56 Contrast *Re F.G. (Films) Ltd.* [1953] 1 W.L.R. 483 and *Firestone Tyre and Rubber Co. Ltd. v. Lewellin* [1957] 1 W.L.R. 464, H.L. which suggest that in tax cases there may be a greater readiness on the part of the English courts to hold that a foreign company is carrying on its business in the U.K. through its British subsidiary.

(1)   When the court is construing a statute, contract or other document.

(2)   When the court is satisfied that a company is a "mere façade" concealing the true facts,

(3)   When it can be established that the company is an authorised agent of its controllers or its members, corporate or human.

And (2) only is a true example of lifting the veil; in (1) and (3) the separate personality of the company is not denied but the practical effect on the parties' rights and liabilities is the same as if it had been. The court cannot lift the veil merely because it considers that justice so requires.[57] Nor, unless the case falls within one or both of circumstances (1) and (2), can it have regard to the economic reality that most company groups are operated as if they were a single entity.

When the case falls within (1)—an "interpretation case"—the court may have regard to the economic reality and treat a group as if it were one entity if that is how the group operates. This gives scope for a measure of judicial activism by judges especially if they are prepared to adopt a purposive construction.[58] In doing so they will not be constrained by a need to find that the company is a mere façade[59] as they will if they are to act under (2).

The difficulty about (2) is the lack of guidance on the principles for determining whether a company is a mere façade. The holding by the Court of Appeal in *Cape* that motive might be highly relevant is helpful. It also seems clear that a company can be a façade even though it was not originally incorporated with any deceptive intention; what counts is whether it is being used as a façade at the time of the relevant transactions. But, apart from that, uncertainty and difficulties, remain.[60] If only for that reason, it is regrettable that the Court of Appeal and the House of Lords refused in *Cape* to give leave to appeal. It is to be hoped that the Lords will be afforded another opportunity of reviewing the law in this field. Having

---

[57]   See *Cape* [1990] Ch. at p. 537. English judges (apart from Lord Denning) have shown a marked reluctance to operate any such formula (for another example see Chap. 24, below, in relation to the rule in *Foss* v. *Harbottle*)—somewhat to the surprise of laymen who think that that is what judges are for.

[58]   *e.g.* to treat a new company as the same as its predecessor — as the C.A. did in *Willis* v. *Assn. of Universities of the Commonwealth* [1965] 1 Q.B. 140.

[59]   See above,

[60]   *e.g.*: there are devices often employed by landlords to try to ensure that their tenants do not have the protection of statutory tenants under the Rent Acts. In *Antoniades* v. *Villiers* [1990] 1 A.C. 417, H.L. the landlord resorted to the device of incorporating in the lease a clause reserving to himself or his nominees a right to share occupation of a one-bedroom flat let to a young couple. This was held to be a mere sham and the landlord's efforts failed. In *Hilton* v. *Plustile* [1989] 1 W.L.R. 149, C.A. *per dis* at *ibid* 310 H.L. the device used was to interpose between the landlord and the real tenant a shelf company the sole purpose of which was to be the ostensible tenant. The company was held not to be mere façade. Yet in both cases the motives were identical and the means seemingly equally deceptive.

invented the "façade" test it behoves the Lords to tell us what it means. Perhaps one factor suggesting that a subsidiary is a mere façade for its parent is that the subsidiary is obviously under-capitalised for the role that it is ostensibly performing as an independent entity. In the United States this is regarded as an important factor, as it was here in *Re F.G. Films Ltd.*[61]

Regarding circumstance (3), while it may be possible to establish that in particular transactions a subsidiary has acted as the authorised agent of its parent (or vice versa) any prospect of establishing that it has general authority to carry on the latter's business is remote.

Hence while statutory inroads into the corporate entity principle continue to increase those by the judiciary have contracted.[62]

RATIFICATION OF DEFECTIVE CORPORATE ACTS

The matter to which we now turn relates not to lifting the veil but rather to the related question of raising the curtain over the internal operations of a company. As such, this seems to be an appropriate chapter in which to deal with what is a matter of considerable practical importance.

In a number of cases the question has arisen whether something less formal than a resolution duly passed at a properly convened meeting of the members can be regarded as equivalent to a resolution of the members in general meeting. In a comparatively early case[63] a strong Court of Appeal held in a judgment delivered by Lindley L.J. that:

"Individual assents given separately may preclude those who have given them from complaining of what they have sanctioned, but for the purpose of binding a company in its corporate capacity individual assents given separately are not equivalent to the assent of a meeting."[64]

In a series of later cases, however, the courts have come to recognise that "individual assents given separately" by all the members entitled

61 [1953] 1 W.L.R. 483.
62 Note also the dictum of Browne-Wilkinson V.C. in *Tate Access Inc. v. Boswell* [1991] Ch. 512 "If people choose to conduct their affairs through the medium of corporations, they are taking advantage of the fact that in law those corporations are separate legal entities ... In my judgment controlling shareholders cannot for all purposes beneficial to them insist on the separate identity of such corporations and then be heard to say the contrary" [when is it disadvantageous]; at p. 531 H.
63 *Re George Newman Ltd.* [1895] 1 Ch. 674, C.A. The court also suggested that, in any case, the acts assented to were *ultra vires* and later cases have distinguished it on that ground.
64 At p. 686.

to vote are "equivalent to the assent of a meeting" and that the assent may be no more than passive acquiescence in the result. This development started with a recognition that a resolution of a board meeting bound the company, notwithstanding that it was beyond the directors' powers, when the directors were the company's only members and all were present.[65] It was then extended to a recognition that the members might waive the normal period of notice for convening meetings[66]—a view adopted and extended by the companies legislation.[67] That also recognised that articles of association could effectively provide that a written resolution signed by all the members entitled to vote at general meetings was equivalent to one passed at a general meeting and, in the case of private companies, Table A Part II of the 1948 Act so provided and the latest Table A of 1985 so provides in the model articles for *all* companies limited by shares.[68] In relation to private companies, as a result of the Companies Act 1989 this now applies irrespective of any provision in the articles since, subject to a few qualifications, anything which could be done by a resolution in general meeting or a class meeting may be effectively done by written agreement of all members entitled to attend and vote and irrespective of the type of resolution.[69] And the courts have recognised that there need be no sort of "meeting" or "resolution," or, indeed, unanimous agreement of *all* members. It suffices if all the members entitled to vote on the matter concerned have informally ratified or acquiesced and this seems to be so irrespective of the nature of the resolution and the reduction[72] he was entitled to refuse confirmation unless and until the size of the majority that would have been needed had the formalities been observed.[70]

The only discordant note is that sounded by Nourse J. (as he then was) in *Re Barry Artist Ltd*.[71] This case concerned a resolution signed by all the members as a special resolution for the reduction of the company's capital. Though conceding that this was an effective resolution, the judge held that, on an application to confirm the resolution was passed at a meeting. After an hour-and-a-half's

65 *Re Express Engineering Works Ltd*. [1920] 1 Ch. 466, C.A.
66 *Re Oxted Motor Co. Ltd*. [1921] 3 K.B. 32.
67 Companies Act 1985, s.369(3) and (4) repeating the 1948 Act, s.133(3). The consent of 95 per cent. suffices (except for an AGM) and a private company may by an elective resolution reduce it to 90 per cent.
68 Table A 1985 Art. 53. It is impracticable to use this procedure in the case of a widely-held public company but not all plcs are widely held.
69 See Chap. 5, pp. 103, 104 above.
70 *Parker & Cooper Ltd. v. Reading* [1926] Ch. 975; *Re Pearce Duff & Co. Ltd*. [1960] 1 W.L.R. 1014; *Re Duomatic Ltd*. [1969] 2 Ch. 365; *Re Bailey Hay & Co. Ltd*. [1971] 1 W.L.R. 1357; *Re Gee & Co (Woolwich) Ltd*. [1975] Ch. 52; *Cane v Jones* [1980] 1 W.L.R. 1451; *Re Moorgate Mercantile Holdings Ltd*. [1980] 1 W.L.R. 227 at 242 G; *Multinational' Gas Co. v. Multinational Gas Services* [1983] 1 Ch. 258, C.A.
71 [1985] 1 W.L.R. 1305.
72 Under what are now ss.136 and 137 of the Companies Act 1985.

argument he relented with great reluctance but warned that he "would not be prepared to do so in any similar case in the future." It is difficult to see why a unanimous written resolution should be regarded as any more objectionable in relation to capital reductions than in any other matter. In the light of the new section 381A(6) it clearly is permissible in relation to private companies and there is no apparent reason why it should be impermissible in relation to a public company with only a few members[73].

What is not wholly clear is whether, in any circumstances, something less than agreement of all members entitled to vote can be treated as equivalent to a resolution passed at a general meeting. *Obiter dicta* in a decision of the Privy Council in 1937[74] suggest that it cannot. The decision which, at first sight, comes closest to holding that something less will suffice is *Re Bailey Hay & Co. Ltd.*[75] There, notice of a meeting to consider a resolution to wind up the company had been given which was one day short of the required period of notice. The meeting was attended by all five members and the resolution was passed, two voting in favour, and three abstaining since they did not consider that they knew sufficient about the company's financial position to judge whether it was necessary to wind it up. Had they voted against the resolution it would have been defeated. Shortly afterwards one of the three discovered that the notice had been inadequate and expressed the view that he and his two fellow abstainers should reserve the right to dispute the validity of the liquidator's appointment. Not until some three months later did he draw the inadequacy of the notice to the attention of the liquidator. And, apparently, the liquidator was not told that the validity of his appointment was disputed until, three years later, he applied to the court for a declaration that certain payments made by the company to one of the three abstainers were void as fraudulent preferences and was met with the defence that the company was not and never had been in liquidation.

The judge[76] rejected this "bold defence" on two grounds. The first was that, in his view, all the members had agreed to the winding up resolution since they had suffered it to be passed with knowledge of their power to stop it. This ground, therefore, lends scant support for

---

[73] There may also be a singularly anomalous statutory exception: s.121 of the Act empowers a company to make certain innocuous alterations to its share capital (not involving a reduction of capital) by ordinary resolution and subs. (4) specifically provides that "the powers conferred by this section must be exercised by the company in general meeting". The wording of s.381A makes it clear that this does not prevent a private company from proceeding by a written resolution but it is arguable that a public one cannot, even though it has only a few members so that it would be practicable to do so.

[74] *E.B.M. Co. Ltd. v. Dominion Bank* [1937] 3 All E.R. 555 (recently cited with apparent approval by the H.L. in *Williams & Humbert v. W. & H. Trade Marks* [1986] A.C. 368 at 429).

[75] Above, n. 70.

[76] Brightman J. (later Lord Brightman).

the view that less than 100 per cent. assent can ever suffice. But the second ground comes closer to doing so. This was that the delay in asserting that the liquidation was invalid gave rise to the doctrine which we lawyers quaintly continue to describe as "laches." Laches has affinities with estoppel[77] but seems to be wider in its scope. It is particularly useful where, as in the instant case, and in many other corporate irregularities, there is no period of limitation within which actions have to be brought. Lord Blackburn, in *Erlanger v. New Sombrero Phosphate Co.*[78] described it as:

> "a doctrine which, if founded on mere delay, must be tried upon principles essentially equitable and invoked only where it would be practically unjust to give a remedy ... because one party has by his conduct and neglect ... put the other party in a situation in which it would not be reasonable to place him if the remedy was afterwards to be asserted."

Citing and relying on this description, the judge held that in the instant case it would be "practically unjust" to the creditors and liquidator of the company to allow the sort of relief sought by the defendant.[79] As expressed, this too does not support the proposition that anything less than unanimity will suffice to make the actions of the members an act of the company itself; seemingly it merely bars a remedy if claimed by those guilty of laches and, in contrast with unanimous agreement, does not validate the transaction which remains liable to attack by anyone with *locus standi* who is not guilty of laches.

Nevertheless, in the present case the practical effect of laches was much the same as validation since no one else had any interest in attacking its validity. This, however, will not always be so. Creditors as well as members may sometimes have *locus standi* to complain of corporate irregularities; and, in relation to widely-held public companies, it will be almost impossible to establish that all the members had sufficient knowledge of the facts to make it possible to say that they had been neglectful in failing to complain about them. If such knowledge has to be established in the case of all entitled to complain, the company will often be vulnerable indefinitely. Happily hints can be found that the courts might be prepared to hold that it could be "practically unjust" to allow anyone to complain of an irregularity if an unreasonable length of time had elapsed since the

77 Under which, as Lindley L.J. recognised in *Re George Newman Ltd.*, "Individual assents given separately may preclude those who have given them from complaining of what they have sanctioned"; see above, p. 134.
78 (1878) 3 App.Cas. 1218, P.C at 1279.
79 At pp. 1367, 1368.

irregularity occurred.[80] If that is so, laches, unlike estoppel would not merely ban proceedings by particular complainants but, like unanimous agreement of members, would, in effect, validate the transaction.

The foregoing decisions on the effect of unanimous members' agreement have continued to stress that it is effective only when the transaction in question is not *ultra vires* the company. But, in the light of the virtual abolition of the *ultra vires* doctrine by the Companies Act 1989,[81] generally this is no longer relevant. Where the transaction would be valid under the provisions of the Act if taken by a resolution in general meeting it will be equally valid if agreed to by the members without a formal meeting.

---

[80] See *Phosphate of Lime Co.* v. *Green* (1871) L.R. 7 C.P. 43, where it was held that "acquiescence" by members of a company could be established without proving actual knowledge by each individual member so long as each could have found out if he had bothered to ask, and *Ho Tung* v. *Man On Insurance Co.* [1902] A.C. 232, P.C., where articles of association, which had never been adopted by a resolution but had been acted on for 19 years and amended from time to time, were held to have been accepted and adopted as valid and operative articles.
[81] See below, Chap. 8.

CHAPTER 7

THE COMPANY'S ORGANS AND OFFICERS

THE preceding chapters attempted to show that a company is itself a legal person, with an existence independent of that of its members. Yet it remains an artificial person; its policy can be formulated and decided upon only by individual human beings, and can be put into effect and carried out only by human agencies.[1] Just as the legal position of unincorporated associations depends largely on the law of agency (especially is this so in connection with partnerships in which each partner automatically becomes the agent of the others and, as a necessary result, stands in a fiduciary position towards his co-partners) so also the law of agency is equally at the root of company law. But agency principles have undergone a number of modifications in their application to companies. The present chapter discusses the nature of these agencies and the relationship between them; the succeeding chapter will consider the extent to which a company may be held liable for their acts. Detailed consideration of the duties which they owe to the company and its members is left for later consideration.[2]

How a Company's Organs are Appointed

The application of agency principles to companies meets an initial difficulty: since the company is an artificial person how is it to appoint its agents? This problem does not arise in connection with unincorporated societies for the question there is simply whether the members (natural persons) have appointed other persons as their agents. But, with a corporation, it is the incorporated company, not its members, which is the principal and somehow certain acts have to be regarded as those of the company itself if only in order to enable it to appoint agents. The early law of corporations seems to have tried to avoid this dilemma by a resort to formalism—the acts of the corporation were those which were authenticated by its common seal. This, however, merely begged the question without solving it, for someone had to affix the seal and if it was affixed without lawful authority the corporation would not be bound. Moreover the insistence on the use of a seal which was appropriate only to contractual liability was, even there, totally unworkable under

---

[1] "The company itself cannot act in its own person, for it has no person; it can only act through directors and the case is, as regards those directors, merely the ordinary case of principal and agent": *per* Cairns L.J. in *Ferguson* v. *Wilson* (1866) L.R. 2 Ch. 77 at 89.

[2] See Part Five, below.

modern conditions[3] and has now been abrogated both as regards individuals[4] and companies.[5]

Hence a more satisfactory solution was found by regarding the decisions of the majority of the members of the company in general meetings[6] as the acts of the company itself.[7] But this rule too has had to be supplemented since it is normally impossible for all day-to-day decisions to be taken in general meeting. In practice the initial constitution of the company will provide for the appointment of a board of directors and expressly delegate all powers of management to it.[8] In such circumstances the theory seems to be that the company, as such, has, in its constitution, appointed its agents and clothed them with authority; the act which gives birth to the company operates as an appointment and delegation by the company.

It will be observed that authority to exercise the company's powers is delegated, not to individual directors, but only to the directors as a board; although it may be sub-delegated by the board to individual managing directors and to other officers.[9] Between the company and the board and the officers there is a relationship akin to agency, but there is none between the company and the members or between the members *inter se*. This is in marked contrast with the partnership in which each member becomes an agent of the others. The absence of any such relationship in the case of a company is one of its distinctive features and one which is essential if a public company is to perform its economic role.

The Board of Directors

All registered companies must now have directors and normally there must be at least two, though one suffices for a private company

[3] As recognised by the Corporate Bodies Contracts Act 1960.
[4] Law of Property (Miscellaneous Provisions) Act 1989.
[5] Companies Act 1985 ss.36, 36A and 36B (as substituted by the 1989 Act).
[6] The functioning of general meetings is described in Chap. 19. Additionally, the unanimous decision of all the members entitled to vote, though not taken in general meeting, may be regarded as the act of the company: see above, at pp. 134–138.
[7] *per* Hardwicke L.C. in *Att.-Gen.* v. *Davy* (1741) 2 Atk. 212: "It cannot be disputed that wherever a certain number are incorporated a major part of them may do any corporate act; so if all are summoned, and part appear, and part of those that appear may do a corporate act . . . it is not necessary that every corporate act should be under the seal of the corporation . . ." This principle is at the root of the rule in *Foss* v. *Harbottle* (1843) 2 Hare 461 (see Chap. 24, below) in which Wigram V.-C. (at p. 493) referred to the members in general meetings as "the supreme governing body."
[8] Companies Clauses Consolidation Act 1845, s.90; Table A in the Companies (Tables A–F) Regs. 1985 (S.I. 1985 No. 805 as amended by S.I. 1985 No. 1052), art. 70. This Table A is hereinafter referred to as "Table A 1985." It must be borne in mind that it applies only to companies incorporated since the 1985 Act (without registering articles which exclude it) and to post- or pre-1985 companies which adopt it after 1985. Many, perhaps most, companies still have articles based on Table A of the 1948 Act or a still earlier Companies Act.
[9] Table A 1985, arts. 72 and 84.

or one registered before 1929.[10] On initial registration the company must send to the Registrar of Companies particulars of the first directors[11] with their signed written consents to act. Thereafter he must be sent particulars of any changes with signed consent to act by any new directors.[12] The registrar must cause receipt of these notifications to be "officially notified" in the Gazette.[13] The company must also maintain a register giving particulars of its directors,[14] Hence the public can obtain information about who the directors are either from Companies House or from the company's registered office.

The Act itself says little more about the means of appointing the directors, leaving this to the articles of association. These normally provide for retirement by rotation of a certain proportion and for the filling of the vacancies at each annual general meeting.[15] The Act then provides that each appointment shall be voted on individually[16] except in the case of a private company or unless the meeting shall agree *nem. con.* that two or more shall be included in a single resolution. There is nothing in the Act to provide that an ordinary resolution suffices to elect a director, but this is the normal practice.[17] However appointed, a director can be removed by ordinary resolution[18] in addition to any other means of removal that may be provided in the articles.[19] It is not uncommon in private companies for certain directors not to retire by rotation but to be appointed for life, or for as long as they hold some other office,[20] but these, too, can now be removed from their directorships by ordinary resolution.

It will therefore be appreciated that a member holding 51 per cent. of the voting shares can be sure of electing the whole of the board or, at any rate, of having a veto over the constitution of the whole of the

10 s.282.
11 s.10, and Sched. 1.
12 s.288(2).
13 s.711. This formality, somewhat pointless under English practice, is required to comply with the First Company Law Directive.
14 ss.288, 289. It is no longer necessary to state the names of the directors on the company's letter-heading but if it states any it must state all: s.305.
15 Table A 1985, art. 73. It is customary to empower the directors themselves to fill a casual vacancy and to appoint additional directors within the maximum prescribed by the articles (*ibid.* art. 79). Normally directors appointed by the board come up for re-election at the next A.G.M. (*ibid.*).
16 s.272. This is designed to prevent the members being faced with the alternative of either accepting or rejecting the whole of a slate of nominees.
17 But there is nothing to prevent articles providing that directors can be appointed by a particular class of shareholders, by debenture holders or, indeed by third parties. Under the memo. and arts. of the Securities and Investments Board (a company limited by guarantee) all board members are appointed and dismissible by the Secretary of State and the Governor of the Bank of England (acting jointly) neither of whom is a member of the company.
18 s.303. See below, pp. 153 *et seq.*
19 These may, *e.g.* empower certain of the directors to remove others (see *Bersel Manufacturing Co. Ltd.* v. *Berry* [1968] 2 All E.R. 552, H.L.) or provide for vacation of office on a request by his co-directors to resign: *Lee* v. *Chou Wen Hsien* [1984] 1 W.L.R. 1202, P.C.
20 *e.g.* that of managing director or other executive office: see Table A 1985, art. 84.

board. There is, in England, nothing comparable to the system of "cumulative voting," which is optional or compulsory in many States of the U.S.A. and which affords the shareholder the possibility of board representation proportional to his holding.[21] This system has now been extended, on an optional basis, to some other Common Law countries, but, though it has its advocates it seems unlikely to be introduced here. More likely, perhaps, is the introduction, at least for the larger companies, of compulsory worker directors and, perhaps, of a two-tier board structure.[22] Either of these developments would involve substantial amendments of the legal position as set out in this chapter.[23]

Unless the articles so provide, directors need not be members of the company. At one time it was customary so to provide,[24] but now the possibility of a complete separation of "proprietors" and "managers" is recognised and Table A no longer provides for a share qualification. If, however, one is needed under the articles, the shares must be taken up within two months and his office will be vacated if they are not, or if they are later relinquished.[25]

Articles commonly provide for the vacation of office by directors in certain circumstances, including resignation, prolonged absence from board meetings or insanity.[26] The Cohen Committee also tried to ensure that directors should normally retire when they attained the age of 70,[27] but as finally enacted this provision is so riddled with exceptions that it has proved of little value.[28] Nor, it seems, is any minimum age required; presumably infant directors must be old enough to sign the required consent to act but that seems to be the only legal restraint.[29] Indeed, in contrast with the company

[21] Briefly, the number of votes which each shareholder has is multiplied by the number of directors to be elected and he can "cumulate" his votes on one or some nominees only instead of spreading them over the slate. This is of little benefit to a member with only a handful of votes but it does mean that one who holds one-third of the voting shares should secure one-third representation on the board and that one with 51 per cent. should secure only one-half and not, as under our system, be able to elect the whole board.

[22] See Chap. 4 (pp. 62, 73) above.

[23] The Bullock Committee (see *ibid.*) recognised that the introduction of worker-elected directors even to a unitary board would not only necessitate amendments to what is now s.303 relating to removal of directors but would need to be accompanied by mandatory legal provisions delegating powers of management to the board and altering the present division of powers between the board and the members in general meeting: Cmnd. 6706, Chap. 8.

[24] Companies Act 1929, Table A, art. 66.

[25] Companies Act 1985 s.291. The two month period runs from the declaration of the result of the vote electing the director: *Holmes* v. *Keyes* [1959] Ch. 199, C.A.

[26] Table A 1985, art. 81. But except as authorised by the articles the directors cannot exclude one of their number from the board and can be restrained by injunction from so doing (at any rate if the directorship carries fees): *Hayes* v. *Bristol Plant Hire Ltd.* [1957] 1 W.L.R. 499.

[27] Cmd. 6659, para. 131.

[28] s.293. Note that the age limit does not apply to private companies unless subsidiaries of public ones (subs. (1)), that it can be excluded by the articles (subs. (7)), and that an over-age director can always be appointed if "special notice" (see below) is given (subs. (5)).

[29] A practical restraint is that if the infant was very young there would, presumably, be a "shadow director" behind him.

secretary,[30] no positive qualifications are required of directors—though, as we shall see, they may be disqualified on the ground of misconduct or unfitness. Nor need directors be natural persons; a body corporate can be appointed[31] and this has sometimes been done to enable a parent company to maintain complete control of a subsidiary by becoming its director.[32]

Sometimes the articles entitle a director to appoint an alternate director to act for him at any board meeting that he is unable to attend. The extent of the alternate's powers and the answer to such questions as whether he is entitled to remuneration from the company or from the director appointing him will then depend on the terms of the relevant article.[33] Some doubts have been expressed regarding the exact status of an alternate director and it was suggested to the Jenkins Committee that his position should be regulated in the Act. However the Committee thought this unnecessary as they were satisfied that he was "in the eyes of the law in the same position as any other director."[34] The Committee also thought it unnecessary to do anything about the growing and potentially misleading practice of giving employees status without responsibility by appointing them "special" or "associate" directors.[35] The directors need not be so called; for the purposes of the Companies Act "director" includes any person occupying the position of director, by whatever name called,[36] and directors of some guarantee companies are still called "governors" or the like.

De Facto and Shadow Directors

While, *de jure*, people cannot be directors unless they have been properly appointed, they may, as we shall see later,[37] be able to bind the company although they have not. Moreover, they may be subject to liability as if they were directors because they have assumed that position,[38] or because an increasing number of legislative provisions expressly apply not only to directors, but also to "shadow directors," *i.e.* persons "in accordance with whose directions or instructions the

---

30 See below p. 162.
31 This is forbidden in some other countries and the Jenkins Committee recommended that it should be banned here: Cmnd. 1749, para. 84. It is somewhat surprising that this recommendation has not been implemented since liquidators, administrators and receivers must be natural persons.
32 In the light of s.213 and s.214 of the Insolvency Act 1986 (see above pp. 110–115) it is less likely to be done now.
33 See Table A 1985, arts. 65–69 which, if adopted, go far to clarify the alternate's position.
34 Cmnd. 1749, para. 83.
35 *Ibid.* para. 82. One difficulty is that it would be necessary to make exceptions for descriptions such as "director of research."
36 s.741(1).
37 Below Chap. 8 at pp. 186–188.
38 *Re Lo-Line Electric Motors Ltd.* [1988] Ch. 477 (a decision on disqualification orders; below).

directors of the company are accustomed to act" otherwise than only because "the directors act on advice given .. in a professional capacity."[39] The difference between liability as a *de facto* director and as a shadow director is that the former has openly acted as if he had been validly appointed, whether or not there are other, properly appointed, directors, whereas the definition of shadow director "presupposes that there is a board of directors who act in accordance with instructions from someone else, the eminence grise or shadow director."[40] The last thing that the latter will want is to advertise the fact that he is exercising this improper influence and nor will the proper directors, who are breaching their duties by acting as his puppets.[41]

Disqualification of Directors

In certain circumstances a court order may be made disqualifying for a specified period a person from acting as a director (or, indeed, as a liquidator or administrator of a company or as a receiver or manager of its property or from being in any way concerned in its promotion, formation or management) unless the court grants leave.[42] The legal provisions relating to this are now consolidated in the Company Directors Disqualification Act 1986, which classifies the circumstances in which such an order may be made under three heads: (i) disqualification for misconduct in relation to a company; (ii) disqualification for unfitness; and (iii) other cases of disqualification. Included in (i) are cases where the person concerned has (a) been convicted of an indictable offence in connection with a company[43]; (b) committed persistent breaches of companies legislation relating to the delivery of documents or returns to Companies House[44], and (c) participated in fraudulent trading[45] or other fraud or breach of duty which comes to light in the course of winding up.[46] In any of these cases an application for a disqualification order may be

[39] Companies Act 1985, s.741(2), Insolvency Act 1986, s.251, Company Directors Disqualification Act 1986, s.22(4) and (5); Financial Services Act 1986 s.207 (definition of "director").

[40] *Re Lo-Line Electric Motors Ltd.*, (above, n. 38) at p. 489.

[41] And, by failing to include him in the returns and register required by ss.288 and 289 (see above p. 141) they will render the company and the officers liable to default fines (under s.288(4)) since, for the purposes of those sections, a shadow director is classed as a director of the company.

[42] Company Directors Disqualification Act 1986 s.1. The order may relate to all or any of these various offices or activities. The period of disqualification runs from the date of the order (s.1(1)) and if there is an existing extant order the period must run concurrently with it (s.1(3)). Hence if the person concerned is serving a prison sentence the period cannot be made to run from the time when he is released; *R. v. Bradley* [1961] 1 W.L.R. 398, C.A.

[43] *Ibid.* s.2.

[44] ss.3 and 5 (which deal with continuous defaults in differing, but overlapping, ways, having been culled from a variety of prior legislation).

[45] *i.e.* an offence (whether or not there is a conviction) under (now) Companies Act 1985 s.458: see above p. 110.

[46] s.4.

made by the Secretary of State or the Official Receiver, or by the liquidator or any past or present member or creditor of any company in relation to which the person concerned is alleged to have offended.[47] The court has a discretion whether or not to make an order, which may provide for disqualification for a maximum of 15 years in cases (a) and (c) or 5 years in case (b).

Class (ii) deals with two cases where the person concerned may not necessarily have committed any specific offence—though if he has that may be taken into consideration, whether or not he has been convicted[48]—but has shown himself to be unfit to be concerned in the management of a company.[49] Under section 6 there are new provisions whereby the court *must* make a disqualification order for not less than 2 or more than 15 years if satisfied that the person concerned has been a director[50] of a company which has at any time become insolvent[51] (whether while he was a director or subsequently) and that his conduct was such as to make him unfit to be concerned in the management of a company. Application for an order under this section can be made only by the Secretary of State or, if he so directs, by the Official Receiver.[52] If it appears to the Official Receiver, or to the liquidator or to an administrator or an administrative receiver that the conditions of section 6 are satisfied, he must report the matter to the Secretary of State[53] who may require him to furnish all relevant information.[54] Similarly, under section 8, if, as a result of an Inspectors' report[55] or an investigation by officials of his Department,[56] the Secretary of State considers it expedient in the public interest that a disqualification order should be made against any person who is or has been a director of any company, he may apply to the court for such an order. The maximum period of disqualification is, again, 15 years but there is no prescribed minimum.

---

47 s.16(2).
48 s.1(4).
49 Under s.9 the court is required to have regard in particular to the matters prescribed in Schedule I to the Act in determining unfitness.
50 Which includes a "shadow director" as it does in relation also to ss.7–9, s.22(4) and (5).
51 *i.e.* has gone into insolvent liquidation, or has had an administrator or administrative receiver appointed: s.6(2). Without the leave of the court, an application for an order cannot be made after the expiration of two years from the date when the company became insolvent: s.7(2). Hence, if an administrator or administrative receiver is appointed, but later the company goes into liquidation, the 2 years run from the date of the original appointment: *Official Receiver v. Nixon, The Times*, 16 Feb., 1990 (C.A.)
52 s.7(1). An official receiver is an officer of the DTI's Insolvency Service attached to the court. For the procedure generally, see the Insolvent Companies (Disqualification of Unfit Directors) Proceedings Rules 1987 (S.I. 1987 No. 2023).
53 s.7(3).
54 s.7(4).
55 Under s.437 of the Companies Act or ss.94 or 177 of the Financial Services Act 1986 (as amended by the Companies Act 1989); see Chap. 25 below.
56 Under s.447 or s.448 of the Companies Act or s.94 or s.177 of the Financial Services Act (as amended); see *ibid.*

The Act's "other cases" relate to: (a) participants in fraudulent or wrongful trading[57] (the court may add to a declaration of liability to contribute, a disqualification order whether or not that has been applied for[58]); (b) undischarged bankrupts (it is an offence to act as a director or to be concerned in the promotion, formation, or management of a company, without leave of the court[59]); and (c) persons who have failed to pay under a county court administration order which has accordingly been revoked.[60]

The Act provides for a register of disqualification orders.[61] In view of this one might have expected it also to provide that a company commits an offence if it appoints as a director anyone who was disqualified; but it does not. Nor, in contrast with a "disqualification direction" under section 59 of the Financial Services Act, does it expressly impose any duty on the company "to take reasonable care not to employ a person in contravention of the order."[62] It simply provides (perhaps more effectively) that the disqualified person incurs criminal penalties[63] and that any other person involved in the management of a company, who acts or is willing to act on his instructions knowing him to be disqualified, is personally liable for debts of the company contracted while the disqualified person so acts.[64]

Greater use is now being made of these salutary provisions,[65] which go some way to make up for the fact that no qualifications are required for appointment as a director, by weeding out those who have proved to be glaringly unfit.

The first case concerning the new provisions in the Disqualification Act to have reached the Court of Appeal is *Re Sevenoaks Stationers (Retail) Ltd.*[66] where the court reviewed the decisions of courts of first instance[67], particularly in relation to mandatory disqualification under section 6. The court held that:

(a)   The permitted period of 2–15 years disqualification should be regarded as divided into three brackets. The top bracket

---

[57] See ss.213 or 214 of the Insolvency Act 1986: above Chap. 6 at pp. 110–115.
[58] s.10.
[59] s.11.
[60] s.12.
[61] s.18. See also the Companies (Disqualification Orders) Regs. 1986 (S.I. 1986 No. 2067).
[62] F.S. Act. s.59(6).
[63] Company Directors Disqualification Act, s.13. Where the "person" is a body corporate its officers in default may also commit an offence; s.14.
[64] *ibid.* s.15. See above p. 115.
[65] Disqualification Orders notified to the DTI rose from 112 in 1986–87 to 197 in 1987–88, 332 in 1988–89 and 318 in 1989–90: *Companies in 1989–90,* Table D. I.
[66] [1991] Ch. 164, C.A. (In a second case to do so the Court held by a majority that s.16(1), requiring not less than 10 days notice to be given to the culprit of the intention to apply (for a disqualification order, was directory and not mandatory and that failure to do so did not render the application void or voidable: *Secretary of State for Trade & Industry v. Langridge* [1991] Ch. 402, C.A.: *pet.dis.* [1991] 1 W.L.R. 606, H.L.).
[67] Which revealed the interesting but slightly disturbing information that the High Court was imposing shorter periods of disqualification than the County Courts.

(10–15 years) should be reserved for particularly serious cases (*e.g.* when the culprit had already suffered a period of disqualification). The middle bracket (6–10 years) was appropriate in serious cases which did not merit the top bracket, and the minimum period (2–5 years) in cases which were not very serious.

(b) A person should not be disqualified on the basis of charges which had not been put to him but which had only emerged in the course of the hearing of the application (for the disqualification order).

(c) In assessing the degree of seriousness it was relevant to consider whether the company had been kept going, when it was known that it was insolvent, by paying only those creditors who were particularly pressing thus, in effect paying them out of money due to the creditors who were less aggressive, but that in this respect no distinction should be drawn (as some Chancery judges had thought) between debts due to the Crown and those due to trade creditors.

(d) "Unfitness" did not demand dishonesty; incompetence or negligence in a marked degree sufficed.[68]

In a subsequent High Court decision[68a] on an application under section 8, the judge applied (a) and (d) to a case where a director of a run-down, but solvent, public company, "treating the company as his own and ignoring the shareholders had embarked on a course of action which was *ultra vires* and which involved a number of persistent and deliberate breaches of important statutory provisions," and ignored "complaints by shareholders and the auditors" until the Registrar and the DTI took action.[68b] The judge regarded it as "a serious case meriting being subsumed in the middle bracket" but, understanding that it was the first case of its type,[68c] thought it would "suffice to place it the top of the minimum bracket" and disqualified for only 5 years.

Division of Powers Between the General Meeting and the Board

Until the end of the nineteenth century it seems to have been generally assumed that the principle remained intact that the general

---

[68] As in the instant case where the director, a chartered accountant, had not been dishonest but had been woefully negligent, including failing to ensure that the companies he controlled kept proper accounts. But the court reduced the period of disqualification from the 7 years ordered by the Chancery judge at first instance, to 5 years because of a failure to observe (c) above.

[68a] *Re Samuel Sherman plc* [1991] 1 W.L.R. 1070.

[68b] At p. 1086.

[68c] Should this have been regarded as a relevant consideration? The object of disqualification is to protect the public from directors' unfitness not further to punish directors for any offences they may have committed.

meeting was the supreme organ of the company and that the board of directors was merely an agent of the company subject to the control of the company in general meeting. Thus, in *Isle of Wight Railway v. Tahourdin*,[69] the court refused the directors of a statutory company an injunction to restrain the holding of a general meeting, one purpose of which was to appoint a committee to reorganise the management of the company. Cotton L.J. said:

"It is a very strong thing indeed to prevent shareholders from holding a meeting of the company when such a meeting is the only way in which they can interfere if the <u>majority</u> of them think that the course taken by the directors, in a matter intra vires of the directors, is not for the benefit of the company."[70]

In 1906, however, the Court of Appeal in *Automatic Self-Cleansing Filter Syndicate Co. v. Cuninghame*,[71] made it clear that the division of powers between the board and the company in general meeting depended in the case of registered companies entirely on the construction of the articles of association and that, where powers had been vested in the board, the general meeting could not interfere with their exercise. The articles were held to constitute a contract by which the members had agreed that "the directors and the directors alone shall manage."[72] Hence the directors were entitled to refuse to carry out a sale agreement adopted by ordinary resolution in general meeting. *Tahourdin's* case was distinguished on the ground that the wording of section 90 of the Companies Clauses Act 1845 was different—though that section does not in fact seem to have been relied on in the earlier case.

The new approach, though cited with apparent approval by a differently constituted Court of Appeal in 1908,[73] did not secure immediate acceptance[74] but since *Quin & Axtens v. Salmon*[75] it appears to have been generally accepted that where the relevant articles are in the normal form exemplified by successive Tables A, the general meeting cannot interfere with a decision of the directors unless they are acting contrary to the provisions of the Act or the articles.[76]

[69] (1883) 25 Ch.D. 320, C.A.
[70] At p. 329.
[71] [1906] 2 Ch. 34, C.A.
[72] *Per* Cozens-Hardy L.J. at p. 44.
[73] *Gramophone & Typewriter Ltd. v. Stanley* [1908] 2 K.B. 89, C.A.; see especially, *per* Fletcher Moulton L.J. at p. 98, and, *per* Buckley L.J. at pp. 105–106 (despite the fact that the then current edition of his book took the opposite view).
[74] *Marshall's Valve Gear Co. v. Manning Wardle & Co.* [1909] 1 Ch. 267.
[75] [1909] 1 Ch. 311, C.A.; [1909] A.C. 442, H.L.
[76] But for contrary views, see Goldberg (1970) 33 M.L.R. 177; Blackman (1975) 92 S.A.L.J. 286; and Sullivan (1977) 93 L.Q.R. 569. And see Chap. 11 at pp. 287, 288, below, for the related dispute on the effect of what is now s.14 of the Act.

In *Shaw & Sons (Salford) Ltd.* v. *Shaw,*[77] in which a resolution of the general meeting disapproving the commencement of an action by the directors was held to be a nullity, the modern doctrine was expressed by Greer L.J. as follows[78]:

"A company is an entity distinct alike from its shareholders and its directors. Some of its powers may, according to its articles, be exercised by directors, certain other powers may be reserved for the shareholders in general meeting. If powers of management are vested in the directors, they and they alone can exercise these powers. The only way in which the general body of the shareholders can control the exercise of the powers vested by the articles in the directors is by altering their articles, or, if opportunity arises under the articles, by refusing to re-elect the directors of whose actions they disapprove.[79] They cannot themselves usurp the powers which by the articles are vested in the directors any more than the directors can usurp the powers vested by the articles in the general body of shareholders."

And, in *Scott* v. *Scott*[80] it was held, on the same grounds, that resolutions of a general meeting, which might be interpreted either as directions to pay an interim dividend or as instructions to make loans, were nullities. In either event the relevant powers had been delegated to the directors, and until those powers were taken away by an amendment of the articles the members in general meeting could not interfere with their exercise. As Lord Clauson[81] rightly said, "the professional view as to the control of the company in general meeting over the actions of directors has, over a period of years, undoubtedly varied."[82]

A remarkable feature of this development was that it came about in relation to companies in which the provisions of the relevant article were identical with, or based on, versions of Table A which, far from supporting the full extent of the case-law, would seem to contradict it. Tables A of both the 1929 Act[83] and the 1948 Act,[84] having provided that, subject to the Act and the articles, the business of the company should be managed by the directors who might exercise all

77 [1935] 2 K.B. 113, C.A.
78 At p. 134.
79 They can now remove the directors by ordinary resolution: Companies Act 1985, s.303 below.
80 [1943] 1 All E.R. 582. See also *Black White and Grey Cabs Ltd.* v. *Fox* [1969] N.Z.L.R. 824, N.Z.C.A., where the cases were reviewed, as they were by Plowman J. at first instance in *Bamford* v. *Bamford* [1970] Ch. 212, C.A.
81 At p. 585D. Lord Clauson was sitting as a judge of the Ch.D.
82 This is clearly seen if the judgments in the above cases are compared with that in *Foss* v. *Harbottle* (1843) 2 Hare 461; see especially at pp. 492–495.
83 Table A 1985, art. 67.
84 *Ibid.* art. 80.

such powers as were not required to be exercised in general meeting, went on to qualify this by:

" ... *subject nevertheless to any regulation of these articles, to the provisions of the Act and to such regulations, being not inconsistent with the aforesaid regulations or provisions, as may be prescribed by the company in general meeting*[85]; but no regulation made by the company in general meeting shall invalidate any prior act of the directors which would have been valid if that regulation had not been made."

This, one would have thought, could only mean that the powers of the directors could be curtailed for the future by a resolution in general meeting[86]—though an act already undertaken by the directors could not be invalidated thereby. The decisions fail to give any satisfactory explanation for the words italicised,[87] which seem to have been deprived of any meaning.

However, in the present Table A[88] these words have been changed. The new version of the relevant article reads:

"Subject to the provisions of the Act, the memorandum and the articles *and to any directions given by special resolution*,[89] the business of the company shall be managed by the directors who may exercise all the powers of the company. No alteration of the memorandum or articles and no such direction shall invalidate any prior act of the directors which would have been valid if that alteration had not been made or that direction had not been given ... ".[90]

This is an affirmation of the case law; but with a clarification or qualification in that it recognises that the general meeting may curtail the future powers of the directors by a special resolution whether that formally alters the memorandum or articles or merely gives "directions." Companies which incorporate under the 1985 Act and those incorporated under earlier Acts which adopt new articles are likely to follow the new formula.

85 Italics supplied.
86 As pointed out in the publications cited in n. 76 above.
87 Though judges have tried: see Loreburn L.C. in [1909] A.C. at p. 444 and Lord Clauson in [1943] 1 All E.R. at p. 585 A–D.
88 *i.e.* Table A 1985, art. 70.
89 Italics supplied.
90 Art. 70 further states that "The powers given by this regulation shall not be limited by any special power given to the directors by the articles" [thus excluding any risk of the application of the *inclusio unius, exclusio alterius* rule] and that "a meeting of directors at which a quorum is present may exercise all powers exercisable by the directors."

It cannot be confidently predicted that the new formula will not raise new questions. For example, can a "direction" by special resolution effectively compel the directors to enter or not to enter into a transaction which is clearly part of the general management of the company's business? Presumably it can, because the Act does not state that the management *has* to be vested in the directors[91]; the articles could provide otherwise. But would the members then be "directors" within the meaning of the Act which defines "director" as including "any person occupying the position of director, by whatever name called"? Not, presumably, unless all or a substantial part of "management" was removed and vested in the members. Would it make any difference if the board had already resolved that the transaction should not, or should, be entered into? Would that resolution be "a prior act" of the directors which, under article 70, the special resolution cannot invalidate? Probably it would. But the special resolution would not "invalidate" it. The directors' resolution would remain valid as a resolution of the directors; what the special resolution would direct (validly it seems) is that the directors should not act upon it. If, however, they had already acted upon it by entering into a binding contract on behalf of the company, the special resolution could not invalidate that. On the other hand, if the resolution had been that the transaction should not be entered into, the special resolution could, it would seem, force them to enter into it—assuming that that was still practicable.[92]

It is not clear whether the enhancement of the status of the board of directors vis-a-vis the general meeting is wholly salutary. Where the company is a public one it probably is, since management cannot be undertaken by a vast body of small shareholders and will not be undertaken by large institutional investors. Moreover, there is now an increasing number of situations in which the Act or The Stock Exchange requires major transactions to be ratified in general meetings.[93] Even so it seems strange that the members in general meeting can dismiss the board by an ordinary resolution[94] but cannot take a less extreme step except by a special resolution. And it is stranger still in the case of most small private companies which, as the courts have recognised,[95] are essentially incorporated partnerships. In them, one would have thought, the rule should be that unless otherwise agreed, "any differences arising as to ordinary matters connected with the partnership business may be decided by a

---

[91] As Corporation Laws of the USA do, and as it is arguable that we should have to comply properly with EC Company Law Directives.

[92] Seemingly if, in *Shaw & Son (Salford) Ltd.* v. *Shaw* or *Scott* v. *Scott*, above, the relevant article had been equivalent to art. 70 of the new Table A and the resolution had been a special resolution, the decision in the former would have been the same but, in the latter, different.

[93] See Chap. 21 at pp. 575 *et seq* below.

[94] s.303: see below p. 153 *et seq* below.

[95] See Chap. 24 at pp. 662 *et seq* below.

majority of the partners, but no change may be made in the nature of the partnership business without the consent of all existing partners."[96] That is very different from article 70 of Table A; and, although the members may have legal remedies if their interests are being ignored by those quasi-partners who are the directors, it is clearly a handicap to them when they invoke those remedies.[97]

What is needed, if we cannot have a special Act for such companies, is model articles adapted to their needs. This perhaps we may get as a result of the 1989 Act[98] which inserted a new section 8A in the 1985 Act empowering the Secretary of State to prescribe by regulations a Table G appropriate for "partnership companies," (defined as companies limited by shares "whose shares are intended to be held to a substantial extent by or on behalf of its employees"). This Table will presumably fundamentally alter the Table A division of powers between the board and the members in relation to those private companies which adopt it.[99]

Default Powers of the General Meeting

Despite what has been said above, it seems that if for some reason the board cannot or will not exercise the powers vested in them, the general meeting may do so. On this ground, action by the general meeting has been held effective where there was a deadlock on the board[1]; where there were no directors[2]; where an effective quorum could not be obtained[3] or the directors were disqualified from voting.[4] Moreover, although the general meeting cannot normally abort legal proceedings commenced by the board in the name of the company,[5] it still seems to be the law that the general meeting can, in some circumstances, commence proceedings or ratify unauthorised proceedings already commenced by someone on behalf of the company if the directors fail to pursue the claim.[6] These exceptions

[96] Partnership Act 1890, s.24(8).
[97] See Chap. 24 at pp. 662 *et seq* below.
[98] 1989 Act, s.128.
[99] Table A is inappropriate to private companies intending to adopt the "elective regime." But the proponents of Table G seem to have in mind employee share-ownership rather than a Table appropriate to elective regime private companies.
[1] *Barron v. Potter* [1914] 1 Ch. 895. Contrast situations in which a board cannot do what the majority of the directors want because of the opposition of a minority acting within its powers under the articles: see, e.g. *Quin & Axtens v. Salmon* [1909] A.C. 442, H.L. and the recent decision of Harman J. in *Breckland Group Holdings v. London & Suffolk Properties* [1989] B.C.L.C. 100.
[2] *Alexander Ward & Co. v. Samyang Navigation Co.* [1975] 1 W.L.R. 673, H.L.Sc., *per* Lord Hailsham at 679 citing the corresponding passage from the 3rd edition of this book.
[3] *Foster v. Foster* [1916] 1 Ch. 532.
[4] *Irvine v. Union Bank of Australia* (1877) 2 App.Cas. 366, P.C.
[5] See *Breckland* case: n. 1 above. Even if the company had an article equivalent to Table A 1985, art. 70 (above) a "direction" by special resolution would seemingly be an ineffective attempt to "invalidate a prior act of the directors."
[6] See Chap. 24 below.

are convenient, but difficult to reconcile in principle with the strict theory of a division of powers. Their exact limits are not entirely clear.[7]

It is generally assumed that it is perfectly in order for the board of directors, if it so wishes, to refer any matter to the general meeting either to ratify what the board has done or to enable a general meeting to decide on action to be taken. It is quite clear, as was affirmed by the Court of Appeal in *Bamford* v. *Bamford*,[8] that an act of the directors which is voidable because, for example, it is in breach of their fiduciary duties, can be ratified by the company in general meeting if the act is within the powers of the company and the meeting acts with full knowledge and without oppression of the minority. It is, perhaps, less clear whether the board, without taking a decision on a matter within its powers, can initially refer it to the general meeting for a decision there. In an elaborate discussion at first instance in the *Bamford* case,[9] Plowman J. had held that the general meeting then had power to act under the residual powers, but he suggested that this might depend on the terms of the memorandum and articles of the company concerned. The Court of Appeal considered that this question was irrelevant to the issue before them and expressed no view on it. It seems absurd if the directors are forced to take a decision and then to ask the general meeting to whitewash them, but perhaps the safest course is for them to resolve on action "subject to ratification by the company in general meeting."

If the directors have purported to exercise powers reserved to the company in general meeting their action can be effectively ratified by the company in general meeting. And for the purpose of ratifying past actions of the board, as opposed to conferring powers on the board for the future, it is not necessary to pass a special resolution altering the article; normally an ordinary resolution will suffice.[10]

Removal of Directors by the General Meeting

One way in which the members can exercise ultimate control is by getting rid of the present directors and by appointing others more compliant. But until the 1948 Act this depended on the existence of powers to do so in the articles or on the members' ability to alter the articles.[11] In the absence of either, all they could do was to refrain

---

[7] In the words of Megarry J., "there are deep waters here"; *Re Argentum Reductions (U.K.) Ltd.* [1975] 1 W.L.R. 186, at p. 189.

[8] [1970] Ch. 212, C.A.

[9] *Ibid.*

[10] *Grant* v. *U.K. Switchback Rys.* (1888) 40 Ch.D. 135, C.A.

[11] Which requires a three-quarters' majority of those voting. Under Table A of the 1929 Act a director could be removed by extraordinary resolution (a provision repeated in most articles at that time) but this too requires a three-quarters' majority.

from voting for the reappointment of directors if and when they came up for re-election. However, under section 303 of the Companies Act 1985, re-enacting section 184 of the 1948 Act, a director, subject to certain conditions, can be removed by ordinary resolution at any time. This expressly applies notwithstanding anything in the articles or in any agreement between the company and the director.[12] Notwithstanding this, it has been held by the House of Lords in *Bushell* v. *Faith*[13] that its object can be frustrated by a provision in the articles attaching increased votes to a director's shares on a resolution to remove him. This apparently indefensible decision can perhaps be justified on the ground that in a small private company[14] which is, in effect, an incorporated partnership, it is not unreasonable that each "partner" should, as under partnership law, be entitled to participate in the management of the firm in the absence of his agreement to the contrary and to protect himself against removal by his fellow partners. Moreover it has been recognised that the removal of a director in the case of such "quasi-partnerships" (as they have come to be called) may so strike at the essential underlying obligations of the members to each other as to justify the compulsory winding-up of the company on the ground that it is "just and equitable" to do so.[15] Nevertheless, the decision has been much criticised[16] and would have been reversed by the aborted Companies Bill 1973. At present, however, it remains the law and is probably likely to do so since, as we have seen,[17] the Government has used this device in relation to some of its privatisation measures.

Moreover, the section provides some pretty stringent conditions. Special notice has to be given of any resolution to remove a director[18] (that is to say the proposer must give 28 days' notice to the company of his intention to propose the resolution[19]) and the company must

12 s.303(1).
13 [1970] A.C. 1099, H.L. The shares in a private company were held equally by three directors and the articles provided that in the event of a resolution to remove any director the shares held by that director should carry three times their normal votes, thereby enabling him to outvote the other two. It was held that: "There is no fetter which compels the company to make voting rights or restrictions of general application and—such rights or restrictions can be attached to special circumstances and to particular types of resolution": *per* Lord Upjohn at 1109.
14 A similar article would scarcely be practical in most other cases and normally a public company with such an article would not be listed on The Stock Exchange: *Yellow Book*. Section 9, Chap. 1, para. 4.3.
15 See *Re Westbourne Galleries Ltd*. [1973] A.C. 360, H.L., and Chap. 24 below. It also seems that the court could enjoin the breach of a binding agreement between members on how they should vote on any resolution to remove a director, thus, in effect, affording another method of circumventing s.303.
16 See the forthright dissenting opinion of Lord Morris of Borth-y-Gest at p. 1106 and Prentice (1969) 32 M.L.R. 693 (a note on the C.A.'s judgments).
17 At p. 77 above. By providing for it in the enabling legislation, the Stock Exchange ban (see n. 14 above) is avoided since that is qualified by "where not otherwise provided by law."
18 s.303(2).
19 s.379. The company must then give notice to the members in the notice convening the meeting or, if that is not practicable, by newspaper advertisement or other mode allowed by the articles, normally not less than 21 days before the meeting: *ibid*.

supply a copy to the director, who is entitled to be heard at the meeting.[20] Further, he may require the company to circulate any representations which he makes.[21] The object of these restrictions is to prevent a director from being deprived of an office of profit on a snap vote and without having had a full opportunity of stating his case.[22] This is fair enough. A more serious restraint on the members' powers of dismissal is the provision that the section shall not deprive a director of any claim for compensation or damages payable in respect of the termination.[23] If there is a contract of service between him and the company, as will be the case with managing and other executive directors, the probability is that the members will be able to sack him only at the risk of imposing on the company liability to pay damages or a sum fixed by the contract as compensation. This, it may be said, is also fair, because the company has freely bound itself by contract. But so far as the entry into service agreements is concerned it is normally the directors who will have the power to appoint and fix the terms of service of the executive directors.[24] The members may therefore find that the directors have entrenched themselves by contracts of service, as a result of which the company has to pay them substantial sums if it exercises its statutory power to dismiss them by ordinary resolution—or indeed dismisses them in any other way[25] other than for serious misconduct.

Formerly the members might know nothing about these contracts of service. In these respects their position has now improved; the contracts have to be available for their inspection[26] and, if the contract is for more than five years, during which it cannot be terminated by notice by the company, prior approval by a resolution of the general meeting is required.[27] As directors of public companies are unaccountably reluctant to have their service contracts submitted for approval by members of their companies, this has served to place some limit on the extent to which they entrench themselves. It must be emphasised, however, that the dismissed director will have a legal claim for damages only if he has a binding contract entitling him

20 s.304(1). In this case a private company cannot use a written resolution under s.381A; a meeting has to be held.
21 s.304(2) and (3).
22 But apparently he can be deprived of this protection if the articles contain an express power to remove a director by ordinary resolution and the company acts under that power; s.304(2) and (3) are expressly limited to removals "under this section."
23 s.303(5).
24 Table A 1985, art. 84.
25 The board of directors can normally terminate a director's contract of service as an executive but, under Table A, so can the general meeting by removing him as a director: see *ibid.*
26 s.318.
27 s.319. It may also be necessary in some circumstances to obtain members' approval if compensation for loss of office is paid on termination resulting from a sale of the undertaking or a takeover: see further Chap. 27 at pp. 738–741 below.

either to hold his position for a fixed term or to be dismissed only after a prescribed or reasonable notice.

As will be pointed out later,[28] the articles alone do not constitute a contract between the company and a director. He will have to show that there is a separate contract of service or for services, whether formal or informal.[29] If there is such a contract, the company cannot evade its terms by altering the articles and if the alteration gives the company a power of dismissal contrary to the terms of an existing agreement, the exercise of this power will constitute a breach of contract.[30] This is so even though the articles at the time of his appointment provided that an "appointment shall be automatically determined if he ceases from any cause to be a director," since, on an appointment for a given period, there is an implied undertaking that the company will not during that period revoke his appointment as director.[31] If, however, the director's contract does not contain any provisions about its duration and the articles of association at the time of his appointment provide that it shall cease automatically on his ceasing to be a director, it appears from the decision of the Court of Appeal in *Read* v. *Astoria Garage (Streatham) Ltd.*,[32] that on his ceasing to be a director from any cause his contract will also be terminated without that being a breach of contract. Accordingly it would seem that the company in such circumstances can sack a managing director (without breaking the contract) by dismissing him as a director under section 303 (or under any other power in the articles) and that he can resign his directorship and then walk out without any period of notice—a surprising result.

The relevant decisions related to companies with articles equivalent to Table A of the 1929 Act. This dealt only with the appointment of a director as "managing director" or "manager" and provided that the appointment should "be subject to determination ipso facto if he ceased from any cause to be a director."[33] Table A of the 1948 Act contained a similar article[34] but added a further one[35] which read: "A director may hold any other office or place of profit under the company . . . in conjunction with his office of director for such period

---

28 Chap. 11 at pp. 282 et seq.
29 For the complications which are liable to occur in the latter event, see *James* v. *Kent* [1951] 1 K.B. 551, C.A., and *Pocock* v. *A.D.A.C. Ltd.* [1952] 1 All E.R. 294n.
30 *Southern Foundries* v. *Shirlaw* [1940] A.C. 701, H.L.; *Shindler* v. *Northern Raincoat Co. Ltd.* [1960] 1 W.L.R. 1038 (Diplock J.). In the light of the observations in the earlier case it seems that the court will not grant an injunction to restrain the alteration of the articles. See *Cumbrian Newspapers* v. *Cumberland Co.* [1987] Ch. 1 on which see further Chap. 20 at pp. 545–547 below.
31 See *ibid.*
32 [1952] Ch. 637, C.A.
33 Art. 68.
34 Art. 107, which omitted "or manager" and changed "be subject to determination ipso facto" to "be automatically determined."
35 Art. 84(3).

and on such terms ... as the directors may determine ... ," and which said nothing about termination following automatically on the cessation of the directorship.

It would appear, therefore, that in the case of companies with relevant articles equivalent to Table A of the 1929 or 1948 Act (and there are still plenty of them about) *Read v. Astoria Garage* (until overruled by the House of Lords) will apply to a director who is appointed managing director[36] but not to one appointed to any other executive position. If the position is, say, that of secretary of the company, dismissal from his directorship obviously ought not to amount to dismissal as secretary. But if the "office" is that of an executive director (assuming that an executive director is not necessarily a "managing director" within the meaning of the articles) the distinction between managing directors and other executive directors seems bizarre.

Happily the position seems to be better in relation to companies with articles equivalent to Table A 1985. This merges the two relevant articles of the 1948 Table A into one Article 84 which reads as follows:

"Subject to the provisions of the Act, the directors may appoint one or more of their number to the office of managing director or to any other executive office under the company and may enter into an agreement or arrangement with any director for his employment by the company or for the provision by him of any services outside the scope of the ordinary duties of a director. Any such appointment, agreement or arrangement may be made upon such terms as the directors determine and they may remunerate any such director for his services as they think fit. *Any appointment of a director to an executive office shall terminate if he ceases to be a director but without prejudice to any claim for damages for breach of the contract of service between the director and the company* ..."[37]

The words italicised are not free from difficulty[38] but it is submitted that, although the *appointment* ceases if the director ceases to be a director,[39] the *contract* with him is to be interpreted without any other reference to the article so that, if the contract says nothing

---

36 Or "manager" if the 1929 Table A applies (but can a "director" who is a "manager" be other than a "managing director"?)

37 Italics supplied.

38 *e.g.* why does the earlier part refer 'to contracts of service or for services" while the later part refers only to contracts of service?

39 So that if one of the directors is also the secretary he will apparently cease to be that also (but can, of course, be reappointed secretary and, if not, will be entitled to damages).

about its duration, it will normally be treated as lawfully determinable only by giving reasonable notice.[40] In other words, *Read v. Astoria Garage* does not apply to companies with an article equivalent to Table A 1985, article 84. If this submission is rejected, the revised version will have made things worse by extending the decision from managing directorships to all offices held by a director, including that of secretary.

Executive and Non-Executive Directors

It will have been apparent from the foregoing that directors may be either non-executive or executive. The former are directors expected to do little or nothing other than to attend a reasonable number of board meetings and, perhaps, some of the committees that the board may establish.[41] As such they will be modestly rewarded by directors' fees resolved upon by the company in general meeting.[42] Executive directors are those who, in addition to their roles as directors hold some executive or managerial position to which, as we have seen, they are appointed by the board, which will determine their emoluments and "perks."[43] Between them and the company there must therefore be some sort of contract although, even in the case of public companies, it may be no more formal than a board resolution communicated to the director or an exchange of letters. In the case of small private companies (quasi-partnerships) there may well be nothing in writing at all; the member directors will work out what each is to do and decide from time to time how much the company can afford to pay and how it should be divided between them.

The top executive directors are the managing director or directors. In the case of public companies, however, the growing practice is not to call all of them "managing directors" but to describe one as "Chief Executive,"[44] a description frequently preceded by "Chairman and" (unless the board elects a non-executive director as its chairman). This is a development with which draftsmen of Table A have not caught up. And indeed it is rare to find any reference in articles to a "chief executive"; the assumption is that a power to appoint a managing director includes a power to call him or her a chief executive instead.

---

[40] Which in the case of executive directors of public companies would probably be six months to a year and often more in the case of managing directors.

[41] The articles invariably make provision for delegation to committees: see Table A 1985 art. 72.

[42] *Ibid.* art. 82.

[43] *Ibid.* art. 87. It was held in *Re Richmond Gate Property Co.* [1965] 1 W.L.R. 335 that in the absence of a determination there can be no claim on a quantum meruit. But see (1965) 28 M.L.R. 347 and (1966) 29 M.L.R. 608.

[44] The practice in the U.S.A. is to call him the "President" but in the U.K. this title does not imply any executive responsibilities but is sometimes conferred as an honorary title on a retiring chief executive.

Public companies generally have both executive and non-executive directors and are encouraged to have a reasonable proportion of the latter. Their position, however, can be somewhat invidious since the executive directors will inevitably know so much more about the company's business. Hence effective non-executives are difficult to find[45] though some worthy souls collect an ever increasing number of such directorships, often, apparently, without regard to the possibility that there must be some limit to the number in which any man or woman can be really effective.

A question which sometimes arises is whether it is permissible for the board to give contracts to non-executive directors providing emoluments additional to their fees. The answer seems to be that if the director is not intended to undertake any work for the company other than to perform the modest role for which the company has elected him, it cannot be justified as a bona fide exercise of the board's business judgment but will be an improper device to entrench the director[46] or to pay him more than the fees that the general meeting has resolved upon for that work. If, however, he is to "undertake any services outside the scope of the ordinary duties of a director,"[47] (for example, to be the board's chairman or deputy chairman or to act as a consultant in matters in which he has particular expertise albeit without becoming a full-time or part-time executive) that seems unobjectionable (as article 84 of Table A 1985 implies) unless the articles otherwise provide.

However directors, like trustees, are not entitled to any remuneration unless the articles or a resolution of the company provides for it (as the articles always do except in the case of charitable companies) and the provisions of the articles must be strictly observed. Thus when a director with special expertise was appointed a member of a committee of the directors to act for the company in connection with a take-over and the committee agreed to his receiving additional remuneration on terms which enabled him to claim and be paid £5.2m., it was held[48] that he had to return it to the company. Under the relevant articles, special remuneration could be granted only by the full board. Nor was he entitled to be paid anything on a *quantum meruit* or otherwise since that would conflict with the articles.[49]

Exercise of Directors' Powers

Where powers are conferred on the directors under articles such as those considered above in the Tables A, they are conferred upon the

[45] Inspired by the Bank of England, an organisation, PRONED (an acronym for "promotion of non-executive directorships") has been set up to help find them.
[46] See further, Chap. 21 at pp. 556, 557 below.
[47] Table A 1985, art. 84 above.
[48] *Guinness plc* v. *Saunders* [1990] 2 A.C. 663, H.L.
[49] See further on this case, Chap. 21 at pp. 562, 563, 569 below.

directors collectively as a board. Prima facie, therefore, they can be exercised only at a board meeting of which due notice has been given and at which a quorum is present. In contrast with general meetings, where the procedure is laid down in some detail,[50] directors are normally left very much to settle their own procedure.[51] But, unless the regulations provide to the contrary, due notice must be given to all of them and a quorum must be present at a meeting[52] which must be convened as such. Notice here merely means reasonable notice having regard to the practice of the company,[53] and if all in fact meet without notice they may waive this requirement if they wish, but are not bound to do so.[54] And although majority decision prevails, a meeting of the majority without notice to the minority is ineffective, for it could be that the persuasive oratory of the minority would have induced the majority to change their minds.[55] But if all are agreed, a meeting may be a waste of time and hence it is usual to provide that a resolution in writing signed by all the directors shall be as valid and effectual as if it had been duly passed at a meeting.[56]

It follows that prima facie neither an individual director nor any group of directors has any powers conferred on him or them, and it seems that in the absence of an express authorisation in the articles or other appropriate constitutional document the board will not be able to appoint executive agents or servants[57] of the company but must not delegate the exercise of its discretion. Although it is very doubtful whether the board of a registered company ought any longer to be regarded as a delegate, nevertheless, the maxim *delegatus non potest delegare* is regarded as applying.[59]

Today, in the case of public companies it is normally the executive directors who manage the business of the company, with the board as a whole exercising only a supervisory role. To some extent therefore the practice of English public companies resembles that of

[50] Chap. 19, below.
[51] See Table A 1985, arts. 88–98.
[52] It seems clear that this does not necessarily involve meeting under one roof so long as they can discuss and vote: *Byng v. London Life Association Ltd.* [1990] 1 Ch. 170, C.A. (see below Chap. 19, pp. 525–527) which related to a general meeting. With the aid of modern technology a meeting is possible despite the fact that physically the "meeters" are far apart. Nevertheless articles commonly provide that notice of meetings need not be given to a director who is absent from the U.K.: Table A 1985, art. 88.
[53] *Browne v. La Trinidad* (1887) 37 Ch.D. 1, C.A. If the practice is for the directors to meet at fixed times, further notice may be unnecessary.
[54] *Barron v. Potter* [1914] 1 Ch. 895.
[55] Per Jessel M.R. in *Barber's Case* (1877) 5 Ch.D. 963, C.A., at p. 968; and see *Re Portuguese Consolidated Copper Mines* (1889) 42 Ch.D. 160, C.A.
[56] Table A, 1985, art. 93.
[57] *Cartmell's Case* (1874) L.R. 9 Ch.App. 691.
[58] But it seems that in the absence of an express power (which the articles invariably confer) one of the directors must not be appointed: *Kerr v. Marine Products* (1928) 44 T.L.R. 292.
[59] By contrast, in the U.S.A. the board of directors is generally regarded as possessing original and undelegated powers, which are capable of delegation.

not.[63]

Continental companies with two-tier boards—despite the hostility which the English business world customarily displays towards the suggested introduction of the two-tier system. There are, however, major differences. Under the Continental system there is no overlapping membership of the supervisory board and the management board. In contrast, in England executives on the unitary board normally outnumber the non-executives and, even if they do not, tend to dominate it because of their closer acquaintance with the company's affairs. Moreover, the division of powers between the various organs of the company is left to be determined not by the law but by provisions in the articles of association and by the extent and terms of the delegation to executives which the board has chosen to make. Hence there is nothing in the law which ensures that the board holds the whiphand over the executives. Admittedly, it is still customary for the terms of appointment, even of chief executives and managing directors, to provide that they shall perform such duties and exercise such powers as from time to time are assigned to them by the board. When that is so the board can maintain a firm grip on them and curtail the range of their activities as it sees fit. But Table A articles[60] expressly permit delegation "either collaterally with or to the exclusion of their own powers." If the delegation was made to the exclusion of the board's own powers, until it was revoked[61] the effect quite clearly ought to be that both the board, in respect of its residual powers not delegated and the executive director should be treated as primary organs of the company. But, as we shall see from the next chapter, although the courts are prepared to recognise that executives may be organs rather than mere agents,[62] the legislature is

The Company Secretary

A word must be said about another important officer of the company—the secretary.[64] Speaking generally the secretary's functions are purely ministerial and administrative and he is not, as secretary, charged with the exercise of any managerial powers. As was said in one case[65]:

---

[60] Table A, 1948, art. 109; Table A 1985, art. 72.

[61] Table A expressly recognises that the delegation may be revoked by the board but, even if the relevant articles did not, it would be implicit in the general delegation of the company's powers to the board. The revocation might, however, be a breach of the executive's contract: see above. And query what the position would be if the powers exclusively sub-delegated included those to appoint and dismiss executives.

[62] pp. 193–197 below.

[63] p. 197 below.

[64] The position of another important official—the auditor—is discussed in Chap. 18, below.

[65] *Per* Pennycuick V.C. in *Re Maidstone Buildings Provisions Ltd.* [1971] 1 W.L.R. 1085, at 1092.

"So far as the position of a secretary as such is concerned, it is established beyond all question that a secretary, while performing the duties appropriate to the office of secretary, is not concerned in the management of the company. Equally I think he is not concerned in carrying on the business of the company."

On the other hand it is he that will be charged with the primary responsibility of ensuring that the documentation of the company is in order, that the requisite returns are made to Companies' House, and that the company's registers are properly maintained.[66] Moreover it is he that will in practice be referred to in order to obtain authenticated copies of contracts and resolutions decided upon by the board, and the articles will generally provide that he is one of those in whose presence the company's seal (if it has one) is to be affixed to documents.[67]

The Act provides that every registered company must have a secretary who must not be the sole director.[68] It also provides that anything required to be done by a director and the secretary shall not be done by the same person acting as both.[69] But the secretary can be appointed with less formality than a director; the appointment will be made by the board—not by the general meeting—and any officer of the company may be authorised by the board to act in the absence of a formally appointed secretary.[70] Further it has been recognised that those dealing with the company will be concerned to know who the secretary is, and hence the register of directors has been expanded into a register of directors and secretaries. Copies of the particulars in this register must be filed at Companies' House and are available for inspection by the public both there and at the company's office.[71]

As a result of back-bench pressure, a new provision was inserted in the 1980 Act requiring qualifications for secretaries of public companies. This is now section 286 of the 1985 Act, which provides that it is the duty of directors to take all reasonable steps to secure that the secretary or each joint secretary of such a company "is a person who appears to them to have the requisite knowledge and experience to discharge the functions of secretary of the company" and who, in addition, fulfils requirements regarding previous experience or membership of specified professions or professional bodies.

[66] Sometimes a separate professional firm is appointed to act as registrar to maintain the registers of members and debentureholders.
[67] Table A 1985, art. 101. Generally, too, he will be authorised to countersign cheques.
[68] s.283(1) and (2).
[69] s.284.
[70] s.283(3).
[71] ss.288 and 290.

Although all this amounts to little more than saying that the directors should not appoint someone unless they think he is capable of undertaking the task, it is interesting as a further recognition of the rising professional status of the secretary—and renders it still more anomalous that no qualifications are required of directors (an anomaly of which the Institute of Directors is very conscious).

Despite this statutory recognition of the increasingly important status of the secretary the courts until recently continued to treat him as a subordinate servant, without ostensible authority to commit the company by his actions apart from such matters as the engagement of clerical staff. However, in *Panorama Developments (Guildford) Ltd.* v. *Fidelis Furnishing Fabrics Ltd.*,[72] the Court of Appeal held the defendant company liable to a car hire company where the secretary had fraudulently ordered self-drive cars for his own use but ostensibly for the business purposes of his employers. In the words of Lord Denning M.R.[73]:

"But times have changed. A company secretary is a much more important person nowadays than he was in 1887.[74] He is an officer of the company with extensive duties and responsibilities. This appears not only in the modern Companies Acts, but also by the role which he plays in the day-to-day business of companies. He is no longer a mere clerk. He regularly makes representations on behalf of the company and enters into contracts on its behalf which come within the day-to-day running of the company's business. So much so that he may be regarded as held out as having authority to do such things on behalf of the company. He is certainly entitled to sign contracts connected with the administrative side of a company's affairs, such as employing staff, and ordering cars and so forth. All such matters now come within the ostensible authority of a company's secretary."

It is arguable, therefore, that the secretary has also graduated as an organ of the company; he is an officer of the company with substantial authority in the administrative sphere and with powers and duties derived directly from the articles and the Companies Act. And in the performance of his statutory duties he is clearly entitled to resist interference from the members, board of directors or managing director. Where he differs from them is that he has no responsibility for corporate policy, as opposed to playing an administrative role in ensuring that the policy decisions are implemented.

---

[72] [1971] 2 Q.B. 711, C.A.
[73] At pp. 716–717.
[74] The reference is to *Barnett, Hoares and Co.* v. *South London Tramways Co.* (1887) 18 Q.B.D. 815, in which Lord Esher M.R. said: "A secretary is a mere servant; his position is that he is to do what he is told, and no person can assume that he has any authority to represent anything at all . . . "

Organs of Ailing Companies

Since the aim of this book is to deal primarily with healthy, rather than sick, companies, this chapter has concentrated on the organs of a company while it remains a solvent going concern. When, however, it has become insolvent or needs for some other reason to cease business, the organs described above are likely to be largely superseded by another organ—an administrative receiver,[75] an administrator,[76] or a liquidator.

A description of these "crisis organs" (to coin a collective description) is left to later chapters.[77] Here it suffices to say that, when any of them is appointed, the management of the company's business vests in him and is carried on for the following purposes: in the case of an administrative receiver, to realise the appointing creditor's charge over the company's undertaking and assets; in the case of an administrator, to restore, if possible, the company's fortunes and to avoid its liquidation; and, in the case of the liquidator, to achieve an orderly winding up. In each case the role of the board of directors (and of any executive directors if their services are retained) will cease to be dominant and will generally be vestigial. The role of the general meeting, too, will alter and, except in the case of a member's voluntary liquidation, will be greatly reduced.

The position of the crisis organs differs from that of the normal organs in another important respect. As we have seen, the method of appointment and the powers of the latter depend on the company's memorandum and articles and on resolutions of the general meeting and of the board of directors,[78] rather than on statutory provisions. In contrast, the position in these respects of the crisis organs depends on statutory provisions[79]; exclusively in relation to administrators and liquidators and largely in relation to administrative receivers.[80]

---

[75] The new description given to a "receiver and manager" by the Insolvency Act 1986, Part III.

[76] A new type of officer introduced by the Insolvency Act, Part II.

[77] In the case of administrative receivers, to Chap. 16 dealing with Company Charges and in the case of administrators and liquidators to Chap. 28.

[78] The Second Company Law Directive (which we purported to implement in 1980) requires in its Art. 2.d that the constitution of a public limited company with a share capital shall give information concerning the "allocation of powers," among the company's organs in so far as that is not "legally determined." It is difficult to see how perusal of U.K. memoranda and articles is likely to give that information.

[79] And, of course, on reported decisions interpreting those provisions.

[80] In relation to an administrative receiver it depends also on the terms of the instrument under which he is appointed.

CHAPTER 8

AGENCY AND ULTRA VIRES

As pointed out in the previous chapter, one consequence of the artificial nature of a company as a legal person is that inevitably decisions for, and actions by, it have to be taken for it by natural persons. Decisions on its behalf may be taken either (a) by its primary organs (the board of directors or the members in general meeting) or (b) by officers, agents or servants of the company; acts done on its behalf will perforce be by (b). In either event a question may arise as to whether the decisions or acts have been taken or done in such a way that they can be attributed to the company.

Basically the answer to this question depends on normal principles of the Law of Agency. These principles can be summarised as follows:

(i) A principal is bound by the transactions on his behalf of his agents or servants if the latter acted within either

   (a) the actual scope of the authority conferred upon them by their principal prior to the transaction or by subsequent ratification[1]; or

   (b) the apparent (or ostensible) scope of their authority.[2]

(ii) A principal, *qua* employer, may also be vicariously liable in tort for acts of his employees which, though not authorised, are nevertheless within the scope of their employment but, in general, is not criminally liable for their acts.[3]

Obviously, application of these principles is more complicated when the principal is a body corporate which cannot confer authority on agents or servants except through the action of natural persons who constitute its organs or agents. But to those inevitable complications

---

[1] Actual authority may be conferred expressly or impliedly. Authority to perform acts which are reasonably incidental to the proper performance of an agents' duties will be implied unless expressly excluded and an agent who, on previous occasions, has been allowed to exceed the actual authority originally conferred upon him may thereby have acquired actual authority to continue so to act. Ratification of a contract entered into by an agent in excess of his authority enables the principal to sue the other party if the agent had disclosed that he was acting for an identifiable principal.

[2] This consists of (i) the authority which a person in his position and in the type of business concerned can reasonably be expected to have and (ii) the authority which the particular agent has been held out by the principal as having unless, in either case, the other party knows or ought to have known that the agent was not actually authorised. The liability of the principal in both cases rests on estoppel; but in case (i) the principal cannot be estopped unless the other party knows that the agent is acting as agent whereas in case (i) the other party may believe the agent to be the proprietor of the business and the principal, having allowed him to appear as such, is estopped from denying his power so to act: see *Watteau v. Fenwick* [1893] 2 Q.B. 346.

[3] Unless he has initiated, or participated in, the crime.

English Company Law added others which were not inevitable. Happily, two of these additional complications have now been largely removed as a result of the Companies Act 1989. Unhappily, however, they cannot be wholly ignored; partly because their removal was not retrospective, so that they will continue to be relevant in relation to transactions entered into prior to the coming into operation of the relevant provisions of the 1989 Act,[4] but mainly because the new statutory provisions cannot be properly understood without an appreciation of the earlier position with which those provisions had to deal. Nevertheless they can now be disposed of relatively briefly.

ULTRA VIRES

The first of the two former complications was the *ultra vires* doctrine in its relation to companies. *Ultra vires* is a Latin expression which lawyers and civil servants use to describe acts undertaken beyond (*ultra*) the legal powers (*vires*) of those who have purported to undertake them. In this sense its application extends over a far wider area than Company Law. For example, those advising a Minister on proposed subordinate legislation will have to ask themselves whether the enabling primary legislation confers *vires* to make the desired regulations.

In its application to bodies of persons *ultra vires* is habitually used in three different senses which ought to be kept distinct. When used in the strict sense, essentially what is in question is whether the body as such has capacity to act. Unless the body is incorporated, and thus has a personality distinct from its members, this question will normally not arise; the body is simply an association of human beings all or most of whom will have full capacity. Hence *ultra vires* in this sense does not arise in relation to partnerships. And the early case of *Sutton's Hospital*[5] is generally taken to have established that it also has no application to chartered corporations despite the fact that they do have a legal personality distinct from that of their members.[6] In these cases the only question is whether those who have acted are deemed to be authorised to do so in accordance with the normal

---

[4] Those who are faced with such transactions will need a more detailed account than will be found in this edition.

[5] (1612) 10 Co.Rep. 1a.23a.

[6] See *British South Africa Co.* v. *De Beers* [1910] 1 Ch. 354, C.A.; *Bonanza Creek Gold Mining Co.* v. *R.* [1916] 1 A.C. 566, P.C.; *Jenkin* v. *Pharmaceutical Society* [1921] 1 Ch. 392; *Pharmaceutical Society* v. *Dickson* [1970] A.C. 403. H.L. The A.-G. may take proceedings to restrain it from abusing its charter or for forfeiture of the charter if it exceeds the objects for which it was chartered; meanwhile its acts remain fully effective. But the strict *ultra vires* doctrine applies if the corporation is granted under statutory powers which restrict the activities which the corporation may carry on: *Hazell* v. *Hammersmith & Fulham L.B.C.* [1990] 2 Q.B. 697, C.A.; [1991] 2 W.L.R. 372, H.L. and cases there cited. Anomalously the doctrine applies to trade unions although they are not incorporated: see *Taylor* v. *N.U.M.* (1985) 14 I.R.L.R. 99; and Wedderburn (1985) 14 I.L.J. at 127–129.

agency principles summarised above. Nevertheless, it is customary to say that when those so acting (for example, the governing body) have exceeded their authority they have acted *ultra vires*. Thirdly, the courts have an unfortunate habit of describing as *ultra vires* any activity which a company cannot lawfully undertake (for example one which infringes the capital maintenance provisions dealt with in Chapters 9 and 10).

It was not until the latter part of the nineteenth century that it was clearly established that the strict type of *ultra vires* applied to companies. Until 1844 the most common type of company—the deed of settlement company—had no corporate personality; that was enjoyed only by chartered companies (to which the strict doctrine did not apply) and by companies directly incorporated by statute (a rare breed until the railway boom). After the Joint Stock Companies Act 1856, deed of settlement companies became superseded by registered incorporated companies with limited liability and memoranda of association which had to specify their objects.[7] Only then were the courts forced to decide whether or not the *ultra vires* doctrine applied. And in the landmark decision in *Ashbury Carriage Company v. Riche*[8] the House of Lords finally decided that it did. If a company, incorporated by or under a statute, acted beyond the scope of the objects stated in the statute or in its memorandum of association, such acts were void as beyond the company's capacity even if ratified by all the members. The House, mindful no doubt of the abuses that had occurred at the time of the South Sea Bubble, thought that the decision would not only prevent trafficking in company registrations but would afford some protection to members and creditors who had to face the risk of loss if the company became insolvent in the course of its known and declared business but should not have to face the risk that it might embark on wholly different activities.

It was not, however, a decision that proved popular with the business world which, with the aid of its advisers, sought means of circumventing it. This was done by ensuring that the objects clauses of memoranda of association did not follow the succinct models in the Tables to successive Companies Acts but instead specified a profusion of all the objects and powers[9] that the ingenuity of their advisers could dream up. The courts sought to narrow the scope of the resulting *vires* by distinguishing between "objects" (in the sense of

---

[7] See Chap. 3 above.

[8] (1875) L.R. 7 H.L. 653. In relation to statutory companies it had become generally accepted that the *ultra vires* rule applied but that all the members could effectively ratify an *ultra vires* act. Shortly afterwards it was decided that they could not: *A.-G. v. Great Eastern Railway* (1880) 5 App.Cas. 473, H.L.; *Baroness Wenlock v. River Dee Co.* (1885) 10 App.Cas. 354, H.L.

[9] The model memoranda in the Tables show that it had not been the intention that powers should be specified and the House of Lords in *A.-G. v. Great Eastern Railway*, above, held that every ancillary power reasonably incidental to the specified objects was to be implied.

types of business) and "powers" and, applying the *ejusdem generis* rule of construction, ruling that the powers could be used only in relation to the objects. But that too was circumvented by the device of ending the "objects" clause by stating that each of the specified objects or powers should be treated as independent and in no way ancillary or subordinate one to another,[10] and, at a later date, by also inserting a power "to carry on any other trade or business whatsoever which can, in the opinion of the board of directors, be advantageously carried on by the company in connection with or as ancillary to any of the above businesses or the general business of the company . . . ".[11]

The result of these devices was to destroy any value that the *ultra vires* doctrine might have had as a protection for members or creditors; it had become instead merely a nuisance to the company and a trap for unwary third parties. The nuisance to the company was reduced somewhat when the Companies Act 1948 made it possible for objects clauses to be altered without the need to obtain the court's consent.[12] But all too often companies launched into new lines of business without realising that changes in their objects clauses were needed and, as a result, wholly innocent people who had granted them credit might find themselves without a remedy.[13] So might the company on contracts which it had entered into, for, as a crowning absurdity, it seems that, such contracts being void, in contrast with the normal rules in cases of incapacity not only could the incapable company not be sued but it could not sue the other party.[14]

---

[10] The House of Lords in *Cotman v. Brougham* [1918] A.C. 514 felt reluctantly compelled to uphold the validity of such a provision, with the result that it was held to be *intra vires* for a rubber company to underwrite an issue of shares of an oil company by virtue of an "independent" general power to underwrite securities. But as recently as 1969 it was held by the C.A. that whatever the memorandum might say a power to borrow could not be treated as an independent object: *Introductions Ltd. v. National Provincial Bank* [1970] Ch. 199, C.A. which concerned a company incorporated at the time of the Festival of Britain in 1951, with the object of providing foreign visitors with accommodation and entertainment but which later devoted itself solely to pig-breeding (an activity which those who drafted its memorandum had not foreseen) and granted its bank a debenture to secure the substantial overdraft which built up prior to its insolvent liquidation. It was held to have acted *ultra vires* so that the bank could not enforce the debenture or claim in the liquidation.

[11] A provision upheld in *Bell Houses Ltd. v. City Wall Properties Ltd.* [1966] 2 Q.B. 656, C.A. See also *Newstead v. Frost* [1980] 1 W.L.R. 135, H.L., where the company had a general object "To carry on business as bankers, capitalists, financiers, concessionaires and merchants . . . and generally to undertake and carry out all such obligations and transactions as an individual capitalist may lawfully undertake and carry out." It was held that this made it *intra vires* to enter into a partnership with Mr. David Frost which minimised his U.K. tax on earnings in the U.S.A.

[12] Prior to that Act the objects clause could be altered for one or more of seven specific reasons by a special resolution subject to its confirmation by the court. Thereafter confirmation by the court was not needed unless dissenting members petitioned within 21 days.

[13] See, *e.g. Introductions Ltd. v. National Provincial Bank*, above, and *Re Jon Beauforte (London) Ltd.* [1953] Ch. 131.

[14] See *Bell Houses Ltd. v. City Wall Properties Ltd.* at first instance [1966] 1 Q.B. 207 and the discussion by the C.A. at [1966] 2 Q.B. at 693, 694.

Moreover the legal position became still more confused because courts failed to draw a clear distinction between strict *ultra vires* (in the sense of the company's lack of capacity) and illegality or lack of authority of the company's officers or agents. Moreover, they held that an activity not bona fide designed to enhance the financial prosperity of the company would necessarily be *ultra vires*: "charity" it was said "cannot sit at the boardroom table" and "there are to be no cakes and ale except for the benefit of the company."[15] This did not necessarily ban charitable (or, indeed, political) donations or the grant of pensions to retired employees; while the company remained a going concern all that might well be good for business.[16] But in *Parke v. Daily News*,[17] it was held that to use the proceeds of sale of the defunct *News Chronicle* and *Star* newspapers to compensate employees who lost their jobs was *ultra vires* since the company's business had ended. This led to an outcry and belatedly to legislative action on this particular point.[18] But the general confusion continued, until later decisions[19] narrowed the formerly perceived scope of *ultra vires* and showed that many of the cases which had been decided on the assumption that they raised that issue should have been decided as involving only excess of the directors' authority or breach of their duty to act bona fide in the interests of the company.[19a]

A further complication was that although *ultra vires* transactions were said to be void, the question whether a third party was affected by the voidness depended in some circumstances on the state of his knowledge. This, though perhaps difficult to justify in principle, was eminently reasonable. If, for example, a company had power to borrow or to buy office furniture (as almost every company has, expressly or by implication) a third party cannot be expected to check that the money or furniture is to be used by the company for an *intra vires* object. But, unfortunately, the protection thus afforded was

---

[15] *Hutton v. W. Cork Ry.* (1883) 23 Ch.D. 654, C.A., *per* Bowen L.J. at 673.
[16] *Evans v. Brunner Mond & Co.* [1921] 1 Ch. 359; *Re Lee Behrens & Co.* [1932] 2 Ch. 927.
[17] [1962] Ch. 927.
[18] Companies Act 1980, s.74. Now 1985 Act, s.719 and Insolvency Act 1986, s.187: see pp. 184, 185 below.
[19] *Charterbridge Corporation Ltd. v. Lloyds Bank* [1970] Ch. 62; *Re Halt Garage Ltd.* [1982] 3 All E.R. 1016; *Re Horsley & Weight Ltd.* [1982] Ch. 442, C.A.; *Rolled Steel Ltd. v. British Steel Corp.* [1986] Ch. 246, C.A.; *Brady v. Brady* [1988] BCLC 20, C.A., revd. [1989] A.C. 755, H.L. They established, it is thought, that (i) *ultra vires* should be restricted to the question whether the company has acted within its capacity, (ii) this depended solely on the construction of its objects clause, (iii) if it had acted within those objects and the express and implied powers, the act was *intra vires*, whether or not it was done bona fide for the benefit of the company and for a proper purpose (that was relevant only in connection with the related question of whether the organ which acted for it had authority to do so), (iv) an exercise of an express power could never be *ultra vires* unless, perhaps, the power was not stated to be an independent object, and its exercise was undertaken in pursuance of activity beyond its objects.
[19a] Yet, despite the exhortations of the C.A. in *Rolled Steel*: see *per* Browne-Wilkinson L.J. at [1986] Ch. at pp. 302G–303A, the courts are still apt to describe unlawful reductions of capital as *ultra vires* the company: see, *e.g. Aveling Barford Ltd. v. Perion Ltd.* [1989] B.C.L.C. 626 at 631b.

often illusory. This was because of the second of the, now discarded, complications which the courts introduced.

CONSTRUCTIVE NOTICE

This second rule, established even before the strict *ultra vires* doctrine was held to apply, was that anyone dealing with a registered company was deemed to have notice of the contents of its "public documents." Precisely what that included was never wholly clear[20] but it certainly included the memorandum and articles of association,[21] thus introducing a further distinction between partnerships and companies. It meant that anyone having dealings with a company was deemed to have knowledge of the contents of its objects clause. In *Re Jon Beauforte (London) Ltd.*[22] (where the insolvent company's stated objects were to manufacture veneered panels) a combination of actual knowledge of the business being carried on by the company and of constructive notice of its stated objects resulted in all but one of its creditors' claims being *ultra vires*. Even the claim of the supplier of heating fuel, who argued that this would have been needed whatever the company's business, was met by the answer that he had actual knowledge of the present nature of the business, since the fuel had been ordered on the company's notepaper which described it as "veneered panel manufacturers", and constructive knowledge that this was *ultra vires*! The result, therefore, of this constructive notice rule was that where the businesses being carried on by the company were known to the third party and, whether he actually knew it or not, were *ultra vires*, he would be unable to sue the company. And, as already pointed out, nor, it seems, would the company be able to sue him. The only remedy of either would be to recover money or property paid or transferred under the void transaction to the extent to which it was possible to trace it[23] or, in the case of a lender, to be subrogated to the claims of *intra vires* creditors to the extent that his money had been used to pay them.[24]

[20] Presumably one was not deemed to have knowledge of everything in the annual returns that companies have to file at Companies House.

[21] *Royal British Bank v. Turquand* (1856) 6 E. & B. 327, Exch.Ch.; *Ernest v. Nicholls* (1857) 6 H.L.C. 401, H.L.

[22] [1953] Ch. 131. Some of the creditors had in fact obtained judgments against the company in default of appearance or by consent but this did not avail them since the courts had not specifically adjudicated on the *ultra vires* issue and nor had there been any bona fide compromise on that issue.

[23] Either in law or in equity: see *Sinclair v. Brougham* [1914] A.C. 398, H.L.; *Re Diplock* [1948] Ch. 465, C.A. affd. *sub nom. Minister of Health v. Simpson* [1951] A.C. 251; and the helpful discussion in *Agip (Africa) Ltd. v. Jackson* [1991] Ch. 547, C.A.

[24] *Sinclair v. Brougham*, above: *Re Airdale Co-op. Worsted Society* [1933] 1 Ch. 639. The difficulties that could be faced by a liquidator of a company, particularly if it had carried on both *intra* and *ultra vires* businesses, were horrendous.

In relation to *ultra vires*, improperly so called, where the directors or other organs or agents of the company acted beyond their authority, the effect of the constructive notice rule was mitigated by yet another refinement of normal agency principles. Under the so-called rule in *Royal British Bank* v. *Turquand* (on which see more below) although those dealing with a company were deemed to have notice of the contents of its memorandum and articles, they were not required to satisfy themselves that all the internal regulations set out therein had been complied with. This, however, was no help when the transaction was beyond the company's capacity.

The 1972 Reforms

That the strict *ultra vires* doctrine in relation to companies should be abolished had long been recognised. But we made very heavy weather of doing so, partly because it took us long to recognise that it would do little good to abolish it unless we also abolished the constructive notice doctrine.[25] So long as that remained, the only consequence of abolishing *ultra vires* would be that, while transactions outside the company's stated objects and powers would not be void because of the company's incapacity, they would not bind the company, unless ratified by the company in general meeting, since they would be beyond the actual and apparent authority of the company's organ which acted on its behalf.

It was not until our entry into the EC that we belatedly did anything effective and then only to the minimum extent thought necessary to comply with our obligations under the First Company Law Directive.

Section 9(1) of the European Communities Act 1972, later re-enacted as section 35 of the Companies Act 1985 attempted to dispose of all the problems posed in two short subsections, the first of which provided that, in favour of a person dealing with a company in good faith, any transaction decided on by the directors should be deemed to be within the capacity of the company and free from any limitations under the memorandum and articles on the directors' powers, and the second of which relieved the other party of any obligation to inquire about those matters.

Although this was a considerable step forward it was widely criticised as failing fully to implement the Directive and as leaving much to be desired on policy grounds. It covered only "transactions

[25] This was the excuse for not implementing, in 1948, the Cohen Committee's recommendation that, in favour of third parties, companies should have all the powers of a natural person: 1945 Cmd. 6659, para. 12. There was less excuse for not implementing those of the Jenkins Committee: 1962 Cmnd. 1749, paras. 35–42, which would have abolished constructive notice also.

decided on by the directors,"[26] and protected only a third party "dealing with the company in good faith."[27] And it did nothing to protect the company against invocation of *ultra vires* by the other party.[28] The few reported cases[29] on the section show that the courts did their best to construe it sensibly and consonantly with the Directive, but it was recognised that more needed to be done. Hence, anticipating further company legislation in 1989, the Department of Trade and Industry commissioned Professor Dan Prentice to undertake a review of the position and to make recommendations. His report, delivered in 1986, was circulated as a Consultative Document,[30] and what the Department described as a "refined," (*i.e.* a more complicated but less far-reaching) version of his recommendations was enacted in the Companies Act 1989.

The 1989 Reforms

(a) *Objects clauses*

Professor Prentice had recommended that companies should be afforded the capacity to do any act whatsoever and should have the option of not stating their objects in their memoranda. Unfortunately this straightforward solution was not adopted, notwithstanding the precedents for it in some other common law countries. Some of those countries, however, were not subject to two complications which arose here. First, our companies, as we have seen,[31] are not necessarily "business corporations"; on the contrary most of those limited by guarantee are formed to enable the advantages of corporate personality and limited liability to be obtained by those undertaking activities which are not the carrying on of business with a view of profit. Such companies are entitled to dispense with "Ltd." as the suffix to their names[32] and many of them are recognised, both by

[26] Many, and in the case of public companies most, transactions will not in fact be decided on by the board of directors. Art. 9.1 of the Directive (corresponding to s.35(1)) refers to "acts done by the organs," and "organs" was certainly intended to cover more than the board of directors. Moreover, Art. 9.2 further provides that: "The limits on the powers of the organs of the company, arising under the statutes [*anglice* memorandum and articles] or from a decision of the competent organs, may never be relied on as against third parties, even if they have been disclosed."

[27] This expression had been deliberately omitted from the Directive because its meaning varied between Member States.

[28] The Directive does not specifically deal with this point, presumably because prior to the entry of the common law countries it did not occur to anyone concerned with the Directive that any legal system could be so asinine as to allow a third party to invoke *ultra vires* against the company.

[29] The main ones are: *International Sales & Agencies Ltd. v. Marcus* [1982] 2 C.M.L.R. [1982] 3 All E.R. 551 (the former report is the better); *Barclay's Bank v. TOSG Trust Fund* [1984] BCLC at 16–18 (the *ultra vires* point was not pursued on appeal [1984] 2 W.L.R. 49, C.A. and [1984] A.C. 626, H.L.); *T.C.B. Ltd. v. Gray* [1986] Ch. 621 affd. [1987] Ch. 458, C.A.

[30] *Reform of the Ultra Vires Rule: A Consultative Document* (The DTI has the unhelpful habit of circulating Consultative Documents which bear neither date nor reference number.)

[31] See Chap. 1, pp. 10, 11 above.

[32] See Chap. 11, pp. 268, 269 below.

the Charity Commission and by the Inland Revenue, as charities. In all these cases the Department of Trade and Industry and, in the case of charities, the Charity Commission and the Inland Revenue, will need to be satisfied that they have stated objects and keep within them. But that need not have prevented the adoption of Professor Prentice's recommended solution which would have permitted companies to register objects if they wanted to and which was expressly not intended to derogate in any way from the relevant authority's powers to intervene.[33]

The second complication (from which non-EC countries are free) was that the Second Company Law Directive requires that, in the case of public companies, the statutes or instruments of incorporation shall state the objects of the company.[34] But total abolition of limitations on capacity was in no way dependent on abolition of objects clauses and, if the Directive precluded the latter, it certainly did not preclude the former. In deciding not to go that far the Department may have been influenced by the argument that there are, obviously, certain acts, (*e.g.* marriage, the procreation of children and, according to a recent decision,[35] the driving of a lorry) which an artificial person is physically unable to do. But physical inability should not be confused with legal incapacity. The author of this book is still regarded as of full legal capacity but he is acutely aware that there are many acts which he never was able to perform, and some which he can perform no longer.

Whatever the reasons may have been, what the 1989 Act did[36] was rather different. First, without amending section 2 of the 1985 Act, which requires the objects of the company to be stated in its memorandum, it inserted a new section 3A providing (a) that a statement that the company's object is to carry on business as a "general commercial company" means that its object is to carry on any trade or business whatsoever, and (b) that then the company has "power to do all such things as are incidental or conducive to the carrying on of any trade or business by it." And secondly, it substituted a new section 4 providing simply that a company may, by special resolution, alter its memorandum with respect to the statement of the company's objects but that if an application is made under section 5 the alteration is not to have effect except in so far as it is confirmed by the court.

The object of section 3A is to encourage the use of simple general statements of objects. So far as objects in the sense of types of business are concerned, it may perhaps succeed in that aim in the

---

[33] As the Charity Commission and the Inland Revenue manage to do when the charity is run by natural persons of full capacity under a trust instead of through a body corporate.
[34] Art. 2.1(*b*).
[35] *Richmond Borough Council* v. *Pinn & Wheeler Ltd.* [1989] R.T.R. 354.
[36] By its s.110.

case of some companies limited by shares[37] and it could be a boon to the marketers of shelf companies.[38] It is doubtful, however, whether it will lead to the hoped-for disappearance of the present long list of what are really powers but which are stated to be independent objects. It seems more likely that, regrettably, the present practice will continue of naming certain businesses at the beginning of the objects clause, following that with a long list of specific "independent" powers[38a], and adding a general statement on the lines of section 3A(b)—perhaps expressing it subjectively (*i.e.* "all such powers as, *in the opinion of the directors*,[39] are incidental or conducive . . .") rather than objectively as the section does. If that fear proves well-founded, objects clauses may become still longer.

The importance of the new section 4 is in what it omits, namely the former provision that alteration of the objects is to be for one or more of seven specified reasons only. That had long been a pretty ineffective restraint since it could be ignored unless there was a likelihood that there would be an application under section 5. That section remains unchanged[40] and entitles holders of 15 per cent. of the company's issued share capital or any class of it or, if the company is not limited by shares, 15 per cent. of the members[41] (provided in either case that they have not consented to, or voted for, the resolution[42]) to apply to the court within 21 days of the passing of the resolution which then does not take effect except to the extent that it is confirmed by the court.[43] Previously the court was constrained to refuse confirmation unless it was satisfied that the alteration could be justified under one of the seven reasons[44] and might refuse even if it was—though in that event it would be likely instead to exercise one of the wide powers given to it.[45] Now it has a

---

[37] It is wholly inappropriate for guarantee companies.

[38] On which see Chap. 11 at pp. 277, 278 below.

[38a] There is, however, a school of thought which argues that on the wording of s.3A a company cannot be a "general commercial company", unless that is stated as its sole object. If that is held to be correct, it is not likely to encourage the use of the section. Surely a company formed to acquire an existing business can state that as one of its objects as well as that of carrying on business as a general commercial company. And cannot it expressly exclude certain types of business?

[39] As in *Bell Houses Ltd.* v. *City Wall Properties Ltd.* p. 168, n. 11 above.

[40] Notwithstanding that the anomalies in the section mentioned in nn. 41 and 42, *below*, were pointed out by the Jenkins Committee in 1962 with recommendations that they be removed: Cmnd. 1749, paras. 49(i) & (iii).

[41] Or a similar proportion of holders of debentures, secured by a floating charge first issued prior to 1 Dec., 1947: s.5(2)(b) and (8). Notice of the proposed special resolution has to be given to such debenture holders: s.5(8); notice to the trustees for them will not do: *Re Hampstead Garden City Trust Ltd.* [1962] Ch. 806. But anomalously, such notice does not have to be given to members without rights to attend and vote at the meeting so that they may not learn of the resolution until it is too late to exercise their right to apply to the court.

[42] This has the unfortunate effect that a nominee shareholder who has voted in favour on the instructions of some of his beneficiaries, but against on the instructions of others, cannot apply on behalf of the latter.

[43] s.4(2).

[44] *Re Hampstead Garden City Trust*, above.

[45] These include powers: to impose such terms and conditions as it sees fit and to adjourn in order that arrangements may be made to its satisfaction; to order the

discretion in all cases and, in the light of the statutory acceptance, by the new section 3A, of generalised objects clauses and the fact that the change will have been approved by the requisite three-fourths majority of those voting, the court is unlikely to refuse confirmation save in very exceptional circumstances. Under section 6 (also unchanged) the validity of the alteration cannot be challenged on any ground unless proceedings are taken, under the section or otherwise, within 21 days of the passing of the resolution.[46]

(b) *Virtual abolition of ultra vires*

Having thus attempted to simplify objects clauses (probably in vain) and (more successfully) to make it easier to alter them, the second step taken was to attempt to remove the consequences of exceeding any limitations on a company's capacity without actually admitting that it had full capacity. This the 1989 Act did[47] by substituting for the original section 35 of the 1985 Act new sections 35, 35A and 35B.

Subsection (1) of the new section 35 reads as follows:

"(1) The validity of an act done by a company shall not be called into question on the ground of lack of capacity by reason of anything in the company's memorandum."[48]

This is obviously an improvement on the former section 35(1). Unlike that, it deals discretely with the effects of lack of capacity instead of attempting, with confusing consequences, to deal in the same subsection also with acts in excess of directors' powers. It omits the former words "in favour of a person dealing with a company" and thereby does not merely remove the uncertainties flowing from "dealing with" but makes it clear that neither the company nor a third party can any longer invoke strict *ultra vires*. Had the section stopped there the only question that would have remained was whether the acts done failed to bind the company because those acting for it had acted outside their actual or apparent authority. Short of admitting that companies have full legal capacity we could hardly have done better.

purchase of the interest of dissentients (s.5(4)); to provide for that purchase by the company, even if that involves a reduction of capital; to alter the memorandum and articles (s.5(5)); and to require the company not to make further alterations to the memorandum and articles without the court's leave: s.5(6).

46 s.6(4) and (5). s.6(1), (2) and (3) provide for notice to the Registrar whether no application is made (in which case a printed copy of the amended memorandum also has to be delivered to him) or if an application is made (in which case once an order is made an office copy of it and, if it alters the memorandum, a printed copy of the memorandum as altered, will also have to be delivered to him).

47 By its s.108.

48 Note that this is not restricted to the *objects clause* of the memorandum; it applies, for example, to a separate clause saying that the company shall *not* undertake certain types of business and to any provision in the memorandum imposing limitations on the company's powers and thereby on its "capacity."

In fact, however, the section went on to add qualifications.

Subsection (2) provides:

"(2) A member of the company may bring proceedings to restrain the doing of an act which but for subsection (1) would be beyond the company's capacity; but no such proceedings shall lie in respect of an act done in fulfilment of a legal obligation arising from a previous act of the company."

But for an idiosyncrasy of English Company Law this subsection would not have been necessary. If the proposed act breaches the provisions of the memorandum or articles it would necessarily be a breach of the company's constitution and in excess of the actual authority of those so acting. Hence a member ought to be able to bring proceedings to restrain that act from being undertaken. But, owing to the so-called rule in *Foss v. Harbottle*, he generally cannot. That notorious rule is dealt with more fully in a later chapter.[49] Here it suffices to say that normally the only proper plaintiff to restrain corporate irregularities is the company itself, acting through its appropriate organ which, as we saw in the previous chapter, is likely to be the board of directors or, on their default, the general meeting. There are, however, exceptions to this rule, a well-established one being that a single member may sue to restrain an act that is *ultra vires*. Subsection (2) preserves that exception.

However, under the proviso to subsection (2) a member cannot bring proceedings to restrain an act of the company which, but for subsection (1) would be beyond its capacity, if that act is to be done in fulfilment of a legal obligation arising from a previous act of the company. Hence if, say, the company has entered into a contract which is beyond its powers, but which, as a result of subsection (1), cannot be questioned, the company cannot be restrained from performing its obligations to a bona fide third party under that contract. If, however, that contract was one under which, say, the company, bought an option to purchase, a member could take proceedings to restrain it from exercising the option since it would not be under a legal obligation to do so.

The second qualification is made by subsection (3), which provides that:

"(3) It remains the duty of the directors to observe any limitation on their powers flowing from the company's memorandum and action by the directors which, but for subsection (1), would be

[49] Chap. 24.

beyond the company's capacity may only be ratified by the company by special resolution.

A resolution ratifying such action shall not affect any liability incurred by the directors or any other person; relief from any such liability must be agreed to separately by special resolution."

This subsection was included because of the Government's declared policy to abolish *ultra vires* in relation to external relations but, so far as possible, to maintain the status quo for internal relations between the company and its directors. Had that been carried to its logical conclusion it would have been provided that ratification by the company should not affect any liability which the directors had incurred to the company by causing it to enter into a transaction beyond its powers under its memorandum. Rightly recognising that this would go too far, it is instead provided that, in this case (in contrast with ratifying an act within the company's capacity but beyond the directors' actual or apparent authority—when an ordinary resolution suffices)[50] a special resolution is needed and, if this is to absolve "the directors or any other person," from liability which, but for subsection (1), they would have incurred, there must, it seems, be both a special resolution ratifying the transaction and a separate special resolution agreeing to absolve them.

There might have been some justification for this if the adverse consequences or moral blameworthiness were necessarily greater where the directors had caused the company to act in excess of its capacity than when they had exceeded their authority. But that is not the case. A better solution might have been to require a special resolution in both cases.

However subsection (3) qualifies subsection (1) only in respect of the *liabilities* which the directors and "other persons" (words presumably inserted to catch officers of the company who participated in the directors' act). It enables their action, which formerly could not be ratified even by the unanimous consent of the members, to escape liability only if their action is ratified by a special resolution in accordance with the subsection. It does not detract from the protection afforded to the other party to the transaction. Under subsection (1) it cannot be called into question on the grounds of lack of capacity . . . ." So far as he is concerned, ratification by special resolution is of relevance only if it took place before any legal obligation to him was incurred (in which event it would preclude a member from bringing an action under subsection (2)) or when he is unprotected by section 35A because he has acted in bad faith (in which event the members would be unlikely to ratify).

---

50 *Grant* v. *U.K. Switchback Rys.* (1880) 40 Ch.D. 135; s.35A (below) does not affect this when only absence of authority is involved.

(c) *Lack of authority and constructive notice*

These two matters are intertwined and were dealt with by inserting four new sections into the 1985 Act. These are sections 35A and 35B (inserted, like the substitute section 35, by section 108 of the 1989 Act) and section 711A (inserted by section 142) in Part XXIV of the Act).

Subsection (1) of section 35A provides:

"(1) In favour of a person dealing with a company in good faith, the power of the board of directors[51] to bind the company, or authorise others to do so, shall be deemed to be free of any limitations under the company's constitution."[52]

This, too, is an improvement on the wording of the former section 35 in that it omits the restriction to "transactions decided on by the directors"[53] and thus recognises that many transactions will be decided upon by executive officers appointed by the board of directors. But it is not free from difficulties. The first difficulty is that, as we saw in the previous chapter, our Companies Acts have never said what the powers of directors are; this is left to the constitution, *i.e.* normally the memorandum and articles of association.[54] To make sense of the subsection it seems that it has to be read as if it said:

"In favour of a person dealing with the company in good faith the board of directors shall be deemed to have authority to exercise all the powers of the company, except such as the Act requires to be exercised by some other organ, and to authorise others to do so, notwithstanding, in either event, any limitations in the company's constitution on the board's authority."

Only if the courts so construe it,[55] will it achieve its aim.

---

[51] Under Prof. Prentice's Proposals this would have read "the board of directors *or any individual director*" (see his Report, Chap. IV, para. 50(iii)). This would have improved the position of a third party (see pp. 188–190 below) and would, it is submitted, have given effect to the intention of the Directive.

[52] The substitution of "constitution" for the former "memorandum or articles" recognises that the sections apply to companies within the meaning of ss.680 & 718 of the Act (see pp. 293 *et seq.*) and that these will probably not have memoranda and articles.

[53] Lawson J. in *International Sales & Agencies Ltd.* v. *Marcus*, n. 29 above, felt able to treat a single effective director as "the directors" within the meaning of the former version of the section. Under the new one, if the company has a board of directors, it will hardly be possible to construe "board of directors", as including a managing director or chief executive; he is one of the "others" whom the board has power to authorise to bind the company. Yet he would almost certainly be an "organ" of the company within the meaning of Art. 9,1 of the First Company Law Directive. If, as permitted in relation to private companies, there is only one director, he will, however, be "the board of directors."

[54] See Chap. 7 above.

[55] Which they should since they can refer to the Directive in aid of interpretation: *Lister* v. *Forth Dry Dock* [1990] 1 A.C. 456, H.L..

A more serious objection is that section 35A(1) fails to afford any protection when the third party has dealt with another organ of the company. There are companies which, under their constitutions, reserve certain powers to the general meeting and the general meeting is unquestionably an organ of the company within the meaning of the First Company Law Directive. It should also be noted that, whereas the section says that in favour of a person dealing with the company the board shall be deemed to have power to authorise other persons to bind the company, it does *not* say that the board shall be deemed to have exercised that power. To the consequences of that we shall revert later.[56]

Subsection (1) of section 35A retains the expressions ("dealing with the company" and "in good faith") which caused some difficulty in the earlier version of section 35. But happily subsection (2) gives help in their interpretation. It provides:

"(2) For this purpose—

(a) a person "deals with" a company if he is a party to any transaction or other act to which the company is a party;

(b) a person shall not be regarded as acting in bad faith by reason only of his knowing that an act is beyond the powers of the directors under the company's constitution; and

(c) a person shall be deemed to have acted in good faith unless the contrary is proved."

Subsection (2)(a) provides a straightforward test of whether a person is "dealing with a company." He will be, so long as he is a party to a transaction (e.g. a contract) or an act (e.g. a payment of money) to which the company is also a party. It no longer matters whether the person is an insider or an outsider as it did under the *Turquand* rule.[57] A member or employee of the company is more likely than a complete outsider to know when an act is beyond the board's authority. But knowledge is not decisive of bad faith. That is expressly stated in subsection (2)(b). If he knew, the likelihood is that he acted in bad faith, and if he did not know the likelihood is that he acted in good faith. But that is all. As Nourse J. concluded on the wording of the former section, good faith is a subjective test: "A person acts in good faith if he acts genuinely and honestly in the circumstances of the case."[58] And, as in the former version of section 35, a person is presumed to have acted in good faith unless the contrary is proved.[59]

56 See pp. 188–192 below.
57 See p. 182 below. And as it still does if the other party is a director or connected with a director: see s.322A, below, pp. 181, 182.
58 *Barclays Bank Ltd.* v. *TOSG Trust Fund* [1984] BCLC at 18.
59 But, on the authority of a case decided on the 1972 version of the provisions but seemingly unaffected by the latest version, the onus is on the third party to establish that he "dealt with" the company: *International Sales & Agencies Ltd.* v. *Marcus* [1982] 2 C.M.L.R. 46; [1982] 3 All E.R. 551.

Section 35A(3) makes it clear that "any limitation under the company's constitution" includes not only a limitation in the memorandum and articles (or the equivalent) but also one deriving from an agreement or resolution of the members or a class of members even if it does not formally alter the memorandum or articles themselves. That such resolutions should be expressly covered is the more necessary because, as we have seen in the previous chapter,[60] in companies with an article corresponding to Article 70 of Table A, 1985, it is possible for the general meeting to curtail the directors' powers by "directions" given by special resolution.

Subsections (4), (5) and (6) are equivalent to subsections (2), (3) and (4) of the new section 35 except that subsections (4) and (5) omit any reference to ratification. Hence, an act in excess of the directors' powers or officers' authority can be ratified by ordinary resolution,[61] although if the act is beyond the *company's* powers, it will need under section 35(3) to be a special resolution if it is to relieve the directors from liability.

Turning now to section 35B, this provides that:

"A party to a transaction with a company is not bound to enquire as to whether it is permitted by the company's memorandum or as to any limitation on the powers of the board of directors to bind the company or authorise others to do so."

On its own this adds little to what is already implied in sections 35 and 35A and stops far short of totally abolishing the doctrine that those having dealings with a company are deemed to have notice of its public documents. That further step, however, is taken by the new section 711A, subsection (1) of which provides that:

"(1) A person shall not be taken to have notice of any matter merely because of its being disclosed in any document kept by the registrar of companies (and thus available for inspection) or made available by the company for inspection."

The result of this is that those dealing with the company are no longer deemed to have notice of the contents of any document[62] merely because it is one of the company's documents available for inspection at Companies House or the company's registered office.[63] Of particular importance in the present context is the fact that thereby they are not saddled with notice of anything in the

[60] At pp. 150, 151 above.
[61] See n. 50, above.
[62] Defined in subs. (3) as including "any material which contains information" (*e.g.* on a computer).
[63] On rights of public inspection see Chap. 17 below.

memorandum and articles, or of special resolutions or of anything on the register of directors and secretaries. Subsection (1) is, however, qualified by subsection (2) which reads:

"(2) This does not affect the question whether a person is affected by notice of any matter by reason of a failure to make such inquiries as ought reasonably to be made."

At first glance this might appear seriously to diminish the protection afforded by section 35A to a person dealing with the company in good faith. That, however, is not so. Under section 35A, in favour of such a person "the power of the board of directors to bind the company or authorise others to do so" is deemed to be free of any limitation and he is not regarded as acting in bad faith "by reason only of his knowing that an act is beyond the powers of the directors." In his case, section 711A is relevant only in situations where section 35A does not protect him because it is not the board of directors that has exceeded its powers but the officer of the company through whom he dealt with the company. In saying that, it is not suggested that a failure to make such inquiries as ought to be made may not be evidence of bad faith; if he has deliberately decided not to make inquiries, knowing that, if he does, it is likely to confirm his suspicions that the board is exceeding its powers, that may well be treated as equivalent to actual knowledge and, in consequence, as probable bad faith. But negligent failure to make inquiries cannot, in itself, constitute bad faith.

(d) *Transactions involving directors*

The new section 322A, which the 1989 Act[64] inserts in the 1985 Act Part X (enforcement of fair dealing by directors) constitutes an important qualification to sections 35 and especially 35A. It applies where the transaction exceeds a limitation on the powers of the board of directors under the company's constitution and the other parties include a director of the company or its holding company, or a person connected with[65] such a director, or a company with which such a director is associated.[66] In such circumstances the transaction is voidable at the instance of the company[67] and, whether or not it is avoided, such parties and any director who authorised the transaction, knowing that it exceeded the board's powers, are liable to

64 By its s.109.
65 As defined in s.346(2) & (3).
66 As defined in s.346(4).
67 s.322A(1) and (2): *cf.* ss.320–322 (substantial property transactions involving directors, etc.) under which some such transactions are voidable at the instance of the company unless the arrangements have first been approved by the general meeting: see Chap. 21, pp. 580, 581 below. s.322A(4) provides that nothing in the section shall exclude "the operation of any other enactment or rule of law by virtue of which the transaction may be called in question, or any liability to the company may arise."

account to the company for any gains they make and to indemnify the company against any loss it suffers.[68] The transaction ceases to be voidable in any of the four events[69] set out in subsection (5) but this, apparently, does not affect the company's right to be indemnified,[70] at any rate unless the transaction is ratified by the company in general meeting "by ordinary or special resolution or otherwise as the case may require."[71] Presumably this means that, if the transaction exceeds the company's capacity, ratification must be in accordance with section 35(3), *i.e.* by a special resolution but that an ordinary resolution suffices if it is otherwise beyond the board's authority so that section 35A only is relevant.[72] The section does not affect the operation of section 35A in relation to any party to the transaction other than a director or a person with whom he is connected or associated but where that other party is protected by section 35A the court may make such order affirming, severing or setting aside the transaction on such terms as appear to be just.[73]

The effect of section 322A, therefore, is to preserve to some extent the distinction, drawn in relation to the rule in *Royal British Bank v. Turquand*[74] between "insiders" who are not protected by that rule and "outsiders" who are. But the meaning of "insider" is now clearly defined as it was not in relation to the *Turquand* rule.

(e) *Charitable companies*

The 1989 Act also makes special provision regarding charitable companies. It amends, by its section 111, not the Companies Act 1985, but the Charities Act 1960, into which it inserts new sections 30A, 30B and 30C the effect of which is to provide modifications in their case of the new sections 4, 35, 35A and 322A of the Companies Act.

The broad effect of section 30A seems to be that where a charity is a company or other body corporate having power to alter its constitution, no exercise of that power which has the effect of the body ceasing to be a charity will affect the application of any of its

---

68 s.322A(3).
69 (a) *restitutio in integrum* is no longer possible, (b) the company has been indemnified, (c) rights of a bona fide purchaser for value (other than a party to the transaction) would be affected or (d) the transaction is ratified by the company.
70 This seems to follow from subss. (3) and (5).
71 subs. (5)(d).
72 But it could mean that liability to account for gains and to indemnify against losses remains despite ratification. There is a similar obscurity in ss.320–322 (major property transactions): see below, pp. 581, 582.
73 Subs. (7).
74 See below, p. 186. In a case on the *Turquand* rule (*Hely-Hutchinson v. Brayhead* [1968] 1 Q.B. 549) Roskill J., as he then was, held that a director was an "insider" only if the transaction with the company was so intimately connected with his position as a director as to make it impossible for him not to be treated as knowing of the limitations on the powers of the officers through whom he dealt. s.322A contains no such qualification.

existing property unless it bought it for full consideration in money or money's worth. In other words, although the company is not prevented from changing its objects (so long as it obtains the prior written consent of the Charity Commission[75]) in such a way that they cease to be exclusively for charity, its existing property obtained by donations continues to be held for charitable purposes only.[76] In effect, the company will be in an analogous position to an individual trustee of a charitable trust; part of its property will be held for charitable purposes only and part of it not. And, presumably, it will have to segregate the former.[77]

The new section 30B(1) of the Charities Act provides that sections 35 and 35A of the Companies Act do not apply to acts of a company which is a charity except in favour of a person who either (i) gives full consideration in money or money's worth and does not know that the act is not permitted by the company's memorandum or is beyond the powers of the charity or (ii) does not know that the company is a charity. Under subsection (2), however, subsection (1) does not affect the title of any person who subsequently acquires an interest in property transferred by the company so long as he gave full consideration and did not have actual notice of the circumstances affecting the validity of the transfer. It is clear that "know," in subsection (1) connotes actual (not constructive) knowledge and subsection (3) provides that in any proceedings the burden of proving knowledge lies on the party alleging it. That burden, especially in relation to whether he knew that the company was a charity, should be lightened if the company complies with section 30C.[78] This requires a company, which is a charity, but has a name which does not include the word "charity" or "charitable," to state on all business documents in English in legible characters that it is a charity. Proof that the party concerned has received such documents should go a good part of the way to discharging that burden.

Finally section 30B(4) provides that, in the case of a company which is a charity, ratification of an act under the Companies Act, section 35(3) or to which section 322A applies shall be ineffective without the prior written consent of the Charity Commission.

75 s.30A(2).
76 One cannot say "on charitable trusts" because it seems that a charitable corporation does not hold its property on a trust in the strict sense; see *Liverpool Hospital* v. *A.-G.* [1981] Ch. 193 and cases there reviewed. These are waters too deep to be fathomed here.
77 The result seems to be that if the Charity Commission consents to a change of objects which results in the company being empowered to undertake both charitable and non-charitable activities, any future donations which it receives will not be regarded as charitable donations *vis-à-vis* either the donors or the company unless the donors specifically direct that the gifts are to be held by the company for its charitable objects. In practice, donations to it are likely to dry up since the *company* will no longer be recognised by either the Commission or the Revenue as a charity.
78 If it fails to comply, it will commit an offence and it and its officers will be liable to fines in accordance with section 349(2)–(4) of the Companies Act: s.30C(3).

Though the new sections inserted in the Companies Act apply equally to Scotland, the Charities Act 1960 does not extend to Scotland. Hence, section 112 of the 1989 Act makes provisions comparable to sections 30A–30C applying to Scotland only.

(f) *Provision for employees*

Mention has already been made of the special provisions made by the Companies Act 1980 to reverse the effect of the decision in *Parke v. Daily News*.[79] Those provisions subsequently became section 719 of the Companies Act 1985 and section 187 of the Insolvency Act 1986. The 1989 Act did not alter these—though section 719 now sits rather uncomfortably with the new sections. It provides that the powers of a company include "if they would not otherwise do so apart from this section," power to make provision for employees or former employees of the company or any of its subsidiaries in connection with the cessation or transfer of the undertaking of the company or that subsidiary.[80] This power may be exercised notwithstanding that it is not in the best interests of the company.[81] Before the commencement of the winding up of the company,[82] it may be made out of profits available for dividend.[83] But, if made "by virtue only of subsection (1)" it may be exercised only if sanctioned by an ordinary resolution of the company or, if the memorandum or articles so require, a resolution of some other description or compliance with other formalities in accordance with those requirements.[84]

Unless the memorandum or articles have made special provisions regarding this matter (and none of the 1985 Tables does) a board of directors is likely to find some difficulty in construing this section in the light of the new sections 3A, 35 and 35A. Presumably neither the new general purpose objects clause permitted by section 3A nor a similar clause at the end of the list of objects and powers[85] will suffice to authorise the board to exercise the power without the sanction of a resolution of the general meeting. But, under section 719(3), this resolution can, in the absence of contrary provision in the memorandum or articles, be an ordinary resolution, whereas under section 35 it would have to be a special resolution. Presumably section 719, dealing with a specific situation, prevails over section 35, with the apparent result that, if the memorandum includes a specific power to provide for employees and this is a power not excluded in the articles from those which can be exercised by the board, it will be

79 [1962] Ch. 927. See p. 169 above.
80 s.719(1).
81 s.719(2).
82 Then s.187 of the Insolvency Act confers similar powers on the liquidator.
83 s.719(4).
84 s.719(3).
85 *Parke* v. *Daily News* had held that when the trade or business of the company is ending, gratuitous generosity cannot be "incidental or conducive to the carrying on of any trade or business by it."

able to exercise it without the sanction of the general meeting,[86] and that, if the memorandum does not include such a power, an ordinary resolution will suffice notwithstanding section 35(3).

In any event, the employees[87] once they have received their golden handshakes will be protected (unless they are directors[88]). The only risk they run is that a member will intervene,[89] or that the company will go into liquidation,[90] before any decision has been made.

THE RESULTING POSITION

The objective of the foregoing statutory changes was to draw the sting of the *ultra vires* and constructive notice doctrines, thus improving the position of those who dealt with the company externally, while making as few alterations as possible to the position as between the company and its members, directors and other agents. This limited objective appears to have been achieved reasonably satisfactorily. But it did not attempt to provide a complete code defining when a third party can safely assume that those dealing with him on behalf of a company have power to bind the company.

Normally, as a result of the new sections, if a transaction with a third party acting in good faith is effected on behalf of a company by the board of directors or by a person who, in fact, the board has authorised, the transaction will bind the company. But, except where the company is very small or the transaction is very large, the third party will probably not have had dealings through the board. His dealings will, more often in practice, be with someone who is an executive of the company or even a comparatively lowly employee of whom the members of the board of directors may never have heard. Nor will the third party be likely to know whether in fact that executive or employee has actually been authorised by the board. Is he then entitled to assume that the board has, in fact, authorised that person to bind the company? And that the board has imposed no limitations on the exercise of that person's authority? And what is his position if in fact there is no legally constituted board of directors? The new sections 35A and 35B give no answers. For them we have to

---

[86] The transaction will be one within the powers of the company apart from s.719 and not one which it could exercise only by virtue of subs. (1); and, the directors will be authorised by the articles.

[87] They will be ''dealing with'' the company within the meaning of s.35A.

[88] When s.322A will apply.

[89] Under s.35(2) or s.35A(4).

[90] Under s.187 of the Insolvency Act the liquidator may implement any decision previously made by the company and if none has, may, after all the company's liabilities have been met, exercise a similar power to that which the company had by virtue only of s.719. But he must receive the sanction of members and, on a winding up by the court, any creditor or member may apply to the court.

turn to the basic common law principles of agency[91] as refined in relation to companies by the rule in *Royal British v. Turquand*.[92]

The rule in Turquand's case

This rule was enunciated by the courts to mitigate the effects of the constructive notice doctrine. As that doctrine has now been abolished the rule is no longer often of direct relevance when the third party has dealt with the company through the board of directors.[93] Its importance now is in situations where, instead, the third party's dealings have been with some officer or agent other than the board. To this, however, there is an exception, best illustrated by the leading case of *Mahoney v. East Holyford Mining Co.*[94] in which the rule was first upheld by the House of Lords. The question to be decided was whether the liquidator of an insolvent company could recover from its bank money paid on cheques drawn on the company's account. The company's articles provided that cheques should be signed in such manner as the directors should determine. The bank had received a copy, signed by the "secretary," of an alleged board resolution that cheques should be signed by any two of three named "directors" and by the secretary. The cheques had been signed by those named. In fact, the directors had never been formally appointed and no formal directors' or members' meetings had ever been held. The Lords took the opinion of the judges and upheld their unanimous conclusion that the liquidator could not recover. As Lord Hatherly said[95]:

"When there are persons conducting the affairs of the company in a manner which appears to be perfectly consonant with the articles of association, those so dealing with them externally are not to be affected by any irregularities which may take place in the internal management of the company."

Dealing with the board or those authorised by it

Lord Hatherly's dictum, (substituting, now, "perfectly normal" for "perfectly consonant with the articles of association") remains, it is submitted, the guiding principle which the courts should bear in mind in interpreting the new statutory provisions. And it affords an answer to one of the questions that those provisions leave unanswered: "the

[91] Summarised with, it is hoped, sufficient accuracy for present purposes at p. 165, nn. 1 and 2 above.
[92] (1856) 6 E. & B. 327, Exch.Ch.
[93] As in the *Turquand* case itself. There, under the company's deed of settlement, the board could borrow on bonds such sums as from time to time should be authorised by a resolution of the company in general meeting. The court held that a third party "finding that the authority might be made complete by a resolution ... would have a right to infer the fact of a resolution authorising that which on the face of the document appeared to be legitimately done": at p. 332. Today he would be protected by the new sections.
[94] (1875) L.R. 7 H.L. 869.
[95] At p. 894.

board of directors" for the purpose of the new sections means "the persons occupying the position of the board of directors" whether or not they have been validly appointed.

For that proposition there is, indeed, additional statutory, support. The Companies Acts[96] have long provided that: "The acts of a director or manager[97] are valid notwithstanding any defect that may afterwards be discovered,[98] in his appointment or qualification."

To this the 1985 Act added:

"and this provision is not excluded by section 292(2) (void resolution to appoint)."[99]

This, however, seems to add little to the protection afforded by the common law rule[1] since the House of Lords had held in *Morris v. Kanssen*[2] that it applies only when there has been a valid appointment which has not been vacated and not where there has been "no appointment." This presumably still remains the law (subject to the new statutory exception) despite the difficulty, illustrated by the case itself,[3] of distinguishing between the two situations.

It can no longer be argued that a person having dealings with a company is deemed to have notice of who the true directors are (this being shown by its "public documents," *i.e.* by the register of directors required to be maintained by the company and the notices of changes therein which it is required to send to Companies House[4]). The new section 711A disposes of that argument. It does not, however, dispose of a possible argument based on section 42 of

---

[96] Now s.285 which applies only to registered companies. It is normally supplemented by an article on the lines of Table A 1985, Art. 92 which, however, could not be invoked by a third party unless he actually knew of it and had relied upon it. Note also s.382(2) and (4) which could strengthen reliance on the *Turquand* rule when minutes of meetings have been kept.

[97] The "or manager" is probably only a relic of the days when "manager" was sometimes the name given to a director. Especially in the light of the recent addition to this section (s.292 relates only to the appointment of directors) it is unlikely that any court would construe it as including "sales manager" or the like.

[98] This apparently means "discovered by the other party": *Kanssen v. Rialto (West End) Ltd.* [1944] Ch. 346, C.A. But this point was left open by the H.L.: *sub nom. Morris v. Kanssen* [1946] A.C. 459.

[99] s.292 requires each director's appointment to be voted on individually, (unless the meeting otherwise agrees nem. con.) and says that otherwise the resolution is void.

[1] Except that the section can be relied on by the director himself (*Channel Collieries Trust v. Dover Light Rly. Co.* [1914] 2 Ch. 506, C.A.) whereas under the *Turquand* rule, as an insider, he normally could not.

[2] Above, n. 98.

[3] There an originally valid appointment had expired without being renewed and this was treated as "no appointment at all" when the director continued to act as such. ss.288 and 709. But if the directors with whom the third party dealt were those shown on the register at the material time, and that was known to and relied on by the third party, it might further enhance his protection as a holding out by the company that they were the directors (unless there had been a change within the previous 14 days: see s.288(2)). A similar estoppel by holding out (see below, pp. 191, 192) might occur if the company was one which still names its directors on its notepaper. This was formerly required by the Companies Act 1948, s.201, but is not under s.305 of the 1985 Act which replaced it.

the Act.[5] That section provides that a company is not entitled to rely against other persons on the happening of certain events which have not been officially notified in the *Gazette*, unless these events are actually known by him at the material time. Among these events are changes among the directors. It could be argued that section 42 implies that if the events are notified in the *Gazette*, the company can rely on them. However it would be absurd if section 42 was held to have that effect and the Court of Appeal has held that it does not.[6]

Hence, a third party, who has dealt with the company through its board of directors (*de jure* or *de facto*) or with someone authorised by that board, will be protected so long as he has acted in good faith. The combined effect of the new sections and the *Turquand* rule produces that result.

Dealing with officers not so authorised

What of the more common case where the third party has not dealt with the board or an agent authorised by the board? If the third party acted in good faith he is entitled to rely on the fact that the board had unlimited power to authorise another person to exercise the powers of the company. But the new sections do not say that he is entitled to assume that the board has done so or that, to the extent that it has done so, it has not imposed any limitations on that person. Yet in many, perhaps most, cases unless he is entitled to make some such assumptions the new statutory provisions will be precious little help to him. But if he is to be entitled to make any such assumptions it can only be by reliance on the general law of agency and the rule in *Turquand*'s case and not on section 35A of the Act. This needs emphasizing because it seems often to be overlooked. Equally, however, it would be absurd if he could safely assume, say, that authorisation to sell the company's premises had been conferred on the office-boy, the lift attendant or someone who had no apparent connection with the company.[7] Despite the apparent width of the *Turquand* rule as expressed in the dicta in *Turquand* and *Mahony* quoted above[8] (and despite the fact that the rule has now been freed from the limitations on it under the constructive notice doctrine) the later cases on the *Turquand* rule make it clear that these assumptions can be made only in one or both of two sets of circumstances in each of which a very similar result would be reached by applying normal principles of agency.

The first, and more common, set of circumstances is where the person through whom the third party dealt occupies a position in the

---

[5] Originally s.9(4) of the European Communities Act, implementing Art. 3.5 of the First Directive.

[6] *Official Custodian* v. *Parway Estates* [1985] Ch. 151.

[7] In these extreme cases the company would, no doubt, have little difficulty in persuading the court that the third party had not dealt in good faith.

[8] See p. 186, text and n. 93 above.

company[9] such that it would be usual for an occupant of that position to have authority to bind the company in relation to the transaction concerned. If that is so, the third party dealing with the company in good faith will be entitled to assume that that person has authority unless he knows the contrary or knows of facts which would have put a reasonable person on inquiry.[10] Thus if the person acting for the company is its chief executive or managing director, then, despite the fact that the Act refuses to treat him as an "organ" of the company equivalent to the board of directors, unless there are suspicious circumstances, or the transaction is of such magnitude as to imply the need for board approval, he may safely be assumed to be authorised. In practice, he will probably have actual authority[11] but even if he has not he will have ostensible authority and his acts will bind the company.[12]

Much the same applies to other executive directors except that if the descriptions of their posts suggest particular areas of responsibility ("finance director," "sales director" or the like) they cannot be assumed to have authority outside those areas. Even though individual non-executive directors have no managerial responsibility unless the board delegates it to them[13] they may be assumed to have some individual authority, beyond that of sharing in the exercise of the board's collective authority at meetings of the board or its committees. It is usual, for example, for them to be authorised signatories of the company's cheques[14] or attesters of the affixing of its seal.[15] And the new section 36A[16] (which removes the need for a company to have a common seal[17]) provides that in favour of a purchaser[18] a document shall be deemed to be duly executed by a company if it purports to be signed by a director and the secretary or

[9] Whether formally appointed to it or merely allowed by the company to assume it; that is a matter of "internal management."
[10] When dealing with someone other than the board or someone authorised by it, the third party is not necessarily protected merely because he acted in good faith. If there are suspicious circumstances, he should, as under s.711A, "make such inquiries as ought reasonably to be made" and he will be protected only if the suspicions of a reasonable person would be allayed by the answers to his inquiries: *Underwood Ltd. v. Bank of Liverpool* [1924] 1 K.B. 715, C.A.; *Houghton & Co. v. Nothard, Lowe & Wills* [1927] 1 K.B. 48, C.A.; affd., on other grounds, [1928] A.C. 1, H.L.
[11] *Hely-Hutchinson v. Brayhead Ltd.* [1968] 1 Q.B. 549, C.A.
[12] *Freeman & Lockyer v. Buckhurst Park Properties Ltd.* [1964] 2 Q.B. 480, C.A.; especially the judgment of Diplock L.J. at 506.
[13] *Rama Corporation v. Proved Steel & General Investments Ltd.* [1952] 2 Q.B. 147.
[14] See *Mahoney v. Holyford Mining Co.*: above.
[15] Articles normally provide that the seal shall be affixed only pursuant to a resolution of the board or a committee of the board and attested by a director and the secretary or a second director: Table A 1985, Art. 101. But this seems clearly to be a matter of the company's internal management despite suggestions to the contrary in *S. London Greyhound Racecourses Ltd. v. Wake* [1931] 1 Ch. 496: see *County of Gloucester Bank v. Rudry Merthyr Colliery Co.* [1895] 1 Ch. 629, C.A.
[16] Inserted by the 1989 Act, s.130(2).
[17] s.36A(3).
[18] Defined as "a purchaser in good faith for valuable consideration [including] a lessee, mortgagee or other person who for valuable consideration acquires an interest in property."

by two directors and that, where it makes it clear on its face that it is intended to be a deed, to have been "delivered."[19]

Moreover, it is not uncommon for the board of directors to allow one of their number to assume the position of managing director even though he has never been formally appointed to that position and in these circumstances the courts have treated him as if he were the managing director.[20] Some decisions have even suggested that a non-executive chairman of the board has, as such, individual authority equating with that of a managing director.[21] But why the right to take the chair should imply a right to manage out of the chair is difficult to understand and the proposition has been doubted.[22]

When the third party deals with an officer or employee below the level of director the position is more problematical and, until recently, the courts have shown a marked reluctance to recognise any ostensible authority even of a manager.[23] But this is now changing and it may be taken that a manager, even if he does not have actual authority, will generally have ostensible authority to undertake everyday transactions relating to the branch of business which he is managing (though probably not if they are really major transactions[24]) and that the secretary will similarly have such authority in relation to administrative matters.[25] Indeed, almost every employee of a trading company must surely have apparent authority to bind the company in some transactions, though the extent of that may be very limited. For example, the men or women behind the counter in a departmental store clearly have apparent authority to sell the goods on display for cash and at the marked prices. Whether their apparent authority extends beyond that (for example, to accept a cheque not

[19] s.36A(6). This extends s.74 of the L.P.A. 1925.

[20] See, e.g. *Biggerstaff* v. *Rowatt's Wharf Ltd.* [1896] 2 Ch. 93, C.A.; *Clay Hill Brick Co.* v. *Rawlings* [1938] 4 All E.R. 100; *Freeman Lockyer* v. *Buckhurst Park Properties Ltd.*, above.

[21] *B.T.H.* v. *Federated European Bank* [1932] 2 K.B. 176, C.A.; *Clay Hill Brick Co.* v. *Rawlings*, above. It is a popular misconception, shared by lawyers and laymen alike (and apparently by the legislature: see 1985 Act (Sched. 6, Pt. 1, para. 3) that the chairman is some sort of overlord and remunerated as such; he often is but may be merely an ornamental figurehead.

[22] In *Hely-Hutchinson* v. *Brayhead* [1968] 1 Q.B. 549, C.A., *per* Roskill J. at first instance at p. 560D, and Lord Wilberforce at p. 586G.

[23] *Houghton & Co.* v. *Nothard, Lowe & Wills* [1927] 1 K.B. 246, C.A., affd. on other grounds [1928] A.C. 1, H.L.; *Kreditbank Cassel* v. *Schenkers* [1927] 1 K.B. 826, C.A.; *S. London Greyhound Racecourses* v. *Wake* [1931] 1 Ch. 496; see also the observations of Willmer L.J. in *Freeman & Lockyer* v. *Buckhurst Park Properties Ltd.* [1964] 2 Q.B. at 494.

[24] See *Armagas Ltd.* v. *Mundogas S.A.* [1986] A.C. 717, H.L. There an employee who bore the title of "Vice-president (Transportation) and Chartering Manager" was held not to have authority to bind his company to charter-back a vessel which it was selling. But there were complicating factors in that case for the employee was colluding with an agent of the other party in a dishonest arrangement and did not purport to have any general authority to bind the company but merely alleged that he had obtained actual authority for that particular transaction.

[25] *Panorama Developments Ltd.* v. *Fidelis Furnishing Fabrics Ltd.* [1971] 2 Q.B. 7111, C.A. (above, p. 163). How far, if at all, his apparent authority extends to the commercial side of the company's affairs is still unclear; see, *per* Salmon L.J. at p. 718.

supported by a cheque-card or to take goods back if the customer returns them) we shall probably never know, for it is unlikely to be litigated—at any rate against the customer. But clearly the fact that, under section 35A, the board of directors might have authorised them to exercise all the company's powers (including that to sell the store itself) cannot estop the company from denying that it has done anything so crazy. Hence, when the employee or agent of the company does not occupy a position in the company in which it would be usual for him to have delegated authority to bind the company in relation to the transaction concerned, the company will not be bound, unless he has actual authority or has, in some other way, been held out as having authority to bind it in relation to that transaction.

The fact that, prior to the recent reforms, the third party was deemed to have notice of the contents of the memorandum and articles did not mean that he could rely on something in those documents to estop the company from denying the authority of an officer of the company who would not usually have had authority. Constructive notice was a negative doctrine curtailing what might otherwise be the apparent scope of the authority and not a positive doctrine increasing it.[26] The position may be different, however, if the third party had actual knowledge of the memorandum and articles and had relied on some provision in them. What, however, is clear is that mere knowledge that the board of directors might have delegated does not estop the company from denying that it has done so. It would be necessary for the other party also to establish that it had authority to enter into the contract sought to be enforced.

Obviously, it will be unlikely that the board will so conduct itself if it has neither conferred that authority nor decided to ratify what the agent has done. It is, no doubt, theoretically possible to conceive of a provision in the memorandum or articles which, if known to and relied on by the third party, might estop the company, but there seems to be no reported case in which that has occurred. If this sort of estoppel is to be relied on it will generally be because of conduct by the company's organs and not because of any provision in its

---

[26] Any doubt on this point was finally dispelled by the C.A. in *Freeman & Lockyer v. Buckhurst Park Properties Ltd.*, above; see especially Diplock L.J. at [1964] 2 K.B. at 504. It had formerly led to much judicial (and academic) disputation: see *Houghton v. Nothard Lowe & Wills* [1927] 1 K.B. 826, C.A.; *B.T.H. v. Federated European Bank* [1932] 2 K.B. 176; *Clay Hill Brick Co. v. Rawlings* [1934] 4 All E.R. 100; *Rama Corporation v. Proved Tin & General Investments* [1952] 2 Q.B. 147; and, finally, *Freeman & Lockyer v. Buckhurst Park Properties Ltd.*, above. For the academic discussion see (1934) 50 L.Q.R. 469; (1956) 11 Univ. of Toronto L.J. 248; (1966) 30 Conv.(N.S.) 128; (1969) 18 I.C.L.Q. 152.

[27] Per Diplock L.J. in *Freeman & Lockyer v. Buckhurst Park Properties*, above, at p. 508. See also Atkin L.J. in *Kreditbank Cassel v. Schenkers* (above) at p. 844.

memorandum or articles. An example is afforded by *Mercantile Bank of India* v. *Chartered Bank of India*.[28] There the board of directors had caused the company to appoint agents under powers of attorney which authorised them to borrow on the security of charges on the company's property. The directors imposed limits on the extent to which those agents could borrow but these limitations did not appear in the powers of attorney. A charge to secure a borrowing in excess of the limitations was held to bind the company in favour of a lender who had relied on the powers of attorney.

An officer or agent of the company cannot, however, confer ostensible authority on himself by representing that he has actual authority.[29] It can be conferred only by conduct of the company, acting through an organ or agent of the company, such as the board or the managing director, with actual or apparent authority to make representations as to the extent of the authority of the company's officers or agents. If the company has made such representations on which the third party has acted in good faith, the company may be estopped.[30]

It will therefore be seen that protection afforded to a third party who has dealt with an employee is considerably less than that afforded to one who has dealt with the board of directors, or with someone actually authorised by the board. The statutory reforms have improved his position by the modifications of *ultra vires* and constructive notice but section 35A helps him only to the extent that he may safely assume that the board had power to delegate to that employee. That will not protect him unless the board has actually done so or is estopped from denying that it has or has ratified what he did. If it has not, he will be unprotected unless the employee has acted within his apparent authority; and he will lose that protection not only if he has not acted in good faith but also if he negligently failed to make proper inquiries or if he actually knew or ought to have known that the officer had exceeded his authority.

There is one further respect in which the statutory reforms may lead to clarification of a grey area of the law. The cases establish that in some circumstances a third party becomes a constructive trustee of any property of the company which passes to him under a transaction

---

28 [1937] 1 All E.R. 231. The headnote is misleading in suggesting that it was the fact that the articles expressly empowered the board to delegate by powers of attorney (which today would be implied and, under s.35A, an exclusion in the articles would not affect a bona fide third party) that brought about the estoppel. It was the powers of attorney that did so. The only relevance of the articles (of which, at that time, third parties were deemed to have notice) was that they did not preclude the grant of such powers of attorney.

29 *Armagas Ltd.* v. *Mundogas S.A.* [1986] A.C. 717, H.L.: see p. 190 n. 24 above.

30 Contrary to what was thought at one time, this is so even if the officer or agent has forged what purported to be a document signed or sealed on behalf of the company: *Uxbridge Building Society* v. *Pickard* [1939] 2 K.B. 248, C.A., explaining dicta in *Ruben* v. *Great Fingall Consolidated* [1906] A.C. 439, H.L.; *Kreditbank Cassel* v. *Schenkers*, above; and *S. London Greyhound Racecourses* v. *Wake*, above.

which is in breach of the directors' fiduciary duties. But what has been unclear is precisely what those circumstances are.[31] The new emphasis in section 35A on lack of good faith should enable the courts to hold that the sole criterion is that the third party has acted in bad faith.[32]

THE ORGANIC THEORY

Thanks to the recent statutory reforms there are now fewer situations in which companies will be able to escape liability for acts undertaken on their behalf. But there are some types of liability which demand actual fault of the principal or master himself. Does this mean that a company can never be liable in such cases since it has no "self"? In *Lennard's Carrying Co. Ltd. v. Asiatic Petroleum Co. Ltd.*,[33] a ship-owning company, *Lennard's*, had sought, under section 502 of the Merchant Shipping Act 1894, to limit its liability to *Asiatic*. This it could do only if the injury to the latter was incurred without *Lennard's* "actual fault or privity." The fault was that of *Lennard's* managing director. The House of Lords rejected *Lennard's* attempt, Viscount Haldane L.C. saying[34]:

"[A] corporation is an abstraction. It has no mind or will of its own any more than it has a body of its own; its active and directing will must consequently be sought in the person of somebody who for some purposes may be called an agent but who is really the directing mind and will of the corporation, the very ego and centre of the personality of the corporation . . . If Mr. Lennard was the directing mind of the company then his action must . . . have been an action which was the action of the company itself . . . "

But he emphasised that the fault or privity must be:

"of somebody who is not merely an agent or servant for whom the company is liable upon the footing *respondeat superior*, but

31 See, e.g. *Selangor United Rubber Estates Ltd. v. Cradock* (No. 3) [1968] 1 W.L.R. 1555; *Karak Rubber Co. v. Burden* (No. 2) [1972] 1 W.L.R. 602; *Belmont Finance Corp. Ltd. v. Williams Furniture Ltd.* [1979] Ch. 250, C.A.; *International Sales & Agencies Ltd. v. Marcus* [1982] 2 C.M.L.R. 46; *Rolled Steel Ltd. v. British Steel Corp.* [1986] Ch. 246, C.A.; *Smith v. Croft* (No. 2) [1988] Ch. 114; *Agip (Africa) Ltd. v. Jackson* [1990] Ch. 265.
32 Which, in this context, should mean participating knowingly in an act of the directors which constitutes a breach of their fiduciary duties and not merely an act in excess of their authority. This, as revealed in the Debates under probing by Lord Wedderburn, was, it seems, the Government's intention: see O.R. (H.L.) Vol. 505, cols. 1234–1247 (6 Apr. 1989).
33 [1915] A.C. 705, H.L.
34 At pp. 713, 714.

somebody for whom the company is liable because his action is the very action of the company itself."[35]

Here, therefore, the English judiciary recognised the distinction between "organs" and "agents" more clearly than the English legislature has yet done notwithstanding that it is fundamental to the company laws of our Continental partners[36] and reflected in the Company Law Directives which we have purported to implement.[37] And it has proved to be a concept useful both in civil and criminal cases.

Civil cases

One example of its use in civil law can be found in *Bolton (Engineering) Co. Ltd. v. Graham & Sons*[38] where the question was whether the landlord company had effectively terminated a business tenancy because it intended to occupy the premises for the purpose of its own business. No formal general or board meetings had been held to decide on its intentions in that regard but its executive directors had clearly manifested that intention and that was held to be a sufficient indication of the company's mind. Quoting Lord Haldane, in *Lennard's* case, Denning L.J. said[39]:

"A company may in many ways be likened to a human body. It has a brain and nerve centre which controls what it does. It also has hands which hold the tools and act in accordance with directions from the centre. Some of the people in the company are mere servants and agents who are nothing more than hands … and cannot be said to represent the mind and will. Others are directors and managers who represent the directing mind and will of the company and control what it does. The state of mind of these managers is the state of mind of the company and is treated by the law as such."

Other examples occur in relation to the test of a company's residence[40] and to inducing a breach of contract.[41] The theory also

[35] This decision was followed in *H.M.S. Truculent* [1954] P. 1, where the Third Sea Lord was held to be the "directing mind" of the Admiralty, and in *The Lady Gwendolen* [1965] P. 294, where it was emphasised that the "directing mind" need not necessarily be a director.

[36] Particularly Germany, where Haldane, in his youth, had studied.

[37] But, in doing so, have, in effect, recognised it only in respect of the board of directors.

[38] [1957] 1 Q.B. 159, C.A. (the H.L. refused leave to appeal [1957] 1 W.L.R. 454). See also *Sevenarts Ltd. v. Busvine* [1968] 1 W.L.R. 1929, C.A.

[39] At p. 172.

[40] This normally depends on where the company's "head and brains" are located.

[41] Inducing an "organ" of the company to cause the company to break a contract is equivalent to inducing the company itself, and a tort whether or not the organ itself acts wrongfully; *Thomson & Co. v. Deakin* [1952] Ch. 646, C.A.

seems the true justification for holding, as has been done in a number of recent cases[42] that, if the court makes an order against a company, its controllers will also be in contempt of court if they wilfully fail to take effective steps to ensure that the order is obeyed. Although the language used in the judgments[43] tends to suggest that the courts regard this as an example of "lifting the veil" it is submitted that it is rather an application of the organic theory involving no disregard of the corporate entity. It could also help in determining whether a principal is deemed to have knowledge of information known to one of his agents who, however, is not the agent acting for him in that transaction.[44] If it is known to the board of directors or to the manager of that area of the company's business, then, in favour of a person dealing with the company in good faith, the company should be deemed to know—but not otherwise.[45] But the courts have refused to apply the theory in relation to their own procedure, for they have insisted that a company cannot appear in person.[46] Hence not even the chief executive, formally authorised by a board resolution, will be allowed to represent the company in a High Court action,[47] a rule which appears to serve no purpose other than to protect the monopoly of the legal profession.

Criminal cases

However, it is in the sphere of criminal law that the organic theory has had its major impact. Whether any useful purpose is served by making companies themselves criminally liable has been much debated[48] but has now been answered in the affirmative except where the crime is one in which the *actus reus* is such that an artificial person is physically unable to commit it,[49] or, as in the case of

42 See, *e.g.* A.-G. *for Tuvalu* v. *Philatelic Corpn.* [1990] 1 W.L.R. 926, C.A.; *Tate Access Floors Inc.* v. *Boswell* [1991] Ch. 512, but contrast *Re Supply of Ready Mixed Concrete* [1991] 3 W.L.R. 707, C.A.

43 See especially [1991] 2 W.L.R. at 318H–319A.

44 See *Armstrong* v. *Strain* [1952] 1 K.B. 232, C.A.

45 But as yet there is no reported English decision which so holds.

46 *Tritonia Ltd.* v. *Equity & Law Life Assce.* [1943] A.C. 584, H.L.

47 In the county court greater freedom is allowed: *Kinnall* v. *Harding* [1918] 1 K.B. 408.

48 See, *e.g.* Winn (1929) 3 Camb. L.J. 398; Welsh (1946) 62 L.Q.R. 345; Glanville Williams, *Textbook of Criminal Law* (2nd ed. 1983) pp. 974–977; Leigh, *The Criminal Liability of Corporations in English Law* (1969); Law Commission's Working Paper No. 44 (1972) and Law Com. 143 (1985). Also debated was whether the strict *ultra vires* doctrine applied to criminal liability but the overwhelming weight of academic opinion was that it had no application and there are no modern reported cases where the contrary was argued. It also seems to have no application to those torts where liability of the master is dependent on whether the servant has acted within the scope of his employment: *Campbell* v. *Paddington Corp.* [1911] 1 K.B. 869.

49 *e.g.* bigamy or sexual offences. In a recent case it was held, rather surprisingly, that a company could not be convicted of driving a lorry without a permit contrary to GLC regulations, since only a human being could drive a vehicle: *Richmond-on-Thames B.C.* v. *Pinn & Wheeler Ltd.* [1989] R.T.R. 354.

murder, where it carries a mandatory period of imprisonment,[50] or where the offence is statutory and corporate liability is clearly excluded.[51] This, however, is a recent development in relation to offences which require *mens rea*, as well as an *actus reus*, and was reached only as a result of the organic theory. Except in the case of statutory offences of absolute liability or where the statute made it clear that masters were to be vicariously liable for the crimes of their servants, it was generally assumed until 1944[52] that companies, having no minds of their own, could not have guilty ones. But in three cases reported in that year[53] companies were convicted of offences clearly requiring *mens rea* and prosecutions for such offences have now become commonplace.[54] The application here of the organic theory was recognised by the House of Lords in the leading case of *Tesco Supermarkets Ltd.* v. *Nattrass*[55] where, however, it was held that a shop manager, one of several hundred in the company's employ, could not be regarded as an "organ" of the company but was merely its servant or agent for whose acts the company could be liable criminally only on the basis of *respondeat superior* or express statutory provision.

The rationale

As Lord Reid pointed out in the *Tesco* case, to describe the organic theory as an example of treating the company as the alter ego of its controllers (or vice versa) would be misleading. Unlike some examples of lifting the veil[56] (where the controllers are made liable for acts of the company because the company is their alter ego) under the organic theory the company is made liable not because the controllers are its alter ego but because they are an organic part of the company's ego itself. Whether they are, depends on whether they have control and managerial discretion, either generally over the company's business or over that particular part of it to which the transaction relates.[57]

---

[50] But, both in this and the previous exception, companies could be held liable as accessories.

[51] When insider-dealing was made a criminal offence it was deliberately restricted to individuals: see Company Securities (Insider Dealing) Act 1985. See below, Chap. 23.

[52] But there were earlier signs of the change in a civil case, *Triplex Glass Ltd.* v. *Lancegaye Safety Glass Ltd.* [1939] 2 K.B. 395, C.A., and Winn (later Winn L.J.) had, with remarkable prevision, enunciated the modern view in his article (n. 48 above) published in 1929.

[53] *DPP* v. *Kent & Sussex Contractors Ltd.* [1944] K.B. 146; *R.* v. *ICR Haulage Ltd.* [1944] K.B. 551, C.C.A.; *Moore* v. *Bresler* [1944] 2 All E.R. 515. In these decisions there was no express reference to Haldane's dictum but subsequent cases have expressly relied on it, either directly or via Denning L.J.'s judgment in *Bolton (Engineering) Co. Ltd.* v. *Graham & Sons* (above, p. 194 n. 38).

[54] A recent example, far from commonplace, was the (unsuccessful) prosecution for manslaughter of the company which owned the cross-Channel ferry that sank at Zeebrugge with the loss of 193 lives.

[55] [1972] A.C. 153, H.L.; see especially the illuminating speech of Lord Reid.

[56] See Chap. 6 above.

[57] See, in particular, *Bolton (Engineering) Co. Ltd.* v. *Graham & Sons* (above p. 194 n. 38) and *Tesco Supermarkets Ltd.* v. *Nattras*, above n. 55.

This organic theory has been carried to the logical conclusion that a company and an individual, who is its directing will, cannot be successfully indicted for conspiracy since this requires the meeting of two or more minds.[58] But it has not been carried to absurd extremes. If those who constitute the head and brains are engaged in defrauding the company they cannot successfully defend a civil action by the company[59] or a criminal prosecution[60] by saying "we were the controlling organs of the company and accordingly the company knew all about it and consented." Were such a defence to prevail it would wholly negate the duties which the organs owe to the company. So far as concerns the internal relationship between the company and its organs, dishonest acts directed against the company by its organs are not attributed to the company—though they may well be in favour of a third party dealing with the company in good faith.

CONCLUSION

A company's liability to third parties no longer depends solely on principles of agency or *respondeat superior*. Section 35A, though it does not use the word "organ," has, in effect, recognised that the board of directors is not a mere agent of the company but an organic part of it so that third parties can treat acts of the board as acts of the company itself. The section, however, has not, it seems, gone so far as to treat any other officers of the company as its organs. If third parties deal with the company through another officer they will not be entitled, under section 35A, to treat his acts as those of the company itself and the company will be bound only if that person is acting within his actual or apparent authority (or, where relevant, within the scope of his employment) or the company ratifies what he has done or the company is estopped. The courts, however, have gone further. They have recognised that where managerial powers have been delegated by the board to other officers, those officers also may be treated as organs, rather than agents or servants, of the company so that their acts can be regarded as those of the company itself and not merely as acts of the officers for which it is liable vicariously. As yet, however, they have adopted that theory only in relation to tortious and criminal liability of the company and in cases of contractual liability have generally been content to apply normal agency principles modified only by the *Turquand* rule and, now, by the statutory reforms.

58 *R.* v. *McDonnell* [1966] 1 Q.B. 233.
59 *Belmont Finance Corp.* v. *Williams Furniture Ltd.* [1979] Ch. 250, C.A.
60 *A.-G.'s Reference (No. 2 of 1982)* [1984] Q.B. 624, C.A.; *R.* v. *Phillipou* (1989) 89 Cr.App.R. 290, C.A.

On the face of it, it is anomalous that when an executive of the company signs a contract on behalf of the company its liability depends upon whether he has acted within the actual or apparent scope of his authority as an agent of the company, whereas if he negligently or fraudulently injures a third party, the company may be liable civilly or criminally on the basis that the company itself has acted. But this has come about because the courts have felt that, in the latter case, the company ought to be made liable even though on normal principles of vicarious liability it would not be. In contractual cases, however, normal principles of agency as elaborated by the Rule in *Turquand's* case work well enough.

Even where the organic theory comes into operation, normal principles of agency and vicarious liability seem to apply to some extent. The company's chief executive will presumably not be regarded as acting as an organ of the company when he goes off with his mistress "on a frolic of his own" in the company's car. Moreover, the new statutory rules and the courts' organic theory only apply externally and do not affect the liabilities of the organs in their internal relationships with the company; the members of the board are still regarded *vis-à-vis* the company as its fiduciary agents whose liability to the company the Act specifically preserves.

The present position may be somewhat lacking in coherent logic and a few ghostly relics of *ultra vires* continue to haunt us, but at last we seem to have reached a pragmatic result which is generally defensible.

CHAPTER 9

THE RAISING AND MAINTENANCE OF CAPITAL

MEANING OF CAPITAL

THE concept of capital is of fundamental importance to a proper understanding of company law in general, and in particular to an appreciation of the distinction between individual traders and partnerships on the one hand, and incorporated limited liability companies on the other. Unhappily "capital" is a word of many different meanings,[1] and even in the legal, economic[2] and accounting senses with which we are concerned, it is used loosely and to describe different concepts at different times, although its users do not always recognise the fact.

Expressed at its simplest, we may say that whenever anyone starts a business he will put certain property into it. This property may be tangible—money, land, furniture or stock-in-trade—or intangible—patents, copyrights, trade secrets or the goodwill and connection of a going concern. Whatever the form of this property it will probably be convenient to place a monetary value upon it, if for no other reason than because this will facilitate the preparation of accounts and enable the proprietor to see what return he is getting for the property sunk in the business. Especially is this so if two or more persons are trading in partnership; the monetary valuation of their respective contributions will then become desirable in order to quantify the shares in which they are respectively entitled. Hence the owners of the business start with a fund of capital and their aim is to use this fund so that it increases and provides profits. These profits may either be taken out by the proprietors, or left in the business which, in the latter case, will start the next trading period with a larger capital. Of course, the object of the proprietors may be defeated; the assets may not be increased by profits but diminished by losses. In this event the business will start the next year with a reduced capital unless the proprietors decide to bring in further assets.

So far as concerns the business of an individual trader or partnership this concept of capital is merely a matter of convenience and accounting practice. Except to the extent that the bankruptcy, and tax laws and those regulating particular activities require accounts to be kept and profits or losses to be calculated, there is no legal requirement that the assets brought into the business should be given

---

[1] cf. capital punishment, capital letter, capital ship, capital city, capital of a pillar, capital and labour, capital and income, and "capital!"

[2] No attempt is here made to deal with the economist's analysis of capital; such an attempt would take us into the higher flights of economic theory for which the writer has no qualifications.

199

a money value and credited to the proprietors as their capital, and there is nothing to prevent capital being increased or withdrawn by the proprietors at any time. If they decide that the business is over-capitalised they are free to withdraw part of the assets and reduce the capital accordingly. Since the proprietors are fully liable without limitation of liability it makes little difference to creditors whether their personal wealth is treated as business capital or not; it remains liable for payment of debts in any event. The trust to be reposed in the proprietors has therefore little relation to the capital in the business as such. It does not even depend solely on the present wealth of the proprietors; third parties may be prepared to place trust in them because of their character and reputation irrespective of their existing fortunes, for, like Sir Walter Scott, they may be willing to slave for the rest of their lives to discharge the liabilities of the business.

With an incorporated company limited by shares all this is altered. But, unless trust is reposed in it, it will be unable to survive in competition with its rivals. It may need to raise by loans more money than that subscribed by its members, or to buy on credit; in any event it will be vital, if it is to dispose of its goods or services, that third parties shall be able to trust it properly to fulfil its contracts. The creditworthiness of the company depends on the adequacy of its capital,[3] and this being so it is essential that capital should be more clearly defined and inviolable than is the case with an individual or partnership.

Hence the law has worked out certain principles relating to the raising and maintaining of capital. In effect, capital has ceased to be a name given to the fluctuating net worth of the business and has become a yardstick fixing the minimum value of the assets which must be raised initially and then, so far as possible, retained in the business. These principles have no application to unlimited companies and have been worked out in relation only to companies limited by shares—though most of them apply to the few remaining companies limited by guarantee and having a share capital. They are primarily intended for the protection of creditors (and it is upon this aspect that the following discussion concentrates) but, as was the now defunct *ultra vires* rule, are also designed to protect shareholders, present and future, against action by the directors which might covertly diminish the value of their shares as long-term investments.

Until recently these principles were largely judge-made and were lax in comparison with those of the Civil Law countries of the EC. As a result of the need to implement[4] the Second Company Law Directive they are now mainly statutory and far stricter. Although the

---

[3] And the high rate of failure of small private companies is due to the fact that so many of them are under-capitalised.
[4] Originally by the Companies Act 1980.

Directive only compelled us to adopt these principles in respect of public companies, an option of which we took some advantage, the opportunity was seized to rationalise, in relation to both public and private companies, the former confusing mixture of judge-made law and statutory glosses and exceptions, so that something approaching a comprehensive code of the law relating to share capital can now be found in Parts IV and V of the Companies Act 1985.[5]

RAISING CAPITAL

Authorised Share Capital

In the case of a company with a share capital (unless it is an unlimited company) its memorandum must "state the amount of the share capital with which [it] proposes to be registered and the division of that share capital into shares of a fixed amount."[6] These amounts are normally expressed in United Kingdom currency. But, as was held in *Re Scandinavian Bank*,[7] except for the "authorised minimum"[8] required (now) in the case of a public company, they can be denominated in a foreign currency or in a number of different currencies.[9] Even if denominated in United Kingdom currency, the "fixed amount" of each share can be too small to be legal tender (for example a half-penny[10]). The amount of the authorised capital in itself is of no importance as an indication of creditworthiness.[11] All that the foregoing long-standing statutory provisions achieve is to prescribe the maximum number of shares which the company can issue without increasing its authorised capital and the nominal value which it has chosen to place upon the shares into which the share capital is divided.[12] It is not even true to say, as one tends to,[13] that the nominal value of the shares fixes the maximum liability of the

[5] However these Parts contain sections dealing with some matters (*e.g.* "pre-emptive rights," class rights, and debentures) which are here dealt with in later chapters of this book.
[6] s.2(5)(a).
[7] [1988] Ch. 87.
[8] See below p. 208.
[9] As the Scandinavian Bank wished and was permitted, to do. According to the evidence of the Registrar, at least 125 English registered companies already had foreign currency share capital and, probably, two had multi-currency share capital. What appears not to be permissible is to denominate a share as, for example, "£1 or DM3"; it must be one or the other.
[10] And one public company listed on The Stock Exchange has its share capital divided into shares with a nominal value of 0.1p.
[11] Since the unsophisticated may not realise this and be misled by the (apparently) impressive amount of the authorised capital, if, on the company's stationery or order forms, there is any reference to the amount of its share capital it must be to paid-up capital: s.351(2).
[12] And, if authorised by the articles, the authorised capital can be increased, and the nominal value of its shares can be increased or diminished by consolidation or sub-division. An ordinary resolution suffices: s.121.
[13] See pp. 11, 12 above. It does, however, fix their minimum liability since shares cannot be issued at a discount.

shareholders; shares may be, and frequently are, issued at a premium which they will be contractually liable to pay.[14]

Issued Share Capital

All that is of any importance (and it may be very little in the case of a private limited company) is its issued capital. It was established by the courts in the 19th century[15] that shares must not be issued at a discount to their nominal par value. This is now stated in the Act,[16] which specifically provides that if the shares should be so issued the allottee is liable to pay to the company the amount of the discount with interest.[17] Payment by way of commissions, brokerage or the like to any person in consideration of his subscribing or agreeing to subscribe is prohibited, even if the shares are issued at a premium,[18] except to the limited extent permitted by section 97.[19] Hence those dealing with the company have some assurance that the company has received, or will be entitled to receive, from its members payment of the price at which the shares are issued and that this price is not less than the nominal value of the issued capital. Formerly it was common for shares to be issued on the basis that part of the price would be paid on allotment and the balance when called upon, thus introducing a distinction between paid-up capital and uncalled capital. Today the price is almost invariably payable on or shortly after allotment except that, to encourage small investors to respond to privatisation issues, payment in such cases may generally be made in two or three instalments, spread over about two years. Long-term uncalled capital (though it could be a valuable indication of creditworthiness since, in effect, it affords a personal guarantee by the members)[20] is now virtually a thing of the past.[21] How far those dealing with a limited company can derive comfort from the assurance that its paid-up capital has been raised depends on that capital being more than

---

[14] But, as we shall see (pp. 207–209 below) the premium is not technically *share* capital though it is now treated for most purposes as if it was.
[15] Finally by *Ooregum Gold Mining Co.* v. *Roper* [1892] A.C. 125, H.L. It was there held that discounts were forbidden even though the existing shares of the same class were quoted at a discount. This does not mean that a company whose existing shares stand at a discount cannot issue any more; it can by exercising the powers under s.121 (n. 12 above) to create shares of a different class which can be issued at or above this nominal value because of their preferential rights.
[16] s.100.
[17] A subsequent holder is also liable, jointly and severally, unless he is, or claims through, a purchaser for value without notice of the contravention (s.112(1) and (3)) but, unlike the original allottee, he may be granted relief under s.113, on which see pp. 206, 207 below.
[18] s.98.
[19] s.98.
[20] As amended by the F.S. Act 1986.
[21] The Act still provides (ss.120 and 124(b)) that a limited company may determine that any part of its uncalled capital shall not be called-up except in the event and for the purposes of its winding up and formerly banks, and the like, often took advantage of this.
[21] For obvious reasons long-term investors in public companies fight shy of partly paid shares. Not infrequently, however, members of private companies are lax in actually paying for their shares.

negligible. As we shall see,[22] this is now necessarily the case in relation to public companies. But it is not so in relation to private ones which may carry on business with a paid-up capital of £2 or even less.[23]

Moreover payment does not have to be in cash; it can instead be made in kind[24] and very frequently is.[25] But, except (now) in relation to public companies, it seems that the parties' valuation of the non-cash consideration will be accepted as conclusive[26] unless its inadequacy appears on the face of the transaction[27] or there is evidence of bad faith.[28] Hence on an issue for a non-cash consideration it is possible to "water" the shares by agreeing to accept payment in property which is worth less than the nominal value of the shares. The only protection against this in relation to private companies is that, under what is now section 88, companies have to send the Registrar a "Return of Allotments" which distinguishes between shares allotted for cash and those allotted for non-cash and that, in relation to the latter, this return has to be accompanied by the relevant contract, or particulars of it if it is oral. However the wording of the section suggests that this is intended for the protection of the Revenue[29] rather than the public and, in any case, it is often avoidable by the device of two ostensibly distinct agreements between the proposed allottee and the company—one for him to supply the company with property or services for £X and the other for him to subscribe for shares at the price of £X.[30]

Until the Companies Act 1980, implementing the Second Company Law Directive, the foregoing rules were all that the law prescribed regarding raising share capital.[31] Then, however, in what probably amounts to the most fundamental adoption so far by English

22 See pp. 207 below.
23 See p. 12 n. 38 above.
24 s.99(1) restates the general rule that "shares allotted by a company may be paid-up in money or money's worth (including goodwill and know-how)" but this is followed by exceptions and qualifications relating to public companies only.
25 For example, when the proprietor of a business incorporates it by transferring the undertaking and assets to a newly formed company in consideration of an allotment of its shares.
26 *Re Wragg* [1897] 1 Ch. 796, C.A.
27 *Re White Star Line* [1938] Ch. 458.
28 *Tintin Exploration Syndicate* v. *Sandys* (1947) L.T. 412.
29 By ensuring that any appropriate stamp duty is paid: see s.88(2)(*b*)(i), (3) and (4).
30 The company and the other party, then exchange cheques or rely on mutual set-off. Such an arrangement was held in *Spargo's Case* (1873) L.R. 8 Ch.App. 407 to be an issue for cash and s.738(2) appears to confirm that it is. Technically, a bonus issue (see below p. 210) is a non-cash issue and, although for the purposes of many of the sections referred to in what follows it is expressly treated as if it was not, this is not so in relation to s.88. On a bonus issue it will not be practicable to adopt the avoiding device (hence Table A 1985 art. 110(d)). Nor, presumably, would the courts allow it to be adopted to evade the statutory provisions regarding non-cash issues by public companies. This seems to be confirmed by the fact that in Hoffmann J.'s discussion of those statutory provisions in *Re Bradford Investments* [1991] B.C.L.C. 221 and 688, that possibility was not mentioned.
31 Apart from the rationalisation in the 1948 Act of the treatment of share premiums: see below p. 207–209.

Company Law of Civil Law practices, there was a long overdue tightening-up *in relation to public companies*. The changes fall under two heads: (1) far stricter rules relating to issues for a non-cash consideration and (2) prescription of a minimum share capital.

Public companies: non-cash issues or transactions

A public company may not accept, in payment for its shares or any premium on them, an undertaking by any person that he or another will do work or perform services for the company or any other person.[32] If it should do so, the holder of the shares[33] is liable to pay the company an amount equal to the nominal value of the shares plus the premium or such part of that amount as has been treated as paid up by the undertaking.[34] Nor may it allot shares as fully or partly paid-up if the consideration is *any* sort of undertaking which need not be performed until after five years from the date of the allotment.[35] If the undertaking should have been performed within five years but is not, payment in cash then becomes due immediately.[36] And (though this is of minimal importance[37]) shares taken by a subscriber to the memorandum of association in pursuance of his undertaking in the memorandum must be paid for in cash.[38]

Finally, the possibility of "share-watering" by placing an inflated value on the non-cash consideration is tackled by requiring it to be independently valued. Under section 103 a public company may not allot shares as fully or partly paid-up (as to their nominal value or any premium) otherwise than in cash unless:— (i) the consideration has been valued in accordance with section 108, (ii) a report is made to the company in accordance with that section during the six months immediately preceding the allotment and (iii) a copy is sent to the proposed allottee.[39] To this there are exceptions in relation to bonus issues[40] and in relation to most types of takeovers and mergers[41] or schemes of arrangement with creditors.[42] But, in other cases, if the allottee has not received the copy of the valuation report or there is some other contravention of section 103 or 108, which he knew, or

---

[32] s.99(1) and (2). But neither these sections nor ss.102 and 103 (below) prevent the company from enforcing the undertaking: s.115. If a private company wishes to convert to a plc such undertakings must first be performed or discharged: s.45(3).
[33] Including not only the registered holder but also the beneficial owner: s.99(5).
[34] s.99(2) and (3). Bonus issues are excluded: s.99(4).
[35] s.102. If contravened the consequences are similar to those for contravention of s.99.
[36] s.102(5) and (6). And see s.45(4) regarding a private company converting to a plc.
[37] The English practice is for two persons to subscribe for only one share each and the subscribers are generally two clerks of the professional advisers (who will hold each share as a nominee for the promoters): see Chap. 11, p. 276 below. The promoters themselves may suffer more serious consequences under ss.104 and 105: below.
[38] s.106.
[39] s.103(1).
[40] s.103(2).
[41] s.103(3)–(5). The rules of the Take-over Panel, or The Stock Exchange will normally ensure that there has been professional assessment of value in such cases.
[42] See s.103(7) as amended by the Insolvency Act 1986.

ought to have known, amounted to a contravention, once again he is liable to pay in cash with interest.[43]

Under section 108 the valuation has to be made by a person "qualified to be appointed, or continue to be, an auditor of the company."[44] He may, however, arrange for and accept a valuation from another person who appears to him to have the requisite experience and knowledge and who is not an employee or officer of any company in the group.[45] In practice, therefore, the report will be by the company's auditor supported by another professional valuation of any real property or other consideration which the auditor does not feel competent to value on his own. The report has to go into considerable detail[46] and must support the conclusion that the aggregate of the cash and non-cash consideration is not less than the nominal value and the premium.[47]

A private company proposing to convert to a public one cannot evade these valuation requirements by allotting shares for a non-cash consideration shortly before it re-registers as a public one. In such a case, the Registrar cannot entertain the application to re-register unless the consideration has been valued and reported on in accordance with section 108.[48]

In addition, during an initial period of two years from the date when the company was entitled to carry on business as a public company, sections 104 and 105 apply similar valuation requirements to certain transactions with anyone who was a subscriber to the memorandum on the company's formation or a member of it on its conversion to a public company. The transactions in question are those under which such a person is to transfer to the company (or to anyone else) a non-cash asset[49] and the price to be paid (in cash or kind) by the company is equal in value at the time of the agreement to one tenth or more of the company's nominal issued capital at that time.[50] This is aimed at a mischief rather different from that tackled by section 103; not at an issue of shares by the company at a concealed discount but at a purchase by the company of property from the promoters at an excessive price.

Unless the transaction is in the ordinary course of the company's business or the agreement is entered into under the supervision of the court,[51] the following conditions will have to be complied with:

---

43 s.103(6).
44 s.108(1). For these qualifications, see Chap. 18, pp. 477–483 below.
45 s.108(2) and (3).
46 See s.108(4)–(7). Subs. (7) deals with the complication where the consideration payable to the company is partly for the shares and partly for some other consideration given by the company.
47 s.108(6)(d).
48 s.44.
49 As is a subsequent holder unless he is or claims through a purchaser for value without notice: s.112. See *Re Bradford Investments*, above n. 30.
50 Defined in s.739.
51 s.104(1), (2) and (3).

(i)   the consideration to be received by the company and any consideration (other than cash[52]) to be given by the company must be independently valued under section 109, which adapts section 108 to meet this different situation[53];

(ii) the valuer's report must have been made during the six months immediately preceding the agreement;

(iii) the terms of the agreement must have been approved by an ordinary resolution; and

(iv) not later than the giving of the notice of the meeting at which the resolution is to be proposed, copies of the agreement must have been circulated to members and to the other party to the agreement.[54]

If these conditions are not fulfilled, the agreement, so far as not carried out, is void.[55] Moreover, the company can normally recover the consideration given by it or its value.[56] If the agreement included provision for the allotment of the company's shares, that provision is not void but the consequences are similar to those on contravention of section 103.[57]

Whether the valuation is under section 103 or 104, the valuer is entitled to require from the officers of the company such information and explanation as he thinks necessary[58] and it is an offence if false or deceptive replies are made knowingly or recklessly.[59] However, when, under sections 99, 102, 103, 105 or 112 or by virtue of an undertaking given to the company, a person is liable to pay-up shares he may apply to the court to be relieved of that liability and the court may exempt him to the extent that it considers just and equitable.[60] But the court must have regard to two "overriding principles," namely:

(a)   that a company which has allotted shares should receive money or money's worth at least equal in value to the aggregate of the nominal value of those shares and the value of the premium or, if the case so requires, so much of that aggregate as is treated as paid-up, and

---

52 If the consideration includes an issue of shares, s.103 will also have to be complied with: s.104(5)(*b*).
53 The value of the consideration to be received by the company is the value of the non-cash asset, if that is to be transferred to it, or the value of the advantage to the company if the non-cash asset is to be transferred to another person: s.104(5)(*a*).
54 s.104(4).
55 s.105(1)(*a*) and (2).
56 But, if the other party has received the valuer's report, only if he knows or ought to have known of the contravention: s.105(1)(*b*) and (2).
57 s.105(1)(*b*) and (2).
58 s.110(1).
59 s.110(2) and (3).
60 s.113(1) and (2).

(b) that when the company would, if the court did not grant exemption, have more than one remedy against a particular person it should be for the company to decide which remedy it should remain entitled to pursue.[61]

Public companies: minimum capital

The "authorised minimum" share capital of a public company is £50,000 or such other sum as the Secretary of State may specify by statutory instrument.[62] In practice most public companies and all those whose shares are listed will have a considerably larger share capital than the minimum. A company formed as a public company cannot commence business until it has satisfied the Registrar that it has issued and allotted shares to the nominal value of not less than the authorised minimum,[63] of which at least one quarter[64] and the whole of any premium has been paid up either in cash or (to the extent permitted and subject to the independent valuation as described above) in kind.[65] He has similarly to be satisfied that these conditions are met when a private company re-registers as a public one.[66] The formalities that have to be complied with in order that he may be satisfied are described in Chapter 11 below. On any subsequent issue of shares the same requirements regarding payment-up have to be met, i.e. the shares must be paid-up at least to the extent of one quarter of their nominal value and the whole of any premium.[67]

Share premiums

Prior to 1948, when companies issued shares at a premium, (i.e. at above their nominal value) the premiums were treated totally differently from share capital. Share capital was regarded as

[61] s.113(5). For other matters which the court should take into account, see subss. (3) and (4). When proceedings are brought by one person, (e.g. a holder of the shares) against another (e.g. the original allottee) for a contribution in respect of liability the court may adjust the extent (if any) of the contribution having regard to their respective culpability in relation to that liability: s.113(6) and (7). And see s.113(8) for exemption from liability under s.105(2).
[62] s.118(1). Should an increase be specified, the S.I. may require any public company with capital less than that specified to conform or to convert to a private company:
[63] s.118(2).
[64] s.117(1) and (2).
[65] In view of the unpopularity of partly paid shares (see above n. 21) the strong probability is that the full nominal value will be paid up.
[65] s.101. This does not apply (see s.101(2)) to shares allotted under an employees' share scheme (defined in s.743) but unless they are paid up to that extent they may not be taken into account in determining the nominal value of allotted share capital:
[66] s.117(4).
[66] ss.43–45.
[67] s.101. If the company allots a share in contravention of s.101 it is treated as if this sum had been received (s.101(3)) and the allottee (and any subsequent holder, unless he is, or claims through, a purchaser for value without notice—see s.112) is liable to pay it with interest: s.101(4). Neither subs. (3) nor (4) applies to an issue of a bonus share unless the allottee knows or ought to have known of the contravention: s.101(5).

determined by the nominal par value of the shares; if they had been issued at a price above par the excess was not "capital" and, indeed, constituted part of the distributable surplus which the company, if it wished, could return to the shareholders by way of dividend.[68] This was ridiculous. If the price paid for the shares was £100,000, the true capital of the company was £100,000 and it should have made no difference to the company or to the shareholders whether the £100,000 was obtained by issuing 100,000 £1 shares at par or by issuing 10,000 £1 shares at £10. This absurdity, however, was mitigated by section 56 of the 1948 Act, now replaced by section 130 of the 1985 Act. This provides that a sum equal to the aggregate amount or value of the premiums shall be transferred to a "share premium account" which, in general, has to be treated as if it were part of the paid-up share capital.[69] But, anomalously, it is still necessary to refer expressly to both, and for the company, in its annual accounts and reports, to distinguish between them. What, if it were not for arbitrary par values, would be a single item—capital— has to be treated as two distinct items, albeit for most purposes treated identically.

Moreover the two are not treated as wholly identical. Section 130 provides for two "exceptions"[70] and two "reliefs."[71] The first exception is that a company may apply the share premium account in paying up bonus shares. It would, of course, be impossible thus to apply issued capital but to apply share premium account is wholly unobjectionable since the only effect is to convert it, or a part of it, to share capital proper. The second exception is that it may be applied in writing off the company's preliminary expenses or the expenses of, or the commissions paid or discount allowed on, any issue of the company's shares, or in providing for the premium payable on redemption of debentures of the company. It is difficult to justify this second exception (and the reference to "discount allowed on any issue of shares" is puzzling since payment of such a discount is now proscribed in relation to both public and private companies.[72] The exceptions, however, are not of great importance. More important (and more interesting) are the "reliefs."

Section 130 (as did its predecessor, section 56) expressly applies to issues at a premium "whether for cash or otherwise." The result of this was held to be that if, say, on a merger one company (A) acquired the shares of another (B) in consideration of an issue of A's own shares and the true value of B's shares exceeded the nominal value of those issued by A, a share premium account had to be

---

[68] *Drown v. Gaumont British Corpn.* [1937] Ch. 402.
[69] s.130(1) and (3).
[70] s.130(2).
[71] s.130(4).
[72] s.100: see p. 202 above. And commissions are permitted only to the limited extent provided in ss.97 and 98.

established in respect of the excess.[73] The result of this was that B's undistributed profits formerly available for distribution by way of dividend ceased to be distributable. This caused something of a furore in commercial circles which, in such circumstances, wanted to continue to avoid that consequence by employing so-called "merger," instead of "acquisition," accounting.[74] Although the decision was thought to be correct by the majority of the legal and accountancy professions there was at least one well-known set of Chambers which disputed it. Hence, relying on Opinions obtained to be employed, thus avoiding the creation of a share premium account. However, in 1980 the question was again litigated and the earlier decision fully upheld.[76] Faced with two decisions, the Chambers had to capitulate but joined the City in demanding that some relief should be afforded in the envisaged Companies Act 1981. This, to the extent thought to be reasonable and consonant with the Second Company Law Directive, was forthcoming. Hence, sections 131 and 132 now provide for "merger relief" (section 131) and "relief in respect of group reconstructions" (section 132).

The general effect of section 131 is that section 130 does not apply when, pursuant to a merger arrangement, one company has acquired at least 90 per cent. of each class of equity shares of another in exchange for an allotment of its equity shares at a premium. The general effect of section 132 is to exclude the application of section 130 in the case of issues at a premium by a wholly-owned subsidiary in consideration of a transfer to it of non-cash assets by another company in the group comprising the holding company and its wholly-owned subsidiaries. If section 132 applies, section 131 does not.[77] The Secretary of State is empowered by section 134 to make regulations providing further relief from section 130 in relation to premiums other than cash premiums or for modifying any relief provided by sections 131–133.

Increase of capital

"Capital," in the sense of the net worth of a business, will fluctuate from time to time according to whether it makes profits and ploughs

[73] *Head & Co. Ltd.* v. *Ropner Holdings Ltd.* [1952] Ch. 124.
[74] These alternative methods of accounting are explained in paras. 7–12 of the new Sched. 4A inserted by the 1989 Act.
[75] One of the few advantages of a divided profession is that, by shopping around, solicitors can generally obtain Counsel's Opinion supporting the course which their clients want to pursue.
[76] *Shearer* v. *Bercain Ltd.* [1980] 3 All E.R. 295.
[77] Anyone wishing to take advantage of these reliefs will need to study carefully the sections themselves in the light of the supplementing provisions in s.133; they are more complicated than the above summary may imply. (Note that the erroneous cross-reference (to s.132(4) instead of s.132(8)) in s.131(1) was corrected by Sched. 19, para. 1 of the 1989 Act).

them back or suffers losses. But a company's capital, *i.e.* the issued share capital plus share premium account (if any) does not automatically fluctuate to reflect this. It remains unaltered until increased by a further issue of shares, which must be made in conformity with the rules dealt with above, or reduced in accordance with the rules dealt with below.[78] While a reduction is potentially dangerous, an increase of capital is to be encouraged and merely involves increasing the authorised share capital, if all that has been issued, and finding one or more persons willing to take up the new shares. If, however, the company has made profits and not distributed them as dividends, a normal issue of further shares will not bring the "capital" of the company into balance with the net worth of the company. Although it will increase the share capital and the share premium account (if any), the price received will initially increase the net assets to a corresponding extent and it will still be necessary in the balance sheet to have a further (notional) liability in order to balance the "assets" and "liabilities." This is normally described as a "reserve," an expression which may confuse those unaccustomed to accounting practice since it may suggest (falsely) that the company has set aside an actual earmarked fund to meet some potential or actual liability.

The only way in which a profit-rich company can effectively bring its "capital" more into line with its increased capital, in the sense of its net worth, is by making a "bonus" or "capitalisation" issue[79] to its shareholders. The former expression is likely to be used by the company when communicating with its shareholders (in the hope that they will think that they are being treated generously by being given something for nothing) and the latter when communicating with the workforce (which might otherwise demand a bonus in the form of increased wages). In fact such an issue is merely a means of capitalising reserves by using them to pay-up shares newly issued to the shareholders. For example, suppose that before the issue the net worth (taking book values) of the company was £2M and the issued capital one million shares of £1 each. The shares, on book values, will be worth £2 each.[80] The company then makes a one-for-one bonus issue paid up out of the share premium account or free reserves. The only effect on a shareholder is that for each of his former £1 shares worth £2 he will now have two £1 shares each worth £1.[81] And the only effect on the company is that, insofar as the bonus

[78] At pp. 211 *et seq.*

[79] The two expressions mean the same thing and, indeed, so does a third ("scrip" issue) which is sometimes used.

[80] This does not mean that listed shares will be quoted at that price; that will depend on many other factors, including in particular the expected future profits and dividends. And the book values, of fixed assets in particular, may not reflect their present values.

[81] The *quoted* price, is not likely to fall by a half because it is to be expected that the company will seek to maintain approximately the same rate of dividend per share as before the issue.

issue is paid up out of share premium account, that, as part of the "capital yardstick," is reduced or eliminated and replaced by issued share capital and, insofar as it is paid out of free reserves, these are reduced or eliminated and, again, replaced by issued share capital.

To a small extent the same effect can be achieved by the practice, increasingly common among listed companies, of allowing the shareholders to opt to take shares in lieu of dividends. This may appeal to shareholders whose concern is capital appreciation only. But it has disadvantages unless the dividends are very large; fractions of shares cannot be allotted, shareholders will, under our present archaic system, end up with lots of share certificates for small numbers of shares, and they will be liable to tax as if they had received the cash dividend. Nor is it likely to result in any simplification and rationalisation of the company's capital structure.

Maintenance of capital

Clearly all the foregoing provisions regarding raising of capital would be pointless if the company, having raised capital, had complete freedom to reduce it. But here we are faced with the ambiguity of the expression "capital." In saying that it should not be reduced, do we mean that the notional liability shown under that head in the company's balance sheet should not be reduced? If so, there is no difficulty about that; all that is needed is to say so or, indeed, merely to provide no means whereby that can be done. Or does it mean, instead or in addition, that the company must not allow the value of its net assets to fall below the figures representing "capital?" In fact, as finally enacted as a result of implementing the Second Company Law Directive,[82] it now means (at any rate in relation to public companies) something approaching both of these possibilities without, however, going quite so far as either.

Formal reductions of capital

Generally speaking, the capital yardstick represented by issued share capital plus share premium account (and, as we shall see shortly, any capital redemption reserve[83]) cannot be reduced except under an order of the court. By what is now section 135 of the 1985 Act, a company may, if so authorised by its articles,[84] reduce its share capital "in any way"[85] so long as confirmation by the court is obtained under sections 136-138 (dealt with in Chapter 26 below). Not only may the capital yardstick then be reduced[86] but that may be

[82] Initially by the Companies Act 1980.
[83] See below pp. 216, *et seq.*
[84] If the articles do not so authorise, it can alter them by passing a special resolution.
[85] s.135(1).
[86] Thus, perhaps, enabling the company to resume the payment of dividends which might otherwise be prohibited by the dividend rules; see below Chap. 10.

accompanied by a repayment of capital to the shareholders,[87] thus reducing both the capital yardstick (a notional liability) and the assets of the company to a corresponding extent.

If the result of the reduction thus made is that the nominal value of a public company's allotted share capital falls below the authorised minimum, the court's order is not registered by the Registrar, and so does not become effective,[88] until the company re-registers as a private company.[89]

Loss of capital

The mere fact that the company incurs losses so that the value of its net assets falls below the capital yardstick does not mean that it must cease trading. It would be going too far to demand that since it will still be fully solvent in every sense so long as its true assets exceed its true liabilities and it is able to pay its debts as they fall due. The only immediate effect of the loss of capital is that normally the company will not be able to pay dividends. However, in the case of a public company, section 142 requires that if the net assets[90] become half or less of its called-up share capital it must, within 28 days of that becoming known to a director, convene an extraordinary general meeting for not later than 56 days thereafter "for the purpose of considering whether any, and if so what, steps should be taken to deal with the situation."[91] Since the general meeting is not compelled to take any steps and is given no greater powers than it would otherwise have, the requirement seems somewhat fatuous[92] but a director who knowingly and wilfully authorises a failure to comply is liable to a fine.[93]

Acquisition of its own shares

It was held by the House of Lords in the 19th century that a company could not purchase its own shares, even though there was an express power to do so in its memorandum, since this would result in a reduction of capital.[94] Assuming that on purchase the shares

---

87 See s.135(2)(c). It may also extinguish or reduce any uncalled capital (s.135(2)(a)) but in both such circumstances there are special protections (in s.136(3)–(6)) for creditors.

88 s.138(2).

89 s.139.

90 "Net assets" for the purposes of s.142 is not defined. Presumably it has the same meaning as elsewhere, *i.e.* "the aggregate of the company's assets less the aggregate of its liabilities (liabilities to include any provision for liabilities or charges within paragraph 89 of Schedule 4)": see ss.152(2) and 264(2). Or should the words in brackets be omitted?

91 s.142(1) and (3).

92 We were required to enact it, in respect of public companies, by the Second Company Law Directive but we did not extend it to private companies, most of which are mainly financed by bank overdrafts repayable on demand (and thus "liabilities") so that they might have had to convene such a meeting almost immediately after they were launched.

93 s.142(2).

94 *Trevor v. Whitworth* (1887) 12 App.Cas. 409, H.L.

were cancelled and nothing put in their place this would necessarily reduce the capital yardstick represented by issued share capital and could also be regarded as objectionable as a diversion of the company's assets to the shareholder whose shares were purchased. Nevertheless the rule thus laid down was stricter than in some Common Law countries (for example the United States and Canada) and many Civil Law ones (and than was required by the Second Directive). Nor did either objection apply if, for example, the shares were given to the company and held by a nominee for it,[95] or if a company with uncalled capital forfeited shares for non-payment of calls—as has always been recognised as permissible. Moreover, increasingly over the years the legislation has empowered the courts to order a company to buy its shares in certain circumstances.

By the Companies Acts 1980 and 1981 the rule and an extended number of exceptions to it were codified and are now to be found in sections 143–181 of the 1985 Act. The following pages of this chapter attempt to explain their effect, not always adopting the order in which they appear in the Act.

Section 143(1)[96] lays down the general rule that a company "shall not acquire its own shares whether by purchase, subscription or otherwise." If it purports to do so, the company and every officer in default is liable to a fine and the purported acquisition is void.[97] This, however, is subject to the succeeding provisions of the Act. Section 143(3) mentions five exceptions some of which are elaborated or qualified in later sections. These five are:

(i)   the acquisition of fully paid shares otherwise than for valuable consideration,[98]

(ii)   the redemption or purchase of shares in accordance with sections 159 to 181,[99]

(iii) the acquisition of shares on a formal reduction of capital confirmed by the court.[1]

(iv) the purchase of shares in pursuance of an order of the court under section 5 (contested alteration of objects),[2] section 54 (litigated objection to conversion from public to private company),[3] sections 459–461 (relief to members unfairly prejudiced),[4] or

---

[95] Held to be permissible in *Re Castiglione's Will Trust* [1958] Ch. 549.
[96] Which applies to a company, public or private, whether limited by shares or by guarantee if it has a share capital.
[97] s.143(2).
[98] Thus adopting *Re Castiglione's Will Trust*, above, and apparently extending it by not compelling the vesting of the shares, if fully paid, in a nominee for the company.
[99] See pp. 215–226 below.
[1] See p. 211 above and Chap. 26 below.
[2] See Chap. 8 at p. 174 above.
[3] See Chap. 11 at p. 290 below.
[4] See Chap. 24 at pp. 662 *et seq.* below.

(v)   forfeiture of shares (or acceptance of their surrender) for non-payment of calls.

Section 144 then contains further provisions relating to cases where (a) shares are issued to a nominee of the company or (b) are acquired by the nominee from a third party as partly paid. In either of such cases the shares are to be treated as held by the nominee for his own account and the company as having no beneficial interest in them; the nominee is liable to pay them up (as to their nominal value and any premium) when called upon to do so.[5] Section 145 provides certain exceptions principally designed to deal with problems faced by public companies in relation to shares acquired by the trustees of a company's employees' share scheme or pension scheme.[6]

Sections 146–149 deal with the treatment of the shares held by or for a public company when the acquisition of them is not void under section 143. In most cases, under section 146 the shares, or any interest of the company in them must be disposed of or the shares cancelled before the end of "the relevant period"[7] which, according to the circumstances in which they were acquired, is either one year or three years.[8] If cancelled, the issued share capital must be reduced by the nominal value of such shares.[9] This, under section 147, can be done by a resolution of the general meeting without the need for a formal reduction of capital. But if the effect is to reduce the allotted capital below the authorised minimum the company must apply for re-registration as a private company[10] in accordance with section 147(3) and (4).[11]

Furthermore, so long as the shares are held by or for the company no voting rights may be exercised and any purported exercise is void.[12] Were it not for this, the directors would be able to decide on how the shares should be voted, thus enhancing their own voting strength as shareholders. And if the value of the shares is shown in the company's balance sheet as an asset,[13] an amount equal to the value of the shares (or, where appropriate, the value to the company

[5] s.144(1). If he was a subscriber to the memorandum he and other subscribers become jointly and severally liable, as do the directors at the time of acquisition in other cases (s.144(2)) but the court may grant relief similar to that under s.113 (above p. 206): s.144(3) and (4).
[6] These problems were originally tackled by the Companies (Beneficial Interests) Act 1983: see now the 1985 Act, ss.145, 146 and 148 and Schedule 2. The acquisition of such shares is likely to be financed by the company and the company may have a residuary beneficial interest in them which, under Schedule 2, may be disregarded.
[7] s.146(1) and (2).
[8] s.146(3).
[9] s.146(2).
[10] If it fails to do so it is nevertheless treated as if it was a private company so far as offering of its shares are concerned and the company and its officers in default are liable to fines: s.149.
[11] s.146(2)(b).
[12] s.146(4).
[13] s.148(4). It is not normal practice to show them as assets.

of its interest in them) must be transferred out of profits available for dividend to a reserve not available for distribution.

Section 148(1) and (2) applies provisions similar to those of sections 146, 147 and 149 to a private company which re-registers as a public one at a time when its shares were held by or for it, but with the modification that "the relevant period" for the purposes of section 146 runs from the date of re-registration.

Redeemable shares

Far more extreme examples of exceptions to the rule that a company limited by shares may not acquire its own shares, are afforded by what is now Part V, Chapter VII, of the Act[14] dealing both with redemption of shares issued as redeemable and with purchase of shares whether or not issued as redeemable. We deal first with redeemable shares, which have been permissible since the Companies Act 1929. This introduced a method whereby redemption could take place without a reduction of the capital yardstick—a method which was adopted when, many years later,[15] companies were empowered to purchase their own shares, whether or not they were issued as redeemable.

Prior to the 1981 Act only preference shares could be issued as redeemable. Now, however, section 159 of the 1985 Act provides that a company, if authorised by its articles, may issue shares of any class which are to be redeemed or are liable to be redeemed, whether at the option of the company or the shareholder.[16] They may not be issued unless the company also has issued shares which are not redeemable.[17] Nor may they be redeemed until they are fully paid.[18] Section 159A[19] makes it clear that all the terms of redemption and the manner in which it is to be undertaken must be dealt with by provisions in the company's articles except to the extent that they are prescribed by the Act.[20]

Subject to an exception relating to private companies,[21] they can be redeemed only out of distributable profits or out of the proceeds of a fresh issue of shares made for the purpose.[22] And any premium

[14] ss.159–181.
[15] By the Companies Act 1981.
[16] s.159(1).
[17] s.159(2). This minimises the risk that redemption might result in the company having no members—though there are no very strong reasons why that should matter if s.24 of the Act and s.122(1)(e) of the Insolvency Act 1986 were repealed.
[18] s.159(3). Thus avoiding redemption wiping out the personal liability of the holders in respect of uncalled capital.
[19] Inserted by the 1989 Act, s.133(2).
[20] s.159A supersedes the original s.160(3).
[21] s.171: see below p. 222.
[22] s.160(1).

payable on redemption must be paid out of distributable profits.[23] On redemption the shares are cancelled and the issued share capital reduced by their nominal amount.[24] But the authorised capital is not reduced and can be utilised either for the new issue for the purpose of the redemption or for a future issue.[25] When redeemed out of the proceeds of a fresh issue the capital yardstick will be maintained as a result of the issue. This, however, is not so if shares are redeemed out of profits. The effect of that method is that not only are the company's assets reduced by the repayment to the shareholders but, without more, so would be the issued share capital.

The answer found to avoid that result is now stated in section 170. It provides that if shares are wholly redeemed out of profits the amount by which the issued share capital is diminished shall be transferred to a reserve called "the capital redemption reserve",[26] and that, if they are redeemed partly out of profits and partly out of the proceeds of a new issue and the aggregate amount of those proceeds is less than the nominal value of the shares redeemed, the amount of the difference shall be so transferred.[27] Like share premium account this reserve is treated as if it was paid-up capital of the company but may be applied in paying up a bonus issues,[28] thus converting it to paid-up share capital. Unless and until this is done the "capital" will consist not just of issued share capital plus share premium account (if any) but of issued share capital plus share premium account (if any) plus capital redemption reserve. The result is that the company's former "capital" is not reduced (although, if the redemption is out of profits, the company will have a smaller amount (if any) of distributable profits out of which to pay dividends.) There is no reduction of the capital yardstick; one type of "capital" is substituted for another.

As a result of the reforms introduced by the 1981 Act, there are circumstances in which the foregoing capital maintenance requirements on redemption are relaxed in relation to private companies. But as the provisions in question apply both to redemption and to purchases other than redemptions, they are left for consideration in what follows.

[23] s.160(1)(*g*). But where the shares were issued at a premium any premium payable on redemption may be paid out of the proceeds of a fresh issue up to an amount equal to the aggregate of the issue premiums or the current amount of the share premium account, whichever is the less, the share premium account being appropriately reduced: s.160(2).
[24] s.160(4).
[25] s.160(5).
[26] s.170(1). Prior to the 1981 Act this was misleadingly called "the capital redemption reserve *fund*" which was apt to lead students into believing that companies could not redeem shares out of distributable profits unless these totalled at least twice the redemption price. This, of course, is not so. The capital redemption reserve is, and always was, merely a notional liability not an earmarked fund of assets.
[27] s.170(2) but with an exception in relation to private companies: ss.170(3) and 171 below.
[28] s.170(4).

Purchase of own shares

Until the 1981 Act, redemption of preference shares was the only type of purchase by a company of its own shares permitted by English Law without a court order. So far as capital maintenance is concerned there was no reason for so restricting it; the solution adopted in relation to redeemable shares could equally well be applied to other purchases. But undoubtedly the opportunities for other abuses are then greater; for example the directors, by causing the company to repurchase shares of other members could, without any personal expense, enhance the value of their own holdings and their control of the company. But these dangers too could be guarded against and it was widely felt that the former restrictions were anachronistic. Hence, in 1980 the Department of Trade published a Consultative Document (a Green Paper)[29] canvassing the possibility of widening a company's powers. This met with an enthusiastic reception and was implemented by the 1981 Act,[30] both in relation to private companies and, to the extent permitted by the Second Company Law Directive, to public companies. The power has been widely used by both and seems to have given rise to few problems.[31]

The essential difference between redemption and purchase is that, under the latter, agreement of the parties (the selling shareholder and the buying company) will be needed at the time of the purchase. Neither party can force the other to sell or buy if he or it does not want to and if he or it does want to, the terms and conditions will have to be agreed at the time of the purchase. In contrast, as we have seen, in the case of redeemable shares the terms and conditions of redemption will have been set out in advance in the company's articles at the time the shares were issued. Subject to that difference, the two transactions are, broadly speaking, treated alike.

Section 162 provides that: subject to the following provisions, a company, if authorised to do so by its articles, may purchase its own shares (including redeemable shares[32]); that sections 159 and 160 apply as they do to redemptions; but that a repurchase cannot be made if the result would be that there were no longer any members of the holding non-redeemable shares.[33] Similarly, section 170, relating to the establishment of the capital redemption reserve, expressly applies to both redemptions and purchases; in other words, on a purchase "capital" has similarly to be maintained. And, in

29 *The Purchase by a Company of its own Shares:* Cmnd. 7944.
30 Now 1985 Act, Part V, Chap. VII which contains provisions relating to both redemption and purchase.
31 But an essential first step is to clear the transaction with the Inland Revenue to ensure that it will not be regarded as a "distribution" giving rise to payment of advance corporation tax by the company and of income tax by the sellers on the whole of the purchase price.
32 Thus enabling the company to "redeem" them prior to a date fixed in the terms and conditions if it can do so at a lower price.
33 *cf.* s.159(2) and n. 17 above.

contrast with the practice in the United States, shares which are re-purchased have to be cancelled[34] and cannot be held as "treasury shares" which can be re-sold by the company. It was decided not to countenance the latter practice, which, in effect, would have enabled a company to trade as a market-maker in its own shares and which would have given rise to accounting and tax complexities.

However, in relation to matters other than capital maintenance, stricter provisions apply to purchases. These provisions vary according to whether the purchase is to be an "off-market" or a "market" purchase, as these terms are defined in section 163.[35] For practical purposes what this means is that if The Stock Exchange[36] has listed the relevant shares or afforded facilities for dealings in them to be undertaken on its Unlisted Securities Market[37] and the purchase is so made it is a "market purchase"; otherwise it is not. Market purchases create fewer risks of abuse since the rules of The Exchange will apply and purchases will be effected at an objectively determined market price. If there is no market, a shareholder who needs to sell is likely to find that the company (or it's directors) is the only potential purchaser and the shareholder will have to accept the price that it is prepared to pay.

Off-market purchases

Under section 164 an off-market purchase can be made only in pursuance of a contract the terms of which have been authorised by a special resolution of the company before it is entered into.[38] The authorisation can subsequently be varied, revoked or renewed by a like resolution.[39] In the case of a public company the resolution must specify a date on which it is to expire and that date must not be later than 18 months after the passing of the resolution.[40]

Moreover, on any such resolution, whether of a public or private company, a member, any of whose shares are to be purchased, may not exercise the voting rights of those shares and if the resolution would not have been passed but for his votes the resolution is ineffective.[41] This is an interesting (and rare) example of the extension of the rule that directors must not vote at directors'

34 s.162(2) applying s.160(4) and (5).
35 As amended by the F.S. Act 1986.
36 The section refers to "any recognised investment exchange" other than "an overseas investment exchange." There are other recognised investment exchanges in the UK but not, at present, any dealing with shares, as opposed to their related futures and options.
37 See below Chap. 13.
38 s.164(1) and (2).
39 s.164(3).
40 s.164(4).
41 s.164(5) which also provides (a) that it applies whether the vote is on a poll or by a show of hands, (b) that, notwithstanding any provision in the company's articles, any member may demand a poll and (c) that a vote and a demand for a poll by a member's proxy is treated as a vote and demand by the member. For the adaptations when a private company uses a written resolution under s.381A, see Sched. 15A, para. 5(2).

meetings on matters in which they have a personal financial interest—a rule which normally does not apply to members voting as such. The resolution is also ineffective unless a copy of the contract or a memorandum of its terms is available for inspection by members at the meeting and for not less than 15 days before it is held.[42] The same requirements apply on a resolution to approve any variation of the contract.[43]

Section 165 provides that a company may purchase in pursuance of a "contingent purchase contract," *i.e.* one which does not amount to a binding contract to purchase shares but under which the company may become entitled or obliged to purchase them.[44] Similar requirements regarding prior approval of the contract by special resolution have to be observed.[45] Hence, although the Act does not expressly say so,[46] a purchase under a contingent purchase contract cannot be effected as a market purchase of traded options or futures since prior approval of the terms of individual market contracts is impracticable.[47] Where contingent purchase contracts may be particularly useful is to enable the company to bind or entitle itself to purchase the shares of a director or employee when his employment ends, or, as an alternative to the creation of a new class of redeemable shares, to meet the requirements of a potential investor in an unquoted company who wants assurance that he will be able to find a purchaser if he needs to realise his investment.

Market purchases

Under section 166 a company (which, in practice, will be a public one) cannot make a market purchase of its own shares unless the making of such purchases has first been authorised by the company in general meeting.[48] An ordinary resolution suffices[49] but, as in the case of a special resolution,[50] a copy of this and of any other resolution required by the section has to be sent to the Registrar within 15 days.[51] The authorisation may be general or limited to shares of any particular class or description and may be conditional or

[42] s.164(6). The names of members holding shares to which the contract relates must be disclosed. For adaptations when a written resolution under s.381A is used, see Sched. 15A, para. 5(3).
[43] s.164(7). For adaptations, see *ibid.*
[44] s.165(1).
[45] s.165(2) and s.164(3)-(7) which it expressly applies.
[46] And, indeed, the definition of "contingent purchase contract" seems wide enough to cover those types of traded options and futures relating to shares under which actual delivery may be required (though it rarely is) as opposed to contracts for differences which have to be settled in cash.
[47] See *Market purchases*, below.
[48] s.166(1). As in the case of off-market purchases, the authority may be varied, revoked or renewed by a like resolution: s.166(4). As regards listed companies, see *Yellow Book*, Section 5, Chap. 2, para. 30.4.
[49] Presumably to enable the company to act quickly (21 days' notice is needed for a special resolution but 14 days' suffices for an ordinary resolution).
[50] s.380.
[51] s.166(7).

unconditional[52] but it must specify the maximum number of shares to be acquired, the maximum and minimum prices[53] and a date on which it is to expire which must not be later than 18 months after the passing of the resolution.[54]

In the case of market purchases there is no requirement for the prior approval by members of the actual contracts of purchase.[55] What, in practice, will happen is that the company in general meeting will pass a resolution that x number of shares may be purchased at prices within a stated bracket, and the board of directors will instruct the company's stockbrokers to buy on The Stock Exchange when quoted prices make that possible.

Additional safeguards

Section 167(1) provides that the rights of a company under a contract to purchase its own shares are not capable of being assigned. This, once again, is designed to minimise the risk that the company will speculate in its own shares or attempt to rig the market. And, by section 167(2), an agreement by the company to release its rights under an off-market purchase is void unless approved in advance by a special resolution in relation to which the requirements of section 164(3) to (7) are observed.[56] The sort of abuse struck at here is when the company has agreed, contingently or otherwise, to purchase the shares of a director who, when the time to complete the purchase arises, finds that he has made a bad bargain and persuades his fellow directors to release him. A variation of the contract would require prior approval by special resolution; so should a release. There is no similar requirement in the case of market purchases; it is not needed since a bargain once struck on The Stock Exchange cannot be cancelled at the whim of the parties.[57]

As we have seen, the price for any of its shares purchased by the company must normally be paid out of distributable profits or the proceeds of a new issue of shares made for the purpose.[58] Section 168 applies a similar, but stricter, rule to any payment (other than the purchase price) made by the company in consideration of:

(a) acquiring any right (for example an option) to purchase under a contingent purchase contract,

---

[52] s.166(2).
[53] These may be determined either by specifying particular sums or by providing objective formulae for calculating the prices: s.166(6).
[54] s.166(3) and (4). But the purchase may be completed after the expiry date if the contract to buy was made before that date and the authorisation permitted the company to make a contract which would or might be executed after that date.
[55] But the members will, as a result of s.169 (below p. 221) be able to find out precisely what was done.
[56] In the case of a private company which has proceeded by a written resolution, see the adaptations in Sched. 15A.
[57] But if, in consideration of a payment made by the company, the contract is reversed, s.168 will apply.
[58] See above, p. 217.

(b) the variation of any off-market contract, or

(c) the release of any of the company's obligations under any off-market or market contract.

Although such payments are not strictly part of the purchase price,[59] none of them is normal expenditure in the course of the company's business but rather a distribution to a member or members, and the payment would not have been made but for the fact that the company was minded to agree to purchase its shares. Such payments ought therefore to be treated, so far as practicable, in the same way as the purchase price. It is highly unlikely that a company would contemplate making a new issue of shares for the purpose of financing any such payment.[60] Hence the section provides that they must be paid for out of distributable profits only. If this is contravened, in cases (a) and (b) above, purchases are not lawful, and in case (c) the release is void.[61]

Finally, section 169 provides Company Law's traditional prophylactic—disclosure of precisely what has occurred. It requires both detailed returns to the Registrar within 28 days of the delivery to the company of shares purchased by it[62] and retention by the company of contracts, or memoranda of them, for 10 years at its registered office where they are to be open to inspection by any number and, if it is a public company, by any other person.[63]

Private Companies: redemption or purchase out of capital

It was recognised that it would frequently be impossible for a private company to redeem or purchase its own shares unless it could do so out of capital[64] and without having to incur the expense of a formal reduction of capital with the court's consent. The whole concept of raising and maintaining capital is, in relation to such companies, of somewhat dubious value and will remain so unless and until a prescribed minimum share capital (realistic but, no doubt, less than that for public companies) is introduced in relation to them also. Hence it was decided that, subject to safeguards, they should be empowered to redeem or buy without maintaining the former capital yardstick. The relevant provisions are now contained in sections 171 to 177 of the 1985 Act.

[59] Though, in case (a), the division of the total price between that paid for the option and that paid on its exercise may be arbitrary.

[60] Which, in case (a) and perhaps (b), would be made some time before any actual purchase and which in cases (a) and (c) might never be made at all.

[61] s.168(2) which qualifies "not lawful" by "under this Chapter" thus recognising that it may be "lawful" under provisions not included in Part V, Chapter VII of the Act; e.g. where a court so orders under s.461.

[62] s.169(1)–(3).

[63] s.169(4)–(9) as amended by 1989 Act, s.143(2) in relation to subs. (5).

[64] This was particularly so prior to the relaxation of the tax provisions which discouraged "close companies" from retaining profits.

Section 171 provides that, subject to what follows, a private company may, if so authorised by its articles, make a payment in respect of the redemption or purchase of its shares otherwise than out of its distributable profits or the proceeds of a fresh issue of shares.[65] The extent of any such payment (a "payment out of capital"[66]) must, however, be restricted to what the section describes as "the permissible capital payment".[67] Subsections (3)–(6) define how one calculates what the permissible capital payment is and what adjustments to the company's issued capital and undistributable reserves have to be made when it is used. The permissible capital payment is the amount by which the price that the company has to pay (A) exceeds its "available profits"[68] and the proceeds of any fresh issue made for the purposes of the redemption or purchase (B). It is only if, and to the extent that, A exceeds B that a capital payment may be made.[69] If the permissible capital payment is less than the nominal value of the shares redeemed or purchased the amount of the difference must be transferred to the capital redemption reserve,[70] but if it should be more than that nominal value, the amount of the issued share capital and undistributable reserves[71] may be reduced by sums not exceeding in the aggregate the extent of the excess.[72]

Section 172 deals with the meaning of "available profits" for the purposes of section 171. Subsection (1) states that it means "the company's profits which are available for distribution (within the meaning of Part VIII[73])." However, it then goes on to say that for the purposes of section 171 "it shall be determined ... in accordance with the following subsections instead of sections 270 to 275 in that Part." As in the case of the latter,[74] the profits must be calculated on the basis of specified items as shown in the "relevant accounts" of the company,[75] but in this case, these accounts must be specifically prepared for the purpose of determining the permissible capital payment and must give the position as at a date within a period of three months ending with the date of the statutory declaration which the directors are required to make under section 173.[76] The available profits so determined have then to be treated as reduced by any

[65] s.171(1).
[66] s.171(2).
[67] s.171(3).
[68] See s.172, below.
[69] s.171(3).
[70] s.171(4) and (6).
[71] *i.e.* paid up share capital, share premium account, and capital redemption reserve (and any "revaluation reserve" on which see Chap. 10 below).
[72] s.171(5) and (6). The overall effect of s.171 is to ensure that neither the permissible capital payment nor the reduction of the capital yardstick is greater than is necessary.
[73] *i.e.* the dividend rules, on which see Chap. 10 below.
[74] See pp. 251 *et seq.* below.
[75] s.172(2).
[76] s.172(2), (3) and (6).

lawful distributions made by the company since the date of the accounts and before the date of the statutory declaration.[77]

Further safeguards

The effect of the foregoing concessions is that a private company may be able to make a return to one or more of its members which will exhaust its accumulated profits available for dividend and reduce both its assets and its capital yardstick. This presents potential dangers both to the members and to the creditors, present and future, of the company. Hence safeguards are needed, additional to those prescribed under the sections of the Act already dealt with, and these are provided by sections 173 to 177.

Section 173(1) states that, subject to any order of the court under section 177, payment by a private company for the redemption or purchase of its shares is not lawful unless the requirements of sections 173, 174 and 175 are satisfied. The first step required is that the directors must make a statutory declaration specifying the amount of the permissible capital payment and stating that, having made full inquiry into the affairs and prospects of the company, they have formed the opinion[78] that:

(a) immediately following the payment there will be no grounds on which the company could then be found unable to pay its debts, and

(b) for the year following, the company will be able to continue to carry on business as a going concern and to pay its debts as they fall due throughout that year.[79]

This declaration must be in the prescribed form[80] and contain such information with respect to the nature of the company's business as may be prescribed.[81] Annexed to it there must be a report by the company's auditors stating that they have enquired into the company's affairs, that the amount stated as the permissible capital payment is, in their view, properly determined in accordance with section 171 and 172 and that they are not aware of anything to indicate that the opinion expressed by the directors is unreasonable.[82] Section 173(2) then requires the capital payment to be authorised by a special resolution of the company (or a written resolution under

---

[77] s.172(4) and (5); "Distributions" include payments made for the purchase of its share, or under s.168, above, and any lawful financial assistance under s.154 or s.155: below pp. 226 *et seq.*
[78] A director who makes such a declaration without having reasonable grounds for the opinion commits an offence: s.173(6).
[79] s.173(3) and (4).
[80] Form No. 173.
[81] s.173(5).
[82] *Ibid.*

section 381A). Under section 174 this resolution must be passed on, or within a week immediately following, the making of the statutory declaration and the payment out of capital must be made no earlier than five nor more than seven weeks after the date of the resolution.[83] Once again,[84] the member of the company whose shares are to be redeemed or bought may not vote and if he does the resolution will be ineffective if it would not have been passed without his votes.[85] It will also be ineffective unless the statutory declaration and auditors' report were available for inspection by members attending the meeting.[86]

To protect creditors, section 175 requires that within a week following the passing of the resolution the company must cause to be published in the Gazette and, unless it notifies each of its creditors in writing, in an "appropriate national newspaper,"[87] a notice giving details about the resolution and the intended purchase or redemption out of capital and stating that any creditor may within five weeks of the resolution apply to the court under section 176 for an order prohibiting the payment.[88] Not later than the date of the first publication of the notice the company must deliver to the Registrar a copy of the directors' statutory declaration and the auditors' report and the originals of these must be kept at the company's registered office for the next five weeks and be open to inspection by any member or creditor.[89]

Section 176 entitles any member of the company, who has not consented to or voted for the resolution, and any creditor of the company, within five weeks of the passing of the resolution to apply to the court for the cancellation of the resolution.[90] The company must then forthwith give notice to the Registrar and, within 15 days from the making of any order, deliver an office copy of it to the Registrar.[91] On the hearing of any such application the court is given the widest powers by section 177. For example it can cancel the resolution, confirm it, or make such orders as it thinks expedient for the purchase of dissentient members' shares or for the protection of creditors, and may make alterations in the company's memorandum and for the reduction of its capital.[92]

83 s.174(1).
84 *cf.* s.164(5) above p. 218.
85 s.174(2) and see subss. (3) and (5).
86 s.174(4). Here again Sched. 15A prescribes the adaptations when the company has used a written resolution: para. 6.
87 *i.e.* an English or Scottish "national" according to whether the company is registered in England and Wales or in Scotland: s.175(3).
88 s.175(1) and (2).
89 s.175(4), (5) and (6). If inspection is refused, the company and its officers are liable to fines and the court may order an immediate inspection: s.175(7) and (8).
90 s.176(1) and (2).
91 s.176(3).
92 *cf.* the powers of the court on an application under s.5 (alteration of objects) or ss.459–461 (unfair prejudice).

Supplementary provisions

Finally, Chapter VII deals with certain questions which can arise in relation to redemption or purchase, whether by public or private companies and in the case of the latter, whether or not the redemption or purchase is out of capital. For example section 179 empowers the Secretary of State to modify by regulations certain of the foregoing provisions[93] and section 180 contains a few transitional provisions relating, in particular, to the redemption of preference shares created prior to the 1981 Act. Only section 178 needs more than a mention in a book of this sort. That section deals with questions which could well have arisen prior to the 1981 Act in relation to redeemable preference shares, but upon which there was no clear authority, and which became of increasing importance on the introduction of new powers to purchase shares and to redeem equity shares.

The first such question is: What are the remedies of a shareholder if the company does not perform the contract to redeem or purchase his shares? This may occur because it decides to break the contract or because it cannot lawfully perform it since the new issue of shares has not raised the proceeds expected and the company has inadequate available profits.[94] Section 178 (which applies when a company has, after the coming into force of the 1981 Act, issued redeemable shares or agreed to purchase any of its shares[95]) provides first that the company is not liable in damages in respect of any failure on its part to redeem or purchase.[96] It was thought that damages were not an appropriate remedy; that would result in the seller retaining his shares in, and membership of, the company and yet recovering damages (paid perhaps out of capital) from the company.[97] Instead the section provides[98] that the shareholder shall retain any other right to sue the company but that the court shall not grant an order for specific performance (perhaps a more appropriate discretionary remedy) "if the company shows that it is unable to meet the costs of redeeming or purchasing the shares in question out of distributable profits."[99] Apart from making it clear that the right to sue for specific performance is a right that the shareholder retains, the section gives

---

[93] This power is becoming increasingly common in legislation especially when, as here, new practices are being introduced. For a still wider power, see s.117 of the 1989 Act: above p. 106.

[94] The company could, presumably, protect itself from being in breach by expressly providing in the contract that the purchase is conditional upon its having the needed proceeds or sufficient profits. But then, perhaps, the contract would have had to be approved as a "contingent purchase contract?"

[95] s.178(1).

[96] s.178(2).

[97] But the abolition of the rule in *Houldsworth* v. *City of Glasgow Bank* (1880) 5 App.Cas. 317, H.L. Sc. by the new s.111A suggests that this is no longer regarded as objectionable.

[98] s.178(3).

[99] This ignores the possibility that it has adequate proceeds of a fresh issue but has nevertheless decided to break the contract. Surely the seller should then be entitled to specific performance?

no indication of what "other rights" he might have. There is little doubt that these would include the right to sue for an injunction restraining the company from making a distribution of profits which would have the effect of making it unlawful for the company to perform its contract.

The second and related question which section 178 answers is: What is the position if the company goes into liquidation before the shares have been redeemed or purchased? Generally the terms of redemption or purchase may then be enforced against the company and when the shares are accordingly redeemed or purchased, they are cancelled.[1] This, however, is not so if the terms of redemption or purchase provided for performance to take place at a date later than that of the commencement of the winding-up; nor, if during the period beginning with the date when redemption or purchase was to take place and ending with the commencement of the winding-up, the company did not have distributable profits equal in value to the redemption or purchase price.[2] Moreover even if these exceptions do not apply, the shareholder will gain little or nothing by enforcing the contract if the winding up is an insolvent liquidation since any claim in respect of the purchase price is postponed to the claims of creditors—and, indeed, to those of other shareholders whose shares carry rights (whether as to capital or income) which are preferred to the rights as to capital of the shares to be redeemed or purchased.[3] Subject to that, however, his claim as a creditor ranks ahead of those of other members as such.[4]

Financial Assistance by a Company for the Purchase of its Shares

Superficially, for a company to provide finance to enable someone else to buy its shares may seem to resemble a purchase by the company itself and to be similarly objectionable as reducing the company's capital.[5] In fact it raises completely different issues and in

[1] s.178(4). Hence in respect of these shares the seller will cease to be a member or "contributory" and will become a creditor in respect of the price.

[2] s.178(5).

[3] s.178(6).

[4] *Ibid.* The overall effect is that when he is entitled to enforce the contract, (*i.e.* when subs. (4) applies and neither exception in subs. (5) does) his claim in the liquidation for the price is deferred to the claims of all other creditors but, if there is anything left after they have been paid in full, he is preferred to the claims of members unless they hold shares of a class which ranks ahead of his (in which event his claim is deferred to theirs). Note that subs. (7) was repealed on the rationalisation of the rules regarding claims for interest by the Insolvency Act 1986, s.189.

[5] The Greene Committee, (1926 Cmd. 2657), on whose recommendation the ban on the practice was imposed by the 1929 Act, thought that it offended against the spirit, if not the letter, of the rule in *Trevor v. Whitworth*, but the Jenkins Committee commented that had the ban "been designed merely to extend that rule we should have felt some doubt whether it was worth retaining": (1962) Cmnd. 1749, para. 173. Nevertheless in the 1985 Act it still appears in Part V which is entitled *Share Capital, Its Increase, Maintenance and Reduction.*

no way affects "capital" in the sense of issued share capital, share premium account or capital redemption reserve; nor does it necessarily result in a reduction of the value of the company's net assets.[6] Nevertheless it is a practice which is open to the gravest abuses[7]—abuses which have continued to this day despite prohibiting legislation—originally section 45 of the 1929 Act which was re-enacted with amendments as section 54 of the 1948 Act. That section, despite its relative brevity, became notorious as unintelligible and liable to penalise innocent transactions while failing to deter guilty ones. The Jenkins Committee[8] suggested an alternative approach very similar to that now adopted in relation to private companies, but at the time no action was taken on that suggestion and, when the Second Company Law Directive was adopted, it became impracticable in relation to public companies.[9]

However, in 1980 two reported cases[10] caused considerable alarm in commercial and legal circles, suggesting, as they did, that the scope of the section was even wider, and the risk of wholly unobjectionable transactions being shot down even greater, than had formerly been thought. Hence it was decided that something had to be done about it in the 1981 Act which was then in preparation. Probably more midnight-oil was burnt on this subject than on all the rest of that Act and the resulting elaborate provisions are certainly some improvement on section 54. They are now to be found in Part V, Chapter VI (sections 151 to 158) of the 1985 Act.

The prohibition

Sections 151 and 152 apply to both public and private companies, but subject to a relaxation in relation to private companies if they comply with sections 153 to 158. The earlier legislation did not distinguish between assistance given prior to the acquisition and that given afterwards. Section 151 does. Its subsection (1) says that, subject to the exceptions in section 153,

---

[6] If the assistance is in the form of an adequately secured loan it merely substitutes one asset for another of equal or greater value.

[7] Particularly (but not exclusively) in relation to take-overs on which see Chap. 27 below. The classic abuse is financing the take-over by a bridging loan and immediately repaying it by raiding the coffers of the cash-rich company which is taken over: on variations of this see *Selangor United Rubber Estates v. Cradock* (No. 3) [1968] 1 W.L.R. 1555; *Karak Rubber Co. v. Burden* (No. 2) [1972] 1 W.L.R. 602; and *Wallersteiner v. Moir* [1974] 1 W.L.R. 991, C.A. (*per. diss.*) [1975] 1 W.L.R. 1093, H.L. A more sophisticated abuse is where the target company lends money to, or indemnifies against loss, known sympathisers who buy its shares; or where, on a share-for-share offer, either or both of the target and predator companies do so to maintain or enhance the quoted price of their own shares. Even if the predator does not provide financial assistance it runs the risk that its sympathisers may become its "associates" and fall foul of the Takeover Code; this cost *Guinness* an extra £95m on its take-over of *Distillers*.

[8] (1962) Cmnd. 1749, paras. 170–186.

[9] See Art. 23 of the Directive.

[10] *Belmont Finance Corpn. v. Williams Furniture Ltd.* (No. 2) [1980] 1 All E.R. 393, C.A.; *Armour Hick Northern Ltd. v. Whitehouse* [1980] 1 W.L.R. 1520.

"where a person is acquiring or is proposing to acquire[11] shares in a company, it is not lawful for the company or any of its subsidiaries[12] to give financial assistance directly or indirectly for the purpose of that acquisition before or at the same time as the acquisition takes place."

Subsection (2) provides that, subject to the same exceptions, when a person has acquired shares in a company and any liability has been incurred (by him or any other person[13]) for that purpose it is not lawful for the company or any of its subsidiaries to give financial assistance, directly or indirectly, for the purpose of reducing or discharging that liability.

Section 152 contains specific definitions of various expressions used in Chapter VI. Among those that are of relevance in understanding section 151, the first is the extremely wide meaning given to "financial assistance."[14] In addition to such obvious assistance as gifts, loans, guarantees, releases, waivers and indemnities,[15] it includes: any loan *or other* agreement under which the obligations of the company giving the assistance are to be fulfilled before the obligations of another party to the agreement[16], and the novation of a loan or of such other agreement; or the assignment of rights under it.[17] If the assistance is of one or more of those types listed in section 152(1)(*a*)(i), (ii) or (iii) it is irrelevant whether or not the net assets of the company are reduced by reason of the assistance.[18] However, paragraph (a) concludes with "(iv) any other financial assistance given by a company, the net assets[19] of which are thereby reduced to a material extent, or which has no net assets."[20] The effect of this is that, even if the financial assistance does not fall within the specific types that the draftsman, and those instructing him, were able to

---

[11] In contrast with the former s.54, which used the expression "purchase or subscription," the new section refers to "acquire" or "acquisition" thus extending the ambit of the section to non-cash subscriptions and exchanges.

[12] The sections do not apply to financial assistance by a holding company for the acquisition of shares in its subsidiary; in such a case there is less likelihood of prejudice to other shareholders or to creditors.

[13] Thus, if A lends B £1m to enable B to make a take-over of a company and C guarantees repayment, it will be unlawful for any financial assistance to be given by the company, when taken over, to A, B or C towards the repayment of the £1m.

[14] s.152(1)(*a*).

[15] Other than one in respect of liability resulting from the company's neglect or default, (*e.g.* the customary indemnity given to underwriters of a share issue): s.152(1)(*a*)(ii).

[16] *e.g.* where a company which is a diamond merchant sells a diamond to a dealer for £100,000, payment to be 12 months hence, the intention being that the dealer will sell the diamond at a profit or borrow on its security thus putting him in funds to acquire shares in the company.

[17] s.152(1)(*a*)(iii).

[18] In some cases, (*e.g.* gifts) they will be; in others, (*e.g.* loans or guarantees) they may or may not.

[19] Defined as "the aggregate of the company's assets, less the aggregate of its liabilities" and "liabilities" includes any provision for anticipated losses or charges: s.152(2).

[20] s.152(1)(*a*)(iv).

foresee, it will nevertheless be unlawful if the company has no net assets or if the consequence of the assistance is to reduce its net assets "to a material extent."

Clearly "materiality" is to be determined to some extent by the relationship between the value of the assistance and the value of the net assets; assistance worth £50 would reduce the net assets materially if they were only £100 but immaterially if they were £1m. But how far is that to be taken? A company with net assets of £1m might regard a reduction of £1m as immaterial, but it seems unlikely that judges (most of whom are not accustomed to disposing of £millions) would so regard it.

Assistance, however, will not be unlawful unless it is "financial."[21] Merely giving information (even financial information) is not financial assistance.[22]

The second definition in section 152 which is relevant to section 151(2) is to be found in section 152(3). It provides that a reference to a person incurring a liability includes

"his changing his financial position by making an agreement or arrangement (whether enforceable or unenforceable and whether made on his own account or with any other person[23]) or by any other means,"

and it adds that reference to a company giving financial assistance to reduce or discharge a liability incurred for the purposes of acquiring shares includes giving assistance for the purpose of wholly or partly restoring the financial position of the person concerned to what it was before the acquisition. This results in an enormous extension of the normal meaning of "liability" and seems to mean that before a company can give any financial assistance to *any* person (whether or not the acquirer) it must assess his overall financial position before and after the acquisition[24] and if, afterwards, it has deteriorated, must refrain from any form of financial assistance which is not covered by one of the exceptions—at any rate if there is a causal connection between the deterioration and the acquisition.

The exceptions

Section 153 provides a number of exceptions to the prohibitions. Those in subsections (3),[25] (4) and (5)[26] are more or less what one

---

21 The wording of s.152(1)(*a*) emphasises this.
22 But reimbursement of the costs of digesting and assessing the information could be.
23 The words "or with any other person" are somewhat puzzling; one would have expected "or that of any other person." Can there be an agreement or arrangement which is not made with some other person? And, if there can, would it not be covered by "or by any other means?"
24 The difficulty of doing this after a take-over is mind-boggling.
25 As amended by the I. Act 1986.
26 The F.S. Act 1986 added a new subs. (4)(*bb*) and a new subs. (5) extending the ambit of the exception relating to employees' share schemes.

would have expected. They include allotment of bonus shares, transactions under other sections of the Act in accordance with a court order and redemptions or purchases of shares in accordance with Part V, Chapter VII of the Act.[27] Also excepted are lending money in the ordinary course of business when lending is part of the company's ordinary business, and contributions to employees' share schemes and the like[28]; but, in the case of a public company, only if it has net assets[29] which are not thereby reduced or, to the extent that they are thereby reduced, if the assistance is provided out of distributable profits.[30] It should be noted, however, that also excluded is "a distribution[31] of a company's assets by way of dividend lawfully made or a distribution made in the course of a company's winding-up."[32] Hence, if those taking over a company, obtain control, they may be able lawfully to recoup the whole or part of the cost of doing so out of dividends paid by the company or by putting it into liquidation. But the dividends must be lawfully made in strict accordance with the rules in Part VIII of the Act and the provisions of the company's articles.[33]

The main change which section 153 makes to the former section 54 is to be found in section 153(1) and (2) intended to allay the fears aroused by the two decisions in 1980.[34] Subsection (1) says that section 151(1) does not prohibit a company from giving financial assistance if:

(a) the company's principal purpose in giving the assistance is not to give it for the purpose of acquisition of shares of the company or its holding company, or, if the giving of the assistance for that purpose is but an incidental part of some larger purpose of the company, and

(b) the assistance is given in good faith in the interests of the company.

Subsection (2) provides similarly that section 151(2) does not prohibit assistance given subsequently to the acquisition if:— (a) the principal

---

27 s.153(3).
28 s.153(4) and (5) (as amended by s.132 of the 1989 Act).
29 For this purpose (*cf.* s.152(2)) "net assets" means the amount by which the aggregate of the company's assets exceeds its liabilities, taking those amounts to be as stated in the company's accounting records, and "liabilities" includes provisions for expected liabilities or losses: s.154(2).
30 s.154(1). "Distributable profits," for the purposes of the Chapter is defined in s.152(1)(*b*) as "profits out of which the company could lawfully make a distribution equal in value to that assistance," including, if the assistance comprises a non-cash asset, any profit available for the purpose of a distribution in kind under s.276: see Chap. 10 at p. 256 below.
31 As defined in s.263(2): s.152(1)(*c*). On s.263(2) see below Chap. 10 at p. 244.
32 s.153(3)(*a*).
33 See below Chap. 10.
34 *Belmont Finance Corpn. v. Williams Furniture Ltd.* (No. 2) and *Armour Hick Northern Ltd. v. Whitehouse*: above p. 227, n. 10.

purpose is not to reduce or discharge any liability incurred for the purpose of acquiring such shares, or the reduction or discharge of any such liability is but an incidental part of some larger purpose of the company, and (b) the assistance is given in good faith in the interests of the company.

On the meaning of these difficult subsections[34a] we now have an authoritative ruling from the House of Lords in the case of *Brady* v. *Brady*,[35] a case remarkable both because of the extent of the judicial disagreement to which it gave rise and because it was ultimately decided on a ground not argued in the lower courts. It related to prosperous family businesses, principally concerned with haulage and soft drinks. The businesses were run and owned in equal shares by two brothers, Jack and Bob Brady, and their respective families, through a parent company, T. Brady & Co. Ltd. (Brady's), and a number of subsidiary and associated companies. Unfortunately Jack and Bob fell out, resulting in a complete deadlock. It was clear that unless something could be agreed amicably, Brady's would have to be wound-up—which was the last thing that anyone wanted. It was therefore agreed that the group should be re-organised, sole control of the haulage business being taken by Jack and that of the drinks business by Bob. As the respective values of the two businesses were not precisely equal, this involved various intra-group transfers of assets and shareholdings which became increasingly complicated as the negotiations proceeded. It suffices to say that, in the end, one of the companies had acquired shares in Brady's and the liability to pay for them thus incurred was to be discharged by a transfer to it of assets of Brady's. Bob, however, contended that further valuation adjustments were needed and refused to proceed further unless they were made. Jack then started proceedings for specific performance which Bob defended on various grounds which were ultimately reduced to two; (i) that the transfer would be *ultra vires*[36] and (ii) that it would be unlawful financial assistance under section 151. Only the second concerns us here.

It was conceded that the transfer of assets would be unlawful financial assistance under section 151(2) unless, in the circumstances,

---

[34a] Which hardly seem to be compatible with art. 23 of the Second Directive.

[35] [1989] A.C. 755, H.L. This case is an illustration (of which *Charterhouse Investment Trust* v. *Tempest Diesels Ltd.* [1987] BCLC 1, is another) of how, all-too-often, parties agree in principle to a simple arrangement which on the face of it raises no question of unlawful financial assistance but then refer it to their respective advisers who, in their anxiety to obtain the maximum fiscal and other advantages for their respective clients, introduce complicated refinements which arguably cause it to fall foul of s.151. In the *Charterhouse* case, where the former s.54 applied, Hoffmann J., by exercising commonsense in interpreting the meaning of "financial assistance," was able to avoid striking down an obviously unobjectionable arrangement. But the elaborate definition of that expression in the present s.152 leaves less scope for commonsense.

[36] The case has been cited in the previous chapter in relation to *ultra vires* (at p. 169 n. 19) but has now been overtaken by the reforms in the Companies Act 1989. With one exception all the judges held the transaction not to be *ultra vires*.

that was disapplied by section 153(2). On the face of it one might have thought that the circumstances afforded a classic illustration of the sort of situation that section 153(1) or (2) was intended to legitimate. And, at first instance, that view prevailed. In the Court of Appeal,[37] however, while all three judges thought that the conditions of paragraph (a), relating to "purpose," were satisfied, the majority thought that those of paragraph (b), relating to "good faith in the interests of the company," were not. In contrast, in the House of Lords[38] it was held unanimously that paragraph (b) was complied with but that (a) was not. Hence the contemplated transfer would be unlawful financial assistance if carried out in the way proposed.

Lord Oliver, in a speech concurred in by the other Law Lords, subjected the wording of paragraph (a) to detailed analysis.[39] He pointed out that "purpose" had to be distinguished from "reason," or "motive" (which would almost always be different and wider) and that paragraph (a) contemplated alternative situations. The first is where the company has a principal and a subsidiary purpose; the question then is whether the principal purpose is to assist or relieve the acquirer or is for some other corporate purpose. The second situation is where the financial assistance is not for any purpose other than to help the acquirer but is merely incidental to some larger corporate purpose. As regards the first alternative, he accepted that an example might be where the principal purpose was to enable the company to obtain from the person assisted a supply of some product which the company needed for its business.[40] As regards the second, he offered no example, merely saying that he had:

"not found the concept of 'larger purpose' easy to grasp" but that "if the paragraph is to be given any meaning that does not provide a blank cheque for avoiding the effective application of section 151 in every case, the concept must be narrower than that for which the appellants contend."[41]

The trial judge, and O'Connor L.J. in the Court of Appeal,[42] had thought that the larger purpose was to resolve the deadlock and its inevitable consequences and Croom-Johnson L.J.[43] had found it in the need to reorganise the whole group. But if either could be so regarded, it would follow that, if the board of a company concluded

37 [1988] BCLC 20, C.A.
38 [1989] A.C. 755, H.L.
39 [1989] A.C. at pp. 778, *et seq.* Agreeing with O'Connor L.J. in the C.A. ([1988] BCLC at 25) he described the paragraph, with commendable restraint, as "not altogether easy to construe."
40 A situation envisaged by Buckley L.J. in his judgment in the *Belmont Finance* case [1980] 1 All E.R. at 402, as giving rise to doubts under the former s.54.
41 At p. 779.
42 [1988] BCLC at p. 26.
43 *Ibid.* at p. 32.

in good faith that the only way that a company could survive was for it to be taken-over, it could lawfully provide financial assistance to the bidder—the very mischief that the legislation was designed to prevent.

The logic is, of course, impeccable and the House of Lords is infallible. But the result seems to reduce section 153(1) and (2) to very narrow limits indeed and to make one wonder whether the midnight-oil burnt on the drafting of the two subsections has achieved anything worthwhile.

Having reached the foregoing conclusion "with a measure of regret"[44] the House gave permission for Jack to raise further points of law not argued in either of the courts below.

The successful argument on these proceeded as follows: When an arrangement can be implemented in alternative ways, one lawful and one unlawful, it is to be presumed that the parties intend it to be carried out in the lawful manner unless it is clear that they have agreed on the other. There was nothing in the terms of the arrangement which prevented its being implemented perfectly lawfully under the relaxation for private companies to which we turn next. Brady's (and each of the other companies involved) was a private company with ample distributable profits and thus able lawfully to effect the arrangement under the relaxed regime for private companies.[44a] Hence, upon obtaining an undertaking to comply strictly with the terms of the sections 155 to 158 it was declared that the proposed transaction was not unlawful.[45] Having regard to the wealth of legal and accountancy talent available to the parties, it seems almost incredible that this course had not occurred to anyone earlier.[46]

Relaxation for private companies

While the Second Company Law Directive curtailed our freedom in relation to public companies, it did not in relation to private companies and, therefore, as in the case of purchase of shares, it was possible for us to adopt a more relaxed regime for them based on that suggested by the Jenkins Committee.[47] This was done by what

[44] [1989] A.C. at p. 781.
[44a] In a later case, *Plant v. Steiner* [1989] 5 B.C.C. 352, the parties failed to establish the "wider purpose" exception and were not able to take advantage of the private company relaxation.
[45] *Ibid.* at pp. 782, *et seq.*
[46] It seems to suggest that the professions are still not as familiar with the relevant provisions introduced in 1981 as they ought to be and perhaps justifies what readers may regard as the overlong treatment here. It was suggested by Lord Oliver that in fact the explanation was not ignorance of the law but a misunderstanding of the facts, it having been thought that "the transfers alleged to infringe the section had already taken place rather than being ... still uncompleted": at p. 782. But why then did Jack sue for specific performance?
[47] See p. 227 above.

are now sections 155–158. While sections 152–153, dealt with above, apply to private companies, the prohibitions in section 151 do not if a private company is able to proceed instead under sections 155–158.

These sections maintain the basic principle that "financial assistance may only be given if the company has net assets, which are not thereby reduced or, to the extent that they are reduced, if the assistance is provided out of distributable profits."[48] There is also a restriction on the use of the sections by subsidiary private companies in a group with public companies.[49] Subject to that, however, the conditions are not unduly onerous—though somewhat time-consuming.

The first step is for the directors of the company and, where the assistance is for the acquisition of shares in its holding company, the directors of the holding company and any intermediate holding company, to make statutory declarations (similar to those required when private companies seek to redeem or purchase their shares out of capital[50]) complying with section 156.[51] Under the latter section these declarations must identify the person to whom the assistance is to be given[52] and must state that, in the directors' opinion, immediately following the assistance there will be no grounds on which the company could then be found unable to pay its debts; and either

(a) if it is intended to commence the winding-up of the company within 12 months of the assistance, that it will be able to pay its debts in full within 12 months of the commencement, or

(b) in any other case, that the company will be able, during the year following the assistance, to pay its debts as they fall due.[53]

Each declaration must have annexed to it a report of the company's auditors stating that they have enquired into the state of affairs of the company and that they are not aware of anything to indicate that the directors' opinion is unreasonable in the circumstances.[54]

[48] s.155(2). "Net assets" are as defined in s.154(2) and "distributable profits" as defined in s.152(1)(b), above.
[49] s.155(3). This is intended to prevent the relaxation being abused by indirectly enabling public companies to avail themselves of it.
[50] See pp. 221–224 above.
[51] s.155(6).
[52] s.156(1).
[53] s.156(2). They are required to take into account actual, contingent and prospective liabilities like a court determining whether a company should be wound up on the ground that it is unable to pay its debts: s.156(3) as amended by the Insolvency Act 1986.
[54] s.156(4). *British & Commonwealth Holdings v. Quadrex Holdings* [1989] Q.B. 942 C.A., illustrates how delays in obtaining the declaration and report may wreck a corporate reorganisation scheme.

The second step is to secure the approval of the assistance by a special resolution (or written resolution under section 381A) of the company proposing to give it.[55] This can be dispensed with if the company is a wholly-owned subsidiary[56] (when it could serve no purpose[57]) but, if the shares to be acquired are of its holding company, the latter and any intermediate holding company (other than a wholly-owned subsidiary) must also approve by special (or written) resolution.[58] These special resolutions must be passed on, or within a week of, the day on which the directors made the statutory declarations,[59] and are not effective unless the declarations and auditors' reports are available for inspection by members at the meetings.[60]

The third step is to deliver to the Registrar a copy of each statutory declaration and annexed auditors' report. This has to be done within 15 days of the declaration and, if a special (or written) resolution of that company is required,[61] must be accompanied by a copy of the resolution which, like any other special (or section 381A) resolution, has to be delivered to the Registrar under section 380.[62]

Where any special (or section 381A) resolution was needed, the approved financial assistance must not be given before the expiration of four weeks beginning with the date on which the resolution was passed or, if more than one was passed, the date on which the last of them was passed, unless each member entitled to vote at general meetings voted in favour.[63] This is to provide time for members who did not consent or vote in favour to apply to the court to cancel the resolution under section 157.[64] If there is an application under that section the financial assistance must not be given before the final determination of that application unless the court otherwise directs.[65] Nor, unless there is such an application and the court otherwise directs, may it be given after the expiration of eight weeks from the time when the directors of the company proposing to give the assistance made their statutory declaration or, where declarations were made by the directors both of that company and of any of its holding companies, after the expiration of eight weeks from the date

55 s.155(4).
56 *Ibid.*
57 See the definition of "wholly owned subsidiary" in s.736(6) as substituted by the 1989 Act.
58 s.155(5).
59 s.157(1).
60 s.157(4)(a). For adaptations when a written resolution is used under s.381A, see Sched. 15A, Para. 4.
61 A special (or written) resolution of at least one company will be required unless the financial assistance is to be given by a wholly-owned subsidiary for the acquisition of its own shares (which the holding company will be able to stop if it wants to).
62 s.156(5).
63 s.158(2).
64 See below.
65 s.158(3).

of the earliest declaration.[66] This is to prevent the assistance being given so long after the statutory declaration and auditors' report that they can no longer be relied on. If no resolution was needed, or if all members voted in favour, the assistance may be given immediately after the delivery to the Registrar of the statutory declaration and auditors' report but must not be given after the expiration of the eight week period, unless the court otherwise orders.[67]

Under section 157, which corresponds to sections 176 and 177 in relation to redemption or purchase by a private company out of capital (except that it protects only members and not creditors[68]) an application may be made to the court for the cancellation of the resolution:

(a) by the holders of not less in the aggregate than 10 per cent. in nominal value of the company's issued share capital or any class of it, or

(b) if the company is not limited by shares,[69] by not less than 10 per cent. of the company's members.

But it cannot be made by any member who has consented to, or voted in favour of, the resolution.[70] The court must either confirm or cancel the resolution, in either event being afforded the widest powers comparable to those under section 177.[71]

Civil remedies for breach of the prohibition

The only sanctions prescribed by the Act for breaches of section 151 are, fining the company[72] and fining or imprisoning, (or both) its officers in default.[73] But more important are the consequences in civil law resulting from the fact that the transaction is unlawful. Unfortunately precisely what these consequences are has vexed the courts both of England and of other countries which have adopted comparable provisions[74] and it is a pity that the 1981 Act did not

---

[66] s.158(4).
[67] This is the effect of s.158(2) and (4).
[68] Creditors are protected by ss.155(1) and 156, above.
[69] The company whose shares are to be acquired will be a company limited by shares but a subsidiary giving financial assistance for the purchase of shares of its holding company might be limited by guarantee.
[70] s.157(2).
[71] s.157(3) which, unlike s.177, does not set out these powers but incorporates them by applying s.54(3)–(10) relating to applications to cancel a resolution converting a public to a private company (on which see Chap. 11 p. 290 below).
[72] Since s.151 is intended to protect the company and its members and creditors it is difficult to conceive of a more inappropriate sanction than to reduce the company's net assets (still further than the unlawful financial assistance may have done) by fining the company.
[73] s.151(3). See also s.156(7) making directors liable to fines for making statutory declarations without having reasonable grounds for the opinions expressed.
[74] For a valuable account of the Australian and New Zealand decisions see Farrar: *Company Law* (3rd ed., 1991) at pp. 198–200.

attempt to clarify the position as, to some extent, the 1989 Act did in relation to acts by the board of directors in excess of the company's objects or the board's powers.[75]

What has caused the curious wording of section 151 and its predecessors. Since somewhat curious wording of section 151 and its predecessors. Since the object of the section is to protect the company and its members and creditors, one would have expected it to say that it is not lawful for any person who is acquiring or proposing to acquire shares of a company to receive financial assistance from the company or any of its subsidiaries; that would have pointed the courts in the right direction to work out the consequences. But instead the courts in the right direction to work out the consequences. But instead it declares that it is unlawful for the company to give the assistance, and follows that by imposing criminal sanctions on the company and (the one thing that makes good sense) on the officers of the company who are in default. This could be taken to imply (and was so taken by Roxburgh J. in *Victor Battery Co. Ltd. v. Curry's Ltd.*[76]) that the object was not to protect the company but to punish it and its officers by imposing fines (the maximum then being only £100!). This calamitous decision continued to be accepted in England, and was cited with apparent approval by Cross J. (subsequently a Law Lord) 20 years later,[77] though rejected by the Australian Courts whose decisions helped those in England eventually to see the light. The decision has now been disapproved or not followed in a series of cases[78] and is accepted to be heretical.

Freed from the fetters of that heresy the courts have since given the section real teeth and it is submitted that the following propositions can now be regarded as reasonably well established:

(a) *An agreement to provide unlawful financial assistance being unlawful is unenforceable by either party to it.* This proposition is undoubted and infallible authority for it is the decision of the House of Lords in *Brady v. Brady.*[79]

(b) *However, the illegality of the financial assistance given or provided by the company normally does not taint other connected transactions,* such as the agreement by the person assisted to acquire the shares; it would be absurd if, for example, a take-over bidder who has been given financial assistance by the company, or by a subsidiary of the company, could escape from the liability to perform

---

[75] See Chap. 8, above. Under s.277, a shareholder who has received a distribution paid in contravention of Part VIII of the Act (Chap. 10 below) is liable to repay it if he knew or had reasonable grounds for believing that it was paid in contravention of that Part but that section expressly does not apply to financial assistance in contravention of s.151 or in respect of redemption or purchase: see s.277(2).

[76] [1946] Ch. 242.

[77] *Curtis's Furnishing Stores Ltd. v. Freedman* [1966] 1 W.L.R. 1219. But he ignored it in *S. Western Mineral Water Co. Ltd. v. Ashmore* [1967] 1 W.L.R. 1110.

[78] *Selangor United Rubber Estate Ltd. v. Cradock (No. 3)* [1968] 1 W.L.R. 1555; *Heald v. O'Connor* [1971] 1 W.L.R. 497; and Lord Denning M.R. in *Wallersteiner v. Moir* [1974] 1 W.L.R. at 1014H–1015A.

[79] Above.

purchase contracts which he has entered into with the shareholders. Clearly he cannot.

(c) *This, however, may be subject to a qualification if the obligation to acquire the shares and the obligation to provide financial assistance form part of a single composite transaction.* The obvious example of this would be an arrangement in which someone agreed to subscribe for shares in a company (or its holding company) in consideration of which the company agreed to give him some form of financial assistance. In such a case the position apparently depends on whether the terms relating to the acquisition of shares can be severed from those relating to the unlawful financial assistance. If they can, those relating to the acquisition can be enforced. If they cannot, the whole agreement is void.

The authorities supporting this proposition are the decisions of Cross J. in *South Western Mineral Water Co. Ltd. v. Ashmore*[80] and of the Privy Council in *Carney v. Herbert*.[81] In essence the facts of both were that shares of a company were to be acquired and payment of the purchase price was to be secured by a charge on the assets of, in the former case, that company and, in the latter, its subsidiary. The agreed security was, of course, unlawful financial assistance. In the former case, the shares had not been transferred or the charge executed; in the latter, they had. In the former it was held that unless the sellers were prepared to dispense with the charge (which they were not) the whole agreement was void and that the parties must be restored to their positions prior to the agreement. In the latter it was held that the unlawful charge could be severed from the sale of the shares and that the sellers were entitled to sue the purchaser for the price. Despite the different results, the Privy Council judgment, delivered by Lord Brightman, cited with approval the decision of Cross J. in the earlier case. In both cases a fair result seems to have been arrived at and certainly one preferable to that for which the assisted share-purchaser contended in *Carney*, namely that he should be entitled to retain the shares without having to pay for them.[82] It is therefore to be hoped that even in a single composite transaction the courts will permit severance or order *restitutio in integrum* unless there are strong reasons of public policy[83] why the whole transaction should be treated as so unlawful as to preclude the court from offering any assistance to any party to it.

(d) *If the company has actually given the unlawful financial assistance, that transaction will be void.* The practical effect of that depends on the nature of the financial assistance. If it is a mortgage,

80 [1967] 1 W.L.R. 1110.
81 [1985] A.C. 301, P.C., on appeal from the Sup. Ct. of N.S.W.
82 Yet Lord Brightman seemed to think that this would be the consequence if severance was not possible: see [1985] A.C. at 309.
83 In support of this caveat, see [1985] A.C. at pp. 313 and 317.

guarantee or indemnity of the like, the party to whom it was given cannot sue the company upon it.[84] It is he who suffers,[85] and the company, so long as it realises in time that the transaction is void, need do nothing but defend any hopeless action that may be brought against it. If, however, the unlawful assistance was a completed gift or loan, the company will need to take action if it is to recover what it has lost. And a long line of cases has established that, in most circumstances, this it will be able to do.[86]

Its claim may be based on misfeasance, when recovery is sought from the directors or other officers of the company, or on restitution, conspiracy,[87] or constructive trust, when the claim is against them or those to whom the unlawful assistance has passed or who have otherwise actively participated in the unlawful transaction. The most popular basis seems to be constructive trust[88]; the argument being that the directors committed the equivalent of a breach of trust when they caused the company's assets to be used for the unlawful purpose and the recipients became constructive trustees thereof.

What is still not wholly clear is precisely what degree of fault has to be established if claims on any of the grounds are to succeed. The earlier decisions held that the company's officers would be liable on a misfeasance claim even though they had no idea that the transaction was unlawful,[89] and that other participants would be liable if they had knowledge, actual or constructive, which should have led them to realise that they were taking part in an unlawful or dishonest activity.[90] The more recent decisions suggest that (as seems to be the case with participants in acts of the directors in excess of the

84 See the cases discussed under (c) and *Heald* v. *O'Connor* [1971] 1 W.L.R. 497, where the unlawful assistance was a mortgage on the property of the company whose shares were being acquired, the purchaser guaranteeing the payment of sums due under the mortgage. The mortgage was unlawful. Hence the purchaser escaped liability on the guarantee (though that was lawful) since no payments were lawfully due under the mortgage. It would have been different had the guarantee been an indemnity.

85 Since the mortgage is illegal and void (not merely voidable) presumably a bona fide purchaser of it without notice could not enforce it either.

86 *Steen* v. *Law* [1964] A.C. 287, P.C.; *Selangor United Rubber Estates* v. *Cradock* (No. 3) [1968] 1 W.L.R. 1555; *Karak Rubber Co.* v. *Burden* (No. 2) [1972] 1 W.L.R. 602; *Wallersteiner* v. *Moir* [1974] 1 W.L.R. 991, C.A.; *Belmont Finance Corp.* v. *Williams Furniture Ltd.* (No. 2) [1980] 1 All E.R. 393, C.A.; *Smith* v. *Croft* (No. 2) [1988] Ch. 114; *Agip* (Africa) *Ltd.* v. *Jackson* [1991] Ch. 547, C.A.

87 The state of confusion arising from conflicting views on whether there are still two alternative grounds of civil liability for conspiracy, *i.e.* (i) employment of unlawful means or (ii) a predominate purpose to injure the plaintiff (the traditional view) or only one, (*i.e.* (ii), (see *Metall und Rohstoff A.G.* v. *Donaldson Lufkin & Jenrette Inc.* [1990] 1 Q.B. 391, C.A.; and *Derby & Co.* v. *Weldon* (No. 5) [1989] 1 W.L.R. 1244) has now been resolved by the H.L. in *Lonrho plc* v. *Al Fayed* [1991] 3 W.L.R. 188, H.L. in favour of the traditional view.

88 Which may enable the company to "trace" the assets of which it has been deprived.

89 "[W]here directors have used their directorial powers to part with moneys of their company in a manner or for a purpose which the law forbids, it is not a defence ... to plead merely that they acted in ignorance of the law." *Steen* v. *Law*, above, at p. 300.

90 See the *Cradock* and *Burden* cases: n. 86 above.

company's powers[91]) the essential condition for liability is bad faith. And, notwithstanding *Steen v. Law*, it may be that the same test should apply in an action against officers based on misfeasance. An officer commits an offence under section 151 only if he is "in default,"[92] *i.e.* when he "knowingly and wilfully authorises … the contravention."[93] Even if that is established, the court may relieve him of civil liability if he has acted honestly and reasonably and ought fairly to be excused.[94] The probability is that an officer who has acted in good faith will not be "in default" (and, even if he is, he may be excused).

(e) *In the light of propositions (a)–(d) it would also seem to follow that if the unlawful assistance given by the company is a loan secured by a mortgage or charge on the borrower's property*[95] *then, so long as the company has rights of recovery from the borrower under proposition (d), it should be able to do so by realising its security.* This would certainly be so if the mortgage or charge could be severed from the unlawful loan—which, however, might be regarded as impossible since the consideration given for the mortgage or charge *was* the unlawful loan. But, since the effect of the recent case law is to recognise that the object of section 151, despite its wording, is to protect the company, the courts ought not to boggle at the conclusion that the security given to the company can be realised to recover what is due to it by the borrower.

It will therefore be seen that we have come a long way from the time when it was believed that the only likely sanctions were derisory fines on the company and its officers in default. These developments have caused the banking community some alarm, for there is no doubt that banks could find themselves caught out—as indeed they have been in the past.[96] The fact that money passing in the relevant transactions is likely to do so through banking channels inevitably exposes banks to risks.[97] But, if the above propositions are correct, these risks will generally be avoided so long as banks (or, in practice,

[91] See Chap. 8, pp. 192, 193 above. In principle it seems that the two situations should be treated alike; they are distinguishable only in that breach of s.151 is a criminal offence, while the other, without more, is not.
[92] s.151(3).
[93] s.730(5).
[94] s.727(1).
[95] Unless the company is a public company and the charge is on shares in it, for then the charge may be void under s.150: see below.
[96] See, *e.g.* the *Cradock* and *Burden* cases, above.
[97] But they are afforded special protection since section 151 does not invalidate a loan: "where the lending of money is part of the ordinary business of the company", and the loan is "in the ordinary course of its business": s.153(4). This, as interpreted in *Steen v. Law* above, only avails banks and similar "moneylending" institutions (and then only if the transaction is in the ordinary course of that business). It does not avail a company which may incidentally lend money and may be expressly empowered to do so in its objects clause. But it recognises that it would be absurd if, on a public issue of shares by one of the major High Street banks, its branches had to refuse to honour applicants' cheques if they were customers who had been granted overdrafts.

their managers) act in good faith—or do not behave with such naivety and gullibility that a court cannot accept that they have so acted. Apart from that, perhaps the greatest risk they run is that they may innocently lend money on the security of a debenture with a charge on a company's property, which, unbeknown to the bank, was issued by the company to enable the borrower to raise finance for the purpose of acquiring its shares or those of its holding company and which is therefore unlawful and void. But that is no more than the risk, which any lender faces, that there may be a defect in the borrower's title to the property offered as security.

Charges to a company on its shares

If, except as above, a company cannot purchase its own shares, one might have supposed that equally it cannot take a mortgage or charge on such shares. This, however, was not the view taken by the English courts and it was not uncommon for articles of association to provide that the company should have a lien on its shares, not only in respect of any money due in payment for the shares but for any sums due to the company from shareholders in any capacity.[98] However, the Second Company Law Directive took a different view which was implemented by the 1980 Act—though in relation to public companies only. The relevant section (now section 150 of the 1985 Act) provides that a lien or other charge on its own shares is void[99] unless:

(i) the shares are not fully paid and the charge is for any amount payable in respect of the shares,[1] or

(ii) the company's ordinary business includes the lending of money, providing credit or the bailment of goods under a hire-purchase agreement

and the charge arises in connection with a transaction entered into in the ordinary course of its business.[2]

The position of private companies remains unchanged.

CONCLUSION

This discussion of the raising and maintaining of capital is logically incomplete without a discussion of the extent to which a company can distribute its assets to its members by way of dividend; for much of what has gone before is an essential prelude to that. But this chapter

[98] If, however, the shares were to be listed on The Stock Exchange the latter would not permit that.
[99] s.150(1).
[1] s.150(2).
[2] s.150(3). This protects hire purchase finance companies.

is already over-long and it seems better to postpone that to the next chapter.[3] But one concluding observation:

It will have been apparent from the foregoing pages that what makes the concept of share capital unnecessarily complicated and confusing is the insistence that shares shall be given a fixed nominal value and that the amount of the company's share capital shall be determined exclusively by that nominal value. The nominal value of a share need not bear any relationship to its true value even at the time of its issue and is most unlikely to do so after the company has been trading for some time. Nor, does the nominal value of issued share capital provide the yardstick for determining whether the company can lawfully make a distribution to its members. When shares have been issued at a premium that will depend on the amount of the issued share capital plus its share premium account and, when shares have been redeemed or repurchased, on the aggregate amount of its issued share capital plus its share premium account plus its capital redemption reserve.

All this could be avoided if, like some countries (notably the USA and Canada) we permitted the issue of no-par-value shares. In 1954 the Gedge Committee recommended the legalisation of no-par equity shares[4] and in 1962 the Jenkins Committee[5] recommended it in respect of any class of shares. An attempt was made to introduce legislative provisions to that effect in what became the 1967 Act; but without success. And there is now little likelihood of their being introduced since nominal par values are required under the EC Directives. This is regrettable; particularly so in the light of the Government's efforts to increase individual share ownership, for no-par would render the true position more readily intelligible to unsophisticated investors and protect them from being misled.[6] There would, however, be little point in introducing them unless they were made compulsory.[7] If par and no-par existed side-by-side, confusion would be worse confounded and the unscrupulous would continue to adopt par shares when they wished to mislead.

---

[3] The Act goes still further by postponing it from Part V to Part VIII.
[4] Cmd. 9112. The Committee had been appointed to consider this one topic.
[5] Cmnd. 1749, para. 32–34.
[6] *e.g.* (as in an actual case) by describing shares as 9¹/₂ per cent. £1 Preference Shares and issuing them to the public at £1.25, (with the result that the true rate of dividend on the price paid was only 7.6 per cent. and, on a winding-up or the return of capital, only £1 per share was repayable).
[7] As in the Ghana Companies Code 1963 (Act 179) s.40.

CHAPTER 10

CAPITAL AND DIVIDENDS

THE elaborate rules dealt with in the previous chapter would achieve their primary purpose only if they controlled the extent to which any return of the company's assets could be made to its members. As that chapter should have shown, this they do if the return is of capital not only when that is by a formal reduction of capital approved by the court but also when it is by a redemption or purchase by the company of its shares or by the company giving financial assistance for the subscription or purchase of its shares. But a far more common type of distribution to shareholders is in the form of periodical dividends. It defeats the purpose of the capital maintenance rules if dividends can be paid despite the fact that the value of the net assets of the company is, or would become as a result of the payment, less than the value of the capital yardstick of issued share capital plus share premium account (if any) plus capital redemption reserve (if any).

PRE-1981 POSITION

Nevertheless under the largely judge-made law prevailing prior to the 1980 Act that was not prevented. True, the courts declared that dividends must not be paid out of capital. But that was meaningless; "capital" as an item in the company's accounts exists only as a notional liability and nothing can be paid out of a liability—actual or notional. More meaningfully, they declared that dividends could be paid only out of profits; but then discovered that "profits" was an elusive and baffling concept better left to accountants and businessmen.

Unfortunately, however, when litigation ensued it had to be decided by lawyers after listening to the expert evidence of accountants. The result was often one which baffled lawyers, accountants and businessmen alike.

What the courts seem to have decided can be briefly summarised as follows:

(a) So long as the properly presented accounts of the company showed a trading profit for the accounting period (normally a year) that could be distributed by way of dividend without regard to losses made in previous years; in other words "nimble dividends," as the Americans describe payments in such circumstances, were permissible.

(b) A realised profit made on the sale of a fixed asset[1] could also be so distributed and, according to the English courts[2] (but not the Scottish[3]) so could an unrealised profit on a revaluation of fixed assets.

(c) Accumulated profits of previous years could also be so distributed unless they had been capitalised by a bonus issue or transfer to the capital redemption reserve.

Had companies taken full advantage of these rules (which fortunately most public companies did not) it would have made nonsense of the whole capital concept. Happily, the Second Company Law Directive made it incumbent on us to tighten up our rules—at any rate in relation to public companies[4]—and this the 1980 Act did in relation to both public and private companies but to a greater extent as regards public ones. The resulting legislative provisions, as amended by the 1981 Act, are now to be found in Part VIII of the 1985 Act.[5]

PRESENT POSITION

Part VIII starts with section 263 which applies to companies whether public or private and to any distribution of its assets to its members, whether in cash or otherwise, except[6]

(a) an issue of shares as fully or partly paid bonus shares,
(b) redemption or purchase of a company's own shares in accordance with Chapter VII of Part V of the Act,[7]
(c) a formal reduction of capital, and
(d) a distribution of assets on a winding-up.

And it declares that a company shall not make a distribution not so excluded except "out of profits available for the purpose."[8] It then defines "profits available for the purpose" as the company's

---

[1] *i.e.* its land, buildings, plant, office furniture, etc., as opposed to current assets turned over in the course of its trade.
[2] *Dimbula Valley (Ceylon) Tea Company v. Laurie* [1961] Ch. 353, not following the Scottish decision cited in n. 3.
[3] *Westburn Sugar Refineries v. I.R.C.* 1960 S.L.T. 297; [1960] T.R. 105. Both the English and the Scottish courts accepted that such profits could be used to pay-up a bonus issue. Buckley J. in *Dimbula* did not see how that could be possible unless the profits were distributable by way of dividend.
[4] It enunciated the basic principle that "No distribution to shareholders may be made when ... the net assets are, or following such distribution would become, lower than the amount of the subscribed capital plus those reserves which may not be distributed under the law or the statutes", (art. 15.1(*a*)) and prescribed detailed rules to give effect to that principle.
[5] *i.e.* ss.263–281 (as amended by the 1989 Act).
[6] s.263(2)(*a*), (*b*), (*c*) and (*d*).
[7] On which see Chap. 9 above.
[8] s.263(1).

"accumulated realised profits, so far as not previously utilised by distribution or capitalisation, less its accumulated, realised losses, so far as not previously written off in a reduction or reorganisation of capital duly made."[9] This results in two fundamental changes of the three rules summarised above.[10]

First, no longer may "nimble dividends" be paid out of profits for the year, ignoring losses for previous years; there must be a surplus of profits for the current and past years (so far as they are retained) over losses for those years (so far as they have not been lawfully written off). Secondly, the profits must be realised; although unrealised profits can be applied to pay up a bonus issue,[11] they no longer be used to pay a dividend.[12]

It will be observed that, for the purpose of section 263, no distinction is drawn between revenue (trading) profits and capital profits. Such a distinction is relevant only in the case of "investment companies,"[13] or when the company's articles restrict dividends to payments out of revenue profits only.[14] The sole test for the purposes of section 263, applicable to both public and private companies, is whether there are accumulated realised profits net of accumulated realised losses.

The main difficulty about this is precisely how one determines whether at a particular date there are realised profits or losses and in the Act's attempt to define those terms for the purposes of the accounting provisions in Part VII there is a note of frustrated desperation.[15] Nor have prolonged efforts successfully ensured that the profits or losses shown are adjusted to take account of inflation.[16] A further difficulty is that annual accounts for years prior to 1981 did not necessarily have to distinguish between realised and unrealised profits or losses. This, however, is dealt with by subsection (5) of section 263 which says that if the directors after making all reasonable

9 s.263(3). This is "subject to the provision made by sections 265 and 266 for investment and other companies" on which see below pp. 247–250.

10 At p. 243–244.

11 This being excepted by s.263(2)(a) above. But unrealised profits cannot be used to pay up amounts unpaid on issued shares for this would conflict with the policy of ss.98 and 99 (see Chap. 9 pp. 202, 203 above and is not a payment from 'sums available for this purpose" within the meaning of s.99(4); nor can they be used to pay up debentures (s.263(4)) which, though it would not be a distribution to members as such, would be even more objectionable: s.263(4).

12 *i.e. Westburn* is adopted rather than *Dimbula*: see nn. 2 and 3 above.

13 See ss.265 and 266: below pp. 247–250.

14 s.281 expressly recognises that the memo. and arts. may restrict, though they cannot widen, the sums out of which, or the cases in which, a distribution may be made.

15 s.262(3) (as inserted by the 1989 Act) says: "References in this Part to 'realised profits,' and 'realised losses,' in relation to a company's accounts, are to such profits or losses of the company as fall to be treated as realised for the purpose of those accounts in accordance with principles generally accepted as at the time when the accounts are prepared, with respect to the determination for accounting purposes of realised profits or losses," *i.e.* the legislature, as the judges had done, tries to leave it to the accountants. But the subs. goes on to recognise that in some cases the Act makes specific provision, to which the foregoing is "without prejudice."

16 The optional "alternative accounting rules" referred to in Chap. 17 at p. 458, do not go so far in that direction.

enquiries are unable to determine whether a particular profit or loss made before December 22, 1980 was realised or not they may treat the profit as realised or the loss as unrealised,[17] thus giving the company the benefit of the doubt.

As a result of section 263, the law, in relation to both public and private companies, now goes much of the way towards adopting the basic principle prescribed for public companies by the Second Directive. But it does not go all the way; it would still permit a public company to pay a dividend notwithstanding that its net assets are, or will be as a result of the payment, worth less than the amount of the issued share capital and undistributable reserves. Hence, in relation to public companies, we had to go further.

Public companies

The necessary extension is made by section 264. This provides that a public company may not make a distribution at any time unless, in addition to compliance with section 263, the amount of its net assets is not less than its called up share capital and undistributable reserves and would not become less as a result of the distribution.[18] For this purpose "net assets" means the aggregate of the company's assets,[19] less the aggregate of its liabilities and, although "liabilities" means real liabilities (and not notional ones like "free reserves") it includes "provisions" within the meaning of paragraph 89[20] of Schedule 4.[21] Moreover "undistributable reserves" includes not only those which companies are prohibited by the Act from distributing, *i.e.* (a) share premium account and (b) capital redemption reserve (which, as we saw in the previous chapter, are treated for most purposes as share capital) but also:

"(c) the amount by which the company's accumulated unrealised profits, so far as not previously utilised by capitalisation,[22] … exceed its accumulated unrealised losses (so far as not previously written off in a reduction or reorganisation of capital duly made) and

(d) any other reserve which the company is prohibited from distributing by any other enactment (other than one contained in this Part) or by its memorandum or articles."[23]

---

[17] This is an example of a specific provision to which s.262(3) is "without prejudice": see above n. 15. Other examples are in ss.268(1), 269, 275 and 276: see below.
[18] s.164(1). This, like s.263 (see n. 13 above) is subject to the modifications in ss.265 and 266 in relation to "investment companies."
[19] Not including uncalled share capital: s.264(4).
[20] *i.e.* "any amount retained as reasonably necessary for the purpose of providing for any liability or loss which is either likely to be incurred or certain to be incurred but uncertain as to amount or as to the date on which it will arise."
[21] s.264(2).
[22] Except by a post-1980 transfer to capital redemption reserve and thus falling under (b).
[23] s.264(3).

Reserves of class (c) and (d) differ from (a) and (b) dealt with in the previous chapter, (*i.e.* share premium account and capital redemption reserve) in that they cannot be reduced except by a formal reduction of capital or by their being converted into issued share capital by a bonus issue. Nevertheless for the purpose of the capital yardstick measuring the extent to which the company can make distributions to members, they have, while they remain, to be treated as constituents of that yardstick.

Class (c) reserves would include the so-called "revaluation reserve" which companies, under the accounts rules in Schedule 4,[24] may have to set up when there is a revaluation of fixed assets.[25] An amount may be transferred from that reserve (i) to the profit and loss account, if previously charged to that account or it represents realised profits or (ii) on capitalisation by a bonus issue. The reserve is then reduced to the extent that the amounts transferred to it are no longer needed for the purposes of the valuation method used; but except to that extent it is an irreducible reserve.[26]

Class (d) reserves include those which banks and similar financial institutions under legislation relating to them, may be required to maintain and those that a company may be required to establish by a provision in its memorandum or articles. The extent to which such reserves can be reduced will then depend on the provisions of the enactment or memorandum and articles as the case may be.

Investment companies

The rules in sections 263 and 264 are modified by section 265 in relation to "investment companies" (as defined in section 266) which meet certain conditions. Basically, an investment company is one, the business of which "consists of investing its funds mainly in securities with the aim of spreading investment risk and giving members of the company the benefit of the results of the management of its funds."[27] Today this aim is largely met by unit trusts so far as small investors are concerned. At present, unit trusts established in the United

24 Sched. 4 para. 34, as amended by 1989 Act, Sched. 1 para. 6.
25 On which see further s.275 and pp. 255, 256 below.
26 Sched. 4, para. 34(3)(3A) and (3B).
27 s.266(2)(*a*). They are generally known as investment trust companies but "trust" is a misnomer and the result of an historical accident. Such collective investment schemes were established in the U.K. though the medium of the trust in the early 1870s. Jessel M.R. held, in *Sykes* v. *Beadon* (1879) 11 Ch.D. 170, that they were illegal as partnerships with more than 20 members. Despite this, one continued to operate as a trust and, in *Smith* v. *Anderson* [1880] 15 Ch.D. 247, persuaded the C.A. to over-rule Jessel's decision. In the meantime, all the others had either been wound up, or converted themselves into companies which became known as investment trust companies. It was not until the early 1930s that unit trusts (inspired by the analogous "Massachusetts trusts" of the U.S.A. (where they have since been superseded by incorporated bodies known as "mutual funds") returned to the U.K., since when their numbers have grown astronomically.

Kingdom operate not as bodies corporate but through the medium of a trust.[28] The underlying investments are vested in trustees (normally a trust corporation such as a bank or insurance company) but managed by a management company which also sells and repurchases the "units" at prices which must bear a close relationship to the value of their proportion of the total portfolio. Thereby an investor can acquire at a fair price a beneficial interest in a wide spread of investments in a way which he could not if he invested his modest savings directly.[29] These unit trusts have no fixed capital (they are "open-ended") and rules regarding raising and maintaining capital have no application to them. They are regulated not by the Companies Act but by the Financial Services Act 1986,[30] and rules and regulations made under it.

Sections 265 and 266 are not dealing with them, but only with investment companies.[31] Such companies are ordinary registered "closed-end" companies. As companies, their share capital may be divided into different classes, thereby affording investors in their equity shares the advantages of "gearing" in a bull market. But the market price of their shares need not bear any close relationship to the value of the underlying securities and, in fact, in the post-War years they have always been quoted at a substantial discount to that value (at times as great as 20 to 30 per cent.). In consequence, some have been wound up, been converted into unit trusts or been acquired by pension funds. A substantial number still remain however.

The modifications of the dividend rules in their case do not apply to all, so called, investment trust companies but only to those which:

(a) are public companies that have given notice to the Registrar of their intention to carry on business as "investment companies"[32] and have not withdrawn that notice[33];

(b) have their shares listed on a recognised stock exchange in the United Kingdom, (*i.e.* The Stock Exchange)[34].

[28] The UCITS Directive (see Chap. 4 p. 65 above) permits either the trust or the corporate form (so long as the investments are held by a custodian) and it is intended to legislate to permit the formation of the latter in the U.K.. At present corporate-based schemes are practicable only in relation to "single property schemes" operating under S.I. 1989 No. 28, made under the F.S. Act.
[29] The present Government, however, believes that individual direct investment is more desirable than collective indirect investment and, by tax incentives, is encouraging the hybrid Personal Equity Plans (PEPs) whereby the individual investor has a personal portfolio (with, in practice, a lesser spread) but managed for him by a qualified professional.
[30] F.S. Act, Part I, Chapter VIII.
[31] More commonly described as "investment trust companies": see n. 27 above. Many of them have their registered offices in Scotland; Scottish solicitors played a major role in the birth and development of such companies.
[32] s.266(1).
[33] s.266(1) and (3).
[34] s.265(4)(a) as amended by the F.S. Act.

(c) do not have holdings in a company (other than another investment company) which represent more than 15 per cent. in value of their portfolios[35];

(d) prohibit in their memoranda or articles the distribution of capital profits[36]; and

(e) have not retained (except when Part VIII requires them to do so[37]) in any accounting period more than 15 per cent. of the income derived from securities.[38]

If these conditions are met, in addition to a distribution authorised by sections 263 and 264, the company may distribute the excess of its accumulated realised revenue profits over its accumulated revenue losses (whether realised or not) so long as the result is not that the value of its assets[39] is below one-and-a-half times the aggregate of its liabilities.[40] Here, therefore, a distinction *is* drawn between revenue profits and capital profits, the rationale being that investors in investment companies have a legitimate expectation that they will receive a share of the dividends paid to the company on the shares in its portfolio.

The price paid for this concession is that it cannot distribute capital profits and cannot normally plough back more than 15 per cent. of the income derived from securities,[41] coupled with the requirement that there must be at least a 50 per cent. surplus of assets over liabilities. This seems a more than adequate safeguard against the risk of insolvency. Indeed that risk is minimal in the case of investment companies.[42] Unless they are managed with reckless extravagance or invest in highly speculative securities or only in companies operating in a foreign country, the Government of which expropriates those companies' assets without compensation, it is almost impossible for investment companies to become insolvent—though their members may lose some of the capital that they invested.

Section 267 empowers the Secretary of State to extend sections 265 and 266 from companies investing mainly in securities to those "whose principal business consists of investing their funds in securities, land, or other assets with the aim of spreading investment risk and giving their members the benefit of the results of the

[35] s.265(2)(*b*).
[36] s.265(2)(*b*). And see s.265(4)(*b*) under which the company will lose the rights afforded by s.265(1) if it does make such a distribution or applies any unrealised profits to pay up debentures or amounts unpaid on its issued shares.
[37] *e.g.* when its accumulated losses preclude a distribution.
[38] s.266(2)(*d*).
[39] Which must not include uncalled share capital: s.265(3).
[40] s.265(1). "Liabilities" includes provisions within the meaning of para. 89 of Sched. 4 (see n. 20 above): s.265(2).
[41] This price is extracted to protect the Inland Revenue rather than members or creditors.
[42] Or unit trusts.

management of the assets."[43] This, no doubt, will be used to extend the concession to companies managing real property portfolios[44] and the like.

Other special cases

It suffices here merely to draw attention to the special treatment of certain other types of company. Section 279[45] relates to what Part VII of the Act (accounts and audit) calls "special category companies" (banking, shipping and insurance companies) to which modified accounts rules apply with the result that Part VIII makes appropriate modifications to sections 264 to 275 by section 279 and Schedule 11 to the Act.

In addition, a more fundamental modification is made by section 268 in relation to insurance companies carrying on "long-term business," (*i.e.* life assurance and pensions) instead of, or, in the case of "composite" companies as well as, "general business" (fire, household, motor, marine, etc.).[46] Under the insurance company legislation such a company has to maintain a separate life fund or funds in respect of long-term business. Section 268 provides that any surplus on life funds, as shown by an actuarial investigation,[47] when properly transferred to the profit and loss account, is to be treated as a realised profit, that any deficit is to be treated as a realised loss and that any other profit or loss arising from that business is to be left out of account for the purposes of the dividend rules.

Development costs

Normally, development costs are not shown as an asset in the company's accounts[48] and they can be only if the reasons for so doing are explained in a note to the accounts. Section 269 provides that the amount of the costs is then to be treated as a realised loss for the purposes of section 263 and as a realised revenue loss for the purposes of section 265.[49] This, however, does not apply to any part of that amount representing an unrealised profit made on a revaluation of those costs or if there are special circumstances justifying their not being treated as a realised loss and, in the notes to

[43] s.267(1).
[44] "Single property schemes" (whether corporate-based or trust-based) would presumably continue to be dealt with under S.I. 1989 No. 28: see n. 28 above.
[45] As substituted by 1989 Act, Sched. 10 para. 8.
[46] Life assurance (essentially a form of investment) is fundamentally different from general insurance (essentially a protection against calamities) and accordingly the EC Life Insurance Directives ban the formation of new composite insurance companies but, as yet, existing ones have not been forced to separate.
[47] In relation to life assurance it is the company's actuary, rather than its auditor, that is the watch-dog—but guarding those assured rather than the shareholders.
[48] Normally research costs and development costs are not distinguished and it is not permissible to treat research costs as an asset.
[49] s.269(1).

the accounts, an explanation is given of the circumstances relied on to justify the directors' decision to that effect.[50]

RELEVANT ACCOUNTS

It will have been apparent from the foregoing that, in determining whether there are profits from which distributions can be made in accordance with the rules, what counts are the relevant figures in the company's accounts. Nevertheless, the provisions relating to accounts and audits in Part VII of the Act need to be supplemented by additional provisions in Part VIII, if only because companies may make distributions at a time when there are no, or no justifying, annual accounts prepared under Part VII. Accordingly sections 270 to 276 contain additional accounting provisions for determining whether a distribution may be made by a company "without contravening sections 263, 264 or 265."[51]

They start with a statement that the amount which may be distributed is to be determined by reference to the following items in the "relevant accounts":

(a) profits, losses, assets and liabilities,

(b) provisions of any of the kinds referred to in paragraphs 88 and 89[52] of Schedule 4, and

(c) share capital and reserves (including undistributable reserves).[53]

The relevant accounts for this purpose are normally the company's last annual accounts, prepared and presented to the members in accordance with Part VII of the Act.[54] When that is so, the distribution is lawful so long as it is justified by reference to those items[55] and the accounts have been properly prepared in accordance with the Act, or have been properly prepared subject only to matters not material for determining whether the distribution would be

50 s.269(2).
51 s.270(1).
52 Para. 88 refers to provisions for depreciation of assets. For para. 89 see n. 20 above.
53 s.270(2).
54 s.270(3). Among the amendments to Part VII made by the 1989 Act are two new sections 252 and 253 which enable members of a private company, subject to stringent conditions, to elect to dispense with laying accounts and reports before a general meeting so long as they are sent to members and others in accordance with s.238(1) (though a member or the auditor may then require a meeting to be held). When such an election operates the wording of ss.270(3) and (4) and 271(4) is modified accordingly: see s.252(3).
55 *i.e.* item (*a*) (*b*) and (*c*) above.

lawful.[56] These accounts must have been duly audited and, if the auditors' report is qualified, the auditors must also state in writing whether the respect in which the report was qualified is material in determining whether the distribution would be lawful. This statement must have been laid before the company in general meeting, or sent to the members when there is an election to dispense with a meeting.[57]

In two cases, however, special accounts will be needed. The first is where the distribution would contravene section 263, 264 or 265 if reference was made only to the last annual accounts. In that event the company will have to prepare additional "interim accounts." The second is where it is proposed to declare a dividend during the company's first accounting period or before any accounts have been presented in respect of that period. In that event it will have to prepare "initial accounts." The interim or initial accounts must be "those necessary to enable a reasonable judgment to be made as to the amounts of items mentioned" in section 270(2).[58] So far as *private* companies are concerned, that is the only requirement laid down in Part VIII regarding interim or initial accounts; presumably it was thought that it sufficed in relation to them and that it would be unreasonable to impose on them the specific obligations (which include auditing in relation to initial accounts) appropriate (and necessary to comply with the Directive) in relation to public ones.

Before turning to these latter obligations one point needs to be stressed. The use of the expression "interim accounts" might lead one to suppose that such accounts are needed whenever it is proposed to declare interim or special dividends in addition to the normal dividend for the year. That is not so. So long as the company has duly complied with its obligations under Part VII in respect of its annual accounts for the past year it can, in the current year, pay interim or other special dividends in addition to the final dividend for that year so long as these dividends, in total, do not exceed the amount (as determined from the relevant annual accounts) which it can distribute without contravening sections 263, 264 or 265.[59] It is only when the last annual accounts would not justify a proposed payment that it is necessary to prepare interim accounts. This might

[56] s.271(1) and (2). Subs. (2) specifically refers to the need to ensure that the balance sheet and profit and loss account present "a true and fair view."
[57] s.271(3) and (4) (and see n. 54 above). This statement may be made whether or not a distribution is proposed at the time when the statement is made and may refer to all or any types of distribution; it will then suffice to validate any distributions of the types covered by the statement: s.271(5). The need for the auditors' statement is frequently overlooked and if the company has gone into liquidation before the omission is discovered it seems that nothing can be done to render the distribution lawful: *Precisions Dippings Ltd.* v. *Precisions Dippings Marketing Ltd.* [1986] Ch. 447, C.A.
[58] s.270(4).
[59] See s.274, below p. 254.

occur, for example, when a realised profit had been made on the sale of fixed assets after the date of the last annual accounts and the company wanted to distribute part or all of it to its shareholders without waiting until the next annual accounts are prepared. It could also occur if the net trading profits in the current year are seen to be running at a rate considerably higher than formerly and the directors wished to give the shareholders early and concrete evidence of this by paying an immediate interim dividend.[60] In both these examples the last year's accounts might well not justify the payment and would have to be supplemented by interim accounts. Normally, however, it will not be necessary to prepare interim accounts merely because the company pays quarterly or half-yearly interim dividends in anticipation of the final dividend for the year to be declared by the company when the year's accounts are presented.[61]

As regards both interim and initial accounts, section 272 (interim accounts) and section 273 (initial accounts) specifically provide that in the case of a *public* company the accounts must have been properly prepared in accordance with Schedule 4, with such modifications as are necessary because the accounts are not prepared in respect of the company's accounting reference period, or have been so prepared subject only to such matters as are not material for determining whether the proposed distribution would contravene the relevant section.[62] In particular, the balance sheet and the profit and loss account must give a "true and fair" view.[63] And, like annual accounts, a copy of the accounts must be delivered to the Registrar[64] with an English translation if they are in a foreign language.[65] Initial accounts must be audited and, if the auditors' report is qualified, must, as in the case of annual accounts,[65] be accompanied by a written statement on whether the qualifications are material in relation to determining whether section 270 is complied with.[67] There are no such auditing requirements in relation to interim accounts.[68] Hence a public company with listed shares is unlikely to be put to much additional expense in preparing interim accounts when they are needed since it will have to prepare half-yearly financial statements in order to comply with The Stock Exchange's listing regulations.[69] Unless the requirements of sections 270 to 273 are duly complied with

60 As articles normally authorise them to do: see Table A 1985 art. 103.
61 See Table A 1985, art. 102, under which the dividend "shall not exceed the amount recommended by the directors."
62 ss. 272(2) and (3), 273(2) and (3).
63 ss. 272(3), 273(3).
64 ss. 272(4), 273(6).
65 ss. 272(5), 273(7).
66 See ss. 271(3)–(5), above p. 252.
67 s. 273(4)(5) and (6).
68 But, in contrast with initial accounts, there will be published audited annual accounts which the interim accounts supplement.
69 *Yellow Book*, Section 5, Chapter 2, para. 23.

the distribution will be deemed to contravene sections 263 to 265 and the distribution will be unlawful.[70]

Section 274 deals, in respect of both public and private companies, with the method of applying section 270 in relation to successive distributions in reliance on the same relevant accounts, whether they be annual, interim or initial. As previously mentioned,[71] such reliance is permissible, but all previous such distributions have to be treated as added to that proposed for the purpose of determining whether the latter will be lawful. For this purpose, "distributions" include not only dividends but also payments, made since the date when the relevant accounts were prepared, in respect of financial assistance for the acquisition of the company's shares[72] or as the purchase price for the acquisition by the company of its own shares[73] (unless such payments were lawfully made otherwise than out of distributable profits[74]).[75]

Additional provisions on calculation of profits or losses

Reference has already been made to the difficulties of calculating profits or losses and of determining whether or not they are realised. Section 275 contains further provisions, mostly of a somewhat technical character, designed to help. Section 275 is something of a rag-bag. It deals mainly with the effects of a revaluation of fixed assets but contains two subsections of wider impact. The first of these is subsection (1) which says that for the purposes of sections 263 and 264 a "provision" of any kind mentioned in Schedule 4 paragraphs 88 and 89[76] is, with one exception,[77] to be treated as a realised loss. The second is subsection (3)[78] which provides that if there is no record of the original cost of an asset, or a record cannot be obtained without unreasonable expense or delay, for the purpose of determining whether a company has made a profit or loss in respect of that asset its cost is to be taken as the value ascribed to it in the earliest record made since its acquisition by the company.

The exception, mentioned above, to subsection (1) relates, as do the remaining subsections, to the main subject of the section. It excludes from the "provisions" to be treated as a realised loss "one

---

[70] s.270(5).
[71] See p. 252 above.
[72] On which see Chap. 9 at pp. 226 *et seq.* above.
[73] On which see Chap. 9 at pp. 217 *et seq.* above.
[74] Or, in the case of financial assistance, do not reduce its net assets or increase its net liabilities: s.274(2)(c).
[75] s.274(2) and (3). These subss. are deemed to be included in Chap. VII of Part V (redemption or purchase of shares) for the purpose of the Secretary of State's powers under s.179 to make regulations modifying that Chapter: s.274(4).
[76] See nn. 20 and 52 above.
[77] See below.
[78] It is not altogether clear why this subsection was necessary since Sched. 4, para. 28, says the same thing.

in respect of a diminution in value of a fixed asset appearing on a revaluation of all the fixed assets of a company or all its fixed assets, other than goodwill." Clearly, if all fixed assets are revalued what is important is the overall resulting profit or loss and it would be anomalous to treat a "provision" in respect of the unrealised loss on one of them as a realised loss. On the other hand, it is important (particularly where the revaluation produces a profit (normally a more likely result so far as real property is concerned) that the directors should not pick and choose which fixed assets are revalued but should reconsider the value of all of them. The reason for excluding "goodwill" (which prior to 1981 was treated as neither fixed nor current) is that in the accounts it may be shown as an asset only to the extent that it "was acquired for valuable consideration"[79] (so that it is essentially a balancing item representing the excess of the price paid for a business over the value of its other net assets) and it must be written off within a period chosen by the directors and explained in a note to the accounts.[80]

When a revaluation produces a profit rather than a loss it will be an unrealised profit unless and until the asset is disposed of. When that occurs any actual profit realised may be transferred to the profit and loss account and it becomes part of the distributable profits out of which dividends may be paid. Until then the method adopted for valuing it in the accounts will differ somewhat according to whether the company adopts the historical costs rules set out in Part II Section B of Schedule 4 or the alternative accounting rules set out in Section C.[81] In the former case the value will be shown as the original cost less provision for depreciation where appropriate[82]; in the latter it will be shown as the latest valuation figure, less depreciation of that figure, and any profit or loss shown by the valuation will be credited or debited (as the case may be) to the "revaluation reserve,"[83] referred to above,[84] the effect being that part of what would be a "provision" under historical cost accounting becomes a "reserve" under the alternative rules. To the foregoing, however, subsection (2) of section 275 makes one concession applying whichever accounting rules are adopted. If, on the revaluation, an unrealised profit is shown and thereafter the asset continues to be depreciated to a greater extent than would have been the case if that unrealised profit had not been made,[85] an amount equal to the excess may be treated

[79] See Sched. 4, Balance Sheet Formats 1 and 2, note 3.
[80] Sched. 4, para. 21. Treatment of goodwill—particularly where a company with valuable brand names is acquired—is at present a subject of heated debate in accountancy circles.
[81] Which attempts to meet some of the problems caused by inflation.
[82] Sched. 4, paras. 17–19.
[83] Sched. 4, paras. 31–34.
[84] p. 247 above.
[85] Which will be the case if it continues to be depreciated at the same rate but upon the increased value.

for the purposes of sections 263 and 264 as a realised profit made over the period of the depreciation subsequent to the revaluation.

What precisely is meant by "a revaluation of all the fixed assets" for the foregoing purposes? In practice there is unlikely to be anything in the nature of a detailed revaluation with professional assistance of all the fixed assets (or of all of them except goodwill). That will probably occur only in relation to the company's freehold and leasehold premises and perhaps not all of them. That practice is permitted by section 275 subject to compliance with the fairly strict conditions in subsections (4), (5) and (6). Subsection (4) provides that any consideration by the directors of the value of a fixed asset at a particular time can be treated as a revaluation but only if the directors are satisfied that the aggregate value of such assets as have not actually been revalued is not less than the aggregate amount at which they are shown in the company's accounts[86] and that is stated in a note to the "relevant accounts."[87]

Distributions in kind

Distributions within the meaning of Part VIII can be made in kind as well as in cash.[88] Section 276 then makes another (though minor) exception to the general rule that distributions can be made only out of realised profits. It provides that if a distribution is of, or includes, a "non-cash asset"[89] and any part of the stated value of that asset in the relevant accounts represents an unrealised profit, it will nevertheless be treated as if it were a realised profit for the purposes of determining whether the distribution is lawful and whether that profit can be included in, or transferred to, the profit and loss account despite the fact that Schedule 4[90] provides that that can be done only with realised profits. The reason for this section was to facilitate de-mergers which had been rendered practicable without adverse tax consequences by the Finance Act 1981. Such operations will often involve distributions of the property or shares of the de-merging company or of other companies in the same group. These distributions might be impossible to the extent needed unless some

---

86 s.275(5).
87 s.275(6). The note has to be somewhat more elaborate than the summary in the text above.
88 s.263(2), above p. 244. Whether this is so in respect of "distributions" excluded by s.263(2)(b) from those to which Part VIII applies is not wholly clear. If the terms of redemption of redeemable shares provided for their redemption otherwise than in cash there seems to be nothing in Part V, Chapter VII to prevent that (but if the consideration was another class of share, those redeemed would be "convertible" rather than "redeemable" shares). As regards purchase of shares, the wording of the relevant sections which refer throughout to "purchase" and not "exchange,") appears to require the company to pay cash.
89 Defined in s.739 as "any property or interest in property other than cash; and for this purpose 'cash' includes foreign currency." When shares are denominated in foreign currency (see Chap. 9 at p. 201) dividends are likely to be paid in that currency—though they do not have to be unless the articles so provide.
90 Paras. 12(a) and 34(3)(a).

unrealised profits relating to the non-cash assets concerned could be treated as realised (and, in a sense, it can be said that the distribution by the de-merging company is equivalent to a realisation). However, the concession is not restricted to de-mergers and advantage of it could be taken whenever a non-cash distribution is made.

Effects of the "relevant accounts" rules

The fact that normally the legality of the distribution will have to be supported by accounts is certainly some protection against distributions to the members which place the creditors, present or future, at risk. Particularly is this so when the accounts concerned have to be audited, as is normally the case; they are then more likely to be accurate than if matters were left to the creative accountancy of the company's officers and scrutiny by the directors through rose-tinted spectacles. This is so despite the fact that accountancy is not an exact science and, as post-mortems after take-overs have frequently revealed, auditors of comparable expertise and reputation, faced with the same books of account, may arrive at widely different conclusions on what the "true and fair" results are.

A further consequence is that the answer to the question whether and what dividend can lawfully be paid depends primarily on the situation as at the date of accounts which, if the "relevant accounts" are the latest annual accounts, is likely to be at least seven months before the dividend is actually paid.[91] Hence the wording of sections 263, and, especially, 264 and 265, is somewhat misleading. It suggests that whether a distribution can lawfully be made depends upon the company having the requisite profits (and, in the case of public companies, net assets) available at the time of payment and not on the position some months before.

What then is the position if, before the date of actual payment, the directors realise that the company is not going to meet those conditions at that time? The normal practice regarding dividend payments is that reflected in article 102 of Table A 1985, *i.e.* "Subject to the provisions of the Act, the company may by ordinary resolution declare dividends in accordance with the respective rights of the members but no dividend shall exceed the amount recommended by the directors." The directors will make their recommendation in the notice of the meeting[93] at which dividends are to be declared. Whether they should, in the light of their then knowledge, not recommend a dividend will depend on the nature of that knowledge. If they have discovered that the relevant accounts were so seriously

91 See s.244 (as inserted by 1989 Act).
92 Note also art. 103 as regards their own powers to pay interim dividends.
93 Normally the AGM. If a private company has elected to dispense with meetings presumably the recommendation will be made when the accounts are sent to the members.

inaccurate that they did not in fact give a true and fair view of the state of the company's affairs and its profits or losses at the time the accounts were signed,[94] they clearly should not recommend a dividend, and, should withdraw any recommendation they have made; for the dividend, if paid would be unlawful.[95] If however, the relevant accounts truly reflected the position as at their date and the only reason why the requisite conditions are no longer met is some calamity occurring thereafter, payment of the dividend would not seemingly, be unlawful—unless the effect of paying it would be to reduce the company to insolvency.[96] That is not to say that the originally proposed dividend should necessarily be declared and paid; if the directors would not have recommended it had they foreseen what was to befall, it clearly would be wiser and safer if it were not declared.

CONSEQUENCES OF UNLAWFUL DISTRIBUTIONS

In contrast with unlawful financial assistance for the purchase by a company of its own shares[97] (where the Act provides only for criminal sanctions, leaving the courts to work out the civil law consequences) no criminal sanctions are provided in the case of unlawful distributions covered by Part VIII but something (though precious little) is said about the civil consequences. This is done by section 277 which provides that when a distribution[98] is made to a member which he then knows, or has reasonable cause to believe, is made in contravention (in whole or in part) of Part VIII he is liable to repay it or, if the distribution was otherwise then in cash, its value.[99] In other words, the payment, though "unlawful," is neither void nor voidable but can nevertheless be recovered from any recipient of it who knew or ought to have known that it was unlawful.

---

[94] This seems to have been the position in relation to Ferranti International in 1989 when it discovered that a massive sum had apparently been misappropriated from the assets of its American subsidiary.

[95] ss.270(3), 271(2) and (3), 272(2) and (3). And the accounts should be revised; there are now statutory provisions for this: see ss.245–245C.

[96] This, assuming that the payment was justified by the "relevant accounts," would not be one which the Act specifically makes unlawful but the pre-1980 case-law presumably survives: for an interesting illustration see *Peter Buchanan Ltd.* v. *McVey* (1950) [1955] A.C. 516, H.L. (Ir.) at pp. 521–522. It would certainly render the directors vulnerable to claims based on misfeasance (or on "wrongful trading" (see Chap. 6 pp. 110–115 above) and clearly they should not exercise their own discretion to pay interim dividends: *Lagunas Nitrate Co.* v. *Schroeder & Co.* (1901) 85 L.T. 22.

[97] See Chap. 9 p. 236 above.

[98] Other than financial assistance for the acquisition of the company's own shares given in contravention of s.151 or any payment made in respect of the redemption or purchase of shares in the company s.277(2).

[99] s.277(1).

Except in relation to small private companies (which rarely pay dividends) it is obviously unlikely that the prescribed actual or constructive knowledge could be established unless the member was an officer of the company.[1] Hence the occasions when the section will bite are likely to be few. It is true that the section further provides that it is "without prejudice to any obligations imposed apart from this section on a member of a company to repay a distribution unlawfully made to him"[2] but it is difficult to identify any such obligation on members, as such, in respect of dividends.[3]

A more powerful civil sanction is the possibility of recovering from the directors and other officers who were responsible for the making of the unlawful distribution. Clearly they may well have broken their duties of care and diligence and possibly those of good faith[4] and in that event the extent of their liability will not be limited to what they themselves have received by way of unlawful dividend but will extend to restoration of the loss which the company suffered as a result of the unlawful payments.[5] But in practice it is unlikely that action will be taken against them by the company unless there is a change in those controlling the company or unless it goes into liquidation,[6] administration or receivership. Until any of these events occur, nothing is likely to happen, except perhaps an attempt to recover damages for alleged professional negligence against the firm of auditors that reported on the relevant accounts.[7]

CAPITALISATION AND THE DIVIDEND RULES

The final section of Part VIII to which reference needs to be made is section 278. But a short preamble is necessary. As we have seen,

---

[1] It seems fanciful to suppose that any court would hold that "Sid" and "Aunt Agatha" should study the relevant accounts and the documents accompanying them and read with understanding Part VIII of the Act to check that their dividends are lawfully payable.

[2] s.277(2).

[3] At common law, shareholders appear to be liable to repay only if they actually knew that the dividend was unlawful and it seems clear that, at best, the common law liability is no greater than that under s.277: see *Moxham* v. *Grant* [1900] 1 Q.B. 85, C.A. But in the *Precision Dippings* case (p. 252 n. 57 above) the C.A. avoided the need to construe what is now s.277(1) by holding that the unlawful payment was *ultra vires* (an example of the continuing loose use of that expression (see Chapter 8 above) and that the recipient of the dividend (the company's parent) was liable, as a constructive trustee, to restore it. See also *Re Cleveland Trust* [1991] B.C.L.C. 424.

[4] On which see Chap. 21 below.

[5] *Dovey* v. *Cory* [1901] A.C. 477, H.L.

[6] When a misfeasance summons under what is now s.212 of the Insolvency Act 1986 might be successful: *Re Sharpe, Re Bennett* [1892] 1 Ch. 154, C.A.

[7] Another possibility, of greater theoretical than practical importance, is that a member, if he acted in time, could obtain an injunction to restrain the company from paying an unlawful dividend. In such a case action by a member on behalf of the company would not seem to be precluded by the *Foss* v. *Harbottle* rule on which see Chap. 24 below.

prior to 1981, according to the English courts whether profits could be capitalised by making a bonus issue depended on there being profits out of which a dividend could be paid.[8] Now, however, a clear distinction is drawn between profits which can be distributed (generally only net realised profits) and profits which can be capitalised. Accordingly Part VIII of the Act excludes, from its definition of "distributions,"[9] an "issue of shares as fully or partly paid bonus shares."[10] The only remaining connection between capitalisation and distributable profits is that once profits are capitalised, whether by a bonus issue or by a transfer to the capital redemption reserve, they cease to be profits and become, in the first case, share capital, and, in the second case, "undistributable reserves." This will affect the ability to pay dividends, both because the former profits are no longer "distributable profits"[11] and because, in relation to public companies, the capital yardstick will have been increased thereby.[12]

So far so good. But then comes section 278 which at first sight is curious and misleading. It provides that where, before December 1980, a company was authorised by its articles to apply its unrealised profits in paying up bonus shares "that provision continues (subject to any alteration of the articles) as authority for those profits to be so applied after that date." This seems to imply, in contradiction of what is said above, that only a company, with pre-1981 articles which expressly authorised it, can capitalise unrealised profits. In fact, however, the object of the section is not that at all.

Why it was thought (rightly) that some such provision was needed is because of the idiosyncrasies of English Companies Acts which, as we saw in Chapter 7, frequently empower companies to do various things but leave it to the companies' articles to say when, whether and through which of their organs they shall do it. Part VIII affords an example of this. It prescribes when, so far as the Act is concerned, dividends may or may not be paid and makes it clear that companies may, and in some cases must,[13] capitalise profits. But it expressly recognises that its provisions are "without prejudice to … any provision of a company's memorandum or articles restricting the sums out of which or the cases in which a distribution may be made."[14] Nor does it say anything about which organs of a company are to

---

[8] See above p. 244 n. 2.

[9] *i.e.* "Any distribution of a company's assets to its members whether in cash or otherwise"; s.263(2). What makes a bonus issue a "distribution of a company's assets to its members" is not the issue of the shares (a company's shares are not its assets) but the fact that the company parts with its assets in paying them up.

[10] s.263(2)(*a*).

[11] For the purposes of s.263.

[12] Thus increasing the restrictive impact of s.264.

[13] *i.e.* where a company is required to transfer profits to capital redemption reserve or to the revaluation reserve.

[14] s.281.

exercise its powers to distribute profits or to capitalise them. Hence articles invariably contain provisions about these powers.[15] Since, prior to the 1980 Act, it was believed that profits, whether realised or unrealised, could be distributed, it was customary for the capitalisation article to refer to "profits available for dividend."[16] If nothing had been done, companies with such articles would have lost the right to capitalise unrealised profits when the 1980 Act (now section 263 of the 1985 Act) made them not "available for dividend." Hence the Act did two things. It first inserted[17] a new article 128A in Table A 1948 which enabled a company formed thereafter with Table A 1948 to capitalise any or all of its reserves. This, however, did not help those formed prior to the coming into force of that Act, most of which would probably not have realised that they had lost the ability to capitalise unrealised profits unless they altered their articles. Secondly, therefore, it contained a provision corresponding to the present section 278, the intention being to entitle such companies to continue to be authorised to capitalise unrealised profits without having to alter their articles. It is a pity that this intention could not have been more clearly expressed.[18]

However, as regards companies with an article equivalent to Table A 1985, article 110, there is no problem; it is carefully worded so as to enable the directors, with the authority of an ordinary resolution of the company, to capitalise profits "whether or not they are available for distribution."

CONCLUSION

While, perhaps, lawyers and businessmen, may fairly complain that not all the present capital maintenance and dividend rules, described in this and the previous chapter, are expressed in a way which is readily intelligible to anyone other than a specialist corporate accountant, at long last we have rules which on the whole are logical and sensible. For this we have to thank our membership of the EC. It should again be emphasised, however, that while these rules afford protection against the risk that a public company's assets will not be milked by distributions to its members to the detriment of its

---

15 Table A 1948, arts. 114–122 (dividends) and 128, 129 (capitalisations); Table A 1985, arts. 102–108 (dividends) and 110 (capitalisations).
16 As did art. 128 of Table A 1948.
17 Companies Act 1980 Sched. 3.
18 Particularly as the wording ignores the fact that unrealised capital profits of a Scottish registered company would not have been "profits available for dividend" unless and until the Scottish courts overruled *Westburn Sugar Refineries* v. *IRC* 1960 S.L.T. 297; [1960] T.R. 105: see p. 244 nn. 2 and 3 above. Section 278 achieves its object only if one assumes that *Westburn* was wrong on this point and *Dimbula Valley (Ceylon) Tea Company* v. *Laurie* [1961] Ch. 353, right (a view which few share).

creditors, they afford little protection in relation to private companies—and will not do so unless they too are required to raise and maintain a minimum capital and are made subject to section 264. Of that there is no immediate likelihood.

It must also be repeated that, in the case of most private companies, members who are also directors extract their rewards in the form of remuneration which will be paid whether or not there are profits or the members' capital is intact.[19] Moreover, in practice, companies (public or private) raise their working capital not only in the form of share capital but also from borrowings, secured or unsecured. When this loan capital is raised by an issue of secured debenture-stock or unsecured loan-stock, the subscribers will not think of themselves as wholly different animals from the members who have subscribed for shares.[20] But in law they will be wholly different—they will be creditors not members. And the rules relating to the raising and maintenance of capital or to distributions will have no application. Loan capital is a true liability, and, as such, it may reduce the company's net assets and payment of interest on it may reduce the distributable profits.[21] To that extent it affects the application of the rules relating to capital maintenance and to distributions to members—but not otherwise. And when the loan capital is secured on the undertaking and assets of the company, it may seriously reduce the protection which the capital concept is supposed to afford to trade creditors against the dangers of limited liability.

This is not to suggest that the capital concept is a chimaera; only that it still has its limitations.

[19] And members who are not directors will be lucky if they are paid anything.
[20] As the Act seems to recognise, since provisions relating to debentures are included in Part V notwithstanding that this is entitled "Share Capital, Its Increase, Maintenance and Reduction."
[21] On the other hand from the company's viewpoint operating on borrowings may prove a sound investment since (a) it will hope to earn more from employment of the money borrowed than the interest it has to pay, (b) the interest will be deductible in assessing its income for tax purposes, and (c) the money it will ultimately have to repay will, almost certainly, be worth less in real terms than the sum borrowed.

Part Three

FORMATION AND FLOTATION OF COMPANIES

INTRODUCTION

THIS Part deals with the problems which have to be faced on the company's birth. Chapter 11 considers the steps necessary to secure the company's incorporation and the questions which then arise. Chapter 12 considers the position of the individuals who are responsible for the incorporation and their duties towards the new-born company. Chapter 13 (Flotations) indicates the methods whereby a public company raises its capital from the public. Formerly flotation commonly preceded formation; the promoters would publish a prospectus inviting subscription from the public and the company would be formed only if these invitations were successful. Today, however, this order is invariably reversed; the company is formed first and, after incorporation, "floats-off" its capital. Hence the order of these three chapters.

CHAPTER 11

FORMATION OF COMPANIES

As we have seen today there are three basic types of incorporated company—statutory, chartered and registered, and the formalities attending formation vary fundamentally as between each type. Detailed consideration is necessary only in respect of the last, companies registered under the Companies Act, for these are overwhelmingly the most common and important.

STATUTORY COMPANIES

These are formed by the promotion of a private Act of Parliament. Details of the procedure therefore appertain to the field of Private Bill legislation rather than to a manual of company law and the reader who is concerned in the formation of such a company should refer to the specialised works on the former topic. In practice the work is monopolised by a few firms of solicitors who specialise as parliamentary agents and by a handful of counsel at the parliamentary bar. The numbers of both promotions and specialist practitioners are dwindling, having regard to the curtailment of work resulting first from nationalisation and now from privatisation, both of which are achieved under Public Acts.

CHARTERED COMPANIES

It is unlikely that there will be any further creations of chartered trading companies but the grant of charters to charitable or public bodies is not uncommon. The procedure in such cases is for the promoters of the body to petition the Crown (through the office of the Lord President of the Council) praying for the grant of a charter, a draft of which is normally annexed to the petition. If the petition is granted the promoters and their successors then become "one body corporate and politic by the name of—and by that name shall and may sue or be sued plead and be impleaded in all courts whether of law or equity . . . and shall have perpetual succession and a common seal."

265

Sometimes a charter will be granted to the members of an existing guarantee company registered under the Companies Acts in which event the assets of the company will be transferred[1] to the new chartered body, and the company wound up unless the Registrar can be persuaded to exercise his power to strike it off the register under section 652 of the Companies Act, thus avoiding the expense of a formal liquidation.[2]

REGISTERED COMPANIES

In the vast majority of cases the company, whatever its objects, will today be formed under the Companies Act, and it may be helpful to set out the practice in such cases in some detail.

Choice of type

The promoters will first have to make up their minds which of the several types of registered company they wish to form, since this may make a difference to the number and types of documents required, and will certainly affect their contents.

First, they must choose between a limited and an unlimited company.[3] The disadvantage of the latter is that its members will ultimately be personally liable for its debts and for this reason they are likely to be wary of it if the company intends to trade. If, however, the company is merely to hold land or investments, the absence of limited liability may not matter and may confer certain advantages, for example, as regards returning capital to the members and escaping from having to give publicity to the company's financial position. The absence of limited liability may also render the company more acceptable in certain circles (for example, the turf).

If they decide upon a limited company they must then make up their minds whether it is to be limited by shares or by guarantee, and as already explained,[4] this is really a matter which will be decided for them by the purpose which the company is to perform. Only if it is to be a non-profit-making concern are they likely to form a guarantee company which is especially suited to a body of that type.

Overlapping these distinctions, but closely bound up with them, is the further point of whether or not the company should have a share

---

[1] It is understood that it is not the practice of the Revenue to claim ad valorem stamp duty thereon.
[2] See Chap. 28 at pp. 773–775, below.
[3] An alternative, which in practice is very rarely adopted, is a limited company with unlimited liability on the part of the directors: s.306. A similar type of association is of considerable importance in some other legal systems, *e.g.* the German Kommandit-Gesellschaft auf Aktien and the French société en commandite par actions.
[4] See Chap. 1 above.

capital. If, as is most probable, the company is to be limited by shares this question does not arise. Likewise if it is to be limited by guarantee.[5] But if the company is unlimited it may or may not have its capital divided into shares. Once more, the decision is dependent on the company's purpose; if the company is intended to make and distribute profits a share capital will be appropriate.

They will further have to make up their minds whether the company is to be a public or private one. As we have seen,[6] public and private companies essentially fulfil different economic purposes; the former to raise capital from the public to run the corporate enterprise, the latter to confer a separate legal personality on the business of a single trader or a partnership. Once again, therefore, the choice will in practice be clear-cut and normally it will be to form a private company. The incorporators may have the ultimate ambition of "going public" but, as we have seen,[7] rarely will they be in a position to do so immediately. If, however, they are, then the company will have to be a company limited by shares, the memorandum of association will have to state that it is to be a public company and special requirements as to its registration will have to be complied with.[8] Any other type of company will, perforce, be a private company. Theoretically therefore, the incorporators will have a choice of five types:

(i) a public company limited by shares
(ii) a private company limited by shares
(iii) a private company limited by guarantee and without a share capital
(iv) a private unlimited company having a share capital
(v) a private unlimited company not having a share capital.

In practice, however, the choice is likely to be between (ii) and (iii) and will be determined for them according to whether they want the company to trade for the profit of the members or to perform some charitable or quasi-charitable purpose.

Name of company

The incorporators must next decide on a suitable name. This is of some importance in identifying an artificial person[9] and the Act

---

[5] Since the coming into force of the Companies Act 1980 no further companies limited by guarantee and having a share capital can be formed: s.1(4).
[6] Chap. 1, above.
[7] See p. 106 above.
[8] s.1(3).
[9] Though less so now that the Registrar has to allot each company a registered number (s.705) which it has to state on its business letters and order forms: s.35(1)(a).

provides that it must be stated in the memorandum of association,[10] on the company's seal,[11] on business letters, negotiable instruments, and order forms[12] and must be affixed outside every office or place of business.[13] It is advisable, therefore, that it should be kept as short as possible. Nor, once the company has been registered, can it change its name as informally as can a natural person.

Major changes in the law relating to company names[14] were made by the Companies Act 1981 and the present position is now set out in Part I Chapter II of the Act[15] under which a name can no longer be refused registration merely because it is considered to be undesirable. There are, nevertheless, still restrictions on freedom of choice. The first of these is the obvious one, already referred to,[16] that if the company is a limited company its name must end with the prescribed warning suffix—"limited"—if it is a private company or "public limited company" if it is a public one.[17] These expressions may be abbreviated to "Ltd" or "plc"[18] and the company may subsequently use those abbreviations even if it has registered with the full suffix.[19]

To the requirement that a private limited company must have "limited" at the end of its name, section 30 provides an exemption in relation to a company limited by guarantee, the objects of which are to be "the promotion of commerce, art, science, education, charity or any profession",[20] and the memorandum of which forbids the distribution of profits or income and requires its assets on a winding up to be transferred to a body with like objects. Prior to the Act of 1981 a licence from the Department had to be obtained if this exemption was to be enjoyed.[21] This caused the Department a

---

[10] s.2.

[11] s.350 (if it decides to have one: see s.36A(3) inserted by the 1989 Act).

[12] s.349. See Chap. 6 at p. 116 above.

[13] s.348. And note s.351(3) and (4) regarding English translations of Welsh suffixes.

[14] And business names (the former register of busines names was abolished).

[15] i.e. ss.25–34.

[16] See pp. 12, 13 above.

[17] s.25. If, however the company's memorandum states that its registered office is to be situated in Wales, the Welsh equivalents ("cyfyngedig" or "cwmni cyfyngedig cyhoeddus") may (not must) be used instead. Where they are used the fact that the company is limited or a plc must be stated in English on business communications and at each place of business: s.351(3) and (4). It is an offence for any person to use any of the suffixes in carrying on business if the person is not a limited company or a public limited company: ss.33 and 34.

[18] s.27 (the Welsh equivalents are "cyf" or "c.c.c."). The abbreviations can be adopted whenever a company "by any provision of this Act is either required or entitled to include in its name" the prescribed suffix. But it will, of course, have to state in full in its memorandum that the liability of its members is limited and, if such be the case, that it is to be a public company.

[19] Or, presumably, vice versa though the section does not say so.

[20] Anomalously the objects have to be to "promote" rather than to "regulate" a profession. Hence to enable SIB to dispense with "limited," the Financial Services Act had specifically to extend ss.30 and 31 to "designated agencies" under that Act: FS Act 1986 Sched. 9 para. 2.

[21] At that time licences could be granted to companies other than those limited by guarantee, though in practice it was only guarantee companies that applied for them. Any company limited by shares which may have obtained an exemption retains it under the new provisions: see s.30(2).

considerable amount of somewhat pointless labour.[22] The new system avoids much of that since the Registrar may accept a statutory declaration that the necessary conditions are fulfilled and may (and normally will) refuse to register without the suffix unless such a declaration is delivered to him.[23] From the company's point of view, exemption has the additional advantage that it also exempts from the requirements of the Act relating to the publication of its name[23a] and the sending of lists of members to the Registrar with its annual return under section 364A (4).[24] It does not, however, exempt it from the requirement to state on business letters and order forms that it is a limited company.[25] When the company is a charity (in the legal sense of that term) and its name does not include the word "charity" or "charitable" it will also have to state that it is a charity in all business communications whether or not it has dispensed with "Ltd."[26]

More important than what the name must contain is what it must not. Certain expressions are banned.[27] Thus the name must not include, except at the end, any use of "limited," "unlimited," "public limited company" or their abbreviations or Welsh equivalents.[28] And the name must not be the same as any name already on the Registrar's index of names.[29] This is likely to present the severest obstacle because there are some 915,000 names on that index. Hence a Smith, Jones, Brown or Robinson who has carried on an unincorporated business under his name may have difficulty in finding an available way of continuing to use that name on incorporating the business.[30]

Two further prohibitions differ somewhat from the foregoing since they depend upon the opinion of the Secretary of State (which means the Registrar in the first instance). If, in his opinion, the name is such

22 When the Jenkins Committee asked the representatives of the Board of Trade why they wished to continue to perform this task their reply was "We have been doing it for a long time and have got rather to like it": Minutes of Evidence, 20th Day, Q6886.

23 s.30(4) and (5). If it subsequently appears to the S. of S. that the conditions for exemption are not being observed he may direct the company to change its name (by a resolution of the directors) so that it ends with "Limited": s.31(2).

23a Under ss.348, 349.

24 s.30(7).

25 s.351(1)(d). This somewhat reduces the value of the cachet which the absence of "limited" is thought to confer but its effect is usually minimised by putting the statement inconspicuously at the bottom of the notepaper.

26 Charities Act 1960, s.30 as inserted by Companies Act 1989.

27 s.26(1)(a), (b) and (c).

28 This is primarily to prevent any blurring of the warnings implied by "Ltd." or "plc" but the inclusion of "unlimited" (for which, incidentally, there is no authorised abbreviation) would presumably prevent a moneylender from incorporating as "Unlimited Loans Ltd."

29 In determining whether one name is the same as another, words such as "the," and "and Company" are to be ignored: s.26(3) and see s.28(2).

30 Those with less common surnames can often surmount this difficulty by, for example, inserting an appropriate place-name: e.g. Gower (Hampstead) Ltd.

that its use would constitute a criminal offence[31] or be "offensive,"[32] it cannot be adopted.

Certain other names may be adopted only with the express approval of the Secretary of State. These are names which, in his opinion, would be likely to give the impression that the company is connected in any way with the Government or a local authority[33] or which include any word or expression for the time being specified in regulations made under section 29.[34] That section empowers the Secretary of State to specify the words or expressions for which his approval is required and, in relation to any of them, to state the Government Department or other body which has to be asked whether it objects and, if so, why. The relevant regulations[35] list some 90 words[36] and, in relation to about a third of them, specify a body which has to be invited to object.[37] The person making the statutory declaration of compliance[38] then has to send to the Registrar, when the incorporation documents are lodged, a statement, that the body has been asked and a copy of any response.[39]

It will therefore be apparent that it may be difficult to find a name acceptable to both the incorporators and the Registrar or Secretary of State. But until it is achieved, it will be impossible to complete the documents required to obtain registration and unsafe to order the stationery which the company will need once it is registered. We have never introduced a system comparable to that in some other common law countries whereby a name can be reserved for a prescribed period. Prior to 1981, however, it was possible and usual to write to the Registrar submitting a name (or two or three alternative names) and asking if it was available. If the reply was affirmative it was usually safe to proceed so long as one did so promptly. Now, however, the incorporators or their professional advisers will have to search the index[40] and make up their own minds.

Even if they do secure registration under a particular name they cannot be certain that they will not be forced to change it. The main

31 s.26(1)(d). e.g. a name which holds out the company as carrying on a business which requires a licence or authorisation which the company does not have.
32 s.26(1)(e).
33 s.26(2)(a).
34 s.26(2)(b).
35 The Company and Business Names Regs. 1981 (S.I. 1981 No. 1685) and the amending Regs. 1982 (S.I. 1982 No. 1653). In addition, the Registrar has published Notes of Guidance on Company and Business Names and on Sensitive Words and Expressions (NG 8 and 9).
36 Mainly those implying some official or representative status but ranging from "Abortion" to "Windsor" and including, for example, "University," "Polytechnic" and "Stock Exchange." A listed word should be avoided unless the incorporators are prepared to face delay and possible rejection.
37 e.g. if the name includes "Charitable," or "Charity," the Charity Commission must be asked; if "Dental" or "Dentistry," the General Dental Council; and if "Windsor" (because of its royal associations) the Home Office or the Scottish Home and Health Dept.
38 See below p. 277.
39 s.29(2) and (3).
40 And, ideally, also the Register of Trade Marks to ensure that the name proposed is not someone's registered trademark.

risk is that the Secretary of State, under section 28(2), will, within 12 months of the company's registration, direct it to change its name on the ground that it: "is the same as, or in the opinion of the Secretary of State, *too like*[41] a name appearing at the time of registration in the registrar's index of company names . . . or which should have appeared in that index at the time."

The object of section 28(2) is two-fold: (a) to enable a mistake to be rectified, when the name of an existing company has been registered either because the name had not then been entered on the index, or because the fact that it was the same as that of the new company had escaped detection, and (b) to extend, by the words italicised above, the ambit of "the same as" to "too like" that of another. If another company finds that the new company is trading with a name so similar to its own as to cause confusion and face it with unfair competition, that company can, as a cheaper alternative to a "passing-off action" complain to the Registrar asking that the Secretary of State should exercise his powers to direct the new one to change its name.[42] If the Secretary of State does so, the company will have to comply within such period as he may direct. But this course will be effective only if the complaint is in time for a direction to be made within 12 months of registration of the second company. Otherwise the only remedy available to the first company will be a passing off action[43] which will not be successful merely because the two names are identical or "too like." It will have to be established that both companies are carrying on the same of type of business and that the second is, in effect, cashing in on the reputation of the first and appropriating its goodwill and connection.[44] If that is established the new company will be enjoined from continuing to trade under that name and will either have to go out of business or change its name. Any company can now do the latter by passing a special resolution[45] but the new name will have to pass the same tests as those for a name selected on original registration.[46]

The Secretary of State may also direct the company to change its name if it appears to him that misleading information has been given in connection with the company's registration with a particular name or that undertakings or assurances have been given for that purpose which have not been fulfilled[47] and in this case the direction may be

---

41 For a case where the names were not thought "too like" although they were sufficiently alike to have caused a petitioning creditor to obtain a winding up order against the wrong company with damaging consequences to it, see *Re Calmex Ltd.* [1989] 1 All E.R. 485.

42 35 directions were made in 1989–90. *Companies in 1989–90* Table D4.

43 Unless the name conflicts with the older company's registered trademark, in which event it may also have a right of action in that respect.

44 See, *e.g. Tussaud v. Tussaud* (1890) 44 Ch.D. 678: *Panhard et Levassor v. Panhard Levassor Motor Co.* [1901] 2 Ch. 513.

45 s.28(1).

46 *I.e.* ss.26 and 27 apply.

47 This is likely to arise only when approval of the name has been obtained under ss.26(2) or 30.

given within five years of registration.[48] And, finally, he may at any time direct it to change its name if, in his opinion, it gives so misleading an indication of the nature of the company's activities as to be likely to cause harm to the public.[49] Little or no use of this power has been made; undoubtedly the names of many companies give totally misleading indications of the nature of their activities but this, on its own, has apparently not been thought "likely to cause harm to the public."

On a change of name, whether voluntarily or because of a direction, the Registrar enters the new name on the register in place of the old and issues an amended certificate of incorporation.[50] The change is effective from the date on which that certificate is issued.[51] But the company remains the same corporate body and the change does not affect any of its rights or obligations or render defective any legal proceedings by or against it.[52]

The effect of the statutory provisions is to afford a registered company something approaching an exclusive right to corporate trading under its registered name,[53] since another company should not be registered with the same name and may be forced to change its name if that is too like the name. That, however, does not protect it against the use of the name by unincorporated businesses. These are free from any statutory restraints so long as they use the true names of their proprietors.[54] Alternatively, subject to observing the provisions of the Business Names Act 1985 regarding disclosure of the identity of the proprietors,[55] they can adopt any business name so long as it is not one of those which are prohibited or require the approval of the Secretary of State.[56]

There is nothing in the Business Names Act 1985 which empowers the Secretary of State to direct the change of a business name because it is the same as, or too like, the name of an existing business, corporate or incorporate. However, if a registered company carries on any business under a name other than its own (for example because it has acquired an existing business with a goodwill attached to its name) it too will have to comply with the provisions of the Business Names Act, by disclosing on all business documents and at

---

[48] s.28(3).
[49] s.32.
[50] See on this certificate, pp. 278–281 below.
[51] ss.28(6) and 32(5).
[52] ss.28(7) and 32(6). Hence contracts entered into prematurely under the new name will not be pre-incorporation contracts on which, under s.36C, the individual who acted would be personally liable (see Chap. 12 at pp. 306–310). But if the new name was used prior to the date of the issue of the certificate (or the old name used thereafter) there would be a risk of personal liability under s.349(4): see Chap. 6 at pp. 116–117 above.
[53] Hence companies have sometimes been registered in order to obtain an exclusive right to use a name which the incorporators think they might wish to trade under at some future date. And recently someone has apparently registered companies with the names of well-known firms of solicitors which he then offers to sell to the firms!
[54] Business Names Act 1985, s.1.
[55] *Ibid.* s.4.
[56] *Ibid.* ss.2 and 3 (equivalent to ss.26(2) and 29 of the Companies Act).

all its business premises its corporate name and an address in Great Britain at which documents can be served.[57] A breach of this obligation is not only an offence[58] but may prevent the company from suing on its contracts.[59]

Finally, in relation to company names, it should be mentioned that the controls exercisable under sections 26 and 27 of the Companies Act are extended by section 694 of that Act to the name under which overseas companies may trade from a place of business in Great Britain.[60] While the Secretary of State cannot compel a foreign company to change its corporate name, the section empowers him to prevent trading here under that name and to approve another which, for the purposes of our law, is treated as if it were the corporate name.

The Memorandum and Articles

The next step is to prepare the memorandum and articles. The Companies Act provides that, as regards each of the various types of company,[61] these documents shall be in the form specified by regulations[62] made by the Secretary of State "or as near to that form as circumstances admit."[63] This, however is treated with considerable latitude and so long as the documents submitted are in the same basic form as that specified and contain what the Act prescribes,[64] the widest variations of content are permitted.[65] Thus, as we have seen,[66] the practice has long been to produce memoranda much lengthier than the prescribed forms because of inflated objects clauses—a practice which conceivably may change as a result of the reforms of the *ultra vires* doctrine by the Act of 1989.

The present Regulations[67] contain five Tables of which Table A, prescribing model articles for a company (whether public or private) limited by shares, is the most important and differs in its effect from

[57] *Ibid.* s.4.

[58] *Ibid.* ss.4(6), (7) and 7.

[59] *Ibid.* s.5.

[60] This closes a loophole of which advantage was formerly taken; see, *e.g. Wallersteiner v. Moir* [1974] 1 W.L.R. 991, C.A., where the Liechtenstein registered "Rothschild Trust" had no connection with the well-known merchant banks.

[61] Except in relation to an unlimited company without a share capital when there are no prescribed forms.

[62] Under earlier Companies Acts the forms were Scheduled to the Act (but alterable by regulations) which made them more readily accessible (unless they were so altered).

[63] s.3 (as regards the memorandum) and s.8 (as regards articles).

[64] ss.2 and 7(2).

[65] Gaiman v. *National Association for Medical Health* [1971] Ch. 317.

[66] Above pp. 172–175.

[67] The Companies (Tables A to F) Regs (S.I. 1985 No. 805 as amended by S.I. 1985 No. 1052). The new s.8A, inserted by the 1989 Act, envisages an additional Table G containing articles appropriate for "partnership companies." This, presumably, will take account of the fact that most such companies are likely to be private companies which take advantage of the new ss.366A, 379A, 381A, 381B and 382A; see above Chap. 7 at p. 152.

the others. Such a company does not have to register articles[68] (as opposed to the memorandum) and, if it does not, Table A (as in force at the date of the company's registration) becomes its articles.[69] Even if it does register articles, in so far as these do not exclude or modify Table A, its provisions will apply. Furthermore, it, and any other type of company (which will have to register articles) may, in them, adopt by reference any provisions of Table A.[70] In contrast, the model articles in Table C (relating to a company limited by guarantee without a share capital), Table D (relating to a company limited by guarantee and with a share capital[71]) and Table E (relating to an unlimited company having a share capital) are merely models which cannot be adopted by reference and will not apply to fill lacunae in the registered articles. Tables C and D also include model forms of memoranda for the types of company to which they relate as does Table B (for a private company limited by shares) and Table F (for a public limited company).

Before preparing the memorandum and articles, the draftsmen will need to obtain, from the promoters, information on matters such as the following:

1. *The nature of the business.*[72] This will be required in connection with the objects clauses of the memorandum unless the promoters are content to adopt the general purpose formula in section 3A.[73]

2. *The amount of nominal capital and the denomination of the shares into which it is to be divided* (assuming, of course, that it is to have a share capital). These will need to be stated in both the memorandum and articles. For the articles the draftsman will also require to know if the shares are to be all of one class and, if not, what special rights are to be attached to each class,[74] as these should be set out in the articles, but preferably not in the memorandum.[75] The capital of a public company will have to be not less than the authorised minimum.

3. *Any other special requirements which deviate from the normal as exemplified by the appropriate Table.* The most likely matters are quorums, and the minimum and maximum numbers of directors.

With the aid of this information the draftsman should have no difficulty in preparing drafts based on precedents from his own

---

68 s. 7(1).
69 s. 8(2).
70 s. 8(1).
71 Although these cannot now be formed, it has been thought necessary to retain this Table to ensure that those registered prior to 1981 maintain the appropriate forms of memoranda and articles.
72 Particular care will need to be taken if it is intended that the company shall obtain the advantage of charitable status. The courts will not look outside the memorandum to discover what the objects are, though it may look at surrounding circumstances to determine whether the stated objects are charitable: *Incorporated Council of Law Reporting v. Att.-Gen.* [1972] Ch. 73, C.A.
73 See Chap. 8 pp. 173, 174 above.
74 See further, Chaps. 14 and 20, below.
75 See Chap. 20, below.

experience, reference books, and the Tables. Moreover, most law stationers have their own standard forms set up in print, adaptation of which will reduce printing charges.

The main question for consideration is the extent to which Table A is to be adopted. The option of not registering any articles, which is permissible when the company is limited by shares, is rarely chosen because most companies on initial registration will be private ones and the incorporators will wish to include the sort of restrictions on freedom to transfer shares, which were a pre-condition for qualifying as a private company prior to the Companies Act 1980. The restrictions in Table A are limited to giving the directors a right to refuse to register a transfer when the shares are partly paid or the company has a lien upon them.[76] When the incorporation is a partnership or family business what will be wanted is an absolute discretion to reject transfers and, probably, provisions requiring the shares to be offered to the existing shareholders if a member wishes to sell. A common practice is to register articles which substitute alternative provisions for certain Table A provisions but adopt the rest. This reduces the length of the document and the printing costs.[77] But if this is done, care should be taken to specify exactly which provisions of Table A are excluded and not leave this to implication by some such formula as "Table A shall apply except in so far as it is varied by or inconsistent with the following provisions"—a formula which inevitably leads to trouble.

Unless economy is a serious consideration, however, it is far better to exclude Table A completely and to have self-contained articles, even if, as will almost certainly be the case, these in most respect merely duplicate the provisions of the Table. By so doing, the company's officer will not be faced with the task of extracting its regulations from two separate documents, one of which, Table A, may become progressively less accessible—for it will be appreciated that it is the Table extant at the time of incorporation which continues to govern.[78] Adoption of Table A is therefore often a false economy, particularly as the larger firms of company solicitors have their own standard forms which are kept in print by their stationers, thus minimising the costs to their clients.

In the case of a company whose memorandum states that its registered office is to be in Wales it is now permissible for the memorandum and articles (and other documents that have to be

---

[76] Table A 1985, art. 24.

[77] Articles must be printed: s.7(2). The Act specifically requires memoranda to be printed only when they are subsequently altered (s.6(1)(a)) but, in practice, both documents are printed and bound up together. Section 706 provides for prescription of the form, size, durability etc. of any documents delivered to the Registrar and s.707 facilitates the use of modern technology (on which see the D.T.I. *Guidance Note on Company Information on Magnetic Tape*, N.G. 24).

[78] This is often overlooked when new articles are adopted; it is the original, not the current Table A which should be expressly excluded.

delivered for registration) to be in Welsh, but they have to be accompanied by certified English translations when delivered for registration.[79]

The distinction between the memorandum and the articles of association has already been dealt with.[80] The effect of the two documents as between the members and the company will be considered later.[81]

Lodgment of documents

The final step is to lodge certain documents at the Companies' Registry.[82] The first of these documents—the memorandum and articles must each have been signed by at least two persons,[83] whose signatures must be attested by a witness.[84]

If the company has a share capital each subscriber to the memorandum must write opposite his name the number of shares he takes and must not take less than one.[85] In practice he will merely subscribe for one share in the first instance, irrespective of the number which he eventually intends to acquire, and more often than not clerks in the solicitors' office will sign as subscribers rather than the true promoters. On lodging the memorandum and articles they must be accompanied by two documents in the forms prescribed,[86] i.e. the *Statement of Particulars of the Directors and Secretary and Situation of Registered Office* and the *Declaration of Compliance.* The first of these[87] is required by section 10 of the Act. Under its subsection (2) the Statement must contain the names and "requisite particulars",[88] of the first directors and secretary of the company. An appointment made by the articles is void unless the appointee is named in the Statement.[89] The Statement may be signed either by or on behalf of the subscribers to the memorandum[90] but it must include

---

79 s.21.
80 Chap. 1, p. 14 above.
81 pp. 282–288, below.
82 Since 1976 this has been, for English and Welsh companies, at the Companies Registration Office, Maindy, Cardiff. Prior to that, the registry was at Companies House, City Road, London EC1, and search facilities have been retained there.
83 Presumably one will suffice when the Directive on Single Member Companies is implemented.
84 ss.1(1), 2(6) and 7(3)(6). *Semble,* an infant can be a subscriber (*Re Laxon & Co.* (No. 2) [1892] 3 Ch. 555, C.A.) as can an alien resident abroad: *Reuss v. Bos* (1871) L.R. 5 H.L. 176. If more than the minimum number subscribe the memorandum they must also subscribe the articles.
85 s.2(5).
86 The various prescribed forms are in the Companies (Forms) Regs 1985 (S.I. 1985 No. 854 (as amended)). This adopts, wherever possible, the helpful practice of numbering forms by the number of the relevant section of the Act. The forms are obtainable from any law stationer.
87 Which combines in one form what were formerly two.
88 See Sched. 1 to the Act (as amended by the 1989 Act).
89 s.10(5). Table A 1985 makes no provision for the first appointments which, in effect, can be made only by naming the appointees in the Statement and obtaining their signed consents.
90 When the memorandum is lodged by their agent, (*e.g.* the solicitor or accountant) the Statement must give his name and address: s.10(4).

a consent to act signed by each person named.[91] Finally, the Statement must also specify the intended situation of the company's registered office on incorporation. The memorandum will have stated whether this is to be in England and Wales or in Scotland[92] but it will not state its actual address which can be moved within the relevant country as the company decides so long as notice is given to the Registrar within 14 days.[93] But the company must, at all times, have a registered office to which all communications and notices may be addressed.[94]

The second of the two documents, the Declaration of Compliance, is required by section 12(3) and consists of a statutory declaration in the prescribed form, by either the solicitor or a director or secretary named in the Statement required under section 10, declaring that all the requirements of the Act in respect of registration and of matters precedent and incidental to it have been complied with.[95] Unless the Registrar is satisfied that the foregoing requirements have been complied with he is not entitled to register the company[96] but he may accept the declaration as sufficient evidence of compliance.[97]

Normally these will be the only documents required and all that will be needed in addition is payment of the registration fees.[98] However, as we have seen, a second declaration may be needed if the company is a guarantee company which wishes to dispense with "limited"[99]: and a further Statement will be required if the company's proposed name is one on which a Government Department of other body has to be consulted.[1]

Purchase of a shelf-company

If the incorporators have no immediate special requirements regarding the company's constitution or name, but want their business to be incorporated as rapidly as possible as a private company limited by shares, an alternative to registering a new company is to buy one off-the-shelf from one of the agencies which provide this service. This alternative is increasingly being adopted, somewhat to the horror of traditional company lawyers. Its great advantage is speed because all the incorporators have to do is to pay the agency and to take transfers of the subscribers' shares and

[91] s. 10(3).
[92] s.2. This determines the company's domicil and cannot be altered except as provided in s.2(2) as regards Welsh companies.
[93] s.287.
[94] *Ibid.* And the address must appear on its business letters and order forms:
[95] s.351(1)(a).
[96] s.12(3).
[97] s.12(1).
[98] s.12(3). And normally will unless a flaw is apparent from the documents lodged.
[99] See Companies (Fees) Regs 1988 (S.I. 1988 No. 887). The fee for initial registration is still only £50, despite the recent abolition of Capital Duty.
[1] pp. 268, 269 above.
p. 270 above.

custody of the company's registers. They will, of course, then have to send to the Registrar notices of changes of the directors and secretary (with the required consents) and of the situation of the registered office. Any other changes, (e.g. alterations of the articles or a change of name) can be effected at leisure. The main disadvantage is that until they make changes, the company's name is unlikely to bear any relationship to them or to the business being carried on. But with the recent virtual abolition of the ultra vires rule and the introduction of the all-purpose objects clause[2] there should be less risk that the objects clause of the memorandum of association will prove inappropriate.

Registration and Certificate of Incorporation

If the Registrar is satisfied that the requirements for registration are met and that the purpose for which the incorporators are associated is "lawful,"[3] he issues a certificate of incorporation signed by him or authenticated under his official seal.[4] This states that the company is incorporated and, in the case of a limited company that it is limited[5]; it is, in effect, the company's certificate of birth as a body corporate on the date mentioned in the certificate.[6] Section 13(7) declares that the certificate is conclusive evidence:

"(a) that the requirements of this Act in respect of registration and matters precedent and incidental to it have been complied with and that the association is a company authorised to be registered and is duly registered under this Act,[7] and

(b) if the certificate contains a statement that the company is a public company, that the company is such a company."

The functions of the Registrar in deciding whether or not to register the company are administrative, rather than judicial, but a refusal to register can be challenged by judicial review, albeit with

---

[2] s.3A inserted by the 1989 Act.
[3] See s.1(1) which permits incorporation only by "any two or more persons associated for a lawful purpose." This is interpreted as banning both purposes which are criminal and those which are regarded as contrary to public policy: R. v. Registrar of Joint Stock Companies [1931] 2 K.B. 197, C.A.; R. v. Registrar of Companies, ex p. HM's Attorney General, below p. 279 n.12. In the light of the decision in Yuen Kun Yeu v. A-G of Hong Kong [1988] A.C. 175, P.C., it seems clear that a member of the public subsequently defrauded by the company could not successfully sue the Registrar on the ground that he was negligent in registering the company (or, in the case of a public company, issuing the trading certificate).
[4] s.13(1) and (2). He also causes notice of the issue to be published in the Gazette (s.711(1)(a)) allots the company a registered number (s.705), and enters its name on the index of company names (s.714).
[5] s.13(1).
[6] s.13(3).
[7] It has been held to be conclusive as regards the date of incorporation even when that was clearly wrong: Jubilee Cotton Mills v. Lewis [1924] A.C. 958, H.L.

scant hope of success.[8] However, normally, the registration of a company cannot be challenged because of the conclusive effect of the certificate. This, happily, has rendered English Company Law virtually immune from the problems arising from defectively incorporated companies which have plagued the United States and many Continental countries.[9] But the decided cases on section 13(7) (or its predecessors under earlier Acts) and the recent review of them by the Court of Appeal in a case[10] concerning the, then, comparable provision relating to a certificate of registration of a charge on a company's property, show that this immunity is not complete. Since section 13 and its predecessors in earlier Companies Acts are not expressed to bind the Crown, the Attorney-General can apply to the court and may obtain certiorari to quash the registration.[11]

This was successfully done in R. v. *Registrar of Companies, Exp. H.M.'s Attorney-General*,[12] where a prostitute had succeeded in incorporating her business under the name of "Lindi St Claire (Personal Services) Ltd." (the Registrar having rejected her first preference of "Prostitutes Ltd." or "Hookers Ltd." and shown no enthusiasm for "Lindi St Claire (French Lessons) Ltd.") and, with scrupulous frankness, specified its primary object in the memorandum as "to carry on the business of prostitution."[13] The court, on judicial review at the instance of the Attorney-General, quashed the registration on the ground that the stated business was unlawful as contrary to public policy.[14] It is unlikely, however, that the Attorney-General (or any other Crown servant) will take action unless public policy is thought to be involved and will not do so if all that has occurred is a technical breach of the formalities of incorporation.

---

[8] R. v. *Registrar of Joint Stock Companies* [1931] 2 K.B. 197, C.A. where an application for mandamus to order the Registrar to register a company formed for the sale in England of tickets in the Irish Hospital Lottery was rejected on the ground that the Registrar had rightly concluded that such sales were illegal in England.

[9] See Drury, *Nullity of Companies in English Law* (1985) 48 M.L.R. 644. The First Company Law Directive contains three Articles dealing with Nullity.

[10] R. v. *Registrar of Companies, Exp. Central Bank of India* [1986] Q.B. 1114, C.A. Reversing the decision at first instance; the C.A. held that, even on judicial review, the effect of s.98(2) of the Companies Act 1948, under which the certificate of registration of a charge was "conclusive evidence that the requirements—as to registration have been satisfied," was to make evidence of non-compliance inadmissible, thus precluding the court from quashing the registration. As a result of the 1989 Act the certificate of registration of a charge is now conclusive only as regards the date when particulars were delivered: s.397(5).

[11] *Bowman v. Secular Society* [1917] A.C. 406, H.L. where, however certiorari was denied as the Society's purposes were held not to be unlawful.

[12] (1980) now reported in [1991] BCLC 476.

[13] Had she been less frank, for example by stating the primary object as "to carry on the business of masseuses and to provide related services," she would probably have got away with it.

[14] Notwithstanding that, as she indignantly protested, she paid income tax on her earnings. Since prostitution can be carried on without necessarily committing any criminal offence and since she continued, without incorporation, to practise her profession (for which she has become a well-known spokeswoman), some may think that this was an example of the "unruly horse" of public policy unseating its judicial riders.

Nevertheless there is one other situation in which the certificate does not seem to be conclusive of valid incorporation. This results from what is now section 2(2) of the Trade Union and Labour Relations Act 1974 (repeating similar provisions in earlier Acts) which declares that the registration of a trade union under the Companies Acts, shall be void.[15] In the past, parties other than the Crown have been held entitled to rely on this; for example as a defence to a claim by a registered company whose objects make it a trade union. The reported cases[16] related to versions of what is now section 13(7) which were less comprehensive and which were not thought to cover substantive matters but only ministerial acts leading to registration.[17] Hence, it seems doubtful if they would be followed today. However, the researches of Mr. Drury[18] have unearthed a more recent example of a company's removal from the register because its objects made it a trade union. The company in question was one formed by junior hospital doctors to represent their interests. It was later realised that its objects made it a trade union within the statutory definition. The Department of Trade took the view that section 2(2) of the 1974 Act overrode what is now section 13(7) of the Companies Act and accordingly the Registrar removed the company from the register for "void registration."[19] This, apparently, was done without any court order[20] and without challenge by the doctors. Presumably this action by the Registrar could be regarded as having been taken on behalf of the Crown and as the correction of a mistake which he, or one of his predecessors, had made and therefore as rectifiable.[21]

Hence, it now seems probable, but not certain, that in no circumstances can anyone other than the Crown plead the nullity of a registered company unless and until it has been removed from the register as a result of action by or on behalf of the Crown. Removal as a result of that action is tantamount to a declaration that it never existed as a corporate body.[22] This is not likely to be a satisfactory

---

[15] This contained an exception for "special register" unions—a category now obsolete though legislation continues to ignore that: see s.124 of the 1989 Act which inserts a new subs. (9) in the Trade Union and Labour Relations Act 1974, which refers to "a trade union, which…is a company within the meaning of the Companies Act 1985."

[16] *Edinburgh & District Water Manufacturers Asscn. v. Jenkinson* [1903] 5 Sessions Cases 1159; *British Asscn. of Glass Bottle Manufacturers v. Nettlefold* [1911] 27 T.L.R. 527 (where, however, the company was held not to be a trade union).

[17] (1911) 27 T.L.R. at 528, 529.

[18] *loc. cit.* n. 9, above, at pp. 649, 650.

[19] See *Companies in 1976* Table 10.

[20] Notwithstanding that the First Company Law Directive provides by Art. 11.1(*a*) that "Nullity must be ordered by a decision of a court of law."

[21] But, presumably, unless the company agreed, he could not take this action unless the incorporation was void (as in the case of a trade union or where the purposes were unlawful), rather than voidable (which would seem to be the case where, for example, registration had been secured by fraudulent misrepresentations).

[22] Whether this retrospective effect could be avoided by the A-G asking for relief in the nature of scire facias (instead of certiorari) is obscure. The writ itself seems to have been abolished by the Crown Proceedings Act 1947, s.13 and Sched. 1, and it was always doubtful whether it was available in relation to statutory incorporations.

outcome if it has in fact been carrying on business as what both its members and its creditors believed to be a registered company[23], it should be wound up[24] rather than declared never to have existed.[25] All that can be said with some assurance is that Mr. Drury[26] is right in concluding that, although cases of nullity of incorporation may be rare in England, they do happen and when they do the present law is unclear, unsatisfactory and not wholly consistent with our obligations under the First Company Law Directive which we purported to implement in 1972. Remedial legislative action is needed[27] and it is a pity that the opportunity to provide it was not taken in the Companies Act 1989 which remedied defects in relation to the analogous problem of ultra vires.

Commencement of Business

From the date of registration mentioned in the certificate of incorporation, the company, if it is a private company, becomes "capable forthwith of exercising all the functions of an incorporated company." But when it is registered as a public company this is "subject . . . to section 117 (additional certificate as the amount of allotted share capital)."[28] In order to ensure that the company complies with the stringent requirements imposed on a public company regarding the allotment of the minimum share capital, as already described in Chapter 9, it must not do business or exercise any borrowing powers until the Registrar has issued it with a certificate (commonly known as a "trading certificate") or it has re-registered as a private company.[29] Unless it does one or the other within a year from incorporation, it may be wound up by the Court and the Secretary of State may petition.[30]

[23] Their rights and obligations would be seriously affected (especially when the company was registered with limited liability) contrary to the First Company Law Directive, Art. 12.3.

[24] As the First Directive appears to envisage: see Art. 12.2.

[25] But as what? As a registered company, which it ostensibly is? Or as an unregistered company under Part V of the Insolvency Act 1986?

[26] *Loc. cit.* p. 279 n. 9 above.

[27] And if, under the present registration procedures, there is still a risk that a mistaken date of registration might appear on the certificate (as occurred in *Jubilee Cotton Mills v. Lewis*, above p. 278, n. 7) consideration should be given either to reversing the effect of that decision or to clarifying the inter-relationship between s.13 and s.36C on pre-incorporation contracts: see Chap. 12 at pp. 307 *et seq.* Under s.13(3) the company is incorporated "as from the date of incorporation mentioned in the certificate." If the company was registered on 3 January 1992 but, by a mistake, which so many of us make in January, the certificate read "1991," it would appear that any contracts made in the name of the company before it was in fact formed would bind the company and not, as under s.36C, the persons purporting to act for the company!

[28] s.13(4).

[29] s.117(1). In the more usual case where original registration was as a private company but it later converts to a public one, similar requirements will first have to be met (see ss.43–48) but there is no suspension of business during the process of conversion: below pp. 288–290.

[30] Insolvency Act 1986 ss.122(1)(b) and 124(4)(a).

In order to obtain the trading certificate the company must apply in the prescribed form supported by a statutory declaration in the prescribed form signed by a director or the secretary of the company.[31] This statutory declaration must state that the nominal amount of the allotted share capital is not less than the authorised minimum and must specify the amount paid up, the preliminary expenses and to whom they were paid or payable, and any payment or benefit to a promoter and what it was for.[32] The Registrar may accept this statutory declaration as sufficient evidence of the matters stated in it.[33] He may, however, have rather more information to go on, since within one month of allotting the shares the company will have had to deliver another document, the Return of Allotments, required by section 88 and, as regards any shares issued for a non-cash consideration, a copy of the valuation report required by sections 103 and 108.[34] Hence, only if he issues the certificate before the latter documents are filed will be need to rely solely on the bald statement in the statutory declaration that the minimum capital has been duly allotted. If satisfied, he has to issue the certificate.[35]

The certificate is "conclusive evidence that the company is entitled to do business and exercise any borrowing powers."[36] However, by analogy with the decisions referred to above[37] in relation to the certificate of incorporation, it appears that, as this section is not expressed to bind the Crown, the Registrar's decision could be quashed on judicial review at the instance of the Attorney-General.[38] This, in contrast with quashing registration, would not have the undesirable effect of nullifying the incorporation. A more likely course, however, would be for the Secretary of State, if he had grounds for suspecting that the share capital had not been properly allotted, to institute an investigation under Part XIV of the Act[39] and, if his suspicions proved well-founded, petition the court to wind up the company under section 124 or 124A of the Insolvency Act.

Contractual effect of the memorandum and articles

Section 14 of the Act provides that the memorandum and articles, "shall, when registered, bind the company and its members to the same extent as if they respectively had been signed and sealed by each member, and contained covenants on the part of each member to observe all" their provisions, and that money payable by a

[31] s.117(2).
[32] s.117(3).
[33] s.117(5).
[34] s.111. On ss.103 and 108, see Chap. 9 at pp. 204–207 above.
[35] s.117(2).
[36] s.117(6).
[37] See pp. 278–281 above.
[38] See p. 279 above.
[39] See Chap. 25 below.

member to the company under the memorandum or articles shall be in the nature of a specialty debt.

The wording of this section can be traced back with variations to the original Act of 1844 which adopted the existing method of forming an unincorporated joint stock company by deed of settlement (which did, of course, constitute a contract between the members who sealed it) and merely superimposed incorporation on registration. The 1856 Act substituted the memorandum and articles for the deed of settlement and introduced a provision on the lines of the present section. Unhappily, full account was not taken of the vital new factor (namely that the incorporated company was a separate legal entity) and the words "as if . . . signed and sealed by each member" did not have added to them "and by the company." This oddity has survived into the modern Acts (with the result that debts due *from* the company to a member under the contract are not specialty debts).[40] Despite the odd wording, however, certain points are clearly established.

First, the memorandum and articles constitute a contract between the company and each member.[41] But it is a contract with various special characteristics. Section 14 expressly provides that it is "subject to the provisions of this Act."[42] Those provisions include sections which permit of alterations of the memorandum and articles of association by means of a special resolution. Thus, a member enters into a contract on terms which are alterable by the other party,[43] rather in the same way as a member of a club agrees to be bound by the club rules as validly altered from time to time, or a workman agrees to be employed on the terms of a collective agreement as occasionally varied by the employers and his trade union. Nor can the memorandum or articles be rectified by the court if they do not truly reflect the agreement between the company and its members.[44] And formerly it was widely believed that a member's remedies against the company for breach of the statutory contract were restricted to actions for an injunction or declaration or for a liquidated sum due to him as a member and that the effect of the decision in *Houldsworth*

---

[40] Hence sums due as repayment of share capital become statute-barred on the lapse of the shorter period applicable to simple contracts, in contrast with those due on express contracts under the company's seal, such as bonds or debentures: *Re Compania de Electricidad de Buenos Aires:* [1980] Ch. 146 at 187.

[41] *Hickman* v. *Kent or Romney Marsh Sheepbreeders' Assoc.* [1915] 1 Ch. 881, where Astbury J. reviewed earlier cases in a judgment which has become the *locus classicus.* An article providing for a reference to arbitration of disputes between members and the company was held to be contractually binding.

[42] Articles cannot therefore contract out of the statutory requirement in s.183(1) (which expressly operates, "notwithstanding anything in the company's articles") for a written instrument for the transfer of shares: *Re Greene* [1949] Ch. 333, C.A.

[43] *Shuttleworth* v. *Cox* [1927] 2 K.B. 9, C.A., *per* Atkin L.J. at p. 26; *Malleson* v. *National Insurance and Guarantee Corporation* [1894] 1 Ch. 200, *per* North J. at p. 205.

[44] *Scott* v. *Frank Scott (London) Ltd.* [1940] Ch. 794, C.A. On the power of the court to rectify the share register, see below p. 386.

v. City of Glasgow Bank[45] was to preclude him from suing for damages for breach of contract while he remained a member of the company. In view, however, of the new section 111A[46] inserted by the 1989 Act that is no longer a tenable view.

Secondly, the contract is enforceable among the members *inter se.* The principal occasions on which this question is likely to be important arise when articles confer on members a right of pre-emption or first refusal when another member wishes to sell his shares[47] or, more rarely, impose a duty on the remaining members or the directors to buy the shares of a retiring member.[48] A direct action between the shareholders concerned is here possible; and for the law to insist on action through the company would merely be to promote multiplicity of actions and involve the company in unnecessary litigation.

Thirdly, the decisions have constantly affirmed that the section confers contractual effect on a provision in the memorandum and articles only in so far as it affords rights or imposes obligations on a member qua member.[49] As Astbury J. said in the *Hickman* case[50]:

"An outsider to whom rights purport to be given by the articles in his capacity as such outsider, whether he is or subsequently becomes a member, cannot sue on those articles, treating them as contracts between himself and the company, to enforce those rights."

The same applies to the contract between the members *inter se.*[51] On the wording of the section it would be difficult to interpret it as creating a contract with anyone other than the company and the members. Furthermore, there is obvious sense in restricting the ambit of the section to matters concerning the affairs of the company.[52] But there is no obvious justification in the statutory wording for still further restricting it to matters concerning a member in his capacity

---

45 (1880) 5 App.Cas. 317, H.L.
46 "A person is not debarred from obtaining damages or other compensation by reason only of his holding or having held shares in the company or any right to apply or subscribe for shares or to be included in the company's register in respect of shares."
47 *Borland's Trustee* v. *Steel* [1901] 1 Ch. 279 (member seeking declaration that rights of pre-emption in articles were valid). *cf. Lyle & Scott* v. *Scott's Trustees* [1959] A.C. 763, H.L.
48 *Rayfield* v. *Hands* [1960] Ch. 1, where Vaisey J. was prepared to make an order in effect for specific performance.
49 But not necessarily qua shareholder; in *Lion Mutual Marine Insurance* v. *Tucker* (1883) 12 Q.B.D. 176, C.A., the provision concerned the members' liabilities qua insurers.
50 [1915] 1 Ch. 881 at 897.
51 *London Sack & Bag Co.* v. *Dixon & Lugton* [1943] 2 All E.R. 763, C.A.
52 If the solicitor had slipped into the articles, to which he and his wife were the subscribers, a provision to the effect that he and his wife should no longer be bound to cohabit, it would be absurd if this were treated as a deed of separation.

of member.[53] It may not matter much that the result is that a provision that a promoter, who becomes a member, cannot enforce a provision that the company shall reimburse the expenses he incurred,[54] or that solicitor, who becomes a member, cannot enforce a provision that he shall be the company's solicitor.[55] What does matter is that it apparently prevents a member who is also a director or other officer of the company from enforcing any rights purporting to be conferred by the articles on directors or officers. Only if he has a contract extraneous to the articles will he have contractual rights and obligations *vis-à-vis* the company or his fellow members. This, as we have seen in relation to directors' contracts of service,[56] does not mean that such an extraneous contract may not be interpreted in the light of the articles or adopt provisions in them but it presumably does mean (though there seems to be no reported decision to that effect) that a non-executive director without any express or implied contract with the company cannot sue to recover directors' fees.

It is highly anomalous to treat directors as "outsiders" since for most purposes the law treats them as the paradigm "insiders" (which members, as such, are not) and they will breach their fiduciary duties and duties of care if they do not act in accordance with the memorandum and articles. It also produces some strange results. *Hickman's case*[57] concerned a provision in the articles stating that any dispute between the company and a member should be referred to arbitration and this was enforced as a contract. But in the later case of *Beattie* v. *Beattie Ltd.*[58] where there was a similar provision, the Court of Appeal, relying on the dictum in *Hickman*, held that a dispute between a company and a director (who was a member) was not subject to the provision because the dispute was admittedly in relation to the director qua director. In the still later case of *Rayfield* v. *Hands*,[59] the articles of a private company provided that a member intending to transfer his shares should give notice to the directors "who will take the said shares equally between them at a fair value." A member gave notice but the directors refused to buy. Vaisey J. felt able to hold that the provision was concerned with the relationship between the member and the directors as members and ordered them to buy.[60]

This difficult concept of "member in his capacity of member" has not been carried by the courts to what might be its logical conclusion, *i.e.* that, since a member need not be a shareholder[61] (or, more

---

[53] Courts have, however, put a similar construction on "member" in what is now s.459 (members' remedy against unfair prejudice): see Chap. 24 below.
[54] *Re English & Colonial Produce Co.* [1906] 2 Ch. 435.
[55] *Eley* v. *Positive Life Association* (1876) 1 Ex.D. 88, C.A.
[56] Chap. 7 at p. 156 above.
[57] Above n. 41.
[58] [1938] Ch. 708, C.A.
[59] [1960] Ch. 1.
[60] What he would have held if one of the directors had not been a member is unclear.
[61] He cannot be a shareholder if the company has no share capital.

rarely, a shareholder a member[62]) the statutory contract does not embrace matters appertaining to him as a shareholder only. Rights conferred by the articles to attend general meetings, to speak thereat and to vote on a show of hands are clearly rights qua member.[63] Rights to vote on a poll seem to be a mixture of both membership and shareholder rights since the number of votes exercisable will normally depend on the number of shares held as well as on membership. But rights to a return of capital,[64] to payment of a dividend duly declared and payable,[65] or to receive a share certificate[66] appear to affect a member solely as shareholder. Happily it has never been doubted that the statutory contract applies to all these cases.[67]

However, in addition to these relatively straightforward examples, section 14 is also important in relation to the rights of members in restrain corporate irregularities and to the so-called Rule in *Foss v. Harbottle*. This Rule is discussed in some detail in Chapter 24. Here it suffices to say that, subject to certain exceptions, if the irregularity complained of is a wrong done to the company, the company acting, normally, through its board of directors, is the only proper plaintiff in an action to prevent, or recover in respect of, the wrong, and that when, in exceptional circumstances, an individual member is allowed to sue he must do so in a "derivative action" suing on behalf of himself and the other members and joining the company as a defendant. None of this applies, however, if his personal rights have been infringed. In that event the only restriction is that he may not be allowed to sue if the irregularity complained of is one which could be put right by an ordinary resolution of the company.

In 1957, Lord Wedderburn, in his seminal article on *Foss v. Harbottle*,[68] pointed out that, in *Quinn & Axtens Ltd. v. Salmon*,[69] the Court of Appeal and the House of Lords allowed a managing director, suing as a member, to obtain an injunction restraining the company from completing transactions entered into in breach of the company's articles which provided that the consent of the two managing directors was required in relation to such transactions.

[62] He need not be a member if he holds share warrants to bearer: see below pp. 384, 385.
[63] As in *Pender v. Lushington* [1877] Ch.D. 70.
[64] As in *Re Compania de Electricidad de Buenos Aires* [1980] Ch. 146, above p. 283 n. 40.
[65] As in *Wood v. Odessa Waterworks Co.* (1889) 42 Ch.D. 636.
[66] As in *Burdett v. Standard Exploration Co.* (1899) 16 T.L.R. 112.
[67] Nor was it argued in *Rayfield v. Hands* that the provision did not relate qua member to the member disposing of his shares. It also seems to be assumed that a provision in the articles entitling the holders of a class of shares to appoint a director is enforceable as a s.14 contract between the class members and the company. Where debentureholders are given such a right it will normally be prescribed in the debentures and therefore enforceable as a contract extraneous to the memorandum and articles.
[68] *Shareholders' Rights and the Rule in Foss v. Harbottle*, [1957] Camb. L.J. 193, especially at pp. 210–215. See also Beck (1974) 22 Can.B.R. 157 at 190–193.
[69] [1909] 1 Ch. 311, C.A.; affd. [1909] A.C. 442, H.L.

This, in effect, showed that a member had a personal right to require the company to act in accordance with its articles, which right could be enforced by the member even though the result was indirectly to protect a right which was afforded to him (or presumably anyone else) in some other capacity. If this is correct the supposed principle, that there is a statutory contract between the company and its members only in respect of matters affecting members qua members, is effectively outflanked—though presumably it still applies to the statutory contact between members *inter se*.

As we have seen, this has not caused the judges to cease to express the orthodox view[70] which, on the whole, continues to be espoused in the text-books. It has, however, led to a fascinating and continuing debate in the law reviews,[71] in which the contributors, Goldberg, G. N. Prentice, Gregory and Drury, favour the Wedderburn view rather than the orthodox one but seek to refine it. Goldberg does this by narrowing Wedderburn's formulation so that it would provide that a member of a company has a contractual right under section 14 to have any affairs of the company conducted by the particular organ of the company specified in the Act or the company's memorandum or articles, even if its enforcement has the effect of indirectly, enforcing outsider rights. That, he argues with force, would produce a conclusion desirable on policy grounds and would not conflict with decisions such as those in *Ely* v. *Positive Life Assurance* or *Beattie* v. *Beattie*, neither of which concerned what organ should conduct the company's affairs. Prentice takes a broadly similar view but expresses it somewhat differently. He argues that a member qua member can sue the company to compel it to observe those provisions which relate to the company's constitutional powers and their exercise, even if that indirectly enforces his rights as an outsider, and that the company can sue a member on any provision of the memorandum and articles relating to him qua member whether or not the provision relates to such constitutional matters. Gregory flatly denies that there is any extant rule that the statutory contract arises only when it affects members qua members and contends that the Court of Appeal decision in *Beattie* v. *Beattie* was plainly wrong in the light of the earlier House of Lord's decision in *Quinn & Axtens* v *Salmon*,[72] and Drury's conclusion is essentially similar to that of Wedderburn but

---

70 But Wedderburn can point to later decisions which afford support for his interpretation of *Quinn & Axtens*: see, e.g. *Re Harmer Ltd.* [1959] 1 W.L.R. 62 at 85 and 89 (C.A.), *Re Richmond Gate Property Co.* [1965] 1 W.L.R. 335, (see (1965) 28 M.L.R. 347 and (1966) 29 M.L.R. 608 at 612; *Hogg* v. *Cramphorn* [1967] Ch. 254; *Bamford* v. *Bamford* [1970] Ch. 212; *Re Sherbourn Park Residents Co. Ltd.* (1986) 2 BCC 99,528; *Breckland Group Holdings* v. *London & Suffolk Properties* [1989] B.C.L.C. 100 (see (1989) 52 M.L.R. 401 at 407, 408); *Guinness plc* v. *Saunders* [1990] 2 A.C. 663, H.L.

71 See, pro. tem, Goldberg, (1972) 33 M.L.R. 362; G. N. Prentice, (1980) 1 Co.Law 179; Gregory, (1981) 44 M.L.R. 526; Goldberg, (replying) (1985) 48 M.L.R. 121; and Drury [1986] Camb. L.J. 219.

72 In this he is not supported by Goldberg: see (1985) 48 M.L.R. 121.

with the gloss that an individual member should not be able to enforce rights relating to him as an outsider in disregard of the views and interests of other members, so that the matter should ultimately be decided, like other matters of internal management, by the members in general meeting.[72a]

There, for the present, the matter rests and this book is not the appropriate place to carry the debate further. What clearly is needed is either a review of all the relevant authorities by the House of Lords or a revised version of section 14. And the latter would probably be desirable even if there were a definitive ruling by the Lords since, on the present wording of the section, it is difficult to see how any interpretation could cure all its imperfections. At the very least the section needs to be re-drafted so that it says that the memorandum and articles constitute a contract between the company, its members, directors and other officers and also provides that whether that contract is sought to be enforced by or against the company, it should be treated similarly, either as a simple contract or as a contract under seal.

Re-Registration of an Existing Company

A company may wish, at some stage, to convert itself into a company of a different type. This, in most cases, it may do without the expense of effecting a complete re-organisation of the types referred to in Chapter 26, below, and without having to form a brand new company. The circumstances and methods whereby conversions may be achieved are now collected together in Part II of the Act.

(i) Private company becoming public

Under sections 43 to 48 a private company limited by shares can become re-registered as a public company, by passing a special resolution that it should be so re-registered and applying to the Registrar in the prescribed form signed by a director or the secretary, accompanying the application by a number of documents designed to enable the Registrar to satisfy himself that the minimum capital requirements for a public company are complied with.[73] The special resolution must alter the memorandum of association to state that the company is to be a public company and must make such further alterations as are necessary to comply with the provisions of the Act in relation to public companies[74] (including the change of the suffix to

[72a] This gloss would seemingly come close to reducing the member's personal right to his position in a derivative action: *Smith* v. *Croft (No. 2)* [1988] Ch. 114, discussed Chap. 24 at pp. 656–660 below.
[73] s.43(1).
[74] s.43(2).

its name from "Ltd." to "plc"[75]) and it must also make any needed alterations to its articles of association.[76]

The documents that must accompany the application are copies of:

(a) the altered memorandum and articles;

(b) a balance sheet dated not more than seven months before the application and the auditors' report thereon, which must be "unqualified",[77]

(c) a written statement by the auditors that that balance sheet showed that at its date the company's net assets were not less than the aggregate of its called up share capital and undistributable reserves;

(d) when, since the balance sheet date, shares have been allotted otherwise than for cash, the valuation report required under sections 103 and 108;[78]

(e) a statutory declaration by a director or secretary of the company confirming that the special resolution has been passed, that the conditions of sections 44 and 45 have been complied with, and that no change has occurred since the balance sheet date resulting in the net assets becoming less than the called up capital and undistributable reserves.[79]

and these documents must be supported by

If the Registrar is satisfied that the company may be re-registered as a public company,[80] he issues a new certificate of incorporation,[81] the alterations in the memorandum and articles take effect, and the company becomes a public company.[82] In effect, the certificate is a combined certificate of incorporation and trading certificate which would have been needed had the company been initially registered as a public company.

If the private company, which wishes to convert to a public one, is an unlimited company it will, of course, have to become limited that being one of the essential elements of the definition of a public company. This, by virtue of section 48, it is enabled to do in the

[75] Or the Welsh equivalents.
[76] s.43(2)(c).
[77] Defined in s.46, as amended by the 1989 Act.
[78] See pp. 204–207 above.
[79] s.43(3).
[80] He may accept the statutory declaration as sufficient evidence (s.47(2)) but must not issue the certificate if it appears that the court has made an order confirming a reduction of capital bringing the company's allotted share capital below the authorised minimum: s.47(3).
[81] Which is conclusive evidence that the requirements have been met: s.47(5). On "conclusiveness," see pp. 278–280 and 282 above.
[82] s.47(4).

conversion operation—and rather more simply than if it first re-registered as limited under (iv) below, and subsequently re-registered under section 43 as a public company. It merely has to add to the special resolution that the liability of the members is to be limited and what its share capital is to be and to make the appropriate alterations in the company's memorandum.[83]

(ii) Public company becoming private

To convert from public to private (an operation which must not be confused with "privatisation" in the sense of de-nationalisation) is comparatively simple unless there is disagreement among the members. Under section 53 it can convert to a private company limited by shares or by guarantee[84] by passing a special resolution making the necessary alterations to the memorandum and articles and applying, in the prescribed form, to the Registrar with a copy of the amended memorandum and articles. But special safeguards are prescribed since loss of public status may have adverse consequences to the members, especially as regards their ability to dispose of their shares. Hence, under section 54, members who have not consented to, or voted in favour of, the resolution can, within 28 days of the resolution, apply to the court for the cancellation of the resolution if they can muster the support of:

(a) holders of not less than 5 per cent. in nominal value of the company's share capital or any class of it; or

(b) if the company is not limited by shares,[85] not less than 5 per cent. of the members; or

(c) not less than 50 members.

The Registrar must not issue a new certificate of incorporation until the 28 days have expired without an application having been made or, if it has been made, until it has been withdrawn or dismissed and a copy of the court order delivered to the Registrar.[86] The Court has powers similar to those on an application under sections 4 and 5 in relation to a resolution altering a company's objects.[87] Unless the

[83] s.48(2).

[84] For obvious reasons it cannot, by this simple process, convert to an unlimited company: s.53(3). Nor can it become a company limited by guarantee but with a share capital: s.1(4).

[85] This is somewhat puzzling since, until the Registrar issues a new certificate, the company remains a public company (s.55(2)) which it could not be unless it had a share capital. Presumably (b) is to cater for an "old public company", which has still not re-registered under the transitional provisions, now in the Companies Consolidation (Consequential Provisions) Act 1985, ss.1–9. As there can now be few, if any, such companies that have not re-registered under the transitional provisions either as plcs or as private companies, this book ignores them.

[86] s.53.

[87] s.54(5), (6), (7) and (8).

court cancels the resolution, the Registrar issues a new certificate of incorporation with the usual conclusive consequences.[88]

A public company will have to re-register as a private company if, under section 137,[89] the court makes an order confirming the reduction of its capital which has the effect of reducing the nominal amount of its allotted share capital below "the authorised minimum." In such circumstances that order will not be registered and come into effect (unless the court otherwise directs) until the company is re-registered as a private company.[90] The court may (and, in practice will) authorise this to be done without the need to resort to section 53. Instead of the company having to pass a special resolution, the court will specify in the order the alterations to be made in the memorandum and articles[91] and, on application in the prescribed form signed by a director or the secretary, accompanied by a printed copy of the memorandum and articles as so altered,[92] the Registrar will issue the new certificate of incorporation.[93] In this case there can be no application to the court by dissenting members[94] since the company has no option but to become private.

(iii) Limited company becoming unlimited

The conversion which presents the greatest dangers to the members is, obviously, that from a limited company to an unlimited one. Nevertheless it is not completely banned since the members of a small private company may legitimately conclude that forfeiting the advantages of limited liability is worthwhile, as enabling them to operate with much the same flexibility (particularly as regards withdrawal of their capital) and privacy of their financial affairs as a partnership, while yet retaining all the advantages of corporate personality other than limited liability. Hence, under section 49 a private limited company[95] may re-register as an unlimited company if all the members agree.[96] As with other conversions, an application, in the prescribed form and signed by a director or the secretary, has to be lodged with the Registrar, together with supporting documents.[97] The application must set out the alterations to be made in the memorandum and articles,[98] and the supporting documents needed are[99]:

88 s.55.
89 See Chap. 9 at pp. 211, 212 above and Chap. 26 at p. 691 below.
90 s.139(1) and (2).
91 s.139(3).
92 s.139(4).
93 s.139(5).
94 Under s.54, above.
95 s.49(3).
96 s.49(8)(*a*) and (5).
97 s.49(4).
98 s.49(5), (6) and (7).
99 s.49(8).

(a) the prescribed form of assent signed by or on behalf of all the members[1];

(b) a statutory declaration by the directors, confirming that assent and stating that they have taken all reasonable steps to satisfy themselves that each person who signed on behalf of a member was empowered to do so;

(c) a printed copy of the altered memorandum; and

(d) if articles have been registered (as they normally will have been) a printed copy of them incorporating any alterations.

The Registrar then issues a new certificate of incorporation with the usual conclusive effect.[2]

(iv) Unlimited company becoming limited

In this, the converse of case (iii), it is not the members who need special safeguards but the creditors. Surprisingly, however, in section 51 of the Companies Act under which this conversion is effected (unless it is combined with a conversion from a private to a public company under section 43, *i.e.* under (i) above) the only protection afforded them is that the new suffix, "Ltd.," to the company's name should alert them to the fact that it has become a limited company. Their real protection is afforded by what is now section 77 of the Insolvency Act 1986, which applies whether the conversion is achieved under section 43 or 51.[3] The effect of this is that those who were members of the company at the time of its re-registration remain potentially liable in respect of its debts and liabilities contracted prior thereto if winding up commences within three years of the re-registration.[4]

Section 51 permits re-registration as a company whether limited by shares or by guarantee. The first step is the passing of a special resolution stating which of these the company is to be and making the necessary alterations to its memorandum and articles.[5] A copy of this must (like all special resolutions) be forwarded to the Registrar within 15 days. With it, or subsequently, an application in the prescribed form, signed by a director or the secretary, and accompanied by printed copies of the altered memorandum and

---

[1] Including the personal representatives of any deceased member and the trustee in bankruptcy of any member: s.49(9). In the event of the company's subsequent liquidation, a past member is not liable to contribute to its assets to a greater extent (if any) than if the conversion had not occurred: Insolvency Act 1986, s.78.

[2] s.50.

[3] Insolvency Act s.77(1).

[4] *Ibid.* s.77(2)–(4) which, in a somewhat confusing manner, make the necessary adjustments to s.74 regarding the respective obligations of past and present members.

[5] s.51(1), (2), (3).

articles must be lodged with the Registrar[6] who then issues a new certificate of incorporation with the usual conclusive consequences.[7]

Ban on vacillation between limited and unlimited

What a company is not permitted to do is to chop and change more than once between limited and unlimited. Once a limited company has been re-registered as unlimited it cannot again re-register as a public company under section 43[8] or as a limited company under section 51[9] and once an unlimited company has been re-registered as a limited company under section 51, it cannot be re-registered as an unlimited company under section 49.[10] There is, however, no ban on switching back and forth between private limited company and public limited company.

TREATMENT OF UNREGISTERED COMPANIES

A matter which has caused the Department of Trade and Industry and Parliamentary Counsel agonies disproportionate to its practical importance is how to deal with "unregistered companies," *i.e.* bodies not formed under our past or present companies' legislation.[11] The solution has been to deal with them in four ways, only two of which, the third and fourth, require more than a mention here. The first has been to apply to all bodies incorporated and having a place of business in Great Britain[12] (other than (a) those formed under a public general Act, (b) those not formed for the purposes of gain, and (c) those exempted by a direction of the Secretary of State) an ever increasing number of the provisions of the Companies Act.[13] The second has been to subject to the winding up jurisdiction of the courts[14] a still wider range of bodies, corporate or unincorporated.[15]

The third has been to include in the Companies Act special provisions whereby unregistered companies can re-register under the Act. The object of this is to enable (and, indeed to encourage) the few remaining companies formed by deeds of settlement, private Acts

---

6 s.51(4) and (5).
7 s.52.
8 s.43(1).
9 s.51(2).
10 s.49(2) and (3).
11 Companies formed under earlier companies' legislation are, if still surviving, subject to all the present provisions of the Act (see ss.675–677) except to the extent that these expressly provide (as occasionally they do) that they shall not apply to companies formed prior to a stated date.
12 And to any surviving unincorporated bodies entitled by virtue of letters patent to any privilege conferred by the Chartered Companies Act 1837 (s.718(4)).
13 s.718 and Sched. 22 (as amended by the 1989 Act) and the Companies (Unregistered Companies) Regs. 1985 (S.I. 1985 No. 680).
14 Insolvency Act 1936, Part V.
15 *i.e.* "any association and any company" except a railway company incorporated by Act of Parliament: *ibid.* s.220.

of Parliament or letters patent to register under the Companies Act without having to form a new company and wind up the old one. The modus operandi is dealt with in Chapter II[16] of Part XXII of the Act as supplemented by Schedule 21.[17] Subject to various qualifications and exceptions, any such company with two or more members may register under the Act as an unlimited company, or as a company limited by shares or by guarantee.[18] A distinction is drawn between companies which were "joint stock companies" (essentially those with a share capital)[19] and others. Only the former may register as companies limited by shares[20] and may do so either as private companies or, if they comply with the normal conditions for registration as a public company and for obtaining a trading certificate, as public companies.[21] On registration, a deed of settlement company may substitute a memorandum and articles of association for the deed of settlement but need not do so.[22] The procedural requirements for registration are a cross between those required for initial registration and for re-registration as a different type of company under the provisions dealt with above[23] and there are similar controls over company names.[24] On registration the Registrar issues a certificate which has the usual conclusive consequences.[25] The details of the effect of registration, provisions for the automatic vesting of property, savings for existing liabilities and rights and similar matters are dealt with in Schedule 21.[26]

The fourth solution is that applied to what the Act calls "oversea companies," namely companies incorporated outside Great Britain but which establish a place of business (as opposed to merely doing business) here. Oversea companies are dealt with in Part XXIII of the Act,[27] Chapter I of which requires such companies to deliver to the Registrar for registration certain particulars within one month of establishing the place of business,[28] and to give him notice of any changes.[29] The particulars required include a copy of the company's constitution with an English translation and details of the directors

---

16 *i.e.* ss.680–690. Only the salient features are dealt with here.
17 As amended by the 1989 Act.
18 s.680.
19 s.683.
20 ss.680(3), 684.
21 s.685.
22 s.690. The Stock Exchange when, as a result of the City's "Big Bang," it re-registered as a limited company initially retained its deed of settlement.
23 ss.681, 684, 685 and 686.
24 ss.682, 687.
25 s.688.
26 s.689. See, in particular, Sched. 21 paras. 5 and 6 on how certain provisions in its constitution (unless, in the case of a deed of settlement company, it substitutes a memorandum and articles) have to be treated in future as if they were in a memorandum.
27 ss.691–703N, as amended by the 1989 Act.
28 s.691. The date on which the place of business was established must be stated in a statutory declaration: s.691(1)(b)(iv).
29 s.692.

and secretary and of a person or persons resident in Great Britain authorised to accept service on behalf of the company.[30] In addition, requirements, similar to those relating to companies incorporated here, apply in respect of publicity of the company's name at places of business and on business communications but with the need also to state the country of the company's incorporation.[31] And, as we have seen, there is also control over the name in which the company may carry on business in Great Britain.[32]

Chapter II of Part XXIII, as substituted by the 1989 Act,[33] requires oversea companies to prepare, and to deliver to the Registrar, the like accounts and directors' and auditors' reports as would be required if the company were registered under the Act.[34] This, however, is subject to certain adaptations in section 701 and to the power in section 700 whereby the Secretary of State may by order (a) modify those requirements in relation to oversea companies or (b) exempt an oversea company from those requirements or such of them as are specified in the order. This power has been exercised by the Oversea Companies (Accounts) (Modifications and Exemptions) Order 1990.[35]

Under Chapter III[36] of Part XXIII, inserted by the 1989 Act,[37] an oversea company is subject, as respects charges on its property in Great Britain, to detailed requirements regarding registration of those charges similar to those required of an English company.[38]

Moreover, like any foreign company with a sufficient connection with this country[39] for the English Courts to have jurisdiction to wind it up, it will be liable to be wound up, as an unregistered company, under Part V of the Insolvency Act 1986.[40]

---

[30] s.695 ensures that it will always be possible to serve process or notice so long as there is "a place of business established by the company in G.B."

[31] s.693.

[32] s.694: see p. 273 above.

[33] 1989 Act Sched. 10, para. 13.

[34] s.700. For those requirements, see Chap. 17 at pp. 453 *et seq.*

[35] S.I. 1990 No. 440.

[36] ss.703A–703N.

[37] 1989 Act, Sched. 15.

[38] See Chap. 16 below. The amended version of these provisions resulting from the 1989 Act cures the former absurdity that a foreign company which had not filed documents with the Registrar under what is now Chapter I of Part XXIII, (*e.g.* because it had not established a place of business in G.B.) had nevertheless to register such charges with the Registrar who would have no file on the company in which to do so. s.703A(3) introduces the concept of "a registered oversea company," (*i.e.* "an oversea company which has duly delivered documents ... under section 691 and has not subsequently given notice ... under section 694(4) that it has ceased to have an established place of business" in G.B.) and restricts registration of charges to "registered oversea companies."

[39] On which see *Re Compania Merabello S.A.* [1973] Ch. 75 at 91, 92; and *Re A Company (No. 00359 of 1987)* [1988] Ch. 210.

[40] See particularly Insolvency Act ss.221(2) and (5) and s.225.

CHAPTER 12

PROMOTERS

MEANING OF "PROMOTER"

IF, in a psycho-analyst's consulting room, we were asked to say what picture formed in our minds at the mention of the expression "company promoter," most of us would probably confess that we envisaged a character of dubious repute and antecedents who infests the commercial demi-monde[1] with a menagerie of bulls, bears, stags, and sharks as his familiars, and who, after rising to affluence by preying on the susceptibilities of a gullible public, finally retires from the scene in the blaze of a sensational suicide or Old Bailey trial.[2] In other words, we should envisage someone whose profession it was to form bogus companies and foist them off on the public to the latter's detriment and his own profit. Such figures have existed and it is probably too much to hope that they will ever be entirely eradicated, but even in their Edwardian heyday they formed only the minutest fraction of those whom the law classifies as promoters. A much more typical, if less romantic, example, would be the village grocer who converts his business into a limited company. He, of course, is in no sense a professional company promoter, always and increasingly a rare bird,[3] but he would be the promoter of his little company, and a moment's thought will make it clear that the difference, however great, between him and a professional promoter is basically one of degree rather than of kind. Both create or help to create the company and seek to sell it something, whether it be their services or a business. Both are obviously so placed that they can easily take advantage of their position by obtaining a recompense grossly in excess of the true value of what they are selling.[4] The only difference is that the grocer is less likely than the professional to abuse his position since he will probably continue to be the majority shareholder in his company, whereas the promoter, if a shareholder at all, will intend to off-load his holdings on to others as soon as possible.

It will have been apparent from the foregoing that the expression "promoter" covers a wide range of persons. Indeed it is still wider.

---

[1] Somehow associated in our minds with "the curb."
[2] It is perhaps a tribute to the law that we definitely picture him as coming to a sticky end; cf. Lord MacNaghten in *Gluckstein v. Barnes* [1900] A.C. 240, H.L. at 248.
[3] As pointed out in the next chapter, the handling of public issues is now virtually monopolised by reputable merchant bankers. It is the close scrutiny by these and The Stock Exchange as much as the rigour of the law which has caused the virtual disappearance of the old-time promoter.
[4] A good (or rather, bad) example of the modus operandi is *Re Darby* [1911] 1 K.B. 95.

Both the professional promoter and the village grocer are promoters to the fullest extent, in that each "undertakes to form a company with reference to a given project, and to set it going and ... takes the necessary steps to accomplish that purpose."[5] But a person may be a promoter who has taken a much less active and dominating role; the expression may, for example, cover any individual or company that arranges for someone to become a director, places shares, or negotiates preliminary agreements.[6] Nor need he necessarily be associated with the initial formation of the company; one who subsequently helps to arrange the "floating off" of its capital (in the manner explained in the next chapter) will equally be regarded as a promoter.[7] On the other hand, those who act in a purely ministerial capacity, such as solicitors and accountants, will not be classified as promoters merely because they undertake their normal professional duties[8]; although they may if, for example, they have agreed to become directors or to find others who will.[9]

Who constitutes a promoter in any particular case is therefore a question of fact.[10] The expression has never been clearly defined either judicially[11] or legislatively, despite the fact that it is frequently used both in decisions and statutes. So far as the promoter himself is concerned this imposes no particular hardship; as we shall see, his duty is merely to act with good faith towards the company and this he should do whether legally compelled or not. But from the point of view of the company the vagueness of the term is apt to be embarrassing when legislation requires promoters to be named or transactions with them to be disclosed.[12]

Duties of promoters

The early Companies Acts contained no provisions regarding the liabilities of promoters, and even today they are largely silent on the subject, merely imposing liability for untrue statements in listing

---

[5] Per Cockburn C.J. in *Twycross v. Grant* (1877) 2 C.P.D. 469, 541, C.A.

[6] cf. *Bagnall v. Carlton* (1877) 6 Ch.D. 371, C.A.; *Emma Silver Mining Co. v. Grant* (1879) 11 Ch.D. 918, C.A.; *Whaley Bridge Printing Co. v. Green* (1880) 5 Q.B.D. 109; *Lydney & Wigpool Iron Ore Co. v. Bird* (1886) 33 Ch.D. 85, C.A.; *Mann v. Edinburgh Northern Tramways Co.* [1893] A.C. 69, H.L.; *Jubilee Cotton Mills v. Lewis* [1924] A.C. 958, H.L. and cases cited, below.

[7] *Lagunas Nitrate Co. v. Lagunas Syndicate* [1899] 2 Ch. 392, 428, C.A.

[8] *Re Great Wheal Polgooth Co.* (1883) 53 L.J.Ch. 42.

[9] *Lydney & Wigpool Iron Ore Co. v. Bird* (1886) 33 Ch.D. 85, C.A.; *Bagnall v. Carlton* (1877) 6 Ch.D. 371, C.A.

[10] For an excellent discussion of this question, see Gross, (1970) 86 L.Q.R. 493, and his book *Company Promoters* (1972).

[11] For attempts, in addition to Cockburn C.J.'s description (above), see those of Lindley J. in *Emma Silver Mining Co. v. Lewis* (1879) 4 C.P.D. 396, 407, and of Bowen J. in *Whaley Bridge Printing Co. v. Green* (1880) 5 Q.B.D. 109, 111.

[12] e.g. under s.117(3)(d) (see Chap. 11 p. 282 above) and the *Yellow Book*, Section 2, Chap. 1, para. 2.13, Section 3, Chap. 2, para. 2.20 and Section 10, Chap. 1, para. 7.

particulars or prospectuses to which they were parties.[13] The courts, however, were conscious of the possibilities of abuse inherent in the promoter's position and in a series of cases in the last quarter of the nineteenth century they laid it down that anyone who can properly be regarded as a promoter stands in a fiduciary position towards the company with all the duties of disclosure and accounting which that implies; in particular he must not make any profit out of the promotion without disclosing it to the company. The difficulty, however, is to decide how he is to make this disclosure—the company being an artificial entity. The first leading case on the subject, *Erlanger* v. *New Sombrero Phosphate Co.*[14] suggested that it was his duty to ensure that the company had an independent board of directors and to make full disclosure to it. In that case Lord Cairns said[15] that the promoters of a company:

"stand ... undoubtedly in a fiduciary position. They have in their hands the creation and moulding of the company; they have the power of defining how, and when, and in what shape, and under what supervision, it shall start into existence and begin to act as a trading corporation ... I do not say that the owner of property may not promote and form a joint stock company and then sell his property to it, but I do say that if he does he is bound to take care that he sells it to the company through the medium of a board of directors who can and do exercise an independent and intelligent judgment on the transaction. ..."

This rule, however, was obviously too strict; an entirely independent board would be impossible in the case of most private and many public companies, and since *Salomon* v. *Salomon*[16] it has never been doubted that a disclosure to the members would be equally effective. In that famous case it was held that the liquidator of the company could not complain of the sale to it at an obvious over-valuation of Mr. Salomon's business, all the members having acquiesced therein. "After Salomon's case I think it impossible to hold that it is the duty of the promoters of a company to provide it with an independent board of directors if the real truth is disclosed to those who are induced by the promoters to join the company."[17] But the promoter cannot escape liability by disclosing to a few cronies, who constitute

[13] F.S. Act 1986, ss.150–152; 166–168 (replacing s.43 of the Companies Act 1948 and ss.67, 68 of the 1985 Act which date back to the Directors' Liability Act 1890 passed as a result of *Derry* v. *Peek* (1889) 14 App.Cas. 337, H.L.). But note s.150(6) which makes it clear that in respect of mis-statements in listing particulars a promoter is in no worse position than any other person responsible for the listing particulars.
[14] (1878) 3 App.Cas. 1218, H.L.
[15] At p. 1236.
[16] [1897] A.C. 22, H.L.: see Chap. 5 above.
[17] *Per* Lindley M.R. in *Lagunas Nitrate Co.* v. *Lagunas Syndicate* [1899] 2 Ch. 392, C.A. at 426.

the initial members, when it is the intention to float off the company to the public or to induce some other dupes to purchase the shares. This was emphasised by the speeches of the House of Lords in the second great landmark in the development of this branch of the law—*Gluckstein* v. *Barnes*.[18] "It is too absurd," said Lord Halsbury with his usual bluntness, "to suggest that a disclosure to the parties to this transaction is a disclosure to the company. ... They were there by the terms of the agreement to do the work of the syndicate, that is to say, to cheat the shareholders' and this, forsooth, is to be treated as a disclosure to the company, when they were really there to hoodwink the shareholders."

The position therefore seems to be that disclosure must be made to the company either by making it to an entirely independent board or to the existing and potential members as a whole. If the first method is employed the promoter will be under no further liability to the company, although the directors will be liable to the subscribers if the information has not been passed on in the invitation to subscribe; indeed, if the promoter is a party to this invitation,[19] he too will be liable to the subscribers.[20] If the second method is adopted disclosure must be made in the prospectus, or otherwise, so that those who are or become members, as a result of the transaction in which the promoter was acting as such, have full information regarding it. A partial or incomplete disclosure will not do; the disclosure must be explicit.[21]

It is sometimes stated that the duty of a promoter may be even heavier than that of making full disclosure of any profit made. The suggestion is that if he acquires any property after the commencement of the promotion he is presumed to do so as a trustee for the company so that he must hand it over to the company at the price he gave for it, unless he discloses not merely the profit which he proposes to make but also informs the company of its right to call for the property at its cost price. In theory this is undoubtedly sound. If the promoter broke his duty by attempting to acquire the property beneficially when he should have acquired it for the unborn company,[22] then his breach of duty was not merely failure to disclose his profit but was his attempted expropriation of the company's property. Indeed, if this is the situation it appears that nothing short of unanimous consent of all the shareholders of the company when

---

18 [1900] A.C. 240, H.L. at 247.
19 In which event he will find some difficulty in persuading the court that the directors were truly independent of him.
20 See above n. 13 and Chap. 13 below.
21 *Gluckstein* v. *Barnes*, above.
22 There seems to be no objection in principle to the establishment of a trust in favour of an unborn company—for there can certainly be a trust in favour of an unborn child and this might have alleviated the problem of pre-incorporation contracts dealt with below at pp. 306–310, but the decisions display a reluctance to invoke this principle: *cf. Natal Land Co.* v. *Pauline Syndicate* [1904] A.C. 120, P.C.

formed should entitle the promoter to retain his ill-gotten gains,[23] for not even a resolution of a general meeting can authorise an expropriation of the company's property.[24] But in fact the English decisions cited in support of this suggestion[25] do not go anything like so far (although certain dicta in them do[26]). There seems to be no case in which, *full disclosure of the profit having been made*, the promoter has been held liable to account. The judgments acknowledge the possibility that the promoter may have acquired the property as trustee, but they seem to require something more than the mere acquisition of property after the commencement of the promotion with the intention of re-selling it to the company.[27] In principle it should suffice if the company can show that the promoter acquired the property for himself when it was his duty to acquire it for the company.[28] But in practice all seems to turn on the intentions of the promoter at the time of purchase; on whether he intended to buy for himself *for re-sale to the company or to buy initially *for* the company.*[29] In the former case his only duty is to disclose; in the latter he cannot subsequently change his mind and seek to act as vendor rather than as trustee.

It will be observed that the promoter's duty to the company, even apart from statute, is not merely to refrain from wilfully false statements but actively to disclose the whole truth. His duty to the company is to be contrasted with that which he owes towards people invited to subscribe for the company's shares. At common law his duty to the latter was merely to refrain from falsehoods,[30] and, even as a result of statutory intervention, it is doubtful if there is a positive duty to disclose all material facts.[31]

It seems clear that a promoter cannot effectively contract out of his duties by inserting a clause in the articles whereby the company and the subscribers agree to waive their rights.[32] Moreover Article 11 of the Second Company Law Directive was intended to ensure that when a public company acquired a substantial non-cash asset[33] from

---

[23] *cf. Cook v. Deeks* [1916] 1 A.C. 554, P.C.
[24] See Chap. 22, below.
[25] *Tyrrell v. Bank of London* (1862) 10 H.L.C. 26; *Re Ambrose Lake Tin Co.* (1880) 14 Ch.D. 390, C.A.; *Re Cape Breton Co.* (1885) 29 Ch.D. 795, C.A., affd. *sub nom. Cavendish Bentinck v. Fenn* (1887) 12 App.Cas. 652, H.L.; *Ladywell Mining Co. v. Brookes* (1887) 35 Ch.D. 400, C.A.
[26] See especially (1887) 35 Ch.D. at 413.
[27] See especially, *Omnium Electric Palaces v. Baines* [1914] 1 Ch. 332, C.A.
[28] *cf. Cook v. Deeks*, n. 23 above.
[29] See especially, *per* Sargant J. in [1914] 1 Ch., 347.
[30] *Derry v. Peek* (1889) 14 App.Cas. 337, H.L.
[31] This matter is dealt with more fully below in Chap. 13, where it is pointed out, at pp. 324, 325, that in practice the liability has become almost as extensive.
[32] *Gluckstein v. Barnes*, above; *Omnium Electric Palaces v. Baines* [1914] 1 Ch., 247, *per* Sargant J. Such "waiver" clauses used to be common and, except as regards actual misrepresentations (on which see Misrepresentation Act 1967, s.3), there is still no statutory prohibition of them: s.310 (invalidating exemption clauses) only covers officers and auditors.
[33] One for which the consideration paid by the company was equal to one-tenth or more of the company's issued share capital.

its promoters within two years of its entitlement to commence business, an independent valuation of that asset and approval by the company in general meeting should be required. But, as we have seen,[34] as implemented by the United Kingdom[35] this applies only to acquisitions from the subscribers to the memorandum who need not be the true promoters and generally are not.[36] However, when a private company re-registers as a public one (a more common occurrence than initial formation as a public company) a similar requirement applies to such acquisitions from anyone who was a member on the date of re-registration[37] and that may well catch a promoter. This, therefore, affords an additional statutory protection[38] against the risk that promoters will seek to off-load their property to the company at an inflated price.

Remedies for breach of promoters' duties

Since the promoter owes a duty of disclosure to the *company*, the primary remedy against him in the event of breach is for the company to bring proceedings for rescission of any contract with him or for the recovery of any secret profits which he has made. So far as the right to rescind is concerned, this must be exercised on normal contractual principles, that is to say the company must have done nothing to show an intention to ratify the agreement after finding out about the non-disclosure or misrepresentation[39] and *restitutio in integrum* must still be possible.[40] In view of the wide powers now exercised by the court to order financial adjustments when directing rescission, it is doubtful whether the *restitutio in integrum* rule operates as any real restraint, at any rate where the promoter has been fraudulent or where he himself is responsible for the dealings alleged to have resulted in restitution being impossible.[41] The only circumstances where this requirement seems likely to impose a serious limitation is where innocent third parties have acquired rights to the property concerned, and even there a monetary adjustment will often enable the third parties' rights to be satisfied.[42] The mere fact that the

34 Chap. 9 at pp. 205, 206 above.
35 Now s.104(1), (2) and (4)–(6).
36 See Chap. 11 at p. 289 above.
37 s.104(3)–(6).
38 But one which can be avoided by the promoters ceasing to be members prior to the re-registration.
39 *Lagunas Nitrate Co. v. Lagunas Syndicate* [1899] 2 Ch. 392, C.A. Here again "the company" must mean the members or an independent board; clearly ratification by puppet directors cannot be effective.
40 *Re Leeds & Hanley Theatre of Varieties* [1902] 2 Ch. 809, C.A.; *Steedman v. Frigidaire Corp*. [1933] 1 D.L.R. 161, P.C.; *Dominion Royalty Corpn. v. Goffatt* [1935] 1 D.L.R. 780 (Ont.C.A.), affd. [1935] 4 D.L.R. 736 (Can.S.C.).
41 *Erlanger v. New Sombrero Phosphate Co.* (1878) 3 App.Cas. 1218, H.L., and *Spence v. Crawford* [1939] 3 All E.R. 271, H.L. These cases suggest that the courts have more restricted powers of financial adjustment when there is no fraud: *sed quaere,* cf. *Armstrong v. Jackson* [1917] 2 K.B. 822.
42 As, perhaps, in *Re Leeds & Hanley Theatre of Varieties,* above, where the property had been mortgaged to a bank.

contract had been performed never seems to have destroyed the right to rescind a contract of this type[43] and since the Misrepresentation Act 1967 any suggestion to that effect seems unarguable.[44]

If the contract is rescinded the promoter's secret profit will normally disappear as a result, but if he has made a profit on some ancillary transaction there is no doubt that this too may be recovered. Moreover, a secret profit may be recovered although the company elects not to rescind. The classic illustration of this is *Gluckstein v. Barnes*[45] itself. In that case a syndicate had been formed for the purpose of buying and reselling Olympia, then owned by a company in liquidation. The syndicate first bought up at low prices certain charges on the property and then bought the freehold itself for £140,000. They then promoted a company of which they were the directors, and to it they sold the freehold for £180,000 which was raised by a public issue of share and debentures. In the prospectus the profit of £40,000 was disclosed. But in the meantime the promoters had had the charges on the property repaid by the liquidator out of the £140,000 and thereby made a further profit of £20,000. This was not disclosed in the prospectus, though reference was there made to a contract, close scrutiny of which might have revealed that some profit had been made. Four years later the new company went into liquidation and it was held that the promoters must account to the company for this secret profit.

There is, however, authority for saying that if the property on which the profit was made was acquired before the promoter became a promoter, there can be no claim for the recovery of the profit as such.[46] According to this view it may be necessary for this purpose to make the, admittedly difficult, determination of the exact moment of time at which the promotion began.

Normally however, this rule works fairly enough. If the company freely elects to affirm the purchase, there would be an element of injustice in making the promoter disgorge the whole of the difference between the price at which he bought—perhaps many years previously—and that at which he sold. No doubt the court could assess the market value at the date of the sale and on that basis force

[43] [1900] A.C. 240, H.L. And see *Jubilee Cotton Mills v. Lewis* [1924] A.C. 958, H.L.
[44] *Re Ambrose Lake Tin Co.* (1880) 14 Ch.D. 390, C.A.; *Re Cape Breton Co.* (1885) 29 Ch.D. 795, C.A., affd. sub nom. *Cavendish Bentinck v. Fenn* (1887) 12 App.Cas. 652, H.L.; *Ladywell Mining Co. v. Brookes* (1887) 35 Ch.D. 400, C.A.; *Re Lady Forrest (Murchison) Gold Mine* [1901] 1 Ch. 582; *Burland v. Earle* [1902] A.C. 83, P.C.; *Jacobus Marler Estates v. Marler* (1913) 85 L.J.P.C. 167n.; *Cook v. Deeks* [1916] 1 A.C. 554 at pp. 563, 564, P.C.; *Robinson v. Randfontein Estates* [1921] A.D. 168 (S.Afr.S.C.App.Div.); *P. & O. Steam Nav. Co. v. Johnson* (1938) 60 C.L.R. 189 (Austr.H.C.).
[45] As pointed out in the 10th Report of the Law Reform Committee (Cmnd. 1782), paras. 6–9, the extent, if any, of any such rule was doubtful except as regards contracts relating to land. The Misrepresentation Act 1967 is based on this Report.
[46] s.1 of that Act expressly provides that a contract can be rescinded for misrepresentation notwithstanding that the misrepresentation has become a term of the contract or that the contract has been performed.

the promoter to account, but this, it has been argued,[47] would be to make a new contract for the parties. On the other hand, the rule could work grave injustice to the company on the rare occasions when *restitutio in integrum* had become impossible so that the company had lost the right to rescind through circumstances beyond its control. In practice the courts avoided this injustice either by finding that the promoter was fraudulent, and accordingly liable to an action for deceit, or that the promotion had commenced when he acquired the property; indeed, they have often found both.[48] They have even suggested that, in the absence of common law fraud, the promoter would be liable in damages for his failure to disclose,[49] or for negligence in allowing the company to purchase at an excessive price,[50] the damages being the difference between the market value and the contract price. As a result of the Misrepresentation Act 1967 there is a clear legal basis for awarding damages in all cases where the promoter has made an actual misrepresentation and cannot prove that he had reasonable ground to believe and did believe up to the time the contract was made, that the facts represented were true.[51] When there is any misrepresentation the Misrepresentation Act makes any exclusion clause ineffective to bar any remedy, "except in so far as it satisfies the requirement of reasonableness. . . ."[52]

In addition to the remedies of the company, the promoter may be liable to those who have acquired securities of the company in reliance on mis-statements in listing particulars or prospectuses to which the promoter was a party. The remedies available against him are the same as those against the officers of the company or others responsible for the listing particulars or prospectuses and are dealt with in Chapter 13 below.

Remuneration of promoters

A promoter is not entitled to recover any remuneration for his services from the company unless there is a valid contract to pay

---

47 *Re Cape Breton Co.* (1885) 29 Ch.D. 795, C.A.

48 *Re Olympia, Ltd.* [1898] 2 Ch. 153, affd. *sub nom. Gluckstein v. Barnes*, above; *Re Leeds and Hanley Theatre of Varieties*, above. But the mere non-disclosure of the amount of the profit is not misrepresentation: *Re Lady Forrest (Murchison) Gold Mine* [1901] 1 Ch. 582; *Jacobus Marler Estates Ltd. v. Marler* [1913] 85 L.J.P.C. 167n.

49 *Re Leeds and Hanley Theatre of Varieties*, above; see especially, *per* Vaughan Williams L.J. [1902] 2 Ch. at 825.

50 *Per* Lord Parker in *Jacobus Marler Estates v. Marler* (1913) 85 L.J.P.C. at p. 168.

51 Misrepresentation Act 1967, s.2(1). Moreover, under s.2(2) damages may be awarded in lieu of rescission.

52 *Ibid.* s.3, as substituted by s.8 of the Unfair Contract Terms Act 1977, s.11 of which defines the requirements of reasonableness for this purpose as "the terms shall have been a fair and reasonable one to be included having regard to the circumstances which were, or ought reasonably to have been, known to or in the contemplation of the parties when the contract was made." The onus is on those seeking to show that the requirement is satisfied: ss.8 and 11.

between him and the company. Indeed, without such a contract he is not even entitled to recover his preliminary expenses or the registration fees.[53] In this respect the promoter is at the mercy of the directors of the company. Until the company is formed it cannot enter into a valid contract[54] and the promoter therefore has to expend the money without any guarantee that he will be repaid. In practice, however, recovery of preliminary expenses and registration fees does not normally present any difficulty. Former Tables A[55] contained an express provision authorising the directors to pay them[55] and, although this did not constitute a contract between the company and the promoter,[56] it empowered the directors to repay expenses properly incurred.[57] The corresponding article of Table A 1985[58] omits this express provision; presumably it was thought to be unnecessary. And this surely must be correct; the whole tenor of the Act assumes that preliminary expenses properly incurred will be borne by the company[59] and that the general delegation of the company's power to the board of directors suffices.

It may well be however, that the promoter will not be content merely to recover his expenses; certainly if he is a professional promoter he will expect to be handsomely remunerated. Nor is this unreasonable. As Lord Hatherly said,[60] "The services of a promoter are very peculiar; great skill, energy and ingenuity may be employed in constructing a plan and in bringing it out to the best advantages." Hence it is perfectly proper for the promoter to be rewarded, provided, as we have seen, that he fully discloses to the company the rewards which he obtains. The reward may take many forms. The promoter may purchase an undertaking and promote a company to repurchase it from him at a profit, or the undertaking may be sold directly by the former owner to the new company, the promoter receiving a commission from the vendor. A once-popular device was for the company's capital structure to provide for a special class of deferred or founders' shares which would be issued credited as fully paid in consideration of the promoter's services.[61] Such shares would

[53] *Re English and Colonial Produce Co.* [1906] 2 Ch. 435, C.A.; *Re National Motor Mail Coach Co.* [1908] 2 Ca. 515, C.A.

[54] *Kelner v. Baxter* (1866) L.R. 2 C.P. 174; *Natal Land Co. v. Pauline Syndicate* [1904] A.C. 120, P.C. Nor can it ratify a preliminary contract purporting to be made on its behalf: *ibid.* It must enter into a new contract and this ought to be by a deed since the consideration rendered by the promoter will be past.

[55] See, *e.g.* Table A, 1948 art. 80.

[56] See Chap. 11 at p. 285 above.

[57] *Re Rotherham Alum Co.* (1883) 25 Ch.D. 103, C.A.; *Re Englefield Colliery Co.* (1877–78) 8 Ch.D. 388, C.A.

[58] Art. 70.

[59] See, *e.g.* s.117(3)(c) regarding the need to state the amount of the preliminary expenses in the statutory declaration leading to the issue of the trading certificate: above p. 282.

[60] In *Touche v. Metropolitan Ry. Warehousing Co.* (1871) L.R. 6 Ch.App. 671, 676.

[61] The promoter should obtain a contract with the company prior to rendering the services, for past services are not valuable consideration: *Re Eddystone Marine Insurance* [1893] 3 Ch. 9, C.A. Hence if the services are rendered before the company was formed the promoter will have to pay for the shares. Moreover, in the

normally provide for the lion's share of the profits available for dividend after the preference and ordinary shares had been paid a dividend of a fixed amount. This had the advantage that the promoter advertised his apparent confidence in the business by retaining a stake in it; but all too often his stake (which probably cost him nothing anyway) was merely window-dressing. And if, in fact, the company proved an outstanding success the promoter might do better than all the other shareholders put together. Today, when the trend is towards simplicity of capital structures, founders' shares are out of favour and, in general, those old companies which originally had them have got rid of them on a reconstruction.[62] A more likely alternative is for the promoter to be given warrants or options entitling him to subscribe for shares at a particular price, (*e.g.* that at which they were issued to the public) within a specified time. If the shares have meanwhile gone to a premium this will obviously be a valuable right.

Preliminary contracts by promoters

Until the company has been incorporated it cannot contract or enter into any other act in the law. Nor, once incorporated, can it become liable on or entitled under contracts purporting to be made on its behalf prior to incorporation,[63] for ratification is not possible when the ostensible principal did not exist at the time when the contract was originally entered into.[64] Hence preliminary arrangements will either have to be left to mere "gentlemen's agreements" or the promoters will have to undertake personal liability. Which of these courses will be adopted depends largely on the demands of the other party. If our village grocer is converting his business into a private company of which he is to be managing director and majority shareholder he will obviously not be concerned to have a binding agreement with anyone. In such a case a draft sale agreement will be drawn up and the main object in the company's memorandum will be to acquire his business as a going concern "and for this purpose to enter into an agreement in the terms of a draft already prepared and

case of a public company an undertaking to perform work or supply services will no longer be valid payment: s.99(2), Chap. 9 at p. 204 above. But provided the shares are given a very low nominal value this may not be a serious snag.

62 There have been many interesting battles between holders of founders' shares and the other members. If the holdings of founders' shares are widely dispersed there is obviously a risk of a block being acquired on behalf of the other classes in the hope of outvoting the remaining founders' shareholders at a class meeting to approve a reconstruction. To safeguard their position, in a number of cases the founders' shareholders formed a special company and vested all the founders' shares in it, thus ensuring that they were voted solidly at any meeting.

63 *Kelner* v. *Baxter* (1866) L.R. 2 C.P. 174; *Natal Land Co.* v. *Pauline Syndicate* [1904] A.C. 120, P.C.

64 Contrast the position when a public company enters into transactions after its registration but before the issue of a trading certificate (s.117(8), above Chap. 11 at p. 281) or when a company changes its name (above Chap. 11 at p. 272).

for the purpose of identification signed by. . . ." When the incorporation is complete the seller will ensure that the agreement is executed and completed.

If, however, promoters are arranging for the company to take over someone else's business, the seller will certainly, and the promoters will probably, wish to have a binding agreement immediately. In this event the sale agreement will be made between the vendor and the promoters and it will be provided that the personal liability of the promoters is to cease when the company in process of formation is incorporated and enters into an agreement in similar terms, which, once again, will be referred to in the memorandum.

Agreements of this nature will be a necessary feature of nearly every incorporation, and not only must the promoters make full disclosure to the company but, in addition, the company must give particulars of them in any listing particulars or prospectuses.[65] Generally speaking, all material contracts must be disclosed unless entered into more than two years previously and in particular all those relating to property acquired or to be acquired by the company.

Companies' pre-incorporation contracts

What, in practice, is a not infrequent source of trouble is that those engaged in the formation of a company cause transactions to be entered into ostensibly by the company but before it has in fact been formed. As we have seen, the company, when formed, cannot ratify or adopt the contract,[66] but prior to the European Communities Act 1972 the legal position of the promoter and the other party seemed to depend on the terminology employed. If the contract was entered into by the promoter and signed by him "for and on behalf of XY Co. Ltd." then, according to the early case of *Kelner* v. *Baxter*,[67] the promoter would be personally liable. But if, as is much more likely, the promoter signed the proposed name of the company, adding his own to authenticate it, (*e.g.* XY Co. Ltd., AB Director) then, according to *Newborne* v. *Sensolid (Great Britain) Ltd.*,[68] there was no contract at all.

[65] See Chap. 13 below.
[66] Unless it enters into a new contract. This, of course, does not mean that, in the absence of a new contract, the company or the other party can accept the delivery of the goods or payment without being under any obligation. See below at pp. 308, 309.
[67] See nn. 54 and 63 above. If two (or more) promoters each enter into pre-incorporation contracts that will not in itself make them partners or liable as such on contract entered into by the other: *Keith Spicer Ltd.* v. *Mansell* [1970] 1 W.L.R. 333, C.A.
[68] [1954] 1 Q.B. 45, C.A. In that case it was the promoter who attempted to enforce the agreement but it appears that the decision would have been the same if the other party had attempted to enforce it, as was so held in *Hawkes Bay Milk Corporation Ltd.* v. *Watson* [1974] 1 N.Z.L.R. 218, *cf. Marblestone Industries Ltd.* v. *Fairchild* [1975] 1 N.Z.L.R. 529. But it is difficult to see why the promoter should not be liable for breach of implied warranty of authority.

However, on the entry of the United Kingdom to the European Community we had to implement Article 7 of the First Company Law Directive which reads:

"If, before a company being formed has acquired legal personality, action has been carried out in its name and the company does not assume the obligations arising from such action, the persons who acted shall, without limit, be jointly and severally liable therefor unless otherwise agreed."

This initially was implemented by section 9(2) of the European Communities Act 1972 which, on the 1985 Consolidation became section 36(4) of the 1985 Act and which, as a result of the reform of the law relating to company contracts generally,[69] has now been replaced by section 36C(1) and supplemented by a new subsection (2). Subsection (1) reads:

"(1) A contract which purports to be made by or on behalf of a company at a time when the company has not been formed, has effect, subject to any agreement to the contrary, as one made with the person purporting to act for the company or as agent for it, and he is personally liable on the contract accordingly."

This, it was hoped,[70] would put paid to the former alleged distinction between purporting to act for the unformed company and appending a signature purporting to authenticate that of the putative company. This at least, seems to have been achieved, not only because of its provisions but also because the Court of Appeal in three more recent decisions now seems to regard the alleged distinction as having been a mistaken view of the common law.

The first of these decisions was that in *Phonogram Ltd.* v. *Lane.*[71] While Lord Denning M.R. thought that the distinction had been eradicated by the section, Oliver L.J. took the view, which later decisions have adopted, that the question whether the contract purports to be made by or on behalf of the company depends on the construction of the contract as a whole.[72] This decision also established that "subject to any agreement to the contrary" means an express agreement and not one that can be inferred. Such an "agreement" could presumably be either (a) a term in the contract

69 1989 Act s.130, substituting new ss.36–36C in the 1985 Act.
70 But Prentice in (1973) 89 L.Q.R. 518 feared that it might not. Though on this point later events have shown that it has been achieved, his criticisms of the section (and those of Green in (1984) 47 M.L.R. 671) have, as we shall see, proved to be all too well-founded.
71 [1982] Q.B. 938 C.A.
72 At p. 945.

itself expressly negating any liability on the part of the promoter[73] or providing that the promoter's liability would cease if the company, when formed, entered into a contract in similar terms or (b) by a subsequent agreement releasing the promoter from liability.

The second Court of Appeal decision was in *Rover International Ltd. v. Cannon Films Ltd.*[74] This concerned the *rights* (not liabilities) of the *company* after its formation. It will have been noticed that neither the Directive nor section 36C says anything about that or about the rights of the promoters (except that the Directive expressly contemplates that the company may "assume" the obligations after it is formed). So far as the promoter is concerned the common law position appears to be that if the promoter is liable under the contract he becomes entitled to enforce the contract.[75] Does the same apply when the promoter becomes liable as a result of section 36C? This question might have been answered if section 36C had been relevant in the *Rover* case but unfortunately it was not because, as Harman J. pointed out at first instance, section 36C applies only to companies registered in Great Britain.[76] It is submitted, however, that if the promoter is, under section 36C, liable under the contract the other party must also be liable to perform his obligations under it; otherwise there would be a "contract" without any mutuality.

What is disturbing is that the Court in *Rover* dealt with the case on the basis that it was governed exclusively by English domestic common law without any consideration of what the position was under the law of Guernsey where Rover was in course of incorporation. If, under its law, the promoter or the company on its formation would have been liable on the pre-incorporation contract, surely the English courts should have followed Guernsey law as the law of the place of incorporation? If not the position would be particularly anomalous when the country of incorporation was an EC member State[77] which has or should have implemented the Directive; it defeats the harmonising intention of Article 7 unless the laws of all member States apply to it all EC companies, at any rate in respect of their actions in the EC.

However, the Court in *Rover* held that, on a construction of the agreement, the clear intention and belief of both parties was that it was a contract with the unformed company and *not* with or through

---

[73] That, however, ought to be effective only if the other party knew that the company did not exist. If he thought it had been formed he could reasonably assume that it was no more than an express statement of the legal position of an agent who acts for a disclosed principal.

[74] [1989] 1 W.L.R. 912 C.A.

[75] Above, n. 68.

[76] [1987] B.C.L.C. 540 at 543h–544b. s.36C has been applied to "unregistered companies," Companies (Unregistered Companies) Regs. 1985 (S.I. 1985 No. 680 as amended by 5.8.1990 No. 438) but not to "oversea companies" even if they have established a place of business in G.B.

[77] Which Guernsey, except for certain limited purposes, is not.

the promoter. Hence it was wholly void. But money paid under it was recoverable as money paid under a mutual mistake, (*i.e.* that the company had already been incorporated at the time of the agreement) and for a consideration that had wholly failed and Rover was entitled to claim a *quantum meruit* for services that it rendered after its incorporation.

The conclusion in the third case, *Cotronic U.K. Ltd.* v. *Dezonie*[78] was somewhat similar. There the original company had been struck off the Register under what is now section 652.[79] In ignorance of this it went on trading for some years and, while doing so, entered into the relevant contract. Years later, when it was realised that the original company had ceased to exist, another company with the same name was registered and continued the trade. It was held that the transaction could not be regarded as a pre-incorporation contract but was one which was wholly void since at the time of the transaction there was no company in existence or in course of formation. However, recovery on a *quantum meruit* basis was allowed.[80]

Before leaving subsection (1) of section 36C and by way of introduction to its subsection (2) attention should be drawn to a major difference in wording between subsection (1) and Article 7 of the Directive which it purports to implement. Article 7 applies to pre-incorporation "actions"; subsection (1) only to "contracts". In most cases, no doubt, the "action" will be the entry into or performance or non-performance of a contract; but not always and subsection (1) hardly seems to amount to full implementation of Article 7.

The 1989 Act amended section 36C by adding subsection (2) which reads as follows:-

"2. Subsection (1) applies:

  (a) to the making of a deed under the law of England and Wales,

and

  (b) to the undertaking of an obligation under the law of Scotland

as it applies to the making of a contract."

This subsection appears to have introduced an anomalous distinction between the position in England and Wales and that in Scotland. As a result of (b) Scotland seems to have come close to a full

---

78 [1991] B.C.L.C. 721, C.A.
79 On which see Chap. 28 at pp. 773-775 below.
80 Two months later the C.A. was faced with *Badgerhill Properties Ltd* v. *Cottrell* [1991] B.C.L.C. 805 which was concerned not with a pre-incorporation contract but with one in which it was unclear whether the contract was entered into by an individual under a trade name or by his company under that trade name: *i.e.* it concerned not s.36C but ss.36 and 36A; but much reliance was placed on the decisions dealt with above.

implementation of Article 7. England and Wales, however, have done so only to the extent that obligations arising from a deed are now expressly covered.

It will therefore be seen that the statutory reforms have introduced as many questions as they have solved. An even more serious flaw is that they have done nothing to make it simpler for companies to "assume" the obligations of a pre-incorporation transaction. While one can understand that the Directive preferred to leave that to each member State, it is lamentable that we have not got round to doing anything about it.

Many common law countries have recognised, either by judge-made law or by statute that a company when formed can effectively elect to adopt pre-incorporation transactions purporting to be made on its behalf without the need for a formal novation and that the liability of the promoter ceases when the company adopts it. In 1962 the Jenkins Committee recommended[81] that we should do likewise (and clause 6 of the aborted Companies Bill 1973 would have implemented that recommendation) but we have still not done so. We have tried to make promoters personally liable on pre-incorporation transactions unless it is otherwise agreed or unless the company, after its incorporation, adopts the transaction. But at present the only way in which the company can adopt it is by entering into a post-incorporation agreement in the same terms. Even if the company does so, that will not relieve the promoters of personal liability (at any rate while the new agreement remains executory[82]) unless they are parties to the new agreement which expressly relieves them of liability under the pre-incorporation agreement. The need for all this is frequently overlooked. This may not matter much if all those concerned remain able and willing to perform their obligations under the pre-incorporation agreement. But it can be calamitous if one or more of them becomes insolvent or wants to withdraw because changes in market conditions have made the transactions disadvantageous to him or them.

As pre-incorporation transactions are inevitable features of every new incorporation we ought to make it as easy as possible to achieve what the parties intend (or would have intended if they had realised that the company was not yet incorporated and had understood the legal consequences). In this case, if not generally, the legal technicality that ratification dates back to the date of the transaction so that it is not effective unless, at that time, the ratifying person existed and had capacity to enter into the transaction, should not apply.

[81] Cmnd. 1749, para 44.
[82] If the contract has been fully performed by the company, after incorporation, and by the other party, that clearly will end any liability under the contract.

CHAPTER 13

FLOTATIONS

INTRODUCTION

THIS chapter is concerned with a subject which is now rightly regarded as a branch of Securities Regulation rather than Company Law. When Part V of the Financial Services Act is brought into operation the statute law will be wholly in that Act and in rules made under it and not, as formerly, in the Companies Act. Nevertheless it is not a subject which books on Company Law can ignore; students of that subject need to have some understanding of how public companies go about raising their share and loan capital from the investing public and of the legal regulations that have to be complied with when they do. An elaborate discussion of this specialised branch of legal practice is inappropriate in a book of this sort but on outline is essential.

Unfortunately this cannot be undertaken satisfactorily in a revision of this book if it is to be published, as planned, by 1992. This is because of the situation mentioned earlier,[1] resulting from the belated adoption of all the relevant EC Directives and of the decision to delay full implementation until there has been a thorough review of the present Parts IV and V of the Financial Services Act and of the regulations needed thereunder. Only when that has been completed will a revised Part V be brought into operation. In consequence, it may be misleading to describe the legal regulations as they now are[2] since they are likely to be different before the publication of this edition or very soon thereafter. However, in the circumstances, the least unsatisfactory course seems to be to proceed on the assumption that the legal regulation of listed issues, (*i.e.* Part IV of Act and the present listing rules of The Stock Exchange in the *Yellow Book*) will remain substantially unchanged and that the legal regulation of unlisted issues will be broadly as provided in the original Part V as amended by the Companies Act 1989.

In addition to the foregoing explanation of why this chapter is more than usually unsatisfactory, a brief description of the role and status of The Stock Exchange[2a] is needed as an introduction to what

---

[1] Chap. 4 at p. 65.
[2] Except to say that it is a confusing mess in relation to unlisted issues where the antiquated "prospectus provisions" of the Companies Act remain for the time being unrepealed and applicable.
[2a] Its official name is "The International Stock Exchange of the United Kingdom and The Republic of Ireland Limited" but its role in relation to the Republic is being shed and the intention is then to change its name to "The London Stock Exchange." Throughout this book, it is called "The Stock Exchange."

follows. As a result of the City of London's "Big Bang" and the Financial Services Act,[3] The Exchange has completed its transformation from a club to a statutory-recognised regulatory body. Its status is, however, very different from that of other self-regulating organisations and bodies recognised under that Act. They, in relation to the authorisation and supervision of their members' investment business, are subject to the surveillance of the Securities and Investments Board (SIB). The Exchange, in contrast, is the "competent authority," for the purposes of the EC Listing Directives and that Act, in relation to the regulation of officially listed issues. As such it is not subject to the surveillance of SIB. On the other hand, whereas formerly it was both a recognised stock exchange and also "a recognised association of dealers in securities"[4] whose members were thereby authorised to carry on investment business, it has now shed the latter role. For that authorisation, its members have to be directly authorised by SIB or by membership of an appropriate recognised SRO which, in this case, will be the Securities and Futures Authority (the SFA).

Alarmed by the growth of public issues of securities which were not listed, The Stock Exchange decided in 1980 also to operate a regulated lower-tier market[5] (supplementing that in securities officially listed) which it called the Unlisted Securities Market (U.S.M.)[6] As a result of this and of the coming into operation of the Financial Services Act, domestic issues to the general public of securities, not listed or dealt in on the U.S.M., have virtually dried up except for those designed to afford the tax advantages of Business Expansion Schemes.

One other introductory point: the new legislation[7] seeks to avoid the use of the expressions "public issue" or "public offer" because no-one has succeeded in defining satisfactorily what "public" means in this context. Unfortunately it is difficult to find another shorthand expression which conveys what types of issue are meant (*i.e.* general offers to members of the public, however selected).[8] Hence the expression continues in common use and will not be eschewed in this chapter.

[3] See Chap. 3 at p. 53 above.

[4] Under the, soon to be wholly repealed, Prevention of Fraud (Investments) Act 1958.

[5] And, for a short time, two such markets. After "Big Bang" The Exchange introduced a "third market" primarily to meet the assumed needs of "greenfield" companies without a track record. This did not prove as successful as the U.S.M. and was merged with the latter in 1990 (but permission may be given under S.E. r.535–2 for matched bargains in shares of unadmitted companies to be put through The Exchange).

[6] This is not an over-the-counter (OTC) market, such as exists in N. America. There had been attempts by those firms which sponsored public issues of unlisted securities to establish a regulated OTC market here but these came to naught and many of the sponsoring firms have disappeared, leaving The Exchange with a virtual monopoly.

[7] In contrast with the old: see Companies Act 1985, Part III Chap. 1.

[8] Offers by a public company to its existing members are not excluded but a more relaxed regime has always been applied to issues restricted to them.

Methods of Public Offering

A company may have a choice of various methods whereby its securities can be offered to the public. In practice, it will normally engage the services of an issuing house (a merchant bank) and a stockbroker as sponsors of the issue and the method chosen will depend on their advice. One of the changes resulting from "Big Bang" is that, whereas formerly there were a small number only of British merchant banks specialising in this work as members of the Issuing Houses Association (and an even smaller number as members of the still more elite Accepting Houses Committee) there is now a far wider choice of British and multi-national concerns. While this has resulted in increased competition between them, so that they may have to expose themselves to a "beauty contest" to persuade the company to engage them rather than one of their rivals, it is less clear that it has led to reductions in the charges that they demand.[9]

Initial offers

On an initial public offering, a company's choice of method will be severely restricted. If the issue is of any size it will have to proceed by way of an offer for sale or subscription[10] coupled with an introduction to listing (or admission to the U.S.M.). An offer without an introduction will rarely be commercially practicable since the securities will then lack liquidity. And an introduction without an offer will not raise any new money for the company. Hence, unless the company's securities have somehow become sufficiently widely held (which is unlikely but conceivable[11]) to make it possible to raise the new money needed by a rights or open offer[12] to its existing shareholders, the only option will normally[13] be an Offer for Sale with an introduction to listing. That will prove to be an expensive and time consuming operation. The company's finance director (and probably other executives) and representatives of the issuing house and of the company's and the issuing house's solicitors will for weeks or months devote most of their time to working as a planning team. At a later stage the services of the New Issues Department of one of the major banks will generally need to be enlisted to handle applications and the preparation and despatch of allotment letters.

---

[9] It has always been denied that there was ever any sort of price-fixing cartel but issuers, appalled by the proposed charges of their first choice, who shopped around to find another that would charge less, generally suffered disappointment—and probably still do.

[10] Generally this will be an offer for sale by the sponsoring issuing house which will have agreed with the company to subscribe. Hence, we hereafter describe it as an "offer for sale."

[11] Since the Companies Act 1980 there has been no upper limit on the number of members of a private company and the F.S. Act will make it easier for it to raise capital without having to comply fully with Part IV or V of that Act.

[12] On which see below, pp. 317–319.

[13] Unless a "Placing" is permitted by The Stock Exchange: see below pp. 315–317.

The offer will have to be made by a lengthy prospectus (or "listing particulars", as that is now called when the securities are to be listed) which will have to be published in the form of a circular and as an advertisement in newspapers. To ensure that the issue is fully subscribed, arrangements will have to be made for it to be underwritten. Today this is normally achieved by the sponsoring issuing house agreeing to subscribe for the whole issue and for it, rather than the company, to make the offer. In major offerings, such as the Government's privatisation issues, a syndicate of issuing houses may be employed. The issuing house or houses will endeavour to persuade other financial institutions to sub-underwrite. Ultimately the cost of all this, including the commissions payable to underwriters and sub-underwriters, will have to be borne by the company.

The most ticklish decision that will have to be made is the price at which the securities should be issued and, for obvious reasons, this is normally left to the last possible moment. If it proves to have been set too low, so that the issue is heavily over-subscribed, the company will be unhappy, while, if it is set too high so that much of the issue is left with the underwriters, it is they who will be unhappy since their commission rates will have assumed that they will end up with a handsome profit and not be left with securities that, initially, they cannot sell except at a loss. Nor, probably, will the company be best pleased since it is generally believed that an under-subscribed issue will reduce the company's prospects of raising further capital in the future.[14] The nightmare of all concerned is that there will be an unforeseen stock-market collapse between the date of publication of the prospectus and the opening of the subscription list.[15] The sweet dream is that the issue will be modestly over-subscribed and that trading will open at a small premium.

If the issue is over-subscribed it will obviously be impossible for all applications to be accepted[16] in full. Hence, the prospectus or listing particulars will need to say how that situation will be dealt with. Normally this will be by accepting in full offers for small numbers of shares and scaling down large applications, balloting sometimes being

---

[14] In a report by a SE Committee (*Initial Public Offers*) published in February 1990 (and hereinafter referred to as *The "Ross Russell Report"*) it was suggested that there is scope for research (Business Schools please note) "to see whether a company's prospects of returning to the capital markets are indeed prejudiced ...": at p. 11. The only obvious reason why they might be, is that the sponsoring houses who have burnt their fingers might be reluctant to risk that again. But in view of what they charge they surely should take the rough with the smooth, especially as it is they who will have decided on what the issuing price should be.

[15] Which came true in the case of one of the privatisation issues on the "Crash of 1987." Yet thousands of small investors continued to put in applications notwithstanding that the media were warning them that trading would open at a massive discount.

[16] The so-called "Offer" is normally not an offer (as understood in the law of contract) which on acceptance becomes binding on the offeror. It may be in the case of a rights issue (see below) but on an Offer for Sale it is an invitation to make an offer which the issuer may or may not accept.

resorted to. The company will probably wish to achieve a balance between private and institutional investors. To succeed in that aim multiple applications by the same person will probably be expressly prohibited.[17] An abuse which also needs to be guarded against is that "stags" will apply but seek to withdraw and stop their cheques if it seems likely that dealings will not open at a worthwhile premium to the offer price. As we shall see[18], the legal regulations have struck at this practice but what perhaps is more likely to discourage it is that the offer documents will require applications to be accompanied by cheques for the full amount of the securities applied for, the cheques being cleared immediately on receipt and any refund sent later. This means that an applicant may not only fail to get all or any of the shares he hoped for but may, for a period, lose the interest that he was earning on his money.[19]

The offer price is normally stated as a fixed and pre-determined amount per share. It can however, be determined under a formula stated in the offer.[20] Or applicants can be invited to tender on the basis that the shares will be allocated to the highest bidders (this however is rarely used in relation to issues of company securities). Nevertheless, a variation of it became popular in the early 1980s. Under this, a minimum price will be stated and applicants invited to tender at or above that price, an issue price then being struck at the highest price which will enable the issue to be subscribed in full, all successful applicants paying the same price, and those applicants who tendered below the striking price being eliminated. This, however, did not prove to have the advantages expected of it and is now seldom used—though it still has its advocates.[21]

Obviously, the expense of an Offer for Sale plus introduction to listing is prohibitive unless a very large sum of money is to be raised. The Stock Exchange was concerned about this and the *Ross Russell Report* made some interesting suggestions which led to important changes of the listing rules in December 1990 allowing greater use of an alternative method known as a Placing.

Under this method the sponsor obtains firm commitments, mainly from its institutional-investment clients (instead of advertising an offer to the general public) coupling this with an introduction to listing. The absence of the need for newspaper advertisements, "road-shows" and the like makes this a much less expensive

---

17 Breaches are difficult to detect where applications are made in different names but that abuse will doubtless become less common now that culprits have been successfully prosecuted. The decision that they had committed a criminal offence and not merely a breach of contract was something of a surprise both to them and others.

18 See P. 341 at n. 55 below.

19 This causes bona fide applicants who are unsuccessful understandable resentment.

20 As is common in euro-security issues which are addressed to "professionals" rather than to the public: see below pp. 319-321.

21 See the *Ross Russell Report*, pp. 17 & 18, where the pros and cons are summarised.

procedure. On the other hand, it prevented the general public from acquiring shares at the issue price. Hence the Exchange had been reluctant to permit it except in the case of small issues and, when it did, normally insisted that 25 per cent. was made available to the market when trading began.

Now, however, there has been a considerable relaxation. As an alternative to an offer for sale, a marketing by a new applicant for listing to raise up to £30 million may be made by a placing effected by one of two methods according to whether more than £15 million is to be raised. If not, the company may choose to have the issue placed wholly with the clients of the sponsoring member firm.[22] If, however, it seeks to raise more than £15 million,[23] it may choose to have parts of the issue[24] placed with clients of the member firm but must ensure that the balance is marketed either by an offer for sale or by what is called "an intermediaries offer."[25] The latter means that the balance will be placed by the sponsoring member firm not solely with their own clients but with some of their competitors who, in turn, will place them with their clients.

The basic provisions relating to such intermediaries offers are expressed in the *Yellow Book* as recommended guidelines[26] but, so far as a sponsoring member firm is concerned, with the warning that if it "chooses to allocate securities to intermediaries otherwise than in accordance with the following guidelines it should have a valid commercial or other reason for doing so and may be called upon to explain and justify that reason to" The Exchange.[27] The guidelines provide that if 10 or more intermediaries apply for securities the sponsoring member firm will be expected to allocate securities to at least 10 of them and that, if less than 10 apply, should allocate to all of them. If the demand is such that applications have to be scaled down, it is recommended that this shall be done pro rata according to the size of each intermediary's application. The member firm is also "expected to announce the result of the intermediaries offer prior to the commencement of dealings", on The Stock Exchange.[28] The intermediaries are also "expected" to "undertake to the sponsoring

22 But, without special permission, there must be at least one market maker independent of the sponsoring member firm, at least 5 per cent. of the securities must be offered to it and the places must number at least 100: *Yellow Book*, Section I. Chapter 3, para. 2.5.

23 There must be at least two market makers independent of the sponsors, at least 5 per cent. must be offered to them and there must be at least five placees for each million placed: *ibid.* para. 2.6.

24 Up to 75 per cent. of the securities or £15 million whichever is the less: *ibid.* para. 2.6.

25 *Ibid.*

26 Presumably because the conduct of business by authorised persons under the F.S. Act (which both the member firms and the intermediaries will be) is a matter for regulation by SIB and the SFA rather than by The Stock Exchange.

27 *Ibid.* para. 2.8.

28 *Ibid.* And, as in the case of all issues, the member firm will, on the conclusion of the issuing have to furnish The Exchange with a completed distribution statement: see *ibid.*, para. 2.10 and Sched. 2 to Section 2, Chapter I.

member firm to avoid grey market dealing"[29] and the intermediary "must allocate securities to its clients at the issue price but will be permitted to charge such clients a commission."[30]

Accordingly, an intermediaries offer affords the issuing company with a new[31] alternative to an Offer for Sale which should be only marginally more expensive than a straightforward placing and one which has the advantage that it is more likely to result in a wide spread of shareholders and a more active and competitive subsequent market. And, assuming that intermediaries obey the rules, such members of the general public as are clients of the applicant intermediaries will be afforded an opportunity to get in at the issue price.

It should also be mentioned that straightforward placings are allowed more readily in the case of issues of debenture stock[32] and in certain other special circumstances.[33]

Subsequent offers

Once a company has made an initial public offering it will have additional methods whereby it can raise further capital and, even if it proceeds by an Offer for Sale, this will be less expensive if the securities issued are of the same class as those already admitted to listing or to the U.S.M. More often, however, it will make what is called a Rights Issue and, if it is an offering of equity shares[34] for cash, it will generally have to do this unless the company in general meeting otherwise agrees. This is because of the provisions of sections 89–96 of the Companies Act (discussed in the next chapter[35]). The object of those provisions is to protect the existing shareholders from having their aliquot share of the equity diluted without their consent. Hence the sections require that they be offered pre-emptive rights to subscribe in proportion to their existing holdings.

The practice is to make a rights issue at a price which represents a discount (often substantial) to the quoted price of the existing shares, thus increasing the likelihood that the rights will be taken up either by the existing shareholders or by those to whom they have renounced their rights.[36] Nevertheless it is customary for the issue to be underwritten, not only to guard against the risk of a market crash

---

[29] *i.e.* making a market in the securities prior to the commencement of dealings on The Stock Exchange. Presumably the member firm should not allocate to an intermediary unless it obtained such an undertaking.

[30] Section I Chapter 3, para. 2.9.

[31] New so far as the U.K. is concerned: it resembles methods commonly employed in N. America.

[32] *Yellow Book*, Section 1, Chapter 3, para. 2.11.

[33] *Ibid.* para. 2.12.

[34] Rights issues may be made of non-equity securities but in their case it is optional.

[35] At pp. 364–369 below.

[36] The shareholders will receive renounceable "letters of right" corresponding to renounceable allotment letters that successful applicants receive on an Offer for Sale.

but also because there will always be some shareholders who, out of apathy or because they have moved from their registered addresses or because the rights are being quoted at a minimal or no premium, have neither taken up nor renounced their rights.[37]

In one sense a rights issue is considerably less expensive than an Offer for Sale; circulating the shareholders is cheap in comparison with publishing a lengthy prospectus in national newspapers and mounting a sales-pitch to attract the public. But in another sense it may be dearer; if the issue price is deeply discounted the company will have to issue far more shares (on which it will be expected to pay dividends) in order to raise the same amount of money as on an Offer.

Analogous to, but distinguishable from, rights issues are Open Offers. Under these an offer is made to the company's existing security holders, not necessarily pro rata to their existing holdings and not affording them rights to renounce. Such offers are less common than rights issues[38] and, when they relate to cash offers for equity securities, will be practicable only if the offer is pro rata or pre-emptive rights have been waived in accordance with the statutory provisions referred to above. Other methods of issue which can be used in appropriate circumstances, include exchanges or conversions of one class of securities into another, issues resulting from the exercise of options or warrants, and issues under employee share-ownership schemes—though these will not necessarily raise new money for the company. Nor, of course, will capitalisation issues, dealt with in Chapters 9 and 10 above.

Two other types of issue deserve mention. The first of these is a Vendor Consideration Issue, *i.e.* one made as consideration for, or in connection with, an acquisition of property.[39] If the vendor is willing to take by way of consideration an allotment of equity shares of the acquiring company, there will be no need to offer the existing equity shareholders pre-emptive rights; the issue to the vendor is not for cash.[40] But investors, and institutional ones in particular, became alarmed at the extent to which vendor consideration issues were being used even when the vendor wanted cash and the acquiring company raised it by a new issue of equity shares without offering its shareholders pre-emptive rights. The *modus operandi* was a tripartite arrangement whereby the vendor sold in consideration of an allotment of shares which a merchant bank then placed on behalf of the vendor who thereby received the desired cash. This had

[37] In one rights issue in 1990 only 6 per cent. of the rights were taken up and 94 per cent. left with the underwriters.
[38] Their use is not encouraged by The Stock Exchange: see *Yellow Book*, Section 1, Chapter 3, para. 5.1 and 5.2.
[39] Frequently on a take-over or merger but not necessarily so.
[40] And it would, of course, be impracticable to offer the shares to the existing shareholders on like terms.

advantages for all the parties (the company because it made it easier for it to adopt merger accounting[41]). And so long as the acquiring company did not have to increase its authorised capital and its directors had been given general authority to issue capital[42] all this could usually be done without any reference to its members in general meeting. However, in 1987 a committee consisting of representatives of listed companies, institutional investors and The Stock Exchange produced Guidelines which, if observed will appease The Stock Exchange and the institutions but which, if not followed, the company will need to discuss with the investment committees of the National Association of Pension Funds and the Association of British Insurers and to obtain their prior approval if trouble is to be avoided. Approval may involve what is known as a "claw-back" arrangement. Under this, instead of the merchant bank placing the shares with its associates, it will first make what is known as a "Vendor Rights Offer" enabling the acquiring company's share-holders to take up their pro-rata entitlement at the issue price.

The second type is a Euro-Security Issue. Such an issue is sometimes used by a major company as a means of raising capital by an international offering of what are variously described as "euro-bonds," "euro-securities" or "euro-currency securities." "Euro" is a misnomer since the securities and the methods of issue have no particular connection with either Europe as a whole or with the EC[43]—except that the largest concentration of the primary dealers is in London, that in so far as there is a regulatory or representative body, it is the Association of International Bond Dealers (the AIBD) with headquarters in Switzerland, and that issues are generally listed on the Luxembourg Stock Exchange.[44] The only reason for listing, is that under the laws of some countries certain institutions may not invest in unlisted securities; transactions do not take place on any stock exchange for the market is exclusively an international "over-the-counter" one, conducted by telephone or telex (and largely dominated by American and Japanese investment banks).

Originally the securities traded were pure debt securities—hence the original term "euro-bonds." But increasingly those of companies have come to contain an equity element—hence the growing use of "euro-equities" or "euro-securities."[45] No one as yet has succeeded in satisfactorily defining such securities; or is ever likely to, for the

41 See Chap. 9 at p. 209 above.
42 See Chap. 14 at pp. 362, 363 below.
43 It has been suggested that "euro" came to be adopted because that formed part of the name of the first body that made such an issue—but that seems to be apocryphal. The probable explanation is that it was adopted by American investment banks to distinguish such issues from U.S.A. domestic issues.
44 Somewhat to the chagrin of The Stock Exchange; but Luxembourg is cheaper and is said to adopt a more "pragmatic" attitude to applications for listing.
45 Terminology varies (The Stock Exchange favours "euro-currency" which, mislead-ingly, suggests that (the securities are necessarily denominated in ecus.) This book uses "euro-securities."

securities themselves do not have any unique features which distinguish them from other bonds or debentures, with or without conversion or similar rights to a share in the equity. Their distinguishing mark is the way in which they are marketed on issue and here the best attempt so far to distinguish them from other international issues is that in Article 3(f) of the Prospectus Directive,[46] which reads:

"Euro-securities shall mean transferable securities which:—are to be underwritten and distributed by a syndicate, at least two of the members of which have their registered offices in different states,—are offered on a significant scale in one or more States other than that of the issuer's registered office, and—may be subscribed for or initially acquired only through a credit institution[47] or other financial institution."[48]

All one need add is that the value of the business conducted on the market is enormous (far greater than that on any stock exchange); that when trading starts[49] it will normally be in lots exceeding $(US) 25,000; and that there are efficiently organised clearing systems.

When we turn (as we are about to) to the legal regulation of public issues little will be said about euro-issues. This is because the attitude of the United Kingdom (and of other countries) has been studiously to exclude them from regulation;[50]—an attitude acquiesced in by the European Commission. The arguments of the AIBD and its members which have led to this "hands-off" treatment are (i) that the market is used by "professionals only" and (ii) that if attempts were made to regulate it more strictly the centre of its operations would move from London to somewhere else in the European time zone,[51] (say Zurich) thus depriving the United Kingdom (and, perhaps, the Community)[52] of one of its more valuable financial assets. Neither argument is convincing. While it is true that the primary distributions will be to "professionals only," as a result of secondary dealings euro-securities can, and sometimes do, end up in the hands of private investors.[53] Nor is it really believable that the major dealers would uproot

---

[46] Directive 89/298/EEC.

[47] EC-ese for "banks."

[48] This is an improvement on U.K. efforts such as F.S. Act s.152(6) (see below p. 347 n. 89) but does not seem adequately to distinguish "euro" issues from other international offers such as those undertaken on some of the Government's privatisation issues.

[49] Which it frequently does before the listing particulars are even filed at the Luxembourg Exchange.

[50] Apart from the need for those dealers carrying on business in the U.K. to be authorised to carry on investment business.

[51] Since the euro-market is a global 24 hour market it is important that its centre should be in the time-zone midway between that of Japan and the U.S.A.

[52] Switzerland is not a member of the Community.

[53] While a minimum price of $25,000 would deter many private investors, on the secondary market odd-lots are obtainable for as little as $500. And "pools" or mutual funds afford another avenue.

themselves from London and flee to Switzerland; only gross over-regulation would cause them to contemplate that. Nevertheless, until there is a major scandal in the market (so far there have only been relatively minor ones) the likelihood is that it will remain the most lightly regulated of the world's major capital markets.

Legal Regulation of Public Issues

The legal regulations which will have to be complied with are laid down in the Financial Services Act and in rules and regulations made thereunder.[54] The contents of both the primary and secondary legislation are constrained by four principal EC Directives.[55] The Act can paraphrase the Directives, so long as the result is the same as that prescribed by the Directives, and can supplement them to the extent that they permit. So can the secondary legislation to the same extent so long as the Act so permits.

The Stock Exchange, as "the competent authority" for the purposes of the Listing Directives, has made full use of the powers which it believes it has and, by its listing rules in the *Yellow Book*, has not only adapted the wording of the Directives to practice in the United Kingdom, but, treating the Listing Directives as "minimum standards" rather than "co-ordinating" Directives,[56] has added further requirements. The danger is that thereby it may have prescribed requirements which do not fully implement, or which conflict with, the Directives. So long as they do not conflict with the Act, their validity is not impaired so far as domestic English law is concerned. But, if the European Commission were to think that we have breached our Community obligations, it could object and the Secretary of State could direct The Exchange to put matters right.[57] Indeed, an individual adversely affected might argue that he was entitled to treat the relevant provision of the Directive as directly effective and enforceable by him.[58] That would be a difficult

---

[54] It is assumed that by the time this edition is published the former provisions in the Companies Act will have been wholly superseded; see p. 311 above.

[55] See Chap. 4 at p. 65 above. The four are; Directive 79/279/EEC (co-ordinating the conditions for admission to official stock exchange listing); Directive 80/390/EEC (co-ordinating the requirements for the drawing-up, scrutiny and distribution of listing particulars); Directive 82/121/EEC (on information to be published on a regular basis by companies admitted to listing); and Directive 89/298/EEC (on prospectuses for initial public offerings of securities which are not already listed on a stock exchange in the member State). Here these will be described respectively as the "Admission to Listing Directive", "the Listing Particulars Directive", the "Continuing Obligations Directive" and the "Prospectus Directive", and the first three collectively as the "Listing Directives." The Prospectus Directive impinges on and amends the Listing Directives (especially the Listing Particulars Directive). There are also two amending Directives, (87/345/EEC and 90/211/EEC; the latter dealing with mutual recognition of listing particulars and of prospectuses, implemented by S.I. 1991 No. 823 and *Yellow Book*, section 8, Chapter 2).

[56] This is clearly right in relation to the Continuing Obligations Directive but distinctly dubious in the case of the other two Listing Directives, both of which are expressly described as "co-ordinating" though with certain powers to add or subtract.

[57] See F.S. Act s.192 (as substituted by the Companies Act 1989).

[58] See Chap. 4, at pp. 58 (n. 21) and 65 above.

Flotations

argument to refute, since The Stock Exchange must surely now be regarded as an organ of the State and the Listing Directives as sufficiently clear and precise as to be capable of direct effect (we originally implemented them by appending them verbatim to Regulations[59] which made them United Kingdom law[60]). However none of this has yet happened and probably never will.[61] Much the same applies to unlisted issues admitted to the Stock Exchange's U.S.M. Under the missing position until Part V is revised,[62] whether or not the issue is admitted to the U.S.M., the company will have to publish a prospectus which complies with the antiquated Schedule 3 of the Companies Act; the Exchange cannot grant an effective certificate of exemption under section 76 of that Act since that applies only if the securities are to be "listed."[63] The account which follows assumes that Part V has been brought fully into operation and the provisions of the Companies Act repealed.

A. Listed Issues—Statutory Provisions

The statutory provisions are to be found in Part IV of the Financial Services Act in relation to listed issues and in Part V in relation to unlisted issues. Unfortunately it is unsafe to assume that so long as the provisions in the relevant Part are complied with there are no sections in other Parts of that Act that must also be observed. In fact a number of sections in its Part I may well be relevant. A prospectus (or "listing particulars" as at present it is called when the securities are to be officially listed) is "an investment advertisement," as defined in section 57, inviting the entry into an "investment agreement," as defined in section 44(9), and is also "an advertisement in respect of investment business" for the purposes of section 48(2)(e). This normally can be ignored so long as the prospectus complies with Part IV or V;[64] but is relevant if it does not. And, even if it does comply, objectionable selling practices may fall foul of section 47[65] or 56.

(i) Admission to Listing. The first section in Part IV (section 142) provides that "no investment to which this section applies" (in practice all types of securities likely to be issued by a company[66] to

[59] S.I. 1984 No. 716.
[60] See pp. 58 and 65 above.
[61] This, however, is not to deny that it is arguable that some provisions of the *Yellow Book* are not wholly consistent with the Directives and that the present introductory Chapter of the *Yellow Book* gives the impression that The Stock Exchange has a wider discretion to reject an application for listing, notwithstanding that it complies with the Directives, than the Directives seem to afford.
[62] See p. 311 n. 2 above.
[63] Unless the prospectus has been approved in another member State in which case it will be deemed to comply with the Companies Act's provisions so long as certain conditions are complied with: see the Companies Act 1985 (Mutual Recognition of Prospectuses) Regs 1991 (S.I. 1991 No. 823).
[64] See ss.58(1)(d) and 48(5).
[65] See p. 349 below.
[66] Parts IV and V apply to issues by bodies other than companies but here we are concerned only with the latter.

the general public) "shall be admitted to the Official List of The Stock Exchange except in accordance with the provisions of this Part.... " Section 143 requires the application to be made to the "competent authority," (*i.e.* The Stock Exchange[67]) in such manner as the listing rules made by it may require and says that application must not be made without the consent of the issuer of the securities, (*i.e.* the company). The latter requirement precludes major share-holders from off-loading to the public without the concurrence of the company and ensures that the company and its directors will have to accept responsibility for the listing particulars. It also provides that no application shall be made in respect of securities to be issued by a private company.[68]

Section 144, having stated that The Exchange shall not admit any securities to the Official List unless it is satisfied that its listing rules, and any other requirements imposed by it, are complied with,[69] goes on to provide that such rules may require the submission, approval and publication of listing particulars or, in such cases as may be specified by the rules, the publication of another document.[70] The section also states that an application may be refused if The Exchange considers that admission would be detrimental to the interests of investors or if the company has failed to comply with the obligations to which it was subject by virtue of official listing in another member State.[71] Subsection (6)[72] says that when securities have been admitted "their admission shall not be called in question on the ground that any requirement or condition for their admission has not been complied with." It is interesting to contrast this wording with that in the Companies Act relating to the conclusiveness of certificates of incorporation.[73] That says that such certificates are conclusive evidence that all the requirements have been observed. Section 144(6) of the Financial Services Act avoids saying more than that once securities have been admitted to listing, the admission cannot be questioned even if any of the requirements have not been complied with—a much more sensible provision.

Section 145 provides that The Stock Exchange may, in accordance with its listing rules, discontinue or suspend the listing of any securities. The difference between the two is that if the listing is discontinued, which can be done only if The Exchange "is satisfied

[67] It was formerly its Council until the Exchange re-registered as a limited company in 1991.
[68] Thus, with s.170 (below), preserving the long-standing ban on private companies issuing their securities to the public.
[69] Subs. (1).
[70] Subs. (2). This recognises that there are some cases where publication of full listing particulars is unnecessary.
[71] Subs. (3). This complies with arts. 10 and 11 of the Admission to Listing Directive.
[72] Subs. (4) and (5) in effect provide that if the application is not granted within six months of its submission or a request for further information, it shall be deemed to refused.
[73] On which see Chap. 11 at pp. 278-281 above.

that there are circumstances which preclude normal regular dealings in the securities,"[74] the securities cease for all purposes to be listed. Suspension, on the other hand, can occur in a wider range of circumstances provided in the listing rules and the securities remain "listed securities" for the purposes of The Exchange's control over the company under section 153.[75] Suspension (often at the request of the company's board) occurs not infrequently and is the only effective sanction which The Exchange has over listed companies (as opposed to its member firms). Unfortunately the main sufferers are the innocent shareholders who, until the suspension is lifted, are deprived of a market for their shares and may be left in the dark about what is going on. The Act does not specifically re-state Article 15.1 of the Admission to Listing Directive which requires member states to "ensure that decisions refusing admission to listing or discontinuing listing shall be subject to the right to apply to the courts." It is clear, however, that there is such a right by way of judicial review.

(ii) Listing particulars. As heretofore, in the case of most new issues the company will have to submit to The Stock Exchange a very lengthy and detailed document which is both an integral part of the application for listing and of the offer which it proposes to make to the public. It corresponds with what was formerly called a "prospectus"—as it still is in relation to unlisted issues.

The Listing Particulars Directive prefaces its detailed requirements regarding the contents of listing particulars by a general statement in Article 4.1 that:

"The listing particulars shall contain the information which, according to the particular nature of the issuer and the securities . . , is necessary to enable investors and their investment advisers to make an informed assessment of the assets and liabilities, financial position, profits and losses, and prospects of the issuer and of the rights attaching to such securities."[76]

And Article 4.2 requires member States to ensure that this obligation is incumbent on those responsible for the listing particulars. This comes close to making contracts resulting from public offers, contracts of the utmost good faith demanding disclosure by the offerors of all material facts. In principle, this has much to commend

[74] Subs. (1).
[75] Subss. (2) and (3). See below pp. 328, 329.
[76] Art. 11.1 of the Prospectus Directive provides similarly in respect of prospectuses for unlisted issues.

it—and indeed seems to go no further than the view adopted by the English courts in the nineteenth century.[77] However the prospect of finding such an open-ended obligation laid down by statute caused shivers to run down the spine of the City Establishment.

Nevertheless, laid down it is by section 146(1) of the F.S. Act. However, the section seeks to give the Directive's requirement greater precision without offending against its spirit (or so it is hoped). Hence, subsection (2) provides that the information which, under subsection (1) has to be included, is limited to that within the knowledge of any person responsible for the listing particulars or which it would be reasonable for him to obtain by making enquiries. And subsection (3) allows regard to be had not only to the nature of the issuer and of the securities but also: to the nature of the persons likely to consider acquiring the securities, to the knowledge which their likely professional advisers may be expected to have; and to information available by virtue of its publication under statutory requirements or those of The Stock Exchange or other recognised investment exchange. The *Yellow Book*, instead of including in its rules any specific provisions regarding this general obligation, merely says that: "Issuers are reminded that section 146 of the Act contains a general duty of disclosure to which they must in addition have regard."[78]

Under section 147, if after the preparation of listing particulars and before dealing commences there is any change significant for the purposes of making an informed assessment, the company must submit to The Exchange supplementary listing particulars for approval and, if they are approved, must publish them in accordance with The Exchange's listing rules. The same applies if there is any such change to supplementary listing particulars. If the company is unaware of any change it is not required to comply with this obligation but any person responsible for the listing particulars who does know of it is under a duty to notify the company. Supplementary listing particulars must not be confused with preliminary "pathfinder" or subsequent "mini" prospectuses[79]; unlike the latter they are "listing particulars" to the same extent as the original listing particulars.

---

[77] "Those who issue a prospectus, holding out to the public the great advantages which will accrue to persons who will take shares . . . and inviting them to take shares on the faith of the representations therein contained, are bound to state everything with strict and scrupulous accuracy and not only to abstain from stating as fact that which is not so, but to omit no one fact within their knowledge, the existence of which might in any degree affect the nature, or extent, or quality of the privileges and advantages which the prospectus holds out as inducements to take shares"; *per* Kindersley V.-C. in *New Brunswick & Canada Ry. Co. v. Muggeridge* (1860) 1 Dr & Sm. 363 at 381. This "golden legacy," (as the dictum was described by Page Wood V.-C. in *Henderson v. Lacon* (1867) L.R. 5 Eq. 249 at 262) was adopted by Lord Chelmsford in *Central Ry. of Venezuela v. Kisch* (1867) L.R. 2 H.L. 99 at 113.

[78] *Yellow Book*, Section 3, Chapter 1, para. 1.4.

[79] See below pp. 327, 328.

Section 148 permits The Exchange to authorise the omission from listing particulars of any information which would otherwise be required by section 146 if its disclosure would be (a) contrary to the public interest or (b) seriously detrimental to the company (provided, however, that its omission would not be likely to mislead as to facts essential in order to make an informed assessment) or (c) the issue is of bonds or debentures of a class specified in the listing rules and disclosure is unnecessary for persons of the kind who may be expected normally to buy or deal in them.[80] As regards (a) The Exchange is entitled to rely on a certificate from the Secretary of State or the Treasury,[81] that disclosure would be contrary to the public interest.

Although it is the responsibility of The Stock Exchange to ensure that the listing particulars comply with the Act and The Exchange's listing rules, section 149 preserves the time-honoured requirement that a copy of the prospectus, (*i.e.* the listing particulars and any supplementary listing particulars) must be delivered to the Registrar of Companies on or before the date of publication and that the particulars shall state that this has been done. This makes some sense when the company is incorporated in the United Kingdom,[82] or when it has established a place of business there so that, under Part XXIII of the Companies Act,[83] the Registrar should have a file on the company. But, in other cases it is difficult to see what purpose it serves. Indeed, section 149, as worded, could produce absurdities even in the case of a foreign company with an established place of business in the United Kingdom. In the case of a company incorporated in the United Kingdom the section provides, as one would expect, that the copy shall be delivered to the Registrar of that part of the United Kingdom in which it was incorporated. But, in any other case, it may be delivered to any United Kingdom Registrar.[84] Hence a foreign company with an established place of business in Northern Ireland could, it seems, make an issue there but deliver a copy of the listing particulars to the Registrar of England and Wales or of Scotland.

Sections 150 to 152 deal with liability to compensate for false or misleading statements in listing particulars, and are dealt with later in this chapter in relation to liabilities generally. And as section 154 is

---

[80] (a) and (b) are permitted by art. 7(*b*) of the Listing Particulars Directive and (c)—mainly a "euro-security exception"—presumably by art. 10.
[81] Even if they are themselves responsible for the listing particulars! In the case of issues of company securities this is only likely to occur in relation to privatisation issues, where, one would have thought, a similar proviso to that in (b) ought to apply.
[82] Putting the statement on the listing particulars is liable to suggest, falsely, that thereby the offer has some sort of Governmental approval. But the information in it may be of interest to those searching the company's file at Companies' House.
[83] Or the corresponding provisions of the N. Ireland Companies Act.
[84] s.149(2).

logically related to what has gone before we turn to it before section 153.

(iii) Pathfinder and mini prospectuses. In practice on a major public issue there will be preliminary advertisements of the forthcoming offering. These may go beyond a mere announcement that an issue is to be made and may amount to what is generally described as a "pathfinder" prospectus designed to test (and to arouse) interest in subscribing. Furthermore, in some cases contemporaneously with the publication of the listing particulars a "mini-prospectus" (summarising the essential information in the particulars) may be published and copies sent to all those who have expressed an interest in response to the pathfinder prospectus.

Both pathfinder and mini-prospectuses can perform a useful purpose and have done so in relation to the Government's privatisation issues. But extended use of them could be highly dangerous and defeat the whole object of ensuring that the public is not invited to subscribe except in reliance on approved listing particulars. Unfortunately the present position is confusing. The Listing Particulars Directive provides by Article 22 that:

"Where listing particulars are or will be published—the notices, bills, posters and documents announcing this operation and indicating the essential characteristics of [the] securities, and all other documents relating to their admission and intended for publication by the issuer or on his behalf, must first be communicated to the competent authorities. The latter shall decide whether they should be submitted to scrutiny before publication.

The aforementioned documents must state that listing particulars exist and indicate where they are being, or will be, published. . . ."

This must surely mean that both a pathfinder prospectus (at any rate if it "indicates the essential characteristics" of the securities) and a mini-prospectus must be communicated to the competent authority before publication and must not be published until listing particulars "exist." The way in which it has been implemented by section 154(1) and by the listing rules produces that result in relation to mini-prospectuses but not, in relation to pathfinder prospectuses. Section 154(1) provides that "no advertisement or other information of a kind specified in the listing rules shall be issued in the United Kingdom unless the contents ... have been submitted to the competent authority and that authority has either; (a) approved those contents, or (b) authorised the issue of the advertisement without such approval." The Stock Exchange, the competent authority, by recent

Flotations

amendments to its listing rules[85] has "specified" what are the types of advertisements and information for the purposes of section 154 and these expressly include mini-prospectuses.[86] As regards these, the former rules have been clarified. While The Exchange is not prepared to approve such documents it may authorise their publication providing they include: (i) only statements of a factual nature drawn from listing particulars; (ii) a statement that listing particulars have been published[87] which alone contain full details, (iii) a statement that the directors are satisfied that the mini-prospectus contains a fair summary of the listing particulars, stating their date and the addresses at which copies are available to the public, and (iv) a statement that the issue of the document has been authorised by The Exchange without approval of its contents.[88] However, as regards pathfinder prospectuses it is expressly provided that "press releases and draft or pathfinder listing particulars are not regarded as falling in" the specified categories.[89] The effect seems to be that they do not have to be communicated to The Exchange and that they are to be regarded as falling outside Part IV of the Act. This does not mean that they are wholly unregulated; sections 47 and 57 in Part I of the Financial Services Act will clearly apply to them. But how, in the absence of a requirement to communicate them to the competent authority, this result can be regarded as compliance with the Directive is difficult to see.

Hence, in regard to pathfinder prospectuses in particular, the position is disturbing—as is the overall result. It is easy enough for a recipient of a pathfinder prospectus to obtain an application form and to apply without ever having seen the listing particulars or taken professional advice—most small investors in the privatisation issues probably did just that. Should not The Exchange be required to approve both pathfinder and mini-prospectuses? It is on them that those most in need of protection will rely.

(iv) Continuing Obligations of Listed Companies. Prior to the nomination of The Stock Exchange as the "competent authority" for the purposes of the Listing Directives, The Exchange imposed continuing obligations on listed companies, by requiring them, as a condition of admission to listing, to enter into a listing agreement, thereby making the obligations contractually binding. The disadvantage of this was that, as the rules were changed from time to time, the obligations might vary as between one company and another

85 *Yellow Book*, Section 2, Chapter 1, para. 9 and Chapter 3, para. 3.11.
86 *Ibid.* Section 2, Chapter 1, para. 9(c).
87 This is stricter than the Directive which requires only that listing particulars must "exist" (whatever that may mean) and will be published. But The Exchange reserves the right to refuse: *ibid.* Section 1, Chapter 1, para. 15.
88 *Yellow Book*, Section 2, Chapter 3, para. 3.11.
89 *Ibid.* Chapter 1, para. 9.

according to the date of the company's admission to listing. Section 153 of the Act now empowers The Exchange to lay down such requirements in the listing rules as subordinate legislation, thus making the use of agreements unnecessary, and this expressly applies to companies whether or not their listing was before or after the coming into force of Part IV.[90] Section 153(1) states that The Exchange may by its listing rules specify requirements to be complied with by listed companies and the action which The Exchange may take in the event of non-compliance, adding that this action may include publishing the fact that the company has contravened the rules and that, if the contravention was failure to publish required information, The Exchange itself may publish that information. Hence the listing rules in the *Yellow Book* can, and do, both implement the Continuing Obligations Directive and, since that is only a "minimum-standards" Directive,[91] add very substantially to its requirements by including those which were formerly made effective by listing agreements.

(v) **Supplementary provisions.** The concluding provisions of Part IV can be disposed of very briefly. Section 155 empowers The Stock Exchange to charge fees for applications for, and retention of, listing, section 156 contains formal and evidentiary requirements regarding listing rules and section 157 empowers the Secretary of State to transfer the functions of "competent authority" from The Stock Exchange to another body, either at the request of The Exchange or if it appears to him that it is not doing its job properly.[92]

B. *Listing rules*

The *Yellow Book*, a loose-leaf publication,[93] is divided into ten Sections most of which contain several Chapters. In general the rules relating to companies (as opposed to other issuers) are to be found in Chapter 1 or 2 of each Section. It may be important to know whether a particular rule is one which The Exchange is required to make in order to comply with the Listing Directives or whether the rule is made of its own volition. In relation to the latter, The Exchange will

90 s. 153(2).

91 "The member States may subject companies to obligations more stringent than those provided by this Directive or to additional obligations provided that they apply generally to all companies or to all companies of a given class"; Continuing Obligations Directive, art. 3. And as regards continuing obligations under the Admission to Listing Directive, see its art. 5.2.

92 These are the customary provisions applying to bodies to which, under the F.S. Act, the Secretary of State has delegated powers; the power to transfer functions is known as "the nuclear deterrent" since it is never likely to be used.

93 The present edition is dated 1984 but has been very substantially amended, particularly in 1990–91. A completely new edition is promised but no date has been given for this. There are often substantial time-lags between notices of rule changes coming into immediate effect and the dates when replacement pages of the *Yellow Book* itself are circulated to subscribers.

have power to waive compliance with the rule whereas in relation to the former it will not, except to the extent that that is expressly permitted by the Directives. Hence, in Section 3, Chapter 2 (contents of listing particulars) and Section 5 (continuing obligations) the derivation of each rule is indicated by a marginal note.[94]

(i) Application for listing. The general conditions for admission to listing are explained in Section 1. The applicant company must appoint a member firm of The Exchange to sponsor the application. The firm is responsible for ensuring that The Exchange is given all information that should be brought to its notice and for lodging all supporting documents and is the channel of communication for discussions with The Exchange.[95] Normally, the expected market value of the securities must not exceed a prescribed minimum,[96] the securities must be freely transferable,[97] and the company must have published accounts for the 3 years preceding the application,[98] which accounts must have been "independently audited in accordance with standards . . . appropriate for companies of international standing and repute."[99] Listing particulars or other offering documents must not be published until they have received the formal approval of The Exchange.[1] The detailed application procedure is laid down in Section 2 (and its Schedules 1–5). It involves the submission of copies of a formidable number of documents and observance of a strict time-table if admission is to be obtained before dealings are planned to begin. Chapter 3 of section 2, is of particular importance for it deals with the extent to which the expensive operation of newspaper publication is compulsory.[2]

(ii) Contents of Listing Particulars. Section 3 of the *Yellow Book* purports to deal with the contents of listing particulars but in fact also contains provisions exempting from the need for listing par-ticulars[3]—a matter which seems more logically to belong to Section 2. Nor is the arrangement of Section 3 as user-friendly as it might

---

94 The abbreviations used are explained in, respectively, the heading to Section 3, Chapter 2 and the second para. of the Introduction to Section 5, Chapter 1.
95 *Yellow Book*, Section 1, Chapter 1, para. 4. As we have seen, an issuing house also will probably sponsor. All sponsors "should satisfy themselves that the company is suitable to be listed . . . and pay particular attention to the composition of the board . . .," satisfying themselves that it will comply with a listed company's continuing obligations: *ibid.* para. 5.
96 *Ibid.* Chapter 2, para. 3.
97 *Ibid.* para. 4. And all securities of the same class must be listed: para. 9.
98 *Ibid.* para. 5. It was formerly five years but has been reduced to three which is all that the Admission to Listing Directive requires.
99 *Ibid.* para. 6.
1 *Ibid.* para. 16.
2 There are now numerous exceptions to the requirement to publish in two national newspapers.
3 Section 3, Chapter 1, para. 5. The most important of these exemptions is where the issue is of securities of the same class as those already listed and increases them by less than 10 per cent.: para. 5.4. For the anomalous consequences, see below p. 345.

be—though for that the Listing Particulars Directive (which it implements) is more blameworthy than The Exchange. Chapter 1, having dealt with some general matters, proceeds to detail what items of information set out in Chapter 2 have to be included in listing particulars in different circumstances, what additional items have to be included in particular cases, and what, in particular cases, can be omitted. Chapter 2 (which can broadly be regarded as providing a comprehensive list of the information required on an Offer for Sale of equity shares by a company which is not already listed) requires information to be given on:

The issuer, persons responsible for listing particulars, the auditors and other advisers (Part 1)

The securities (Part 2)

General information on the company's objects and capital (Part 3)

The group's activities (Part 4)

Financial information about the company or group (Part 5)

The Management (Part 6)

Recent developments and prospects (Part 7)

Of particular importance are the requirements of Parts 5 and 7. What is required under the former are accounts, normally for the past three financial years, and an accountant's report thereon. Under Part 7, information on the group's prospects for at least the current financial year must be given and, if this includes a profit forecast,[4] the assumptions upon which the directors have based it must be stated and the accounting policies examined and reported on by the reporting accountants. The issuing house (or, if none, the sponsoring member firm) must in addition report whether it has satisfied itself that the forecast has been stated after careful enquiry.[5]

While the effect of the new rules has been to make listing particulars even longer than prospectuses formerly were, the principal difference is in respect of arrangement and lay-out rather than in the nature of the information that they must contain. All that perhaps needs specific mention here is that the information must include "a summary of the principal contents of each material contract (not . . . entered into in the ordinary course of business) by any member of the group within the two years immediately preceding the publication of the listing particulars . . ." and a statement of where the contract may be inspected.[6] The question whether contracts are "material" can raise sensitive issues and is one on which the company's directors

---

[4] It is not compulsory to include forecasts but it is customary to do so notwithstanding that their record for accuracy is unimpressive. Their omission is likely to attract comment and to diminish the impact of the particulars as a selling document.

[5] Section 3, Chapter 2, Part 7, para. 7.2.

[6] Section 3, Chapter 2, Part 3, paras. 3.16, 3.17.

are likely to seek legal advice—and, indeed, one which the lawyers should raise with the directors. If the directors do not want to disclose any particular contract that is cogent evidence that it is material.

Before leaving listing particulars, one further general point needs to be made. Increasingly it is coming to be recognised that the extent of the disclosure required to be made in prospectuses can be reduced if information relating to the company is already in the public domain. This is reflected both in the Act[7] and in The Exchange's listing rules which, are less stringent when there are further issues by a company which is already listed, and which, for example, provide that, when companies transfer to listing from the U.S.M., The Exchange, in considering requests for derogations from items not arising from the Directives, will take into account the regulatory standards and controls to which U.S.M. companies are subject.[8]

(iii) **Continuing obligations.** The *Yellow Book* rightly emphasises in its first Chapter, that: "A most important condition for listing is acceptance of the continuing obligations which will apply following admission."[9] These obligations are set out in Section 5 of the *Yellow Book* and supplemented by Section 6 which relates to acquisitions and realisations and to take-overs and mergers. As already pointed out they go much further than is required by the Admission to Listing and the Continuing Obligations Directives. Indeed, not only do they prescribe what information has to be given by listed companies to The Exchange, members of the company, and the public, but, in many respects, they supplement the provisions of the Companies Act regarding the duties of directors and controllers. For example, Section 5 includes a "model code for securities transactions by directors of listed companies:"[10] and companies are required to adopt rules "no less exacting than those of the model."[11] Even more important are the rules in Section 6, especially those relating to major acquisitions or realisations.[12] These are divided into six classes[13] in relation to some, the rules require not merely notification to, but approval by, the members[14] and, in the case of some so-called "Class

[7] F.S. Act s.146(3)(*d*): see p. 325 above.

[8] *Yellow Book* Section 3, Chapter 1, para. 6.1. See also para. 6.2 and Section 8.

[9] Section 1, Chapter 1, para. 9. This goes on to say that such obligations are set out in section 5. This ignores the all-important Section 6 the *vires* for most of which must, surely, also derive from s.153 of the F.S. Act.

[10] *Yellow Book*, section 5, Chapter 2, pp. 5.41–5.46.

[11] *Ibid.* para. 44. The Exchange cannot directly impose legal obligations on directors but only on "issuers," (*i.e.* the company): s.153 above. But it could put the directors on its "black-list" if they breached the company's rules.

[12] Section 6, Chapter 1.

[13] *Ibid.* para. 2.

[14] This is so in relation to "Super Class 1 transactions" (*Ibid.* paras. 2 and 3), "Class 4 transactions" (paras. 7.1) and very substantial acquisitions or reverse takeovers (para. 8).

4 transactions," (*i.e.* those with a director, substantial shareholder or an associate of either) the "Class 4 party" may be required to abstain from voting.[15]

(iv) Miscellaneous. The remaining Sections of the *Yellow Book* deal with special cases: Section 7 with euro-securities (notwithstanding that listing in London is rare); Section 8 with foreign companies; Section 9 with articles of association and documents of title to securities; and Section 10 with special types of issuers, (*i.e.* property companies, mineral companies, investment companies and unit trusts[16])

In this brief *tour d'horizon*, designed only as a guide through the *Yellow Book*, no more needs to be said.

C. *Unlisted Issues*

The legal regulation of unlisted issues can be dealt with more briefly, both for reasons already explained[17] and because the present provisions of Part V of the Financial Services Act follow closely those of Part IV. Where they diverge, this is mainly because the regulations of unlisted issues have to deal with a problem which does not arise when an issue is to be listed. In the latter case, there is no doubt that regulation is needed because the general public will be able to acquire the securities, if not at the issue price at any rate at the quoted prices once dealings on The Exchange commence. However, in relation to unlisted issues, unless there is another organised market on which the securities are to be traded (and in the United Kingdom there is at present no organised OTC market) it is only when the securities are to be admitted to The Stock Exchange's U.S.M. (which is really a form of lower-tier listing) that one has a similar indication that the securities are being made available to the public. Otherwise, another test has to be found for distinguishing between issues which need to be stringently regulated in the interests of the public and those which do not. The Prospectus Directive ducks this.[18] It admits in its preamble that: "so far, it has proved impossible to furnish a common definition of the term 'public offer' and all its component parts" but nevertheless restricts its requirements to "offers to the public," leaving the member States to put their own interpretation upon it.

The objective of the Prospectus Directive, as its preamble makes clear, is to ensure that, when an unlisted public issue is made,

---

15 *Ibid.* para. 7.2, last sub-para.
16 Unit Trusts can be listed; but few are since the managers, not the market-makers: see p. 248 above.
17 Above p. 311.
18 Except that art. 2 excludes certain types of offer, in some cases obviously because they are not fairly to be regarded as made "to the public": see art 2(a), (b), (h) and, perhaps, (c).

information similar to that required in listing particulars is made available except that "less detailed information can be required so as not to burden small and medium-sized issuers unduly." What that seems to ignore is that on unlisted issues the public is at greater risk of being misled, if only because the Prospectus Directive does not require member States to provide for prior scrutiny of prospectuses.[19] Moreover, it also ignores the fact that some information, not needed if the issue is to be listed, is of vital importance if it is not. In particular the public need to be told what arrangements (if any) have been made to provide a trading market for the securities and to what extent these ensure that they will be able to sell their shares at a fair price. And, if there is no such market, they need a warning in bold type that they may not be able to dispose of their securities at any price unless the issue is to be admitted to the U.S.M. Past experience has shown that rules to this effect are vital and it is to be hoped that that will be recognised in the review of Part V now taking place.

Statutory Provisions

As already explained, Part V of the Financial Services Act has not, at the time of writing, been brought into operation and will be further amended before it is.[20] However, it is likely to remain basically in its present form since the nature of the requirements of the Prospectus Directive[21] were known at the time of its enactment.

Part V begins with section 158, much of which corresponds (for example in relation to the "securities" to which it applies) with section 142 of Part IV. But it contains two important subsections which have no direct counterpart in section 142. The first of these is subsection (4) which provides that for the purposes of Part V an advertisement offers securities if:

"(a) it invites a person to enter into an agreement for, or with a view to, subscribing for or otherwise acquiring or underwriting any securities; or

[19] The Commission wanted it to, but its attempts to make member States see reason were unavailing. But prospectuses are not entitled to mutual recognition throughout the E.C. unless they are pre-vetted.
[20] It has already been prospectively amended by the Companies Act 1989 and the summary which follows assumes that these amendments will also have been brought into operation.
[21] It was originally intended to be the first of the four principal Directives, containing the basic requirements for all public offer prospectuses which would be supplemented by the other three if the securities were listed. It still bears signs of its origins but applies "to transferable securities which are offered for the first time in a member State provided that these securities are not already listed on a stock exchange situated or operating in that member State"; art. 1. Since, under the U.K. system, The Exchange does not admit to listing until the public offer has been made it seems that we shall have to revert to the position prior to the implementation of the listing Directives and to call listing particulars "prospectuses" as well.

(b) it contains information calculated to lead directly or indirectly to a person entering into such an agreement."

This is considerably wider than "listing particulars" for the purposes of Part IV and indeed, than "prospectuses" for the purposes of Part V; it clearly includes as a result of (b) all forms of pathfinder and mini-prospectuses.[22] The other such subsection is subsection (6) which says that in Part V "approved exchange" means "a recognised investment exchange[23] approved by the Secretary of State for the purposes of this Part of the Act."

(i) Issues admitted to an approved exchange. When issues are to be officially listed, Part V has no operation. But, as we have seen, The Stock Exchange also has an organised lower-tier market,[24] the U.S.M. If the securities are to be admitted to dealings on that, the issue is clearly a public issue requiring regulation but this can be left to The Stock Exchange. Hence section 159 provides that no person shall issue or cause to be issued in the United Kingdom[25] an advertisement offering any securities on their admission to dealings on an approved exchange unless (a) a prospectus containing information about the securities has been submitted to and approved by The Exchange and delivered to the Registrar of Companies or the advertisement is such that no agreement can be entered into in pursuance of it until it has been so submitted, approved, and delivered, or (b) a prospectus has been delivered for registration within the previous 12 months and the approved exchange certifies that it is satisfied that persons likely to consider acquiring the securities will have sufficient information from that prospectus and any information published in connection with the admission. The points that need to be noted are:

(a) The section draws a distinction between prospectuses and other "advertisements":

(b) The prospectus has to be approved by The Exchange (notwithstanding that this is not mandatory under the Directive), and

(c) The result of this section (supplemented by sections 161(3), 162(3) and 164) is to enable the Secretary of State to place

---

22 And letters inviting underwriting if these can be regarded as "advertisements" as defined in s.207(2).

23 *i.e.* recognised under s.37 of the Act. These include not only The Stock Exchange (and various U.K. financial and commodity future exchanges) but also certain overseas exchanges recognised under that section and s.40.

24 As have some overseas exchanges.

25 An advertisement is treated as issued in the U.K. if it is directed to persons in the U.K. or made available to them otherwise than in a newspaper or periodical published and circulating principally outside the U.K. or broadcast principally for reception outside the U.K.: s.207(3).

The Stock Exchange, in relation to U.S.M. issues, in very much the same position as in relation to listed issues (except that its relevant rules will, as at present, be in the *Green Book* (as revised) instead of the stricter *Yellow Book*).

(ii) Other issues. Issues which are not to be dealt in on an approved exchange raise more difficult problems. The attempted solutions begin in section 160(1) which provides that, subject to what follows, no person shall issue or cause to be issued in the United Kingdom an advertisement which is a "primary or secondary offer" unless (a) he has delivered to the Registrar a prospectus expressed to be in respect of the offer or (b) the advertisement is such that no agreement can be entered into pursuance of it until a prospectus has been delivered to the Registrar.

The distinction here drawn between primary and secondary offers does not relate to that between initial distributions and secondary marketing. A primary offer is one made by or on behalf of the company,[26] whereas a secondary offer is one made in certain circumstances by a security holder on his own behalf.[27] The aim is the same as that of the former section 58 of the Companies Act 1985, *i.e.* to prevent avoidance of the need for a prospectus by the device of a private sale to a third party with a view to his then offering them to the public. Like that former section, it first does this by applying the ban in subsection (1) to any advertisement inviting persons to enter into an agreement for, or with a view to, acquiring securities or containing information calculated to lead directly or indirectly to their doing so, if the advertisement was issued or caused to be issued by a person who has acquired the securities with a view to issuing such an advertisement.[28] That is presumed to be the motive if the advertisement was issued within six months after the issue of the securities or before they had been paid for in full.[29] Section 160 then extends the former provisions in section 58 in three respects. First, the Companies Act required a prospectus only if the offer was for "subscription," (or, in some cases, "subscription or purchase") which was held to imply an acquisition for cash.[30] This is no longer so. Section 160 uses the word "acquire" or its derivatives,[31] or, when "subscribe" is used to indicate that an original allotment by the company is meant (and not an acquisition from a security holder) is careful to qualify it by "whether or not in cash."[32] Secondly, its scope is extended to a person who acquired the securities from someone

26 s.160(2).
27 s.160(3).
28 s.160(3)(*a*).
29 s.160(4).
30 *Governments Stock Investment Co. v. Christopher* [1956] 1 W.L.R. 237.
31 See s.160(3).
32 See s.160(2).

other than the company with a view to advertising them; but only if the securities had not been admitted to dealings on an approved exchange, or held by a person who acquired them as an investment and without any intention that they should be so advertised.[33] And thirdly, it also extends the ban to a person who is a "controller[34] of the company, or who has been a controller in the previous 12 months, and who is acting with the consent or participation of the company, in issuing the advertisement."[35]

Section 160(5) disapplies subsection (1) in relation to a secondary offer if a prospectus has been delivered in accordance with that subsection in respect of an offer of the same securities made in the previous six months by the company or by another person making a secondary offer. This corresponds with section 159(2) except that there is not the additional protection of a certificate by an approved exchange.

(iii) Exemptions and Exceptions. As a result of amendments made by section 198 the Companies Act 1989, new subsections (3) of section 159 and (6) of section 160 make both sections subject to the "exemptions" under a new section 160A and to the "exceptions" in section 161. Section 160A empowers the Secretary of State to make the needful rules distinguishing and exempting those offers which can be excluded from regulation because they are not regarded as offers to the general public.

Under subsection (1) the Secretary of State may by order exempt advertisements issued in such circumstances as may be specified in the order and which (a) appear to him to have a private character, whether by reason of a connection between the company and those to whom they are addressed[36] or otherwise; (b) appear to him to deal with investments only incidentally,[37] (c) are issued to persons appearing to him to be sufficiently expert to understand any risks involved[38] or (d) are such other classes of advertisements as he thinks fit.[39] Further, under subsection (2) he may similarly exempt, in

---

33 s.160(3)(b).
34 *i.e.* a person who, either alone or with his associates, controls 15 per cent. or more of the votes of the company or its holding company: s.207(5).
35 s.160(3)(c). As it is unlikely that the will be able to comply with the rules relating to the contents of prospectuses without the participation and consent of the company this is virtually equivalent to an absolute ban unless one of the exemptions or exceptions applies.
36 An obvious example would be the existing security holders.
37 *e.g.* advertisements of sales of businesses which imply that the transactions might be achieved by a sale of the share capital rather than of the undertaking and assets.
38 *i.e.* the time-honoured "professionals only" exemption, the difficulty with which is the impossibility of preventing such advertisements getting into the hands of "amateurs."
39 This totally unfettered discretion makes (a) (b) and (c) otiose, but their inclusion is presumably to make (d) look less outrageous and to curb extravagant use of it by pointing at the possibility that the courts, applying the *eiusdem generis* rule of construction (but what is the common genus of (a), (b) and (c)?) might hold it to be beyond the S of S's powers.

whatever circumstances, an advertisement which relates to securities appearing to him to be of a kind that can be expected normally to be bought or dealt in only by persons sufficiently expert to understand any risks involved.[40] Finally, subsection (3) provides that an order under subsection (1) or (2) may require the observance of such requirements as are specified in the order.

A subsequent section (170), having, in subsection (1), provided that no private company may issue or cause to be issued in the United Kingdom any advertisement offering its securities,[41] contains, in subsections (2) (3) and (4)[42], identical enabling powers in relation to private companies.[43]

The "exceptions" in section 161 have a different and largely technical purpose. Subsection (1) makes it clear that neither section 159 nor 160 applies to any advertisement offering securities conditional upon their admission to listing in accordance with Part IV and that section 159 does not apply if the securities have been so listed in the previous 12 months and the approved exchange certifies that persons likely to consider acquiring them will have sufficient information. A slightly more elaborate subsection (3) provides similarly where securities have been admitted to dealings on an approved exchange.

Section 161(2) provides that neither section 159 nor 160 applies to an advertisement mentioned in section 58(2). This is an example of the unfortunate fact, already referred to,[44] that Parts IV and V do not contain comprehensive provisions regarding public issues. Section 58 provides exceptions to section 57 which requires investment advertisements to be issued only by or with the approval of "an authorised person" (i.e. a firm authorised as fit and proper to undertake investment business). Section 58(2) disapplies this in relation to advertisements inviting subscriptions in cash if the advertisement consists either of a prospectus registered in accordance with Part V or contains only: the name and address of the company; the nature of the investments and their number, nominal value and price; a statement that a prospectus is or will be, available; and instructions for obtaining a copy.[45] Publication of such an advertisement is accordingly excluded from any control so long as it says no more than that. If, however, it contains more information it will not

[40] This appears to be designed to permit a blanket exemption of all offers of euro-securities.
[41] cf. s.143(3) above.
[42] This may help private companies to raise shares or loan capital and even to obtain admission to the U.S.M. if The Stock Exchange is prepared to allow that.
[43] s.58(3) and (4) contain similar provisions enabling orders to be made exempting from s.57 (see below) and these have already been exercised by S.I. 1988 No. 316 and S.I. 1988 No. 716 which are likely to provide the initial model for similar orders under s.160A when Part V is brought into operation.
[44] See p. 322 above.
[45] i.e. is a "micro" pathfinder prospectus.

be excluded from section 57 and will have to be issued or approved by an authorised person. But it will not be subject to sections 159 or 160 so long as it is such that no agreement can be entered into in pursuance of it until a prospectus has been submitted to and approved by the approved exchange and delivered for registration to the Registrar (when section 159 is relevant)[46] or delivered for registration (when section 160 applies).[47]

The result is that the regulation of advertisements (other than "prospectuses") in relation to unlisted issues which are not to be dealt in on the U.S.M. is frighteningly lax; at best the only scrutiny to which they will be subject is that of the authorised person. At present, the principal examples of such issues are those designed to obtain the tax advantages of Business Expansion Schemes. And, as regards these, S.I.B. has made rules under section 48 regulating the conduct of authorised persons in relation to their advertisements.[48] This, however, can only be a stop-gap solution for there are no grounds for assuming that there will not be a renewed outbreak of other types of issue.

Finally, section 161(4) provides that if it appears to the Secretary of State that the law of a foreign country provides investors in the United Kingdom with equivalent protection to that provided by Part IV or V in respect of securities dealt in on exchanges in that country he may by order specify circumstances in which sections 159 and 160 are not to apply to advertisements offering those securities in the United Kingdom.

(iv) **Form and content of prospectuses.** In contrast with listing particulars, where details of the contents are left to The Stock Exchange as competent authority, section 162(1) provides that prospectuses for unlisted issues "shall contain such information and comply with such requirements" as may be prescribed by rules made by the Secretary of State. In other words, the rule-making authority is the DTI. However, under subsection (2) the rules may make provision whereby compliance with requirements imposed by the law of a foreign country is treated as compliance with the D.T.I. rules. Moreover, under subsection (3), if it appears to the Secretary of State that an approved exchange has rules and practices in respect of prospectuses relating to securities dealt in on the exchange which provide investors with at least equivalent protection, he may direct that any such a prospectus shall be subject to its rules instead of his. This complements section 159(1)(a) and will enable amended rules in The Stock Exchange's *Green Book* to continue to apply to issues admitted to the U.S.M., thereby placing The Exchange in relation to

46 See s.159(1).
47 See s.160(1).
48 See The Financial Services (Conduct of Business) (BES Investments) Rules 1989.

such issues in much the same position as in relation to listed issues.[49] In both cases the contents of the prospectus will be subject to The Exchange's rules and, the prospectus will have to be submitted to and approved by The Exchange.[50] In other cases however, under the present provisions of Part V no independent body (other than the Registrar who cannot do more than check formal compliance) will have an opportunity or an obligation to pre-vet it.

Section 163 repeats the general duty of disclosure in similar terms to section 146 of Part IV, section 164 makes provisions regarding supplementary prospectuses similar to those in section 147, and section 165 enables the Secretary of State to confer on an approved exchange power to authorise the omission of information on the same grounds as those in section 148.[51] These sections are followed by sections 166 to 168 dealing with compensation for false or misleading statements in prospectuses. These are, in substance, identical with sections 150–152 and both will be dealt with when we turn to liabilities generally.[52] So will section 171 (contraventions) which has no direct counterpart in Part IV.

Section 169 also has no counterpart in Part IV. It confers a further rule-making power on the Secretary of State, namely to make rules:

"(a) regulating the terms on which securities may be offered by an advertisement to which [Part V] applies, and

(b) otherwise regulating the conduct of the issuer with a view to ensuring that persons to whom the offer is addressed are treated equally and fairly."[53]

And it adds that rules may "in particular, make provision with respect to the giving of priority as between persons to whom an offer is made and with respect to commissions."[54]

The need for, and object of, this section is not immediately apparent but it seems to be designed primarily to enable certain provisions in the former prospectus provisions of the Companies Act, which are repealed and not replaced by the Financial Services Act, to be re-introduced by rules in relation to non-listed issues (on the assumption, presumably, that The Stock Exchange as the competent authority will be able to do likewise in relation to listed ones). One

[49] But the DTI will first make its detailed rules (complying with the requirements of the Prospectus Directive) and then decide whether it is satisfied that the *Green Book* provides equivalent protection. Control over The Exchange in this capacity is easier to exercise than in relation to its role as competent authority in respect of listed issues as it will not involve use of the "nuclear deterrent" of withdrawing its recognition as an approved exchange.
[50] In the case of U.S.M. issues under s.159(1)(a).
[51] Under s.148, The Exchange, as competent authority, has that authority conferred upon it directly by statute; under s.165, as an approved exchange, it has it only if the S. of S. so directs.
[52] pp. 342, *et seq.* below.
[53] s.169(1).
[54] s.169(2).

such section is the former section 82 of the 1985 Act. Subsections (1)–(6) of that section provided for a "waiting period" of at least three working days between the publication of a prospectus and the opening of the subscription lists, thus ensuring that the public had time to consider the prospectus and media comment thereon and to take professional advice. And subsection (7) provided that until the expiration of that period applications should be irrevocable.[55]

Another such provision which needs to be preserved is the former section 86. This provided that, if the prospectus stated that an application has been or would be made for the issue to be listed on any stock exchange, an allotment of the securities was void, unless an application was duly made and granted, and the company and its directors were liable to repay the subscription money with interest and, in the meantime, required to hold it in a separate bank account.[56] To preserve this valuable protection to subscribers and to extend it from cases where the statement relates to listing to those where it relates to admission to the U.S.M. provisions in both Parts IV and V are needed. In relation to listed issues this cannot be left to The Stock Exchange because, unless the company is already listed, its rules will never become binding on the company and, even if it is listed, will not be directly binding on its directors; indeed, if no application for listing is made, The Exchange may know nothing about it.[57]

The clue to what is intended by the cryptic reference to "commissions" in subsection (2) of section 169 is afforded by amendments to section 97 of the Companies Act 1985 (mentioned in Chapter 9[58]) by the Companies Act 1989. These amendments deleted the former maximum limit of 10 per cent. which a company could pay by way of commission to any person in consideration of his subscribing, procuring or agreeing to subscribe and substituted a requirement that such commissions could be paid only subject to any conditions imposed by rules made under section 169(2) of the Financial Services Act and within any limit imposed by them or, if none, not exceeding 10 per cent. or the rate authorised by the articles, whichever is less. But what is envisaged by the "provisions with respect to the giving of priority as between "persons to whom an offer is made"" remains a mystery to those not privy to the Government's thinking (or at least to the writer).[59]

---

[55] This is the "anti-stag" provision mentioned at p. 315 above.
[56] This has been held to result in its being held on trust for the subscribers who are accordingly not left solely to their claims as creditors against the company and its directors: *Re Nanwa Gold Mines* [1955] 1 W.L.R. 1080).
[57] There seems to be no case for retaining s.83 which the F.S. Act repeals and s.84 will presumably remain in the Companies Act.
[58] At p. 202 above.
[59] It may be that it is thought that such matters cannot be dealt with solely by rules of conduct made by SIB and its recognised SROs (since these apply only to authorised persons and not to an issuing company as such) so that D.T.I. rules are needed. (The Consultative Document published in July 1990, confirms this guess.)

In any event, it seems clear that rules made under section 169 ought to apply to both listed and unlisted issues and hence that this section ought not to be only in Part V which applies exclusively to an investment "which is not listed or the subject of an application for listing in accordance with Part IV."[60]

The U.S.M. Requirements

These are at present, and will doubtless remain, set out in The Stock Exchange's *Green Book*, as revised in the light of the D.T.I.'s rules and the overall review now taking place. All that can usefully be said at the present juncture is that The Exchange, is likely to continue to rely, to a greater extent than in the case of listed issues, on the sponsoring member firm, both in relation to applications for admission and subsequent surveillance of the company, and that the requirements will be less strict as regards size of issues, width of distribution and length of the company's track record.

Liabilities in Relation to Public Issues

The company and others concerned in making a public issue may find themselves liable, civilly and criminally, if they fail to comply with the statutory provisions, or induce subscriptions by false or misleading representations, or engage in other improper practices. These potential liabilities are of particular importance in relation to issues which are not to be listed or dealt in on an approved exchange since they then provide the only sanctions for breaches of the rules.

(i) *Failure to comply with requirements under Part IV or V*

Non-compliance with the procedural requirements is dealt with differently in the two Parts; in Part IV in relation to two sections only (sections 149 and 154), in Part V in relation to several sections in a single comprehensive section 171. The reason for this is that when the securities are to be listed, non-compliance can usually be left to be dealt with by The Stock Exchange. That, however, is not so when the contravention is a failure to deliver a copy of the listing particulars to the Registrar (an official of the D.T.I. not of The Exchange) in accordance with section 149. Hence section 149(3) provides that the company and any person who is party to the publication of the particulars is liable, on failure to comply, to a fine. Similarly, if, contrary to section 154, an advertisement or other information is published in connection with an application for listing without its having been submitted to, and its publication authorised by, The Exchange, statutory sanctions need to be provided since The Exchange may have no jurisdiction over culprits that are not its

[60] s.158(1).

member firms. Hence section 154(2) provides that if the culprit is an authorised person he shall be deemed to have breached the rules of conduct to which he is subject as an authorised person, thus rendering him liable to the risk of losing his authorisation and to possible civil liability under section 61 or 62 of the Financial Services Act. The company itself will normally not be an authorised person but it, and others, may well be responsible for the contravention and, if so, under subsection (3), it and those others, will be guilty of an offence and liable to fines or, in the case of individuals, to imprisonment. However, under subsection (4) a person who issues, in the ordinary course of a business other than investment business, (*e.g.* as publisher of a newspaper or periodical) an advertisement or other information to the order of another person is not guilty if he proves that he believed on reasonable grounds that its issue had been authorised by The Exchange.

Apart from these two sections it is only in relation to false or misleading statements that Part IV provides sanctions, essentially identical with those in Part V. Non-compliance with the requirements of Part V is dealt with in a necessarily different but, seemingly, unnecessarily convoluted, manner in section 171. This says, first, that if an authorised person:

(a) contravenes section 159 or 160 or rules made under section 169,

(b) contravenes any requirement under an order made under section 160A or 170, or

(c) on behalf of a private company, causes to be issued an advertisement which it is prohibited from issuing by section 170, he is to be treated as having breached the rules of conduct to which he is subject as an authorised person.[61]

Secondly, it provides that if the company or any other non-authorised person contravenes any of the sections, rules or requirements mentioned in (a) and (b) above, he is liable to a fine or imprisonment.[62] If the contravention is of (c) above, the company and the other person are treated in the same way as if they had contravened section 57 of the Act.[63] The consequences of that are again that they will commit a criminal offence.[64] Moreover, any resulting agreement will be unenforceable against the other party, who will be entitled to his money back and compensation for loss sustained,[65] unless the court grants relief.[66] As if that were not

[61] s.171(1). And see s.171(6) below.
[62] s.171(3). And again see s.171(6).
[63] s.171(2).
[64] s.57(3). Unless subs. (4) applies to him.
[65] s.57(5), (6), (7), (9) and (10).
[66] Under s.57(8).

enough, section 171 further provides that any contravention to which the section applies shall be actionable at the suit of any person who suffers loss, "subject to the defences and other incidents applying to actions for breach of statutory duty."[67]

The section does, however, make two concessions. First a person who, in the ordinary course of non-investment business, issues an advertisement to the order of another person does not commit an offence under subsection (3) if he proves that he believed on reasonable grounds that neither section 159 nor 160 applied to the advertisement or that one of those sections had been complied with in respect of the advertisement.[68] But, as worded, this does not protect him against potential civil liability.[69] The second concession is that a person is not to be regarded as having contravened section 159 or 160 by reason only of a prospectus not having complied fully with the requirements of Part V as to form and content.[70] This, however, is expressly "without prejudice to any liability under section 166" (to which we turn next); *i.e.* it protects against a mere breach of section 162,[71] or rules made thereunder but not against liability for a false or misleading prospectus.

(ii) *Compensation for misleading particulars or prospectuses*

Both Parts IV and V repeat and improve upon provisions dating back to the Directors Liability Act 1890, passed as a result of the decision in *Derry v. Peek*[72] which exposed the inadequacy of the common law tort of deceit as a remedy for investors who suffered loss as a result of misleading prospectuses. The present provisions are sections 150–153 in Part IV and 166–168 in Part V, which in substance are virtually identical. Their effect can be summarised as follows:

(a) Liability to compensate. Subject to the exemptions in (b) below, those responsible for the listing particulars or the prospectus (or supplementary particulars or prospectus) are liable to pay compensation to any person who has acquired any of the securities to which it relates and suffered loss as a result of any untrue or misleading statement in it or of the omission of any matter required to be included under the Act or rules made thereunder.[73] The same applies

[67] s.171(6). It would have been helpful to indicate what these (apparently peculiar) "defences" and "incidents" are.
[68] s.171(4).
[69] Under subs. (6). Surely it should be if the defence can be established?
[70] s.171(5).
[71] Above p. 339.
[72] (1889) 14 App.Cas. 337, H.L.
[73] ss.150(1) and 166(1). Where the rules require information regarding a particular matter or a statement that there is no such matter, an omission to do either is to be treated as a statement that there is no such matter: ss. 150(2) and 166(2).

when a person has suffered loss as a result of a failure to publish supplementary particulars when that is required under section 148 or 164.[74]

This is a considerable improvement,[75] on the former section 67 of the Companies Act 1985. That applied only to persons who had "subscribed," i.e. acquired the securities from the company and for cash.[76] It therefore excluded both those who bought on the market when dealings commenced and those who, on a take-over, exchanged their shares in one company for those in another.[77] Now anyone who has acquired,[78] the securities whether for cash or otherwise and whether directly from the company or by purchase on the market and who can show that he suffered loss as a result of the misstatement or omission,[79] will have a prima facie case for compensation.[80] In addition, whereas the former version applied only to misleading "statements" the new sections specifically include "omissions" also.

In one respect, however, sections 150 and 166 are defective in a way in which the former section 67 was not. The new sections apply only to statements or omissions in listing particulars or prospectuses. Section 67 applied only to a prospectus but that was defined as every document "offering to the public for subscription or purchase any shares in or debentures of a company."[81] As we have seen, the new Act distinguishes between those offer documents which are listing particulars or prospectuses and those which are merely other "advertisements." Public offers can be made in some circumstances by documents which are not treated as listing particulars[82] or

74 ss.150(3) and 166(3).
75 Except in one respect: see the next para. of text.
76 Governments Stock Investment Co. v. Christopher, [1956] 1 W.L.R. 237.
77 As in Governments Stock Investment Co. v. Christopher, above.
78 "Acquire" includes contracting to acquire them or any interest in them: ss.150(5) and 166(5).
79 He will have to establish a causal connection between the misstatement or omission and the loss but not necessarily that he himself relied on the misstatement. A market purchaser will have the gravest difficulty in establishing the causal connection if he bought after the true facts became public knowledge or after such a lapse of time that the particulars or prospectus would no longer have any influence on the market price.
80 It seems that the measure of compensation corresponds to that of damages in tort, i.e. to restore him to his former position: Clark v. Urquhart [1930] A.C. 28, H.L.(N.I.).
81 See Companies Act 1985, s.744. (But their contents were prescribed only in the case of certain types of prospectuses resembling those which are listing particulars or prospectuses under the F.S. Act.)
82 See Yellow Book, Chapter 1, para. 5. The most important example is rights or other issues which increase the class of shares already listed or admitted by less than 10 per cent.: ibid. para. 5.4(a). According to the recent decision at first instance in Al Nakib Investments v. Longcroft [1990] 1 W.L.R. 1390 shareholders who took up their rights in reliance on a misleading rights circular might have a remedy at common law in respect of loss they suffered in consequence; but if they purchased more shares on the market in reliance on the circular they would have no remedy in respect of that since the only purpose of such a circular is to enable shareholders to consider the rights offer (applying Peek v. Gurney (1873) L.R. 6 H.L. 377, H.L.) and is beyond the scope of any duty of care owed by those responsible for the circular (following Caparo v. Dickman [1990] 2 A.C. 605, H.L.).

prospectuses. Section 150 or 166[83] will not avail investors in such cases. This defect will doubtless be corrected as a result of the review of Parts IV and V. What seems to be needed is to ensure that all documents making what section 160 describes as a primary or secondary offer (whether or not the securities are to be listed or dealt in on an approved exchange) come within the scope of section 150 or 166.

(b) Defences. Sections 151 and 167 then provide persons responsible for the misstatement or omissions with, what the headings to the sections describe as "exemptions," but which are really defences that may be available if a claim for compensation is made.

The overall effect of these defences is that the defendant escapes liability under section 150 or 166 if, but only if, he can satisfy the court (a) that he reasonably believed[84] that there were no misstatements or omissions and that he had done all that could reasonably be expected to ensure that there were not any and that, if any came to his knowledge, they were corrected in time or (b) that the plaintiff acquired the securities with knowledge of the falsity of the statement or of the matter omitted.[85] This not only reverses the onus of proof which, at common law, the plaintiff would have to discharge but considerably curtails the defences which, at common law, defendants would have under the increasingly narrow view taken by the courts of the extent of the duty of care owed to those who rely on a prospectus.[86]

(c) Persons responsible. Parts IV and V then deal with the sensitive question of who are "persons responsible." Sections 152(1) and 168(1) provide that they are:

(a) the issuer, (*i.e.* normally the company)—a further improvement on earlier versions which did not afford a remedy against the company itself,

(b) the directors of the company,

(c) each person who has authorised himself to be named, and is named, as having agreed to become a director, whether immediately or at a future time,

---

[83] Nor will s.57 since the document will be excluded as one which is "required or permitted" . . . by listing rules under Part IV . . . or by an approved Exchange under Part V . . .''; s.58(1)(*d*)(ii).

[84] He may have to satisfy the court that his belief continued until such time had elapsed that he ought reasonably to be excused: see ss.151(1)(*d*) and 167(1)(*d*).

[85] It is hoped that this summary will be more helpful than a tedious repetition of each subsection.

[86] See below p. 352.

(d) each person who accepts, and is stated as accepting, responsibility for, or for any part of, the particulars or prospectus,[87] and

(e) each other person who has authorised the contents of the particulars or prospectus or any part of it.

Without further qualification this would make almost everybody who had played any part in the preparation of the listing particulars or prospectus responsible for the whole of it. Accordingly, its scope is narrowed by the subsequent subsections. Subsection (2) provides that a person is not responsible under (c) if the document was published without his knowledge and consent and, when he became aware of it, he forthwith gave reasonable public notice of that. Subsection (3) restricts the responsibility of a person under (d) or (e) to that part of the document for which he has accepted responsibility or has authorised, and only if it is included substantially in the form and context to which he agreed. The somewhat opaque subsection (4) is designed to avoid duplication of responsibility when, as described at page 319 above, "claw-back" arrangements and a vendor rights issue are made to preserve the pre-emptive rights of equity shareholders; the general effect is to enable each of the companies involved, and its directors, to be held responsible only for the parts which relate to that company.

Subsection (5) of each section enables an approved exchange on which the securities are to be listed or dealt in to exclude a director from responsibility under paragraph (b) or (c) by certifying that, by reason of his having an interest or of other circumstances, it was inappropriate for him to be responsible. It would clearly be unreasonable to face a director with the alternative of resigning or accepting responsibility for a document in the preparation of which he would be unable to play any part because of a conflict of interest or, for example, illness or absence abroad on the company's business. (yet this seems to be the position if the securities are not to be listed or dealt in on an approved exchange.[88]) Section 152(5) also excludes paragraphs (b) and (c) on a euro-security issue[89] which would be quite monstrous but for the fact that no one seems to rely on the prospectus in relation to such issues.

Sections 152(8) and 168(7) provide that nothing in either section shall be construed as making a person responsible by reason only of his giving advice in a professional capacity. This is generally regarded

87 *i.e.* the reporting accountant and any other "experts."
88 It is not clear that s.162 or s.169 affords the *vires* to put this right.
89 Described as an issue of "international securities" and defined (inadequately) in s.152(6). The absence of these provisions in s.168 is presumably because the securities will be listed—albeit in Luxembourg not London.

as excluding the lawyers involved[90]—though confidence in this belief may be misplaced; the leading firms of solicitors admittedly carry on investment business, "arrange," as well as "advise" and are authorised persons under the Act. It clearly does not exclude the sponsoring member firm or issuing house. It is unlikely, however, that a misled investor will be able to glean from the listing particulars or prospectuses who (in addition to the company, the directors and named experts) are persons responsible. All that is likely to appear at the beginning of the document are particulars regarding the directors and a declaration that they:

"accept responsibility for the information contained in this document. To the best of the knowledge and belief of the Directors (who have taken all reasonable care to ensure that such is the case) the information contained in this document is in accordance with the facts and does not omit anything likely to affect the import of such information."[91]

This hardly seems to comply fully with the Listing Particulars and Prospectus Directives which require details of, and a declaration by, "persons responsible,"[92] which is surely intended to mean all such persons. Failure to name them all is unimportant so long as the company and its directors are able to meet any claims for compensation but, if they are not, investors may find difficulty in identifying the other responsible person who may well be worth powder-and-shot.

Attention should also be drawn to sections 150(4) and (6) and 154(5). Section 150(4) says that the section "does not affect any liability which any person may incur apart from this section," but section 150(6) limits the effect of that by providing that no person, by reason of being a promoter or otherwise, shall incur any liability for failing to disclose in listing particulars information which he would not have had to disclose if he had been a person responsible for those particulars or, if he was a person responsible, which he would have been entitled to omit by virtue of section 148. Hence, it seems, section 150 pre-empts and overrules any duty which a promoter or other fiduciary might be under to disclose in the listing particulars of matters additional to those required under sections 146–148 and the *Yellow Book*. Similarly, under section 154(5) where The Stock Exchange has approved the contents, or authorised the

[90] Though they seem to be less enthusiastic than formerly in being named prominently on the front of the listing particulars or prospectus.
[91] *Yellow Book*, Section 3, Chapter 2, Part 1, paras. 1.6 and 1.7. In "exceptional cases" The Exchange may require other persons to join in the declaration but this is unusual.
[92] Listing Particulars Directive, Annex, Schedule A, Chap. 1, paras. 1.1 and 1.2; Prospectus Directive, Art. 11, paras. 2a and 2b.

issue, of a mini-prospectus the persons issuing it or responsible for it will not incur any liability by reason of any statement in or omission from it, if it and the listing particulars taken together would not be likely to mislead those likely to acquire the securities in question. The Companies Act 1989 added to both sections additional words the effect of which is to make it clear that the exclusion of liability extends to any liability to another party whether for damages or rescission of any agreement.

There are no similar provisions in Part V.

(iii) *Section 47 of the Financial Services Act*

Some of the relevant provisions in other Parts of the Act have already been mentioned but a further word needs to be said about section 47 and the exception to its subsection (2) placed, singularly infelicitously,[93] in section 48. Subsection (1) of section 47 is a revised version of section 13 of the repealed Prevention of Fraud (Investments) Act 1958. Under it, it is a criminal offence knowingly or recklessly to make a statement promise or forecast or to conceal material facts for the purpose of inducing, or reckless as to whether it may induce, any other person to enter into or refrain from entering into an investment agreement or to exercise or refrain from exercising any rights conferred by an investment. This is a useful weapon in the prosecutor's armoury since only recklessness (not fraud) needs to be established and promises and forecasts (not just statements or omissions of facts) are covered.

Subsection (2) is new.[94] It reads:

"(2) A person who does any act or engages in any course of conduct which creates a false or misleading impression as to the market in, or the price or value of, any investments is guilty of an offence if he does so for the purpose of creating that impression and of thereby inducing another person to acquire, dispose of, subscribe for, or underwrite those investments or to refrain from doing so, or to exercise or refrain from exercising any rights conferred by those investments."

To this, subsection (3) provides a defence if he proves that he reasonably believed that his act or conduct would not create an

---

[93] s.47 applies to "any person" but s.48 only to conduct of business by authorised persons (see s.48(1)). Yet s.48(7) and (7A) purport to disapply s.47(2) by rules made under s.48 and to empower the S. of S. to amend subs. (7) by orders. The basic mistake was placing provisions relating to misconduct by *any person* in a Chapter of the Act dealing primarily with conduct of business by authorised persons.

[94] It was borrowed, though not verbatim, from the Federal securities legislation of the USA.

impression that was false or misleading.[95] The section says nothing about civil liability and it was a disputed question whether the former section, corresponding to subsection (1), gave rise to a civil action at the suit of the victim. Now the position seems to be that he cannot sue directly under section 47(1) or (2) for breach of statutory duty.[96] If, however, the offence is committed by an authorised person and involves a contravention of the rules of conduct to which that person is subject, there could be a civil remedy under section 62 of the Act.[97] Moreover, SIB could, under section 61, apply to the court, on behalf of the victims generally, for an injunction and restitution order against any person who had contravened section 47[98] and against an authorised person who had contravened the rules of conduct to which he was subject.[99]

Section 47(2) is aimed particularly at market manipulation. To what extent that is a common law offence is unclear[1] but it appears to be if false rumours are passed or "false and fictitious acts" are undertaken with the object of causing a rise or fall of market prices.[2] It clearly is an offence under the new section.

There is, however, a widespread practice in America and on international public issues, whereby a form of manipulation (given the less-pejorative name of "stabilisation") is engaged in, and which is permitted, subject to strict conditions, in order to enable the sponsors of the issue to stabilise the price of the securities during the issue period. A variety of devices can be employed for this purpose, most of which would fall foul of section 47(2). Stabilisation has not been customary in relation to United Kingdom domestic issues,[3] (there is less need for it than in the United States where the issuing and underwriting procedures take longer). However, it was strongly represented that it was vital that it should be permissible on major euro-security and other international issues. Hence section 48(7) and (7A)[4] provide that section 47(2) shall not be deemed to be

---

[95] In which case it is difficult to see how the prosecution could have discharged its onus of proof under subs. (2).

[96] In the context of an Act which specifically provides a civil remedy when that is intended, this seems to be the inevitable conclusion. On the other hand, the facts may give rise to civil liability at common law.

[97] See s.62(1) and (2).

[98] See s.61(1)(a)(ii).

[99] s.61(1)(a) and (3)–(7).

[1] It may become clearer, as a result of the prosecutions arising from the Guinness affair, which occurred before s.47(2) was brought into force.

[2] See *R.* v. *Beranger*, (1814) 3 M. & S. 67 (where there had been a conspiracy to cause the price of "gilts" to rise by mounting an elaborate charade designed to spread false rumours that Napolean had died) and *Scott* v. *Brown Doering & Co.* [1892] 2 Q.B. 724.

[3] Though analogous devices have clandestinely been employed in relation to take-overs or in order to stabilise or de-stabilise the share prices of the predator or target company.

[4] The former amended, and the latter added, by the Financial Services (Stabilisation) Order 1988 (S.I. 1988 No. 717) made by the S. of S. under his powers conferred by s.48(8).

contravened by anything done for the purpose of stabilising if it is done in conformity with rules made under section 48[5] and during a limited period starting with the date of the first public announcement of an offer which states the minimum price at which the securities are to be sold and ending on the 30th day after the closing date for applications. Moreover the offer must be made on the occasion of admission to dealing on The Stock Exchange or on an exchange of repute outside the United Kingdom and the sum to be raised must be at least £150m or the equivalent in other currency.[6]

(iv) *Liabilities under other legislation or at common law*

In addition to liabilities under the Financial Services Act there is always the possibility that there will be contraventions of provisions in other Acts, such as the Companies Act[7] or the Theft Act, or at common law. This is particularly likely when there have been false or misleading statements in listing particulars or prospectuses and sections 150 and 166 (above) expressly recognise this by saying in their respective subsections (4) that: "This section does not affect any liability which any person may incur apart from this section." At common law[8] if there have been misrepresentations there are likely to be remedies in tort or contract available to a misled investor entitling him to damages or rescission or both. Formerly, there was one peculiarity when the defendant was the company because the decision of the House of Lords in *Houldsworth* v. *City of Glasgow Bank*[9] apparently established that a shareholder could not recover damages from the company unless he had first rescinded and thus ceased to be a member of the company. Happily any such rule has now been abolished by section 131 of the Companies Act 1989 which inserts a new section 111A in the 1985 Act declaring that:

"A person is not debarred from obtaining damages or other compensation from a company by reason only of his holding or having held shares in the company or any right to apply or subscribe for shares or to be included in the company's register in respect of shares."[10]

---

[5] For the rules, see SIB's Financial Services (Conduct of Business) Rules 1987 (by 1992 likely to be substantially amended) r. 4.18 and Part 10 (the substance of which is unlikely to be much changed). Their principal aims are (a) to ensure that potential investors are warned if there is a possibility of stabilisation and (b) to regulate the manner in which it may be undertaken.

[6] In the case of euro-security issues no actual dealings will take place on any stock exchange but the amount raised is likely to be £billions rather than millions (see above pp. 319, 320) and the listing in Luxembourg will meet the admission requirement.

[7] *e.g.* of its s.151: see Chap. 9 pp. 227, *et seq*, above.

[8] Or as a result of the Misrepresentation Act 1967.

[9] (1880) 5 App. Cas. 317. See also *Re Addlestone Linoleum Co.* (1887) 37 Ch.D. 191, C.A.

[10] The wording of the section (and its insertion in a Chapter of the Act dealing with allotments) seems to assume that the rule applied only to "shareholders" and not to other members, (*e.g.* of a guarantee company) who were not members.

Hence normal common law principles apply and there seems to be no justification for prolonging this chapter by discussing them; they are better left to books on Contract or Tort. But one observation should perhaps be made in relation to claims at common law based on alleged negligence of those responsible for offer documents or of those who have advised the company or potential investors. The ambit of liability for negligence, which had widened between 1932 (when Lord Atkin delivered his seminal speech in *Donoghue v. Stevenson*[11]) and 1977 (when Lord Wilberforce delivered his in *Anns v. Merton Borough Council*[12]) has since undergone a continuing contraction, especially where, as here, the damage suffered is economic rather than physical.[13] This has not dammed the flood of actions and reported cases—the favourite targets being accountants who have prepared, audited or reported on the company's accounts—but it has certainly diminished the chances of a successful outcome for the plaintiffs.

CONCLUSION

There is little doubt that the new regime for the regulation of public issues is an improvement on the old. But, at present, it falls far short of the ideal to which, it is hoped, it will be brought closer as a result of the overall review now being undertaken. Attention has been drawn to some of its present defects in the course of the foregoing discussion. Perhaps the most serious of these is the inadequate control of pathfinder prospectuses, especially when the issue is not to be officially listed or admitted to the U.S.M. Unless control is tightened there is a grave risk of a renewed outbreak of pathfinder prospectuses for unlisted issues, which extol the advantages of the proposed issue without adequate disclosure of its risks and which invite the recipients to respond on a tear-off slip saying how many shares they wish to acquire when the prospectus is registered. When it is, they may then be sent a mini-prospectus which tells them little more than how to obtain copies of the full prospectus if they want to. No independent authority will have approved either the pathfinder or mini-prospectus—only the "authorised person" who is sponsoring the offer. And, it seems, not even the final prospectus need be pre-vetted. Sight seems to have been lost of one of the basic philosophies of the Act—that "prevention is better than a cure." And a misled

[11] [1932] A.C. 562. H.L.(Sc.).
[12] [1978] A.C. 728. H.L. which the H.L. has now held to have been wrongly decided: *Murphy v. Brentwood D.C.* [1991] 1 A.C. 398, H.L.
[13] *Caparo plc v. Dickman* [1990] 2 A.C. 605, H.L. (on which see Chapter 18 at pp. 491 *et seq.* below); see also the still more disturbing decision at first instance in *Al Nakib Investments v. Longcroft* [1990] 1 W.L.R. 1390; and *Al Saudi Banque v. Clarke Pixley* [1990] Ch. 313.

investor will often have no "cure" unless section 150 or 166 applies to the document that has misled him.

In addition there seem to be more fundamental flaws. Neither Part IV nor Part V of the Act deals discretely with listed or unlisted issues respectively. Nor, in combination, do they deal comprehensively with the regulation of public issues; other relevant sections are to be found in Part I of the Act dealing with investment advertisements and inducing entry into investment agreements. Too many different regulatory bodies with different (and possibly conflicting) rules may become involved—in the case of unlisted issues, the DTI, The Stock Exchange, SIB and one or more SROs.

What we surely need is the nearest possible approach to a single comprehensive code for all public issues, with a single regulatory and rule-making authority[14]; the present overlapping rules and roles of different authorities are a recipe for disaster.

---

[14] If the need for pre-vetting of all offer documents was recognised, the appropriate body to undertake it would seem to be The Stock Exchange in the case of issues to be listed or admitted to the U.S.M. and SIB in other cases.

Part Four

A COMPANY'S SECURITIES

CHAPTER 14

THE NATURE AND CLASSIFICATION OF COMPANY SECURITIES

FREQUENT references have been made to the securities which a company can issue. It is now necessary to look a little more closely at the exact nature of these securities and to indicate the various forms they may take.

They fall into two primary classes which legal theory tries to keep rigidly separated but which in economic reality merge into each other. The first of these classes is described as shares; the second as debentures. The basic legal distinction between them is that a share constitutes the holder a member of the company,[1] whereas the debenture holder is a creditor of the company but not a member of it.

LEGAL NATURE OF SHARES

What, then, is the exact juridical nature of a share? At the present day this is a question more easily asked than answered. In the old deed of settlement company, which was merely an enlarged partnership with the partnership property vested in trustees, it was clear that the members' "shares" entitled them to an equitable interest in the assets. It is true that the exact nature of this equitable interest was not crystal clear, for the members could not, while the firm was a going concern, lay claim to any particular asset or prevent the directors from disposing of it. Even with the modern partnership, no very satisfactory solution to this problem has been found, and the most one can say is that the partners have an equitable interest, often described as a lien, which floats over the partnership assets throughout the duration of the firm, although it crystallises only on dissolution. Still, there is admittedly some sort of proprietary nexus (however vague and ill-defined) between the partnership assets and the partners.

At one time it was thought that the same applied to an incorporated company, except that the company itself held its assets as trustee for its members.[2] But this idea has long since been

---

[1] A person may, however, become a member without being a shareholder—the company may not have a share capital.

[2] *Child* v. *Hudson's Bay Co.* (1723) 2 P. Wms. 207. As in the case of partnerships it was clear long before the express statutory provisions to this effect (see now s.182(1) (a)) that shares were personally and not really even if the company owned freehold land.

rejected. Shareholders have ceased to be regarded as having equitable interests in the company's assets; "shareholders are not, in the eyes of the law, part owners of the undertaking."[3] As a result the word "share" has become something of a misnomer, for shareholders no longer share any property in common; at the most they share certain rights in respect of dividends, return of capital on a winding up, voting, and the like.

Today it is generally stated that a share is a chose in action.[4] This, however, is not helpful, for "chose in action" is a notoriously vague term used to describe a mass of interests which have little or nothing in common except that they confer no right to possession of a physical thing, and which range from purely personal rights under a contract to patents, copyrights and trade marks.

It is tempting to equate shares with rights under a contract, for as we have seen[5] the memorandum and articles of association constitute a contract of some sort between the company and its members and it is these documents which directly or indirectly define the rights conferred by the shares. But a share is something far more than a mere contractual right *in personam*. This is sufficiently clear from the rules relating to infant shareholders, who are liable for calls on the shares unless they repudiate the allotment during infancy or on attaining majority,[6] and who cannot recover any money which they have paid unless the shares have been completely valueless.[7] As Parke B. said,[8]

"They have been treated, therefore, as persons in a different situation from mere contractors for then they would have been exempt, but in truth they are purchasers who have acquired an interest not in a mere chattel, but in a subject of a permanent nature . . . ,"[9]

The definition of a share which is, perhaps, the most widely quoted is that of Farwell J. in *Borland's Trustee* v. *Steel*.[10]

---

[3] *Per* Evershed L.J. in *Short* v. *Treasury Commissioners* [1948] 1 K.B. p. 122, C.A.
[4] See, *e.g.*, *per* Greene M.R. in [1942] Ch. p. 241, and *Colonial Bank* v. *Whinney* (1886) 11 App.Cas. 426, H.L.
[5] Above, Chap. 11 at p. 282 *et seq.*
[6] *Cork & Brandon Ry.* v. *Cazenove* (1847) 10 Q.B. 935; *N.W. Ry.* v. *M'Michael* (1851) 5 Exch. 114. If they repudiate during infancy it is not clear whether they can be made liable to pay calls due prior thereto: the majority in *Cazenove's* case thought they could, but Parke B. in the later case (at p. 125) stated the contrary.
[7] *Steinberg* v. *Scala (Leeds) Ltd.* [1923] 2 Ch. 452, C.A.
[8] (1851) 5 Exch. at p. 123.
[9] Later he suggested that the shareholder had "a vested interest of a permanent character in all the profits arising from the land and other effects of the company" (p. 125). This can hardly be supported in view of later cases.
[10] [1901] 1 Ch. 279 p. 288. Approved by C.A. in *Re Paulin* [1935] 1 K.B. 26, and by H.L. *ibid., sub nom. I.R.C.* v. *Crossman* [1937] A.C. 26. See also the other definitions canvassed in that case.

"A share is the interest of a shareholder in the company measured by a sum of money, for the purpose of liability in the first place, and of interest in the second, but also consisting of a series of mutual covenants entered into by all the shareholders inter se in accordance with [section 14]. The contract contained in the articles of association is one of the original incidents of the share. A share is not a sum of money ... but is an interest measured by a sum of money and made up of various rights contained in the contract, including the right to a sum of money of a more or less amount."

It will be observed that this definition, though it lays considerable and perhaps disproportionate stress on the contractual nature of the shareholder's rights, also emphasises the fact that he has an interest *in* the company. The theory seems to be that the contract constituted by the articles of association defines the nature of the rights, which, however, are not purely personal rights but instead confer some sort of proprietary interest in the company though not in its property. The company itself is treated not merely as a person, the subject of rights and duties, but also as a *res*, the object of rights and duties.[11] It is the fact that the shareholder has rights in the company as well as against it, which, in legal theory, distinguishes the member from the debenture holder whose rights are also defined by contract (this time the debenture itself and not the articles) but are rights against the company and, if the debenture is secured, in its property, but never in the company itself. Farwell J.'s definition mentions that the interest of a shareholder is measured by a sum of money. Reference has already been made to this[12] and it has been emphasised that the requirement of a nominal monetary value is an arbitrary and illogical one which has been rejected in certain other common law jurisdictions. The nominal value is meaningless and may be misleading, except in so far as it determines the minimum liability. Even as a measure of liability, it is of less importance now that shares are almost invariably issued on terms that they are to be fully paid up on or shortly after allotment and are frequently issued at a price exceeding their nominal value. But reference to liability is valuable in that it emphasises that shareholders *qua* members may be under obligations to the company as well as having rights against it.

This analysis may seem academic and barren, and to some extent it is, for a closer examination of the rights conferred by shares and debentures will show the impossibility of preserving any hard and fast

---

[11] "A whole system ... has been built up on the unconscious assumption that organisations, which from one point of view are considered individuals, from another are storehouses of tangible property": Arnold, *The Folklore of Capitalism*, p. 353.

[12] Above, Chaps. 9 & 10.

distinction between them which bears any relation to practical reality. Nevertheless the matter is not entirely theoretical, for in a number of cases the courts have been faced with the need to analyse the juridical nature of a shareholder's interest in order to determine the principles on which it should be valued. The most interesting of these cases is *Short v. Treasury Commissioners*[13] where the whole of the shares of Short Bros. were being acquired by the Treasury under a Defence Regulation which provided for payment of their value "as between a willing buyer and a willing seller."[14] They were valued on the basis of the quoted share price, but the shareholders argued that, since all the shares were being acquired, stock exchange prices were not a true criterion and that either the whole undertaking should be valued and the price thus determined apportioned among the shareholders, or the value should be the price which one buyer would give for the whole block, which price should then be similarly apportioned. The courts upheld the method adopted and rejected both the alternatives suggested, the first because the shareholders were not "part owners of the undertaking" and the second because the regulation implied that each holding was to be separately valued. It was conceded that had any individual shareholder held a sufficient block to give him "control" of the company then he might have been entitled to a higher price than the total market value of his shares,[15] since he would then have been selling an item of property—control—additional to his shares. But as no one shareholder had control to sell, the Government was able to acquire control of the company's assets for a fraction of their true value (and for a fraction of what it would have had to pay on a take-over bid[16]).

One thing at least is clear: shares are recognised in law, as well as in fact, as objects of property which are bought, sold, mortgaged and bequeathed. They are indeed the typical items of property of the modern commercial era and particularly suited to its demands because of their exceptional liquidity. To deny that they are "owned" would be as unreal as to deny, on the basis of feudal theory, that land is owned—far more unreal because the owner's freedom to do what he likes with his shares in public companies is likely to be considerably less fettered. Nor, today, is the bundle of rights making up the share regarded as equitable only. On the contrary, as the next chapter will show, legal ownership is recognised and distinguished from equitable ownership in much the same way as a legal estate in

[13] [1948] 1 K.B. 116 C.A., affd. [1948] A.C. 534, H.L.
[14] This popular formula is much criticised by economists who argue with some force that the willingness of the buyer and seller depends on the price and not vice versa.
[15] Hence in *Dean v. Prince* [1953] Ch. 590 (reversed on the facts [1954] Ch. 409, C.A.) Harman J. held that the "fair value" of a block of shares conferring control must include something above the "break-up" value of the assets, in respect of this control.
[16] On which, see Chap. 27 below.

land is distinguished from equitable interests therein. Nor must this emphasis on the proprietary and financial aspects of a shareholder's rights obscure the important fact that his shareholding causes him to become a member of an association, normally with rights to take part in its deliberation by attending and voting at its general meetings.

THE PRESUMPTION OF EQUALITY BETWEEN SHAREHOLDERS

The typical company—one limited by shares—must issue some shares, and the initial presumption of the law is that all shares confer the same rights and impose the same liabilities. As in partnership[17] equality prevails in the absence of agreement to the contrary. Normally the shareholders' rights will fall under three heads: (i) dividends, (ii) return of capital on a winding up (or authorised reduction of capital) and (iii) attendance at meetings and voting, and unless there is some indication to the contrary all the shares will confer the like rights to all three. So far as voting is concerned this is a comparatively recent development, for, on the analogy of the partnership rule, it was long felt that members' voting rights should be divorced from their purely financial interests in respect of dividend and capital, so that the equality in voting should be between members rather than between shares. A stage intermediate between these two ideas was reflected in the Companies Clauses Act 1845[18] which provided that in the absence of contrary provision in the special statute every shareholder had one vote for every share up to ten, one for every additional five up to a hundred and one for every ten thereafter, thus weighting the voting in favour of the smaller holders. However, attempts to reduce the proportion of voting rights as the size of holdings increased were doomed to failure since the requirement could be easily evaded by splitting holdings and vesting them in nominees. It is now recognised that if voting rights are to vary, separate classes of shares should be created so that the different number of votes can be attached to the shares themselves and not to the holder. Even today, however, the older idea still prevails on a vote by a show of hands, when the common law rule is that each member has one vote irrespective of the number of shares held; a rule which, although it can be altered by the constitution, is normally maintained,[19] if only because the number of a human being's hands cannot be more than two.

---

[17] Partnership Act 1980, s.24(1).
[18] s.75.
[19] For the law and practice regarding voting at meetings, see Chap. 19, below.

For many years it was thought that in the absence of express provision in the original constitution the continued equality of all shares was a fundamental condition which could not be abrogated by an alteration of the articles so as to allow the issue of shares preferential to those already issued.[20] This idea was, however, finally destroyed in *Andrews v. Gas Meter Co.*[21] which established that in the absence of a prohibition in the memorandum, the articles could be altered so as to authorise such an issue.

There is a similar presumption of equality in relation to shareholders' liabilities but it too can be altered by provisions in the memorandum and articles. In the case of a company limited by shares, normally the only liability imposed on a shareholder as such will be to pay up the nominal value of the shares and any premium in so far as payment has not already been made by a previous holder. This, however, does not mean that all the shares, even if of the same nominal value and of the same class, will necessarily be issued at the same price, or that, even if they are, all shareholders will necessarily be treated alike as regards calls for the unpaid part. Section 119 provides that a company if so authorised by its articles may: (a) make arrangements on an issue of shares for a difference between shareholders in the amounts or times of payments of calls; (b) accept the whole or part of the amount remaining unpaid although it has not been called up; or (c) pay a dividend in proportion to the amount paid up on each share where a larger amount is paid up on some shares than on others.[22] Subject to that, however, calls must be made *pari passu*.[23]

Directors' authority to allot shares

The principle of equal treatment was carried a stage further when the Second Company Law Directive[24] was implemented by the Companies Act 1980. This introduced a system whereby existing shareholders had, in some circumstances, to be afforded pre-emptive rights on an issue of further shares. But as a preliminary to an explanation of the statutory pre-emption provisions it is necessary first to refer to a further reform introduced at the same time, *i.e.* to restrictions placed on the authority of directors to allot shares at their whim and pleasure. This was dealt with relatively simply in what is

[20] *Hutton v. Scarborough Cliff Hotel Co.* (1865) 2 Dr. & Sim. 521.
[21] [1897] 1 Ch. 361, C.A.
[22] Table A 1985 appears to authorise (a) only (see art. 17) probably rightly in view of the complications which (b) and (c) would cause a public company.
[23] *Galloway v. Halle Concerts Society* [1915] 2 Ch. 233.
[24] The principle itself was affirmed in art. 42: "For the purposes of the implementation of this Directive the laws of the member States shall ensure equal treatment to all shareholders who are in the same position."

now section 80 of the 1985 Act to which the 1989 Act added section 80A. Section 80 provides that directors shall not exercise any power of the company to allot shares in the company or rights to subscribe for, or convert into, shares in the company unless they are authorised to do so by the company in general meeting[25] or by the company's articles.[26] This in itself would have achieved little. What makes it more meaningful is that any such authority, whether given in the articles or by a resolution, must state the maximum number of securities which can be issued under it[27] and the date at which the authority will expire. That date must not be later than 5 years from the date of the relevant resolution or, if conferred in the original articles, from the date of incorporation,[28] though it may be renewed by the company in general meeting for successive periods not exceeding 5 years.[29] Moreover, it may at any time be varied or revoked by an ordinary resolution even if that involves an alteration of the articles.[30] Authority may be given for a particular exercise of the power or for its exercise generally (a distinction of some importance in relation to pre-emptive rights) and may be unconditional or subject to conditions.[31] Contravention of the section does not affect the validity of any allotment made[32] but any director, who "knowingly and wilfully" permits it, is liable to a fine.[33]

Section 80 is one of the provisions that a private company may relax by an elective resolution under section 379A.[34] If it does so the provisions of section 80A apply instead of those in subsections (4) and (5) of section 80 and the authority can be given for any fixed period or indefinitely though it can be revoked at any time.[35] Should the elective resolution cease to have effect, if the authority has lasted for 5 years or more before the election it expires forthwith: otherwise it has effect as if it had been given for a fixed period of 5 years.[36]

---

[25] *i.e.* by an ordinary resolution, which in the case of a private company can be a written resolution signed by all the members entitled to vote: s.381A. But a copy of it has to be sent to the Registrar under s.380: s.80(3).

[26] s.80(1). This does not apply to shares taken by subscribers to the memorandum or shares allotted in pursuance of an employees' share scheme (s.80(2)) but otherwise it applies to all classes of shares and all types of issues. The section describes those shares and rights to which it applies as "relevant securities" (not to be confused with "relevant shares," in ss.89–96 dealing with pre-emptive rights).

[27] In relation to allotments of rights to subscribe or to convert, what has to be stated is the maximum number of shares that can be allotted pursuant to the rights: s.80(6).

[28] s.80(4). But, if the authority so given permitted the directors to make an offer or agreement which would or might require an allotment to be made after the authority expired and the directors make such an offer or agreement before the authority expires, they may allot accordingly: s.80(7). But for this, directors who had lawfully allotted rights such as options, warrants or convertible bonds might find themselves precluded from allotting the shares when the rights were exercised.

[29] s.80(5).

[30] s.80(4).

[31] s.80(3).

[32] s.80(10).

[33] s.80(9).

[34] See Chap. 5, p. 105 above.

[35] s.80 A(2) and (3).

[36] s.80A(7).

Pre-emptive rights

In contrast with the relative simplicity of sections 80 and 80A, the provisions relating to pre-emptive rights (now sections 89 to 96) are complicated and confusing. However, the basic principle which they enshrine is simple enough and is stated with admirable clarity in note 37.1 to the comparable rule of The Stock Exchange[37] in relation to its listed companies:

"Importance is attached to the principle that a shareholder should be able to protect his proportion of the total equity by having the opportunity to subscribe for any new issue for cash of equity capital or securities having an equity element."

That is what sections 89 to 96 seek to achieve. But to understand the substantive provisions it is necessary to look first at certain definitions in section 94.

In contrast with sections 80 and 80A which apply to all issues, whether for cash or otherwise, and to rights to all classes of shares,[38] the ambit of the pre-emptive provisions extends only to issues for cash of "equity securities" as defined (by a somewhat tortuous process) in section 94. Subsection (2) of that section says that "equity security" means "a relevant share" in the company (other than one taken by a subscriber to the memorandum or a bonus share) or the right to subscribe for or convert into "relevant shares" in the company. Subsection (5) defines "relevant shares" as: "shares in the company other than— (a) shares which as respects dividends and capital carry a right to participate only up to a specified amount[39] in a distribution,[40] and (b) shares which are held by a person who acquired them in pursuance of an employees' share scheme or, in the case of shares which have not been allotted, are to be allotted in pursuance of such a scheme."

And sub-section (4) defines "relevant employee shares" as "shares of the company which would be relevant in it but for the fact that they are held by a person who acquired them in pursuance of an employees' share scheme"

In the light of these definitions, section 89(1) becomes intelligible. What it provides is that a company proposing to allot equity securities

---

[37] *Yellow Book,* Section 5, Chapter 2, para. 37.
[38] Other than subscribers' shares and those subject to an employees' share scheme.
[39] There is no upper limit to this amount (and it would be impracticable to set one) with the result that it is possible to prescribe amounts so high that the holders would in fact be entitled to the whole or the lion's share of the equity (unless subsequent issues were made without affording them pre-emptive rights).
[40] The test under (a) of whether or not shares are "relevant," (*i.e.* "equity capital" as defined in s.744) depends solely on their financial rights; voting rights are irrelevant. Pre-emptive rights are particularly important in relation to non-voting equity shares since sections 80 and 80A afford their holders no protection and they will have no say on whether the proposed issue should be made.

shall not allot them to any person unless it has first offered, on the same or more favourable terms, to each person who holds relevant shares or relevant employee shares, a proportion of those equity securities which is as nearly as practicable equal to his existing proportion in nominal value of his aggregate holdings of relevant shares and relevant employee shares.[41] The effect of this is that equity shares, or rights to them, can be allotted as subscribers' shares, bonus shares or pursuant to an employees' share scheme[42] without first offering pre-emptive rights. But, if equity shares or rights to them are to be issued in other circumstances, they first have to be offered to all equity shareholders in proportion to their holdings whether or not these were acquired as subscribers' shares, bonus shares or pursuant to an employees' share scheme. This is clearly as it should be. Employees' share schemes for example would be unworkable if, every time a further allotment was to be made pursuant to them, all equity shareholders had to be offered pre-emptive rights. If, however, equity shares have been allotted under the scheme, the holders should have the same rights to protect their proportion of equity as any other shareholder.

All this is on the assumption that the proposed issue is exclusively for cash,[43] when it is proposed to allot shares as consideration payable to the vendor on the acquisition of a business or real property it would be impossible to make an offer to the existing shareholders on the same terms.[44]

Only one pre-emptive offering has to be made; if it is not accepted in full, shares not taken up may be allotted to anyone;[45] accepting existing shareholders do not have to be given further pre-emptive rights in respect of those unaccepted shares. The procedure whereby the pre-emptive offer is to be communicated to the shareholders is laid down in section 90. The offer must be in writing, must state a period of not less than 21 days within which it can be accepted and withdrawal of the offer before the end of the stated period is forbidden.[46] In effect, when section 89 applies, the company if it wishes to issue equity shares for cash, has to do so by a rights issue, as described in chapter 13[47] or a similar process if it is a private company.

---

[41] On a date specified in the pre-emptive offer, which date must not be more than 28 days before that of the offer: s.94(7).

[42] Even if those scheme members may be entitled to renounce or assign their rights so that, if they do, the shares when allotted will not be "held in pursuance of the scheme."

[43] See s.89(4).

[44] But if an issue for cash of equity securities is made in order to raise the money to pay for the acquisition, pre-emptive rights (unless they have been disapplied under s.91 or s.95, below) will have to be offered. And see Chap. 13 at p. 319 above.

[45] s.89(1) (b). But in the case of listed companies see p. 368 below.

[46] This, being a statutory provision, over-rides the common law rule that an offer may be withdrawn until it has been accepted.

[47] At pp. 317, 318 above.

However, despite section 89, the statutory pre-emptive rights are far from being entrenched; in certain circumstances they can be modified or waived. Under section 91, the need to offer pre-emptive rights may be excluded by a provision in the memorandum or articles of a private company—either wholly or in relation to allotments of a particular description.[48] This seems unfortunate since pre-emptive rights are particularly needed in relation to those private companies which are essentially incorporated partnerships and it is difficult to see why, here, the Act could not have treated private companies in the same way as public ones.[49]

Section 95 deals with the position of public companies and with private companies to the extent that they have not excluded the statutory provisions in their memoranda or articles. The position differs according to the extent of the authority which has been conferred on the directors. If the directors are authorised generally they may also be given power, by the articles or by the resolution, to allot equity securities as if section 89(1) did not apply or applied with such modifications as the directors determined.[50] When they are authorised, whether generally or in relation to a particular allotment, the company may resolve by special resolution that section 89(1) shall not apply to a specified allotment under that authority or shall apply with such modifications as are specified in the resolution.[51] In either event, the power to exclude or modify pre-emptive rights ceases with the expiration or revocation of the authority conferred under section 80,[52] (or 80A) though it can be renewed by special resolution when, and to the extent that, the authority is renewed.[53] However a special resolution required under the section may not be proposed unless it has been recommended by the directors, and there is circulated to members entitled to notice of the meeting a written statement by the directors of their reasons for making the recommendation, the amount to be paid to the company in respect of the proposed issue, and the directors' justification of that amount.[54]

The result of sections 91 and 95 is that the statutory pre-emptive rights can be disapplied with relative ease and afford an individual

[48] s.91(1). A provision in the memorandum or articles which is inconsistent with s.89(1) or any subsection of s.90 has effect as an exclusion of that subsection: s.91(2).
[49] Happily Table A 1985 does not disapply pre-emptive rights and appears to contain nothing that is inconsistent with them.
[50] s.95(1). Whereupon "sections 89 to 94 have effect accordingly," *i.e.* only to the extent that they are consistent with the disapplication in the articles or resolution.
[51] s.95(2). Again with like consequences to those in s.95(1).
[52] s.95(3). But with a like power to that in s.80 (see n. 28 above) to permit allotments in pursuance of a contract entered into prior to the expiration of the authority: s.95(4).
[53] s.95(3).
[54] s.95(5). Any person who knowingly or recklessly permits the inclusion of a statement misleading in a material particular commits an offence: s.95(6). Where a private company uses a written resolution in accordance with ss.381A and 381B the directors' statement has to be supplied to each relevant member at or before the time when the resolution is supplied to him for signature: Sched.15B para. 3.

equity shareholder precious little assurance that his existing pre-emptive rights will be preserved unless his shares carry sufficient votes to block the passing of a special resolution. Nor will he necessarily be able to prevent his share of the equity from being diluted even if he is offered pre-emptive rights; he may not be able to afford to buy more shares but cannot prevent the new issue being made unless he has voting control.[55]

A further complication dealt with in the sections relates to the effect on sections 89 to 96 when there are different classes of equity shares and a provision in the memorandum or articles that pre-emptive offers of shares of each class shall be made to members of that class. Under section 89(2) and (3) the company may allot shares in accordance with that provision which is not to be treated as inconsistent with section 89(1) within the meaning of section 91. Nor is such a provision invalidated because the method of communicating the offer differs from that prescribed by section 90; but the procedure laid down by that section supersedes that provided in the memorandum or articles.[56] Furthermore, section 96 provides for pre-emptive procedures operative before 22 June 1982. One problem here is that now, if pre-emptive provisions other than those prescribed in the Act are to apply, they must be in the memorandum or articles[57] whereas previously they could have been provided in other ways, for example in an agreement between the shareholders or as part of the terms of issue of the shares. Hence section 96 has to provide savings of "pre-1982 pre-emptive requirements" imposed "whether by the company's memorandum or articles *or otherwise.*"[58] In the case of a public company subject, at the time of its registration or re-registration, to a pre-1982 pre-emptive requirement, sections 89 to 95 do not apply to an allotment of the equity securities which are subject to such a requirement.[59] In the case of a private company, a pre-1982 pre-emptive requirement is to be treated as if it were in its memorandum or articles so long as it remains a private company.[60]

Finally, a civil (but not a criminal) sanction is provided by section 92. When there has been a contravention of subsection (1) of section 89 or of any of subsections (1) to (6) of section 90 or of a provision to which subsection (3) of section 89 applies, the company and every officer of it who knowingly authorised or permitted the contravention are jointly and severally liable to compensate any person, to whom

---

55 Though he might have remedy under s.459: see *Re A Company (No. 007623 of 1986)* [1986] BCLC 362; *Re Sam Weller Ltd.* [1990] Ch. 682; Chap. 24 below; and Burridge, *Wrongful Rights Issues* (1981) 44 M.L.R. 40.
56 s.90(7).
57 See ss.89(2) and 91.
58 s.96(2).
59 s.96(1).
60 And, except in the case of a public company registered as such or its original incorporation, a pre-1982 pre-emptive requirement relating to a particular class of shares is to be treated as if it was in the memorandum or articles: s.96(3).

an offer should have been made under the subsection or provision, for any loss, damage, costs or expenses.[61] Where under section 95, the statutory provisions are validly modified by a company resolution this will equally apply to a contravention of the modified provisions since "sections 89 to 94 have effect accordingly."[62]

Where the company is listed on The Stock Exchange the protection afforded shareholders is greater than under the Act. In the first place, The Exchange's rules require that the authority to dispense with an offer of pre-emptive rights shall not last beyond the expiration of 15 months or until the next annual general meeting whichever occurs first.[63] Secondly they require a listed company to obtain the consent of its shareholders if any of its major subsidiaries makes an issue for cash of securities having an equity element which would materially dilute the percentage equity interest of the company and its shareholders in that subsidiary.[64] Thirdly while both the Act and The Stock Exchange rules allow fractional entitlements to be ignored[65] they differ as regards the treatment of rights that are not taken up. The effect of section 89(1) is that the shares concerned may then be offered to anybody. Under The Stock Exchange rules regarding rights issues, the rights must normally be sold for the benefit of the non-accepting shareholders unless arrangements to the contrary have been specifically approved by the shareholders in general meeting and The Stock Exchange has been consulted.[66] However, where the amount to which the shareholders will be entitled is small, they may be sold for the benefit of the company or, if no premium exists, allotted to the underwriters.[67] Another difference between the Act and The Stock Exchange rules is that the latter specifically permit pre-emptive offers to exclude holders of shares when the directors "consider it necessary or expedient ... on account of either legal problems under the laws of any territory or the requirements of any recognised regulating body or any other stock exchange."[68] The nearest

---

61 s.92(1). Proceedings must be commenced within 2 years of the filing of the relevant return of allotments under s.88 or, where rights to subscribe or convert are granted, within 2 years from the grant: s.92(2).

62 See s.95(1) and (2), under which ss.89 to 94 "have effect accordingly."

63 *Yellow Book*, Section 5, Chapter 2, para. 37 n. 37.1. Under the Act the combined effect of ss.80 and 95 is that it may last for 5 years though it can be revoked by ordinary resolution at any time.

64 *Ibid.* para. 37 (b)

65 s.89(1) (which only requires the offer to be *"as nearly as practicable"* equal to his proportion) and *Yellow Book*, Section 5, Chapter 2, n. 37.2(a). Hence, if there is a one-for-ten rights issue, a shareholder with, say, 475 shares will be offered only 47 new shares.

66 *Yellow Book*, Section 1, Chapter 3, para 4.3.

67 *Ibid.*

68 *Yellow Book*, Section 5, Chapter 2 n. 37.2(b). This is primarily designed to deal with the situation where a company has shareholders resident in the U.S.A. Under the Federal securities legislation it may have to register with the S.E.C. if it extends the offer to such shareholders. Hence the present practice is to exclude such shareholders and to preclude those to whom the offer is made from renouncing in favour of a US resident. This practice was upheld in *Mutual Life Insurance of N.Y. v. Rank Organisation* [1985] BCLC 11, but a fairer arrangement would surely be for the rights of the American shareholders to be sold for their benefit?

approach to this in the Act is section 93 under which sections 89 to 92 are "without prejudice" to any enactment by virtue of which the company is prohibited (either generally or in specified circumstances) from offering or allotting equity securities to any person. This however is designed to make it clear that offer must not be made to those whose shares are subject to a restriction order under Part XV of the Act;[69] for the situation to which The Stock Exchange rule is directed, companies have to rely on the "as nearly as practicable" in section 89 (1), and *Mutual Life Insurance of N.Y. v. Rank Organisation*.[70]

CLASSES OF SHARES

As will have been apparent, the prima facie equality of shares can be modified by dividing the share capital into different classes with different rights as to dividends, capital or voting or with different nominal values. By permutations of these various incidents the number of possible classes is limited only by the total number of shares.

On the whole it is not the present fashion for public companies to complicate their capital structures by having a large number of share classes—though much ingenuity is displayed in devising the most attractive methods of marketing issues and in creating types of company securities, other than shares but with rights to convert into shares.[71] But, in the case of public and private companies, there may well be two or three different classes and sometimes more. The division of shares into classes and the rights attached to each class will normally be set out in the company's memorandum or articles (generally the latter) but, in contrast with the Companies Acts of some other common law countries, that is not compulsory.[72] Instead steps have been taken to ensure that the classes and their rights can be ascertained from the company's public documents. The effect of what is now sections 128 of the Act[73] is that if particulars of such rights are not set out either in the memorandum or articles, or in a resolution or agreement (a copy of which has to be sent to the Registrar under section 380) they must be given in a statement, in the

---

[69] On which see Chap. 23 at pp. 622-624 below.
[70] See n. 68.
[71] It is beyond the scope of this book to do more than draw attention to a further recent (and disturbing) development, namely the extent to which investors are being beguiled into including in their investment portfolios "futures," options, and contracts for differences whereby they speculate in, or bet on, fluctuations in the price of shares or indices of such prices.
[72] Except as regards rights of redemption: see s.159A (Chap. 9 at p. 215 above).
[73] Originally s.33 of the 1980 Act, section 129 contains similar provisions regarding companies without a share capital. In their case there will be no question of differences in respect of rights to dividends or return of capital but the members may nevertheless be of different classes in respect of voting rights.

prescribed form, sent to the Registrar within a month of allotment of the shares.[74] If a class is assigned a name or other designation, that too must be given in the statement.[75] The same applies if and when there is any variation of the class rights.[76]

Preference shares

Where the differences between the classes relates to financial entitlement, *i.e* to dividends and return of capital, the likelihood is that they will be given distinguishing names, though these may be no more informative than "preference" and "ordinary," (perhaps, in the case of the former, preceded by "first" or "second" where there are two classes of preference shares). If a potential investor should assume that "preference" means that he should prefer them to the ordinary shares he would be sorely in need of professional advice. The advice that he would receive would probably not be couched in terms of relative merits and de-merits of preference and ordinary shares but of "prior charges" and "equities". And if the client's needs suggested the former, he would probably be advised to invest not in shares but in debentures. For preference shares may often be virtually indistinguishable from debentures except that they afford less assurance of getting one's money back or a return on it until one does. On the other hand, if in addition to being "preferential" they are also "participating" they may be a form of equity shares with preferential rights over the ordinary shares (and in consequence should be, and often are, designated "preferred ordinary").

As will have been apparent from the discussion on pre-emptive rights, this borrowing by the stock markets of an expression "equities" derived from the activities of Courts of Chancery[77] has in turn been borrowed by the companies' legislation in its definition of "equity securities" and "equity share capital."[78] Under these definitions, participating preference shares will be equity shares if they participate in distributions "beyond a specified amount." Whether they do, will depend upon the construction of the memorandum, articles or other instrument creating them. So will the

---

[74] s.128(1). This statement is not required if shares are allotted which are uniform with shares previously allotted in all respects except in relation to dividends during the 12 months following the new allotment: s.128(2).

[75] s.128(4).

[76] s.128(3). The question of how class rights may be varied is left to Chap. 20 since it essentially concerns the extent to which class rights of members (whether or not shareholders) may be varied. Here it suffices to warn that the drafting of the Act (which assumes that, when a company has a share capital, any class rights will be attached to the shares rather than to the holder of them) has faced the courts with problems: see *Cumbrian Newspapers Group Ltd. v. Cumberland Newspaper Co. Ltd.* [1987] Ch. 1.

[77] This borrowing (probably unconscious) from "equity of redemption" is more excusable than that of "trust" to describe monopolies.

[78] See above pp. 364–369.

determination of whether they have other rights (for example voting) or of whether their preferential dividend, is cumulative (in the sense that if passed in one year it must nevertheless be paid in a later one before any subordinate class receives a dividend) or non-cumulative (in the sense that the dividend once passed, is lost for ever). Unfortunately, in the past the drafting of the creating documents has often been deplorably lax.[79] Hence the courts have had to evolve various canons of construction which, even more unfortunately, have fluctuated from time to time, thus over-ruling earlier decisions and defeating the legitimate expectations of investors who purchased preference shares in reliance on the construction adopted earlier.[80] In former editions of this book the story of these vacillations was traced, in some detail,[81] starting with the virtually irreconcilable decisions of the House of Lords[82] and the Court of Appeal[83] relating to the winding-up of the *Bridgwater Navigation Company* in 1889–91. Since, at long last, a reasonably clear finale now appears to have been reached, there is no longer a justification for that indulgence, especially in view of the present unpopularity of preference shares. It suffices to summarise what the present canons of construction appear to be.

Canons of construction

1. Prima facie all shares rank equally. If, therefore, some are to have priority over others there must be provisions to this effect in the terms of issue.

2. If, however, the shares are expressly divided into separate classes (thus necessarily contradicting the presumed equality) it is a question of construction in each case what the rights of each class are.[84]

3. If nothing is expressly said about the rights of one class in respect of either (a) dividends, (b) return of capital, or (c) attendance at meetings or voting, then, prima facie, that class has the same rights in that respect as the residuary ordinary shares. Hence a preference as to dividend will not imply a preference as to capital (or vice versa).[85] Nor will an exclusion of participation in dividends beyond a fixed preferential rate necessarily imply an exclusion of participation in

---

[79] Even to the extent of simply providing that the share capital is divided into so many X% Preference Shares and so many Ordinary Shares and issuing them without further clarification.

[80] The classic illustration is the over-ruling, by the H.L. in *Scottish Insurance* v. *Wilsons & Clyde Coal Co.* [1949] A.C. 462, of the C.A. decision in *Re William Metcalfe Ltd.* [1933] Ch. 142.

[81] 4th ed. (1979) pp. 414–421.

[82] *Birch* v. *Cropper* (1889) 14 App.Cas. 525, H.L.

[83] *Re Bridgewater Navigation Co.* [1891] 2 Ch. 317, C.A.

[84] *Scottish Insurance* v. *Wilsons & Clyde Coal Co.* above n. 80; *Re Isle of Thanet Electric Co.* [1950] Ch. 161, C.A.

[85] *Re London India Rubber Co.* (1868) L.R. 5 Eq. 519; *Re Accrington Corp. Steam Tramways* [1909] 2 Ch. 40.

capital (or vice versa) although it will apparently be some indication of it.[86]

4. Where shares are entitled to participate in surplus capital on a winding up, prima facie they participate in all surplus assets and not merely in that part which does not represent undistributed profits that might have been distributed as dividend to another class.[87]

5. If, however, any rights in respect of any of these matters are expressly stated. that statement is presumed to be exhaustive so far as that matter is concerned. Hence if shares are given a preferential dividend they are presumed to be non-participating as regards further dividends,[88] and if they are given a preferential right to a return of capital they are presumed to be non-participating in surplus assets.[89] The same clearly applies to attendance and voting[90], if they are given a vote in certain circumstances, (e.g. if their dividends are in arrears) it is implied that they have no vote in other circumstances.

6. The onus of rebutting the presumption in 5 is not lightly discharged and the fact that shares are expressly made participating as regards either dividends or capital is no indication that they are participating as regards the other—indeed it has been taken as evidence to the contrary.[91]

7. If a preferential dividend is provided for, it is presumed to be cumulative.[92] This presumption can be rebutted by any words indicating that the preferential dividend for a year is to be payable only out of the profits of that year.[93]

[86] This is implied in the speeches in the *Scottish Insurance* case, above, and in *Dimbula Valley (Ceylon) Tea Co. Ltd. v. Laurie* [1961] Ch. 353.

[87] *Dimbula Valley (Ceylon) Tea Co. Ltd. v. Laurie*, above: *Re Saldean Estate Co. Ltd.* [1968] 1 W.L.R. 1844. These cases "distinguished" *Re Bridgwater Navigation Co.*, above, (on the basis that the contrary decision of the C.A. depended on the peculiar wording of the company articles) but it is thought that *Bridgwater* can now be ignored; in *Wilsons & Clyde Coal Co.* Lord Simonds pointed out the absurdity of supposing that "parties intended a bargain which would involve an investigation of an artificial and elaborate character into the nature and origin of surplus assets": [1949] A.C. at 482.

[88] *Will v. United Lankat Plantations Co.* [1914] A.C. 11, H.L.

[89] *Scottish Insurance v. Wilsons & Clyde Coal Co.* above; *Re Isle of Thanet Electric Co.*, above.

[90] *Quaere* whether attendance at meetings and voting should not really be treated as two separate rights. It seems, however, that express exclusion of a right to vote will take away the right to be summoned to (or presumably to attend) meetings: *Re MacKenzie & Co. Ltd.* [1916] 2 Ch. 450. If, under this canon, they have votes but the articles do not say how many, the effect of s.370(6) appears to be that they have one vote per share or, if their shares have been converted to stock (on which see pp. 366, 367 below) per each £10 of stock and that if the company has no share capital each member has one vote.

[91] *Re National Telephone Co.* [1914] 1 Ch. 755; *Re Isle of Thanet Electric Co.*, above and *Re Saldean Estate Co. Ltd.*, above. This produces strange results. If as the H.L. suggested in the *Scottish Insurance* case, the fact that shares are non-participating as regards dividends is some indication that they are intended to be non-participating as regards capital (on the ground that the surplus profits have been appropriated to the ordinary shareholders) where the surplus profits belong to both classes while the company is a going concern, both should participate in a winding up in order to preserve the status quo.

[92] *Webb v. Earle* (1875) L.R. 20 Eq. 556.

[93] *Staples v. Eastman Photographic Materials Co.* [1896] 2 Ch. 303, C.A.

8. It is presumed that even preferential dividends are payable only if declared.[94] Hence arrears even of cumulative dividend are prima facie not payable in a winding up unless previously declared.[95] But this presumption may be rebutted by the slightest indication to the contrary.[96] When the arrears are payable, the presumption is that they are to be paid provided there are surplus assets available, whether or not these represent accumulated profits which might have been distributed by way of dividend,[97] but that they are payable only to the date of the commencement of the winding up.[98]

The effect of applying these canons of construction has been, as Evershed M.R. pointed out,[99] that over the past 100 years

"the view of the courts may have undergone some change in regard to the relative rights of preference and ordinary shareholders … and to the disadvantage of the preference shareholders whose position has … become somewhat more approximated to [that] of debentureholders."

Unless preference shareholders are expressly granted participating rights they are unlikely to be entitled to share in any way in the "equity" or to have voting rights except in narrowly prescribed circumstances. Yet they enjoy none of the advantages of debentureholders; they receive a return on their money only if profits are earned (and not necessarily even then), they rank after creditors on a winding-up and they have less effective remedies against the company. Suspended midway between true creditors and true members they get the worst of both worlds.

Ordinary shares

Ordinary shares (as the name implies) constitute the residuary class in which is vested everything after the special rights of preference

---

[94] *Burland* v. *Earle* [1902] A.C. 83, P.C.; *Re Buenos Ayres Gt. Southern Ry.* [1947] Ch. 384; *Godfrey Phillips Ltd.* v. *Investment Trust Ltd.* [1953] 1 W.L.R. 41. *Semble*, therefore, non-cumulative shares lose their preferential dividend for the year in which liquidation commences: *Re Foster & Son* [1942] 1 All E.R. 314; *Re Catalina's Warehouses* [1947] 1 All E.R. 51. But, if the terms clearly so provide, a prescribed preferential dividend may be payable so long as there are adequate distributable profits in accordance with Chap. 10 above: *Evling* v. *Israel & Oppenheimer* [1918] 1 Ch. 101.

[95] *Re Crichton's Oil Co.* [1902] 2 Ch. 86, C.A.; *Re Roberts & Cooper* [1929] 2 Ch. 383; *Re Wood, Skinner & Co. Ltd.* [1944] Ch. 323.

[96] *Re Walter Symons Ltd.* [1934] Ch. 308; *Re F. de Jong & Co. Ltd.* [1946] Ch. 211, C.A.; *Re E. W. Savory Ltd.* [1951] 2 All E.R. 1036; *Re Wharfedale Brewery Co.* [1952] Ch. 913.

[97] *Re New Chinese Antimony Co. Ltd.* [1916] 2 Ch. 115; *Re Springbok Agricultural Estates Ltd.* [1920] 1 Ch. 563; *Re Wharfedale Brewery Co.*, above, not following *Re W.J. Hall & Co. Ltd.* [1909] 1 Ch. 521.

[98] *Re E. W. Savory Ltd.*, above.

[99] *Re Isle of Thanet Electric Co.* [1950] Ch. at p. 175.

classes, if any, have been satisfied. They confer a right to the "equity" in the company and, in so far as members can be said to own the company, the ordinary shareholders are its proprietors, It is they who bear the lion's share of the risk and they who in good years take the lion's share of the profits (after the directors and managers have been remunerated). If, as is often the case, the company's shares are all of one class, then these are necessarily ordinary shares, and if a company has a share capital it must perforce have at least one ordinary share whether or not it also has preference shares. It is this class alone which is unmistakably distinguished from debentures both in law and fact.

But as we have seen, the ordinary shares may shade off imperceptibly into preference, for, when the latter confer a substantial right of participation in income or capital, or *a fortiori* both, it is largely a matter of taste whether they are designated "preference" or "preferred ordinary" shares. Moreover, distinctions may be drawn between ordinary shares, ranking equally as regards financial participation, by dividing them nevertheless into separate classes with different voting rights. In this event they will probably be distinguished as "A" "B" "C" (etc.) ordinary shares. Many public companies have issued non-voting A ordinary shares. By this device control may be retained by a small proportion of the equity leading to a further rift between ownership and control. This disturbing development (a response to the threat of take-over bids[1]) gave rise to demands that The Stock Exchange should refuse to list such shares, or, failing that, that the legislature should intervene. The Jenkins Committee was divided on this issue. The majority took the view that the case for banning non-voting ordinary shares had not been made out but that such shares should be clearly labelled[2] and that their holders should be entitled to receive notices of all meetings so as to be kept informed.[3] A minority of three recommended that all equity shareholders should have a right to attend and speak at meetings and that there should be a prohibition on the listing of non-voting or restricted-voting equity shares.[4] No legislative action has been taken on either recommendation.[4a] However opposition of

---

[1] See Chap. 27, below. After the initial battle in the 1950s for control of Savoy Hotel Ltd, the capital of the company was reorganised so that £21,198 B ordinary stock could outvote £847,912 A ordinary stock. There the A stock had voting rights but the votes were so weighted that over 97 per cent. of the equity could be outvoted by the remainder! Over 40 years later, despite changes in the share capital, the balance of power remains much the same and the continued efforts of the holders of a large majority of the equity to wrest control from the minority have not succeeded. However at the end of 1989 a truce was declared when the majority was allowed representation on the board.

[2] The Stock Exchange requirements now provide that non-voting shares must be so designated and that the designation of equity shares with restricted votes must include the word "restricted voting" or "limited voting": *Yellow Book*, Section 9 Chapter I, para. 11.

[3] Cmnd. 1749, paras. 123–140.

[4] *Ibid*. pp. 207–210.

[4a] But see n. 2 above.

institutional investors has caused issues of non-voting shares to be less frequent and many companies have enfranchised their non-voting shares.

Redeemable Shares

As we have seen,[5] all classes of shares may now be issued as redeemable in accordance with Part V Chapter VII of the Act. When that is done those that are redeemable necessarily constitute a class separate from those not issued as redeemable even though they may be identical in every other respect. In contrast with the power of a company to purchase its own shares in accordance with that Part,[6] the power to issue redeemable equity shares has been little used and when redeemable shares are to be found they will normally be preference shares. If the terms of redemption merely provided for their redemption at par, their holders would be highly vulnerable; for if interest rates fell since the date of issue it would clearly pay the company to redeem them and to borrow money at a lower rate of interest than the fixed dividend. This, following the House of Lords decision in *Scottish Insurance* v. *Wilson & Clyde Coal Co*[7] was, in effect, done by capital reductions even though the shares were irredeemable and quoted at above par, for the Lords decided in that case and in *Prudential Assurance* v. *Chatterley-Whitfield Collieries*[8] in the same year, that the courts had to confirm the reductions since the preference shareholders were being treated in strict accordance with their class rights.[9] The obvious unfairness of this led to the practice of providing, on issues of non-participating preference shares by public companies, that on redemption or any return of capital the amount repaid should be tied to the average quoted price in the months before. This, so-called "Spens formula,"[10] affords reasonable protection in the case of listed companies but preference shareholders in unquoted companies still remain at risk.

Special classes

Although in most cases the shares of a company will fall into one or other of the primary classes of preference or ordinary, it is, of

---

[5] Chap. 9, p. 215 above.
[6] *Ibid* pp. 217 *et seq.* above.
[7] [1949] A.C. 462.
[8] [1949] A.C. 512.
[9] Though, in the first case, only as a result of its over-ruling of the decision of the C.A. in *Re William Metcalf Ltd.* [1933] Ch. 142.
[10] Named after its inventor. See also the limitations on purchases for redemption by the company. *Yellow Book*, Section 9. Chapter 1 para. 8 and the comparable provisions regarding loan stock in *ibid* Chapter 2 para. 1.

course, possible for the company to create shares for particular purposes and containing terms which cut across the normal classifications. An example of this is afforded by employees' shares. Frequent references have already been made to "employees share schemes." Under the present definition of such schemes,[11] the beneficiaries of them may include not only present employees of the company concerned, but also employees, or former employees, of it or any company in the same group, and the spouses, widows or widowers, children or step-children under the age of 18, of any such employees. When employees' share schemes first came to be introduced here, the normal practice was to create a special class of shares with restricted rights regarding, in particular, votes and transferability; only in relation to share option schemes, designed as incentive to top management, were ordinary voting equity shares on offer. Now, however, that is usual in all cases[12] in order that employees' share schemes may enjoy the special tax concessions conferred on "approved profit-sharing schemes" or "approved savings-related share option schemes." Hence today such schemes will rarely lead to the creation of a special class of share; it is only in relation to their allotment, financing, and provision for re-purchase by the company or the trustees of the scheme that there will be special arrangements which the Act facilitates by exclusions from the normal restrictions on purchase of own shares and on the provision of finance by a company for the acquisition of its shares.[13]

Unclassified shares

In recent years it has become common, when the whole of the stated authorised share capital is not intended to be issued initially, to designate the unissued shares as "unclassified shares." This practice, borrowed from the United States, recognises that until shares are issued they confer no rights at all, and that the rights ultimately attached to them depend on the company's decision at the time when they are issued.

Conversion of shares into stock

Once the shares or any class of them are fully paid, the company may convert them into stock;[14] in other words the company may merge the relevant share capital, say 10,000 shares of £1 each into

---

[11] s.743.
[12] But it would be rare indeed for this to have led to employees controlling a large public company—as has occurred in the USA.
[13] See Chap. 9 at pp. 214, 230. And note also the special treatment in relation to pre-emptive rights: above p. 365.
[14] s.121(2)(c). Stock can be re-converted into shares: *ibid.*

£10,000 of stock. Formerly, when each share had, throughout its life, to bear a distinctive number, there were practical advantages in so doing. But the Companies Act 1948 (now the 1985 Act, section 182(2)) enables numbers to be dispensed with once shares are fully paid. Since, in relation to shares (as opposed to debentures[15]) there were no other practical advantages in conversion, this now rarely takes place though many major public companies which date back to before the 1948 Act still have stock. For the purposes of the Act "shares" includes "stock"[16] and the distinction between them is merely a source of confusion.[17]

LEGAL NATURE OF DEBENTURES

The difficulty in the case of shares is to fit them into any normal legal category; but one is unlikely to be left in doubt whether something is or is not a share. The converse is the case in relation to debentures. The legal relationship between a company[18] and its debentureholders is simply the contractual relationship of debtor and creditor, coupled, if the debt is secured on some or all of the company's assets, with that of mortgagor and mortgagee. In contrast with a shareholder, the debentureholder is in law not a member of the company having rights in it, but a creditor having rights against it. In reality, however, the difference between him and a shareholder may not be anything like as clear-cut, for the debenture may give the holder a contractual right:—to appoint a director; to a share of profits (whether or not available for dividend); to repayment at a premium; to attend and vote at general meetings[19] and even to convert his debentures into equity shares.[20] Moreover, where the debenture is secured by a floating charge on all the undertaking and assets of the

---

[15] See below pp. 380, 381.

[16] s.744.

[17] As the Jenkins Committee recognised: Cmnd. 1749 para. 473. The Companies Bill 1973 would have banned future conversions.

[18] The word "debenture" is not restricted to securities of companies or bodies corporate. Clubs not infrequently issue debentures and the name may even be applied to bonds issued by an individual; *e.g.* to those issued by the Tichborne Claimant to finance his attempt to establish his right to the Tichborne inheritance: Lord Maugham (the Law Lord, not the novelist) was one of many who have written accounts of this fascinating chapter in legal and social history: See his *The Tichborne Case* (1936).

[19] But his vote should not be counted if the Act requires the resolution to be passed by "members"—as in the case of extraordinary or special resolutions: s.378(1) and (2). In which case he will be holding an "equity security" (see p. 364 above) and when he exercises the right will become an equity shareholder. To issue at a discount debentures which can be immediately converted into shares of the full par value would be a colourable device to evade the prohibition on issuing shares at a discount (*Moseley* v. *Koffyfontein Mines* [1904] 2 Ch. 108, C.A.) but appears to be unobjectionable if convertible only when the debentures are due for repayment at par since the shares will then be paid up in cash "through the release of a liability of the company for a liquidated sum": s.738(2).

company, he will have a legal or equitable interest in the company's business, albeit of a different kind from that of its shareholders.[21]

Difficulty of defining

The difficulty, however, is to determine whether or not the transaction between the debtor company and the creditor is such as to make the latter a debentureholder, for no one has yet succeeded in defining "debenture." As Chitty J. lamented over a century ago:

"I cannot find any precise definition of the term, it is not either in law or commerce a strictly technical term, or what is called a term of art."

It is, nevertheless a term frequently used in statutes—including the Companies Act which contains, in Part V, Chapter VIII, seven sections[22] under the heading *Debentures* as well as frequent references throughout the Act to debentures and debentureholders. One would therefore expect to find an attempt to define what debentures are. But all one gets is:

"In this Act, unless the contrary intention appears ... 'debenture' includes debenture stock, bonds and other securities of a company, whether constituting a charge on the assets of the company or not."[23]

This attempt to "define" by inclusions has been carried a stage further by the Financial Services Act which, for its purposes, employs both inclusions and exclusions.[24] While neither Act can be said to

[21] *Levy v. Abercorris Slate & Slab Co.* (1887) 37 Ch. p. 260 at 264. See also Lindley J. in *British India Steam Navigation Co. v. I.R.C.* (1881) 7 Q.B.D. at 172 and Warrington L.J. in *Lemon v. Austin Friars Trust* [1926] Ch. 1 (C.A.) at p. 17 and the H.L. in *Knightsbridge Estates Co. v. Byrne* [1940] A.C. 613.

[22] ss.190–197.

[23] s.744. A "definition" which has remained substantially unchanged since the 1929 Act.

[24] Sched. 1, para. 2 of the F.S. Act says that "debentures" means:— "Debentures, including debenture stock, loan stock, bonds, certificates of deposit and other instruments creating or acknowledging indebtedness ....
Note This paragraph shall not be construed as applying—
(a) to any instrument acknowledging or creating indebtedness for, or for money borrowed to defray, the consideration payable under a contract for the supply of goods or services;
(b) to a cheque or other bill of exchange, banker's draft or a letter of credit, or
(c) to a bank note, a statement showing a balance in a current, deposit or savings account or (by reason of any financial obligation contained in it) to a lease or other disposition of property, inheritable security or an insurance policy."
The inclusion of "certificates of deposit" is interesting since it was generally thought that they were not "debentures"; hence the need for the Protection of Depositors Act 1963 (now superseded by the Banking Act 1987).

define what is the primary meaning of "debentures," both give some pointers to what, both in law and in commerce, would, for most purposes be regarded as their essential feature; namely, that debentures are a type of transferable security (in this respect resembling shares) whereby a company can raise finance in the form of loan capital instead of share capital.

In practice, the absence of a precise definition has given rise to surprisingly few problems and to even fewer reported cases. That may change; for, in recent years, developments in banking and commercial circles have led to the invention of a remarkable array of new and highly sophisticated types of "securitised" loan investments as a result of which finance, which would formerly have been raised by a straightforward bank loan (for most purposes not a debenture) may be obtained through the issue of instruments, some of which for most purposes unquestionably are debentures and others of which may or may not be.

However, if the courts display the commonsense approach that the House of Lords did in the one relevant reported case of any importance, the probability is that we shall get by without much trouble. That case, *Knightsbridge Estates Ltd.* v. *Byrne*[25] concerned a mortgage on houses, shops and a block of flats by a company to secure a loan of £310,000. The loan was to be repayable by 80 half-yearly instalments spread over 40 years but became immediately repayable if the mortgagor should sell the equity of redemption. The company was forbidden from selling any of the properties free from the mortgage or from granting leases for more than 3 years without the consent of the mortgagee. Five years later the company wished to pay off the mortgage in full and argued that the term making the mortgage irredeemable for 40 years was void as a clog on the equity of redemption. Under what is now section 193 of the Act,

'a condition contained in debentures ... is not invalid by reason only that the debentures are thereby made irredeemable or redeemable only on the happening of a contingency (however remote) or on the expiration of a period (however long) any rule of equity to the contrary notwithstanding."

The question therefore was whether this mortgage was a debenture. The speeches in the House of Lords pointed out that one would have expected to find this section in a Part of the Act dealing with company charges[26] rather than in that dealing with debentures,[27] for the mortgage would not be a "debenture," for the and accepted that the mortgage would not be a "debenture," notwithstanding.

25 [1940] A.C. 613.
26 Where, indeed, it (and s.196) should be; the trouble is that there is no Part dealing with Company Charges—only one dealing with Registration of Charges.
27 *Per* Lord Romer at p. 628.

purposes of some of the other sections.[28] Nevertheless, it was held that the legislative intention must have been to exclude from the equitable rule any mortgage by a company. In the words of Lord Romer,[29]

"if it is thought desirable that debentures in their popular meaning may be made irredeemable, it would seem to be both absurd and inconsistent to forbid a company to make its ordinary mortgages of land also irredeemable."

Accordingly the mortgage was a "debenture" for the purposes of section 193.

The normal debenture, however, is very different from a single mortgage of land. It generally consists of one of a series of securities ranking *pari passu* with each other. The expression "debenture" is applied indiscriminately to the instrument creating or evidencing the indebtedness and to the debt itself and the bundle of rights vested in the holder to secure its payment. These rights, as we have seen, may include a charge on all or some of the company's assets. If there is no such charge it will normally be described as a "bond" or a "loan note," but, as the "definitions" in the Companies Act and the Financial Services Act at least make clear, it will in law be a "debenture." When there is a charge, it will probably be a floating charge, the peculiar features of which are left to Chapter 16 on Company Charges.

Debenture Stock

Reference has already made to the, largely meaningless, distinction between "shares" and "stocks."[30] There is a similar distinction between "debentures" and "debenture stock" but here it is far from meaningless and debenture stock has considerable practical advantages. If a public company wishes to raise £1m, it could seek to do so by an issue of a series of, say £1, £10, £100, or £1000 debentures, each representing a separate debt totalling in aggregate £1m. This would result in an enormous bundle of paper for the company to process and subscribers to handle. And, if a subscriber for a single debenture wanted to sell half of it, he would not be able to make a legal transfer of that half. If, however, the company creates £1m of

[28] *Per* Viscount Maugham at p. 624. Clearly such a mortgage does not have to be registered in the company's register of debentureholders under s.190 in addition to registration of the mortgage under Part XII.
[29] At p. 629. The other Law Lords concurred with the speeches of Lords Maugham and Romer.
[30] Above pp. 376, 377.

debenture stock it can issue it;[31] to subscribers in such amounts as each wants,[32] giving each a single certificate[33] and he can sell and transfer any fraction of it.[34] A further advantage is that whereas with a series of debentures with a charge on the company's assets it will be necessary to say expressly in each debenture that it is one of a series each ranking pari passu in respect of the charge,[35] debenture stock achieves that result without express provision.

Trustees for debenture holders

The deed required on the creation of debenture stock may be a deed poll executed by the company alone, but it is now invariable practice[36] for the deed to be made with trustees. This, too, is normally done when there is an issue of a series of debentures. In other words, trustees, normally a trust corporation,[37] are interposed between the company and the debentureholders. Any charge can then be in favour of the trustees who hold it on trust for the debentureholders. Such an arrangement has many advantages.

In the first place it will enable the security to be by way of specific legal mortgage or charge on the company's land as well as by way of equitable floating charge on the rest of the assets. Clearly the ideal security is one so constituted, but a legal interest cannot be vested in thousands of debentureholders,[38] nor can the deeds be split up amongst them. If, however there are trustees, the legal mortgage can be vested in them, on trust for the beneficiary debentureholders, and the trustees retain custody of the title deeds. Again, if there is to be a specific charge on shares in subsidiary companies (which may be a necessary precaution) trustees are needed in order that someone independent of the holding company shall be able to exercise the voting rights attached to the shares.

Secondly, it will provide a single corporation or a small body of persons charged with the duty of watching the debentureholders'

31 Debenture stock can be created de novo; there is no need to create debentures and then to convert them to debenture stock as there is in relation to shares and stock.
32 In practice there is likely to be a prescribed minimum amount which can be subscribed for or transferred.
33 A simple document of one sheet, similar to a share certificate, in contrast with a debenture which will, unless there is a trust deed (see below) have to set out all the terms.
34 But see n. 32 above.
35 Without this their respective priorities might depend on the dates when each debenture was issued.
36 Except with unsecured loan stock.
37 Formerly it was common for banks to undertake this work but they have tended to fight shy of it since *Re Dorman Long & Co.* [1934] Ch. 635 drew attention to the conflict of interest and duty which might arise when the bank was both a creditor in its own right and a trustee. Today, therefore, the duties are generally undertaken by other trust corporations, such as insurance companies, though sometime by the separate trustee companies formed by certain banks. Very occasionally individual trustees are still employed.
38 Since 1925 a legal estate in land cannot be vested in more than four persons.

interests and of intervening if they are in jeopardy. This is obviously far more satisfactory than leaving it to a widely dispersed class of persons each of whom may lack the skill, interest and financial resources required if he is to take action on his own.[39] It will also be possible, by the trust deed, to impose on the company additional obligations, regarding the submission of information and the like, which might not otherwise be practicable. Similarly, the trustees can be empowered to convene meetings of the holders in order to acquaint them with the position and to obtain their instructions.

Complaints have been made in the past that the trustees are all too often content to act as passive recipients of their remuneration rather than as active watchdogs. The Cohen Committee admitted that these complaints were not altogether unfounded[40] but all that has resulted is section 192 of the Act which invalidates provisions in trust deeds (or elsewhere) which purport to exempt a trustee from, or to indemnify him against, "liability for breach of trust where he fails to show the degree of care and diligence required of him as a trustee having regard to the provisions of the trust deed conferring on him any powers, authorities or discretions."[41] There is here a conspicuous contrast with the stricter rules under Federal legislation in the United States and with the duties imposed on trustees of unit trusts under the Financial Services Act.

---

[39] Although there are trustees, an individual stockholder can take steps to enforce the security but he is not regarded as a creditor with the latter's personal remedies against the company: *Re Dunderland Iron Ore Co.* [1909] 1 Ch. 446.

[40] Cmd. 6659, paras 61–64.

[41] But note the exceptions and qualifications in subss. (2)–(4). In the case of listed debt securities, The Stock Exchange requires that, unless it otherwise agrees, there must be a trustee or trustees, at least one being a trust corporation with no interest in, or relation to, the company which might conflict with the position of trustee; and, unless the debenture holders have a general power to remove and appoint trustees, any appointment must be approved by an extraordinary resolution of the holders. It also specifies provisions which trust deeds must contain: *Yellow Book*, Section 9, Chap. 2.

CHAPTER 15

ACQUISITION AND DISPOSAL OF COMPANY SECURITIES

Because of the peculiar nature of company securities, particularly shares[1] their acquisition and disposal raise issues which need to be dealt with as a branch of Company Law. This Chapter discusses the most important of them. It describes the present position but draws attention under the heading **De-materialisation of Listed Securities** to the aims of the TAURUS project which may be achieved shortly after this edition is published and which will change the position markedly so far as concerns fully paid securities of listed companies.

BECOMING A SHAREHOLDER

The Act assumes that, in the case of a company with the share capital, becoming a shareholder is the same as becoming a member. That is not necessarily so in relation to the few surviving companies limited by guarantee and having a share capital.[2] And there is no inherent reason why it should be so with companies limited by shares; indeed a very sensible method of promoting voluntary "co-determination"[3] would be to provide means whereby employees could become members without also having to buy shares in the company, thus risking the loss of their savings as well as their jobs if their employer-company becomes insolvent. But while the Act does not specifically prohibit a constitution on those lines, it clearly does not contemplate it.

The basic principle which the Act lays down[4] is that to become a member, and thereby a shareholder, there must be agreement and entry on a register of members which every type of registered company is required to maintain and which, in relation to a company with shares is also a register of shareholdings.[5] Until entry on the register an acquirer is not, in law, yet a member or shareholder. To this, there are two exceptions. The first relates to subscribers' shares. Each subscriber to the memorandum of a limited company with a

---

[1] Which, as we saw from the last chapter, are difficult to place in any traditional type of "property."
[2] Such companies can no longer be formed: see s.1(4).
[3] See Chap. 4, at p. 63 above.
[4] s.22. On which, see *Re Nuneaton Football Club*, [1989] BCLC 454, C.A., holding that "agreement" requires only assent to become a member.
[5] ss.352–362.

share capital is required to take at least one share and against the name of each must be shown the number of shares that he takes.[6] The subscribers are then "deemed to have agreed to become members of the company and on its registration shall be entered in such in its register of members."[7] The effect of this has been held to be that, even if the company omits to put them on the register they become members and holders of the number of shares stated.[8] This is of little importance since in practice only two shares will be subscribed for.

The second exception relates to share-warrants to bearer. Section 188[9] provides that a company, if so authorised by its articles, may issue with respect to any fully-paid shares a warrant stating that the bearer of the warrant is entitled to the shares specified in it. If similarly authorised, it may provide, by coupons attached to the warrant or otherwise, for the payment of future dividends.[10] Title to the shares specified then passes by manual delivery of the warrant,[11] which is a negotiable instrument.[12] On their issue, the company removes from its register of members the name of the former registered holder and merely states the fact and date of the issue of the warrant and the number of shares (or amount of stock) to which it relates.[13] The bearer of the warrant from time to time is unquestionably a shareholder but to what extent, if at all, he is a member of the company depends on a provision to that effect[14] in the articles.[15] Hence shareholding and membership are not necessarily co-terminous if share warrants are issued. However, again subject to the articles, the bearer of the warrant is entitled, on surrendering it for cancellation, to have his name and shareholding re-entered on the register.[16] In practice this second exception is unimportant because bearer securities have never been popular with

[6] s.2(5)(b) and (c).

[7] s.22(1). Since it is the invariable practice for the memorandum to conclude with "We, the subscribers . . . agree to take the number of shares shown opposite our respective names" one would have thought that they had expressly agreed and that no "deeming" came into it. But perhaps it was thought necessary to preclude any argument that one cannot have a binding agreement with a company which does not yet exist: see Chap. 12 at pp. 305, 306. But see n. 4 above where the member's "assent" was after the formation.

[8] *Evans' Case* (1867) L.R. 2 Ch.App. 247; *Baytrust Holdings Ltd.* v. *I.R.C.* [1971] 1 W.L.R. 1333 at 1355–56. But if the company allots all the authorised share capital to others the courts have had to accept the inevitable consequence that the subscribers did not become members or shareholders: *Macley's Case* (1875) 1 Ch.D. 247; *Baytrust Holdings Ltd.* v. *I.R.C.*, above, where a statement to this effect in an earlier edition was cited with approval.

[9] As substituted by Sched. 17, para. 6 of the 1989 Act.

[10] s.188(3).

[11] s.188(2).

[12] *Webb, Hale & Co.* v. *Alexandria Water Co.* (1905) 21 T.L.R. 572.

[13] s.355(1).

[14] Table A 1985 contains no provisions at all about share warrants.

[15] A "bearer of a share warrant may, if the articles so provide, be deemed a member of the company within the meaning of this Act, either to the full extent or for any purposes defined in the articles": s.355(5).

[16] s.355(2).

English investors or English companies and are rarely issued and hardly ever in respect of shares, as opposed to bearer bonds, (*i.e.* debentures) which are sometimes issued to attract Continental investors who have a traditional liking for securities in bearer form. It is fortunate that bearer shares are such a rarity for if they became common it would play havoc with many provisions of the Act.[17]

The register

Since, in practice, shares in British companies are "registered" and not "bearer" and since the process of becoming (or ceasing to be) a member and shareholder is incomplete until entry on the register, the statutory provisions regarding its maintenance are of importance. In summary, they are as follows:

In addition to showing the name and address of every member and the date on which he was registered as a member or ceased to be a member,[18] in the case of a company with a share capital the register must also state the number and class[19] of shares (or amount of stock) held by him and the amount paid-up on each share.[20] The register may be kept at the company's registered office or at another office of the company or at the office of professional registrars to which the company has delegated this task,[21] but, if kept otherwise than at the company's registered office, notice must be given to the Registrar of the place where it is kept and of any change of that place.[22] If the company has more than 50 members then, unless the register is kept in such form as to constitute an index of names of the members, such an index must also be kept in the same place as the register. The register and index have to be open for inspection during business hours by any member without charge and by any other person on payment of a small fee and a copy of it or any part of it has to be supplied to anyone on payment of a modest charge.[23] This

17 *e.g.* those relating to purchase of own shares (see Chap. 9 at pp. 217–226 above, and, especially, those relating to disclosure of share-ownership and dealings: see Chap. 23 at pp. 619–624 below.
18 s.352(1). The entry may be removed after 20 years of his ceasing to be a member: s.352(6).
19 In the case of a company without a share capital but with different classes of membership the register now has to state the class to which each member belongs: s.352(4). This fills the lacuna revealed in *Re Performing Right Society Ltd.* [1978] 1 W.L.R. 1197.
20 s.352(3)
21 s.353(1). Use of professional registrars (normally a subsidiary of a clearing bank) is now usual in the case of listed public companies. Where it is adopted, the professional registrar is liable to the same penalties for default in compliance with the statutory provisions as if it were an officer of the company: s.357.
22 s.353(2) and (3). The place must be in England or Wales if the company is registered in England and Wales or in Scotland if it is registered in Scotland. But if the company carries on business in one of the countries specified in Sched. 14 to the Act it may cause to be kept an "overseas branch register" in that country, a duplicate of which will also be maintained with the principal register: see Sched. 14, Part I.
23 s.356.

is a legitimate help to any member who wishes to communicate with any of his fellow members and to a take-over bidder. But unfortunately it also enables traders who wish to attempt to sell their wares by "junk-mail," or telephone calls, to obtain, more cheaply than in any other way, a "sucker-list" of potential victims by buying a copy of the membership register of, say, British Telecom or British Gas.

A company may close the register for any time or times not exceeding in total 30 days in any year.[24] Advantage of this can be taken by widely-held public companies to enable them temporarily to freeze the list of those who are entitled to receive an annual dividend or to vote at an annual general meeting.

The register is "prima facie evidence of any matters which are by this Act directed or authorised to be inserted in it."[25] It is not, however, conclusive evidence for, as we have seen, membership is dependent both on agreement to become a member and entry in the register and if the entry does not truly reflect the agreement or there was no valid agreement the register ought to be rectified. Hence section 359 provides a summary remedy whereby, if:

"(a) the name of any person is without sufficient cause entered in or omitted from a company's register of members, or

(b) default is made or unnecessary delay takes place in entering on the register the fact of any person having ceased to be a member,

the person aggrieved or any member of the company, or the company may apply to the court for rectification of the register."[26]

This wording is defective because it ignores the fact that the register is not just a register of members but also a register of shareholdings and that a likely error is in the amount of a member's shareholding. However commonsense has prevailed and in *Re Transatlantic Life Assurance*[27] Slade J. felt able to hold that "the wording ... is wide enough in its terms to empower the court to order the deletion of some only of a registered shareholder's shares."[28] It must follow that it is similarly empowered to order an addition to the registered holding.[29]

[24] s.358. It must give notice of this in a newspaper "circulating in the district in which the company's registered office is situated."

[25] s.361.

[26] s.359(1).

[27] [1980] 1 W.L.R. 79. The case arose because the allotment of some shares was void because Exchange Control permission had not been obtained as at that time was necessary.

[28] At p. 84F-G.

[29] But the wording of s.359(1) ought to be amended to make it clear that the court can rectify "any matters which are by this Act directed or authorised to be inserted in" the register. A court following Slade J. would presumably so construe the subsection but its present wording would mislead anyone unfamiliar with his judgment.

On an application the court may decide any question relating to the title of any person who is a party to the application whether the question arises between members or alleged members,[30] or between members or alleged members on the one hand and the company on the other hand,[31] and may decide "any question necessary or expedient to be decided for rectification. . . . ."[32] Moreover, the court may order payment by the company of "damages sustained by any party aggrieved.""[33]

There is some uncertainty as to the extent to which the company can rectify the register without an application to the court. But in practice here again common sense prevails. Sections 352, 354 and 355 clearly envisage, and indeed demand, alterations without which the register could not be kept up to date and fulfil its purpose, and although there is no express provision for alterations of members' addresses that takes place all the time. Indeed it would be quite absurd if companies cannot correct any mistake if all interested parties agree.

It must be emphasised, however, that although the register provides prima facie evidence of who its members are and what their shareholdings are, it provides no evidence at all, either to the company or anyone else, of who the beneficial owners of the shares are. The registered member may well be a trustee or nominee but of that the company neither knows nor is entitled to let anyone know; for "No notice of any trust, expressed, implied or constructive shall be entered on the register or be receivable by the Registrar" in the case of companies registered in England and Wales.[34] It has now been recognised that often the company, and indeed the regulatory authorities and the public, may need to be able to find out who the beneficial owners are and other sections, dealt with later,[35] seek to enable them to find out. But the register with which we are presently concerned is of little help; in the case of a listed company the majority of the shares will probably be registered in the names of nominees.

---

30 *e.g.* when A and B are disputing which of them should be the registered holder.

31 *e.g.* when there is a dispute between the company and A or B on whether either should be.

32 s.359(3).

33 s.359(2). "Compensation" would clearly be a better word than "damages" and "party aggrieved" is an expression which courts have constantly criticised, but apparently without convincing Parliamentary Counsel responsible for drafting Government Bills.

34 s.360. The omission from this section of Scotland is not because, as English lawyers tend (mistakenly) to believe, Scots law (as a Civil Law system) does not recognise trusts. On the contrary it is because the traditional Scottish practice is for trustees to be registered as "trustee disponees." This, apparently, does not affect the relationship between the company and the registered trustees (the company is no more concerned with what the trusts are than it would be if this section did apply) but it affords the beneficiaries greater protection *vis-à-vis* the trustees since it identifies the holding as that of a trust. It would seem to have much to commend it.

35 See Chap. 23 below at pp. 609–624.

The register, like other records that a company is required to maintain, may be kept either in bound books or by recording the matter in any other way[36] and, in particular, may be on a computer or other electronic device so long as the material can be reproduced in legible form and is so reproduced for purposes of inspection or supply of a copy.[37] It is also subject to the powers of the Secretary of State to make provision by regulations as to obligations of a company under the Act to make documents available for inspection or to provide copies of them.[38] The wording of the section[39] suggests that this power could not be used to restrict the right to inspect or obtain copies, for example by requiring good cause to be shown thus preventing share registers being used as "sucker-lists,"[40] but is intended to ensure that the matter is reproduced in a way which is as "user-friendly" as possible without imposing undue burdens on the company.[41]

Acquisitions from the company

Shares may be acquired either (a) from the company itself on an issue by it[42] or (b) by taking a transfer from an existing shareholder. Dealing first with (a), the normal *modus operandi* in the case of new issues by public companies has been described in Chapter 13: a would-be shareholder will apply in response to the prospectus, listing particulars or circular; if the application is accepted he will be sent an allotment letter[43]; and this completes the needful agreement to become a member and shareholder.[44] But he will not yet be either, since he will not, at that stage have been "entered on the register" and, it may be that he never will be. In practice, the letter of allotment will be renounceable; *i.e.* for a short period stated in it, his rights can be renounced in favour of someone else. Printed on the back of the letter there will be forms enabling the allottee to

36 s.722.
37 s.723. See Companies (Registers and Other Records) Regs. (S.I. 1985 No. 724) made under its subs. (4)).
38 s.723A, inserted by the 1989 Act. See the Companies (Inspection and Copying of Registers, Indices, and Documents) Regs. 1991, S.I. No. 1998.
39 See in particular subss. (1), (2), (3) and (6).
40 See p. 386 above.
41 Subs. (1) refers only to the obligation of the company and says that if it fails to comply with the regulations it shall be deemed to have refused inspection or failed to have supplied a copy. Nowhere in the section is there anything to suggest that regulations can impose conditions on the applicant.
42 Or, of course, by subscribing the memorandum of association though that is an option available only to the promoters and the advisers.
43 For the purposes of the Act "shares shall be taken . . . to be allotted when a person acquires the unconditional right to be included in the company's register of members in respect of those shares": s.738(1). If that right is conditional, say, upon a further payment, the allotment letter will not be an "allotment" in that sense; it will be equivalent to a letter of rights on a rights issue: see Chap. 13 at pp. 317, 318.
44 See p. 383 above.

renounce, and the person to whom they are ultimately renounced to confirm that he accepts the renunciation and agrees to be entered on the register. Normally the original allottee will not insert the name of the person to whom they are to be renounced and the effect is then to produce something similar to a short-term share warrant to bearer; it is not a negotiable instrument but once the renunciation is signed by the original allottee, the rights can be assigned by manual delivery of the allotment letter without a formal transfer. Before the stated period ends, however, it will be necessary for the name of the ultimate holder to be inserted, his signature obtained, and the allotment letter lodged with the company or its registrars.

Only when the allottee[45] or the ultimate person to whom his allotment has been renounced, has been entered on the register will anyone became a shareholder and member. And even then he will find difficulty in selling his shares until, later still, he receives a share certificate affording the only evidence of his title to the shares that he will be able to produce under the present antiquated system.[46]

Becoming a member and shareholder on an issue by a private company (or a closely-held public company whose shares are not listed or dealt in on the U.S.M.) is subject to the same legal requirements of agreement plus entry on the register but in practice both will be achieved with less formality and, in the case of private companies, without the issue of allotment letters. If someone wants to become a shareholder and the company wants him to, he will be entered on the register and issued with a share certificate without more ado.

Acquisitions from a shareholder

We now turn to the second method of becoming a member and shareholder, *i.e.* by taking a transfer of shares from an existing member and shareholder. Once again, the transaction will not be complete until the transferee is entered on the company's register as the holder of the shares (and until then the transferor will not cease to be a member or the legal holder of the shares). Neither the agreement to transfer nor delivery of a signed transfer form will pass the legal title.[47] Registration can be confidently expected to occur in due course unless the company's articles impose restrictions on the transferability of its shares. This is most unlikely if the shares are

---

[45] If the original allottee does not wish to sell his rights he need do nothing apart from retaining the allotment letter in safe custody until he ultimately receives a share certificate.
[46] But see under *Dematerialisation of Listed Shares* later in this chapter.
[47] But the beneficial interest may pass to the transferee prior to registration. See pp. 398 *et seq*, below.

listed[48] but very probable if the company is a private one. If there are any restrictions, a purchaser should not pay until he is satisfied that he will be registered, for there is no implied warranty to that effect by the seller.[49] In other circumstances all that needs to be done if the transaction is a domestic one, whereby, say, a shareholder transfers his holding as a gift to a member of his family or sells it to an acquaintance, is for the transferor to hand over to the transferee a signed share transfer[50] together with the share certificate which the transferee will lodge with the company and the register will then be amended by adding the transferee and noting that the transferor has ceased to be a member or shareholder in respect of the shares.[51]

Generally, however, anyone wishing to buy or sell listed shares will want to do so at the best price obtainable and for that purpose to use the facilities of The Stock Exchange instead of himself seeking out a willing counterparty. He will then enlist the services of a member firm of The Stock Exchange. The former mandatory distinction, between brokers, who acted only as agents for their clients, and jobbers who acted only as market-making principals, has disappeared; as a result of "Big Bang", firms may now act as either, so long as they disclose to the client whether they are acting as agents or principals. By pressing the appropriate buttons on their office computers linked to The Exchange's automated quotations system (SEAQ) they can execute their clients' instructions at the best available price quoted by market-makers in the shares concerned. They will then notify their clients by sending them contract notes—a "bought" note in the case of a purchase and a "sold" note in the case of a sale—accompanied, in the case of a purchase, by a request for payment prior to the next settlement date (unless they are already holding their client's funds) or, in the case of a sale, by a transfer form for signature and return and a request for the share certificate (unless they already hold it).

If the transferor bothers to read the transfer form he will find that it differs slightly from the one that he would have used if he transferred his shares to his wife or children. It will bear the heading TALISMAN and will purport to transfer the shares to "SEPON

---

[48] *Yellow Book*, Section 1, Chapter 2, para. 4 and Section 9, Chapter 1, para. 1.2.

[49] His only obligation is not to do anything to prevent the purchaser, or someone claiming through the purchaser, from being registered: *Hooper v. Herts*, [1906] 1 Ch. 549, C.A.

[50] As a result of the Stock Transfer Act 1963 it is not necessary for the transferee to sign unless the shares are only partly paid.

[51] Alternatively the two documents may be lodged by the transferor (s.183(4)) and in the case of a gift this might well be done. On a sale, however, the purchaser will normally want to receive documents on payment. For a mild complication where the certificate covers more shares than are being transferred: see below under *Certification of Transfers*. It is unlawful for the company to register a transfer unless "a proper instrument of transfer has been delivered to it": s.183(1). This was primarily designed to ensure that payment of stamp duty on the transfer was not evaded by provisions in the company's articles dispensing with the need for a written document.

Ltd." This is because The Stock Exchange, from, 1979 onwards, began to modernise its clearing-system by introducing progressively what is known as TALISMAN.[52] This now covers all market deals in fully paid listed shares or loan stock. The detailed working of this system is of little interest or concern to the investing public, or to readers of this book. It suffices to say that SEPON is the subsidiary company of The Exchange which acts as its clearing-house. It holds a pool of the securities of each listed company and on dealings on The Exchange each seller transfers to SEPON, thus momentarily augmenting its pool and out of it SEPON transfers the appropriate amount of shares to each purchaser.[53] The transfer forms which the company will receive for registration enable it to amend its register in the light of the transactions. But the securities, while passing in and out of the SEPON pool are as "fungible" as a sum of money. While this is a considerable improvement on the former method, it does nothing to reduce the paper-work involved or to shorten the time before a buyer is entered on the company's register and receives his share certificate—which will take weeks and sometimes months. For some 25 years it has been recognised that the overall settlement system is antiquated in comparison with that of other major financial centres and that, if The Exchange is to maintain and enhance its position as one of the World's major international exchanges, further and more radical reforms are needed. Happily at long-last something is being done.

Dematerialisation of listed securities

What is proposed is generally described as the "dematerialisation" of shares. The proposals were outlined in a publication of The Stock Exchange in March 1990 entitled "*Project TAURUS: A prospectus for settlement in the 1990s*" (hereinafter referred to as *Project Taurus*). The intention was to introduce by the end of 1993 a system, TAURUS,[54] complementing TALISMAN, whereby, once a bargain in fully-paid listed securities was struck, the buyer would become, and the seller, in respect of the shares sold, would cease to be, a member and shareholder. This would no longer depend on entry on, or removal from, the individual company's register and share certificates would become a thing of the past.[55] Instead, holdings and dealings would be recorded electronically in an account, corresponding to a bank account, with one of a number of "account operators,"

---

[52] Its introduction was facilitated by the Stock Transfer Acts of 1963 and 1982, the Stock Transfer (Additional Forms) Order 1979 (S.I. 1979 No. 277) and the Stock Exchange (Completion of Bargains) Act 1976; as amended by s.194 of the F.S. Act 1986.

[53] Shares held in the pool are registered in the name of SEPON but share certificates are not issued to it.

[54] "Transfer and automated registration of uncertificated stock."

[55] The UK would thus become the first completely "certificateless" major international securities market: see *Project Taurus*, pp. 7 & 8.

linked to TAURUS, from whom shareholders would be able to obtain at any time documentary evidence of the state of their accounts. Apart from this, and, presumably, apart from the need for member firms to send their clients "bought" or "sold" contract notes, the whole process would be paperless. And, moreover, it would be far less labour-intensive and much more rapid especially as the present 14-day settlement would be replaced by a rolling 3-day settlement.[56]

TAURUS will have a far more noticeable impact on investors than did TALISMAN. And it will take private investors some time to get used to it. But they should welcome it if in fact their dealings cost them materially less than at present.[57] It is clear that further legislative changes will be needed before TAURUS is introduced[58] but precisely what these will be remains to be worked out. However section 207 of the Companies Act 1989 enables such changes to be made by regulations. Indeed, that section is worded exceptionally widely and would empower the Secretary of State to undertake root-and-branch reforms of the whole process of transferring shares, whether or not these were listed on an exchange. The likelihood, however, is that the transfer of shares which are not listed, or admitted to dealings on the U.S.M.[59] (or other recognised investment exchanges) will be left unchanged.[60] Hence it remains necessary to explain in further detail the present legal provisions and to highlight some of the problems to which they can give rise.

Share certificates

Section 185(1) of the Act provides that, unless the terms of issue of the securities otherwise provide, a company shall, within two months of allotment or receipt of a transfer, complete and have ready for delivery certificates resulting therefrom. To this there are certain

---

56 *Ibid.* p. 12.
57 They presently feel hard-done-by since the abolition of fixed commissions in 1983 has meant that while the commissions paid by institutional investors have been substantially reduced, private investors (formerly subsidised by institutional investors) have to pay rather more.
58 Thus causing further mutilation of the 1985 consolidation.
59 Neither the *Ross Russell Report* nor *Project Taurus* makes any reference to U.S.M. stocks but presumably both TALISMAN and TAURUS will be extended to them in due course?
60 In May 1991 the D.T.I. published a Consultative Document containing over 150 pages of draft Uncertificated Securities Regulations. This came too late for this edition but one comment must be made. If the final version of the Regulations follows this draft, it seems clear that we shall not enjoy, at any rate until many years hence, anything approaching "a completely certificateless securities market." Under the draft, companies which want to join TAURUS must pass a special resolution choosing to do so and may join in respect of some classes of their securities and not others. Hence it seems that, in respect of listed securities, the old and the new systems will operate side-by-side in respect of the same company. Why can we never adopt comprehensive simplifying reforms instead of confusing half-measures?

exceptions in subsections (2) to (4). These are designed to deal with the situations where, under the TALISMAN system, a certificate is not issued to a particular type of transferee[51], or the company is entitled to and does refuse to register a transfer.

Section 186, as substituted by the Companies Act 1989, provides:

"A certificate under the common seal of the company (or, in the case of a company registered in Scotland, subscribed in accordance with section 36B) specifying any shares held by a member is—

    (a) in England and Wales, prima facie evidence, and

    (b) in Scotland, sufficient evidence unless the contrary is shown,

of his title to the shares."

The wording of this is very curious, since it suggests that the section applies only if the certificate is under the common seal. This, however, cannot be correct since section 36A, inserted by the 1989 Act, provides that a company need not have a common seal[62] and that whether it has or not "a document signed by a director and the secretary of the company or by two directors and expressed (in whatever form of words) to be executed by the company has the same effect as if executed under the common seal of the company."[63] Moreover, section 40 (as amended by the 1989 Act) enables a company, which has a common seal, instead to use for sealing documents evidencing securities, an "official" seal which is the replica of its common seal with the addition of the word "Securities." Hence the section 186 applies so long as the certificate is authenticated as executed by the company by the use of the common seal, the official seal or signatures of two directors or one director and the secretary (or, in the case of Scottish companies, under the still wider provisions of section 36B).[64]

Since, like the membership register, a share certificate is prima facie evidence only, it is far from being a document of title in the sense that a share warrant is. Where there is a conflict between the register and the certificate, the former is stronger prima facie evidence than the latter but neither is decisive; ownership of the shares depends on who is *entitled* to be registered. Suppose, say, that A, who is registered and is entitled to be registered, loses his

61 *e.g.* SEPON. Nor need a certificate be issued if shares are allotted to another recognised investment exchange or its clearing house: s.185(4).
62 s.36A(3). This was part of the general abolition of the need for deeds to be sealed: s.1 of the Law of Property (Miscellaneous Provisions) Act 1989.
63 s.36A(4). There are comparable provisions for Scotland in s.36B which require only signature by a director, the secretary, or any person authorised to subscribe so long as the signature is witnessed. The other differences between English and Scottish law in this respect appear to be terminological only.
64 But why this could not have been stated more clearly is baffling.

certificate, obtains a duplicate from the company[65] and transfers to B who is registered by the company. Subsequently A finds the original certificate and, either because he has forgotten about the sale to B or because he is a rogue, then purports to sell the shares to C. The company will rightly refuse to register C whose only remedy will be against A (who may by this time be a man-of-straw) unless he can successfully invoke against the company the so-called doctrine of *estoppel by share certificate.*

A share certificate will contain two statements on which the company will know that reliance may be placed. The first is the extent to which the shares to which it relates are paid up. The second is that the person named in it was registered as the holder of the stated number of shares. The company may be estopped from denying either statement if someone in reliance upon it has changed his position to his detriment. This will rarely benefit an original recipient of the incorrect certificate because receipt of his certificate normally marks the conclusion of the transaction and is not something on which he relied in deciding to enter into it and because he should be aware of the true facts. But in exceptional circumstances it may do so.[66] More commonly it may afford a transferee who, in reliance on the transferor's share certificate, has bought what he believed, wrongly, to be fully-paid shares a defence if the company makes a call upon him.[67] The company will also be estopped if the transferee has relied on a false statement in his transferor's certificate that the transferor was the registered holder of the shares on the date stated in the certificate.[68] But the certificate is not a statement that the named shareholder has continued to be a shareholder since that date.[69] Hence the company will not be estopped in the example given above; it has not made any false statement.

[65] Companies do this readily enough so long as the registered holder makes a statutory declaration regarding the loss and supplies the company with a bank indemnity against any liability it may incur. Since the risk is negligible (see below, n. 69) and what banks charge for this service is not, this must be a profitable activity for the banks.

[66] In *Balkis Consolidated Co. v. Tomkinson* [1893] A.C. 396, H.L., the facts were similar to the example in the text, except that the company (wrongly) issued a certificate to C but (rightly) did not put him on the register. When C tried to sell the shares to D the company (rightly) refused to register the transfer to D, and C, to complete his bargain, had to buy other shares in the company. It was held that C could recover from the company the price he had paid.

[67] *Burkinshaw v. Nicholls* (1878) 3 App.Cas. 1004, H.L.; *Bloomenthal v. Ford* [1897] A.C. 156 H.L. If the reason why the shares were not fully paid up is because of a contravention of the provisions regarding payment in ss.97 *et seq.* of the Act (see Chap. 9 above at p. 202) a bona fide purchaser and those securing title from him will be exempted from liability to pay calls by virtue of s.112(3) and will not have to rely on estoppel.

[68] *Dixon v. Kennaway & Co.* [1900] 1 Ch. 833. This, in contrast with resisting a call, may seem to be committing the heresy of using estoppel as a sword rather than a shield. The justification is that a purchaser who has bought from the registered owner has a prima facie right to be registered in his place and that the company is estopped from denying that the transferor was the registered owner.

[69] *Rainford v. James Keith & Blackman Ltd.* [1905] 2 Ch. 147, C.A. "The only representation is that at the date of the certificate the person named therein was the

Already the estoppel doctrine has little or no relevance to transactions on The Stock Exchange under the TALISMAN system; The Exchange and the member firms will ensure that the parties get what they have bargained for. And when TAURUS is in operation, it will cease, with the disappearance of share certificates,[70] to have any relevance to off-market dealings in listed shares of companies which have joined TAURUS.[71]

Certification of transfers

If only to explain what section 184 of the Act is all about a brief reference is needed to a further aspect of the present system. A seller will be unwilling to part with the transfer and share certificate until the buyer has paid the price but an off-market buyer will be unwilling to pay until he gets both documents. This presents no problem if the seller has a certificate or certificates representing the precise amount sold to a single buyer. There is a difficulty, however, if the seller is disposing of only part of his holding represented by a certificate or if he is disposing of all his holding but to several buyers. To solve the problem a practice grew up of lodging the certificate or certificates with the company or its registrars who endorsed each transfer with a statement that certificates covering the transaction had been lodged. Delivery of a certificated transfer is treated by a buyer and by the company as equivalent to delivery of a transfer and the relevant certificate. On registration by the company a buyer receives a new certificate and the seller a balance certificate for any shares he retains.

Unfortunately confidence in this practice was somewhat sapped when the House of Lords decided that, if the officer of the company who certified the transfer did so fraudulently and for his own purposes when sufficient share certificates had not in fact been lodged, the company was not liable.[72] However an attempt was made to restore confidence in it by what is now section 184. This makes it clear that certification, like a share certificate, is not a representation that the transferor has title to the shares[73] but is a representation that certificates covering the transaction had been lodged.

70 "The private investor will no longer need to safeguard certificates or pay indemnity fees for duplicates if they are lost": *Project Taurus* at p. 10.
71 But just as banks may be estopped from denying the accuracy of bank statements so, presumably, might an "account operator" if it gave an inaccurate statement of an investor's account on which he acted to his detriment.
72 *George Whitechurch Ltd.* v. *Cavanagh* [1902] A.C. 117, H.L. The decision appears to have been based upon the prevailing belief at the time that an agent or servant so acting would necessarily be doing so outside the scope of his employment and his actual or apparent authority. That belief was later shown to be mistaken in *Lloyd* v. *Grace Smith & Co.* [1912] A.C. 716, H.L. However, when, in relation to certification, the question was again taken to the H.L. in 1934 it held that it was bound to follow its previous decision in the *Whitechurch* case: *Kleinwort, Sons & Co.* v. *Associated Automotive Machine Corpn.* (1934) 50 T.L.R. 244, H.L.
73 s.184(1).

representation that certificates have been produced to the company showing a prima facie title and that the company will be liable to compensate any person who acts on the faith of it, provided that it was issued by someone authorised by the company to issue certificated transfers and was signed by someone authorised to sign.[74]

Restrictions on transferability

Of far greater practical importance are questions which may arise when the company's articles of association impose restrictions on the freedom of transferability of its shares. Except in relation to partly paid shares this is unlikely in the case of public companies[75]; but is almost invariably done in relation to private companies. Generally, the directors will be empowered to refuse to register transfers and frequently this will be accompanied by provisions affording the other members or the company[76] rights of pre-emption, first refusal or even compulsory acquisition. Such provisions require the most careful drafting if they are to achieve their purpose; and have not always received it, thereby facing the courts with difficult questions of interpretation. However, the following propositions can, it is thought be extracted from the voluminous case law.

(a) The extent of the restriction is solely a matter of construction of the articles of association. But, since shareholders have a prima facie right to transfer to whomsoever they please, this right is not to be cut down by uncertain language or doubtful implications.[77] If, therefore, it is not clear whether a restriction applies to any transfer or only to a transfer to, say, a non-member,[78] or to any type of disposition or only to a sale[79] the narrower construction will be adopted.

(b) On the other hand the courts will not carry a literal construction of the articles so far as to defeat their obvious purpose. In one case[80] the articles conferred a right of pre-emption on the other shareholders when any shareholder was "desirous of transferring his ordinary shares." Certain shareholders sold their shares to a take-over bidder, received the purchase price and gave him irrevocable proxies to vote on their behalf, but, in the light of the

---

[74] s.184(2) & (3). The text attempts accurately to summarise the singularly tortuous subsections. If, as the wording suggests, the persons concerned must have *actual* authority the position is still less than satisfactory.
[75] See n. 48 above.
[76] Acquisition by the company itself will, of course, be lawful only if it is able to comply with the conditions enabling a private company to buy its own shares: see above Chap. 9 at pp. 217–226. Less usually the provision may impose an *obligation* on other members to buy.
[77] Per Greene M.R. in *Re Smith & Fawcett Ltd.* [1942] Ch. 304, C.A., at p. 306.
[78] *Greenhalgh v. Mallard* [1943] 2 All E.R. 234, C.A.; *Roberts v. Letter "T" Estates Ltd.* [1961] A.C. 795, P.C.
[79] *Moodie v. Shepherd (Bookbinders) Ltd.* [1949] 2 All E.R. 1044 H.L.Sc.
[80] *Lyle & Scott Ltd. v. Scott's Trustees* [1959] A.C. 763, H.L.Sc.

articles, transfers were not to be lodged for registration. The House of Lords held that in the context "transferring" obviously meant assigning the beneficial interest and not the technical process of having a transfer registered.[81] The shareholders had clearly manifested an intention to sell their shares and could not continue with the sale without giving the other shareholders a right to exercise their option under the articles. But this decision was distinguished in a later case[82] where, in all relevant respects, the wording of the article was similar but the shares were held by the executors of a deceased shareholder. The administration of the estate was completed and the executors now held the shares as bare trustees for two beneficiaries. Neither had any wish that the shares should be transferred to him but it was argued that, on the basis of the House of Lords' decision, the passing of the beneficial interest to them was a "transfer" of which notice should have been given, thus entitling other members to acquire the shares at a fair price. Vinelott J. and the Court of Appeal refused to construe the provisions as extending to that situation.

(c) Where the regulations confer a discretion on directors with regard to the acceptance of transfers, this discretion, like all the directors' powers, is a fiduciary one[83] to be exercised bona fide in what they consider—not what the court considers—to be in the interest of the company, and not for any collateral purpose. But the court will presume that they have acted bona fide, and the onus of proof of the contrary is on those alleging it and is not easily discharged.[84]

(d) If, on the true construction of the articles, the directors are entitled to reject only on certain prescribed grounds and it is proved that they have rejected on others, the court will intervene.[85] And interrogatories may be administered to determine on which of certain prescribed grounds the directors have acted, but not as to their reasons for rejecting on these grounds,[86] and not if the articles provide, as they often do, that they shall not be bound to state their reasons.[87] If the directors do state their reasons the court will investigate them to the extent of seeing whether they have acted on the right principles and will overrule their decision if they have acted on considerations which should not have weighed with them, but not merely because the court would have come to a different

---

81 This distinction is all too often overlooked in the drafting of the relevant article.
82 *Safeguard Ltd.* v. *Nat. West Bank* [1981] 1 W.L.R. 286, [1982] 1 W.L.R. 589, C.A.
83 For a fuller discussion of director's fiduciary duties, see Chap. 21 below.
84 In *Re Smith & Fawcett Ltd.* above, the directors refused to register but agreed that they would register a transfer of part of the shareholding if the transferor agreed to sell the balance to one of the directors at a stated price. It was held that this was insufficient evidence of bad faith but it might today be "unfairly prejudicial" under s.459: see Chap. 24 below.
85 *Re Bede Steam Shipping Co.* [1917] 1 Ch. 123, C.A.
86 *Sutherland* v. *British Dominions Corpn.* [1926] Ch. 746.
87 *Berry & Stewart* v. *Tottenham Hotspur Football Co.* [1935] Ch. 718.

conclusion.[88] If the regulations are so framed as to give the directors an unfettered discretion the court will interfere with it only on proof of bad faith[89] and since the directors will not be bound to disclose either their grounds or their reasons, the difficulty of discharging the onus of proof is especially great.

(e) If, as is normal, the regulations merely give the directors power to refuse to register, as opposed to making their passing of transfers a condition precedent to registration,[90] the transferee is entitled to be registered unless the directors resolve as a board to reject. Hence in *Moodie v. Shepherd (Bookbinders) Ltd.*[91] where the two directors disagreed and neither had a casting vote, the House of Lords held that registration must proceed. The directors have a reasonable time in which to come to a decision,[92] but since section 183(5) of the Act imposes an obligation on them to give to the transferee notice of rejection within two months of the lodging of the transfer, the maximum reasonable period is two months.[93]

The positions of transferor and transferee prior to registration

In the case of an off-market transaction it may be of importance to determine the precise legal position of the transferor and transferee pending registration of the transfer which, if there are restrictions on transferability may never occur. As we have seen, only if and when the transfer is registered, will the transferor cease to be a member and shareholder and the transferee will become a member and shareholder. However, notwithstanding that registration has not occurred, the beneficial interest in the shares may have passed from the transferor to the transferee. In the case of a sale the transaction will normally go through three stages:– (1) an agreement (which, particularly if a block of shares conferring de facto or de jure control is being sold, may be a complicated one) (2) delivery of the signed transfer and the certificate by the seller and payment of the price by the buyer and (3) lodgment of the transfer for registration by the company. Notwithstanding that the transfer is not lodged for

[88] *Re Bede Steam Shipping Co.,* above; *Re Smith & Fawcett Ltd.,* above. Indeed, if there are rights of pre-emption at a fair price to be determined by the auditors the court can investigate the adequacy of this price only if the auditors give a "speaking valuation" stating their reasons: *Dean v. Prince* [1954] Ch. 409, C.A.; *Burgess v. Purchase & Sons Ltd.* [1983] Ch. 216.
[89] *Re Smith & Fawcett Ltd.,* above; *Charles Forte Investments Ltd. v. Amanda* [1964] Ch. 240.
[90] It is common to state that transfers have to be passed by the directors but under normal articles that is not so (see, *e.g.* Table A arts. 24 and 25) and in the light of s.183(4) and (5) it is doubtful if the articles could make the directors' approval a condition precedent.
[91] [1949] 2 All E.R. 1044, H.L.Sc.
[92] *Shepherd's Case* (1866) L.R. 2 Ch.App. 16.
[93] *Re Swaledale Cleaners Ltd.* [1968] 1 W.L.R. 1710, C.A. And normally it seems that they will not be treated as acting unreasonably if they take the full two months: *Re Zinotty Properties Ltd.* [1984] 1 W.L.R. 1249 at 1260.

registration or registration is refused, the beneficial interest in the shares will, it seems, pass from the seller to the buyer at the latest at stage (2) and, indeed will do so at stage (1) if the agreement is one which the courts would order to be specifically enforced.[94] The seller then becomes a trustee for the buyer and must account to him for any dividends he receives and vote in accordance with his instructions (or appoint him as his proxy).[95] This, however, begs several questions. The first arises because at stage (2) delivery of the documents may not necessarily be matched by payment of the full price; the agreement may have provided for payment by instalments[96] and the seller will then retain a lien on the shares as an unpaid seller. This will not prevent an equitable interest passing to the buyer but the court will not grant specific performance unless the seller's lien can be fully protected[97] and until paid in full he is entitled to vote the shares as he thinks will best protect his interest.[98] Instead of being a bare trustee his position is analogous to that of a trustee of a settlement of which he is one of the beneficiaries.

The second begged question is whether the foregoing can apply when the articles provide for rights of pre-emption or first refusal when a shareholder wishes to dispose of his shares. In such a case the transferor (perhaps with the full knowledge of the transferee[99]) has breached the deemed contract under section 14 between him and the company and his fellow shareholders. There are observations of the House of Lords in *Hunter* v. *Hunter*[1] to the effect that accordingly the transfer is wholly void even as between the transferor and transferee. However, in two later cases[2] courts have refused to follow this and, it must surely be right (at any rate if the price has been paid) that the buyer obtains such rights as the transferor had. This will not benefit the buyer if all the shares are taken up when the transferor is compelled to make a pre-emptive offer, but it does not

[94] The fact that the agreement is subject to fulfilment of a condition beyond the control of the parties will not prevent it from being specifically enforceable, notwithstanding that the condition has not been fulfilled, if the party for whose benefit the condition was inserted is prepared to waive it. In *Wood Preservation Ltd.* v. *Prior* [1969] 1 W.L.R. 1077, C.A., where the condition was for the benefit of the buyer, the court was prepared to hold that the seller ceased to be "the beneficial owner" on the date of the contract notwithstanding that the buyer did not become the beneficial owner until he later waived the condition. In the interim, beneficial ownership was, apparently, in limbo!

[95] *Hardoon* v. *Belilios* [1901] A.C. 118, P.C.

[96] The normal practice then is to provide that the transfer and share certificate shall be held by a stake-holder and not lodged for registration until released to the buyer on payment of the final instalment.

[97] *Langen & Wind Ltd.* v. *Bell* [1972] Ch. 685.

[98] As in *Lyle & Scott Ltd.* v. *Scott's Trustees* [1959] A.C. 763, H.L.Sc., above n. 80.

[99] *Musselwhite* v. *Musselwhite & Son Ltd.* [1962] Ch. 964.

[1] [1936] A.C. 222 H.L.

[2] *Hawks* v. *McArthur* [1951] 1 All E.R. 22; *Tett* v. *Phoenix Property Co.* [1986] BCLC 149, where the C.A. was not required to rule on this point because the appellants did not argue that the decision on it at first instance was wrong.

follow that all of them will be taken up and, if not, the transferee has a better claim to those shares not taken up than has the transferor.

When the transaction is not a sale but a gift there need be no agreement. Even if there is, it will not be legally enforceable under English law because there will be no valuable consideration and because under the so-called rule in *Milroy v. Lord*[3] "there is no equity to perfect an imperfect gift." One might have supposed, therefore, that if the donor has chosen to make the gift by handing to the donee a signed transfer and the share certificate, rather than by a formal declaration of trust in favour of the donee, the gift would not be effective unless and until the transfer was registered. In two modern cases,[4] however, it has been held that so long as the donor has done all he needs to do, the beneficial interest passes from him to the donee.[5]

Priorities between competing transferees

In the case of off-market transactions questions may also arise in determining the priority of purported transfers of the same shares to different people. In answering these questions the courts[6] have relied on two traditional principles of English property law: *i.e.* (1) that as between two competing holders of equitable interests, if their equities are equal the first in time prevails and (2) that a bona fide purchaser for value of a legal interest takes free of earlier equitable interests of which he as no notice at the time of purchase. In applying these principles to competing share transfers, a transferee prior to registration is treated as having an equitable interest only but registration converts his interest into a legal one.[7] Hence if a registered shareholder, A, first executes a transfer to a purchaser, B, and later to another, C, while both remain unregistered B will have priority over C. If, however, C succeeds in obtaining registration before B, he will have priority over B so long as he had no notice, at the time of purchase, of the transfer to B. If C did have notice, although he has been registered his prima facie title will not prevail over that of B who will be entitled to have the register rectified (assuming that there are no grounds on which the company could

---

3 (1862) 4 De G., F. and J. 264.

4 Both, purely coincidentally apparently, named *Re Rose*, respectively reported in [1949] Ch. 78 and [1952] Ch. 499, C.A.

5 Thus, until the transfer is registered, placing the donee in the same position as if the donor had instead made a declaration of trust.

6 The leading cases are *Shropshire Union Ry. v. R.* (1875) L.R. 7 H.L. 496; *Société Generale v. Walker* (1885) 11 App.Cas. 20, H.L.; *Colonial Bank v. Cady* (1890) 15 App.Cas. 267, H.L. Among more recent decisions, see *Hawks v. McArthur*, above n. 2, and *Champagne Perrier-Jouet v. Finch & Co.* below n. 18.

7 Notwithstanding a suggestion by Lord Selbourne (in *Société Generale v. Walker*, above, at p. 28) that "a present absolute right to have the transfer registered" might suffice, it seems that nothing less than actual registration will do. In *Ireland v. Hart* [1902] 1 Ch. 521 the transfer had been lodged for registration and the directors had no power to refuse but it was held that the legal interest had not passed.

refuse to register B) and in the meantime C's legal interest will be subject to the equitable interest of B.[8] If both transfers were gifts, the position would presumably be different; the gift to B[9] would leave A without any beneficial interest that he could give to C and, not being a "purchaser," C could not obtain priority by registration; his legal interest, on his becoming the registered holder, would be subject to the prior equity of B.

It should perhaps be pointed out once again that even registration affords only prima facie evidence of title. If the registered transferor, A, was not entitled to the shares, what will pass when he transfers to B or C is not, strictly speaking, either a legal or equitable interest but only his imperfect title to it which will not prevail against the true owner. If, for example, the transfer to A was a forgery the true owner will be entitled to be restored to the register.[10] Hence a transferee can never be certain of obtaining an absolute title in the case of an off-market transaction. But his risk is slight so long as he promptly obtains registration of the transfer. And this he can do unless there are restrictions on the transferability of the shares or unless there are good reasons for failing to apply for registration.

The principal example for the latter occurs when the shareholder wants to borrow on the security of his shares. This can be done by a legal mortgage, under which the shareholder transfers the shares to the lender (who registers the transfer) subject to an agreement to re-transfer them when the loan is repaid. Generally, however, this suits neither party; the lender normally has no wish to become a member and shareholder of the company and the borrower does not want to cease to be one. Hence a more usual arrangement is one whereby the shareholder deposits with the lender his share certificate and, often, a signed blank transfer, this usually being accompanied by a written memorandum setting out the terms of the loan. The result is to confer an equitable charge which the lender can enforce by selling the shares if he needs to realise his security. Custody of the share certificate is regarded as the essential protection of the lender[11] and it is not clear precisely how continuation of this popular method of providing security will be practicable in relation to uncertificated

---

[8] *France v. Clark* (1884) 26 Ch.D. 257, C.A.; *Earl of Sheffield v. London Joint Stock Bank* (1888) 13 App.Cas. 332, H.L.; *Ranford v. James Keith & Blackman* [1905] 2 Ch. 147, C.A.

[9] So long as it has been "perfected"—as interpreted in the two *Re Rose* cases: see above p. 400 n. 4.

[10] The transferee will have no remedy against the company based on estoppel by share certificate: it made no false statement: see p. 394 above. The Forged Transfers Acts 1891 and 1892 enabled companies to adopt fee-financed arrangements for compensating innocent victims of forged transfers but this is purely voluntary and seems to have been virtually a dead-letter since its inception.

[11] Banks usually grant their clients overdrafts on the security of an equitable charge by a deposit of share certificates without requiring signed blank transfers.

[12] Shares not listed or dealt in on the U.S.M. are rarely accepted as security for loans because of their illiquidity and, usually, restrictions on their transferability. Banks will instead want a charge on the undertaking and assets of the company itself plus, probably, personal guarantees of the members or directors.

listed securities[12] on the introduction of TAURUS[13]—short of repealing section 360 of the Act and requiring "account operators" to note equitable interests.[14] If that were done the lender's protection would be enhanced.

The Company's lien

As we have seen,[15] a public company is no longer permitted to have a charge or lien on its shares except (a) when the shares are not fully paid and the charge or lien is for the amount payable on the shares, or (b) the ordinary business of the company includes the lending of money or consists of the provision of hire-purchase finance and the charge arises in the course of a transaction in the ordinary course of its business. Neither exception is of much importance in the present context. Hence it is only in respect of private companies that problems are still likely to arise when their articles provide, as they frequently do, that "the company shall have a first and paramount lien on shares, whether or not fully-paid, registered in the name of a person indebted or under any liability to the company." Since the decision of the House of Lords in *Bradford Banking Co. v. Briggs, Son and Co.*[16] it appears to be accepted that the effect of such a provision is that:

(a) Once a shareholder has incurred a debt or liability to the company, it has an equitable charge on the shares of that shareholder to secure payment which ranks in priority to later equitable interests and, it seems to earlier ones of which the company had no notice when its lien became effective; and (b) in determining whether the company had notice,[17] section 360 has no application; if the company knows of the earlier equitable interest (because, for example, a transfer of the shares has been lodged for registration even if that is refused) it cannot improve its own position to the detriment of the holder of that known equitable interest.

---

[13] Unless something is done to preserve this simple (and relatively inexpensive) method of mortgaging shares TAURUS despite its many advantages, will not be loved by private investors. The D.T.I.'s Consultative Document (see p. 392 n. 60 above) tackles this in draft reg. 77 but query whether the result will satisfy both lender and borrower.

[14] At present a company will reject any notice to it, pointing to s.360 (see above p. 387) and to its common-form article worded even more widely: see Table A 1985, art. 5 (which, however, seems to add nothing to the courts' interpretation of the section). There is a procedure under R.S.C. Ord. 50 (revised, in the light of the Charging Orders Act 1979, by the Supreme Court (Amendment) Rules, S.I. 1980 No. 629 and S.I. 1982, No. 111) whereby holders of equitable interests can require a company to give them notice of any application to register a transfer of the shares and enabling them to apply to the court. But little use seems to be made of this by equitable chargees.

[15] Chap. 9 at p. 241 above.

[16] (1886) 12 App.Cas. 29, H.L.

[17] It is not altogether clear why notice should be relevant. Since the company's lien is merely an equitable interest, its priority vis-à-vis another equitable interest should depend on the respective dates of their creation. But the decisions seem to assume that the company's lien will have priority over an equitable interest if the company has not received notice of the latter.

An interesting modern illustration is afforded by *Champagne Perrier-Jouet* v. *Finch & Co.*[18] There the company's articles provided for a lien in the above terms. One of its shareholders[19] had been allowed to run up substantial debts to the company resulting from trading between him and the company and it had been agreed that he could repay by instalments. Another creditor of the shareholder subsequently obtained judgment against him and a charging order on the shares by way of equitable execution. It was held that the company's lien had become effective when the debts to it were incurred (even though they were not then due for repayment) and as this occurred before the company had notice of the charging order,[20] the company's lien had priority.[21]

As this case shows, an equitable charge on shares in a private company with articles conferring a lien on the company is likely to be an even more undesirable form of security than shares in private companies always are. It may, however, be the only security obtainable, for an attempt to obtain a legal charge will almost certainly be frustrated by the refusal of the directors to register the transfer. If, *faute-de-mieux*, it has to be accepted, notice should immediately be given to the company, making it clear that this is a notice which it cannot disregard in relation to any lien it may claim, and an attempt should be made to obtain information about the amount, if any, then owed to the company.

Transmission of shares by operation of law

The Act[22] recognises that shares may be transmitted by operation of law and that, when this occurs, the prohibition on registering unless a proper instrument of transfer has been delivered does not apply.[23] The principal examples of this are when a registered shareholder (a) dies or (b) becomes bankrupt. As regards (a), the Act further provides that a transfer by the deceased's personal representative, even if he is not a member of the company, is as valid as if he had been.[24] The company is bound to accept probate or letters of administration granted in any part of the United Kingdom

18 [1982] 1 W.L.R. 1359.
19 He had also been a director and it was argued that the debt he incurred to the company was a loan unlawful under what is now s.330(1) so that the company could not have a valid lien. It was held that it was not a loan; it would, however, today be "a quasi-loan" as defined in s.331 and as such unlawful if the company was a "relevant company," (*e.g.* a subsidiary of a public company) as defined in s.331.
20 It also ante-dated the charging order but the court seems to have regarded the date of notice as decisive: see at p. 1367 B-E.
21 It was also held that if the company enforced its lien by selling the shares it would have to comply with provisions in the articles conferring pre-emptive rights on the other members of the company.
22 And see Table A 1985, arts. 29-31.
23 s.183(2).
24 s.183(3).

as sufficient evidence of the personal representative's entitlement.[25] However, he does not become a member unless he elects to apply to be registered and is registered as a member. In the meantime, the effect is, as Table A, article 31 puts it, that he has

"the rights to which he would be entitled if he were the holder of the share, except that he shall not, before being registered as the holder of the share, be entitled in respect of it to attend or vote at any general meeting of the company or at a separate meeting of the holders of any class of shares in the company."

If the shares are those if a listed company this anomalous position can be ended rapidly because, unless the shares are not fully paid, there will not be any restrictions on transferability and the personal representative will either obtain registration of himself or execute a transfer to a purchaser or to the beneficiaries. In relation to a private company, however, it may continue indefinitely and prove detrimental to the personal representative, the deceased's estate and sometimes, the company. The personal representative may suffer because it may not be possible for him fully to wind up the estate and to obtain a discharge from his fiduciary responsibilities. The estate may suffer because it may be impossible for the personal representative to sell the shares at their true value, especially if any attempt to dispose of them would trigger rights of pre-emption or first refusal.[26] The company may suffer because, as we have seen,[27] unless such rights have been most carefully drafted, they will not come into operation so long as no action regarding registration is taken by the personal representative and because, if the company had only two members and directors, the death of one may mean that no quorate meetings can be held,[28] and the company may face a petition to wind it up.[29] Clearly in relation to private companies

---

[25] s.187. If it does so without such production of the grant it may become liable for any tax payable as a result of the transmission (*NY Breweries Co. v. Att.-Gen.* [1899] A.C. 62, H.L.) but in the case of small estates, companies may be prepared to dispense with production of a grant if the Revenue confirms that nothing is payable. If the deceased was one of a number of jointly registered members, the company, on production of a death certificate will have to recognise that he has ceased to be a member and shareholder and that the others remain such. But the whole beneficial interest in the shares will not pass to them unless they and the deceased were beneficial owners entitled jointly rather than in common.

[26] If there are any restrictions on transfers when Table A, art. 30 applies, all the articles relating to restriction on transfers apply both to a notice that the personal representative wishes to be registered and to a transfer from him.

[27] *Safeguard Ltd. v. Nat. West Bank,* above p. 397 n. 82.

[28] This might benefit the personal representative and the estate if the only restriction was a power of the directors to refuse to register transfers, for, if no directors' meeting could be held, transfers lodged by the personal representative or a transferee from him would be entitled to registration after two months of application: see *Re Swaledale Cleaners Ltd. v. Re Zinotty Properties Ltd.* above p. 398 n. 93.

[29] Under the Insolvency Act 1986, s.122(1)(e).

reform of this branch of the law is urgently needed. At the least, this should include an obligation on directors who refuse to register personal representatives or transferees from them to state their reasons.[30] All that statutory reforms have done as yet is to make piecemeal extensions of the remedies afforded to members so that they can be invoked by personal representatives of members.[31]

The position on bankruptcy of an individual shareholder[32] is broadly similar. His rights to the shares will automatically vest in the trustee in bankruptcy as part of his estate.[33] But, as in the case of a personal representative, until he elects to become registered and is, he will not become a member of the company entitled to attend meetings and to vote. In contrast, however, with the position on the death of a member, the bankrupt will remain a member and be entitled to attend and vote—though he will have to do so in accordance with the directions of the trustee. Hence there will, in this case, be no reduction in the membership of the company. As in the case of personal representatives, the company's articles will probably provide that any restrictions on transferability apply on any application to be registered and to any transfer by him[34] and these restrictions may handicap the trustee in obtaining the best price on a sale of the shares, particularly if the articles confer pre-emption rights.[35] If a personal representative or trustee in bankruptcy elects to be registered, and is, he becomes personally liable for any amounts unpaid on the shares and not merely representationally liable to the extent of the estate. Trustees in bankruptcy, but not personal representatives, may disclaim onerous property,[36] which the shares might be if they were partly paid or subject to an effective company lien.

Applicability to debentures

The foregoing discussion in this chapter has been primarily directed to the acquisition and disposal of shares. But much of it is equally

---

[30] As recommended by the Jenkins Committee (1962) Cmnd. 1749, para. 212(g).

[31] See, in particular, s.459(2), which makes it possible for personal representatives to invoke the "unfairly prejudicial" remedy which might well be effective if it could be shown that the directors were exercising their powers to refuse transfers in order to enable themselves or the company to acquire the shares of deceased members at an unfair price: see Chap. 24 below.

[32] On winding up of a corporate shareholder there is no transmission of the company's property; it remains vested in the company but most of the directors' powers to manage it pass to the liquidator.

[33] Insolvency Act 1986, ss.283(1) and 306. But not if the shareholder held his shares as a trustee for another person: *ibid.* s.283(3)(a).

[34] See Table A, 1985, art. 30. Both this article and art. 31 expressly apply to both personal representatives and trustees in bankruptcy.

[35] In *Borland's Trustee v. Steel Bros.* [1901] 1 Ch. 279, a provision in the articles that in the event of a shareholder's bankruptcy (or death) his shares should be offered to a named person at a particular price was held to be effective and not obnoxious to the bankruptcy laws.

[36] Insolvency Act 1986, s.315. Disclaimer puts an end to the interest of the bankrupt and his estate and discharges the trustee from any liability: *ibid.* s.315(3).

applicable to debentures and many of the statutory provisions expressly apply equally to them, though it is clear that when they do so "debentures", is usually used in its narrow sense of debenture stock or a series of identical debentures and not in its wider meaning of a single mortgage, charge or bond.[37] So far as the former are concerned, the Act (as does the Financial Services Act) assumes that public issues of debentures will be undertaken by the same methods as issues of shares and it provides that a contract to take up debentures, like one to take up shares, may be enforced by an order for specific performance.[38] It also assumes that debentures or debenture stock will be transferred in much the same way as shares. Hence subsections (1), (2), (5) and (6)[39] of section 183 (relating to the need for written transfers, except when the transmission is by operation of law, and to the recognition of personal representatives) expressly apply. So do sections 184 (certification of transfers) and 185 (duty to issue certificates). And estoppel, similar to estoppel by share certificate, clearly could arise from statements in certificates of debenture stock or in debentures.

One could also be faced with problems, similar to those in relation to shares, regarding equitable and legal ownership of debentures and the priority of competing transferees. But the great difference here is the lesser role played by registration. Unlike the membership register a company is not compelled to maintain a register of debenture-holders. The Act assumes that a company probably will maintain a register if it issues debenture stock or a series of debentures and the Act contains provisions, similar to, but not identical with, those relating to the membership register, concerning where the register shall be kept[40] and who shall be entitled to inspect and obtain copies of it.[41] But it says nothing about the register being evidence of ownership, and it is not clear what role, if any, it plays in converting an equitable interest into a legal one. On general principles relating to assignments of choses-in-action, a transfer of a debenture should be an equitable assignment only, until it becomes a legal assignment when the company receives notice of it. In principle, therefore, the legal interest should pass from transferor or transferee when the company is given notice of it, and that date, rather than the later date of actual registration, should be the relevant one in determining its priority over earlier unnotified transfers.

Other differences flow from the fact that whereas the rights of shareholders depend mainly on the provision of the company's articles, which will have been drafted in the interests of the company,

[37] See Chap. 14 at pp. 378–380 above.
[38] s.195.
[39] But not subss. (3) and (4) which relate only to "members" which debenture-holders are not.
[40] s.190.
[41] s.191.

those of debentureholders depend upon the terms of a contract between lender and borrower and its terms will have to be acceptable to the lender. Hence in practice there will be no problems arising from restrictions on transferability or from a company's lien; debentures will invariably provide that the money expressed to be secured will be paid, and that the debentures are transferable, free from any equities or claims between the company and the original or any intermediate holder.[42] Another contrast with shares is that if shares are redeemed or re-purchased by the company they have to be cancelled, whereas the Act provides that, unless it is otherwise agreed, redeemed debentures may be re-issued with their original priority.[43] The great contrast, however, is that debentures secured by charges on the company's property throw up problems regarding the priority between conflicting charges. These problems are dealt with in the next chapter.

[42] Without this, debentureholders and their transferees would be in grave danger, for a debenture, unless in bearer form and thus a negotiable instrument, would, as a chose-in-action, be transferable only subject to the state of the account between the company and the transferor. As stressed throughout this chapter, neither shares (unless in the form of share warrants to bearer) nor debentures (unless bearer bonds) are negotiable instruments like bills of exchange. Although the Admission to Listing Directive requires listed shares and debt securities to be "freely transferable" (Scheds. A & B II 2) this is interpreted as "freely negotiable" and not as prescribing that they must be "negotiable instruments" in the full sense.

[43] s.194. Note subs. (3) which is designed to remove the technical difficulties revealed in *Re Russian Petroleum Co.* [1907] 2 Ch. 540, C.A. when a company secures its overdraft on current account by depositing with the bank a debenture for a fixed amount.

CHAPTER 16*

COMPANY CHARGES

Borrowers are often obliged to provide security for the repayment of their debts and in this respect a company is no different from any other borrower. Almost invariably debentures issued by a company will be secured by a charge over the company's assets. However, there are sufficiently unique features associated with the granting of security by a company that justify it being treated as a separate topic. In particular, the floating charge is practicable only if created by a body corporate,[1] there is a separate system for the registration of company charges,[2] there are distinct statutory procedures for the enforcement of the floating charge,[3] certain provisions of the Insolvency Act 1986 affecting company charges are unique to corporate insolvency,[4] and the floating charge can be used tactically in order to veto the making of an administration order.[5] Coupled with these, the granting of security by a company is subject to the law relating to corporate capacity and director's duties.[6] As regards these latter matters, it will be assumed for the remainder of the chapter, unless the contrary is stated, that a company has capacity to grant the security and that the directors were not acting in breach of their duty to the company or exceeding their authority. Some comment is also needed on nomenclature. "Charge," "security," or "security interest" will be used interchangeably in the sense in which charge is defined in the Companies Act 1985, namely as any form of security, fixed or floating, over a company's property present or future.[7]

THE LEGAL NATURE OF SECURITY INTERESTS

It is necessary to deal briefly with what is a complex area of the law and that is the types of security interests recognised by English law.[8] Some knowledge of this topic is essential in order to understand the nature of the rights conferred on a secured charge holder, the

* *As stated in the Preface, this chapter has been contributed by Professor D.D. Prentice to whom I am deeply indebted. L.C.B.G.*
[1] See pp. 96–97.
[2] See pp. 425 *et seq.*
[3] See pp. 436 *et seq.*
[4] In certain situations there are analogues in the case of personal bankruptcy.
[5] See Insolvency Act 1986, s.9(3) and p. 747 below.
[6] See pp. 166, *et seq.* and Chap. 21.
[7] Companies Act 1985, s.395(2) (introduced by Companies Act 1989, s.93). As will be seen later, "charge" can have a more restricted technical meaning in equity.
[8] There is a considerable volume of literature on this vast and vexed topic. See Oditah, *Legal Aspects of Receivables Financing*, Chap. 1 and Goode, *Commercial Law*, Chap. 25 for helpful analyses.

priorities of charges, and the system for the registration of company charges. Although a number of security interests are clearly accepted as being recognised by English law, there is some doubt at the penumbra as to what constitutes a security interest and, in particular, as to whether there is a *numerus clausus* of such interests. Browne-Wilkinson V.-C., without claiming that it was comprehensive, accepted the following as a description of a security interest:

"Security is created where a person ('the creditor') to whom an obligation is owed by another ('the debtor') by statute or contract, in addition to the personal promise of the debtor to discharge the obligation, obtains rights exercisable against some property in which the debtor has an interest in order to enforce the discharge of the debtor's obligation to the creditor."[9]

This brings out what is perhaps the essential feature of a security interest, namely, that ultimately it gives the holder of the security a proprietary claim over assets, normally the debtor's, to secure payment of the debt. The position of a secured creditor is to be contrasted with that of an unsecured creditor who merely has a personal claim to sue for the payment of his debt and to invoke the available legal processes for the enforcement of any judgment that he may obtain.[10]

Security interests can be divided broadly into consensual and non-consensual securities. As the name implies, consensual security interests arise by way of agreement of the parties. There is general acceptance that as regards consensual security English law recognises at least the following: the mortgage, the charge, the pledge and the lien.[11] In contrast to consensual security interests are those security interests that arise by operation of law. The classification of this category is not free from difficulty but it includes at least a common law lien and a lien arising by operation of law.[12]

It is not possible in a text of this nature to go into the details of security interests in any great depth but a number of questions arise with respect to the creation of such interests by a company.

9 *Bristol Airport Plc. v. Powdrill* [1990] Ch. 744 at 760. The only significant refinement that one might want to add to this description is that the property of a third party can also be made available by way of security. See also *Re Curtain Dream plc.* [1990] BCLC 925 at 935-937; *Welsh Development Agency v. Export Finance Co. Ltd.* [1992] BCLC 148; Insolvency Act 1986, s.248.
10 See Goode, *op. cit.*, at 710-711. An unsecured creditor may be able to invoke certain types of court procedures which make a party's assets security for his claim: for the nature of these procedural securities see Goode, *op. cit.*, at 732-733.
11 See Bell, *Modern Law of Personal Property in England and Ireland*, Chap. 5; Oditah, *op. cit.*, at 85-88; Goode, *Legal Problems of Credit and Security* (2nd. ed.), at 10-15.
12 Bell, *op. cit.*, at 138-141. Section 246 of the Insolvency Act 1986 deprives certain types of merely possessory liens of effect against an administrator or liquidator; *Re Aveling Barford Ltd.* [1989] 1 W.L.R. 360 at 364-355

(i)   First, is the charge fixed or floating? An example of the fixed charge is the mortgage and no more need be said about it here. The floating charge will be dealt with later.

(ii)   Second, is the interest created by the charge equitable or legal? This has a bearing on the priorities of different chargees and of course the equitable charge holder can be defeated by the bona fide purchaser for value

(iii) Third, is the security interest possession in the sense that possession, either actual or constructive, of the property subject to the security is necessary in order to confer a security interest on the security holder? Obviously, if all security interests were possessory it would make secured borrowing virtually impossible as a debtor would be deprived of the ability to use the assets subject to the security in the course of business (but English law has for long recognised non-possessory security interests). The classic example of a possessory security is the pledge which involves the pledgee (the security holder) taking possession of the goods of the debtor (the pledgor) until the debt is paid or the pledgee takes steps to enforce the pledge. The lien also in many situations is possessory although it is possible to have a non-possessory lien.

(iv)   Fourth, what type of "proprietary" interest is vested in the chargee by the charge? This has a direct bearing as to remedies. The remedies of the floating charge holder will be dealt with in greater detail later. But some brief comment is needed on the remedies available to the holders of other types of security interests. First is to be contrasted the mortgage and the charge and in this context charge is being used in its technical meaning and not in the broader sense set out at the beginning of this chapter. Although the words "charge" and "mortgage" are often used interchangeably, there is technically an essential difference between them: "a mortgage involves a conveyance of property subject to a right of redemption, whereas a charge conveys nothing and merely gives the chargee certain rights over the property as security for the loan."[13] The essential difference between an equitable charge and a mortgage is as regards remedies; since a charge, unlike the mortgage, does not involve a conveyance of a proprietary interest, a chargee cannot foreclose or take possession. The remedy of a chargee is to apply to the court for an order for sale or for the appointment of a receiver.[14]

[13] See *Re Bond Worth Ltd.* [1980] Ch. 228 at 250. Such a charge is however a present existing charge. For some of the difficulties in distinguishing an equitable charge from a mortgage in terms of the quality of the security granted see Oditah, *op. cit.*, at 94–96.

[14] See Megarry and Wade, *The Law of Real Property* (5th ed.) at 953. The point is that a chargee does not have an estate.

The principal remedy of a pledgee is that of sale of the pledged goods and he can also sub-pledge the goods.[15] A lien holder merely has the right to detain the goods subject to the lien until the debt has been paid.[16]

(v) Fifth, is the security interest one that is created by the act of the parties or is it one created by operation of law? This point has already been referred to above. It is of critical importance with respect to the registration of company charges since charges created by a company over its assets are treated differently from charges over a company's assets arising other than by the creation of the company. This point will be dealt with in greater detail later.

(vi) Lastly, is the charge registrable under the provisions for the registration of company charges. Again this will be dealt with in greater detail later.

The above is a very compressed survey of what constitutes a security interest. To complicate the picture even further, there are a number of other devices which, although not strictly security interests in the sense of vesting some type of proprietary interest in the creditor or which give him possessory control over assets of the debtor company, nevertheless act as security. These devices often put a creditor in a position superior to that of other unsecured creditors in the event of a company's insolvent liquidation. Two illustrative examples of such devices are (i) the negative pledge clause in unsecured lending and (ii) retention of title by a seller of goods. The first of these is an agreement by a debtor company and its unsecured creditor that the company will not create any securities which have priority to the claim of the creditor. Although this does not vest a security interest in the creditor, it has been claimed (rightly) that it "behaves"[17] like a security interest since it is an attempt to preclude the debtor from freely using its assets and thus, as with a security interest, it provides the creditor with a measure of protection. The retention of title is an arrangement whereby the seller of goods retains title to the goods until at least the buyer of the goods pays for them.[18] Some of the problems raised by this type of security will be dealt with later in the discussion on registration.[19]

---

[15] See Bell, *op. cit.*, at pp. 136–137.

[16] The lienee will normally have the right to sell by contract and where this is the case some argue that it is tantamount to a pledge. Other charge holders may of course take subject to the lien: *George Barker (Transport) Ltd. v. Eynon* [1974] 1 W.L.R. 462.

[17] See Oditah, *op. cit.*, at 11. For a list of other types of quasi-security interests see Oditah, *ibid.*, at 11. See also Goode, *op. cit.*, Chap. 25.

[18] See generally, McCormack, *Reservation of Title*. This, rightly it is submitted, is seen as a matter of commercial substance as being a chattel mortgage securing a loan: Diamond, *A Review of Security Interests In Property* (DTI, 1989), at para. 3.6; *Welsh Development Agency v. Export Finance Co. Ltd.* [1991] BCLC 936 at 950; [1992] BCLC 148.

[19] There are also self-help remedies such as set-off, abatement, rejection of goods and forfeiture of deposit, all of which firm up the position of a creditor: see Harris, *Remedies in Contract and Tort* (1988), Chap. 2.

The purpose of taking security

There are a number of compelling reasons for a creditor to obtain a charge and not rely solely on his personal action against a debtor company. First, in the event of the insolvency of a company a secured creditor will at least have priority to unsecured creditors and will, according to the seniority of his claim, have priority over any less senior security holders. This is a direct consequence of the fact that a security interest confers some type of proprietary interest on its holder. Priority-gaining in the event of a company's liquidation is one of the principal reasons for taking security.[20] Second, the secured creditor may have the right of pursuit. This arises where a company in violation of the rights of a chargee disposes of the property subject to the charge and it entitles a chargee to pursue his claim into the proceeds of the disposition.[21] Third, a security interest gives its holder the right of enforcement. What this entails is that once a charge becomes enforceable, the chargee may thereupon take whatever steps are available to enforce the charge since English law places no significant impediments in the way of the right of enforcement of a charge.[22] This right of enforcement is further enhanced by the fact that English insolvency law permits a chargee to remain outside the insolvency proceedings and to enforce his charge independently of such proceedings.[23] Lastly, a charge affords a chargee a measure of control over the business of the debtor company. The company may have to report regularly to the chargee and if the company gets into financial difficulties, the chargee may be made privy to management decisions.[24] In addition, the charge may be so all-embracing that it confers on the chargee as a matter of fact the exclusive right to supply the debtor company with credit. A charge will obviously deter a second financier from providing the company with funds where its charge would rank after a charge that the company has already created over its assets. Also, unsecured creditors will often be deterred from seeking a winding-up since such creditors would readily appreciate the futility of such action where the company's assets were charged up to the hilt.[25]

[20] See Cork Report, Chap. 35.
[21] He may also be able to assert a claim against the property subject to the security unless it is acquired by a bona fide purchaser for value.
[22] The right has to some extent been circumscribed by statute: See Insolvency Act 1986, s.11(3) and s.43.
[23] *Sowman* v. *Samuel (David) Trust Ltd.* [1978] 1 W.L.R. 22; *Re Potters Oils Ltd.* [1986] 1 W.L.R. 201. Also, by remaining outside the insolvency proceedings the chargee will not be subject to the rules of insolvency set-off (no proof no set-off): see *Re Norman Holding Co. Ltd.* [1991] 1 W.L.R. 10.
[24] Although the chargee has to be careful not to become a shadow director and thus, *e.g.*, potentially liable under the Insolvency Act 1986, s.214.
[25] See generally Wood, *Law and Practice of International Finance,* Chap. 6 which sets out the reasons for various types of bond covenants that can be taken by a creditor.

The floating charge

The general nature of a floating charge has already been explained[26]; it is an equitable charge on some or all of the company's present and future property which leaves the company free to deal with the property subject to the charge in the ordinary course of business. Such a charge is, therefore, a particularly valuable means whereby a business concern can raise money without removing any of its property from the business. Also, it facilitates the granting of security over assets which in the normal course of a company's business are circulating, for example, stock in trade. The charge remains floating and the company free to use the assets subject to the charge until the charge is converted into a fixed charge. This is referred to as the crystallisation of the charge. The normal crystallising event is the taking of steps to enforce the charge but there are others and these will be dealt with later.[27] No particular form of words is necessary to create a floating charge; it suffices if the intention is shown (a) to impose a charge on assets both present and future, (b) the assets are of such a nature that they would in changing in the ordinary course of the company's business, and (c) the company is free to continue to deal with the assets in the ordinary course of its business.[28] The phrase "ordinary course of business" is construed widely[29]; it may even cover the sale of the company's whole undertaking in exchange for securities in another company provided such sale is authorised by the objects clause in the company's memorandum.[30]

---

[26] See pp. 96–97. For valuable analyses of the floating charge see Goode, *Commercial Law*, Chap. 28; Gough, *Company Charges*, Chap. 2. Floating charges and receivers in Scotland are dealt with by Part XVIII of the 1985 Act and Part III, Chap. II of the 1986 Act.

[27] See p. 417.

[28] *Re Yorkshire Woolcombers' Association Ltd.* [1903] 2 Ch. 284 at 295; *Illingworth v. Houldsworth* [1904] A.C. 355, H.L. In practice it is usual to state specifically that the charge is "by way of floating charge" but it suffices if it is expressed to be on the "undertaking" or the like: *Re Panama Royal Mail Co.* (1870) L.R. 5 Ch. App. 318; *Re Florence Land and Public Works Co.* (1879) 10 Ch. D. 530, C.A.; *Re Colonial Trusts Corp.* (1880) 15 Ch. D. 465. The fact that a charge is called a "fixed" charge does not necessarily make it so; if the company is free to use the assets in the normal course of its business then it will be treated as a floating charge: *Re Armagh Shoes Ltd.* [1984] BCLC 405, Ch.D. (N.I.).

[29] See *Hamilton v. Hunter* (1982–83) 7 A.C.L.R. 295; *Re Bartlett Estates Pty Ltd.* (1988–89) 14 A.C.L.R. 512 where the court found that the company had acted outside its normal course of business. To be affected by this, the person dealing with the company will probably have to be aware of this fact.

[30] *Re Borax Co.* [1901] 1 Ch. 326, C.A. It is important to note that the company in that case had not ceased to carry on business. It is not clear whether because of s.35 of the 1985 Act the disposition of a company's assets in a manner not authorised by its objects would result in the person who acquires an interest in the assets taking them subject to the floating charge at least if he has notice. However, s.35 deals with the issue of validity of the transaction whereas the question under discussion is one of priority between the floating charge holder and the person who acquires the property outside the company's normal course of business. In this latter situation the question should be determined by the normal rules of priority.

For a clear grasp of the nature of a floating charge, two important factors must be kept in mind. First, probably the most significant feature for identifying the floating charge is that the company retains management autonomy with respect to the assets subject to the charge. Thus the essence of the charge is not determined by the nature of the property over which it is created but rather by the degree of freedom accorded to the company to deal with this property in the normal course of business. This is illustrated by *Siebe Gorman & Co. Ltd. v. Barclays Bank Ltd.*[31] Where the court held that a fixed charge had been created in favour of a bank over book debts (in this case bills of exchange)[32] where the charge provided that the company could not charge or assign these debts and, most importantly, had to pay the proceeds into an account with the chargee bank which the company could not operate without the consent of the bank. It was the absence of the ability to use the book debts in the normal course of business that deprived the charge of the character of being floating.[33] However, the fact that there is some restriction on the power of the company to deal with assets subject to a charge does not preclude it from being a floating charge. To preclude a charge from being a floating charge, the restriction must substantially deprive the company of the power to deal with its assets in the normal course of business.

The second factor of importance with respect to the nature of a floating charge is that although a floating charge relates to future assets it is a present charge and not a future one. In *Re Margart Properties Ltd.*[34] a bank enforced its floating charge after the commencement of the company's winding-up and the liquidator argued that the payment of the proceeds of the realisation was invalid because of what is the equivalent of section 127 of the Insolvency Act 1986 which invalidates any disposition of a company's property after the commencement of winding up. The argument failed for the very good reason that the disposition of the company's property took place when the charge was created[35] and not when the charge was enforced; the floating charge is an existing charge and not one arising in the future when the charge is enforced or when it crystallises.

31 [1979] 2 Lloyd's Rep. 142; *cf. Re Atlantic Computer Systems plc.* (No.1) [1991] BCLC 606 at 623–625.

32 See *Dawson v. Isle* [1906] 1 Ch. 633.

33 Cf. *Re Brightlife Ltd.* [1987] Ch. 200 where the court held that a floating charge had been created where the company could pay the proceeds of charged book debts into its bank account and use them in the normal course of business.

34 [1985] BCLC 314 (this was a decision of the Supreme Court of New South Wales but it is submitted that it reflects English law): see also *Re French's (Wine Bar) Ltd.* [1987] BCLC 499; *Evans v. Rival Granite Quarries Ltd.* [1910] 2 K.B. 979 at 999 ("A floating security is not a future security; it is a present security . . . .").

35 This of course only determines the relationship between the company and the floating charge holder and does not provide an answer to issue of priority as between charges.

Vulnerability of the floating charge

The holder of a floating charge is not solely concerned with the rights which it provides against the company but equally importantly he is concerned with the priority it provides against other charge holders. As regards the latter aspect, the floating charge provides less than perfect security. Because of the management autonomy accorded to the company with respect to the charged assets, the company can create security interests that have priority to the floating charge[36]; a floating charge will be deferred to any subsequent fixed legal or equitable charge created by the company over its assets.[37] Similarly, if debts due to the company are subject to a floating charge, the interest of the floating charge holder will be subject to any lien or set off that the company creates with respect to the charged assets prior to crystallisation,[38] for a floating charge is not regarded for this purpose as an immediate assignment of the chose in action,[39] it becomes such only on crystallisation.[40] If a creditor has levied and completed execution[41] the debentureholders cannot compel him to restore the money, nor, until the charge has crystallised, can he be restrained from levying execution.[42] The floating charge holder will take the company's property subject to the rights of anyone claiming by title paramount, so that a landlord can re-enter and can distrain on chattels in the leased premises if rent is unpaid, notwithstanding that the chattels are comprised in a charge which has crystallised.[43] But if a receiver has been appointed by the court, the court's leave must be obtained, for it is then in possession through its officers.[44]

To firm up their security against subsequent security interests created by the company and which would otherwise have priority, floating charges almost invariably contain a provision that restricts the right of the company to create charges that have priority to or rank

---

[36] The charge holder runs the risk that the company may dissipate the assets subject to the charge which arguably is the most serious risk that the charge holder faces.

[37] *Wheatley* v. *Silkstone and Haigh Moor Coal Co.* (1885) 29 Ch. D. 715. See also *Robson* v. *Smith* [1895] 2 Ch. 118 at 124 (any dealing with the property subject to a floating charge "will be binding on the debentureholders, provided that the dealing be completed before the debentures cease to be merely a floating security").

[38] Even though, if *George Barker (Transport) Ltd.* v. *Eynon* [1974] 1 W.L.R. 462 C.A. is rightly decided, the lien or set off has not actually accrued.

[39] *Biggerstaff* v. *Rowatt's Wharf* [1896] 2 Ch. 93, C.A.; *Rother Iron Works Ltd.* v. *Canterbury Precision Engineers Ltd.* [1974] Q.B. 1, C.A. ; *George Barker (Transport) Ltd.* v. *Eynon* [1974] 1 W.L.R. 462, C.A.

[40] See *Cretanor Maritime Co. Ltd.* v. *Irish Marine Management Ltd.* [1978] 1 W.L.R. 966, C.A. where the company's assets were subject to an injunction, against their removal from the jurisdiction, obtained by an unsecured creditor. On the application of the holder of the debenture whose charge had crystallised the court discharged the injunction. See also *Capital Cameras Ltd.* v. *Harold Lines Ltd.* [1991] 1 W.L.R. 54 (successful application of a receiver to dismiss a *Mareva* injunction).

[41] Seizure alone does not suffice: *Norton* v. *Yates* [1906] 1 K.B. 112, C.A.

[42] *Evans* v. *Rival Granite Quarries* [1910] 2 K.B. 979, C.A.

[43] *Re Roundwood Colliery Co.* [1897] 1 Ch. 373, C.A.; *Rhodes* v. *Allied Dunbar Pension Services Ltd.* [1989] 1 W.L.R. 800, C.A.

[44] Leave will normally be granted unless the company is in liquidation, in which case s.128 of the Insolvency Act 1986 applies: *Re Oak Pits Colliery Co.* (1882) 21 Ch. D. 322, C.A.

Company Charges

equally with the floating charge (called a negative pledge clause).[45] Such restrictions, which are quite common but strictly construed, limit the company's actual authority to deal with its assets and accordingly remove the basis on which floating charges are postponed to later charges. Nevertheless, it has been held that they may may still be postponed to later mortgages, notwithstanding the limitation of the company's actual authority. If the later mortgage is legal, the mortgagee will obtain priority by virtue of his legal interest unless he has notice not only of the floating charge but also of the restriction in it.[46] If it is equitable, the chargee may be preferred on the ground that the company has been allowed to represent that it is free to deal with the assets in the normal course of business as though they were unencumbered. For example, if the title deeds are left with the company, an equitable mortgagee by deposit will take priority.[47] Most of the problems in this area have now been resolved by the requirement that undertakings by a company not to create subsequent charges having priority to an existing charge have to be registered in the company's register of charges and this will constitute notice to any person who is taking a charge which also has to be registered.[48] Whatever the nature of protection provided by registration, it is also a wise precaution for a chargee to deprive a company of the title deeds to its properties—this is another advantage of having trustees who can take possession of the deeds.

Some limit was placed on the company's power to create charges having priority to the floating charge by the decision of Sargant J.[49] that a company could not create a floating charge on the same assets ranking in priority to or *pari passu* with the original floating charge. This decision was subsequently approved by the Court of Appeal,[50] but limited to cases where the assets comprised in both charges are the same, and it appears that a general floating charge on the whole of the undertaking may be postponed to a subsequent floating charge on a particular class of assets where the first charge contemplates the creation of the later charge.[51] In Scotland, however, where the same property (or any part of the same property) is subject to two floating charges they rank according to the time of registration unless the

[45] *Brunton v. Electrical Engineering Corp.* [1892] 1 Ch. 434; *Robson v. Smith* [1895] 2 Ch. 118.
[46] *English & Scottish Mercantile Investment Co. Ltd. v. Brunton* [1892] 2 Q.B. 700, C.A.
[47] *Re Castell & Brown Ltd.* [1898] 1 Ch. 315; *Re. Valletort Sanitary Steam Laundry* [1903] 2 Ch. 654.
[48] s.415(2)(*a*) (introduced by s.103 of the 1989 Act). This assumes that the subsection has been brought into effect. s.464(1)(*a*) of the 1985 Act provides that a floating charge created by a company registered in Scotland may contain such a provision.
[49] *Re Benjamin Cope & Co.* [1914] 1 Ch. 800.
[50] *Re Automatic Bottle Makers Ltd.* [1926] Ch. 412, C.A.
[51] *Re Automatic Bottle Makers Ltd.* above, implies that this depends on the wording of the charge and of the express provision, if any, relating to the creation of further charges.

instruments creating the charges otherwise provide.[52] Also, where the company subsequent to granting a floating charge containing a negative pledge provision purchases property leaving part of the purchase secured by a mortgage, the mortgage will take priority, even if the mortgage has actual notice so long as what the company acquired was the equity of redemption subject to the mortgage.[53]

Given the vulnerability of the floating charge the question arises as to why a creditor should bother to obtain one. While obviously the fixed charge accords superior protection, there are sound reasons for taking a floating charge. First, where a subsequent holder of a registrable charge is deemed to have notice of a negative pledge clause then this accords priority to the floating charge holder. Second, the charge provides security against unsecured creditors. Third, the floating charge holder will be able to take steps to enforce the charge and, as will be seen, this accords him considerable control over the company's affairs. Fourth, the holder of a floating charge will have some measure of control over the company even without taking any steps to enforce it.[54] Lastly, the holder of a floating charge will be able to block the appointment of an administrator.[55]

Crystallisation

Crystallisation is the term used to describe the process by which a floating charge is converted into a normal fixed charge. A crystallised charge will bite on all the assets covered by the charge since normally a floating charge does not provide for crystallisation over part only of the assets to which it relates.[56] The effect of crystallisation is to deprive the company of the autonomy to deal with the assets subject to the charge in the normal course of business. The events of crystallisation, on which there is general agreement, are[57] (i) the making of a winding up order,[58] (ii) the appointment of an

[52] s.464(3) and (4) of the 1985 Act (as amended by s.140 of the 1989 Act). But when the first chargee receives written notice of the registration of the later charge his priority is restricted to present advances and future advances which he is legally required to make plus interest and expenses: s.464(5).

[53] *Abbey National Building Society v. Cann* [1991] 1 A.C. 56, H.L. This directly addresses the issue of priority but does not, however, deal with the separate issue of registration and hence voidness. It is submitted that there is a sufficient degree of involvement by the company so as to make the charge one "created" by it and thus void for non-registration if not registered within 21 days of its creation: see *Tatung (U.K) Ltd. v. Gortex Telesure Ltd.* (1989) 5 BCC 325 at 327, *et seq*.

[54] See p. 412.

[55] See Goode, *Legal Problems of Credit and Security* (2nd. ed.), at p. 50 where these points are developed.

[56] Gough, *op. cit.*, at 89–92. There is no reason why partial crystallisation should not be provided for by agreement. It is submitted that *Robson v. Smith* [1895] 2 Ch. 118 is not authority against this since the floating charge in that case did not confer any such right.

[57] See Goode, *Legal Problems of Credit and Security* (2nd, ed.) at 59–77.

[58] *Wallace v. Universal Automatic Machines* [1894] 2 Ch. 547, C.A.; *Re Victoria Steamboats Ltd.* [1897] 1 Ch. 158. Even if the winding-up is for purposes of reconstruction: *Re Crompton & Co.* [1914] 1 Ch. 954. It is the making of the order and not, for example, the presentation of the petition since there is always the chance that the court will decline to make the winding-up order. In Scotland the charge crystallises on the commencement of the winding-up of the company: section 463 (as amended) of the 1985 Act.

administrative receiver,[59] (iii) the company's ceasing to carry on business,[60] (iv) the taking of possession by the debentureholder[61] and (v) the happening of an event expressly provided for in the debenture, often referred to as "automatic crystallisation." Automatic crystallisation is not a term of art but covers at least two situations which at first blush appear dissimilar; one is where the charge is made to crystallise on the happening of an event provided for in the charge without there being any need for a further act by the chargee[62] and the other is where the charge is made to crystallise on the serving of a notice of crystallisation on the company. However, these events have one important common feature and that is they will normally not be known to a person dealing with the company and therefore it seems appropriate to treat them together. Although there was some doubt as to the validity of automatic crystallisation provisions, the matter seems to be settled beyond dispute by the judgment of Hoffman J. in *Re Brightlife Ltd.*[63] upholding the validity of a provision enabling the floating charge holder to serve a notice of crystallisation on the company. He saw crystallisation as being a matter of agreement between the parties and on this reasoning there can be no objection to a charge being made to crystallise on the happening of a specified event. In so far as insolvency law is committed to the principle that property within the apparent ownership of the company should be treated as the company's in the event of its insolvent liquidation,[64] permitting party autonomy to effect automatic crystallisation undermines this policy. It has been claimed that automatic crystallisation is unfair in the sense that it could prejudice subsequent chargees who do not know, and indeed who may have no way of knowing, that the charge has crystallised.[65] Whether this is indeed the case is not clear cut. As Professor Goode has pointed out, the fact that the charge has crystallised will affect the relationship between the chargee and the company but it does not necessarily affect a third party since if the company is left free to deal with the assets in the normal course of its business then the chargee

---

[59] *Evans v. Rival Granite Quarries Ltd.* [1910] 2. K.B. 979. The same applies to the appointment of a receiver by the court.

[60] *Re Woodroffes (Musical Instruments Ltd.)* [1986] Ch. 366 (it is the cessation of business and not ceasing to be a going concern assuming the latter is different).

[61] *Evans v. Rival Granite Quarries Ltd.* [1910] K.B. 979 at 997.

[62] The crystallising event could, for example, be the failure by the debtor to pay any moneys due or to insure the charged property.

[63] [1987] Ch. 200.

[64] English insolvency law is not wholeheartedly committed to this policy but to some extent it achieves it by requiring registration of non-possessory securities. It does not, however, require registration of title retention clauses and assets in possession of the company which are subject to a trust do not form part of the company's assets in a winding-up.

[65] It is common when taking a fixed charge or purchasing an asset of the company to serve on it inquiries as to whether any floating charge has crystallised. This provides limited protection since the company can lie or, more likely, it may not appreciate that the charge has crystallised.

should be estopped from denying the company's authority to do so.[66] Even if this argument is unsuccessful, it should be kept in mind that it is not all security interests which will be prejudiced by automatic crystallisation but only those lacking priority to a crystallised floating charge.[67] Lastly, the matter may now be dealt with by statute as the Secretary of State can pass regulations requiring notice to be given to the Registrar of events which affect the nature of the security under a floating charge and can provide that the happening of such events shall be ineffective until the prescribed particulars have been delivered.[68]

It is unclear as to whether the making of an administration order crystallises a floating charge. Arguably the appointment of an administrator for the more advantageous realisation of the company's assets than a winding-up has this effect since this constitutes a virtual cessation of business. Although there is no authority on this, it is submitted that this is not the case since the provisions on administration (particularly the right of the floating charge holder to block the appointment of an administrator[69]) obviously envisage that crystallisation must arise from the act of the floating charge holder or the terms of the charge.[70] Also, it would frustrate an administration where an administrator is appointed for the purpose set out in section 8(3)(a) of the 1986 Act.

There are certain events that do not cause crystallisation. Default in the payment of interest or capital are not crystallising events[71] although, given the validity of an automatic crystallising clause, there is no objection in principle to a charge by its terms being made to crystallise on the happening of a stipulated event of default. However, even though default may not result in crystallisation the

66 Goode, *op. cit.*, at 70–71; a similar point is made by Gough, *op. cit.*, at 104–105. For this approach to work, the company must be treated as free to deal even though the charge is ignorant that the charge has crystallised.
67 The primary charges in this category are the subsequent equitable chargee, chargee over chattels and execution creditors: see Gough, *The Floating Charge: Traditional Themes and New Directions* in Finn (ed.) *Equity and Commercial Relationships* 239 at 262.
68 s.413 (introduced by s.102 of the 1989 Act). This does not completely dispose of the problem since registration only affects a person taking a charge which has to be registered: see p. 413.
69 See p. 747. Floating charges normally contain a provision enabling the chargee to appoint an administrative receiver if a petition for the appointment of an administrator is presented. See Insolvency Act 1986, Sched. 11, para. 1 which inserted such a clause in floating charges created before the Act came into effect.
70 Where a charge has crystallised it is unclear if it can be decrystallised by the charge holder renewing the company's licence to deal: see Lightman and Moss, *The Law of Receivers of Companies* at 3–13. It is difficult to see why re-crystallisation should not be treated as the creation of a new charge since it constitutes an alteration of the chargee's proprietary interest. What is clear is that the reverse would appear not to be possible, namely, the subsequent flotation of a fixed charge as a floater as otherwise this would enable the rights of the preferential creditors to be overridden. Also, if crystallising events are made registrable, this would be an argument against permitting re-crystallisation.
71 *Government Stock and Other Securities Investment Co. Ltd.* v. *Manila Ry. Co. Ltd.* [1897] A.C. 81.

company will be in breach of contract and the chargee will have appropriate contractual remedies. In many situations the chargee may have a contractual remedy even though the charge has not crystallised; for example, the holder of an uncrystallised charge can always "intervene and obtain an injunction to prevent the company from dealing with its assets otherwise than in the ordinary course of its business."[72] The crystallisation of an earlier floating charge does not crystallise a subsequent floating charge since the subsequent chargee may pay off the earlier charge or agree to indemnify the company which continues to carry on business despite the crystallisation of the earlier charge with respect to any liability incurred towards the earlier chargee.[73]

Statutory limitations on the floating charge

There are certain statutory provisions that further add to the vulnerability of the floating charge. These provisions relate to (i) preferential creditors—which affects the priority of the charge; (ii) defective floating charges—which affects the validity of the charge; (iii) the right of an administrator to override a floating charge— which affects the enforcement rights of the charge; (iv) costs of the liquidation—which diminishes the assets available for the floating charge holders. It is proposed to deal with these matters seriatim.

(i) **Preferential creditors** As a matter of policy, insolvency law has to determine (a) what constitutes insolvency proceedings and (b) whether any particular class of creditors should be given protection in the insolvency of a company[74] and accorded a statutory preference over some or all of the company's creditors.[75] The relevance of this policy to the rights of floating charge holders is that the procedure for enforcement of a floating charge is to some extent treated as an insolvency proceeding.[76] Also, as already pointed out, debentureholders with a floating charge closely resemble shareholders and form a class of those interested in the company rather than of those who merely have claims against it. Consequently it has been thought unjust that they should obtain priority over employees (one of the categories of preferential creditor) who have priority to the

---

[72] *Re Woodroffes (Musical Instruments) Ltd.* [1986] Ch. 366 at 378.
[73] *Re Woodroffes (Musical Instruments) Ltd., ibid.* It would follow from this that the crystallisation of a later floating charge would not crystallise an earlier one. It is important to note that crystallisation does not affect priorities: see Picarda, *The Law Relating to Receivers, Managers and Administrators* (2nd.ed.) at 36–39.
[74] The same policy decisions have to be made with respect to bankruptcy: see, *e.g.* Insolvency Act 1986, s.336 dealing with the matrimonial home.
[75] This of course constitutes a departure from the normal principle of insolvency law that the pre-insolvency entitlements of creditors should be respected in liquidation: see p. 771.
[76] *e.g.* the enforcement of the floating charge is dealt with in Part 3 of the Insolvency Act 1986; administrative receivers have to be qualified insolvency practitioners (s. 230(2)); and s.247(1) defines insolvency as including the appointment of an administrative receiver.

shareholders in the event of the company's liquidation.[77] Hence it is provided that on winding up, a voluntary arrangement, or appointment of an administrative receiver under a floating charge,[78] preferential debts, which include certain payments to employees, will have priority over the claims of ordinary creditors and shall similarly have priority over any floating charge. The preferential debts of the employees are set out in Schedule 6 to the Insolvency Act 1986 and include four months' wages and accrued holiday remuneration.[79] In the case of a floating charge the relevant date for quantifying the preferential debts is the date of the appointment of the receiver by the debentureholders.[80] Anyone who has advanced money for the payment of the employee debts which would have been preferential is subrogated to the rights of the employee.[81] It is important to note that the preferential creditors are given priority where a receiver is appointed with respect to a charge "which, as created, was a floating charge".[82]; thus the fact that the charge has crystallised at the time a receiver is appointed does not result in preferential debts being denied their statutory priority.[83] The Secretary of State for Employment is required to pay employees unpaid remuneration and other entitlements and entitled to recover this in priority to the debentureholder.[84]

More controversially, the Crown for certain unpaid taxes and other levies is also accorded the status of preferential creditor. It is argued

77 Another argument made in favour of employees is that they have no way of obtaining security for the payment of their salary which is normally made after the provision of the services. This is not strictly correct since money to pay employees could be placed in a trust account to be paid on the appropriate date. But this would be cumbersome and as a matter of practice does not happen.

78 ss.40, 175, 386 of and Sched. 6 to the Insolvency Act 1986 and s.196 of the 1985 Act. s.40 of the 1986 Act and s.196 of the 1985 Act are the most relevant for the subordination of the floating charge.

79 See paras. 9 and 10 of Sched. 6.

80 s.387(4)(a) of the 1986 Act. For the date of the appointment see s. 33 of the 1986 Act.

81 Sched. 6, para. 11 to the 1985 Act. This enables the company to be kept going where it is in financial difficulties but there is some chance that it can trade out of its difficulties. For case law on the previous statutory provisions see *Re Primrose (Builders) Ltd.* [1950] Ch. 561; *Re Rutherford (James R.) & Sons Ltd.* [1964] 1 W.L.R. 1211; *Re Rampgill Mill Ltd.* [1967] Ch. 1138.

82 s.40(1) of the 1986 Act.

83 Under the old law the crystallisation of the charge prior to the appointment of a receiver resulted in the preferential creditors being denied their priority: see *Re Brightlife Ltd.* [1987] Ch. 200 This alteration of the old law has made an automatic crystallising clause less attractive.

84 Employment Protection (Consolidation) Act 1978, ss.122–123 and 125: the entitlement is to eight weeks' arrears of pay, holiday pay, compensation for the basic (but not the compensatory) award for unfair dismissal, for failure to give the statutory period of notice and unpaid contributions to an occupational pension scheme. The Secretary of State is subrogated to the employee's rights as a preferential creditor (s.125): *Re Urethane Engineering Products Ltd.* [1991] BCLC 48, C.A. This type of wage-earner protection fund enables the employee to be promptly paid and accords the administrative receiver or liquidator a certain freedom to realise the assets of the company: see *The Law Reform Commission of Australia* (Discussion Paper No. 32), Chap. 14; see generally Davis, *Acquired Rights, Creditors' Rights, Freedom of Contract, and Industrial Democracy* (1990) 9 Y.B.E.L. 21.

that these are debts owed to the community and as such should be accorded a preference. This was roundly rejected by the Cork Committee who considered that the wrong done to individual creditors could well outweigh any prejudice to the community in depriving the Crown of its preference.[85] As regards withholding taxes, (e.g. VAT and PAYE), where the company acts as a tax collector rather than a taxpayer, the Cork Committee considered that the Crown should be given a preference as other creditors had no legitimate expectation of payment from this source. The Insolvency Act 1986 embodies these reforms and the Crown's preferred position is confined to taxes or social security contributions collected by the company for transmission to the Government.[86]

The provisions relating to the payment of preferential creditor creates a statutory duty and if a debentureholder or a receiver realises assets he will be personally liable to the extent of these assets if preferential creditors are not paid.[87] Where the company can exercise the right of set-off against a preferential creditor who is also owed a non-preferential debt by the company, the set-off must be exercised against the debts rateably in proportion to the amounts of the preferential and non-preferential claims of the creditor.[88]

(ii) **Defective floating charges** It has also been thought unjust to allow an unsecured creditor to obtain priority to other creditors by obtaining a floating charge when he realises that liquidation is imminent. The temptation and the opportunities to attempt to salvage something out of the wreck are particularly great in the case of the directors themselves. So long as assets remain available they will have caused the company to borrow on mortgage, but when the company's credit is exhausted they may attempt to keep the company afloat by themselves making unsecured loans to it. Finding that their efforts are doomed to failure, what more natural than that they should cause the company to execute a floating charge in their favour to secure the loans so that if anything is left, after the claims of the prior chargees are satisfied, they take it rather than the unsecured creditors?[89] To

[85] Cork Committee Report, Chap. 32.
[86] See the 1986 Act, Sched. 6, paras. 1–8. Levies under the E.C.S.C. Treaty are also given a preference: see para. 5. Where the holder of a fixed and floating charge exercises his rights under s.101 of the L.P.A. 1925 any surplus must be paid to the liquidator: Re G. L. Saunders Ltd. [1986] 1 W.L.R. 215. Had there been another floating charge holder in that case the outcome would have been different. For an erudite discussion of this issue see Picarda, The Law Relating to Receivers, Managers and Administrators (2nd ed.) at pp. 253–256.
[87] I.R.C. v. Goldblatt [1972] Ch. 498.
[88] Re Unit 2 Windows Ltd. [1985] 1 W.L.R. 1383. If the company's assets are insufficient to meet the claims of the preferential creditors, such creditors rank equally and their claims must abate in equal proportions: s.175(2) of the 1986 Act.
[89] In some cases the company has been deliberately floated with the intention of defrauding creditors by granting floating charges to the promoters and then winding up: see Cohen Report, Cmd. 6659, para. 148.

prevent this, section 245 of the Insolvency Act 1986[90] provides that a floating charge created in favour of an unconnected person within 12 months[91] of the commencement of the winding-up or the making of an administration order[92] shall be invalid (except to a prescribed extent) unless it is proved that the company was solvent immediately after the creation of the charge.[93] If these conditions are not satisfied the charge is valid only to the extent of any cash, goods or services supplied to the company,[94] or the discharge of any liability of the company, where these take place "at the same time as, or after, the creation of the charge."[94a] This phraseology was held by Hoffmann J. in *Re Shoe Lace Ltd.*[94b] to import contemporaneity and not causality. The question was whether the reasonable business man would have considered that the new value was extended at the same time as the execution of the charge and not whether the new value was extended because of the existence of the charge. In many ways the latter approach would be preferable since the essential question is whether the charge was intended to secure some new value and the requirement to register it within 21 days of its creation would suffice to protect those dealing with company. Hence those who take a floating charge from a company which cannot be proved to be solvent,[95] and which does not survive for a further year, cannot thereby obtain protection in respect to their existing debts, but only to the extent that they provide the company with new value[96] and thus increase the assets available for other creditors. The directors, in the example given previously, cannot retrospectively convert themselves into secured creditors in respect of moneys which they have previously advanced without demanding security. Nor will it avail them to advance further money on a floating charge on the understanding that this is to be used to repay existing loans; a creditor cannot by use of the floating charge transmute an unsecured

[90] This applies to Scotland: s.245(1).
[91] The period was three months in the 1908 Act and six months in the 1929 Act: each was found to be inadequate in view of the ingenuity displayed in staving off liquidation.
[92] s.245(3)(b) and (5).
[93] The test of solvency is that laid down in s.123 of the 1986 Act.
[94] The value of the goods or services is their market value: s.245(6).
[94a] s.245(2)(a) and (b).
[94b] To be reported in [1992] BCLC. Contrast *Re Columbian Fireproofing Co. Ltd.* [1910] 1 Ch. 758 which as Hoffmann J. pointed out was decided under slightly different statutory language.
[95] There is nothing in the section to displace the normal rule that he who asserts must prove and thus the burden of proof would be on the liquidator or administrator. This should cause no great hardship as they will normally have sufficient information to found their action.
[96] For interesting illustrations of the way in which the rule in *Clayton's Case* ((1816) 1 Mer. 572) may protect a bank when the charge secures a current account, see *Re Thomas Mortimer Ltd.* (1925) now reported at [1965] Ch. 186n; *Re Yeovil Glove Ltd.* [1965] Ch. 148, C.A. The Cork Committee recommended that *Re Yeovil Glove Ltd.* be reversed by statute (paras. 1561–1562) but why this should be so is far from clear since the bank by permitting the company to continue to draw on its overdrawn account is providing it with new value: see Goode, (1983) 4 Co.L. 81.

into a secured debt by attempting to manipulate the saving provisions of section 245.[97] It is important to note that not all value is "new value" for the purpose of section 245 as the latter is confined to money, goods or services and excluded are, for example, intellectual property and rights under a contract.[98]

Where the floating charge is in favour of a "connected person" it is easier for an administrator or liquidator to challenge the charge. The period within which the charge is vulnerable is two years after its creation[99] and there is no need to show that at the time the charge was created the company was insolvent. The definition of connected person is somewhat complex but it includes a director, the director's relatives and companies within a group.[1]

The statutory limitations in (i) and (ii) only apply to floating charges and not to fixed charges. The policy justification for this has been questioned. The Cork Committee considered that section 245 should not be extended to fixed charges since the charge would relate to the company's existing assets whereas the floating charge could cover future assets.[1a] Why this should make a critical difference is far from clear since a company can create a fixed charge of accounts receivable or a mortgage of future property. The exclusion of fixed charges from section 245 arguably reflects the favouritism shown to secured creditors in English company law, although to make a secured charge subject to the claims of preferential creditors would obviously affect both the terms of credit and the amount of credit available, and this may justify the present position. A fixed charge may of course be attacked as a preference where it is given to secure past value[2] but not as a transaction at an undervalue since the assets of the company are not diminished by the creation of the charge.[3] Both these statutory limitations may affect companies other than those registered under the Act if, but only if, they are being wound up under it.[4]

[97] *Re Destone Fabrics Ltd.* [1941] Ch. 319 (this would now be a transaction with a connected person on which see below); *Re G. T. Whyte & Co. Ltd.* [1983] BCLC 311. It is submitted that the transactions in these cases would not fall within s.245(2)(b) as there would be no discharge as a matter of substance of the debts at the time of the creation of the charge. Contrast *Re Mathew Ellis Ltd.* [1933] Ch. 458, C.A. The test seems to be whether the company receives what is genuinely new value.

[98] See Goode, *Principles of Corporate Insolvency Law*, at p. 181.

[99] s.245(3)(a).

[1] See ss.249 and 435 of the 1986 Act and p. 582.

[1a] Cmnd. 8558 at paras. 1494 and 1553. The other reason given was that the extension of s.245 to fixed charges would compel creditors to seek repayment if security could not be granted. This argument could also be applied to the restriction in s.245 to obtaining a floating charge.

[2] For preferences see p. 771. The principal difference between preferences and defective floating charges is that the time within which a preference in favour of an unconnected person can be challenged is six months. Also a preference can involve a diminution of the company's assets whereas a floating charge constitutes a claim on them.

[3] *Re M. C. Bacon Ltd.* [1990] BCLC 324.

[4] *i.e.* a floating chargee who appoints a receiver of a statutory or chartered company will not be subject to the claims of preferential creditors unless the company goes into compulsory liquidation under Part V of the 1986 Act.

(iii) The third statutory limitation on the right of a floating charge holder is section 15 of the Insolvency Act 1986 which empowers an administrator to sell property subject to a charge which as created was a floating charge without the need to obtain a court order.[5] As protection, the floating charge holder is given the same priority with respect to any property representing directly or indirectly the property disposed of as he would have had with respect to the property subject to the floating charge.[6] However, this qualification of the floating charge holder's rights does not constitute a serious erosion of the rights of the floating charge holder since he can block the making of an administration order by appointing an administrative receiver.[7]

(iv) The last statutory limitation on the rights of the floating charge relates to costs of the liquidation. It is a principle of insolvency law that the expenses of a company's liquidation are payable out of the assets of the company in priority to all other claims.[8] And since these costs can be substantial, it is important to determine what constitutes the company's assets out of which such costs can be paid. In *Re Barleycorn Enterprises Ltd.*,[9] the court held that assets subject to a floating charge constituted assets of the company for the purpose of paying the costs of the liquidation. These costs, combined with the claims of the preferential creditors, entail a substantial erosion of the entitlement of the floating charge holder.[10]

Registration of charges

Introduction Part XII of the Companies Act 1985 contains provisions requiring a company to register certain charges with the Registrar of Companies. This requirement has been a feature of the Companies Acts since 1900.[11] The present provisions were introduced by Part IV of the Companies Act 1989 which inserted a new Part XII into the 1985 Act and it is to the 1989 interpolations that reference will be

5 s.15(1) and (3). For the power of the administrator to override a fixed charge see p. 754.
6 Where the charge has crystallised, the priority will be that of a fixed equitable charge.
7 s.9(3) of the 1986 Act; *Re Croftbell Ltd.* [1990] BCLC 844.
8 For voluntary winding up see section 115 of the 1986 Act; this section has been held to be a priority section and does not deal with the question of what constitutes properly incurred expenses in a liquidation: see *Re M. C. Bacon Ltd.* [1991] Ch. 127. The position as regards court-ordered winding up is not so explicit but a combination of section 156 and Insolvency Rules 1986, rr. 4.218 and 4.220 produces this effect.
9 [1970] Ch. 465.
10 Attempts to extend the *Barleycorn* decision have not been successful. In *Re M. C. Bacon Ltd.* [1991] Ch. 127 the court held that the costs of the liquidator in bringing an action under s.214 of the 1986 Act and to challenge a transaction as a preference were not costs of realising the company's assets and thus did not enjoy the priority accorded to such expenses in a winding-up. See also, s.19(4) & (5) of The 1986 Act.
11 First introduced by the Companies Act 1900, s.14.

made throughout this chapter.[12] For some time to come, there will obviously be two systems for the registration of charges operating side by side since the 1989 reforms are not retrospective. Other than to draw attention to salient differences, it is not proposed to deal with the pre-1989 system in any detail.

Registration of charges fulfils a range of purposes. It provides a picture of the state of the incumbrances on a company's property, something which is obviously of interest to those contemplating entering into a secured lending transaction with the company. Registration is also of interest to credit analysts, liquidators, receivers, shareholders, and prospective investors. In addition, registration operates to protect the security holder by providing him with a certain degree of protection as to the validity and priority of his charge once it is registered; this in turn benefits the company by enabling it to give the chargee the guarantee of such protection.[13] Also, if registration creates, at the minimum, a presumption that the charge has been validly registered, this facilitates the chargee assigning the charge either outright or by way of security. It is to be doubted if unsecured trade creditors have much, if any, interest in the state of encumbrances on a company's property as they normally will only be interested in whether the company can pay its debts as they fall due.

The mechanics of registration It is the duty of the company to submit prescribed particulars[14] of a charge requiring registration to the Registrar[15] who, in turn, is under a statutory obligation to maintain a register setting out these particulars.[16] The register is in the form of a file and the person seeking registration does not have to submit the original charging documents.[17] This type of notice filing is intended to be simple, inexpensive and expeditious and to put persons on notice[18] that a charge has been registered so that they can take whatever steps they consider appropriate to protect their interests. The register of

---

[12] These are to be brought into effect in July 1992 (the date of implementation has been repeatedly extended). These provisions also apply to Scotland: see s.92 of the 1989 Act. The appropriate register is set out in section 395(4) (introduced by s.93 of the 1989 Act).

[13] See Diamond, *A Review of Security Interests in Property* (DTI, 1989), Chap. 21.

[14] For the definition of prescribed particulars see s.415(1) (introduced by s.103 of the 1989 Act).

[15] s.398(1) (introduced by s.95 of the 1989 Act); the normal practice is for the chargee's solicitors to register the charge and s.398(1) provides that any person interested in the charge may register it.

[16] s.397 (introduced by s.94 of the 1989 Act).

[17] This differs from the pre-1989 position which required delivery of the instrument (if any) by which the charge was created. Section 413 (introduced by s.102 of the 1989 Act) empowers the Secretary of State to require by regulation that the instrument by which any charge is created be submitted to the Registrar of Companies at the time of registration.

[18] See p. 432 on the effect of registration. Whether the goal of simplicity is achieved will very much depend on the regulations setting out the prescribed particulars.

charges is open for public inspection and any person for a fee is entitled to a certified copy of it.[19]

What has to be registered Section 396, which sets out the charges that have to be registered, enumerates a list of registrable charges and any charge not on the list does not have to be registered. It would equally be possible to require the registration of all charges (with perhaps some specified exceptions) but this approach, while guaranteeing comprehensiveness, is not free from difficulties. It is not possible to predict the types of security interests that will be created in the future and requiring registration of some such unforeseen interests could be unnecessarily burdensome; even with respect to the known types of legal charge, particularly those conferring the right to possession, it would produce overkill; and lastly it is claimed that to require the registration of all charges could dry up certain types of secured borrowing.[20] Also, at the end of the day there may not be a great deal of difference between a system which requires all charges subject to exceptions to be registered as opposed to the present one which requires specified charges to be registered subject to the power of the Secretary of State to add to or delete from their number.[21]

The purpose of the registration provisions is to "secure the registration of charges on a company's property."[22] Section 395 contains a generic definition of what constitutes a charge and a partial definition of what constitutes property. Charge is defined as any form of security interest not arising by operation of law[23] and property is defined as including future property.[24] As was pointed out earlier, there is some uncertainty as to what constitutes a security interest; it is submitted that the courts will adopt something along the lines of the definition of Sir Nicolas Browne-Wilkinson V.-C. set out at the commencement of this chapter.[25] The uncertainties caused by what constitutes a security interest are greatly reduced by the fact, as pointed out above, that it is a *numerus clausus* of charges that has to be registered so if the charge is not within the list it is not registrable. Most of the major types of charge have to be registered and these on

---

[19] Companies Act 1985, s.709 (introduced by s.126 of the 1989 Act).
[20] See Jenkins Committee at para. 301; Diamond Report, *op. cit.*, at para. 23.1.6. This could happen if the security interest in transient and thus the need to register it could curtail its usefulness.
[21] Such a power is contained in s.396(4) (introduced by s.93 of the 1989 Act).
[22] s.395(1) (introduced by s.93 of the 1989 Act).
[23] s.395(2).
[24] s.395(2). s.395(3) makes it clear that for the purpose of registration it does not matter where the property is situated.
[25] See p. 409. *Quaere* would the court in this context find, as did the court for the purpose of s.11(3)(c) of the 1986 Act, that the right of re-entry for non-payment of rent constituted the enforcement of a security: *Exchange Travel Agency Ltd.* v. *Triton Property Trust plc* [1991] BCLC 396. It is submitted that it probably will not as security has to be given a purposive interpretation for the purpose of section 11(3)(c).

any definition are clearly security interests. Thus charges on land,[26] charges on goods,[27] charges on intangible movable property,[28] a charge for securing an issue of the company's debentures[29] and a floating charge[30] have to be registered. Intangible movable property includes a charge on the book debts of the company or those assigned to it[31] but the Act contains no definition of what constitutes a book debt.[32] Registration is also required of any property acquired by a company which is subject to a charge of a class requiring registration.[33]

What need not be registered There are a range of charges that do not need to be registered. Charges arising by operation of law (to be contrasted with those created by the company) fall into this category.[34] Also excluded from registration are (i) a charge on goods where the chargee is entitled to possession of the goods or of a document of title to them,[35] (ii) a deposit of a negotiable instrument by way of security to secure payment of a book debt[36] and (iii) a lien on subfreights.[37] The first is excluded because possession by the chargee will render the asset unusable by the company as security in favour of another creditor[38], the second because registration would

be a charge for rent or for the payment of some other periodical sum).

[26] s.396(1)(a) (excluded is a charge for rent or for the payment of some other periodical sum).

[27] s.396(1)(b); and see also s.396(2)(b) (introduced by s.93 of the 1989 Act) the section headed "What need not be registered."

[28] s.396(1)(c).

[29] s.396(1)(d); for the meaning of issue or series of debentures see s.419(1) (introduced by s.104 of the 1989 Act). Such a debenture is not a book debt; s.396(2)(e).

[30] s.396(1)(e).

[31] s.396(1)(c)(iii). There are certain exclusions which will be dealt with later.

[32] Book debts are debts owed to the company and in a credit economy they are obviously of economic significance. The common law definition of book debts is debts which a trader would in the ordinary course of business in question enter into well-kept books whether or not the entry is so made: see *Shipley v. Marshall* (1863) 14 C.B. (N.S.) 566; Oditah, *op. cit.*, at 19–32. Professor Diamond recommended that the term book debts be replaced by more modern terminology such as "receivables" and that the Act contain a definition of receivables along the lines of "debts due to or to become due to the company in respect of goods supplied or to be supplied or services rendered or to be rendered by the company in the course of the company's business" (Diamond Report, *op. cit.*, at para. 23.9.22). A charge under a contingent debt, such as the proceeds of an insurance policy, is not registrable as a book debt: see *Paul & Frank Ltd. v. Discount Bank Overseas Ltd.* [1967] Ch. 348; *cf. Re Brush Aggregates Ltd.* [1983] BCLC 320.

[33] s.398(1). See also the sub-heading "Other registers" at p. 441 below.

[34] s.395(2). This would include an unpaid vendor's lien: see *London and Cheshire Insurance Co. Ltd. v. Laplagrene Property Co. Ltd.* [1971] Ch. 499; *cf. Re Wallis and Simmonds (Builders) Ltd.* [1974] 1 W.L.R. 391. But if a registrable charge is created and is not registered, the lender cannot avoid the consequences of a failure to register by claiming to be subrogated to the unpaid vendor's lien on the ground that the money advanced was used by the company to pay the vendor of land: *Burston Finance v. Speirway* [1974] 1 W.L.R. 1648.

[35] s.396(1)(b); see also section 396(2)(c) which qualifies this.

[36] s.396(2)(f).

[37] s.396(2)(g). This under the pre-1989 reforms was registrable as a charge on book debts: see *Re Welsh Irish Ferries Ltd.* [1986] Ch. 471.

[38] It is important to note that it is only the "right" to possession and not actual possession that is relevant. However, if the chargee permits the company to retain possession of the assets then he may find his priority defeated by the company charging or disposing of the asset to a third party.

destroy the negotiability of the instrument; and the third because these interests arise and disappear quite quickly and registration would be simply too burdensome and provide little new information as those dealing with charterers would normally assume the existence of such charges.[39] Also not included are fixed charges on bank accounts[40] and, more importantly, fixed charges on shares held in a subsidiary. As to the latter, the Jenkins and Diamond Reports took diametrically opposed positions. Diamond came out against such registration on the grounds, *inter alia*, that it could mislead in circumstances where shares subject to a fixed charge are held in a company which becomes a subsidiary after the charge has been created.[41] This is an undoubted problem, but to use it to preclude registration of a charge of shares in a subsidiary is to make the best the enemy of the better. Lastly, it must always be kept in mind that there will be no need to register financing devices which the law of personal property does not treat as charges; for example, title reservation.

The question remains as to whether the register of charges maintained by the Registrar of Companies accurately reflects the extent of the incumbrances on a company's property. Although not exhaustively comprehensive, it does give a reasonably accurate picture and its most serious defects arise not from the register as such but because English law lacks a satisfactory system for classifying personal property security interests. Also, at the end of the day it is arguable that all that the register needs to show are the principal charges over the company's property since anyone dealing with the company can seek to find out the full extent to which the company's property has been charged once put on notice that *some* charges have been created. There is always the chance that the company will not give honest answers but the extent to which debtor dishonesty is a danger should not be exaggerated.

Effect of (i) non-registration (ii) late registration and (iii) defective registration

(i) **Non-registration** Failure to comply with the various registration requirements leads, as one would expect, to liability to fines. But the most potent sanction is that non-registration in the register maintained by the Registrar of charges created by the company (as opposed to existing charges on property acquired by the company)

[39] Diamond, *op. cit.*, at para. 23.4.15.
[40] A deposit at the bank would normally not be a book debt, although not necessarily in all situations: see *Re Permanent Houses (Holdings) Ltd.* [1988] BCLC 583; *Northern Bank Ltd.* v. *Ross* [1991] BCLC 401, C.A. (N.I.).
[41] Diamond report, *op. cit.*, at para. 23.8.

destroys the validity of the charge.[42] Unless the prescribed particulars of the charge are delivered to the Registrar within 21 days of the creation[43] of the charge, it will be void against the administrator, liquidator, or any person who for value acquires an interest in or right over the property subject to the charge.[44] The charge is void whether or not the event which gave rise to its voidness occurred during or after the end of the 21-day period.[45] And it is submitted that it will be void even against a subsequent chargee who has notice.[46] The sufferer is, of course, the chargee, not the company; hence the provision previously mentioned allowing any person having an interest in the charge to register it. If, however, the company or the chargee fails to do so[47] the consequences are grave indeed for the chargee; in effect, he loses his security. To reduce this hardship the Act provides that if the charge is void to any extent for non-registration the whole of the sum thereby secured becomes immediately repayable on demand.[48] This, of course, also provides the company with an incentive to register.

As between two registrable charges which have not been registered within 21 days, the first to register will obtain priority[49] and a charge is not void against a person taking an interest in property which is made expressly subject to the charge.[50] It is important to note that a void charge still remains valid against the company and there is no reason why the chargee should not take steps to enforce it. An unsecured creditor has no standing to prevent the holder of a void charge from enforcing it[51] but, somewhat anomalously, such a creditor gets protection against an unregistered charge if the company goes into liquidation or administration. Since an administrator and liquidator (particularly the latter) are more or less statutory trustees for unsecured creditors, it could be argued that there is nothing anomalous about this. This, however, begs the question of what are the "trust" assets. The justification for this is probably that it provides the chargee with an additional incentive to ensure that his charge is registered.

[42] More accurately, it is the failure to deliver particulars of the charge to the Registrar that results in the charge being rendered void but this will be referred to as non-registration. Non-registration in the company's own register has no such sanction.
[43] For what constitutes the date of creation see s.414 (introduced by s.103 of the 1989 Act) and s.419(2) (introduced by s.104 of the 1989 Act).
[44] s.399; these events are referred to as "relevant events": see s.399(2) (introduced by s.95 of the 1989 Act).
[45] s.399(1). S.399(1) would preclude the type of reasoning that occurred in *Watson v. Duff, Morgan and Vermont (Holdings) Ltd.* [1974] 1 W.L.R. 450.
[46] *Re Monolithic Building Co.* [1915] Ch. 643, C.A.; *Midland Bank Trust Co. Ltd. v. Green* [1980] Ch. 590.
[47] This happens surprisingly often; *e.g.* because of failure to realise that the charge is of the registrable class, or because both the company and the lender assume that the other will register.
[48] s.407 (introduced by s.99 of the 1989 Act).
[49] s.404 (introduced by s.99 of the 1989 Act).
[50] s.405 (introduced by s.99 of the 1989 Act).
[51] *Re Ehrmann Bros. Ltd.* [1906] 2 Ch. 697, C.A.

(ii) **Late registration** Failure to register a charge within the 21-day period does not preclude its subsequent registration; a charge can be registered outside the 21-day period at any time prior to the company's liquidation or the appointment of an administrator without the need to obtain a court order.[52] However, for a chargee such an out-of-time registration has risks. First, there is the risk that a subsequent chargee will be registered first and thus gain priority.[53] Secondly, if the company is insolvent when the charge is registered out of time, it is vulnerable to challenge by the administrator or the liquidator. Broadly speaking, it can be challenged in the same way as a floating charge or a preference can be challenged under the Insolvency Act 1986.[54] The court has no jurisdiction to order that a charge registered out of time has priority to a charge which has already been registered.[55]

(iii) **Defective registration** It may be that the charges register fails to disclose accurately particulars of the charge; for example, it may contain inaccurate particulars of the amount secured, or the property subject to the charge.[56] This can have important consequences for the charge holder. Where the registered particulars of a charge[57] are not complete and accurate, the charge is void to the extent of the rights not disclosed as against an administrator, liquidator or a person who acquires for value an interest or right over the property subject to the charge.[58] The court has a curative power.[59] (i) as against an administrator and liquidator, if it is satisfied that the inaccuracy did not prejudice any unsecured creditor or that no person became an unsecured creditor during the period when the registered particulars were defective[60] and (ii) as against a person who acquires an interest, if that person was not misled by the unregistered particulars.[61] The broad effect of this is that a defect will normally be cured as against the administrator and liquidator (since normally unsecured creditors will not normally rely on the register of charges)

---

52 s.400 (introduced by s.95 of the 1989 Act). This marks an important departure from the previous law which required a court order.
53 See p. 432 on the effect of registration.
54 See pp. 422 and 771.
55 For an example of this being done under the old law see *Re R. M. Arnold & Co. Ltd.* [1984] BCLC 535; *Re Fablehill Ltd.* [1991] BCLC 830; *Re Chantry House Development plc* [1990] BCLC 813.
56 See Prentice, *Defectively Registered Charges* (1970) 34 Conv.(N.S.) 410 where the case law on the pre-1989 position is collected.
57 Defined as particulars submitted for registration: see section 415(3) (introduced by s.103 of the 1989 Act).
58 s.402 (introduced by s.97 of the 1989 Act). This is one of the most significant alterations on the 1989 Act. Under the previous law the charge was not prejudiced by defects on the register whatever their provenance.
59 The court does not have jurisdiction to order partial effectiveness.
60 s.402(4)(a). If the company is a trading company it is inconceivable that no person will have become a creditor when the particulars were defective. Also, employees' wages will normally be paid in arrears and hence they will be creditors.
61 s.402(5).

but not against persons who acquire an interest (who will normally rely on the register of charges). There is one defect that will not affect the chargee[62] and that is one which is caused by the Registrar's officials, happily a rare event. This is because (as we have seen)[63] registered particulars means the particulars delivered for registration and where these are accurate the chargee will not be prejudiced by any defects arising from transcribing the submitted particulars on to the register.[64]

Effect of registration

Registration does not cure any flaw in the charge itself as between the parties so that the validity of the charge remains challengeable by the company. In addition, registration does not create a priority point in the sense that the chargee is guaranteed priority from the date of registration; this is because if A registers have charge on 21 January he has no guarantee that the company has not created a charge prior to this which may be registered within 21 days and thus have priority. Registration does, however, have considerable importance:

(i) first, while registration may not be a priority point, failure to register, as we have seen, renders the charge void and therefore registration is a necessary, although not sufficient, condition to obtain priority;

(ii) second, where on registration of a charge the Registrar (as he can be required to do)[65] issues a certificate of registration stating the date on which particulars of a charge were delivered to him, this is made conclusive evidence that the particulars were delivered no later than the date stated on the certificate and a presumption that they were delivered no earlier.[66] This certificate is of critical importance since the date of delivery of the particulars is determinative of whether the

---

[62] An inaccuracy of the name of the chargee is not a relevant inaccuracy for the purpose of s.402: see subsection (6). Chargee is defined as the person entitled to exercise the security rights conferred by the charge (section 419(1)) and this will often be the person to whom the charge has been transferred by way of security and who will not be registered as chargee. The reason for subsection (6) is to facilitate the use of secured debentures as security by the debentureholder since an assignee by way of security of such an interest normally would not seek registration as holder of the security.

[63] See p. 431, n. 57 supra.

[64] Whether the Registrar would be liable to anyone suffering damages must be open to doubt despite Ministry of Housing and Local Government v. Sharp [1970] 2 Q.B. 223: see Davis v. Radcliffe [1990] 1 W.L.R. 821, H.L. and the cases cited therein; Banque Keyser Ullmann S.A. v. Skandia (U.K.) Insurance Co. Ltd. [1990] 1 Q.B. 665 at 796–798 (on appeal, [1991] 2 A.C. 449).

[65] s.397(3).

[66] s.397(5). This constitutes a major change from the pre-1989 position which made the certificate conclusive evidence that the charge had been validly registered: see Re C. L. Nye Ltd. [1971] Ch. 442; Exeter Trust Ltd. v. Screenways [1991] BCLC 888. Also under the previous law the validity of the certificate could not be challenged by judicial review: R. v. Registrar of Companies, ex p. Central Bank of India [1986] Q.B. 1114. See also Chap. 11 at pp. 278–281.

charge has been registered within 21 days after the date of its creation. In addition, the certificate enhances the liquidity of the security interest since an assignee of the interest will want to be assured that the charge has been validly registered. However, the certificate does not constitute, as it did under the pre-1989 position, [67] conclusive evidence that the charge has been validly registered. Because it was felt necessary to deal with the uncertainties that this would create for those acquiring the interest of a chargee of a company's assets, and also to enhance the transferability of charges created by companies,[68] section 406[69] provides that a chargee in exercising a power of sale[70] may dispose of property freed of any interest which has arisen because the charge has become void against an administrator, a liquidator or a person who has acquired an interest in it.[71] In addition, a purchaser from the chargee is not concerned to determine whether the charge has become void.[72] Section 406 also sets out the order in which the proceeds of sale must be distributed; broadly, distribution must be in favour of security holders in order of priority but any residue has to be returned to the company and not to the holder of the void charge.[73] To take an example, a person taking a lien on subfreights is not affected by the register since this is not a registrable charge but a person taking a floating charge would be.[74]

(iii) thirdly, and perhaps most importantly, any person taking a registrable charge over the company's property (and only to such persons) will have notice of any matter requiring registration and disclosed.[75]

Modifications to the register

Provision is made for the registration of further particulars relating to a charge,[76] something of some importance given the effect of defective registration on the rights of the chargee. If the Registrar finds that the further particulars are in order, he must note the date of their receipt and send to the company and any person interested in the charge a copy of the particulars and the date on which they were

---

[67] See previous note.
[68] The ability to transfer a charge created by a debtor is to the advantage of both the debtor and the chargee.
[69] Introduced by s.99 of the 1989 Act.
[70] It is important to note that the section only applies where the chargee is exercising a power of sale.
[71] See generally on this Ferran and Mayo, *Registration of Company Charges—The New Regime* [1991] J.B.L. 152, at 158–161.
[72] s.406(1). Purchaser is defined as a person who in good faith and for valuable consideration acquires an interest in the property: s.406(4)(c).
[73] s.406(2). However, the holder of the void charge would be entitled to exercise his rights under section 407.
[74] s.416 (introduced by s.103 of the 1989 Act).
[75] It is submitted that s.711A(2) (introduced by s.143 of the 1989 Act) does not apply in this situation and the issue of notice with respect to charges is dealt with exclusively by s.416.
[76] s.401 (introduced by s.96 of the 1989 Act). See also s.408 (introduced by s.100 of the 1989 Act) on delivery of particulars relating to the issue of debentures.

delivered.[76a] As regards the registration of futher particulars a number of points need to be emphasised. First, section 401 applies to provisions which supplement or vary the particulars of an existing charge and therefore in some situations it will be necessary to distinguish between this and the creation of a new charge.[76b] Second, there is no time period within which the particulars have to be delivered and no criminal sanction for failure to deliver them. The only consequences will be those relating to the effect of omissions and errors in the registered particulars. This is to be contrasted with the requirements as to registration on the creation of a new charge and the consequences of late registration of such a charge. Third, the Registrar's certificate will be given the same effect as regards further particulars as it has with respect to the creation of a charge.[76c] A memorandum of satisfaction that the charge has been discharged can also be registered[77]; it must be signed by both the chargee and the company and if a fraudulently signed memorandum is registered it is submitted that it will not affect the chargee as it would not be a "duly" signed memorandum.[78] Both particulars and memorandum of satisfaction have to be signed by the chargee and the company and there is provision to obtain a court order where one of the parties refuses to sign the particulars.[79]

Enforcement of debentures—receivers

The methods of enforcing a security interest depend upon the nature of the rights which it confers and are often in no way peculiar to company law. However, company law does provide a distinct procedure for the enforcement of a floating charge by the appointment of an administrative receiver. Almost invariably the first step in the enforcement of a charge is for the debentureholders or their trustee to obtain the appointment of a receiver.[80] This appointment will normally be made by the debentureholder under an express or implied[81] power in the debenture, or by the court. Where the appointment is pursuant to a provision in the debenture then it must be clear that the conditions justifying the appointment have

[76a] s.401(3) and (4).
[76b] If the variation has the effect of turning an unregistrable charge into a registrable charge then it will be treated as the creation of a new charge: s.419(2).
[76c] See s.397(5) and s.415(3). It is unclear how s.401 will interlink with charges registered before the reforms of 1989 were introduced.
[77] s.403 (introduced by s.98 of the 1989 Act).
[78] See s.403(3).
[79] s.417 (introduced by s.103). Presumably the power in s.417(2) would, for example, enable the court to protect the chargee against prejudice caused by the company's refusal to sign a charge.
[80] If the state of the company is so parlous that it is doubtful whether there will be enough to cover the receiver's remuneration it may be necessary for the trustees to take possession. If the "debenture" is just an ordinary mortgage of particular property the debentureholder may, of course, exercise his power of sale without the preliminary step of appointing a receiver.
[81] *i.e.* under the L.P.A. 1925, s.101 when applicable.

arisen otherwise the receiver will be a trespasser and also liable for conversion.[82] Once the conditions for the enforcement of a charge have arisen English law places few constraints on the right of the security holder to enforce his charge and in this respect it is pro-security holder. Thus if the chargee is entitled to payment on demand he is not required to give the company a reasonable time in which to raise the funds to make payment and is only required to give the company time in which to effect the mechanics of payment.[83] In addition the chargee is not obliged to refrain from exercising his rights merely because by doing so he could avoid loss to the company[84] nor does failure to exercise them when the security is declining in value constitute a breach of any duty that he may owe to the company.[85] If nothing has occurred to render the security enforceable but the debentureholder's position is nevertheless in jeopardy, an application to the court may be necessary, for the court has a discretionary power to appoint a receiver in such circum-stances.[86] The normal procedure is for one of the debentureholders, on behalf of himself and all other holders to commence a debentureholder's action, the first step of which will be the appointment of a receiver. "Jeopardy" will be established when, for example, execution is about to be levied against the company,[87] or when it proposes to distribute to its members its one remaining asset.[88] It would be tempting to say that, when there is a floating charge, "jeopardy" should be assumed whenever the circumstances make it unreasonable, in the interests of the debentureholder, that the company should retain power to dispose of the property subject

[82] Where the appointment is defective the court can order the person making the appointment to indemnify the receiver: s.34 of the 1986 Act. See also s.232 which deals with the validity of acts of a defectively appointed administrative receiver and s.234 dealing with the seizure or disposal of property by an administrative receiver which does not belong to the company and generally *Re London Iron and Steel Co. Ltd.* [1990] BCLC 372; *Welsh Development Agency v. Export Finance Co. Ltd.* [1992] BCLC 148.

[83] *Bank of Baroda v. Panessar* [1987] Ch. 335; this is normally a matter of hours during normal banking hours. In addition the company may be estopped by its conduct from challenging the validity of the appointment of a receiver and the appointment of a receiver on invalid grounds may be subsequently cured if grounds justifying the appointment are subsequently discovered: *Bank of Baroda* at 512 and *Byblos Bank SAL v. Al-Khudairy* [1987] BCLC 232 respectively. There is no need for the debentureholder to specify the exact sum due in any demand: see *NRG Vision Ltd. v. Churchfield Leasing Ltd.* [1986] 1 BCLC 624.

[84] *Re Potters Oils Ltd.* [1986] 1 W.L.R. 201; *Standard Chartered Bank Ltd. v. Walker* [1982] 1 W.L.R. 1410.

[85] *China and South Sea Bank Ltd. v. Tan* [1990] 1 A.C. 536, P.C.; of course it will always be in the commercial interests of the chargee to exercise his rights if the security is declining in value. On other aspects of the receiver's duties to the company and others see p. 438.

[86] But the court will not normally have any power to appoint a receiver unless the debentures are secured by a charge: *Harris v. Beauchamp Bros.* [1894] 1 Q.B. 801, C.A.; *Re Swallow Footwear Ltd., The Times*, October 23, 1956. Also the court will not imply a term into a debenture empowering a chargee to appoint a receiver where his security is in jeopardy: see *Cryne v. Barclays Bank plc* [1987] BCLC 548, C.A.

[87] *McMahon v. North Kent Co.* [1891] 2 Ch. 148; *Edwards v. Standard Rolling Stock* [1893] 1 Ch. 574; and see *Re Victoria Steamboats Co.* [1897] 1 Ch. 158.

[88] *Re Tilt Cove Copper Co.* [1913] 2 Ch. 588.

to the charge. This is in fact the statutory definition under Scottish law,[89] but the English decisions hardly go so far, for the fact that the assets on realisation would not repay the debentures in full has been held insufficient.[90]

In cases where appointment out of court is possible this is certainly preferable from the viewpoint of the debentureholders as a body. The procedure in a debentureholders' action is lamentably expensive and dilatory, since the receiver, as an officer of the court, will have to work under its closest supervision and constant applications will have to be made in chambers throughout the duration of the receivership, which may last years if a complicated realisation is involved. Since the 1986 Act allows a receiver, even though appointed out of court, to obtain the court's directions,[91] it is difficult to envisage circumstances in which an application to the court can be justified if the cheaper alternative is available, and the professional adviser who recommended it would be laying himself open to grave risk of criticism. In the discussion which follows it will be assumed that what is being referred to is a receiver appointed out of court. A receiver appointed out of court can be either a receiver or an administrative receiver, the difference between them being that the latter is a receiver appointed under a charge which as created was a floating charge.[92]

Function and status of receiver and administrative receiver

Part III of the 1986 Act regulates both types of receiverships, although the provisions applicable to them are not identical. As the administrative receiver is unique to company law (and is probably the most common type of receiver appointed with respect to companies) it is proposed to concentrate on this type of receiver. The 1986 Act views the appointment of an administrative receiver as being in some respects similar to insolvency proceedings and regulates it accordingly. Thus administrative receivers must be qualified to act as insolvency practitioners[93] and can only be removed from office by the court.[94] Also, like the liquidator, the administrative receiver can compel those involved in the affairs of the company to provide him with information relating to the company's affairs[95] and is also obliged to report to the Secretary of State if he forms the opinion

89 s.122(2) of the 1986 Act.
90 *Re New York Taxicab Co.* [1913] 1 Ch. 1.
91 s.35.
92 s.29(2) and s.251 of the 1986 Act. As to whether there can be more than one administrative receiver (other than joint appointments) see Oditah, *Lightweight Floating Charges* [1991] J.B.L. 49.
93 s.388(1) of the 1986 Act. A body corporate, an undischarged bankrupt, or a person disqualified to act as a director may not act as an insolvency practitioner: see s.390(1) and (4). For other receivers see ss.30 and 31.
94 s.45(1) of the 1986 Act; they can resign, *ibid.*
95 ss.47 and 236; *Re Aveling Barford Ltd.* [1989] 1 W.L.R. 360; *Cloverbay Ltd. (Joint Administrators) v. B.C.C.I. S.A.* [1991] Ch. 90.

that the conduct of a director makes him unfit to act as a director of a company.[96] However, the appointment of a receiver must not be equated with that of a liquidator: (i) where a receiver is appointed the company need not go into liquidation[97] and if it does the same person who acted as receiver will normally not be appointed liquidator; (ii) liquidation is a class action designed to protect the interests of the unsecured creditors whereas, as we shall see, receivership is designed to protect the interests of the security holders who appointed the receiver and it is for this reason that a receiver can be appointed even where the company is in liquidation[98]; (iii) liquidation terminates the trading power of the company[99] whereas this is not the case with receivership; (iv) a liquidator has power to disclaim onerous property,[1] something not possible in the case of receivership; (v) a liquidator in a compulsory winding up is an officer of the court[2] whereas this is not the case with a receiver unless appointed by the court[3]; (vi) lastly, it is easier to obtain recognition of liquidation as opposed to receivership in proceedings in foreign courts.[4] These are the most important differences but there are others particularly with respect to liability on contracts.[5]

An administrative receiver might be considered to be the agent of those who appointed him but this is not the case; section 44 of the 1986 Act makes him the agent of the company.[6] The reason for this is to avoid those who appointed the administrative receiver being treated as mortgagees in possession[7] or being held liable for the receiver's acts which would be the case were the receiver to be treated as their agent.[8] As many have pointed out, the receiver's agency is a peculiar form of agency. This is because the primary responsibility of the receiver is to protect the interests of the security holders and to realise the charged assets for their benefit.

96 Companies Directors Disqualification Act 1986, section 7(3)(d).
97 See Insolvency Act 1986, s.247(2). Although generally a receiver should not be seen as a doctor but rather an undertaker.
98 Also without the leave of the court legal proceedings cannot be brought against the company: see s.130 of the 1986 Act.
99 *Re Potters Oil Ltd.* [1986] 1 W.L.R. 201.
1 See s.178 of the 1986 Act.
2 *Parsons v. Sovereign Bank of Canada* [1913] A.C. 160.
3 It is contempt of court to interfere with the exercise of power by a court-appointed receiver without the leave of the court.
4 s.72 of the 1986 Act permits an English or Scottish receiver to act throughout Great Britain provided local law permits this.
5 See p. 439.
6 Also the debenture will invariably provide that irrespective of the type of receiver appointed by the charge holder he is to be the agent of the company. A receiver appointed by the court is not an agent of anyone but an officer of the court: see *Moss SS. Co. v. Whinney* [1912] A.C. 254, H.L.
7 The duties of a mortgagee in possession are onerous: see Megarry and Wade, *The Law of Real Property* (5th ed.) at pp. 942-943.
8 If the chargee interferes with the receiver's discharge of his duties this could, provided the interference is sufficiently pervasive, result in the chargee being treated as the agent of the chargee: see *American Express International Banking Corp. v. Hurley* [1985] 3 All E.R. 564.

The powers of the administrative receiver are extensive and he will have complete control over the management of the company.[9] In addition he can apply to the court for an order empowering him to dispose of property subject to a prior charge.[10] In the exercise of his powers a receiver is under a duty to the debtor company to take reasonable care to obtain the best price reasonably possible at the time of sale[11]; this duty is also owed to a guarantor of the company's debts.[12] However, as the receiver in exercising his power of sale is in a position analogous to that of the mortgagee, he is not obliged to postpone sale in order to obtain a better price or to adopt a piecemeal method of sale.[13] The basis of the receiver's duty set out above was initially considered to involve the extension of the common law of negligence to supplement equity,[14] but the courts now treat it as something which flows from the nature in equity of the relationship between the mortgagee and mortgagor.[15]

A person dealing with an administrative receiver in good faith is not bound to inquire if the receiver is acting within his powers.[16] Unlike a winding-up,[17] the board of directors does not become *functus officio* on the appointment of a receiver but the directors' powers are substantially superseded since they cannot act so as to interfere with the discharge by the receiver of his responsibilities and accordingly their powers are suspended "so far as is requisite to enable a receiver to discharge his functions."[18] Given the extent of the powers of the administrative receiver, the directors will have a minuscule aperture within which they are free to exercise their powers. However, they do possess certain residual powers and, for example, it has been held that they can bring an action on behalf of the company against a debentureholder for the improper exercise of his powers.[19] This authority has been doubted because of the conflict

[9] s.42 of the 1986 Act confers on an administrative receiver the powers set out in Schedule 1 to the Act in so far as they are not inconsistent with the terms of the debenture. There are 23 powers enumerated and they are very wide; for example, number 14 confers on an administrative receiver "Power to carry on the business of the company." An ordinary receiver does not have such powers but normally they will be conferred on him by appointing him as a manager.

[10] s.43 of the 1986 Act. The rights of the security holder are protected in the same way as they are under section 15: see p. 425.

[11] *Cuckmere Brick Co. Ltd. v. Mutual Finance Ltd.* [1971] Ch. 949; *Bishop v. Bonham* [1988] 1 W.L.R. 742.

[12] *Standard Chartered Bank Ltd. v. Walker* [1982] 1 W.L.R. 1410; *American Express International Banking Corpn. v. Hurley* [1985] 3 All E.R. 564.

[13] *Tse Kwong Lam v. Wong Chit Sen* [1983] 1 W.L.R. 1349.

[14] See Lightman and Moss, *op. cit.*, Chap.7.

[15] *Parker-Tweedale v. Dunbar Bank Plc* [1991] Ch. 12, C.A. (mortgagee owes no duty to beneficiary of mortgaged property).

[16] s.42(3). If an administrative receiver is seen as being an organ of the company, then this provision is not in compliance with Article 9(2) of the First Directive.

[17] See pp. 768 and 770.

[18] *Re Emmadart Ltd.* [1979] Ch. 540 at 544; see also *Gomba Holdings UK Ltd.* v. *Homan* [1986] 1 W.L.R. 1301.

[19] *Newhart Developments Ltd. v. Co-operative Commerical Bank Ltd.* [1978] Q.B. 814, C.A. (it is important to note that in that case the company was indemnified for any costs that it might incur).

that would arise were the receiver and the directors to have different views on whether an action should be brought and also on the handling of any counterclaim.[19a] Whatever the status of the *Newhart*[19b] decision, it is clear that it will be confined to very narrow limits since to allow any such action would interfere with the primary duties of the receiver to protect the interests of the security holder.[19c] Also, as the directors remain in office, the receiver would probably be under an obligation to provide the directors with the information that they need to know to enable them to comply with their reporting obligations under the Companies Act.[20] The receiver will be obliged at the end of his receivership to hand over to the company any documents belonging to the company but not those brought into existence for the discharge of his own professional duties or his duties to the chargee.[21]

The receiver's liability with respect to contracts

This raises two separate issues. The first relates to contracts already in existence when the receiver is appointed. As the administrative receiver is the agent of the company, his appointment does not terminate the company's contracts. Thus, for example, contracts of employment are not terminated unless the receiver does something which is inconsistent with the continuation of the contract,[22] for example a sale of the company's business.[23] The receiver is not, however, obliged to fulfil existing contracts and because of this it is claimed that in this regard he is better placed than the company which of course must stand by its contracts.[24] The reason for this is one of priorities; if the receiver were obliged to fulfil existing

[19a] *Tudor Grange Holdings Ltd.* v. *Citibank N.A.* [1992] Ch. 53. As Browne-Wilkinson V.-C. pointed out in that case, it would be more appropriate for receivers or their appointor to use s.35 of the 1986 Act.

[19b] It could be argued that the right to bring an action against the debentureholder could not be an asset covered by the charge. This, however, proves too much since it would mean that the directors would always be in a position to bring an action against the debentureholder even when the special factors in *Newhart* were not present. And while this argument rightly emphasises the scope of the receiver's authority it fails to give effect to his functions. Also the agency of the receiver may have sufficient content to impose on him a duty to seek redress against a debentureholder in appropriate cases.

[19c] See also *Gomba Holdings U.K. Ltd.* v. *Homan* [1986] 1 W.L.R. 1301; *Watts* v. *Midland Bank plc* [1986] BCLC 15 (a case which illustrates that since the power to use the corporate name in litigation is normally vested in the directors a shareholder will normally be precluded from bringing a derivative action against a receiver).

[20] *Gomba Holdings (U.K.) Ltd.* v. *Homan* [1986] 1 W.L.R. 1301; see also pages 1305–1306 where Hoffmann J. points out that equity may impose on a receiver a duty to account which is wider that his statutory obligations.

[21] *Gomba Holdings U.K. Ltd.* v. *Minories Finance Ltd.* [1988] 1 W.L.R. 1231, C.A.

[22] *Griffiths* v. *Secretary of State for Social Services* [1974] Q.B. 468. The appointment of the receiver by the court does terminate contracts of service: *Reid* v. *Explosives Co. Ltd.* (1887) 19 Q.B.D. 264.

[23] *Re Foster Clark's Ltd.'s Indenture Trusts* [1966] 1 W.L.R. 125.

[24] *Airlines Airspares Ltd.* v. *Handley Page Ltd.* [1970] Ch. 193. The receiver cannot interfere with existing equitable rights of a third party, for example under a contract which is specifically enforceable: see *Freevale* v. *Metrostore (Holdings) Ltd.* [1984] Ch. 199 and cf. *Ash & Newman Ltd.* v. *Creative Devices Research Ltd.* [1991] BCLC 403.

contracts it would mean that the unsecured creditors would be in a position to require fulfilment of their contracts before the receiver could realise the security. Such an outcome would place priorities on their head and, accordingly, the receiver should be seen as acting in the right of the debentureholder.[25] However, although unclear, it may be that the receiver has a limited duty to continue to trade where this would not jeopardise the chargee's interests and a failure to do so would impose gratuitous damage on the company.[26] Not to extend his duty in this way would stretch the pro-creditor bias of receivership to ridiculous lengths.

Where the receiver enters into a new contract this will be binding on the company. More importantly, the receiver is liable on any contract that he enters into on behalf of the company unless the contract otherwise provides.[27] As regards contracts of employment, it is provided that he is to be liable on any contract of employment adopted by him but nothing he does or omits to do in the first 14 days of his appointment is to be taken as adoption of the contract.[28] What this means is far from clear. Adoption is different from novation and also appears to be distinguishable from merely acting as though the contract were binding on the company. What it appears to import is some positive act which is short of entering into a new contract and as such it does not fit neatly into the conceptual apparatus of contract law.

Publicity of appointment and reports

Where a receiver or manager is appointed then this must be stated in various business documents relating to the company.[29] Also all receivers have to make prescribed returns to the Registrar[30] and the administrative receiver has to report to creditors including unsecured creditors.[31] A receiver who fails to comply with his reporting obligations can be ordered to do so[32] and, more importantly, he can be disqualified from acting as a receiver or manager.[33] There is no similar obligation to report where a debentureholder enters into

25 See *Edwin Hill* v. *First Federal Finance Corporation Plc* [1989] 1 W.L.R. 225; as this makes clear the question is whether the chargee has a superior right to the person with a contractual claim and the answer to this will normally be in the affirmative.
26 See Lightman and Moss, *op. cit.*, at pp. 94–96; *Knight* v. *Lawrence* [1991] BCC 411 at 418: "Though he may be appointed by one party his function is to look after the property of which he is a receiver for the benefit of all those interested in it."
27 s.44(1)(b) of the 1986 Act. He is entitled to indemnification out of the assets of the company (s.44(1)(c)) and can also contract for indemnification by those who appointed him (s.44(3)). See s.37 of the 1986 Act for other receivers.
28 s.44(1)(b) and (2). This was intended to reverse the effect of the judgment in *Nicoll* v. *Cutts* [1985] BCLC 322. In *Re Specialised Mouldings Ltd.* (13 February 1987) the court held that the receiver could serve a notice of non-adoption on the employees.
29 s.39 of the 1986 Act.
30 s.38 (receivers) and s.48 (administrative receivers) of the 1986 Act.
31 s.48 of the 1986 Act.
32 s.41 of the 1986 Act. Also of relevance are the Insolvency Rules 1986, Part 3.
33 Company Directors Disqualification Act 1986, ss.1(1)(c), 3 and 22(7); see *Re Artic Engineering Ltd. (No. 2)* [1986] 1 W.L.R. 686.

possession and it has been recommended that this omission be corrected.[34]

Other registers

There are a number of other registers that are relevant with respect to certain specialist charges; the most important of these registers are those maintained under the Land Registration Act 1925 and the Land Charges Act 1972. It is not intended to go into them in any detail here.[35] It is important to note that a company must itself maintain a register of charges which is more extensive than that maintained by the Registrar of Companies (since it covers all charges irrespective of type) but failure to register a charge in it does not invalidate the charge.[36]

[34] Jenkins Committee, para. 306(k).
[35] See Diamond Report, Chap. 12. Registration in these registers does not eliminate the need to register in the companies register should it be a type of charge that needs to be so registered.
[36] s.411 (introduced by s.101 of the 1989 Act); the company must also keep a copy of every instrument of charge at its registered office. This is open for inspection and copies can be obtained on payment of a fee: see section 412 (introduced by s.101 of the 1989 Act).

Part Five

INVESTOR AND CREDITOR PROTECTION

INTRODUCTION

THE purpose of this Part is to consider the protection afforded to investors in, and creditors of, a company. Many of the matters discussed appear in the Companies Act under the heading "Management and Administration," and the orthodox textbook arrangement is to consider them merely as aspects of the company's internal machinery. Such subjects as accounts, audits, meetings and resolutions could well be dealt with in this way, for even in the absence of mandatory legal rules business convenience would demand the voluntary adoption of very similar practices. But in the case of companies these practices have been converted into legal regulations because this has been thought necessary to protect those interested in the company and those having dealings with it. And, from the viewpoint of the lawyer, their primary importance lies in their effectiveness as a means of avoiding disputes and preventing injustices. Hence the discussion which follows is deliberately directed towards this aspect of them.

The danger of this approach is that it may give the erroneous impression that companies are constantly embroiled in internecine strife, and that investors and creditors are habitually maltreated by dishonest or incompetent company controllers. On the contrary, the majority of limited companies, both public and private, are honestly and conscientiously managed. The succeeding chapters consider the extent to which the legal rules conduce to this desirable result and provide adequate redress in the case of the small number of companies less scrupulously and competently operated. If they suggest that the legal sanctions against the abuse of power by company controllers are not wholly adequate, it must be remembered that it is but rarely that power is abused. The British believe that they have a genius for constitutional government with a minimum of constitutional laws, and for working majority rule without oppression of minorities. Until recently company law, with its relative freedom from stringent regulations, reflected this national belief. It can hardly be said to do so any longer. But no system can wholly protect fools from their own folly or from the knavery of others, and the advantages of trying to do so as fully as possible have to be weighed against the disadvantages of imposing fetters on business conducted honestly and efficiently.

The problems of protecting (a) investors, both shareholders and debentureholders, and (b) creditors, cannot be kept entirely distinct. Of the additional safeguards now to be considered the primary one,

444

both to investors and creditors, is the publicity which, to a greater or lesser extent, attends the functioning of the company. Hence it forms the subject of the first chapter of this Part.

CHAPTER 17

PUBLICITY AND ACCOUNTS

On the basis that "forewarned is forearmed" the fundamental principle underlying the Companies Acts has been that of disclosure. If the public and the members were enabled to find out all relevant information about the company, this, thought the founding fathers of our company law, would be a sure shield. The shield may not have proved quite so strong as they had expected, and in more recent times it has been supported by offensive weapons, such as inspections or investigations instigated by the Department of Trade and Industry.[1] But, basically, disclosure still remains the principal safeguard on which the Companies Acts pin their faith, and every succeeding Act since 1862 has added to the extent of the publicity required, although, not unreasonably, it varies according to the type of company concerned.

This publicity is mainly secured in four ways:

(a) by official notification in the Gazette;
(b) by provisions for registration at Companies House;
(c) by compulsory maintenance of various registers and the like by the company; and
(d) by compulsory disclosure of the financial position in the company's published accounts and by attempting to ensure their accuracy through a professional audit.

In these ways, and in certain others of less importance which will be referred to briefly, members and the public (which, for practical purposes, means creditors and others who may subsequently have dealings with the company and become its members or creditors) are supposed to be able to obtain the information which they need to make an intelligent appraisal of their risks, and to decide when and how to exercise the rights and remedies which the law affords them.

Official notification

This is a concept relatively new to English company law having been introduced by section 9 of the European Communities Act 1972 to comply with the First Company Law Directive. As a result of that

---

[1] See Chap. 25 below.

and later Directives there are now many cases in which the Registrar must cause to be published in the Gazette[2] notice that he has received for registration various types of documents.[3] The notice merely records the name and registered number of the company, the nature of the document and the date of its receipt. To see the document itself it will be necessary to resort to Companies House or the company itself. Nor is it an effective method of notifying the members, creditors or the general public, few of whom read the Gazette.[4] When it is thought vital that members or creditors should receive notice, the Act requires them to be given notice by the company; in relation to the general public the best that can be done is to require publication in newspapers.

Registration at Companies House

The most common method of obtaining information about a company is by searching its file at Companies House in Cardiff or London (or Edinburgh if the company is registered in Scotland). Most of the information (and more besides) could be obtained from the company itself but generally the first step will be to Companies House. At one location it is possible to inspect not only the file of the company known to the searcher but also those of any related companies that this inspection reveals. And, especially perhaps, it enables searches to be undertaken without any of the companies knowing about it.

It is unnecessary, and would make tedious reading, to list all the sections of the Act which require a company to deliver documents for registration. Many such sections have been mentioned already. Here it suffices to say that the aim is to ensure that a company is required to do so when it is thought that the matter is one that the public needs to know. Hence a search of its file should enable reasonably up-to-date information to be obtained on such matters as: its constitution (the memorandum and articles, as amended); its officers; the address of its registered office[5]; its issued share capital[6]; charges on its property[7]; and, in most cases, its latest annual accounts.[8]

Subject to the payment of a fee prescribed from time to time by statutory instrument,[9] any person is entitled to inspect and to obtain

---

[2] The London or the Edinburgh Gazette according to the place of registration of the company: s.744.

[3] s.711 (which lists the documents in question).

[4] It is not read by the populace but is scanned by credit-agencies and the like.

[5] This is important since it is there that process can be served upon it.

[6] The returns of allotments (see Chap. 9 at p. 203 above) will show to whom the shares were originally allotted but not in whose names they are now registered as a result of transfers; for that, inspection of the membership register is needed unless the latest annual return (see below) is sufficiently recent for the searcher's purpose.

[7] This may give a more reliable indication of creditworthiness, or the lack of it, than the filed accounts which are unlikely to be as up-to-date.

[8] See below at pp. 453, *et seq.*

[9] s.708.

copies of "any records kept by the registrar for the purposes of the Companies Acts"[10]; no distinction is drawn between the rights of members and inspection by other persons.[11] And a copy of any registered document, duly certified by the Registrar "is in all legal proceedings admissible in evidence as of equal validity with the original document and as evidence of any fact stated therein of which oral evidence would be admissible."[12]

Annual Returns

In addition to the documents which have to be delivered to the Registrar shortly after[13] the occurrence of the events which they record, every company is required to make an Annual Return. As well as a means of publicising information this is a document of some importance administratively, since without it the register would be cluttered, to a greater extent than it is, with files of moribund companies[14] abandoned by their members. Failure to file the annual return alerts the Registrar and enables him to take appropriate steps leading to the companies' removal from the register.[15]

As a source of information, the return collates much that should have been delivered for registration when the relevant transactions occurred, so that a searcher may find it unnecessary to search back beyond the latest annual return on the file. It also enables some additional or more recent[16] information to be obtained. The 1989 Act substituted a new and somewhat simplified Chapter III (Annual Return) for that in the original Part XI of the 1985 Act. Briefly summarised the effect of the new Chapter is as follows:

Every company, whether or not it is required to file annual accounts, must deliver to the Registrar successive returns in the prescribed form made up to its "return date," *i.e.* the anniversary of its incorporation or, if its last return was made up to a different date, the anniversary of that date. This must be signed by a director or the

---

10 s.709 (inserted by the 1989 Act) subs.(1).

11 Nor could there be, since the Registry's officials are not in a position to check the credentials of searchers or of those on whose behalf they are acting, more often than not searches will be undertaken by solicitors, articled clerks or by professional agencies).

12 s.709(3).

13 A helpful reform would be to standardise so far as possible the periods within which the various documents are supposed to be delivered; at present they vary greatly, and often for no obvious reason, between 7, 14, 21 and 28 days and "one month."

14 Such companies should not be confused with "dormant companies" (see below pp. 471, 472) which may have legitimate reasons for remaining registered.

15 Also, the fee for registering the return may help to finance Companies House. But the present fee can barely cover the cost of registering and hardly seems large enough to discourage people from allowing their moribund companies to cumber the register.

16 *e.g.* the annual return should be delivered within 28 days after the "return date" to which it is made up whereas the annual accounts, even if filed timeously, are likely to be made up to a date some 7 months before (and more in the case of private companies).

secretary of the company and must be delivered within 28 days after the return date.[17] If a proper return is not so delivered the company is guilty of an offence and liable to a fine and a daily default fine so long as the contravention continues.[18] And any director or the secretary of the company is similarly liable unless he shows that he took all reasonable steps to avoid the commission or continuance of the offence.[19]

Section 364 specifies the "general" information which the return must state. This includes the address of the company's registered office[20] and particulars of the directors[21] and secretary.[22] It also, and this is new, includes "the type of company and its principal business activities,"[23] the type to be "given by reference to the classification prescribed for the purposes of this section,"[24] while the principal business activities "may be given by reference to categories of any prescribed system of classifying business activities."[25] Also new is the requirement that a private company which has elected under the substituted section 252 to dispense with the laying of accounts before a general meeting or, under section 366A, to dispense with the holding of annual general meetings, must so state in the return.[26]

If the company has a share capital, in addition to the general information the return must give the "particulars of share capital and shareholders" specified in section 364A. This enables much the same information to be obtained as that obtainable from the company's membership register[27] but only as at the return date. If up-to-date particulars are needed, the searcher will have to inspect, or obtain a copy of, the company's membership register. But, to enable the searcher to know where the register is kept, if that is not at the registered office, the general part of the return has to state where that is.[28] In the case of a company without share capital the return will give no particulars of the members; to ascertain that, resort must be to the company.

[17] s.363(1) and (2).
[18] s.363(3). The contravention continues until there is delivered a return which complies both in form and content: s.363(2) and (5)(a).
[19] s.363(4). This, however is but one of the many sanctions that can be invoked: see n.30 below. And note that, under the Company Directors Disqualification Act, Sched. I, para. 4(f), failure to make annual returns is one of the matters relevant to determination of unfitness of directors.
[20] s.364(1)(a).
[21] And (optimistically—see Chap. 7, pp. 143, 144) includes a shadow director although he is not an authorised signatory of the return: s365(3).
[22] s.364(1)(c)–(f).
[23] s.364(1)(b).
[24] s.364(2). See The Companies (Forms Amendment No. 2 and Companies Type and Principal Business Activities) Regs. (1990 S.I. No. 1766) made on the authority of no less than 8 sections of the Act.
[25] s.364(3). See ibid.
[26] s.364(1)(i).
[27] s.364A(3)–(6). Subs (6) relieves companies of the need to include a full replica of the membership register more often than once every three years so long as all changes have been stated in each of the two preceding returns.
[28] s.364(1)(g) and likewise as to any register of debentureholders: ibid (h).

However, section 365(1) empowers the Secretary of State by regulations[29] to "make further provision as to the information to be given in a company's annual return, which may amend or repeal the provisions of sections 364 and 364A." So further changes seem likely.

The principal weakness of these provisions is that companies (especially, but not exclusively, private ones) are deplorably dilatory in delivering returns to the Registrar so that at any one time a majority of companies are in arrear to a greater or lesser extent. However, in recent years a blitz on such companies has been mounted[30] with the result that there has been some improvement. Nevertheless, if a creditor, with grounds for suspecting that a company is in financial difficulties, makes a search he is all too likely to find that no recent annual returns or accounts have been filed.

Companies' Registers and Records

Most of the information obtainable from Companies House can instead be obtained from the company and so can further information especially if the searcher is a member of the company. Nevertheless a member, even of a private company, unless he is also a director is not entitled, as he would be if he were a member of a partnership, to inspect the books and records of the company except to the extent that the Act specifically provides.[31] But there are an increasing number of documents and registers which he, and, indeed, other persons, are entitled to inspect (in the case of a member generally without payment) and to obtain copies on payment. These include, for example, directors' contracts of service,[32] and the registers of:—the directors and secretary,[33] directors' holdings of, and dealings in, the company's securities,[34] and (in the case of a public company)

---

[29] To be made by statutory instrument subject to annulment by a resolution of either House of Parliament: s.365(2).

[30] In 1989–90 there were 2359 prosecutions and 1245 convictions for failure to forward annual returns (and 4443 prosecutions and 2513 convictions for failure to deliver accounts). 2,800 directors of 1763 companies were involved in proceedings relating to annual returns and accounts and 1558 directors of 1005 companies were convicted: *Companies in 1989–90*, Table D2 and note 2. If companies are as dilatory in replying to correspondence as they are in filing returns they may find that the Registrar has struck them off the register under s.652 as "defunct," with serious and expensive consequences even if they succeed in getting restored to the register under s.653. In 1989–90 some 1400 companies were restored to the register under this or other sections: see *ibid.* Table C1. A further weapon in the authorities' armoury is s.713 which can lead to defaulting companies and directors finding themselves in contempt of court.

[31] Hence in *Butt v. Kelson* [1952] Ch. 197, C.A. it was held that the beneficial owners of shares of a company could not compel the trustee, who was a director of the company, to produce the company's books for their inspection.

[32] s.318. These can be inspected by any member without payment, but not by any other person.

[33] ss.288–290. These can be inspected by any person without payment and copies may be obtained, in the case of a member without payment.

[34] s.325 and Sched. 13, Part IV, paras. 25 and 26. The position is the same as in n. 33.

the register of 3 per cent. shareholders.[35] The last two registers afford important information, not obtainable from Companies House, in relation to beneficial ownership and not just registered ownership, and are particularly valuable to a searcher who suspects that some major transaction, (*e.g.* a take-over bid) is in the offing. Furthermore, the register of charges which the company is required to maintain may be more illuminating than that at Companies House since it must now contain entries of all charges on the company's property whether or not they require to be registered at Companies House and copies of any instrument creating or evidencing a charge must also be kept.[36] Both the register and the copies are open to inspection by any creditor[37] or member without payment and by any other person on payment, copies being obtainable on payment.[38]

The maximum fees that companies can charge for inspection or copies are now prescribed by regulations (the former practice of stating them in the primary legislation did not work well in an inflationary climate) and these regulations[39] clarify the obligations of companies regarding inspection and copies.

Other methods

Before turning to the all-important Accounts, mention must be made of other methods whereby information about a company is required to be disseminated. One which the Act employs in relation to information which can be briefly conveyed, is to require it to appear on all business communications of the company. Thus its name, number, the fact that its liability is limited (if such be the case) and the address of its registered office must be stated on all business letters or order forms. Again, if the company is listed, it will be subject to additional duties to keep its security holders and, indeed the public, informed of all major developments and if it does not The Exchange may publish the information.[40]

Apart from legally required publicity there is media publicity which may occur whether the company wants it to or not.[41] All the national

[35] See pp. 609–619 below. Here again the position is the same regarding inspection and copies (see s.219) save for the limited exception in s211(9).

[36] s.411. The company may be faced with a difficult task in deciding whether the transaction, (*e.g.* a retention of title on a sale of goods) creates a "charge."

[37] This equating of creditors with members is unusual but makes sense here. Note, however, that neither "creditor" nor "member" includes a person who is contemplating becoming a creditor or member: if he searches, as he should before he has committed himself he will have to pay if the company insists.

[38] s.412.

[39] The Companies (Inspection and Copying of Registers, Indices and Documents Regs. 1991 (1991 S.I. No. 1998) made under s.723A: see p. 388 above.

[40] See Chap. 13, above, and *The Yellow Book* Section 5. And note s.329 of the Act which imposes an obligation on listed companies to notify The Stock Exchange of any reported transaction in its listed shares which a director is required to report to the company under s.324 or 328 (for entry on the register maintained under s.325: see n. 34 above) and expressly empowers the Exchange to publish it.

[41] It will welcome publicity only if the news is good but in that event it will probably have to pay for its inclusion as an advertisement.

newspapers and many of the provincial ones now devote an increasing number of columns to "City" or "Business" matters. The columnists have keen noses for scandals and once their interest is aroused they follow the scent with sleuth-like pertinacity and commendable disregard of the risks of suits for defamation.[42] The result may be that, what a company had hoped to treat as a minor domestic matter which could be brushed under the carpet, is exposed to the harsh light of day. This may not always be in the best interests of the company but as, on the whole, the Press acts in this area[43] with reasonable restraint, it generally is in the best interests of investors and the public.

Finally, it should be pointed out that one of the grounds on which under section 432[44] the Secretary of State may appoint inspectors to investigate and report on the affairs of a company is that "the company's members have not been given all the information with respect to its affairs which they might reasonably expect"[45]—whether or not that information is such that they have an express statutory right to be told it. A failure to give such information might also be relevant on a petition to wind-up the company on the "just and equitable" ground[46] or to grant relief on the ground that the affairs of the company are being conducted in a manner unfairly prejudicial to members.[47]

(a) that the price of limited liability ought to be the maximum possible disclosure of information regarding the company's financial position,

Accounts

A staggering transformation has occurred in the course of the 20th Century in the ambit of statutory provisions regarding company accounts, as will be apparent to anyone who compares the exiguous provisions in the 1908 Act with the profusion of sections and Schedules in the Companies Act 1985 as amended, supplemented and re-arranged by the 1989 Act. This has resulted from the recognition

---

[42] This attitude may not always be shared by their editors or the papers' proprietors. The only special protection that newspapers have is that 'fair and accurate reports of general meetings of public companies are not actionable in the absence of malice so long as any reasonable explanation or correction is published: Defamation Act 1952 s.7 and Sched. 11. This adds little to the general defences of justification, fair comment and qualified privilege. However, even if the paper decides not to publish, the journalist may alert the regulatory authorities.

[43] In contrast with exposure of sexual peccadilloes, when there tends to be an assumption that it must be in the public interest to publish whatever appeals to the prurient interests of the public.

[44] See Chap. 25 at pp. 678, 679 below.

[45] s.432(2)(d).

[46] Insolvency Act s.122(1)(g). See Chap. 24 below at pp. 662–668 and 670–672.

[47] Companies Act s.459. See Chap. 24 below at pp. 662–670.

(b) that within the EC that information ought to be presented in a standardised fashion so that like can be compared with like irrespective of the member State in which the company was incorporated, but

(c) that some concessions regarding (a) should be afforded to small companies so as to relieve them of burdens and expense that they might find intolerable.[48]

All this chapter attempts is to offer guidance on how to find the way through the statutory provisions[49] which, understandably, tend to be expressed in accountants' language rather than that of lawyers. The United Kingdom chose dutifully to implement the Fourth Directive on Company Accounts without waiting, as some other member States did, for the adoption of the Seventh Directive on Group Accounts. Hence, when the latter was implemented by the 1989 Act, Part VII of the Act and the related Schedules needed copious revision and the opportunity was seized to undertake a major re-arrangement of the Schedules.[50] Despite taking two bites, the implementation of the Directives was achieved with less trauma than in some other member States whose existing requirements were less advanced than those of the United Kingdom. Particularly was this so because the British accountancy profession played a more constructive role in the preparatory stages of the two Directives than our professional bodies had hitherto taken in relation to EC proposals. We even succeeded in securing the adoption of our basic principle that accounts must present a "true and fair view"—notwithstanding that we were unable to explain precisely what that expression meant.

Accounting records

This chapter concentrates primarily on accounts as a means of publicising information and hence on the annual accounts through which that publicity is achieved. But Part VII of the Act starts with a prescription of a company's obligation to maintain current accounting records; and logically enough, because, although these are not open

[48] The extent of proposition (c) is controversial since the failure-rate of small companies is greater.

[49] Reference has already been made to some of the relevant provisions particularly in Chap. 6 in relation to group accounts, in Chaps. 9 and 10 in relation to raising and maintaining capital and to dividends, and in Chap. 13 in relation to public issues. This chapter concentrates on accounts as a means of publicising information and on those statutory provisions on the construction of which lawyers are likely to be asked to advise.

[50] These Schedules now are Sched. 4 (form and content of company accounts); Sched. 4A (form and content of group accounts); Sched. 5 (disclosure of information: related undertakings); Sched. 6 (disclosure of information: emoluments and benefits of directors and others); Sched. 7 (matters to be dealt with in directors' reports); Sched. 8 (exemptions for small and medium-sized companies); Scheds. 9 and 10 (special provisions for banking and insurance companies and groups), and Sched. 10A (supplementary provisions on parent and subsidiary undertakings).

to inspection by members or the public,[51] unless they are kept it will be impossible for the company to produce verifiable annual accounts. Hence section 221 provides that every company shall keep records sufficient to show and explain the company's transactions, to disclose, with reasonable accuracy at any time, its financial position and to enable its directors to ensure that any balance sheet and profit and loss account will comply with the provisions of Part VII.[52]

The records must contain day-to-day entries of all money received or expended and of the matters to which that related and a record of the company's assets and liabilities.[53] If the company's business involves dealing in goods the records must also contain a statement of stock held at the end of the financial year and statements of stocktakings from which that was prepared, and, except in the case of goods sold in the ordinary course of retail trade, statements of all goods sold or purchased, in sufficient detail to enable the other party to be identified.[54]

A company which has a subsidiary undertaking to which these requirements do not apply[55] must take all reasonable steps to secure that the subsidiary keeps such records as will enable the directors of the parent company to ensure that any balance sheet and profit and loss account prepared under Part VII complies with the Act's requirements.[56]

Failure to comply with the section renders every officer of the company[57] who is in default guilty of an offence[58] unless he shows that he acted honestly and that, in the circumstances in which the company's business was carried on, the default was excusable.[59]

Section 222 provides that accounting records are at all times to be open for inspection by officers of the company.[60] If any such records are kept outside Great Britain,[61] there must be sent to Great Britain (and be available for inspection there by the officers) records which will disclose with reasonable accuracy the position of the business in question at intervals of not more than six months and will enable the directors to ensure that the company's balance sheet and profit and loss account comply with the Act.[62] All required records must be

51 See p. 451 above.
52 s.221(1).
53 s.221(2).
54 s.221(3).
55 e.g. because it is a foreign subsidiary or a partnership.
56 s.221(4).
57 But not the company itself.
58 Punishable by fine or imprisonment or both: s.221(6).
59 s.221(5).
60 s.222(1). And note the even wider rights of the auditors (s.389A(1)) and of the DTI or inspectors under Part XIV of the Act on which see below Chap. 25 below.
61 e.g. because the company has a branch outside G.B.
62 s.222(2) and (3). The penalty for non-compliance is the same as that in s.221: s.222(4).

preserved for three years if it is a private company or for six years if it is a public one.[63]

Annual accounts

Part VII then turns to matters concerning annual accounts. Sections 222–225 prescribe how a company's "financial year" is to be determined. Despite its name it is not a calendar year or, necessarily, a period of 12 months. What period it is depends on its "accounting reference period", as determined in accordance with section 223, which in turn depends on its "accounting reference date" as determined in accordance with sections 224 and 225. We therefore start with sections 224 and 225.

Under section 224 a company may at any time before the end of nine months from the date of its incorporation give notice to the Registrar specifying what its accounting reference date is to be.[64] If it fails to do so, in the case of a company incorporated before April 1990,[65] the reference date is 31st March[66] and, in the case of a company incorporated thereafter, it is the last day of the month in which it was incorporated.[67] This date determines the date on which its accounting reference period ends in each calendar year.[68] But it will not necessarily begin 12 months before. A company's first accounting reference period must be a period of not less than six months or more than 18 months beginning with the date of its incorporation and ending with its accounting reference date.[69] It is only its subsequent accounting reference periods that have to be of 12 months duration beginning immediately after the end of the previous accounting reference period and ending on the accounting reference date.[70] Moreover section 224 is "subject to the provisions of section 225"[71] which permit a company by notice in the prescribed form to specify a new accounting reference date in relation to the current reference period and subsequent ones.[72] Indeed, if the change is to enable the accounting reference periods of parent and subsidiary undertakings to coincide or because an administrator has been appointed, it may operate in respect also of the immediately preceding accountancy reference period.[73] Any such notice must state

---

[63] s.222(5). An officer of the company is liable to imprisonment or a fine or both if he fails to take all reasonable steps to secure compliance or intentionally causes any default. If there has been villainy, destroying all records of it is all too likely.
[64] s.224(2).
[65] The date when these provisions of the 1989 Act came into operation.
[66] As under the former version of s.224.
[67] s.224(3).
[68] s.224(4) and (5).
[69] s.224(4).
[70] s.224(5).
[71] s.224(6).
[72] s.225(1).
[73] s.225(2). But, unless there is an administration order in force, notice cannot be given in respect of a preceding accounting reference period if the time for laying the accounts for that period has already expired: s.224(5).

whether the current (or preceding, when allowed) reference period is to be shortened, so that it will end on the first occurrence of the accounting reference date, or lengthened, so that it will end on its second occurrence,[74] but unless an administration order is in force the period cannot be extended so as to exceed 18 months.[75] Nor, normally, can an accounting reference period be extended if it has already been extended during the previous five years.[76]

The end-product, as stated in section 223, is that the company's first "financial year" begins with first day of its first accounting reference period,[77] (*i.e.* the date of its incorporation) and ends on the last day of the reference period and that subsequent financial years begin with the day immediately following the end of the previous financial year and end with the last day of its next accounting reference period[78] "*or on such other date not more than seven days before or after the end of that period as the directors may determine.*"[79] But for the words italicised "financial year" and "accounting reference period" would mean exactly the same thing; as it is they need not. But the difference cannot be more than seven days, since although the next financial year begins from the end of the last, it has to end within seven days of the next accounting reference period.

As we have seen, the Directives compel us to apply group accounting to undertakings which are not necessarily companies.[80] Accordingly section 223(4) provides that, in relation to one that is not, references to its financial year are to any period in respect of which its constitution or the law under which it is established requires a profit and loss account to be made up. And, finally section 223(5) provides that the directors of a parent company shall secure that, except where there are good reasons to the contrary, the financial years of each of its subsidiaries coincide with that of the parent company. Unless this is so any form of meaningful group accounting is difficult to achieve.

Form and content of annual accounts.

Section 226 imposes on the directors of every company the duty to prepare for each financial year of the company a balance sheet and a profit and loss account (its "individual accounts"[81]) and section 227

74 s.225(3).
75 s.225(6).
76 s.225(4). But this does not apply if the object is to make the periods of parent and subsidiaries coincide, or if an administration order is in force, or if the S. of S. agrees: *ibid.*
77 s.223(2).
78 s.223(3).
79 s.223(3) and (4). Since nobody is required to do anything on the end date it is not immediately apparent why this liberty is needed but presumably it is to enable the directors to choose a date on which published prices of investments and of exchange rates will be available.
80 See Chap. 6 at p. 119 above.
81 s.226(1).

imposes a like duty on directors of a company which is a parent company additionally to prepare a consolidated balance sheet and profit and loss account ("group accounts")[82] The basic and over-riding principle is that the balance sheets must give a true and fair view, in the case of individual accounts "of the state of affairs of the company at the end of the financial year"[83] and in the case of group accounts "of the state of affairs as at the end of the financial year of the undertakings included in the consolidation as a whole, so far as it concerns the members of the company."[84] Similarly the profit and loss accounts must give a like view of the profit or loss of the company or of the undertakings included in the consolidation for the financial year again "so far as it concerns, the members." These latter words may be thought puzzling; accounts are intended to protect creditors as well as members. But so long as English law refuses to recognise that parent companies are under a legal as well as a moral obligation to meet the debts of their subsidiaries the group accounts are largely irrelevant so far as creditors are concerned since they normally have resort only against the individual company with which they have dealt.

Subject to the foregoing, the form and content of the balance sheets and profit and loss accounts and additional information provided by way of notes[85] must comply with Schedule 4[86] in relation to individual accounts and with Schedule 4A[87] in relation to group accounts.[88] Pursuant to the Directives' aim to promote comparability of the accounts of companies of the various member States, companies are required to adopt one of two prescribed formats for the balance sheet and one of four for the profit and loss account but in doing so they may use either the prescribed "historical cost accounting rules"[89] or the "alternative accounting rules" which pay greater recognition to the impact of inflation by a type of current cost accounting.

Such is the importance attached to the true-and-fair principle that, when compliance with the relevant Schedule and other provisions of the Act would not be sufficient to give a true and fair view, the

[82] s.227(1) & (2).
[83] s.226(2).
[84] s.227(3).
[85] Scheds. 4 and 4A and later sections of the Act provide for what information must or may be in notes instead of in the accounts themselves and Scheds. 5 and 6 make additional provisions for notes, the proliferation of which has been a feature of the last 50 years.
[86] Which was amended but not wholly replaced by the 1989 Act.
[87] Newly inserted by the 1989 Act. Essentially, Sched. 4 applies with adaptations, Sched. 4A, para. 1(1) providing that: "Group accounts shall comply so far as practicable with the provisions of Sched. 4 as if the undertakings included in the consolidation ('the group') were a single company" and para. 6 providing for the elimination of inter-group transactions.
[88] ss.226(3) and 227(4).
[89] Which most English companies choose.

necessary additional information must be given in the accounts or notes to them.[90] And if, in special circumstances, compliance with a provision of the Schedules would be inconsistent with the requirement to give a true and fair view the directors must depart from that provision to the extent necessary, giving, in a note to the accounts, particulars of the departure and the reasons for, and effect of, it.[91]

Although normally every parent company must prepare consolidated group accounts which must include all its subsidiary undertakings, there are narrowly defined exceptions. Under section 228 when a parent company is itself a subsidiary and its immediate parent is established under the law of a member State, it may, if certain conditions are fulfilled, be exempt from the requirement to prepare group accounts. But these conditions are strict. The exemption applies only (a) if the company is a wholly-owned subsidiary or (b) if the parent holds more than 50 per cent. of its shares and the other shareholders[92] have not served notice requesting the preparation of group accounts[93] and the company's securities are not listed on a stock exchange in any member State.[94] Moreover strict conditions are laid down[95] to ensure that the company is included in consolidated accounts drawn up and audited in accordance with the Seventh Directive and made available to the British public.

Similarly in certain circumstances a subsidiary may, under section 229, be omitted from the consolidation. This is so, for example, if its inclusion is not material for the purposes of giving a true and fair view[96] or if, in effect, the parent is not able to exercise dominance over the subsidiary[97] or holds its interest in the subsidiary exclusively with a view to resale,[98] or the information necessary for group accounts cannot be obtained without disproportionate delay or expense.[99] And a subsidiary must be excluded from the consolidation if its activities are so different from those of the rest of the group that its inclusion would be incompatible with the obligation to give a true and fair view.[1]

Under section 230 certain derogations from the provisions of Schedule 4 apply to the individual accounts of a parent which is required to prepare consolidated accounts (and has done so) thereby rendering those provisions otiose.

[90] ss.226(4) & 227(5).
[91] ss.226(5) & 227(6).
[92] Holding more than half of the remaining shares or 5 per cent. of the total shares:
s.228(1)(b).
[93] s.228(1).
[94] s.228(3).
[95] s.228(2).
[96] s.229(2). But two or more undertakings may be excluded on this ground only if
taken together they are immaterial: *ibid.*
[97] s.229(3)(a).
[98] s.229(3)(c).
[99] s.229(3)(b).
[1] s.229(4).

Section 231 requires information specified in Schedule 5 to be given in notes to the accounts regarding what are referred to in the headings to the section and the Schedule as "related undertakings",—an expression which the Act does not define but which includes parent and subsidiary undertakings,[2] associated undertakings,[3] joint ventures, and undertakings in which the company has a substantial holding.[4] Similarly section 232 requires the information specified in Schedule 6, regarding the emoluments and other benefits of directors and their associates, to be given in notes to the accounts.[5]

The annual accounts must be approved by the directors and signed on behalf of the board by a director.[6] If the approved accounts do not comply with the Act, every director who was a party to their approval and who knows that they do not comply or is reckless as to whether or not they comply is guilty of an offence and every director at the time the accounts were approved is taken to be a party to their approval unless he shows that he took all reasonable steps to prevent their approval.[7] Furthermore if there is a breach of the requirements as to signature of the balance sheet the company and every officer in default is guilty of an offence.[8]

The directors' report

Under section 234 the directors must, in addition, prepare a report for each financial year. This must contain a fair review of the development of the business of the company and its subsidiaries during the financial year and the position at the end of it, must state what amount (if any) they recommend should be paid as dividend, and what amount (if any) they propose to carry to reserves.[9] In addition it must give the names of all persons who at any time during the financial year were directors of the company and its subsidiaries and describe the principal activities of the company and its subsidiaries and any changes therein during the course of the year.[10] Furthermore, it must give additional information on the matters mentioned in Schedule 7 to the Act.[11]

---

[2] Defined in s.258 and Sched. 10A. See Chap. 6 at pp. 119, 120 above.
[3] Defined in Sched. 4A para. 20 and dependent on the holding of a "participating interest" as defined in s.260: see Chap. 6 at p. 120 above.
[4] See Chap. 6 *ibid.*
[5] Thereby supplementing Part X of the Act (enforcement of fair dealing by directors).
[6] s.233(1). The signature must be on the balance sheet (s.233(2)) and every published copy of it must state the name of the signatory (s.233(3)). The copy delivered to the Registrar must also be signed on behalf of the board by a director (though not necessarily the same one): s.233(4).
[7] s.233(5). A director whose primary defence is that he did not know and was not reckless would be ill-advised to attempt to show alternatively that he took all reasonable steps to prevent approval since unless he knew or suspected that the accounts did not comply he would have no reason for trying to prevent their approval.
[8] s.233(6).
[9] s.234(1).
[10] s.234(2).
[11] s.234(3) & (4).

Schedule 7[12] is divided into five parts, some of which require information which goes far beyond the purely financial. Thus Part III requires information to be given about the employment, training and promotion of disabled persons, Part IV about the company's arrangements for health, safety and welfare of employees, and Part V about "employee involvement," *i.e.* the extent to which employees are systematically given information, consulted, and encouraged to join employee share schemes. None of these is relevant to an appraisal of the company's financial position. Nor, indeed is the requirement in Part I for separate disclosure of the amounts of charitable or political donations; in view of the minimal amounts needed to trigger this requirement and the modest amounts normally donated, they would very rarely be material to a true and fair view of its financial affairs.[13] It is, however, a recognition that employees are entitled to information regarding the financial health of their employers and that the public and the Government should be enabled to judge to what extent the company is recognising social obligations[14] and complying with social legislation.

The auditors' report

The final document that has to accompany the annual accounts is the auditors' report thereon. This has to be addressed to the company's members[15] and to state whether in the auditors' opinion the annual accounts have been properly prepared in accordance with the Act and, in particular, whether they give a true and fair view.[16] The report must also state whether the auditors consider that the information given in the director's report is consistent with that in the annual accounts and, if they are not satisfied, they must say so in the report.[17] In preparing this report they must carry out such investigations as will enable them to form an opinion on (a) whether proper accounting records have been kept by the company[18] and whether proper returns adequate for their audit have been received from branches which they have not visited[19] and (b) whether the

---

12 As amended by the 1989 Act, generally in minor respects only but note paras. 2, 2A, 2B and 5A.
13 Nor does disclosure of political contributions do much to assuage the resentment of the trade unions that they can contribute (generally to the Labour Party) only out of a political fund raised from those of their members who "contract in", whereas companies can contribute (generally to the Conservative Party directly or indirectly) with no more than subsequent disclosure.
14 Or, more probably in the case of Part III, the extent to which it is not.
15 s.235(1).
16 s.235(2).
17 s.235(3).
18 See s.221, above.
19 This would include records required from branches outside G.B. under s.222 above, but is not restricted to them. A company with retail outlets throughout G.B. may need initially to keep some records at each branch and although these may be collated at the head office the auditors will need to satisfy themselves that the accounts at head office are based on adequate and accurate returns from the branches.

company's individual accounts are in agreement with the accounting records and returns.[20] If they are not of those opinions they must say so.[21] If they have failed to obtain all the information and explanations which, to the best of their knowledge and belief, are necessary for the purpose of their audit their report must so state. Moreover, if the requirements of Schedule 6 (disclosure of emoluments and benefits of directors) are not complied with in the accounts, "the auditors shall include in their report, so far as they are reasonably able to do so, a statement giving the required particulars."[22]

The auditors' report must state the names of the auditors and be signed by them[23] and their names must be stated on all issued copies of the report.[24] The copy delivered to the Registrar must also be signed by the auditors.[25] And, now that the Act expressly recognises that a firm, as such, may be appointed[26] and that increasingly accountancy firms are incorporated, it is expressly stated that what is then required is a signature in the name of the firm by a person authorised to sign on its behalf.[27]

Publicity of accounts and reports

The next group of sections deals with the various types of publicity that have to be given to the annual accounts and reports. It starts with section 238 but it may be more illuminating to start here with section 240 which draws a distinction between the publication of "statutory accounts," (*i.e.* the annual accounts and reports considered above, copies of which have to be delivered to the Registrar under section 242) and "non-statutory accounts," (*i.e.* any other purported balance sheet or profit and loss account dealing with a financial year[28] of the company or group).[29] Section 240 seeks to ensure that recipients of the latter will not confuse them with statutory accounts. If a company publishes[30] any of its statutory accounts they must be

---

[20] The group accounts will be based in those of the individual undertakings in the group and not all of them will necessarily be audited by the same firm.
[21] s.237(1) and (2).
[22] s.237(4). This is an extension of the normal role of auditors. It is the directors' responsibility to prepare full and accurate accounts—not the auditors'. But this subs. requires the auditors in effect to correct the accounts.
[23] s.236(1).
[24] s.236(2).
[25] s.236(3).
[26] See Chap. 18 below. It had long been the general practice to appoint in the firm name but only as a result of the 1989 Act is it fully recognised that the firm may be "a person corporate or unincorporate."
[27] s.236(5). If there is a contravention of subs. (1) (2) or (3) the company and any officer of it who is in default is guilty of an offence and liable to a fine.
[28] Half-yearly financial statements, which are required by *The Yellow Book* in the case of listed companies, are not "statutory" nor are they "non-statutory accounts" since they do not relate to a financial year.
[29] s.240(5).
[30] For the purposes of the section "a company shall be regarded as publishing a document if it publishes, issues or circulates it, or otherwise makes it available for public inspection in a manner calculated to invite members of the public generally, or any class of members of the public, to read it": s.240(4). This clearly covers the methods of publication dealt with below—and others besides, (*e.g.* a radio or TV

accompanied by the auditors' report[31] and if it is required to prepare statutory group accounts it may not publish its (statutory) individual accounts unless they are accompanied by its statutory group accounts.[32] In contrast, any publication of non-statutory accounts must be accompanied by a statement indicating: (a) that they are not statutory accounts, (b) whether statutory accounts have been delivered to the Registrar, (c) whether the auditors have reported on those statutory accounts, and (d) whether any such report was qualified or contained a statement under section 272 or 273.[33] An auditors' report under section 235 must not be published with any non-statutory accounts.[34] The sections to which we next turn are concerned with publication of the "statutory" accounts only.

First, section 238(1) provides that any member, holder of the company's debentures[35] and any person who is entitled to receive notice of general meetings shall, not less than 21 days before the accounts are to be laid before the general meeting under section 241, be sent copies of them. This is subject to the minor exceptions in subsections (2) and (3), and to adaptations when a private company has validly elected under section 252 to dispense with laying of accounts before general meetings or when shareholders of listed companies have elected under section 251[36] to receive summary financial statements instead. If copies are sent less than 21 days before, they may be deemed to have been duly sent if so agreed by all the members entitled to attend and vote.[37]

Secondly, section 239 entitles any member or debentureholder to be furnished, on demand and without charge, with a copy of the last accounts in addition to that to which he is entitled under section 238.[38]

Thirdly, under section 241 the statutory accounts must be laid before the company in general meeting (unless the company is a private one which has elected to dispense with this requirement under section 252). Section 244 provides that this normally has to be done within 10 months after the end of the accounting reference period to which the accounts relate (if it is a private company) or within six months (if it is a public one).[39] But there are concessions in respect

---

31 ... advertisement announcing the publication of annual accounts and where they can be inspected).
32 s.240(1).
33 s.240(2).
34 s.240(3). When under s.254, below, an unlimited company is exempt from delivering statutory accounts the wording of (b) is amended appropriately: see s.254(4).
35 s.240(3).
36 In this and the later sections "debenture" is clearly used in its popular sense of a series of debentures or debenture stock and would not include a mortgage or one of the company's properties: see Chap. 14, at pp. 377, 380 above.
37 s.238(4).
38 See below, at pp. 467–469.
39 If he wants any more copies he can, of course, get them (on payment) from Companies House.

of the first accounting reference period,[40] or on a change of the accounting reference date,[41] or in the case of a company carrying on business or having interests outside the British Isles.[42] Moreover, the Secretary of State may allow an extension in special circumstances.[43]

Fourthly, copies of the annual accounts and reports have to be delivered to the Registrar under section 242. This has to be done before the end of the time allowed for laying them before the general meeting[44] and if any of the documents is not in the English language a certified translation must be annexed.[45]

Compliance with section 242 is the most important of the four since it is the one which makes the statutory accounts available to the general public. While all four have provisions for penalties for non-compliance, those in section 242, as supplemented by section 242A, are the most stringent. If the requirements of section 242 are not complied with on time, any person who was a director immediately before the end of the time allowed is liable to a fine and, for continued contravention, to a daily default fine.[46] Furthermore, under subsection (3) if the directors fail to make good the default within 14 days after the service of a notice requiring compliance,[47] the court, on the application of the Registrar or any member or creditor of the company, may make an order directing the directors or any of them to make good the default within such time as may be specified[48] and may order them to pay the costs of and incidental to the application. Any person charged with an offence under the section has a defence if he can prove that he took all reasonable steps for securing that the accounts were delivered in time.[49] But, to spike the guns of barrack-room lawyers, it is expressly stated that it is not a defence to prove that the documents prepared were not in fact prepared in accordance with the Act.[50]

To these criminal sanctions against directors, section 242A adds civil penalties, against the company. The amount of the penalty, recoverable by the Registrar, varies according to whether the company is private or public and to the length of time that the

40 s.244(2).
41 s.244(4).
42 s.244(3).
43 s.244(5).
44 s.242(1) and (2). In the case of a private company which has dispensed with laying they must be delivered to him before they are sent to the members and others under s.238 above: s.252(3).
45 s.242(1). Note also s.243 under which in some circumstances the accounts of a foreign or unincorporated subsidiary undertaking that have been excluded from consolidation under s.229(4) may have to be delivered as well.
46 s.242(2).
47 The subsection does not say who may serve such a notice so presumably anyone can: but in practice it is likely to be the Registrar who does so—though the subs. makes it pretty clear that a member or creditor certainly could.
48 If they fail to do so they will be in contempt of court and liable to imprisonment.
49 s.242(4).
50 s.242(5). A similar express provision appears in s.241 (above) and in s.242A (below).

default continues; the minimum being £100 for a private company and £500 for a public company when the default is for not more than three months and the maximum £1000 for a private and £5,000 for a public company when the default exceeds 12 months.[51] There are obvious attractions in affording the Registrar an additional weapon in the form of a penalty recoverable by civil suit to which there is no defence once it is shown that accounts have not been delivered on time. But in principle it seems inexcusable to penalise the company for breach of a duty not owed by it but by its directors and intended to protect, among others, the company and its members.[52] Moreover the amount of the penalty seems derisory—at any rate in the case of public companies—and it is difficult to believe that, as a deterrent against failing to file on time, this new sanction will prove any more effective than those that the Registrar formerly had and still has.[53]

Revision of defective accounts

Another innovation by the 1989 Act is the introduction of statutory provisions regarding the correction of defective accounts. It has never been doubted that if directors discover that the accounts that they have presented are defective they can, and should, correct them. But there had been no statutory provisions regarding it. Now we have such provisions concerning both voluntary revisions (section 245) and revisions under compulsion (sections 245A–245C).

Section 245 provides that if it appears to the directors that any annual accounts of the company or any directors' report[54] did not comply with the provisions of the Act they may prepare revised accounts or a revised report.[55] If copies of the previous accounts or report have been laid or delivered the revisions must be confined to the correction of those respects in which they did not comply with the Act and the making of any consequential alterations.[56] The section provides that the Secretary of State may make provisions by regulations in relation to revised accounts and reports[57] which, in particular, may:—make different provisions according to whether the previous documents are replaced or merely supplemented by a statement of corrections; deal with the functions of the auditors; require the directors to take specified steps in relation to circulation to members and others entitled under section 238; laying before a

---

51 s.242A(2).
52 The company could, presumably, sue the directors to recover its loss resulting from their default. But unless the company goes into liquidation, administration or receivership this will not happen.
53 The figures quoted in n. 30 at p. 451 above show that failure to deliver accounts is even more common than failure to deliver annual returns (and that this is not due to any reluctance to prosecute).
54 Obviously they cannot revise the *auditors'* report.
55 s.245(1).
56 s.245(2).
57 s.245(3).

general meeting and delivery to the Registrar; and the application of provisions of the Act (including penalties).[58]

Under section 245A, where copies of the annual accounts have been sent out, laid, or delivered to the Registrar and it appears to the Secretary of State that there is or may be a question whether they comply with the Act he may give notice to the directors indicating the respects in which it appears to him that the question may arise[59] and specifying a period of not less than one month for the directors to give him explanations or prepare revised accounts.[60] If at the end of the specified period, or such longer period as he may allow, they have not satisfied him in one way or the other, the voluntary process ends and he may apply to the court.[61]

Section 245B provides that, as an alternative to an application to the court by the Secretary of State, such an application may be made "by any person authorised by him for the purposes of this section."[62] In either case, the court may declare that the accounts do not comply and may order the directors to prepare revised accounts. The order may give directions on: auditing, the revision of the directors' report or any summary financial statement,[63] steps to be taken to bring the order to the notice of persons likely to rely on the original accounts, and on such other matters as the court thinks fit.[64]

Finally, section 245C deals with the authorisation of "any other person" for the purposes of section 245B. The Secretary of State may authorise any person appearing to him:— (i) to be "fit and proper," and (ii) to have an interest in, and satisfactory procedures directed to, securing compliance by companies with the accounting provisions and for receiving and investigation complaints.[65] Authorisation may be general or in respect of particular classes of case.[66] Such authorisation has been conferred on the new Financial Reporting Review Panel,[67] a subsidiary of the Financial Reporting Council.[68]

---

[58] s.245(4). See the Companies (Revision of Defective Accounts and Reports) Regs. 1990 (S.I. 1990 No. 2570).
[59] s.245A(1).
[60] s.245A(2).
[61] s.245A(3). The section can be invoked in relation to revised accounts as well as to the original versions: s.245A(4).
[62] s.245B(1). Notice of the application must be given to the Registrar by the applicant: s.245B(2).
[63] See s.251 below.
[64] s.245B(3). And the court may order that all or part of the costs and expenses shall be borne by such of the directors as were party to the approval of the defective accounts (which every director at the time when they were approved is deemed to be unless he shows that he took all reasonable steps to prevent their being approved): s.245B(4). But the court should have regard to whether a director knew or ought to have known that the accounts did not comply and may exclude one or more of the directors from the order or require payment of different amounts by different directors: s.245B(5).
[65] s.245C(1).
[66] s.245C(2).
[67] S.I. 1991 No. 13.
[68] The body, supported by public funds, which is independent of the professional accountancy bodies, and which has the wider remit of promoting best practice in financial reporting.

Exemptions, exceptions and special provisions

The 1989 Act substitutes a new Chapter II, headed as above, in Part VII of the Act. It is mainly concerned with concessions to smaller companies and with the special treatment (not dealt with here) of banking and insurance companies and groups. But it also includes an interesting innovation in relation to companies listed on The Stock Exchange and to this we turn first.

Summary financial statements

Under the new section 251, a company, any of whose shares are officially listed, need not, in such circumstances as are specified by regulations[69] and subject to complying with conditions so specified, send copies of the accounts and reports to members[70] but may instead send them a summary financial statement,[71] derived from the company's annual accounts and directors' report, in such form and containing such information as may be specified in the regulations.[72] In fact, various conditions are laid down in the section itself; in particular that the nature of the document must be made clear, and that it must contain a statement by the company's auditors of their opinion on whether the statement is consistent with the accounts and reports and complies with the section and the regulations. It must also state whether the auditors' report was qualified or unqualified and, if it was qualified, must set out the report in full with any further material needed to understand the qualification.[73] Use of the section is purely optional and even if the company adopts it each member must be sent copies of the full accounts and reports if he wants to receive them.[74]

The importance that the Government place on this section is shown by the fact that it was among the first provisions of the 1989 Act to be brought into operation and the regulations made under it were among the first to be published. The commendable objectives were (i) to present private investors[75] with a document which they might find more helpful to them than the full statutory accounts, (ii) to reduce an appalling waste of paper, since undoubtedly a great many such investors consign the glossy brochures containing the accounts to their waste-paper baskets after only the most cursory of glances (if any) and, perhaps, (iii) to reduce the company's postage—though it is

---

69 The Companies (Summary Financial Statements) Regs., (S.I. 1990 No. 515).
70 Curiously, the obligation under s.238 to send the full accounts to debenture holders still remains and they are not entitled to a copy of the summary financial statement: s.251 does not apply if it is only the company's debenture stock that is listed.
71 s.251(1).
72 s.251(3).
73 s.251(3). s.240 (above) does not apply: s.251(7).
74 If it contained a statement under s.237(2) or (3) that too must be set out: s.251(4). s.251(2). And the regulations may make provisions as to the manner in which it is to be ascertained whether a member wishes to receive them: *ibid.*: see Reg. 6.
75 Institutional and professional investors will obviously wish to continue to receive the full accounts.

unlikely that any saving on that could be commensurate with the cost of preparing an additional document and, in effect, having it audited.

It will be interesting to see whether these objectives are attained. As regards the first, it seems unlikely. A perusal of the Regulations suggests that the summary will be a pretty lengthy one and expressed in equally impenetrable accountants' and lawyers' jargon. What most private investors need is not a summary (which is generally less intelligible than the document it summarises) but an explanation; and this they will not get. This is openly admitted by the Regulations which require that the summary should state prominently that "This summary financial statement does not contain sufficient information to allow for a full understanding of the results ... and state of affairs ... For further information, the full annual accounts, the auditors' report on those accounts and the directors' report should be consulted."[76] And the statement encourages those who have received it to ask in addition for the free copy of the latest statutory accounts by requiring that it must contain a conspicuous statement of their rights under section 239.[77]

As for the conservation aim, there will initially be a greater, not a lesser, consumption of paper, if members are to be persuaded to be content with the summary, it will be necessary to undertake what the Regulations call a "relevant consultation" which involves sending to each member both the full accounts for the financial year and a summary financial statement plus a postage-paid card on which he can make his choice for the future.[78] If he does nothing, he will be deemed to have opted for the summary statement.[79] Hence there is likely thereafter to be some saving of paper in future years[80] so long as most members do not also demand copies of the full accounts under section 239. But one cannot help thinking that a far greater contribution to the preservation of the World's rain forests would be made if companies could be persuaded to make their annual brochures less glossy and to print them on re-cycled paper.

The other points to note on the Regulations are: (i) that advantage cannot be taken of the section if a provision, "however expressed," of the company's memorandum or articles requires copies of the full accounts to be sent to members or which prohibits the sending of summary financial statements[81] (ii) that provisions, similar to

[76] Reg. 5(e) and (f).
[77] Reg. 5(g).
[78] Reg. 6(3).
[79] Reg. 6(1)(b).
[80] Mainly, one suspects, because a great many will fail to return the card. But each subsequent summary statement must be accompanied by a pre-paid card entitling them to obtain full accounts: Reg. 5(h).
[81] Reg. 4(1). But note the concession to companies with an article equivalent to art. 127 of Table A 1948 in respect of a financial year beginning prior to 1990: Reg. 4(2). They will, however, need to amend their articles if they want to use s.251 in future years.

those in relation to the full accounts, apply to approval by, and signature on behalf of, the directors of the summary, and (iii) that, up to the end of 1991, most listed companies do not seem to have opted to adopt the innovation.[82]

Small and medium-sized companies or groups

The first four sections of Chapter II of Part VII replace, with amendments, the concessions to smaller companies originally afforded by the 1981 Act as permitted by the Fourth Company Law Directive. To qualify as "small" or "medium-sized" in any financial year a company must meet the qualifying conditions in that year and its previous financial year (if there was one).[83] These conditions in the case of individual company accounts are that the company must satisfy at least two of three requirements relating to the maximum size of: (i) its turnover, (ii) its "balance sheet total"[84] and (iii) the average number of its employees during the year.[85]

Even if it meets these conditions, it will not be entitled to the concessions unless, at no time during the year, has it, or any member of the group of which it is a member, been a public company, a banking or insurance company or an authorised person under the Financial Services Act[86] and, if it is a parent company, unless the group qualifies as a small or medium-sized group.[87] The conditions for qualification as a small or medium-sized group are broadly similar except that the maximum size of each of the three criteria is greater.[88]

If, in accordance with the foregoing, a company is eligible as a small or medium-sized company, the concessions to which it is entitled are:

(a) exemption from the requirements of paragraph 36A of Schedule 4;

(b) exemptions to the extent provided by Schedule 8 with respect to the delivery of individual accounts to the Registrar under section 242[89]; and

(c) exemption from the requirement to prepare group accounts in respect of a year in which the group headed by the company is a small or medium-sized group

---

[82] Reg. 5(c) and (d).
[83] s.247(1) and (2).
[84] In effect, the value of its gross assets as shown in the balance sheet.
[85] s.247. The maxima permitted are greater for qualification as "medium-sized" than for "small" but the extent of the concessions much less: see below.
[86] s.246(3) and (4).
[87] s.246(5).
[88] ss.248 and 249.
[89] s.246(1).

so long as the auditors have reported that in their opinion the company is entitled to the exemptions and their report is attached to the company's individual accounts. [90]

Only (a) and (b) require a brief explanation. As regards (a), the new paragraph 36A of Schedule 4 provides:

"It shall be stated whether the accounts have been prepared in accordance with applicable accounting standards and particulars of any material departure from those standards and the reason for it shall be given."

For many years the Accounting Standards Committee (the ASC) of the accountancy bodies had been producing valuable Statements of Standard Accounting Practice (SSAPs) and had done its best to ensure that they were observed—not always successfully since the Statements had no statutory recognition. [91] Now they have. A later section (section 256) defines them as "statements of standard accounting practice issued by such body or bodies as may be prescribed by regulations" and goes still further by empowering the Secretary of State to make grants, [92] "to or for the purposes of bodies concerned with (a) issuing accounting standards, (b) overseeing and directing the issuing of such standards or (c) investigating departures from such standards or from the accounting requirements of this Act and taking steps to secure compliance with them." [93] As a result, the former ASC has been converted into another recognised body, the Accounting Standards Board as another subsidiary company of the Financial Reporting Council. [94] The case for exempting small and medium-sized companies from the obligation to comply with the Standards does not appear to be particularly strong; but exempted they are. [95]

As regards (b) it should be noted that all it does is to permit small and medium-sized companies to prune the accounts to be delivered to the Registrar and thus made public. Far from relieving the companies from burdens and expense it adds to them; for those companies that

90 s.248.
91 Except to the extent that they embodied "generally recognised accounting principles," which Sched. 4 sometimes required to be observed but which are rather different from "Standards."
92 This represents a considerable U-turn by the Government which had insisted that the regulatory bodies set up under the Financial Services Act should be financed from fees payable by those regulated. There, the only support from public funds is in relation to the Tribunal plus a pump-priming loan by the Bank of England to SIB, now being repaid out of SIB's fee-generated income.
93 s.256(3).
94 See n. 68, p. 466 above.
95 This does not necessarily mean that they will ignore the standards; if the accounts are professionally prepared and audited it is likely that the standards will be observed by those companies which want small to be beautiful.

take advantage of it will have to prepare two distinct sets of accounts and reports, the full version to circulate to their members and the expurgated version to be made available to the general public.[96] What it does, in effect, is to enable such companies to conceal from outsiders detailed information regarding profitability and turnover, something of which they have a (much exaggerated) fear that it will be used by their competitors to the company's disadvantage. It represents, however, a retreat from the basic principle that the price of limited liability should be full financial disclosure—a principle which after a long struggle, was adopted in the 1967 Act. This retreat goes far in relation to small companies because, under Part I of Schedule 8, they are wholly exempt from delivering copies of the profit and loss account[97] and the directors' report[98] while the balance sheet and the information that has to be given in notes to the accounts can be substantially abbreviated.[99] In contrast, under Part II of Schedule 8, medium-sized companies have to deliver a copy of the full balance sheet, and a profit and loss account which, however, can combine various items prescribed by Schedule 4 under a single item (gross profits)[1] and can omit particulars of turnover.[2]

Dormant companies

The one type of company which can totally dispense with the provisions of the Act relating to auditing of the accounts is a so-called "dormant company." Under section 250 it is treated as dormant "during a period in which ... there is no transaction which is required by section 221[3] to be entered in the company's accounting records; and a company ceases to be dormant on the occurrence of such a transaction."[4] The most obvious and common example of such a company is a "shelf company"[5] while it remains on the shelf. But there may be legitimate reasons for incorporating a company which is intended to remain dormant indefinitely or for retaining on the

---

95 Moreover, under para. 7 of Sched. 8 a company wishing to take advantage of the exemptions will have to add to the balance sheet which it delivers a statement that advantage is being taken of the exemptions and the grounds on which, in the opinion of the directors, the company is entitled to the exemptions and, under para. 8, will have to obtain from the auditors a special report stating that in their opinion the company is so entitled and that the accounts are properly prepared in accordance with the Schedule. That special report must reproduce the full text of the auditors' report and if it was qualified must contain any further matter necessary to understand the qualification.

96 *Ibid.* para. 4. But see n. 96 above regarding paras. 7 & 8 which require them to make special statements and to deliver a special report.

97 Sched. 8, para. 2.

98 Sched. 8, para. 4.

99 para. 3.

1 para. 5.

2 para. 6.

3 See above. p. 455.

4 s. 250(3). "For this purpose there shall be disregarded any transaction arising from the taking of shares by a subscriber to the memorandum in pursuance of an undertaking of his in the memorandum." *ibid.*

5 See Chap. 11 at p. 277 above.

register a company which for the time being has ceased to carry on business but which the members may wish to use at some time in the future for the same or some different business.

A company does not obtain the exemption merely by being dormant. In addition it must have passed a special resolution making itself "exempt"[6] and that resolution may not be passed if it is a public company, a banking or insurance company or an authorised person under the Financial Services Act.[7] If the company has been dormant from the time of its formation, the special resolution will be effective if passed before the first general meeting at which accounts are to be laid. If it has been dormant since the end of the previous financial year and it is entitled in respect of its individual accounts to the exceptions conferred on a small company by section 246 (or would be so entitled but for being a member of an ineligible group) and it is not required to prepare group accounts for that year, the resolution is effective if passed at a general meeting at which the accounts for that year are to be laid.[8] Moreover, not only is the dormant company then entitled to the exemption from auditing but, if it would have been entitled to the exemptions of a small company under section 246 but for the fact that it is a member of an ineligible group, it will also be entitled to those exemptions[9]; until it ceases to be dormant or no longer qualifies to make itself exempt under section 250.[10]

It hardly needs saying that if there is no audit there will not be any auditors' report to be sent to members, laid before a general meeting, or delivered to the Registrar. This is recognised in the section[11] which, however, requires the copy of the balance sheet delivered to the Registrar to state immediately above the signature that the company was dormant throughout the year.[12]

Private companies: dispensing with laying accounts

The elective regime for private companies introduced by the 1989 Act[13] enables a private company to elect to dispense with the laying of accounts and reports before a general meeting in accordance with section 241.[14] So long as the documents have been sent to all those entitled to attend a general meeting in accordance with section 238,[15] it is a pointless farce to require a formal general meeting to be held in order that they may be "laid" unless a member wants to raise

---

[6] s.250(1).
[7] s.250(2). Every authorised person under the F.S. Act is required to keep audited accounts whether he is an individual, a partnership or a company.
[8] s.250(1).
[9] s.250(4)(d).
[10] s.250(5).
[11] s.250(4)(a) (b) & (c).
[12] s.250(4)(c). The Registrar should also have received a copy of the special resolution under s.380(4).
[13] See Chap. 5 at p. 105 above.
[14] See p. 463 above.
[15] *Ibid.*

questions about them at a meeting,[16] or the auditors want to have an opportunity of talking to the members about them. Hence section 252 provides that a private company (whether or not small or medium-sized) may elect (by elective resolution in accordance with section 379A)[17] to dispense with the laying of accounts,[18] and this dispensation applies in respect of the financial year in which the election is made and to subsequent financial years so long as it remains in force.[19] References in other provisions of the Act to laying of accounts are then to be read as references to the sending of copies under section 238.[20]

However, the rights of any member or of the auditors to insist on a general meeting are entrenched by section 253. This requires that the accounts sent to members under section 238 shall be sent not less than 28 days before the end of the period allowed for laying and delivery of them[21] and shall be accompanied by notice of their right to require them to be laid before a general meeting.[22] Before the end of the 28 days any member or auditor may serve notice on the company requiring a meeting to be held for that purpose.[23] If the directors do not, within a further 21 days, proceed duly to convene the meeting,[24] the person who gave notice may himself do so.[25] The meeting must be convened in the same way, as nearly as possible, as that in which meetings are to be convened by the directors and must be held not later than 3 months from the date of service of the notice.[26] Any reasonable expenses incurred by the person who gave notice have to be made good to him by the company and recouped by the company out of any fees or other emoluments of the directors in default.[27]

Unlimited companies

In general, the accounting provisions of Part VII of the Act apply to every company, limited or unlimited. But, in the case of the latter it has been recognised that as regards the obligation, now in section 242, to deliver accounts and reports to the Registrar (thus making them available to the public) they (like partnerships) are entitled to

16 In the case of smaller private companies he can usually do so without the need for a formal meeting.
17 On which see Chap. 5 at p. 105 above.
18 s.252(1).
19 s.252(2). When it ceases to have effect, s.241 applies to the financial year in which that occurs and subsequent financial years: s.252(4).
20 s.252(3).
21 Under ss.238 and 242, above. Under those sections the period allowed is not less than 21 days before.
22 s.253(1). Formal notice to the auditors is not needed; they will have copies of the accounts and will know of the elective resolution and what their rights are.
23 s.253(2).
24 Which they shall be deemed not to have done if they give notice convening a meeting but for a date more than 28 days from the notice: s.253(6).
25 s.253(3).
26 s.253(4).
27 s.253(5).

exemption. However, inroads into that exemption, have been made when they are part of a group. Section 254(1) provides that the directors of an unlimited company are not required to deliver accounts and reports to the Registrar if certain conditions are met.[28] These conditions are that at no time during the relevant accounting reference period—

(a) has the company been, to its knowledge, a subsidiary undertaking of an undertaking which was then limited, nor

(b) have there been, to its knowledge, rights exercisable by or on behalf of two or more limited undertakings which if exercisable by one of them would have made the company a subsidiary of it, nor

(c) has the company been a parent company of an undertaking which was then limited.[29]

The reason for the inclusion of "to its knowledge" in (a) and (b) and its exclusion from (c) is that a subsidiary could well be ignorant, through no fault of its own, that it is a subsidiary, whereas a parent company ought to know what subsidiaries it has. The object of (b) is to require delivery of the accounts of an unlimited company if two or more limited companies would, if they had been a single entity, have been the parent of the unlimited company under the criteria in section 258,[30] although technically the unlimited company is not a subsidiary of any of them.

The only other exclusion from the exemption is that it does not apply if at any time during the relevant accounting period the unlimited company carried on business as the promoter of a trading stamp scheme within the meaning of the Trading Stamps Act 1964.[31] To single out such companies seems curious; one would have thought that there is a stronger case for excluding unlimited companies which are authorised persons under the Financial Services Act.[32]

Banking and insurance companies

The remaining sections[33] of Chapter II of Part VII deal with the special provisions applying to banking and insurance companies.

[28] s.254(1).
[29] s.254(2).
[30] On which see Chap. 6 at pp. 119, 120.
[31] s.254(3).
[32] As in ss.246(3), 248(2), s250(2). The other exclusions in those sections are unlikely to be relevant in relation to s.254 (an unlimited company cannot be a public company) but an unlimited company (or a partnership) could be an authorised person and might well be a subsidiary undertaking in a group. If so, the public should surely be entitled to access to its accounts?
[33] ss.255–255D. These, and Sched. 9, are now in course of amendment implementing E.C. Directives. See in particular The Companies Act 1985 (Bank Accounts) Regs. 1991, S.I. No. 2705, implementing Directive 86/635/EEC.

these may prepare their accounts in accordance with Schedule 9 (as amended) instead of Schedule 4.

Supplementary provisions

The 1989 Act adds a new Chapter III, under the above heading, to Part VII. This contains section 256 (accounting standards) already referred to in this chapter.[34] It also contains section 258 and 259 which, in conjunction with Schedule 10A, define "parent and subsidiary undertakings" and section 260, defining "participating interest." These have been dealt with in Chapter 6 above.[35] Attention should, however, be drawn to sections 257 and 261. The former affords the Secretary of State the widest powers to modify, by Regulations, any of the provisions of Part VII.[36] If they are made more onerous an affirmative resolution of each House of Parliament is needed[37]; if not, they are effective unless annulled by a resolution of either House.[38] Section 261 clarifies the position of notes to the accounts; references in the Act to the accounts; include any notes to the accounts containing information which the Act requires to be given and which it requires or allows to be given in a note to the accounts.[39] Such notes may be included in the accounts or in separate documents annexed thereto.[40]

CONCLUSION

There is no doubt that members and creditors (actual or potential) of companies are afforded ample opportunities to obtain a great deal of financial and other information about the companies concerned. What is questionable is whether they make the best use of this information, particularly of that which, if they were competent to extract it, could be deduced from the companies' published accounts. This may not matter too much if they have professional advisers on whom they could rely. These advisers are more likely to be accountants, rather than lawyers whose principal role in this repect is likely to be in advising on the interpretation of the statutory provisions rather than on the financial state of the companies which the information reveals. But any worthwhile advice on the latter is dependent on the accuracy of the information disclosed. Hence the

34 See P. 470 above.
35 At pp. 118–121 above.
36 s.257(1) and (4).
37 s.257(2).
38 s.257(3).
39 s.261(2).
40 s.261(3).

importance of audits by competent and independent auditors—to which we turn in the next chapter.

CHAPTER 18

AUDITORS

MANY references to the role of auditors have been made in earlier chapters[1] and it has been stressed that their role is a vital one. If reliance is to be placed on accounts, it is essential that they should be true and fair and that is more likely to be the case if someone independent of the company has vetted them and certified that they are. If, however, that certification is to be relied on, the scrutineer must be competent as well as independent. Hence the Companies Acts have attempted to ensure that company auditors are both.

In the original version of the Companies Act 1985 provisions relating to audits and auditors were to be found in Part VII, and in Part XI, Chapter V. They still are. But, in addition, in implementation of the Eighth Company Law Directive on the qualifications of company auditors, the 1989 Act not only amends Part VII and Part XI Chapter V but also contains in its Part II some thirty sections dealing with eligibility to be appointed as a company auditor. In contrast with most of the provisions of the 1989 Act, its Part II did not make textual amendments to, or insertions in, the Companies Act 1985; these sections are self-standing substantive provisions. What will happen to them when and if there is a new official consolidation of the Companies Act is unclear. But it will not be a happy solution if there is, say, a consolidated Companies Act 1993 which excludes, but leaves on the statute-book, an emasculated Companies Act 1989 consisting of thirty sections numbered 24 to 54.[2]

The main purposes of these sections[3] "are to secure that only persons who are properly supervised and appropriately qualified are appointed company auditors, and that audits by persons so appointed are carried out properly and with integrity and with a proper degree of independence."[4] Subsequent sections then deal successively with eligibility, recognition of supervisory bodies and of professional qualifications, duties of recognised bodies, offences, and "supplementary provisions." The general effect is to subject auditors to a somewhat similar regime to that applying to authorised persons under the Financial Services Act (or to insolvency practitioners under the Insolvency Act). All that can be attempted in this chapter (written before all the needed regulations have been published) is a description of the salient points. It should, however, be pointed out

---

[1] Especially in Chaps. 9, 10 and 17.
[2] At any rate unless that residue of the Act is renamed the Companies (Eligibility of Auditors) Act, (*cf.* the Company Securities (Insider Dealing) Act) or the Company Auditors Qualification Act, (*cf.* the Company Directors Disqualification Act).
[3] Which follow immediately ss.1–23 substituting new sections of Part VII of the 1985 Act.
[4] 1989 Act, s.24(1).

by way of introduction that in fact it will not resemble the financial services regime as closely as was originally envisaged. The sections follow the precedent of the Financial Services Act by conferring functions on the Secretary of State and then, by section 46, empowering him to delegate nearly all of them to a body corporate established for the purpose. On delegation to it, this would have resulted in there being a body corresponding to SIB under the Financial Services Act, which would perform the role of recognition and surveillance of the lower-tier bodies corresponding to the SROs and RPBs under that Act. In the light of the extent to which the accountancy bodies[5] already collaborated in matters of mutual concern it was thought that they would welcome this solution. But in fact they did not.

Hence, for the foreseeable future there will be no general delegation of the Secretary of State's functions under these sections and section 46 can be ignored. Instead the new regulatory bodies,[6] are recognised by, and are answerable to the Secretary of State.

Elegibility of auditors

A person is eligible for appointment as auditor of a company only if he is a member of a recognised supervisory body and is eligible for the appointment under the rules of that body.[7]

As already mentioned,[8] an individual or a firm[9] may now be appointed as auditor.[10] Section 26 of the 1989 Act deals with the effect of an appointment of a partnership, which under English law (but not Scottish) is not a legal person. Despite that, an appointment of a firm is, unless the contrary appears, an appointment of the partnership as such and not of the individual partners[11] and, when the composition of the partnership changes, the appointment extends to the successor partnership so long as its composition is substantially the same and it succeeds to substantially the same practice.[12] The same applies if the partnership ceases and a former partner, who is eligible, succeeds to the practice.[13] Where no one succeeds under the foregoing provisions, the appointment may, with the consent of the

---

5 *i.e.* the Institute of Chartered Accountants in England and Wales, the Institute of Chartered Accountants of Scotland, the Chartered Association of Certified Accountants and the Institute of Chartered Accountants in Ireland (which covers both the Republic and N. Ireland) which collaborate through the Consultative Committee of Accountancy Bodies (the C.C.A.B.).
6 Including the new Financial Reporting Review Panel and the Financial Reporting Council mentioned in Chap. 17 at p. 466 above.
7 1989 Act. s.25(1). The four bodies mentioned in n. 5, above, plus the Association of Authorised Public Accountants are recognised as supervisory bodies.
8 See Chap. 17 at p. 462 above.
9 1989 Act s.25(2).
10 In that Act (and in this chapter) "he" and "him" are used whether the person is an individual or a firm.
11 *Ibid.* s.26(2).
12 *Ibid.* s.26(3)(*a*) and (4).
13 *Ibid.* s.26(3)(*b*) and (4).

company, be extended to a partnership or other person eligible for the appointment which succeeds to the business of the former partnership or to such part of the business as is agreed by the company to include the appointment.[14][15]

A person is ineligible for appointment on the ground of lack of independence if he is an officer or employee[16] of the company or a partner or employee of such an officer or employee or, in the case of the appointment of a partnership, if any member of the partnership is ineligible on these grounds. And, he is also ineligible if any of these grounds apply in relation to any associated undertaking[17] of the company.[18]

Clearly an employer-employee relationship is far from being the only type of relationship which might impair the independence of the auditors, *e.g.* a debtor-creditor relationship or a substantial share-holding in the company[19] might do so. Hence section 27(2) empowers the Secretary of State to specify by regulations such connections "between him and any associate[20] of his and the company or any associated undertaking of it" which will also render him ineligible.

No person may act as a company auditor if he is ineligible for appointment[21] and if he becomes ineligible he must vacate office and forthwith give notice in writing to the company that he has vacated office by reason of ineligibility.[22] Contravention is an offence punishable by a fine[23] which may increase daily if he continues to act though ineligible.[24]

14 *Ibid.* s.26(5).
15 In the text, the paraphrase of s.26 has distinguished between changes of composition and cessations, since this seems helpful to an understanding of a somewhat complicated section. The section does not do so since, technically, any change in composition causes a cessation of the former partnership. The whole section would be unnecessary (with the possible exception of subs. (5)—and the Scots presumably manage happily without that) if English law had had the sense to follow the Scots by recognising the legal personality of a partnership.
16 s.27(1) expressly states that for this purpose an auditor is not to be regarded as an "officer or employee." This hardly needs saying, for if he was he would become ineligible once appointed. And the definition of "officer" in the Companies Acts ("officer—includes a director, manager or secretary": 1985 Act. s.744) would seem to exclude auditors. Nevertheless they have been held to be "officers" for the purpose of what is now s.212 of the Insolvency Act (summary remedy against delinquents): *Re London & General Bank (No. 1)* [1895] 2 Ch. 166, C.A.; *Re Kingston Cotton Mills (No. 1)* [1896] 1 Ch. 6, C.A.
17 *i.e.* a parent or subsidiary undertaking of the company: 1989 Act s.27(3).
18 *Ibid.* s.27(1).
19 Though the shareholding might make the auditor a more diligent watchdog over the members' interests—but members are not the only people whose interests he should protect.
20 As defined in *ibid.* s.52.
21 1989 Act. s.28(1).
22 *Ibid.* s.28(2).
23 *Ibid.* s.28(3). It is a defence for him to show that he did not know and had no reason to believe that he was ineligible: s.28(5). This might well be shown when the ineligibility flowed from action by the company or by one of its associated undertakings or by one of his partners or associates.
24 *Ibid.* s.28(4).

If an auditor proves to have been ineligible during any part of his audit, the Secretary of State may direct the company to appoint another (eligible) auditor in his place, either to carry out a second audit or to review the first and to report (giving reasons) whether a second audit is needed.[25] If a second audit is recommended, the company must comply.[26] The Registrar has to be sent a copy of the direction and of any report and the provisions of the 1985 Act applying to the first audit apply to the second "so far as is practicable."[27] If the original auditor knew that he was ineligible the company is entitled to recover from him any costs incurred in complying with the direction or recommendation.[28] But if the company has failed to comply with the direction or recommendation it is liable to a fine on a basis similar to that applying to the ineligible auditor.[29]

Educational qualifications

There is a marked difference between the regulation of the financial services industry (except in respect of those firms that are authorised by virtue of membership of recognised professional bodies) and that of the accountancy profession when acting as company auditors. In the case of the former it is, unfortunately, not yet possible to prescribe educational training and qualifying examinations as an essential precondition in all cases of "fitness and properness" for authorisation. But section 30–34 and Schedules 11 and 12 of the 1989 Act do this in respect of company auditors.[30]

In addition to being a member[31] of a supervisory body which has been recognised in accordance with section 30, as supplemented by sections 35–53 and Schedule 11,[32] a person is not eligible for

---

[25] *Ibid.* s.29(1).

[26] *Ibid.* s.29(2).

[27] *Ibid.* s.29(3) and (4). The extent of the practicability will depend on whether the ineligibility is discovered before the accounts and reports have been sent out, laid and delivered to the Registrar. If it is, the statutory provisions can be fully complied with by substituting the second auditor's report for the first's. Even if it is too late for that, the report of the second auditor has to be delivered to the Registrar (see s.29(3)) and presumably copies should be sent to the members—at any rate if it differs from the first auditors' report.

[28] *Ibid.* s.29(7).

[29] *Ibid.* s.29(5).

[30] It is also possible to do so relation to the authorisation of insolvency practitioners under Part XIII of the Insolvency Act 1986 and this is done to the extent that the recognised professional body that authorises them must, as a condition of recognition, have adequate rules ensuring that applicants for authorisation "meet acceptable requirements as to education and practical training and experience." Insolvency Act, ss.391(2)(b) and 393(2)(b). There is, however, nothing comparable to the detailed statutory prescription in ss.30–34 and Scheds. 11 and 12 of the 1989 Act.

[31] "Membership" includes "persons who, whether or not members of the body, are subject to its rules in seeking appointment or acting as company auditors": 1989 Act s.30(2).

[32] Supervisory bodies will not be recognised unless they have rules and resources for effective monitoring and enforcement and for investigation of complaints: Sched. 11 Part II.

appointment as a company auditor unless he holds "an appropriate qualification." For this purpose sections 31–34, as supplemented by sections 35–53 and Schedule 12, deal with recognised qualifying bodies and recognised professional qualifications.

The role of the *qualifying* bodies is to provide courses and examinations in accountancy leading to an approved qualification. A body may apply to the Secretary of State for an order declaring a qualification offered by it to be a recognised professional qualification. But an order will not be made unless the Secretary of State is satisfied that the requirements of Schedule 12 regarding entry, theoretical instruction, professional experience, examinations[33] and rules regarding monitoring, are met.[34] There seems to be no reason why a recognised supervisory body should not also be a recognised qualifying body if it is able and willing to perform both roles; indeed it seems that the five recognised supervisory bodies[35] will also be the initial qualifying bodies.

However, a recognised professional qualification is not the only "appropriate qualification" without which a person is ineligible. A "grandfather" provision is needed to prevent all those formerly qualified from having to qualify anew. Hence section 31 of the 1989 Act provides that a person qualified under the former section 389(1)) before 1990 by virtue of membership of one of the four, then recognised, accountancy bodies remains qualified[36] and that a person so qualified under that section, otherwise than by virtue of such membership, shall be treated as holding an approved qualification for 12 months from the date when section 25 came into force and shall continue thereafter to be so treated if, within that time, he notifies the Secretary of State that he wishes to retain the benefit of his qualification.[37] There is also a concession to someone who, before 1990, started a course leading to a professional qualification in

---

[33] The subjects on which theoretical knowledge must be tested by examinations, part at least of which must be written, may be prescribed by regulations made by the Secretary of State under Sched. 12 para. 7: see The Company Auditors (Examinations) Regs: S.I. 1990 No. 1146. These seem innocuous but the extent of the control which could be exercised by the Secretary of State for *Trade and Industry* over courses and examinations "requiring a standard of attainment at least equivalent to that required to obtain a degree from a university or similar establishment in the U.K." (Sched. 12 para. 7(1)) may cause shivers to run down academic spines. But note that exemption from subjects in the examination may be granted to someone who "has passed a university or other examination of equivalent standard in that subject or holds a university or equivalent qualification in it." Sched. 12, para. 7(2).
[34] *Ibid.* para. 9.
[35] See p. 378 n. 7 above.
[36] 1989 Act, s.31(1)(a).
[37] *Ibid.* s.31(2). If he fails to give notice in time, he may be excused if there was good reason for the failure and he genuinely intends to practise as an auditor in G.B.: s.31(3). But note that a person previously qualified only for the audit of unquoted companies: *ibid* s.34(1) and (2). And other enactments, (e.g. the F.S. Act) referring to eligibility for appointment as a company auditor do not include such a person: s.34(4).

accounting offered by a United Kingdom body and successfully completed it before 1996, but only so long as the Secretary of State is satisfied that the qualification was equivalent to a "recognised professional qualification."[38]

In addition, section 33 provides a further type of recognised qualification of which section 31[39] has to take account. Under section 33 the Secretary of State may declare that a person qualified to audit accounts under the law of a specified country outside the United Kingdom, or one who holds a specified professional qualification recognised under the law of such a country, shall be regarded as holding "an approved overseas qualification."[40] Such approval is dependent on satisfying the Secretary of State that the overseas qualification affords an assurance of professional competence equivalent to that afforded by a recognised professional qualification[41] and the declaration may be made subject to his holding additional qualifications ensuring that he has an adequate knowledge of United Kingdom law and practice relevant to the audit of accounts.[42]

Among the duties which are imposed on the recognised bodies is that of maintaining a register of qualified company auditors. The Secretary of State is required to make regulations about the register, inspection of it and the obtaining of copies.[43] He has also to make regulations requiring recognised supervisory bodies to keep, and make available to the public, information about firms eligible for appointment as company auditors.[44]

Attention must be drawn to certain provisions in Schedule 11 which provide the answer to a question which may have puzzled readers. When, as will normally be the case, a firm, corporate or unincorporated, is appointed as auditors how does one ensure that the firm is qualified not only by membership of a recognised supervisory body (which presents no difficulty) but also by compliance with the educational and training requirements of a recognised qualifying body? One cannot educate or train a firm; but only individual members of it. This is not, as one would have expected, dealt with in a section of the 1989 Act itself but by paragraphs 4 and 5 of Schedule 11. These provide that the supervisory body as a condition for its recognition must have rules which ensure that a person is not eligible for appointment unless, in the case of an individual, he holds an appropriate qualification and that, in the case of a firm: (i) the individuals responsible for company audit work on behalf of the firm hold appropriate qualifications, and

38 *Ibid.* s.31(4) and (5).
39 *Ibid.* s.31(1)(c).
40 *Ibid.* s.33(1).
41 *Ibid.* s.33(2).
42 *Ibid.* s.33(4).
43 *Ibid.* s.35.
44 *Ibid.* s.36.

(ii) the firm is controlled by qualified persons.[45] A firm which has ceased to comply may, however, be permitted to remain eligible for not more than three months.[46] "Controlled by qualified persons" means that a majority of the members hold appropriate qualifications and, when the firm is managed by a management body, that a majority of that body is qualified also.[47]

The foregoing covers only a part of the provisions of Part II of the 1989 Act[48] but sufficient, perhaps, to convey an impression of this new system for ensuring that auditors are properly qualified and which has now replaced section 389 of the Companies Act 1985.[49]

Appointment of auditors

We now turn to the new and amended sections 384–394A which sections 118–123 of the 1989 Act insert as Chapter V of Part XI (Auditors) of the 1985 Act.[50]

The first set of sections deals with appointment of auditors. Every company, other than a dormant one, must appoint an auditor or auditors.[51] Except in the case of a private company which has elected to dispense with the laying of accounts[52] or with annual appointments,[53] this must be done at each general meeting at which the accounts and reports are to be laid and the appointment must be from the conclusion of that meeting until the conclusion of the next such meeting.[54] This is designed not merely to emphasise that it is to the members that auditors are to report and to ensure that the company has auditors at all times but also to enhance the auditors independence from the directors. However, the first auditors of the company must be appointed before the first general meeting at which accounts are to be laid and accordingly the first auditors may be, and, in practice invariably are, appointed by the directors[55] to hold office until that general meeting when the directors will recommend re-appointment and the meeting, almost invariably, will agree. Normally, those auditors will continue to be re-appointed until they wish to retire or the directors want to get rid of them.

[45] *Ibid.* Sched. 11, para. 4(1). This does not prevent the supervisory body from imposing more stringent requirements: para. 4(2).

[46] Para. 4(3). Thus giving it the opportunity, on a change in its membership, to make arrangements whereby it will comply.

[47] Para. 5, of which the text is a brief summary omitting various qualifications.

[48] They confer powers on the S of S to ensure compliance by the recognised bodies (ss.37–41), and include matters such as offences (s.47 and Sched. 14, which provides a regime analogous to that applying to recognised SROs under F.S. Act).

[49] See The Companies Act 1989 (Eligibility for Appointment as Company Auditor) (Consequential Amendments) Regs. 1991 S.I. No. 1997.

[50] Hereafter references to sections are to those of the 1985 Act, as so amended, unless the contrary is stated.

[51] s.384.

[52] Under s.252, above Chap. 17 p. 463.

[53] Under s.386 below.

[54] s.385(1) and (2).

[55] s.385(3). If they fail to do so a general meeting may: s.385(4).

In the case of a private company which has elected to dispense with laying of accounts, the foregoing provisions are adapted by requiring appointment within 28 days after the day on which copies of the accounts are to be sent to members under section 238.[56]

A private company may elect (by an elective resolution under section 379A) to dispense with the obligation to appoint auditors annually.[57] If such an election is in force, the auditors, once appointed, are deemed to be reappointed for each succeeding financial year unless a resolution has been passed under section 293[58] ending their appointment.[59] If an election ceases to be in force the auditors then holding office continue to do so until others are appointed under section 385 or 385A.[60] If, then or thereafter, they cease to hold office, no account can be taken of any loss of the opportunity of further deemed re-appointment in assessing the amount of any compensation or damages payable for loss of office.[61]

In default of any appointment of auditors when they are required, the Secretary of State may appoint to fill the vacancy and the company must give notice to him, within one week of the end of the time for appointing auditors, that his power to do so has become exercisable.[62] In addition, the directors or the company in general meeting may fill a casual vacancy[63] and until it is filled the surviving or continuing auditor or auditors may continue to act.[64] If a casual vacancy is to be filled by a resolution of the general meeting or by a resolution to re-appoint a person who was appointed by the directors, "special notice"[65] has to be given to the company and it must give notice of it to the person proposed to be appointed and, if the casual vacancy was caused by the resignation of an auditor, to him also.[66]

Subsection (1) of section 388A states the obvious—that a dormant company which is exempt from the provisions of Part VII of the Act relating to audit of accounts is also exempt from the obligation to appoint auditors. The subsequent subsections deal with the less obvious question of precisely what occurs if the exemption ceases. In

---

[56] s.385A. But see subs. (2) and (3) if notice is given under s.253(2) requiring the accounts for a particular year to be laid.
[57] s.386(1).
[58] See below. Or unless a resolution has been passed under s.250 dispensing with audits as a "dormant company": see Chap. 17 at p. 471 above.
[59] s.386(2).
[60] s.386(3).
[61] s.386(4). If account were taken of it, the auditors would be paid more just because the company had elected to dispense with annual re-appointment.
[62] s.387.
[63] s.388(1). In practice the directors will do so.
[64] s.388(2). If a firm has been appointed in accordance with the provisions of s.25 of the 1989 Act, the effect of its s.26 (see above p. 478) will normally be to minimise the risk of there being a casual vacancy.
[65] *i.e.* 28 days notice to the company of the intention to move it: s.379, on which see Chap. 19 at p. 509 below, and *cf.* Chap. 7 at pp. 153–155.
[66] s.388(3) and (4).

the normal situation, where accounts have to be laid,[67] the directors may appoint auditors at any time before the next general meeting at which accounts are to be laid and the auditors so appointed hold office until the conclusion of that meeting.[68] If, however, the company is a private company which has elected to dispense with laying[69] the directors may appoint at any time before the expiration of the period provided by section 385A[70] and the auditors hold office until the end of that period.[71] If the directors fail to appoint, the company in general meeting may do so.[72]

Rights of auditors

Section 237 in Part VII of the Act[73] having imposed statutory duties on the auditors in relation to the preparation of their reports, sections 389A and 390, as inserted in Chapter V of Part XI,[74] confer on them statutory rights which they need in order to perform these duties. Under section 389A they have a right of access at all times to the company's books, accounts and vouchers and are entitled to require from the company's officers such explanations as they think necessary for the performance of their duties as auditors[75] and an officer commits an offence if he knowingly or recklessly makes to the auditors a statement which conveys or purports to convey any information or explanation which is misleading, false or deceptive in any material particular.[76] Similarly, a subsidiary undertaking incorporated in Great Britain and the auditors of that body are under a duty to give to the auditors of any parent company such information and explanations as they require for the purposes of their duties as auditors of that parent company.[77] Moreover a parent company having a subsidiary undertaking not incorporated in Great Britain must, if required by its auditors to do so, take such steps as are reasonably open to it to obtain such information and explanations from the subsidiary.[78]

---

67 *i.e.* when s.385, above, applies.
68 s.388A(2) and (3).
69 *i.e.* when s.385A, above, applies.
70 Or the beginning of the general meeting if one has been demanded; s.388A(2) and (4).
71 Or the end of the meeting: s.388A(4).
72 s.388A(5).
73 See Chap. 17 p. 462 above.
74 On a new consolidation an effort really ought to be made to bring the sections relating to duties and rights together in one Chapter of the Act.
75 s.389A(1).
76 s.389A(2).
77 s.389A(3). The subsidiary, its officers in default and its auditors may commit an offence if they do not comply. If the offence is by an unincorporated body (*e.g.* an auditing partnership) s.734 applies (*i.e.* it is treated as if it was incorporated): s.389A(5).
78 s.389A(4). The parent and its officers in default commit an offence if they fail to comply.

Under section 390, auditors are entitled to receive all notices and other communications relating to general meetings, to attend any general meeting and to be heard on any part of the business which concerns them as auditors.[79] In view of the fact that most private companies are likely to use written resolutions in accordance with section 381A rather than those passed at a meeting and that many of them will elect to dispense with laying accounts before general meetings, this would be ineffective as a means of strengthening the role of the auditors as watchdogs of the members' interests unless the auditors could insist upon a meeting being held. Hence, in relation to laying accounts, section 253(2), as we have seen,[80] entitles an auditor to insist on a meeting being held. And, as regards written resolutions under section 381A, section 381B affords the auditors a like right if the resolution concerns them as auditors. This is reinforced by section 390(2) which reiterates that they are entitled to attend any such meeting and to be heard on any part of the business which concerns them as auditors. It also makes it clear that if the auditors are a firm (corporate or unincorporated) the right to attend and to be heard is exercisable by an individual authorised by it in writing.[81]

As regards public companies, the value of the auditors' right to attend meetings is diminished by the fact that, as we shall see later[82] the result of the meeting will, in practice, generally be determined by proxy votes lodged before the meeting is held. Hence the right is virtually worthless unless the auditors are able to get their views across to the members before proxies are lodged. This, as we shall see,[83] they may be able to do if they are prepared to resign or if it is proposed to remove them.

Remuneration of auditors

Section 390A provides that when auditors are appointed by a general meeting[84] (which, under sections 384–388[85] sooner or later they will generally have to be) their remuneration shall be fixed by the company in general meeting or in such manner as the general meeting shall determine.[86] This too is intended to emphasise that the auditors are the members' watchdogs rather than the directors' lapdogs. But in practice it serves little purpose since the members normally adopt a resolution proposed by the directors to the effect that the remuneration shall be agreed by the directors. And when the

[79] s.390(1).
[80] Chap. 17 at p. 473 above.
[81] s.390(3).
[82] Chap. 19 below.
[83] Below pp. 487–490.
[84] The effect of s.381A(4) is presumably that this includes a case when a private company has appointed by a written resolution under that section.
[85] Above pp. 483, 484.
[86] s.390A(1).

auditors are appointed by the directors or the Secretary of State, the remuneration is to be fixed by them or him.[87] A more effective protection, perhaps, is that the amount of the remuneration, which includes expenses and benefits in kind (the monetary value of which has to be estimated) has to be shown in a note to the annual accounts,[88] thus enabling the members to criticise the directors if the amount seems to be out-of-line.[89]

The new section 390B recognises that very frequently the directors will arrange for the firm of auditors to undertake advisory or similar functions in addition to that of auditing, that for this they will be separately and additionally remunerated, and that section 390A does not require disclosure of the amount of that remuneration. Hence section 390B empowers the Secretary of State to make regulations[89a] requiring the disclosure of remuneration of auditors or their associates "in respect of services other than those of auditors in their capacity as such." Unfortunately this section does not tackle the root of the problem[90] which is that undertaking such services may be incompatible with their independence as auditors and that, even if it is not, it will increase the value to the firm of the auditorship and thus make the firm the more reluctant to do anything which will render it likely that the board of directors will seek to get rid of them as auditors. This problem is one that the supervisory bodies, and the Secretary of State, should tackle and it is to be hoped that they will. Unless it is tackled, the supervisory bodies will not have "adequate rules and practices designed to ensure that persons are not appointed company auditors in circumstances in which they have any interest likely to conflict with the proper conduct of their audit—a condition for recognition as a supervisory body.[91]

Removal and resignation of auditors

As in the case of directors,[92] "a company may be ordinary resolution at any time remove an auditor from office notwithstanding anything in any agreement between it and him."[93] But in relation to

[87] s. 390A(2).
[88] s. 390A(3), (4) and (5).
[89] Generally they criticise only if the amount seems abnormally high; they should perhaps be more alarmed if it is abnormally low.
[89a] See the Regs. made by 1991 S.I. No. 2128.
[90] An increasingly worrying problem as the major firms of accountants, themselves or through associated companies, offer a full range of financial services to their corporate clients, the profits from which may be greater than that earned from audit work.
[91] 1989 Act, Sched. 11 para. 7(1). Another vexed question which the regulations will need to answer is in what circumstances the auditors, notwithstanding their duty of confidentiality, should immediately inform the regulatory authorities of misbehaviour that they have detected. If directors are party to a fraud, informing the board will merely alert the culprits.
[92] s. 303. See Chap. 7 at pp. 153–155 above.
[93] s. 391(1). If such a resolution is passed, the company must within 14 days give notice of it to the Registrar: s. 391(2).

the removal of an auditor special safeguards are needed not only to protect him, but to protect the company from being deprived of an auditor whose fault in the eyes of the directors may be that he has rightly not proved subservient to their wishes. Hence, not only has special notice[94] to be given to the company of a resolution to remove an auditor or not to re-appoint him,[95] but notice of the proposed resolution has to be given to the auditor and to the person that is to be appointed in his place.[96] The auditor is entitled to make written representations which, if received in time have to be sent to the members with the notice of the meeting,[97] and which, if not received in time, have to be read out at the meeting.[98] If the resolution is passed, he still retains his rights under section 390, above, in respect of the general meeting at which his term of office would otherwise have expired or at which it is proposed to fill the vacancy caused by his removal.[99] Nor does his removal deprive him of any right to compensation or damages to which he may be entitled under the contract between him and the company in respect of the termination of his appointment as auditor or any appointment terminating with that as auditor.[1]

In other words, a company cannot remove an auditor against his will without facing a serious risk of a row at the general meeting (and, in the case of a listed company, adverse Press publicity) and, probably, payment of compensation.

It has been argued that this indefinite entrenchment of the existing auditors is not desirable, since it is liable to lead to an excessively cosy relationship between the company's management and the auditors, and that accordingly there should be a prescribed maximum period for which the same firm can hold office. But, so far, that argument has not prevailed.

However, no auditor will want to retain office if relations between him and the management of the company have become seriously strained. It is therefore essential that he should not resign his office without ensuring that any matters which have caused him concern will not be brushed under the carpet. Hence section 392 provides that although an auditor may resign by depositing a notice in writing to that effect at the company's registered office, the notice is not effective unless it is accompanied by the statement required by

---

[94] In accordance with s.379.
[95] s.391A(1).
[96] s.391A(2).
[97] The auditor should ensure that it is received in time since otherwise members may return proxy forms before they see his representations.
[98] s.391A(3) (4) and (5). But see subs. (6) regarding restraint by the court if the section is being abused "to secure needless publicity for defamatory matter." This is less likely than under the corresponding s.304(4) when a director is removed under s.303.
[99] s.391(4).
[1] s.391(3).

section 394.[2] The latter section provides that where an auditor ceases to hold office for any reason,[3] he shall deposit at the company's registered office a statement of any circumstances connected with his ceasing to hold office which he considers should be brought to the attention of members or creditors, or, if he considers that there are no such circumstances, a statement to that effect.[4] If the statement is of circumstances which the auditor considers should be brought to the attention of members or creditors, the company must, within 14 days of its deposit, either send copies of it to any person who, under section 238,[5] is entitled to be sent copies of the accounts[6] or apply to the court[7] and notify the auditor that it has done so.[8] Unless the auditor receives such a notification within 21 days, he must, within a period of a further seven days send a copy of the statement to the Registrar[9] thus making it available to creditors and the public generally. If the company applies to the court which is satisfied that the auditor is using the statement to secure needless publicity for defamatory matter it must direct that the statement need not be sent out and may order the company's costs to be paid, in whole or in part, by the auditors.[10] The company must then send to members or debentureholders a statement setting out the effect of the order.[11] If the court is not so satisfied the company must within 14 days of the decision send copies of the auditor's statement to members, debentureholders and any of the persons entitled to receive notice of general meetings,[12] and notify the auditor who must thereupon send the Registrar a copy of his statement.[13] Failure of the auditor or the company to comply is an offence.[14]

Furthermore, where an auditor's notice of resignation is accompanied by a statement of circumstances which he considers should be brought to the attention of members or creditors, he may under

2 s.392(1). A copy of the notice must be sent to the Registrar within 14 days of its deposit: s.392(3). An effective notice ends the auditor's term of office on the date of its deposit or such later date as may be specified in it: s.392(2).
3 Except, presumably, if he is an individual and he dies. It may have been thought that this can be ignored now that auditors are likely to be a firm which has two or more partners or is a body corporate. It is also unlikely that the circumstances of his death will be such as should be brought to the attention of members or creditors—unless, say, a fraudulent employee of the company whom he was about to expose had laced his mid-morning coffee with a lethal dose of poison.
4 s.394(1). In cases of failure to seek re-appointment the statement has to be deposited not less than 14 days before the time allowed for next appointing auditors and in other cases (except that of resignation) within 14 days after he ceases to hold office: s.394(2).
5 See Chap. 17 at p. 463 above.
6 This includes members and debentureholders but not other creditors.
7 s.394(3).
8 s.394(4).
9 s.394(5).
10 s.394(6).
11 *Ibid.*
12 This would include the new auditor (if he had been appointed) and any continuing joint auditor.
13 s.394(7).
14 See s.394A for details.

section 392A deposit with the notice a signed requisition calling upon the directors forthwith to convene an extraordinary general meeting for the purpose of receiving and considering such explanation of the circumstances of his resignation as he may wish to place before the meeting.[15] He may also require the company to place before that meeting (or one at which his term of office would have expired but for his resignation) his statement of the circumstances.[16] The directors must convene the meeting promptly, and, in the notice of it, state the fact that the statement has been made and send a copy of it to every member if it is received in time.[17] Hence, persuading auditors to retire or not to stand for re-appointment cannot be effectively used as a means of muzzling the auditors.

Finally, section 393 empowers any members of a private company which has elected to dispense with the annual re-appointments to deposit at the registered office of the company not more than one notice in each financial year proposing that the appointment of the auditors be brought to an end.[18] The directors must thereupon convene a meeting for a date not later than 28 days after the deposit of the notice to consider a resolution enabling the meeting to decide whether the auditors' appointment should be ended.[19] If the decision is that it should, the auditors are deemed not to be reappointed on the next occasion when otherwise they would be so deemed under section 386.[20] Indeed, if the member's notice was deposited within 14 days after the accounts and reports were sent to members under section 238, any deemed re-appointment for the year following that to which those accounts related ceases to have effect.[21] This section prevails notwithstanding any agreement to the contrary between the company and its auditors and, as under section 386(4),[22] no compensation or damages are payable to the auditors by reason of the appointment being terminated under it.[23]

Auditors' negligence

Having reviewed, in this and the previous chapter, the statutory provisions relating to company accounts and their audit, something

[15] s.392A(1) and (2).
[16] s.392A(3).
[17] s.392A(4) and (5). If this statement was received too late for the company to comply, the auditor can require it to be read at the meeting and this is without prejudice to his right to be heard orally, in accordance with s.390, as if he was still the auditor: s.392A(6) and (8). There is the customary power of the court to ban defamatory matter: s.392(7).
[18] s.393(1).
[19] s.393(2). If the directors fail to do so, the member may, as under s.253 (Chap. 17 at p. 473), himself convene the meeting and recover from the company his reasonable expenses: s.393(4) (5) and (6).
[20] s.393(3).
[21] *Ibid.*
[22] See p. 484 above.
[23] s.393(7).

needs to be said about the auditors' potential civil liability if they are negligent in the performance of their duties. Although it is the directors who are responsible for the published accounts, the auditors are more likely to be worth powder-and-shot[24] if they can be shown to have been negligent in certifying the accuracy of those accounts. Moreover, in contrast with directors, they are required to display the care and skill of professionals.

Hence at any one time in recent years, actions against auditors attempting to recover billions of pounds or dollars have been proceeding not only in England but in countries from Hong Kong in the East to the Pacific Coast of N. America in the West. The reported decisions in common law jurisdictions were reviewed by the House of Lords in the recent case of *Caparo Industries plc v. Dickman*[25] and, as a result of its unanimous decision, the ambit of the duty of care owed by auditors has been somewhat clarified so far as English law is concerned—and in a way which will give greater comfort to auditors[26] than to investors.

As a result of *Caparo* it seems that the present position can be summarised in the following propositions:

Proposition 1. As pointed out by Lord Jauncey,[27] three matters clearly emerge from the statutory provisions dealt with in this and the previous chapter:

"(1) that the responsibility for the preparation of accounts giving a true and fair view of the company's financial state is placed fairly and squarely on the shoulders of the directors;

(2) that the role of the auditors is to provide an independent report to the members on the proper preparation of the balance sheet and profit and loss account and as to whether those documents give a true and fair view. . . . Their role is thus purely investigative rather than creative;

(3) that the company's accounts, including the auditors' report, will be furnished to all members of the company as well as to debentureholders and any persons entitled to receive notice of general meetings. The accounts will of course also be available to

---

24 Especially because they will be covered by professional indemnity insurance though it is becoming more difficult and expensive to obtain full cover.

25 [1990] 2 A.C. 605. H.L. The preliminary issue on which *Caparo* reached the H.L. was whether, on the facts pleaded, a claim against the auditors could succeed. Two directors were also being sued for alleged fraud.

26 Less so, perhaps, to the big international firms which also operate in countries that take a wider view of the scope of the duty of care, (e.g. N. Zealand and some States of the USA).

27 [1990] 2 A.C. at p. 660.

any member of the public who chooses to examine the company's file in the office of the Registrar of Companies."

Proposition 2. The Act imposes certain specific duties on the auditors in relation to the preparation of their report,[28] and confers upon them specific rights to obtain information from the directors and officers of the company.[29] While the speeches in *Caparo* do not deal specifically with the effect of those statutory duties and rights, it seems clear that (a) failure to observe them does not give rise to civil liability for breach of statutory duty as such[30]; but (b) they cannot be waived or reduced by any provision in the contract between the company and the auditors[31] and (c) failure to observe them would be a failure to take due care.

Proposition 3. The statutory provisions establish a relationship between those responsible for the accounts (the directors) or for the report (the auditors) and some other class or classes of persons and this relationship imposes a duty of care owed to those persons. Among these "persons" is the company itself, to which, apart altogether from the statutory provisions, the directors are in a fiduciary relationship and the auditors in a contractual relationship by virtue of their employment by the company as its auditors.

Proposition 4. However, the statutory provisions do not establish such a relationship with everybody who has a right to be furnished with copies of the accounts or report or, *a fortiori*, with everybody who has a right to inspect, or obtain, copies of them. If a relationship other than that with the company is to be established under the statutory provisions it can be only with members (and perhaps debenture-holders[32]) and, even in their case, the scope of the resulting duty of care extends only to the protection of what, for the moment, may be described as those persons' corporate powers to safeguard their

[28] s.237, above Chap. 17, pp. 461, 462.

[29] s.389A, above p. 485.

[30] The speeches in *Caparo* assumed that actions will be at common law, in tort or contract.

[31] Apart from the fact that the duties are statutory, s.310 (see Chap. 21 below pp. 572–575) would make any such provision void. Nor, it is submitted, could the auditors defend themselves in an action based on their alleged negligence by arguing that proper performance of the directors' and officers' duties was a condition precedent to the performance by the auditors of their duties. They could, however, assume that the directors and officers were trustworthy until they had reason to suspect the contrary: see the oft-quoted dictum of Lopes L.J. in *Re Kingston Cotton Mill (No. 2)* [1896] Ch. 279. C.A. at pp. 288–289 that an auditor is: "a watch-dog not a bloodhound. He is justified in believing tried servants of the company in whom confidence is placed by the company. He is entitled to assume that they are honest and to rely on their representations provided that he takes reasonable care." [But if] "there is anything calculated to excite suspicion he should probe it to the bottom . . ."

[32] See below p. 495.

interests in the company. That does not include their powers to buy further shares in the company even if it is a perusal of the annual accounts and reports that led them to do so.[33]

Proposition 5. In so far as a duty of care is owed to members as a result of the statutory provisions it is owed to them collectively, not individually, and in practice will normally be enforced by an action by the company which, if successful, will restore it, and hence its members collectively, to the position that they would have been in had the breach of duty not occurred.

Proposition 6. To establish a duty of care either as an individual or as a member of an identifiable class, specifically in connection with a particular transaction or transactions of a particular kind (e.g. in a prospectus inviting investment[34]) and that the plaintiff would be very likely to rely on it for the purpose of deciding whether or not to enter upon that transaction or upon a transaction of that kind."[35]

To establish a duty of care owed under proposition 4 or 5, or to establish any duty of care to other persons there must be an additional "special" relationship with the person who suffered loss as a result of relying on the accounts or report. To succeed in establishing that, the plaintiff (who in this case will be the person or class of persons who have so relied—and not the company itself) must show that the defendant knew that the accounts and report—

"would be communicated to the plaintiff

---

[33] This was the specific point that had to be determined in *Caparo.* The C.A. had held unanimously that auditors owed no duty of care to members of the public who, in reliance on the accounts and reports, bought shares (in the absence of a special relationship—see proposition 6 below) but, by a majority, that they did owe such a duty to existing shareholders who, in such reliance, bought more shares The H.L. held unanimously that, in the absence of a "special relationship," a duty of care did not extend to either.

[34] As pointed out in Chap. 13, above at pp. 344, 345, where the prospectus is "listing particulars" or a "prospectus" within the meaning of Part IV or V of the Financial Services Act, the statute law has gone beyond the common law which will normally be irrelevant. But it remains highly relevant at present in relation, e.g. to circulars on a rights issue: See *Al-Nakib Investments Ltd.* v. *Longcroft,* [1990] 1 W.L.R. 1390.

[35] *Per* Lord Bridge at p. 621 E.F. This was clearly the unanimous view, adopting the dissenting judgment of Denning L.J. in *Candler* v. *Crane Christmas & Co.* [1951] 2 K.B. 164, C.A. (which already had been adopted unanimously by the H.L. in *Hedley Byrne & Co.* v. *Heller* [1964] A.C. 465) and affirming the decision of Millett J. in *Al Saudi Banque* v. *Clark Pixley* [1990] Ch. 313, but rejecting the wider views expressed in *JEB Fasteners Ltd.* v. *Marks Bloom & Co.* [1981] 3 All E.R. 289 and in *Twomax Ltd.* v. *Dickson, McFarlane & Robinson,* 1982 S.C. 113, and by the majority of the N.Z.C.A. in *Scott Group Ltd.* v. *McFarlane* [1978] N.Z.L.R. 553. *cf. Smith* v. *Eric S. Bush* [1990] 1 A.C. 831, H.L. where, applying a similar test of proximity and foresight, it was held that a surveyor employed by a building society or local authority owed a duty of care to the purchaser/mortgagor of a house as well as to the mortgagee for whom the survey was undertaken.

Proposition 7. Whether the action is brought by the company under proposition 3 or by others under proposition 4, 5 or 6 the plaintiffs will have to show, if they are to recover damages, that they have suffered a quantifiable loss which was caused by a breach of the particular defendant's duties of care.

Comments

A brief commentary on the foregoing propositions is needed because they beg certain questions and, in so far as they are gleaned from the speeches in *Caparo*, they depend upon the view there taken on the purpose of the statutory provisions—a view which is certainly not self-evident from the present wording of those provisions. First, then: What was their view of that purpose? And by what chain of reasoning was it reached?

The most detailed account of the chain of reasoning was given in the speech of Lord Oliver.[36] He pointed out that when, at the beginning of the Century, provisions regarding accounts and audits were first introduced, they provided only for audited accounts to be laid before general meetings and for the auditor's report to be read at those meetings. Clearly, therefore, the original purpose was to give the general body of shareholders[37] the information which they needed for the informed exercise of such powers as they could exercise at general meetings. In the light of the subsequent development of the relevant legislative provisions it could no longer be said that:

"the purpose of making such information available is solely to assist those interested in attending general meetings to an informed supervision and appraisal of the stewardship of the company's directors; for the requirement to supply audited accounts to, for instance, preference shareholders having no right to vote at general meetings and to debentureholders cannot easily be attributed to any such purpose."[38]

Nevertheless Lord Oliver could not:

"discern in the legislation any departure from what appears to be the original, central and primary purpose of these provisions, that

[36] At pp. 630–632.
[37] Throughout the speeches (except that of Lord Jauncey) in *Caparo*, the expression "shareholders" was used instead of "members," the expression used in the Act. On the assumption that "shareholders" were referred to in the speeches only because in *Caparo* the members were shareholders, in the foregoing propositions "members" has been substituted. It can hardly have been the intention of the H.L. to exclude members of companies without a share capital.
[38] At p. 631 E–F.

is to say, the informed exercise by those interested in the property of the company, whether as proprietors of shares in the company or as holders or rights secured by a debenture trust deed, of such powers as are vested in them by virtue of their respective proprietary interests."[39]

In particular he found it "difficult to believe" that the requirement to file accounts and the auditors' report with the Registrar "could have been inspired also by consideration for the public at large."[40]

The other speeches, however, adopted a formulation different from Lord Oliver's conclusion that the duty of care is owed to shareholders *and debentureholders* to the extent needed to protect "the exercise of such powers as are vested in them by virtue of their respective proprietary interests." They make no mention of debentureholders and Lord Bridge describes the scope of the duty of care as that needed to protect the shareholders' "opportunity to exercise their powers in general meeting to call the directors to book and to ensure that errors in management are corrected."[41] Lord Jauncey said much the same.[42] This seems to hark back to the "original" purpose of the statutory provisions and to disregard completely the present wording of them.[43]

Lord Bridge, having said that:

"The shareholders of a company have a collective interest in the company's proper management and in so far as a negligent failure . . . to report accurately on the state of the company's finances

[39] *Ibid.* This, admittedly does lend credence to the possibility that he may have intended to exclude members of companies not having a share capital (notwithstanding n. 37 above). But surely all members of unlimited companies without a share capital have "proprietary" rights equivalent to those of partners and members of guarantee companies have such rights even if it is only that of sharing in the surplus assets on the liquidation (unless the company is a charity or one which has dispensed with the suffix "Ltd"). Moreover, his formulation, if interpreted strictly, would also exclude all holders of unsecured debentures or of a series of debentures secured otherwise than by a trust deed.

[40] At 632 A.B. But what other purpose could it have had? And the legislature, when by the 1967 Act, it removed the exemption from filing formerly enjoyed by some private companies, was well aware that it did so to implement the recommendation of the Jenkins Committee (Cmnd. 1749 para. 61) that "all companies which are incorporated with the privilege of limited liability" should be required to "file their accounts with the Registrar of Companies *for the benefit of those who may have dealings with them*" (itals supplied). Admittedly, on the optimistic assumption that most accounts and audits will be prepared with due care, having access to accounts may be a benefit to "persons having dealings with" most companies most of the time. But, if the information is misleading and if this was due to a want of due care, is it fanciful to suppose that the legislature would have expected that those who had negligently prepared the poisoned chalice would be liable to compensate those who swallowed the potion?

[41] At p.626 C, D.

[42] At p.661, 662.

[43] It also seems to display a somewhat exaggerated confidence in what the shareholders of a listed company will, in practice, be able to achieve at a general meeting held shortly after they have received the accounts and report.

deprives them of an opportunity to exercise their powers in general meeting . . . the shareholders ought to be entitled to a remedy,"[44]

went on to say:

"But in practice no problem arises in this regard since the interest of the shareholders . . . is indistinguishable from the interest of the company itself and any loss suffered by the shareholders, *e.g.* by the negligent failure of the auditor to discover and expose a misappropriation of funds by a director of the company, will be recouped by a claim against the auditors in the name of the company, not by individual shareholders."[45]

This, however, seems to ignore three considerations:

(1) In a simple case where the negligence is a failure to detect the misdeeds of a single officer or employee, the directors, if they have not been as negligent as the auditors, may well cause the company to take action. But if the directors too are negligent, and especially if they have been fraudulent, they certainly will not. In practice no action will then be taken by the company unless and until there is a change of control because the company has gone into liquidation or receivership, or an administrator has been appointed or it has been taken-over.

(2) An action in the name of the company will lead, if successful, to recovery of damages by the company, thereby enuring for the benefit of those persons who have interests in it at the date of the recovery. In the case of a listed company, or any company that has been taken-over, the members will then be different from those who were members at the date of the breach of duties. Those who were members at that time and those who have become members thereafter will benefit by the recovery (new members probably undeservedly) but those who have ceased to be members will not. In contrast, if the members at the time of the breach could sue directly (normally in a representative action) those who were damaged by the breach would recover, and those who were not would not obtain an undeserved windfall.

(3) If an action can only be brought in the name of the company (which Lord Bridge seems to imply) it is tantamount to saying that the duties are owed only to the company and the whole discussion in the speeches (and here) about the extent of the duty of care owed to

[44] At p. 626 C, D.
[45] *Ibid.*

shareholders is misguided. Propositions 3, 4, and 5 should be merged into a single proposition 3 reading:

"The statutory provisions impose a duty of care owed only to the company itself."

This would certainly make for simplicity. But it is a somewhat startling conclusion not hinted at in the other speeches.

It will have been apparent from the foregoing comments that the writer is unhappy about some aspects of propositions 4 and 5. But for *Caparo*, his view would have been that the effect of the statutory provisions in the light of their historical development is that auditors owe a duty of care to all those to whom their report is required to be sent (or at least to members to whom their report is addressed) and that if they breach that duty those who in reliance on their report enter into any transaction which the auditors ought reasonably to have foreseen, and suffer loss which would not have been sustained but for the auditors' breach of duty, they are liable accordingly. That view, however, is no longer tenable.

Three comments are needed on proposition 6:

(1) Whereas *Caparo* establishes that a member who has brought more shares in reliance on misleading annual accounts or reports cannot, on that account alone, recover damages from the negligent directors or auditors, the decision does not definitely decide that the same applies to a member who, in response to the accounts and the auditors' report on them, *sells* his shares. However, the emphasis in the speeches on the contrast between "investment decisions" and what, in proposition 4, is described as "the exercise of corporate powers,"[46] suggests that the result would be the same. But both Lord Bridge[47] and Lord Oliver[48] expressly leave this open. And, clearly there is a strong probability, as the directors and auditors will foresee, that accounts which paint a gloomy picture of the company's financial position will lead shareholders to cut their losses by selling—this is their only speedy remedy and one which is normally taken by shareholders, whether institutional or private.[49]

(2) The later decision at first instance in *Al Naktib Investments Ltd. v. Longcroft*[50] prompts the question: What precisely is meant by

---

[46] An attempt to encapsulate the two formulae above.
[47] At p. 626, 627. But see below for his comments on "causation."
[48] "It is unnecessary to decide the point on this appeal but I can see more force in the contention that one purpose of providing the statutory information might be to enable the recipient to exercise whatever rights he has in relation to his proprietary interest ... by way of disposing of that interest"; at p. 653 E, F.
[49] They are less likely to increase their holdings merely because the accounts paint an excessively rosy picture.
[50] [1990] 1 W.L.R. 1390.

"specifically in connection with a particular transaction or transactions of a particular kind, (*e.g.* in a prospectus inviting investment)?"[51]

In *Al Nakib* a rights circular accompanied by audited accounts had "invited investment," the company's purpose being to raise new money by the rights issue. The plaintiff had taken up his rights and, in addition, purchased further shares on the market. From his viewpoint both were investment decisions of precisely the same kind and the directors and auditors must have realised that the second transaction was one that some shareholders were "very likely to enter upon."[52] Yet it was held that since that transaction was not within the company's purpose of raising new money, the plaintiff had no remedy in relation to it. This followed the old case of *Peek v. Gurney*[53], which held that an investor who, in reliance on a false prospectus, bought shares on the market had no remedy—a decision which seemed outmoded once prospectuses specifically stated that one of their purposes was to lead to admission to listing on The Exchange and which has now been rejected by statute law. It is to be hoped that *Al Nakib*, which resurrects it, will be reviewed by a higher court. Legislation in preparation may, perhaps, overrule it in relation to its particular facts,[54] but its contagion may spread unless it is overruled.

(3) Two subsequent decisions of the Court of Appeal, in *McNaughton Ltd. v. Hicks Anderson & Co.*,[55] and *Morgan Crucible & Co. v. Hill Samuel & Co.*[56] have wrestled with the problem whether, and if so when, the needed "special relationship" could be established between the directors and auditors of a target company and a take-over bidder. Clearly there can be no such relationship until the bidder has identified itself; if it is to arise it must be as a result of what has occurred thereafter. Hence in the *McNaughton* case the bidder's action against the target's auditor was dismissed, applying *Caparo*, since nothing had occurred thereafter to establish a special relationship and known reliance on the draft accounts which he had prepared. However in the *Morgan Crucible* case, a differently constituted Court, reversing Hoffmann J. at first instance, refused to strike out, as disclosing no cause of action, a claim by a successful bidder against the target's financial advisers, directors and accountants, alleging that they had induced the bidder to raise its bid by reiterating the accuracy of their

---

[51] As used by Lord Bridge and quoted in proposition 6 at p. 493 above.
[52] Indeed they doubtless hoped that the shareholders would do so; purchases on the market would support the share price and thereby make it more likely that all the rights would be taken up.
[53] (1873) L.R. 6 H.L. 377.
[54] See Chap. 13 at pp. 345, 346 above.
[55] [1991] 2 Q.B. 113, C.A.
[56] [1991] Ch. 295, C.A.

(allegedly) negligent profit forecasts. The Court held that, if the bidder could establish these allegations, it had an arguable case which should be allowed to proceed. The parties then reached an out-of-court settlement.

The fact that the published accounts do not show a true and fair view despite the auditors' report, does not cause either the company or the shareholders collectively any immediate pecuniary loss. All it does is to deprive them of knowledge which might have afforded them an opportunity to take remedial action to recover losses already incurred by the company, and, more importantly in practice, to prevent a continuance of mismanagement or fraud. The pecuniary value to be placed on that lost opportunity depends upon the degree of likelihood that action would have been taken and that it would have led to recovery of damages or cessation of the malpractice. Often that likelihood will be minimal, especially when those at fault included the directors. Then, it would seem, to establish any loss the plaintiff would have to show on the balance of probabilities that, had, say, the auditors' report been properly qualified, action would have been taken which would have led to the removal of the directors. And to recover any substantial damages he would further have to establish a probability that the ill-consequences of the former directors' negligent or fraudulent reign would have been effectively remedied. The difficulties of establishing all this are obvious.

The difficulties may be less when individuals in a special relationship have rights of action under proposition 6. But they may arise there too. Thus in *JEB Fasteners Ltd.* v. *Marks Bloom & Co.,*[57] Woolf J. held that although all the conditions necessary for success other than causation had been established, the plaintiff failed on that since he would have entered into the transaction (a take-over) even if the accounts on which he had relied had presented a wholly true and fair view of the company's financial position, his main object having been to secure the managerial skills of two executive directors.[58] And in *Caparo,* Lord Bridge suggested that if a shareholder in a listed company suffered a loss as a result of selling his shares at an undervalue attributable to an undervalue of the company's assets in the audited accounts, the loss would be caused not by reliance on the auditors' report but by the "depreciatory effect

Finally, a comment on the questions of causation and measure of damages mentioned in proposition 7. These questions did not arise directly in *Caparo* and little was said about them in the speeches. But they raise intractable problems in the present context.

---

57 [1981] 3 All E.R. 289; *affd.* on other grounds [1983] 1 All E.R. 583, C.A.
58 Who, in fact, resigned!

of the report on the market value of the shares before ever the decision of the shareholder to sell was taken."[59]

CONCLUSION

The final part of this chapter can be summed up in one sentence: Anyone involved, either as plaintiff or defendant, in a suit based upon alleged negligence in the preparation or auditing of the annual accounts has stepped into a minefield which, despite *Caparo*, has still not been comprehensively mapped.

However, the earlier part of the chapter has shown that the status of company auditors has in the course of this century been transformed from that of somewhat toothless strays given temporary house-room once a year, to that of trained rottweilers, entitled to sniff around at any time and, if need be, to bite the hands that feed them. As a result the quality of most company audits has improved, even if the likelihood of recovery, in cases where audits are defective, has not.

[59] [1990] 2 A.C. at 627A. The result seems to be that (a) if the shareholder is able to have his "sell" order executed before the market has reacted to the accounts, he will have suffered no loss by relying on the accounts, while (b) if it is not executed until after the market has reacted, that reaction has broken the chain of causation between his reliance and his loss. This amounts to saying that reliance on the accounts by one type of recipient of them (the market-makers) destroys the causal connection between reliance and loss in relation to others (the members). Can that really be right?

CHAPTER 19

GENERAL MEETINGS

As will have been apparent from previous chapters, it is no longer realistic to say that the ultimate control of a company rests with the general meeting and that it is the primary organ of the company.[1] Nevertheless there are many transactions which, under the Act, cannot be entered into without a resolution of the company in general meeting (and some which also require a resolution of a class or of classes of members). Moreover, under the accounting provisions discussed in Chapter 17, a general meeting, at which the annual accounts and the directors' and auditors' reports will be laid, must normally be held annually, thus affording the members an opportunity of questioning the directors on their stewardship and, if they have got their tackle in order in time, of taking further action if dissatisfied.

Hence, general meetings afford members a measure of protection of their investment in the company. To assess the extent to which it is effective, an appreciation is needed of how such meetings are convened and conducted. This depends to some extent on the regulations of the particular company but in practice there is considerable uniformity; indeed there has to be because the Act prescribes basic rules which have to be observed.

The annual general meeting

The Act provides that a company shall in each year (*i.e.* each calendar year, not every 12 months[2]), hold an annual general meeting (AGM) specified as such in the notices convening it,[3] and not more than 15 months must elapse between one annual general meeting and the next.[4] But it suffices if the first annual meeting is held within 18 months of formation even though this is not in the first or second year of incorporation.[5] Until the 1989 Act this was the only exception to the need to hold AGMs each year. But now, as we saw in Chapter 17[6] the new section 366A enables a private company to elect to dispense with AGMs[7] unless a member demands that one

[1] See Chap. 7 above.
[2] *Gibson v. Barton* (1875) L.R. 10 Q.B. 329.
[3] s.366(1).
[4] s.366(3).
[5] s.366(2).
[6] At p. 472.
[7] s.366A. When this is done the company will also dispense with laying of the accounts before a general meeting and with annual reappointment of auditors. But the members' (and auditors') rights to a meeting are protected: see Chaps. 17 and 18 above.

be held.[8] If, when an AGM should be held, there is default in doing so[9] not only are the company and any officers in default liable to fines, but the Secretary of State on the application of any member may call or direct the calling of a meeting[10] which, normally, will be deemed to be an AGM.[11]

Rather surprisingly the Act does not say precisely what business must be transacted at the AGM. But the presentation of the accounts and reports and the appointment of auditors must normally be undertaken at regular intervals, and the company's articles will almost certainly provide for other matters of an annually recurring nature. Indeed, the ordinary business of an AGM is best indicated by Article 52 of Table A 1948[12] which implies that it is the declaration of dividends, consideration of the accounts and the directors' and auditors' reports, the appointment of directors in place of those retiring, and the appointment and fixing of the remuneration of auditors. These are the things which have to be done in respect of each financial year and which it is envisaged will be done at the AGM.

The AGM is the one occasion when members can be sure of having an opportunity of meeting the directors and of questioning them on the accounts, on their report, and on the company's financial position and prospects. It is at this meeting that, normally, a proportion of the directors will retire and come up for re-election, and at which the members may be able to try to exercise their only real power over the board—that of dismissal. Moreover, it may afford members an opportunity of moving resolutions on their own account. Most of these things could, of course, be done at other general meetings, but the members who want to raise these matters may not be able to insist upon the convening of other meetings. The AGM is valuable to them because the directors can be made to hold it whether they want to or not.

It must be emphasised that the business of an annual general meeting need not be restricted to the ordinary matters specified above. The AGM is a general meeting, and anything that can be done at a general meeting can be undertaken at the AGM. There is, for example, no reason why a special resolution or an extraordinary resolution should not be considered.[13]

---

[8] See s.366A(3) & (4).

[9] s.91; If an AGM is held after the prescribed time, voting rights are determined as at the actual date of the meeting; not as they would have been if the meeting had been held at the proper time: *Musselwhite v. Musselwhite & Sons Ltd.* [1962] Ch. 964.

[10] s.367. It may give directions about the conduct of the meeting: subss. (1) & (2).

[11] s.367(4) & (5).

[12] The distinction drawn between "ordinary" and "special" business of an AGM has disappeared from Table A 1985.

[13] This point is emphasised for there seems to be a widespread belief that the AGM should be restricted to ordinary business and that if, *e.g.* a special or extraordinary resolution is to be considered, an extraordinary general meeting should be convened even if this is to be held at the same time and place.

Extraordinary general meeting

A company's regulations commonly provide that any meeting other than the AGM shall be called an extraordinary general meeting, and that it may be convened by the directors whenever they think fit. In the absence of any further statutory requirement the regulations would probably stop there, for the management would like nothing better than to be able to call meetings when it suited them, but to be under no obligation to do so when it did not. But the Act provides[14] that the directors must convene a meeting on the requisition of holders of not less than one-tenth of the paid-up capital carrying voting rights.[15] If they fail to do so within 21 days of the deposit of the requisition, the requisitionists, or any of them representing more than half of the total voting rights of all of them, may themselves convene the meeting,[16] and their reasonable expenses must be paid by the company and recovered from fees payable to the defaulting directors.[17] A former weakness of this provision was that although the directors would be in default unless they took prompt steps to convene a meeting there was nothing to stop them from convening it for a date in the distant future. This abuse, however, has at long last been put right by the 1989 Act which inserts a new subsection providing that the directors shall be deemed not to have duly convened a meeting if they convene it for a date more than 28 days after the date of the notice.[18] Moreover, under section 170(1) and (3) if the company's articles make no provision for calling general meetings by members, two or more members holding not less than one-tenth of the issued share capital (whether or not they have voting rights) or, if the company does not have a share capital, not less than 5 per cent. of the members may call a meeting without having to requisition one.

These provisions work reasonably well in the case of small private companies, but in a public company with a large and dispersed membership it may be a matter of considerable difficulty and expense for one member to enlist the support of sufficient of his fellow-members to be able to make a valid requisition. The requisition must state the objects of the meeting[19] and, unless the articles otherwise provide, it will be impossible to insist on anything else being included in the notice of the meeting.[20]

---

14 s.368(1).
15 Or, if the company has no share capital, members representing not less than one-tenth of the voting rights s.368(2). Note that in the case of a company with a share capital in which some shares have more than one vote no regard is paid to this so far as concerns powers to requisition a meeting.
16 s.368(4).
17 s.368(6).
18 s.368(8). Thus, 28 years (and six Companies Acts) later, implementing a recommendation of the Jenkins Committee (Cmnd. 1749 para. 458).
19 s.368(3).
20 *Ball* v. *Metal Industries Ltd.*, 1957 S.C. 315. Section 376, below, does not help because it applies only to resolutions to be moved at AGMs.

As we have seen, the Secretary of State may cause an AGM to be held if the directors fail to convene it. A wider power, exercisable in respect of either type of general meeting, is conferred on the court "if for any reason it is impracticable to call a meeting … in any manner in which meetings of that company may be called or to conduct the meeting in manner prescribed by the articles or this Act." This power may be exercised by the court "of its own motion or on the application—(a) of any director of the company or (b) of any member who would be entitled to vote at the meeting," and the meeting can be "called, held and conducted in any manner the court thinks fit."[21] The "court may give such ancillary or consequential directions as it thinks and these may include a direction that one member of the company present in person or by proxy be deemed to constitute a meeting."[22]

These provisions go some way towards solving the problems which can arise when the members of a small private company have been reduced to one or none.[23] But what seems to be needed is to widen the class of those who may apply to the court, which (unless the company is involved in litigation before it) will not act "on its own motion" because it will know nothing about the matter. As a minimum, it ought, surely, to be expressly provided that "member" includes the personal representative of a deceased member. The provisions can also be used if it is clear that were a meeting to be held on the requisition of a member the other members would render it abortive by ensuring that there was no quorum.[24]

As pointed out in relation to directors' meetings,[25] thanks to modern technology it is no longer necessary that a meeting should require all those attending to be in the same room. If more turn up than had been foreseen a valid meeting can still take place if proper arrangements have been made to direct the overflow to other rooms

---

21 s.371(1) & (3), *cf.* s.367, above, which confers similar powers on the S.of S. in respect of AGMs only.
22 s.371(2).
23 Normally, "meeting" pre-supposes at least two persons getting together: *Sharp v. Dawes* (1876) 2 Q.B.D. 26., C.A. (where the only member present solemnly proposed a vote of thanks to himself as chairman!); *Re London Flats Ltd.* [1969] 1 W.L.R. 711 and *Re Shanley Contracting Ltd.* (1980) 124 Sol. J. 239 (notwithstanding that the one member held proxies from others). But *cf. East v. Bennett Bros* [1911] 1 Ch. 163 (where one member held all the shares of a class) and *Neil M'Leod & Sons Ltd.*, 1967 S.C. 16 (which Oliver J. in *Re Shanley Contracting Ltd.* declined to follow)
24 *Re El Sombrero Ltd.* [1958] Ch. 900 where the applicant shareholder held 900 of the company's 1000 shares, the remaining 100 being held by the two directors whom the applicant wished to remove in exercise of his statutory powers under what is now s.303. The court directed that one member present in person or by proxy should constitute a quorate meeting. This decision was applied in *Re Opera Photographic Ltd.* [1989] 1 W.L.R. 634 where there were two directors, their shareholdings being 51 per cent. and 49 per cent. respectively. A meeting, requisitioned by the holder of 51 per cent. for the purpose of removing the other director, had been convened but rendered inquorate by the latter's failure to attend.
25 Chap. 7 at p. 160 n. 52 above.

with adequate audio-visual links enabling everyone to participate in the discussion to the same extent as if all had been in the same room.[26] But this, it seems, does not go quite so far as it may in relation to meetings of directors who are allowed to regulate their proceedings with greater freedom and less formality. In their case there seems no difficulty in regarding them as having resolved on something if they do so as a result of a discussion between them conducted on audio-visual links however physically far apart they may have been. It is more difficult to regard a decision of the members arrived by a like method as having been taken at *a* general meeting. However, in the case of a private company, much the same result could be achieved through the use of written resolutions and "fax" machines so long as all the members agreed to the resolutions.[27]

Notice of meetings

Prior to the 1948 Act, the length of notice of meetings, and how and to whom notice should be given, depended primarily on the company's regulations. The only statutory regulation which could not be varied was that 21 days' notice was required for a meeting at which a special resolution was to be proposed. In other cases the Act of 1929 provided that, unless the articles otherwise directed (which they rarely did) only seven days' notice was needed. This far too short a time for opposition to be organised.[28] Hence, it is now provided by section 369 of the 1985 Act that any provision of a company's articles shall be void in so far as it provides for the calling of a meeting by a shorter notice than 21 days' notice in writing in the case of an annual general meeting or a meeting for the passing of a special resolution, or 14 days' notice in writing in other cases.[29] The company's articles may provide for longer notice but they cannot validly provide for shorter.[30] However, if a meeting is called on shorter notice than the Act or the articles prescribe, it is deemed to be duly called if so agreed, in the case of an AGM, by all the members entitled to attend and vote and, in the case of an extraordinary meeting by "a requisite majority,"[31] *i.e.* "a majority holding not less than 95 per cent. of the shares giving a right to attend and vote at the meeting: or, in the case of a company not having a share capital, 95 per cent. of the total votes of all the

[26] s.381A.
[27] *Byng* v. *London Life Association Ltd.* [1990] Ch. 170, C.A. See below pp. 525–527.
[28] Particularly as the period might be reduced still further by provisions requiring proxy forms to be lodged in advance of the meeting.
[29] Seven days in the case of unlimited companies: s.369(1).
[30] s.369(2). There has been disagreement between the English and the Scottish courts on whether "days" means "clear days," (*i.e.* excluding the day of giving the notice and the day on which the meeting is to be held). The English courts hold that it does: *Re Hector Whaling* [1936] Ch. 208.
[31] s.369(3).

members."[32] This applies even if a special resolution is to be passed[33] so long as the members appreciate that they are being asked to consent to short notice of that resolution.[34] Moreover, as a result of amendments made by the 1989 Act, a private company may, by an elective resolution,[35] reduce the prescribed 95 per cent. to not less than 90 per cent.[36]

Apart from prescribing the minimum periods of notice and that it must be in writing, the Act leaves it to the company's articles to provide how it shall be given. What it does, however, is to say that in so far as the articles of the company do not make other provision in that behalf "notice shall be served on every member of it in the manner in which notices are required to be served by Table A (as for the time being in force)".[37] Hence, except to the extent that companies make "other provision in that behalf" they will, as regards giving of notice, be required to comply with Table A 1985 or, as that is amended or replaced, with the then current version, while remaining in respect of other matters subject to the Table A at the date of incorporation (to the extent that they have adopted it or, in the case of companies limited by shares, not excluded it).[38] The reason, presumably, for adopting this half measure rather than making statutory provisions is that had the latter been done the provisions would have had to deal with exceptional cases (such as that where holders of share warrants to bearer are entitled to attend and vote).[39] Table A can and does ignore such cases and assumes that the company's register of members will give the names and addresses of all members. It deals comprehensively with that[40] but with that only; if companies behave exceptionally it is left to them to make appropriate provisions in their articles.

The salient points to note in the present Table A provisions are:

(i) Notice may be given to a member personally[41] or by sending it by post addressed to him at his registered address or by leaving it at that address. Notices to joint shareholders are to be given to the one first named in the register and this is sufficient notice to all joint holders. A member whose registered address is outside the United

---

32 s.369(4).
33 s.369(2) makes this clear and it is repeated in s.378(3).
34 *Re Pearce Buffalo Ltd.* [1960] 1 W.L.R. 1014.
35 Under s.379A.
36 ss.369(4) and 378(3). It will be appreciated that in the case of a typical small private company there would often not be a 95 per cent. majority if one member did not consent. And that will be so even with the reduction to 90 per cent.
37 s.370(1) and (2).
38 Which is liable to be overlooked by companies with Table A arts. earlier than the current one.
39 The usual practice is to give notice by a newspaper advertisement. On listed companies see *The Yellow Book*, Section 9, Chap. 1, para. 8.
40 Arts. ss.111–125.
41 *i.e.* by handing it to him (not telling him orally for the Act requires notice in writing).

Kingdom, is entitled to receive notice only if he gives the company an address within the United Kingdom at which notices may be given to him.[42]

(ii) If a member attends the meeting, in person or by proxy, he is deemed to have received notice[43]; and if, before a transferee of shares is entered on the register, notice has been given to someone through whom the transferee derives title, that is effective notice to the transferee.[44]

(iii) Proof that an envelope containing a notice was properly addressed, prepaid and posted is conclusive that that notice was given; and the notice shall be deemed to be given[45] at the expiration of 48 hours[46] after the envelope containing it was posted.[47]

These regulations may be thought to give greater weight to the administrative convenience of the company than to the protection of members (but that is what articles of association often do) and especially is this so in the light of article 39[48] of Table A which provides that the accidental omission to give notice of a meeting to, or the non-receipt of a notice by, any person entitled to receive notice shall not invalidate the proceedings at that meeting.[49]

Contents of notices

The notice will obviously have to say where the meeting is to be held and on what day and time. If, having despatched the notices, the company finds it necessary to alter the arrangements it will have to notify members of the change before the expiration of the minimum period of notice prescribed by the Act or the articles of the company. The members are entitled to that length of notice in order to make arrangements to attend if they want to and it does not follow that a member who, say, has arranged to attend a meeting at the Barbican at 12 noon will be able instead to attend it at The Cafe Royal at 2.30 pm.[50]

The notice, equally obviously, will have to indicate the object of the meeting; unless a member knows that, he cannot be expected to decide whether or not to attend. But how specific must the notice be?

[42] Art. 112.
[43] Art. 113.
[44] Art. 114.
[45] Under the original version this was followed by "unless the contrary is proved" but these words were deleted by S.I. 1985 No. 1052.
[46] This is optimistic even for 1st Class post (but it was "24 hours" under Table A 1948).
[47] Art. 115.
[48] There is a similar provision in earlier Tables.
[49] This, of course, would not cover the deliberate omission to give notice to a troublesome member, nor does it cover a deliberate omission based on a mistaken belief that a member is not entitled to attend the meeting: *Musselwhite* v. *Musselwhite & Son Ltd.* [1962] Ch. 964. But, if the omission is "accidental," it applies even if the meeting is called to pass a special resolution: *Re West Canadian Collieries Ltd.* [1962] Ch. 370.
[50] See *Byng* v. *London Life Association Ltd.* [1990] Ch. 170, C.A., below pp. 525–527.

If the meeting is an AGM at which all that is to be undertaken is what former Tables A described as "ordinary business,"[51] all that is necessary is to list those matters. If, however, resolutions on other matters are to be proposed it is customary to set out the resolutions verbatim and to indicate that they are to be proposed as special, extraordinary, elective, or ordinary resolutions as the case may be. In the case of special and extraordinary resolutions it has been held that the effect of section 378, defining such resolutions, is that the notice must specify "either the text or the entire substance of the resolution."[52] In relation to other matters all that seems to be necessary is a fair statement of "the general nature of the business to be transacted"[53] in sufficient detail to enable the members to decide whether or not to attend and vote.[54] But the directors should ensure that, if the effect of the proposed business will be to confer a personal benefit on the directors, that should be made clear either in the notice or in a circular[55] sent with it.[56]

Notice of members' resolutions

In times past the requirement of notice rendered largely illusory the power of individual shareholders to move their own resolutions at AGMs, for there was no way in which they could compel the board to include notice of them in the notice of the meeting. Hence they might have themselves to undertake the task of giving notice—a laborious and expensive operation in relation to a widely-held public company. Only if they were able to requisition a meeting could they be sure that the notice given by the board would include their resolutions.[57]

Their position is now strengthened by section 376.[58] Under that section members representing not less than one-twentieth of the total voting rights or 100 members holding shares on which there has been paid up an average sum per member of not less than £100[59] may require the company to give notice of their resolutions which can then be considered at the next AGM.[60] The section ensures that

51 See p. 502 above.
52 *Re Moorgate Mercantile Holdings Ltd.* [1980] 1 W.L.R. 227 at 242 F. This related to a special resolution but the wording of the section is identical in all material respects as regards extraordinary resolutions and, seemingly, elective resolutions under s.379A(2)(*a*).
53 Table A 1985, art. 38.
54 Contrast *Choppington Collieries Ltd.* v. *Johnson* [1944] 1 All E.R. 762, C.A. with *Bachellor & Sons* v. *Batchellor* [1945] Ch. 169.
55 On circulars. See below p. 510.
56 *Kaye* v. *Croydon Tramways Co.* [1989] 1 Ch. 358, C.A.; *Tiessen* v. *Henderson* [1889] 1 Ch. 861; *Baillie* v. *Oriental Telephone Co.* [1915] 1 Ch. 503; *Prudential Assurance* v. *Newman Industries Ltd.* (No. 2) [1981] Ch. 257, [1982] Ch. 204, C.A.
57 And then only if their resolutions were set out in their requisition: see p. 503 above.
58 Re-enacting s.140 of the 1948 Act.
59 *i.e.* normally half the number required to requisition a meeting under s.368, above, but here regard is had to multiple voting rights: *cf.* p. 503 n. 15 above.
60 s.376(1)(*a*) and (2).

notice of the resolution will be given to members[61] and that the directors cannot argue that the nature of the resolution is not one that could properly be dealt with at an AGM.[62] However the company is not bound to give notice unless the conditions stated in section 377 are met. These conditions are that the requisition, duly signed, must be deposited at the registered office of the company at least six weeks before the AGM[63] and a sum tendered which is reasonably sufficient to meet the company's expenses in giving effect to it.[64] These expenses should be small since, unless the requisitionists want to accompany the resolution with a reasoned statement,[65] all that will be involved is an addition to the notice. Whatever the additional expenses are, the requisitionists will have to pay them unless the company otherwise resolves.[65]

Special notice

As we have seen, in certain circumstances a type of notice, unimaginatively and unhelpfully designated "special notice" has to be given, the principal examples[67] being when it is proposed to remove a director or to remove or not to reappoint the auditors. In the light of the discussion of these examples in Chapters 7[68] and 18[69] respectively, little more needs to be said here except to emphasise that special notice is a type of notice very different from that discussed hitherto in this chapter. It is not notice of a meeting given *by* the company but notice given *to* the company of the intention to move a resolution at the meeting. Under section 379, where any provision of the Act requires special notice of a resolution, the resolution is ineffective unless notice of the intention to move it has been given to the company at least 28 days before the meeting.[70] The company must then give notice (in the normal sense) of the resolution, with the notice of the meeting or, if that is not practicable,[71] either by newspaper advertisement or by any other

---

[61] s.376(3), (4) and (5). But less detail is required in relation to members not entitled to notice of the meeting: s.376(5).

[62] s.376(6). In the U.S.A. where, under the Federal Securities Legislation, stockholders may have still wider powers to bring their resolutions before general meetings, companies frequently attempt to frustrate efforts of "consumer", "equal opportunity" or "environmental" activists to move resolutions on the company's practices by arguing that they are not matters which can be discussed at general meetings. s.376(6) would appear to render this unarguable here and pressure groups have raised such issues at AGMs—though less frequently than in the U.S.A.

[63] But the board cannot frustrate the requisitionists by convening a meeting for less than six weeks after the deposit of the requisition: s.377(2).

[64] s.377(1).

[65] As they can: see under "Circulars" below.

[66] s.376(1).

[67] For another, see s.293(5) relating to the appointment or re-appointment of a director aged over 70.

[68] At pp. 154, 155.

[69] At p. 488.

[70] s.379(1). This applies whether the resolution is proposed by the board or by a member. But the notice is effective if the meeting is called for a date 28 days or less after special notice has been given, s.379(3).

[71] *e.g.* if notices of the meeting have already been despatched.

method allowed by the articles, at least 21 days before the meeting.[72] All this achieves in itself is to ensure that the company and its members have plenty of time to consider the resolution but as we have seen, in the two principal cases where special notice is required[73] supplementary provisions enable protective steps to be taken by the directors or auditors concerned.

Circulars

In practice, the notice of a meeting will be of a formal nature but, if anything other than ordinary business is to be transacted, it will be accompanied by a circular explaining the reasons for the proposals and giving the opinion of the board thereon. Normally, therefore, the circular will be a reasoned case by the directors in favour of their own proposals or in opposition to proposals put forward by others. In deciding whether the nature of the business has been adequately described, the notice and circular can be read together.[74] But the circular must not misrepresent the facts; there have been many cases in which resolutions have been set aside on the ground that they were passed as a result of a "tricky" circular.[75]

If there is opposition to the board's proposals, the opposers will doubtless wish to state their case and a battle of circulars will result. It is here, however, that the superiority of the board's position becomes manifest. Even if the directors do not directly control many votes they are for the moment in control of the company and they can get their say in first and use all the facilities and funds of the company in putting their views across. They will have had all the time in the world in which to prepare a polished and closely reasoned circular and with it they will have been able to dispatch stamped and addressed proxy forms in their own favour. And all this, of course, at the company's expense.[76]

Until the 1948 Act members opposing the board's resolution or proposing their resolutions had none of these advantages and, still, only timid steps have been taken towards counteracting the immense

[72] s.379(2). But it seems that this notice has to be given only if the resolution is to be put on the agenda and that the mover cannot compel the company to do this unless he can and does invoke s.376, above: *Pedley v. Inland Waterways Ltd.* [1971] 1 All E.R. 209, *sed quaere.*
[73] See pp. 154, 155 and 487, 488 above.
[74] *Tiessen v. Henderson* [1899] 1 Ch. 861 at p. 867; *Re Moorgate Mercantile Holdings Ltd.* [1980] 1 W.L.R. 227 at 242F.
[75] *Kaye v. Croydon Tramways Co.* [1898] 1 Ch. 358, C.A.; *Tiessen v. Henderson* [1899] 1 Ch. 861; *Baillie v. Oriental Telephone Co.* [1915] 1 Ch. 503, C.A.; and see *Prudential Assurance v. Newman Industries Ltd.* (No. 2), [1981] Ch. 257, [1982] Ch. 204, C.A. In the case of listed shares there is a further safeguard in the requirement that copies (and sometimes drafts) of circulars shall be sent to The Stock Exchange: see *Yellow Book* Section 5, Chapter 2 paras. 30 and 34.
[76] *Peel v. L.N.W. Ry.* [1907] 1 Ch. 5, C.A. For an excellent description of the relative weakness of the opposition, see *per* Maugham J. in *Re Dorman Long & Co.* [1934] 1 Ch. 635 at pp. 657–658.

advantage enjoyed by those in possession of the company's machinery. Such steps as have been taken are included in sections 376 and 377. As we have already seen, section 376 entitles members holding one-twentieth of the votes or 100 members holding shares on which there has been paid up an average of £100 each, to use the company's machinery for circulating resolutions to be moved at AGMs. It further entitles them to require the company to circulate statements not exceeding 1,000 words in length[77] with respect to any business to be dealt with at *any* meeting.[78] Members can therefore now use the company's machinery for the dispatch of circulars whether in support of their own resolutions or in opposition to any proposals of the board. In the case of circulars it suffices if the requisition is deposited with the company not less than a week before the meeting.[79]

In practice, however, this provision is of limited value. The expense still has to be borne by the members[80]—unless the company otherwise resolves[81]—and no substantial saving will result from the use of the company's facilities except in the case of a circular which can go out at the same time as the notices. In other cases, for example, when the circulars are designed to oppose proposals already forwarded by the board, little extra cost will be incurred by acting independently of the company and this will have a number of advantages. It will avoid any difficulty in obtaining sufficient requisitionists and will prevent delay, which may be fatal if notices of the meeting have already been dispatched. It will also obviate the need to cut the circular to 1,000 words and will enable the opposition to accompany it with proxies in their own favour.[82] Moreover, and from a tactical point of view this is vital, the board will not obtain advance information about the opposition's case, nor be able to send out at the same time a circular of its own in reply.

Hence members determined to do battle with the board may be better advised to disregard section 376 in relation to circulars. But whether they do so or not they start with severe handicaps, the least

---

[77] Contrast the vaguer formula in the provisions relating to removal of auditors or directors where representations are to be "not exceeding a reasonable length."
[78] s.376(1)(b). As under the provisions relating to auditors and directors the court can excuse the company from circulating matter designed to "secure needless publicity for defamatory matter": s.377(3).
[79] s.377(1)(a)(ii).
[80] s.376(1).
[81] *Ibid.* The company is likely so to resolve if the members' resolution is passed (which is unlikely) and may conceivably do so even if it is lost. In cases where it has not so resolved there have sometimes been disputes on precisely what are properly to be regarded as "the company's expenses in giving effect" to the requisition. *e.g.* does it include the costs of a circular opposing the members' resolution? It ought not to.
[82] There is clearly no reason why the members' circular should not invite recipients to cancel any proxies previously given to the board but it seems that the company could refuse to despatch the members' proxy forms unless, perhaps, the words in them were counted against the 1000 words allowed.

of which is that they will have to draw on their own funds, not on those of the company. Victory normally goes to those who first state their case and first solicit proxies. Unless the board is so foolish as to part with the initiative by failing to comply with a valid requisition for a meeting, it is almost invariably the board that will strike the first blow. In a public company with a large and dispersed membership this is normally sufficient to ensure victory.[83]

Proxies

It will have been apparent from the foregoing that proxies play a vital part in modern company meetings. At common law attending and voting had to be in person,[84] but it early became the normal practice to allow these duties to be undertaken by an agent or "proxy."[85] Until the 1948 Act, however, the right to vote by proxy at a meeting of a company was dependent upon express authorisation in the articles. In practice this was almost invariably given; but not infrequently it was limited in some way, generally by providing that the proxy must himself be a member. Where there was such a limitation the scales were further tilted in favour of the board, for a member wishing to appoint a proxy to oppose the board's proposals might find difficulty in locating a fellow member prepared to attend and vote on his behalf. It has also been customary to provide that proxy forms must be lodged in advance of the meeting. While this is a reasonable provision, in as much as it is necessary to check their validity before they are used at the meeting,[86] it too could be used to favour the board if the period allowed for lodging was unreasonably short. Moreover, as already pointed out, it had become the practice for the board to send out proxy forms in their own favour with the notice of the meeting and for these to be stamped and addressed at the company's expense.

For all these reasons, although proxy voting gave an appearance of stockholder democracy, this appearance was deceptive and in reality the practice helped to enhance the dictatorship of the board. In recognition of this The Stock Exchange requires that listed companies

[83] The only effective opposition is likely to come from institutional investors who probably hold large blocks and whom the board will endeavour to woo. Where those institutions are hostile small shareholders may obtain protection under their umbrella. But *cf Re Old Silkstone Collieries Ltd.* [1954] Ch. 169, C.A. (at 191–192), for a case where their approbation was likely to lull the other shareholders into unwarranted apathy. In the U.K. attempts to form investor protection associations to protect the interests of private investors have not proved successful.

[84] *Harben v. Philips* (1883) 23 Ch.D 14, C.A., and see *Woodford v. Smith* [1970] 1 W.L.R. 806, *per* Megarry J. at p. 810.

[85] The word "proxy" is used indiscriminately to describe both the agent and the instrument appointing him.

[86] In the U.S.A., where there is no such practice, the meeting may be deliberately prolonged for days in order to enable more proxy votes to be obtained by high-pressure solicitation.

shall send out "two-way" proxies, *i.e.* forms which enable members to direct the proxy whether to vote for or against any resolution.[87]

The statutory provisions relating to proxies are now to be found in section 372 of the Act. Any member entitled to appoint another person (whether a member of the company or not) as his proxy to attend and vote instead of himself and, in the case of a private company, to speak at the meeting.[88] But, unless the articles otherwise provide: (a) this does not apply to a company not having a share capital,[89] (b) a member of a private company is not entitled to appoint more than one proxy to attend on the same occasion[90] and (c) a proxy is not entitled to vote except on a poll.[91]

The shareholders must be informed of their rights to attend and vote by proxy in the notice convening the meeting.[92] Moreover, if proxies are solicited at the company's expense the invitation must be sent to all members entitled to attend and vote[93]; the board cannot invite only those from whom it expects a favourable response. Finally, it is no longer permissible to provide that proxy forms must be lodged more than 48 hours before a meeting or adjourned meeting.[94]

It cannot be said, however, that these provisions have done much to curtail the tactical advantages possessed by the directors. They still strike the first blow and their solicitation of proxy votes is likely to meet with a substantial response before the opposition is able to get under way. Even if their proxies are in the "two-way" form, many members will complete and lodge them[95] after hearing but one side of the case, and only the most intelligent or obstinate are likely to

---

[87] *Yellow Book*, Section 5, Chapter 2, para. 36. Notwithstanding recommendations that this should be a statutory requirement in all cases (*e.g.* by the Jenkins Committee, Cmnd. 1749 para. 464) it is still not. But Table A 1985 includes two forms of proxy, one of which gives the proxy complete discretion (art. 60) and the other, a two-way proxy which can be used "where it is desired to afford members an opportunity of instructing the proxy how he shall act" (art 61).

[88] s.372(1). The Jenkins Committee recommended that this should apply also to a public company: Cmnd. 1749, para. 463. But this recommendation has not been implemented, apparently because it is feared that meetings would be unduly prolonged if professional advocates could be briefed to represent the various factions at a meeting of a public company. This seems rubbish for, so long as action is taken in time to ensure that the advocate will be entered on the register before the meeting; all each faction needs to do is to transfer one share to its advocate.

[89] If the articles of a guarantee company follow Table C 1985 they will "otherwise provide": see arts. 1 and 8.

[90] Table A 1985 otherwise provides: art. 59.

[91] s.372(2). He can, however, demand a poll: see below.

[92] s.372(3).

[93] s.372(6). Overruling as regards registered companies *Wilson v. L.M.S. Ry.* [1940] Ch. 393. C.A.

[94] s.372(5). Hence proxies may now validly be lodged between the original date of the meeting and any adjournment for more than 48 hours.

[95] Encouraged by the fact that postage is prepaid: see below p. 530 n. 99. Most two-way proxies provide that if neither "for" nor "against" is deleted the proxy will be used as the proxy thinks fit, (*i.e.* as the board wish): Table A 1985, art. 61. The Stock Exchange requires this to be expressly stated: *Yellow Book*, Section 5, Chapter 2, para. 36. n. 2.

withstand the impact of the, as yet, uncontradicted assertions of the directors. It is, of course, true that once opposition is aroused members may be persuaded to cancel their proxies, for these are merely appointments of agents and the agents' authority can be withdrawn[96] either expressly or by personal attendance and voting.[97] But in practice this rarely happens.

Articles commonly provide that a vote given by a proxy shall be effective notwithstanding the revocation, by death or otherwise, of the authority, provided that the company has not received notice of the revocation,[98] and they sometimes specify that such notice must be received not later than so many hours before the meeting. Such provisions are clearly effective as between the company and the member, and it has even been held that the company must disregard notice of revocation received out of time.[99] On the other hand it does not prevent the member from attending and voting in person and the company must then accept his vote instead of the proxy's.[1] And, on ordinary agency principles, it is clear that as between the member and his proxy a revocation is always effective if notified to the proxy before he has voted.[2]

The final question of interest relating to proxies is whether they are compelled to exercise the authority conferred upon them. Unless there is a binding contract or some equitable obligation compelling them to do so, the answer appears to be in the negative. Normally there is only a gratuitous authorisation imposing no positive obligation on the agent, but merely a negative obligation not to vote contrary to the instructions of his principal if he votes at all.[3] But there may be a binding contract, if, for example, the proxy is to be remunerated. Or there may be a fiduciary duty, if, for example, the proxy is the member's professional adviser. Although the directors are not normally in a fiduciary relationship to individual members, it seems that if they are appointed proxies and instructed how to vote they must obey their instructions.[4] If it were otherwise the two-way proxy would be valueless, for the board would only use the favourable proxies and ignore the others. Similarly anyone who

---

[96] Unless it is an "authority coupled with an interest," (*e.g.* when given to a transferee prior to registration of his transfer) or is an irrevocable power of attorney under the Powers of Attorney Act 1971, s.4.

[97] *Cousins* v. *International Brick Co.* [1931] 2 Ch. 90, C.A.

[98] Table A, 1985 art. 63.

[99] *Spiller* v. *Mayo (Rhodesia) Development Co. Ltd.* [1926] W.N. 78.

[1] *Cousins* v. *International Brick Co.,* above.

[2] Unless the agency is irrevocable, see n. 96 above.

[3] This was discussed, but not decided, in *Oliver* v. *Dalgleish* [1963] 1 W.L.R. 1274, which also left open the question of how far the company is concerned to see whether the proxy is obeying his instructions.

[4] *Per* Uthwatt J., in *Second Consolidated Trust* v. *Ceylon Amalgamated Estates* [1943] 2 All E.R. 567, at p. 570. So held in the case of proxies solicited under an order of the court in connection with a scheme of arrangement in *Re Dorman Long & Co.* [1934] Ch. 635 (this case contains an admirable discussion of the general problems of proxy voting). But in both the cases the proxy holders were present at the meeting; *quaere* whether they can be compelled to attend: see [1934] Ch. pp. 664–665.

solicits proxies stating that he will use them in a certain way or as instructed, will, it is thought, be under a legal obligation to do as he has stated. But failing any such statement or definite instructions from his principal he will have a discretion and if he exercises it in good faith he will not be liable, whichever way he votes or if he refrains from voting.

Corporations' representatives

Since a company or other corporation is an artificial person which must act through agents or servants, it might be supposed that, when a member is another company, it could attend and vote at meetings only by proxy. This, however, is not so. Section 375 provides that a body corporate may, by a resolution of its directors or other governing body,[5] authorise such person as it thinks fit to act as its representative at meetings of companies of which it is a member (or creditor) and that the representative may exercise the same powers as could the body corporate if it were an individual.[6] It is therefore preferable for a company to attend and vote by representative rather than by proxy, for the representative is in a stronger position since he may speak even at meetings of public companies, and vote on a show of hands as well as on a poll.

Conduct of meetings

The discussion under this heading is focussed primarily on meetings of public companies. Small private companies in most cases are likely to take advantages of the concessions in the 1989 Act and to pass any needed resolutions by written resolutions and to dispense even with AGMs. But, even so, they may not always be able to avoid holding meetings. Written resolutions are effective only if signed by, or on behalf of all the members who would be entitled to attend and vote if a meeting was held,[7] and cannot be used in relation to a resolution under section 303 removing a director or under section 391 removing an auditor.[8] Moreover, the auditors may insist on a meeting being held if the resolution concerns them as auditors."[9] An elective resolution also has to be agreed to by all the members entitled to attend and vote and, even if it is, it will not necessarily prevent a member from insisting on an AGM.[10] Hence dispensing with meetings presupposes continued harmony between the members. All too often this breaks down at some stage in the lives of private

5 e.g. its liquidator: *Hillman* v. *Crystal Bowl Amusements Ltd.* [1973] 1 W.L.R. 162.
6 This is really a statutory example of an officer acting as an organ of the company rather than as a mere agent.
7 s.381A.
8 s.381A(7) and Sched. 15 A, Part I.
9 s.381B.
10 s.366A(3).

companies and the meetings, which will then have to be held to attempt to resolve the disagreements, are likely to be particularly bitter. The observance of the rules will then be just as important as in relation to public companies.

In relation to public companies, although the result of any disputed resolution is in reality generally determined in advance through the system of proxy votes, the meeting still has to be held. At the meeting the board and the opposition will have an opportunity of repeating the arguments already expressed in their circulars, often succeeding in generating a surprising amount of heat considering that both sides know that it is little more than shadow boxing; little, but nevertheless more, for a mistake at the meeting may still dash the cup of victory from the lips of the triumphant party since a breach of the regulations governing the conduct of the meeting may cause any resolutions passed to be invalid.[11] Nor are meetings merely a means of passing resolutions, they also give the members an opportunity of asking questions either out of a genuine desire for information for its own sake, or as a tactical move in the next stage of the battle. And, of course, meetings may be, and most often are, held when there is no battle at all, and here they afford an opportunity for the management to report to the members and for the latter to congratulate or commiserate with the former on the results of their labours. Unhappily meetings are rarely attended by more than a handful of members unless there is some dispute, and then the only real excitement arises from the attempts by the party that has lost the battle of circulars to trap the other into some formal irregularity or into revealing information which may enable the validity of the notices to be attacked as misleading or incomplete.

It is therefore necessary in relation to all types of company to ensure that the rules for the conduct of meetings are scrupulously observed. What these rules are will depend on the regulations of the company construed in the light of the common law as to the conduct of meetings generally. Here attention can be drawn only to the most important matters which will require attention.

Quorums

The first essential is to ensure that a quorum is present, for without a quorum no resolutions can be passed. It is not clear whether, if the articles are silent on the question, a quorum must remain present throughout or whether it suffices if it is present at the beginning of the meeting. Under the wording of earlier Tables A[12] the English

---

[11] For a recent example, see *Byng v. London Life Association Ltd.*, below pp. 526, 527.

[12] "No business shall be transacted at any general meeting unless a quorum is present *at the time when the meeting proceeds to business*" (italics supplied): Table A 1948 art. 53.

courts held that it sufficed that a quorum was present at the time when the meeting began,[13] even though some members left before all the business had been conducted (provided that at least two remained so that it could still be regarded as a meeting).[14] But under the wording of Table A 1985[15] it is clear that a quorum must be present throughout. As, however, it is the English practice to prescribe very small quorums,[16] except in relation to class meetings,[17] this is of not great importance in the case of general meetings of public companies though it can be in relation to those of private ones. Table A 1985 also provides that if a quorum is not present within half-an-hour of the time appointed, or if the meeting becomes inquorate, the meeting shall stand adjourned to the same day in the next week at the same time and place or to such time and place as the directors shall determine.[18]

Chairman

The next step is to provide a chairman to preside over the meeting. Who he shall be depends on the company's articles and if those are silent the members present may elect a chairman.[19] Table A 1985 sensibly takes the view that the chairman ought to be a member of the board and accordingly provides that the chairman of the board, or, in his absence, some other director nominated by the directors, shall preside but if neither is present (and willing to act) within 15 minutes after the time appointed, the directors present shall elect one of their number, and, if only one is present, he shall be chairman if willing.[20] Only if all this fails to produce a willing member of the board[21] will the members present have any say in the matter.

The position of chairman is an important and onerous one, for he will be in charge of the meeting and will be responsible for ensuring

---

13 *Re Hartley Baird Ltd.* [1955] Ch. 143, not following *Henderson* v. *James Outit & Co. Ltd.* (1894) 21 R (Ct. of Sess.) 674, Sc.
14 *Re London Flats Ltd.* [1969] 1 W.L.R. 711.
15 Art. 40 (which omits the words italicised in the former article quoted at n. 12.) and art. 41 which says that the meeting shall be adjourned if during the meeting a quorum ceases to be present.
16 Under Table A 1985 "two persons entitled to vote upon the business to be transacted, each being a member or a proxy for a member or a duly authorised representative of a corporation"; art. 40. If the articles make no provision, two members personally present are a quorum: s. 370(4). *cf.* the U.S.A. where large quorums are commonly required and it is not unknown for a disgruntled minority, whose presence is needed for a quorum, if it expects to be outvoted to stay away or to walk out before the vote—which has been known to lead to fisticuffs.
17 See below p. 528.
18 Art. 41. Table A 1948, art. 54, distinguishes between meetings requisitioned by members (which are dissolved if a quorum is not present within half-an-hour) and others (which stand adjourned as in the text above) and which adds that the members present at the adjourned meeting shall constitute a quorum (but presumably only if there are at least two).
19 s. 370(5).
20 Table A 1985 art. 42. Table A 1948 is substantially to the same effect.
21 Which is unlikely unless all the directors have travelled together to the meeting and met with a serious accident on the way.

that its business is properly conducted. This may entail taking snap decisions on points of order, motions, amendments and questions, often deliberately designed to harass him, and upon the correctness of his ruling the validity of the action may depend.[22] He will probably require the company's legal adviser to be at his elbow, and this is one of the occasions when even the most cautious lawyer will have to give advice without an opportunity of referring to the authorities.[23]

Resolutions

A reader who has got this far will appreciate that a meeting may have to deal with any one or more of four types of resolution—ordinary, extraordinary, special and, in the case of a private company, elective. But it may be helpful to remind him or her of the differences between them.

An ordinary resolution is one passed by a simple majority of those voting, and is used for all matters not requiring another type of resolution under the Act or the articles. An extraordinary resolution is one passed by a three-fourths majority but no special period of notice is needed.[24] Under the Act an extraordinary resolution is required only for certain matters connected with winding up,[25] or when class meetings are asked to agree to a modification of class rights.[26] A special resolution is also one passed by a three-fourths majority, but 21 days' notice must be given of the meeting at which it is to be proposed.[27] A special resolution is required before any important constitutional changes can be undertaken; and as a result of the legislation in the 1980s the number of such cases has greatly increased. In the case of both extraordinary and special resolutions the notice of the meeting must specify the intention to propose the resolution as an extraordinary or a special resolution, as the case may be.[28]

In all these three cases the requisite majority is of the members entitled to vote and actually voting either in person or by proxy

[22] For the sort of situation with which the chairman may have to cope if the members of a public company turn up in far larger numbers than the board has foreseen, see the recent case of *Byng v. London Life Association Ltd.* [1990] Ch. 170, C.A. (below pp. 526, 527) where his well-meaning efforts were in vain and the company had to convene a new meeting.

[23] He should appear to be sure of his ground even if he is not and pray that the rule in *Foss v. Harbottle* (below, Chap. 24, p. 643 *et seq.*) will make it difficult for any of his rulings to be effectively attacked.

[24] s.378(1).

[25] See especially Insolvency Act. s.84(1)(c).

[26] s.125(2)(b).

[27] s.378(2). But shorter notice can be agreed to by a majority of 95 per cent. in nominal value of holders of shares giving a right to attend and vote or, in the case of a company not having a share capital, a majority of not less than 95 per cent. of the total voting rights at the meeting of all members: s.378(3). A private company may elect, by an elective resolution, that not less than 90 per cent. will suffice: *ibid.*

[28] s.378(1) and (2).

where proxy voting is allowed. This may and, in the case of a public company normally will, be much less than a majority of the total membership, and may even be less than a majority of the members present at the meeting, for those who refrain from voting are ignored.[29] To take an extreme case: A meeting of a company with 500,000 preference shares without voting rights, and 500,000 ordinary shares each with one vote, is attended only by five ordinary shareholders, four with one share each and one with a hundred shares. If on a poll a resolution is voted for by three of the holders of one share and against by the fourth shareholder with one share, the holder of the hundred shares abstaining, the resolution will have been duly carried even if it is an extraordinary or special resolution, notwithstanding that only three out of a total of one million shares, three out of five hundred thousand total votes and three out of one hundred and four votes exercisable at the meeting, have actually been polled in its favour. As we shall see later,[30] the procedure of voting on a show of hands, unless a poll is effectively demanded, may produce even greater anomalies.[31]

In relation to the new type of "elective resolution" (relevant only to private companies[32]) the position is very different. Such a resolution is ineffective unless:

"(a) at least 21 days notice in writing is given of the meeting, stating that an elective resolution is to be proposed and stating the terms of the resolution and (b) the resolution is agreed to at the meeting, in person or by proxy, by all the members entitled to attend and vote at the meeting."[33]

In other words, there must be unanimous agreement of all members entitled to vote whether or not they are present or represented at the meeting.

Amendments to proposed resolutions

Problems on amending a resolution notified in the notice of the meeting may arise in two circumstances. The first is where the proposer of the resolution wants to amend it prior to the meeting.

---

[29] s.378(5). states this expressly as regards extraordinary and special resolutions and the same applied to the simple majority needed for ordinary resolutions.
[30] Below, p. 522.
[31] So may multiple votes attached to the shares of a particular holder: *Bushell* v. *Faith* [1970] A.C. 1099, H.L.
[32] And, under s.379A(1), enabling them to elect to relax the requirements on the duration of the directors' authority to allot shares (s.80A); to dispense with the laying of accounts (s.252); to dispense with holding AGMs (s.366A); to reduce the majority required to agree to short notice of meetings (ss.369(4) and 378(3)); to dispense with annual appointment of auditors (s.386); or to dispense with such other requirements as may be specified by regulations made under the 1989 Act s.117.
[33] s.379A(2). It may be revoked by an ordinary resolution: s.379A(3).

This will be possible only if it is practicable to give valid notice of the amended resolution. That is most unlikely if the proposer is a member rather than the board and unlikely even if the proposer is the board unless the company has a small membership willing to consent to short notice under section 369(3) and (4) or section 373(3). Normally there is nothing that can be done except either to withdraw the resolution (and start all over again) or to seek to amend the resolution at the meeting. Obviously the latter alternative would be preferred if practicable.

The second circumstance is where a member wishes to move at the meeting an amendment to a resolution proposed by the board, by another member or by himself. This, one might have supposed, would be entirely legitimate so long as the amendment was not such as to take the resolution beyond the scope of the business notified to the members in the notice of the meeting. However, as a result of the decision of Slade J. in *Re Moorgate Mercantile Holdings Ltd.*[34] it seems that, in relation to special, extraordinary and elective resolutions, no amendment can be made if it in any way alters the substance of the resolution as set out in the notice. Grammatical and clerical errors may be corrected, or words translated into more formal language, and, if the precise text of the resolution was not included in the notice,[35] it may be converted into a formal resolution, provided always that there is no departure whatever from the substance as stated in the notice.[36]

The learned judge thought that his decision was desirable on policy grounds,[37] as well as being demanded by the terms of the Act, and that it would prevent the substantial embarrassment to the chairman of the meeting and to any persons holding "two-way" proxies on behalf of absent members,[38] that any less strict rule would cause. This however ignores the greater embarrassment which the company may face if the legal position is not understood at the time and put right by starting again. The company will then act upon the resolution until, sometime in the future, a disgruntled member seeks to take

[34] [1980] 1 W.L.R. 227. The case concerned the confirmation of a special resolution reducing the company's share premium account which had been "lost." The notice of the meeting proposed that the whole of it (£1,356,900.48) "be cancelled." Before the meeting was held it was realised that £327.17 resulting from a recent share issue could not be said yet to have been "lost." Accordingly, at the meeting the resolution was amended and it was resolved that the share premium a/c be reduced to £327.17. Confirmation was refused on the ground that the resolution had not been validly passed. But in a later case (unreported, but see (1991) 12 Co. Law pp. 64, 65), where the facts were virtually identical, a reduction was confirmed because the "substance," (*i.e.* the amount of the reduction) remained unchanged.

[35] Rather surprisingly, Slade J. thought that the language of what is now s.378(2) did not require this be done (at pp. 240H–241A). But that of s.379A(2), which requires notice of a meeting to pass an elective resolution to state "the terms of the resolution," (see above p. 519) seems to demand that the actual resolution be stated. In all three cases it is good (and almost universal) practice to do so.

[36] At p. 242C.

[37] At pp. 242A–243.

[38] At p. 243F.

advantage of its invalidity. The company will then have to fall back on the uncertain defences of laches, acquiescence or waiver.[39] As a result of the companies' legislation of the 1980s there are now many more than the "about ten circumstances"[40] where special resolutions are needed and it is not unlikely that some, which companies believe to have been passed, are technically invalid. At present thousands of private companies are passing elective resolutions. If the notice is of a single such resolution dispensing with all five requirements[41] which can be dispensed with under section 379A but at the meeting this is amended by, say, deleting the election in respect of section 80A, the resolution will, it seems, be invalid.[42]

Slade J. emphasised that his decision had no relevance to ordinary resolutions and that in relation to them the criteria for permissible amendments might well be wider.[43] This is clearly so if the precise terms of the resolution are not set out in the notice but come within a statement of "the general nature of the business to be transacted at the meeting."[44] But even if the terms of an ordinary resolution are set out in the notice it seems that some amendments may be made at the meeting and that if the chairman refuses to allow a permissible amendment to be moved the resolution will be invalid.[45] It is submitted that an amendment is permissible if, but only if, the amended resolution is such that no member who had made up his mind whether or not to attend and vote and, if he had decided to do so, how he should vote, could reasonably adopt a different attitude to the amended version.[46] The criticisms of that test by Slade J.[47] apply equally to an ordinary resolution but it is difficult to find any other test short of applying to ordinary resolutions that applied to special and extraordinary resolutions, *i.e.* that no amendment of substance however trivial may be made. And does the suggested test really face the chairman and two-way proxy-holders with the substantial embarrassments that Slade J. foresees?[48]

There may, nevertheless, be one type of ordinary resolution to which the stricter rule applies. This is when special notice of the resolution is required. The wording of section 379 bears a close

39 For these deep waters, see Chap. 6 at pp. 134 *et seq.* above.
40 [1980] 1 W.L.R. at 242H.
41 See n. 32 above.
42 If the company realises this it can easily put matters right by, for example, getting all the members to sign a written resolution under s.381A—but it is unlikely that it will realise that it needs to do so.
43 At p. 242H, citing *Betts & Co. Ltd.* v. *Macnaghten* [1910] 1 Ch. 430.
44 Table A 1985, art. 38.
45 *Henderson* v. *Bank of Australasia* (1890) 45 Ch.D. 330, C.A.
46 This was the advice given to the chairman in the *Moorgate* case see [1980] 1 W.L.R. at p. 230A.
47 *Ibid.* at p. 243 D-G.
48 If the articles say (as does Table A art. 82) that directors' fees shall be such as "the company may by ordinary resolution determine" and the directors give notice of an ordinary resolution to increase the fees by £10,000 p.a. surely a member should be entitled to move an amendment to reduce the increase (though the directors clearly should not be permitted to move an amendment to increase it further).

resemblance to that of sections 378 and 379A and makes it arguable that no amendment of substance however trivial, can be made to the resolution stated in the special notice. Hence, if, say, special notice has been given of a single resolution to remove all the directors[49] (under section 303) or both of two joint auditors (under section 391A) an amendment seeking to exclude from the resolution some or one of them may be impermissible. If so, this seems a regrettable emasculation of such powers as members have (and which the relevant sections were intended to enhance) and also seems unfair to the directors or auditors whom the members may wish to retain.[50]

Voting

Unless the company's regulations otherwise provide, voting is in the first instance on a show of hands, *i.e.* those present indicate their views by raising their hands. Recognising the limitations of human anatomy, regulations generally provide for one vote only per person on a show of hands, irrespective of the number of shares held. Moreover, there is no statutory obligation to allow proxy votes on a show of hands and it is not usual to do so.[51] For both these reasons the result on a show of hands may give a very imperfect picture of the true opinion of the meeting. If the resolution is uncontroversial a vote by show of hands will probably suffice and will save time and trouble, and on such matters the chairman's statement that the resolution is carried will normally be undisputed.[52] But on any disputed question a poll will almost certainly be demanded[53] by a member, or by the chairman if a resolution proposed by the board has been defeated on a show of hands (as may well be the case since it is probably only the opposition which will have attended in person in any strength). It is therefore of considerable importance to decide whether such a demand is effective.

The regulations of companies invariably direct that a demand by the chairman shall be effective.[54] This again strengthens the position of the directors, for they run no risk of not being able to use their

[49] This seems to be permissible—the singular "director" includes the plural—and s.292 relates only to voting on *appointments*, not to *removals.*
[50] Nor should proxy holders have any doubts on how they should vote. If instructed to vote for the resolution they would vote against the amendment but, if that was passed, for the amended resolution. If instructed to vote against, they would vote for the amendment but against the resolution as amended. If given a discretion they would exercise it.
[51] Unless the proxy holders are physically segregated from the members personally present it may, in a well-attended meeting, be difficult to enforce this in practice.
[52] s.378(4) provides, in the case of special and extraordinary resolutions, that the chairman's declaration shall be conclusive. Table A, 1985, art. 47, provides generally that the chairman's decision when recorded in the minutes shall be conclusive.
[53] It is a question of construction of the relevant article whether a poll can be demanded before there has been a vote on a show of hands: *Carruth v. I.C.I.* [1937] A.C. 707, H.L. at pp. 754–755; *Holmes v. Keyes* [1959] Ch. 199, C.A.
[54] Table A 1985, art. 46.

full voting power. Further, the Act[55] provides that the articles must not exclude the right to demand a poll on any question, other than the election of a chairman or the adjournment of the meeting; nor must they make ineffective a demand by not less than five members having a right to vote, or by members representing not less than one-tenth of the total voting rights or holding shares having a right to vote on which a sum has been paid up on all the shares conferring that right. Further, a proxy may demand or join in demanding a poll. This makes it impossible for the articles to hamstring a sizeable opposition by depriving them of their opportunity to exercise their full voting strength. Nevertheless, it may still mean that the members who on a poll can outvote all the others will (if less than five) never have an opportunity of doing so because they cannot effectively demand a poll. If, in the example given at page 519, above, the four holders with one share each had voted in favour and the holder of 100 shares had voted against, the special resolution would have been validly passed on a show of hands and the unfortunate dissentient would have had no right (unless the articles were more liberal than the Act) to demand a poll so as to reverse this decision. If a member wants to be absolutely safe, he should split his holdings among five nominees.[56] It is, however, the duty of the chairman to exercise his right to demand a poll so that effect is given to the real sense of the meeting, and, if he realised what the position was, it seems that he would be legally bound to direct a poll to be taken.[57]

If a poll is demanded the company's articles may provide how it shall be taken; if they do not the chairman will have to decide. Usually the members and proxies present will sign lists or slips indicating whether they vote for or against and the number of votes that they are polling.[58] In the case of a small private company this should present no problem; the poll can be taken, the result declared and the meeting then proceed to the next item on the agenda. But in the case of a large public company this will probably not be practical. Hence the detailed regulations in Table A.[59] These provide that a

55. s.373. In the absence of anything in the regulations any member may demand a poll (*R. v. Wimbledon Local Board* (1882) 8 Q.B.D. 459, C.A.), and, of course, the articles may be more generous than s.373: see Table A, 1985 art. 46 which entitles two members, rather than the statutory five, to demand a poll.

56. It will be no use appointing five different proxies, for these will all represent one member and only be counted as one for the purpose of demanding a poll. Indeed, in the particular example quoted, the only result would be that the member would have disfranchised himself completely since his vote would not be counted at all on the show of hands!

57. *Second Consolidated Trust v. Ceylon Amalgamated Estates* [1943] 2 All E.R. 567 (in this case the chairman held proxies (without which there would have been no quorum) which if voted would have defeated the resolutions passed on a show of hands.

58. They are not bound to exercise all their votes nor need they vote them all in the same way: s.374. This is designed to enable trustees or nominees to give effect to the directions of the beneficial owners.

59. See Table A 1985, arts. 48–53. Future references to Table A are to that of 1985 unless otherwise stated.

demand for a poll may (but only with the consent of the chairman) be withdrawn before the poll is taken and that, the decision on the show of hands stands if it is withdrawn.[60] If the poll is demanded on the election of a chairman[61] or on a motion for an adjournment, it will obviously be necessary to take the poll immediately.[62] Otherwise it may be taken forthwith or at such time and place as the chairman directs (not being more than 30 days ahead) and the meeting may proceed on other matters on the agenda.[63] What normally happens is that the poll will be taken forthwith but, in accordance with article 49 of Table A, the chairman will appoint scrutineers (who need not be members[64]) and fix a time and place for the declaration of the result. Whether the poll itself is postponed or only the declaration of the result, it seems that the meeting itself is not regarded as adjourned, so that, if the articles provide that proxies shall be lodged at least 48 hours before a meeting or adjourned meeting—as Table A does[65]—further proxies cannot be lodged even if the poll itself is postponed unless the articles otherwise provide.[66] This Table A does, but the proxies must be lodged not less than 24 hours before the time appointed for taking the poll if that is more than 48 hours after it was demanded.[67]

At common law, the chairman does not have a second or casting vote in the event of a tie, except, it seems, that if he has votes as a member which he has not cast he may do so to resolve the deadlock.[68] But articles normally provide that he shall be entitled to a casting vote, in addition to any other vote he may have, whether on a show of hands or a poll.[69]

It will be noted, (a) that the need to check proxy forms and votes cast makes it impossible to have a secret ballot[70] and (b) that, unless the articles specifically provide for it,[71] voting by postal ballot is not permissible.[72] The latter may be thought strange since clearly such a referendum would be a better way of obtaining the views of the

---

60 Art. 48.
61 Under Table A articles, this is unlikely to arise: see p. 517 above.
62 Art. 51. And to declare the result before the meeting can proceed. The chairman should presumably exercise his inherent power to adjourn (see below p. 526) if it is clear that the result cannot be determined that day.
63 Art. 51. Unless, presumably, the other matters are dependent on the result of the poll.
64 It will often be better to employ independent professionals.
65 Art. 62(a).
66 *Jackson v. Hamlyn* [1953] Ch. 577.
67 Art. 62(b). If the poll is to be taken less than 48 hours after the demand, proxies may be delivered to the chairman, secretary or a director at the meeting at which the poll was demanded: art. 62(c). Hence members present in person at the meeting but who will not be able to attend the poll in person, are enabled to vote by proxy.
68 *Nell v. Longbottom* [1894] 1 Q.B. 767 at 771.
69 Table A art. 50.
70 But the identity of the voters will not be known by the directors if independent scrutineers are appointed.
71 Which is unusual except in the case of clubs or other associations formed as companies limited by guarantee.
72 *McMillan v. Le Roi Mining Co.* [1906] 1 Ch. 338.

members. But the fiction is preserved that the result is determined after oral discussion at a meeting although everybody knows that in the case of public companies the result is normally determined by proxies lodged before the meeting is held.[73]

Adjournments

One situation in which it may be necessary to adjourn is when the meeting is inquorate; this has been dealt with above[74] and presents few problems. What may present many is the converse case where those attending the meeting are too many rather then too few, and the meeting becomes chaotic. It is this situation that has given rise to litigation in recent years. Before dealing with the reported cases, of which the latest is *Byng* v. *London Life Association Ltd.*[75] (where the earlier decisions were reviewed by the Court of Appeal) it should be emphasised that an adjournment of a meeting is to be distinguished from an abandonment of it.[76] In the latter case the meeting ends. If a new meeting is convened, new business, as well as any unfinished at the abandoned meeting, may be undertaken so long as proper notice is given of both. In contrast, if a meeting is adjourned, the adjourned meeting can undertake only the business of the original meeting[77] or such of it not been completed at that meeting. Indeed, it was thought necessary specifically to provide by what is now section 381 of the Act that where a resolution is passed at an adjourned meeting it shall "for all purposes be treated as having been passed on the date on which it was in fact passed and is not to be deemed to be passed on any earlier date."[78] On the means whereby a meeting may be adjourned, article 45 of Table A 1985, provides that:

"The chairman may, with the consent of a meeting at which a quorum is present[79] (and shall if so directed by the meeting) adjourn the meeting from time to time and from place to place, but no business shall be transacted at an adjourned meeting other than

---

[73] As was well said in an American case (*Berendt* v. *Bethlehem Steel Corpn.* (1931) 154 Atc. 321 at 322) statements made to a meeting of proxy holders fall "upon ears not allowed to hear and minds not permitted to judge: upon automatons whose principals are uninformed of their own injury."

[74] See Table A, art. 45, below. But a meeting can be adjourned despite the fact that it was not a meeting at which any substantive resolution could be passed: see *Byng's* case above. This must be right for otherwise an inquorate meeting could not be adjourned, as all Tables A have provided that they can.

[75] [1990] Ch. 170, C.A.

[76] At p. 517.

[77] One of the criticisms of the chairman in *Byng's* case was that he had not given sufficient consideration to the possibility of abandoning rather than adjourning.

[78] Were it otherwise the company might unavoidably contravene the obligation to deliver to the Register a copy of the resolution within 15 days of its passage, as required, in the case of a considerable number of resolutions, under s.380.

[79] On the position where a quorum is not present, see p. 517 above.

business which might properly have be transacted at the meeting. When a meeting is adjourned for 14 days or more, at least seven clear days notice shall be given specifying the time and place of the adjourned meeting and the general nature of the business to be transacted. Otherwise it shall not be necessary to give any such notice."

As there was a similar article in Tables A 1929 and 1948 it can safely be assumed that it, or something to the same effect, is likely to be found in the articles of nearly all existing companies. The effect of the first part of the article is that normally it rests with the members present in person or by proxy at the meeting to decide whether the meeting shall be adjourned. The chairman can suggest that the meeting shall be adjourned and, if the members consent (by a show of hands or on a poll if validly demanded) the meeting will then stand adjourned. Alternatively the members can resolve on a adjournment on the motion of a member and, if this is passed, again the meeting will stand adjourned, since the meeting will then have "directed" the chairman to adjourn it. Basically this gives effect to the common law rule under which the chairman has no general right to adjourn a meeting if there are no circumstances preventing its effective continuance.[80] However, the primary duty of the chairman is to ensure, so far as possible, that the meeting conducts its business in an orderly manner and if, say, tempers have become heated and the proceedings are in danger of becoming unruly, the chairman has a common law power and duty to adjourn the meeting to allow tempers to cool. But the power and duty must be exercised bona fide for the purpose of facilitating the meeting and not as a ploy to prevent or delay the taking of a decision to which the chairman objects.[81]

Is, then, the effect of an article corresponding to Table A 1985, article 45, to exclude this common law power to adjourn, on the basis that *inclusio unius, exclusio alterius?* In *Byng's* case, the Court of Appeal held that it is not. But, reversing the decision at first instance, the court held nevertheless that the chairman's adjournment was invalid. The facts of that case were that the company, knowing that the meeting convened to pass a special resolution needed to carry out a merger, was likely to be unusually well-attended,[82] booked Cinema I at the Barbican Centre and overflow rooms there which were intended to have audio-visual links with the cinema. The meeting was convened for 12 noon on 19 October 1988. As a precaution against the meeting over-running the duration for which the cinema was

[80] *National Dwellings Society v. Sykes* [1894] 3 Ch. 159; *John v. Rees* [1970] Ch. 345 (which concerned, not a company meeting, but one of a Divisional Labour Party); *Byng v. London Life Asscn. Ltd.,* above. n. 75.
[81] If the chairman purports to adjourn for such a reason the meeting may elect another chairman and continue: *ibid.*
[82] The proposed merger had aroused some opposition and critical press comments.

available, a room with a capacity of 800 was booked at the Cafe Royal for 1.30pm to 5pm that afternoon. Far more members turned up at the Barbican than the cinema and over-flow rooms could accommodate and the audio-visual links were not working. At 12.30 the chairman purported to open the meeting despite the fact that members were still trying to get in. Those that had succeeded protested about the conditions—though they seem to have remained surprisingly good-humoured. At about 12.30, after one member had proposed a vote of no-confidence in the board, the chairman, having taken legal advice, purported to adjourn the meeting to 2.30 at the Cafe Royal. Far fewer members than had attended at the Barbican turned up at the Cafe Royal but those that did passed the special resolution. The plaintiff, a member of the company, brought an action against the company and the chairman, claiming a declaration that all proceedings and the resolution were invalid and an injunction restraining the company from acting on them. With commendable rapidity the action, both at first instance and on appeal, was disposed of by 21 December 1988. The Court of Appeal held:

(i) that the meeting at the Barbican was not a meeting in the sense of one at which business could be validly undertaken but was one which could be adjourned;

(ii) that notwithstanding an article corresponding to article 45 of Table A 1985 the chairman could have adjourned if the common law conditions justifying that had been met;

(iii) but that those conditions had not been met because the chairman, though he had acted in good faith, had failed: (a) to take into account relevant facts (namely that it was not until 31 March 1989 that the merger had to be completed, that some members who had attended at noon at the Barbican would not be able to do so at 2.30 at the Cafe Royal and would not be able to arrange proxies for the adjourned meeting) and (b) to consider the alternative course of abandoning the meeting and starting again.

Hence the action succeeded; and the company had to start again—some two months later[83] than if the meeting had been abandoned.

It will be noted that, under the final part of Table A article 45, no notice has to be given if a meeting is adjourned for less than 14 days. Clearly if the adjournment is a temporary one and the meeting is resumed at the same place on the same day, this is fair enough; but otherwise it seems unfair to members who may, perhaps through no fault of their own, have found themselves unable to attend the

---

[83] And somewhat poorer—the defendants were ordered to pay the costs of both hearings at which each side was represented by a silk and junior instructed by a major City firm.

meeting as they had intended. As a result they may not know that it has been adjourned and may be prevented from exercising their rights to attend the adjourned meeting. If the meeting has attracted the interest of the media they may find out in time. But not necessarily; for example, if in *Byng's* case, a member, delayed in transit to the meeting, had not reached the Barbican until after 1pm and had found the cinema deserted (the officers of the company then being on their way to the Cafe Royal) he would have assumed that the meeting had been concluded.

Class meetings

In addition to general meetings it may be necessary to convene separate meetings of classes of members or debentureholders (for example, to consider variation of rights) or of creditors (for example, in connection with a reconstruction or in a winding up). Here again, the rules to be observed will depend on the company's articles construed in the light of the general law relating to meetings. Statute law is generally silent, but sections 372 (proxies) 374 (voting on a poll) 375 (representation of corporations), and 381 (resolutions passed at an adjourned meeting) are expressed to cover also meetings of any class of members (but not debentureholders) and section 125, on variation of class rights of shareholders,[84] contains specific provisions regarding class meetings for that purpose. The main point to note is that whereas the prescribed quorums for general meetings are minimal, those for class meetings are usually substantial in respect of the proportion of capital which has to be represented.[85] In practice, very similar arrangements are incorporated in debenture trust deeds to regulate the conduct of meetings of debentureholders.

At class meetings all members other than those of the class ought to be excluded, but if for convenience a joint meeting is held of the company and all separate classes, followed by separate polls, the court will not interfere if no objection has been taken by anyone present.[86]

Minutes of meetings

Section 382 requires every company to cause minutes of all proceedings of general meetings[87] to be entered in books kept for

---

84 Dealt with in the next chapter.
85 Under s.125, two persons holding or representing by proxy at least one-third in nominal value of the issued shares of the class: s.125(6)(*a*). But at an adjourned meeting one person holding shares of the class or his proxy suffices: *ibid*. This makes sense only if the adjournment is because there was no quorum at the original meeting.
86 *Carruth v. I.C.I.* [1937] A.C. 707, H.L.
87 And of directors' meetings.

that purpose.[88] Such minutes, if purporting to be signed by the chairman of the meeting or of the next succeeding meeting, are evidence of the proceedings[89] and, until the contrary is proved, the meeting is deemed to be duly convened and held.[90] Section 382A now further provides that when a written resolution is agreed to in accordance with section 381A, a record of it shall be entered in the minute book in the same way as minutes of proceedings of a general meeting[91] and that any such record, if purporting to be signed by a director or the secretary of the company, shall be evidence of the proceedings in agreeing to the resolution which, until the contrary is proved, shall be deemed to have complied with the requirements of the Act.[92]

The minute-books of meetings held after October 1929 must be kept at the company's registered office and be open to inspection there by any member without charge. A member is also entitled to obtain a copy of such minutes on payment of a prescribed charge.[93] However, the minute-books are not open to the public; they form part of the company's internal administration.

It should be noted that sections 382, 382A and 383 apply only to resolutions passed at meetings and to written resolutions agreed to under section 381A which applies only to private companies. As we have seen[94] a written resolution may be effective even in relation to a public company if it has been agreed to by all the members entitled to attend and vote.[95] But it seems that these do not have to be recorded in the minute-books. Note also that although minute-books are not open to the public, an ever-increasing number of resolutions, whether or not recorded in the minute-books become available to the public because, under section 380, copies of them have to be sent to the Registrar within 15 days. This applies not only to resolutions passed at general meetings but to agreements of all the members which would otherwise have to be passed by a special, extraordinary or elective resolution[96] and not only to those resolutions but also to

88 s.382(1).
89 s.382(2). But not conclusive, as they are when the chairman has declared that a special or extraordinary resolution has been passed or defeated on a show of hands: s.378(4) above p. 522, n. 52. Table A, art. 47 extends that to such a declaration on any type of resolution so long as it is minuted. In *Kerr v. Mottram Ltd.* [1940] Ch. 657, Simonds J. held that an article purporting to extend conclusiveness to signed minutes of any matter was effective in the absence of fraud. But his reasoning (that because the forerunner of s.374(4) had that effect so must an article which went considerably further) is unconvincing.
90 s.382(4).
91 s.382A(1).
92 s.382A(2).
93 s.383 as amended.
94 See Chap. 6, pp. 134, *et seq.*
95 Table A art. 53 so provides and s. 381C(2) expressly states that s.381A does not derogate from any "rule of law." It is impracticable for a widely held public company to avail itself of such an article but not all public companies are widely held and those that are may cease to be after a take-over or management buy-out.
96 s.380(4)(bb), (c), (d).

some ordinary resolutions and directors' resolutions.[97] Moreover (and this tends to get overlooked) a copy of any such resolution or agreement for the time being in force must be embodied in or annexed to every copy of the articles issued thereafter.[98]

CONCLUSION

General meetings are intended to be the means whereby the members exercise control over the management. In the case of small private companies, where there is generally no separation of "ownership" and "control," formal general meetings rarely perform a useful purpose and the reforms instituted by the 1989 Act, enabling such companies, if all the members agree, to pass any needed resolution by agreeing to them in writing and to dispense even with AGMs, are eminently sensible. But, if and when there ceases to be identity between membership and directorship, their general meetings are more likely than in the case of large public companies to prove an effective way of enabling the majority of the members to exercise control over the directors and, in the last resort, to remove and replace them. Only if the directors hold a majority of the votes in general meeting will they be able to ignore the wishes of the members.

In contrast, in relation to public listed companies, general meetings have proved a singularly ineffective way of making directors answerable to the general body of members who have no wish to play any role in the administration of the company and who, in most cases, will not attend general meetings[99] unless their investment has proved so disappointing that they relish the opportunity of attending a meeting to tell the company's management what they think of it. Even then, most of them will decide instead to cut their losses by selling their shares if that is still possible. It is only institutional shareholders that the directors have to fear; if they get together the board can probably be ousted (but generally they too prefer to cut their losses if they cannot persuade the management to mend its ways). Subject to that and to the risk of an unwelcome take-over bid, the boards of widely-held public companies are self-perpetuating

---

[97] s.380(4)(e)-(k).
[98] s.380(2).
[99] A survey of the general meetings of 55 major listed companies during the ten years 1960–69 revealed that: the average attendence was 80 members (approximately 27 out of every 10,000 shareholders); the voting capital represented, rarely exceeded 1 per cent. of the total; large institutional investors did not normally attend; rarely did companies receive back more than 20 per cent. of the proxy forms that they had sent and that figure fell dramatically if postage was not pre-paid; almost all proxies that were returned were in favour of the proposed resolutions; AGMs lasted on average 23 minutes with only three questions asked; and out of some 500 meetings only on two occasions had shareholders attempted to propose or amend a resolution—in both cases unsuccessfully: Midgley (1974) 114 Lloyds Bank Rev, 24.

oligarchies which control the general meeting rather than it controlling them.

This, however, does not mean that the need to hold general meetings fulfils no useful purpose. Directors of public companies do not relish the prospect of facing embarrassing questions[1] from shareholders at the AGM (however ill-attended it may be) and that may operate as a mild deterrent against directorial excesses. But, as a means of making the board answerable to an informed membership or of ensuring that members have an effective veto on major corporate action it is wholly ineffective—though the legislature seems to assume the contrary by adding ever more circumstances where the consent of a general meeting is required.

[1] *e.g.* "if, as the accounts show, the company's profits have halved why have the directors' emoluments been increased far beyond the rate of inflation?"

CHAPTER 20

VARIATION OF INVESTORS' RIGHTS

THIS chapter discusses whether and to what extent the rights of investors, whether they hold shares or debt securities of a company, can be varied or abrogated by the company without their individual consent. At first sight it might be thought that there could be no question of that. Their rights are essentially contractual and a contract cannot be varied without the consent of both parties. But, particularly in the case of members' rights, it is not as simple as that.

MEMBERS' RIGHTS

In determining to what extent a member's rights are variable by the company a number of sections of the Act are relevant. First, there is section 2(7) which provides that a company may not alter the conditions contained in its memorandum except in the cases, in the mode and to the extent for which express provision is made by the Act. This is a relic of the time when the distinction between memoranda and articles was that the former were generally unalterable. Now, in one way or another, all the provisions which have to be included in the memorandum are alterable except that which states whether the company is registered in England and Wales or in Scotland.[1]

Secondly, there is section 9 which provides that, subject to the provisions of the Act and to the conditions contained in the memorandum, a company may by special resolution alter its articles.[2] The effect of this is that, except to the extent that the Act itself imposes additional conditions or formalities which have to be complied with before the special resolution is effective and subject to there being no resulting conflict between the altered article and the memorandum,[3] a company has a statutory power to alter its articles and cannot rid itself of that power.[4]

---

[1] Thus making its domicil (but not its residence) unalterable. But it may in fact be able to achieve even that if another country is prepared to allow it to re-register there.

[2] s.9(1). s.9(2) specifically states that the alterations so made are (subject to the Act) as valid as if originally contained in the articles and are subject in like manner to alteration. This, of course, does not mean that the alteration is retrospective in the sense that the validity of earlier transactions has to be determined on the assumption that the articles were then what they have become as a result of the alteration, but it does mean that thereafter the alteration is effective in relation to existing members and creditors except as provided in s.16, below.

[3] If there is, the memorandum will prevail but in construing the memo. the original articles and the memo may be read together to resolve an ambiguity in the memo: see *Re Duncan Gilmour & Co. Ltd.* [1952] 1 All E.R. 871 and authorities there cited. In any event normally all that will be needed is to amend the memo as well (under s.17 below).

[4] But see below at pp. 545–547.

Thirdly, section 16 says that a member is not bound by an alteration made in the memorandum or articles after the date on which he became a member if, and so far as, the alteration (a) requires him to acquire more shares than the number held by him at the date on which the alteration was made; or (b) in any way increases his liability as at that date to contribute to the company's share capital or otherwise to pay money to the company.[5] This applies notwithstanding anything in the memorandum or articles but does not apply if the member agrees in writing, whether before or after the alteration, to be bound by it. This, strictly speaking, does not relate to an attempted alteration to the member's *rights* but it does at least protect him from an increase in his financial liabilities.

Fourthly, section 17 provides that a provision contained in a company's memorandum which could lawfully have been in the articles can be altered by special resolution. This, however, is subject to four limitations:

(i) dissenting members have a right (similar to that afforded under sections 5 and 6 when the objects clause of the memorandum is altered[6]) to apply to the court for the resolution to be cancelled, in which event the alteration does not have effect except to the extent that it has been confirmed by the court[7];

(ii) it is subject to section 16, above, and to cases when, under Part XVII,[8] a court has ordered that a provision of the memorandum shall be unalterable unless it consents[9];

(iii) it does not apply when the memorandum itself provides for or prohibits the alteration of the provision[10]; and

(iv) it "does not authorise any variation or abrogation of the special rights of any class of members."[11]

Of these limitations (iii) and (iv) are the most important; (iii) because it makes it possible to entrench provisions by including them in the memorandum and expressly providing in the memorandum that they shall be unalterable, and (iv) because, even in the absence of an

---

[5] The final words of (b) do not seem to have given rise to litigation in England, as they have in N. Zealand (which copied them) in relation to agricultural co-operatives. It is surprising that they have not caused difficulties in England, *e.g.* in relation to management companies formed by the owners or tenants of "condominiums" or blocks of flats. If the memo and arts. purport to impose an obligation on members of the company to pay it specified sums for maintenance and insurance, an increase from time to time would seem to fall foul of the section.
[6] See Chap. 8 above.
[7] s.17(1).
[8] See Chap. 24 at pp. 662, *et seq.* below.
[9] s.17(2)(*a*).
[10] s.17(2)(*b*).
[11] *Ibid.*

express prohibition, section 17 does not permit class rights, if set out in the memorandum, to be altered.

Finally, Part V, Chapter II of the Act contains, under the heading Class Rights, five sections (125–129). Mention has already been made of sections 128 and 129 in Chapter 14.[12] They provide that if a company allots shares[13] or creates a class of members[14] with rights that are not set out in the memorandum or articles, or in a resolution or agreement which is required under section 380 to be sent to the Registrar, a statement must be sent setting out those rights, as must a statement of any alteration of them. The curious feature of Part V, Chapter II, is that although these sections recognise that there may be class rights, and alterations of them, whether or not the company has a share capital, the remaining sections (125–127) deal only with the variation of class rights of *shareholders* and say nothing about how class rights of members who are not shareholders may be varied.

The explanation of this curiosity is that the sections were introduced into the Companies Acts at different times and for different reasons. The object of sections 125–127 was to clarify the extent to which class rights of shareholders could be varied. Until the beginning of the present century the extent to which the rights which shareholders enjoyed could be varied, was in doubt. Even if there was initially only one class of shares it was widely believed that shareholders had contractual rights which could not be varied without their consent—a belief that was not wholly irrational since their rights will not necessarily be set out in the memorandum or articles (when they could be regarded as arising solely from the statutory contract under what is now section 14[15]) but may depend on the terms of issue and could therefore be regarded as specific contractual rights independent of the statutory contract. This belief in the sanctity of financial rights of shareholders was, however, finally rejected by the Court of Appeal in *Andrews* v. *Gas Meter Co.*[16]

Nevertheless the legislation from then onwards until 1980 seems consistently to have assumed that while there was no special sanctity attached to shareholders' general rights there was as regards their class rights when the company had more than one class of shares. Thus, all Tables A from that of 1908 until that of 1985 have contained articles essentially the same as that in Table A 1948 art. 4, *i.e.*

---

[12] At pp. 369, 370 above.
[13] s.128.
[14] s.129.
[15] See Chap. 11 at pp. 282–288 above.
[16] [1897] 1 Ch. 361, C.A. where it was held that a company with only one type of shares could resolve to create and issue preference shares notwithstanding that this would necessarily affect the rights of the existing shareholders. See also *Allen* v. *Gold Reefs of W. Africa* [1900] 1 Ch. 656, C.A. where it was held that a company could alter its articles so as to impose a lien on shares of existing holders in respect of existing debts.

"If at any time the share capital is divided into different classes of shares, the rights attached to any class (unless otherwise provided by the terms of issue of the shares of that class) may . . . be varied with the consent in writing of the holders of three-fourths of the issued shares of that class or with the sanction of an extraordinary resolution passed at a separate general meeting of the holders of the shares of that class . . . ."[17]

This wording implies that, but for that provision, the rights could not be varied by the company. Similarly, when what is now section 17 was enacted by the 1948 Act, there was, as we have seen, an express provision that it did not authorise "any variation or obligation of the special rights of any class of members."

However, what were the clearest indications of the legislature's understanding are the forerunners[18] of the present section 127 which afforded a dissenting minority a right to apply to the court to cancel a variation of their class rights but which expressly applied only if the variation was made pursuant to a provision in the memorandum or articles. As Scott J. conceded in *Cumbria Newspapers Group Ltd.* v. *Cumberland & Westmorland Herald Ltd.*[19] the section prior to its amendment by the 1980 Act (when what is now section 125 was also enacted) "made little or no sense except on the footing that in the absence of some variation of rights provision class rights could not be varied at all." Accordingly earlier editions of this book[20] argued that that was indeed the position. However the contrary view, that the effect of what is now section 9 was to enable a company by special resolution to alter class rights without the consent of the class unless the rights were set out in the memorandum, was widely held in the profession and was adopted by Scott J.[21]

All this is now water-under-the-bridge so far as companies with a share capital are concerned because section 125, as construed in the *Cumbria Newspapers* case, has dealt satisfactorily and comprehensively with their position.[22] But unfortunately nothing has been done to clarify the position regarding variation of class rights of members of companies not having a share capital. What is now section 125 first

[17] The words in brackets were deleted when what is now s.125 was enacted by the 1980 Act. Table A 1985 has no equivalent article, recognising that in the light of s.125 it is unnecessary.
[18] s.61 of the 1929 Act and s.72 of the 1948 Act.
[19] [1987] Ch. 1 at p. 20A.
[20] See 4th ed. pp. 563–564 to which Scott J. did full justice but rejected its conclusions, citing Viscount Simonds' remark in *Kirkness* v. *Hudson & Co. Ltd.* [1955] A.C. at 714 that "the beliefs or assumptions of those who frame Acts of Parliament cannot make the law"; at p. 21A.
[21] But he accepted that where there is a variation of rights clause similar to art. 4 of Table A 1948 "it may fairly be said to be implicit that rights attached to a class of shares cannot be varied, at least by the members themselves, otherwise than by the procedure there laid down."; at p. 190E.
[22] See below.

appeared in the Companies Act 1980 and was designed belatedly to implement recommendations of the Jenkins Committee.[23] What is now section 128 was enacted at the same time. It was then realised that the latter section needed to be supplemented by another to deal with registration of newly created class rights of members of companies without a share capital and accordingly what is now section 129 was enacted in the 1981 Act. But it never seems to have occurred to anyone that the equivalent of section 125 needed to be supplemented by comparable provisions relating to such companies.[24] As a result we have to distinguish between variation of shareholders' class rights and variation of class rights of members who are not shareholders.

Shareholders' class rights

Section 125 begins by explaining that: "This section is concerned with the variation of rights attaching to any class in a company whose share capital is divided into shares of different classes."[25] This clearly covers the normal situation in which a company's share capital is expressly divided into separate classes. But does it cover also cases where nominally the shares are of the same class but special rights are conferred on one or more members without attaching those rights to any particular shares held by that member or members? This was the question facing Scott J. in the *Cumbria Newspapers* case.[26] Two companies, publishing rival provincial weekly newspapers in an area where it had become apparent that only one was viable, entered into an arrangement designed to ensure that one of the companies (company A) would publish that one newspaper but that it would issue 10 per cent. of its ordinary share capital[27] to the other company (company B). Company B was anxious to ensure that the paper should remain locally owned and controlled and to this end the articles of company A were amended in such a way as to confer on company B pre-emptive rights in the event of any new issue of shares by company A or on a disposal by other shareholders of their shares in company A. These rights were not attached to any particular shares but on company B by name. Further, another new article provided that: "If and so long as [company B] shall be the holder of not less than one-tenth in nominal value of the issued ordinary share capital of" company A, company B "shall be entitled from time to

23 (1962) Cmnd. 1749, paras. 188–198.
24 As the author had been a member of the Jenkins Committee, and was an adviser on company law to the DTI in 1980 and 1981, he must share the blame.
25 s.125(1).
26 Above n. 19.
27 It also had preference shares but nothing turned on that. Clearly an attempt to vary their rights would have been subject to the equivalent of s.125 from 1981 onwards.

time to nominate one person to be a director of" company A. Company A's articles had adopted article 4 of Table A 1948.[28] Eighteen years later, company A's directors proposed to convene a general meeting to pass a special resolution deleting the relevant articles. Company B thereupon applied to the court for a declaration that company B's rights were class rights that could not be abrogated without its consent and for an injunction restraining company A from convening or holding the meeting to pass the special resolution.

Scott J. pointed out that special rights contained in articles could be divided into three categories.[29] First, there are rights annexed to particular shares. The classic example of this is where particular shares carry particular rights not enjoyed by others, *e.g.* in relation to "dividends and rights to participate in surplus assets on a winding up."[30] These clearly were "rights attached to [a] class of shares" within the meaning of section 125(1) and article 4 of Table A 1948. He also held that this category would include cases where rights were attached to particular shares issued to a named individual but expressed to determine upon transfer by that individual of his shares.

The second category was where the articles purported to confer rights on individuals not in their capacity as members or shareholders.[31] Rights of this sort would not be class rights for they would not be attached to any class of shares.[32] But company B's rights did not fall within this class; the articles in question were "inextricably connected with the issue to the plaintiff[33] and the acceptance by the plaintiff of the ordinary shares in the defendant."[34]

This left the third category: "rights that, although not attached to any particular shares were nonetheless conferred upon the beneficiary in the capacity of member or shareholder of the company."[35] In his view, rights conferred on company B fell into this category.[36] But did they come within the words in section 125(1) "rights attaching to any class of shares?" After an analysis of the various legislative provisions and of the anomalies which would result if they did not,[37] he concluded that the legislative intent must have been to deal comprehensively with the variation or abrogation of shareholders' class rights and that he should therefore construe section 125 as

28 Quoted on p. 535 above.
29 [1987] 1 Ch. at pp. 15A–18A.
30 At p. 15.
31 He instanced *Eley* v. *Positive Life Assurance Co.* (1875) 1 Ex.D. 20, on which see Chap. 11 at p. 285 above. It seems clear that in such a case the individual will have no enforceable rights in the absence of an express contract with the company additional to the articles.
32 At pp. 16A–E.
33 *i.e.* company B.
34 At p. 16G.
35 At p. 16G.
36 At pp. 16A–17A.
37 At p. 17. He instanced as other examples, *Bushell* v. *Faith* [1970] A.C. 1099 (above p. 154) and *Rayfield* v. *Hands* [1960] Ch. 1. (above p. 285).

applying to categories one and three.[38] He accordingly granted the declaration sought.[39]

This decision is greatly to be welcomed since it makes admirable sense. The pity of it is that there is no way in which sections 125 and 127 can be construed as applying to class rights in companies without a share capital.

The effect of sections 125–127

Section 125(2) deals with the most common situation, *i.e.* that in which the rights are attached to a class of shares otherwise than by the memorandum. If the articles do not contain provisions with respect to the variation[40] the rights may nevertheless be varied[41] but only if (a) the holders of three-quarters in nominal value of the issued shares of that class consent in writing or (b) an extraordinary resolution passed at a separate general meeting of the holders of shares of that class sanctions the variation and (c) in either case, any additional requirements, however imposed,[42] are complied with. In other words, what was formerly the optional article 4 of Table A 1948 is now a statutory provision applying in this situation in the absence of an express variation of rights clause. Moreover, under subsection (3), in two circumstances the provisions of subsection (2) have to be complied with even if there is provision in the memorandum or articles for the variation. This is so if the variation of the rights is connected with (i) the giving, variation, revocation or renewal of an authority to the directors to allot shares under section 80[43] or (ii) with a special resolution for a formal reduction of capital under section 135.[44] In either of these cases the company cannot take advantage of a laxer variation of rights clause in its memorandum or articles (or insert such a clause)[45] in order to remove or reduce the rights of a class in relation to the authority or reduction.

Subsection (4) starts with the situation: (a) where rights are attached by the memorandum and the articles contain a variation of

[38] At p. 22 F, G.
[39] But he refrained from granting an injunction on the ground that this would "prevent the company from discharging its statutory duties in respect of the convening of meetings" (instancing s.368—though there had not in fact been any requisition by its members under this section). The result was therefore that company A could hold the meeting if it wished but, if the resolution was passed, it would nevertheless be ineffective in the light of the declaration unless company B consented.
[40] Since there is no variation of rights clause in Table A 1985 this is likely to become increasingly common.
[41] In this section and in any variation of rights clause in the company's memo or arts. "variation" includes "abrogation" except when the context otherwise requires: s.125(8).
[42] *i.e.* whether in the memo or arts. (which would be unlikely since it is difficult to envisage how there could be any such requirement without that being "a provision with respect to the variation") or in the terms of issue, a resolution or an agreement.
[43] See Chap. 14, p. 363 above.
[44] See Chap. 9, pp. 211, 212 above and Chap. 26 at pp. 689–692 below.
[45] See s.125(7) below.

rights clause which had been included in the articles at the time of the company's incorporation, or (b) with that in which the rights are attached, *otherwise than in the memorandum*, and the articles contain a variation of rights clause *whenever first so included*. In either case, so long as the variation is not connected with either of the two transactions referred to in subsection (3)(c), the rights can be altered in accordance with the provision in the articles.

If, however, the rights are attached by the memorandum and neither it nor the articles contain provision with respect to their variation, then, under subsection (5), they can be varied only if all the members of the company agree to the variation. This, it will be noted,[46] requires not merely the consent of the class of shareholders whose rights are to be varied but of all members of the company. And that is a valuable protection because one of the weaknesses of that afforded by class meetings is that if one class (say, the ordinary shareholders) would benefit by the variation of the rights of another (the preference shareholders) those who hold both classes may, at the meeting of the preference shareholders, out-vote those who do not.[47]

Moreover by subsection (7), any alteration of a variation of rights clause in a company's articles or the insertion into the articles of any such clause is to be treated as a variation of class rights. This, of course, does not preclude the alteration or insertion of such a provision by special resolution at a time when there is only one class of shares. But, once there is another class, class consents in accordance with the foregoing will be needed.

Finally, as an additional precaution it is expressly provided by subsection (6) that the provisions of section 369 (length of notice of meetings), section 370 (meetings and votes), sections 376 and 377 (circulation of members' resolutions) and the provisions of the articles as to general meetings[48] shall, so far as applicable and with such modifications as are necessary, apply to any meetings required by the section, or otherwise, in relation to variation of rights, except that the quorum, other than at an adjourned meeting, shall be two persons holding or representing by proxy one-third in nominal value of the issued shares of the class or at an adjourned meeting[49] one person holding shares of the class or his proxy and that any holder or his proxy may demand a poll. Section 126 merely states the obvious, that

46 The use here of "members" rather than "shareholders" is presumably to take account of the few remaining companies limited by guarantee and having a share capital (where some members may not be shareholders) and to exclude the need for consent of holders of share warrants to bearer unless the articles treat them as members.

47 In which event, however, if the variation is connected with a transaction requiring the court's consent it may be refused: see, *e.g. Re Holders Investment Trust* [1971] 1 W.L.R. 583.

48 On all of which see Chap. 19 above.

49 As suggested above (Chap. 19 p. 528 n. 85) this ought to be amended to make it clear that it applies only if the adjournment was because of the absence of a quorum.

nothing in section 125(2)–(5) derogates from the powers of the court under sections 4–6,[50] 54,[51] 425,[52] 427,[53] or 459–461.[54]

Section 127,[55] however, is of greater interest. It affords a dissenting minority of not less than 15 per cent. of the issued shares of a class[56] whose rights have been varied in manner permitted by section 125, a right to apply to the court to have the variation cancelled.[57] Application must be made within 21 days after the consent was given or the resolution passed but can be made by such one or more of their number as they appoint in writing.[58] Once such an application is made the variation has no effect unless and until it is confirmed by the court.[59] If, after hearing the applicant "and any other persons who apply to the court to be heard and appear to the court to be interested,"[60] the court is satisfied that the variation would unfairly prejudice[61] the shareholders of the class represented by the applicant, it may disallow the variation but otherwise must confirm it.[62] It is expressly provided that "the decision of the court is final,"[63] which presumably means that it cannot be taken to appeal.[64]

The dearth of reported cases on section 127, and earlier versions of it, suggests that applications under it are used rarely if at all. Nevertheless it probably serves a useful purpose in specifically drawing the attention of boards of directors to the need to ensure that variations of class rights treat classes fairly. But should they

50 Chap. 8 at pp. 174, 175 above.
51 Chap. 11 at p. 290 above.
52 Chap. 26 at pp. 696–701 below.
53 *Ibid.*
54 Chap. 24 at pp. 662 *et seq.,* below.
55 Already referred to at p. 535 above.
56 Provided that they have not consented to or voted in favour of the resolution—an unfortunately worded restriction which effectively rules out nominees who have not exercised all their votes in one way.
57 s.127(1) and (2).
58 s.127(3).
59 *Ibid.*
60 This clearly includes representatives of other classes affected and of the company itself.
61 This is the same expression as that used on ss.459–461 (see Chap. 24 below) which would seem to provide a better alternative remedy not demanding 15 per cent. support and strict time limits and with a wider range of orders that the court can make.
62 s.127(4). The company must within 15 days after the making of an order forward a copy to the Registrar: s.127(5).
63 s.127(4).
64 This was certainly the intention of the Greene Committee on whose recommendation the section was based: Cmd. 2657, para. 23. But the need for speedy finality seems no greater than on an application under ss.459–461 in which there is no such provision and cases can be, and have been, taken to the H.L. But if the application is struck out on the ground that subs. (3) is not complied with, that can be taken to appeal and was in *Re Suburban Stores Ltd.* [1943] Ch. 156, C.A. See also *Re Sound City (Films) Ltd.* [1947] Ch. 169 which seems to be the only other officially reported case on s.127 and its predecessors. Cases in which it might have been invoked, (*e.g. Rights & Issues Investment Trust v. Stylo Shoes Ltd.* [1965] Ch. 250) have been taken instead under ss.459–461 or earlier versions of those sections. Under the original version of s.217 in the 1929 Act an application had to be made within seven days of the variation, rather than the present 21 days, which made it virtually impossible for a dissenting minority in a large public company to get its tackle in order unless it had done so prior to the meeting in anticipation of their defeat at that meeting.

ignore that warning they are more likely to face an application under sections 459–461 rather than under section 127.

What constitutes a "variation"

What the various sections do not make clear is precisely what constitutes a variation of class rights. Indeed they obfuscate that by referring in one section [65] to a variation of "the special rights of any class" but elsewhere to a variation of "the rights attached to a class of shares." [66] The use of the former expression in section 17 seems on the face of it to imply that class rights attached by the memorandum are protected only to the extent that they are rights unique to that class (unless they are protected by an express provision prohibiting their alteration). In the light of section 125, however, that seems not to be the case. That section, however, has not removed all anomalies and uncertainties. Prior to the enactment of the section it seems to have been widely assumed that variation of class rights in accordance with an article equivalent to Table A 1948 article 4 required class consent only of the class whose rights were being altered in a manner adverse to that class. Thus, if there were two classes of ordinary shares, one of which had restricted voting rights or none at all, the separate consent of that class was not necessary if what was proposed was the enfranchisement of their shares without any reduction of their other rights in order to compensate the other class for the reduction in their proportion of voting power. [67] But it is very difficult to believe that "variation" (even if coupled with the statement that it includes "abrogation") can reasonably be construed as "*adverse* variation" and it is submitted that, to avoid any subsequent attack on the validity of the resolution, the formal consent of the benefitted class should be obtained.

What, however, was more serious, was the extraordinarily narrow construction placed by the courts on what constituted a variation of rights. The House of Lords in *Adelaide Electric Co.* v. *Prudential Assurance* [68] held that the alteration in the place of payment of a preferential dividend from England to Australia did not vary the rights of the preference shareholders notwithstanding that the Australian pound was worth less than the English. A subdivision [69] or

65 s.17(2)(*b*).

66 ss.125 and 127. See also Table A 1948 art. 4.

67 Nor, it seems, would the separate consent of a class with one vote per share be needed if another with one vote per hundred shares was to be given one vote per share. On the construction placed by the courts on the meaning of "variation" (see the cases cited in nn. 68–77 below), their rights to one vote per share would not be "varied."

68 [1934] A.C. 122, H.L.

69 *Greenhalgh* v. *Arderne Cinemas* [1946] 1 All E.R. 512, C.A., where the result of the sub-division was to deprive the holder of one class of his power to block a special resolution.

increase[70] of one class of shares was held not to vary the rights of the other notwithstanding that the result was to alter the voting equilibrium of the classes. When preference shares were non-participating as regards dividend but participating as regards capital on a winding up or reduction of capital, a capitalisation of undistributed profits in the form of a bonus issue to the ordinary shareholders was not a variation of the preference shareholders' rights notwithstanding that the effect was to deny them their future participation in those profits on winding up or reduction.[71] A reduction of capital by repayment of irredeemable preference shares in accordance with their rights on a winding up was not regarded as a variation or abrogation of their rights.[72] Nor, was an issue of further shares ranking *pari passu* with the existing shares of a class.[73] And, where there were preference and ordinary shares, an issue of preferred ordinary shares ranking ahead of the ordinary but behind the preference was not a variation of the rights of either existing class.[74]

Presumably the courts will continue to follow this restrictive interpretation of variation of rights clauses in memoranda and articles and will apply it in relation to section 125, for there is nothing in the wording of that section which constrains them to do otherwise. It is true that the decisions suggest that the terms of variation of rights clauses could be expressed so as to afford protection against action additional to a variation or abrogation as construed by the courts. But very clear wording will have to be used if such a provision is to be construed as affording any greater safeguards. In *White v. Bristol Aeroplane Co.*[75] and *Re John Smith's Tadcaster Brewery Co.*,[76] the

[70] *White v. Bristol Aeroplane Co.* [1953] Ch. 65, C.A.; *Re John Smith's Tadcaster Brewery* [1953] Ch. 308, C.A.

[71] *Dimbula Valley (Ceylon) Tea Co. v. Laurie* [1961] Ch. 353. And see the startling decision in *Re Mackenzie & Co. Ltd.* [1916] 2 Ch. 450 which implies that a rateable reduction of the nominal preference and ordinary capital (which participated *pari passu* on a windingup) did not modify the rights of the preference shareholders notwithstanding that the effect was to reduce the amount payable to them by way of preference dividend while making no difference at all to the ordinary.

[72] *Scottish Insurance Corp. v. Wilson & Clyde Coal Co.* [1949] A.C. 462, H.L.; *Prudential Assurance Co. v. Chatterly Whitfield Collieries* [1949] A.C. 512, H.L., and this is so even if they are participating as regards dividends: *Re Saltadean Estate Co. Ltd.* [1968] 1 W.L.R. 1844; *House of Fraser v. AGCE Investments Ltd.* [1989] A.C. 387, H.L.Sc. (this, of course, does not apply if they are expressly given special rights on a reduction of capital). But contrast *Re Old Silkstone Collieries Ltd.* [1954] Ch. 169, C.A. where confirmation of the repayment was refused because it would have deprived the preference shareholders of a contingent right to apply for an adjustment of capital under the coal nationalisation legislation.

[73] This is expressly provided in Table A, 1948 art. 5 (but not in Table A 1985). But the position seems to be the same in the absence of express provision: see the cases cited above, but contrast *Re Schweppes Ltd.* [1914] 1 Ch. 322, C.A., which, however, concerned s.45 of the 1908 Act, which forbade "interference" with the "preference or special privilege" of a class.

[74] *Hodge v. James Howell & Co.* [1958] C.L.Y. 446, C.A., *The Times*, December 13, 1958.

[75] [1953] Ch. 65, C.A.

[76] [1953] Ch. 308, C.A.

relevant clauses referred to class rights being "affected, modified, dealt with or abrogated." At first instance Danckwerts J.[77] held that a bonus issue to the ordinary shareholders could not be made without the consent of the preference shareholders because, although their rights would not be abrogated or varied, they would be "affected" since their votes would be worth less in view of the increased voting power of the ordinary shareholders. But the Court of Appeal reversed his decisions. They said that the rights of the preference shareholders would not be affected; the rights themselves—to one vote per share in certain circumstances—remained precisely as before. All that would occur was that their holders' enjoyment of those rights would be affected. If that eventuality was to be guarded against, more explicit wording would have to be used.

It seems, therefore, that if section 125 is effectively to prevent class rights from being "affected as a matter of business,"[78]—which one would have supposed is what businessmen would want—it is necessary to find a formula for a variation of rights clause which will expressly operate in any event which affects any class of shareholders (as opposed to the rights attached to their shares) or the enjoyment of their rights (as opposed to the rights themselves). In the absence of such a clause in Table A, adoption of such clauses is unlikely. This seems less than satisfactory. In every case where the voting equilibrium is upset it is clear that class rights are "affected as a matter of business," and it is strange to protect a class from having its votes halved while refusing to protect it when the votes of the other class are doubled; the practical effect is the same in both cases.

Class rights of members not shareholders

As we have seen,[79] the Act does nothing to clarify the position regarding the variation of class rights of members who are not shareholders. As a result the present position in their case seems to be as follows:

(1) The only relevant statutory provision remains section 17(2) under which "special rights," if attached to a class of members by the *memorandum*, cannot be varied or abrogated under section 17. Unless "special rights" is to be interpreted as meaning rights unique to the class (which, in the light of section 125 it clearly does not mean if the rights are attached to shares and which, it is submitted, it cannot mean here

---

[77] Only his judgment in the latter case is fully reported: see [1952] 2 All E.R. 751.
[78] The words are those of Greene M.R. in *Greenhalgh* v. *Arderne Cinemas* [1946] 1 All E.R. at 518.
[79] p. 536 above.

either[80]) the result is that members' class rights, if attached by the memorandum can be altered only to the extent permitted under the case law prior to the 1948 Act. That established that such alterations of class rights were permissible only in accordance with a variation of rights clause in the memorandum or, perhaps, in the original articles registered with the memorandum.[81] Hence, it seems that that remains the position. If the class rights in the memorandum are varied under such a variation of rights clause, dissenting members will have a right to apply for its cancellation under section 127 but not under section 17(1) and (3) since that applies only to "alterations made under this section"[82] and the alteration would not have been so made. This, however, is of little moment since a member, if unfairly prejudiced, will have a better remedy under sections 459–461.

(2) If, however, class rights are not attached by the memorandum but by the articles (the more usual situation) or otherwise[83] then, assuming that the courts follow the dicta of Scott J., in the *Cumbrian Newspapers* case[84] on the position prior to the enactment of section 125, the company will be able to vary the rights by a special resolution[85] and without the need for class consents. If, however, the articles contain a variation of rights clause, even if it is expressed as enabling (rather than as restricting) as in former Tables A, then "it may fairly be said to be implicit … that rights cannot be varied … otherwise than by the procedure thus laid down."[86] That, at least, gives the members of the class some protection. And, in any event, they have the protection of sections 459–461 if they are able to establish that a variation is unfairly prejudicial to them.

The contrasts between variation of class rights of shareholders and of members who are not shareholders are highly anomalous. Particularly is this so when, as is usual, the rights are set out in the

80 If it did, it would presumably mean that those unique rights could not be varied under s.17 but that other class rights could unless that was prohibited by the memorandum.
81 *Re Welsbach Gas Light Co.* [1904] 1 Ch. 87, C.A., where the memo expressly referred to variation in accordance with a provision in the articles. Two Scottish cases went further, holding that it sufficed if the clause was in the original articles: *Oban Distilleries Ltd.* (1903) 5 F. 1140; *Marshall Fleming & Co. Ltd.* 1938 S.C. 873. Since the Scottish view has been adopted by the legislature in s.125(4)(a), the English courts can be expected to follow suit. Whether they would feel able also to adopt by analogy s.125(5), validating a variation agreed to by all the members, is less clear but unanimous agreement plus the abolition of *ultra vires* has presumably produced the same result.
82 This seems to be the effect of the application of s.5(1) by s.17(3).
83 *e.g.* under the terms of issue.
84 [1987] Ch. 1: see above.
85 On which the class affected may not be entitled to vote.
86 [1987] Ch. at p. 19D.

articles and the articles do not contain a variation of rights clause (as will become increasingly common since neither Table A nor Table C contains such a clause). Whereas in the *Cumbrian* case, class consents were required and, under section 125, would have been required even if there had been no express variation of rights clause, had the company been one without a share capital, class consents would not have been needed. Yet the protection which the class rights were designed to protect were essentially of voting rights and board representation, both of which are equally important whether or not the company has a share capital.[87]

Protection by contract

One way in which members (and others) can protect their rights in or against the company is by having an enforceable agreement, either with the company or with the other members or with both, independent of the statutory deemed contract under section 14. In the case of the other type of investor—the debentureholder—the latter's rights will, in fact, depend on such a contract; but there is no reason why such a contract should not be entered into by a member or why it should not be designed to afford additional protection of his rights *qua* member or shareholder. Where, however, the contract is with the company, one is faced with two apparently conflicting principles: (1) that a company, like any other person, cannot with impunity break its contracts and (2) that a company cannot contract-out of its statutory power under section 9 to alter its articles by special resolution.

This was another matter facing Scott J. in the *Cumbrian* case, for an alternative argument of the plaintiff company was that there had been a contract between it and the defendant company under which the latter had agreed that the relevant articles would be inserted and it was an implied term of that agreement that those articles would not be removed. Having found for the plaintiff that class rights were created which could be varied only in accordance with section 125, it was not necessary to deal with that alternative; but since it had been fully argued he expressed his views on it. He concluded[88]: (1) that there had been no such agreement between the two companies and that, even if there had been, a term that the articles would not subsequently be amended could not be implied; (ii) that a company cannot by contract deprive its members of their rights to alter the articles by special resolution[89]; (iii) that if a company does contract

---

[87] And there is no reason why a newspaper should not be published by a company without share capital—many companies limited by guarantee are in fact publishers of journals.
[88] [1987] Ch. at pp. 23, 24.
[89] Citing *Punt v. Symons & Co.* [1903] 2 Ch. 506.

that its articles will not be altered, nonetheless its members are entitled to requisition a meeting and pass a special resolution altering the articles; and, (iv) that if the articles are validly altered the company cannot be prevented from acting on the altered articles even though so to act may involve it in a breach of its contract.

For these conclusions he cited part of the well-known dictum of Lord Porter in *Southern Foundries Ltd. v. Shirlaw*,[90] *i.e.*:

"A company cannot be precluded from altering its articles thereby giving itself power to act upon the provision of the altered articles . . . but so to act may nevertheless be a breach of contract if it is contrary to a stipulation in a contract validly made before the alteration."

What Scott J. did not quote was the second part of that dictum, in which Lord Porter added:

"Nor can an injunction be granted to prevent the adoption of the new articles. In that sense they are binding on all and sundry; but for the company to act upon them will nevertheless render it liable in damages if such an action is contrary to the previous engagements of the company."

This certainly suggests that the only remedy of the other party to the contract is damages and that an injunction or specific performance cannot be granted even though damages are not an adequate remedy.[91] Scott J.'s judgment, had it stopped at the statement "the company cannot be prevented from acting on the altered articles" would have implied that he shared that view. But in fact he went on to say that, while an injunction could not, in his view, be properly granted so as to prevent the company from discharging its statutory duties in respect of the convening of a meeting he could "see no reason why it should not, in a suitable case, be injuncted from initiating the calling of a general meeting with a view to the alteration of the articles."[92] This goes somewhat further than the view expressed in earlier editions of this book[93] which was that, while a company cannot be restrained from exercising its statutory power to alter its articles, it could be restrained from acting upon the altered

---

[90] [1940] A.C. 701, H.L. at 740.
[91] But *Southern Foundries Ltd. v. Shirlaw* was concerned with the dismissal of a managing director in breach of his ten-year contract. Clearly, there the only remedy would be damages since to grant an injunction would be tantamount to ordering specific performance of a contract for personal services.
[92] At p. 24D.
[93] See 4th ed. at p. 559. But the extension is warmly welcomed.

articles in breach of its contract if damages were not an adequate remedy. Injunctions certainly have been granted in such circumstances[94] and to deprive the other party of the appropriate contractual remedy is tantamount to allowing the company to benefit from its breach of contract.

As an alternative to an agreement with the company it may be possible for members to protect their rights by an agreement between themselves. Normally this will be practicable only if there is a small number of shareholders or a small number of large shareholders. In either of those events an agreement between them, as to how they will vote at general meetings and, say, that they will support each other's nominees for election to the board, may enable them to consolidate their control. Whereas the directors, standing as they do in a fiduciary relationship to the company, may not be able to fetter their discretion as to how they will vote at directors' meetings, there is nothing to stop members (even those who are directors) from doing so in relation to voting at general meetings. But, in the case of shareholders in a public company they will have to bear in mind that such an agreement may result in their becoming members of a "concert party" requiring notification to, and registration by the company of their holdings and dealings under Part VI[95] of the Act as if the members of the concert party were a single shareholder.

A more sophisticated arrangement, not uncommon in the United States but less used in the United Kingdom, is to set up what is generally described as a voting trust. Under this, in effect, voting rights are separated from the financial interest in the shares, the former being held and exercisable by trustees while the latter remains with the shareholders.

DEBENTUREHOLDER'S RIGHTS

The protection of the rights of the other type of investor—the debentureholder—is obviously much greater than that of a member's rights under the articles since a debenture confers contractual rights independent of the company's articles. It is, nonetheless, possible that those contractual rights might be affected as a result of the exercise by the company or the general meeting of its statutory powers. If, for example, the debenture provided that the holder should be entitled to appoint a director of the company and if a provision to that effect

[94] *e.g.* in *Baily* v. *British Equitable Assurance Co.* [1904] 1 Ch. 374, C.A. where it was held that a company could be restrained from adopting new articles which infringed the rights of its policyholders (the decision was reversed by the H.L. [1906] A.C. 35, on the ground that the provisions of the articles, and hence the power to alter them, had been incorporated in the terms of the policies) and *British Murac Syndicate* v. *Alperton Rubber Co.* [1915] 2 Ch. 186.

[95] See Chap. 23 at pp. 615–618 below.

was inserted in the company's articles, a question similar to that discussed in relation to shareholders might arise on whether an attempt to delete that provision could be restrained by injunction.[96] But this would rarely be a live question for the breach would normally entitle the debentureholder to require his debt security to be repaid and, if it was secured by a charge on the company's property, to enforce his security. This he would do rather than sue for damages for the breach. While the value of his rights may depend on the continued prosperity of the company, particularly if the debenture is unsecured loan stock, he is normally not subject, as is a shareholder, to any serious possibility that his rights will be varied by the company by corporate action without his consent.

To this, however, there are two exceptions. The first is that, if the debenture is one of a series or is debenture stock, its terms may provide for the variation of the holders' rights with the consent of a prescribed majority of the holders or an extraordinary resolution of the holders. In such a case, while he will not be vulnerable to action by the company or its members as such, he will be vulnerable to that of the requisite majority of his fellow debentureholders who may have interests conflicting with his because they are also shareholders or directors. In such circumstances he will not have the protection of sections 459–461 which apply only to "members."[97] However, as we have seen,[98] where there is a series of debentures or debenture stock there will almost invariably be independent trustees who should ensure that any proposed variations are fair and are fully and fairly explained in the circulars seeking the needed consents.

The second exception is that the powers of a debentureholder to enforce his security may be seriously curtailed if the court makes an administration order under Part II of the Insolvency Act 1986.[99] Such an order will not be made if a debentureholder has already appointed an administrative receiver unless the court is satisfied that the debentureholder has consented to the order being made or is not satisfied that the security under which the administrative receiver was appointed could not be challenged under certain provisions[1] of that Act.[2] If, however, an order is made, any administrative receiver must vacate office as must a receiver of any part of the company's property if the administrator requires him to do so.[3] Thereafter, so long as the administrative order remains in force there is a complete moratorium

[96] Even if it could, it seems clear that an injunction could not be granted to restrain the general meeting from removing his nominated director under s.303.

[97] Nor, of course, will ss.125–127 afford protection (they apply only to shareholders).

[98] Above Chap. 14 at pp. 381, 382.

[99] See Chap. 28 at pp. 743–760.

[1] *i.e.* Insolvency Act ss.238–240 (transactions at an undervalue or preferences); s.242 (gratuitous alienations); s.243 (unfair preferences); or s.245 (avoidance of floating charges): see *ibid.*, and Chap. 16 above.

[2] *Ibid.* s.9(3).

[3] *Ibid.* s.11(1)(b) and (2).

on any type of enforcement against the company without the consent of the administrator or the leave of the court.[4]

While an administrative order does not destroy or vary the debentureholder's rights, it does mean that his powers to enforce those rights are suspended and that any realisation of the property on which he has a charge will not rest with him or with an insolvency practitioner chosen by him (and whose primary aim will be to realise it at a price sufficient to discharge the debenture) but with one appointed by the court, whose primary aim will normally be to achieve "the survival of the company, and the whole or any part of its undertaking, as a going concern"[5] and so that if any parts of the undertaking have to be disposed of, it will be on the best terms obtainable in the interests of creditors and members as a whole.

VARIATIONS UNDER RECONSTRUCTIONS

This chapter has concentrated on variation of investors' rights under what may be termed internal corporate action. As we shall see in a later chapter,[6] variations may also occur under formal reductions of capital or schemes of arrangement involving, normally, court confirmation. All that needs mention at this stage is that there too emphasis is placed on protection of class rights and that "classes" in that context may have a wider connotation than it has in relation to classes of members in the context of this chapter.

[4] *Ibid.*, s.11(3).
[5] *Ibid.*, s.8(3)(a).
[6] Chap. 26 below.

CHAPTER 21

DIRECTORS' DUTIES

THE two preceding chapters have dealt with the means whereby investors can exercise such control as they have over the company by attending and voting at meetings, and with the legal limitations on the powers of those meetings to vary the rights of investors without their individual consents. But, as we saw in an earlier chapter,[1] the general meeting is merely one of the company's two primary organs and most of the company's powers are not vested in it but in the board of directors. And, as we also saw, the directors exercise these powers either directly or through managers appointed by them. It is therefore of vital importance to see what duties are owed by directors and managers in the exercise of their powers. It is to this that we now turn.

It is often stated that directors are trustees and that the nature of their duties can be explained on this basis. It is easy to see how this idea arose. Prior to 1844 most joint stock companies were unincorporated and depended for their validity on a deed of settlement vesting the property of the company in trustees.[2] Often the directors were themselves the trustees and even when a distinction was drawn between the passive trustees and the managing board of directors the latter would quite clearly be regarded as trustees in the eyes of a court of equity in so far as they dealt with the trust property.

With directors of incorporated companies the description "trustees" was less apposite but it was not unnatural that the courts should extend it to them by analogy. For one thing, the duties of the directors should obviously be the same whether the company was incorporated or not; for another, courts of equity tend to apply the label "trustee" to anyone in a fiduciary position. Nevertheless, to describe directors as trustees seems today to be neither strictly correct nor invariably helpful.[3] In truth, directors are agents of the company rather than trustees of it or its property. But as agents they stand in a fiduciary relationship to their principal, the company. The duties of good faith which this fiduciary relationship imposes are virtually identical with those imposed on trustees, and to this extent the description "trustee" still has validity. It is when we turn to the duties of care and skill that the trustee analogy breaks down. The duty of

---

[1] Chap. 7.
[2] Chaps. 2 and 3.
[3] *Re City Equitable Fire Insurance Co.* [1925] Ch. 407, *per* Romer J. at p. 426.

the trustees of a will or settlement is to be cautious and to avoid risks to the trust fund. The managers of a business concern must, perforce, take risks in an attempt to earn profits for the company and its members. Hence the duties of directors can conveniently be discussed under two heads: (1) fiduciary duties of loyalty and good faith (analogous to the duties of trustees *stricto sensu*), and (2) duties of care and skill (differing fundamentally from the duties of normal trustees).

FIDUCIARY DUTIES

General equitable principle

The basic principle is the same as that applying to any other fiduciary and discussed in works on Trusts and Agency. Such duties have, indeed, already been dealt with briefly in connection with another type of fiduciary peculiar to company law, the promoter.[4] But the relevant rules have received particular elaboration in relation to directors and the practical importance of the subject makes it desirable to discuss it here in greater detail.[5]

In the first place it should be noted that whereas the authority of the directors to bind the company as its agents normally depends on their acting collectively as a board,[6] their duties of good faith are owed by each director individually. One of several directors will not as such be an agent of the company with power to saddle it with responsibility for his acts, but he will be a fiduciary of it. To this extent, directors again resemble trustees who must normally act jointly but each of whom severally owes duties of good faith towards the beneficiaries.

Secondly, the fiduciary duties are owed to the company and to the company alone. The difficulties which may be caused by treating a metaphysical entity as the beneficiary, in whose interests the directors must act, are referred to later.[7] Here it suffices to emphasise that, in general, the directors owe no duties to the individual members as such, or, *a fortiori*, to a person who has not yet become a member—such as a potential purchaser of shares in it. This principle

---

[4] Chap. 12 above.
[5] An attempt in the 1978 Companies Bill to codify directors' duties proved abortive, to the regret of those of us who believe that a comprehensive statutory re-statement of those duties would make it more likely that they are observed; a belief strengthened by the fact that the main reason for giving up the attempt was the impossibility of obtaining agreement of the legal profession on precisely what the duties are.
[6] Chaps. 7 & 8 above.
[7] Below, pp. 554–556.

is regarded as firmly established by the much-criticised decision in *Percival* v. *Wright*,[8] where directors purchased shares from their members without revealing that negotiations were in progress for a sale of the undertaking at a favourable price.[9] This, however, does not mean that directors can never stand in a fiduciary relationship to the members; they well may if they are authorised by the latter to negotiate on their behalf with, for example, a potential take-over bidder.[10] And far less than the establishment of an agency relationship may suffice, particularly, as an important New Zealand decision illustrates,[11] in the case of a family company, "depending upon all the surrounding circumstances and the nature of the responsibility which in a real and practical sense the director has assumed towards the shareholder."[12] Nor, as we shall see, does it necessarily follow that if they make a personal profit as a result of the use of inside information in dealings in the company's securities they will not break their fiduciary duty to the company and be liable to account to it.

The *Percival* v. *Wright* rule was severely criticised by the Cohen Committee,[13] and forthrightly rejected by the Jenkins Committee in one of its bolder moods.[14] After much vacillation, the 1980 Act[15] provided criminal sanctions against directors (and other "insiders") who make use of price-sensitive information in dealings in their companies' securities but this in no way modified the general principle that it is to the company, and not to its members individually,[16] or to anyone else, that the directors stand in a fiduciary relationship. It seems that directors of a holding company do not even owe duties to its subsidiary, at any rate when that has an independent board of directors.[17]

---

8 [1902] 2 Ch. 421. This applies even if all the shares are owned by a holding company with whom the directors have service contracts: *Bell* v. *Lever Bros.* [1932] A.C. 161, H.L.

9 The actual decision may be defensible because the shareholders had approached the directors and asked them to buy their shares.

10 *Briess* v. *Woolley* [1954] A.C. 333, H.L.

11 *Coleman* v. *Myers* [1977] 2 N.Z.L.R. 225 (N.Z.C.A.). In the Supreme Court (*ibid.*) Mahon J. had held that *Percival* v. *Wright* was wrongly decided but the C.A. distinguished it.

12 *Per* Woodhouse J. at p. 324. And see his elaboration at 324–325 and *per* Cooke J. at p. 330. Their views were adopted by Browne-Wilkinson V.-C. in *Re Chez Nico (Restaurants) Ltd.* [1991] B.C.C. 736 at 750.

13 Cmd. 6659, paras. 86 and 87.

14 Cmnd. 1749, paras. 89 and 99(*b*).

15 See now the Company Securities (Insider Dealing) Act 1985, as amended by the Financial Services Act 1986: below Chap. 23.

16 Even to a member who is the controlling shareholder such as the holding company: *Pergamon Press Ltd.* v. *Maxwell* [1970] 1 W.L.R. 1167. And if the subsidiary's directors merely act in the interests of the holding company ignoring those of the minority shareholders, those shareholders may have a remedy under s.459 (see Chap. 24 at pp. 662 *et seq.*): *Scottish Co-operative Wholesale Society* v. *Meyer* [1959] A.C. 324, H.L.

17 *Lindgren* v. *L. & P. Estates Ltd.* [1968] Ch. 572, C.A. But *cf.* the dicta of Lords Simonds and Keith in *Scottish Co-operative Wholesale Society* v. *Meyer*, at pp. 343 and 362.

Thirdly, these duties, except in so far as they depend on statutory provisions expressly limited to directors, are not so restricted but apply equally to any officers of the company who are not so restricted to act on its behalf[18] and in particular to those acting in a managerial capacity.[19] Fourthly, the duties attach from the date when the director's appointment takes effect[20] but do not necessarily cease when his appointment ends; for example, he may be restrained from using to the prejudice of the company confidential information acquired when he was a director.[21]

In applying the general equitable principle to company directors four separate rules have emerged. These are: (1) that directors must act in good faith in what they believe to be the best interests of the company; (2) that they must not exercise the powers conferred upon them for purposes different from those for which they were conferred; (3) that they must not fetter their discretion as to how they shall act; and (4) that, without the informed consent of the company, they must not place themselves in a position in which their personal interests or duties to other persons are liable to conflict with their duties to the company.

1. Acting in good faith

In most cases compliance with the rule that directors must act honestly and in good faith is tested on commonsense principles, the court asking itself whether it is proved that the directors have not done what they honestly believed to be right, and normally accepting that they have unless satisfied that they have not behaved as honest men of business might be expected to act. Directors are required to act "bona fide in what they consider—not what a court may consider—is in the interests of the company. . . ."[22] On the face of it, this duty is simply to display subjective good faith. But, notwithstanding that it is for the directors and not the court to consider what is in the interests of the company, they may breach that duty notwithstanding that they have not acted with conscious dishonesty but have failed to direct their minds to the question whether a

18 *i.e.* to those who are the company's agents, and who therefore stand in fiduciary capacity towards it, as opposed to those who are merely its servants, who do work for it but co not act on its behalf. That the latter's duties of good faith are somewhat less extensive seems clearly established: *Bell* v. *Lever Bros.* [1932] A.C. 161, H.L. But servants, too, owe duties of fidelity which in most respects amount to much the same: *cf. Reading* v. *Att.-Gen.* [1951] A.C. 507, H.L. These, however, depend upon the normal law of master and servant and present no peculiarities in the company law field.

19 This sentence, in an earlier edition, was approved by the Canadian Supreme Court in *Canadian Aero Service* v. *O'Malley* (1973) 40 D.L.R. (3d) 371 at 331.

20 In *Lindgren* v. *L. & P. Estates Ltd.*, above n. 17, the C.A. rejected an argument that a "director-elect" is in a fiduciary relationship to the company.

21 See *Industrial Development Consultants Ltd.* v. *Cooley* [1972] 1 W.L.R. 443; *Canadian Aero Services Ltd.* v. *O'Malley*, above n. 19; *Island Export Finance Ltd.* v. *Umunna* [1986] BCLC 460 (where it was pointed out that otherwise "a director, provided he does nothing contrary to his employer's interests while employed, may with impunity conceive the idea of resigning so that he may exploit some opportunity of the employees and, having resigned, proceed to exploit it for himself."

22 Per Lord Greene M.R. in *Re Smith & Fawcett Ltd.* [1942] Ch. 304 at 306, C.A.

transaction was in fact in the interests of the company. A good illustration of this is afforded by Re W. & M. Roith Ltd.[23] There the controlling shareholder and director wished to make provision for his widow. On advice he entered into a service agreement with the company whereby on his death she was to be entitled to a pension for life. On being satisfied that no thought had been given to the question whether the arrangement was for the benefit of the company and that, indeed, the sole object was to make provision for the widow, the court held that the transaction was not binding on the company.[24]

But what exactly is meant by saying that they must act in the interests of the company? Despite the separate personality of the company it is clear that directors are not expected to act on the basis of what is for the economic advantage of the corporate entity, disregarding the interests of the members.[25] They are, for example, clearly entitled to recommend the payment of dividends to the members and are not expected to deny them a return on their money by ploughing back all the profits so as to increase the size and wealth of the company. If, as will normally be the case, the directors themselves are shareholders, they are entitled to have some regard to their own interests as shareholders and not to think only of the others. As it was happily put in an Australian case, they are "not required by the law to live in an unreal region of detached altruism and to act in a vague mood of ideal abstraction from obvious facts which must be present to the mind of any honest and intelligent man when he exercises his powers as a director."[26]

Until the 1980 Act it seemed that the only interests to which the directors were entitled to have regard were the long-term interests of the members. As it had become a cliché, repeated in the chairman's speech at almost every AGM of a public company, that "this company recognises that it has duties to its members, employees, consumers of its products and to the nation," this was somewhat anachronistic and was modified, and was now sections 309 and 719 of the Act and section 187

23 [1967] 1 W.L.R. 432. But cf. *Charterbridge Corpn.* v. *Lloyds Bank* [1970] Ch. 62, where the directors of a company forming part of a group had considered the benefit of the group as a whole without giving separate consideration to that of the company alone. It was held that "the proper test ... in the absence of actual separate consideration must be whether an intelligent and honest man in the position of a director of the company concerned could ... have reasonably believed that the transactions were for the benefit of the company"; at p. 74.

24 Following *Re Lee, Behrens & Co. Ltd.* [1932] 2 Ch. 46. See also *Alexander v. Automatic Telephone Co.* [1900] 2 Ch. 56, C.A.; but cf. *Lindgren v. L. & P. Estates Ltd.* [1968] Ch. 572, C.A., where it was held that there had been no failure to consider the commercial merits.

25 In connection with members voting in general meetings, Evershed M.R. in *Greenhalgh* v. *Arderne Cinemas* [1951] Ch. 286, C.A., said, at p. 291, "the phrase 'the company as a whole' does not (at any rate in such a case as the present) mean the company as a commercial entity as distinct from the corporators." This seems equally true in the present context.

26 *Mills* v. *Mills* (1938) 60 C.L.R. 150 (Aust. H.C.), *per* Latham C.J. at p. 164; cf. Dixon J. at pp. 185–186.

of the Insolvency Act 1986. The two latter sections have been dealt with sufficiently in Chapter 8.[27] What is relevant in the present context is section 309. Under that, the matters to which directors[28] are to have regard in the performance of their functions "include the interests of the company's employees in general, as well as the interests of its members."[29] However subsection (2) provides that: "Accordingly, the duty imposed by this section on the directors is owed by them to the company (and the company alone) and is enforceable in the same way as any other fiduciary duty owed to a company by its directors" which means that the employees as such have no means of enforcing it.

This grudging recognition that the interests of the company include those of its workforce has not been extended. The courts have even been reluctant to recognise that the directors have any right, let alone duty, to have regard to the interests of creditors. But it cannot be right to deny that the interests of the company in all circumstances mean those of members and employees only. If the company's capital has been lost the members have no financial interest in the company. The directors must, in those circumstances, have regard to the interests of debentureholders and other creditors and, if they do not, but continue the company's business while it runs into insolvency, they are likely to find themselves held guilty of fraudulent or wrongful trading. As Lord Diplock said in *Lonrho Ltd.* v. *Shell Petroleum*[30]: "it is the duty of the board to consider ... the best interests of the company. These are not exclusively those of its shareholders but may include those of its creditors."[31] And so long as the company remains a going concern the company's best interests may well be served by having regard to the other interests; dissatisfied customers and an aggrieved public or Government Department are not conducive to the future prosperity of the company. Hence it is generally possible to justify charitable donations and even political contributions.[32]

27 At pp. 169 and 184 above. They empower a company to make gratuitous provision for employees on the cessation of a company's business even though that "is not in the best interests of the company."

28 Including shadow directors: s.309(3).

29 s.309(1).

30 [1980] 1 W.L.R. 627. H.L.

31 [1980] 1 W.L.R. 634f. See also *Walker* v. *Wimborne* (1976) 50 A.L.J.R. 446 (Aust. H.C.), noted (1977) 40 M.L.R. 226.

32 Though these have to be disclosed in the accounts and are actively encouraged by the Government, there is still no statutory power to make such gifts and, it seems, "charity has no business to sit at boards of directors *qua* charity": *per* Bowen L.J. in *Hutton* v. *W. Cork Ry.* (1883) 23 Ch.D. at p. 673. But a gift by a company such as I.C.I. for scientific education can easily be justified (*Evans* v. *Brunner Mond & Co.* [1921] 1 Ch. 359); one for famine relief in Eritrea would be more difficult to justify in law except on the cynical basis that it was good advertising. For an example of the more liberal attitude in the U.S.A., see *Theodora Holding Co.* v. *Henderson* (1969) 257 Atl. 2d. 398, (Del. Ch.). The political contributions disclosed by companies suggest that boards find no difficulty in justifying them, presumably on the basis that the policy of the political party or pressure group would be good for the company's business. And conceivably the stated objects of the company might include that of making political contributions: *cf. Re Horsley & Weight* [1982] Ch. 442, C.A.

The rule that directors are supposed to have regard primarily to the long-term interests of members and employees may also pose difficulties for directors who are appointed by a particular class of security holders.[33] The obvious intention is that then they shall pay particular attention to the interests of that class whether that be of members or creditors. Yet this, it seems, they must not do. This, indeed, seems to require them to "live in an unreal region of detached altruism and to act in a vague mood of ideal abstraction from obvious facts."[34]

2. *Proper purpose*

If directors exercise their powers for purposes other than those for which they were conferred, it could be said that they have exceeded their authority and are liable accordingly. But it probably makes for clarity to distinguish between an excess of authority and an act which prima facie is within the powers delegated to them but which they have abused by exercising it for an improper purpose. The former hardly seems to be a breach of the fiduciary duty of good faith; the latter is.[35] Often the improper purpose will be to feather the directors' own nests or to preserve their own control, in which event it will be a breach of the duty, already considered, to act honestly for the benefit of the company as a whole. But it is clear that notwithstanding that directors have acted honestly in what they believe to be the benefit of the company they may nevertheless be liable if they have exercised their powers for a purpose different from that for which the powers were conferred upon them.[36]

[33] "There is nothing wrong in it. It is done every day. Nothing wrong, that is, so long as the director is left free to exercise his best judgment in the interests of the company . . .": *per* Denning M.R. in *Boulting v. A.C.T.A.T.* [1963] 2 Q.B. 606 at 626. For a recent illustration see *Kuwait Bank v. National Nominees Ltd.* [1991] 1 A.C. 187, P.C. where a bank which held 40 per cent. of the shares of a company had appointed as directors of one of that company's subsidiaries two of its employees whom the bank continued to pay in respect of the time spent as such directors. It was held that although they "owed a duty to their employer, the bank," . . . in the performance of their duties as directors of the company," their primary duty when acting as directors was to the company (at p. 319H) and in the performance of their duties they "were bound to ignore the interests and wishes of their employer, the bank": at 320C.

[34] See *Mills v. Mills*, n. 26 above. The Ghana Companies Code 1973 (Act 179) provides by its s.203(3) "In considering whether a particular transaction or course of action is in the best interests of the company as a whole, a director, when appointed by, or as a representative of, a particular class of members, employers or creditors, may give special, but not exclusive, consideration to the interests of that class." This attempted to face the facts of life while continuing to ban the obnoxious practice of mandating representatives on how they should vote (on which see the report of the Bullock Committee on Industrial Democracy (1977), Cmnd. 6706, Ch. 8 para. 40).

[35] If the purpose is illegal or contrary to public policy the transaction will be ineffective on that ground rather than as a breach of the fiduciary duty: see *Pharmaceutical Society v. Dickson* [1970] A.C. 403, H.L. (restraint of trade).

[36] See *Howard Smith Ltd. v. Ampol Ltd.* [1974] A.C. 821, P.C. at 834, citing *Fraser v. Whalley* (1864) 2 H.C.M. & M. 10; *Punt v. Symons & Co. Ltd.* [1903] 2 Ch. 506; *Piercy v. S. Mills & Co. Ltd.* [1920] 1 Ch. 77; *Ngurli v. McCann* (1954) 90 C.L.R. 425 (Aust. H.C.); *Hogg v. Cramphorn Ltd.* [1967] Ch. 254 at 267.

The legal position was reviewed by the Privy Council in *Howard Smith Ltd. v. Ampol Ltd.*,[37] which considered the decisions on this subject of courts throughout the Commonwealth. It concerned, as have most of the cases, the power of directors to issue new shares.[38] It was argued that the only proper purpose for which such a power could be exercised was to raise new capital when the company needed it.[39] This was rejected as too narrow.[40] It might be a proper use of the power to issue shares to a larger company in order to secure the financial stability of the company[41] or as part of an agreement relating to the exploitation of mineral rights owned by the company.[42] If so, the mere fact that the incidental (and desired) result was to deprive a shareholder of his voting majority or to defeat a take-over bid would not be sufficient to make the purpose improper.[43] But if, as in the instant case, the purpose was found to be simply and solely to dilute the majority voting power so as to enable an offer to proceed which the existing majority was in a position to block,[44] the exercise of the power would be improper despite the fact that the directors were not motivated by a desire to obtain some personal advantage. Moreover, when:

"'a dispute arises whether directors ... made a particular decision for one purpose or for another, or whether, there being more than one purpose, one or another purpose was the substantial or primary purpose, the court ... is entitled to look at the situation objectively.... If it finds that a particular requirement, though real, was not urgent or critical at the relevant time, it may have reason to doubt, or discount, the assertions of individuals that they

---

37 Above n. 36. The judgment was delivered by Lord Wilberforce.
38 This particular example should have become less common in the light of ss.80, 89-96 restricting the authority of directors to issue shares: see Chap. 14 at pp. 362, 363 above. But the principle applies generally. For examples in relation to other powers, see, *Stanhope's Case* (1866) L.R. 1 Ch.App. 161, and *Mansty's Case* (1873) 17 S.J. 745 (forfeiture of shares); *Galloway v. Halle Concerns Society* [1915] 2 Ch. 233 (calls); *Bennet's Case* (1854) 5 De G.M. & G. 284 and *Australian Metropolitan Life Asscn. Co. Ltd. v. Ure* (1923) 33 C.L.R. 199, Aust. H.C. (registration of transfers); *Hogg v. Cramphorn Ltd.*, above (loans). See also *Lee Panavision Ltd. v. Lee Lighting Ltd.* [1991] B.C.C. 610, C.A.
39 This has often been assumed and the directors had apparently been so advised and sought, unsuccessfully, to show that this was their purpose. The only other possible motives (held to be the true ones) were to destroy the existing majority and to enable a more favourable take-over bid to proceed. Even the latter was held not to be a proper purpose since the right to dispose of shares is an individual right not a corporate one: at pp. 837-838.
40 At pp. 835-836.
41 *Harlowe's Nominees Pty Ltd. v. Woodside Oil Co.* (1968) 121 C.L.R. 483, Aust. H.C.
42 *Teck Corpn. Ltd. v. Miller* (1972) 33 D.L.R. (3d) 288, B.C. Sup.Ct.
43 The test is what the substantial or primary purpose was: *Hirsche v. Sims* [1894] A.C. 654, P.C.; *Hindle v. John Cotton Ltd.*, 1919 56 S.L.T. 625; *Mills v. Mills* (1938) 60 C.L.R. 150, Aust. H.C.
44 Or, conversely, to block a bid: *Winthrop Investments Ltd. v. Winns Ltd.* [1975] 2 N.S.W.L.R. 666, N.S.W., C.A.

acted solely to deal with it, particularly when the action they took was unusual or even extreme."[45]

3. *Unfettered discretion*

We now turn to certain objective standards which must be complied with notwithstanding the presence of good faith and proper motive. Before dealing, under the next head, with the more important of these, there is one which is often ignored but which appears to exist and to need mention. Since the directors' powers are held by them as fiduciaries of the company they cannot, without the consent of the company, fetter their future discretion. Thus, it seems clear as a general principle, despite the paucity of reported cases on the point,[46] that directors cannot validly contract (either with one another or with third parties) as to how they shall vote at future board meetings.[47] This is so even though there is no improper motive or purpose (thus infringing the previous rules) and no personal advantage reaped by the directors under the agreement (thus infringing the succeeding rule).

This, however, does not mean that if, in the bona fide exercise of their discretion, the directors have entered into a contract on behalf of the company, they cannot in that contract validly agree to take such further action at board meetings as are necessary to carry out that contract. As was said in a judgment of the Australian High Court[48]:

"There are many kinds of transaction in which the proper time for the exercise of the directors' discretion is the time of the negotiation of a contract and not the time at which the contract is to be performed. ... If at the former time they are bona fide of opinion that it is in the best interests of the company that the transaction should be entered into and carried into effect, I can see no reason in law why they should not bind themselves to do whatever under the transaction is to be done by the board."[49]

Indeed, it may be that if there is a voting agreement between all the members and directors which provides that they shall vote together at all meetings, whether general meetings or directors'

[45] At p. 832.
[46] But see *Clark v. Workman* [1920] 1 Ir.R. 107 and an unreported decision of Morton J. in the *Arderne Cinema* litigation, below, Chap. 22, at p. 599 and the Scottish decision in *Dawson International plc v. Coats Paton plc*, 1989 S.L.T. 655 (1st Div.) where it was accepted that an agreement by the directors would be subject to an implied term that it did not derogate from their duty to continue to act bona fide in the interests of the company.
[47] Contrast the position of shareholders who may freely enter into such voting agreements: above Chap. 20 at pp. 545–547.
[48] *Thorby v. Goldberg* (1964) 112 C.L.R. 597 (Aus.H.C.).
[49] *Ibid*, per Kitto J. at pp. 605–606.

meetings, the parties to it will be bound *inter se*,[50] and only if there are other members or directors will they be able to complain.[51]

On much the same principle, the board must not, in the absence of express authority, delegate their discretions to others.[52] But in practice wide authority to delegate is invariably conferred by the articles.[53]

4. Conflict of duty and interest

As fiduciaries, directors must not place themselves in a position in which there is a conflict between their duties to the company and their personal interests or duties to others. Good faith must not only be done but must manifestly be seen to be done; and the law will not allow a fiduciary to place himself in a position in which his judgment is likely to be biased and then to escape liability by denying that in fact it was biased. It will be convenient to consider its application in three connections. And first, in relation to transactions with the company, where it has received its most detailed working out.

(a) **Transactions with the company.** By the middle of the 19th Century it had been clearly established that the trustee-like position of directors was liable to vitiate any contract which the board entered into on behalf of the company with one of their number. This principle receives its clearest expression in *Aberdeen Ry.* v. *Blaikie*[54] in which a contract between the company and a partnership of which one of the directors was a partner was avoided at the instance of the company notwithstanding that its terms were perfectly fair. Lord Cranworth L.C. said on that occasion[55]:

"A corporate body can only act by agents, and it is, of course, the duty of those agents so to act as best to promote the interests of the corporation whose affairs they are conducting. Such agents have duties to discharge of a fiduciary nature towards their principal. And it is a rule of universal application that no one, having such duties to discharge, shall be allowed to enter into engagements in which he has, or can have, a personal interest conflicting, or which possibly may conflict, with the interests of

---

[50] *cf.* Menzies J., *ibid.* p. 616.
[51] This was discussed, but not clearly settled, by the Canadian Supreme Court in *Ringuet* v. *Bergeron* [1960] S.C.R. 672, where the majority held the voting agreement valid because, in their view, it related only to voting at general meetings. The minority held that it extended also to directors' meetings and was void, but they conceded that the position might have been different had all the members originally been parties to the agreement: see at p. 677.
[52] *Cartmell's Case* (1874) L.R. 9 Ch.App. 691.
[53] See Chap. 7 above, at p. 160.
[54] (1854) 1 Macq.H.L. 461 (H.L. Sc.).
[55] At pp. 471–472.

those whom he is bound to protect. ... So strictly is this principle adhered to that no question is allowed to be raised as to the fairness or unfairness of a contract so entered into. ..."

Later cases have added little to the general principle thus enunciated.[56] It applies not only to transactions directly with the directors but also to those in which they are in any way interested, whether because they benefit personally, however indirectly, or because they are subject to a conflicting duty.[57] The principle is the same as that applying to promoters and already discussed,[58] but the burden of it falls more heavily upon directors. As we have seen, promoters can enter into transactions with the company if they make full disclosure of all material facts either to an independent board or to the members of the company. Any transaction which the company then enters into with the promoter will be valid and enforceable. The same applies to a transaction with any agent of the company other than a director.[59] But the directors themselves cannot escape so easily. Disclosure to themselves is ineffective even if the interested directors refrain from attending and voting, leaving an independent quorum to decide, for the company has a right to the unbiased voice and advice of every director.[60] Hence, in the absence of express provision in the company's articles, the only effective step is to make full disclosure to the members of the company and to have the contract entered into or ratified by the company in general meeting.

This need for approval in general meeting was expressly recognised by section 29 of the first Joint Stock Companies Act of 1844. However, this section disappeared from the Act of 1856, to be replaced only by an article in the optional Table[61] to the effect that any director, directly or indirectly interested in any contract with the company (except an interest merely as shareholder of another company) should be disqualified and vacate office—a provision borrowed from the provisions in the Companies Clauses Consolidation Act of 1845.[62] Similar provisions for disqualification have caused

---

56 Except to recognise that, as we shall see below, the duty may, within limits, be waived or modified by provisions in the company's articles.
57 *Transvaal Lands Co.* v. *New Belgium (Transvaal) Land and Development Co.* [1914] 2 Ch. 488, C.A.; *Boulting* v. *A.C.T.A.T.* [1963] 2 Q.B. 606, C.A., *per* Upjohn L.J. at pp. 635–638. The rule is for the protection of the company and cannot be used by the director as a shield to protect himself against a third party: *Boulting* v. *A.C.T.A.T.*
58 Above, Chap. 12, p. 298, *et seq.*
59 *e.g.* the company's solicitor: see *Regal (Hastings) Ltd.* v. *Gulliver* [1942] 1 All E.R. 378; [1967] 2 A.C. 134n., H.L.; below, p. 565.
60 See *Benson* v. *Heathorn* (1842) 1 Y. & C.C.C. 326, *per* Knight-Bruce V.-C. at pp. 341–342, and *Imperial Mercantile Credit Assocn.* v. *Coleman* (1871) L.R. 6 Ch.App. 558, C.A., *per* Hatherley L.C. at pp. 567–568.
61 Then Table B (art. 47) which later became Table A.
62 ss.85–87. These provisions were borrowed from the Municipal Corporations Act 1835, s.28; it was not unnatural to apply to statutory companies running public utilities the same rules as those for local authorities.

difficulty in the case of public authorities; they seem even less appropriate in the case of purely commercial ventures. Yet they remained in all Tables A until the 1948 Act.

It is not surprising that these strict rules were not acceptable to the business community. Hence it soon became the practice to attempt to modify them by provisions in the articles. So far as the disqualifying rules were concerned this was easy; they had no common law or equitable basis and all that was necessary was to exclude or modify Table A. And in the case of registered companies formed under the 1948 and subsequent Acts not even that is needed, for the post-1948 Tables omit the former disqualifying clause.

The basic equitable principle was, and is, the more serious snag. Contracts with directors, such as service agreements, became increasingly common, and contracts in which the directors were interested, for example as directors of another company, more common still. And the directors were unwilling to suffer the delay, embarrassment and possible frustration entailed by having to submit all such contracts to the company in general meeting. But just as the normal restraints on trustees can be modified by express provisions in the will or deed under which they were appointed,[63] so (within limits) can the normal fiduciary duties of directors be modified by express provision in the company's constitution. Such provisions have become common-form in the articles of registered companies.

Alarmed by the increasing ambit of these clauses, the legislature intervened.

(b) Statutory duty to declare interests. Section 149 of the 1929 Act placed directors under a duty to declare their interests in a contract or proposed contract with the company at a meeting of the directors. This section became section 199 of the 1948 Act and an amended version, which extends its ambit from "contracts" to "contracts, transactions or arrangements," is now section 317 of the 1985 Act. Discussion of its precise terms is left until later in this chapter,[64] when the various statutory extensions of the general equitable principle are dealt with. Here it is only necessary to note that the only express sanction securing its observance is that the errant director is liable to a fine[65] but that nothing in the section "prejudices the operation of any rule of law restricting directors from having an interest" in transactions with the company.[66]

---

63 The most common example is a "charging clause" enabling professional trustees and their firms to charge fees for acting as trustees or executors.
64 See pp. 576-578 below.
65 s.317(7).
66 s.317(9).

The inter-relation between this section and the general equitable principle was considered by an unusually strong Court of Appeal[67] in *Hely-Hutchinson* v. *Brayhead Ltd.*[68] and by the House of Lords in the recent case of *Guinness* v. *Saunders*.[69] In both, the articles of association provided (as do Tables A 1948[70] and 1985[71]) that a director might be interested in, and should not be liable to account to the company for benefits resulting from transactions with the company provided that he disclosed his interest in accordance with the section. In both cases he had entered into such a transaction without declaring his interest. Both decisions accept that if a director fails to declare his interest the transaction is voidable at the instance of the company and any benefits received by the director are recoverable by the company if it acts while it is still possible to restore both parties to their former positions.[72] It is also implicit in the judgments that if he has duly declared his interest[73] the transaction will not be voidable despite the fact that the company has not specifically consented to his placing himself in a position where his interest conflicts with his duty to the company.

What these cases do not make wholly clear, however, is what the position is if the director has not declared his interest and the enabling article makes no reference to his duty to do so. Earlier editions of this book[74] took the view that in those circumstances the contract would be voidable under the equitable principle since, although articles could contract-out of the need for the ad hoc consent by the company, they could not contract out of the statutory

---

[67] Lord Denning M.R. and Lords Wilberforce and Pearson.
[68] [1968] 1 Q.B. 549, C.A.
[69] [1990] 2 A.C. 663, H.L. This was one of the many cases—civil and criminal—arising from the hotly contested take-over battle for Distillers which Guinness won. Mr. Ward, an American lawyer, and a Guinness director had played a valuable role as a member of the ad hoc committee of the board set up to plan Guinness's strategy and tactics. After the victory he submitted an invoice for special remuneration of £5.2m, based on an agreement by the committee that if the Guinness bid was successful he should be remunerated at the rate of 0.2 per cent. of the value of the bid. The £5.2m was paid to him but when the full board learnt of it they caused Guinness to sue Mr. Ward for its recovery and, at first instance and in the C.A. obtained summary judgment on the ground that he had not disclosed his interest in accordance with s.317: [1988] 1 W.L.R. 863, C.A. In the *Hely-Hutchinson* case, *restitutio in integrum* was no longer possible. However the appeal was dismissed on a new ground. Namely that, under Guinness's articles, remuneration of directors could be determined only by the board and could not be delegated to a committee. Hence there was no contract with Mr. Ward, the £5.2m belonged in equity to Guinness and had to be restored. Nor had he any legal entitlement to a *quantum meruit* or to an "equitable allowance" under *Boardman* v. *Phipps*; below pp. 568–569.
[70] Art. 84.
[71] Art. 85. This does not specifically mention s.317 but says: "Subject to the provisions of the Act and provided that he has disclosed to the directors the nature and extent of any interest of his, a director may . . ."
[72] Which in both cases it was not.
[73] And complied with any other conditions in the articles; *e.g.* that he should not vote (or be counted in the quorum) on any matter in which he is interested: see Table A 1985, arts. 94, 95. As regards listed companies, see *Yellow Book Section 9, Chapter 1*, para. 4.1.
[74] 4th ed. p. 586.

duty. That seems to be the view of most of the judges in the two cases.[75] But Lord Goff in *Guinness* v. *Saunders* and, perhaps, Lord Pearson in *Hely-Hutchinson* v. *Brayhead* took a rather different view which, although it led to the same result in the cases before them, would lead to a different one in the circumstances presently under consideration. Lord Pearson said[76]:

"It is not contended that section 199[77] in itself affects the contract. The section merely creates a statutory duty of disclosure and imposes a fine for non-compliance. But it has to be read in conjuction with [the article]. If a director makes or is interested in a contract but fails to disclose his interest, what happens to the contract? Is it void or is it voidable at the option of the company, or is it still binding on both parties, or what? I think the answer must be supplied by the general law, and the answer is that the contract is voidable at the option of the company."

In *Guinness* v. *Saunders*, Lord Goff, having quoted that dictum, said[78]:

"On this basis I cannot see that a breach of section 317 ... had itself any effect upon the contract[79] between Mr. Ward and Guinness. As a matter of general law to the extent that there was a failure by Mr. Ward to comply with his duty of disclosure *under the relevant articles*[80] of Guinness ... the contract was no doubt voidable under the general law to which Lord Pearson refers."

It would seem to follow that if the article did not make it a condition that the interest should have been declared,[81] Lord Goff would hold that the contract would be unimpeachable, even though the interest was not declared. That seems to be a regrettable conclusion and one which the legislature surely could not have intended. It would mean that a director could profit at the expense of

75 In *Hely-Hutchinson* v. *Brayhead*, *per* Lord Denning [1968] 1 Q.B. at 585; and *per* Lord Wilberforce, *ibid.* at 589, but perhaps not of Lord Pearson. In *Guinness* v. *Saunders*, *per* Fox L.J. (with whose judgment Glidewell L.J. and Sir Frederick Lawton concurred) at [1988] 1 W.L.R. 868, 869 (see especially "It seems to me that section 317(1) must be regarded as imposing a duty which has consequences in the civil law in addition to the penalty of a fine;", at 869G); *per* Lord Templeman (with whose speech Lords Keith and Brandon concurred) at [1990] 2 A.C. 694D. It is impossible to tell whose side Lord Griffith is on as he expressed agreement with the speeches of both Lords Templeman and Goff.
76 [1968] 1 Q.B. at 594.
77 Of the 1948 Act which was then the relevant one.
78 [1990] 2 A.C. at 697.
79 This was said at the stage of his speech where he was dealing with the effect of the breach of s.317 and before he concluded that there was no contract with Mr. Ward.
80 *Itals* supplied.
81 As article 85 of Table A 1985 does. But there is nothing to stop companies from adopting articles which do not.

the company notwithstanding that he had breached his statutory duty as a director.[82] It may be, however, that too much is being read into the different formulations. In both of the cases the articles required compliance with the section and the judges did not have to consider what the position would otherwise have been and may well not have directed their minds to it.[82a]

(c) Disclosure of misconduct. This seems a convenient place to mention another curious feature of the fiduciary duties of directors. One might have supposed that these duties required disclosure by the directors of their own misconduct at any rate where that was relevant to any proposed transaction between the company and the directors. Yet the leading case of *Bell v. Lever Bros. Ltd.*[83] is taken to have determined that they are under no such duty. What makes this the more anomalous is that executive directors may be under a duty to disclose the misconduct of other employees, even though in so doing they may inevitably have to disclose their own.[84]

(d) Use of corporate property, opportunity or information. Another and most important, consequence of the principle, that directors must not place themselves in a position where their fiduciary duties conflict with their personal interests, is that they must not, without the informed consent of the company, use for their own profit the company's assets, opportunities or information. And this prohibition is one that it has not proved so easy to avoid by provisions in the company's articles.[85]

Misuse of corporate assets generally presents no particular problem[86]; even the most unsophisticated director should realise that he must not use the company's property as if it was his own (although even this is frequently overlooked or ignored in a

[82] The possibility of having to pay a fine is an inadequate preventative particularly as it is unlikely that he will be prosecuted.
[82a] It is clear from a still more recent case that the apparent divergence of views is causing difficulties. In *Lee Panavision Ltd.* v. *Lee Lighting Ltd.* [1991] B.C.C. 620, (Harman J. and C.A.) Harman J. discussed it (at pp. 626F–627H) but the C.A. declined an invitation to do so (at 637 E, G).
[83] [1932] A.C. 161, H.L. The company which, in ignorance that the directors had misbehaved so seriously that the company would have been entitled to dismiss them summarily (and would have done so) was held to be not entitled to recover the substantial sums paid to them on their retirement.
[84] *Sybron Corpn.* v. *Rochem Ltd.* [1984] Ch. 112, C.A. following *Swain v. West (Butchers) Ltd.* [1936] 3 All E.R. 261, C.A.
[85] An article such as art. 85 of the 1985 Act might be effective in some situations, but not in all, and only if the director "has disclosed to the directors the nature and content of any material interest of his" which, as the cases discussed below illustrate, it is not very likely that he will be able and willing to do.
[86] Except the problem of knowing when "corporate assets" end and "corporate information," or "corporate opportunity," begin. The present law does not clearly draw a distinction between them and the decisions frequently treat the latter as "belonging" to the company. *i.e.* as being its "property" or "asset." As we shall see the distinction may be important in relation to authorisation or ratification by the company.

"one-man" company). *Guinness* v. *Saunders*[87] may be regarded as an example of this; although Mr. Ward thought he was entitled to the £5.2m of Guinness's funds it was held that he had no right to it and therefore had to return it to Guinness.

It is misuse of corporate information or a corporate opportunity—in practice the two are likely to overlap—which gives rise to difficulties. A decision which illustrates both the questions which may arise and the extreme severity of the law is that of the House of Lords in *Regal (Hastings) Ltd.* v. *Gulliver*.[88] The facts, briefly, were as follows: Company A owned a cinema and the directors decided to acquire two others with a view to selling the whole undertaking as a going concern. For this purpose they formed company B to take a lease of the other two cinemas. But the lessor insisted on a personal guarantee from the directors unless the paid-up capital of company B was at least £5,000 (which in those days was a large sum). The company was unable to subscribe more than £2,000 and the directors were not willing to give personal guarantees. Accordingly the original plan was changed; instead of company A subscribing for all the shares in company B, company A took up 2,000 and the remaining 3,000 were taken by the directors and their friends. Later, instead of selling the undertaking, all the shares in both companies were sold, a profit of £2. 16s. 1d. being made on each of the shares in company B. The new controllers then caused company A to bring an action against the former directors to recover the profit they had made.

It will be observed that this claim was wholly unmeritorious. Recovery by the company would benefit only the purchasers, who, if the action was successful, would recover an undeserved windfall resulting in a reduction in the price which they had freely agreed to pay.[89] It also appears that the directors had held a majority of the shares in company A so that there would have been no difficulty in obtaining ratification of their action by the company in general meeting[90]; but acting, as it was conceded they had, in perfect good faith and in full belief in the legality and propriety of their actions it had not occurred to them to go through this formality. It was also clear that the directors had not deprived the company of any of its property.[91] (unless information can be regarded as property[92]), or, seemingly, robbed it of an opportunity which it might have exercised

87 Above, p. 562.
88 [1942] 1 All E.R. 378; [1967] 2 A.C. 134n. A case which, because it was decided during the War and then reported only in the All E.R., was frequently overlooked until it was included in the L.R. 25 years later.
89 Only one of their Lordships seemed to be disturbed by this—Lord Porter at [1967] 2 A.C. 157.
90 See the cogent editorial note in [1942] 1 All E.R. at 379. It was conceded that had this been done, there could have been no recovery: see further on this question Chap. 22 below.
91 Thus bringing the case within the "corporate asset" basis of liability.
92 On this vexed question, see the differing views of the Law Lords in *Boardman* v. *Phipps* [1967] 2 A.C. 46, H.L.: below pp. 568, 569.

for its own advantage; the 3,000 shares in company B had never been the company's property and, on the facts as found, the company could not have availed itself of the opportunity to acquire them. Because of this the court of first instance and a unanimous Court of Appeal had dismissed the action. But a unanimous House of Lords[93] reversed this decision. Following the well-known cases on trustees[93] it was held that the directors were liable to account once it was established "(i) that what the directors did was so related to the affairs of the company that it can properly be said to have been done in the course of their management and in utilisation of their opportunities and special knowledge as directors; and (ii) that what they did resulted in a profit to themselves."[94]

This may well be thought to be carrying equitable principles to an inequitable conclusion. Nor does this account exhaust the anomalies inherent in the decision. The chairman (and, apparently, the dominant member) of the board, instead of agreeing himself to subscribe for shares in company B, had merely agreed to find subscribers for £500. Shares to that value had, accordingly, been taken up by two private companies of which he was a member and director, and by a personal friend of his. It was accepted that the companies and friend had subscribed beneficially and not as his nominees and, accordingly, he was held not to be under any liability to account for the profit which they had made.[95] The company's solicitor also escaped; though he had subscribed for shares and profited personally he could retain his profit because he had acted with the knowledge and consent of the company exercised through the board of directors. The directors themselves could avoid liability only if a general meeting had ratified, but the solicitor, not being a director, could rely on the consent of the board. And this, despite the fact that the board had acted throughout on his advice. Hence the two men most responsible for what had been done escaped liability, while those who had followed their lead had to pay up.

What seems wrong with the application of the basic principle in this case is that recovery was not from all the right people and, more especially, was in favour of quite the wrong people.[96] Had it not been for the change of ownership it might well have been equitable to order restoration to the company, thus, in effect, causing the directors' profits to be shared among all the members. Certainly it is generally salutary to insist that directors shall not derive secret benefits from their trust. And it is probably well that this should apply whether or not any actual loss is suffered by the company, and

---

[93] Notably the leading case of *Keech* v. *Sandford* (1726) Sel. Cas. Ch. 61.
[94] *Per* Lord MacMillan at [1967] A.C. 153.
[95] The companies and friend had not been sued. Could recovery have been obtained from them had they been joined as parties?
[96] Some American jurisdictions, in like circumstances, allow what is there known as "pro rata recovery" by those shareholders who have not profited. We, unfortunately, lack any such procedure.

whether or not it is deprived of an opportunity of benefiting itself. To allow directors to decide that the company shall not accept the opportunity and then to accept the opportunity themselves might impose too great a strain on their impartiality.

Of the many subsequent decisions that have followed or commented on the *Regal* case, three are of particular interest: *Industrial Development Consultants* v. *Cooley*,[97] *Canadian Aero Service* v. *O'Malley*[98] (a decision of the Canadian Supreme Court in which the judgment was delivered by Laskin J.—later the C.J.) and *Boardman* v. *Phipps*.[99] The facts in the first two cases were very similar. In both the companies concerned had been eager to obtain, and in negotiation for, highly remunerative work in connection with impending projects. In both it was unlikely that the companies would have obtained the work, but in each there was a director whose expertise the undertaker of the project was anxious to obtain. Accordingly each of the directors concerned resigned his office and later joined the undertaker of the project, in *Cooley* directly, in *Canadian Aero Service* indirectly through a company formed for the purpose which entered into a consortium with the undertaker. In both they were held liable to account for the profits which they made.[1]

In *Cooley* liability was based on misuse of information,[2] the defendant having, while managing director, obtained information and knowledge that the project was to be revived and deliberately concealed this from the company and taken steps to turn the information to his personal advantage. It was irrelevant that the approach had been made to him and that his services were being sought as an individual consultant and would be undertaken free from any association with the company.[3] "Information which came to him while he was managing director and which was of concern to the plaintiffs and relevant for the plaintiffs to know, was information which it was his duty to pass on to the plaintiffs."[4] It might be

97 [1972] 1 W.L.R. 443 (Roskill J.).
98 [1973] 40 D.L.R. (3d) 371 (Can. S.C.).
99 [1967] 2 A.C. 46, H.L.

1 In *Canadian Aero Service* the award of $125,000 was described as "damages" but was upheld on the basis that it should be "viewed as an accounting for profits or, what amounts to the same thing, as based on unjust enrichment": (1973) 40 D.L.R. (3d) at 392.

2 Roskill J. presumably chose this rather than the more obvious loss of opportunity because the chance that the company could have secured the opportunity was minimal: Roskill J. assessed it at not not more than 10 per cent.: [1972] 1 W.L.R. at 454.

3 So that, "in one sense, the benefit … did not arise because of the defendant's directorship: indeed, the defendant would not have got this work had he remained a director": [1972] 1 W.L.R. at 451.

4 *Ibid.* It would follow that even if the defendant had not used the information himself he would have been liable in damages for breach of duty if the company could have proved that it suffered loss as a result of the failure to disclose. Suppose he had been a director of two companies to each of which the information was relevant: would he have been liable to both if he did not disclose to either and liable to one if he disclosed to the other?

remarkable that the plaintiffs should receive a benefit which "it is unlikely that they would have got for themselves had the defendant complied with his duty to them" but "if the defendant is not required to account he will have made a large profit as a result of having deliberately put himself into a position in which his duty to the plaintiffs who were employing him and his personal interests conflicted."[5]

In *Canadian Aero Service*, the decision was based firmly on misuse of a corporate opportunity. On this Laskin J. said[6]:

"An examination of the case-law ... shows the pervasiveness of a strict ethic in this area of the law. In my opinion this ethic disqualifies a director or senior officer from usurping for himself or diverting to another person or company with whom or with which he is associated a maturing business opportunity which his company is actively pursuing[7]; he is also precluded from so acting even after his resignation where the resignation may fairly be said to be prompted or influenced by a wish to acquire for himself the opportunity sought by the company, or where it was his position with the company rather than a fresh initiative which led him to the opportunity which he later acquired."

It seems, however, that he would have favoured a flexibility, greater than English case law allows, when testing the conduct of directors against "the general standards of loyalty, good faith and the avoidance of a conflict of duty and self-interest."[8]

In the third case, *Boardman v. Phipps*,[9] the two defendants were not company directors but a trustee and the solicitor to the trust who had acted as agents of the trustees in relation to a company in which the trust had a substantial but minority shareholding that was not proving a satisfactory investment. They eventually decided that the best course would be to try to obtain control of the company by making a take-over bid for the other shares and, if that was successful, then to make a capital distribution. As there were obvious difficulties in the trustees using the trust fund in bidding, they obtained, as they thought, the informal consent of all the trustees and beneficiaries to bid on their own behalf and at their own expense. Unfortunately they did not, as the court held, adequately explain

[5] At p. 453.
[6] (1973) 40 D.L.R. (3d) at 382.
[7] But *quaere* whether the company need be "actively pursuing" it. The test rather seems to be whether the company has not decided whether or not the company shall pursue it and, if not, that the director may: see below.
[8] At p. 391, where he enumerated some of the many factors which in his view were relevant. *cf.* Gareth Jones in (1968) 84 L.Q.R. 472 who argues persuasively that fiduciaries should not be liable to account unless they have not acted honestly or they have been unjustly enriched. Contrast Beck in Zeigel (ed.) *Studies in Canadian Company Law*, Vol. II, Chap. 5.
[9] n.99 above.

their proposed course of action to the plaintiff, one of the beneficiaries. After long and skilful negotiations with the other shareholders they succeeded in acquiring their shares at prices between £3 and £4. 10s. per share (mainly the latter). Thereafter the company made distributions totalling £5. 17s. 6d. per share which still left each share worth, on asset value, more than £3 per share. Hence the trust, with 8,000 shares, did well; but the defendants, with some 22,000 shares, did even better—making a profit of over £75,000. It was held, following *Regal*, that they had to account to the plaintiff for a proportion of that profit corresponding to his fraction of the beneficial interest (8/15s.) in the trust fund.

However, and this is the interesting feature of the decision, it was also held that in taking the account the defendants were entitled to payment on a liberal scale for their work and skill but for which the profit would not have been made. But it seems that the courts will permit such an equitable allowance only in very exceptional circumstances. In *Guinness* v. *Saunders*[10] Mr. Ward contended that, if not entitled to retain the whole £5.2m, he should at least be entitled to some allowance for his undoubtedly valuable and skilful work. But on a variety of grounds[11] the courts rejected his plea; indeed Lord Goff expressly left open the question "whether any such allowance might ever be granted by a court of equity in the case of a director of a company as opposed to a trustee." To do so might "be said to involve interference by the court in the administration of the company's affairs . . . "[12]

One question which these decisions do not answer but which was posed in *Regal*, is: Does the equitable principle involve "the proposition that, if the directors bona fide decide not to invest their company's funds in some proposed investment, a director who thereafter embarks his own money therein is accountable for any profits he may derive therefrom?"[13] The one circumstance in which it is clear that there is no such liability is where the company has duly authorised the act of the director; *i.e.* has not merely decided that the company shall not avail itself of the information or opportunity but also decided that the director may. However, although that authority could be conferred by the board on an officer of the company who is

10 [1990] 2 A.C. 663, H.L.: see p. 562 n. 65 above.
11 The C.A. because it could have no application when the director had become a constructive trustee of the company's property (see [1988] 1 W.L.R. at 870H–871a); Lord Templeman because "the law cannot, and equity will not, amend the articles of Guinness. The court is not entitled to usurp the functions conferred on the board by the articles" see [1990] 2 A.C. at 689); and Lord Goff because the jurisdiction to award an allowance should not be exercised if to do so would be to encourage fiduciaries to put themselves in a position where their duties conflicted with their interests, as Mr. Ward had done by "agreeing to provide his services in return for a substantial fee of the size of which was dependent upon the amount of a successful bid by Guinness." As Lord Goff pointed out, it was still open to the full board to pay Ward appropriate remuneration if it thought fit: see *ibia.* at pp. 701, 702.
12 *Ibid.* at p. 701.
13 *Per* Lord Russell (quoting Greene M.R.) at [1967] A.C. p. 152.

not a director,[14] the board cannot confer it on the directors themselves; only the general meeting, or the agreement of all the members entitled to vote, can do so. But suppose it is not all the directors who want to take advantage of the opportunity but only one (or some) of them. Can the board effectively authorise him to do so? There is powerful support from the Privy Council decision in *Queensland Mines Ltd.* v. *Hudson*,[15] for the view that it can. There, "the board of the company knew the facts, decided to renounce the company's interest … in the venture and assented to Mr. Hudson [the managing director] doing what he could with [it] at his own risk and for his own benefit."[16] It was held that, although the venture ultimately proved profitable, the managing director was not liable to account. This has been criticised on the ground that the decision should have been taken either by a completely independent board with Hudson playing no part or by the general meeting.[17] Normally, no doubt, that is correct but on the facts it seems an over-technical objection since the only members of the company were two companies, each represented on the board and fully aware of the company's "early interest in the venture and of the manner and circumstances of the company's escape."[18]

It is therefore submitted that if the board has taken a bona fide decision that the company should reject the opportunity on its merits, it may then permit one (or more) of its members to take it up.[19] If, however, that director has any intention to ask for permission he should declare his interest at the meeting and absent himself from the discussion of the matter. Failing that, the board's decision to consent should be submitted for ratification, after full disclosure of material facts, by a general meeting or by all the members entitled to attend and vote.

Suppose, however, that at the time of the directors' meeting the director had no intention of taking up the opportunity, but subsequently decided that he would like to do so. It is submitted that he cannot without full disclosure of all material facts (which may well be different from those at the time of the company's decision to

[14] *New Zealand Netherlands Society v. Kuys* [1973] 1 W.L.R. 1127 P.C. where an opportunity to publish a newspaper had come to the secretary of an incorporated society as a result of his position. With full knowledge of the facts the society, which initially provided some financial support, had agreed that it should be published by him beneficially and at his own risk.

[15] [1978] 52 A.L.J.R. 379, P.C. In this case, unlike *Regal, Coony, Canadian Aero* and *Boardman*, there had been a bona fida decision that the company should renounce the opportunity on its merits. In the other cases the opportunity was not taken up on the alleged, but dubious, ground that it was impossible for the company to do so.

[16] Lord Scarman at p. 403.

[17] (1979) 42 M.L.R. 711.

[18] Lord Scarman at p. 404.

[19] But, in such circumstances, a court is likely to take a deal of persuading that the board's decision to reject the opportunity was taken bona fide in the interests of the company rather than in that of their fellow director—especially if he has a powerful personality.

renounce) and that, if still a member of the board, he should play no part in its deliberations on the matter.

(e) Competing with the company. One of the most obvious examples of a situation which might be expected to give rise to a conflict between a director's interests and his duties is where he carries on or is associated with a business competing with that of the company. Certainly a fiduciary without the consent of his beneficiaries is normally strictly precluded from competing with them and this is specifically stated in the analogous field of partnership law.[20] Yet, strangely, it is by no means clear on the existing case law that a similar rule applies to directors of a company.[21] Indeed, it is generally stated that it does not, and there appears to be a definite, if inadequately reported, decision that a director cannot be restrained from acting as a director of a rival company.[22] And it has been said that "What he could do for a rival company he could, of course, do for himself."[23] This view is becoming increasingly impossible to support. It has been held that the duty of fidelity flowing from the relationship of master and servant may preclude the servant from engaging, even in his spare time, in work for a competitor,[24] notwithstanding that the servant's duty of fidelity imposes lesser obligations than the full duty of good faith owed by a director or other fiduciary agent. How then, can it be that a director can compete whereas a subordinate employee cannot? Moreover it has been recognised that one who is a director of two rival concerns is walking a tight-rope and at risk if he fails to deal fairly with both.[25]

In *Thomas Marshall (Exporters) Ltd.* v. *Guinle*[26] a managing director had specifically agreed in his service contract not to engage in any other business without the company's consent or to disclose confidential information. He was alleged to have done both and to have diverted the company's business to himself and, later, to have unilaterally repudiated the contract by resigning without notice. Megarry V.-C. held that on these facts he had breached his duties of fidelity and good faith and that the express obligations in his service contract survived his repudiation of that contract. Interim injunctions

---

[20] Partnership Act 1890, s.30.
[21] It clearly does not apply to members, even in a private company, for members, as such, are not fiduciaries, s.429.
[22] *London & Mashonaland Exploration Co.* v. *New Mashonaland Exploration Co.* [1891] W.N. 165, approved by Lord Blanesburgh in *Bell* v. *Lever Bros.* [1932] A.C. 161 at 195, H.L.
[23] *Per* Lord Blanesburgh, *ibid.*
[24] *Hivac Ltd.* v. *Park Royal Scientific Instruments Ltd.* [1946] Ch. 169, C.A. If correct it must apply to an executive director: see *Scottish Co-op Wholesale Society Ltd.* v. *Meyer* [1959] A.C. 324, H.L., *per* Lord Denning at p. 367.
[25] See, *per* Lord Denning in *Scottish Co-op Wholesale Society* v. *Meyer,* above, at pp. 366–368. This concerned an application under what is now s.459 (on which see Chap. 24 below) but Lord Denning obviously had doubts whether the *Mashonaland* case was still good law.
[26] [1978] 3 W.L.R. 116; [1978] I.C.R. 905.

were granted restraining him from dealing with the company's customers and from disclosing any confidential information or trade secrets. Because of the express agreement not to compete and because of his diversion of the company's business, this decision is less than a clear authority for the proposition that competing per se is a breach of duty. But it strongly suggests that it is, at any rate in the case of executive directors, and illustrates that it will almost inevitably lead to other breaches of duty.

In arguing that a director who carries on a business which competes with that of his company inevitably places himself in a position where his personal interest will conflict with his duty to the company it is not being contended that he will necessarily have breached his fiduciary duty; he will not if the company has consented so long as he observes his subjective duty to the company by subordinating his interests to those of the company. Nor is it being suggested that there is anything objectionable in his holding other directorships so long as all the companies have consented if their businesses compete. But in both cases consent is unlikely if he is a full-time executive director or if the extent of the competition is substantial. And even if the consent is given the director is likely to be faced with constant difficulties in avoiding breaches of his subjective duty of good faith to the company or companies concerned. He may be able to subordinate his personal interests to those of a single company but it is less easy to reconcile conflicting duties to more than one company.

STATUTORY INTERVENTIONS

Although the equitable principle has not been codified, there has been considerable statutory intervention regarding particular applications of it, notably in what are now sections 310 to 347 of the Act.

Section 310

Section 310[27] is the successor to section 205 of the 1948 Act. Prior thereto it had been generally accepted that provisions in articles might effectively exempt officers of the company from liability to it provided, at any rate, that the officers were not guilty of fraud or wilful default.[28] Now this section provides that "any provision, whether contained in a company's articles or in any contract with the company or otherwise,"[29] which purport to exempt any officer or

[27] Implementing a recommendation of the Greene Committee: Cmd. 2657, paras. 46 & 47.
[28] See *Re City Equitable Fire Insurance Co.* [1925] Ch. 407.
[29] It is not clear whether "or otherwise" relates to "with the company" or to "any provision." If to the latter it would seem to ban such provisions in members' or directors' resolutions.

auditor of a company from, or to indemnifying him against, "any liability which by virtue of any rule of law would otherwise attach to him in respect of any negligence, default, breach of duty or breach of trust of which he may be guilty in relation to the company" shall, except as provided in subsection (3),[30] be void.[31] On the face of it, this seems clearly to ban provisions in articles such as those which, as we have seen, purport to exempt directors from the most likely applications of the duty not to place themselves in a position in which their personal interests or duties to the company. But these provisions have continued to appear in Tables A 1948 and 1985 and, as such, must presumably be taken to be valid and effective—as, indeed, highly authoritative decisions have assumed.[32] How a provision, such as Table A 1985, article 85, can be reconciled with section 310 has led to a considerable volume of literature[33] but not to any explanation by the English courts until Vinelott J. wrestled with it in the recent case of *Movitex Ltd.* v. *Bulfield*.[34]

His explanation draws a distinction between (1) "the over-riding principle of equity" that "if a director places himself in a position in which his duty to the company conflicts with his personal interest or duty to another, the court will set aside the transaction without enquiring whether there was any breach of duty to the company" and (2) the director's "duty to promote the interests of [the company] and when the interests of [the company] conflicted with his own to prefer the interests of [the company]." While any proposed modification of (2) would infringe section 310, the shareholders of the company in formulating the articles can exclude or modify the application of (1) "the over-riding principle of equity." In doing so they do not exempt the director from, or from the consequences of, a breach of duty owed to the company."[35]

Earlier editions of this book[36] accepted that there was a distinction between (a) the over-riding principle that a director must not place himself in a conflicting position and (b) the director's subjective duty to act bona fide in the interests of the company. They also accepted that, seemingly, the former (but not the latter) could be excluded or modified by the articles. To that extent the views expressed were in accord with those of Vinelott J. (though, in contrast with his, they failed to offer any rational explanation of how that could be

30 See below pp. 574, 575.
31 s.310(1) and (2).
32 See, *e.g. Hely-Hutchinson* v. *Brayhead*, and *Guinness* v. *Saunders* above pp. 562–564.
33 See, in addition to the company law textbooks, Baker, [1975] J.B.L. 181; Birds (1976) 39 M.L.R. 394; Parkinson, [1981] J.B.L. 335; and Gregory (1982) 98 L.Q.R. 413.
34 [1988] B.C.L.C. 104.
35 *Ibid.* 120–121d.
36 4th ed. p. 601.

reconciled with section 310). But his conclusions go much further. If it be a fact that a director is under no *duty* not, without the company's consent, to place himself in a position where his interests conflict with his duty, then it presumably follows that, even if there is no contracting-out in the articles, the director's only duty is to declare his interest (with liability to a fine if he does not) under section 317 when it applies.[37] Hence, it would seem that if the director has placed himself in a position where a serious conflict is inevitable, the company will not be able immediately to dismiss him without liability to pay damages for breach of his service agreement if he has one. To avoid that liability it will have to wait until it can prove that the director has actually breached his duty to prefer the company's interests to those of himself or of others to whom he owes duties.[38] This seems an undesirable conclusion on policy grounds.

The fact is that at present it seems impossible to reconcile section 310 with exclusions of the "over-riding equitable principle" by articles such as articles 85 and 86 of Table A 1985 without doing violence to the section and producing undesirable results. A possible solution might be to translate those articles (appropriately amended) into sections of the Act itself and to amend section 310 so as to exclude from its ambit any transactions permitted under those sections. If section 317 was also amended to meet the criticisms made below[39] this would produce a result defensible on policy grounds.[40]

A further query that has arisen in relation to section 310 is whether subsections (1) and (2) apply only to exemptions and indemnifications from liability to the company or also to indemnifications by the company of liabilities incurred to third parties by an officer or auditor acting in relation to the company. The writer's view is that, reading the section as a whole[41] it is reasonably clear that they apply to the latter also; but some take the opposite view and it would be well to remove any doubt.

As a result of the 1989 Act, subsection (3) now provides, first that the section does not prevent a company from purchasing and maintaining for an officer or auditor insurance against any liability under subsections (1) and (2). This was inserted as a result of representations that public companies were finding it difficult to persuade people to accept directorships in the light of increased risks

---

[37] See above. It does not apply unless the conflict arises from a director's interest in "an actual or proposed contract, transaction or arrangement with the company": see below p. 576.

[38] But it is perhaps reconcilable with the dictum of Cranworth L.C. in *Aberdeen Ry.* v. *Blaikie* (see above) and would seem to be the position if there is a contracting-out in the articles wide enough to cover the type of conflict (but then at least there is a semblance of "consent" by the company).

[39] See below at pp. 576–578.

[40] And the result for which Birds contends (*loc. cit.* n. 33 above) but which cannot, surely, be achieved without statutory intervention.

[41] Particularly having regard to the new subs. (3) inserted by the 1989 Act: see below.

of liability (for example, for "wrongful trading" under subsection 214 of the Insolvency Act 1986) unless the companies could offer (and pay for) insurance against such risks.[42] If a company does take out such insurance that must be disclosed in the directors' annual report.[43]

Secondly, subsection (3) provides that the section does not prevent a company from indemnifying an officer or auditor against any liability incurred by him in defending any proceedings (civil or criminal) in which judgment is given in his favour or he is acquitted, or if the court grants him relief under section 144(3) or (4)[44] or under section 727.[45]

Enforcement of Fair Dealing

Part X of the Act contains sections, most of which are derived from those in the 1980 Act, designed to render more effective the "enforcement of fair dealing by directors."[46] This it does in three ways. First, an increased number of transactions with directors are prohibited outright; secondly, certain transactions with directors require the prior approval of the general meeting; and thirdly, increased disclosure is required of transactions undertaken with or by the directors. In general, the sections apply only to directors (not to other officers) but, as so often, "directors" includes "shadow directors," except that, for the purposes of most of the sections[47] in Part X, "a body corporate is not to be treated as a shadow director of any of its subsidiary companies *by reason only*[48] that the directors of the subsidiary are accustomed to act in accordance with its directions or instructions."[49]

(a) Tax-free emoluments. Section 311 makes it unlawful for a company to pay remuneration to a director (whether as a director or otherwise) free of income tax or varying according to his income tax or his tax rate. Apart from the difficulty of calculating precisely what

[42] This is, to some extent, beneficial to the companies since without insurance the errant directors are less likely to be worth powder-and-shot. The case for allowing companies to insure their auditors is less obvious, for auditors will be covered by their own professional indemnity insurance, the cost of which will be indirectly borne by their clients out of the fees charged. If two rival insurance companies cover the risk it may make life more difficult for auditors.
[43] Sched. 7, para. 5A, inserted by s.137(2) of the 1989 Act.
[44] See Chap. 9 at p. 214 n. 5 above.
[45] The court's general power to grant relief to officers or auditors who have acted honestly and reasonably and ought fairly to be excused.
[46] The words of the heading of Part X.
[47] *i.e.* ss.319, 320-322 and 330-346.
[48] Itals supplied. This wording implies that the parent company could be a shadow director of the subsidiary if there were other reasons. But it is difficult to see how, since "shadow director" is defined as "a person in accordance with whose directions or instructions the directors of the company are accustomed to act" (s.741(2)). Hence, unless to directors are so accustomed a person cannot be a shadow director.
[49] s.741(3).

the company would be liable to pay,[50] a provision for such payments is objectionable since what appeared to be a modest remuneration could prove to be exorbitant. Hence any provision for such a payment takes effect as if the net sum for which it purports to provide was a gross sum subject to income tax.[51]

Sections 312–316 relate to payments to directors, ostensibly as compensation for loss of office, on the occasion of a transfer of undertakings or a take-over. They are dealt with in Chapter 27.[52]

(b) Declarations of interest. Section 317, relating to declarations of interests, has already been referred to more than once in this chapter,[53] but it needs to be looked at in greater detail, if only to indicate its inadequacies.

Section 317(1) provides that it is the duty of a director, who is in any way, whether directly or indirectly, interested in a contract or proposed contract with the company, to declare the nature of his interest at a meeting of the directors of the company. This subsection refers only to "contracts" and, moreover, to contracts "with the company." Hence, on its own, it covers only one of the many situations in which a director may have an interest conflicting with that of the company. However, as a result originally of the 1980 Act, it has been widened considerably by what are now subsections (5) and (6). The former provides that a reference in the section to a "contract" includes "any transaction or arrangement (whether or not a contract) made or entered into on or after 22nd December 1980." The latter adds that for the purposes of the section a transaction described in section 330[54] made by a company for a director or a "connected person"[55] of that director shall be treated (whether or not it is prohibited by section 330) as a transaction or arrangement in which the director is interested.[56] Accordingly a declaration of interest is now required more often. But the section still does not apply to all conflict situations. It applies only to interests in transactions or proposed transactions *with* the company and to

[50] It would depend on the precise terms of the provision, his other income and his family situation and in calculating his taxable income the net sum would have to be grossed-up since the benefit he received by having it paid net of tax would be a taxable benefit.
[51] Which means that his remuneration would probably be less than it would have been had he not tried it on.
[52] At pp. 738–741 below.
[53] Particularly in connection with its inter-relationship with provisions in the articles enabling directors to be interested in transactions notwithstanding the equitable principle: see pp. 561–564 above.
[54] The effect of that section is dealt with below at pp. 582, 583.
[55] As defined in s.346.
[56] Accordingly in this book when citing or summarising the provisions of s.317, "transactions" has been substituted for "contracts."

transactions described in section 330 that are *by* the company. It would not apply, for example, to the use of a corporate opportunity or of corporate information which is not, or has not reached the stage of becoming a transaction or proposed transaction with the company.

All that subsection (1) requires is a declaration at a meeting of directors of "the nature of" the director's interest (not of all material facts or even of the extent of his interest). On the other hand, it appears to require a declaration even if the extent of the interest is so minimal as to be immaterial. However, if the company has an article corresponding to article 85 of Table A 1985 a director will be permitted to have personal interests in company transactions but only "subject to the provisions of the Act and provided that he has disclosed to the directors the nature and extent of any material interest of his." The result appears to be that he will then have to comply with section 317 and also to disclose to the board the extent of his interest if material.

Section 317(2) provides that in the case of a proposed transaction the declaration shall be made at the meeting of the directors at which the question of entering into the transaction is first taken into consideration or, if the director was not at that meeting, at the next meeting held after he became so interested. It has often been assumed[57] that the effect of this is that a declaration of interest is required only if the transaction is one that is "taken into consideration by the directors"—which, of course, is unlikely except in the case of major transactions. But that view is thought to be mistaken. The duty imposed by subsection (1) is not so qualified. And subsection (2) goes on to say that, in a case where the director becomes interested in a transaction after it is made, the declaration shall be made at the first meeting of the directors after he becomes interested—again without any reference to whether the transaction has been, or is to be, "taken into consideration by the directors." Hence it is thought that a declaration is required in the case of all relevant transactions whether or not they would otherwise come before the board.

However, subsection (3) provides an avenue which directors can take to protect themselves from breaching the statutory duty. It provides that a general notice given to the directors of the company by a director to the effect:

(a) that he is a member of a specified company or firm and is to be regarded as interested in any transaction after the date of the notice with that company or firm, or;

---

[57] *e.g.* in earlier editions of this book and in the Report of the Jenkins Committee which made recommendations accordingly, Cmnd. 1949, paras. 95 and 99(c).

(b) that he is to be regarded as interested in any transaction after the date of the notice with a specified person who is "connected" with him within the meaning of section 346,[58]

is deemed to be a sufficient declaration of interest.

Under subsection (4) that is so only if notice is given at a meeting of the directors or the director takes reasonable steps to ensure that it is brought up and read at the next directors' meeting. Even so there is an undoubted weakness.[59] If all that the director needs to do is to declare that he is a member of another company and that suffices in respect of all subsequent transactions, he will not have to add, if that be the case, then or subsequently, that, say, he is also a director whose remuneration varies with the company's annual profits. Nor, it seems, if at the time of the notice he held only 100 shares and mentioned that in the notice, would he have to give notice if he increased his holdings even if that gave him a controlling interest.

Of the remaining subsections it is only necessary to mention that subsection (8) applies the section to shadow directors with appropriate adjustments to the method of making the declaration of interest and that subsection (9) states that the section does not derogate from any rule of law restricting directors from having an interest in transactions with the company.

(c) **Restraints on directors' remuneration.** Sections 318 and 319 deal with the obvious openings for abuse flowing from the fact that whereas the members of the company have some control over directors' fees they had, until recently, none over the total emoluments paid to a director in the form of salaries, bonuses, contributions to pension schemes and compensation for loss of office.[60] Members could, of course, glean some information from the annual accounts[61] but there was precious little they could do about it beyond complaining at the AGM that it was grossly excessive in total and that the emoluments of the chairman and chief executive were positively obscene. In effect, the directors could vote themselves long-term service agreements in the case of executive directors, and generous contracts for consulting and similar services in the case of non-executives. Now some restraints are imposed by these two

---

[58] In effect, members of his immediate family and companies which he or they control.
[59] A weakness not to be found in art. 86(a) of Table A 1985. And art. 86(b) sensibly provides, as s.317 does not, that an interest of which a director has no knowledge and of which it is unreasonable to expect him to have knowledge, shall not be treated as an interest of his. At present we have a defective s.317, improved by an optional Table A if companies choose to adopt it; not a satisfactory solution.
[60] Except when ss.312–315 apply, on which see Chap. 27 at pp. 738–741 below.
[61] Chap.17 above at p. 460.

sections on the liberality with which directors assess the value of each other's services.

Section 318 requires every company to keep a copy of the service agreement (but not of an agreement for services) of each director[62] of the company or its subsidiary or a memorandum of its terms if the agreement is not in writing.[63] The copy or memorandum must be kept either at the registered office, or at the place where its register of members is kept, or at its principal place of business if that is situated in that part of Great Britain in which the company is registered.[64] All such copies and memoranda must be kept at the same place[65] and the company must notify the Registrar of the place where they are kept.[66] The copies and memoranda must be open to inspection by any member of the company without charge.[67] If inspection is refused the court may order an immediate inspection.[68] In practice not much use is made of the rights of inspection conferred by this section even in the case of public companies.[69] More use would no doubt be made of it if the right to inspect were extended from members to employees, to whose interests the directors are required to have regard in the exercise of their duties to the company[70]; but any such proposal would undoubtedly cause howls of protest as a gross breach of confidentiality.

More effective, however, is section 319. This prohibits any term whereby any director is to be employed, whether under a contract of service *or for services*,[71] which may last for more than 5 years without being terminable[72] by the company or terminable only in specified circumstances,[73] unless the term is first approved by a resolution of the company in general meeting.[74] If approval is sought, a written memorandum of the proposed agreement has to be

---

[62] Including a shadow director.
[63] s.318(1). This does not apply if the contract requires the director to work wholly or mainly outside the U.K. but the company must then keep instead a memorandum giving the director's name and the provisions of the contract relating to its duration: s.318(5). There is also an exception for contracts having less than 12 months to run: s.318(11).
[64] s.318(3).
[65] s.318(2).
[66] s.318(4).
[67] s.318(7).
[68] s.318(9). And the company and every officer in default are liable to fines for any contravention of the section: s.318(8).
[69] In the case of small private companies there will probably not be any prior agreements regarding emoluments: the member-directors will just decide from time to time how much to pay themselves.
[70] s.309, above p. 555.
[71] s.319(7)(*a*): *itals* supplied.
[72] *i.e.* terminable without that being a breach of contract: see Chap. 7 at pp. 155-158 above.
[73] s.319(1) and (2). In the case of a director of a holding company it applies to any employment within the group (as defined in s.319(7)(*b*) and "director" includes a shadow director (s.319(7)) other than the holding company: s.741(3).
[74] s.319(3). But note the restriction in s.319(4) on the types of "company" to which it applies and that it does not apply to a wholly-owned subsidiary—when it would be farcical.

made available for inspection without charge by members at the company's registered office during a period of not less than 15 days before the meeting and at the meeting itself.[75] If a term, prohibited in the absence of approval in general meeting, is included in the agreement in contravention of the section, the term is void to the extent that it contravenes the section and the agreement is terminable at any time by reasonable notice by the company.[76]

Since directors of public companies have a rooted antipathy to exposing their service agreements to debate and possible rejection by a general meeting of the members, this has largely eradicated long-term service agreements not determinable by the company until the directors reach retirement age or later. Legal ingenuity has, however, devised agreements, popularly known as "5 year rollers," which are not caught by the section but which ensure that when and if they are terminated by the company, the agreement will have about five years to run.

(d) Substantial property transactions. Sections 320–322 similarly require substantial property transactions with directors to be approved in advance by the company in general meetings. Under section 320(1), except as provided in section 321, a company is prohibited from entering into any arrangement whereby a director[77] of the company or its holding company, or a person connected with[78] such a director, is to acquire[79] from the company or the company is to acquire from any such person, one or more non-cash assets[80] "of the requisite value," unless the arrangement is first approved by a resolution of the company in general meeting and, if the director or connected person is a director of the holding company, by a resolution in general meeting of that company. Under subsection (2) the present "requisite value," is anything exceeding £100,000 or 10 per cent. of the company's net assets if more than £2,000.[81]

To the need for approval in general meetings there are exceptions in section 321. The only ones needing mention[82] are: (a) inter-group transfers when the property is to be acquired by a holding company

---

[75] s.319(5). Although only members are entitled to inspect it (and are not entitled to take copies) it may be difficult to prevent its salient points being leaked to and published by the press.

[76] s.319(6).

[77] Again including a shadow director.

[78] Defined in s.346.

[79] Defined in s.739(2) as including the creation or extinction of an estate or interest in, or right over, any property and the discharge of any person's liability other than for a liquidated sum.

[80] Defined in s.739(1) as meaning "any property or interest in property other than cash."

[81] The original figures were doubled by 1990 S.I. No.1393 made under s.345. The value of the net assets is to be determined by the latest accounts or, if none have been laid, by reference to its called-up share capital: s.320(2).

[82] s.321(1) corresponds to s.319(4) mentioned in n. 74 above.

from one of its wholly-owned subsidiaries, or vice-versa, or by one wholly-owned subsidiary from another wholly-owned subsidiary of that holding company,[83] and (b) arrangements entered into by a company which is being wound up otherwise than by a members' voluntary winding up.[84]

Section 322 in effect provides that an arrangement which contravenes section 320, or any transaction entered into in pursuance of it, is to be treated much as it would be under the general equitable principle when there has been no modification of that principle by provisions in the company's articles; *i.e.* it is voidable at the instance of the company unless it is too late to avoid it[85] or the arrangement has been affirmed within a reasonable time by a general meeting.[86]

Under subsection (3) the other party and any director of the company who authorised the arrangement, or any transaction in pursuance of it, is liable to account to the company for any gain which he has made, and (jointly and severally with any others liable under the section) is also liable to indemnify the company from any loss resulting from the arrangement or transaction. Subsection (3) is without prejudice to any liability imposed otherwise than under it and the liability arises whether or not the arrangement or transaction has been avoided in pursuance of subsection (1).[87] However, under subsection (2), if the company has been indemnified, pursuant to subsection (3), for the loss or damage suffered by it, it cannot subsequently avoid the contract even though *restitutio in integrum* is still possible.[88]

It will be noted that the section does not preclude the director from voting as a member at a general meeting to approve or affirm. But, in the case of a listed company, The Stock Exchange may require him not to.[89]

Section 322A was inserted by the 1989 Act as a result of its reforms of the law relating to ultra vires. As such it has already been dealt with in Chapter 8.[90] Here all that is necessary is a reminder that it relates to transactions (cash or non-cash) in which the parties include the company and a director of the company or its holding company

83 s.321(2)(a).
84 s.321(2)(b), *i.e.* in a winding up in which the liquidator will not have been appointed by the members on the nomination of the directors.
85 s.322(1) and (2)(a) and (b).
86 s.322(2)(c). When the director is concerned as director of the holding company affirmation is required of both a general meeting of the company party to the transaction and a general meeting of its holding company.
87 s.322(4).
88 And if an arrangement contravening s.320 has been entered into with a person connected with a director, the director is not liable under subs. (3) if he shows that he took all reasonable steps to secure the company's compliance with the section: s.322(5). Nor is the connected person, or another director who authorised the arrangement or transaction, if he shows that, at the time the arrangement was made, he did not know the relevant circumstance constituting the contravention: s.322(6).
89 The *Yellow Book*, Section 6, Chapter 1, para. 7.2 (last sub-para.).
90 At pp. 181, 182.

or a person connected with such a director or a company with which the director is associated.[91] If the transaction exceeds the powers conferred on the board by the company's constitution, the transaction is voidable at the instance of the company and the director[92] must account for his gains—essentially as under section 322.

Sections 323–329 are left until we turn to to the question of insider dealing in Chapter 23.[93] However, it should here be pointed out that they play a wider role in that, by requiring the holdings of, and dealings in, the securities of the company by its directors or their families, they may afford valuable information in judging the extent to which the directors are fulfilling their duty to subordinate their personal interests to that of the company.

(e) Loans, quasi-loans and credit transactions. Restraints on making loans to directors date back to the 1948 Act but sections 330–344 extend them, especially in relation to public companies.

Subject to the exceptions in sections 332–338,[94] section 330(2) and (3) prohibit a company from making a loan to a director of it or of its holding company or from entering into any guarantee[95] or providing any security in connection with a loan made by any person to such a director.[96] Further, a "relevant company," (*i.e.* any company which is part of a group which contains a public company[97]) is prohibited from:

(a) making what the Act calls a "quasi-loan,"[98] to a director of the company or of its holding company;

(b) making a loan or quasi-loan to a person connected with such a director; or

(c) entering into any guarantee or providing any security in connection with a loan or quasi-loan made by any other person to such a director or connected person.[99]

The object of extending the prohibition, so far as relevant companies are concerned, is to catch transactions resulting in debts to the company which are not technically "loans." Essentially, quasi-loans are transactions, to which the company is a party, resulting in a

91 "Connected" and "associated" are defined in s.346.
92 Or connected or associated person.
93 At pp. 609–613.
94 s.330(1).
95 Which includes an indemnity: s.331(2).
96 s.330(2).
97 s.331(6) which defines "relevant company" rather more elaborately than in the text.
98 Defined, in a complicated fashion, in s.331(3) which describes the company as "the creditor," and the director or his connected person as "the borrower." The text attempts to describe the effect of the statutory definitions in terms more immediately intelligible. This, it is hoped, renders it unnecessary, in relation to either quasi-loans or credit transactions, to go into the intricacies of s.331(9).
99 s.330(3).

director or his connected person obtaining some financial benefit for which he is liable to make reimbursement to the company. If, for example, a public company agrees that its managing director may at all times retain £50,000 of the company's money to provide a "float" out of which to meet expenses of world-wide trips on the company's business (instead of his having to reclaim expenses from the company) that will be an unlawful quasi-loan.[1]

Section 330(4) similarly prohibits a company from entering into a "credit transaction" with such director or his connected person or from guaranteeing or providing security in connection with a credit transaction with him by any other person. A credit transaction is one under which the director or his connected person is supplied with goods or sold land under a hire-purchase agreement or conditional sale agreement; or in which land or goods are let or hired out to him in return for periodical payments, or land, goods or services are supplied to him on the understanding that full payment is to be deferred.[2]

Section 330(6) prohibits the company from arranging the assignment to it, or the assumption by it, of any rights, obligations or liabilities of a transaction which, if entered into by the company, would have contravened subsection (2), (3) or (4). Nor, under section 330(7), may a company take part in any arrangement whereby another person enters into a transaction which, if it had been entered into by the company, would have contravened section 330(2), (3), (4) or (6), and the other person pursuant to the arrangement obtains any benefit from the company or group.

Finally, section 330(5) provides that the purpose of sections 330-346 "director" includes a shadow director.[3]

To each of these prohibitions, sections 332-338 provide certain exceptions. In a book of this sort it is not necessary to go into detail. It suffices to say that their general effect is to exclude certain transactions which are small,[4] short-term,[5] inter-group,[6] or in the ordinary course of the company's business and on its normal terms,[7] but provided, in most cases, that the aggregate amount or value of that transaction and of that outstanding on earlier such transactions (the "relevant amounts") does not exceed a prescribed figure.[8]

---

[1] But it would not have been unlawful if the float had been more modest and s.337 (below) had been complied with.
[2] s.331(7).
[3] But, as in the following sections, excluding a holding company: s.741(3).
[4] See s.334 as regards small loans.
[5] See s.332 as regards short-term quasi-loans.
[6] See s.333 as regards inter-group loans and s.336 as regards transactions for the benefit of the holding company.
[7] See s.335 and, as regards money-lending companies, s.338.
[8] The figures in the original version of the Act have been at least doubled (to account for inflation) either by the 1989 Act or by S.I. 1990 No. 1393 and are at the time of writing: in ss.332(1) and 334(1), £5,000; in s.335(1), £10,000; in s.337(3), £20,000; and in s.340(7), £100,000.

Section 339 prescribes how the "relevant amounts" are to be ascertained and section 340 how the "value" of transactions is to be determined.

Specific mention should, however, be made of section 337. This says that a company is not prohibited by section 330 "from doing anything to provide a director with funds to meet expenditure incurred or to be incurred by him for the purposes of the company or for the purpose of enabling him properly to perform his duties as an officer of the company."[9] But it then severely limits that concession by requiring either that prior approval of the general meeting is obtained after disclosure of the matters stated in subsection (3)[10]; or, if such approval is not given at or before the next AGM, that the funds will be repaid within six months after the AGM. Moreover, a relevant company must not enter into any such transactions if the aggregate of the relevant amounts exceeds £20,000.[11] Hence, there is now a curb on the abuses, disclosed in several Inspectors' reports, whereby directors draw freely on the company's funds, making it difficult to determine at any time precisely what is the extent of their indebtedness to the company.

Under section 341, breaches of section 330 give rise to civil remedies[12] similar to those under section 322 (for breaches of section 320) and under section 322A. There are also criminal penalties under section 342.

Generally, the types of transaction mentioned in section 330 which are lawfully undertaken under the exceptions will require to be disclosed in the annual accounts.[13] But the accounts of authorised banking institutions or their holding companies, prepared in accordance with Schedule 9, are not required to do so. However, such a company must, by section 343, maintain a register of such transactions[14] and make available, at its registered office for at least 15 days before the AGM, and at the AGM, a statement containing particulars of such transactions during the financial year.[15] This statement must have been examined and reported on by the auditors and their report must be annexed and must state whether in their opinion it contains the particulars required. If, in their opinion, it does not, they must include in their report a statement of those

9 s.337(1). Nor does it "prohibit a company from doing anything to enable a director to avoid incurring such expenditure": s.337(2). But most such "things," (*e.g.* supplying him with a company car) would not normally be transactions caught by s.330.
10 *i.e.* the purpose of the expenditure, the amount provided by the company and the extent of the company's liability under any connected transaction: s.337(4).
11 s.337(3).
12 The company is entitled to avoid the transaction, to indemnity against loss, and to recovery of profits made by the director or his connected person.
13 Under Sched. 6 of the Act.
14 s.343(1), (2) & (3).
15 s.343(4) & (5).

particulars so far as they reasonably can.[16] Under section 344, section 343 is disapplied in relation to transactions for a person who, at no time during the financial year, owed the company more than £2,000 in respect of all such transactions.[17]

The unfair prejudice remedy. Before leaving the statutory interventions, mention must again be made to sections 459–461[18] which afford members a remedy in the event of conduct of the company which is unfairly prejudicial to the interests of its members generally or of some part of its members. This remedy is dealt with more fully in Chapter 24,[19] below, but deserves mention here because, though it does not directly affect the duties of directors, it does so indirectly.[20]

COMMON LAW DUTIES OF CARE AND SKILL

This subject can be disposed of briefly, for there is a striking contrast between the directors' heavy duties of loyalty and good faith and their light obligations of skill and diligence. Here, as already pointed out,[21] the trustee analogy breaks down, for what is required of a cautious trustee is somewhat different from what an enterprising director needs to display. The law might, no doubt, have demanded of directors a degree of diligence comparable to that of trustees—a high degree particularly where they are paid.[22] But the law cannot be too far in advance of public opinion, and public opinion has come to recognise that non-executive directorships are often little more than sinecures, requiring, at the most, attendance at occasional board meetings. But if, in this respect, directors are not trustees they are certainly agents. Does the law of agency offer a guide? In agency it is customary to draw a distinction between those exercising a particular trade or profession, who must display a degree of diligence and skill comparable with that of reasonably competent and conscientious members of that trade or profession,[23] and other agents who are

---

[16] s.343(6) and (7).

[17] s.344(1). And s.343(4) and (5) do not apply to a bank which is a wholly owned subsidiary of a U.K. company: s.344(2).

[18] As amended by the 1989 Act.

[19] At pp. 662 *et seq.*

[20] If unfair prejudice is established, the order of the court is likely to be detrimental to some or all of the directors who have caused or allowed the company so to conduct itself. In effect, the sections impose an additional "duty," supplementing the fiduciary duties, *i.e.* to ensure that the company's affairs are not conducted in a manner unfairly prejudicial to any of the members.

[21] Above pp. 550, 551.

[22] *National Trustees Co. of Australasia v. General Finance Co. of Australasia* [1905] A.C. 373, P.C.; *Re Windsor Steam Coal Co.* [1929] 1 Ch. 151, C.A.

[23] As in the case of auditors: see Chap. 18 at pp. 490 *et seq.* above.

merely expected to display such skill as they possess and such diligence as would be displayed by a reasonable man in the circumstances.

Is a directorship a profession within the meaning of this distinction? In favour of this view it may be argued that a directorship is a recognised office of profit. But, once again, the courts have had to face the facts, and the facts are that the possession of a title is sometimes regarded as a greater qualification for office than any amount of business acumen and drive, and that the ordinary part-time non-executive director is only expected to display such skill (if any) as he happens to possess, and such attention to duty as he can. The position differs radically with holders of other offices under the company. Full-time employees are obviously bound to devote their whole time and attention (during usual office hours) to the business of the company, and professionally qualified executive directors are expected to display the normal skill of members of their professions. Full-time executive directors are also expected to display similar diligence but it is not yet clear whether there is, so far as they are concerned, any objective standard of *skill* to which they must measure up. The evolution of a class of company managers is one of the distinctive features of the present epoch, but the courts hardly seem prepared to recognise that it has attained professional status and standards.[24]

The judges have faced a further difficulty. Whereas their training and experience may make them well equipped to adjudicate on questions of loyalty and good faith, they move with less assurance among complicated problems of business administration. Hence, they display an understandable reluctance to interfere with the directors' business judgment—a reluctance of which many examples will be found throughout the whole area of company law.[25] Perhaps, too, they are conscious of the possible unfairness of attempting to substitute their hindsight for the directors' foresight, and are therefore unwilling to condemn directors even though events have proved them wrong.

Re City Equitable Fire Insurance Co.[26] reduced the effect of the case law to the following three propositions and, nearly 50 years later, they still appear fairly to reflect the position at common law.

[24] Note the speeches of the Law Lords in *Holdsworth & Co. v. Caddies* [1955] 1 W.L.R. 352 (also reported 1955 S.C., H.L., 27), H.L. Sc. refusing to recognise the "conception of a stratification of a position as managing director," to use the phrase of Lord Kilmuir L.C. p. 356.

[25] "There is no appeal on merits from management decisions to courts of law; nor will courts of law assume to act as a kind of supervisory board over decisions within the powers of management honestly arrived at": *Howard Smith Ltd.* v. *Ampol Ltd.* [1974] A.C. 821, P.C. at 832.

[26] [1925] Ch. 407 at 428 *et seq.* The case went to appeal only in respect of the auditor's liability and it is only in that respect that the judgment can technically be said to have been upheld by the C.A.

1. *A director need not exhibit in the performance of his duties a greater degree of skill than may reasonably be expected from a person of his knowledge and experience.*

This proposition lays down the standard of skill to be exhibited in such actions as the director undertakes. It prescribes a test which is partly objective (the standard of the reasonable man), and partly subjective (the reasonable man is deemed to have the knowledge and experience of the particular individual).

2. *A director is not bound to give continuous attention to the affairs of his company. His duties are of an intermittent nature to be performed at periodical board meetings, and at meetings of any committee of the board upon which he happens to be placed. He is not, however, bound to attend all such meetings, though he ought to attend whenever in the circumstances he is reasonably able to do so.*

Whereas, in the present stage of legal development, proposition 1 probably applies equally to managing directors, this second proposition clearly does not. It is directed solely to holders of non-executive directorships from whom nothing more is expected than attendance at meetings. And though it is said that they ought to attend these meetings whenever they can, the cases suggest that this is little more than a pious hope. [27] As in other walks of life, if anything is going wrong there are great advantages in "not being there." The director who stays away runs the risk of not being reappointed when he next comes up for re-election, but little risk of liability for what is done in his absence. Here, as throughout this branch of the law, questions of causation are of paramount importance; if a director is party to a decision to take a particular course of action it may be possible to show that this led to loss by the company, [28] but it will be next to impossible to show that his laziness was the cause of the damage or that the action would have been different had he attended. [29]

However, it may be that today the courts would require a degree of diligence somewhat greater than that suggested in the old

[27] In *Re Denham & Co.* (1883) 25 Ch.D. 752, the director had not attended any meetings for four years, and, in *The Marquis of Bute's Case (Re Cardiff Savings Bank)* [1892] 2 Ch. 100) a trustee of a savings bank had not attended for even longer (but there were 50 trustees); each escaped liability. In the latter case Stirling J. said (p. 109): "Neglect or omission to attend meetings is not, in my opinion, the same thing as neglect or omission of a duty which ought to be performed at those meetings."

[28] Observe how, in the *City Equitable* case, specific losses were pleaded as flowing from particular acts or omissions. A director who attends board meetings and rubber-stamps the chairman's recommendations runs a far greater risk than one who does not attend at all: see *Selangor United Rubber Estates Ltd. v. Cradock (No. 3)* [1968] 1 W.L.R. 1555 at 1614.

[29] This is well brought out in the opinion of Learned Hand J. in the American case of *Barnes v. Andrews* (1924) 298 Fed. 614.

decisions. Certainly, today most public companies expect all their directors to do some homework to familiarise themselves with the company's operations and also expect non-executive directors to play an active role on their internal audit committees.

3. *In respect of all duties that, having regard to the exigencies of business and the articles of association, may properly be left to some other official, a director is, in the absence of grounds for suspicion, justified in trusting that official to perform such duties honestly.*

Since directors as such are not required to possess any particular accomplishments and since the successful running of a business requires a measure of skill, ignorant directors must obviously rely on expert officials. These officials are the agents and servants of the company, not of the directors. Hence, the directors are not responsible vicariously for their misdeeds. If a director is to be made liable, it can only be on the basis of his personal negligence,[30] and, as proposition 3[31] recognises, it is not negligent to trust an employee whose previous conduct has given no ground for suspicion. Duties must not once again the particular circumstances are relevant. Duties must not be entrusted to an obviously inappropriate or unqualified official; the handling of the investments of a finance company must not be left to the office boy. One of the grounds on which the *City Equitable* directors were held to have broken their duties was that they had allowed the managing director to usurp functions not delegated to him, and had permitted the company's stockbrokers to retain large sums without security in a manner more appropriate to bankers than to brokers.

Although the *City Equitable* directors were held to have fallen short even of these somewhat lowly standards,[32] they escaped because of a provision in the articles absolving them from liability other than for wilful default. Now Section 310 specifically bans such

---

[30] This may change. The proposed Fifth Company Law Directive (and the proposed Statute for a European Company) provides at present that all members of the board shall be jointly and severally liable to compensate the company for loss sustained as a result of breach of duty by any one of them but so that a director may be exonerated if he proves that no fault is attributable to him personally: art. 14, paras. 2 & 3.

[31] Which is fully supported by the decision of the H.L. in *Dovey v. Cory* [1901] A.C. 477, H.L.

[32] Romer J. also thought that the auditor had been negligent but this question was left open by the C.A. In what seems to be the only reported English case in recent years in which directors have been held liable for negligence (in contrast with the spate of cases on auditors' liability) three directors (one executive and two non-executive) all of whom had considerable accountancy and business experience and two of whom were chartered accountants, were held liable: *Dorchester Finance Co. v. Stebbings*, decided in 1977 but not reported until [1989] BCLC 498. The company was a wholly-owned subsidiary, thus limiting the role which non-executive directors could perform, but unfortunately for them what they had done was to turn up at the office from time to time to sign blank cheques on the company's accounts.

provisions exempting from negligence.[33] However, it has been made clear, as a result of the amendment by the 1989 Act to section 310(3), that it does not prohibit the company from purchasing and maintaining insurance indemnifying him against liability for negligence.[34]

Statutory interventions

Although the common law duties of care and skill may have stagnated here too there have been statutory interventions which indirectly extend the ambit of such duties. Particularly important are section 214 of the Insolvency Act (on "wrongful trading")[35] and the provisions of the Company Directors Disqualification Act 1986.[36] Under the former a director who knew or ought to have known that there was no reasonable prospect of the company avoiding going into insolvent liquidation but nevertheless failed to take reasonable steps to minimise risk to its creditors and customers may find that his negligence leads to his being made liable to contribute to the company's assets. He may, in addition, be disqualified for a considerable period from acting as a director or manager of any company. These sanctions are more likely to encourage care and diligence than the possible liability for damages.

CONCLUSION

The foregoing description of the duties of directors has implied that their duties of loyalty and good faith are exceptionally strict and their duties of care, skill and diligence exceptionally lax. While that is generally true, it is something of an over-simplification. So long as directors act in good faith, which is not too much to ask of them, the general equitable principle, modified as it will be in practice by the articles, should not often weigh too heavily upon them; the specific statutory duties are probably more onerous than the common law and equitable ones. The common law duties of care, skill, and diligence are admittedly lax—but this is inevitable unless and until company directorship is recognised as a profession with professional standards.

There are, however, two major difficulties regarding enforcement of duties whether they be strict or lax. The first is that directors' duties apply to what they do as directors without prior consent or subsequent ratification by the company in general meeting. It is therefore important to see whether and to what extent those voting at

---

33 See pp. 572–575 above.
34 See pp. 574–575 above.
35 See Chap. 6 at pp. 110–115 above.
36 See Chap. 7 at pp. 144–147 above.

general meetings, which will include the directors if they are members, are subject then to comparable duties to subordinate their personal interest to those of the company. This is among the matters dealt with in the next chapter. The second difficulty is procedural. Duties are of little value unless they can be, and are, enforced. Hence, after a chapter (23) on Insider Dealings, the various means of doing so and how far they are effective are discussed in Chapters 24 and 25.

CHAPTER 22

MEMBERS' DUTIES

In the last chapter we saw that although directors or officers of the company may be acting within the powers conferred upon them by the company, they owe certain duties, notably of good faith, in the exercise of those powers. The present chapter discusses whether in any circumstances there are comparable duties on those connected with the company when not acting as directors or officers of it. They will, of course, be liable if they knowingly participate in a breach of "trust" by the director or officers.[1] Hence the controlling shareholders cannot with impunity install men of straw as dummy directors and use them to bleed the company. It will, however, be difficult to prove that in any particular transaction the directors have acted merely as puppets for others who have pulled the strings.[2] Those responsible for drafting the Acts seem to have toyed with the idea of shifting responsibility on to the shoulders of the true masters of the company's destiny since, as we have seen, for the purpose of a growing number of sections "director" includes a shadow director in accordance with whose directions or instructions the directors of a company are accustomed to act. There is, however, little evidence that this has achieved very much beyond making the banks more reluctant to support companies in financial difficulties lest the discipline that they would wish to impose on the directors might cause them to be regarded as shadow directors with potential liability for wrongful trading if the company goes into insolvent liquidation despite the support.

VOTING AS MEMBERS

Scattered throughout the reports are statements that members must exercise their votes "bona fide for the benefit of the company as a whole,"[3] a statement which suggests that they are subject to precisely the same basic principle as directors. But, it seems, this is highly misleading, and the decisions do not support any such rule as a

---

[1] Or without lawful excuse induce them to break any contractual duties which they owe the company: *Jasperson* v. *Dominion Tobacco Co*, [1923] A.C. 709, P.C.; *Torquay Hotel Co.* v. *Cousins* [1969] 2 Ch. 106, C.A.; *cf. Boulting* v. *A.C.T.A.T.* [1963] 2 Q.B. 606, C.A.

[2] That this is a serious problem is apparent from a number of Inspectors' Reports.

[3] The original source of this oft-repeated but misleading expression seems to be Lindley M.R. in *Allen* v. *Gold Reefs of W. Africa* [1900] 1 Ch. at 671.

591

universal principle. On the contrary, it has been repeatedly laid down that votes are proprietary rights, to the same extent as any other incidents of the shares, which the holder may exercise in his own selfish interests even if these are opposed to those of the company.[4] He may even bind himself by contract to vote or not to vote in a particular way and his contract may be enforced by injunction.[5]

In all these respects the position of the shareholder is in striking contrast with that of the director. If it were the case that the general meeting could only operate in a few residual matters reserved to it by the company's constitution[6] this would not be unduly serious. But, as we have seen,[7] the general meeting is regarded as having power to act in place of the board if for any reason the board cannot function. If, therefore, a proper quorum cannot be obtained at a directors' meeting or there is a deadlock on the board, the general meeting may act instead.[8] Furthermore, what would otherwise be a breach of the directors' duties may, as we have seen,[9] in some circumstances be authorised or ratified by the company in general meeting. This may be so although the transaction relates to the ordinary management of the company and is therefore primarily a matter for the board of directors.[10] As a result, the activities of general meetings may indirectly extend over the whole sphere of the company's operations, and ultimate control revert to shareholders who are free from duties of good faith to which the directors are subject.

What is more startling still is that the directors themselves, even though personally interested, can vote in their capacity of share-holders at that general meeting.[11] And this is so even as regards the transactions which, under Part X of the Act,[12] require the prior approval of the company in general meeting.[13] As a consequence, when the directors have *de facto* control they can, subject to what

[4] *North-West Transportation v. Beatty* (1887) 12 App.Cas. 589, P.C.; *Burland v. Earle* [1902] A.C. 83, P.C.; *Goodfellow v. Nelson Line* [1912] 2 Ch. 324.
[5] *Greenwell v. Porter* [1902] 1 Ch. 530; *Puddephatt v. Leith* [1916] 1 Ch. 200—in which a mandatory injunction was granted.
[6] See above, Chap. 21.
[7] *Ibid.*
[8] *Barron v. Potter* [1914] 1 Ch. 895; *Foster v. Foster* [1916] 1 Ch. 532; *Alexander Ward & Co. Ltd. v. Samyang Navigation Co. Ltd.* [1975] 1 W.L.R. 673, H.L. But see *Breckland Holdings Ltd. v. London & Suffolk Properties Ltd.* [1989] BCLC 100.
[9] See Chap. 21.
[10] *Irvine v. Union Bank of Australia* (1877) 2 App.Cas. 366, P.C.; *Grant v. UK Switchback Ry.* (1888) 40 Ch.D. 135, C.A.; *Hogg v. Cramphorn Ltd.* [1967] Ch. 254; *Bamford v. Bamford* [1970] Ch. 212, C.A.
[11] *N.W. Transportation Co. v. Beatty* (1887) 12 App.Cas. 589, P.C.; *Burland v. Earle* [1902] A.C. 83 at 93, P.C.; *Harris v. A. Harris Ltd.*, 1936 S.C. 183 (Sc.); *Baird v. Baird & Co.*, 1949 S.L.T. 368 (Sc.). And see the remarkable case of *Northern Counties Securities Ltd. v. Jackson & Steeple Ltd.* [1974] 1 W.L.R. 1133 where it was held that although, to comply with an undertaking given by the company to the court, the directors were bound to recommend the shareholders to vote for a resolution they, as shareholders, could vote against it if so minded.
[12] See Chap. 21 at pp. 579–581 above.
[13] For the rare statutory exceptions, see ss.164(5) and 174(2) under which a shareholder whose shares are to be purchased by the company must refrain from voting on the resolutions approving such a purchase: Chap. 9 at pp. 218 and 214 above.

follows, disregard their fiduciary duties at their pleasure, provided that they are prepared openly to disclose what they propose to do, and force through a confirming resolution by the exercise of their own votes supplemented, if need be, by their control of the proxy voting machinery. It is true that if the transaction to be ratified is one which has increased their voting power the court may order that the increased votes shall not be exercised but it will not, apparently, prevent them from exercising their original votes.[14]

Clearly, therefore, some restraint must be put on the power of those able to command a majority vote. And in fact it is clear that, in some circumstances, the courts will intervene to annul[15] the resulting resolution and to restrain what is generally described as a fraud on the minority.

Meaning of fraud on the minority

The exact meaning of the expression "fraud on the minority" is not easy to determine. But at least it is clear that both "fraud" and "minority" are used somewhat loosely. There need not be any actual deceit; if there were, those on whom it was practised would have a common law remedy against those who had wilfully deceived them. "Fraud" here connotes an abuse of power analogous to its meaning in a court of equity to describe a misuse of a fiduciary position. Nor is it necessary that those who are injured should be a minority; indeed, the injured party will normally be the company itself,[16] though sometimes those who have really suffered will be a class or section of members, not necessarily a numerical minority, who are outvoted by the controllers.[17] It has been said to cover certain "acts of a fraudulent character"—in the wider sense just described—of which "familiar examples are when the majority are endeavouring directly or indirectly to appropriate to themselves money, property or advantages which belong to the company or in which the other shareholders are entitled to participate."[18] Most of the cases in which the principle has actually been applied appear to fall within one of the following three classes (a)–(c), though there may be a wider class discussed under head (d).

[14] *Hogg* v. *Cramphorn Ltd.*, above; *Bamford* v. *Bamford*, above. In *Mason* v. *Harris* (1879) 11 Ch.D 97, C.A., James L.J. remarked (p. 109) that no procedure existed for submitting such matters to the vote of independent shareholders only and suggested that, at least in certain types of cases, this might afford the best solution. See also Beck, (1975) 53 Can. Bar Rev. 771 at 785–787.

[15] It seems clear that a resolution only impeachable as a fraud on the minority is merely voidable and will be valid until successfully attacked: cf. *Borland's Trustee* v. *Steel Bros.* [1901] 1 Ch. 279 and the observations thereon in *Brown* v. *British Abrasive Wheel Co.* [1919] 1 Ch. 290.

[16] As in (a) and (b), below. These cases, therefore, should properly be described as frauds *on the company*.

[17] As in (c) and (d), below.

[18] Per Lord Davey in *Burland* v. *Earle* [1902] A.C. 83 at 93, P.C.

Before embarking on a discussion of these heads it should be pointed out that the importance of the concept of fraud on the minority has in the present and other contexts been greatly reduced by the remedy available to members under what is now section 459 of the Act and which is dealt with more fully in Chapter 24. When that remedy was first introduced by the 1948 Act it was available only when the company was being conducted "in a manner oppressive to some part of the members." That being so it could not be used when all that was objected to was a particular transaction. However, it now applies both to conduct "unfairly prejudicial[19] to the interests of its members generally or of some part of its members" and to "any actual or proposed act or omission of the company [which] is or would be so prejudicial." Hence fraud on the minority has been largely subsumed in the wider concept of unfair prejudice. Nevertheless if all a member wants is to enjoin or strike down a particular resolution, it is still the normal practice to apply for an injunction or declaration rather than to invoke section 459.

(a) *Resolution permitting expropriation of company property*

The classic example of this is *Menier v. Hooper's Telegraph Works*.[20] There the defendants, a rival concern, held a controlling interest in the company which it was alleged that they had exercised so as to compromise a pending action to their own advantage and had then put the company into liquidation, leaving them in possession of the company's assets to the exclusion of the minority. It was held that such action could be enjoined at the suit of the minority. This case was followed in *Cook v. Deeks*,[21] in which the directors had diverted to themselves contracts which they should have taken up on behalf of the company. By virtue of their controlling interests they secured the passing of a resolution in general meeting ratifying and approving what they had done. It was held that they must be regarded as holding the benefits of the contracts on trust for the company, for "directors holding a majority of votes would not be permitted to make a present to themselves."[22] The same may apply when the present is not to themselves but to someone else.

Where, then, is the line to be drawn between those cases where shareholder action is improper, and those in which shareholder action has been upheld? How, in particular, can one reconcile *Cook v. Deeks* with the many cases in which the liability of directors has been held to disappear as a result of ratification in general meeting,

19 "Oppression" has been dropped.
20 (1874) L.R. 9 Ch.App. 350.
21 [1916] 1 A.C. 554, P.C.
22 At 564.

notwithstanding the use of their own votes?[23] Why, in *Regal (Hastings) Ltd.* v. *Gulliver*,[24] did the House of Lords say that the directors would not have been liable to account for their profits had the transaction been ratified, while, in *Cook* v. *Deeks*, the Privy Council made them account notwithstanding such ratification? A satisfactory answer, consistent with commonsense and with the decided cases, is difficult (and perhaps impossible) to provide.[25]

The solution may be that a distinction is to be drawn between (i) misappropriating the company's property and (ii) merely making an incidental profit for which the directors are liable to account to the company. *Cook* v. *Deeks* came within (i) for it was the duty of the directors to acquire the contracts on behalf of the company and accordingly when they themselves acquired them they did so as constructive trustees of the company. On the other hand, in *Regal (Hastings) Ltd.* v. *Gulliver* the directors did not misappropriate any property of the company; they had instead profited from information acquired as directors of the company and made use of an opportunity of which the company might have availed itself.

Until the decision of the Court of Appeal in *Rolled Steel Products Ltd.* v. *British Steel Corporation*[26] it was widely believed that for a company to give away its property was *ultra vires* and void so that even the agreement of all its members could not ratify it. But in the light of that decision and of the reforms of the *ultra vires* doctrine by the 1989 Act that view is untenable. The most that can now be argued is that if the transaction which the directors seek to have ratified by the general meeting is a misappropriation of the company's property the resolution must be passed "bona fide in the interests of the company" as illustrated by the decisions cited above. But in the light of sections 320[27] and 322A[28] of the Act it seems doubtful whether those decisions would be followed today. Both sections make voidable certain transactions in which directors are interested and which are thought to be particularly objectionable. Both lay down how those transactions can be approved or ratified by the company in general meeting and neither says that the resolutions have to be passed "bona fide in the interests of the company." It seems unlikely that the courts would add that requirement to those prescribed by the Act. Admittedly not every case of expropriation will necessarily fall within either section but if there is no such requirement in relation to

23 *e.g. N.W. Transportation Co.* v. *Beatty* (1887) 12 App.Cas. 589. P.C.; *Burland* v. *Earle* [1902] A.C. 83, P.C.; *A. Harris* v. *Harris Ltd.*, 1936 S.C. 183 (Sc.); *Baird* v. *Baird & Co.*, 1949 S.L.T. 368 (Sc.).

24 [1942] 1 All E.R. 378; [1967] 2 A.C. 134n., H.L.; above, Chap. 21, p. 565 *et seq.*

25 It has troubled a number of other writers: see, in particular, Wedderburn, [1957] Cam.L.J. 194, [1958] *ibid.* 93; Afterman, *Company Directors and Controllers* (1970), pp. 149 *et seq.*; Beck, in Ziegel (ed.), *Canadian Company Law*, Vol. II, pp. 232–238, and Sealy, [1967] Cam.L.J. 83, pp. 102 *et seq.*

26 [1986] Ch. 246, C.A.: see Chap. 8 at p. 169 n. 19 above.

27 See Chap. 21 at p. 580 above.

28 See Chap. 8 at pp. 181, 182 above.

transactions regarded as particularly objectionable, it is difficult to see why there should be in relation to transactions that were not so regarded.

(b) *Resolutions relieving directors' liability*

As pointed out in the previous chapter the overriding principle that directors shall not place themselves in positions of conflict can be modified by provisions in the articles of association. But the articles cannot relieve the directors from their duty to act bona fide in the interests of the company. Nor can a resolution of the company in general meeting. But suppose that the directors have entered, or propose to enter, into a transaction which is obviously in their interest but which they are not satisfied is necessarily in the interests of the company. Can they then protect themselves from liability by referring the matter to the general meeting for ratification or prior approval? The answer might be that the transaction can be validated and the directors released from liability if (a) all material facts are disclosed in the notice of the meeting or in a circular accompanying the notice and (b) it can be shown that the resolution was passed "bona fide in the interests of the company." So far as (a) is concerned, it is undoubtedly a precondition for the validity of such a resolution[29] and indeed of any resolution. But, as we shall see when, in Chapter 24 below, "fraud on the minority" is further explored as an alleged exception to the rule in *Foss* v. *Harbottle*, so far as (b) is concerned the courts now seek to find other means (more realistic than requiring members when voting to subordinate their interests to those of the company) to ensure that the decision of the meeting reflects the views of disinterested members.[30] Moreover here again recent statutory reforms make it unlikely that any such principle as (b) can apply. Under the new section 35 of the Act if the directors have breached their duty to observe limitations on their powers in the memorandum of association they can be released from liability by a special resolution. As has been argued in relation to sections 310 and 322A, it seems unlikely that the courts would imply a further precondition that the resolution must be shown to have been passed "bona fide in the interests of company" or that they would do so in relation to resolutions releasing the directors from liability for other breaches of their duties.

(c) *Resolutions to expropriate members' shares*

Resolutions falling under this head seem to the writer to present a stronger case for requiring members voting for such a resolution to consider whether it is in the best interests of the company. But, once

[29] *Prudential Assurance* v. *Newman Industries (No. 2)* [1982] Ch. 204, C.A.: see below at pp. 647–654.
[30] *Smith* v. *Croft (No. 2)* [1988] Ch. 114: see below at pp. 656, *et seq.*

again, it is not clear whether they are required to do so. The relevant authorities start with *Brown* v. *British Abrasive Wheel Co.*,[31] a decision at first instance in which a public company was in urgent need of future capital which shareholders, holding 98 per cent. of the shares, were willing to put up but only if they could buy out the 2 per cent. minority. Having failed to persuade the minority to sell, they proposed a special resolution adding to the articles a provision to the effect that any shareholder was bound to transfer his shares upon a request in writing of the holders of 90 per cent. of the shares. Although such a provision could have been validly inserted in the original articles,[32] and although the good faith of the majority was not challenged, it was held that the addition of such a provision in order to enable the majority to expropriate the minority could not be for the benefit of the company as a whole but was solely for the benefit of the majority. Hence an injunction was granted restraining the company from passing the resolution.

This decision, however, was almost immediately "distinguished" by the Court of Appeal in *Sidebottom* v. *Kershaw Leese & Co.*[33] There a director-controlled private company had a minority shareholder who had an interest in a competing business. Objecting to this, the company passed a special resolution adding to the articles a provision empowering the directors to require any shareholder who competed with the company to sell his shares at a fair value to nominees of the directors. This was upheld on the basis that it was obviously beneficial to the company. In contrast, shortly thereafter in *Dafen Tinplate Co.* v. *Llanelly Steel Co.*,[34] it was held at first instance that a resolution inserting a new article empowering the majority to buy out any shareholder as they thought proper, was invalid as being self-evidently wider than could be necessary in the interests of the company.

So far, all the decisions had implied that a resolution adding to the articles a provision enabling the shares of a member to be expropriated would be upheld only if it was passed bona fide in the interests of the company and that this was to be judged not just by the members but also by the court. However, in *Shuttleworth* v. *Cox Bros. Ltd.*,[35] a case concerning not expropriation of shares but the removal of an unpopular life director, the Court of Appeal, in upholding the validity of a resolution inserting in the articles a provision that any director should vacate office if called upon to do so by the board, held that it was for the members, and not the court, to

[31] [1919] 1 Ch. 290.
[32] *Phillips* v. *Manufacturers Securities Ltd.* (1917) 116 L.T. 209; in *Borland's Trustees* v. *Steel Bros.* [1901] 1 Ch. 279 an even wider article was inserted with the agreement of all the members.
[33] [1920] 1 Ch. 154, C.A.
[34] [1920] 2 Ch. 124.
[35] [1927] 2 K.B. 9, C.A.

determine whether the resolution is for the benefit of the company and that the court will intervene only if satisfied that the members have acted in bad faith.[36] If the same applies to expropriation of shares, it is difficult to understand why what is now section 429 of the Act[37] was needed. That section[38] enables a take-over bidder who has acquired 90 per cent. or more of the target company's shares to acquire compulsorily the remainder. There would have been no need for that section if a bidder, having acquired a controlling interest, could then cause the target company to insert in its articles a similar power. But, as we have seen,[39] "the beliefs or assumptions of those who frame Acts of Parliament" are an unsafe guide to what the law actually is. More significant, perhaps, are the decision and observations of the Court of Appeal in *Re Bugle Press*.[40] There the holders of 90 per cent. of the shares, who wished to buy out the remaining 10 per cent. but who must have been advised not to attempt to proceed by the simple expedient of inserting an enabling power in the articles, formed another company and vested their shares in it. It then made a bid for the remaining 10 per cent. and, when the bid was rejected, purported to exercise the power under section 209 of the 1948 Act (corresponding to section 429 of the present Act). The court refused to countenance this, declaring that to allow existing shareholders to use the section as a device to get rid of a minority whom they did not happen to like would be contrary to "fundamental principles of company law."[41]

(d) *A general principle?*

It therefore appears that in relation to certain types of resolution, (particularly those mentioned in (c) above) the members in general meeting are subject to a sort of fiduciary duty which is expressed in similar terms to that applying to directors, namely that the members must act "bona fide in the interests of the company." But those types purport to be illustrations of a general principle which applies whenever the members are called upon to vote at general meetings,[42] thus contradicting the statement at the beginning of this

---

36 The court conceded that if the resolution was such that no reasonable man could consider it for the benefit of the company as a whole that might be a ground for finding bad faith. *ibid.* at pp. 18, 19, 23, 26 & 27. Another, it is submitted, would be if the majority was trying to acquire the shares of the minority at an obvious undervalue.
37 Formerly s.209 of the 1948 Act.
38 Dealt with in Chap. 27 at pp. 732–738 below.
39 In relation to the discussion of *Cumbrian Newspapers Group v. Cumberland and Westmorland Herald* [1987] Ch 1; see Chap. 20 at pp. 536–538, above.
40 [1961] Ch. 270, C.A.
41 *Ibid. per* Evershed M.R. at p. 287 and Harman L.J. at pp. 287, 288. But it is not easy to detect any such "fundamental principle" in Evershed's judgment in *Greenhalgh v. Arderne Cinemas* [1951] Ch. 286; see below.
42 It has been suggested that it applies only to resolutions altering the memoranda or articles but, although most of the reported cases concern such resolutions, there seem to be no reasons or authorities for drawing any such distinction.

chapter,[43] that votes by a member can be exercised in what he considers are his own best interests. This leaves unanswered a number of questions. How far does the general principle extend? What exactly is the relationship between fraud on the minority and acting bona fide in the interests of the company? And what precisely does "bona fide in the interests of the company" mean in this context?

An attempt to answer these questions was made by the Court of Appeal in *Greenhalgh v. Arderne Cinemas Ltd.*[44] This case marked the conclusion of a 10-year battle between the plaintiff, Greenhalgh, and one Mallard and his associates who had enlisted the aid of Greenhalgh when the company needed financial support. As a result Greenhalgh then became the controlling shareholder and a director. However, after a few years, thanks to an adroit series of manoeuvres orchestrated by Mallard (which had already led to no less than six actions, three of which had been taken to the Court of Appeal)[45] Greenhalgh had been ousted from his control and his seat on the board. But he was still a shareholder and, as such, had pre-emptive rights under the articles if any other shareholder wanted to sell to a non-member. This the Mallard faction now wished to do because Mallard had negotiated a deal with another entrepreneur to take over the company. To enable the deal to go through, they had to circumvent Greenhalgh's pre-emptive rights and this they sought to do by amending the articles by a special resolution which provided that, despite the pre-emptive rights, "any member may, with the sanction of an ordinary resolution ... transfer his shares ... to any person named in such resolution as the proposed transferee and the directors shall be bound to register any transfer which has been so sanctioned." Having secured the passage of this special resolution they then passed an ordinary resolution sanctioning transfers to the purchaser. Thereupon Greenhalgh instituted this, his seventh action, claiming a declaration that the resolutions were invalid as a fraud on the majority and had not been passed bona fide in the interests of the company as a whole. This, too, went to the Court of Appeal.

In his judgment,[46] Evershed M.R., though critical of the conduct of Mallard, held first that the resolutions were not a fraud on the minority. He then went on to consider whether the resolutions were nevertheless invalid as not having been passed bona fide in the

43 See pp. 591, 592 above.
44 [1951] Ch. 286, C.A. and [1950] 2 All E.R. 1120 where the judgment of Evershed M.R. is reported more fully.
45 The three are: *Greenhalgh v. Mallard* [1943] 2 All E.R. 234, C.A.; *Greenhalgh v. Arderne Cinemas Ltd.* [1946] 1 All E.R. 512, C.A.; and *Greenhalgh v. Mallard* [1947] 2 All E.R. 255, C.A. A fuller account of the whole saga was recounted in earlier editions (4th ed. at pp. 624–627) but is omitted here as largely of historical interest only; it is thought that today anyone treated as Greenhalgh was would be able to nip it in the bud by invoking s.459: see Chap. 24 below.
46 With which Asquith and Jenkins L.JJ. concurred.

interests of the company, clearly assuming that, if not, they would be invalid on that ground. This, if correct, seems to put paid to the belief that bona fides has to be shown only if the transaction would otherwise have been a fraud on the minority. In a dictum which has been widely cited in judgments throughout the Commonwealth, he said[47]:

"In the first place it is now plain that 'bona fide for the benefit of the company as a whole' means not two things, but one thing.[48] It means that the shareholder must proceed on what, in his honest opinion is for the benefit of the company as a whole. The phrase, 'the company as a whole' does not (at any rate in such a case as the present) mean the company as a commercial entity; it means the corporation as a general body. That is to say the case may be taken of an individual hypothetical member and it may be asked whether what is proposed is, in the honest opinion of those who voted in its favour, for that person's benefit."

This formula seems to be the same as that applying to directors[49] except that the "hypothetical member" is a novel refinement. On the face of it, what this is saying is that whenever members vote on a resolution they must ask themselves whether the proposal is beneficial not only to themselves but to a hypothetical member who, presumably, has no personal interest apart from that of being a member and (if such be the case) a shareholder.[50] If their honest answer is that it would not be in the hypothetical member's interest they should vote against (if they vote at all) and, presumably, if their answer is that it would be for the hypothetical member's interest they should vote for it (if they vote at all) even though convinced that it would be against their own interests. If that is correct the only safe course seems to be for every member to refrain from voting unless he is satisfied that he is the paradigm hypothetical member—for no one has yet suggested that a member is bound to exercise his votes.[51]

One can see that such a conclusion might conceivably be reasonable (a) in relation to a small family concern which was, in reality, an incorporated partnership and (b) in relation to directors voting as members at general meetings. But in other situations it seems utterly unrealistic. Even if the onus of proof that members had

47 [1951] Ch. at 291.
48 *i.e* not "(i) bona fide" and (ii) "for the benefit of the company as a whole" but a single "bona fide for the company as a whole."
49 See Chap. 21 above.
50 This interpretation was expressly adopted by McLelland J. in *Australian Fixed Trusts Pty. Ltd. v. Clyde Industries Ltd.* [1959] S.R.(N.S.W.) 33 at p. 56.
51 In this respect there would seem to be a difference between the position of a member and that of a director at a directors' meeting; the latter, if present at the meeting, could not, by abstaining, evade his duty to act in the interests of the company.

not asked themselves the suggested question was placed on those attacking the validity of the resolution, there would be little difficulty in the case of a resolution voted on at a meeting of a large public company in finding numerous Sids and Aunt Agathas honest enough to confess that it had never occurred to them to ask themselves anything of the sort. The impracticality of the formula suggested by Evershed M.R. seems to have worried him; for he went on to say:

"I think that the matter can, in practice, be more accurately and precisely stated by looking at the converse and by saying that a special resolution of this kind would be liable to be impeached if the effect of it were to discriminate between the majority shareholders and the minority shareholders, so as to give the former an advantage of which the latter were deprived."

That, however, seems to go to the other extreme; for all it appears to do is to reiterate that members of the same class must generally be treated alike. That principle[51a] seems to have no connection with the concept of "bona fide in the interests of the company" unless what Evershed M.R. meant was that resolutions could be impeached if they were intended to enable the majority to deprive the minority (but not the majority) of an advantage. But clearly he did not mean that. In all the cases cited under head (c) that is precisely what the majority had done. In some, it was held that the resolution could not be impeached since it was in the interests of the company as a whole, while in others the resolution was impeached because it was not in the company's interests. In none was there any overt distinction, in the resolution itself, discriminating against the minority.

In the instant case the Court held that, whichever of the Evershed tests was applied, the resolutions were unimpeachable. Faced with that and the earlier decision of the Court of Appeal in *Shuttleworth* v. *Cox* one might have supposed that the last nail had been driven into the coffin of bona fides in relation to members' resolutions. Not so. *Re Holders Investment Trust*[52] concerned a capital reduction scheme requiring the confirmation of the court. Confirmation was refused because the resolution of a class meeting of the preference shareholders had been passed as a result of votes of trustees who held a large block of the preference shares but a still larger block of ordinary shares. Had the refusal been on the ground that the court was not satisfied that the scheme was fair to both classes there would have been nothing remarkable about the decision; as we shall see

51a But which Goulding J., in *Mutual Life* v. *Rank Organization* [1985] BCLC 11, held did not mean that there could be no discrimination so long as directors acted fairly as between different shareholders.
52 [1971] 1 W.L.R. 583.

later[53] the courts, which normally regard a majority vote of members as cogent evidence that the scheme is fair, are rightly hesitant to do so where the majority vote of one class has resulted from the votes of members who also belong to another class. But Megarry J. approached the matter on the basis that he first had to be satisfied that the resolution of the preference shareholders had been validly passed bona fide in the interest of that class. He held that it had not, because the trustees had taken advice as to how, as trustees, they should vote and had been advised that in the interest of their beneficiaries they should vote for the resolution. This they did, admittedly without any consideration of what was in the best interest of the preference shareholders as a whole.[54] This case is also interesting in that it confirms the view taken in an earlier case[55] that in relation to class meetings it is the interest of the class rather than that of "the company as a whole" that has to be considered. In that respect, therefore, there is another difference between members and directors since the latter have to exercise their powers in the interest of the company as a whole even if they are appointed by the members of a particular class.

More remarkable, perhaps, is the later and much criticised decision of Foster J. in *Clemens v. Clemens Bros. Ltd.*[56] That case concerned a private company in which the plaintiff held 45 per cent. of the shares and her aunt, who, unlike the plaintiff, was one of the five directors (and the dominant one) held 55 per cent. Resolutions were passed at a general meeting, by the aunt's votes, to issue further shares to the other directors and to trustees of an employees' share-ownership scheme. The result was to reduce the plaintiff's holding to under 25 per cent., thereby depriving her of her negative control through her power to block a special or extraordinary resolution and reducing the value of her pre-emptive rights under the articles if another shareholder wished to sell. Foster J. set the resolutions aside saying[57]:

53 Chap. 26.
54 Contrast *Rights & Issues Investment Trust v. Stylo Shoes Ltd.* [1965] C.A. 250 where there was an unsuccessful attack on the validity of a resolution which, on the issue of further shares to one class, increased the votes of another class to preserve the existing balance of control. That other class had refrained from voting and the court, adopting the terminology both of the then version of the present s.459 and of Evershed's alternative formula, held that there had been no "oppression" of, or "discrimination" against, some part of the members. Both classes had decided that it was for the benefit of the company to preserve the existing balance.
55 *British American Nickel Corpn. v. O'Brien* [1927] A.C. 369, P.C. which seems to suggest that the obligation of a class member to consider the interest of the class as a whole is greater than that of a member voting at a general meeting to consider the interest of the company as a whole. There seems to be no reason why that should be so and there is nothing in the judgment of Megarry J. to suggest that there is any such difference.
56 [1976] 2 All E.R. 268. See the note in (1977) 40 M.L.R. 71 where his decision is described as "heart-warming" (at p. 71) but as subverting "the present basis of the law by displacing the principles of majority rule" (at p. 73).
57 At p. 282.

"They are specifically and carefully designed to ensure not only that the plaintiff can never get control of the company but to deprive her of what has been called her negative control. Whether I say that these proposals are oppressive to the plaintiff, or that no one could reasonably believe that they are for her benefit, matters not."

Here, in effect, the judge substituted for Evershed's hypothetical member an actual minority member and held that the majority had to consider whether the resolutions were for her benefit. In reaching this rather startling conclusion the judge was obviously influenced by section 210 of the 1948 Act (the predecessor of the present section 459) as his reference to "oppression" shows. But the plaintiff was not proceeding under section 210 and at that time would probably not have succeeded had she done so. But now she could succeed under section 459 if the court was satisfied, as Foster J. obviously was, that the resolutions were "unfairly prejudicial" to her.

CONCLUSIONS

What conclusions (if any) can be drawn from the foregoing discussion of the case law? Only, it is submitted, that the twin concepts of "fraud on the minority" and "bona fide in the interests of the company" are obsolete and meaningless in relation to activities by members. They were invented by the judges to curb the worst excesses of majority rule and at the time of their invention they were needed in the light of the then statute law. Now, however, because of recent statutory reforms[58] they are needed no longer. In most cases anything that they achieve can be achieved better by a petition under section 459. If the innate conservatism of members of the English legal profession causes some of them to continue to regard section 459 as providing a remedy of last resort only, it is high time that they were persuaded to the contrary. The only advantage of applying directly for an injunction or declaration rather than by petition under section 459 is that, when suing in a derivative action on behalf of the company,[59] the plaintiff may be able to obtain immediate security for his costs whereas under section 459 he apparently cannot do so unless and until the court authorises him (as it can[60]) to bring civil proceedings in the name and on behalf of the company. That

---

[58] These include not only s.459 but also provisions protecting shareholders, *e.g.* on issues of new equity shares: see Chap. 14 at pp. 362–369 above—though pre-emptive rights are inadequately protected in the case of private companies as they can too easily be excluded.

[59] See Chap. 24 at pp. 656, 657 below.

[60] See s.461(2)(c).

disadvantage could be removed by a simple amendment to section 459 or to the rules of court. Unless and until that is done there is no great harm in allowing proceedings for an injunction or declaration to continue, so long as the courts cease to base their decisions on the wholly unrealistic vague concept of fraud on the minority and the wholly unrealistic pretence that it is meaningful to require members (except perhaps of a quasi-partnership private company) to ask themselves when they vote whether they are doing so for the benefit of the company as a whole.

In all the cases reviewed above, if the courts, instead of having to ask themselves whether there was a fraud on the minority or whether the resolution had been passed "bona fide in the interests of the company" had simply had to consider whether the members or some of them were being unfairly prejudiced, it can scarcely be doubted that they would have found that an easier question to answer. Indeed, in the more recent of the cases reviewed above they have come very close to asking themselves just that.[61] In many, perhaps most, of the cases the results would have been the same, but in some it would undoubtedly have been different—and preferable on policy grounds. What therefore is being suggested is that the true position can be summarised as follows:

1. Fraud on the minority is a misleading concept which should be abandoned.

2. There is no principle that members as such are ever required to act "bona fide in what they believe to be in the best interests of the company as a whole." That is a principle restricted to fiduciaries which members, as opposed to directors, are not.

3. There is, however, a general principle that a resolution of a general or class meeting[62] is invalid if it can be shown that it is unfairly prejudicial to the whole or some part of the members or of the class.

4. If satisfied that the resolution is unfairly prejudicial the court should so declare whether proceedings are brought under section 459[63] or otherwise.

5. The onus of proof that the resolution is unfairly prejudicial is on the plaintiff but the weight of the burden varies according to the circumstances. It is light in the case of class meetings where the resolution has been passed by the votes of members who were also members of another class or, indeed, in the case of any resolution

---

[61] As they also have in relation to fraud on the minority as an exception to the rule in *Foss* v. *Harbottle*: see Chap. 24 below at pp. 643–662 and especially, *per* Templeman J. in *Daniels* v. *Daniels* [1978] Ch. 406 and *Estmanco* v. *G.L.C.* [1982] 1 W.L.R. 2, *per* Megarry V.-C.
[62] Or a written resolution.
[63] Which has the advantage that the court then has a wider range of orders that it can make: see Chap. 24 pp. 662–670 below.

which would not have been passed but for the votes of members shown to have personal interests conflicting with that of the company. In other cases the burden is heavy if the resolution has been passed by a clear majority.

This, it is submitted, would be a clarification and rationalisation towards which the courts are moving and which they can reach without doing violence to any authoritative decision.

DUTIES OTHER THAN IN RELATION TO VOTING

Hitherto this chapter has concentrated on the case law relating to voting as members. Increasingly, however, restrictions are being placed on their freedom to exercise their proprietary rights in any way they like. Examples occur when a shareholder seeks to increase his holding by a "dawn raid"; he will then have to comply with the Take-over Panel's *Rules on Substantial Acquisitions of Shares*.[64] If his shareholdings reach certain thresholds he finds himself under restrictions on further acquisitions prescribed by the *Code on Take-overs and Mergers*[65] and may be obliged to make a mandatory general offer at the maximum price that he has paid.[66] Thereby, we have gone some way towards recognising that the premium paid for a purchase of control should be shared among all the selling shareholders and not enjoyed only by those whose holdings were large enough to command the higher price. The courts of some jurisdictions in the United States have reached a similar conclusion on the basis that controllers owe fiduciary duties to the minority.[67] While the English courts have not recognised that (except to the limited extent dealt with above) the Take-over Code comes close to doing so in take-over situations.[68]

[64] Appended to the *Code on Take-overs and Mergers*. See Chap. 27 at pp. 708, 709, below.

[65] See *Code* rule 5.

[66] *Code* rule 9.

[67] See, e.g. *Perlman v. Feldmann* (1955) 219 Fed. 2d. 173 (*cert. denied* 349 U.S. 952); *Jones v. Ahmanson & Co.* (1969) 460 Pac. 2d. 464 (Cal. S.C.). In the latter Traynor C.J. said that in California "the courts have often recognised that majority shareholders, either singly or acting in concert to accomplish a joint purpose, have a fiduciary responsibility to the minority and to the corporation to use their ability to control the corporation in a fair, just and equitable manner. . . . Any use to which they put the corporation or their power to control the corporation must benefit all shareholders proportionately. . . ."

[68] But note that the Code makes concessions when control is obtained by a purchase from a single shareholder: rule 5.2. It has been argued that in such circumstances "the minority is in exactly the same position as it was before the sale except that the control is to be exercised by B instead of A"; *per* Kuper J. in *United Trust Pty. Ltd. v. S. African Milling Co.* 1959 (2) S.A. 426 (Wits P.D.) at 433–434. Nevertheless it means that B by paying A a premium on the market price may obtain control of A's assets worth far more and that the minority will not share in the premium paid to A and may find itself locked in to a company controlled by a new master intent on stripping it of its assets.

In addition, the Act now provides for disclosure of share ownership so that members can no longer be certain that they will be able to conceal the extent of their holdings by registering them in the names of nominees. And the Companies Securities (Insider Dealing) Act 1985 may impose sanctions upon them if they obtain undisclosed price-sensitive information which they use to their advantage in market dealings in the company's securities. These related topics raise wider issues and deserve a separate chapter (the next) to themselves.

THE previous chapter discussed the "quasi-fiduciary" duties allegedly imposed on members when acting as such. We now turn to the restraints on insider dealing which affect a far wider range of persons who obtain unpublished price-sensitive information about a company's securities and use it for their own profit. This is a practice which most countries have now recognised to be objectionable,[1] but which until quite recently was a way of life. The first country to tackle it effectively was the United States.[2] In the United Kingdom, we agonised over it for several decades, but did not legislate against it until 1980. Before turning to the present statutory provisions making it a criminal offence, reference must be made to certain other restraints on indulging in the practice.

NON-STATUTORY RESTRAINTS

(i) General equitable principles

Those most likely to have confidential price-sensitive information affecting the securities of a company are its directors and officers. As pointed out in Chapter 21[3] if they make use of it for their personal advantage they will breach their fiduciary duties to the company and be liable to account to it for any profits they have made. In practice, however, it is unlikely that the company will call them to account unless and until there is a change of control. If this occurs as a result of a take-over, those who will benefit from any recovery of the profits are the successful take-over bidders and not the members of the company at the time of the directors' breach—as *Regal (Hastings) Ltd.* v. *Gulliver*[4] illustrates. If only one director has committed the

---

[1] For a contrary view still espoused by some people, see Manne, *Insider Trading and The Stock Market* (1966). The argument, in a nutshell, is that the more dealings there are resulting from price-sensitive information the more "efficient" the market will be. Another argument, which most find equally implausible, is that insider dealing is a "victimless" offence in which one party may make an immoral gain but the counterparty will not suffer a loss.

[2] On which see Loss, *Fundamentals of Securities Regulation* (2nd ed. 1988 with current supps.) pp. 541–589 and 723–810.

[3] At pp. 564–570 above.

[4] [1967] 2 A.C. 134n, H.L. See pp. 565, 566 above.

breach, the others may cause the company to take action against him—as in *Industrial Development Consultants Ltd.* v. *Cooley*[5]—but most public companies are likely to avoid damaging publicity by persuading the errant director to resign "for personal reasons" and to go quietly.

It is also possible that, for example, in relation to a take-over,[6] the directors may place themselves in the position of acting as agents negotiating on behalf of the individual shareholders and thereby, despite *Percival* v. *Wright*,[7] owe fiduciary duties to the shareholders. If so, they would breach those duties if they persuaded any shareholder to sell to them at a price which they knew (and the shareholders did not) was materially lower than that which the bidder was likely to offer. It is, however, highly unlikely that the directors would do that so blatantly; if they did it at all, it would be by dealing, through a nominee, on a stock exchange so that no seller would be able to link up his sale with a purchase by a director.[8]

Hence the general equitable principle is, on its own, rarely an effective deterrent.

(ii) The Stock Exchange's model code

A somewhat more effective restraint in relation to directors of listed companies is The Stock Exchange's *Model Code for Securities Transactions by Directors*.[9] For reasons already explained,[10] this is not directly binding on directors but is a model which listed companies are required to adopt with such refinements as are thought necessary. In practice it is normally adopted virtually verbatim. Its importance is that, in addition to emphasising that in no circumstance should directors deal when they are forbidden from doing so under the Insider Dealing Act, it prescribes that they should not do so within a period of two months preceding the preliminary announcement of the company's annual results or of the announcement of the half-yearly results and should in relation to all dealings give notice beforehand to the board's chairman or a committee of directors appointed specifically for the purpose. Directors of listed companies are scared of breaching these prescriptions for, if they are found out (which they will be unless they also breach the disclosure provisions of the Companies Act) they run grave risk of finding themselves on

---

5 [1972] 1 W.L.R. 443: above, Chap. 21, p. 567.
6 In relation to which insider dealing is most likely to take place.
7 [1902] 2 Ch. 421: see Chap. 21, p. 552 above.
8 But it would be an offence under the Insider Dealing Act and a breach of The Stock Exchange's *Model Code* and of the *Code on Take-overs and Mergers*: see below.
9 Appended to Section 5, Chapter 2, of the *Yellow Book*.
10 See Chap. 13, at p. 332 above.

The Exchange's black-list of persons unacceptable as directors of listed companies.

(iii) **Statutory provisions**

The statutory provisions attack insider-dealing in three ways. First, by providing for the disclosure of dealings by those most likely to have unpublished price-sensitive information, namely the directors, and their families and associates, and major shareholders. Secondly, by empowering companies to find out who are the true owners of their shares. The provisions regarding both these are in the Companies Act. And thirdly, by making it a criminal offence to deal on a recognised stock exchange while in possession of such unpublished information. The provisions relating to this originated in the Companies Act 1980, but on the 1985 consolidation were removed to the Company Securities (Insider Dealing) Act 1985.[11] We deal first with the disclosure provisions in the Companies Act.

(a) *Disclosure of dealings by directors or their families*

This type of disclosure is dealt with in Part X of the Act, many provisions of which have been dealt with in Chapter 21.[12] Its section 323 was, in effect, our first limited attack on insider dealing by prohibiting directors from buying put or call options in the listed securities of the company or another in the same group; a practice which could conceivably be undertaken without the director making use of his price-sensitive information but which is likely to involve just that.

Part X of the Act does not forbid directors from buying or selling other types of the company's securities; on the contrary, it is generally regarded as desirable that they should show their confidence in the company by becoming shareholders of it and as unreasonable to prevent them from realising their investment if they need to. But it does require them to disclose their holdings and dealings. By section 324(1) a person who becomes a director is obliged to notify the company in writing of (a) his interest in any shares or debentures of the company or of any other company in the same group and of the number or amount of each class in which he is interested. Thereafter, under section 324(2), he is under a like obligation to notify the company of: (a) any event occurring while he is a director as a result of which he becomes or ceases to be so interested; (b) his entering into any contract to sell any such shares or debentures and (c) any assignment by him of a right granted to him to subscribe for any such shares or debentures. The notification must state the number or amount and class of the securities involved.

[11] Herein referred to as "the Insider Dealing Act."
[12] At pp. 575–585 above.

A detailed Schedule 13 to the Act amplifies the two subsections. The salient points to note are that: (a) "Interested in" is defined elaborately and widely. In general, it includes an interest "of any kind whatsoever,"[13] and whether actual or contingent.[14] It extends to shares or debentures held not by the director but by any body corporate of which he is a shadow director or is entitled to exercise or control the exercise of one-third or more of the voting power at general meetings.[15] There are, however, certain exceptions,[16] of which, perhaps, those of most general importance relate to nominees and to trustees. When securities are held by nominees, the nominees are not deemed to be "interested"[17]; it is the person for whom the nominee holds as a bare trustee who is. Hence, while a director cannot escape notification by vesting his shares in nominees, he will not have to notify if he holds the shares as a nominee for another person (not being a member of his family[18]). If, however, he holds them as trustee of a family trust (of which all the beneficiaries are not absolutely entitled[19]) he will have to notify.[20] Whether or not he is a trustee, he will have to notify if he is one of the beneficiaries unless his interest is only in reversion to that of another person entitled to the income during his (or another person's) life.[21] There are also, under the Schedule or the Companies (Disclosure of Directors' Interests) (Exceptions) Regulations,[22] exceptions in relation to special types of trust where it would be unreasonable[23] or unnecessary[24] to require notification. Part II of Schedule 13 prescribes the period within which notification has to be made. In relation to section 324(1), (*i.e.* on the director's initial appointment) the period allowed is normally five days beginning on the day after that on which he becomes a director.[25] Owing, however, to the width of the definition of "interest" it could be that the director will not know until later that he has a notifiable interest.[26] In that event

---

13 Sched. 13, Part I, para. 1.
14 *Ibid.* paras. 1–8.
15 *Ibid.* para. 4.
16 *Ibid.* paras. 9–13. Under s.324(3) other exceptions may be added by statutory instrument—and have been; see S.I. 1985 No. 802 below.
17 They are "bare trustees" excluded by *ibid.* para. 10.
18 See s.328 below.
19 So that the trustee is a "bare" trustee.
20 But, if he wishes, he can indicate that his interest is merely as a trustee: see Sched. 13, para. 23 below.
21 *Ibid.* para. 9.
22 S.I. 1985 No. 802.
23 *e.g.* where the interest is in units of an authorised unit trust, the portfolio of which happens to include shares in the director's company: Sched. 13, para. 11(*a*).
24 See Sched. 13, paras. 11(*b*), (*c*) and 12 and Regs. 2 and 3.
25 Sched. 13, para. 14(1).
26 This could easily happen as a result of the extension in s.327 to interests of his spouse and his infant children. If a husband and wife are living apart they may well not acquaint each other with their investment decisions or the directorships which they hold. Nor will a teenager necessarily tell his parents that he has subscribed for shares in a privatisation issue of shares in a company of which his father or mother is a director.

the five days begin on the day after he finds out.[27] In relation to section 324(2), (*i.e.* as regards subsequent acquisitions or cessations of his interest) there are similar periods of five days beginning the day after the occurrence or, if he did not then know of the occurrence, beginning the day after he finds out.[28] In all cases Saturdays, Sundays and bank holidays in any part of Great Britain[29] are to be disregarded.

Part III of Schedule 13 is entitled "Circumstances in which obligation imposed by section 324 is not discharged." This is a euphemism. What it in fact does is to add the requirement which directors are likely to find the most distasteful; namely that the price or other consideration paid or received must be disclosed in the notification—a requirement which section 324 studiously avoids saying. It also requires certain other information in some circumstances[30] but disclosure of the price is the bitterest pill to swallow.

Returning to section 324 itself, subsection (5) says that the obligation to notify is not discharged unless the notification is expressed to be given pursuant to section 324. The object of this is to help the company's secretariat in maintaining the register required under section 325 (to which we are about to turn). Subsection (6) crams two unrelated matters into a single sentence: (1) the section applies to shadow directors as to directors; and (2) the section does not require notification in relation to shares in a wholly-owned subsidiary. Since all the wholly-owned subsidiary's shares will necessarily be owned by the holding company or its other wholly-owned subsidiaries or by bare nominees for it or them,[31] notification by it of transactions relating to its shares would serve no purpose.[32]

Finally subsection (7) says that any person who fails to discharge within the proper period an obligation to notify or who, in purported compliance, makes a statement which he knows to be false or makes it recklessly is guilty of an offence.[33]

Under section 325 every company has to keep a register in which must be entered the information received from each director and the date of the entry.[34] The company is also obliged, when it grants to a director a right to subscribe for its shares or debentures, to enter on

27 Sched. 13, para. 14(2).
28 Sched. 13, para. 15(1) and (2).
29 Since Scottish bank holidays are not identical with those in England and Wales this may afford directors one or two (undeserved) extra days.
30 Sched. 13, paras. 17, 19.
31 See s.736(2) as inserted by the 1989 Act.
32 And would, in general, be excluded anyway under Sched. 13. All that is relevant are transactions in the holding company's shares, and in wholly-owned subsidiaries' debentures.
33 For which he can be prosecuted only with the consent of the Secretary of State or the DPP: ss.324(8) and 732.
34 s.325(1) and (2).

the register the date on which the right was granted, the period during, or the time at which, it is exercisable, the consideration (or, if none, that fact) and a description of the securities involved, their number or amount and the price or consideration to be paid when the rights are taken up.[35] When the rights are exercised by the director the company must enter against his name on the register the number or amount of shares or debentures, the names of the persons in whose names the securities are registered and the number or amount in the name of each.[36]

Part IV of Schedule 13 prescribes how the register shall be kept and contains the customary provisions for its inspection and the obtaining of copies.[37] The company has to fulfil its obligations within three days beginning with the day after the obligation arises.[38] The nature and extent of the director's interest must, if he so requires, be recorded[39] but this does not put the company on notice as to the rights of any person.[40] Section 326 imposes liability to fines on the company, and any officer of it in default, in the event of failure by the company to comply with section 325 or Part IV of the Schedule.

Section 327 extends the banning of dealings in options in the company's shares[41] to dealings by the spouse or infant children or step-children of the director and section 328 similarly extends the ambit of section 324. But whereas section 327 does so by making those members of the director's family personally liable on a contravention of the prohibition,[42] section 328 does so by requiring the director himself to notify and imposes no liability on the spouse or children. The broad effect of section 328 is that sections 324 and 325 are to be construed as if any reference in them to a director's interest included any interest of his spouse or infant children. It matters not that the director himself has no personal interest or whether or not he has tipped them off; his only protection is that, if they have acted without telling him, he will not have to notify the company until he finds out.[43]

By section 329 a further obligation is imposed on listed companies. If a notification relates to shares or debentures listed on The Stock

35 s.324(1) and (3). This would apply on a rights issue (if the director was already a shareholder) and to a grant of warrants or options.
36 s.325(4).
37 See Chap. 17 at pp. 451, 452 above. It also has to be produced at the commencement of the company's AGM and to remain open and accessible to any person attending the meeting: Sched. 13, para. 29.
38 With the exclusion of Saturdays, Sundays and bank holidays: Sched. 13, para. 22. Ten days are allowed for dispatch of copies.
39 Sched. 13, para. 23.
40 *Ibid.* para. 24.
41 By s.323, mentioned at p. 609 above.
42 Inevitably so, since s.323 bans the transactions instead of merely requiring, as s.324 does, that they be disclosed. But the spouse or children have a defence if they can prove that they had no reason to believe that the other spouse or their father or mother was a director of the company: s.327(1).
43 See nn. 27 and 28 above.

Exchange,[44] the company must, before the end of the next working day,[45] notify The Exchange of that matter and The Exchange may publish it in any way it thinks fit. This not only helps The Exchange to detect breaches of its Model Code[46] but helps also in relation to its role as detector of possible offences under the Insider Dealing Act.

(b) *Disclosure by substantial shareholders*

This type of disclosure resembles in many ways that dealt with in (a) above, but it appears in a different Part of the Act,[47] applies to a wider range of security holders but to a narrower range of companies and securities, and has slightly different aims. Whereas the provisions dealt with under (a) apply to all types of company and to all classes of their shares and debentures, this second type applies only to public companies, to shares (not debentures) and only to shares carrying the right to vote. Whereas both may apply to directors (so that those of public companies may have to make two separate notifications in respect of a single transaction) this second type is not concerned with directors as such but with all persons who have acquired an interest in a substantial proportion of the voting capital. Its aim is not only to deter insider dealing but also, and primarily, to preclude a take-over bidder from secretly building up a holding sufficiently substantial to launch a bid which will take the company and the market by surprise. Unfortunately while the provisions relating to type (a) are difficult enough,[48] those relating to type (b) are probably the most impenetrable of any in the Act.[49] This is particularly regrettable since the need to comply with one or both sets of provisions arises frequently and those concerned ought to be able to work out whether or not they are required to disclose without having to rush to their lawyers—who may prove to be as uncertain as they are and whose only advice may be "when in doubt, disclose." In the account that follows all that is attempted is to offer a simplified map, hoping thereby to help those who enter the swamp to avoid sinking without trace.

The basic principle of type (b) is simple enough. Once any person has acquired an interest in a prescribed proportion of the voting shares he comes under an obligation to notify the company and thereafter to do so if there is any increase or decrease in that

44 Or any other recognised investment exchange other than an overseas exchange within the meaning of the Financial Services Act.
45 This is not quickly enough for The Stock Exchange which requires "immediate" notification: *Yellow Book*, Section 5, Chapter 2, para. 16.3.
46 See p. 608, above.
47 In Part VI (entitled Disclosure of Interests in Shares) instead of Part X (entitled Enforcement of Fair Dealing by Directors).
48 Even more so than the summary in the text may have suggested.
49 The need to implement in 1992 a relevant EC Directive (88/627/EEC) will not lead to its being made less impenetrable because implementation can (and will) be achieved by minor amendments only.

proportion.[50] At present the prescribed proportion is 3 per cent.[51] Despite the fact that the provisions relate only to shares carrying votes at any general meeting,[52] the relevant percentage is not of the votes but of the nominal value of the shares carrying votes. When there is only one class of such shares this would produce the same result but it would not do so if, for example, there were two classes of different nominal values, but both carrying the same number of votes per share. Section 198(2)(a) is generally interpreted as going further than is needed to deal with that situation and to require notification if over 3 per cent. of any class of voting shares is acquired, even if that is far less than 3 per cent. of the total votes.[53]

A shareholder may, however, have considerable difficulty in determining whether from time to time his shares do constitute 3 per cent. or more of the issued voting share capital (particularly now that companies may purchase their own shares which thereupon cease to be issued share capital). Moreover, when directors have authority to issue more shares he may not know how many they have issued. Indeed, since, as we shall see, he may have attributed to him interests in shares held by others[54] he may not even know how many shares he is deemed to be interested in. To meet these difficulties the provisions[55] make the obligation to notify dependent on his knowledge.[56] The notification must be made within two days of his becoming aware of it[57] and the provisions lay down what it must contain,[58] what the company must do about putting the information on a separate register,[59] and regarding rights to inspect it and to obtain copies.[60] These provisions are broadly similar to those relating to the register of directors' holdings. So are those relating to what are regarded as "interests" in shares[61] and to the inclusion of family[62] and corporate interests.[63]

On the other hand, sections 204–206 have no counterpart in the provisions relating to directors' shareholdings. These sections are

---

[50] ss.198–200: s.201 was repealed by the 1989 Act.
[51] s.199. Reduced from the former 5 per cent. by the 1989 Act. Three per cent. may sound insignificant but it can represent an investment of millions of pounds in relation to a major listed company. The percentage may be varied by regulations made under s.210A.
[52] Including those on which voting rights are temporarily suspended, (*e.g.* under ss.216 and 454, below, pp. 622–624).
[53] If this is the effect, it is a pity that a provision said to be "for the avoidance of doubt" could not have expressed it more clearly.
[54] See nn. 61–63 below.
[55] Borrowing the solutions adopted regarding directors' interests.
[56] See ss.198(1), (3) & (4) and 199(2).
[57] s.202(1) and (4) which, as amended by the 1989 Act, substitutes two days for the former five.
[58] s.209.
[59] ss.211, 217 & 218. If the person concerned is a director he will have to make two separate notifications and be entered on two distinct registers.
[60] s.219.
[61] ss.207–209.
[62] s.203(1).
[63] s.203(1)–(4).

designed to prevent the evasion of the need to notify dealings by the use of what have come to be known as "concert parties." There is nothing illegal or improper in a number of persons acting in concert in attempting to acquire or to maintain control of a company. It becomes objectionable only if that fact is concealed and the holdings of each member of the concert party are not notified until they reach the 3 per cent. threshold notwithstanding that in combination the holdings may have exceeded it long before. To prevent this evasion has been the aim of both the legislation and of the Panel's *Code on Take-overs and Mergers*.

Unfortunately it has not as yet proved possible to agree upon a definition of "concert party,"[64] common to both the Act and the Code. As an introduction to the Act's provisions it is helpful to look first at the definition in the Code which is comparatively simple and more readily intelligible. It says[65]:

"Persons acting in concert comprise persons who, pursuant to agreement or understanding (whether formal or informal) actively co-operate, through the acquisition by any of them of shares in a company to obtain or consolidate control[66] ... of that company,"

and it then goes on to provide that six categories of persons[67] are presumed to be acting in concert unless the contrary is proved. This has not been thought sufficiently precise or "judge-proof" for statutory provisions giving rise to criminal liability. Accordingly the statutory definition is considerably more tortuous—and made the more so in that, unlike the Code, it does not set out to define "acting in concert" but rather to define an arrangement leading to acting in concert, the existence of which arrangement is required to be notified in addition to the dealings under it.

First, section 204(1) provides that in certain circumstances an obligation of disclosure may arise from an agreement, between two or more persons, which includes provision for the acquisition by any one

---

[64] Neither the Act nor the Code in its Rules actually uses the term "concert party," but the latter does so extensively in the Notes.

[65] *Code*, Section C.1. defining "acting in concert." Rule 5 of the Panel's *Rules Governing Substantial Acquisitions of Shares* (the SARs) is even simpler—"Where two or more persons act by agreement or understanding in the acquisition by one or more of them of shares carrying voting rights in a company, or rights over such shares, their holdings and acquisitions must be aggregated and treated as a holding or acquisition by one person for the purpose of the SARs. ... " The Code and the SARs are not primarily concerned with notification (which is left to the Act) but with determining whether certain thresholds have been reached which require a standstill on further acquisitions or a mandatory general bid.

[66] *i.e.* 30 per cent. or more of the voting rights: *Code*, Section C.4.

[67] *i.e.* (i) a company and any others in the group, (ii) a company and any of its directors, (iii) a company and any of its pension funds, (iv) a fund manager and any of its discretionary managed clients, (v) a stockbroker or the financial adviser and persons under the same control, (vi) the directors of the target company.

or more of them of interests in voting shares of a particular public company. Two points arise from the wording of this subsection. (a) The agreement must relate to the acquisition of shares. It does not apply to a voting or other agreement between existing shareholders unless that also requires them to acquire more shares. (b) The subsection refers to the public company whose shares are to be acquired as "the target company." This is liable to mislead. On a take-over bid it is normal to describe the company, whose shares are to be bid for, as the target company. Hence the subsection at first glance appears to apply only if that is the company whose shares are to be acquired. That will usually be the case[68] but the subsection would bite also if, for example, public company A proposed to bid for the shares of public company B on a share-for-share basis and the members of the concert party agreed to support the market price of company A's shares by buying its shares and retaining them until the conclusion of the bid.[69]

However, subsequent subsections in some respects widen, and in others reduce, the ambit of subsection (1). Subsection (5) provides that "agreement" includes "any agreement or arrangement" and that "provisions of an agreement" include "undertakings, expectations or understandings" whether "express or implied and whether absolute or not."[70] Hence the "agreement" need not be an enforceable contract. But subsection (6) introduces a further refinement, somewhat similar to valuable consideration, by providing that section 204 does not apply to an agreement which is not legally binding "unless it involves mutuality in the undertakings, expectations or understandings of the parties to it."[71] This is somewhat mystifying since one would have supposed that if there was such "mutuality" there would be "valuable consideration," making the agreement "legally binding." The object, however, was apparently to make it clear that the mere fact that two or more persons have agreed that one or more of them shall buy and retain voting shares in a public company does not of itself constitute a concert party agreement.[72] Subsection (2)(*a*) says that the section applies only if the agreement "also includes provisions imposing

[68] *e.g.* an agreement by the members of the concert party to support the offeror company by buying shares in the offeree company, and to accept the offer when made; or to support the offeree company by buying its shares and to retain them and not accept the offer (an example of the Code's "consolidation of control").

[69] But it would not cover an agreement to *sell* shares in company B in the hope of causing a fall in the market price of its shares, even if company A agreed to indemnify the members of the concert party from any loss they sustained.

[70] *cf.* the Code's "agreement or understanding (whether formal or informal)."

[71] The subsection also excludes an underwriting or sub-underwriting agreement provided that that "is confined to that purpose and any matters incidental to it."

[72] *e.g.*, Mr. & Mrs. A are advised by their stockbroker that shares in public company B are a sound medium-term investment because its shares are undervalued and it seems a likely target for a take-over bid. Mr. & Mrs. A buy such shares from the broker. This clearly ought not to be a "concert party agreement" between Mr. & Mrs A and the broker. But if it is only subs. (6) that would exclude it (and not subs. (2) or (3)) it does not seem to do so because the agreement *was* "legally binding."

obligations or restrictions on any one or more of the parties to it with respect to their use, retention or disposal of their interests in that company's shares acquired in pursuance of the agreement ....,"[73] And subsection (3) clarifies the meaning of "use" in subsection (2) by saying that it means "the exercise of any rights or of any control or influence arising from" the interests in shares acquired "including the right to enter into any agreement for the exercise or for the control of the exercise of any of those rights by another person." In other words, there must not only be an "agreement" to acquire but also agreement on the use that is to be made of the shares acquired.

No obligation of disclosure arises immediately an agreement has been entered into; it arises only on the first acquisition pursuant to the agreement by any of the parties to it.[74] Thereafter it continues, whether or not further acquisitions take place or the members of the concert party change or the agreement is varied, so long as the agreement continues to include provisions of any description mentioned in subsection (2)(a).

What the disclosure obligations are, is dealt with in sections 205 and 206. Under the former, each member of the concert party is taken for the purposes of disclosure under sections 198–203 to be interested not only in all shares acquired by any member of the concert party but also in any in which other members are interested apart from the concert party agreement.[75] Any notification which a party makes with respect to his interest must state that he is a party to a concert party agreement, must include the names and (so far as known to him) the addresses of the other parties and must state whether or not any of the shares to which the notification relates are shares in which he is interested by virtue of section 204 and, if so, how many of them.[76] And when he makes a notification that he has ceased to be interested in any such shares because he or another member of the concert party has ceased to be a member of the concert party, he must include a statement that he or that other person (identifying him) has ceased to be a member of the concert party.[77] Compliance with this obligation should enable the company and, as a result of its obligation to register notifications,[78] anyone inspecting the register, to ascertain that there is a concert party, who its members are and (though this may take some working out) how

[73] It is this, surely, which would exclude the agreement in n. 72?
[74] s.204(2)(b).
[75] s.205(1), (2), & (3). The effect appears to be that although, under s.204(2)(b), the arrangement becomes a concert party agreement once any interest in shares is acquired in pursuance of it, notification is not required unless and until the total holdings of the concert party members (whether acquired under the agreement or not) reach the 3 per cent. threshold. The provisions would probably be more effective if they required any concert party agreement to be notified once it was entered into, all holdings and transactions of the parties thereafter to be notified.
[76] s.205(4).
[77] s.205(5).
[78] s.211.

many shares the concert party has. But, because a shareholder is obliged to notify only if he knows of his interest,[79] that desired result will not be achieved unless each member of the concert party keeps the other members informed both of all his interests in voting shares of the company at the time of the entry into the concert party agreement and of all changes in his interests (other than those undertaken under the concert party agreement and therefore known to them). This, in effect, is what section 206 requires him to do in writing within two days[80] of his knowing.[81] Section 207 provides when, in such circumstances (or in others when he is deemed to be interested by having attributed to him the interests of another person[82]) he is to be treated as having knowledge.

To conclude this discussion of concert parties all that need be added is that, despite the differences in the Act's and the Code's definitions, in most cases what is a concert party for purposes of the one will be so for the purposes of the other. In both cases, the great difficulty for the regulatory authorities is to prove the existence of a concert party, particularly when the members of it operate outside the United Kingdom.

Before turning to the next set of statutory provisions, mention must be made of two further sections. The first is section 210, subsection (1) of which provides that, if a person authorises an agent to acquire or dispose of voting shares of a public company, he must secure that the agent will notify him immediately of all transactions which may give rise to an obligation of disclosure under Part VI. Most private investors are wholly unaware of this as, probably, are many of the professional agents they employ. Stockbrokers executing their clients' orders immediately notify the latter when they have done so—but an investment manager may not do so until some time later. While a private investor is unlikely, on his own, ever to reach the 3 per cent. threshold for disclosure, he might well join a concert party that did so. It seems therefore that every transaction in voting shares of a public company is one which "*may give rise*" to an obligation of disclosure so that the agent ought always to notify the principal immediately—and arguably commits an offence if he does not![83]

The other subsections of section 210 prescribe the penalties for contravention of the foregoing sections or for knowingly or recklessly making false statements. One such penalty is that the Secretary of State may direct that the shares in respect of which the offence occurred shall be subject to restrictions under Part XV of the Act.[84]

[79] See p. 614 above.
[80] Reduced from the former five days by the 1989 Act.
[81] He is also required to notify them of any change of his address: s.206.
[82] *e.g.* his wife or infant children or a company which he controls.
[83] See s.210(3)(*d*). But the court would probably think he had a "reasonable excuse" (*ibid.*) unless the client had alerted him about what he was up to.
[84] See below, pp. 622–624.

Section 210A, inserted by the 1987 Act, contains wide powers enabling the sections to be amended by statutory instrument. Somewhat surprisingly there is nothing in Part VI corresponding to section 329 under which the company receiving notification of directors' dealings must pass on the information to any stock exchange on which the shares are listed. This, however, is taken care of under The Stock Exchange's regulations[85] when the listing is there.

(c) *Powers of company to ascertain share ownership*

It will be appreciated that all a company may know about the ownership of its shares is in whose names they are registered. In the case of a public company many of its shares are likely to be registered in the names of nominees for the true owners. If the provisions in (a) and (b) above are duly complied with by directors or by 3 per cent. shareholders, the company will, in their case, know who the beneficial owners are. But the "if" is a big "If," especially if the nominees are resident outside the United Kingdom. The board of the company may be able to guess that something is afoot because, say, transfers from the name of one Swiss bank to another are lodged for registration but what that "something" is it cannot tell. Some public companies have sought to meet this problem by provisions in their articles entitling them to demand information on the beneficial ownership, but whether they have or not, all public companies are now afforded statutory powers by sections 212–216.

Section 212 provides that a public company may serve notice on a person whom it knows to be, or has reasonable cause to believe to be, or to have been at any time during the three-years immediately preceding the date of the notice, interested in voting shares of the company. The notice may require that person to confirm that fact and, if so, (a) to give particulars of his own past or present interest; (b) where the interest is a present interest and any other interest subsists or subsisted during the three year period at a time when his own interest did, to give particulars known to him of that other interest; or (c) where his interest is a past interest, to give particulars of the identity of the person to whom that interest was transferred.[86] In cases (a) and (b) the particulars to be given include the identity of persons interested and whether they were members of a concert party or there were any other arrangements regarding the exercise of any rights conferred by the shares.[87] The notice must conclude by

---

[85] *Yellow Book*, Section 5, Chapter 2, para. 16.
[86] s.212(1) and (2). "Interest" bears the same meaning as in ss.203–205 and 208 (but omitting any reference to the interests to be disregarded under s.209): s.212(5).
[87] s.212(3). In the light of the complications of the statutory provisions defining "interests" and "concert party agreements" a lengthy explanation accompanying the notice may be needed if the recipient (particularly if he is a foreigner) is to understand precisely what is being asked of him.

requiring a response to be given in writing within such reasonable time as may be specified in the notice.[88] The initial notice will normally be sent to the person named on the membership register and, if he is the sole beneficial owner of the shares, he will normally say so (at any rate once the likely consequences of refusing to respond are explained to him). But in other cases the notice may merely be the beginning of a long and often abortive paper-chase. If he is a nominee he may well decline to say more than that, claiming that his duty of confidentiality forbids disclosure or, if the nominee is, say, a foreign bank, that the foreign law makes it unlawful to disclose. Ultimately, as a result of the possibility of the freezing and disenfranchisement of the shares,[89] the true ownership may be disclosed—but not always.[90] Such information regarding present interests in the shares as may be elicited as a result of the notice (or a succession of notices as the company follows the trail) must be entered on a separate part of the register maintained for the purposes of sections 198–202.[91]

The Act recognises that members of the company may have a legitimate interest in securing that the company exercises its powers under section 212 even if the board does not want it to (perhaps because the directors or some of them may fear that it may bring to light breaches by them of their obligations to notify their dealings under either or both of section 324 or sections 198–210). Hence, under section 214, members holding not less than one-tenth of the paid-up voting capital may serve a requisition stating that the requisitionists require the company to exercise its powers under section 212, specifying the manner in which those powers are to be exercised[92] and giving reasonable grounds for requiring the powers to be exercised in the manner specified.[93] It is then the company's duty to comply.[94] If it does not, the company and every officer of it who is in default is liable to a fine.[95]

On the conclusion of an investigation under section 214, the company, under section 215, has to prepare a report of the

[88] If the time allowed is unreasonably short, the notice will be invalid: *Re Lonrho plc (No. 2)* [1989] BCLC 309 (which is *not* the same as the decision cited in nn. 17–19 below, also reported as *Re Lonrho (No. 2)* in [1990] Ch. 695.

[89] See s.216 and Part XV of the Act, below.

[90] In some cases the information sought has never been obtained and the shares have remained frozen.

[91] s.213; with the result that the register may contain entries in respect of holdings below the 3 per cent. threshold. The entry is against the name of the registered holder and must state the fact that, and the date when, the requirement was imposed.

[92] In particular, of course, in respect of which shareholdings they require notices to be served.

[93] s.214(1) and (2).

[94] s.214(4). The duty arises "on the deposit of a requisition complying with this section," but presumably the company has a reasonable time within which to dispatch the notice or notices.

[95] s.214(5). Fining the officers in default makes sense; fining the company itself does not.

information received which has to be made available at the company's registered office within a reasonable time[96] after the conclusion of the investigation.[97] If it is not concluded within three months beginning on the day after the deposit of the requisition, an interim report on the information already obtained has to be prepared in respect of that and each succeeding three months.[98] Any report has to be made available for inspection at the registered office[99] and the requisitionists must be informed within three days of the report becoming available.[1]

In addition to the foregoing means of obtaining information about the true ownership of a company, the DTI may intervene in order to do so. In the first instance, if the Secretary of State is persuaded that there may be good reasons for intervening he will probably institute preliminary investigations under the powers conferred on him by section 444. Under this he can require any person whom he has reasonable cause to believe to have, or to be able to obtain, information as to the present and past interests in a company's shares or debentures to give him the information.

If this fails to produce a satisfactory answer he may then appoint inspectors under section 442.[2] He may do so of his own volition[3] or, in the case of a company with a share capital, if application is made either by not less than 200 members or members holding not less than one-tenth of the issued shares, and, in the case of a company without share capital, if the application is by not less than one-fifth of the members.[4] A fully-fledged investigation may afford the best chance of getting at the truth but it is expensive and time-consuming.[5] Hence the amendments to the section made by the 1989 Act provide that the Secretary of State shall not appoint inspectors if he is satisfied that the members' application is vexatious and, if he does appoint, shall exclude any matter if satisfied that it is unreasonable for it to be investigated[6]; and he may require the applicants to give security to an amount not exceeding £5,000, or such other sum as he may specify,[7] for payment of the costs of the

---

96 Not exceeding 15 days: s.215(3).
97 s.215(1). On the meaning of "concluded" see s.215(6).
98 s.215(2).
99 ss.214(7) and 219.
1 s.215(5) and it must remain available for inspection at the registered office for at least six years: s.215(7).
2 As amended by the 1989 Act. This section is directed not merely to determining share and debenture ownership but "the true persons who are or have been primarily interested in the success or failure (real or apparent) of the company or able to control or materially to influence its policy": s.442(1).
3 s.442(2).
4 s.442(3) as inserted by the 1989 Act. He need not appoint if it appears to him that an investigation under s.444 would suffice: s.442(3C).
5 See Chap. 25 below.
6 s.442(3A).
7 By statutory instrument subject to annulment by a resolution of either House of Parliament.

investigation.[8] Furthermore, if it appears to the Secretary of State that there are circumstances suggesting breaches of the sections relating to disclosure of dealings by directors or their families[9] he may, under section 445,[10] appoint inspectors to investigate and report. What makes the foregoing sections more effective than they would otherwise be, is that if a person is convicted of an offence under section 210[11] or there is difficulty in finding out the relevant facts on an investigation under section 442 or 444, he may by order direct that the securities concerned shall, until further notice, be subject to the restrictions of Part XV of the Act.[12] Similarly, if under section 212 a notice is served on a person who is or was interested in shares of the company and he fails to give any information required by the notice, the company may apply to the court for an order directing that the shares in question be subject to the restrictions of Part XV.[13] An order, whether by the Secretary of State or the court, can be made notwithstanding any power in the company's memorandum or articles enabling the company itself to impose similar restrictions.[14]

The restrictions of Part XV (sections 454–457) of the Act are that:

(a) any transfer of the shares, or, in the case of unissued shares, any transfer of the right to be issued with the shares and any issue of them, is void;

(b) no voting rights are exercisable in respect of them;

(c) no further shares may be issued in right of them or in pursuance of an offer made to their holder; and

(d) except in a liquidation, no payment by the company, whether as a return of capital or a dividend may be made in respect of them.[15]

This is a draconian penalty,[16] which may be detrimental to wholly innocent parties, for example bona fide purchasers of, or lenders on

[8] s.442(3B). The costs will not necessarily have to be borne in full by the applicants; only "to such extent (if any) as the S & S may direct": s.439(5), as amended by the 1989 Act.

[9] i.e. type (a) disclosure dealt with at pp. 609–613 above.

[10] As amended by the F.S. Act and the 1989 Act.

[11] i.e. for breach of type (b) disclosure dealt with at pp. 613–619 above.

[12] See ss.210(5) and 445.

[13] s.216.

[14] See ss.210(5), 216(2), 445(1). This seems to be a tacit recognition of the legality and effectiveness of such provisions which, as mentioned at p. 619 above, some companies have inserted in their articles. The Stock Exchange permits such provisions so long as the shares cannot be disenfranchised earlier than 14 days after service of a notice under s.212 (which seems to envisage a curious mixture of the statutory procedure and that of the articles).

[15] s.454(1). And see s.454(2) & (3).

[16] Made the more so since any attempt to evade the restrictions may lead to a heavy fine: s.455.

the security of, the shares, and, as originally enacted, the provisions afforded them inadequate protection. Although the court or the Secretary of State has a discretion whether to make the order since "the clear purpose [of Part VI of the Act] is to give public companies; and ultimately the public at large, a prima facie unqualified right to know who are the real owners of its voting shares" an order should normally be made if that knowledge has not been obtained.[17] If an order was made it had to impose all four restrictions without any qualifications designed to protect innocent parties.[18] Moreover, although the court (or the Secretary of State if he has made the order) could, under section 456, remove the restrictions[19] this normally could be done only by removing all of them "if satisfied that the relevant facts about the shares have been disclosed to the company and no unfair advantage has accrued to any person as a result of the earlier failure to make that disclosure."[20] To this there were (and still are) two exceptions. If "the shares are to be transferred for valuable consideration[21] and the court (in any case) or the Secretary of State (if the order was made under section 210 or 445) approved the transfer" an order could be made that the shares shall cease to be subject to the restrictions.[22] Further, the court, on application by the Secretary of State (unless the restrictions were imposed by the court under section 216) or by the company, might order the shares to be sold,[23] subject to the court's approval as to the terms of the sale,[24] and might then also direct that the shares shall cease to be subject to the restrictions.[25]

---

[17] See *Re Lloyd Holdings plc* [1985] BCLC 293; *Re Geers Gross plc* [1987] 1 W.L.R. 1649, C.A.; *Re Lonrho plc (No. 2)* [1990] Ch. 695. The words quoted are those of Nourse J. in *Re Lloyd Holdings* at p.300, adopted by the C.A. in *Re Geers Gross* and by Peter Gibson J. in *Re Lonrho plc (No. 2)*.

[18] In *Re Lonrho plc (No. 2)*, Peter Gibson J. expressed regret that the court had no power to make an order qualifying the restrictions, being "conscious of the severity of the order and the commercial inconvenience and hardship it may cause to innocent persons affected by the order: [1990] Ch. at p. 708. An advantage of providing powers in the articles is that they could be expressed more flexibly.

[19] On the application of any person aggrieved by an order made by the Secretary of State or his refusal to make an order disapplying the restrictions, or by such a person or the company if the order was made by the court under s.456(1) and (2).

[20] s.456(3)(a).

[21] Originally this read "are to be sold." The C.A. in *Re Westminster Group plc* [1985] 1 W.L.R. 676 felt constrained to hold that this did not enable the court to permit a transfer of restricted shares to a take-over bidder since the offer was an "exchange" and not a "sale." Leave was given to appeal to the H.L., but was not pursued. However, the point was dealt with by an amendment in the 1989 Act.

[22] But the court has a discretion whether to allow the transfer and whether or not also to remove the restrictions; in particular it may continue restrictions (c) and (d) either in whole or in part so far as they relate to rights acquired or offered prior to the transfer: see s.456(6).

[23] Here "sale" was not changed to "transferred for valuable consideration." The only transaction that can be *ordered* is a sale.

[24] s.456(4). The court may then make further orders relating to the conduct of the sale: s.456(5). The proceeds of sale have to be paid into court for the benefit of the persons who are beneficially interested in the shares who may apply for the payment out of their proportionate entitlement: s.457.

[25] But it does not have to remove them and may well continue restrictions (c) and (d) to the extent provided by s.456(6).

Having regard to the observations of Peter Gibson J. in *Lonrho plc (No. 2)*[26] it was felt that someting had to be done about the hardship to innocent third parties. Accordingly section 135 of the 1989 Act enabled the Secretary of State, by regulations made by statutory instrument subject to approval of both Houses of Parliament, to make such amendments to the provisions of the 1985 Act relating to orders imposing restrictions on shares[27] as appeared to him to be necessary or desirable—

"(a) for enabling orders to be made in a form protecting the rights of third parties;

(b) with respect to the circumstances in which restrictions may be relaxed or removed" and

"(c) with respect to the making of interim orders by a court."[28]

The requisite amendments have now been made by The Companies (Dislosure of Interests in Shares) (Orders imposing restrictions on shares) Regulations 1991.[28a] These enable the court or the Secretary of State, as the case may be, if satisfied that an order may otherwise unfairly affect the rights of third parties, to direct that specified acts by such persons or classes of persons shall not constitute a breach of the restrictions and such directions may be given on the making of the order or on a subsequent application to relax or remove the restrictions.[28b] They also empower the court to make an interim order, unconditionally or on such terms as it thinks fit.[28c] This new flexibility is greatly to be welcomed.

THE INSIDER DEALING ACT

Disclosure of dealings, which the foregoing provisions are intended to secure, is only a first step in discouraging insider dealing and helping to detect it when it occurs—which few now doubt that it did on a considerable scale—and indeed still does.[29] Hence most major countries have recognised the need for stronger measures. These range from self-regulation to statutory provisions imposing both civil and criminal penalties. The present British solution, now to be found in the Insider Dealing Act 1985,[30] was to make it a criminal offence

[26] See n. 18 above. His judgment was not delivered until the end of June 1989 by which time the 1989 Bill was nearing its final stages. Hence the resort to a single section to be followed by later detailed Regs.
[27] *i.e.* ss.210, 216, 445 and Part XV of the Act: s.135(2).
[28] Another power which the courts felt they needed.
[28a] S.I. 1991 No. 1646 which came into force on 18th July 1991.
[28b] See, in particular, the new ss.210(5A), 216(1B), 445(1A) and 456(1A).
[28c] s.216(1A).
[29] The possible profits are great, and the risks of exposure relatively slight.
[30] As amended, principally by the F.S. Act 1986 and in minor respects by the 1989 Act and by the Criminal Justice Act 1988. In what follows until p. 638, references to "the Act" are to the Insider Dealing Act (not to the 1985 Act).

but to leave any civil liability to be dealt with under common law (and equity). On the basis that the main objection to insider dealing is that it affects the integrity of the market, it was decided to restrict the offence thus created to dealings on an exchange and, that being so, it was thought there would be little point in providing the other party with a civil remedy since only rarely would that party be able to link a sale or purchase by him with an identifiable counterparty.[31]

The legislation has not proved wholly satisfactory. Some further amendments to it will have to be made in the light of the EC Directive on Co-ordinating Regulations on Insider Dealing (89/592/ EEC). This Directive is a "minimum standards" directive, permitting member States to adopt more stringent or additional provisions,[32] as in some respects our present legislation does. Happily the DTI, in a Consultative Document published in December 1989, announced that the Government "believe that the opportunity created by the implementation should be used to simplify and update the law."[33] That is indeed much to be desired and most of the suggestions in the Document seem eminently sensible. But whether what ultimately emerges will prove to be "simple" remains to be seen. All that is clear is that there is likely to be legislation, shortly after this edition is published,[34] which will make changes to the present position described in what follows. But it is impossible to say precisely what these changes will be.

Under the present law, if a prosecution for an offence under the Insider Dealing Act is to succeed, a considerable number of things have to be established. In effect it has to be proved beyond reasonable doubt that the accused:

(a) was at the material time an individual "insider";

(b) who had inside information;

(c) which was unpublished price-sensitive information;

(d) and who engaged in certain prohibited activities;

(e) with the prescribed mental element (*mens rea*).[35]

If all that can be established, then,

(f) unless one (or more) of the prescribed exclusions applies, he is liable to criminal penalties.

[31] Under The Stock Exchange's TALISMAN system (see Chap. 15 above) his only identifiable counterparty would be SEPON.

[32] Directive Art. 6. The main respect in which the minimum standards go beyond our present legislation is that the Directive extends to dealing in transferable securities of bodies other than companies; *e.g.* to "gilts" and to local authority bonds and stocks.

[33] Consultative Document, para. 2.1.

[34] The Directive provides that it shall be implemented by member States before 1 June 1992.

[35] Namely, "knowingly," a word which is scattered in profusion throughout the sections.

This is very much more elaborate and complicated than the pristine simplicity of section 323 of the Companies Act under which, as we have seen,[36] it is an offence for a director, a shadow director, or a prescribed member of his family, to buy a put or call option on the company's listed shares or debentures. In contrast with that, each of the above elements (a)–(e) has to be established by the prosecution.

(a) *Insiders*

Only individuals, not bodies corporate, are liable to prosecution under the Act. Corporate bodies were excluded, not because it was thought undesirable to make them criminally liable but because of the difficulties that would be faced by merchant banks when one department of the bank had unpublished price-sensitive information about the securities of a client company and other departments had successfully been kept in ignorance of that information by a "Chinese Wall"[37] or otherwise. One of those other departments might deal in the shares, in which event the bank as a single corporate body would arguably have committed an offence had the Act applied to corporate bodies. However, their exclusion does not mean that transactions by corporate bodies can be undertaken with impunity. Such bodies can act only through human agents or organs and if those individuals, with knowledge of the unpublished price-sensitive information, counsel or procure[38] the corporate body to deal, they will have committed an offence assuming that all the elements of it can be established against them.

In addition to being an individual, the accused, if he is to be convicted, must either be (i) a person "connected with" the company to whose securities the unpublished price-sensitive information relates or (ii) an individual who is contemplating or has contemplated making (with or without another person[39]) a take-over of a company[40] or (iii) a public servant who has obtained such information in his official capacity or (iv) an individual who has obtained such information directly or indirectly from (i), (ii) or (iii). Those falling within (i) or (ii) are often described as primary insiders

---

36 See p. 609 above. There, all that has to be proved is that he has bought (though a member of his family has a defence if he can prove that he had no reason to believe that his spouse or parent was a director). To convict him also of a more serious offence under the Insider Dealing Act is much more difficult and there are many more defences.

37 On which see p. 462 below.

38 s.1(7).

39 *e.g.* his company.

40 s.1(5), under which such individuals remain subject to the prohibitions for so long as they know that the fact that an offer is contemplated, or is no longer contemplated, continues to be unpublished price-sensitive information. In contrast an individual who was a connected person ceases to be subject to the prohibition after six months of the severance of the connection: see s.1(1) & (2).

(and so sometimes are those within (iii)[41]) and those falling within (iv) as secondary insiders.

As regards class (i) insiders, section 9 of the Act provides that:

"For the purposes of this Act a person is connected with a company[42] if, but only if,

(a) he is a director of that company or a related company,[43] or

(b) he occupies a position as an officer (other than a director) or employee of that company or a related company or a position involving a professional or business relationship between himself (or his employer or a company of which he is a director) and the first company or a related company which, in either case, may reasonably be expected to give him access to information which, in relation to securities of either company, is unpublished price-sensitive information and which it would be reasonable to expect a person in his position not to disclose except for the proper performance of his functions."

Hence, the first type of "primary" insider is divided into two sub-classes (a) and (b). Those in (a)—directors—are automatically primary insiders whereas those in (b) are not unless it can also be shown that their positions are such that they can be expected to have access to price-sensitive information regarding a company's securities.[44]

As regards "secondary insiders" a far more illuminating description of them, and one which is more commonly used, is "tippees," an expression first used in this context by Professor Louis Loss[45] of the

41 Public servants, dealt with in s.2 (as amended by the F.S. Act) are best treated as a discrete class. Their liability in no way depends on any connection with the company and there need not be one. It depends solely on their having obtained the unpublished price-sensitive information as a result of their official positions: subss. (5) & (6), added by the F.S. Act, define "public servant" (subs. (4)) and authorise the S. of S. to declare by order that persons connected with any body exercising public functions who appear to him likely to have access to unpublished price-sensitive information relating to securities, shall be treated as public servants for the purposes of the section: subss. (5) & (6): see S.I. 1989 No. 2164 which provides that officials of the Bank of England, Lloyds, and the Monopolies and Mergers Commission (but not the Panel on Take-overs and Mergers) shall be so treated.

42 *i.e.* any company, whether or not a company within the meaning of the Companies Act 1985: s.11(*a*).

43 *i.e.* any body corporate which is that company's subsidiary or holding company or a subsidiary of that company's holding company: s.11(*b*).

44 The company's auditors clearly can be expected to. In the case, say, of its solicitors or printers it presumably depends on what sort of work they do for the company. Solicitors would certainly be expected not to reveal information except for the proper discharge of their functions, but unless the company uses them in relation to its public issues, take-overs and the like, they probably cannot be expected to be the recipients of price-sensitive information about its securities. Printers employed by the company to print its annual or half-yearly reports or its prospectuses are clearly "insiders" but not those who print only its advertisements of its products.

45 The *guru* of Securities Regulation, who is rightly proud that the Oxford English Dictionary has credited him with being the parent of "tippee" in this context.

Harvard Law School. They, like public servants, need not be in any sense "insiders" of the company. But, for some reason, they are potentially liable only if the prosecution can show (a) that they knowingly obtained the unpublished price-sensitive information directly or indirectly from another individual who was connected with the company,[46] (b) that they knew or had reasonable cause to believe that that other individual held this information by virtue of being so connected and (c) that they also knew or had good cause to believe that because of the insider's position it would be reasonable to expect him not to disclose the information except for the proper performance of the functions attaching to that position.[47] It will be argued later[48] that this introduction of a concept of breach of confidence is unnecessary and misguided.

However, it was not that particular defect that caused the authorities their first major setback. This occurred in 1988 on a prosecution of a tippee in a Crown Court. A merchant bank acting for a company had told the accused that a take-over of that company had been agreed and that that information was confidential. The accused promptly bought 6,000 of its ordinary shares on The Stock Exchange. This appeared to be the clearest possible example of unlawful insider dealing: the bank was a primary insider, holding the information as such and subject to an obligation not to disclose it except in the proper performance of its functions as such.[49] The accused was aware of that, and knew that information was unpublished and price-sensitive. Yet the prosecution failed. This was because counsel for the accused succeeded in persuading the judge that the primary meaning of "obtain" (the word used in section 1(3)) was "acquire by purpose or effort." Here the accused had not sought out the information but merely received it when the bank offered it.

The result of this decision, if correct, would have frustrated most attempts to convict tippees. Accordingly the Attorney-General referred the points of law to the Court of Appeal[50] which held that, in its context and having regard to the obvious mischief aimed at by section 1(3), "obtained" meant "received."[51] However, pursuant to an application of the accused[52] the Court referred the points of law to the House of Lords, which unanimously affirmed the ruling of the Court.[53] Hence, all was well, but it took a year to establish that.

---

[46] s.1(3), *i.e.* from a primary insider, though apparently he need not know which particular insider.
[47] It is not clear what the position would be if the tippee had reasonable cause so to believe, and did, but was in fact mistaken.
[48] At p. 631 below.
[49] On this see p. 630 below.
[50] Under s.36(1) of the Criminal Justice Act 1972.
[51] *Attorney-General's Reference (No. 1 of 1988)* [1989] 2 W.L.R. 195, 88 Cr.App.R. 191, C.A.
[52] Under s.36(3) of the Criminal Justice Act.
[53] *Attorney-General's Reference (No. 1 of 1988)* [1989] A.C. 971, H.L.

However, other difficulties and complications remain. This is particularly so in relation to take-overs. If the companies are in negotiations relating to a possible take-over of one by the other, the individual directors, officers and advisers of each will almost certainly have highly confidential unpublished price-sensitive information regarding the securities not only of their own company but also of the other. Under the definition of "connected with" in section 9 they will not be "connected with" the other company unless that is already part of the same group.[54] Hence the desired result has to be achieved by tortuous and opaque provisions elsewhere.[55]

The DTI's Consultative Document[56] accepts that "the present definition [of primary insider] is long and complex and experience has shown that there are a number of difficulties with it." Nevertheless it dismisses the obvious and simple solution of rejecting the whole concept of "connected with"[57] and the distinction between insiders and tippees, and providing instead that an individual commits an offence if he engages in any of the prohibited activities knowing that he is in possession of unpublished price-sensitive information. The Document says that: "While simple this could cause damaging uncertainty in the markets as individuals attempted to identify whether or not they were covered."[58] Why this should be so is difficult to understand so long as what is meant by "unpublished price-sensitive information" is clear.

Nor is it understood why the Department should think that a definition of "insider" is needed to identify all those who are likely to have inside information. The object of the Act is not to prevent individuals from occupying positions in which they are likely to have inside information; it is to prevent them from abusing such information when they have it—whether they are likely to have it or not. Those particularly likely to have it[59] should, no doubt, be under an obligation to disclose their deals—but that is taken care of by the provisions of the Companies Act dealt with above. There may also be a case for providing that certain types of transactions, undertaken by those particularly likely to have inside information, raise a presumption that they have made use of it in relation to such

---

54 And hence a "related company": see s.11.
55 See ss.1(5) & (6) and 3(2), the net effect of which seems to be that they must not deal on their own account in the securities of either but that they are not by the Act precluded from counselling or procuring their companies from dealing in order to facilitate the carrying out of the transaction. If a company is to be taken over by individuals (which would be unusual but could occur, *e.g.*, when they were trustees of a pension fund) they are expressly forbidden from dealing in another capacity (s.1(5)) unless to facilitate the transaction (s.3(2)). And the fact that an offer is contemplated or is no longer contemplated is expressly recognised to be price-sensitive information: s.1(6).
56 Para. 2.24.
57 *Ibid.*
58 *Ibid.* The concept has no counterpart in the Directive.
59 *e.g.* directors, shadow directors, 3 per cent. shareholders and their families.

transactions,[60] but the Consultative Document does not consider that possibility.

But at least the Consultative Document suggests some steps in the right direction. Following the provisions of the Directive[61] what it proposes[62] is that a primary insider should be defined as:

"An individual who knows that he has inside information

(a) because he is a director or shadow director of the relevant company; or

(b) because he is a shareholder[63] of that company; or

(c) because he has access to the information as a result of his employment, profession, or duties; or

(d) because at the time when he acquired the information he fell within (a), (b) or (c)."

As the Document says, this seems to produce much the same results as under the present provisions but in a less complicated manner. Furthermore the Document suggests the deletion of the present requirement[64] that the information must be such that the primary insider would be expected not to disclose it except in the proper performance of his duties[65] and of the present provisions[66] whereby individuals connected with the company cease to be insiders six months after their connection with the company has ended.[67] But, under the proposals, the requirement that the information must have been acquired by the primary insider by virtue of his connection with the company will remain, and, in the case of a tippee, so will the need to establish that he knew that the original source of his information was a primary insider—though he need not know which insider it was.[68]

(b) *Inside information*

The present requirements referred to in the immediately preceding paragraph seem to imply that the unpublished price-sensitive information must be "confidential." The proposed removal of the

[60] As, in effect, ss.323 and 327 of the Companies Act do in relation to the purchase of put or call options on the company's securities. In the USA under s.16(b) of the Securities Exchange Act short-swing profits resulting from insiders' purchases and sales within a six-month period have to be disgorged regardless of whether there has been any abuse of inside information; see on this: Loss, *Fundamentals of Securities Regulation* (2nd ed.) pp. 547–582.

[61] Art. 2.1.

[62] Para. 2.26.

[63] It seems, in the light of Art. 2.1 of the Directive, that this envisages any shareholder and not only those with substantial, (*e.g.* 3 per cent.) holdings.

[64] See ss.1(1)(*b*), (2)(*b*), (3)(*b*) and 2(1)(*b*).

[65] Para. 2.16.

[66] s.1(1), (2), (3)(*a*)(i).

[67] Para. 2.27.

[68] Para. 2.28. The present provision says "knows *or had reasonable cause to believe*" (s.1(3)(*a*)(ii)); it is not clear whether it is intended to delete the words italicised.

express provision regarding that[69] would make little difference in most cases because information, held by a primary insider as such and which is unpublished and price-sensitive, will almost certainly be confidential.[70] It is not obvious, however, that confidentiality ought to have any relevance in this context, or why tippees must be shown to have known that the original source of the information was a primary insider. So long as the tippee knows that the information is unpublished and price-sensitive, if he thinks it sufficiently reliable to be acted upon it should surely not be necessary for the prosecution to have to prove that he knew that the source was a primary insider—subject to a duty of confidentiality—something which it may be impossible to prove. All that the Directive seems to require is that the direct or indirect source must be a primary insider.[71]

(c) *Unpublished price-sensitive information*
It is this element which is the essential one. It is defined thus in section 10:

"Any reference in this Act to unpublished price-sensitive information in relation to any securities of a company is a reference to information which—

(a) relates to specific matters relating or of concern (directly or indirectly) to that company,[72] that is to say, is not of a general nature relating or of concern to that company,[73] and

(b) is not generally known to those persons who are accustomed or would be likely to deal in those securities[74] but which would, if it were generally known to them, be likely materially to affect the price of those securities."

On the whole, this seems to be a pretty good and unusually economical definition. But the Consultative Document[75] expresses a preference for the approach of the Directive, which it describes as "simpler and shorter." It contains three elements only[76]: the

---

69 *i.e.* of the requirement that it would be reasonable to expect him not to disclose it except for the proper performance of his functions.
70 The proposed extension of primary insiders to shareholders might make a difference; if Sid and Aunt Agatha are given information as shareholders they will legitimately assume that it is not confidential unless expressly told that it is.
71 Directive Art. 4.
72 *e.g.* that its half-yearly accounts will show a substantial increase or decrease in its profits or that take-over discussions are in progress.
73 Not, for example, that companies in the construction industry are having a bad time or that there has been a collapse on the New York or Tokyo Exchange. In these days of rapid communication these are, in any event, likely to be "generally known" as well as being "of a general nature."
74 This seems to exclude securities traded on what are said to be "professionals only" markets, (*e.g.* the Euro-securities market) so long as the information is generally known to the relevant professionals.
75 Para. 2.15.
76 Art. 1(1).

information (i) must be of a precise nature relating to one or more companies[77] or to one or more transferable securities, (ii) it must not have been made public, and (iii) it must be likely, if made public, to have a significant effect on the price of the security or securities in question. The Document suggests that this makes it clearer than does the Act that the information may relate either to the securities or to the company. Its weakness seems to be that it makes it less clear what is meant by "made public"; but its attraction is that it would seem to make it possible to avoid the present convoluted provisions flowing from the "connected with" concept, particularly in relation to take-overs.[78]

(d) *Prohibited activities*

Assuming that the foregoing elements (a)–(c) are established, then, subject to (e) and (f) below, the following activities are prohibited by section 1 whether undertaken by a primary insider or a tippee:

(i) dealing on a recognised stock exchange in the securities concerned;
(ii) counselling or procuring any other person[79] so to deal;
(iii) communicating the unpublished price-sensitive information to any other person,[80] knowing or having reasonable cause to believe that that, or some other, person will make use of the information for the purposes of doing (i) or (ii).

Section 2, extending the prohibitions to public servants and their tippees, is similar to section 1 but, since the public servant does not have to be "connected with" any company but merely to know that he holds unpublished price-sensitive information relating to the securities of a particular company, it can be (and is) expressed more simply.

The scope of the prohibited activities is widened by sections 4 and 5. The effect of section 4,[81] and its relevant definitions,[82] can be summarised with reasonable accuracy by saying that wherever the Act refers to "dealing on a recognised stock exchange"[83] that has to be

---

[77] The Directive uses the word "issuers" because it extends beyond company securities, as our legislation will also have to: see below at p. 634.
[78] On which see n. 55 above.
[79] Whether or not an "individual."
[80] Again, whether or not an "individual." Although companies or other bodies corporate cannot be prosecuted under the Act, their "tippers" and "tippees" can.
[81] As amended by the F.S. Act.
[82] Of "securities," "listed securities" and "advertised securities" in s.12, and of "deal in securities," and of "off-market dealer," in s.13.
[83] Defined in section 16 as "The Stock Exchange and any other investment exchange which is declared by an order of the S. of S. to be a recognised stock exchange for the purposes of the Act." This enables not only the UK futures and options exchanges to be included but also selected foreign exchanges. Two such orders have been made: S.I. 1989 No. 2165 (NASDAQ) and S.I. 1990 No. 47 (London O.M.).

construed as if it read "dealing on a recognised stock exchange or through an authorised person within the meaning of the Financial Services Act who is making a market in securities which are listed or in respect of which he has advertised his prices." Similarly, under section 5, prohibitions (ii) (counselling or procuring) and (iii) (tipping) are extended to circumstances where the dealings are to be undertaken on a stock exchange outside Great Britain which is not a recognised stock exchange—thus attempting to prevent evasion by dealing through intermediaries on foreign exchanges (which may be less likely to have information that will enable them to detect insider dealing).

The wording of sections 1 and 2 regarding prohibitions (ii) and (iii) results in a consequence which at first sight seems surprising. Whereas those counselled, procured or tipped-off will not commit an offence if they refrain from dealing until after the information has been published, this will not excuse the counsellor, procurer or tipper even if he has expressly embargoed use of the information until after it has been published. Hence if those connected with a company release information to the company's brokers with a warning that the brokers must not act upon it until it has been published by The Stock Exchange, unless they can establish one of the defences under section 3 or 6 (*e.g.* that this was done in order "to facilitate the completion or carrying out of the transaction" to which the information relates[84]), they will have committed an offence. This, however, seems to be a very proper result since by so doing they have (deliberately) enabled the brokers to plan in advance the strategy to adopt once the information is published, thereby gaining a false start on users of the market and affecting the market's integrity.

It is in relation to the prohibited activities that the Consultative Document proposes to make the most important changes—partly because the Directive requires the United Kingdom to do so but also because our present provisions are unsatisfactory. Without resiling from the belief that the basic objection to insider dealing is that it affects the integrity of the markets, the Document concludes that in the light of the growing "internationalisation" of markets and of what are, or arguably are, domestic "investment exchanges," it is becoming impossible to achieve a satisfactory result by defining "exchanges" and limiting the prohibition to dealings on them.[85] The Directive achieves much the same aims in a simpler manner; namely by restricting the ambit of the prohibitions to dealings undertaken through professional intermediaries.[86] It is this approach that the Consultative Document proposes to follow.[87]

[84] See s.3(2) below, p. 636.
[85] Consultative Document, paras. 2.7–2.10.
[86] Art. 2, para. (3). Thus recognising that they constitute "the market" whether they deal on or off exchanges.
[87] Para. 2.10.

At present, our legislation applies only to activities relating to *company securities*.[88] The Directive requires us to go much further,[89] recognising that the integrity of markets is affected by insider dealings in any securities traded thereon. Hence the Document proposes that the ambit of our legislation should be extended to cover government securities ("gilts") and local authority stocks and their "derivatives."[90] Not only will this make for simplicity, enabling a single definition of "securities" to replace those of "securities," "listed securities" and "advertised securities,"[91] it will also remove the obvious anomaly that, at present, section 2 prohibits insider dealing by public servants but not in respect of the securities about which some of them are most likely to have unpublished information.[92] Also, and rightly, it is proposed that unit trusts and traded "contracts for differences" on indices should be covered—but only if the inside information regarding a component of the portfolio or the index would be likely to have a significant effect on the value of the whole.[93]

(e) *Mens rea*

Mention has already been made of the fact that the prosecution will have to prove the accused's knowledge of the existence of various elements of the alleged offence. A primary insider by virtue of being "connected with" the company must be shown to have been "*knowingly* connected with" the company and must *know* that the information is unpublished price-sensitive information; and a tippee must be shown to have *known* that the source of the information was a primary insider and to *know* that it is unpublished price-sensitive information. To prove that someone knows, unless he is willing to admit it, is not easy—though sometimes the facts will raise an almost irresistible inference that he did know.[94] A further difficulty is that in some cases the present provisions do not make it clear who has to know what. For example in section 4(1)(*a*) one would have supposed that it is the person dealing with the off-market dealer who must be shown to have knowledge that the latter was an off-market dealer

[88] Though the meaning of "securities" in many cases includes "any right to subscribe for, or make delivery of, a share or debenture (s.12(*a*)) and as a result of s.13(1A), inserted by the F.S. Act, "deals" includes buying or selling contracts for differences within Sched. 1, para. 9 of the F.S. Act.

[89] *i.e.* to dealings in any "transferable securities" as defined in Art. 1(2).

[90] Para. 2.17. The Government had expressed its intention to do so in its White Paper of January 1985: *Financial Services in the UK* Cmnd. 9472.

[91] Para. 2.18.

[92] *e.g.* officials of the Treasury or the Bank of England in relation to gilts.

[93] Paras. 2.19–2.21.

[94] *e.g.* if he is shown to be a director or officer he will surely be held to know that he was unless *he* can show that for some reason he did not. But if, as proposed, a shadow director becomes a primary insider not only will there be the difficulty of proving that he was a shadow director but the further difficulty of proving that he knew it. If the need for knowledge is maintained in the revision of the Act, should not the accused be required to prove that he did not know?

making a market in advertised securities. However, since the only person previously mentioned in the subsection is the off-market dealer, it seems that he is the one who must know.[95] In some cases, however, the Act requires proof either of knowledge or of "reasonable cause to believe,"[96] thus providing an objective alternative to actual knowledge and one much easier to prove.

(f) Exclusions

The Act then provides a considerable number of exclusions or defences.[97] If the accused is to avail himself of these the onus will be on him to establish that he comes within one or more of them.[98] They are to be found in sections 3, 6[99] and 7.

Section 3 provides first that sections 1 and 2 do not prohibit an individual from "doing any particular thing otherwise than with a view to the making of a profit or the avoidance of a loss (whether for himself or another person) by the use of the information."[1] This is probably the most important of the exclusions because it provides a defence for any type of insider or tippee whereas the others are likely to be available only to special types, mainly to "professionals." It seems to be one of the reasons for the difficulties which prosecutors are finding in persuading magistrates or juries to convict.[2] Although the onus of establishing the defence is on the accused[3] it is not as easily established as one might suppose. On the wording of section 3(1)(a) it should not suffice for the accused to establish that he had a motive additional to that of enabling someone to make a profit or avoid a loss; he should have to establish that the motive could be achieved only by acting when his information was still unpublished and that he could not wait until after the information had been published (or had ceased to be price-sensitive) which it normally would be within a short time. This defence the Consultative Document proposes to retain.[4]

55 Perhaps it was thought that the possibility of an off-market dealer not knowing what he is doing is not as remote as one would wish—but why should that let the accused off the hook? Happily s.4 is likely to be deleted under the Government's proposals.
96 *e.g.* in ss.1(3)(*a*)(ii) and (*b*), (7) and (8) and 2(2)(*b*) and (*c*).
97 Which the Consultative Document proposes to reduce to three only: para. 2.31.
98 *R. v. Cross* (1990) 1 Cr.App.R. 115, C.A.
99 As substituted by the F.S. Act.
1 s.3(1)(*a*). It could be argued that, since our legislation is designed to protect market integrity, the motives of the insider-dealer should be irrelevant; but it may be too harsh to punish someone whose personal circumstances have forced him to act as he did and normally it is unlikely that his activities alone will have much influence on the market.
2 The success rate has been low and even when the accused is convicted the sentence is normally a fine, the amount of which generally seems inadequate in comparison with the gains made. To date only in one case has a custodial sentence been imposed.
3 The attempt in *R. v. Cross* (above, n. 98) to persuade the C.A. that this was not so as regards s.3(1)(*a*) was rejected by the C.A. at p. 121. Nevertheless the conviction was quashed and the case illustrates the difficulty of adequately directing a jury in such cases.
4 Para. 2.31(*a*).

Secondly, section 3 provides a defence for: (i) a liquidator, receiver or trustee in bankruptcy who enters into a transaction in good faith in pursuance of his functions as such[5]; (ii) a recognised market-maker who obtained the information, and could reasonably have been expected to obtain it, in the ordinary course of that business[6]; or (iii) an insider of one company who obtained information about the securities of another because of a transaction, (*e.g.* a take-over) involving both companies and who acts only to facilitate the completion of that transaction.[7] The Consultative Document proposes that (i) and (ii) should be merged in a general defence relating to activities undertaken in good faith by those who have a conflict of obligations. This would certainly reduce the "long list of exceptions [which] could lead to undue confusion and to anomalies"[8] and seems to be an admirable solution if it can be achieved with sufficient precision. Unfortunately it could not embrace (iii) which the Document proposes to retain[9]—but, one hopes, expressed rather more intelligibly.

Section 6[10] provides that no provision of section 1, 2, 4 or 5 prevents an individual from doing anything for the purpose of stabilising the price of newly-issued securities if it is done in conformity with rules made under section 48 of the Financial Services Act and in relation to the types of security, and during the periods, permitted by those rules.[11] The Consultative Document suggests that this too might be taken care of by the proposed general defence afforded to those who have conflicts of obligations. The difficulty is that the rules sometimes "permit," but never "oblige," an individual to stabilise. However, he might, presumably, be under an obligation to the issuer and the underwriters to take advantage of the permission if it was in their interests to do so and in that event it does indeed seem that there would be a "conflict of obligations." But one suspects that there will be pressure for the retention of a defence specific to stabilisation.

Section 7 contains a defence in relation to trustees and personal representatives or, if they are bodies corporate, individuals acting for them. This it does by providing a presumption that they have acted otherwise than with a view to the making of a profit or the avoidance of a loss (whether for themselves or for others[12]) by the use of the

---

5 s.3(1)(*b*).

6 s.3(1)(*d*). Section 3(1)(*c*) contains a similar defence for a "jobber" recognised by The Stock Exchange: but this appears to be an unneeded relic of the original legislation enacted before "Big Bang." The Stock Exchange now has "recognised market makers," not "recognised jobbers."

7 s.3(2).

8 Consultative Document, para. 2.31.

9 *Ibid.* para. 2.31(*b*).

10 As substituted, for the former specific defence of Euro-bond dealers in the original version, by the F.S. Act.

11 On price stabilisation see above, Chap. 13 at pp. 350, 351.

12 In this case, the beneficiaries.

price-sensitive information, provided they have acted on the advice of a person who appeared to them to be an appropriate person from whom to seek such advice[13] and not to be a person prohibited under the Act from dealing in the relevant securities. In other words, if they have acted on impartial professional advice they are presumed to be entitled to the general defence under section 3(1)(*a*). It might appear at first sight that this (rebuttable) presumption is valueless since they clearly have acted "with a view to the making of a profit or the avoidance of a loss" by the beneficiaries. But that is to ignore the words "by the use of that information"; they are presumed to have acted as a result of the advice and *not* as a result of the information. The presumption could be rebutted by showing that the advice was sought in a way which was calculated to produce the advice that would enable them to use their inside information. Spontaneous unsought advice from a stockbroker would protect them and, perhaps, advice on whether they should retain or sell an existing holding. But advice sought by "We are minded to purchase £10,000 of XYZ plc stock but would welcome your advice" clearly would not.

The Consultative Document[14] proposes the deletion of this specific defence, leaving trustees to rely on one or other of the general exceptions if they can bring themselves within it. It argues, rightly, that trustees cannot be compelled to commit a criminal offence even if that is in the interests of the beneficiaries. That argument, however, ignores the fact that, without this specific defence, or something like it, trustees may find themselves unable to undertake transactions needed in the interests of their beneficiaries because one of them has price-sensitive information which prohibits him from undertaking it. In the case of directors, what would occur is that the director would declare that he had a connection with the other company whose securities were concerned and would refrain from playing any part in the decision. But, under an (archaic?) rule of trust law, trustees have to act unanimously. Should not consideration be given to modifying that rule so that in these circumstances the decision could be taken by the other trustees?

Criminal penalties

If all the foregoing hurdles can be jumped, the accused will be liable on conviction on indictment to imprisonment for a term of not more than seven years[15] or, on conviction summarily, for not more than six months and, in either case, to a fine or to both imprisonment

13 *e.g.* the trustees' stockbrokers who are not acting for the company concerned.
14 Para. 2.33.
15 Raised from the former two years by the Criminal Justice Act 1988.

and a fine.[16] Prosecutions can be brought only by, *or with the consent of*, the Secretary of State or the Director of Public Prosecutions.[17] The words italicised enable the Secretary of State to consent to prosecutions by The Stock Exchange, which, for many years past, has been on the watch for movements on its markets which suggested that insider dealing might have taken place, and has carried out preliminary investigations. But formerly if those investigations did not allay its suspicions it could not do more, except sometimes in relation to its own member firms. So far as other possible culprits were concerned it had to hand over its information to the DTI (or the DPP) thus leading to further investigations and delay before prosecutions were launched or, more often, a decision taken not to prosecute. Now it may be enabled to undertake the whole process and may, perhaps, be more willing to prosecute than the DPP.

Investigation by inspectors

There will, however, be cases where the deals were not on The Stock Exchange and others where it lacks the powers needed to obtain the necessary evidence. Here there has been another recent development. Under section 177[18] of the Financial Services Act the Secretary of State is empowered to appoint inspectors with wide inquisitorial powers specifically to investigate and report on whether there have been contraventions of the Insider Dealing Act. This power supplements that under section 442 or 444 of the Companies Act[19] to appoint inspectors to investigate company ownership, an investigation which might incidentally reveal breaches of the Act.[20]

Inspectors appointed under the new section 177 may require any person who is or may be able to give them relevant information (a) to produce any documents in his possession or control relating to the company or its securities, (b) to attend before them, and (c) otherwise to give them all assistance that he is reasonably able to give[21] and the inspectors may examine any such person on oath.[22] A statement made in compliance with any such requirement may be

---

[16] s.8(1). If the accused is convicted summarily, and the accused's profits have exceeded the "statutory maximum" it will not be possible for the fine to match or exceed the profit made by the insider dealing.
[17] s.8(2) as amended by the Companies Act 1989.
[18] As amended by the Companies Act 1989. This, and its supplementary s.178, will on a future reconsolidation presumably be inserted in the Insider Dealing Act where it properly belongs rather than in the F.S. Act (as at present) or in the Companies Act.
[19] See above at pp. 621, 622.
[20] As indeed might investigations under other sections in Part XIV of the Companies Act: see Chap. 25 below.
[21] F.S. Act s.177(3).
[22] *Ibid.* s.177(4).

used in evidence against the maker of it.[23] The person concerned is not required to disclose or produce matter protected by legal professional privilege[24] but bankers may be compelled to breach their normal duties of confidentiality if the Secretary of State specifically authorises the inspectors to make the requirement.[25]

If a person refuses to comply with any such requirement the inspectors themselves cannot compel him to or commit him for contempt of court if he does not. But what they can do under section 178 is to "certify that fact in writing" to the High Court "which may then inquire into the case"[26] and, "if satisfied that he did, without reasonable excuse,"[27] refuse to comply," may (a) "punish him in like manner as if he had been guilty of contempt of court; or (b) direct the Secretary of State to exercise his powers under this section in respect of him."[28]

An interesting illustration of the operation of sections 177 and 178 is afforded by *Re An Inquiry under the Insider Dealing Act.*[29] Alarmed at what appeared to be leaks emanating from one or more public servants in the DTI, Office of Fair Trading or Monopolies and Mergers Commission on whether take-overs were or were not to be referred to the Commission (leaks which seemingly had resulted in insider dealing) inspectors were appointed under section 177. The inspectors became aware that a financial journalist[30] had published

23 *Ibid.* s.177(6). It seems clear that a refusal to answer on the ground that the answer would incriminate him will not in itself be a reasonable excuse under s.178(2) below. If it were, it would defeat the object of the section for the suspected insider dealers are those whom the inspectors will be especially anxious to question.

24 *Ibid.* s.177(7).

25 *Ibid.* s.177(7).

26 Or, of course, if the person to whom the duty is owed consents. *Ibid.* s.177(8) as substituted by the Companies Act 1989.

27 *Ibid.* s.178(1).

28 Under s.178(6) if the contravention or suspected contravention relates to dealings by him on the instructions of another, it is not a reasonable excuse that he did not know the identity of that other, or that he was subject to a foreign law which prohibited him from disclosing without the consent of that other person if he might have obtained that consent or exemption from that law.

29 [1988] A.C. 660, C.A. & H.L.

30 He had not entered into any deals and, by publishing the price-sensitive information he had prevented any further abuse by insider dealers of that information. His position had some affinities with that of the unfortunate Mr. Dirks in the famous *Dirks* case in the U.S.A. (on which see Loss, *Fundamentals of Securities Regulation* (2nd ed.) at pp. 762 *et seq.*). Dirks, a specialist investment analyst of insurance companies' securities, as a result of information offered him by a former employee of a large and respected insurance company and his own subsequent inquiries, had concluded that the company was in fact riddled with fraud. He informed the relevant authorities but none of them would credit it or do anything to investigate. Eventually, in desperation, he told his clients and advised them to sell their holdings in the company—which they did. This led to a collapse in the price of the company's securities and eventually to exposure of the frauds. Thereupon the SEC, instead of giving him a medal, accused him (but not his clients) of breaches of the insider-dealing legislation. He was eventually acquitted but it took him nearly 10 years and resort to the US Supreme Court which held that he was not guilty because he had not breached any fiduciary duty. That is not a precondition of liability under the English legislation and one wonders whether, under that, Dirks would not have been (technically) guilty of a criminal offence.

articles in *The Times* and *The Independent* in which he had stated with uncanny accuracy what decision was going to be announced in each of two take-overs. Hence the inspectors wished to obtain from him information about his source, information which, in accordance with the journalists' creed, he refused to divulge. The inspectors accordingly certified his refusal to the High Court. The effect of the Contempt of Court Act 1981[31] is that a journalist is not compelled to disclose his sources, and is not guilty of contempt if he refuses to do so, unless disclosure is "necessary in the interests of justice, or national security or for the prevention of disorder or crime." Here all turned on whether disclosure was "necessary . . . for the prevention . . . of crime." In the High Court Hoffmann J. held that, in view of the information which the inspectors already had, disclosure was not "necessary for the prevention of crime," and that therefore the journalist had "a reasonable excuse" for refusing. But his decision was reversed by the Court of Appeal and House of Lords and the case remitted to him to decide on the appropriate penalty for contempt.

Civil liability

We presently have insider dealing legislation which, by its proliferation of matters that have to be proved and of defences which may be raised, seems calculated to make it as difficult as possible for the criminal law sanctions against it to be effective—which, however, should be improved if most of the proposals in the Consultative Document are implemented. But the Document does not propose to supplement the present criminal liability by expressly providing the victim of insider dealing with a civil remedy. This is surprising; for the present position in this respect is unsatisfactory. It is not true to say that there is never civil liability; as we have seen,[32] there is little doubt that the company concerned could recover from its fiduciary-insider any profits he made by dealing with the use of unpublished price-sensitive information in the company's securities—whether or not the company had thereby suffered any loss[33] and whether or not an offence under the Act had been committed. Furthermore an "authorised person" under the Financial Services Act is required by the Core Conduct of Business Rules of SIB to comply with the Insider Dealing Act, to ensure that its employees do so and not to act for a client in a transaction which it knows would be an offence by the client.[34] Under the Financial Services Act, if clients of the

---

[31] Passed as a result of Parliamentary disquiet about the effect on media freedom of the decision in *British Steel Corpn.* v. *Granada TV Ltd.* [1981] A.C. 1096, H.L.
[32] At p. 607 above, where it is pointed out that this liability is largely theoretical.
[33] It may well have suffered loss to its reputation.
[34] Core Rule 28. On which see M. Blair, *Financial Services: The New Core Rules*, pp. 121–125.

authorised person suffer loss as a result of a breach of the Rules, there may be a civil remedy under its section 61[35] or 62.[36] And, under section 178(5) of that Act, if the court gives a direction to the Secretary of State under subsection (2)(b) of that section[37] in respect of an authorised person, the Secretary of State may direct that any authorised person who transacts investment business with or on behalf of the unauthorised person shall be treated as having contravened the Rules of Conduct. Hence the combined effect of the two Acts and SIB's Rules may sometimes afford the clients of an "authorised person" compensation in respect of loss sustained as a result of a breach of the Insider Dealing Act to which the authorised person is a party. But if A (not being an "authorised person") is in possession of unpublished price-sensitive information about securities and induces B (with whom he is not in a fiduciary relationship) to buy from, or sell to, A those securities, B will seemingly have no claim for damages or compensation for any loss that B suffers as a result.

The wholly unsatisfactory result at present is that an investor who has suffered loss as a result of the other party's abuse of inside information can recover damages only if the other party is an "authorised person" and is party to a crime which can be established only if a plethora of conditions are met and a plethora of defences rejected. Most of the conditions should have no relevance in relation to civil liability; all that is relevant there is whether one party, knowing that he has unpublished price-sensitive information, has entered into a transaction with another who is ignorant of it, and whether, as a result, the latter has suffered loss. Yet, according to the Consultative Document: "The Government is not at present convinced of the need to modify the civil law in this area."[37] It is to be hoped that it will be convinced by the influential voices expressing the contrary view. Judging from the fear expressed by the financial community of the civil remedy under section 62 of the Financial Services Act, it would be a potent deterrent against insider dealing—and one which would cost public funds little or nothing.

Moreover, section 8(3) of the Insider Dealing Act specifically provides that: "No transaction is void or voidable by reason only that it was entered into in contravention of sections 1, 2, 4 or 5" of the Act, thereby, or so it was generally thought, ensuring that a prohibited transaction is not deemed to be tainted with illegality. But the recent decision of Knox J. in *Chase Manhattan Equities Ltd.* v. *Goodman*[38] holds that this is not so. A contract in breach of the prohibitions in the Insider Dealing Act *is* tainted with illegality and

---

[35] By SIB obtaining a restitution order on their behalf.
[36] By direct actions by "private" clients.
[37] Para. 2.12.
[38] [1991] B.C.L.C. 897.

unenforceable by the party guilty of the criminal offence and the sole object of section 8(3) was to prevent transactions on a stock exchange from being re-opened. While this decision is to be welcomed it cannot be said to leave the overall position clear or satisfactory.

CHINESE WALLS

In conclusion, brief reference should be made to so-called "Chinese Walls," the device invented in the U.S.A. primarily to protect multi-purpose financial firms, against liability for insider dealing, by establishing arrangements designed to prevent knowledge of price-sensitive information held by members of one branch of the business being passed on to members of another branch and the firm itself being deemed to have knowledge of it. Under the present Insider Dealing Act the need for such Walls is somewhat less since, as we have seen, it is only individuals having actual knowledge who can be prosecuted under that Act and the onus of proof of knowledge is on the prosecution. Nevertheless such Walls are a wise precaution against the knowledge being spread throughout the firm and their erection is permissible under the Financial Services Act and the Rules made thereunder.[39] Their effectiveness is, of course, dependent on the Wall proving impenetrable and it has the disadvantage that a client of the firm's corporate financial division which is planning a share-for-share takeover will not take it kindly if the firm's broking arm recommends clients to sell its shares.

[39] In relation, for example, to liability under s.47 of the F.S. Act: see Chap. 13, above.

CHAPTER 24

BREACH OF CORPORATE DUTIES:
LEGAL REMEDIES

When specific duties are imposed by the Act, it frequently states how, by, and against whom, action may be taken to enforce them. When this is so, that has been mentioned in the course of the discussion of the relevant sections. But so far as concerns the common law and equitable duties of directors, members and the company dealt with in earlier chapters in this Part, the Act is generally silent. The purpose of this and the next chapter is to discuss what such remedies are. The obvious one is to invoke the jurisdiction of the courts and with this we start; with a preamble on:

THE RULE IN FOSS V. HARBOTTLE

This famous (or infamous) rule has already been referred to more than once but now has to be dealt with more fully. It was first clearly articulated long ago in the case from which it takes its name[1] and it has since spawned an immense volume of case law and legal literature. The pre-1980 decisions were exhaustively reviewed in the *Newman Industries* litigation[2] and in the light of that[3] it is unnecessary here to repeat that exhausting exercise.[4] Instead it seems best to start with what the Court of Appeal there described as "the classic definition of the rule," namely that in the judgment of Jenkins L.J. in *Edwards* v. *Halliwell*[5] and which the court summarised in the following propositions[6]:

"1. The proper plaintiff in an action in respect of a wrong alleged to be done to a corporation is prima facie the corporation.

2. Where the alleged wrong is a transaction which might be made binding on the corporation and on all its members by a simple majority of the members, no individual member of the corporation is allowed to maintain an action in respect of that matter because, if the

---

[1] (1843) 2 Hare 451.
[2] *Prudential Assurance* v. *Newman Industries (No. 1)* [1981] Ch. 229 (Vinelott J.); *ibid.* (No. 2) [1981] Ch. 257 (Vinelott J.) and [1982] Ch. 224, C.A. The hearing of the latter by Vinelott J. took some 64 days (and 68 cases were cited). In the C.A. it took some 45 days of which four were spent by three L.JJ. taking it in turns to read a seven-chapter written judgment, of which the L.R. reported only Chapters 5 (The Law) and 7 (Conclusions).
[3] Not that, in the end, it spread much light.
[4] The locus classicus of the legal literature remains Wedderburn's article in [1957] Cam.L.J. 194 and [1958] *ibid.* 93. Of the post-Newman literature, see Sealy's devastating critique in Pettet (ed.) *Company Law in Change* (1987) at pp. 1–21 and Sterling in (1987) 50 M.L.R. 468.
[5] [1950] 2 All E.R. 1064, C.A. at 1066–1069. This case concerned a trade union but nothing turned on that.
[6] [1982] Ch. at 210F–211A. The footnotes have been added.

majority confirms the transaction, *cadit quaestio*: or, if the majority challenges the transaction, there is no valid reason why the company should not sue.

3. There is also no room for the operation of the rule if the alleged wrong is *ultra vires* the corporation because the majority of members cannot confirm the transaction.[7]

4. There is also no room for the operation of the rule if the transaction complained of could be validly done or sanctioned only by a special resolution or the like, because a simple majority cannot confirm a transaction which requires the concurrence of a greater majority.

5. There is an exception to this rule where what has been done amounts to fraud[8] and the wrongdoers are themselves in control of the company. In this case the rule is relaxed in favour of the aggrieved minority, who are allowed to bring a minority shareholders' action on behalf of themselves and all others.[9] The reason for this is that, if they were denied that right, their grievance would never reach the court because the wrongdoers themselves, being in control, would not allow the company to sue."

Proposition 1 relates to situations, such as those in *Foss v. Harbottle* itself, in which the alleged wrong is a breach of duty to the company owed, for example, by a director or other officer. Proposition 2, however, is concerned with cases where there has been an irregularity in the operation of the company. Shortly after the decision in *Foss v. Harbottle* its rule was extended to these and the test of whether the irregularity was such that a member could bring an action in respect of it was said to be whether the irregularity was one that could not be rectified by an ordinary resolution.[10] This has

---

[7] Despite the "abolition" of the strict *ultra vires* rule by the 1989 Act this seems to be unaffected as the new s.35(2) expressly entitles a member to bring proceedings to restrain an act which, but for s.35(1) would be *ultra vires*, and under s.35(3) the directors' decision can be ratified only by a special resolution so that exception 4 also applies.

[8] It is clear that "fraud" is here used in the equitable, rather than the legal sense. Indeed it is usual to adopt the expression "fraud on the minority" (discussed in Chap. 22 above) as, in fact Jenkins L.J. did in his judgment in *Edwards v. Halliwell* [1950] 2 All E.R. at 1067A and B.

[9] Nominally the action is so brought but, as we shall see later, the courts now recognise that it is really brought on behalf of the company itself.

[10] *Mozley v. Alston* (1847) 1 Ph. 790; *MacDougall v. Gardiner* (1875) 1 Ch.D. 13, C.A. It was thought that this extension would promote one of the alleged practical advantages of the rule—the avoidance of futile litigation. "If the thing complained of is a thing which in substance the majority of the company are entitled to do, or if something has been done irregularly which the majority of the company are entitled to do regularly, there can be no use in having a litigation about it, the ultimate end of which is only that a meeting has to be called and then ultimately the majority gets its wishes: *per* Mellish L.J. at (1875) 1 Ch.D. at 25. This, as Wedderburn points out, reflects the reluctance of the courts to interfere in majority decisions of partnerships (*loc. cit.* n. 4 above). But it ignores the fact that, in the case of companies, majority decisions of members have to be taken at formal meetings and that, normally, decisions are taken by the directors (and not, as in partnerships by the members) and can be challenged, if at all, only if the members are in a position to insist on a general meeting being held.

led to irreconcilable decisions on what are or are not such irregularities.[11] It has also led to both propositions 1 and 2 being treated as parts of a single rule, subject to the same exclusions or exceptions in propositions 3, 4 and 5 which, if established, enable a member or members to launch a suit instead of the company itself.

A main source of the quagmire into which we now step is proposition 4 which apparently provides an exception or exclusion from both propositions 1 and 2, but to make little sense in relation to either. *Edwards* v. *Halliwell* itself was a case in which there had been an irregularity; the union had purported to increase the members' subscriptions without the passing of a resolution to that effect by a two-thirds majority of the members as required by its rules. The increase was therefore a transaction which could be "validly done or sanctioned only by a special resolution or the like." Jenkins L.J. first held[12] that if the *Foss* v. *Harbottle* rule had any application, the exception from proposition 2 in proposition 4 permitted a member to sue in his own name and on his own behalf. But he then went on to hold[13] that the case fell wholly outside the ambit of the rule since the union's rules conferred personal rights on the members[14] which they were therefore entitled to enforce in a personal action against the union. Whether members have such personal rights clearly cannot depend upon whether or not the irregular action was one which required a "special resolution or the like." That would produce absurd results. It would mean, for example, that, whereas in the recent case of *Byng* v. *London Life Association*[15] a member was able to succeed in an action in his own name and on his own behalf to obtain a declaration that a purported meeting and the special resolutions purporting to have been passed thereat were void, he could not have done so if the void meeting had been convened to pass ordinary resolutions needed to confirm the transaction.

Hence it is difficult to see what proposition 4 achieves in relation to irregularities unless, contrary to general belief, there are two types of

11 See Wedderburn at [1957] Cam.L.J. 213–215, and Smith in (1978) 41 M.L.R. 147.

12 [1950] 2 All E.R. at p. 1067C, E.

13 "In my view this is a case of a kind which is not even within the general ambit of the rule. It is not a case where what is complained of is a wrong done to the union, a matter in respect of which the cause of action would primarily and properly belong to the union . . . The gist of the case is that the personal and individual rights of membership . . . have been invaded by a purported but invalid alteration . . . In these circumstances it seems to me that the rule in *Foss* v. *Harbottle* has no application at all for the members who are suing, sue not in the right of the union but in their own right to protect from invasion their own individual rights as members": at p. 1067F–H and citing, at 1068A,B, Jessel M.R. in *Pender* v. *Lushington* (1877) 6 Ch.D. 70 at 80.

14 In the case of companies, these "personal rights" would presumably flow from the "deemed" contract between the company and its members constituted by the memo and arts. under s.14 of the Act (see Chap. 11 at pp. 282–288 above) and, in relation to the overlapping *ultra vires* exception in proposition 3, from, now, s.35: see Chap. 8 at p. 176 above.

15 [1990] Ch. 170, C.A. discussed in Chap. 19 at pp. 525–527 above.

personal action available to a member; (i) when his personal rights are infringed (which falls wholly outside the *Foss v. Harbottle* rule) and (ii) when the irregularity relates to a transaction requiring a special or extraordinary resolution, when he can bring a personal action notwithstanding that his personal rights are not infringed!

As an exception to proposition 1, proposition 4 presents different, but equal, difficulty. Propositions 3, 4 and 5 are stated in such a way as to imply that any one of them is sufficient to exclude propositions 1 and 2. But that is clearly not so in relation to proposition 1. For the member to be permitted to sue to enforce duties owed to the company, the conditions of proposition 5 have to be met and, if proposition 4 is to have any application it must be as an exception to that exception so that the member will not be able to sue (even though the conditions of proposition 5 are met) if the breach of duty is one which could be sanctioned by an ordinary resolution of the company (whether or not it has been so sanctioned). Since one condition of proposition 5 is that the breach of duty should be one that involves "fraud" (which cannot be sanctioned by an ordinary resolution) this seems to be an unnecessary refinement.

In the light of the foregoing it seems questionable whether it can be correct to treat the rule, as a single, albeit two-part, rule subject to a single list of exceptions in propositions 3–5. There seem to be two distinct rules: (i) the original rule in *Foss v. Harbottle* and (ii) what might better be called the rule in *Mozley v. Alston* or in *MacDougall v. Gardiner*,[16] each with its own exceptions.[17] It has also been questioned whether the exceptions in propositions 3–5 are, in fact, exhaustive; there are dicta in the cases which suggest that there is a further one; namely that the rule will be relaxed whenever the justice of the case so requires.[18]

PERSONAL AND DERIVATIVE ACTIONS

What, however, does seem clear is that a member qua member may have two distinct types of action. The first is a personal action against the company in respect of a breach of the duties which the company owes to him.[19] The second, which is available to him only if the conditions of proposition 5 are met and the court permits it, is what

---

[16] See n. 10 above.

[17] Already it seems to be accepted that the exception in proposition 5 applies only to proposition 1.

[18] See *Foss v. Harbottle* itself, (1843) 2 Hare at 492; *Russell v. Wakefield Waterworks Co.* (1872) L.R. 20 Eq. at 482; *Baillie v. Oriental Telephone Co.* [1915] 1 Ch. at 518; *Cotter v. National Union of Seamen* [1929] 2 Ch. at 9; *Edwards v. Halliwell* [1950] 2 All E.R. at 1067B; *Heyting v. Dupont* [1964] 1 W.L.R. at 851. If these suggestions were adopted (which seems unlikely—see p. 653 below) all the other exceptions could be subsumed in it.

[19] If other members have identical rights, his "personal" action may be on behalf of himself and all other such members (*i.e.* a true representative action).

used to be called a "minority shareholders' action" and to be thought of as a type of representative action on behalf of the members, but which is now given the more illuminating name of "a derivative action"[20] in recognition of what it truly is[21]; namely pursuit of a cause of action derived from, and exercised on behalf of, the company because the alleged wrongdoers control the company, thus preventing the normally appropriate organ (the board of directors or the general meeting) from causing the company itself to pursue it. Later we shall have to look more closely at both these types of action, and particularly at the derivative action. At present, it is merely necessary to note that the fact that there are the two possible types of action can cause doubts and difficulties about which is appropriate in the relevant circumstances and whether both can be combined in a single action; and that successful pursuit of the derivative type is particularly fraught with difficulty because of the need to establish the elusive concepts of fraud-on-the minority[22] and "control"[23] by the alleged wrongdoers.

THE "CALAMITOUS"[24] NEWMAN CASE

The mammoth *Newman Industries* litigation afforded an opportunity for the courts to clear up some, at least, of the foregoing doubts and difficulties. But, although Vinelott J. at first instance seized this opportunity with enthusiasm, the Court of Appeal left his efforts in some disarray. The litigation arose from a transaction between two associated companies *Newman* and *TPG*, each of which was directly or indirectly a substantial minority shareholder of the other. A Mr. Bartlett was Chairman and chief executive of *Newman* and a director and non-executive vice-chairman of *TPG* and a Mr. Laughton was the chief executive of *TPG* and a non-executive director of *Newman* and its vice-chairman. Bartlett and Laughton also wholly-owned a private company holding 35 per cent. of the shares of *TPG* which in turn owned 25.6 per cent. of the shares of *Newman*. In any transaction between *Newman* and *TPG*, Bartlett and Laughton would, therefore, face likely conflicts between their personal interests and their fiduciary duties and between their fiduciary duties to each of the two companies. But *TPG*, unlike *Newman*, was in financial difficulties and faced liquidation or receivership unless prompt steps

20 Borrowed from the U.S.A. where the true nature of this type of action was recognised much earlier.
21 It took an inordinate time for this to be recognised in the U.K. The earliest mention of the term "derivative action" in English legal textbooks appears to have been in 1957 and its first use in reported judgments in *Wallersteiner v. Moir (No. 2)* [1975] Q.B. 373, C.A., *per* Denning M.R. at 390–391 and Scarman L.J. at 407.
22 See Chap. 22 at pp. 593–603 above.
23 On which see Farrar in Pettet (ed.) *Company Law in Change* at p. 39.
24 It was so described by the C.A. at [1982] Ch. at 235C.

were taken. Accordingly Bartlett and Laughton worked out a proposed rescue plan whereby *Newman* would buy substantially the whole of *TPG's* assets (other than its shares in *Newman*) and take over some of its liabilities, the total price payable to a dependent on a valuation of *TPG's* assets by *Newman's* auditors. Under the Stock Exchange regulations such a transaction in which directors were personally interested, had to be conditional on approval by general meetings of both *Newman* and *TPG* and, notwithstanding misgivings by one independent non-executive director of *Newman*, notices and accompanying explaining circulars were sent out. *Prudential*, which held 3.2 per cent. of *Newman's* shares was unhappy about the scheme; it regarded the circular as misleading, and the valuation of *TPG's* assets as inflated. It sought to persuade the *Newman* board to adjourn its meeting until a report had been obtained from an independent merchant bank and the meeting was in fact, adjourned to enable that to be done. But when the report was not ready by the adjourned date, the meeting went ahead and the resolution was passed by a small majority, the shares owned directly or indirectly by *TPG*, Bartlett and Laughton not being voted. *Prudential* then issued a writ against *Newman* claiming, in a personal and non-representative action, a declaration that the transaction had not been duly approved at a valid general meeting because the circular had been tricky and misleading. This action would, seemingly, have presented no serious problems. As in *Edwards* v. *Halliwell*, the plaintiff was alleging that its personal rights, to have the affairs of *Newman* conducted regularly, had been invaded. On the authority of that case, it would have fallen wholly outside the *Foss* v. *Harbottle* rule. But, by the time the case reached the courts *Prudential* must have realised that the claimed declaratory relief alone would be pointless because it was too late to rescind the transaction. Accordingly *Prudential* joined Bartlett and Laughton (and *TPG*) as defendants and claimed declarations that they had conspired, fraudulently and in breach of their fiduciary duties, to injure *Newman* and its members and were liable to pay damages or equitable compensation. This it claimed in four capacities:

(a) in a "personal" action on its own behalf alone;
(b) in a "personal" action in a representative capacity on behalf of all members of *Newman* (other than Bartlett and Laughton);
(c) in a "personal" action in a representative capacity against all members (other than Bartlett and Laughton) at the date of the alleged conspiracy[25];

---

[25] Thus meeting the problem (illustrated, *e.g.* in *Regal (Hastings) Ltd.* v. *Gulliver*, see Chap. 21 at pp. 565, 566 above) that recovery under (b) or (d) would exclude from benefit those members who had left since the date of the conspiracy and that those who had joined after that date would obtain an undeserved windfall.

(d) in a "derivative" action on behalf of *Newman*.

This raised novel problems, both procedural and substantive, particularly in relation to (a), (b) and (c) where, in effect, *Prudential* was attempting to bring personal actions in tort (or its equitable equivalent) committed against the company and therefore, one would have thought, enforceable only by the company[26] or by (d) the derivative action on its behalf if the pre-conditions for that were met. The procedural problems were wrestled with by Vinelott J. in interlocutory proceedings, reported as *Prudential Assurance v. Newman Industries (No. 1)*.[27] He first disposed of an application by Bartlett and Laughton to try as a preliminary issue whether the conditions for a derivative action were met. This he refused because *Prudential* had stated that whatever the result of the derivative action it would also wish to pursue the personal claims and, as there was considerable overlap between all the claims and what was central to all of them was whether the circular was tricky and misleading, he considered that justice and convenience required that the facts should be established before any issue of law was decided.[28] He then went on to consider whether it was permissible[29] for *Prudential* to pursue the personal actions in a representative capacity and held that it was, since this would neither confer a right which would not be available to a member in a separate action nor bar a defence to separate action by a member. But if a declaration was granted each member individually would have to establish what loss, if any, he had suffered.[30]

In the subsequent trial, reported as *Prudential Assurance v. Newman Industries (No. 2)*[31] Vinelott J. took an extremely adverse view of the conduct of Bartlett and Laughton. He concluded his findings of fact by saying: "In my judgment the [rescue] plan ... was a conspiracy, knowingly and wrongfully to injure *Newman* and the shareholders of *Newman*. Each part of the plan ... was in itself such a conspiracy."[32] In the light of this finding, he proceeded to consider the legal issues,[33] dealing first with what loss *Newman* had suffered. This, he concluded, was £445,000 since he thought that, but for the conspiracy, *Newman* would have been able to acquire the *TPG* assets for £445,000 less than it had paid.[34] Secondly, he held that

26 Cp. *Caparo Ltd.* v. *Dickman* [1990] A.C. 605, H.L. discussed in Chap. 18 at pp. 490–498 above. But see Sterling, *The Theory and Policy of Shareholder Action in Tort* (1987) 50 M.L.R. 468.
27 [1981] Ch. 229.
28 *Ibid.* at pp. 233–234. This ruling was later severely criticised by the C.A.
29 Under R.S.C., Ord. 15, r. 4: see below.
30 Applying *David Jones* v. *Cory Bros.* (1921) 56 L.J. 302, C.A.; *Bulmer and Showerings Ltd.* v. *Bollinger S.A. and Lanson* [1978] R.P.C. 79, C.A.
31 [1981] Ch. 257, see n. 2, above, for some frightening details of its length.
32 *Ibid.* pp. 297H–298A.
33 *Ibid.* pp. 298–329.
34 *Ibid.* p. 302.

notwithstanding suggestions to the contrary,[35] a personal action can be joined with a derivative action so long as both arise out of the same transaction.[36] He then turned to the question whether the derivative action was barred by the Foss v. Harbottle rule or fell within an exception to it. In this connection he reviewed at some length[37] the decisions discussed in Chapter 22[38] and drew attention to the interconnection between the two requirements of "fraud-on-the-minority" and "control by the wrongdoers," pointing out that, as argued in earlier editions of this book,[39] if the control is being exercised so as to deprive the company of the power to sue for money due to it by way of damages or compensation, this would seem to be a fraud-on-the-minority indistinguishable from misappropriation of the company's property.[40] However, as it was conceded by Bartlett and Laughton that, on the facts found, Prudential's claim was based on acts of "fraud," whatever meaning was to be attributed to that expression,[41] he did not need to pursue that further.

The central issue, therefore, was "whether a derivative action can be brought against defendants who do not have voting control[42] of the company on whose behalf the derivative claim is brought and, if it can, in precisely what circumstances such a claim will be allowed to proceed."[43] Calling in aid the dicta[44] that there is an additional exception to the rule, namely that it will be relaxed when the interests of justice so require, he concluded:

"I am satisfied on the evidence as a whole that there was no way in which Prudential could have ensured that the question whether proceedings should be brought by Newman would be fairly put to the shareholders or even that a full investigation would be made into all the circumstances surrounding the transaction, including in

[35] In Gore-Browne on Companies 43rd ed. citing Stroud v. Lawson [1898] 2 Q.B. 44, C.A.
[36] At p. 303, distinguishing Stroud v. Lawson, where it was held that a personal action against the directors for fraud in inducing the plaintiff to buy shares could not be joined with a derivative action to recover from them an ultra vires dividend. In contrast, in Newman all the claims arose out of the same transaction, the conspiracy.
[37] At pp. 305–329.
[38] At pp. 593 et seq.
[39] 4th ed. at pp. 630–631.
[40] Counsel for Bartlett and Laughton "very frankly admitted that he could not put forward any valid ground of distinction between a case where the claim by the company is of a proprietary nature and one where it is for damages only, nor between a claim for damages for negligence where the loss to the company is matched by a benefit to those in control [held to be a fraud-on-the minority in Daniels v. Daniels [1978] Ch. 406] and a claim for damages for negligence where the loss to the company is either not matched by any benefit to anybody or is not matched by a benefit to those in control" [held in Pavlides v. Jensen [1956] Ch. 565, not to be a fraud in the minority]: at pp. 316H–317A.
[41] At p. 317A, B.
[42] In the sense of more than 50 per cent. of the votes at a general meeting.
[43] At p. 317C.
[44] See n. 18 above. But for the view of the C.A. see p. 653 below.

particular [the valuation of the *TPG* assets]. In these circumstances, in my judgment *Prudential* have shown that the interests of justice do require that a minority action should be permitted."[45]

In the light of this decision regarding the derivative action it might have been supposed that the personal actions would be dismissed—particularly as *Prudential* had by then indicated that so far as it was concerned it would not wish to pursue them. But for two reasons this was not done. The first was that Vinelott J. considered that there was a theoretical possibility that Newman would take a bona fide decision not to adopt the judgment in its favour.[46] This, at first glance, seems to be putting a novel slant on the concept of "ratification." While one can see that a company might well take a bona fide decision not itself and at its own expense to pursue a claim for damages, it is more difficult to see how it could validly resolve to renounce a judgment in its favour which had been obtained by *Prudential* at the latter's expense.[47] The second reason was that recovery by *Newman* would not benefit those of its shareholders who had sold their shares. Although if those shareholders recovered compensation for any loss they had suffered, it would mean that the individual defendants would have, in effect, to pay twice in respect of the same tort, that element of duplication was, in the judge's view inevitable in the circumstances.[48] Hence he made declarations on all the claims,[49] personal and derivative, but ordered that no further proceedings should be taken on the personal actions without leave of the court and that, in the event of an appeal, all proceedings to enforce the declarations should be stayed until the appeal was concluded. Bartlett and Laughton promptly lodged an appeal which led to the lengthy hearings and the voluminous judgment[50] of the Court of Appeal.[51] It took a view of the facts very different from that of Vinelott J. who had seen and heard the witnesses. In its view there had been no continuous fraudulent conspiracy. However, a dishonest concealment of material facts by Bartlett and Laughton had undoubtedly occurred and for this they were liable to restore to *Newman* any loss that it had sustained as a result.[52]

The court then dealt with the questions of law. It held that all the "personal" claims were misconceived and, indeed, suggested that they had been pleaded and relied on only "because it was feared that

45 See [1981] Ch. at 327B.
46 *Ibid.* at 328.
47 This indeed was the view taken by the board of Newman. But see below at p. 654.
48 See [1981] Ch. at 327.
49 Including that against *TPG* which was held liable as having knowingly benefited from the conspiracy: see at pp. 327, 328.
50 See n. 2 above.
51 [1982] Ch. 204, C.A.
52 Which, however, the C.A. thought could not exceed £45,000 (not £445,000 as Vinelott J. had thought).

the derivative action might be defeated by the rule in *Foss v. Harbottle*."[53] This, however, seems to be going too far; at the time when *Prudential* started proceedings in a personal capacity asking for a declaration that the resolutions of the meeting were invalid, this was undoubtedly a legitimate claim falling, on the authority of *Edwards v. Halliwell*, wholly outside the rule. It was only when such a declaration on its own became pointless, because the transaction had been completed and it was too late to rescind it, that the personal claims became misguided. All concerned can be forgiven for not grasping that; it was somewhat anomalous that, by jumping the gun, *Newman* had caused any former personal rights of members to be effectively destroyed.

However, the court was undoubtedly right in concluding that a member has no personal right to sue directly in respect of a breach of duty owed to the company or in respect of a tort committed against it. Such suits can be brought only by the company itself or in a derivative action under an exception to the *Foss v. Harbottle* rule. The hopes, however, that the court would give some authoritative rulings on the rule and its exceptions, were dashed. The court refused to hear any argument on the topic and the eagerly-awaited climax became an anti-climax. The court refused for this reason: rightly or wrongly Vinelott J. had in *Newman (No. 1)* allowed the derivative action to proceed, and there had been no appeal against that decision. That derivative action had decided that *Newman* was entitled to a judgment in its favour. Hence:

"However desirable it might be in the public interest that we should express our conclusions on Vinelott J.'s analysis of the rule—and what he saw as the exceptions to it, it was necessary for us to bear in mind that the rule has ceased to be of the slightest relevance to the case. It would have been a grave injustice to all parties to increase the already horrendous costs of this litigation by allowing time for argument on an interesting but irrelevant point."[54]

That, however, did not deter the court from making "merely a few reflections of our own thoughts without the benefit of sustained argument. . . ."[55] The first such reflection was that "we have no doubt whatsoever that Vinelott J. erred in dismissing[56] the application to determine as a preliminary issue whether *Prudential* was entitled to sue on behalf of *Newman* in a derivative action. "It cannot have been right to subject the company to a 30-day action (as it was then

53 [1982] Ch. at 225E.
54 *Ibid.* at 220G.
55 *Ibid.* at 221A.
56 In *Newman (No. 1)*.

estimated to be)[57] in order to enable him to decide whether the plaintiffs were entitled in law to subject the company to a 30-day action."[58] But, with respect, this criticism seems a little unfair. At the date of *Newman (No.1.)* everybody was under the impression that the personal claims were alleging that the individual defendants had committed torts against the members personally. At a later stage it ought to have become clearer that the "fraud" was on the company alone but the reason why it took until the appeal in *Newman (No. 2)* for that to be grasped was because, as the Court of Appeal stressed, "discovery was a shambles, there was no proper selection of documents—and the pleadings were never adequately clarified and timeously amended."[59] Once Vinelott J. decided to allow the personal claims to proceed there was no reason to suppose that trial of a preliminary issue regarding the derivative action would shorten the length of the trial as a whole; on the contrary it would probably have lengthened it still further. Secondly, the court cast grave (and probably terminal) doubts in Vinelott J.'s support for the view that there is an exception to the *Foss* v. *Harbottle* rule "whenever the justice of the case so requires." It was "not convinced that this is a practical test, particularly if it involves a full-dress trial before the test is applied."[60] But the preliminary trial favoured by the court is somewhat more "full-dress" than had generally been thought. In contrast with a normal preliminary trial of a point of law, a court should not assume as a fact that every allegation in the statement of claim is true.

"The plaintiff ought at least to be required before proceeding with his action to establish a prima facie case: (i) that the company is entitled to the relief claimed and (ii) that the action falls within the proper boundaries of the exception to the rule in *Foss* v. *Harbottle*."[61]

Presumably, though this was not left entirely clear,[62] this preliminary trial is needed only if an application is made to strike out the action and the court is not required itself to take the point if there is no such application. It also seems to have been the view of the court that unless and until this prima facie case is established, the court should not require the alleged wrongdoers not to vote their shares on any resolution in general meeting purporting to confirm the

---

57 In fact it took over twice that estimate: see n. 2 above.
58 [1982] Ch. at 221B.
59 *Ibid.* at p. 225E.
60 *Ibid.* at p. 22.G.
61 *Ibid.* at 221H-222A.
62 At any rate to the writer. See the discussion at *ibid.* pp. 215-217 of the two *East Pant Du* cases: *East Pant Du Lead Mining Co.* v. *Merryweather* (1864) 2 Hem. & M. 254 and *Atwool* v. *Merryweather* (1868) L.R. 5 Eq. 464 and, more fully, in 37 L.J.Ch. 35.

transaction concerned. If, however, at the end of the day "fraud" is established, such a resolution will be ineffective if passed only as a result of their votes.[63]

Thirdly, agreeing here with Vinelott J., the court stated that it would have been possible for *Newman* for "a proper reason—at a proper board or general meeting to resolve to proceed no further with the claim against Bartlett and Laughton. In that event the plaintiffs [*Prudential*] would not be able to proceed further because a valid release could be pleaded by Bartlett and Laughton."[64] And the explanation of why such a resolution might be "proper" became apparent. Hitherto *Prudential's* costs had been borne by it.[65] But if the derivative action succeeded (as it had) it would, prima facie, be entitled to be indemnified by *Newman*, on whose behalf it had sued, to the extent that costs were not recoverable from Bartlett, Laughton or *TPG*. In these circumstances the independent directors and shareholders of *Newman* might well have concluded that the costs the company was likely to have to pay[66] would greatly exceed any damages it might recover. Although counsel for *Newman* had stated in court that *Newman* would accept the judgment in its favour, the Court of Appeal made it clear that in the circumstances *Prudential* could not expect a full indemnity[67] and it adjourned to a later date for full argument about costs in the Court of Appeal and below. At the adjourned hearing it was announced that all parties had (very wisely) agreed terms of settlement. What precisely these terms were, was not disclosed but it can safely be assumed that all the parties were left considerably worse off.

The aftermath

Subsequent decisions have dutifully followed the obiter dicta of the Court of Appeal in *Newman (No. 2)* regarding the desirability of a trial of a preliminary issue to decide whether a derivative action shall be allowed to proceed. The first case, *Estmanco Ltd. v. G.L.C.,*[68] was decided before the Court of Appeal's judgment had been fully reported, (but the Chancery Division was of course aware of its

---

63 *Ibid.* at p. 217A, B.
64 *Ibid.* at p. 220B, C.
65 *Prudential*, of course, had not needed to apply for a "*Wallersteiner v. Moir* order" on which see below at pp. 656, 657.
66 The newspapers estimated that the total costs incurred already were some £750,000 and damages still remained to be assessed.
67 Nor did the court respond favourably to the invitation "to give judicial approval to the public spirit of [*Prudential*] who, it was said, are pioneering a method of controlling companies in the public interest without involving regulation by a statutory body." On the contrary, it seemed to regard *Prudential* as an interfering busybody attempting to subvert a rule "which is founded on principle but also operates fairly by preserving the rights of the majority": *ibid.* at p. 224. This is not likely to encourage institutional investors to take up the cudgels on behalf of their fellow private investors as they are constantly exhorted to do.
68 [1982] 1 W.L.R. 2.

general terms.) The facts as found by Megarry V.-C. after a 5-day hearing, can be summarised as follows:

The company concerned was a non-profit-making one, incorporated by the G.L.C. as part if its then policy to sell long leases, rather than to grant short-term council lettings, of rehabilitated blocks of flats. The intention was that the company would in due course manage the blocks, but that, until all the long leases were sold, the G.L.C. would retain control; each lessee would become a shareholder but without a vote until then. Thereafter their shares would carry votes and they would then control the company. An agreement under seal to give effect to these arrangements was entered into between the G.L.C. and the company. However, following an election, the G.L.C. decided to change its policy and to revert to letting to applicants on its housing list, retaining permanent control of the management and of the company. This was a breach of the agreement with the company—and was obviously detrimental to its members. Accordingly two directors of the company, commendably acting bona fide in its interest notwithstanding that they were also employees of the G.L.C., [69] caused the company to issue a writ for breach of contract. The G.L.C. thereupon convened a general meeting on short notice, which resolved to apply for leave to discontinue the action, whereupon one of the long leaseholders applied as a minority shareholder to be substituted for the company as the nominal plaintiff to continue it as a derivative action.

Megarry V.-C. accordingly had to choose between (i) an application to kill the action, made by the company acting on a resolution of one of its organs (the general meeting) which resolution had been passed by the controlling shareholders (the G.L.C.) clearly voting primarily in their own interests (as housing authority)—which shareholders are prima facie entitled to do but which in this case purported to reverse a bona fide decision of the board; or (ii) an application by a voteless minority shareholder to continue the action, transformed into a derivative action to be conducted by her on behalf of the company. If he were to choose the latter, he had, under the dicta of the Court of Appeal in *Newman (No. 2)*, to be satisfied that there was a prima facie case that (a) the alleged wrongdoer (the G.L.C.) controlled the company and was exercising its control to frustrate proceedings against it, and (b) that there was fraud-on-the-minority. "Control" was clearly established but (b) was more difficult. However, Megarry V.-C. robustly declared that whatever fraud-on-the-minority might mean it was "wide enough to cover the present case and that if it is not it should now be made wide enough." [70] Hence he granted the minority shareholder's application.

[69] Which the G.L.C., equally commendably, had, on their appointment, given them express authority to do notwithstanding their employment.
[70] At p. 15G.

The later *Smith v. Croft* litigation[71] is of still greater interest and by then the judgment of the Court of Appeal in *Newman (No. 2)* had been reported. This litigation first came before Walton J.[72] on an aspect of the all-important question of costs which had been irrelevant and was not touched on in *Newman.* When, in *Wallersteiner v. Moir (No 2)*,[73] the Court of Appeal first came to realise the true nature of a derivative action, it also recognised that a necessary consequence was that the minority shareholder had no chance of obtaining Legal Aid to pursue the action, since aid was available only to individuals and not to bodies corporate. The court also recognised that it followed that, if the action was successful and, perhaps, even if it was not so long as the nominal plaintiff acted reasonably, he would be entitled to be indemnified by the company in respect of his costs. That, however, was small comfort for someone like Mr. Moir[74] who (in the *Wallersteiner* saga) had brought himself to the verge of financial ruin by his one-man, wholly justified, crusade to expose the machinations of Dr. Wallersteiner. The court accordingly considered what could be done to prevent such hardship in future, and, having rejected by a majority,[75] contingent fees as contrary to public policy, came up with a solution which has since been extensively used by plaintiffs less well-heeled than "the Pru" and the working of which is illustrated by what occurred in *Smith v. Croft.*

There, minority shareholders instituted a derivative action alleging, primarily, that the directors of the company had been paying themselves grossly excessive remuneration. They then applied *ex parte* to a Master of the High Court for an order that the company should indemnify them against the costs of the action down to the conclusion of discovery and disclosure of documents, their intention obviously being then to apply for a further order. Subsequently they took out a summons applying for an order that they should be at liberty to tax their costs already incurred and, thereafter, to tax them at 3-monthly intervals. These applications were supported by an affidavit of a solicitor, instructions to, and an Opinion of, counsel and statements by an accountant. The Master acceded to both requests but restricted the costs payable on the taxations to 60 per cent. From this both sides appealed and the company applied for the *ex parte* order to be set aside—an application which the Master adjourned to the judge—with the result that all these matters came before Walton

---

[71] *Smith v. Croft (No. 1)* [1986] 1 W.L.R. 580; *Smith v. Croft (No. 2)* [1988] Ch. 114. See Sealy [1987] Cam.L.J. 398.
[72] [1986] 1 W.L.R. 580.
[73] [1975] Q.B. 108, C.A.
[74] He had already been taken three times to the C.A.: on unreported interlocutory matters in 1968, in *Wallersteiner v. Moir (No. 1)* [1974] 1 W.L.R. 991, C.A. (pet. dismissed [1975] 1 W.L.R. 1093, H.L.) and now in *ibid.* (*No. 2*) and the action had still not been finally concluded.
[75] Only Denning M.R. was prepared to contemplate a controlled version of that.

J.[76] He took the view that the action was very unlikely to succeed since in the world in which the company operated (it provided film finance) salaries "are so manifestly out of line with that of ordinary mortals, that even fashionable silks feel a twinge of envy from time to time."[77] Moreover the board had commissioned an independent report from a leading firm of chartered accountants on the complaints of the minority shareholders and in the light of that report had decided that it would be contrary to the interest of the company for the action to proceed. To apply the procedure suggested in *Wallersteiner* in such circumstances was, in his view, to create as great a hardship to the company and its members as a whole, as any likely to be suffered by the plaintiff minority. He therefore set aside the original order and allowed the appeal against the second order. Normally, in his view, such orders should not be made until after discovery and then only if the plaintiffs genuinely needed it; if it was to be possible for them to proceed. He also thought that such orders should be made only *inter partes* and with disclosure to the defendants of all evidence on which the plaintiffs intended to rely unless it was covered by legal professional privilege or some other good reason.

Despite this rebuff, the plaintiffs did not capitulate. Indeed, they applied to the Court of Appeal for leave to appeal which was granted but with a direction that the appeal should not be heard until after the hearing in the High Court of an application made by the company and its chairman that the action should be struck out. This application was heard by Knox J. in *Smith* v. *Croft (No. 2)*,[78] He, in accordance with the guidance of the Court of Appeal in *Newman (No. 2)*, tried as a preliminary issue whether there was a prima facie case that (1) the company was entitled to the relief sought and (ii) that the action fell within the proper boundaries of the exception to the rule in *Foss* v. *Harbottle*. As regards the pre-condition that the "wrongdoers" controlled, the plaintiffs seemed to be on strong ground, since directly or indirectly, the "wrongdoers" had well over 50 per cent. of the votes.[79] Their apparent weakness was in establishing that their allegations showed a prima facie case of "fraud." Doubtless for this reason they sought to establish that some of the alleged payments by the defendants to themselves or associated companies were ultra vires (using that term, not in the strict sense of beyond the company's capacity, but in the sense that they were illegal[80]) so that they fell within the exclusion (rather than the exception) to the *Foss* v. *Harbottle* rule. Knox J. had no difficulty in

[76] *Smith* v. *Croft (No. 1)*, n. 71, above.
[77] [1986] 1 W.L.R. at 592C.
[78] n. 71 above. The hearings took 18 days and some 100 decisions were cited in argument.
[79] See [1988] Ch. at 145–147.
[80] See Chap. 8 above.

exposing this as a red-herring. If the payments were indeed *ultra vires*, the plaintiffs in a personal action would have been entitled, had they applied in time, to a declaration or injunction to prevent the payments being made. But the plaintiffs were now seeking to recover on behalf of the company money of which it was alleged to have been illegally deprived. This they could do only in a derivative action and only if the exception to the rule in *Foss* v. *Harbottle* could be established. He considered that there was not a prima facie case that payments made to the directors as remuneration or expenses were illegal and thus ultra vires. However, as regards one payment, made to an associated company, he thought that a prima facie case had been established that it was illegal in that it appeared to be financial assistance for the purchase of the company's shares and illegal under what is now section 151 of the Act.[81] It seems that as a result he might have allowed the action to continue had it not been for the most innovative and slightly surprising part of his judgment relating to "control."

Despite the fact that the alleged wrongdoers had voting control he held that the action should be struck out on the ground that it was clear that a majority of the shareholders independent of both the plaintiffs and defendants did not want it to continue. In his view:

"Ultimately, the question which has to be answered in order to determine whether the rule in *Foss* v. *Harbottle* applies to prevent a minority shareholder seeking relief as plaintiff for the benefit of the company is: Is the plaintiff being improperly prevented from bringing these proceedings on behalf of the company? If it is an expression of the corporate will of the company by an appropriate independent organ that is preventing the plaintiff from prosecuting the action, he is not improperly but properly prevented and so the answer to the question is "No." The independent organ will vary according to the constitution of the company concerned and the identity of the defendants who will in most cases be disqualified from participating by voting in expressing the corporate will.—In this case it is common ground that there would be no useful purpose covered by adjourning to enable a general meeting to be called. For all practical purposes it is quite clear how the votes would be cast . . ."[82]

In so far as this confirms that there is a distinction between rectifying an act and deciding not to sue in respect of it, it is neither novel nor surprising. But what is both, is the apparent introduction of

---

[81] See Chap. 9 above at pp. 227–236.
[82] [1988] Ch. at p. 185A–C.

an exception to the exception to *Foss* v. *Harbottle*,[83] i.e. that notwithstanding "fraud," and "wrongdoer control," a derivative action will be stayed if an independent "organ" of the company has shown that it does not want it to continue and that for this purpose an independent organ may be a majority of a minority acting informally and without the need for a meeting. Some commentators[84] have seen in this a development similar to that in the United States which is supported by the A.L.I.'s *Corporate Governance Project*.[85] Thereby an independent "litigation" committee of the board, assisted by an independent lawyer, reviews and reports on the action, and this report is available to the court which may dismiss the action if satisfied, in the light of that and other evidence before it, that the committee reasonably concluded that the action was contrary to the company's best interests.[86] Certainly Knox J.'s solution is designed to achieve the same aim but, as is still the case in relation to every aspect of derivative actions, in a less sophisticated manner. His solution was practicable in *Smith* v. *Croft* because there were relatively few shareholders and the views of all those who mattered were ascertainable; but it might not have been practicable in the case of a widely held public company.

Knox J. concluded his judgment with four observations,[87] of which, it is greatly to be hoped, heed will be taken if derivative actions are to survive. The first is that, without going to the lengths of leading counsel for the plaintiffs, who had described the procedure of the case as a shambles, he agreed that it had had "unsatisfactory features, not least the length of time taken." One wonders whether the case would not have taken less than the 18 days if it had gone to trial without a determination of the so-called preliminary issue, for then the order of speeches would have matched the onus of proof—which it had not.

Secondly he considered "that there may well be a much stronger case for requiring a prospective plaintiff to have the onus of establishing that his case falls within the exceptions to *Foss* v. *Harbottle* or outside it altogether, than there is for requiring him to show that the company would be likely to succeed if it brought the action. So far as the latter is concerned "it might well be appropriate to apply the usual test which puts the onus on the defendants to establish that the case is effectively unarguable."

[83] In contrast with the distillation of "some guiding principle that is wide enough to comprehend" all the exceptions and exclusions and "yet narrow enough to be practicable and workable," which in *Estmanco* v. *G.L.C.* (above) Megarry V.-C. had expected the courts to find unless ss.459–461 "inhibit that development:" [1982] 1 W.L.R. at 11B, C.

[84] See, *e.g.* Boyle in (1990) 11 Co. Law 3.

[85] See Chap. 4 at p. 72 n. 84 above.

[86] *Principles of Corporate Governance* (Proposed Final Draft (31 March, 1992)) Part VII, Chap. 1, ss.7.07–7.13 (the above summary is somewhat over-simplified).

[87] [1988] C.A. at pp. 189F–190.

Thirdly, amplifying what Walton J. had said in *Smith v. Croft (No. 1)*, he considered that any application for a *Wallersteiner v. Moir* order for costs should be made at the same time as "the plaintiff establishes whatever it is that he has to establish."

And fourthly he said that he believed "it would be helpful for there to be specific procedures laid down, whether by way of rules of court or a practice direction . . . for the initiative and prosecution of actions by minority shareholders to recover on behalf of a company." It would indeed; and some of us[88] have been pleading for this for years. But all our pleas—and so far, those of Knox J.—seem to have fallen on deaf ears. The absence of any specific procedural rules (notwithstanding the recognition, at least for the past 16 years that derivative actions are a discrete class of action) is scandalous. One gets the impression that the Bench as a whole likes the *Foss v. Harbottle* rule so much[89] and derivative actions so little that it is reluctant to recognise any exceptions to the rule when the plaintiff seeks derivative relief (as opposed to personal relief against infringement of personal rights). This is a tenable view for, in the light of the recent cases it can hardly be denied that the derivative action as practised in the United Kingdom is thoroughly unsatisfactory and probably incapable of being made satisfactory short of root-and-branch reforms, of which there seems to be little hope. On the other hand, some remedy is needed, for it cannot be satisfactory that controllers should be able to get away with blue murder. The question is whether, in fact, the remedy under sections 459–461 can always meet the need and to that question we shall return after a closer look at those sections.

Does the same apply in relation to personal actions? It is submitted that it does not, so long as the courts follow Jenkins L.J. in *Edwards v. Halliwell*,[90] and accept that, when a member has personal rights that have been invaded, the *Foss v. Harbottle* rule has no application so that both it and its alleged "exceptions" are irrelevant. The only difficulty then is that when the member's personal rights do not arise from an express contract or a tort but allegedly from a "deemed" contract under the unhappily worded section 14 of the Act, the case law is confusing. If, however, the courts are prepared to recognise that section 14 does confer on each member a personal right to have the affairs of the company conducted in accordance with the provisions of its memorandum and articles and the Act, a

---

[88] Including Sir Jack Jacob (Chief Editor of Supreme Court Practice (the *White Book*) and formerly Senior Master of the Supreme Court (Q.B.D.) and Queen's Remembrancer) who, in the *White Book*, has added to the treatment of representative actions under Ord. 15, r. 12, a helpful note (15/12/5) on their relationship to derivative actions.

[89] See the dictum of the C.A. in *Newman (No. 2)* at [1982] Ch. at p. 224, quoted above in n. 67.

[90] Now affirmed by the C.A. in *Newman* to be the *locus classicus*.

straightforward action for a declaration or injunction may be more appropriate than resort to sections 459-461. It is further submitted, that the question whether the irregularity is "mere" or grave or what sort of resolution is needed to put it right, is irrelevant. To avoid pointless litigation the plaintiff obviously ought to give the company an opportunity to rectify an irregularity capable of rectification.[91] But, if the company denies that there is an irregularity or declines to do anything to rectify it, a member should be entitled to establish the contrary, if he can.

Also for consideration is whether a member suing in a personal capacity in respect of a corporate irregularity, should not be entitled to apply, in the manner suggested by Walton J. in *Smith* v. *Croft (No. 1)*, for a *Wallersteiner* v. *Moir* costs order. It is true that theoretically he might apply for Legal Aid but it is unlikely that he would obtain it, especially if, as is desirable,[92] he sues in a representative capacity.[93] But although the company is a true defendant (not, as in a derivative action, the true plaintiff) it is surely in the interests of the company that its irregularities should be rectified and without such an order they might not be.

Before concluding this discussion of derivative and personal actions, attention should be drawn to three further contrasts between them:

(i) Since a derivative action is discretionary, the court will not permit a member to bring it unless he "comes with clean hands." If he has participated in, or knowingly benefited from, the wrong done to the company, the court is not likely to regard him as qualified to sue on the company's behalf;[94]

(ii) Nor will a member be permitted to bring a derivative action if the company has gone into liquidation; it is then for the liquidator to decide whether the company itself shall sue,[95]

(iii) On the other hand, since a derivative action is on behalf of the company, the plaintiff need not have been a member at

---

[91] This might be done by requiring the "letter before action" to state the grounds on which it was alleged that there was such a irregularity and giving the company a reasonable time to take the steps needed to rectify it.

[92] It ensures that the result is *res judicata* as between the company and those represented, who, if the rights arise under the deemed contract under s.14, will be all the members of the same class.

[93] Since it seems that regard will then be had to the means of those he represents (even though they will not be liable for costs unless they apply to be joined as parties).

[94] *Towers* v. *African Tug Co.* [1904] 1 Ch. 558 on which Lawton L.J. relied in *Nurcombe* v. *Nurcombe* [1985] 1 W.L.R. 370, C.A., at p. 376 in which a wife obtained maintenance in divorce proceedings on the basis of the husband's means and then sought, as a member of a company of which the husband and wife were sole shareholders, to bring a derivative action against him to recover for the company moneys which she alleged that he had misappropriated from the company and which she knew about at the time of the divorce.

[95] *Fargo* v. *Godfroy* [1986] 1 W.L.R. 1134.

the time when the wrong was done to it.[96] In contrast, a member *qua* member can have a personal right of action only if he was a member at the time of the relevant transaction.

Petitions Under Part XVII or for Winding Up

When the forerunner of the present Part XVII was first introduced as section 210 of the 1948 Act it was intended as a remedy for a type of wrong rather different from that where there had been a breach of a specific duty owed by, or to, the company, leading to the possibility of a personal or derivative action. Instead, it was designed to afford a remedy when there had been a course of conduct "oppressive" to some of the members.

Unless this involved some specific breach of duty, the only remedy that the oppressed members formerly had was to petition for a winding up order on the longstanding ground[97] that winding up was "just and equitable." This remedy, originally used mainly in cases where the company was deadlocked had, during the course of the present century, been moulded by the courts into a means of subjecting small private companies to equitable principles derived from partnership law when they were in reality "incorporated quasi-partnerships" so that, for example, the exercise of the legal power of the majority to expel the minority from any say in the management[98] might be a breach of the underlying understanding of the quasi-partners.[99] But, though effective, it was not necessarily a satisfactory remedy; if the company was prospering, it was tantamount to killing the goose that might lay the golden egg.

Hence section 210 of the 1948 Act introduced an alternative whereby any member who complained that the affairs of the company were being conducted in a manner oppressive to some part of the members (including himself) could petition the court which, if satisfied that the company's affairs were being so conducted and that the

[96] *Seaton* v. *Grant* (1867) L.R. 2 Ch.App. 459; *Bloxam* v. *Metropolitan Ry.* L.R. 3 Ch.App. 337 (in both of which the plaintiff had bought shares in order to qualify himself). But he must be a registered member at the time when he brings the action: *Birch* v. *Sullivan* [1957] 1 W.L.R. 1247. It seems that the court could deprive him of the conduct of the action for good cause (*e.g.* a conflict of interest) and substitute for him as plaintiff another member who intervenes and applies for that to be done: see *Estmanco* v. *G.L.C.* [1982] 1 W.L.R. 2 (above) and *Re Services Club Estates Syndicate* [1930] 1 Ch. 78 where that was done in a representative debenture holders' action under what is now Ord. 15, r. 12.

[97] See now Insolvency Act 1986, s.122(g). This, borrowed from a similar ground in the (then uncodified) law of partnership, dates back to the Joint Stock Companies Winding-up Act 1848. It can be invoked by petitioners other than members (*e.g.* creditors) but that is unusual (except on petitions by the Secretary of State: see Chap. 25, p. 685 below).

[98] *e.g.* by securing the passage of a resolution removing them from the board under what is now s.303.

[99] This development culminated in the decision of the H.L. in *Ebrahimi* v. *Westbourne Galleries* [1973] A.C. 360 (see below).

facts would justify the making of a winding up order on the ground that it was just and equitable, but that to wind up the company would be unfairly prejudicial to the oppressed members, could make such orders as it thought fit to put an end to the oppression. The Act also amended the winding up provisions by enacting that a member's petition for a winding up on the just and equitable ground could not be granted if the court was of the opinion that some other remedy was available to the petitioners and that they were acting unreasonably in seeking winding-up instead of pursuing that other remedy.[1] Since then the two remedies have continued to co-exist but the relationship between them has changed as a result of major revisions and extensions to the alternative remedy made principally by the 1980 Act which substituted its section 75[2] for section 210 and which, on the 1985 consolidation, became Part XVII (sections 459–461) of the 1985 Act. Prior to these revisions, apart from two notable exceptions,[3] the courts, particularly those of first instance, had felt constrained to place a narrow construction on section 210 and had shown themselves more ready to exercise their powers to wind up on the familiar just and equitable ground[4] rather than to exercise those under the new section.

This is illustrated by *Ebrahimi* v. *Westbourne Galleries*[5] where the petition was for an order, under section 210, that the respondents should purchase the petitioner's shareholding on such terms as the court should think fit or, failing that, that the company should be wound-up. Plowman J. dismissed the application for an order under section 210 holding that he had to be satisfied (and was not) that there had been a lack of probity and a course of oppressive conduct continued up to the date of the petition and affecting the petitioner qua member. Nevertheless he ordered a winding-up. Only the respondents appealed, with the result that neither the Court of Appeal (which in fact took an even narrower view and granted the respondents' appeal) nor the House of Lords (which restored the winding-up order) were concerned with section 210. One gets the impression that the House of Lords, had it been open to them, would

---

[1] 1948 Act, s.225(2). Now Insolvency Act 1986, s.125(2). Clearly the contemplated "other remedy" was that under s.210 (now ss.459–461) but it was not (and is not) restricted to that; it could be a "personal" or "derivative" action.

[2] Implementing, 18 years later, recommendations made by the Jenkins Committee in 1962 (Cmnd. 1749, paras. 199–212, which summarise the various "mischiefs" aimed at by the revisions).

[3] See *Scottish Co-operative Wholesale Society* v. *Meyer* [1959] A.C. 324, H.L. Sc. and *Re Harmer Ltd.* [1959] 1 W.L.R. 62, C.A. which seem to be the only two reported cases in which the petitioners were successful prior to 1980 (though in many others there had been satisfactory settlements out of court).

[4] Though, Lord Wilberforce in *Ebrahimi* thought that even there the courts had been "too timorous" [1973] A.C. at p. 379. The approval by the H.L. of "just and equitable" as a workable test is to be contrasted with the disapproval by the C.A. in *Newman* of "where the justice of the case requires" as a workable exception to the rule in *Foss* v. *Harbottle*, above.

[5] See n. 99 above.

have been willing to make an order under that section and that the speech of Lord Wilberforce would then have become the locus classicus on section 210 (as well as on the just and equitable ground). Instead we had to wait some 10 years before the legislation made the remedy less susceptible to timorous interpretations.

Section 459(1) now reads as follows:

"A member of a company may apply to the court by petition for an order under this Part on the ground that the company's affairs are being or have been conducted in a manner which is unfairly prejudicial to the interests *of its members generally*[6] or some part of the members (including at least himself) or that any actual or proposed act or omission of the company (including any act or omission on its behalf) is or would be so prejudicial."

This differs from, and improves upon, the former section 210 in four respects:

(i) "Unfairly prejudicial"[7] has been substituted for "oppressive."

(ii) The former need for the conduct to be such as would justify a winding-up order has been removed.

(iii) The words italicised remove the obvious absurdity that, as section 210 had been construed,[8] the remedy was available only if the interests of some (not all) of the members were unfairly prejudiced.[9]

(iv) The remedy is now available where an unfairly prejudicial act or omission by, or on behalf of, the company, has occurred or is threatened.[10]

---

[6] Italics supplied. These words were inserted by the 1989 Act but not, for some reason, brought into operation until 1991.

[7] The Jenkins Committee (Cmnd. 1749, para. 204) recommended this expression since "oppression" was thought to be suggestive of a degree of culpability in excess of what was intended. "Culpability," in the sense of a deliberate intention to injure, now seems to be unnecessary for either s.459 or winding-up on the just and equitable ground.

[8] *Re A Company (No. 00370 of 1983) Exp. Glossop*, [1988] 1 W.L.R. 1068. But see *Re Sam Weller Ltd.*, [1990] Ch. 692.

[9] But it was held in *Re A Company (No. 004475 of 1982) [1983]* Ch. 178 that the members must be affected qua members. If correct this draws an unfortunate distinction between s.459 and winding up on the just and equitable ground to which it clearly does not apply (see *Ibrahimi v. Westbourne Galleries*, above). Fortunately the spate of recent cases seems to have distinguished it out of existence, for it is clear that if a member is admitted to membership on the understanding that he will share in management his interests are prejudiced if he is ousted from management: see, *e.g. Re A Company (No. 002567 of 1982) [1983]* 1 W.L.R. 927 at 933DE; *Virdi v. Abbey Leisure Ltd.* [1990] BCLC 342, C.A. The knotty problem of deciding what precisely is meant by "member qua member" (see Chap. 11 at p. 285 above) now seems to be ignored in this context. But see *Re Cade and Son* [1991] B.C.C. 165 where the prejudice was to a member in his capacity of freeholder of land leased to the company.

[10] Thus making it clear that when a wrong has been done *to the company*, thus unfairly prejudicing the interests of all members, s.459 provides an alternative to a derivative action.

In addition, subsection (2) extends "members" to "a person who has not been registered as a member but to whom shares in the company have been transferred or transmitted by operation of law . . . " (*e.g.* a personal representative or trustee in bankruptcy).[11]

Section 460, as did the former section 210, enables the Secretary of State, after receiving a report from inspectors or having exercised his powers under the sections dealt with in the next chapter, himself to petition under Part XVII.[12] Section 461 deals with the powers of the court on any application under section 459 or 460. These, under section 461(1), are expressed as widely as is possible; if satisfied that the petition is well-founded, the court may "make such order as it thinks fit for giving relief in respect of the matter complained of." Without prejudice to the generality of that, subsection (2) instances: (a) regulating the conduct of the company's affairs in future[13]; (b) requiring the company to refrain from doing an act complained of or to repair an omission complained of; (c) authorising civil proceedings to be brought in the name and on behalf of the company by such person or persons or on such terms as the court may direct; and (d) providing for the purchase of the shares of any member of the company[14] by other members or by the company itself and, in the case of a purchase by the company itself, reducing the company's capital accordingly.[15]

Procedure under Part XVII

Under the rule-making powers conferred by section 461(6),[16] the Companies (Unfair Prejudice Applications) Proceedings Rules 1986[17] have made special rules regarding the procedure to be adopted in relation to petitions under Part XVII—another advantage over derivative actions where, as we have seen, there are none. But

[11] As already pointed out, this is particularly important in relation to personal representatives: Chap. 15 at pp. 404, 405 above.
[12] This he can do in relation to any company liable to be wound up under the Act; s.460(2). Section 459 applies to a slightly less wide category of companies, *i.e.* to companies within the meaning of the Act and, as a result of an amendment made by the Water Act 1989, to statutory water companies: s.459(3).
[13] If the order requires the company not to make any, or a specified, alteration to its memorandum or articles the company then does not have power, without the leave of the court, to make any such alteration (s.461(3)); the provisions of the Act apply to the memorandum and articles as so altered s.461(4); and the company has to deliver a copy of any such order to the Registrar: s.461(5). Whether, if the company did alter the memorandum without the consent of the court and acted upon the altered memo, the act would nevertheless be valid under the new s.35, "abolishing" the *ultra vires* rule (see Chap. 8 above) is an interesting but largely academic question. The combined effect of s.35A and s.461(4) would seem to be to afford protection to a person dealing with the company in good faith.
[14] This is the order most frequently sought: see below.
[15] *i.e.* without the need to comply with Part V, Chapter VII of the Act dealt with in Chapter 9, pp. 217–226 above.
[16] As amended by the Insolvency Acts 1985 and 1986.
[17] S.I. 1986 No. 2000.

unfortunately, all the Rules do is to prescribe the form of the petition, how it shall be served and advertised and what directions the court may give. They then provide that "except so far as is inconsistent with the Act and these Rules, the Rules of the Supreme Court and the practice of the High Court apply to proceedings in the High Court and the Rules and the practice of the county court apply to such proceedings in a county court, with any necessary modifications." This is not as helpful as it might be.[18]

Under the Rules, the petition has "to state the nature of the relief sought" and to pray for that or such other order as the court thinks fit.[19] Nevertheless the practice continued to be to pray in the alternative for winding-up on the just and equitable ground. This was understandable in view of the greater readiness that the courts had displayed to grant that relief; but it is not what the revised legislation intended. Hence, in 1990 a Practice Direction[20] drew attention to "the undesirability of including, as a matter of course, a prayer for winding up as an alternative to an order under section 459. ... It should be included only if that is the relief which the petitioner prefers or if it is considered that it may be the only relief to which he is entitled."[21]

The unfairness requirement

Even in the case of those small companies which can be described as quasi-partnerships it does not follow that every prejudicial act or omission will be "unfair" prejudice (or conduct such as to make it just and equitable to wind-up). The quasi-partners have, after all, chosen to incorporate and must accept the consequences unless in all the circumstances they have been unfairly prejudiced. This has been particularly emphasised by Hoffmann J. who has taken the view that if the articles of the company have made reasonable and fair provision as to what is to occur in the event of a breakdown in the relationship between the quasi-partners it will be neither unfairly

---

[18] See *Re A Company (No. 004175)* [1987] 1 W.L.R. 585, where it was held that the court, until it had been satisfied at the hearing that there was unfair prejudice to the petitioner had no jurisdiction to order an interim payment to the petitioner notwithstanding R.S.C. Ord. 27, r. 3.

[19] See 5(g) of the scheduled form of petition.

[20] See [1990] 1 W.L.R. 490.

[21] The Practice Direction also prescribes that, if a prayer for winding-up is included, the petition should state whether or not the petitioner consents to an order under s.127 of the Insolvency Act in the standard form, and, if not, what modifications he suggests. The standard form provides that transactions in the ordinary course of business between the date of the presentation of the petition and the date of judgment shall not be avoided by the making of the winding-up order (which dates back to the date of petition unless the court otherwise directs). Unless the company is insolvent, or there is misconduct in relation to transactions in the ordinary course of business, the standard form order will obviously be appropriate.

prejudicial nor just and equitable to wind-up so long as the articles have been scrupulously observed.[22]

However, in the recent case of *Virdi v. Abbey Leisure Ltd.*,[23] the Court of Appeal took a somewhat different view. That case, concerned a company, in which the petitioner held 40 per cent. of the shares. The company had been formed for the purpose of purchasing, refurbishing and then selling a night-club. This had been achieved and the proceeds of sale constituted the company's sole asset. Disagreements ensued on what should then happen. The petitioner applied to have the company wound up on the just and equitable ground in order to realise his 40 per cent. of the proceeds of the sale. It was accepted that he had a right to a winding-up order unless he had another remedy which he was unreasonably refusing to use.[24] Hoffmann J. had struck out the petition as an abuse of process since the petitioner had another remedy which he should have used, namely acceptance of an offer from the directors to buy his shares at a price determined, in accordance with the pre-emptive rights in the articles, by an accountant, at a fair price as between a willing seller and a willing buyer. His decision was reversed on appeal and the court also expressed dissent from his views in the earlier cases on section 459 applications.

Calculating a buy-out price

The question of how, and as at what date, a petitioner's shares should be valued if the court orders that he be bought out is an important one since an order that he be bought out is that most commonly asked for on section 459 applications. In practice, the courts have sought to ensure that, if the petitioner is wholly free of blame for the breakdown, his shares will be valued in a way that is fairest to the petitioner.[25] Thus, if the valuation has to be made on an asset basis (as in most cases it will since the company is unlikely to be listed) the court is likely to direct that there shall be no discount because the petitioner's holding is a minority stake not affording control. If the assets of the company have increased since the date of the breakdown, it will normally be fairest for the valuation to be as at the present date unless the respondents can show that the increase is

[22] See *Re A Company (No. 007623 of 1984)* [1986] BCLC 362; *Re A Company (No. 004377 of 1986)* [1987] 1 W.L.R. 102; and *Virdi v. Abbey Leisure Ltd.* below, n. 23.
[23] [1990] BCLC 342; C.A.
[24] Insolvency Act, s.125(2), above.
[25] See, *e.g. Scottish Co-operative Wholesale Society v. Meyer* [1959] A.C. 324, H.L.; *Re Noble & Sons* [1983] BCLC 273; *Re A Company (No. 002567 of 1982)* [1983] 1 W.L.R. 927; *Re Bird Precision Bellows* [1984] Ch. 419, [1986] Ch. 658, C.A.; *Re London School of Electronics* [1986] Ch. 211; *Virdi v. Abbey Leisure*, n. 23 above. In the last of these cases the C.A. thought that winding up was more appropriate than an order under s.459 since it would ensure that the petitioner received his 40 per cent. of the net assets. But this hardly seems to justify forcing a liquidation upon the members who would have to bear the heavier costs of a winding-up.

due to their exceptional efforts. But if, after the petitioner's departure, the value has fallen it may be fairer to adopt the date of the breakdown. If, however, the breakdown is partly the fault of the petitioner, account may be taken of this. Hence, although in contrast with a derivative action, the petitioner does not have "to come with clean hands," on an order under Part XVII (as opposed to a winding-up order) the conduct of the petitioner may nevertheless be material—and not only in affecting the relief which the court grants but, also in that "it may render the conduct of the respondents, not unfair, even if it is prejudicial."[26]

Can Part XVII supersede derivative actions?

The spate of reported cases since the 1980 reforms suggests that resort to Part XVII is rapidly becoming the remedy most commonly used in relation to intra-corporate disputes, at any rate in small private companies. Doubtless it will always be more often invoked in their case than in relation to large public companies, if only because such disputes are more likely to arise within small companies and because "unfair prejudice" is easier to establish in relation to such of those companies as are quasi-partnerships, thus enabling the courts to subject the exercise of legal rights to equitable considerations. Lord Wilberforce in *Ebrahimi v. Westbourne Galleries*[27] instanced, as indications that those equitable considerations apply, the presence of one or more of the following elements:

"(i)   an association formed or continued on the basis of a personal relationship, involving mutual confidence—an element which will often be found where a pre-existing partnership has been converted into a limited company;

(ii)   an agreement, or understanding, that all or some (for there may be 'sleeping' members) of the shareholders shall participate in the conduct of the business; and

(iii)   restriction upon the transfer of the members' interests in the company—so that if confidence is lost, or one member is removed from management, he cannot take out his stake and go elsewhere."[28]

But a Part XVII order is not restricted to such companies and it seems clear that a member of any company will find it easier to

---

[26] See, *per* Nourse J. [1986] Ch. at 222B.
[27] [1973] A.C. 360, H.L. at 379E–C. It seems clear that the indications are relevant to both winding-up and to Part XVII.
[28] In practice he will often not be able, in the case of unlisted companies, "to take out his stake and go elsewhere," even if there are no such restrictions, since it will be difficult to find a purchaser of his shares other than the company or its members (who may be unwilling to pay a fair price unless ordered to do so).

establish unfairly prejudicial conduct than fraud-on-the-minority plus wrongdoer control and all the complications of a derivative action. Yet members still resort instead to derivative actions both in the case of public companies[29] and sometimes, though perhaps less often, even in relation to private ones.[30]

The undoubted intention of section 75 of the 1980 Act (and now of Part XVII) was to provide a possible alternative to a derivative action[31] and what is now section 461(2)(c)[32] was specifically inserted to meet the difficulty that, where a wrong has been done to the company, it may be necessary to sue third parties who are not respondents to the petition. Yet this use of the section seems to have been largely ignored. For that there was, perhaps, some excuse so long as the remedy was restricted to cases where the conduct complained of was unfairly prejudicial to the interests of some part of the members; when a wrong has been done to the company it will be prejudiced if the wrong is not righted. But since the amendment made by the 1989 Act (under which the remedy is available when the interests "*of the whole* or any part of the members" are unfairly prejudiced) there is no such excuse.

Even before that amendment came into operation, the possibility of using Part XVII in relation to wrongs *to* the company had not been wholly ignored. In *Re A Company (No. 005287 of 1985)*[33] shares of a private family company had, originally, all been held by a husband and wife and their four daughters. In 1982, however, they transferred to the husband (H) of one of the daughters sufficient of their shares to give him control. H was alleged by the other three daughters to have managed the company in breach of the agreement made at the time of the transfer and in breach of his fiduciary duties to the company. They therefore petitioned under section 459, claiming, among other relief, an order that he should account to the company for the money that he had improperly extracted from it and should purchase their shares at such price as the court considered appropriate and just. But by the time that the petition first came before Hoffmann J. the plot had thickened. It appeared that H had

---

[29] See, *e.g. Prudential Assurance* v. *Newman Industries*, above, where, it is submitted, if *Prudential* had petitioned under the present s.459, it would have avoided the difficulties it got into and achieved just as much (and saved many weeks of judicial time).

[30] See *Smith* v. *Croft*, above, where the plaintiffs would, no doubt, have been equally unsuccessful under s.459 but at far less expense.

[31] See Jenkins Report, Cmnd. 1749 of 1962, para. 206.

[32] Enabling the court to authorise such proceedings to be taken in the name and on behalf of the company "by such person or persons and on such terms as the court shall direct." This, presumably, would enable the court to direct that such person or persons should be indemnified for their costs by the company (thus, in such a case, meeting the alleged disadvantage that a "*Wallersteiner* v. *Moir* order" is not at present available to petitioners under s.459).

[33] [1986] 1 W.L.R. 281.

sold his shares to a Gibraltarian company, that the undertaking and assets of the family company had been sold for £520,800 (which had seemingly been "laundered" through various bank accounts in off-shore financial centres) and that it and all its former assets and records were untraceable. It was argued on behalf of H that no relief on a petition under Part XVII could be granted against him, since he had ceased to be a member of the company, and therefore the only possible remedy against him was a separate derivative action. Hoffmann J. pointed out how inconvenient this would be, since two actions, based on the same facts and both essentially alleging that the company's affairs had been carried on in a manner unfairly prejudicial to members, would need to be carried on side-by-side. He saw no reason for not construing section 461(1) as other than conferring the widest possible discretion on the court to make "such order as it thinks fit for giving relief in respect of the matters complained of." Hence the petition was allowed to proceed as against both H and the Gibraltarian company which had been joined as a respondent.

It appears from this decision that section 461(2)(*c*) is probably unnecessary and that relief can be ordered on a petition under section 459 against all or any who are joined as respondents whether or not they are or have been members and that the power under section 461(2)(*c*) will be needed only if the third party has not been joined as a respondent to the petition.[34] Accordingly it is possible that, in the not too distant future, derivative actions can be relegated to an historical footnote only.

The wider role of "just and equitable" winding up

Before concluding this discussion of Part XVII and winding-up on the just and equitable grounds, it should be pointed out that although it is now clear that unfairly prejudicial conduct will often give rise to the possible use of either remedy (in which event it will normally be regarded as unreasonable to petition for a winding-up unless there are other grounds for that, and Part XVII should be used) the scope of the two remedies is not wholly co-terminous. A single act or omission may be unfairly prejudicial but is less likely to be regarded as making it just and equitable that the company should be wound up. On the other hand, it may be just and equitable to wind up a company on a member's petition notwithstanding that there was no unfairly prejudicial conduct, act or omission but because, for example, there is a deadlock—which is all too likely to occur where a

---

[34] *e.g.* because his complicity became known only as result of the hearings on the petition.

company has been formed to enable two individuals or companies to undertake a joint enterprise, each having 50 per cent. of the shares and half the seats on the board and with no casting vote by the chairman of any meeting.[35]

It should also be mentioned by way of postscript, that if a company is being wound up, provisions, now in the Insolvency Act, afford additional remedies against delinquent directors and others. Primarily these will be exercisable by the liquidator.[36] But section 212[37] provides a summary remedy when, in the course of a winding-up, it appears that any person, who is or has been an officer, liquidator, administrator[38] or administrative receiver of the company, or is or has been concerned or taken part in its promotion, formation or management, "has misapplied, or retained, or become accountable for any money or other property of the company, or been guilty of any misfeasance or breach of *any fiduciary or other duty*[39] in relation to the company."[40] The court, on the application of the official receiver or the liquidator, or any creditor or (with leave of the court[41]) any member,[42] may examine into the conduct of any such person and compel him to repay, restore or account, or to pay compensation.[43]

It is not suggested that because of this, an unfairly prejudiced member should apply for a winding-up rather than an order under Part XVII; he would probably be regarded as acting unreasonably if he did. But it does mean that, if someone else has put the company into liquidation, a member may, with the leave of the court, be able to apply under section 212 without having to bring himself within an exception to the rule in *Foss* v. *Harbottle*[44] and this he may do

[35] Such arrangements almost invariably lead to trouble sooner or later but they continue to be entered into surprisingly often.

[36] As, *e.g.* in relation to "fraudulent" or "wrongful" trading dealt with in Chap. 6 at pp. 110–115 above.

[37] Replacing s.631 of the 1985 Act which, in turn, replaced s.333 of the 1948 Act. Note also that both members *and creditors* are afforded a remedy similar to s.459 if an administrator manages the affairs of the company in a manner unfairly prejudicial to their interests: Insolvency Act, s.27 on which see Chap. 28 at pp. 758–760 below.

[38] Italics supplied. These words replace "misfeasance or breach of trust" in the earlier versions and implement the recommendation of the Jenkins Committee (Cmnd. 1749, para. 503(d)) "to bring actionable negligence ... within the scope of the section. Negligence had been held not to be covered by the earlier versions: *Re Johnson & Co. (Builders) Ltd.* [1955] Ch. 634, C.A.

[39]

[40]

[41] s.212(1) and (2).

[42] The section, as is customary throughout the winding-up provisions, uses the word "contributory" defined in s.79 in a way which suggests that it does not include a holder of fully paid shares. But it has consistently been held to mean a past or present member, see *Re Anglesea Colliery* (1866) L.R. 1 Ch.App. 555; *Re Aidall Ltd.* [1933] Ch. 323, C.A.; *Re Consolidated Goldfields of New Zealand* [1953] Ch. 689.

[43] s.212(3).

[44] Which, in effect, ceases to have any relevance on a winding-up since the directors' powers will have passed to the liquidator who, with leave of the court, will be able to cause the company itself to sue. But s.212 may be invoked against the liquidator or an administrative receiver if he misbehaves: s.212(2).

"notwithstanding that he may not benefit[45] from any order that the court makes on the application."[46]

CONCLUSION

The two greatest weaknesses of the legal remedies available to members are: (1) that despite the increased amount of information supplied to members in the annual accounts and reports it is not likely to afford them the evidence they will need if they are to launch legal proceedings with any chance of success; and (2) that individual members will be understandably reluctant to incur the costs of litigation. It is in these respects that the administrative remedies available to the Department of Trade and Industry and dealt with in the next chapter, are of paramount importance. Indeed, those remedies may result in members obtaining the relief they seek without more ado or expense to them.

Hence any attempt to draw conclusions as to the adequacy of the available remedies is left until the conclusion of the next chapter.

[45] As he would not, if he was a past member or if the creditors would not be paid in full, even if the application had a successful outcome.
[46] s.212(5).

MANY other countries have recognised that the abuse of corporate power cannot be adequately constrained by leaving it to the company's members to ensure that the controllers behave and to take action in the courts if they do not. They have accordingly set up governmental agencies to exercise a supervisory role, sometimes conferring legislative and judicial, as well as administrative, functions on those agencies. But few of them (not even the United States, which has in the S.E.C. the most powerful of such agencies) have gone so far as we have in empowering them to launch inquisitorial raids on corporate (and even unincorporated) bodies. The fact that we have gone further is not necessarily grounds for pride; it is partly due to the still primitive state of our version of derivative actions and to the appalling cost of litigation in England (not effectively mitigated by Legal Aid and aggravated by our rule that the losing party pays both his and the winner's costs and by our refusal hitherto to countenance contingent fees). Be that as it may, the fact is that Draconian powers have increasingly been vested in the Secretary of State and the Department of Trade and Industry now has a sizeable Investigations Branch which frequently conducts the initial inquisition though it may be hived-off later to outside Inspectors, normally a Q.C. and a chartered accountant.

Originally, appointment of outside Inspectors was the only power that the Secretary of State had. But an announced appointment of Inspectors is likely in itself to cause damage to the company. Hence the Department was reluctant to appoint unless a strong case for doing so could be made out and it normally made inquiries of the board of directors before doing so. Though such inquiries might cause the board to take remedial action they might equally well provide an opportunity for evidence to be destroyed or fabricated. Hence, on the recommendation of the Jenkins Committee,[1] power to require the production of books and papers was added by the 1967 Act, a power which can be exercised with less publicity[2] and which may suffice in itself or lead to a formal appointment of Inspectors if the facts elicited show that that is needed. This power, now conferred by

---

[1] Cmnd. 1749 paras. 213–219.

[2] The Department does not normally announce that it has mounted such an investigation and all information about it is regarded as confidential. This has its disadvantages. If a team of officials is going through the company's books and papers this cannot be concealed from its employees and will soon become known to the Press, thus putting the company under a cloud which may never be dispersed because the ending of the inquiries will not normally be announced or their results ever be published, notwithstanding that the conclusion may be that all is well with the company.

section 447 of the Act[3] is by far the one most commonly exercised.[4] It and the provisions regarding appointment of Inspectors under the Companies Act are now to be found in its Part XIV (sections 431–453).

(1) Investigations by the Department's officials

Under section 447(1)–(3) the Secretary of State may, at any time if he thinks there is good reason to do so, give directions to any company requiring it, at such time and place as are specified in the direction, to produce such documents[5] as may be specified[6] or authorise an officer of his, on producing, if required, evidence of his authority, to produce to that officer any documents which the officer may specify.[7] In practice the latter course is adopted since it avoids the risk of the documents being destroyed or doctored; the officer will arrive without warning[8] at the company's registered office (or wherever else the documents are believed to be held).[9] When it appears to the Secretary of State or to the officer authorised by him that the documents concerned are in the possession of some person other than the company, he has the like power to require that person to produce them.[10]

The requirement to produce documents includes power, if they are produced, to take copies of them or extracts from them and to require any person who produces them, or any other person who is, or was in the past, an officer or employee of the company to provide an explanation of them and, if they are not produced by the person asked, to state to the best of his knowledge where they are.[11]

Failure to comply with any requirement is an offence punishable by a fine[12] but it is a defence to a charge of failure to produce

---

[3] As amended by the 1989 Act, s.63(1)–(7).
[4] In recent years, it has been used more than 130 times each year (157 times in 1989–90) whereas use of any of the other sections has been in single figures and under 15 per annum in all of them combined: see *Companies in 1989–90*, Table 1.
[5] The 1989 Act substituted "documents" for "books or papers" and defined "documents" in a new subs. (9) as including "information recorded in any form and, in relation to information recorded otherwise than in legible form, the power to require its production includes power to require the production of a copy in legible form," (*e.g.* a computer print-out).
[6] s.447(2).
[7] s.447(3).
[8] The investigation is an administrative act to which the full rules of natural justice do not apply: *Norwest Holst Ltd.* v. *Secretary of State* [1978] Ch. 201, (C.A.) at 224. But "fairness" must be observed and directions to produce should be clear and not excessive: *R.* v. *Trade Secretary, ex p. Perestrello* [1981] 1 Q.B. 19 (a case which illustrates the problems that may be met if the documents are not held in the U.K.).
[9] The officer may be accompanied by a policeman with a search warrant: see s.448, below.
[10] s.447(4). But this is without prejudice to any lien that the possessor may have.
[11] s.447(5). Any statements he makes may be used in evidence against him: s.447(8).
[12] s.447(6). The offence is subject to: s.732 (restricting prosecution to the S. or S. or the DPP or with their consent), s.733 (making officers of bodies corporate liable if they connived at, or caused by their neglect, an offence by the body corporate) and s.734 (enabling prosecutions to be brought against unincorporated bodies in the name of the body).

documents, to prove that they were not in the accused's possession or control and that it was not reasonably practicable for him to comply with the requirement.[13] Criminal sanctions are imposed by sections 450 and 451 on any officer of the company who is privy to the falsification or destruction of a document relating to the company's affairs or who furnishes false information.

Section 448,[14] was replaced and strengthened by the 1989 Act.[15] Formerly it applied only to investigations under what is now section 447. But now it applies also to any investigations under Part XIV of the Act, *i.e.* to those by outside Inspectors as well. It nevertheless seems better to deal with it before turning to Inspectors because the full implications of section 447 cannot otherwise be appreciated.

Under subsection (1) of section 448, a Justice of the Peace, if satisfied on information given on oath by the Secretary of State, or by a person appointed or authorised to exercise powers under Part XIV, that there are on any premises documents, production of which has been required under that Part and which have not been produced, may issue a search warrant.

Under that subsection a search warrant cannot be issued unless there has first been a requirement to produce the documents sought. The company thus forewarned, could destroy the documents before the search took place. Hence, the 1989 Act added a new subsection (2) under which a warrant may be issued if the J.P. is satisfied: (a) that there are reasonable grounds for believing that an indictable offence has been committed and that there are on the premises documents relating to whether the offence has been committed, (b) that the applicant has power under Part XIV to require the production of the documents, and (c) that there are reasonable grounds for believing that if production was required it would not be forthcoming but the documents would be removed, hidden, tampered with or destroyed. Though narrowly circumscribed by the need to satisfy the J.P. of conditions (a)–(c), this enables the search for the documents to be undertaken by the police rather than by the (possibly self-interested) officers of the company.

---

[13] s.447(7). s.449 contains detailed provisions regarding the security and confidentiality of documents and information produced under s.447 and the uses to which they can be put.

[14] Note also that there is a power under s.721 whereby (on application of the DPP, the S. of S. or the police) a High Court judge, if satisfied that there is reasonable cause to believe that any person, while an officer of a company, has committed an offence in its management and that evidence of the commission is to be found in any books or papers of, or under the control of, the company, may make an order authorising any named person to inspect the books and papers or require an officer of the company to produce them: see *Re A Company,* [1980] Ch. 138, C.A. (reversed by H.L. *sub nom. Re Racal Communications Ltd.* [1981] A.C. 374, because, under the express provisions of subs. (4), there can be no appeal from the judge and it was held that this included cases where he had erred on a point of law—and, having discovered that other judges had taken a different view, had volunteered leave to appeal!)

[15] 1989 Act, s.54.

The warrant authorises a constable, accompanied by any person named in it and any other constables: to enter the premises using such force as is reasonably necessary; to search the premises and to take possession of any documents appearing to be documents mentioned in subsection (1) or (2); to take such other steps as appear to be necessary for preserving or preventing interference with them; to take copies and to require any person named in the warrant to provide an explanation of them or to state where they can be found.[16] Moreover, in the case of a warrant under subsection (2), if the J.P. is satisfied that there are reasonable grounds for believing that there are also on the premises other documents relevant to the investigation the warrant can also authorise like action in respect of them.[17] The warrant remains in force for a month[18] and documents seized may be retained for three months or, if proceedings are commenced against any person for any criminal offence to which the documents are relevant, until the conclusion of the proceedings.[19] Any person who intentionally obstructs the execution of a warrant or fails without reasonable excuse to provide the explanation of a document or to state where it is to be found, commits an offence.[20]

Part XIV contains further provisions common to both Departmental investigations and to Inspections but these are left until after a description of the latter. What should be emphasised, however, is that an investigation by the Department's officials under section 447 is very far from being merely a preliminary step towards the appointment of Inspectors if the documentary evidence thus discovered justifies that. On the contrary, in most cases it will be the only investigation undertaken and will lead either to a decision that no further action is needed or that some follow-up action should be taken in accordance with (3) below. The time taken to decide may vary from a few days to several months and while it continues the officials will probe deeply and in a way which from the viewpoint of the company is just as traumatic as a formal Inspection.

It should also be mentioned here that sections 82–91 of the Companies Act 1989 contain important new provisions conferring on the Secretary of State and his officers powers similar to those in section 447 of the 1985 Act, which may be exercised at the request of overseas regulatory authorities. These provisions are, in effect, amendments to the Financial Services Act, into which they will, no doubt, one day be incorporated on a reconsolidation. It is beyond the scope of this book to do more than mention their existence and to stress their importance for investor protection generally. One of the

16 s.448(3).
17 s.448(4).
18 s.448(5).
19 s.448(6).   This can be highly inconvenient to the company.
20 s.448(7).   ss.732, 733 and 734 (see n. 12 above) apply to this offence.

greatest problems in this area is that without international collaboration it is impossible to prevent crooks, operating from abroad, from flooding the United Kingdom (and other countries) with invitations to invest in bogus concerns. Mutual assistance between regulators is an essential step towards controlling this abuse and these new powers enable the United Kingdom to play its part and to obtain reciprocal help from the overseas regulators.

Under section 453 of the Act the provisions of Part XIV apply to all bodies corporate which are, or have been, carrying on business here (except for those sections disapplied by its subsection (2)[21] and subject to such modifications and adaptations as may be made by regulations) but this is not effective against the type of crooks referred to in the foregoing paragraph unless, which is unlikely, they have incorporated a company which has established a place of business here.

(2) Investigations by Inspectors

When Inspectors can be appointed

In a wide range of circumstances the Secretary of State is empowered to appoint "one or more competent inspectors[22] to investigate the affairs[23] of a company and to report on them in such manner as he directs." He has a discretion whether or not to do so, except that he must appoint if the court by order declares that the affairs of the company ought to be so investigated.[24]

Under section 431 he may appoint on the application of: (a) in the case of a company with a share capital, not less than 200 members or of members holding not less than one-tenth of the issued shares; (b) in the case of a company not having a share capital, not less than one-fifth of the persons on the company's register of members; or (c) in any case, the company itself.[25] However, appointments under this

---

[21] As amended by 1989 Act, s.70. It disapplies ss.431, 438 and 442–446 but not 447 or 448.

[22] As already mentioned, the usual appointees are a Q.C. and a chartered accountant but less expensive mortals may be appointed in the rarer case when the D.T.I. appoints in relation to a private company.

[23] *i.e.* its business, including its control over its subsidiaries, whether that is being managed by the board of directors or an administrator, administrative receiver or a liquidator in a voluntary liquidation: *R. v. Board of Trade, ex p. St Martins Preserving Co.* [1965] 1 Q.B. 603.

[24] s.432(1). This seems to make the S. of S.'s refusal to appoint reviewable by the court if an application is made to it by anyone with *locus standi* (Ord. 102, r.3(1)(*b*)) and to enable a court, in proceedings before it (*e.g.* on a petition under s.459) to make an order declaring that the company's affairs ought to be investigated by Inspectors. There was formerly another situation in which the S. of S. had to appoint, *i.e.* if the company passed a special resolution declaring that its affairs ought to be so investigated, but this was removed by the 1981 Act.

[25] s.431(2)(*c*). This was added on the deletion by the 1981 Act of the former provision, compelling the S. of S. to appoint if the company resolved by special resolution (see n. 24 above) and enables an application to be instigated by a resolution of the board or, if it refuses to do so, by an ordinary resolution of the company in general meeting.

section hardly ever occur.[26] This is due not only to the fact that before appointing under the section the Secretary of State may require applicants to give security to an amount not exceeding £5,000 for payment of the costs of the investigation[27] but also because the application has to be supported by evidence that the applicants have good reason for the application.[28] If they have, the Secretary of State will normally have power to appoint of his own motion under section 432(2), below, and it is far better for those who have good reasons to draw them to the attention of the Department, requesting that there should be an appointment under that section. That they do so not infrequently is shown by the fact that the most common source of requests for action under section 432(2) is "The Public",[29] which in many, probably most, cases must mean members or employees of the company. Proceeding thus avoids the danger, inherent in section 431, that the malefactors in the company will tamper with the evidence once they learn of possible action under that section and thus frustrate effective intervention by the Department under either sections 447–448 or section 432(2).

Section 432(2) empowers the Secretary of State to appoint Inspectors[30] if it appears to him that there are circumstances suggesting one (or more) of four grounds, the first two of which are:

"(a) that the company's affairs are being conducted or have been conducted with intent to defraud creditors or the creditors of any other person or otherwise for a fraudulent or unlawful purpose or in a manner which is unfairly prejudicial to some part of its members[31]; or

(b) that any actual or proposed act or omission of the company (including an act or omission on its behalf) is or would be so prejudicial, or that the company was formed for any fraudulent or unlawful purpose."

These, it will be observed, adopt the wording of sections 459 and 460 except that, presumably by an oversight, the 1989 Act omitted here to change "some part of the members" (at the end of (a)) to "members generally or some part of the members,"[32] but in addition

[26] There were no appointments under it in the years 1985–1990: *Companies in 1989–90*, Table 1.
[27] s.431(4). The £5,000 can be altered by statutory instrument. In the 1948 Act it was only £100 which, even then, would not have kept a competent Q.C. and chartered accountant happy for the time that most inspections take.
[28] s.431(3).
[29] 306 requests in 1988–89 and 331 in 1989–90. The comparable figures for the next most common source ("Divisions of the DTI") were 229 and 185: *Companies in 1989–90*, Table 2.
[30] Even if the company is in the course of being voluntarily wound up: s.432(3).
[31] "Member" includes a person to whom shares have been transmitted by operation of law: s.432(4).
[32] Arguably, with the absurd result that, strictly speaking, the S. of S. should not appoint Inspectors if he thinks that *all* the members are unfairly prejudiced and therefore cannot, despite the alteration made to ss.459 and 460 (see Chap. 24 at p. 664 above) act under (a) unless he has also acted under s.447 or 448! Since, however, the precise grounds on which he has acted do not have to be stated (see

it enables him to appoint where the company has been operated with intent to defraud creditors or was formed or conducted for a fraudulent or unlawful purpose.

In addition an appointment may be made on the ground:

"(c) that persons concerned with the company's formation or the management of its affairs have in connection therewith been guilty of fraud, misfeasance or other misconduct towards it or towards its member; or

(d) that the company's members have not been given all the information with respect to its affairs which they might reasonably expect."[33]

Under a new subsection (2A), inserted by the 1989 Act, Inspectors may be appointed on terms that any report they make is not for publication, in which case section 437, below, does not apply. Since, under that section, a report does not have to be published unless the Secretary of State thinks fit, it might be thought that subsection (2A) was unnecessary. But it has two advantages; it protects the Secretary of State from pressure to publish even though he is advised that that might prejudice possible criminal prosecutions, and it makes it clear to the proposed appointees that they will not be able to bask in publicity resulting from their efforts.[34]

In recent years appointments under section 432(2) have become less common than they were before the introduction of the powers dealt with under (1) above,[35] which, except in major cases, normally suffice and produce results more rapidly and at less expense.

In addition to the powers of investigation dealt with above, Part XIV of the Act includes provisions regarding investigations of company ownership (sections 442–444) and of dealings in the company's securities (section 446). These, together with the power in section 177 of the Financial Services Act, to investigate insider dealing have been dealt with in Chapter 23.

Conduct of Inspections

The Act itself contains a number of sections on the conduct of Inspections. Under section 433, if Inspectors, appointed to investigate the affairs of a company, think it necessary for the purposes of their investigation to investigate also the affairs of another body corporate

[33] *Norwest Holst v. Trade Secretary* [1978] Ch. 201, C.A.) the omission is probably of no practical importance.
[34] The wording of this implies that members may "reasonably expect" more information than that to which the Act entitles them. But it seems that s.432(2) does not entitle the Secretary of State to appoint merely because the directors or officers of the company appear to have breached their duties of care, skill or diligence: see *SBA Properties Ltd.* v. *Cradock* [1967] 1 W.L.R. 716 (which, however, was concerned with an action by the S. of S. under what is now s.438, below).
[35] It may also tend to make the officers of the company more co-operative. There was only one appointment in each of the years 1985–86 and 1986–87 and two in 1987–88 but the number rose to seven in 1988–89 and there were five in 1989–90: *Companies in 1989–90*, Table 1.

in the same group they may do so and report the results of that so far as it is relevant to the affairs of the company.[36] Under section 434[37] Inspectors have powers, similar to those of officers of the Department under section 447 (above), to require the production of documents.[38] They may also require any past or present officer or agent of the company to attend before them and otherwise to give all assistance that he is reasonably able to give.[39] In addition, they may examine any person on oath[40] and any answer may be used in evidence against him.[41] If any person fails to comply with their requirements or refuses to answer any question put to him by the Inspectors for the purposes of the investigation, the Inspectors may certify that fact in writing to the court[42] which will thereupon inquire into the case and may punish the offender in like manner as if he had been guilty of contempt of court.[43]

The Inspectors may, and, if so directed by the Secretary of State, shall, make interim reports and, on the conclusion of the investigation must make a final report.[44] If so directed by the Secretary of State, they must also inform him of any matters coming to their knowledge as the result of their investigation.[45] When criminal matters have come to light and been referred to the appropriate prosecuting authorities the Inspectors can be directed to discontinue or curtail the scope of their investigation and in that event a final report will be made only if the Inspectors were appointed under section 432(1) in pursuance of an order of the court[46] or if the Secretary of State so directs.[47]

The Secretary of State may, if he thinks fit, forward a copy of any report to the company's registered office and, on request and payment of a prescribed fee, to any member of the company or other body corporate which is the subject of the report, to any person whose conduct is referred to in the report, to the auditors, to the

[36] Most major corporate scandals involve the use of a network of holding and subsidiary companies, the extent of which may only become apparent during the course of the investigation: s.433 avoids the need for a formal extension of the Inspectors' appointment each time they unearth another member of the group.
[37] As amended by the 1989 Act, s.56.
[38] s.434(1), (2) and (6).
[39] s.434(1) and (2).
[40] s.434(3).
[41] s.434(5). Whether or not he was on oath: *London Securities Ltd. v. Nicholson* [1980] 1 W.L.R. 948 (not following *Karak Rubber Co. v. Burden* [1971] 1 W.L.R. 1748). See also *R. v. Seelig, R. v. Spens* (at p. 682 below). The evidence is equally admissible in civil proceedings: see *London Securities v. Nicholson* [1980] 1 W.L.R. 948 where evidence given by the company's auditors to Inspectors was held admissible against the auditors in subsequent proceedings against them by the company for their alleged negligence.
[42] s.436(1) (as substituted by the 1989 Act, s.56).
[43] s.436(2). See on this the discussion of the comparable provision on an investigation of insider dealing under F.S. Act, ss.177 and 178: above Chap. 23 at p. 639.
[44] s.437(1).
[45] s.437(1A) inserted by the F.S. Act.
[46] In which event a copy of the report will be sent to the court: s.437(2).
[47] s.437(1B) and (1C) inserted by the 1989 Act, s.57.

applicants for the investigation[48] and to any other person whose financial interests appear to be affected by matters dealt with in the report.[49] And he may (and generally will, though not until after any criminal proceedings have been concluded[50]) cause the report to be printed and published.[51]

In addition to the foregoing statutory provisions, a number of other matters have been established by practice and case law. Although the Inspectors may be expected to be somewhat more independent and impartial than the Secretary of State or his minions exercising powers under section 447 in the belief that there is good reason for doing so, they too are not regarded as exercising a judicial role but an administrative one. Nevertheless, though the full rules of "natural justice" do not apply, they must act fairly. This involves letting witnesses know of criticisms made against them (assuming that the Inspectors envisage relying on, or referring to, those criticisms in their report) and giving them adequate opportunity of answering. But the Inspectors are not bound to show them a copy of the transcript or a draft of the parts of their report referring to them, so long as they have had a fair opportunity of answering any criticisms of their conduct.[52] In the Notes of Guidance which the Department gives to Inspectors, it is stressed that the object of Inspections is to find facts rather than to express their opinions on the conduct of individuals and that they should seek to avoid the latter especially if expressed in colourful language.[53]

Inspectors sit in private but allow witnesses to be accompanied by their lawyers—although the latter's role is limited since the questioning is undertaken by the Inspectors and neither the witness nor his lawyers can cross-examine other witnesses. Although the range of persons whom the Inspectors may question is very wide,[54] the Act provides that such persons cannot be compelled to disclose or produce any information or document which they would be entitled to refuse on grounds of legal professional privilege except that lawyers must disclose the names and addresses of their clients.[55] A banker's duty of confidentiality is protected more narrowly. Under

---

[48] This is not relevant to Inspections under s.432(2) when the S. of S. appoints of his own motion.

[49] s.437(3).

[50] For an unsuccessful attempt to force the S. of S. to publish while criminal proceedings were still being considered: see *R.* v. *Secretary of State, ex p. Lonrho* [1989] 1 W.L.R. 525, H.L.

[51] s.437(3)(c). Thus making the reports available for purchase from H.M.S.O. by any member of the public so long as the reports remain in print. They often make fascinating reading for anyone interested in "the unacceptable face of Capitalism." *Re Pergamon Press Ltd.* [1971] Ch. 388, C.A.; *Maxwell* v. *D.T.I* [1974] Q.B. 523, C.A.

[53] A temptation which some have found it impossible to resist.

[54] Especially in investigations under s.442 (see s.443(2)), s.444 and under s.177 of the F.S. Act.

[55] s.452. This applies to D.T.I. investigations as well as to Inspections and there are comparable provisions in the F.S. Act and other legislation providing for investigations or Inspections.

section 452(1A) and (1B),[56] nothing in sections 434, 443, or 446 requires any person to disclose anything in respect of which he owes an obligation of confidence by virtue of carrying on the business of banking, unless (a) the person to whom the duty is owed consents, or (b) the duty is owed to the company or other body under investigation, or (c) the making of the requirement is authorised by the Secretary of State, or (d) it is the bank itself that is under investigation.

The main criticism levelled against the conduct of investigations, whether by D.T.I. officials or by Inspectors appointed by the Department, is that persons interrogated feel themselves on trial without the protections normally afforded them. That there may be some justification for this feeling is illustrated by the very recent decision in *R. v. Seelig; R. v. Lord Spens*[57]—one of the criminal proceedings arising from the "*Guinness Affair.*" On the trial of two of the defendants, Henry J. was required to determine as a preliminary issue whether self-incriminatory answers to questions, given earlier to the Inspectors appointed under section 432(2), could be used in evidence against the defendants. Despite the express statutory provision that such answers were admissible,[58] the defendants contended that the evidence should be excluded as a result of provisions in the Police and Criminal Evidence Act 1984 ("the 1984 Act"). They argued that the Inspectors were persons "investigating offences" within the meaning of section 67(9) of the 1984 Act with the result that they were "investigating officers" required to observe the Codes of Practice under that Act and should have cautioned the defendants that their answers might be used in evidence against them. Henry J. ruled that they were not "investigating officers." The defendants argued secondly that nevertheless the evidence should be excluded under section 76(2) of the 1984 Act as having been obtained by oppression or as likely to be unreliable in the light of the failure to give warning of the possible consequences. This too was rejected. And, finally, Henry J. declined to exercise his discretion to exclude the evidence on the ground of unfairness under sections 78(1) or 82(3) of the 1984 Act. While accepting that the defendants were worse placed than the average man being questioned as to a crime, that was due to the fact that the legislature, for good reasons, had in relation to corporate fraud, decided to remove the average man's privilege to remain silent. On the defendants' appeal to the Court of Appeal, all the judge's rulings were upheld.

[56] Inserted by the 1989 Act. Under s.69 under the widened exceptions the bank may find itself compelled to disclose information relating to the accounts of customers who are not themselves under investigation. Again there are comparable provisions in the other legislation.
[57] [1992] 1 W.L.R. 148, C.A. Leave to appeal was refused by both the C.A. and the H.L.
[58] s.434(5).

It should, however, be noted that whether an Inspector was an "investigating officer" within the meaning of the 1984 Act may depend on the type of Inspection. While an Inspector appointed under section 432 "to investigate the affairs of a company" is not primarily "investigating offences," this seems less clear in the case of one appointed, under section 177 of the Financial Services Act, to "carry out such investigations as are requisite to establish whether or not contraventions ..." of sections 1, 2, 4 or 5 of the Insider Dealing Act have occurred.[59]

In general, however, so long as it is accepted that, in this field, the right to silence has to be discarded, criticisms of the fairness of the procedure seem exaggerated. As Henry J. pointed out, in a dictum quoted with approval by the Court of Appeal:[60]

"[G]eneral protections, designed to be wide enough to protect the weak, the inarticulate and the suggestible from having to answer in the strange and hostile environment of a police station, are less obviously needed to protect those likely to be major witnesses in a situation 432 investigation who will usually be intelligent, sophisticated, self-confident and articulate, usually accompanied by lawyers, giving evidence by prior appointment in an environment not so foreign to them."

A more legitimate criticism is that if an investigation, whether by the Department's officials or by Inspectors, reveals what appear to be criminal offences warranting prosecution, it is likely that before any proceedings are launched there will be discussions, and perhaps further inquiries, involving the Department, the DPP, the police and, perhaps the Serious Fraud Office,[61] thus prolonging the agony. Moreover, when civil, rather than criminal, liability is revealed the culprits will have been subjected to an inquisitorial process affording them less protection than the adversarial process to which we still cling in most civil litigation.

A further criticism is that Inspections take too long a time. Attempts have been made to meet this criticism, for example by requiring Inspectors to report within 12 months which, however, they are unlikely to succeed in doing if one of them is a busy Q.C. who is not prepared to devote himself full-time to the task.[62] A major

---

59 But in the *Seelig* and *Spens* case the S. of S., in exercise of his power under s.437(1A) (above p. 682) had required the Inspectors to provide him with "any information you have relating to possible criminal offences and in particular to provide key documents and transcripts of evidence given to you."; see [1992] 1 W.L.R. at 152 E.

60 [1992] 1 W.L.R. at 161 D, E.

61 Despite efforts to ensure greater co-ordination there still appear to be "too many cooks" each determined to have a finger in the pie.

62 Greater use of solicitors, who can more easily delegate other tasks to their partners and staff, might help.

improvement here has been the increased use of investigations by the Department's officials (rather than full-fledged Inspections) but even these may sometimes take many months.

Despite the foregoing, and other legitimate criticisms of Investigations and Inspectors, they seem to be the most effective method yet devised to detect corporate misconduct and to bring to book the perpetrators of it.[63]

(3) Liability for costs of investigations

Under section 439, the expenses of any investigation under Part XIV of the Act[64] are to be defrayed in the first instance by the D.T.I.,[65] but may be recoverable from persons specified in that section, there being treated as expenses such reasonable sums as the Secretary of State may determine in respect of general staff costs and overheads.[66] The persons from whom costs are recoverable include: anyone successfully prosecuted as a result of the investigation[67]; any body corporate in whose name proceedings are brought under section 438[68] to the extent of the amount or value recovered[69]; any body corporate dealt with in an Inspectors' report when the Inspectors were not appointed on the Secretary of State's own motion[70] unless the body corporate was the applicant or except so far as the Secretary of State otherwise directs.[71] Where Inspectors were appointed under section 431 or 442(3) the applicants are liable to the extent, if any, that the Secretary of State directs.[72]

(4) Follow-up to investigations

Following an investigation, the Secretary of State has a number of powers. Apart from the obvious one of causing prosecutions to be mounted against those whose crimes have come to light, he may, as

---

[63] For a recent review of them, see the Report of the House of Commons' Trade and Industry Committee (May 1990 H.M.S.O.).
[64] Which in the case of Inspections are likely to be heavy; of the four under the Companies Act completed in 1989–90, one cost the Department over £1.5m and another over £1m: *Companies in 1989–90*, List B at p. 12 and the total costs of the companies and their officers was probably as great or greater.
[65] This is subject to the power to require security for costs on an appointment of Inspectors under the rarely used s.431 above.
[66] s.439(1) as substituted by s.59 of the 1989 Act.
[67] s.439(2).
[68] On which see (4) below.
[69] s.439(3). And a person ordered to pay costs in a civil action brought under s.438 may also be ordered to pay or contribute to the payment of the costs of the investigation which led to the action: s.439(2).
[70] But under s.431 (above) or s.442(3) (see Chap. 23 at p. 621 above).
[71] s.439(4).
[72] s.439(5) as substituted by s.59 of the 1989 Act. Inspectors appointed otherwise than on the S. of S.'s own motion may, and shall if so directed, include in their report a recommendation about costs: s.439(6). Note also the provisions regarding rights to indemnity or contribution (s.439(8) and (9)) and that the costs may include costs in respect of proceedings under s.438.

we have seen,[73] petition under section 460 for an order under section 461 if unfair prejudice to all or some of the company's members has been revealed. Alternatively or in addition, he may petition for the winding-up of the company under what is now section 124A[74] of the Insolvency Act 1986. Under that section if it appears to him as a result of any report or information obtained under Part XIV of the Companies Act[75] that it is expedient in the public interest that a company should be wound up if the court thinks it just and equitable.

Furthermore, if, from any report made or information obtained under Part XIV, it appears to the Secretary of State that any civil proceedings ought, in the public interest, to be brought by any body corporate, he may, under section 438, himself bring such proceedings in the name and on behalf of the body corporate,[76] indemnifying it against any costs or expenses incurred by it in connection with the proceedings.

As a result of these follow-up powers, the company, its members and its creditors may find that their causes of complaint are ended, or rectified so far as possible, without any further action on their part. But, if not, they should, from the Inspectors' report obtain information of assistance to them should they choose to launch proceedings. Under section 441[77] a copy of any report of Inspectors appointed under Part XIV, certified by the Secretary of State to be a true copy, is admissible in any legal proceedings "as evidence of the opinion of the inspectors in relation to any matter contained in the report and, in proceedings on an application under section 8 of the Company Directors Disqualification Act 1986,[78] as evidence of any fact stated therein."[79] The importance of this, however, seems slight;

---

[73] See Chap. 24 at p. 665.

[74] Inserted by the 1989 Act, s.60(3).

[75] Or under s.94, 105, or 177 of the F.S. Act (or after fraud investigations under s.2 of the Criminal Justice Act 1987 or the Criminal Justice (Scotland) Act 1987 or as a result of information gleaned under s.83 of the 1989 Act in assisting an overseas regulatory agency).

[76] This he can do without first having to petition under s.460, above, and obtaining a court order under s.461(2)(c).

[77] As amended by the Insolvency Acts 1985 and 1986 and the 1989 Act.

[78] See Chap. 7 at pp. 144–147.

[79] Ascertaining the precise meaning of earlier versions of this section caused the courts some difficulty: see *Re Travel and Holiday Clubs Ltd.* [1967] 1 W.L.R. 789; *Re St. Piran Ltd.* [1981] 1 W.L.R. 1300; and *Re SBA Properties Ltd.* [1967] 1 W.L.R. 711; *Re SBA Savings & Investment Bank v. Gasco* [1984] 1 W.L.R. 271. Nor is the present version much clearer except that it appears to rule out any reliance on the report as evidence of facts except in relation to s.8 of the Company Directors Disqualification Act. And, even in relation to that, while the report may be sufficient justification for the S. of S. to apply for a disqualification order on the ground that "it is expedient in the public interest," the court will have to be satisfied that "the director's conduct in relation to the company makes him unfit to be concerned in the management of a company": s.8(2). And does s.441 mean that Inspectors are to be treated as expert witnesses, so that their opinions are admissible as such? Or that their report is admissible only to the extent that their opinions are relevant? Or that their report is admissible as their opinion, for what (if anything) that is worth, despite the fact that it would otherwise be inadmissible as the irrelevant opinions of non-experts?

the real value of an Inspectors' report to a potential litigant is that it will enable him to identify the sources of the evidence on which the Inspectors reached their conclusions, which may enable him to obtain from those sources the evidence he needs.

CONCLUSIONS

The conclusions to be drawn from this and the previous chapter are, it is thought:

(1) If a member has a clear case for saying that a company has breached a duty owed to him personally, so that he has a personal right of action falling completely outside the rule in *Foss v. Harbottle*, it may be sensible for him to sue the company in a personal action. Otherwise he should not resort to the courts until he has drawn the matter to the attention of the D.T.I. with a request that the Secretary of State exercise his investigatory powers;

(2) If that request does not elicit a favourable response[80] he should in no circumstances bring a *derivative* action.[81] If he brings any action it should be by way of a petition under section 459 coupled, if that is a remedy acceptable to him, with a petition for winding-up on the just and equitable ground. A threat to petition may often lead to remedial action being voluntarily taken by the company or to a settlement out of court;

(3) If the company is listed, a member will be well-advised to cut his losses by selling his shares—assuming that he can do so without committing the offence of insider dealing—rather than to litigate. But, if the company is a private one, a sale may not be a practical alternative.

[80] As it may may not; more applications are refused than are granted and there will be reluctance to intervene if the company concerned is a small private company of little public interest.

[81] The alleged advantage of being able to obtain a *Wallersteiner v. Moir* costs order (which has diminished in the light of *Smith v. Croft (Nos. (1) and (2),* see Chap. 24 at pp. 656–661 above) does not outweigh its disadvantages.

Part Six

COMPANIES IN TRAUMA

INTRODUCTION

THIS final Part is concerned with certain major operations which a company may wish, or be forced, to undergo but which the law regards as so fundamental as to require special procedures and a measure of independent supervision. The less traumatic of these operations, dealt with in Chapters 26 and 27, do not necessarily imply that the company is terminally ill; it, or at any rate its business, may well survive—though often under different control. In contrast, those operations referred to in Chapter 28 (administrations and liquidations) are undertaken, in the case of administrations, when major surgery is needed if the company is to have any hope of survival, or, in the case of liquidations, when there are good reasons for voluntary or involuntary euthanasia.

The discussion here of these matters is in outline only (each is a vast subject, demanding a volume to itself). Especially is this so in the case of Chapter 28 which deals with matters now recognised as Insolvency Law rather than Company Law and with the relevant statutory provisions in the Insolvency Act 1986 and not in the Companies Act 1985. They have, nevertheless, implications for Company Law, especially in relation to investor and creditor protection dealt with in Part Five—but, in contrast with that Part, with particular (but not exclusive) emphasis on creditor, rather than shareholder, protection.

ONE difficulty in dealing with the major operations with which this chapter is concerned is the looseness of English legal terminology in this area. The operations are variously described as reductions, reconstructions, re-organisations, schemes of arrangement, amalgamations, mergers, de-mergers, buy-outs, etc. etc. But none of those expressions is a term of art with a clearly defined meaning distinguishing one such transaction from another. In general the expression "reconstruction," "re-organisation," or "scheme of arrangement" is employed when only one company is involved, the last of these terms being more commonly used when the rights of creditors are varied as well as those of the shareholders. Under an "amalgamation" or "merger," two or more companies are merged either by the acquisition of their undertakings and assets by one of them or by a newly incorporated company or, more commonly, by one such company acquiring a controlling shareholding in the others.[1] In English practice most mergers are achieved through take-overs dealt with in Chapter 27. The Act contains various sections under which any of such transactions may be carried out subject to prescribed safeguards which in the case of listed companies may be supplemented by Rules of The Stock Exchange.

(1) Reductions of capital

As we saw from Chapter 9, the Act imposes restraints on the extent to which a limited company with a share capital can reduce that capital. As a general principle it can do so only by a formal reduction of capital confirmed by the court in accordance with sections 135–141.[2] But today a private company will rarely need to resort to that procedure. The main situation in which such a company might wish to reduce capital is when it needs to buy out a retiring member of the company or to return to the personal representatives of a deceased member his share of the capital, but has insufficient profits available for dividend to enable it to do so except out of capital. As pointed out in Chapter 9,[3] when companies were empowered to purchase their own shares special concessions were made to private companies to enable them to do so out of capital and

---

[1] In contrast with the practice in the Civil Law countries of the EC, mergers by transfers of undertakings and assets are unusual: here the normal *modus operandi* is by acquisitions of share capital and most commonly by an agreed or hostile take-over bid (hostile bids are at present virtually impracticable in most other EC countries).
[2] Part V, Chap. IV of the Act.
[3] At pp. 217–226.

without the need for a formal reduction.[4] However in the case of public companies formal reductions may well be necessary or desirable especially in the light of the stricter rules regarding payment of dividends.[5]

Formal reductions are undertaken under Chapter IV of the Part V of the Act. The company must be authorised by the articles to reduce capital. This presents no problems; in the unlikely event that the company is not so authorised, it merely has to alter its articles by a special resolution conferring that authority. It must then pass a special resolution to reduce its share capital and this it may resolve to do "in any way."[6] But the Act envisages that it will normally be either (a) by reducing or extinguishing the amount of any uncalled liability on its shares,[7] or (b) by cancelling any paid up share capital "which is lost or unrepresented by available assets,"[8] or (c) by paying off any paid-up share capital which is in excess of the company's wants. So far as is necessary, it will alter its memorandum by reducing the amount of its share capital and of its shares accordingly.[9]

The company must then apply to the court for an order confirming the resolution.[10] The procedure varies according to whether existing creditors of the company will be affected. This they will be in cases (a) and (c). Then, and in any other case which involves a diminution of liability in respect of unpaid share capital or the payment to any shareholder of any paid up capital and in which the court, having regard to the special circumstances, so directs,[11] a somewhat complicated and expensive procedure, outlined in section 136(3)–(5),[12] may have to be followed to ensure that all creditors have been notified and given an opportunity to object. The difficulty of identifying every one of a fluctuating body of trade creditors is, however, generally avoided by satisfying the court that a sufficient sum has been deposited, or been guaranteed by a bank or insurance company, to meet the claims of all creditors.

[4] ss.171–177.
[5] See Chap. 10 above.
[6] s.135(1).
[7] In the unlikely event (see Chap. 9 at p. 202 above) of its having uncalled capital.
[8] Technically share capital (a notional liability) cannot be "lost" (see Chap. 9, above) but may well be "unrepresented by available assets." However this does not seem to have bothered the courts which have interpreted "lost" to mean that the value of the company's net assets has fallen below the amount of its capital, (*i.e.* its issued share capital, and, if any, its share premium a/c and capital redemption reserve) and that this "loss" is likely to be permanent. If it is likely to be temporary only the court may nevertheless confirm the reduction but may require the company to set up an equivalent non-distributable reserve: see *Re Jupiter House Investments Ltd.* [1985] 1 W.L.R. 975 (where that was required) and *Re Grosvenor Press plc. ibid.* 980 (where, as is more usual, it was not).
[9] s.135(2). No alteration of the memo. will be needed if share premium a/c or capital redemption reserve only are being reduced because neither will be stated in the memo.
[10] s.136(1).
[11] s.136(2) and (6).
[12] And amplified by R.S.C., Ord. 102.

The court, if satisfied that every existing creditor has consented or that his debt or claim has been discharged or secured, may then make an order confirming the reduction on such terms and conditions as it sees fit.[13] But if any creditor has been overlooked and was ignorant of the reduction proceedings and, after the reduction, was not paid and the company goes into insolvent liquidation, the court on the application of that creditor may order members, whose uncalled liability has been reduced, to contribute, as if it had not been, to the extent necessary to pay the creditor.[14] Section 138 contains provisions ensuring that the confirming order is duly registered at Companies House (it does not take effect until it is) and advertised. And section 139 provides that if the effect of the reduction is that the nominal amount of the allotted share capital of a public company is below the "authorised minimum"[15] the order shall not be registered unless the court otherwise directs or the company is first re-registered as a private company (the court may authorise it to be so re-registered without the need for a further special resolution). As a result of the foregoing provisions, existing creditors should be fully protected and future creditors not put at serious risk.[16]

The principal purposes of requiring confirmation by the court are (a) to ensure that the prescribed formalities have been strictly observed and (b) that the reduction treats the company's shareholders fairly. The courts have little difficulty with their role in relation to (a) and perform it with what may seem to be excessive strictness.[17] But in relation to (b), although they constantly affirm that their discretion to confirm will not be exercised unless the reduction is fair and equitable,[18] in practice they normally confirm provided that they are satisfied that the reduction treats the classes of shareholders in strict accordance with their rights, either as they formerly were or as varied in accordance with section 126(3) of the Act, which, as we have seen, demands stricter class consents for a variation if it is connected with a

---

[13] s.137(1). It may also direct that the company shall for a specified period add to its name after "Ltd.," or "plc," the words "and reduced" (s.137(2)) but in practice this is never done at the present day.

[14] s.140. Note also that any officer of the company who wilfully conceals the name of a creditor, or misrepresents the nature or amount of his debt, or is a privy to either, is guilty of an offence: s.141.

[15] See Chap. 9 at p. 209 and Chap. 11 at pp. 281, 282 above.

[16] The latter can obtain knowledge of the company's new capital structure from its documents registered at Companies House, and are not regarded as entitled to any similar protection: *Re Grosvenor Press plc*, n. 8 above.

[17] See, *e.g. Re Moorgate Mercantile Holdings* [1980] 1 W.L.R. 227 (Chap. 19 at pp. 520, 521 above) and *Re Barry Artist Ltd.* [1985] 1 W.L.R. 1305 (Chap. 6 at pp. 135, 136 above).

[18] As Lord President Cooper protested in the Court of Session in *Scottish Insurance Corpn. v. Wilsons & Clyde Coal Company*, 1948 S.C. at 376: "Nothing could be clearer and more reassuring than those formulations of the duties of the court. Nothing could be more disapointing than the reported instances of their subsequent exercise. Examples abound of the refusal of the courts to entertain a plea that a scheme was not fair and equitable, but it is very hard to find in recent time any clear and instructive instance of the acceptance of such an objection."

Reconstructions

reduction of capital.[19] This however, is not, as we have also seen,[20] an effective protection against what most people would regard as unfairness because of the narrow construction which the court have adopted in relation to what are class rights and their variation. Moreover it seems to be clearly established that the courts still have a discretion to confirm a reduction which they regard as fair even if it does not treat classes of shareholders in accordance with their rights, though in that event the onus of satisfying them that the reduction is fair will be on the applicant company.[21] Although it now seems unlikely that the courts would confirm a reduction so blatantly unfair as some of those in the past,[22] it is still difficult to find any English reported case in which confirmation has been refused on the sole ground that it was unfair.[23]

However, a reduction of capital is a very limited form of reconstruction and one which may, and often will, amount to no more than an adjustment of the amount of a company's capital to bring it into closer relationship with reality. While a reduction may have adverse consequences on shareholders, it cannot, on its own, do anything more fundamental. There are, however, other methods which can. One of them, which is not infrequently used in relation to private companies, is provided by what used to be section 287 of the Companies Act 1948 and is now sections 110 and 111 of the Insolvency Act 1986.

(2) Re-organisation under sections 110 and 111 of the Insolvency Act

Under this type of re-organisation the company concerned resolves (a) to go into voluntary liquidation[24] and (b) to authorise by a special

[19] Chap. 20 at p. 538 above.
[20] Chap. 20 at pp. 541–543 above.
[21] *Carruth* v. *I.C.I. Ltd.* [1937] A.C. 707, H.L.; *Re William Jones Ltd.* [1969] 1 W.L.R. 146; *Re Holders Investment Trust* [1971] 1 W.L.R. 583.
[22] Such as that in *Re MacKenzie & Co.* [1916] 2 Ch. 450 where the effect of the special resolution, passed without the class consent of the preference shareholders, was to reduce the amount payable as their preferential dividend to the benefit of the ordinary shareholders!
[23] The nearest approaches are *Re Old Silkstone Collieries Ltd.* [1954] Ch. 169, C.A., where confirmation was refused on the ground that the resolution did not treat the shareholders in accordance with their class rights but the C.A. went on to say that, even if it had, they would have regarded the reduction as unfair, and *Re Holders Investment Trust* (above n. 21) where Megarry J. having held that the resolution of the class meeting was invalid as it had not been passed bona fide in the interests of the class (see Chap. 22 at pp. 601, 602 above) accepted that he had a discretion, notwithstanding that, to confirm the reduction but refused to do so since he was satisfied that it was unfair. But the House of Lords still seems to cling to the belief that if shareholders are treated in accordance with their rights the reduction cannot be "unfair": *House of Fraser plc* v. *AGCE Investments Ltd.* [1987] A.C. 387, H.L. Sc.
[24] Under the former s.287 it had to be a *members'* voluntary liquidation, *i.e.* one in which the directors have made a "declaration of solvency", declaring that all the company's debts will be paid in full within 12 months: see Chap. 28 below. It can now be employed also in a creditors' voluntary liquidation so long as it is sanctioned by the court or the liquidation committee (Insolvency Act, s.110(2)) but that sanction is unlikely to be given unless all creditors are paid in full.

resolution the liquidator to transfer the whole or any part of the company's business or property to another company[25] in consideration of shares or like interests in that company for distribution in specie among the members of the liquidating company. This procedure affords a relatively simple method of reconstructing a single company or of effecting a merger of its undertaking into that of another. In the former case, the other company will be incorporated with a capital structure different from that of the liquidating company and the liquidator will transfer its undertaking to the new company in consideration of an issue of its securities which will be distributed to the members of the liquidating company. A new company may also be formed when the procedure is adopted for the purposes of a merger of two or more existing companies. Alternatively when the arrangement is essentially an agreed take-over by one existing company of another (or others) that existing company may buy the other's undertaking from its liquidator, paying for it by its securities which will be distributed in specie to the liquidating company's members.[26]

Use of this method has the advantage that confirmation by the court is not required.[27] But what it can achieve is somewhat limited. Creditors will be entitled to prove in the liquidation and the liquidator must ensure that their proved claims are met and cannot rely upon an indemnity given by the acquiring company.[28] And, although members' rights will be varied, since it is unlikely that rights under the securities of the other company will be identical with the members' former holdings, it is unsafe to make them seriously less attractive.[29] This is because section 111 provides that any member of the company who did not vote in favour of the special resolution may, within seven days of its passing, serve a notice on the liquidator requiring him either to refrain from carrying the resolution into effect or to purchase his shares[30] at a price to be determined either by agreement or by arbitration.[31] It is normally essential if advantage is

[25] Whether or not the latter is a company within the meaning of the Companies Act: Insolvency Act, s.110(1).

[26] In practice, however, the existing company is much more likely to make a take-over bid to the shareholders of the other companies.

[27] Though the court's sanction may be needed if the company is to be wound-up in a creditors' winding-up.

[28] *Pulsford* v. *Devenish* [1903] 2 Ch. 625. But the sale of the undertaking will be binding on the creditors who will not be able to follow the assets transferred to the transferee company: *Re City & County Investment Co.* (1879) 13 Ch.D. 475, C.A.

[29] *e.g.* by replacing fully paid shares by those that are partly paid.

[30] This is an example, rare under U.K. law (but more widely used in some other common law jurisdictions) of protecting dissenting members by granting them "appraisal rights." The courts will not permit the section by purporting to act under powers in its memo. and arts. to sell its undertaking in consideration of securities of another company to be distributed in specie: *Bisgood* v. *Henderson's Transvaal Estates* [1908] 1 Ch. 743, C.A.

[31] If arbitration has to be resorted to, it has to be undertaken in accordance with the somewhat antiquated provisions of the Companies Clauses Consolidation Act 1845

Continued on next page

to be taken of stamp duty concessions that the membership of the old company and the new should be very largely the same. If a number of the members elect to be bought out[32] there is a grave risk that the re-organisation will have to be abandoned as prohibitively expensive.

(3) Schemes of arrangement

More extreme types of re-organisation can be undertaken under sections 425–427A of the Companies Act 1985. Sections 425–427 replace the former sections 206–208 of the 1948 Act; section 427A (and Schedule 15B[33] which amplifies it) was inserted by the Companies (Mergers and Divisions) Regulations 1987[34] to implement the Third and Eighth Company Law Directives[35] on Mergers[36] and Scissions.[37] When it applies considerably greater formalities and safeguards have to be observed than when sections 425–427 alone are relevant.

Section 425 describes the types of transactions to which it and the other sections apply as "compromises or arrangements between a company and its creditors or any class of them or its members or any class of them";[38] and "arrangement" is expressly stated to include a re-organisation of the company's share capital by the consolidation of shares of different classes or by the division of shares into shares of different classes or by both.[39] This, on the face of it, would suggest that it is wider in its scope than a re-organisation of type (2) only in that it can effect a compromise or arrangement with creditors and not merely with members. But that it is far wider is made clear by section 427 which deals specifically with compromises or arrangements under section 425 proposed for the purpose or in connection with the reconstruction of any company or companies, or the amalgamation of two or more companies.[40] Indeed, the courts have construed "arrangement" as a word of very wide import[41] covering almost every type of legal transaction[42] so long as there is some element of give

---

Continued from previous page

(or, if the winding-up is in Scotland, under the corresponding Scottish Act of the same year). It is not a very satisfactory process because it involves determining what the member would have received on the hypothetical assumption that the liquidation had proceeded without any transfer of the undertaking.

[32] In the case of a widely held company there will, in addition always be some shareholders who cannot be traced or who are too uninterested to do anything so that they too never become members of the new company.

[33] Originally numbered 15A but changed to 15B by the 1989 Act.

[34] S.I. 1987 No. 1991.

[35] See Chap. 4 at p. 61 above.

[36] Directive 78/885/EEC.

[37] Directive 82/891/EEC.

[38] s.425(1).

[39] s.425(6)(b).

[40] s.427(2).

[41] *Re National Bank Ltd.* [1966] 1 W.L.R. 819 at 829; *Re Calgary and Edmonton Land Co.* [1975] 1 W.L.R. 355 at 363; *Re Savoy Hotel Ltd.* [1981] Ch. 351 at 359D–F.

[42] If it involves a reduction of capital, as it often will, this can be sanctioned without the need for separate proceedings under (1) above.

and take[43] and has the approval of the company (or companies) concerned, either through its board or through the members in general meeting.[44]

When the proposed scheme has been formulated, the first step is an application (normally *ex parte*) to the court by the company (or companies)[45] to which the compromise or arrangement relates for the court to order meetings, of the creditors or classes of creditors or members or classes of members, to be summoned.[46] This the court will generally do[47] and will give directions about the length of notice, the method of giving it and the forms of proxy. But it will not, at this stage, give directions or make any decisions on what is a class for this purpose. That is the responsibility of the applicants to deter-mine—and it can be a difficult task, particularly so far as creditors are concerned. Apart from the obvious distinctions between secured debentureholders, unsecured lenders, and trade creditors, what precisely determines whether or not creditors are of the same "class"?[48] Nor is it necessarily simple even so far as members are concerned; for in this context "class" seems to mean something different from what it means elsewhere.[49] The consequences of failing to make a correct determination are serious; the court may refuse to sanction the scheme even though all the meetings have approved it by the requisite majority.

Section 426[50] requires any notice sent out summoning the meetings to be accompanied by a statement explaining the effect of the compromise or arrangement and in particular stating any material interests of the directors (whether in their capacity of directors or otherwise) and the effect on those interests of the scheme in so far as that differs from the effect on the interests of others.[51] Where the scheme affects the rights of debentureholders, the statement must

---

43 *Re NFU Development Trust Ltd.* [1972] 1 W.L.R. 1548 held that the court had no jurisdiction to sanction a scheme whereby all the members were required to relinquish their financial rights without any quid pro quo.

44 *Re Savoy Hotel* above n. 41 where in the course of the long-running battle to wrest control from the holders of a minority of the equity but a majority of the votes, a vain attempt was made to do so by seeking sanction for a scheme which neither the board nor a general meeting had approved.

45 It can instead be made by any member or creditor (so long as the scheme has been approved by the company): see *Re Savoy Hotel* (above nn. 41 and 44) but, if the company is in liquidation or an administrator has been appointed, it must be made by the liquidator or administrator.

46 s.425(1).

47 But, again, see *Re Savoy Hotel*, above, where the court refused to do so.

48 The difficulty is particularly acute in the case of policyholders of an insurance company.

49 *i.e.* in those discussed in Chapters 14 and 20. Here, for example, if some shares of the same class are fully paid and others are not they will be separate "classes." And see *Re Helleric Trust* [1976] 1 W.L.R. 132, below, n. 54.

50 The corresponding earlier section (207) first appeared in the 1948 Act but long before that it was the invariable custom for the notices to be accompanied by a circular and the courts, before sanctioning, needed to be satisfied that it was full and fair and not in any way "tricky."

51 s.426(1) & (2).

give the like statement regarding the interests of any trustees for the debentureholders.[52] If the notice is given by advertisement,[53] the advertisement must include the foregoing statements or a notification of where and how copies of the circular can be obtained[54] and on making application a member or creditor is entitled to be furnished with a copy free of charge.[55] If the scheme is approved at the meetings by a majority in number, representing three-fourths in value,[56] of its creditors and by members present and voting in person or by proxy, the scheme becomes binding on the company and all members and creditors (or all members of the class concerned) and, if the company is in liquidation, on the liquidator, so long as it is sanctioned by the court.[57] But its order sanctioning the scheme does not take effect until a copy is delivered to the Registrar and a copy of it has to be attached to every copy of the company's memorandum of association issued thereafter.[58]

The application for the court's approval is made by petition of the applicants and may be opposed by members and creditors who object to the scheme. In the oft-quoted words of Maugham J.[59] the duties of the court are two-fold:

"The first is to see that the resolutions are passed by the statutory majority in value and number . . . at a meeting or meetings duly convened and held. The other duty is in the nature of a discretionary power[60] . . . [W]hat I have to see is whether the proposal is such that an intelligent and honest man, a member of the class concerned and acting in respect of his interests might normally approve."[61]

Its role, in other words, is very similar to that in the case of reductions of capital under (1) above. However, the courts tend to

[52] s.426(4). If the interests of the directors or the trustees change before the meetings are held the court will not sanction the scheme unless satisfied that no reasonable shareholder or debentureholder would have altered his decision on how to vote if the changed position had been disclosed: *Re Jessel Trust Ltd.* [1985] BCLC 119; *Re Minster Assets, ibid.* 200.

[53] Which will be the only way of notifying holders of share warrants to bearer or of bearer bonds. It may also be necessary to advertise for creditors.

[54] s.426(3).

[55] s.426(5). A default in complying with any requirement of the section renders the company and every officer, liquidator, administrator, or trustee for debentureholders liable to a fine unless he shows that the default was due to the refusal of another director or trustee for debentureholders to supply the necessary particulars of his interest: s.426(6) & (7).

[56] In relation to creditors further difficulties may arise in valuing their claims and thus determining whether the majority does represent three fourths in value. This is a problem met whenever this formula is employed in respect of creditors—as it is throughout the Insolvency Act.

[57] s.425(2).

[58] s.425(3). The latter requirement seems to be an unnecessarily cumbersome and unhelpful way of ensuring that subsequently issued copies of the memorandum reflect any changes of it made by the order.

[59] In *Re Dorman Long & Co.* [1934] Ch. 635.

[60] *Ibid.,* at p. 655.

[61] *Ibid.,* at p. 657.

take their role more seriously and there is greater evidence of a reluctance to rely as heavily on the assumption that if creditors and members "are acting on sufficient information and with time to consider what they are about, and are acting honestly they are . . . much better judges of what is to their commercial advantage than the court can be."[62] Nevertheless when they are unhappy about a scheme there is the same tendency to try to find that there has been some flaw in the procedure rather than to exercise the discretionary power to refuse to sanction on the ground that the scheme is unfair. Although Lord Maugham (as Maugham J. had become) stressed in *Carruth* v. *I.C.I.*[63] that, in the exercise of the court's discretionary role, too much weight should not be placed on majority votes when it can be shown that "the majority of the class has voted, or may have voted, in the way it did because of its interests as shareholders of another class," they are likely to treat this as affecting the validity of the resulting resolutions[64] rather than to rely solely on their own independent judgment that the scheme is unfair.

An advantageous feature of a scheme of arrangement under section 425 is that when it involves the transfer of the whole or any part of the undertaking or property of one company (a "transferor company") to another (the "transferee company") the court may, by the order sanctioning the scheme or a subsequent order, make provision for the automatic transfer of the undertaking and of the property and liabilities[65] of any transferor company to the transferee company and for the allotment or appropriation of the securities of the transferee company.[66] Furthermore the order may provide for: the continuation of legal proceedings pending by or against any transferor company, the dissolution without winding-up of any

62 *Per* Lindley L.J. in *Re English, Scottish & Australian Bank* [1893] 3 Ch. 385, C.A. at 409.
63 [1937] A.C. 707, H.L. at 769.
64 This they may do either by holding that the class had not voted bona fide in the interests of the class (as Megarry J. did in *Re Holders Investment Trust Ltd.* [1971] 1 W.L.R. 583, on an unfair reduction of capital: see above) or, as Templeman J. did on a scheme of arrangement, by holding that proper meetings had not been convened and held because a wholly-owned subsidiary of the transferee company already holding 53 per cent. of the shares to be acquired should not have been regarded as a member of the same class as the other shareholders and accordingly that the court had no jurisdiction to sanction: *Re Hellenic Trust Ltd.* [1976] 1 W.L.R. 123. In both, the courts also declared that they would have declined to exercise a discretion to sanction, in the latter case on the interesting ground that although the scheme was eminently fair to shareholders generally it was not fair to compel those who did not want to, to sell their shares in circumstances where they could not have been compelled to do so under what is now section 429 (see Chap. 27 at pp. 732–738 below) had the transferee company made a take-over offer instead of proceeding by way of a scheme under s.425.
65 As we have seen (Chap. 6 at p. 124 above), it was held in *Nokes* v. *Doncaster Amalgamated Collieries*, [1940] A.C. 1014, H.L. that this did not permit the automatic transfer of contracts for personal services but this has, in effect, been reversed as a result of the Transfer of Undertakings (Protection of Employment) Regs. 1981 (S.I. 1981 No. 1794).
66 s.427(1)–(3)(b). Thus obviating the need to incur the burden and expense of formal transfers and conveyances.

transferor company, the provision to be made for any person who dissents from the scheme[67] and such other matters as are necessary to secure that the scheme is carried out.[68]

However, under the British practice, amalgamations and reconstructions are rarely carried out by means of transfers of undertakings even if section 425 is employed (rather than the more usual take-over bid) and, if the scheme can be carried out by means of transfer of shares rather than undertakings, that solution is likely to be adopted, especially if section 427A would otherwise apply. That section applies only if (a) the arrangement is proposed between a public company and its members or creditors, for the purposes of or in connection with a scheme for the reconstruction of any company or companies or their amalgamation; (b) the circumstances are as specified in one of three "Cases"; (c) the consideration envisaged for any transfers of undertakings is to be shares in the transferee company or companies receivable by the members of the transferor company or companies with or without a cash payment[69] and (d) the public company is not being wound-up.[70] This provides considerable scope for framing the scheme in such a way that it will not have to comply with the considerably stricter requirements which are added to sections 425–427 when section 427A does apply.

The three "Cases" referred to in (b) are[71]:

Case 1. Where the undertaking, property and liabilities of the public company are to be transferred to another public company, other than one formed for the purpose of, or in connection with, the scheme.

Case 2. Where the undertakings, property and liabilities of each of two or more public companies, including the one in respect of which the arrangement is proposed, are to be transferred to a company (whether or not a public company) formed for the purpose of, or in connection with, the scheme.

Case 3. Where, under the scheme, the undertaking, property and liabilities of the public company are to be divided among, or transferred to, two or more companies each of which is either a public company or a company formed for the purposes of, or in connection with, the scheme.[72]

If the scheme is one to which section 427A applies, sections 425–427 have effect subject to the provisions of section 427A and of

[67] Thus enabling the court, if it sees fit, to protect the appraisal rights that the dissentients would have had if the scheme had been carried out under s.110 above. But not much use seems to have been made of this.
[68] s.427(3)(c)–(f).
[69] s.427A(1).
[70] s.427A(4).
[71] s.427A(2).
[72] *i.e.* that type of de-merger known on the Continent as a "scission" and referred to in the Act as a "division."

the lengthy and detailed Schedule 15B.[73] Here it suffices to say that the major additional requirements[74] are:

1. Normally, a draft scheme has to be drawn up by the boards of all the companies concerned, a copy delivered to the Registrar and the latter has to publish a notice of its receipt in the Gazette. All this must be done at least one month before the meetings are held.[75]

2. What has to be stated in the board's circulars required by section 426 is considerably amplified.[76]

3. In addition there generally have to be separate written reports on the scheme to the members of each company by an independent expert appointed by that company or, if the court approves, a single joint report to all companies by an independent expert appointed by all of them.[77] This requirement of an independent report is perhaps the most valuable of the additional requirements. It should help both the members and creditors and the courts in the exercise of their discretionary power to refuse their sanction.[78]

Finally, it should be noted that, when a scheme of arrangement is designed to effect a merger, the Panel and the Code on Take-overs, and Mergers, described in the next chapter, may have roles to play. The Panel's role, however, will then be ancillary to that of the court and will mainly be concerned to ensure that the documentation (as opposed to the time-table) complies with the Code's Rules and that the parties lodge their circulars with it. In such cases the court, as it were, performs the role of referee and the Panel that of linesman.

(4) Voluntary arrangements under Part I of the Insolvency Act

Schemes of arrangement under (3) are available to companies which are insolvent or teetering on the brink of it. But the Cork

[73] As renumbered, and amended in minor respects, by the 1989 Act.
[74] The details differ somewhat according to the "Case" within which the scheme falls, the main differences being between those within Case 1 or 2 (mergers) and Case 3 (divisions).
[75] Sched. 15B, para. 2.
[76] *Ibid.* para. 4.
[77] *Ibid.* para. 5. The matters to be dealt with in the report are specified in some detail. In some respects it resembles the report required (also as a result of EC Directives) when a public company makes an issue of shares paid-up otherwise than in cash: see Chap. 9 at pp. 204–207 above.
[78] As the Scottish courts would, it is believed, confirm from their experience of employing such aid. The English courts are likely to have the auditors' reports and, sometimes, an independent valuation of property but, in circumstances where s.427A does not apply, they are unlikely to have the help of anything comparable to the reports required by Sched. 15B.

Committee[79] felt that something simpler and quicker was needed to enable such companies to avoid or escape from insolvent liquidation by making a composition with their creditors. They expressed the view that an arrangement on the lines that they proposed was "only likely to be used, first, where for some reason it is not appropriate to appoint an administrator and secondly where the scheme is a simple one involving a composition or moratorium or both for the general body of creditors which can be formulated and presented speedily." They were "convinced that the facility to promote such arrangements without the obligation to go to the court will prove of value to small companies ... "[80] Accordingly Part I of the Insolvency Act 1986 provides such a facility.

In contrast with the other types of arrangements discussed in this chapter, this type is primarily designed simply to enable a company to make an arrangement with its creditors. Essentially it relates to Insolvency Law and the statutory provisions are appropriately included in the Insolvency Act rather than the Companies Act.[81] Hence no attempt is made here to describe the procedure in detail. A few comments only need be made.

The first is that although the new type of voluntary arrangement is undoubtedly somewhat simpler than a scheme under section 425, it is not all that simple. The deceptively brief seven sections of Part I cannot be fully understood without reference to the detailed and lengthy Rule 1 of the Insolvency Rules 1986.[82] If employed in an attempt to stave off liquidation or the appointment of an administrator it will be successful only if the creditors by a similar majority to that under section 425 resolve to accept the proposed arrangement and, even if they do, it is all too likely to leave the company without adequate working capital (unless the members are prepared to put up more). If the creditors do not approve, it will merely have added a further step prior to liquidation or administration, and quite an expensive one since a qualified insolvency practitioner has to be engaged as the "nominee" who undertakes the tasks of reporting to the court on the board's proposals, of summoning the meetings, under the court's directions and of implementing the arrangement if approved. Instead of often being a means of avoiding liquidation or administration, as the Cork Committee envisaged,[83] it seems likely to prove more valuable as an additional option available to a liquidator or administrator who may

[79] 1982 Cmnd. 8558, paras. 400–430.
[80] Cmnd. 8558, para. 430. Their recommendations were an adaptation of those relating to individuals implemented in Part VIII of the I. Act.
[81] The same seems less appropriate in relation to arrangements under s.110 of the Insolvency Act: see (2) above. There, as we have seen, the primary aim is to enable a solvent company to re-organise or to amalgamate with another and the fact that a voluntary liquidation is involved is purely incidental.
[82] 1986 S.I. No. 1925 (as amended).
[83] See above.

use it to effect an early settlement with the creditors,[84] leading possibly to the salvage of the company's business.

Although the Cork Committee described their recommended voluntary arrangement as one that could be achieved "without the obligation to go to the court," as enacted this is true only in the sense that in contrast with section 425, the court does not have to confirm the voluntary arrangement; there is however always some court involvement and plenty of opportunities for others.[85] Unless the company is already in liquidation or under administration, a serious weakness is that until approval of the arrangement there is no moratorium on the rights of creditors to enforce their claims. After the board decides to seek a voluntary arrangement it will take weeks before the meetings are held to consider the proposals and during that time the company will be at risk of action by creditors that may scupper the proposals. Nor, even if the proposals are approved, will the voluntary arrangement deprive a secured creditor of his right to enforce his security or a preferred creditor of his right to be paid in priority to non-preferred creditors and to be treated as favourably as other preferred creditors unless, in either case, the creditor agrees.[86]

Despite these limitations some use is being made of voluntary arrangements—though to what extent, if any, they have enabled companies to escape liquidation is unclear. The crying need is that the result of this and other reforms introduced by the Insolvency Act (in particular administration orders[87]) should be closely monitored to assess whether they are in fact achieving their aims. The greatest weakness in Law Reform in the United Kingdom is that, whereas much time and money is spent in deciding what reforms to introduce, little or none is spent on monitoring the results of their implementation.

(5) Other methods

Finally, a further method of achieving a merger or a change of control[88] is by means of a take-over bid and this is, in fact, the most

[84] In that case the liquidator or administrator himself will formulate the proposed arrangement and may act as the "nominee." He may then summon the meetings without reference to the court and undertake the implementation of the arrangement if the meetings approve it. But the Act and the Rules enable the court or the liquidator or administrator to appoint other qualified insolvency practitioners for the whole or part of the nominee's role.

[85] See Insolvency Act, ss.2, 3, 4(6), 5(3) & (4), 6, 7(3) & (5). In particular, even if the arrangement is approved by the requisite majority of members and creditors it may be challenged in court on the ground that there has been some material irregularity in connection with the meetings or that it unfairly prejudices the interests of any creditor or member thus, in effect, extending s.459 in this case from members to creditors: *ibid.* s.4(3) and (4).

[86] *Ibid.* s.4(3) and (4).

[87] The major reform resulting from the Cork Report.

[88] The latter can, of course, sometimes be achieved by an existing minority shareholder or a consortium of shareholders persuading a general meeting to exercise its power under s.303 of the Act to remove the present directors and to appoint nominees of the shareholder or consortium in their place. (This however, in relation to a public

Continued on next page

common method and the one of greatest interest. As such it deserves treatment in a chapter to itself. But, before affording it one, it should, perhaps, be pointed out that occasionally a scheme of arrangement (method (3) above) may be invoked after a take-over bid has succeeded but not the extent that had been hoped: *e.g.* although control in the sense of 50 per cent. plus of the voting rights has been secured, it has not resulted in the target company becoming a wholly-owned subsidiary of the offeror company. In those circumstances the new controllers may seek to achieve that through a later scheme of arrangement.

Continued from previous page
company is unlikely to succeed without the support of institutional investors whose normal practice is to support the incumbent board or to sell their shares if they have lost confidence in it.) Also the company's bankers in their capacity of secured creditors may enforce their security by appointing an administrative receiver (see Chap. 16 above) and thus obtain control but that is not designed to reconstruct the company but to ensure that the bank has priority over other creditors in the company's expected insolvent liquidation.

CHAPTER 27

TAKE-OVERS

As we saw in the previous chapter, mergers or changes of control may be achieved by method $(2)^1$ or $(3)^2$ outlined in that chapter but that by far the most common method is by a take-over bid. The growth of that phenomenon is one of the most conspicuous and controversial developments of the post-War years both in the United Kingdom and other common law countries and one in which the United Kingdom was a pioneer.[3]

The *modus operandi* differs fundamentally from those employed for mergers under methods described in Chapter 26 in that those require corporate action of the companies concerned usually by resolutions in general meetings of all of them. A take-over bid need not. Assuming that there are no restrictions in a company's constitution on the rights of its shareholders to sell their shares,[4] if an offer is made to any shareholder he is able to accept it if he thinks fit. If, as a result, a majority of the voting shares are acquired by the offeror, there will be a change of control of the company[5] and, if the offeror is another company[6] it will become the parent and holding company of the group consisting of the two companies—which we will here describe as the "offeror company" and the "target company."[7] Furthermore if the price offered is to be satisfied wholly or partly in securities of the offeror company there will be a merger of the offeror and target companies similar in effect to one undertaken under method (2) or (3) described in Chapter 26.

The fact that a take-over may need no corporate action by the target company[8] has made it difficult for take-overs to be adequately controlled by provisions in the Companies Act; and indeed provisions

---

[1] *i.e.* under s.110 of the Insolvency Act: see pp. 692–694 above.
[2] *i.e.* under ss.425–427A of the Companies Act: see pp. 694–699 above.
[3] When the author spent 12 months in the U.S.A. in 1954–55 he was surprised to find that take-overs, already common in the U.K., were in the U.S.A. rarely used to obtain control of another company; the popular method being a "proxy fight" with the incumbent board in an attempt to oust it. Now take-overs there are as common as they are in the U.K.—though still, probably, not regulated as effectively and, certainly, very differently.
[4] As there almost certainly will be in the case of private companies.
[5] The successful offeror will be able to remove the former board (s.303) and install his own nominees.
[6] As it generally will be and as the following account assumes it is.
[7] The legislation and the Code on Take-overs and Mergers prefers "offeror" and "offeree" (a recipe for typing errors). If the offer is unwelcome, the target's board will describe the offeror as a "predator."
[8] It will, of course, require such action by the offeror company but so long as (a) that company does not have to increase its share capital,(b) that general authority to issue it has been conferred on the board, and (c) that Chap. 6 of the *Yellow Book* does not require approval by a general meeting, only the board of directors need be involved—and on a contested bid the directors may throw the company's money around without consulting their own shareholders.

in that Act specifically directed to take-overs[9] are still sparse, consisting of sections 314–316 and sections 428–430F,[10] both of which deal with specific problems and not with the general conduct of bids. Formerly regulation of that was left to the Prevention of Fraud (Investments) Act 1939 (or, later, 1958) and to regulations made thereunder. The regulations, however, applied only to take-overs undertaken through the agency of a licensed dealer. In practice, most were conducted through merchant banks, who as "exempted" dealers were a law unto themselves; they were "expected" to observe the regulations, but that expectation was not always fulfilled. Nor were the regulations adequate to curb the excesses in which otherwise respectable business and professional men may indulge in the heat of a take-over battle. Alarmed by what was happening,[11] a City working party published in 1959 a modest set of "Queensberry Rules" entitled *Notes on Amalgamation of British Businesses* which was followed in 1968 by a more elaborate *City Code on Take-overs and Mergers* and the establishment of a Panel[12] to administer and enforce it. It is this Code which has since constituted the main body of "legislation"[13] relating to take-overs, with the Companies Act[14] and the Financial Services Act,[15] and rules and regulations made thereunder, performing an accessory role which has increasingly become relatively less important.[16]

The Code has now grown to a formidable size and to do justice to it demands a large volume.[17] Here all that can be attempted is a brief description of the Panel and the Code, and an indication of the application of the Code's Principles and Rules to each stage of a take-over.

The Panel

The membership of the Panel consists of a chairman, deputy chairman and a "non-representative" member, each nominated by the Governor of the Bank of England, and of representatives of the relevant professional or commercial associations and the SROs

[9] But it does contain provisions which are highly relevant, particularly those on disclosure of shareholdings and dealings, as does the Insider Dealing Act (on both of which see Chap. 23 above) and those in Part V, Chap. VI of the Act (on which see Chap. 9 at pp. 226, *et seq.* above).

[10] On them see pp. 732, *et seq.* below.

[11] Which, in some cases, was horrendous, with rival bidders badgering each of the target's shareholders by night and day telephone calls offering him a special price because, so it was falsely alleged, only his holding was needed to bring that bidder's acceptances to over 50 per cent. In one case the result was that the bidder who eventually succeeded paid prices ranging from £2 to £15 per share.

[12] During the brief life of the "umbrella" Council for the Securities Industry (the CSI) the Panel became "an arm" of the CSI.

[13] Albeit neither primary nor secondary *statutory* legislation: see below.

[14] See above.

[15] See in particular its ss.47, 56, & 57.

[16] Except in relation to criminal liability.

[17] The "bible" is Weinberg & Blank, *Take-overs and Mergers* (1990 ed.).

recognised under the Financial Services Act, and of The Stock Exchange. The day-to-day work is undertaken by an Executive, headed by a Director-General and two Deputy Directors-General. Most of its members[18] are recruited on secondment for two or three years from City institutions but the two Deputy Directors-General have served for many years (and will be sorely missed when they decide to retire). The Panel itself normally meets only when there is an appeal to it from the Executive or when the Executive wishes to remit a matter directly to it. In addition there is an Appeal Committee (headed by a Chairman who has held high judicial office) to which there can be resort by those disciplined for a breach of the Code (or in certain other specified circumstances) or if the Panel grants leave.

The Panel's role is that of a self-regulating body performing legislative, executive and judicial functions. Its status differs from that of the recognised SROs established under the Financial Services Act (or under the Companies Act in relation to auditors or the Insolvency Act in relation to insolvency practitioners) since it is wholly free from any outside surveillance by the DTI or SIB[19] and is the only remaining relic of pure and unsupervised City self-regulation. As such it is something of an anomaly in the post "Big Bang" era and, despite the fact that it has performed its roles with conspicuous success (and to general, if not unanimous, approval) it is questionable whether it will be able for long to retain its present status. Indeed it may well have to change as a result of the proposed EC Directive on Take-overs. The European Commission insists upon Directives being implemented by member States in such a way that their provisions are "legally enforceable"; rules which do not have the force of law may not be regarded as meeting that criterion. The Panel fears that any change in its status would destroy what it regards as its great merits—its ability to act speedily, informally, and flexibly and to waive or adjust its Rules to meet the needs of peculiar circumstances. These fears seem exaggerated; there is no reason why a statutory body should not act likewise so long as the statute is worded so as to permit it to do so.

In fact, the Panel and the Code have already received a considerable measure of recognition both in legislation and by the courts. And breaches of the Code can lead to sanctions which far transcend peer disapproval. Those advising the parties to take-overs now have to be "authorised persons" and if they breach the rules of the Code they run the risk of losing their authorisation. Moreover, since the Rules of SIB and its SROs require them to observe the

18 Including the Director-General.
19 More so even than The Stock Exchange which, in its role of "competent authority," is subject to DTI surveillance and, in its role of a recognised investment exchange, to that of SIB also.

Code, their clients who suffer loss as a result of a breach may have a civil remedy either through SIB suing on their behalf[20] or directly.[21] A more difficult task has been to find effective sanctions against the companies concerned and their directors. The companies may be members of the CBI (one of the bodies represented on the Panel) but the risk of expulsion from that is not likely to deter an offeror or target company from breaching the Code if it sees financial advantage in doing so. A more effective sanction is the withholding of the facilities of The Stock Exchange by the refusal, discontinuance or suspension of listing. That, however, can be more painful to the innocent shareholders than to the guilty controllers and in one notorious case[22] it proved singularly ineffective, despite belated undertakings by the guilty party to behave in future. Now, as a result of discussions between the Panel, the DTI and SIB, the rules of SIB and its SROs require authorised persons to decline to act in a take-over for any person who does not appear likely to comply with the Code. All that seems to be lacking is an express conferment on the Panel of the power to apply for an injunction to restrain a party from breaching the Code. It is difficult to see how the European Commission could then object that the Rules were not legally enforceable. Nor should the Panel reasonably object that it would tarnish its independent self-regulating purity.

In fact, its status in that regard has already been somewhat changed—though in a manner which it has found wholly acceptable. It has been held[23] that the Panel is subject to judicial review but that the courts should be reluctant to nullify its decisions and should normally content themselves with a retrospective review in order to give guidance on how the Panel should proceed in future cases, or to remedy any unfairness done in the instant case in the exercise of the Panel's disciplinary functions.[24] Furthermore the Panel is now designated as an authority with whom regulating authorities under the

[20] F.S. Act, s.61.
[21] *Ibid.* s.62.
[22] Concerning St. Piran Ltd., see the Annual Reports of the Panel for 1981 and 1984.
[23] See *R. v. Take-over Panel, ex p. Datafin plc* [1987] Q.B. 815, C.A.; *R. v. Take-over Panel, ex p. Guinness plc* [1990] 1 Q.B. 815, C.A., 863 C.A. The latter arose out of the battle between Guinness and the Argyll Group to take over Distillers to which reference has been made already: see in particular Chap. 21 at pp. 562, 563 and 569 above. The C.A.'s judgments in both cases repay reading as admirable discussions of the nature of the Panel and its roles.
[24] In the *Guinness* case the Panel, while the take over battle was being waged, had dismissed for lack of evidence Argyll's allegation that a concert party of Guinness and some of its supporters had bought Distillers' shares at a higher price than the bid resulting in a breach of Rule 11 of the Code. A year later the Panel reopened the matter as a result of evidence obtained by inspectors appointed by the DTI. Guinness sought judicial review, alleging unfair procedure by the Executive in connection with the renewed hearings. The court dismissed the complaint (as it had in *Datafin*) though it felt that the Executive had displayed some lack of sensitivity and wisdom. The ultimate result of the renewed hearings by the Panel was that Guinness was ordered to pay Distillers' former shareholders additional sums to make up the price to what it would have been had the Rules been complied with.

Financial Services Act may exchange information and to which documents or information obtained under section 447 or 448 of the Companies Act[25] may be passed.[26] In the light of these developments[27] the Panel is now clearly recognised by the courts, the legislature and the Government as a public body performing public functions on behalf of the State.[28]

The Code

The Code, the current edition of which was published in October 1990, is now a substantial loose-leaf volume of some 180 pages. In the same binders are the *Rules Governing Substantial Acquisitions of Shares* (SARs) for which the Panel is also now responsible and which is closely related to the Code.

The Code consists of an informative Introduction, ten General Principles, definitions of shorthand expressions used in the Rules, the Rules and four Appendices. There are 38 Rules, most of which are divided into several sub-rules. Moreover, in most cases each Definition, Rule or sub-rule has Notes appended, many of which are prescriptive and not just explanatory. The same is true of the four Appendices.

The distinction between the General Principles and the Rules is explained in the Introduction. The Principles are essentially a codification of good standards of commercial behaviour applying in relation to all take-overs. Some of the Rules are examples of the application of those Principles; others are rules of procedure designed to govern specific types of take-over. Both the Principles and the Rules are to be interpreted so as to achieve their underlying purpose, observing their spirit, as well as their letter which the Panel may modify or relax if it considers that in particular circumstances it would operate unduly harshly or inappropriately.[29] When in doubt whether a proposed course of conduct is in accordance with the Code, parties and their advisers are encouraged to consult the Panel's Executive in advance.[30]

The scope of the Code is wide. It covers all types of mergers (including those effected by a scheme of arrangement[31]) in which

25 See Chap. 25 at p. 676 above.
26 Financial Services (Disclosure of Information) (Designated Authorities No. 2) Order 1987 (S.I. 1987 No. 859).
27 See also *R. v. Spens* [1991] 1 W.L.R. 624, C.A. where it was held that although the construction of documents is normally a question of fact for the jury the Code 'sufficiently resembles legislation as to be likewise regarded as demanding construction of its provisions by a judge''; at 632 F.
28 With the result, presumably, that individuals may be able to invoke the proposed Directive on Take-overs in suits against the Panel even if it is not fully implemented by U.K. legislation by the prescribed date. See Chap. 4 at pp. 57, 58 above.
29 Introduction, para. 3(b).
30 *Ibid.* para. 3(a).
31 Though the Panel and the Code will then be constrained by the role played by the court and by ss.425-427A: see Chap. 26 at p. 699 above.

control[32] of a target company is to be obtained or consolidated,[33] and the target company is a public company (whether listed or unlisted) considered by the Panel to be resident in the United Kingdom, the Channel Islands or the Isle of Man.[34] It also applies when the target company is a private company, but only if, within the past 10 years:

(a) its equity capital has been listed on The Stock Exchange;

(b) dealings in its equity capital have been advertised on a regular basis for at least six months;

(c) its equity capital has been afforded facilities for dealings on the U.S.M. or other investment exchange; or

(d) it has filed a prospectus for the issue of its equity shares.[35]

Other private companies are still left to the relevant provisions of the Financial Services Act and the rules and regulations made thereunder.

The basic objective of the Code is to ensure that the shareholders of the target company are treated fairly and equally[36] and given all the information they need in order to decide whether or not to accept the bid. But neither the Panel nor the Code is concerned with the merits of the bid, either in the sense of whether it is one that the shareholders should accept or of whether it is in the public interest that the merger should take place. The former is a question to be answered by the shareholders themselves and the latter by the Office of Fair Trading, the Monopolies and Mergers Commission and the D.T.I. or the European Commission in relation to major "cross-border" mergers.[37]

The SARs

The first step taken by anyone minded to make a take-over bid for a company is likely to be to ensure that he has a sufficiently substantial shareholding in it to act as a launching pad. It is here that

[32] Which is defined as a holding shares carrying 30 per cent. or more of the voting rights, (*i.e.* voting rights attributable to the share capital which are currently exercisable at a general meeting: *Definitions* at p. C6) irrespective of whether that gives *de facto* control: *ibid.* at p. C4. It normally does not apply to bids for non-voting, non-equity shares.

[33] *Introduction* para. 4(*b*).

[34] *Ibid.* para. 4(*a*). Indeed, it also applies to companies resident in the Republic of Ireland if their shares are dealt in on The Stock Exchange. Residence is normally tested by where the company was incorporated and has its head office and central administration.

[35] *Ibid.*

[36] And not, *e.g.*, as they were treated in the pre-Code cases mentioned in n. 11 at p. 704 above.

[37] See Chap. 4 at pp. 74–76 above. As we there saw, these authorities answer it in relation to its effect on competition rather than on other issues, such as whether it is contrary to public policy to permit bidders whose past take-overs have illustrated "the unacceptable face of capitalism" to expand their empires. But the DTI seems to have a distaste for bids by foreign companies in receipt of State aid.

the *Rules Governing Substantial Acquisitions* (the SARs), rather than the Code, may be relevant.

The SARs were promulgated as a result of a "dawn raid" in 1980 in which brokers acting for two mining companies succeeded in obtaining in a few minutes a further 11 per cent. of the shares of another such company (in which the two companies already held over 13 per cent.) by announcing on the floor of The Exchange that they were buyers at a price which was 18 per cent. above the current market price. This was regarded as unfair to shareholders since only the institutional ones were, in practice, able to take advantage of the offer.[38] Hence an effort was made by The Stock Exchange (through instructions to its members), to ensure that nothing comparable occurred again. The result of the SARs (and of the statutory provisions now requiring disclosure of 3 per cent. shareholdings[39]) is to reduce the possibility of surreptitious acquisitions and to ensure that any substantial acquisition of voting capital, except from a single shareholder, must be made either by a take-over bid in accordance with the Code or by a tender offer under Rule 4 of the SARs.[40]

The SARs ensure that the tender offer is made in a way which will give all the shareholders time to take advice and to accept the offer if they want to, and to afford the company's board a breathing space to take stock of the position. The SARs do not apply if the offeror has announced a firm intention to make a bid for control; if it has the Code applies. In practice a tender offer is unlikely to be made if it is intended soon to follow it by a full bid, for the effect of the advertised tender offer which, if it is to succeed, will need to be at a price above the current market one, will cause the latter to rise, at least for so long as the market thinks that a full bid may be in the offing.[41]

The SARs are appended to the Code and, since the demise of the CSI, the Panel is responsible for them.

The Code's Rules

In discussing the Code's Rules we start with the period prior to the actual making of the offer and deal with it rather more fully than

---

38 It also breached the spirit of the Code if it was intended as the first step in a take-over of control.

39 See Chap. 23 at pp. 613 *et seq* above.

40 The type of tender offer required by the SARs resembles that described in Chap. 13 at p. 315 above, except that the offeror invites the shareholders to sell instead of to buy. It may be at a fixed price or subject to a maximum price. In the latter case, if the offer is over-subscribed, a "striking price" will be determined as described in Chap. 13: see SARs, Rule 4.

41 This may suit an offeror buying as an investor or speculator but not one who is contemplating a full bid since it may mean that if that bid is to have any chance of success the price will have to be in excess of that paid on the tender offer.

with what occurs thereafter. This is because the former period is likely to face the directors with particularly intractable problems which raise interesting questions on the relationship between the self-regulating Code and general common law and equitable principles. The Code Rules which apply only to this period are those in its Section D (Rules 1–3) but there are Rules in other Sections that are relevant also.

Preparing to bid

Under Rule 1, the first approach to the target company must be to its board or its advisers. In practice, apart altogether from this Rule, the offeror would normally wish to make such an approach, principally in the hope that discussions will lead to the take-over proceeding as an agreed take-over which will be less expensive and more likely to succeed than a hostile one. The offeror may also hope thereby to obtain further financial information about the target.[42] On such an approach the identity of the ultimate offeror must be disclosed and the board is entitled to be satisfied that it will be in a position to implement an offer in full.

Rule 2.1 emphasises the need for absolute secrecy before any public announcement is made[43] and Rule 2.2 requires such an announcement to be made:

(a) when there is a firm intention to make an offer (that intention[44] not being subject to any pre-condition),

(b) immediately upon any acquisition being made by the offeror or those acting in concert with the offeror which triggers an obligation to make an offer under Rule 9[45]

(c) when, after an approach to the target, it becomes the subject of rumour and speculation or there is an untoward movement in its share price[46]

[42] Although General Principle 2 and Rule 20 forbid the furnishing of information to some shareholders which is not available to all shareholders, both permit the furnishing of information in confidence by the target company to the offeror or vice versa. Under Rule 20.2 any information given to one offeror or potential offeror must on request be given to another even if the latter is less welcome. But some discrimination against the less-welcomed is permitted because it will have to specify precisely what information it wants and is not entitled, by asking in general terms, to receive all the information given to a favoured competitor: Rule 20.2, n. 1. See, however, Rules 20.2, n. 2 and 20.3, designed to counteract the head-start that those mounting a management buy-out will inevitably have over any other competing offeror. Such buy-outs give rise to particular difficulties throughout in view of the inevitable conflicts of interest.

[43] If it is not, insider dealing is almost inevitable.

[44] The offer itself will almost certainly be "conditional," i.e. on its acceptance by a stated proportion of the target's shareholders (normally 90 per cent. or such lesser proportion exceeding 50 per cent. as the offeror may elect to accept).

[45] See below, p. 719.

[46] A movement upward of 10 per cent. or more is regarded as "untoward": Rule 2.2, Note.

(d) when the like occurs prior to the approach and there are reasonable grounds for concluding that it was due to the offeror's actions, whether through inadequate security, purchase of shares, or otherwise;

(e) when discussions are about to be extended beyond a very restricted number of people; or

(f) when, instead of the normal situation in which the initiative has been taken by a potential offeror, a shareholder (or shareholders) or the board of the target company is seeking a purchaser of its shares carrying 30 per cent. or more of the voting rights and the company is the subject of rumour and speculation or an untoward movement has occurred in its share price or the range of potential purchasers is about to be increased beyond a very restricted number.[47]

Once an announcement is made[48] "the offer period" will begin[49] and with it the stricter rules regarding dealings in the shares of the parties.[50]

The board of the offeror will hope that there will be no need to make an announcement until it is possible to make a fuller and firmer announcement[51] under Rule 2.5. This must not be made unless the offeror has every reason to believe that it can and will be able to implement that offer.[52] The reason why the offeror will seek to avoid any earlier announcement is that once any announcement is made the target company will be "in play," as a result of which another bidder may emerge leading to a hotly contested and extremely expensive battle.[53] Hence the offeror will try to negotiate with the target's board so that the first announcement can be that under Rule 2.5 as an agreed take-over with, ideally, a "lock-out" agreement whereby the directors undertake to accept the offer in respect of their own holdings and not to encourage, or collaborate with, any other

---

47 Of these, (f) did not appear in editions prior to that of 1990.

48 The responsibility for an announcement will be that of the offeror prior to an approach to the target's board but thereafter the primary responsibility will normally be that of the target's board and the offeror must not attempt to prevent it from making an announcement or requesting The Stock Exchange temporarily to suspend listing: Rule 2.3(c).

49 See *Definitions* at p. C.5.

50 See Section E of the Code: below, pp. 718, 719.

51 This announcement (in contrast with that under Rule 2.2, (which may amount to no more than that talks are taking place which may lead to a bid: (see Rule 2.4)) bears much the same relationship to the full offer documents (which, if all goes well, will be posted shortly after) as does a mini-prospectus to a full prospectus on an issue of shares: see Chap. 13 at pp. 327–328 above.

52 The financial advisers to the offeror also bear responsibilities in this connection: Rule 2.5. In the report of inspectors appointed to investigate the Al Fayeds' take-over of House of Fraser (the owner of Harrods) the advisers were criticised for not having investigated the offeror's financial resources sufficiently thoroughly.

53 The target's shareholders are likely to obtain the best price for their shares if there is a battle between rival bidders in which each, in the excitement of the fray, increases its offer with reckless abandon (and scant regard to the interests of its shareholders).

potential offeror. This, however, the target's directors are unlikely to agree to unless they are satisfied that a take-over by someone is unavoidable and that they have negotiated the best price that is reasonably obtainable. If not, they will seek a "white knight" that will offer better terms and will not agree to recommend the bid unless and until they have failed.

The duties of the target's board

In relation to the duties of the target's board at this stage the Code contains a number of relevant provisions. Under Rule 3.1 the board is required to obtain competent independent advice[54] on any offer and the substance of that advice must be made known to the shareholders.[55] Independent advice is regarded as of particular importance on a management buyout or an offer by controlling shareholders.[56] The directors should not recommend the acceptance of any offer unless the advice is that the offer is a fair one—and not necessarily even then. Nor need all the directors take the same view: if the board of the target "is split in its views of an offer, the directors who are in a minority should also publish their views", and "the Panel will normally require that they be circulated by the [target] company."[57] If there are any lock-out arrangements such as those mentioned above, these will be referred to in the announcement under Rule 2.5, the notes to which caution that the word "agreement" should be used with the greatest care and not give the impression that persons have committed themselves (for example to accept in respect of their own shares) when in fact they have not and that references to commitments to accept must specify in what circumstances (if any) they will cease to be binding.[58]

In addition, General Principles 7 and 9 are relevant. The former says that after a bona fide offer has been communicated to the board of the target or the board has reason to believe that it is imminent, no action may be taken by the board without the approval of the company in general meeting which could result in the offer being frustrated or to shareholders being denied an opportunity to decide on its merits.[59] This makes it difficult for the existing controllers to

---

[54] Normally from a merchant bank not disqualified under Rule 3.3.
[55] A similar obligation applies to the board of the offeror when the offer is made in a "reverse take-over" (*i.e.* one in which the offeror may need to increase its issued voting equity share capital by more than 100 per cent.: see n. 2 to Rule 3.2) or when the directors are faced with a conflict of interests: Rule 3.2.
[56] Rule 3.1. n. 1.
[57] Note 2 to Rule 25.1.
[58] Notes 1 and 3 to Rule 2.5.
[59] This, however, seems to be restricted to internal corporate action of the sort specified in Rule 21 and, as we have seen (Chap. 4 at p. 76 above) it is not regarded as breached by lobbying the OFT, the Monopolies and Mergers Commission, the European Commission or the DTI seeking to persuade them to take action which will lead to the offer lapsing as a result of Rule 12 below.

erect any of the defences[60] against being ousted from control by an unwelcome take-over unless they have succeeded in doing so, well in advance of a threatened take-over.[61] Principle 9 is of particular importance. It declares that the directors of both the offeror and target companies:

"must always, in advising their shareholders act only in their capacity as directors and not have regard to their personal or family shareholdings or to their personal relationships with the company. It is the shareholders' interests taken as a whole, together with those of employees and creditors which should be considered ... Directors of the [target] company should give careful consideration before they enter into any commitment ... which would restrict their freedom to advise their shareholders in the future. Such commitments may give rise to conflicts of interest or result in a breach of the directors' fiduciary duties."

The overall result seems to be that although the Panel obviously dislikes lock-outs it does not actually ban them[62] but leaves their legality to be determined by the courts on the basis of general legal and equitable principles.[63] But what is the effect of those principles?

In four recent cases the courts have wrestled with that question. The first such case was *Heron International Ltd. v. Lord Grade.*[64] This concerned a take-over of a broadcasting company in which the directors held over 50 per cent. of the voting capital, any transfer of its shares required the consent of the Independent Broadcasting Authority and, under the company's Article 29, the consent of the directors. The latter had given bidder A irrevocable undertakings to accept his offer and A assumed that he had accordingly obtained control. Bidder B then made an offer which admittedly was at a

---

60 Those most commonly employed in the U.K. are through non-voting or weighted voting equity share capital and service agreements which will entitle directors to "golden parachutes" if they are removed. In the U.S.A. a wider and ever-increasing number of defences (with picturesque names—"poison pills," "crown jewels," "PacMan," "shark repellent," etc., etc.) are to be found. Attempts to employ them have given rise to much litigation.

61 Note also Principle 8 which warns that "Rights of control must be exercised in good faith and the oppression of a minority [the Code has not caught up with the legislation's preference for 'unfairly prejudicial' as a substitute for 'oppression'] is wholly unacceptable": hence approval of the shareholders in general meeting (even if one can be convened in time) will not necessarily be effective. See also *Code,* Appendix 3 (Directors' Responsibilities and Conflicts of Interest).

62 Indeed, it expressly recognises that: "Shareholders in companies which are effectively controlled by the directors must accept that in respect of any offer the attitude of their board will be decisive": Note 1 to Rule 25.1. And see n. 5 to Rule 4 which permits directors and financial advisers to deal in such securities contrary to the advice they have given to shareholders so long as they give public notice of their intentions and an explanation.

63 Admirably summarised in General Principle 9, above.

64 [1983] BCLC 244, C.A.

higher price. In the resulting litigation the Court of Appeal, in the course of a written judgment of considerable length, declared[65] that:

"Where directors have decided that it is in the best interests of a company that the company should be taken over and there are two or more bidders the only duty of directors, who have powers such as those in Article 29,[66] is to obtain the best price. The directors should not commit themselves to transfer their own voting shares to a bidder unless they are satisfied that he is offering the best price reasonably obtainable. Where the directors must only decide between rival bidders the interests of the company must be the interests of the current shareholders.[67]

The directors were accordingly ordered to seek advice, and the assistance of the IBA and the Panel, to enable the offer of *B* to be accepted.

However, in *Re A Company*[68] Hoffmann J. took a somewhat different view. There, the essential facts were similar except that the company was a small private company[69] and the application was to strike out a petition under section 459 by a minority shareholder who alleged that he had been unfairly prejudiced on the take-over. Hoffmann J. said[70]:

"I cannot accept the proposition that the board must inevitably be under a positive duty to recommend and take all steps within their power to facilitate whichever is the highest offer. In such a case as the present when the directors propose to exercise their undoubted rights as shareholders[71] to accept the lower offer in respect of their own shares and, for understandable and fully disclosed reasons,

---

[65] Para. 5.11 of the judgment, at p. 265.

[66] In the fourth of the cases (*Dawson International v.Coats Patons* (below), Lord Cullen treated this reference to the article as restricting the whole of this dictum to cases where there are restrictions on transfers, and said that it was "no authority for the proposition that directors are under a positive duty to recommend a bid on the basis that it is the highest bid": 1988 S.L.T. at 861. But while the dictum may not have been part of the *ratio decidendi* (in view of the failure to comply with the article and to obtain the consent of the IBA, the take-over by *A* could have been held ineffective without any discussion of the duties of the directors) it is difficult to construe it as Lord Cullen did.

[67] Surely this sentence cannot be right? The interests of the company must include the interests of the employees (s.309 of the Act) as the Code recognises: General Principle 9 and Rule 24.1.

[68] [1986] BCLC 382.

[69] To which the Code did not apply. Again the directors held 50 per cent. of the votes and had given irrevocable undertakings to accept the first offer.

[70] At p. 389.

[71] This "undoubted right" is one which the C.A. in *Heron v. Grade* had seemingly denied. Hoffmann J.'s view seems more consistent with generally accepted principles (and with the Code which, see above, draws a distinction between advice to the shareholders, which is subject to fiduciary duties, and what controllers decide to do in respect of their own holdings).

hope, in their personal capacities, that a majority of other shareholders will accept it as well, it seems to me that it would be artificial to say that they were under a duty to accept the higher offer."[72]

In a later English decision, *Crowther Group plc.* v. *Carpets International plc.*,[73] Vinelott J. answered some of these problems by holding that undertakings given to a bidder will normally be treated as subject to an implied term that they are conditional upon no better offer being received. The other main point of interest is the argument of the original bidder that if lock-out agreements have been entered into, no subsequent offer can be "better" since acceptance of it would be a breach of contract by the target company, rendering it liable to pay damages, the amount of which would exceed the amount by which the price payable under the later offer exceeded that payable under the former. Hence it was wholly consistent with the directors' fiduciary duties to continue to recommend the original offer! Vinelott J. was unimpressed.

The fourth case, which has already occupied much time in the Scottish Court of Session over the past three years, is *Dawson International plc.* v. *Coats Patons*,[74] in which the recent judgment of Lord Prosser provides the most thorough judicial review to date of lock-outs and of the inter-relationship between the general law and the self-regulating Code. The facts, as found, are worth stating as they are typical of the problems that may arise when there are competing bids.

The board of the textile company, Coats Patons (Coats), had for some time been seeking a merger with some other textile company and had had confidential discussions with other companies, including Vantona Viyella (Viyella). All these discussions proved abortive until, at the end of 1985, Dawson International (Dawson) put out feelers which rapidly resulted in agreement by both boards that Dawson would make a share-for-share offer with a cash alternative, the value of which was thought likely to deter any rival bid. As further assurance, Coats agreed that the take-over would be announced as an agreed merger and that Coats' directors would not seek out, encourage or collaborate with any other bidder, would accept the offer in respect of their own holdings and would recommend their shareholders to accept the bid. As a result of

---

[72] He nevertheless allowed the petition to proceed because there had arguably been "unfairly prejudicial" conduct by the chairman of the target company.

[73] [1990] BCLC 560.

[74] It came first before the court under a Scottish procedure, the nearest English equivalent to which is a motion to strike out a claim on the ground that the facts as pleaded disclose no cause of action. This is reported in 1988 S.L.T. 855 (Outer House) and, on appeal to the First Division, in 1989 S.L.T. 855 and [1990] BCLC 560. The case was then tried by Lord Prosser who delivered a written judgment in March 1991; reported in [1991] B.C.C. 278.

untoward price movements in Coats' shares, it published an announcement[75] that talks were taking place with an unnamed possible bidder, which shortly thereafter was followed by a second and more detailed one[76] by both Dawson and Coats. Broad agreement was also reached on a third joint announcement[77] which it was intended to publish within a few days.

In the meantime Viyella, whose interest had been aroused by the first announcement, approached Coats' merchant bank, indicating that it was eager to make an offer which would be at least as good as any that Dawson was offering. This placed the Coats' board and its advisers in a ticklish position. While they would have preferred Viyella as a suitor (it was considerably larger than Dawson) in view of the agreements with Dawson they felt compelled to give no encouragement to, or collaboration with, Viyella unless and until it made an offer which, price-wise, bettered that of Dawson, and they so informed Viyella. But the latter's difficulty was that until it knew the value of Dawson's offer it could not know what value its offer would have to better. Eventually it did succeed in obtaining from Coats' financial advisers (torn between their conflicting duties to get the best price but not to breach the lock-out agreements) a sufficient indication to make a firm offer to which the Coats' board agreed and told Dawson, somewhat apologetically, that it would not be able to publish the proposed third announcement and why. Instead, an agreed take-over bid by Viyella was jointly announced by it and Coats.[78] Dawson, which had always made it clear that it would not take part in a contested take-over, then withdrew its offer,[79] but understandably incensed, sued Coats seeking to recover the very substantial costs that it had already incurred in relation to its bid and the underwriting of it.

Originally Dawson claimed both in contract and in tort[80] and had joined two of the directors of Coats as defendants. But as a result of Lord Prosser's findings of fact the claims were effectively reduced to those based on alleged breach of the lock-out agreements. It was rightly conceded by Dawson that those lock-outs would cease to bind Coats once an unsolicited better offer was received but it argued that until then they imposed contractual obligations on Coats which it had breached by soliciting, encouraging and co-operating with Viyella. Lord Prosser held that while Coats had not solicited it had, through

---

[75] Under Code Rule 2.2(c).
[76] Also in accordance with Code Rule 2.2.
[77] In accordance with Code Rule 2.5.
[78] And was duly consummated. The merged Coats Viyella has since won a hostile take-over of Tootals—another major UK textile company.
[79] As it was entitled to do under Code Rule 2.7 Note 2, a better offer of a competitor having been posted.
[80] (Sc. "delict"). This was based on alleged misrepresentations that there had been no other potential bidders known by Coats to be "in the wings" when Dawson made its approach. Lord Prosser held that there had been no such misrepresentations: Part IX of his judgment.

its advisers, encouraged and co-operated with Viyella despite its efforts to avoid doing so. He also took the view that a "non encouragement term" would be implied in any agreed take-over since a party, having entered into an agreement, cannot take steps designed to frustrate it.[81] However, and this is the most interesting and novel part of the judgment, Lord Prosser held that when parties are conducting a take-over subject to the Code any statements they make or "agreements" they enter into are normally to be taken as statements of their present intentions in the light of the self-regulating Code and not as legally binding contractual obligations enforceable in the courts (but which, if not honoured, may give rise to sanctions imposed by the Panel if that involves a breach of the Code's General Principles or Rules).[82] Hence he held that no contractual obligation had been breached by Coats and he dismissed the action.[83]

On policy grounds Lord Prosser's view has much to commend it and it should appeal to the Panel which, rightly, is perturbed by the growing extent[84] to which take-overs are leading to litigation. But it is greatly to be hoped that the judgment will be reviewed by the House of Lords so that we have an authoritative ruling for the whole of the United Kingdom. And if "the Prosser view"[85] should be upheld it seems vital that the Panel should review the Code which, as we have seen,[86] is notably unprescriptive so far as lock-out agreements are concerned and which seems to leave such matters to the courts. If the courts are instead to leave it to the Code, companies and their advisers are entitled to clearer guidance than the Code affords them at present. But the fact that the Prosser view would necessarily mean that the result might be different according to whether the take-over was of a company to which the Code applies or of a private company to which it does not, does not seem to be a valid objection. In the case of private companies without public shareholders it may well be more appropriate to leave matters to rules and regulations under the Financial Services Act and to the remedial orders which the courts can make under section 459–461 of the Companies Act if shareholders are unfairly prejudiced. In most such companies the directors will hold over 50 per cent. of the shares and will be entitled to refuse transfers of shares. That being so, whatever may be the position in relation to public companies (and that at present is obscure) it seems absurd[87] to attempt to prevent such directors from selling their shares to whomsoever they prefer or from advising the

---

[81] At Part XIII of his judgment.
[82] At Parts X–XII of his judgment.
[83] This brief summary of the judgment does it less than justice: its Parts IX–XV should be read in full.
[84] Though still to a small extent compared with the U.S.A.
[85] If we may respectfully so describe it.
[86] Pp. 712–713 above.
[87] As it did to Hoffmann J. in *Re A Company* [1986] BCLC 382, above.

Take-Overs

other shareholders to do likewise, so long as the courts can protect the others by appropriate orders under sections 459–461 if they are unfairly prejudiced.

In the meantime, however, all that can be regarded as reasonably well established in the light of these four recent decisions is that:

(1) In advising shareholders whether or not to accept a take-over offer, the directors act as fiduciary organs of the company notwithstanding that the advice may be given by each individual director rather than by the board.

(2) Lock-out agreements given to one bidder normally cease to operate once a better offer is received. But it is not clear whether this is because a term to that effect is to be implied under the "business efficacy" principle or because it would otherwise be a breach of the directors' fiduciary duty not to fetter their discretion in a way which might preclude them from acting at all times bona fide in what they believe to be in the best interests of the company.[88]

Dealings in shares

Section E of the Code imposes certain prohibitions on dealings in the securities of the companies concerned. Prior to the "offer period"[89] the main prohibition is that flowing from the Insider Dealing Act[90] as a result of which anyone with knowledge of the possible take-over will be in possession of price-sensitive unpublished information. This, as we have seen, will not prevent the offeror from continuing to purchase shares of the target but will prevent the target company or any officers of either company from doing so on their own account.[91] However, the Code places restrictions, supplementing those of the SARs, on the extent to which the potential offeror, even before the offer period, may continue to increase its holdings of voting shares in the target. Under Rule 5.1, except as permitted by Rule 5.2, a person who, with others acting in concert with it,[92] holds shares which confer less than 30 per cent. of the voting rights of a company may not acquire further voting shares if that would result in the holding of shares conferring 30 per cent. or more of the votes.[93] Similarly if between 30 per cent. and 50 per cent. is already held, no

[88] It is to be hoped that it is the latter since, presumably, if the former is correct the parties could expressly exclude the implication, whereas under the latter they could not. If the Prosser view were to prevail it would not matter which it was since the agreement would not be legally enforceable. But the Code then should make it clearer whether conduct such as that of Coats is a breach of the Code's Rules.

[89] Which, as we have seen, starts when an announcement is made of a proposed or possible offer.

[90] See Chap. 23 at pp. 624 *et seq.* above. Rule 4.1 of the Code reflects this.

[91] This puts the target company's directors at a temporary disadvantage in defending themselves against an unwelcome bid.

[92] On concert parties see Chap. 23 at pp. 615–618 above.

[93] This bans acquisition of control unless Rule 5.2 applies.

more than an additional 2 per cent, of the voting rights may be acquired in any period of 12 months.[94] This, however, is subject to the exceptions in Rule 5.2 of which the most important are (i) an acquisition from a single shareholder if it is the only acquisition within any period of seven days,[95] and (ii) when the acquisitions are an agreed prelude to an agreed take-over offer.[96]

Once the "offer period"[97] starts and has not ended, the offeror and persons acting in concert with it must not sell any securities in the target company.[98] Moreover during that period disclosure of dealings, additional to and stricter than, that required by the Act, comes into operation.[99]

Mandatory bids

Hitherto we have assumed that the bid is a voluntary one, made by the offeror because it wants to. But it will sometimes have to make a general offer whether it wants to or not—and perhaps at a price higher than it would have contemplated offering. General Principle 10 provides that when control of a company is acquired by a person, or persons acting in concert, a general offer to all other shareholders is normally required and that a similar obligation may arise if existing control is further consolidated.[1] This Principle is spelt out in Rule 9, which also ensures that General Principle 1 (that all shareholders of the same class of a target company must be treated similarly by an offeror) is observed in relation to the general offer.

Under Rule 9.1 when:

(a)   any person acquires shares which (with any shares held or acquired by any persons acting in concert with him) carry 30 per cent. or more of the voting rights of a company; or

94 This restricts consolidation of control, again unless Rule 5.2 applies.
95 Rule 5.2(a). But generally no further acquisitions may then be made (Rule 5.3) and the acquisition must be immediately notified to The Stock Exchange and the Panel (Rule 5.4).
96 Rule 5.2(b), (c) and (d). As Note 2 to Rule 5.2 points out, an acquisition permitted by Rule 5.2 may result in an obligation to make an offer under Rule 9: see "mandatory offers" below. And presumably so might acquisitions covered by Rule 5.1 even if not permitted by Rule 5.2 unless the Panel chose instead to order the acquirer to dispose of the shares concerned.
97 See *Definitions*, P. C.5.
98 Doing so might well be a criminal offence: under s.47(2) of the F.S. Act if the object was to rig the market by causing a fall in the quoted price of the target's shares, thus making the offer more attractive, or under the Insider Dealing Act if information available to the offeror suggested that its offer would not succeed and it wanted to "make a profit or avoid a loss" by selling before the quoted market price fell back when the offer lapsed.
99 In particular 1 per cent. shareholdings (instead of 3 per cent.) must be disclosed (Rule 8.3) and all dealings by the parties or their "associates" (as defined in *Definitions* at p. C.2) must be disclosed to the Panel and, generally, to The Stock Exchange (and, sometimes, to the press) no later than noon on the business day following the transaction.
1 It adds that if an acquisition is contemplated as a result of which a person may incur such an obligation, he must, before making such an acquisition, ensure that he can and will be able to continue to implement such an offer.

(b) any person who, with persons acting in concert with him, already holds not less than 30 per cent. but not more than 50 per cent. of the voting rights and who, alone or with persons acting in concert with him, acquires in any period of 12 months additional shares carrying more than 2 per cent. of the voting rights,[2] then,

unless the Panel otherwise consents, such person must extend offers on the basis set out in Rules 9.3–9.5 to the holders of any class of equity share capital *whether voting or non-voting* and also to the holders of any class of *voting non-equity in which any member of the concert party holds shares.* Offers for the different classes of equity share capital must be comparable[3] and the Panel should be consulted in advance.

The effect of this is that, once acquisitions have secured "control" (circumstance (a)) or substantial acquisitions have been made to consolidate control (circumstance (b)) a general offer must be made, thus giving shareholders an opportunity of quitting the company and sharing in the price paid for the control or its consolidation. Generally the terms of the offer will have to be the same as those which the offeror would have to include if it made a voluntary bid. But in some respects the requirements are stricter. A mandatory bid must not contain any conditions other than that it is dependent on acceptance being such as to result in the bidder holding 50 per cent. of the voting rights[4]; on a voluntary offer, there may well be further conditions.[5] Furthermore a mandatory offer must be a cash offer, or with a cash alternative, in respect of each class of shares and at the highest price paid by the offeror or a member of his concert party within the past 12 months[6]; on a voluntary offer this is so only if

---

[2] The wording of (a) and (b) is very similar to that of Rule 5.1, above, restricting acquisitions. The differences are (i) that Rule 5.1 applies to acquisitions of shares or rights to shares, whereas, in general, Rule 9.1 applies only to acquisitions of shares (but see Note 13 to Rule 9.1) and (ii) that Rule 5.1 is subject to specified exceptions in Rule 5.2 whereas Rule 9.1 is subject only to a blanket "except with the consent of the Panel." A Note on such "dispensations" is appended at the end of Rule 9.

[3] For the meaning of "comparable", see Note 1 to Rule 14.1 applicable to all offers, whether voluntary or mandatory. In relation to non-voting equity (in which a bidder may not be interested unless it wants to ensure that the target company will become its wholly-owned subsidiary) the ratio between the offer values of voting and non-voting must normally be based on the average of the respective mid-market prices over the course of the six months preceding the offer period. This should prevent the non-voting being unduly penalised by the widening of the difference between the market prices for the two classes once there are rumours of a take-over.

[4] Rule 9.3. But, when the offer comes within the provisions for a possible reference to the Monopolies amd Mergers Commission or the European Commission, it must be a condition of the offer that it will lapse if that occurs. But, in contrast with voluntary offers (Rule 12), it *must* be revived if the merger is allowed and, if it is prohibited, the Panel may require the offeror to reduce its holdings to below 30 per cent: Rule 9.4, Note 1.

[5] *e.g.* on a share for share offer that it is conditional on the passing of a resolution by members of the offeror to increase its issued capital.

[6] Rule 9.5. Unless the Panel agrees to an adjusted price in a particular case: see Rule 9.5 Note 3.

shares were purchased for cash and carried 10 per cent. or more of the voting rights of that class, or if the Panel considers that it is necessary in order to give effect to General Principle 1.[7]

Where directors of the target company (or their close relatives and family trusts) sell shares to a purchaser as a result of which the purchaser is required by Rule 9 to make a mandatory offer, the directors must ensure that, as a condition of the sale, the purchaser undertakes to fulfil its obligations under Rule 9 and, except with the consent of the Panel, the directors must not resign from the board until the closing date of the offer or the date when it becomes wholly unconditional, whichever is the later.[8] Nor, except with the consent of the Panel, may a nominee of the offeror be appointed to the board of the target company or exercise the votes attached to any shares it holds in the target company until the formal offer document has been posted.[9]

Section P of the Code (Rule 37) is also relevant. It will be appreciated that, if the target company redeems or purchases its own voting shares, the effect will be to increase the percentage of voting rights carried by the shareholdings of the directors and persons acting in concert with them if their shares are not among those redeemed or purchased. Under Rule 37.1 this will be treated as an acquisition by them and, if their holdings are substantial, may give rise to an obligation to make a mandatory bid. The Panel will normally waive that obligation, but only if there is a vote of the independent shareholders and the procedure set out in the Code's Appendix 1 (the "whitewash" guidance note) is followed.[10] If, however, the board of the target company has reason to believe that an offer may be imminent, from then on and during the course of a take-over, no redemption or purchase of its own shares[11] may take place without the approval of the members in general meeting.[12]

Terms of offers

Section G of the Code contains four Rules (10–13), relating to voluntary offers, on matters which, in relation to mandatory offers, are dealt with in Rule 9. Rule 10 prescribes that it must be a

---

[7] Rule 11.1. Then, too, the Panel has a discretion to agree an adjusted price: Rule 11.2.

[8] Rule 9.6. On "closing dates" see Rule 31, below at pp. 726, 727.

[9] Rule 9.7. It may seem surprising that this is permissible earlier than under Rule 9.6 but it must be remembered that the obligation to make a mandatory offer cannot arise unless the offeror already holds at least 15 per cent. of the votes and it might be unfair to disenfranchise the offeror once it has complied with its obligations to make a general offer.

[10] For the procedure, which is detailed and stringent, see the Appendix. It also applies if the Panel is to be asked to waive an obligation to make a mandatory offer resulting from an issue of new securities as consideration for an acquisition or a cash injection, or in fulfilment of an obligation to underwrite the issue of new securities.

[11] Rule 37.3.

[12] An obvious defence ploy in the case of a hostile bid.

condition of any offer for voting equity share capital which, if accepted in full, would result in the offeror holding over 50 per cent. of the voting rights of the target company, that it will not be declared unconditional as to acceptances unless the offeror has acquired or agreed to acquire (either pursuant to the offer or otherwise) 50 per cent. of the voting rights attributable to (a) the equity share capital alone and (b) the equity share capital and the non-equity share capital combined.[13] It does not specifically state that this may be waived by the Panel but Note 1 makes it clear that, in exceptional circumstances, the Panel may be prepared to do so.

Rule 11, dealing with when a cash offer is required, has already been summarised when dealing with mandatory bids.[14] Rule 12 provides that where an offer (a) comes within the statutory provisions for possible reference to the Monopolies and Mergers Commission or (b) would give rise to a concentration with a Community dimension within the scope of the EC Regulation[15] it must be a term of the offer that it will lapse if there is a reference under (a) or proceedings by the European Commission under (b) before the first closing date of the offer or before it is declared unconditional whichever is the later. As we have seen, by virtue of Rule 9.4, this applies equally to mandatory offers. Rule 12(c) also provides that, except in the case of mandatory offers, the offeror may make the offer conditional upon a decision that there shall be no such references or proceedings or upon that decision being on terms satisfactory to the offeror. When the offer lapses as a result of (a) or (b) the Panel will normally consent to a new offer being made once the merger has been allowed to go forward, without having to wait the normal period of 12 months.[16]

Rule 13 provides that an offer must not be subject to conditions which depend solely on subjective judgments by the directors of the offeror or the fulfilment of which is in their hands.[17]

Section H of the Code (Rules 14–18) relates to terms of offers whether voluntary or mandatory. Under Rule 14, when an offer is made for more than one class of shares, separate offers must be made for each class,[18] and when the target company has more than one

---

[13] cf. Rule 9.3.
[14] See p. 720 above.
[15] EEC/4064/89: see Chap. 4 at p. 75 above. Rule 12 does not cause offers to lapse if they have to be conditional on approval of the take-over by foreign regulatory agencies, (e.g. Federal or State agencies in the U.S.A.). These agencies may take a considerable time to reach a decision, thus playing havoc with the time-limits prescribed by the Code and forcing the Panel to grant extensions.
[16] See Rule 35.1 (below) and Note (a)(iii) thereto.
[17] Note 1 to the Rule concedes that an element of subjectivity may be unavoidable but Note 2 says that an offeror should not invoke any condition so as to cause the offer to lapse unless the circumstances are of material significance to the offeror in the context of the offer (thus precluding the offeror from taking advantage of an immaterial non-fulfilment to extricate itself from the take-over).
[18] Rule 14.2. Thus ensuring that a holder of two classes can accept one and reject the other.

class of equity share capital a "comparable" offer[19] must be made for each whether it carries voting rights or not. The offer for non-voting equity should not be made conditional upon any particular level of acceptance unless the offer for the voting equity shares is conditional upon acceptance of the offer for the non-voting equity.[20] Classes of non-equity need not be the subject of an offer except on a mandatory bid under Rule 9 or when Rule 15 applies.[21] The latter Rule requires that on an offer for equity share capital an appropriate offer or proposal must be made to holders of securities convertible into equity shares.[22]

Except with the consent of the Panel, the offeror may not make any special arrangements, either during an offer or when one is reasonably in contemplation, whereby favourable conditions are offered to some shareholders which are not extended to all of them.[23]

Partial offers

Under the Code's Section 0 (Rule 36) the Panel's consent is needed for partial offers.[24] Consent will normally be given if the offer could not result in the offeror holding 30 per cent. or more of the voting rights of the target company.[25] If it could result in the offeror holding more than 30 per cent. but less than 100 per cent., consent will not normally be granted if the offeror or its concert party has acquired, selectively or in significant numbers, shares in the target company during the previous 12 months or if any shares were acquired after the partial offer was reasonably in contemplation.[26] Nor, without consent, may any member of the concert party purchase any further shares within 12 months after a successful partial bid.[27] If the offer is one which could result in the offeror holding not less than 30 per cent. and not more than 50 per cent. of the voting rights, the offer must state the precise number of shares bid for and the offer must not be declared unconditional unless acceptances are received for not less than that number.[28] And, most importantly, any offer, which could result in the offeror holding more than 30 per cent., must not

---

19 See Rule 14.1, Note 1: see p. 720, n. 3 above.
20 If it is, notwithstanding n. 18, a holder of both should act similarly in respect of both.
21 Rule 14.1.
22 Rule 14.1.
23 It should not normally be made conditional on any particular level of acceptances. It may however be put to the security holders by way of a scheme to be considered at a stockholders' meeting: Rule 15(d).
   Rule 16, Note 1 makes it clear that this bans the not-unknown practice of buying a holding with an undertaking to make good to the seller any difference between the sale price and the higher price of any successful subsequent bid. It also covers cases where a shareholder of the target company is to be remunerated for the part he has played in promoting the offer ("a finder's fee").
24 *i.e.* those in which the offeror bids for a proportion only of the shares or a class of shares.
25 Rule 36.1.
26 Rule 36.2.
27 Rule 35.3.
28 Rule 35.4.

merely be conditional on the specified number of acceptances but also on approval of the offer by shareholders holding over 50 per cent. of the voting rights not held by the offeror and persons acting in concert with it.[29] This consent need not be given at a meeting[30] and is normally secured, as permitted by the Rule, by means of a separate box on the form of acceptance.

Furthermore an offer which could result in the offeror holding shares carrying over 48 per cent. of the votes must contain a prominent warning that, if the offer succeeds the offeror will be free, subject to Rule 36.3, to acquire further shares without incurring an obligation to make a mandatory offer.[31] Each shareholder must be able to accept in full for the relevant proportion of his holding and if shares are tendered in excess of this proportion they must be scaled down rateably.[32] When an offer is made for a company with more than one class of equity capital which could result in the offeror acquiring 30 per cent. or more of the votes, a "comparable" offer must be made for each class.[33] Having regard to the Panel's obvious antipathy to partial offers, and to the stringent conditions to be complied with if it is to consent, such offers are uncommon.

The offer period

Having attempted to describe and explain the major matters relevant to the preparation of the offer we now turn to a briefer description of what then happens and of what Rules then have to be complied with.[34]

The offer document

Rule 30 provides that the offer document should normally be posted within 28 days of the announcement of a firm intention to make the bid. If it is not, the Panel must be consulted.[35] The board of the target company should advise its shareholders of its views on the offer as soon as practicable thereafter and normally within 14 days.[36]

[29] Rule 36.5. This may occasionally be waived if 5 per cent. of the rights are held by a single shareholder: *ibid.*
[30] It might be difficult to achieve the 50 per cent. plus at a meeting, even though proxy voting is permitted. Nor will it always be easy to obtain it by the "box" method because those who are not going to accept will probably not return the acceptance forms and the majority needed is a majority of the whole and not, as in the case of most resolutions, of those voting.
[31] Rule 36.6.
[32] Rule 36.7.
[33] Rule 36.8.
[34] In doing so we shall diverge from the order in which the Rules appear in the Code to an even greater extent than hitherto. The Panel, like all legislative draftsmen, is inhibited from altering the order, and thereby the numbering, since practitioners will have become accustomed to it and will not be pleased if it is changed. The writer of an explanatory textbook is not so inhibited.
[35] Rule 30.1.
[36] Rule 30.2.

The offer will, of course, be a longer and more detailed document than any announcement that may have been made under Rules 2.2 or 2.5.[37] Especially is this so if the offeror or target company is listed, for it will then have to comply with the *Yellow Book*[38] as well as with the Code. Moreover, unless the offer is a pure cash offer—and most are share for share offers[39] although generally with a cash alternative[40]—the offer document will, in effect, be an offer to buy the shares of the target company, demanding full details about that offer, and an offer to pay the purchase price by shares in the offeror company, demanding a prospectus giving details about that company and those shares. On a pure cash offer the detailed information about the offeror's shares will not be needed, but information about the offeror will. In many cases a cash alternative will be provided not by the offeror itself but by the offeror's merchant bank that is underwriting the issue. In that event, this "cash underwritten alternative" will be referred to in the offeror's offer document but probably in such a way as to emphasise that it is a "separate offer."[41]

After a general statement in Rule 23 that shareholders must be given sufficient information and advice to enable them to reach a properly informed decision as to the merits or demerits of an offer and early enough to decide in good time,[42] Rule 24 (divided into 13 sub-Rules) states what financial and other information the offer document must contain and Rule 25 (divided into five sub-Rules) what information must be contained in circulars giving advice by the target company's board. The information required is very much what one would expect in the light of the nature of the documents.

In the case of an agreed recommended take-over with no rival bidders, no more may need stating than the Code requires. But, in the case of a hostile bid or where there are two or more rival bids, each of the companies involved will probably want to make optimistic profit forecasts about itself[43] and to rubbish those of the others. All profit forecasts are unreliable and those made in a take-over battle more unreliable than usual. Hence Rule 28 (with nine sub-Rules) lays down stringent conditions about them. In particular, the forecast

---

37 See pp. 710, 711 above.
38 See its Section 6, Chapter 2.
39 Which the Code describes as "securities exchange offers": *Definitions* at p. C.6. There are many reasons why the bidder would generally prefer a pure share for share offer if it could get away with it; not the least being that, unless the offeror is cash-rich, it will be easier and cheaper to issue paper than to raise the cash.
40 Which the Code frequently insists upon (see above) and which institutional shareholders will expect.
41 See pp. 727 and 736 below.
42 This does not mean that if advised to accept they should promptly do so; on the contrary, they should leave it to the last possible date since, until it is declared unconditional as to acceptances, it is always possible that a rival higher bid will be made.
43 The offeror will not need to do so on a pure cash offer for all the shares; but the target will.

"must be compiled with scrupulous care and objectivity by the directors whose sole responsibility it is" but "the financial advisers must satisfy themselves" that it has been so compiled.[44] The assumptions on which the forecast is based must be stated both in the document and in any press release.[45] Except on a pure cash offer, the forecast must be reported on by the auditors or consultant accountants (and sometimes by an independent valuer[46]) and sent to the shareholders[47] and, if any subsequent document is sent out, the continued accuracy of the forecast must be confirmed.[48] All this is wholly admirable but the evidence does not suggest that it has made such forecasts significantly more reliable. Somewhat similar requirements apply when a valuation of assets is given in connection with an offer.[49] These valuations tend to vary according to whether it is in the interests of the company which engages the "independent" valuer that the value should be high or low; but at least the valuer of real property is likely to have more objective evidence to guide him in the form of prices recently paid for comparable properties.

Acceptances

An offer must initially be open for acceptance for at least 21 days.[50] If this is later extended a new date must be specified unless the offer has already become unconditional as to acceptance, in which case it may be left open until further notice which must be not less than 14 days' notice to shareholders who have not accepted.[51] There is no obligation to extend an offer the conditions of which have not been met by the closing date,[52] but once it has been declared unconditional as to acceptances it must remain open for acceptance for not less than 14 days after the date on which it would otherwise have expired.[53] Apart from that, however, if it is stated that the offer will not be further extended, only in exceptional cases will the Panel allow it to be extended.[54] And, except with the consent of the Panel,

---

44 Rule 28.1.
45 Rule 28.2 (and see the Notes thereto).
46 Rule 28.3.
47 Rule 28.4.
48 Rule 28.5.
49 Rule 29.
50 Rule 31.1. The date so stated is the "first closing date" which has importance in connection with a number of Code Rules.
51 Rule 31.2.
52 Rule 31.3.
53 Rule 31.4. Once non-acceptors know that the take-over is going to be consummated whether they like it or not they may well change their minds and this Rule gives them that opportunity. If, unusually, the offer was unconditional as to acceptances from the outset the extension is not necessary so long as the position is made clear: *ibid.*
54 Rule 31.5. This is not merely because the offeror should not break its promises but to prevent shareholders being pressurised into accepting before the current closing date by false statements that they will lose all chance of availing themselves of the offer unless they accept before that date.

an offer may not be declared unconditional as to acceptances after 60 days from its initial posting.[55]

In some cases the offer may be revised, sometimes more than once. This is particularly likely to occur if there is a contested take-over between two or more bidders. In such circumstances each rival bidder, having already incurred considerable expense, is likely to go on raising its bid and trying to get its new one recommended by the board of the target. Even if it loses the battle it will at least be able to recover part of the expenses out of the profit it will make by accepting the winner's bid in respect of its own holdings. Moreover, even if there is no contest, an offeror may be forced to increase its bid if it or its associates or members of its concert party have acquired shares at above the price of its offer.[56]

If an offer is revised it must be kept open for at least 14 days after the revised offer document is posted.[57] All shareholders who have accepted the original offer are entitled to the revised consideration[58] and new conditions must not be introduced except to the extent necessary to implement an increased or improved offer and with the prior consent of the Panel.[59]

In general the foregoing Rules[60] apply equally to alternative offers in which the target's shareholders are given the option of accepting various types of consideration, (*e.g.* shares, convertible debentures, non-convertible debentures, cash or combinations or different proportions of these.[61] In other words, the shareholders retain their options so long as the offer remains open. But where the value of a cash alternative provided by third parties (*i.e.* a "cash underwritten alternative" mentioned above[62]) is more than half the maximum value of the primary share option the offeror is not obliged to keep that offer open, or to extend it, if not less than 14 days' written notice to shareholders[63] is given reserving the right to close it on a stated date.[64] The reason for this is that the underwriters will be reluctant to remain at risk for an indeterminate period.[65] A disadvantage to an offeror in a contested bid of extending its offer, is that under Rule 34 an acceptor must be entitled to withdraw his acceptance after 21 days from the first closing date of the initial offer

[55] Rule 31.6. But see ss.430A and B in Part XIIIA of the Companies Act (below, pp. 732, *et seq.*) the effect of which may be that non-acceptors get a further chance.
[55] See Rules 6, 9 and 11, above.
[57] Rule 32.1.
[58] Rule 32.3.
[59] Rule 32.4.
[60] *i.e.* those in Rules 31 and 32.
[61] Rule 33.1.
[62] See p. 725 above.
[63] This does not apply to a cash alternative provided to satisfy Rule 9: Rule 33.2, Note 2.
[64] Rule 33.2. But such a notice must not be given if a competing offer has been announced until the competitive situation ends. And the procedure must have been clearly stated in the offer documents and acceptance forms: Rule 24.13.
[65] For the position under Part XIIIA of the Act see pp. 732, *et seq.*

unless by that time the offer has become unconditional as to acceptances. If, therefore, an offeror extends its offer beyond that date it runs the risk that some of those who have accepted its offer will withdraw and switch to the competitor.

Under Rule 17.1, by 8.30 am on the business day following that on which an offer is due to expire or on which it has become unconditional as to acceptances or is revised or extended, an offeror must make an announcement (and, except when the target company is not listed, must inform The Stock Exchange) stating the total number of shares or rights over shares: (a) for which acceptances of the offer have been received, (b) which were held before the offer period and (c) which have been acquired or agreed to be acquired during the offer period. The announcement must specify the percentages of the relevant classes of share capital represented by the figures. Moreover, if any general statements are made by the offeror or its advisers about acceptances, Note 2 to the Rule requires that such an announcement is to be made immediately. Hence, if only to be able to comply, the offeror needs to be in a position at all times to state what the precise position is regarding acceptances and other acquisitions. This is not as easy as it may sound[66] and cases have occurred in which an offer has been declared unconditional as to acceptances when, because of double counting, it should not have been. Notes to Rules 9 and 10 and the *Receiving Agents' Code of Practice*[67] in Appendix 4 to the Code are designed to reduce the risk of such disasters.

Solicitation during the offer period

The advent of the Code and the Panel has in itself done much to reduce the risk of misconduct in the course of take-overs. But recent developments have added a new dimension to the opportunities for high-pressure salesmanship, resort to which is an almost irresistible temptation in the case of a hostile or, especially, a contested take-over. Whereas formerly the only means of communication with the target's shareholders were via written circulars, newspaper advertisements, and meetings with, and calls upon them by visits or telephone, we now have in addition Sound and TV broadcasting and (as the United States has long had) firms specialising in the art of persuading reluctant shareholders. It is increasingly common for the services of such firms to be recruited by the parties or their financial advisers. Rule 19 of the Code is designed to curb the excesses which may result (and sometimes have done).

---

[66] It demands the collaboration of the target company (which will not be given with enthusiasm to an unwelcome or unfavoured offeror) and, usually of The Stock Exchange, plus efficient organisation, supported by modern technology and professional skills on the part of the offeror.

[67] Drawn up by the Panel in consultation with the C.B.I., the banks, and the Institute of Chartered Secretaries and Administrators.

The sub-Rules of particular interest include Rule 19.4 which prohibits the publication of an advertisement connected with an offer unless it falls within one of nine categories, and, with two exceptions,[68] it is cleared with the Panel in advance. The Panel does not attempt to verify the accuracy of statements,[69] but if it subsequently appears that any statement was inaccurate the Panel may, at least,[70] require an immediate correction.[71] This pre-vetting, however superficial, is a powerful disincentive to window-dressing and to "argument or invective."[72] The Rule applies not only to press advertisements (which must not include acceptance or other forms[73]) but also to TV, radio, video, audio-tapes and posters[74] and in each case the advertisement must "clearly and prominently" identify the party on whose behalf it is being published.[75]

The Rule, however, covers only advertising material of which there will be a record. The greater danger arises from unrecorded oral communications, which cannot be vetted in advance or scrutinised afterwards. However, an attempt is made to control these. Rule 19.5 provides that, without the consent of the Panel, campaigns in which shareholders are contacted by telephone may be conducted only by "staff of the financial advisers who are fully conversant with the requirements of, and their responsibilities under, the Code," and it adds that only previously published information which remains accurate and not misleading may be used, and that "shareholders must not be put under pressure and must be encouraged to consult their financial advisers." However, in recognition, no doubt, that the parties will have selected their financial advisers on the basis of their financial expertise and reputation rather than their ability to woo, the Panel may consent to the use of other people, subject to the Panel's approval of an appropriate script which must not be departed from, even if those called upon ask questions which cannot be answered without doing so, and to the operation being supervised by the financial adviser.[76]

Telephone campaigns of the kind envisaged in Rule 19.5 are examples of the practice known as "cold-calling." If the calls are intended to induce those called upon to accept the offer they are

---

[68] A product advertisement, not bearing on the offer (which is not really an exception) and advertisements in relation to schemes of arrangement (when the relevant regulator is the court): see Chap. 26 at p. 699 above.

[69] Time constraints do not permit this to be done; the Panel requires only 24 hours to consider the proof of the advertisement which must have been approved by the company's financial adviser: Rule 9.4, Note 1.

[70] It may also impose a disciplinary penalty.

[71] Rule 19.4, Note 2.

[72] Specifically excluded from exceptions (iii) and (iv) to Rule 19.4.

[73] Rule 19.4, Note 5.

[74] Rule 19.4, Note 4.

[75] Rule 19.4, Note 3.

[76] Rule 19.5, Note 1. It is difficult to see how the financial adviser can supervise effectively unless it insists upon all calls made being recorded on tape; but the Rules and Notes do not require or suggest that.

clearly banned by section 56 of the Financial Services Act (though probably not if the aim is to persuade them to reject it[77]) except to the extent permitted by regulations made by SIB. However, it has been agreed that it would be preferable to leave the regulation in the context of take-overs to the Panel. Accordingly SIB's Common Unsolicited Calls Regulations, which came into force on 1 September 1991, provide by Regulation 6 that the statutory restrictions "are lifted to the extent that the call . . . is made by or under the supervision of an authorised person and in connection with or for the purposes of a takeover or substantial acquisition which is subject to the Takeover Code or to requirements in another member State which afford equivalent protection to investors in the United Kingdom."

With effect from the same date the Panel amended the Code. A new Rule 4.3 provides that any person proposing to contact a private individual or small corporate shareholder with a view to seeking an irrevocable commitment to accept *or refrain from accepting* an offer or contemplated offer must consult the Panel in advance. A new Note 8 to Rule 4.3 states that the Panel will need to be satisfied that the proposed arrangements will provide adequate information as to the nature of the commitment sought and a realistic opportunity to consider whether or not it should be given and with time to take independent advice. It adds that the financial adviser will be responsible "for ensuring compliance with all relevant legislation and other regulatory requirements."[78] Furthermore Note 3 to Rule 19.5 has been amended so that it now reads: "In accordance with Rule 4.3, the Panel must be consulted before a telephone campaign is conducted with a view to gathering irrevocable commitments in connection with an offer. Rule 9.5 applies to such campaigns although, in appropriate circumstances, the Panel may permit those called to be informed of details of a proposed offer which has not been publicly announced. Attention is however drawn to General Principles 2 and 4." Short of a total ban on cold-calling this seems to regulate it in this context as satisfactorily as is reasonably possible—assuming that financial advisers can be relied on to observe the Rules.

Rule 19.6 says that parties, if interviewed on radio or television, should seek to ensure that the interview, when broadcast, is not interspersed with comments or observations made by others in the course of a different interview. It also provides that joint interviews or public confrontations between representatives of the contesting parties should be avoided.

[77] The curious wording of s.56 means that calls are banned only if they result in an "investment agreement" or are made to procure the entry into such an agreement. An agreement to accept a take-over offer is clearly an "investment agreement" as defined in s.44(9); but an agreement to reject it seemingly is not.
[78] This warning ought to frighten the financial adviser!

The more serious problem, arising from meetings with shareholders or those who are likely to advise them, is dealt with in Rule 20.1 which provides that "information about companies involved in an offer must be made equally available to all shareholders as nearly as possible at the same time and in the same manner." [79] Despite this, meetings with institutional shareholders, individually or through their professional bodies, are likely to be held, as, often, are meetings with financial journalists and investment analysts and advisers. Note 3 to the Rule permits this "provided that no material new information is forthcoming and no significant new opinions are expressed." If that really is strictly observed one wonders why anybody bothers to attend such meetings. [80] But many do, and, when a representative of the financial adviser or corporate broker of the party convening the meeting is present (as he must be unless the Panel otherwise consents) he generally seems able to confirm in writing to the Panel (as the Note requires) that this Rule was observed. If such confirmation is not given, a circular to shareholders (and, in the later stages, a newspaper advertisement also) must be published giving the new information or opinions supported by a directors' responsibility statement.

The post-offer period

Except with the consent of the Panel, when an offer [81] has been withdrawn or has lapsed, neither the offeror nor any person who has acted or now is acting in concert with it, may, within the next 12 months:

(a) make another offer for the target company, (b) acquire any shares of the target company which would require an offer to be made under Rule 9, or (c) acquire any shares in the target company if the result would be a holding of over 48 per cent. but less than 50 per cent. of the voting rights of the target. [82] Similar restrictions apply following a partial offer which could result in a holding of not less than 30 per cent. and not more than 50 per cent. of the target's voting rights and whether or not the offer has been declared unconditional. [83] Furthermore, if a person or concert party following a take-over offer holds 50 per cent. or more of the voting rights it must not, within six months of the closure of the offer, make a second offer, or acquire any shares from the shareholders on better terms than those under the previous offer. [84] These provisions prevent the offeror from continuously harassing the target

---

[79] This does not preclude the issue of circulars to their own investment clients by brokers or advisers provided that the circulars are approved by the Panel.

[80] Any refreshment that may be offered at the meeting is rarely such as to provide a powerful inducement.

[81] Or even if no offer has been made but an announcement has been made implying that one is contemplated: Rule 35.1(b).

[82] Rule 35.1(a).

[83] Rule 35.2.

[84] Rule 35.3.

and, while the maximum waiting period is only 12 months, it may enable the target's board to strengthen its defences against further hostile bids by the offeror.

Companies Act provisions

Although in general the Companies Act itself does not regulate the conduct of take-over bids it does nevertheless contain two sets of provisions[85] primarily directed to take-overs. Indeed, one such set[86] relates exclusively to them and, as a result of the Financial Services Act,[87] which substituted a revised version of the sections concerned, now appears in a new Part XIIIA of the Companies Act under the heading "*Take-over offers*." This new Part contains the provisions which have germinated from section 155 of the 1929 Act, enacted when take-overs were in their early infancy and when the Panel and the Code were undreamt of. In Part XIIIA that short and simple section has become no less than nine distinctly complicated ones.

The basic objectives are simple enough. When, as a result of a take-over offer, an offeror has acquired nine-tenths of the share capital of the target company, or nine-tenths of any class of it, then:

(i) the offeror is enabled to acquire the remaining one-tenth on the same terms,[88]

(ii) any shareholder who has not accepted the offeror's offer is enabled to require the transferor to acquire his shares on the same terms.[89]

However, it could be misleading to leave it at that and attention must be drawn to various refinements and qualifications.

Scope of Part XIIIA

In contrast with the Code, Part XIIIA applies to take-overs of any type of company within the meaning of the Act whether it is public or private. As in the case of the Code, the offeror need not be a company though in practice it will usually be a body corporate[90] (or in some cases two or more[91]). The definition of "take-over offer" is somewhat different from that of the Code. It means, for the purposes of Part XIIIA, "an offer to acquire all the shares, or all the shares of any class or classes,[92] in a company (other than shares which at the

---

85 *i.e.* ss.312–316 and 428–430F.
86 ss.428–430F.
87 F.S. Act, s.172.
88 ss.429, 430.
89 ss.430A, 430B.
90 But it could be an unincorporated body *e.g.* the trustees of a pension fund.
91 See s.430D on joint offers.
92 Hence it does not apply to "partial offers": but, where the Code applies, the Panel would not be likely to allow a partial offer which might lead to the acquisition of 90 per cent.

date of the offer are already held by the offeror[93] being an offer on terms which are the same in relation to all the shares to which the offer relates, or, where those shares include shares of different classes, in relation to all the shares of each class."[94]

In a recent case, *Re Chez Nico (Restaurants) Ltd.*,[94a] Browne-Wilkinson V.-C. held that this definition had to be construed strictly, since Part XIIIA enabled a bidder who had acquired 90 per cent of the shares to expropriate the remaining shares, and that accordingly the Part operated only if the bidder had made an "offer" in the contractual sense of the word. In the instant case two directors of the company who were its major shareholders had circulated the other shareholders inviting them to offer to sell their shares to them and indicat-ing the price that those directors would be prepared to pay if they accepted the offers. As a result the directors succeeded in acquiring over 90 per cent. and then sought to acquire the remainder. On an application by one of the remaining shareholders under section 430C (below) the court declared that the directors were not entitled to do so since they had not made any "offer" but instead had invited the shareholders to do so.

While this produced the right result in this instant case[94b] the importation into Company law of the subtle distinctions drawn by the Law of Contract seems regrettable; in Company Law many transac-tions are described as "offers" or "offerings" when strictly they are invitations to make offers.[95] Moreover the decision has adverse consequences to a minority shareholder who, instead of wanting to remain a shareholder in the taken-over company, wishes to exercise his rights under section 430A to be bought out; the effect of the decision is that he will not be entitled to do so if the bidder has proceeded as the directors did in this case.[96]

Attention must also be drawn to another curious effect of this definition of "take-over offer." There is everything to be said for a statutory requirement that a bidder should offer "terms which are the

---

[93] This includes shares which the offeror has contracted to acquire, but not to contracts to accept the offer when made unless the holder has received a payment: s.428(5). Note s.430E regarding shares held by "associates" of the offeror.

[94] s.428(1); "shares" here means shares allotted at the date of the offer but the offer may include shares to be allotted before a specified date: s.428(2).

[94a] [1991] BCC 736.

[94b] See pp. 737, 738 below.

[95] Browne-Wilkinson V.-C. emphasized that his decision was only on the meaning of "take-over offer" for the purposes of Part XIIIA and that he had no doubt that what had occurred would be a take-over offer for the purposes of many statutory or non-statutory provisions. This is certainly true of the non-statutory Code. Indeed, the Panel had treated the *Chez Nico* take-over as subject to the Code (the company had been a plc at the time of the circularisation and remained subject to the Code after its conversion to a private company since, while a public company, it had made a public (BES) offering) but the only penalty that the Panel had imposed was to criticise the two directors for their ignorance of, and failure to observe, the Code: see at p. 743. The decision, however seems to cast some doubt on whether section 314, below, would have applied—as clearly it ought to.

[96] But if he could not petition under s.430C, below, he could petition under s.459 as a member "unfairly prejudiced."

the same in relation to all the shares ... to which the offer relates,"[97] thus adopting the Code's General Principle I. But putting this require-ment in the definition of "take-over offer" again has the effect of depriving the non-accepting minority of their right to be bought out under section 430A if the bidder has failed to observe it.

Buy-out right of offeror

This is dealt with in sections 429 and 430. Subsection (1) of section 429 relates to cases where the take-over has been for shares of one class and subsection (2) to those in which it has been for two or more classes. If the offeror has acquired or contracted to acquire by virtue of acceptances of the offer not less than nine-tenths in nominal value[98] of the shares or class, it may give notice[99] to holders of the shares to which the offer relates but which have not been acquired or contracted to be acquired, stating that the offeror desires to acquire them. In calculating whether the requisite 90 per cent. has been obtained, shares held by the offeror prior to the offer period are ignored; these were not "acquired by virtue of acceptance of the offer." But purchases which he makes during the offer period will be treated as having been so acquired if the price paid does not at that time exceed the value of the consideration specified in the offer or the offer is subsequently revised so that it no longer does so.[1]

The effect of the notice is, under section 430, that the offeror becomes bound to acquire the shares on the final terms of the offer. If the offer gave shareholders alternative choices of consideration, (e.g. shares or a cash alternative) the notice must offer a similar cho-ice and state that the shareholder may, within six weeks from the date of the notice, indicate his choice by a written communication to the offeror and must also state which consideration will apply in de-fault of his indicating a choice.[2] This applies whether or not any time-limit or other conditions relating to choice in the offer can still be

---

[97] An exception to this requirement is permitted if the law of a foreign country precludes an offer there of consideration in the form specified or precludes it except on compliance with unduly onerous conditions, but only if the foreign shareholders are enabled to receive other consideration of substantially equivalent value: s.428(3) and (4). Hence the offeror has to find a way of treating them fairly.

[98] In contrast with the Code, it is the proportion of the share capital (not that of the voting rights) which counts. The main aim of s.429 is to enable and encourage a 100 per cent. take-over resulting in the target becoming the offeror's wholly-owned subsidiary instead of one in which there is a small minority to the embarrassment of the parent and the attendant risks to the minority.

[99] A notice may not be given unless, within four months from the initial date of the take-over offer, the requisite proportion has been obtained and cannot be given later than two months after that proportion was obtained: s.429(3) an additional ground for the decision in *Chez Nico* was that the two directors had not observed this timetable. The notice must be given in the prescribed manner (Form No. 429(4)) and when the offeror gives the first notice he must send a copy of it to the target company with a statutory declaration in the prescribed form (Form No. 429 dec.) stating that the conditions have been satisfied: s.429(4).

[1] s.429(8). In other words, the offeror cannot count towards the 90 per cent. shares which he acquires by offering more than the final offer price but can count those which he was able to buy at less than that price.

[2] s.430(3).

complied with and even if (a) the offer chosen is not cash and the offeror is no longer able to provide it or (b) it was to have been provided by a third party[3] who is no longer bound or able to provide it.[4] The remainder of section 430[5] prescribes in detail the procedure that has to be adopted to ensure that the shares which the offeror is bound to acquire are transferred to it and that the consideration that it is bound to pay reaches the shareholders concerned.[6]

Sell-out rights of shareholders

These are dealt with in sections 430A and 430B which are broadly similar to sections 429 and 430 except that it is the non-acceptors of the take-over offer who can require the offeror to buy them out. There are, however, significant differences of wording. The rights of the offeror under section 429 arise only if as a result of acceptances (or deemed acceptances[7]) nine-tenths of the relevant share capital[8] has been acquired. But the rights of non-acceptors to require the offeror to buy them out arise whenever "at any time before the end of the period within which the offer can be accepted ... (a) the offeror has by virtue of acceptances of the offer acquired or contracted to acquire some (but not all) of the shares to which the offer relates, and (b) those shares, with or without any other shares in the [target] company which he has acquired or contracted to acquire, amount to not less than nine-tenths in value of" the relevant share capital.[9] Hence the rights arise if at the closure of the offer the holdings of the offeror total 90 per cent. or more; and rightly so, for what concerns the shareholder is whether he wants to remain a minority shareholder in a company of which the offeror holds 90 per cent., however that may have been acquired.

Within one month of the closure of the offer, the offeror must give notice, in the prescribed manner,[10] to each shareholder who has not accepted the offer, of the rights exercisable by him under the section and if the notice is given before the closing date of the offer it must state that the offer is still open for acceptance.[11] The notice may specify a period, not being less than three months from the closing date of the offer, within which the rights must be exercised.

---

[3] *i.e.* on a "cash underwritten alternative": see above, pp. 725 and 727.

[4] s.430(4). This adopts and codifies the effect of the decision of Brightman J. in *Re Carlton Holdings Ltd.* [1971] 1 W.L.R. 918, interpreting the corresponding, but less explicit, provisions of s.209(1) of the 1948 Act. But arguments still rage: see below.

[5] subss. (5)–(15).

[6] The main problem that has had to be solved is that many of the non-acceptors of the offer will probably be untraceable. The solution adopted causes the offeror little trouble: see subss. (5)–(8), but the target company may have to maintain trust accounts for 12 years or earlier winding up and then pay into court: subss. (9)–(15).

[7] See s.429(8) above.

[8] s.429(1) and (2). But see s.430C(5) below.

[9] s.430A(1) and (2). There is no equivalent of s.429(8).

[10] On Form 430A.

[11] s.430A(3). This does not apply if the offeror has already given the shareholder a notice under s.429: s.430A(5).

Section 430B, on the effect of the shareholder's requirement that his shares be acquired, is, *mutatis mutandis*, identical with subsections (1)–(4) of section 430.[12] In particular, the same provisions relating to alternative offers apply.[13] It is in this case, rather than in relation to section 429,[14] that the need to provide a choice of all the original alternatives (including a cash underwritten alternative) is so un-popular with offerors and their advisers. And it is, perhaps, rather remarkable and not altogether easy to reconcile with the provisions of the Code. As we have seen, under the Code an offer has to remain open for 14 days after it becomes unconditional as to acceptances.[15] It can be kept open for longer but, even if it is, an offeror is not obliged to keep most types of cash underwritten alternatives open if it has given notice to shareholders that it reserves the right to close them on a stated date being not less than 14 days after the date on which the written notice is given.[16] The effect of section 430B(3) and (4) is virtually to keep the offer open for considerably longer than is required under the Code in all cases where the offer has been 90 per cent. successful. And clearly the parties cannot contract out of the statutory provisions. Nor can the Panel or the Code waive them.

However, it is sometimes argued that sections 430B(3) and (4) do not apply if the cash alternative is described in the offeror's offer document as a separate offer by the underwriting merchant bank. In the light of the section that argument seems unsustainable. The fact is that, as the section and the Code clearly recognise, the offeror's "offer" may and probably will contain a number of separate offers and that some of those offers may be made by third parties. The only way, it is submitted, in which offerors and their merchant banks might be able to achieve their aim is by making no mention at all of a cash underwritten alternative hoping that an independent merchant bank, not acting on behalf of, or paid for its services by, the offeror will come forward and make an offer on its own account to the target's shareholders to buy the shares of the offeror received on the take-over. That is a somewhat unlikely scenario.

Applications to the court

In relation to both buy-outs and sell-outs there is a right to apply to the court under section 430C. Its subsection (1) provides that where the offeror has given a notice to a shareholder under section 429, the shareholder may within six weeks from the date of the notice apply to the court which (a) may order that the offeror shall not be

[12] Provisions corresponding to s.430(5)–(13) are not needed since the shareholder has identified himself and is a willing seller.
[13] A point specifically left open by Brightman J. in *Re Carlton Holdings Ltd.*, above, p. 735 n. 4.
[14] Where the offeror does not have to exercise his rights unless he wants to.
[15] Rule 31.4.
[16] Rule 33.2.

entitled or bound to acquire the shares or (b) specify terms of acquisition different from those of the offer.[17] Under subsection (3) when a shareholder exercises his rights under section 430A an application may be made either by the shareholder or the offeror and the court may order that the terms on which the offeror shall acquire the shares shall be such as the court thinks fit.

At one time, there were a considerable number of such applications, mainly under subsection (1), but with rare exceptions all unsuccessful.[18] It is therefore not surprising that in recent years there seem to have been fewer. Indeed it may be questioned whether there is any need for section 430C in view of sections 459–461. However, section 430C does something to encourage its use by providing specifically that "no order for costs or expenses shall be made against a shareholder[19] unless the court considers that the application was unnecessary, improper or vexatious" or that there has been unreasonable delay in making the application or unreasonable conduct in the shareholder's conduct of the proceedings.[20] This may be regarded as an advantage over proceeding by way of section 459.

Subsection (5) provides that, when an offer has been accepted to the extent necessary for entitling the offeror to give notice under section 429, the court may, on the application of the offeror, permit it to give notice under section 430C notwithstanding that it has been unable after reasonable inquiry to trace one or more of the non-accepting shareholders but the shares that the offeror has acquired or contracted to acquire by virtue of acceptances and those already held by the offeror amount to not less than 90 per cent. But the court must be satisfied that the consideration is fair and reasonable, and that it is just and equitable to do so having regard to the number of shareholders who have been traced but who have not accepted the offer. If such an order is made, the effect is to enable the offeror to invoke section 429 when its total holdings are such as would entitle the shareholders to invoke their rights under section 430A.

On the wording of section 430C it is clear that the court has a discretion whether or not to make an order. In *Re Chez Nico (Restaurants) Ltd.*[20a] Browne-Wilkinson V.-C. made some interesting

---

[17] When an application is pending the procedure for completing the acquisition is suspended: s.430C(2).

[18] The usual fate of applications attacking transactions approved by a substantial majority. The courts on applications under the forerunner of the present Part XIIIA seemed to regard it as scarcely believable that there could be anything wrong with a bid accepted by 90 per cent. For a rare exception see *Re Bugle Press Ltd.* [1961] Ch. 434, C.A. where what is now s.429 was being abused rather than used: see p. 598 above.

[19] In fact it had not been the practice of the courts to order shareholders to pay costs. As in the case of appearing in opposition to a scheme of arrangement, it was generally felt that their appearance was helpful to the court which would otherwise hear only one side of the argument.

[20] s.430C(4).

[20a] [1991] BCC 736; see p. 733, above.

and helpful observations on how he would have exercised his discretion in that case had it been necessary for him to do so. He indicated that he would unhesitatingly have refused to make an order in favour of the two directors having regard to their failure to observe the rules of the Code to which the transaction was subject. On the general duties of disclosure by directors in a take-over situation he expressed his agreement with the views of the New Zealand Court of Appeal in *Coleman v. Myers*[20b] on *Percival v. Wright*[20c] but said that it was unnecessary to decide whether, under the general law, the directors were, in the circumstances, under a duty to make full disclosure to the shareholders; the take-over was subject to the Code's rules and the directors had failed to disclose in accordance with its rules. While the Code "does not have the force of law, in considering for the purpose of section 430C whether the court should exercise its discretion, the Code is a factor of great importance,"[20d] This is a welcome supplement to the views expressed by Lord Prosser in *Dawson International v. Coats Patons*[20e] on the inter-relation of the general law and the Code.

The remaining sections of Part XIIIA deal with certain specific points which, in the past, have caused difficulty. It had been held by the Privy Council on an appeal from Australia that a section similar to the former section 209 of the 1948 Act did not apply when the offer was made by a consortium of offerors.[21] This loophole has now been closed[22] by section 430D which provides that Part XIIIA shall apply with the needed modifications specified in that section.[23] Section 430E deals with the position when shares are held or acquired not by the offeror but by its "associates" as widely defined in its subsections (4)–(8).[24] And, finally, section 430F provides that "shares" shall include securities convertible[25] into, or entitling the holder to subscribe for, shares and that "shareholder" includes the holders of such securities.[26]

Sections 314–316

These sections are in Part X of the Act (Enforcement of Fair Dealing by Directors). They are preceded by sections 312 and 313, the first of which makes it unlawful for a company to give a director

20b See Chap. 21 at p. 552, above.

20c *ibid.*

20d [1991] BCC at pp. 750–751.

20e See pp. 715–717, above.

21 *Blue Metal Industries Ltd. v. Dilley* [1970] A.C. 827, P.C.

22 As it was more promptly in Australia.

23 For the Code's treatment of joint offers, see Rule 4, Note 2.

24 *cf.* the Code's definition: *Definitions* p. C.2 and 3.

25 For the Code's treatment of convertibles, see Rule 5.1, Note 4, Rule 6, Note 6, Rule 9.1, Note 10, and Rule 15.

26 But they do not have to be treated as shares of the same class as that into which they are convertible; nor do different types of securities have to be treated as shares of the same class merely because they are convertible into the same class of share.

of the company any payment by way of compensation for loss of office or as consideration for or in connection with his retirement from office, without particulars of the proposed payment (including its amount) being disclosed to members of the company and the proposal being approved by the company. Section 313 similarly declares it to be unlawful, without such disclosure being made and such approval given, if in connection with the transfer of the whole or any part of the undertaking or property of the company any payment (*by whomsoever made*) is to be made to a director by way of compensation for loss of office or in connection with his retirement. However, neither of these sections is specifically directed to take-overs and neither is likely to be relevant to take-overs of the type dealt with in this chapter.[27]

However, section 314 is specifically directed to take-overs as its side-note indicates—although the word "take-over" is not used in the section itself. It applies when there has been a transfer of shares of a company resulting from:

"(a) an offer made to the general body of shareholders; or

(b) an offer made by or on behalf of some other body corporate with a view to the company becoming its subsidiary or a subsidiary of its holding company; or

(c) an offer made by an individual with a view to his obtaining the right to exercise or control the exercise of not less than one third of the voting power at any general meeting; or

(d) any other offer which is conditional on acceptance to a given extent"[28]

and a payment is to be made (whether by the company or the offeror or by anyone else) to a director of the company "by way of compensation for loss of office or as consideration for or in connection with his retirement from office."[29]

When that is so, it is the director's duty to take all reasonable steps to secure that particulars of the proposed payment are disclosed in or with the offer document sent to the shareholders.[30] If he fails to do so he is liable to a fine (as is any person who has been properly required to include those particulars and has failed to do so).[31] The

[27] s.312 is irrelevant because the wider ss.313 and 314 will apply and s.313 because it will not apply since the take-over will normally be by transfer of shares, not of the company's undertaking or property. But both may be relevant to arrangements undertaken by method (2) or (3) dealt with in Chap. 26.

[28] s.314(1). Though (a), (b) or (c) would almost certainly be a "take-over offer" for the purposes of the Code or Part XIIIA of the Act, this would not necessarily be so in the case of (d).

[29] *Ibid.* For the extended meaning of these quoted words see s.315 below.

[30] s.314(2).

[31] s.314(3).

real deterrent, however, is not the risk of a fine but the consequences flowing from section 315. This provides that if (a) the director's duty is not complied with, or[32] (b) the payment is not, before the transfer of shares, approved by a meeting of the holders of shares to which the offer related,[33] any sum received by the director is held by him in trust for those who have sold their shares as a result of the offer.[34] Here, therefore, the legislation has avoided the absurdity illustrated in *Regal (Hastings) Ltd.* v. *Gulliver*,[35] by providing restitution to those truly damnified, rather than to the company when, in effect, it would result in an undeserved reduction of the price that the successful offeror has paid. Instead, under section 314, the director becomes a trustee for the former shareholders who have sold.

Although sections 312–315 are all expressed to relate only to payments made "for loss of office" or "in connection with retirement from office", the meaning of these expressions is widened in some respects and narrowed in others by section 316. Under its subsection (1) if a payment is made to a director who has lost, or retired from, office in pursuance of any arrangement made either as part of the agreement for the transfer or within one year before or two years after it, and the offeror or target company was privy to the arrangement, the payment is deemed, unless the contrary is shown, to be one to which the sections apply. Furthermore, under subsection (2), if the price to be paid to any such director for his shares is in excess of the price obtainable by other shareholders or if any other valuable consideration is given to the director, the excess price or the value of the gift is deemed to be a payment caught by the sections.[36]

However, these extensions are counterbalanced by subsection (3) which provides that sections 312 to 315 do not include any bona fide payment by way of damages for breach of contract or by way of pension[37] in respect of past services. Hence so long as the directors have rolling five-year service agreements it is normally possible to pay them adequate "golden farewells" without having to get prior approval from the shareholders. Especially is this so because it has been held, by the Privy Council on an appeal concerning the corresponding sections in the New Zealand Act, that they do not

[32] The, grammatically correct, disjunctive "or", in s.315(1) has led some readers to suppose that, if the director has performed his duty under (a), approval under (b) is not required. This, of course, is not so: both must be complied with.

[33] And of "other members of the same class." When the target company has only one class of shares the meeting will be a general meeting of the company. In other cases subs. (2) makes appropriate provisions for class meetings.

[34] s.315(1). The expenses of distributing the sum among those former shareholders must be borne by the director.

[35] See Chap. 21 at pp. 565, 566 above.

[36] This means of evasion by paying more for the shares of a retiring director is unlikely to be tried if the Code applies since it would normally lead to the offer price having to be raised. And for the same reason, if the offeror wants to retain certain directors of the target they will not be paid more for their shares though that would *not* to resign though that would not be caught by the sections.

[37] Widely defined: see s.316(3).

apply to loss of another office held in conjunction with a directorship, for example a managing directorship.[38]

Section 316(4) specifically states that nothing in sections 313 to 315 "prejudices the operation of any rule of law requiring *disclosure*[39] to be made ... of payments made or to be made to a company director." It does not, however, say anything about its not prejudicing any rule of law requiring prior agreement of the members in general meetings to such payments but, in the absence of bad faith on the part of the board, there does not seem to be any such requirement apart from sections 313 to 315.[40]

The loopholes with which the sections are riddled enable their obvious purpose to be easily defeated and they are in need of urgent review.

CONCLUSION

This chapter has not attempted to answer the hotly disputed question of whether, on balance, take-overs are a "good thing" or a bad. The question is an important one and those who are responsible for our present rules—statutory or self-regulating—seem unsure of the answer. Some people would answer it by saying that, while agreed take-overs are not objectionable,[41] hostile or contested ones are.[42] But they will be faced with the riposte that the prospect of a hostile take-over is the one thing that keeps directors on their toes and protects their shareholders from mismanagement, and that contested take-overs secure the best price for the current shareholders. This, however, can be answered by pointing out that the interests of current shareholders are not necessarily the same as those of the public, the company as a whole or the workforce and that concentration on the immediate interests of current shareholders encourages the "short-termism" which is widely believed to be the

---

38 *Taupo Totara Timber Co. v. Rowe* [1978] A.C. 537, P.C. This, with great respect to their Lordships, seems a ridiculous decision—rendering the sections inapplicable to executive directors where they are most needed.

39 itals. supplied.

40 See Chap. 21 above.

41 Since they are merely an alternative to merger by schemes of arrangements in which both offeror and target companies have concurred. But should any type of merger be encouraged? "Big" is not necessarily "beautiful" and the evidence is equivocal on whether, on the whole, merged companies have performed better than the former separate companies did. And is not ambition to extend managerial empires a more common motive than the hope of increased efficiency?

42 Since, as can be illustrated from recent examples, the best of Codes cannot prevent reckless expenditure of time and money in the heat of the battle—or even before the battle starts. The Deputy City Editor of the *Sunday Times* (4 Aug. 1991) reports that: "I.C.I., the chemical company [Britain's biggest] is estimated by City take-over experts to be running up costs of up to £1m a week as it defends itself in the so-called 'phoney war' with Hanson. ... Should Hanson actually launch a bid, the £1m a week expenditure could easily double, say mergers and acquisitions specialists." If true, is this a sensible way of getting out of a recession?

curse of British industry. What may be most difficult to answer is: if one wants to ban hostile or contested bids, precisely how does one propose to do it?

CHAPTER 28

ADMINISTRATIONS, WINDINGS UP AND DISSOLUTIONS

ALTHOUGH, as pointed out in Chapter 5,[1] one of the advantages of a body corporate is that it can live forever, most companies do not. Indeed at present they are being put to death with increasing and alarming frequency because they are unable to pay their debts.[2] If that is their only offence death may seem an unnecessarily extreme penalty (we don't hang individuals who have gone bankrupt). But until the Insolvency Act 1986[3] we had no formal system, such as the South African "judicial management," the Australian "official management," or the American Chapter 11 of the Bankruptcy Act, whereby an attempt can be made to nurse back to health a company presently unable to pay its debts owing to cash flow or similar difficulties. Now we have something similar and the first Part of this chapter deals with that, leaving the funeral rites of liquidation to be described, in brief outline only, in the second and third Parts.

I. ADMINISTRATION ORDERS

Background

This new alternative to liquidation or winding up (the two expressions are used indiscriminately) implements recommendations of the Cork Committee,[4] which were based on its belief in the beneficial results flowing from the appointment, by the holder of a floating charge, of a receiver and manager (now called an "administrative receiver") which has been dealt with in Chapter 16.[5] In most cases an ailing company will have granted its bankers a

---

[1] At pp. 92–94 above.

[2] In the first quarter of 1991, 5,478 companies went into insolvent liquidation in England and Wales, a rise of 77 per cent. over the first quarter of 1990 and the highest figure for 20 years.

[3] In this chapter (except in relation to the last Part on Dissolution and Resurrection) it is the Insolvency Act (not the Companies Act) which is referred to as "the Act" and references to sections are to those of that Act unless the context otherwise requires.

[4] *The Report of the Review Committee on Insolvency Law and Practice*, (1982) Cmnd. 8558.

[5] At pp. 434, *et seq*. It is still possible to appoint a receiver and manager who will not be an administrative receiver within the meaning of the Act because the floating charge and the appointment do not cover "the whole or substantially the whole of the company's property or such of it as would have been substantially the whole of that property but for the fact that some other person has been appointed as receiver," *e.g.* by the holder of a fixed charge on some part of it: s.29(2).

floating charge over all its undertaking and assets and if it becomes unable to meet its obligations the first step will normally be for the bank[6] to appoint an administrative receiver.[7] Since the latter's "primary duty is to realise the assets in the interests of the debenture-holder and his powers of management are really ancillary to that duty,"[8] the administrative receiver will, quite properly, tend to concentrate on realising sufficient of the assets to enable the preferred creditors[9] to be paid and the indebtedness to the debentureholder and the costs of the receivership to be discharged. This, in most cases, will leave little (if anything) to be handed over to a liquidator. Admittedly in a few cases the receiver may have managed so skilfully that the company is restored to solvency and he can then be discharged and the company not put into liquida-tion—but that is very unusual.

However, the Cork Committee regarded the power to appoint administrative receivers as having been "of outstanding benefit to the general public and to society as a whole" since "in some cases they have been able to restore an ailing enterprise to profitability and return it to its former owners," and "in others, to dispose of the whole or part of the business as a going concern"[10] so that, in either case, "the preservation of the profitable parts of the enterprise has been of advantage to the employees, the commercial community, and the general public."[11] The Committee was "satisfied that in a significant number of cases, companies have been forced into liquidation and potentially viable businesses capable of being rescued have been closed down for want of a floating charge under which a receiver and manager could have been appointed."[12] Accordingly, its recommended solution was that the court should be empowered to appoint an administrator, whether or not there was a holder of a floating charge entitled to appoint an administrative receiver, but that the rights of such a holder to appoint an administrative receiver should be preserved so long as the holder elected to do so before an administration order was made.

As a result of the implementation of these recommendations we have a solution which more closely resembles the South African

---

[6] In recent years the banks have been criticised for allegedly acting precipitately, thereby causing companies to be put into receivership followed by liquidation when they might have survived if the banks had not stepped in prematurely.
[7] Alternatively, in the case of a company with debenture stock, the trustees for the debenture stockholders may appoint.
[8] *Per* Hoffmann J. in *Gomba Holdings v. Homan* [1986] 1 W.L.R. 1301 at 1305C.
[9] They have to be paid by the receiver in priority to the holder of the floating charge: see Chap. 16 at pp. 420–422 above.
[10] This, however, can be done in a liquidation since the liquidator is empowered to carry on the business of the company so far as may be necessary for its beneficial winding up, but the sanction of the court is needed in the case of compulsory liquidations: ss.165, 167 and Sched. 4, para. 5.
[11] Cmnd 8558, para. 495.
[12] *Ibid.* para. 496.

"judicial" or Australian "official" management (neither of which seems to have been particularly successful as a rescue operation) rather than the American Chapter 11, which has proved more successful and which affords the ailing company a complete and often lengthy moratorium. However, the new administration procedure is being used to a greater extent than was expected[13] and the number of such appointments is now running at about 250 per annum.[14] This, of course, is minuscule in comparison with the number of insolvent liquidations[15] (most of which were probably preceded by administrative receiverships) but presumably these would have escalated still further had it not been for administrations. What one cannot yet judge is the extent to which they will ultimately save the companies concerned (from going into insolvent liquidation—as some already have—or, failing that, the whole or a substantial part of their businesses to survive as going concerns.[16]

Although the objective of administration is to provide generally something similar to administrative receiverships, there are important differences between the two. Administrators can be appointed only by the court and they are officers of the court who, under the supervision of the court, act in the interests of the company as a whole and in the public interest in its survival if possible. An administrative receiver, in contrast, is normally appointed out of court by the holder of a floating charge and then he is not an officer of the court. And even if he is appointed by the court, his primary duty remains that of realising the company's assets in the interests of the holder of the floating charge.[17]

The statutory provisions relating to administrations are in Part II (sections 8–27) of the Insolvency Act, which, as in relation to receiverships and liquidations, is supplemented by the detailed

13 Because it was thought that, if the company's bankers had a floating charge, they would normally prefer to appoint their own administrative receiver. The fact that now they often seem to be willing to refrain from doing so if administration is proposed may be partly due to sensitivity to the criticisms referred to in n. 6 above. They also now have the assurance that whoever is appointed will be a qualified and licensed insolvency practitioner and not just someone friendly towards the company's management.

14 Mostly companies of some size, rather than quasi-partnership private companies.

15 See n. 2 above.

16 A report by Mark Homan for the Research Board of the Institute of Chartered Accountants in England and Wales, *A Survey of Administration Orders under the Insolvency Act 1986: The Result of Administration Orders made in 1987* (1989), hereinafter cited as the *Homan Report*, found that:—"In 55 per cent of the companies subject to an administration order, all or part of the business has survived as a going concern either in the original company or in new hands. In approximately one in five cases, not only the underlying business but the company itself has survived. Dividends to creditors have averaged 29p in the £."; para. 2.01. But, as that para. emphasizes, 1987 "was a healthy year for business with relatively low levels of insolvency." "We need further surveys for the later years of recession before we can be sure that these "highly successful results" (para. 2.02) are being maintained.

17 But the Act has done something to ensure that the general body of creditors are kept informed about what the administrative receiver is doing: see ss.47-49.

Insolvency Rules,[18] those relating specifically to administrations being in their Part 2.

When administration can be ordered

Section 8(1) provides that if the court:

"(a)   is satisfied that a company is, *or is likely to become*,[19] unable to pay its debts (within the meaning given to that expression by section 123[20] of this Act) and

(b)   considers that the making of an order under this section would be likely to achieve one or more of the purposes mentioned [in section 8 (3)],

the court may make an administration order in relation to the company."

The purposes mentioned in section 8(3) are:

"(a)   the survival of the company, and the whole or any part of its undertaking, as a going concern;

(b)   the approval of a voluntary arrangement under Part I[21] of the Act;

(c)   the sanctioning under section 425 of the Companies Act of a scheme of arrangement[22]; and

(d)   a more advantageous realisation of the company's assets than would be effected in a winding up;

and the order shall "specify the purpose or purposes for which it is made"

It will therefore be seen that the "survival" purpose, (a), on which we have hitherto concentrated, while given priority is not the sole purpose. In practice, most applications allege both (a) and (d) and occasionally (b) or (c).

---

18 S.I. 1986 No. 1925 as amended by S.I. 1987 No. 1919, S.I. 1989 No. 397 and S.I. 1991 No. 380.

19 Italics supplied.

20 That section provides a list of circumstances in which a company is deemed to be unable to pay its debts—the principal ground for winding up by the court: s.122(1)(f). The inclusion of the words italicised above might seem to imply that the court may make an administration order although it would be premature to make a winding up order; but any difference is more apparent than real in the light, for example, of s.123(1)(a) and (2) under which the company need not necessarily be presently unable to pay its debts. The words were presumably included to encourage applications for administration before the company is *in extremis*.

21 See Chap. 26 at pp. 700, 701 above, where it was suggested that voluntary arrangements might work best under an administrator. But in fact relatively little use seems to have been made of them by administrators.

22 See Chap. 26 at pp. 694–699 above.

In an early decision on section 8(3),[23] Peter Gibson J. took the view that the court could make an administration order only if it was satisfied that it was more probable than not that this would achieve one or more of the prescribed purposes. If this view had prevailed it would have been virtually impossible for the court ever to make an order—at any rate for the primary survival purpose (a). However, in a later case[24] Hoffmann J. declined to follow that view, pointing out: (i) that the word "likely" does not necessarily connote a chance better than evens[25]; (ii) that the section requires the court to be "satisfied" of the company's actual or likely insolvency but only to "consider" that the order would be likely to achieve one or more of the purposes; (iii) that it seemed unlikely that Parliament had intended the courts to embark on calculations of cumulative probabilities when the probability that any one of the four purposes on its own was less than evens but the probability that one or other would be achieved was greater than evens; and (iv) that even if the court concluded that it had jurisdiction to make an order it had a discretion not to do so if, weighing all the circumstances, that seemed inappropriate. He therefore concluded that there was a "real prospect" that one or other of the purposes would be achieved. His view was followed shortly thereafter by Vinelott J.[26] and now seems to be generally accepted.[27]

There are, however, further restrictions on the jurisdiction to grant an order. Under section 8(4) an order cannot be made if the company has already gone into liquidation, whether compulsory or voluntary, or if the company is an insurance company.[28] Moreover if at the time of the hearing there is an appointed administrative receiver then, under section 9(3), the court cannot make an order, unless (a) the appointor consents or (b) the court is satisfied that, if an order was made, the floating charge under which the receiver was appointed would be liable to challenge under sections 238–240, 245 or Part XII of the Companies Act—which have been dealt with in Chapter 16.[29]

Section 9 further provides that an application for an administration order shall be made by petition[30] presented either by the company or

23 *Re Consumer & Industrial Press Ltd.* [1988] BCLC 177.
24 *Re Harris Simmons Ltd.* [1989] 1 W.L.R. 368.
25 As in "I think that the favourite, Golden Spurs at 5–1, is likely to win the Derby": at p. 370F.
26 In *Re Primlaks (UK) Ltd.* [1989] BCLC 734.
27 And by Peter Gibson J. in *Re SCL Business Services* [1990] BCLC 98, although he declined to include in his order any "purpose" unless he was satisfied that there was a reasonable prospect of achieving it.
28 But this does not preclude an order being made in respect of a parent company with an insurance subsidiary. s.8(4) also excludes a bank, but this is now misleading since the Banks (Administration Proceedings) Order 1989 (S.I. 1989 No. 1276) applies Part II of the Act to them subject to minor modifications.
29 See pp. 422–425 above.
30 For details of the procedure, see Insolvency Rules, Part 2.

the directors[31] or by a creditor or creditors (including any contingent or prospective creditors)[32] or all or any of them, together or separately.[33] When the petition is presented, notice of it has to be given forthwith to any person who has appointed, or is or may be entitled to appoint, an administrative receiver of the company.[34] Under the Rules, this is to be done by serving on that person and on the receiver, if he has been appointed, a copy of the petition, of the affidavit in its support and of the documents exhibited to it.[35] This should be done at least five clear days before that fixed for the hearing.[36] This affords that person an opportunity to decide whether or not to appoint an administrative receiver (if he has not already done so) and whether or not to consent to the making of an administration order.

However, the courts have held that, under the wide powers conferred by section 9(4) and (5), they may abridge the time for service of the petition and, if necessary, make orders restricting the powers of the directors and of the company in general meeting pending the hearing of the petition. An exercise of these powers may be needed in cases if dire urgency, particularly if there is a risk of the company's assets disappearing before the hearing can take place. Since the reported decisions in *Re A Company No. 00175 of 1987*[37] and in *Re Gallidoro Trawlers Ltd.*[38] such orders have been made with increasing frequency.

---

[31] This rather curious wording appears to mean that application may be made pursuant to a resolution of a general meeting or of the directors, or by all the directors: see, so far as applications by directors are concerned, *Re Equiticorp International plc* [1989] 1 W.L.R. 1010. On presentation by directors it is to be treated for all purposes as a petition by the company: Rule 2.4(3). The petition must state the name and address of the proposed administrator and that he is qualified to act as an insolvency practitioner in relation to the company: Rule 2.4(5).

[32] Or, now, by the clerk of a magistrates' court to enforce fines imposed on the company: s.9(1) as amended by the Criminal Justice Act 1988.

[33] *Re Land & Property Trust plc* [1991] 1 W.L.R. 601, C.A. illustrates the danger that directors run if they allow a petition to be lodged in circumstances which are obviously hopeless. Although the petition was by the company and the directors were not parties Harman J. ordered the directors to pay the costs of a major creditor who had opposed the application and refused leave to appeal. The C.A. held that the normal ban, on appeals against orders regarding costs only unless the judge granted leave did not apply when the order was against non-parties but said nothing in its judgment to suggest that an appeal is likely to succeed.

[34] And to such other persons as may be prescribed: see Insolvency Rules 2.6 and 2.6A. On who may attend the hearing see Rule 2.9.

[35] Rule 2.6.

[36] Rule 2.7(1).

[37] [1987] BCLC 467, Vinelott J. held that the court was entitled to abridge the time for service and that although the court has no power to appoint an interim administrator it could, as he did, produce much the same result by restricting the powers of the directors and appointing an interim manager.

[38] [1991] BCLC 411. In this case, an ex parte application was made by the company's bank which was proposing to file a petition for an administration order. It had a charge on the company's ships but feared that it would be rendered valueless by a sale by the company of its fishing licences. Harman J. declined to appoint an interim manager but decided that the company should not dispose of any of its assets except in the ordinary course of business or with the consent of the proposed administrator or of the court, and he abridged the time for service of the petition to not less than 2 clear days.

Effect of the application

During the period beginning with the presentation of the petition and ending with the making of an order or the dismissal of the petition there is a limited moratorium. Under section 10 no resolution may be passed for voluntary winding up or order made for compulsory winding up by the court.[39] Nor may any steps be taken to enforce any security[40] over the company's property or to repossess goods in its possession under a hire purchase agreement[41] or to take any legal process against the company or its property except with the leave of the court.[42] But this, as we have seen, does not prevent the appointment of an administrative receiver or the carrying out by him of his functions until his appointor consents to the making of the administrative order.[43]

Effect of the order

On the making of an administration order any petition for the company's winding up is dismissed and any administrative receiver vacates office,[44] but a non-administrative receiver of part of the property does not vacate office unless he is required to do so by the administrator.[45] On a vacation of office the receiver's duties cease and he is not required to take any further steps to comply with his duty to pay preferential creditors,[46] but his remuneration and any indemnity to which he is entitled out of the assets of the company are a charge on any property under his control at the time he vacates and are payable in priority to payments to his appointor.[47]

Moreover a more extensive moratorium then comes into effect. Under section 11(3) during the period that the administration order remains in force: (a) no resolution may be passed or order made for the winding up of the company; (b) no administrative receiver of the company may be appointed; (c) no other steps may be taken to enforce any security on the company's property or to repossess goods

39 s.10(1)(a). This, however, does not preclude the presentation of a petition for winding up (see s.10(2)(a)) and in a number of cases the court has been faced at the hearing with petitions for both winding up and administration and has had to decide which (if either) it should order. But no further steps can be taken on the winding up petition until that for the administration order has been heard: *Re A Company (No. 001992 of 1988)* [1989] BCLC 9.
40 Widely defined in s.248. The definition has even been held to include a landlord's right of re-entry; *Exchange Travel v. Triton* [1991] BCLC 396.
41 Which, for the purposes of both ss.10 and 11 include conditional sale agreements, chattel leasing agreements and retention of title agreements: s.10(4).
42 s.10(1)(b) and (c).
43 s.10(2)(b) and (c) and s.10(3).
44 s.11(1). There cannot be an administrator and an administrative receiver in office at the same time.
45 s.11(2).
46 s.11(5).
47 s.11(4).

in the possession of the company under a hire-purchase agreement; and (d) no other proceedings and no execution or other legal process may be taken or continued and no distress may be levied against the company or its property; unless, in case (c) or (d), the administrator consents or the court grants leave on such terms as the court may impose.

It is section 11(3)(c) and (d) that has caused administrators and their advisers particular difficulty. Fortunately they now have some guidance from the two leading cases on administrations, namely the Court of Appeal judgments in *Bristol Airport plc* v. *Powdrill*[48] and, especially, *Re Atlantic Computer Systems (No.1)*.[49] These cases are also of importance in relation to administrations generally for they stress the need for a purposive construction of Part II of the Insolvency Act paying regard to the mischiefs identified by the Cork Committee and which that Part was intended to cure. That is admirable. But unfortunately it does not provide a ready answer to all the problems arising from situations dealt with by section 11(3)(c) and (d) in which there is a potential conflict between the purposes of the legislation, *i.e.* (i) that creditors, secured or unsecured, shall not exercise their rights in a way which might frustrate the purpose of the administration and (ii) that nevertheless such creditors must be treated fairly and, if secured, should not find their status reduced to that of unsecured creditors.

In *Atlantic Computer Systems* the Court of Appeal was disturbed by the increasing number of applications to the courts for leave. It considered that it was the intention of the legislation that, in the first, and ideally the final, instance, such matters should be dealt with by the administrator on applications to him for consent. But this, it recognised, was unlikely to occur unless administrators and their legal advisers had clearer guidance on what is the approach of the courts when application for leave is made so that administrators could adopt the same approach in dealing with applications for consent. Accordingly, with some reluctance, the Court proceeded to give such guidance in what it described as twelve "general observations," hoping thereby that applications to the court would become the exception rather than the rule.[50] The following two paragraphs attempt to summarise the effect of those observations.[51]

---

[48] [1990] Ch. 744, C.A. A case not devoid of humorous facts in which an airport attempted to exercise its statutory right to retain the aircraft of an airline under administration until it had been paid all airport dues payable in respect of the period before its going into administration.

[49] [1991] BCLC 606, C.A. A case, with more complicated facts, concerning the claims of those who had financed the leasing of the computers of a computer-leasing company under administration. Though the judgment of the C.A. is more important than those in *Bristol Airport* it seemed not to have been thought worthy of inclusion in the "official" L.R. but is on its way there: see [1992] 2 W.L.R. 367.

[50] [1991] BCLC at 632 a—e.

[51] *ibid* at 632—634.

Since the prohibitions in section 11 are intended to assist the administrator to achieve the purpose of the administration, it is for the person who seeks leave (or consent) to make out a case for being granted it. If leave is unlikely to impede the achievement of that purpose leave should normally be given. In other cases it is necessary to carry out a balancing exercise, weighing the legitimate interests of the applicant and those of the other creditors of the company.[52] In carrying out that exercise the underlying principle is that an administration should not be conducted at the expense of those who have proprietary rights which they are seeking to exercise except to the extent that this may be inevitable if the purpose of the administration is to succeed and even then only to a limited extent. Thus it will normally be a sufficient ground for granting leave if significant loss would otherwise be suffered by the applicant, unless the loss to others would be significantly greater. In assessing the respective losses all the circumstances relating to the administration should be taken into account[53] and regard paid to how probable they are likely to be. The conduct of the respective parties may sometimes also be relevant.[54]

Similar considerations apply to decisions regarding imposing terms. Powers to do so are expressly conferred when the court grants leave and although section 11 makes no express provision when leave is refused, the court has power to do so, directly by giving directions to the administrator under section 17, or in response to an application by the administrator under section 14, or in exercise of its control over officers of the court. Alternatively, the court may do so indirectly by ordering that the applicant shall have leave unless the administrator is prepared to take steps in the administration specified by the court. Cases where leave is refused on undertakings being given by the administrator are likely to be frequent. The court's observations on terms and its expressed belief that observance by administrators of the guidance will make applications to the courts exceptional necessarily imply that an administrator when granting consent is empowered to impose terms on the applicant and when refusing consent is empowered to give undertakings. This is indeed an admirable example of the use of a purposive construction, for neither is expressly provided in section 11,[54a] which confers such powers only on the court when granting leave. So long as administrators follow the guidelines, applications to the court should be greatly reduced and needed only when mutually acceptable terms cannot be agreed

[52] Citing *Royal Trust Bank* v. *Buchler* [1989] BCLC 130 at 135.
[53] See observation (6) at p. 663(e)(f) of which the text, above, is a somewhat inadequate summary.
[54] Citing, at p. 663, *Bristol Airport* v. *Powdrill*, where leave was refused because the applicant airport had benefited from the administration and delayed in seeking to enforce its right of retention.
[54a] Contrast s.15, below.

by applicants and administrators. In cases where the applicant is the holder of a fully secured fixed or floating charge there should normally be no difficulty in obtaining agreement that the applicant will delay enforcing his security for a reasonable time to enable the administrator to plan his strategy.[54b]

Appointment of administrators

The initial appointment of an administrator will be made by the administration order.[55] If there is only one application under section 9, the court will normally appoint the person proposed so long as he is an insolvency practitioner duly qualified and licensed under Part XIII of the Act[56]—only such persons are eligible for appointment as administrators, liquidators, provisional liquidators or administrative receivers.[57] So long as he was so eligible, the court could hardly reject him as unfit for the job—but it might reject him if it thought that there was a potential conflict of interest (because, for example, he was associated with the former management). If, however, there is more than one application proposing different administrators the court will have to choose between them. Although the Act refers throughout to "the administrator" it is clear that more than one can be appointed as joint administrators[58] and generally two or more are appointed in the case of the larger administrations.[59] If a vacancy occurs by death, resignation or otherwise the court may fill the vacancy by an order[60] made on the application of any continuing administrator, or, if there is none, of a creditors' committee established under section 26, below, or, if no such committee has been established, of any creditor or creditors.[61]

Powers of administrators

The administrator (a) may do all such things as may be necessary for the management of the affairs, business, and property of the

54b See [1991] BCLC at 634d, C.A.
55 s.13(1).
56 And thereby subject to the rules and surveillance of a recognised professional body and to the jurisdiction of the Insolvency Practitioners' Tribunal.
57 s.230. As are nominees and supervisors of voluntary arrangements under Part I: see Chap. 26 at p. 700 above.
58 For some reason the Act and the Rules contain explicit provisions regarding joint administrative receivers but not about administrators.
59 Normally in the same firm of chartered accountants but sometimes in two or more firms. Some solicitors have become licensed insolvency practitioners but this is a field which the legal profession has abandoned to accountants to an even greater extent than in relation to taxation.
60 s.13(2).
61 s.13(3). The Act does not seem to envisage the court appointing on its own motion, presumably on the basis that, if the creditors are not sufficiently interested to do anything about it, it is not for the court to step in. It seems that the directors should then take steps to put the company into liquidation, to protect themselves against accusations of "wrongful trading," unless the company is no longer insolvent.

company and (b) without prejudice to the generality of (a) he has all the powers specified in Schedule 1 to the Act.[62] That Schedule confers 22 specific powers on administrators[63] and a "catch-all" power "to do all other things incidental to the exercise of the foregoing powers." In effect, therefore, the administrator[64] has all the powers normally vested in the board of directors. The directors do not necessarily vacate office, but the administrator has power to remove any director of the company, to appoint any person to be a director of it and to call any meeting of the members or creditors of the company.[65] Hence the administrator can retain directors, executive or non-executive, if he thinks they might be useful and indeed should ensure that there is the minimum number of directors to fulfil their obligations under the Companies Act regarding calling of AGMs and the like to the extent that these duties are not performed by him. But "any power conferred on the company or its officers whether by this Act or the Companies Act or by the memorandum or articles of association, which could be exercised in such a way as to interfere with the exercise by the administrator of his powers, is not exercisable except with the consent of the administrator . . ."[66]

In exercising his powers the administrator is deemed to act as the company's agent,[67] and, in contrast with an administrative receiver,[68] he is not personally liable on contracts which he enters into on the company's behalf.[69] A person dealing with an administrator in good faith and for value is not concerned with whether the administrator is acting within his powers.[70] This would seem to afford third parties much the same protection as they would have obtained, prior to the administration, under the new sections 35-35B of the Companies Act but only so long as in addition to acting in good faith they have given value.[71] In order that persons dealing with the company realise that it is under administration section 12 requires that every invoice, order

---

62 s.14(1).
63 These are the same powers as s.42 confers on administrative receivers except, in their case, to the extent that the powers are inconsistent with the debenture under which they were appointed: see Chap. 16 at p. 438 above.
64 Who may apply to the court for directions in relation to any particular matter arising in connection with the carrying out of his functions: s.14(3).
65 s.14(2).
66 s.14(4).
67 s.14(5). But his relationship with the company is not that of its agent or servant: he is an officer of the court, not of the company.
68 Who, despite the fact that he too acts as agent, is personally liable on contracts he enters into unless they provide to the contrary: s.44(1); see Chap. 16 at p. 440 above.
69 This, one might have thought, would make it more difficult for him to carry on the business of an insolvent company but his power under Sched. 1, para. 3 "to raise or borrow money and grant security therefor over the property of the company" should help and although an administrative receiver also has that power it was a deliberate decision to draw this distinction between administrative receivers and administrators.
70 s.14(6).
71 Which is not a condition of ss.35-35B of the Companies Act: see Chap. 8 above. Presumably it was thought that as the company is insolvent this additional condition was needed to protect creditors.

for goods or business letter on which the name of the company appears shall also contain a statement that the affairs, business and property of the company are being managed by an administrator.

An additional power of an administrator is conferred by section 15[72] which has some affinities with section 11(3).[73] Section 15 deals with two distinct situations. The first is where any part of the company's property is subject to a charge which, when created, was a floating charge.[74] In such a case the administrator is, under subsections (1), (3) and (4), empowered to dispose of the property as if it was not subject to the charge but the holder of the charge has the same priority in respect of any property of the company representing directly or indirectly the property disposed of. In effect the charge is treated as if it is still an uncrystallised floating charge so that the administrator can sell it free from the charge which then attaches to the proceeds of sale.

When, however, the property is subject to any other type of "security," or is held by the company under a "hire-purchase agreement,"[75] the more complicated provisions of subsections (2) and (5)–(8) apply. Under subsection (2), where, on application by the administrator, the court is satisfied that the disposal (with or without other assets) of the property would be likely to promote the purpose or one of the purposes specified in the administration order, the court may by order authorise the administrator to dispose of the property as if it were not subject to the security or to the rights of the owner under the hire-purchase agreement. The court has a discretion whether or not to make such an order and it has been held that in deciding whether or not to do so it should undertake a balancing exercise similar to that on applications under section 11, to decide whether the hardship to the security holder or owner of the goods of making an order would outweigh the detrimental effect on the achievement of the purposes of the administration.[76] Even if the security is a fixed charge the hardship to the holder should be slight. It must be a condition of an order that the net proceeds of the disposal (and, if they prove to be less than the court determined would be realised on a sale in the open market by a willing vendor), such sums as are required to make up the deficiency, have to be applied towards discharging the sums secured.[77] In effect, therefore, the security is retained and the only detriment to the security holder is that he cannot control the timing of the realisation of his security which will be undertaken by the administrator, probably as part of a

[72] Adapted to Scotland by s.16.
[73] See pp. 749–752 above.
[74] *i.e.* it applies notwithstanding that the charge may have crystallised as a result of the administration order or the appointment of an administrative receiver or a receiver and manager, prior to the administration order.
[75] Once again defined, in subs. (9), as including "conditional sale agreements, chattel leasing agreements and retention of title agreements."
[76] *Re ARV Aviation Ltd* [1989] BCLC 664.
[77] See subsection (6) for the position when two or more securities are involved.

larger disposal, instead of by the security holder as a single transaction. In the case of a creditor whose security is a lien or the like without power of sale, his position will be improved since he will have to be treated in effect as if he held a floating charge.

However in relation to liens the overall position seems to be somewhat anomalous. Under section 246 of the Act, which applies to both administrations and winding up, a lien or other right to retain books, papers or other records (other than documents of title) is unenforceable to the extent that it would deny possession of them to the administrator or liquidator. The administrator seems to have an absolute right to obtain possession of such records. In the case of liens on other goods, it seems that the lienor will be in contempt of court if the administrator requires him to give them up, since if he retains them he will be enforcing his security in breach of section 11(3)(c) and (d) unless he promptly applies to the court for leave to retain them.[78] On such an application the court, whether it grants or refuses leave can impose terms on the lienor or the administrator but is not bound to do so.[78a] If, however, the administrator does not need the goods for use in the administration and allows the lienor to retain them until the administrator can sell them with leave of the court under section 15, the court *must* impose the condition in section 15(5) if it grants the administrator leave to sell.

Duties of the administrators

In contrast with the detailed provisions regarding the administrator's powers, all the Act says about his general duties is in one short section 17. This provides that the administrator shall on his appointment take into his custody or control all the property to which the company is, or appears to be, entitled[79]; shall manage its affairs, business and property in accordance with any directions of the court prior to the approval of proposals in accordance with section 24, below; and thereafter in accordance with those proposals[80]; and shall summon a meeting of creditors if requested by one-tenth in value of the creditors or if directed by the court.[81] In addition, specific duties are imposed on him as regards: giving information about his appointment to the company creditors and the Registrar[82]; obtaining a statement of affairs from officers and employees of the company[83];

[78] See *Bristol Airports v. Powdrill* above and *Re Sabre International* [1991] BCLC 470.
[78a] See *Bristol Airports v. Powdrill* (where the court refused leave unconditionally) and *Re Atlantic Computer Systems No.1*: above pp. 750–752.
[79] s.17(1).
[80] s.17(2).
[81] s.17(3).
[82] s.21.
[83] s.22.

and, within three months (or such longer period as the court may allow), sending to the Registrar, the company's members and creditors a statement of his proposals for achieving the purpose or purposes specified in the order and to lay this before a meeting of creditors.[84] If the meeting approves his proposals (with any modifications that he accepts) he must report the result to the court and give notice to the Registrar and to other persons prescribed by the Rules.[85] Thereafter if the administrator proposes to make any revisions which appear to him to be substantial he must convene another meeting of creditors and obtain their approval.[86] At a meeting summoned under section 23 which approves the proposals, the meeting may, if it thinks fit, establish a creditors' committee which may require the administrator to attend before it at any reasonable time and to furnish it with such information relating to the carrying out of his functions as it may reasonably require.[87]

If, however, the administrator's proposals are not approved at the meeting summoned under section 23, this must similarly be reported and the court may "discharge the administration order and make such consequential provision as it thinks fit, or adjourn the hearing conditionally or unconditionally, or make an interim order or any other order that it thinks fit."[88] Normally it will obviously be necessary that the company is put into insolvent liquidation—and as soon as possible. Indeed, except when the efforts of the administrator have enabled the company itself to survive as a solvent going concern, the administration will have to be succeeded by a liquidation if only because (except when the administrator has achieved a successful voluntary arrangement[89]) an administrator has no power to make distributions of dividends to creditors. This is commonly regarded as the greatest weakness of Part II.[90] And unfortunately the wording of the Act and the Rules implies that the winding up will be a compulsory liquidation by the court—the most expensive method.

However, ways have been found for reducing the expense. Almost invariably the liquidator appointed will be the former administrator[91] and the courts have proved willing in an increasing number of cases to countenance a voluntary winding up notwithstanding the wording of the Act—again adopting a "purposive" approach, this time to

---

[84] s.23.
[85] s.24(1)–(4).
[86] s.25.
[87] s.26. This is a somewhat emasculated version of what the Cork Committee recommended; *i.e.* that the creditors "should be required to nominate a Committee which will take office if the court confirms the Order appointing an Administrator or directs that the company should be placed in some form of insolvency proceedings": Cmnd. 8558, para. 513.
[88] s.24(5). If the administration order is discharged, the administrator must send to the Registrar a copy of the order discharging it: s.24(6).
[89] Under Part I of the Act: see Chap. 26 at pp. 699–701 above.
[90] See the *Homan Report* (n.16 above) at paras. 5.20–5.23.
[91] s.140 expressley empowers the court to do so where a winding up order is made immediately upon the discharge of the administrator.

reduce the very real danger that the additional expense of preceding a liquidation by an administration will frustrate the legislative aim by discouraging the use of administrations.

Discharge or variation of administration orders

Section 18 provides that the administrator may at any time apply to the court for the administration order to be discharged or to be varied so as to specify an additional purpose.[92] And he must make an application if "(a) it appears to him that the purpose or each of the purposes specified in the order either has been achieved or is incapable of achievement[93]; or (b) he is required to do so by a meeting of the company's creditors summoned for the purpose."[94] If the order is discharged or varied the administrator must within 14 days send an office copy to the Registrar of Companies and is liable to a fine if he fails to do so without a reasonable excuse.[95]

Vacation of office

The administrator may at any time be removed from office by the court and may, in prescribed circumstances,[96] resign by giving notice to the court.[97] He must also vacate office if he ceases to be qualified to act as an insolvency practitioner in relation to the company or if the administration order is discharged.[98] And, since administrators must be appointed as individuals, his death will also cause a vacation of his office.[99]

When the office is vacated the administrator is released "from all liability both in respect of acts or omissions of his in the

---

92. s.18(1).
93. The wording of this suggests that he is not bound to apply if two or more purposes were specified unless and until it appears to him that both or all purposes have been achieved or are incapable of achievement (if he had to apply when any one of them was achieved or was incapable of achievement "any" would surely have been used instead of "each").
94. s.18(2). On an application under s.18 the court's powers are the same as those under s.24(5) when a report to it is made under that section (see above).
95. s.18(4) and (5).
96. The Rules, (r. 2.53) prescribe ill-health, intention to cease practice as an insolvency practitioner, conflict of interest or a change of personal circumstances which make it impractical to continue to act; but the court may grant leave on other grounds.
97. s.19(1).
98. s.19(2), s.19(4), and (5) contain provisions (similar to those applying to receivers) for protecting his rights in respect of remuneration due and indemnity out of the assets of the company in respect of liability on contracts. The latter is less important than in the case of receivers because he will be personally liable only if he has expressly agreed (see p. 753 above) as he may have had to.
99. This is another reason why firms of practitioners favour joint appointments of two or more of their members: if only one is appointed the firm risks losing the remunerative work on his death.

administration and otherwise in relation to his conduct as administrator,"[1] with effect from, in the case of death, the date when notice is given to the court in accordance with the Rules[2] and in any other case such time as the court may determine.[3] The reason why the date of his release may be later than the date of vacation of office is to ensure that, if liquidation is to follow, the administrator is not released *qua* administrator until he or someone else is appointed as liquidator.

Unfair prejudice by administrator

The final section 27 of Part II of the Act affords a remedy similar to sections 459–461 of the Companies Act.[4] It provides that:

"*At any time when an administration order is in force a creditor or member*[5] may apply to the court by petition for an order under this section on the ground:

(a) that the company's affairs, *business and property* are being *managed, or have been managed, by the administrator* in a manner which is unfairly prejudicial to the interests of its *creditors or members* generally or of some part of its creditors or members (including at least himself); or

(b) that any actual or proposed act or omission of *the administrator* is or would be so prejudicial."[6]

This, in substance, is identical with section 459(1) except as regards the words italicised which differ from those in section 459(1) in order to adapt it appropriately to the period when the business and property of the company are being managed by an administrator. The important change is that, in contrast with section 459, it provides a remedy which is available to creditors as well as members. It should be noted, however, that, in order to use it, the creditors or members must petition while the administration order is in force. Once the order is discharged it will be too late. But, while it is in force, section 27 supersedes section 459 of the Companies Act, even so far as members are concerned, unless the administrator consents or the court grants leave for a petition under the latter section to be commenced or continued.[7]

1 s.20(2). But it does not relieve him from potential liability to the summary remedy, against delinquent directors, administrators *et al.*, under s.212: s.20(3).
2 Under r. 2.54 notice may be given by the deceased's personal representatives, a partner in the deceased's firm who is a qualified insolvency practitioner or by "any person producing to the court the relevant death certificate or a copy of it."
3 s.20(1).
4 See Chap. 24 at pp. 662 *et seq.* above.
5 Which, as in s.459, includes a person to whom shares have been transmitted by operation of law: see s.250; a general provision (which the Companies Act lacks) applying for the purposes of Parts I-VII of the Act.
6 s.27(1). Itals. supplied.
7 No power is conferred on an administrator himself to invoke s.459 (it is not "legal proceedings in the name and on behalf of the company" within the meaning of the Act, Sched. I. para. 5).

Section 27 also provides that an order under it shall not prejudice or prevent the implementation of a voluntary arrangement under Part I of the Act or any scheme of arrangement sanctioned under section 425 of the Companies Act[8]; or the implementation of any proposals approved under section 24 or 25[9] if the application is made more than 28 days after the approval.[10] On the other hand it is expressly provided that "nothing in section 15.[11] is to be taken as prejudicing applications under" section 27.[12] The effect of this seems to be that notwithstanding that the court has made an order under section 15(2) authorising the administrator to dispose of property free from a charge thereon or from the rights of the owner under a hire-purchase agreement the chargee or owner, notwithstanding the protection afforded him by section 15(4) or (5), may petition under section 27 on the ground that the disposition was unfairly prejudicial to him, despite the fact that the court authorised it after deciding that achievement of the purposes of the administration outweighed any detriment to him. This at first glance seems strange but is designed to enable the applicant to complain that the transaction was carried out in a manner unfairly prejudicial if he does so in time.

The orders that the court can make on an application under section 27 are broadly similar to those that can be made under section 461 of the Companies Act on an application under its section 459. They start similarly with a general power to "make such order as it thinks fit for giving relief in respect of the matters complained of ... "[13] and then four particular examples are given.[14] The four are: (a) regulating the future management by the administrator; (b) requiring the administrator to refrain from doing or continuing to do, or from omitting to do, an act in respect of which the petitioner has complained[15]; (c) requiring the summoning of a meeting of creditors or members to consider such matters as the court directs; and (d) discharging the administration order and making consequential provisions.[16] There is nothing similar to the Companies Act, section 461(2)(c) authorising civil proceedings to be taken on behalf of the company (which may seem surprising since the act complained of might be a refusal by the administrator to sue on behalf of the company but the omission is presumably because the court could order him to sue; under section 27(2) or by exercising its inherent jurisdiction over officers of the court). Nor is there anything similar

---

[8] On which see Chap. 26 above.
[9] Above p. 756.
[10] s.27(3).
[11] See pp. 754, 755 above. The same applies in respect of s.16, the Scottish equivalent of s.15.
[12] s.27(5).
[13] s.27(2).
[14] s.27(4).
[15] (a) and (b) correspond with Companies Act, s.461(2)(a) and (b).
[16] (c) and (d) have no counterparts in s.461.

to section 461(2)(*d*) providing for a purchase of the petitioner's shares (which is presumably not regarded as appropriate in the circumstances of an administration of an insolvent company).

At the time of writing, seemingly the only reported case on section 27 is *Re Charnley Davies Ltd. (No. 2)*,[17] where the petitioners were a number of major insurance companies who were creditors of the company and who believed that the administrator had managed the company's business and affairs in a manner which disregarded their interests and those of the creditors generally and that he had realised the company's business precipitately and at a price which was not the best reasonably obtainable. At the hearing Millett J. accepted that that was a complaint which, if established, it was perfectly proper to bring under section 27. But in the course of the hearing it became apparent that all that remained of their complaint amounted, in Millett J.'s words, to "a simple action for professional negligence and nothing more. That, if established, would amount to misconduct; but would neither constitute nor evidence unfairly prejudicial management."[18] In his view the proper course would have been to discharge the administration order and to put the company into compulsory liquidation under a liquidator other than the administrator so that the latter's conduct could be examined under section 212[19] of the Act.[20]

CONCLUSION

It is too early yet to judge whether this well-intentioned attempt to salvage instead of destroying companies in financial difficulties can be regarded as a success or whether the inherent weaknesses will cause it to prove abortive. The two main weaknesses are its dependence on the continued willingness of the banks to allow independent administrators to assume control rather than administrative receivers appointed by them, and the expense of administrations, demanding as they do the employment of one or more administrators and applications to and surveillance by the courts. If, as one suspects, it proves to be the fact that in the vast majority of cases the company itself will be liquidated, administration can nevertheless be regarded as a success if it can be shown that administrators succeed in selling the business as a going concern more often and at a better price than would a liquidator and that the "better" price is sufficiently better to cover the costs of the administration and of the subsequent liquidation. If not, it would seem to be preferable, for all concerned, to put the company into creditors' voluntary liquidation rather than to have what is in effect an initial court administration followed by what is likely to be a winding up by the court.

17 [1990] BCLC 760.
18 [1990] BCLC at 784d.
19 See Chap. 24 at p. 671 below.
20 [1990] BCLC at 784f.

2. WINDING UP

Despite the fact that administrations relate more to Insolvency Law than to Company Law, they have been dealt with relatively fully in the first Part of this chapter because of their novelty and interest and the fact that if they succeed in their primary aim they may enable the company to survive as a solvent concern. This second Part of the chapter is concerned with the winding up process that normally has to be undertaken before a company is dissolved. The provisions relating to this are now to be found almost exclusively[21] in the Insolvency Act and Part IV of the Insolvency Rules,[22] and not in the Companies Act; and rightly so where the company is insolvent. But, although insolvency is the most common reason for winding up, it is far from being the only one and, when the company is fully solvent, it seems, on the face of it, somewhat illogical to treat the process as part of Insolvency Law rather than Company Law. The reason why the legislation relating to liquidation of solvent companies is in the Insolvency Act is probably to avoid duplicating those many provisions that apply whether or not the company is insolvent—to repeat them in the Companies Act would have added substantially to the length of the combined legislation.[23] But it can also be justified as realistic. Once a company goes into liquidation the distinction between shareholders and creditors becomes more than usually difficult to draw; the members' interests will, in effect, have become purely financial interests deferred to those of the creditors.

Types of winding up

The basic distinction is between voluntary winding up and compulsory winding up by the court.[24] But voluntary windings up are subdivided into two types—members' voluntary winding up and

---

[21] But see Companies Act, ss.651–658, below at pp. 773, *et seq.*

[22] Both eschew the use of the word "members" and substitute "contributories," thus giving the misleading impression that it means only members who are called upon to contribute because their shares are partly paid (or in the case of guarantee companies because of the minimal amounts that they have agreed to contribute on a winding up). To avoid this impression, here, "members" has been substituted; but readers should be warned that that too is not wholly accurate for "contributories" also includes past members unless they ceased to be members more than 12 months before the commencement of the winding up: see ss.74 and 76 and *Re Anglesea Collieries* (1866) L.R. 1 Ch. 555, C.A. and *Re Consolidated Goldfields of New Zealand* [1953] Ch. 689.

[23] Duplication has not been avoided without some inficities, not made any happier by the insertion by the Insolvency Act of a new s.735A in the Companies Act under which references in the latter to "this Act" are deemed to include references to a substantial number of sections of the Insolvency Act (and, in some cases, to the whole of the Company Directors' Disqualification Act).

[24] There used to be a further (hybrid) type of voluntary winding up subject to the supervision of the court, but this had ceased to be used and was abolished by the reforms of 1985/86.

creditors' voluntary winding up. In relation to companies registered under the Companies Acts which are dealt with in Part IV of the Insolvency Act,[25] Chapters I and VII–X of that Part relate to all three types, except where it is otherwise stated, Chapters II and V relate to both types of voluntary winding up, Chapter III relates only to members' voluntary winding up, Chapter IV only to creditors' voluntary winding up and Chapter VI only to winding up by the court. This arrangement of the sections is not exactly "user friendly" for it means that, to grasp which sections apply to the type of winding up with which one is concerned, it is necessary to refer to various Chapters of Part IV. Nor is life made easier because other Parts of the Act may also be relevant: for example Part VI on "miscellaneous provisions" and Part VII on "interpretation for first group of Parts."

As their names imply, an essential difference between compulsory winding up by the court and voluntary winding up is that the former does not necessarily involve action taken by any organ of the company itself, whereas voluntary winding up does. The essential difference between members' and creditors' winding up is that the former is possible only if the company is solvent, in which event the company's members appoint the liquidators, whereas, if it is not, its creditors have the whip hand in deciding who the liquidator shall be. In all three cases, and not only, though especially, if the company is insolvent, the winding-up process is not exclusively directed towards realising the assets and distributing the net proceeds to the creditors and, if anything is left, to the members, according to their respective priorities; it also enables an examination of the conduct of the company's management to be undertaken. And this may result in civil and criminal proceedings being taken against those who have engaged in any malpractices thus revealed[26] and in the adjustment or avoidance of various transactions.[27]

Winding up by the court

Under section 122 of the Act a company may be wound up by the court[28] on one or more of seven specified grounds. Of these grounds, by far the most important is ground (f), that the company is unable to pay its debts, and the next most important ground (g), that the court is of the opinion that it is just and equitable that the company

[25] In relation to the winding up of "unregistered companies" (on which see Chap. 11 at pp. 293–295 above) winding up by the court is the only method allowed: see Part V of the Act. A company incorporated outside G.B. which has been carrying on business in G.B. may be wound up as an unregistered company notwithstanding that it has ceased to exist under the law of the country of incorporation: s.225.

[26] See Part IV, Chap. X of the Act.

[27] See Part VI, ss.238–246.

[28] Normally the High Court, but the county court of the district in which the company has its registered office has concurrent jurisdiction if the company's paid-up capital is small and if that county court has jurisdiction in relation to bankruptcy of individuals: s.117.

should be wound up. The latter has been dealt with in Chapter 24 (where we saw that it may be used as a remedy in cases where members are being unfairly prejudiced or there is a deadlocked management) and in Chapter 25 (where we saw that it may be invoked by the Secretary of State following the exercise by him of his investigatory powers). It should be noted that the company itself can opt for winding up by the court, since ground (a) is that the company has by special resolution resolved that the company be so wound up. But normally that is the last thing that those controlling the company will want; it is the most expensive type of winding up and the one in which their conduct is likely to be investigated most thoroughly.[29]

Section 123 affords creditors owed more than £750, a simple means of establishing ground (f), that the company is unable to pay its debts.[30] As in the case of administration orders, creditors are among those who may petition[31] and this they are likely to do once it becomes widely known that the company is in financial difficulties[32], like a petition for the bankruptcy of an individual, a petition for winding up is the creditors' ultimate remedy. The company itself or its directors[33] or members[34] may petition but the court will be reluctant to grant it on ground (f) if it is opposed by a majority of the creditors.

If a winding-up order is made, the first step needing to be taken will be to appoint a liquidator to whom, as in all types of winding up, the administration of the company's affairs and property will pass. In contrast with an individual's trustee in bankruptcy its property does not vest in him[35]; but the control and management of it and of the company's affairs do and the board of directors, in effect, becomes *functus officio*. A liquidator may, indeed, be appointed, before a final order is made, for at any time after the presentation of a winding-up petition the court may appoint a provisional liquidator, normally the official receiver attached to the court.[36]

---

[29] But it might be used if the court is already involved because the liquidation of the company is part of a scheme requiring its sanction in accordance with Chapter 26 above.

[30] By serving a "statutory notice" in accordance with s.123(1)(a).

[31] s.124.

[32] Until then each may try to obtain judgment and levy execution thus getting ahead of the pack.

[33] Prior to the 1985/86 statutory reforms, it was held, somewhat surprisingly, that directors could not apply: *Re Emmerdart Ltd.* [1979] Ch. 540. Now they can. For the interpretation of "the directors" see *Re Equiticorp International plc* [1989] 1 W.L.R. 1010.

[34] But unless the membership has been reduced below two, a member cannot apply unless his shares were originally allotted to him or have been held and registered in his name for at least six months during the 18 months prior to the commencement of the winding up (on which see below) or have devolved on him through the death of a former holder: s.124(2). This is designed to prevent a disgruntled person (*e.g.* an ex-employee) from buying a share and then bringing a winding up petition (or threatening to do so).

[35] Unless the court so orders, as it may: s.145(1).

[36] s.135.

The important role played by official receivers in compulsory liquidations in England and Wales[37] is perhaps the major difference between compulsory and voluntary liquidations.[38] Official receivers are officers of the Insolvency Service, an Executive Agency of the DTI, attached to courts having bankruptcy jurisdiction.[39] Not only will an official receiver normally be the provisional liquidator (if one is appointed) but he will generally be the initial liquidator and often will remain the liquidator throughout. On the making of a winding-up order[40] he automatically becomes liquidator by virtue of his office and will remain so unless and until another liquidator is appointed.[41] He may succeed in ridding himself of the office by summoning separate meetings of the creditors and of the members for the purpose of appointing another liquidator.[42] And if that does not succeed[43] he may decide to refer the need to appoint another liquidator to the Secretary of State who may appoint.[44] But, whenever any vacancy occurs, he again becomes the liquidator until another is appointed.[45]

Whether or not the official receiver becomes the liquidator he has important investigatory powers and duties. When the court has made a winding-up order he may require officers, employees and those who have taken part in the formation of the company to submit to him a statement as to the affairs of the company verified by affidavit.[46] It is his duty to investigate the causes of the failure, and to make such report, if any, to the court as he thinks fit.[47] He may apply to the court for the public examination of anyone who is or has been an officer, liquidator, administrator, receiver or manager of the company or anyone else who has taken part in its promotion, formation or management and must do so, unless the court otherwise orders, if

[37] Scotland manages without them but when the Government, in a desire to reduce civil service manpower and public expenditure, proposed to remove their role in individual bankruptcy there was bitter opposition (not least from the Cork Committee: see Cmnd. 8558, Chap. 14) and the proposal was dropped.

[38] In the latter, their role is principally in relation to disqualification of directors under the Directors Disqualification Act (on which see Chap. 7 at pp. 000 above). They also play a major role in relation to individual bankruptcies which always require a court order, there being nothing comparable to voluntary liquidation except that the individual concerned may, and often will, file his own petition.

[39] Official receivers have the unique distinction of being entitled to act as liquidators notwithstanding that they are not licensed insolvency practitioners under Part XIII of the Act: ss.388(5) and 389(2).

[40] Except when it is made immediately upon the discharge of an administration order or when there is a supervisor of a voluntary arrangement under Part I of the Act (on which see Chap. 26 above at pp. 699–701) when the former administrator or the supervisor of the arrangement may be appointed by the court as liquidator: s.140.

[41] s.136(1) and (2).

[42] See s.136(4) and (5). The nominee of the creditors prevails unless, on application to the court, it otherwise orders (s.139) which it is unlikely to do if the company is insolvent.

[43] Which it may not since both creditors and members may be happy to leave the liquidation to the official receiver since that may prove less expensive.

[44] s.137.

[45] s.136(3).

[46] s.131. See also ss.235 and 236.

[47] s.132.

requested by one-half in value of the creditors or three-quarters in value of the members.[48] And if he is not the liquidator, the person who is must give him all the information and assistance that he reasonably requires for the exercise of his functions.[49]

On the making of a winding-up order the winding up is deemed to have commenced as from the date of the presentation of the petition (or, indeed, if the order is made in respect of a company already in voluntary winding up, as from the date of the resolution to wind up voluntarily[50]). This dating back is important since it can have the effect of invalidating property dispositions[51] and executions of judgments[52] lawfully undertaken during the period between the presentation of the petition and the order,[53] and of affecting the duration of the periods prior to "the onset of insolvency" in which, if certain transactions are undertaken, they are liable to adjustment or avoidance in the event of winding up or administration.[54]

Once a liquidator is appointed, the process of the winding up proceeds very much as it would in the case of a voluntary liquidation since the objective is identical and his functions are the same as those in voluntary windings up, namely[55] "to secure that the assets of the company are got in, realised, and distributed to the company's creditors[56] and, if there is a surplus, to the persons entitled to it."[57] The main difference is that, in a winding up by the court, the liquidator in the exercise of his powers under Schedule 4 to the Act will more often require to obtain sanction of the court before entering into transactions and that throughout he will be subject to the surveillance of the official receiver acting, in effect, as an officer of the court.

Voluntary windings up

In contrast with winding up by the court, voluntary winding up always starts with a resolution of the company. In the unlikely event of the articles fixing a period for the duration of the company[58] or

---

48 ss.133 and 134. It is this public examination that is the most dreaded ordeal, particularly if the company is sufficiently well known to attract the attention of the general public and the Press. But there is a similar provision in relation to individual bankruptcy (s.290) and there is no reason why those who have chosen to incorporate their businesses should escape it.

49 s.143.

50 s.129.

51 s.127.

52 s.128.

53 Which may be considerable if hearings are adjourned, as is not infrequent.

54 See ss.238–245.

55 s.143(1).

56 Giving priority, of course, to preferred creditors as set out in Sched. 6 to the Act.

57 Normally the members (except in the case of non-profit-making or charitable companies) in accordance with their class rights on a winding up.

58 The writer cannot recollect ever coming across a case where this has been done. Charters of incorporation of limited duration are, however, not uncommon.

specifying an event on the occurrence of which it is to be dissolved,[59] all that is required is an ordinary resolution in general meeting.[60] Otherwise what is required is a special resolution that the company be wound up voluntarily,[61] or an extraordinary resolution "to the effect that it cannot, by reason of its liabilities, continue its business, and that it is advisable to wind up."[62] The reason for the resort to an extraordinary resolution is that although it, like a special resolution, requires to be passed by a three-fourths majority of those voting, the meeting can be convened on 14 days' notice rather than 21 and speed may be of the essence when the company is insolvent.[63] Each of these resolutions is subject to section 380 of the Companies Act (*i.e.* a copy of it has to be sent to the Registrar within 15 days[64]) and the company must give notice of the resolution by advertisement in the *Gazette* within 14 days of its passing.[65] A voluntary winding up is deemed to commence on the passing of the resolution[66]; there is no "relating back" as there is in the case of winding up by the court. As from the commencement of the winding up, the company must cease to carry on its business, except so far as may be required for its beneficial winding up,[67] and any transfer of shares, unless made with the sanction of the liquidator, is void, as is any alteration in the status of the members.[68]

Members' winding up

The most important question which the directors of the company will have had to consider prior to the passing of the resolution is whether they can, in good conscience and without dire consequences to themselves, allow the voluntary winding up to proceed as a members', as opposed to a creditors', winding up. In order for that to occur they, or if there are more than two of them, the majority of them, must, in accordance with section 89, make at a directors' meeting[69] a statutory declaration (the "declaration of solvency") to

---

[59] It is possible to conceive of circumstances in which this might be done: *e.g.* when a partnership converts to an incorporated company because its solicitors and accountants advise that this would be advantageous tax-wise, the partners might wish to ensure that it could be dissolved by a simple majority if they were later advised that it would be better to revert to a partnership.

[60] s.84(1)(*a*).

[61] s.84(1)(*b*).

[62] s.84(1)(*c*).

[63] In relation to companies with a very small number of like-minded members this is of theoretical importance only for they will agree on short notice under s.369(3) of the Companies Act and, if a private company, act by a written resolution under its section 381A.

[64] s.84(3).

[65] s.85(1). In Chap. 17 at p. 449 n. 13 above, mention was made of the apparently irrational differences between times allowed for notifications; here we have an example.

[66] s.86.

[67] s.87(1).

[68] s.88. Contrast the wording of the comparable s.127, above, in relation to winding up by the court; that avoids also any disposition of the company's property (unless the court otherwise orders) which s.88 does not.

[69] This, on the face of it rather curious, use of a board meeting as a venue for the making of statutory declarations ensures that all the directors know what is going on.

the effect that they have made a full inquiry into the company's affairs and that, having done so, they have formed the opinion that the company will be able to pay its debts in full, together with interest at the "official rate,"[70] within such period, not exceeding 12 months from the commencement of the winding up, as may be specified in the declaration.[71]

The declaration is ineffective unless:

(a) it is made within five weeks preceding the date of the passing of the resolution, and

(b) it embodies a statement of the company's assets and liabilities as at the latest practicable date before the making of the declaration.[72]

If a director makes the declaration without having reasonable grounds for believing that the company will be able to pay its debts with interest within the period specified in the declaration he is liable to fines and imprisonment[73] and if the debts are not so paid it is presumed, unless the contrary is shown, that he did not have reasonable grounds for his opinion.[74] It therefore behoves the directors to take the utmost care and to seek professional advice before they make the declaration. Especially is this so because, even if the winding up is a members' one, a licensed insolvency practitioner will have to be appointed as liquidator and he is likely to detect whether the declaration was over-optimistic long before the expiration of the 12 months. Formerly small private companies could and often did appoint as liquidator one of the directors and, in effect, continued to proceed much as they would have when a partnership was being dissolved. This is no longer possible[75]; despite the efforts begun by the 1989 Act to reduce the burdens on private companies, the Insolvency Act has increased their burdens as regards winding up even if they are quasi-partnerships.

If the professional liquidator becomes of the opinion that the company will not be able to pay its debts within the stated period, he must summon a meeting of the creditors and supply them with full information in accordance with section 95 and, as from the date when the meeting is held, the winding up is converted under section 96

---

70 *i.e.* whichever is the greater of the interest payable on judgment debts or that applicable to the particular debt apart from the winding up: ss.189(4) and 251.
71 s.89(1). In practice the declaration will play safe and not specify a shorter period than 12 months even if the directors expect that it will be shorter.
72 s.89(2). The declaration must be delivered to the Registrar within 15 days immediately following the passing of the resolution: s.89(3) and (4).
73 s.89(4).
74 s.89(5).
75 But see below at pp. 773–775 for the possible resort to s.652 of the Companies Act.

from a members' to a (insolvent) creditors' voluntary winding up.[76] So long, however, as the liquidator shares the view of the directors (and if they are wise they will have consulted him, as their proposed nominee, before they made the declaration) all should proceed smoothly as a members' winding up. The company in general meeting will appoint one or more liquidators for the purpose of winding up the company's affairs and distributing its assets[77] whereupon "all the powers of the directors cease except so far as a general meeting or the liquidator sanctions their continuance."[78] If a vacancy in the office of liquidator "occurs by death, resignation or otherwise" the company in general meeting may, subject to any arrangement with the creditors,[79] fill the vacancy.[80] If the winding up continues for more than a year,[81] the liquidator must summon a general meeting at the end of the first and any subsequent year or at the first convenient date within three months from the end of the year or such longer period as the Secretary of State may allow.[82] The liquidator must lay before the meeting an account of his acts and dealings, and of the conduct of the winding up during the year.[83]

When the company's affairs are fully wound up the liquidator must "make up"[84] an account of the winding up showing how it has been conducted and the company's property disposed of and must call a final meeting of the company for the purpose of laying before it the account and giving an explanation of it.[85] The fact that this meeting is being called is something which is of wider interest than to members alone for, as we shall see,[86] it will lead to the final dissolution of the company. The Act provides that it shall be called by advertisement in the *Gazette*, specifying its time, place and object and published at least one month before the meeting.[87] Within one week after the

[76] Indeed, it may become a winding up by the court, for a winding up order may be made notwithstanding that the company is already in voluntary winding up and an official receiver, as well as the other persons entitled under s.124, may present a petition: s.124(5). But unless the court, on proof of fraud or mistake, directs otherwise, all proceedings already taken in the voluntary winding up are deemed to have been validly taken: s.129(1).
[77] s.91(1).
[78] s.91(2). As they probably will.
[79] This reference to "creditors" is presumably to cover the case where the members' voluntary winding up forms part of a reorganisation of one of the types dealt with in Chap. 26 above, in which creditors are involved.
[80] s.92(1). The meeting to do so may be convened by any continuing liquidators if there was more than one or by a member: s.92(2).
[81] Which it may, because although the creditors should be paid within 12 months the subsequent distribution of the remaining assets or their proceeds does not have to be completed within any prescribed time.
[82] s.93(1).
[83] s.93(2).
[84] These are the words used in the section but they are not intended to countenance fictitious accounts as they might suggest.
[85] s.94(1).
[86] See pp. 771, 772 below.
[87] What is surprising is that neither the Act nor the Rules seem to require the liquidator to give written notice to the members. If he does not, it is not surprising that the final meeting is frequently inquorate.

meeting he must also send the Registrar a copy of the account and make a return to him of the holding of the meeting.[88]

Creditors' winding up

Here, in contrast with members' winding up, the company is assumed to be insolvent and it is the creditors in whose interests the winding up is undertaken and they who have the whip hand. If no declaration of solvency has been made, the company must cause a meeting of its creditors to be summoned for a day not later than the 14th day after the resolution for voluntary winding up is to be proposed and cause notices to be sent by post to the creditors not less than seven days before the date of the meeting and must advertise it once in the *Gazette* and once at least in two newspapers circulating in the locality in which the company's principal place of business in Great Britain was situated during the previous six months.[89] This meeting must state either (a) the name of a qualified insolvency practitioner[90] who, before the meeting, will furnish creditors with such information as they may reasonably require or (b) a place where, on the two business days before the meeting, a list of the company's creditors will be available for inspection free of charge.[91] Further, the directors must prepare a statement of the company's affairs verified by affidavit and cause it to be laid before the creditors' meeting. The directors must also nominate one of their number to preside at the creditors' meeting—an unenviable task which it is the nominee's duty to perform.[92]

At the respective meetings the creditors and the company may nominate a liquidator and if the creditors do so he becomes the liquidator, unless, on application to the court by a director, creditor or member, it directs that the nominee of the company shall be liquidator instead of, or jointly with the creditors' nominee, or it appoints some other person instead of the creditors' nominee.[93] Provisions, similar in effect, apply when a members' winding up is converted to a creditors' winding up because the liquidator concludes that the company's debts will not be paid in full within the 12 months, except that the obligations of the directors have to be undertaken by the incumbent liquidator.[94]

In a creditors' voluntary winding up,[95] or in a winding up by the court,[96] the creditors may decide at their initial or a subsequent

[88] s.94(3) and (4). If a quorum is not present the liquidator must send instead a return that the meeting was duly summoned and that no quorum was present.
[89] s.98(1).
[90] In practice he will probably be the person that the directors intend to propose to the company meeting for appointment as liquidator.
[91] s.98(2).
[92] s.99.
[93] s.100.
[94] ss.95 and 96.
[95] s.101, and, when a members' is converted to a creditors', winding up, s.102.
[96] s.141.

meeting to establish what used to be called a "committee of inspection" but which the Act now calls a "liquidation committee," and, in the case of a creditors' winding up, may appoint not more than five members of it.[97] If they do so, the company in general meeting may also appoint members not exceeding five in number.[98] However, if the creditors resolve that all or any of those appointed by the general meeting ought not to be members of the committee, the persons concerned will not be qualified to act unless the court otherwise directs.[99]

The functions of a liquidation committee are to be found in the Rules rather than the Act and for present purposes can be summarised by saying that they give the liquidator the opportunity of consulting the creditors and the members without having to convene formal creditors' and company meetings and also provide additional means whereby the creditors and members can keep an eye on the liquidator. In the latter respect, liquidation committees are, perhaps, likely to be more valuable in creditors' voluntary windings up (rather than in windings up by the court) owing to the lesser role played by official receivers.

It may be thought somewhat anomalous that, when the company is insolvent, the members should have equal (or any) representation on the liquidation committee. But the Cork Committee rejected the argument that they should not, because "it is rarely possible to assess the interest of shareholders at the outset of proceedings."[1] This is certainly true. What at the commencement of the winding up would seem to be a clear case of the company's liabilities greatly exceeding its assets (so that the shareholders have no prospective stake in the outcome of the winding up) may turn out otherwise if the winding up is prolonged.[2]

In other respects a creditors' winding up proceeds up to and including the final meetings in much the same way as in a members' winding up.

Conclusion

No attempt has been made here to deal with the many important matters which may arise in the course of winding up, whether by the court or voluntarily; for example how creditors "prove" their debts

[97] s.101(1). In the case of windings up by the court the position under s.141 and Chapter 12 of Part 4 of the Rules is somewhat different and is designed to ensure that, when the official receiver is the liquidator, the committee's functions are performed instead by the D.T.I.'s Insolvency Service and that, if the liquidator is some other person, it is left to him to decide whether to convene a meeting of creditors to establish a liquidation committee (unless one-tenth in value of the creditors require him to do so).

[98] s.101(2).

[99] s.101(3).

[1] Cmnd. 8558, para. 939.

[2] But, unless it is, the reverse is at present likely to be the case, resulting in members' windings up having to be converted into creditors' (or to winding up by the court).

(dealt with in detail by the Rules rather than by the Act). However, a word ought to be said about the position of secured creditors in order to draw attention to the difference between their position on a winding up compared with that during an administration. As we saw, in the latter, unless they have taken steps to enforce their security prior to the administration they may be in difficulties in doing so while it lasts.[3] In contrast, on a winding up, a secured creditor is in the enviable position of having the choice of realising his security and, if this does not raise sufficient to pay him in full, to prove for the balance, or to surrender his security for the benefit of the general body of creditors and prove for the whole debt.[4] Normally, of course, he will adopt the former option.[5]

However, as emphasised in Chapter 16,[6] when his security is a floating charge he may be adversely affected by a winding up (or administration) both because of the inherent nature of such a charge and of the statutory provisions relating to its subordination to the claims of preferred creditors and those relating to adjustment of prior transactions and in particular, avoidance under section 245 of the Act. And it is not only holders of *floating* charges who may find themselves adversely affected. Although section 245 applies only to floating charges, any persons who have obtained benefits from the company prior to the winding up (or administration) may find themselves deprived of them under section 238 as "transactions at an undervalue";[7] or, under section 239, as "preferences";[8] or, under section 244, as "extortionate credit transactions."

3. DISSOLUTION

After winding up

In contrast with the formalities attendant on the birth of a company[9] its death takes place with a singular absence of ceremony. In the case of voluntary liquidations, once the liquidator has sent to the Registrar his final account and return[10] on the expiration of three months from their registration the company is deemed to be dissolved,[11] unless the court, on the application of the liquidator or

---

[3] See pp. 747–752, 754, 755 above.
[4] Rule 4.88. If the winding up follows an administration in which the administrator has exercised his powers under s.15 (above, pp. 754, 755) it would seem that the effect of s.15(4) and (5) will be to preserve the security holder's rights by treating the sums mentioned in those subsections as the security in the winding up.
[5] Unless he is an unusually altruistic creditor or he wants to maximise his votes at a creditors' meeting.
[6] At pp. 420–425 above.
[7] Or in Scotland as "gratuitous alienations": see s.242.
[8] In Scotland as "unfair preferences": see s.243.
[9] See Chap. 11 above.
[10] In accordance with s.94 (members' voluntary) or s.106 (creditors' voluntary).
[11] s.201(1) and (2).

any other person who appears to the court to be interested, makes an order deferring the date of dissolution.[12]

Normally the position is much the same where the winding up is by the court. The liquidator, once it appears to him that the winding up is for all practical purposes complete, must summon a final meeting of creditors[13] which receives the liquidator's report on the winding up and determines whether he shall be released.[14] The liquidator then gives notice to the court and to the Registrar that the meeting has been held and of the decisions (if any) of the meeting. When the Registrar receives the notice he registers it and, unless the Secretary of State, on the application of the official receiver or anyone else who appears to be interested, directs a deferment,[15] the company is dissolved at the end of three months from that registration.[16]

If the official receiver is the liquidator the procedure is the same except that registration is of a notice from the official receiver that the winding up is complete.[17] However, there is a sensible procedure whereby he may bring about an early dissolution if it appears to him that the realisable assets are insufficient to cover the costs of the winding up[18] and that the affairs of the company do not require any further investigation.[19] He must, before doing so, give at least 28 days' notice of his intention to the company's creditors and members and to an administrative receiver if there is one,[20] and, with the giving of that notice, he ceases to be required to undertake any of his duties other than to apply to the Registrar for the early dissolution of the company.[21] On the registration of that application the company becomes dissolved at the end of three months[22] unless the Secretary of State, on the application of the official receiver or any creditor, member or administrative receiver,[23] gives directions to the contrary before the end of that period.

---

[12] s.201(3). It is then the duty of the applicant to deliver an office copy of the order to the Registrar for registration: s.201(4).

[13] The relevant statutory provisions appear to apply to windings up by the court on any ground and whether or not the company is insolvent and not to require any final meeting of the company (as in a voluntary liquidation). If this is correct, it is very curious. In a winding up on the petition of a member on the ground that it is just and equitable, if the company's creditors have been fully paid it is only the members who will have any interest in the result of the winding up.

[14] ss.146 and 172(8).

[15] s.205(3). An appeal to the court lies from any such decision of the Secretary of State: s.205(4).

[16] s.205(1) and (2).

[17] s.205(1)(b).

[18] In Scotland (lacking official receivers) there is a procedure for early dissolution on this ground alone but it involves an application to the court: s.204.

[19] s.202(1) and (2).

[20] s.202(3).

[21] s.204.

[22] s.202(5).

[23] There is an apparent inconsistency between s.202(5) which says that the application can be made by the official receiver "or any other person who appears to the Secretary of State to be interested" and s.203(1) which says that it must be by one of the persons mentioned in the text above. Presumably the Secretary of State will not regard any other person as "interested."

The grounds upon which the application to the Secretary of State may be made are (a) that the realisable assets are in fact sufficient to cover the expenses of the winding up or (b) that the affairs of the company do require further investigation,[24] or (c) that for any other reason the early dissolution of the company is inappropriate.[25] And the directions that may be given may make provision for enabling the winding up to proceed as if the official receiver had not invoked the procedure or may include a deferment of the date of dissolution.[26]

There are no similar provisions for early dissolution on a voluntary winding up; once the company has resolved on voluntary winding up it is expected to go through with it. But if there is a vacancy in the liquidatorship and no one can be found who is willing to accept the office because there is clearly not enough left to pay the expenses of continuing it (no insolvency practitioner will accept office in such circumstances unless someone is prepared to pay him) it is difficult to see how the Registrar could do other than to strike the company off the register as a defunct company, under section 652 of the Companies Act—as, indeed, that section specifically recognises. To that section we now turn because it affords a method whereby a small company can, in practice, often be inexpensively dissolved without any formal winding up. Although it appears in a chapter of the Companies Act headed "matters arising subsequent to winding up" (which therefore has been left in that Act and not transferred to the Insolvency Act) section 652 is in fact something that is extensively used when there has been no winding up.

Defunct companies

Under section 652, if the Registrar has reasonable cause to believe that a company is not carrying on business or in operation, he may send to the company a letter inquiring whether that is so.[27] If within a month of sending the letter he does not receive a reply he shall, within 14 days thereafter, send a registered letter referring to the first letter and stating that no answer to it has been received and that, if an answer to the second letter is not received within one month from its date, a notice will be published in the *Gazette* with a view to striking the company's name off the register.[28] If the Registrar receives a reply to the effect that the company is not carrying on

---

[24] Neither of which is likely to be accepted by the Secretary of State if the official receiver has concluded the contrary.
[25] s.203(2).
[26] s.203(3). There can be an appeal to the court against the S. of S.'s decision: s.203(4).
[27] Companies Act, s.652(1). For meticulous details about how letters and notices are to be addressed, see s.652(7).
[28] *Ibid.* s.652(2). From hereon references to "the Act" are to the Companies Act 1985 unless the context otherwise requires.

business or is not in operation, or if he does not, within one month of sending the second letter, receive any reply, he may publish in the *Gazette* and send to the company by post a notice that at the expiration of three months from the date of the notice the name of the company will, unless cause to the contrary is shown, be struck off the register and the company will be dissolved.[29] At the expiration of the time mentioned in the notice, the Registrar may, unless cause to the contrary is shown, strike the company off the register and publish notice of this in the *Gazette*, whereupon the company is dissolved.[30]

As mentioned in Chapter 17,[31] this section is most commonly used when what has afforded the Registrar reasonable cause to believe that the company is not carrying on business or in operation is the fact that it is in arrear with the lodging of its annual returns and accounts. When so used by the Registrar, it is both a method of inducing those companies that are operating in breach of their filing obligations to mend their ways as well as a method of clearing the register of companies which are indeed defunct. It can, however, specifically be used to deal with the situation referred to above when winding up proceedings have been started but insufficient resources are available to complete them. Section 652(4) says that where the Registrar has reasonable cause to believe either that no liquidator is acting or that the affairs of the company are fully wound up and that the returns required to be made by the liquidator have not been made for a period of six consecutive months, the Registrar shall publish in the *Gazette* and send to the company or the liquidator (if any) a like notice which causes the company to be dissolved.

Moreover it affords companies, and especially small private ones, a method of dissolving without the expense of a formal winding up—an expense which, as already pointed out, the 1985/86 reforms have increased because, even in the case of a members' winding up of a solvent company, a liquidator has to be a qualified and licensed insolvency practitioner.

To take a not uncommon case: an incorporated family business has been carried on effectively by Mr. Jones for the benefit of himself, his wife and children, all of whom are its members and directors. On his death or retirement the rest of the family have no wish to run the business but are unable to find a purchaser of the shares. Instead of a formal winding up by a liquidator, they can sell its assets, discharge its liabilities and divide whatever money remains among themselves by way of directors' remuneration. They can then write, or get their solicitor to do so, to the Registrar explaining that the company is no longer carrying on business, that all the liabilities have been

---

29 s.652(3).
30 s.652(5).
31 At p. 451 at n. 30 above.

discharged and that the company has no remaining assets and asking the Registrar to exercise his powers under section 652. This he should not hesitate to do since the section specifically provides that dissolution under it does not prevent the enforcement of any liability there may be of its former directors or members or preclude the power of the court from winding up the company compulsorily notwithstanding that it has been dissolved. Moreover, as we are about to see, if the need arises a dissolved company can be resurrected under section 651 or 653. In the circumstances envisaged it may be thought somewhat pointless to require the Registrar to go through the formalities of despatching two letters and delaying the dissolution for a few months, but this is a small price to pay to avoid the expense of a formal winding up.

Resurrection of dissolved companies

A contrast between the death of an individual and that of a company is that, without divine intervention but merely by an order of the court, a dissolved company can be resurrected. The courts have found some difficulty in making sense of the statutory provisions empowering them to perform this miracle, particularly because the legislature has, for some reason, chosen to provide two distinct means: one under what is now section 651 of the Companies Act and the other under what is now its section 653. Most people reading the two sections would unhesitatingly conclude that section 651 applies when the company has been dissolved following a formal winding up[32] and section 653 when it has been dissolved under section 652.[33] This was certainly the view of Lord Blanesburgh, in *Morris* v. *Harris*,[34] who said of the predecessor of section 651 that it was "clearly confined to cases where the dissolution succeeds the complete winding up of the company's affairs and cannot take effect at all except at the instance, or with the knowledge, of the liquidator, the company's only executive officer." However, in *Re Belmont & Co. Ltd.*,[35] in which this dictum seems not to have been cited, Wynn Parry J. decided that so long as the applicant could bring himself within the list of those entitled to apply to the court under both sections he could choose either. In the subsequent case of *Re Test Holdings (Clifton) Ltd.*[36] Megarry J. was persuaded by counsel for the Registrar to follow that decision, which had been relied on in many later cases. He did, however, express doubts on whether the

32 See s.651(1) which refers to application by "the liquidator."
33 See s.653(2) which specifically refers to striking-off under s.652.
34 [1927] A.C. 252, H.L. at 269.
35 [1950] Ch. 10.
36 [1970] Ch. 285.

sections reflected a coherent policy and suggested that when the Companies Act was next revised consideration might with advantage be given to that point. Notwithstanding the many subsequent revisions, that suggestion has been taken up only to the extent that the changes made by the Companies Act 1989 to section 651 (but not also to section 653) make sense only on the assumption that the legislature accepts that an applicant does have a choice of either section.

The absence of a "coherent policy" in sections 651 and 653 is vividly illustrated in *Re Wood & Martin Ltd.*[37] and *Re Thompson & Riches Ltd.*[38] In both of these cases the companies concerned had been dissolved as a result of action by the Registrar under what is now section 652. In the first, the company, in blissful ignorance of this (notwithstanding the communications sent to it by the Registrar) purported to pass a resolution for a voluntary winding up, appointing a "liquidator" who had proceeded to realise the assets. When he discovered the flaw in his appointment he applied, under what is now section 651, as "the liquidator of the company or any other person appearing to the court to be interested," for the dissolution to be declared void. Megarry J. held that, although it was necessary to make sense of the section to construe "liquidator" as including a former liquidator, it was impossible to construe it as including someone who, in law, had never been the liquidator. However, it did appear that he was an "other person interested" and he accordingly made the order applied for.

In *Re Thompson & Riches Ltd.* the applicant for an order was a member of the company who, in ignorance (shared, apparently, by all concerned, including the court) of the fact that the company had been struck off, had obtained an order for the winding up of the company by the court and the appointment of the official receiver as provisional liquidator. Presumably it was the official receiver who discovered that the company had long since been struck off. The fact that the winding up was compulsory (rather than voluntary, as in *Re Wood & Martin*) added a complication, since section 652(6)(*b*) says that nothing in its subsection (5) "affects the power of the court to wind up a company the name of which has been struck off the register." Technically, therefore, the winding-up order was not void. Slade J. held that what the applicant should have done was to "follow the common practice adopted in the light of the decision in *Re Cambridge Coffee Room Association Ltd.*[39] by asking for (1) rescission of the existing winding-up order; (2) liberty to amend his petition so as to include an application for restoration of

37 [1971] 1 W.L.R. 293.
38 [1981] 1 W.L.R. 682.
39 [1952] 1 All E.R. 112, where a similar situation had arisen (it is all too common).

the name of the company to the register; and (4) a new winding up order."[40] Instead of adopting this course the applicant had applied[41] under the predecessor of section 651. Slade J., though he thought it would have been preferable to apply under section 653,[42] accepted that in the light of the earlier cases the applicant was entitled to apply under section 651 and he made an order declaring the dissolution void.

In most cases, therefore, applicants will have the choice of applying under either section 651 or 653. The differences between their wording (though less so between their substance) are great. Section 651 provides first that where a company has been dissolved the court may, on the application of the liquidator[43] or any other person appearing to the court to be interested, make an order in such terms as it thinks fit declaring the dissolution to be void. If an order is made "such proceedings may be taken as might have been taken if the company had not been dissolved." The use of the word "proceedings" suggests that all the draftsman was contemplating were legal proceedings by or against the company. But the effect is certainly wider than that since it causes any property of the company which may have vested in the Crown as *bona vacantia* on the company's dissolution to revest in the company.[44] On the other hand the House of Lords[45] has held that it does not, as does an order under section 653,[46] have the effect of validating transactions by or with the company during the period between its dissolution and its restoration. However, it seems that the practice has grown up for applicants, who want restoration to have that effect, to apply under section 651 for an order that the company shall be deemed to have continued in existence as if it had not been struck off and for the court so to order[47] (presumably under the power in section 651(1) to make an order on such terms as the court thinks fit). If an order is made, it is the duty of the applicant to deliver an office copy to the Registrar for registration[48] and the applicant will be liable to fines if he fails to do so.[49]

40 [1981] 1 W.L.R. at 687A.
41 Presumably as a "person interested."
42 Which he could have done as an "aggrieved member": see s.653(1) and (2) below.
43 As Megarry J. had pointed out in *Re Wood & Martin*, above, once the company is dissolved it cannot have a "liquidator" which therefore must be construed as "former liquidator."
44 On this see ss.654–658 dealt with at pp. 783–785 below.
45 *Morris v. Harris* [1927] A.C. 252.
46 See s.653(3) which provides that on the delivery to the Registrar of an office copy of the order made under that section "the company is deemed to have continued in existence as if its name had not been struck off."
47 See *Re Workvale Ltd.* [1991] 1 W.L.R. 294, discussed below. *Morris v. Harris* seems to be ignored; in *Workvale* it was not even cited in argument.
48 As the Registrar should be joined as a respondent unless the company is in liquidation (*Re Test Holdings Ltd.*, above, n. 36, *Re Wood & Martin*, above, n. 37, and *Re Thompson & Riches Ltd.*, above, n. 38) this hardly seems necessary except where the company is in liquidation.
49 s.651(3).

So far, the substance of section 651 is identical with that of the versions in the earlier Companies Acts. But subsections (4)–(7) were newly inserted by section 141(3) of the 1989 Act. Subsection (4) continues the former bar on applications made after the end of two years from the date of the company's dissolution. This is the major contrast with applications made under section 653, where applications can be made up to 20 years after the dissolution. But subsection (4) is expressed to be subject to the remaining subsections and subsection (5) provides that an application made for the purposes of bringing proceedings against the company for damages for personal injuries[50] (including any such claim for funeral expenses[51]) or for damages under the Fatal Accidents Act 1976 may be made at any time, but that no order shall be made on such an application if it appears to the court that the proceedings (herein described as "personal injuries proceedings") would fail by virtue of any enactment[52] as to the time within which proceedings must be brought. Furthermore subsection (6) provides that nothing in subsection (5) affects the power of the court to direct that the period between the dissolution and the order shall not count for the purposes of any such enactment.[53]

To complicate matters further, section 141 of the 1989 Act contains two more subsections which are not inserted in the Companies Act 1985 but are left self-standing in the 1989 Act. Its subsection (4) says that an application may be made under the new section 651(5) in relation to a company dissolved prior to the commencement of section 141,[54] notwithstanding that the time within which the dissolution might formerly have been declared void under section 651 (*i.e.* two years) had expired before that commencement, but that no such application shall be made in relation to a company dissolved more than 20 years[55] before the commencement of the section. Finally section 141(5) provides that except as provided by its subsection (4) none of the amendments made by it applies in relation to a company dissolved more than two years before the section's commencement. The overall effect, therefore, is that applications under section 651 must as formerly be made before the expiration of two years from the dissolution except, now, when the application is

---

[50] Which includes "any disease and any impairment of a person's physical or mental condition": s.651(7).

[51] Under s.1(2)(c) of the Law Reform (Miscellaneous Provisions) Act 1934.

[52] *i.e.* the Limitation Act 1980 (as amended).

[53] This is a power which the courts first assumed in *Re Donald Kenyon Ltd.* [1956] 1 W.L.R. 1397 (a case in which the restoration was under what is now s.653). It is now given statutory recognition where the order is made under s.651.

[54] The date of Royal Assent (16 November 1989): see 1989 Act, s.215(1)(a).

[55] This, otherwise arbitrary, period of 20 years was presumably chosen because applications under s.653 have to be made within 20 years of the dissolution, and so that any possibility of applications for restoration under either section are barred if the dissolution occurred more than 20 years before the commencement of the 1989 Act. But note that it does not impose a 20-years' limitation on applications under section 651 if the dissolution occurs *after* the commencement of the 1989 Act; such an application can be made "at any time."

made for the purpose of bringing personal injuries proceedings against the company. When that exception applies it can be made at any time unless the company was dissolved before 16th November 1989.

The need for the 1989 amendments arose as a result of the special provisions regarding periods of limitation in respect of actions for personal injuries in the Limitation Act 1980 and because of the Third Parties (Rights against Insurers) Act 1930 as interpreted by the House of Lords in *Bradley* v. *Eagle Star Insurance Co.*[56] Under section 11 of the Limitation Act the normal period of limitation in respect of personal injuries proceedings is three years from whichever is the later of (a) the date on which the cause of action accrued, or (b) the date of knowledge by the injured party that he had a cause of action. But section 33 of that Act further provides that the court may direct that these conditions shall not apply if it appears to the court that it would be equitable to allow the action to proceed having regard to the degrees to which the plaintiff would be prejudiced if it were not allowed to continue and the defendant would be prejudiced if it were. These, therefore, are the provisions which the court now has to consider on an application to avoid the dissolution of the company for the purpose of bringing an action against the company in respect of personal injuries.

When the application under section 651 is made in respect of a company which has been dissolved following a winding up, one might have supposed that so long as the company was insured against liability for personal injuries (as it normally will be) there would be no need to avoid its dissolution in the light of the provisions of the Third Parties (Rights against Insurers) Act 1930. Under section 1(1) of that Act, if the assured is a company which has gone into compulsory or voluntary winding up,[57] rights against its insurers vest in the party to whom the company has incurred the liability, whether that was incurred before or after the commencement of the winding up. It would therefore seem wholly pointless to revive the company.[58] But, in *Bradley* v. *Eagle Star Insurance Co.* the House of Lords, affirming earlier decisions of the Court of Appeal, held that the injured party could not proceed directly against the insurers unless and until the existence and amount of the company's liability had been established between the company and the injured party, either by a judgment, arbitration or agreement. That had not been done before the company was dissolved and, once it was, unless the dissolution could be avoided (which in that case it could not, since it had been dissolved far earlier than two years previously) nothing

---

56 [1989] A.C. 1957, H.L.
57 Or, indeed, administrative receivership: s.1(1)(*b*) of that Act.
58 This was the view of Lord Templeman (who dissented in *Bradley* v. *Eagle Star Insurance*: above n. 56).

could be done. Presumably the revisions in the 1989 Act (which was not in operation when the *Bradley* case was decided) were intended to relieve those who had suffered personal injuries from the perceived hardship arising from that decision.

We now have the advantage of the decision of Harman J. in *Re Workvale Ltd.*[59] (the first and, at the time of writing, apparently the only, reported case on the effect of the new section 651(5)). The facts in that case were that in September 1983 an employee of Workvale Ltd. fell off a ladder while working and injured himself. Clearly, therefore, any claim he had against Workvale would be statute-barred under section 11 of the Limitation Act if proceedings were not commenced by September 1986, unless the court allowed it to proceed under section 33 of that Act. A claim was notified to Workvale in November 1983 but shortly thereafter it went into liquidation. The winding up took its normal course and in July 1986 the company was dissolved. In apparent ignorance of this, in September of that year the employee issued a writ, just before the limitation period under section 11 would have expired, and the company's insurers agreed to accept service, on the assumption, presumably, that the Third Parties Act applied—which in the light of *Bradley* it did not. However it would still have been possible, even as the law then stood, for an application to have been made to avoid the dissolution of Workvale (thus enabling matters to be put right) so long as that application was made within two years of the dissolution. Unfortunately the solicitors then acting for the employee were unfamiliar with the Companies Act and did not do so. However, new solicitors who had taken over did so after the 1989 Act commenced.

The application came before Harman J., the original named respondents to the application being the company and the Registrar. The insurance company applied to be joined and the judge allowed that application and also ordered the name of the company to be struck out, since the company did not exist, had not existed since mid-1986, and plainly could not be a proper respondent.[60] Counsel for the insurers then argued that although there was a right to make an application under the new section 651(5) the court had no jurisdiction to make an order since the proceedings would fail by virtue of section 11 of the Limitation Act. This attempt to persuade the judge that, while section 11 was "an enactment as to the time within which proceedings must be brought," section 33 of that Act was not, was given short shrift. The legislative policy laid down in section 33 was that in personal injuries proceedings the court could override the normal period of limitation if it was equitable to do so and the clear policy of the revised section 651(5) of the Companies

[59] [1991] 1 W.L.R. 294.
[60] See at p. 299A, B.

Act was that dissolved companies could be restored to life for that purpose. Hence, Harman J. held that he was required to "consider the discretionary powers under section 33 of the Act of 1980 in order to exercise the discretionary powers granted by section 651(5) of the Act of 1985" and this he found "a very difficult exercise."[61] And not surprisingly; for personal injuries litigation in the High Court is conducted in the Queen's Bench Division, while applications under section 651 are dealt with in the Companies Court of the Chancery Division, the judges of which cannot be expected to be familiar with what Harman J. rightly described as "a mass of practice and a mass of decisions upon the point, most of which, quite rightly,[62] have not been cited."[63] He therefore took the view that unless satisfied to a high degree that the court trying the proposed personal injuries action would refuse to allow it to proceed, he ought to grant the order. Having considered the delay that had occurred in bringing the action (not all of which was the fault of the proposed plaintiff[64]), he concluded that he "should not deprive the applicant *in limine* from seeking to test her luck before a Queen's Bench judge."[65] He accordingly made an order "that the company be restored to the register, its dissolution be declared void, and that it shall be deemed to have continued in existence throughout the period as if its name had not been struck off";[66] but he granted leave to appeal.

This eminently sensible judgment seems likely to be upheld on appeal (if, in fact, one is brought[66a]). The decision does, however, prompt questions which Harman J. did not need to consider. Although the application was plainly made for the purpose of bringing proceedings against the company for damages in respect of personal injuries, there would, it seems, be no indication of that in the order as registered by the Registrar and, even if there were, the order would have the effect of deeming the company to have continued in existence as if its name had not been struck off. Would

---

61 At p. 301B, D.
62 If they had been cited, the hearing of the originating motion to declare the dissolution void would have taken far longer than is expected of such motions. It seems unfortunate that the legislation requires the Chancery court to consider the limitation point. If the court should decide that the intending plaintiff is deprived at an earlier stage of the possibility of pursuing his claim against the company or its insurers merely because the company has been dissolved through no fault of his; and if it decides the contrary, the trial court will have to consider the question all over again and at greater length.
63 At p. 301C.
64 The widow of the employee (the latter having died in August 1990) who had had to obtain letters of administration and legal aid to proceed with the action.
65 At p. 302D.
66 At p. 302E. This he described as the order "as sought by this notice of motion." But that, as reported at p. 295, had also asked that "the period between July 21, 1986 and the date of restoration to the register be excluded from the limitation period in respect of the applicant's claim to damages." That presumably was omitted as it would seemingly have served no purpose in the instant case.
66a The decision has now been affirmed by the C.A., which added to the order the direction which (see n. 66) Harman J. omitted: [1992] 1 W.L.R. 416, C.A.

not therefore anyone else who had a claim against the company, not for personal injuries, be able to pursue it, notwithstanding that he would not have been able to apply under section 651 since, the two-year bar would have applied? The answer seems to be "yes," unless *his* claim was statute-barred. Although the effect of the order would seemingly be that time would have continued to run (unless the order provided to the contrary) his claim might not be statute-barred since the appropriate period of limitation could be substantially longer than the primary three years in respect of personal injuries.

Before leaving section 651 it should be pointed out that our reasons for stating above[67] that the amendments made by the 1989 Act seem to have given tacit approval to the decisions holding that an applicant has a choice of proceeding under either section 651 or 653, are that if an applicant had to proceed under section 653 when the company had been struck off under section 652 he would be in a worse position than an applicant under section 651 since there would be a final bar after 20 years from the dissolution. Although that will normally be more than adequate, it might not be when the injury was an industrial disease. The failure to make similar amendments to section 653 makes sense only on the assumption that the legislature accepted that such an applicant could proceed under section 651.

Turning, then, to section 653. The wording of this is very different and superficially much simpler—though the effect seems to be much the same. It does not say that the court may declare the dissolution to be void but instead provides that if a company or any member or creditor of it feels aggrieved by the company having been struck off, he may apply before the expiration of 20 years from the publication in the *Gazette* of the notice under section 652, and the court may, if satisfied that the company was at the time of the striking off carrying on business or in operation, or otherwise that it is just that the company be restored to the register, order the company's name to be restored.[68] This differs from section 651 (where the application must be made by the liquidator "or any other person appearing to the court to be interested") and is somewhat strange since, although one can reasonably construe "member or creditor" as meaning a "former member or creditor," it is more difficult to see how a non-existent company can "feel aggrieved" or how it can "apply."[69] In practice however, so long as "creditor" includes a contingent or prospective creditor,[70] those who can apply as aggrieved members or creditors are likely to be the same as "any other person appearing to the court to

---

[67] At p. 776 above.
[68] s.653(1) and (2).
[69] Presumably it is envisaged that the former directors or members could cause the presently non-existent company to apply as if it had not been dissolved.
[70] As Megarry J., in *Re Harvest Lane Motor Bodies Ltd.* [1969] 1 Ch. 457, held that it did. But apparently it does not include a transferee or assignee subsequent to the dissolution: *Re Timbique Gold Mines Ltd.* [1961] Ch. 319. But he could, perhaps, apply under s.651 as a "person appearing to the court to be interested."

be interested" who may apply under section 651. And the "otherwise that it is just that the company be restored to the register" seems to afford the court the same wide discretion as under section 651.

Finally, section 653(3) provides that "on an office copy of the order being delivered to the Registrar for registration the company is deemed to have continued in existence as if its name had not been struck off"[71] and the court may by the order give such directions and make such provisions as seem just for placing the company and all other persons in the same position (as nearly as may be) as if the company's name had not been struck off."[72]

A further complication may arise, whether the dissolution has arisen from a formal winding up or from a striking off under section 652. This is because section 654 provides that when a company is dissolved any of its remaining property vests in the Crown[73] as *bona vacantia*, unless the Crown disclaims the property, as it may under sections 656 and 657.[74] If it disclaims, the property does not vest in the Crown but is treated similarly to onerous property disclaimed by a liquidator; *i.e.* any person, other than the company, who has rights or liabilities in respect of it can apply to the court for an appropriate vesting order. Normally, if there has been a formal winding up, all the company's property will have been realised and distributed to the creditors or members.[75] It would, however, be left with property if, on a compulsory winding up in which the official receiver is the liquidator, he has obtained early dissolution under section 202[76] of the Insolvency Act, or if a liquidator has overlooked some reversionary or contingent interest to which the company was entitled and which, after its dissolution, falls into possession. But when a company has been struck off on the assumption that it was no longer in operation or carrying on business, when in fact it is still going strong, it clearly will have assets. Theoretically these will have vested in the Crown as *bona vacantia* on the date of its dissolution, though

---

[71] Thus making it unnecessary for the order to say so, as orders under s.651 will presumably have to if this is what the court intends (as Harman J. did in *Re Workvale Ltd.* above).

[72] As we have seen (p. 778, n. 53 above) although section 653 does not expressly say so, as s.651(6) now does, this enables the court to direct that time shall not run against creditors during the time between the dissolution and the resurrection. The case for doing so when the company has been struck off erroneously under s.652 and has continued to carry on business during that time will be weak unless the applicant creditor has found out that it has been dissolved when he attempts to sue. If he has made no attempt to sue it is difficult to see why time should not continue to run against him.

[73] Or, strictly to the Crown, the Duchy of Lancaster or the Duke of Cornwall, as the case may be: s.654(1).

[74] The latter as amended by the Insolvency Acts 1985 and 1986.

[75] There may, and often will, be unclaimed distributions but a sum sufficient to enable claims to be met should have been paid into the Insolvency Services Account from which those entitled can claim it: Insolvency Regs. 1986 (S.I. 1986 No. 1994), regs. 16, 17 and 33.

[76] See pp. 780, 781 above. Although the assets may be insufficient to pay the costs of a winding up, the company will have assets which will not have been distributed.

in fact nothing is likely to be done by anyone on behalf of the Crown to ensure that the Crown obtains possession of the property since the Registrar and those who rely on him for information will believe that the company had become defunct (and, presumably, had no property) many months before the date of dissolution.[77]

However, section 654(2) provides that section 654(1) "has effect subject and without prejudice to any order made by the court under section 651 or 653." The effect of this is that if a restoration order is made it automatically and retrospectively revests the property in the company.[78] But section 654(2) expressly states that it operates "except as provided by the section next following." This (section 655) provides that the Crown may "dispose of, or of an interest in, any property that has vested in it notwithstanding that an order may be made under section 651 or 653"[79]; but that if such an order is made the Crown shall restore to the revivified company any consideration received on a disposition or its value, or, if no consideration was received, the value of the property,[80] and that on any proceedings arising concerning the liability to restore, the Attorney-General shall represent Her Majesty.[81]

The courts have further protected the Crown by ruling that unless it consents to an order being made under section 651 or 653 the Attorney-General should be made a respondent to the application.[82] What normally happens, however, is that the applicant obtains from the Treasury Solicitor a letter confirming the Crown's consent which is exhibited to the applicant's affidavit.[83] It is not clear from the report of *Re Workvale Ltd.*[84] whether that was done in that case, which was a rare example of one where no one was concerned about any property of the dissolved company (unless the insurance policy could be so regarded); all that was needed there was to revive the

---

[77] It might give such companies a salutary shock and cause them to apply more promptly for restoration to the register, if the Registrar on publishing the notice in the Gazette in accordance with s.652(5) notified the company that its property (if any) had now vested in the Crown.

[78] Often there would be little point in reviving the company unless it had this effect (and the court may refuse to do so "unless there is a real prospect of a surplus to be snatched from the fate of *bona vacantia*": *Re Lindsay Bowman Ltd.* [1969] 1 W.L.R. 1443 at 1448), but presumably the court could provide to the contrary under its power to impose "terms" (s.651(1)) or to "give directions and make ... provisions" under s.653(3).

[79] s.655(1).

[80] s.655(2).

[81] s.655(3) and (4).

[82] *Re Belmont & Co.* [1951] 2 All E.R. 898.

[83] Circumstances in which the Crown could reasonably object to an order being made are rare. In most cases it will not know that the property has vested in it until the application to restore is made and in all cases the only reason why it has received a windfall is because the law insists that property must be vested in someone. The position is to be contrasted with that in *Re Servers of the Blind* [1960] 1 W.L.R. 564 when, after a guarantee company had been wound up and dissolved, a testator died leaving a will under which a legacy was left to the company. Pennycuick J. refused to make an order declaring its dissolution void since the effect of that would have been to deprive the next-of-kin who had become entitled on the lapse of the legacy.

[84] Above, pp. 780, 781.

company so that it could agree the extent of its liability (if any), thus enabling its rights against the insurers to pass to the applicant.

CONCLUSION

The main conclusion to be drawn from this discussion of resurrection of dissolved companies is that it is high time that sections 651 and 653 of the Companies Act were merged into a single section eradicating the real or apparent substantive differences between them[85]; the present dichotomy is a source of nothing but confusion.

---

[85] But with a plea to the draftsman to do so in a way which will cause less difficulty to judges (see [1991] 1 W.L.R. at p. 296C)—and to others.